THE ROUTLEDGE HANDBOOK OF TRANSLATION AND CENSORSHIP

The Routledge Handbook of Translation and Censorship is the first handbook to provide a comprehensive overview of the topic, offering broad geographic and historical coverage, and extending the political contexts to incorporate colonial and postcolonial viewpoints, as well as pluralistic societies. It examines key cultural texts of all kinds as well as audio-visual translation, comics, drama and videogames.

With over 30 chapters, the *Handbook* highlights commonalities and differences across the various contexts, encouraging comparative approaches to the topic of translation and censorship. Edited and authored by leading figures in the field of Translation Studies, the chapters provide a critical mapping of the current research and suggest future directions.

With an introductory chapter by the editors on theorizing censorship, the *Handbook* is an essential reference and resource for advanced students, scholars and researchers in translation studies, comparative literature and related fields.

Denise Merkle is a professor of translation at the Université de Moncton, Canada. She has published broadly on translation and censorship, minority and translation, and the translating subject, as well as (co-)editing collected volumes and journal issues. She is a member of the editorial committee of the journal *TTR: Traduction, Terminologie, Rédaction*.

Brian James Baer is Professor of Russian and Translation Studies at Kent State University. He is founding editor of the journal *Translation and Interpreting Studies*, and co-editor of the Bloomsbury book series Literatures, Cultures, Translation and of the Routledge book series Translation Studies in Translation. He is current president of the American Translation and Interpreting Studies Association and sits on the international advisory board of the Mona Baker Centre for Translation Studies at Shanghai International Studies University and of the Nida Centre for Advanced Study of Translation in Rimini, Italy.

ROUTLEDGE HANDBOOKS IN TRANSLATION AND INTERPRETING STUDIES

Routledge Handbooks in Translation and Interpreting Studies provide comprehensive overviews of the key topics in translation and interpreting studies. All entries for the handbooks are specially commissioned and written by leading scholars in the field. Clear, accessible and carefully edited, Routledge Handbooks in Translation and Interpreting Studies are the ideal resource for both advanced undergraduates and postgraduate students.

THE ROUTLEDGE HANDBOOK OF TRANSLATION AND SEXUALITY
Edited by Brian James Baer and Serena Bassi

THE ROUTLEDGE HANDBOOK OF CORPUS TRANSLATION STUDIES
Edited by Defeng Li and John Corbett

THE ROUTLEDGE HANDBOOK OF INTERPRETING AND COGNITION
Edited by Christopher D. Mellinger

THE ROUTLEDGE HANDBOOK OF TRANSLATION AND SOCIOLOGY
Edited by Sergey Tyulenev and Wenyan Luo

THE ROUTLEDGE HANDBOOK OF CHINESE INTERPRETING
Edited by Riccardo Moratto and Cheng Zhan

THE ROUTLEDGE HANDBOOK OF TRANSLATION AND CENSORSHIP
Edited by Denise Merkle and Brian James Baer

For a full list of titles in this series, please visit www.routledge.com/Routledge-Handbooks-in-Translation-and-Interpreting-Studies/book-series/RHTI

THE ROUTLEDGE HANDBOOK OF TRANSLATION AND CENSORSHIP

Edited by Denise Merkle and Brian James Baer

LONDON AND NEW YORK

Designed cover image: corradobarattaphotos

First published 2025
by Routledge
4 Park Square, Milton Park, Abingdon, Oxon OX14 4RN

and by Routledge
605 Third Avenue, New York, NY 10158

Routledge is an imprint of the Taylor & Francis Group, an informa business

© 2025 selection and editorial matter, Denise Merkle and Brian James Baer;
individual chapters, the contributors

The right of Denise Merkle and Brian James Baer to be identified as the authors of the
editorial material, and of the authors for their individual chapters, has been asserted in
accordance with sections 77 and 78 of the Copyright, Designs and Patents Act 1988.

All rights reserved. No part of this book may be reprinted or reproduced or utilised
in any form or by any electronic, mechanical or other means, now known or
hereafter invented, including photocopying and recording, or in any information
storage or retrieval system, without permission in writing from the publishers.

Trademark notice: Product or corporate names may be trademarks or registered trademarks
and are used only for identification and explanation without intent to infringe.

British Library Cataloguing-in-Publication Data
A catalogue record for this book is available from the British Library

ISBN: 9780367711245 (hbk)
ISBN: 9780367711276 (pbk)
ISBN: 9781003149453 (ebk)

DOI: 10.4324/9781003149453

Typeset in Times New Roman
by Newgen Publishing UK

To Denise Merkle, dedicated teacher, passionate scholar, tireless advocate, and devoted colleague and friend.

CONTENTS

List of Contributors — xi

Introduction: Theorizing Translation and Censorship — 1
Brian James Baer and Denise Merkle

PART I
Illiberal and Religious Contexts — **11**

1 Translation and Censorship in the Arab World and Its Diasporas — 13
Abdel-Wahab Khalifa and Salah Basalamah

2 Suppression and Defiance: Translation and Censorship in Germany — 37
Elisabeth Gibbels

3 Censorship in Modern Iran — 49
Arezou Dadvar

4 Censorship in Russia: Tsarist, Soviet and Post-Soviet Contexts — 64
Natalia Kamovnikova

5 Censorship of Translated Books in Turkey: An Overview — 80
İrem Konca

Contents

PART II
Colonial and Postcolonial Contexts   **93**

6 Cold War Politics in East Africa: Between Translation and Censorship   95
Alamin Mazrui

7 Translation and Censorship in the History of Estonia: Multilingualism, Linguistic Hierarchies and Centres of Power   109
Daniele Monticelli

8 Censorship and Translation in Hispanic South America: The First Translation of the Declaration of the Rights of Man and of the Citizen   126
Álvaro Echeverri

9 Censorship of Translations in Latvia: A Historical Perspective   139
Andrejs Veisbergs

10 Censorship and Translation of Slovene Texts in the Habsburg Monarchy and the Kingdom of Yugoslavia   154
Nike K. Pokorn

11 Translation and Censorship in Ukraine under Russian and Austrian Rule, 1800–1917   165
Oleksandr Kalnychenko and Lada Kolomiyets

PART III
Communist/Socialist Contexts   **177**

12 Censorship and Translation in China   179
Tan Zaixi

13 Censorship in Disguise: The Multiple Layers of Censorship of Literary Works in the GDR   192
Hanna Blum

14 Communist Censorship in Hungary and Beyond   207
Zsófia Gombár

15 Institutional Censorship and Literary Translation in Communist Poland, 1945–1958   222
Kamila Budrowska and Beata Piecychna

Contents

16 Translation and Censorship in Soviet and Independent Ukraine   243
    Lada Kolomiyets and Oleksandr Kalnychenko

17 Translation and Censorship in Romania   261
    Rodica Dimitriu

18 Censorship under Communism in Socialist Slovenia   279
    Nike K. Pokorn

PART IV
Democratic Capitalist Contexts   **289**

19 Censorship and Ideological Manipulation in Intralingual Literary Translation   291
    Manuel Moreno Tovar

20 Censorship and Language Policy: The Case of Canada and Québec   306
    Denise Merkle

21 Market Censorship and Translation   320
    Michelle Woods

22 Translation and Censorship in Wartime: The Case of Canada and the
    United States of America   336
    Denise Merkle and Brian James Baer

PART V
Fascist Contexts   **351**

23 Translating the Enemy in Fascist Italy: The Anthology *Americana*   353
    Christopher Rundle

24 The Censorship of Translations and Foreign Books during the
    Portuguese Dictatorship (1934–1974)   371
    Teresa Seruya

25 Censorship and Performed Translated Drama in Portugal during the
    Estado Novo (1950–1970)   384
    Manuela Carvalho

26 Translation and Censorship in Spain: Focus on Francoism   399
    Maria del Carmen Camus Camus and Cristina Gómez Castro

Contents

27 Censoring Sexuality in Translation: An Overview of Research on Spain (English–Spanish)
José Santaemilia
413

28 Censoring Women's Writing in Translation in Franco's Spain: A View from the Archive
Gora Zaragoza Ninet
432

PART VI
Genre- and Mode-specific Contexts
453

29 Religious Texts, Translation, and Censorship
Jacobus A. Naudé and Cynthia L. Miller-Naudé
455

30 On Translation and Censorship of Children's Literature during the Cold War in Europe
Eliisa Pitkäsalo and Riitta Oittinen
475

31 The Censorship of Comics in Translation: The Case of Disney Comics
Federico Zanettin
489

32 Censorship in Video Game Localisation
Ugo Ellefsen
505

Index
519

CONTRIBUTORS

Brian James Baer is Professor of Russian and Translation Studies at Kent State University. He is founding editor of the journal *Translation and Interpreting Studies*, and co-editor of the Bloomsbury book series Literatures, Cultures, Translation and of the Routledge book series Translation Studies in Translation. He is current president of the American Translation and Interpreting Studies Association and sits on the international advisory board of the Mona Baker Centre for Translation Studies at Shanghai International Studies University and of the Nida Centre for Advanced Study of Translation in Rimini, Italy.

Salah Basalamah is now Chair and Full Professor at the School of Translation and Interpretation, University of Ottawa. His fields of research include the Philosophy of Translation, Translation Rights, Social and Political Philosophy, Postcolonial, Cultural and Religious Studies, as well as Western Islam and Muslims. He is the author of *Le droit de traduire. Une politique culturelle pour la mondialisation* [The Right to Translate. A Cultural Policy for Globalization] (2009) at the University of Ottawa Press. Since 2014, he teaches a multidisciplinary PhD seminar on the diversity of Canadian Muslims at the Institute of Canadian and Aboriginal Studies (ICAS) at the University of Ottawa. He is also a member of the Eco-Translation Network (Edinburgh, Scotland) and of the Nida Center for Advanced Research on Translation (Rimini, Italy). He has two forthcoming books: *A Bergsonian Approach to Translation and Time: Toward Spiritual Translation Studies* (Routledge 2024) and an edited book Translating Modernity (Palgrave Macmillan 2025). For more details, please visit www.basalamah.org.

Hanna Blum is a lecturer at the Department of Translation Studies in Graz. Her main research areas are the translation culture of the GDR, with a focus on 'alltagsgeschichte' of translators and interpreters in East Germany, which was also the topic of her PhD thesis, and postcolonial translation studies.

Kamila Budrowska is a Polish and literary scholar; head of the Department of Comparative Studies and Editing. She is interested in the relationship between Polish literature and politics, with a particular focus on the tasks of censorship. Author of books: *Writers, Literature and Censorship*

Contributors

in Poland. 1948–1958 (translated by P.A. Vickers, Berlin 2020), and numerous articles. She is the scientific editor of the series 'Philological Research on PRL Censorship' and co-editor of the series 'Censorship in the People's Republic of Poland. Archives.' A visiting scholar at the Columbia University of New York (2019) and University of Regensburg (2022).

Maria del Carmen Camus Camus is a senior lecturer at the Universidad de Cantabria (Spain). Her research focuses on the incidence of Franco's censorship in the translations into Spanish in narrative and film. She has published widely on translation and ideology in the context of Franco's dictatorship and has co-authored two volumes on the censorship of gender in translation.

Manuela Carvalho is an assistant Professor in the Department of Portuguese at the University of Macau. Previously, she was a research fellow at the Centre for Comparative Studies at the University of Lisbon, where she led a funded research project on theatre and translation in Portugal. Her main research areas lie within the field of comparative literature, with a particular emphasis on theatre translation and studies in intermediality.

Cristina Gómez Castro is an associate Professor at the University of León (Spain) and co-leader of the TRACE (translation and censorship) research team. Her areas of interest are DTS, (re) translation and censorship, narrative translation and the audiovisual material related to it. She has contributed to international journals and to scholarly volumes.

Arezou Dadvar is associate member of CLESTHIA laboratory at Sorbonne Nouvelle and Persian translator and interpreter for the public service in France. She completed her PhD at Sorbonne Nouvelle University in Translation Studies and was assistant professor of Cultures and societies in Eurasia at the Institut National des Langues et Civilisations Orientales.

Rodica Dimitriu is Professor of Translation Studies at 'Alexandru Ioan Cuza' University of Iași, Romania. Her main research interests include the cultural, ideological and linguistic directions in Translation Studies, as well as literary translation and translator training, but she has also published and edited books and articles in the fields of British literature and ELT. She also coordinates the 'Translation Studies' series at the Institutul European publishing house in Iasi, Romania. Rodica Dimitriu has also coordinated and taken part in several European and Canadian projects devoted to research in Translation Studies or innovative techniques in translator training.

Álvaro Echeverri is assistant Professor in the Department of Linguistics and Translation at the Université de Montréal. His research interests include translation pedagogy, the history of translation in Latin America and translations of translatological texts in English, Spanish and French. He has published several articles in journals such as *TTR*, *Perspectives* and *Meta*.

Ugo Ellefsen is a PhD candidate in the Humanities interdisciplinary program at Concordia University. He teaches translation and translation technology at Concordia University, Université de Montréal, Université du Québec en Outaouais and York University. His research focusses on video game localization and the interplay between games and broader cultural contexts.

Contributors

Elisabeth Gibbels teaches at Humboldt University Berlin, Department for English and American Studies. Her main research interests have been gender, censorship and power. Recent work has focussed on the history of women's translation in Germany.

Zsófia Gombár is the Principal Investigator of the Research Group on Reception and Translation Studies at the University of Lisbon Centre for English Studies (ULICES), where she coordinates the FCT-funded project 'Remembering the Past, Learning for the Future: Research-Based Digital Learning from Testimonies of Survivors and Rescuers of the Holocaust' and leads the University of Lisbon team in the EU-funded project DECONSTRUCT: Digital Education and Campaign to Stand up and Counter Holocaust Distortion and Misinformation. She is also the coordinator of the project 'Intercultural Literature in Portugal (1930-2000): A Critical Bibliography (CECC/ULICES)' with Teresa Seruya and Maria Lin Moniz, and was the initiator and Principal Investigator of the Hungarian research project 'The Reception of English-Language Literature in Hungary, 1945–1989', housed at Savaria University Centre of Eötvös Loránd University. Her primary research areas include censorship studies, translation history and Holocaust education.

Oleksandr Kalnychenko is Associate Professor in Translation Studies of Mykola Lukash Translation Studies Department at V.N. Karazin Kharkiv National University, Ukraine and Researcher of the Slavic Languages Department at Matej Bel University in Banska Bystrica, Slovakia. He edited the re-publication of the works of Oleksandr Finkel, Volodymyr Derzhavyn, Mykola Lukash and Hryhorii Maifet and compiled an Anthology of Ukrainian Translation Thinking of the 1920s-early 1930s. He is a co-editor of the Ukrainian version of John Benjamins' *Handbook of Translation Studies* online and in print.

Natalia Kamovnikova, PhD, is an independent researcher. For over twenty years, she taught translation studies, literature and consecutive and simultaneous interpreting at universities in Russia and the EU. She was a research fellow at Ghent University in 2018 and at the Austrian Academy of Sciences in 2024. Her research is focused on literary translation in the contexts of sur-veillance, censorship, and threat to life. She is the author of the research monograph *Made under Pressure: Literary Translation in the Soviet Union, 1960–1991*, over sixty published academic papers, two manuals on conference interpreting, and an original novel. Natalia is also a practising conference interpreter and translator.

Abdel-Wahab Khalifa is a Senior Lecturer (Associate Professor) in Translation and Interpreting at Queen's University Belfast, with nearly two decades of academic and professional experi-ence. Khalifa holds a double-major PhD in Translation Studies and Arabic from the University of Leeds, focusing on the social history and challenges of publishing Arabic literature translated into English. His research interests encompass a diverse range of topics, including the socio-cultural and historical dimensions of translation and interpreting practices, as well as the role of translation in fostering cultural diplomacy and exchange. Khalifa has delivered invited talks and keynote speeches globally, including appearances at major book fairs such as Frankfurt, London, Thessaloniki, and Abu Dhabi. He has served on the Scientific Committees of various events, including the upcoming EST 2025 Conference, and Advisory Boards for organisations and publications, such as the forthcoming *Routledge Handbook of the Translation Industry*. A Harry Ransom Fellow in the Humanities, he is an executive board member of the Association for Translation Studies in Africa (ATSA) and the IATIS Regional Workshop Committee, and serves on the Editorial Board of *The Translator* and Advisory Boards of several journals, including *Tanwīr*.

Contributors

Lada Kolomiyets is Professor of Translation Studies at the Taras Shevchenko National University of Kyiv and Visiting Professor at Dartmouth College, USA. Former Fulbright Scholar at the U of Iowa and Pennsylvania State U, she is author of several monographs, including *Ukrainian Literary Translation and Translators in the 1920s–1930s* (2013, 2nd expanded ed. 2015), textbooks for graduate students, and is a Scopus author and contributor to collective volumes on translation. Her research is focused on the history and theory of translation and censorship in Ukraine and Eastern Europe and decolonization.

İrem Konca is Assistant Professor of Translation Studies at Bahçeşehir University, Turkey. She received her MA from Boğaziçi University, Department of Translation and Interpreting Studies (2010) and her PhD from KU Leuven, Belgium, Department of Translation and Intercultural Transfer (2022). She was a full-time lecturer at Marmara University and has taught part-time in the Department of Translation Studies at Boğaziçi and Yeditepe Universities. Her research interests include translation history, ideology and censorship in translation and retranslation.

Alamin Mazrui is Professor of sociolinguistics, literature, and comparative cultural studies in the Department of African, Middle Eastern, and South Asian Languages and Literatures at Rutgers University, New Brunswick, New Jersey, USA. He has a special interest in human rights and civil liberties and has written policy reports on these subjects. In addition to his many scholarly publications, Alamin Mazrui is a published Swahili poet and playwright.

Denise Merkle is a professor of translation at the Université de Moncton, Canada. She has published broadly on translation and censorship, minority and translation and the translating subject, as well as (co-)editing collected volumes and journal issues. She is a member of the editorial committee of the journal *TTR – translation, terminology and (w)riting*.

Cynthia L. Miller-Naudé is a senior professor at the University of the Free State, Bloemfontein, South Africa. Her research focuses on pre-modern Hebrew linguistics, the syntax of Shilluk and Bible translation. Since 1992, she has served as translation consultant for Bible translation projects in Sudan, including the Dinka Cam. She co-edits the series Linguistic Studies in Ancient West Semitic (PSU Press) and serves on the editorial boards of *The Bible Translator* and the *Journal for Northwest Semitic Languages*. She formerly served on the Committee on Translation Principles (United Bible Societies) and the Committee on Translation and Scholarship (American Bible Society).

Daniele Monticelli is Professor of Semiotics and Translation Studies at Tallinn University, Estonia. He is co-founder of the History and Translation Network (historyandtranslation.net) and coordinates the Estonian Research Council's grant Translation in History, Estonia 1850–2010: Texts, Agents, Institutions and Practices. He is co-editor of *Between Cultures and Texts: Itineraries in Translation History* (2011), *Translation under Communism* (2022) and *The Rouledge Handbook of the History of Translation Studies* (2024).

Manuel Moreno Tovar is a Doctoral Researcher at the University of Tartu (Estonia). In his project, he reexamines the Jakobsonian concept of intralingual translation and its interface with censorship and manipulation. He works as a translator for the Directorate-General of Translation of the European Commission.

Contributors

Jacobus A. Naudé is a senior professor at the University of the Free State, Bloemfontein, South Africa. His research focuses on pre-modern Hebrew linguistics and religious translation. He co-authored *A Biblical Hebrew Reference Grammar* (Bloomsbury). He co-edits the series Linguistic Studies in Ancient West Semitic (PSU Press) and serves on the advisory boards of *The Bible Translator, Handbook of Translation Studies, Handbook of Terminology, Journal of Northwest Semitic Languages* and National Association of Professors of Hebrew. He served on the translation team of the 2020 Afrikaans Bible translation and as translation consultant for the Dinka Cam Bible (South Sudan, 2024).

Riitta Oittinen holds the title of Docent at the Universities of Tampere and Helsinki, Finland. Her research includes topics such as the verbal and the visual in translating for children, Bakhtin's philosophy, dialogics, multimodality and intervisual translation. Oittinen is a productive artist and has created full illustrations of Carroll's two Alice books.

Beata Piecychna is Assistant Professor at the Faculty of Philology, the University of Bialystok (Poland). She has published papers on translational hermeneutics, philosophy of language, translation pedagogy and cognitive translatology. Her research interests include: philosophical hermeneutics, the hermeneutics of translation, translation theory and embodied aesthetics. Visiting scholar at the University of Cambridge (2019) and University of California in San Diego (2020).

Eliisa Pitkäsalo works as a senior lecturer and a researcher of Translation Studies at Tampere University, Finland and holds the title of Docent at the University of Turku. Her research includes topics such as translating multimodal texts, intersemiotic translation and the interaction between word and image in comics and picture books.

Nike K. Pokorn is Professor of Translation Studies and Chair of English in the Department of Translation Studies at the University of Ljubljana. Her research interests include translation history, directionality in translation and community and healthcare interpreting. She is the author of *Challenging the Traditional Axioms* (Benjamins 2005) and *Post-Socialist Translation Practices* (Benjamins 2012), co-editor with Kaisa Koskinen of *The Routledge Handbook of Translation and Ethics* (2021) and the general editor of the first comprehensive Slovene history of literary translation (*Zgodovina slovenskega literarnega prevoda* 2023).

Christopher Rundle is Professor of Translation Studies at the University of Bologna, Italy; and Research Fellow at the University of Manchester, UK. He is co-editor of the book series Routledge Research on Translation and Interpreting History and co-editor of the journal *inTRAlinea* (www. intralinea.org). He is co-founder of the History and Translation Network (historyandtranslation. net).

José Santaemilia is Full Professor of English at the Universitat de València. His research focuses on gender/sexuality and discourse studies, particularly on the media representation of gender (in) equality through critical discourse analysis and corpus tools. He has also explored topics related to the intersection between gender/sexuality and translation. His work has been published in journals such as the *Journal of the Sociology of Language, Teanga* (The Irish Yearbook of Applied Linguistics), *TTR* (translation, terminology, (w)riting), *Gender and Language, Women's Studies International Forum, Babel, MONTI, Atlantis, TRANS* (Spanish Journal of Translation Studies), *Quaderns* (Journal of Translation), *Spanish Journal of Applied Linguistics* (RESLA), *Perspectives* and others. Some of the publishers where he has chapters: St Jerome Publishing, Multilingual Matters, Routledge, Springer, John Benjamins Publishing, Oxford University Press, Palgrave Macmillan, among others.

Teresa Seruya, a Full Professor (retired since February, 2017) in the Department of Germanic Studies at the Faculty of Letters of the University of Lisbon, teaching German and Austrian literature and culture, history of translation and translation theory, translation methodologies and intercultural communication. She has collaborated with the Catholic University of Portugal. She is responsible (together with M. Lin Moniz and Zsofia Gombár) for the ongoing research project 'Intercultural Literature in Portugal 1930–2000: a Critical Bibliography' within the CECC (Centre for the Study of Communication and Culture), Catholic University of Portugal. She has published on contemporary German literature, migration literature, the history of translation in Portugal, translation and censorship. She is also a literary translator of the following German authors: Goethe, Kleist, Leopold von Sacher-Masoch, Döblin, Thomas Mann, Kafka and, more recently, Arthur Koestler.

Tan Zaixi is a Professor Emeritus of Hong Kong Baptist University, China. He obtained his BA from Hunan Normal University (China), and his master's and doctoral degrees from the University of Exeter (UK). His specialist interests: translation theory, literary translation, cultural politics of translation, translation history.

Andrejs Veisbergs is a Professor of the University of Latvia. His research publications since 1985 amount to more than 430, mainly on Translation and Interpreting, Idioms, Borrowing, Latvian, Language Policies, Language Contacts and Lexicography. He is the author of ten monographs and the biggest Latvian-English Dictionary (1997, Second edition 2005, Third edition 2016, Tilde electronic version 2021). Apart from academic activities he is also the EU accredited interpreter working for various EU institutions and agencies as well as for many high-level one-off occasions.

Michelle Woods is Professor of English at SUNY New Paltz. She is the author of *Kafka Translated* (2014), *Censoring Translation* (2012), and *Translating Milan Kundera* (2006). She is the co-editor of *Teaching Literature in Translation* (2023) and editor of *Authorizing Translation* (2017). Her translations have appeared in *Granta* and *Words Without Borders*.

Federico Zanettin is Full Professor of English Language, Translation and Linguistics at the University of Venezia – Ca' Foscari, Department of Linguistics and Comparative Cultural Studies. He investigates translation-related issues with a focus on methodology, and his interests range from news translation to the translation of comics and corpus-based translation studies. His publications include *Corpora in Translator Education* (St. Jerome 2003, editor, with Silvia Bernardini and Dominic Stewart), *Comics in Translation* (St. Jerome 2008/Routledge 2014, editor), *Translation-driven corpora* (St. Jerome 2012/Routledge 2014), *Communication Skills for International Studies* (Morlacchi 2013), *New Directions in Corpus-Based Translation Studies* (Language Science Press 2015, editor, with Claudio Fantinuoli), *News Media Translation* (Cambridge University Press, 2021) and *The Routledge Handbook of Translation and Methodology* (Routledge 2022, editor, with Chris Rundle). He is co-editor of the journal *inTRAlinea* and serves in the advisory board of The Translator, Translang and Entreculturas.

Contributors

Gora Zaragoza Ninet is an Associate Professor in the Department of English and German, at the University of Valencia (Spain). Her research focuses on feminist translation, and translation and censorship (and reception) of 20th century British women novelists. She has contributed to national and international conferences and published extensively. She has been a guest scholar in leading universities and has coordinated research projects in the field of gender, translation, and censorship. She has recently authored *Traducción y censura de las escritoras ganadoras del Femina Vie Heureuse inglés*, Dykinson, 2023.

INTRODUCTION

Theorizing Translation and Censorship

Brian James Baer and Denise Merkle

In terms of theorizing censorship, there are two general historico-philosophical approaches, which may be designated as pre-Foucauldian and post-Foucauldian. According to the former, censorship is construed as banning access to an entire work or a portion of a work typically with the purpose of protecting public morality or the political status quo. This accords with the American Library Association's definition of censorship as a 'change in the access status of material, based on the content of the work and made by a governing authority or its representatives. Such changes include exclusion, restriction, removal, or age/grade level changes' (ALA 2016). According to this model, censorship is typically divided into a pre-production and a post-production phase: 'Censorship refers broadly to the suppression of information in the form of self-censorship, boycotting or official state censorship before the utterance occurs (preventive or prior censorship) or to punishment for having disseminated a message (post-censorship, negative or repressive censorship)' (Merkle 2002: 9).

According to this conceptualization, censorship is basically an ex post facto phenomenon, imposed on an already formulated thought or completed work, typically by a governing authority. Within this model, one can distinguish among the various mechanisms imposed to restrict access. At a macro-level, the banning of a work can take place covertly—e.g., refusal to publish or translate a work or the surreptitious removal of a work from circulation—or overtly, such as book burnings, which Berkowitz (2021: 9) describes as 'spectacles of power'. On a micro-level, offending or suspicious passages might be blacked out or cut out; the former, referred to in French as *le masque noir* and in Russia as *caviar*, was considered a more advanced form of censorship in that it was restricted to the specific passage. Cutting out a passage, on the contrary, also removed the text on the reverse side of the page, resulting in 'wanton destruction of newsprint' (Skipton and Michelove 1989: 140).

Even banning, however, did not necessarily remove a work from circulation, as 'books that were banned as books found their way into Russia "serialized" in periodicals, and vice versa' (Monas 1961: 194). It was also the case that bans were not always absolute or complete, as a select number of copies might be preserved in special collections for consultation purposes. For example, when Louis-Sébastien Mercier's 1771 novel *L'an 2440: rêve s'il en fut jamais* [The Year 2440: A Dream if Ever There Was One] was placed on the Spanish Index in 1790, it was

DOI: 10.4324/9781003149453-1

The Routledge Handbook of Translation and Censorship

'with a thoughtful caveat, allowing for preservation of consultation copies in the royal library at Madrid' (Vose 2022: 179). In the Soviet Union, some copies of banned books might be kept in *spetskhrany*, access to which was restricted to Party officials or approved researchers. Banned books might also circulate in *samizdat*, a Soviet-era term referring to self-published versions that circulated outside official modes of distribution, and *tamizdat*, referring to editions published abroad. One of the most famous examples of the latter was the publication in Italy of Boris Pasternak's novel *Doctor Zhivago*, which had been banned in the Soviet Union (see Finn and Couvée 2014). It should also be noted that overt bans may have the paradoxical effect of bringing attention to a work, lending it the aura of forbidden fruit and inspiring efforts to make it available through unofficial channels.

While censorship as denial of access has been widely investigated as it relates to age restrictions, as well as restrictions based on gender and social class, only recently has it been studied through the lens of race. Of course, in the United States, the denial of literacy to Black slaves was one way of denying access to written works altogether, but in the Jim Crow era access to books and periodicals was regulated through the library system, which was shaped by racial segregation. For example, some community leaders in Southern towns and cities refused the offer of a Carnegie library—a public library building funded by the industrialist turned philanthropist Andrew Carnegie—because they believed it would require that Blacks be given access (Wiegand 2015). In addition, periodicals produced by and for African and Hispanic communities were often restricted from libraries because they were not included in the *Readers' Guide to Periodical Literature*, produced by the H.W. Wilson Company. Its index of periodicals was typically used by public libraries when selecting their subscriptions (Wiegand 2015). As Steele (2020: 8, fn 2) comments, 'While the segregation of libraries might not be considered censorship by all definitions, it does involve the exclusion of information from people of particular races. Under the American Library Association's definition of censorship (ALA 2016), exclusion is considered to be a form of censorship.'

The study of such forms of restrictive censorship, i.e., forms of censorship that are not carried out by the state, or what Althusser referred to as repressive state apparatuses, but are distributed throughout the social order, or what Althusser referred to as ideological state apparatuses (Althusser 2001), overlaps with what can be described as post-Foucauldian approaches to censorship, referred to by some as New Censorship Theory (see Bunn 2015). According to these approaches, censorship is an integral feature of every discursive field, a manifestation of its distinct distribution and institutionalization of knowledge/power. Among post-Foucauldian approaches, one can include, in addition to the work of Foucault himself, Rancière's notion of consensus, which defines what is sayable in a given society at a given moment (Rancière 2010: 69). Along these lines, censorship refers to 'implicit operations of power that rule out in unspoken ways what will remain unspeakable', functioning through norms that structure and frame the very field of speech (Butler 1997: 130, 140). In this respect, censorship is not an ex post facto phenomenon; rather, it shapes the possibility of speech, resulting, for example, in 'hegemonic non-translation' as 'the dominant (seldom consciously reflected) habitus of the Anglophone supremacist' (Baumgarten 2016: 119). In other words, censorship in this case is not understood as the non-translation of a work that risks offending the powers that be or standards of taste and decency; rather, the translation of works created outside the dominant epistemic regime is simply unimaginable.

Also central to this conceptualization of censorship is the phenomenon of productive censorship, a notion introduced by Foucault that refers to the production of texts under conditions of censorship, that is, texts conceived under with the fact of censorship in mind. Such texts may be designed to be resilient to censorship by cultivating an obscure or baroque style or textual ambiguity. It is interesting in this regard that in tsarist Russia, according to the Statute on Censorship

Introduction

of 9 July 1804, 'Authors (even foreign authors!) were supposed to get the benefit of the doubt in any passage admitting of two possible meanings (Article 21)' (Skipton and Michalove 1989: 141). This would not be the case with Soviet censorship following Stalin's consolidation of power, when the word censorship (*tsenzura*) was replaced in the statutes of 1931 by 'the more genteel, but much more all-embracing, term *kontrol*' (Dewhirst 2002: 22).

That being said, the phenomenon of productive censorship flourished in the Soviet Union, as described by the poet and literary scholar Loseff in his monograph *On the Beneficence of Censorship* (Loseff 1984). Loseff argues that many authors negotiated censorship restrictions by cultivating Aesopian language, embedding in their texts both screens, meant to foreclose politically sensitive readings from the censor, and cues, meant to enable those readings for a select group of 'shrewd readers' (21). Filati (2018: 151) makes a similar point in regard to translation in Fascist Italy: 'Rather than a simple transfer from source to target language, the practice of translation within a "disciplinary mechanism" (Foucault 1977: 197) must of necessity constantly come up with new ways of camouflaging and reconstructing meaning, as the only means to circumvent control and avoid sanction'. Such work is also important in recognizing the active role of readers, something largely overlooked in the early literature on censorship. Recent, archival-based studies of censorship reveal that even in highly repressive regimes, censorship is often porous and negotiated—i.e., 'censorship is never a monolithic structure' (McLaughlin and Munos-Basols 2016: 4)—the effects of censorship are largely unpredictable, and often elaborate networks emerge to evade it.

Much of this general discussion of censorship applies equally to translated and non-translated material. There are distinctions, however, that should be made. First, many state censorship structures distinguish between foreign (imported) and domestic material. In tsarist Russia, for example, postal censorship of foreign correspondence fell under the jurisdiction of the Ministry of Foreign Affairs, while the censorship of domestic correspondence fell under the jurisdiction of the Ministry of Internal Affairs. The censorship of foreign correspondence required translators, who typically acted as censors. Indeed, the translators at the Polish Relay Department (Prikaz) were offended when the head of the Prikaz, the Dutchman Leontii Petrovich Merselius, marked some passages in letters for translation: 'This was insulting for the translators. They knew perfectly well what should be translated and what should not without his help' (Skipton and Michalove 1989: 27). Because the censorship of foreign correspondence, including periodicals, required a knowledge of foreign languages, translator-censors were initially foreign-born individuals and later highly educated Russians, which challenges the popular image of the censor as a narrow-minded *apparatchik*. Indeed, the nineteenth-century lyric poet Fyodor Tiutchev served many years as chief censor at the Ministry of Foreign Affairs of the Russian empire. The journalist Masha Gessen (2005) recounts how her Jewish grandmothers, thanks to their knowledge of foreign languages, including Hebrew, were able to find much-needed employment, as censors, negotiating the ethical quandary of surviving as Jews in the Soviet Union.

An especially remarkable case is that of Alekandr Vasilievich Nikitenko (1804–1877). A well-educated serf in the household of Count Nikolai Sheremetov, Nikitenko was granted his freedom as a young adult and went on to become a literary scholar, a professor of Russian Philology at St. Petersburg University and an ordinary member of the St. Petersburg Academy of Sciences. In 1833, Nikitenko was appointed censor, where he earned a reputation for being relatively liberal. In fact, soon after his appointment, he was arrested and held in jail for eight days for having allowed the release of Victor Hugo's poem 'Enfant, si j'étais roi', translated into Russian by Mikhail Delariu. He was arrested again in 1842 and held for one day in jail for having permitted the publication of Pavel Efebovsk's novella *The Governess* (*Guvernantka* 1842), which mocked the German military police, the Feldjäger. He also argued for the transfer of the censorship agency to the Ministry of Education, but his efforts failed, and the agency was transferred instead to the Ministry of Internal Affairs, responsible for the police and state security. Nikitenko's three-volume diary, published between 1889–1892, has been translated into several foreign languages, but the Russian original was not reissued during the Soviet period.

Also unique to the censorship of translations is the practice of non-translation—i.e., leaving words or passages in the original language—as well as translation into a third language. With sexually explicit material, in particular, restricting access may be attempted through rendering the offending passage in a third language—in modern Europe, this was typically Latin, the language of the educated elite and of science, as it was meant to restrict access to segments of society, such as women, children and the working class, that were seen as more vulnerable to corruption. This was the strategy followed by Sir Richard Burton, who also included other foreign words in the paratextual material accompanying his translation of the *Thousand and One Nights and a Night* (1885), and by the editor Henry Bohn in his Extra Volumes series, dedicated to works that challenged Victorian morality more directly than the books in his Standard Library (O'Sullivan 2010). Additionally, Burton's *Arabian Nights* was initially sold privately, through subscription. Other, more ambivalent forms of restrictive censorship involve euphemism, partial excision and softening or toning down of obscene content. We can describe such forms as ambivalent for, as Reynolds points out, 'The trouble with euphemism is that it is always liable to be taken as innuendo' (Reynolds 2007: 188). In regard to the censorship of audiovisual products, a distinction is often made between dubbing, which may entirely block access to the original language, and subtitling, which leaves the original untouched. The former is, of course, considered more effective in terms of censorship and, indeed, as Dwyer and Uricaru (2009) have shown, subtitling offers opportunities for subversive retranslation that dubbing does not.

In other words, the censorship of translations involves multiple layers of filtration. As O'Sullivan (2009: 77) suggests, 'from the point of view of censorship translation can thus be shown to be more dangerous ground for the reader than so-called original writing because translation is always already mediated'. Indeed, overtly censored and translated texts are similarly double-voiced, as Holquist discusses in his introduction to a special issue of the journal PMLA on censorship:

> Censorship is inescapable as well as arbitrary. And so is an unsettling filiation between censorship and translation: for is it not the primordial undecidability of language as such, the heteroglossia feared by censors, that is also the source of the translator's anxiety? Are not all translations, like Fray de Leon's, acts of censorship in that they, too, are fated to readings performed between the lines? Both censorship and translation are strategies to control meaning that are unavoidably insufficient: the interlinearity characterizing both guarantees in each that something will-always-be left out. (Holquist 1994: 18)

More than something left out, however, both translated and censored texts, and perhaps especially censored translations, allude to the existence of societies with different mores and dispositions, conjuring what Yurchak (2006) refers to as 'imaginary elsewheres', hence the popularity of translated literature, despite censorial intervention, in repressive societies. As Nikitenko notes in his diary in regard to enlightenment efforts in early nineteenth century Russia, 'We also found readers for books such as the legal writings of Johann von Justi and *The Works of the Great and Wise Plato*, in the translation of Sidorovsky and Pakhamov. All of this, of course, did not lead to anything positive but, at least it provoked thought and introduced [readers] to ideas of a better order of things, or mores, customs and lifeways of peoples ahead of us in education' (Nikitenko 1893 (English edition 2002): 48).

Finally, a broad post-Foucauldian understanding of censorship might include the paratextual material accompanying a translation to the extent that it forecloses certain interpretations and enables others, in some cases allowing a work to be published. This is especially relevant for translations as so-called interpretive censorship may allow the text itself to remain more or less intact. This was the case with the poetry of Sappho and Michelangelo in the Soviet Union. The prefaces to those editions insisted that the poets were not queer, allowing the works to avoid radical textual manipulation or bowdlerization—in earlier times, the practice was to omit suspicious passages or replace pronouns in order to heterosexualise the relationships depicted in the poems. Scholarly introductions appear in some cases to have made possible the publication of sexually risqué works, such as Radclyffe Hall's *Well of Loneliness*, which included a short preface by the British sexologist Havelock Ellis—it was banned in Great Britain but was published in the US—and *The Adventurous History of Hsi Men and His Six Wives,* the English translation of the Chinese erotic classic *Chin P'ing Mei,* which included a lengthy introduction by the sinologist Arthur Waley (Qi 2021).

Another approach to the theorization of translation and censorship, which to some extent overlaps with Foucault's, is sociological. Wolf (2006: 10) explains that 'James Holmes' claim of 1972 that "[g]reater emphasis on [social contextualization of translation] could lead to the development of a field of *translation sociology*" (Holmes 1988/1972: 72, Wolf's emphasis), long went unheard.' Bourdieu's work (e.g., 1977, 1990, 1993) in particular contributed to the development of explicit sociological approaches to the study of translation and censorship early in the twenty-first century, starting with the questions: 'To what extent is the translator, as a product of social conditioning, free to choose?' given that 'the many guises of the control of discourse ["repression, morality, blockage, habitus, norms"] invariably implicate the translating subject and [their] reception of the same and the other within a given socio-historical context' (Merkle 2002: 17). Wolf (2006: 10) addresses translation 'as a "socially regulated activity"', whose 'agents participat[e] in and [are] controlled by social networks and shaped by social interactions'. The volume includes the section 'Ideological Pressures on the Production of Translation' that contains a number of chapters dealing with censorship. Wolf (2006) goes on to identify 'three sociologies of translation' (10): 'a sociology of the agents in the translation process', 'a sociology of the translation process' that 'stresses the constraints conditioning the production of translation' and 'a sociology of the cultural product' (11), which alludes to 'the forces responsible for the powerful struggles' in the literary field, a clear reference to Bourdieu's field theory (Bachleitner and Wolf 2004, in Wolf 2006: 11–2). Censorial pressures can therefore be exerted on agents involved in the translation process, during the translation process and on the translation products themselves.

The theoretical discourse on censorship, specifically structural censorship, is in fact notably influenced not only by Bourdieu's sociological theories, but also by Foucault's thought. In terms of sociological approaches to censorship, Foucault utilises the concept of the nineteenth-century Panopticon to illustrate how social structure can influence the communicative behaviour of its members, compelling them to conform to social norms and conventions through self-censorship. The Panopticon, initially conceived by Jeremy Bentham, is an architectural design employed in disciplinary institutions, such as schools, insane asylums, hospitals, factories and prisons, allowing those in charge to continuously observe 'inmates' without being seen, while the 'inmates' constantly surveille one another. The architectural structure instills in them the consciousness of being constantly under surveillance, leading to self-regulation of their behaviour, making external wardens unnecessary (Foucault 1977: 20–1). Foucault posits that this constant visibility 'assures the automatic functioning of power' in inmates. In structural censorship, society functions akin to a panoptic structure, creating an impression among its members that they are perpetually under scrutiny by others, compelling them to self-censor in alignment with dominant norms and conventions (Bourdieu 1977: 192). O'Sullivan (2010) has convincingly applied the 'third-person' effect hypothesis to Victorian publisher Bohn's preemptive self-censorship of classical Latin and Greek writings into English, pointing to Bohn's practice of leaving in the British translations Latin words and phrases, in particular, those that could arouse the ire of morality leagues if translated into English. Only the well-educated members of the society could read classical languages, which denied access to this knowledge to the less well-educated, those deemed to be the most susceptible to corruption.

Foucault's approach to knowledge/power (Foucault 1977) sees censorship as an everyday, socialised and embodied phenomenon, resulting from norms so deeply embedded as to be beyond our perception, causing us to discipline (i.e., self-censor) ourselves without external coercion. This, of course, can be likened to Bourdieu's concept of habitus, which can generally be counted upon to ensure the successful perpetuation of the social order through structural censorship, which compels compliance with social norms and conventions (Bourdieu 1990: 91). In other words, censorship does not originate only from state or religious institutions. Limitations on freedom of expression are not always caused by the direct intervention of the institutional authorities and their official agents of control using overt forms of control to silence contestatory voices. The very structure of every society itself as a dynamic organism can also serve as a major source of censorship. Embedded in the social structure of all communities are certain norms and conventions that put restrictions on what can be expressed and communicated. Although structural censorship is not a new phenomenon, it did not become a focus of attention in TS before the beginning of the twenty-first century, even though Bourdieu wrote about it decades earlier. One possible explanation for this delay, as Kuhiwczak (2011) asserts, is that after the fall of the Berlin Wall, there was so much new documentation available to researchers of easily detectable forms of institutional censorship exercised by different political regimes, e.g., Franco's Spain and the TRACE project's archival work, that it overshadowed the harder to identify forms of structural censorship. However, with the gradual change of the world's political climate and as freedom of expression is increasingly recognised as a universal right, a growing number of 'democratic' countries attempt to avoid overt and violent forms of censorship, making the way for the less visible forms of structural censorship to come to the fore (see, for example, Sapiro 2023).

That said, transgressing the social boundaries that restrict freedom of expression in certain fields, for example, may invite negative reactions from fellow members of the field, who may punish transgressors in various ways (Bourdieu 1977: 38.) Bourdieu (1993) explains that all discursive expression is the product of 'expressive interest' (37) in a given field and the censorship that results from the structure of the field. In other words, the control of discourse varies from one field to another. Yet, generally, discursive expression is the product of a conscious effort to euphemise, which can go as far as silencing, i.e., the limit of censored discourse. Silencing is violent. Bourdieu explains that the concept of 'symbolic violence', defined as a 'gentle, invisible form of violence [...] is never recognised as such, and is not so much undergone as chosen' (Bourdieu 1977: 192). It is perhaps the most insidious aspect of structural censorship insofar as it is 'exercised upon a social agent with his or her complicity' (Bourdieu 1993: 167).

Bourdieu's work on discursive fields underpins the 'new censorship,' particularly his attempt in *Language and Symbolic Power* (Bourdieu 1993: 37) to understand language as a product of the relationship between what he terms the 'linguistic habitus' and the 'linguistic market'. The first

Introduction

implies 'a certain propensity to speak and to say determinate things (the expressive interest) and a certain capacity to speak', referring to both language ability and social competence. The second category covers the 'structures of the linguistic market, which impose themselves as a system of specific sanctions and censorships' (Bourdieu 1993: 37). For Bourdieu, a discursive field has a logic of its own, which distinguishes those who work within it from those outside it. Those within the field control access to it by 'new' competent speakers—be it the literary field, the political field, the theatre field—and this process of initiation requires a '*de facto submission* to the values, hierarchies and censorship mechanisms inherent in the field' (Bourdieu 1993: 176; Bourdieu's emphasis). This is an effect of a field's structures of specialization, which alter the language otherwise available, especially through 'strategies of euphemisation that consist in imposing form as well as observing formalities' (Bourdieu 1993: 137). These structures work to exclude as well as include: to determine who can speak what can be spoken. For Bourdieu, a tension between 'the expressive interest' and censorship thus characterises all discourse.

In her case study of the impact on journalism of the Russian invasion of Crimea, Zeveleva (2020) explores the pertinence of Bourdieusian field theory to understanding how and when direct state censorship is imposed by an invader. She argues that direct state censorship occurs when the traditional field is destabilised and the state institutionalises new rules of the field or rules of the game (Bourdieu 1977) within the field. In the journalistic field in Crimea, after the Russian annexation in 2014, the Russian occupier sought to define new 'rules of the game' by institutionalising censorship through direct control and direct anti-press violence. By contrast, by 2017, Crimean journalists had become familiar with the 'rules of the game' after the dust had settled and they were able to work within the boundaries of what was allowed and sayable through their own strategic actions within the field. As a result, it became less necessary for the Russians to impose direct censorship. In other words, journalists adopted self-censorship when the field became more stable and they began to understand the rules. Zeveleva (2020) concludes that self-censorship is a sign of increased stability within the field. As a result, actors who have learned to understand the new 'rules of the game' within it begin to see the contours of what's possible.

In the Bourdieusian version of structural censorship, the structure of a doxic society leads its members to accept arbitrary social norms and conventions that restrict their communicative behaviour as natural realities; for example, the treatment of female health conditions in Victorian Britain. This naturalization of violence renders external surveillance and overt coercion generally unnecessary since individuals more or less willingly conform. Bourdieu deems this the most perfected form of censorship insofar as individuals are effectively self-censored through internalised forms of perception and expression, and external censorship becomes almost redundant:

> Censorship is never quite as perfect or as invisible as when each agent has nothing to say apart from what he is objectively authorized to say: in this case he does not have to be his own censor because he is, in a way, censored once and for all, through the forms of perception and expression that he has internalized and which impose their form on all his expressions.
>
> (Bourdieu 1993: 138)

The beliefs and actions of translators, among other members of the socio-political, cultural, intellectual and religious elites, along with their respective institutions have controlled access to domestic and foreign ideas, thoughts and values throughout history. Whether voluntary or imposed, control has taken various forms: pre-selection (and exclusion or blockage) of foreign texts, preventive or prior censorship, self-censorship (the result of successful prior censorship) and post-censorship (the failure of initial censorship). Definitions of censorship, therefore, refer not only to conceal-ment and manipulation, but also to exclusion (Cohen 2001: 8) and subversion (Merkle 2010: 109). Cohen (2001: 8) defines censorship as 'the exclusion of some discourse as a result of a judgment by an authoritative agent based on some ideological predisposition'. In addition to censorship legislation on obscenity and sedition, the most prevalent forms of control over discourse are silen-cing by a State, i.e., withdrawing the authority to use one's language (e.g., the reality experienced by many Indigenous groups during colonization) and refusing to translate (or interpret) whether by withdrawing funding or by adopting unilingual language policies. A 'judgment by an authori-tative agent' (Cohen 2001: 8) can be a decision taken by the Church, the government, community groups (e.g., morality leagues), publishers or translators. Their decisions may result in censorship or self-censorship. The decision to exclude a given discourse is based on an overt or internalised 'ideological predisposition.' When ideological predisposition is direct, overt and intentional, it can be identified; however, a 'subtle, systemic discursive process [also] shapes the very boundaries of what can be said' (Cohen 2001: 13), and that process, along with the ideological predisposition underpinning it, can be harder to identify (see Munday 2007: 1973). This subtle and systemic dis-cursive process falls under a broader, socio-discursive understanding of censorship, which is not limited to repressed versus free utterances but includes receivable versus unreceivable discourse (or sayable versus unsayable), in other words what is considered legitimate discourse versus what is considered illegitimate.

Organization of the Volume

The volume was structured so as to highlight a wide variety of systems of censorship in different societies and in different historical periods. We sought to avoid inherited Cold War binaries regarding censorship, which tend to associate the practice with overtly authoritarian societies, construing western democracies as open and free. Post-structural approaches to censorship make such an approach unthinkable on a theoretical level, while studies of market censorship, such as Michelle Woods's *Censoring Translation: Censorship, Theatre, and the Politics of Translation* (2012), reveal that the kind of censorship practised in modern western societies to make texts more appealing to target audiences or to sponsors may result in manipulations no less extensive or distorting than traditional 'political' censorship. We therefore included a section on censorship in democratic capitalist societies, which includes, in addition to a chapter on market censorship, a chapter on wartime censorship in Canada and the US, on censorship and language policy in Canada, and on censorship of intralingual literary works. We also sought to nuance and 'complexify' (see Marais and Meylaerts 2019) the traditional association of cen-sorship with authoritarian states by including sections on religious censorship, censorship in communist states, censorship under fascist regimes, and censorship according to mode or genre, such as comics, video games and children's literature, which are often created with international audiences in mind. Nonetheless, creating categories to describe the potentially endless variety of censorship practices was no easy task, and we readily admit these categories to be overlap-ping, incomplete and perhaps surprising. For example, we included a chapter on Russia's long history of censorship, both under the tsars and under Soviet rule, in the section on illiberal and religious contexts of censorship to underscore the fact that a rather elaborate system of censorship has been more or less a constant throughout Russia's history. As Jakobson notes, 'obtrusive and relentless censorship becomes an essential co-factor in Russian literary history' (1975: 50). By contrast, we included chapters on some countries, such as Slovenia and Ukraine, in two different sections, to underscore significant changes in censorship over the course of

Introduction

these nations' history. We do not, therefore, present this provisional typology as the last word on censorship but rather in the hope that it will initiate scholarly conversations on a topic that is arguably more relevant than ever.

References

Althusser, Louis. 2001. 'Ideology and Ideological State Apparatuses, in *Lenin and Philosophy and Other Essays*. Translated by Ben Brewster. New York: Monthly Review Press, 85–126.

American Library Association (ALA). 2016. 'Challenge Support'. Available at: www.ala.org/tools/challenge support.

Baumgarten, Stefan. 2016. 'The Crooked Timber of Self-reflexivity: Translation and Ideology in the End Times', *Perspectives*, 24(1):115–29.

Berkowitz, Eric. 2021. *Dangerous Ideas: A Brief History of Censorship in the West, from the Ancients to Fake News*. Boston: Beacon Press.

Bourdieu, Pierre. 1977. *Outline of a Theory of Practice*. Translated by Richard Nice. Cambridge and New York: Cambridge University Press.

Bourdieu, Pierre. 1993. *Language and Symbolic Power*. Translated by Gino Raymond and Matther Adamson. Cambridge (UK): Harvard University Press.

Bourdieu, Pierre. 1990. *The Logic of Practice*. Translated by Richard Nice. Cambridge: Polity Press.

Bunn, Matthew. 2015. 'Reimagining Repression: New Censorship Theory and after', *History and Theory*, 54 (February): 25–44.

Butler, Judith. 1997. *Excitable Speech: A Politics of the Performative*. New York: Routledge.

Cohen, Mark. 2001. *Censorship in Canadian Literature*. Montréal and Kingston: McGill-Queen's University Press.

Dewhirst, Martin. 2002. 'Censorship in Russia', in R. Fawn and S. White (eds.), *Russia after Communism, 1991 and 2001*. London: Frank Cass, 21–34.

Dwyer, Tessa and Uricaru, Ioana. 2009. 'Slashings and Subtitles: Romanian Media Piracy, Censorship, and Translation', *The Velvet Light Trap*, 63(Spring): 45–57.

Filati, Rita. 2018. 'Self-censorship under Fascism', *Alif: Journal of Comparative Poetics*, 38: 151–179. Self-Censorship and Fascism - Document - Gale Literature Resource Center.

Finn, Peter and Couvée, Petra. 2014. *The Zhivago Affair: The Kremlin, the CIA, and the Battle Over a Forbidden Book*. New York: Pantheon.

Foucault, Michel. 1977. *Discipline and Punishment: The Birth of the Prison*. Translated by Alan Sheridan. New York: Vintage Books.

Gessen, Masha. 2005. *Ester and Ruzya: How My Grandmothers Survived Hitler's War and Stalin's Peace*. New York: Dial Press.

Holmes, James. 1988. 'The Name and Nature of Translation Studies,' in *Translated! Papers on Literary Translation and Translation Studies*. Amsterdam: Rodopi, 66–80.

Holquist, Michael. 1994. '*Corrupt Originals*: The Paradox of Censorship', *PMLA*, 109(1): 14–25.

Jakobson, Roman. 1975. *Roman Jakobson, Puskin and His Sculptural Myth*. Translated by John Burbank. The Hague: Mouton.

Kuhiwczak, Piotr. 2011. 'Translation and Censorship,' *Translation Studies* 4(3): 358–366.

Loseff, Lev. 1984. *On the Beneficence of Censorship: Aesopian Language in Russian Literature*. Munich: Verlag Otto Sanger in Kommission.

Marais, Kobus and Meylaerts, Reine. 2019. *Complexity Thinking in Translation Studies: Methodological Considerations*. London and New York: Routledge.

McLaughlin, Martin and Munos-Basols, Javier. 2016. 'Introduction: Ideology, Censorship and Translation across Genres: Past and Present', *Perspectives: Studies in Translatology*, 24(1): 1–6.

Merkle, Denise. 2002. 'Presentation', *TTR*, 15(2): 9–18.

Merkle, Denise. 2010. 'Secret Literary Societies in Late Victorian England', in M. Tymoczko (ed.), *Translation, Resistance, Activism*. Amherst and Boston: University of Massachusetts Press, 108–28.

Monas, Sydney. 1961. *The Third Section: Police and Society under Nicholas I*. Cambridge, Massachusetts: Harvard University Press.

Munday, Jeremy. 2007. 'Translation and Ideology', *The Translator*, 13(2): 195–217.

Nikitenko, Aleksandr. 2002. *Up from Serfdom: My Childhood and Youth in Russia, 1804–1824*. Translated by Helen Saltz Jacobson. New Haven: Yale University Press.

O'Sullivan, Carol. 2009. 'Censoring These "Racy Morsels of the Vernacular": Loss and Gain in Translation of Apuleius and Catullus', in E. Ni Chuilleanáin, C. Ó Cuilleanáin and D. Parris (eds.), *Translation and Censorship: Patterns of Communication and Interference*. Dublin: Four Courts Press, 76–92.

O'Sullivan, Carol. 2010. 'Margin and the Third-Person Effect in Bohn's Extra Volumes', in D. Merkle, C. O'Sullivan, L. van Doorslaer and M. Wolf (eds.), *The Power of the Pen: Translation and Censorship in Nineteenth-century Europe*. Berlin and Vienna: Lit Verlag, 119–42.

Qi, Lintao. 2021. 'Translating Sexuality in the Context of Anglo-American Censorship: The Case of *Jin Ping Mei*', *Translation and Interpeting Studies*, 16(3): 416–33.

Rancière, Jacques. 2010. *Dissensus: On Politics and Aesthetics*. London: MPG Books Group.

Reynolds, Matthew. 2007. 'Semi-censorship in Dryden and Browning', in F. Billiani (ed.), *Modes of Censorship and Translation*. Manchester and Kinderhook: St. Jerome, 187–204.

Sapiro, Gisèle. 2023. *The Sociology of Literature*. Translated by Madeline Bedecarré and Ben Libman, Stanford: Stanford University Press.

Skipton, David M. and Michelove, Peter A. 1989. *Postal Censorship in Imperial Russia*. Volume I. Urbana, Illinois: John H. Otten.

Steele, Jennifer Elaine. 2020. 'A History of Censorship in the United States', *Journal of Intellectual Freedom and Privacy*, 5(1): 6–19.

Vose, Robin. 2022. *The Index of Prohibited Books: Four Centuries of Struggle over Word and Image for the Greater Glory of God*. London: Reaktion Books.

Wiegand, Wayne A. 2015. *Part of Our Lives: A People's History of the American Public Library*. New York: Oxford University Press.

Wolf, Michaela. 2006. 'Translating and Interpreting as a Social Practice – Introspection into a New Field', in M. Wolf (ed.), *Übersetzen – Translating – Traduire: Towards a 'Social Turn'?* Vienna and Berlin: Lit Verlag, 9–19.

Woods, Michelle. 2012. *Censoring Translation: Censorship, Theatre, and the Politics of Translation*. London and New York: Continuum.

Yurchak, Aleksei. 2006. *Everything Was Forever Until It Was No More*. Princeton and Oxford: Princeton University Press.

Zeveleva, Olga. 2020. 'Towards a Bourdieusian Sociology of Self-censorship: What We Can learn from Journalists Adapting to Rapid Political Change in Crimea after 2014', *European Journal of Communication*, 35(1): 46–59. https://doi.org/10.1177/0267323119897798.

PART I

Illiberal and Religious Contexts

1

TRANSLATION AND CENSORSHIP IN THE ARAB WORLD AND ITS DIASPORAS

Abdel-Wahab Khalifa and Salah Basalamah

1.1 Introduction and Definitions

1.1.1 Contextualising Translation and Censorship

Translation and censorship have a long and intricate history, with translation often being subjected to censorship by various agents. Translation, with its role in transferring ideas across linguistic and cultural boundaries, is particularly prone to censorial forces seeking to regulate the entry and circulation of foreign content and cultural products. As Merkle et al. (2010) argue, censorship can never be entirely removed from translatorial discourses or discourses about translation. This resonates with Wolf's (2002) assertion that censorship manifests to some degree in all translation practices.

Such interactions between translation and censorship do not occur in a vacuum—they are acts shaped by the socio-political realities and power dynamics of their environment. Meyer (2002: xi) argues that 'censorship may be most powerful when it is least palpable'. Nowhere is this more evident than in the Arab world, where translation has long been impacted by various forms of censorship. From state institutions to religious authorities, from political fervour to cultural concerns, multiple factors collude to regulate translated works circulating within Arab societies. These range from overt and covert government policies, unwritten social norms and even dictated and self-imposed censorship by translatorial agents, including translators themselves. Foreign (and local) cultural products (e.g., literature, films, advertisements and translations) that challenge the status quo or diverge from the predominant narratives run the risk of being sanitised, modified or even blocked outright. While certainly not absolute, this censorial spectre hovers above and permeates translation practices in several Arab countries, affecting content chosen for translation and how it is circulated.

This chapter aims to unveil the multifaceted ways in which censorship affects translations originating from, entering or circulating within the Arab world. Our discussion draws on diverse examples from various Arab nations and genres to highlight prevalent censorship trends. In today's globalised era, the definition of the 'Arab world' has become increasingly complex, as the boundaries demarcating this region become increasingly fluid. For instance, individuals of Arab heritage, like the authors of this chapter, may reside and work outside their ancestral lands yet

DOI: 10.4324/9781003149453-3

remain active contributors to Arabic literary and cultural discourses. Adding complexity, censorship systems vary across Arab countries, even though the majority implement stringent regulatory measures (Saiegh 1994). Despite these complexities, our primary emphasis is on the core issues of translation and censorship, with examples selected for their compelling representation of relevant overarching themes. While we recognise that the full spectrum of translation and censorship experiences in the Arab world is vast, this chapter offers a substantial critical overview, spotlighting dominant censorship trends prevalent throughout the Arab world and their implications for translation, highlighting the key characteristics of translation censorship common throughout the region across different nations, genres and languages. Additionally, we outline various potential research directions, aiming to inspire and encourage further research on the intersection of translation and censorship in the Arab world.

1.1.2   What is Censorship (in Arabic)?

In fields of cultural production, the definition of censorship varies. Many definitions posit that censorship entails suppressing views and ideas that challenge a society's predominant beliefs and norms or those that have the potential to undermine governing authority/ies or the social and ethical systems they uphold. *The Global Arabic Encyclopedia* ('Al-Riqābah' 1999, Vol. 11: 262) offers a more expansive definition, seeing it as a tool to 'control what people are allowed to say, hear, write, read, see or do'. The extent of censorship in a country often mirrors the level of freedom of expression allowed by its governing systems. While freedom of expression is pivotal, it must also have limits and not be absolute; in any society, everyone's rights should be honoured without compromising others. Limiting the production and/or dissemination of translated content that is pornographic, extremist or unsuitable for children could be seen as both desirable and essential. Censorship is not exclusive to autocratic or totalitarian regimes but extends to democratic societies which also implement forms of censorship, primarily based on leaders' convictions about the necessity of societal regulation. However, severe censorship of freedom of expression across all media forms, including translations, is most evident under autocratic regimes (Merkle 2018), in times of political instability (Bourdieu 1990), and conflict and war (Gouanvic 2002). In essence, censorship is the practice by which agents exert their authority to regulate, restrict or ban materials they consider unsuitable or harmful to their societies, people or interests, based on political, religious, moral or cultural considerations, encompassing various media, including all forms of translation. The nature and extent of censorship differ based on a region's laws and cultural norms, and while it often stands at odds with freedom of expression, it can also act as a bulwark for individual rights, public ethics and national security.

As far as translation studies is concerned, translation and censorship are deeply embedded in the socio-cultural and historical fabric of the societies in which they operate. There is no 'one-size-fits-all' approach to understanding translation and censorship. Each culture has its own unique and collective habitus, which shapes and is shaped by its own set of values, norms and historical experiences; the latter inevitably influence its perception and execution of these practices. Furthermore, as societies evolve, so do their cultural and societal norms and, consequently, their translatorial and censorial practices. Therefore, interpretations of translation and censorship are dynamic and can shift with the changing tides of time and societal evolution. Consider, for instance, the recent censorship threats to British editions of Roald Dahl's books, years after their first publication due to changes in socio-cultural norms (Diaz 2023; Taylor 2023). Recognising these distinctions is crucial for a holistic and objective understanding of translation practices and censorship dynamics across different cultural contexts. It is a reminder of the fluidity of cultural

Translation and Censorship in the Arab World and Its Diasporas

concepts and the importance of approaching them with nuance and an open mind. This nuanced understanding brings us to a pivotal point: defining 'censorship' in Arabic, which is key to contextualising and understanding censorial practices in the Arab world.

The Arabic language is renowned for its structured root letter system, where a set of three core letters often generates a series of interconnected words. The concept of 'censorship', represented by the word 'riqābah' (رِقَابَة), originates from the triliteral root 'r-q-b' (ر-ق-ب). From this root, we derive the verb 'raqaba' (رَقَّب) meaning to censor, warn, guard or wait; the noun 'raqbah' (رَقْبَة) which denotes the neck or the beginning of something, but also has several metaphorical connotations including responsibility, execution or setting free; 'taraqub' (تَرَقُّب) indicating waiting or anticipation; 'muraqābah' (مُرَاقَبَة) meaning monitoring or supervision; 'murāqib' (مُرَاقِب) which is an observer or controller; and 'raqīb' (رَقِيب) signifying a censor, guard or protector, with the latter also being one of the 99 names attributed to God in Islam. A collective definition capturing the essence of all the above derivatives related to censorship in Arabic could be: an act or state of vigilance, overseeing, monitoring or protecting, rooted in anticipation and a sense of guardianship or control, usually originating from a pivotal vantage or starting point. Through the derivatives of the word for censorship in Arabic, we discern that the concept intertwines both positive and negative connotations. Although the meaning of censorship in Arabic denotes prohibition, objection, rejection and intellectual property, it also encompasses guarding and protecting. This duality is explored further in the chapter.

Our understanding of censorship is not limited to the outright prohibition or banning of content. It can also manifest as the overwhelming promotion of certain cultural products, coupled with the dissemination of historical inaccuracies and misunderstandings, all of which serve to bolster a specific narrative or worldview. For example, when North African Arab countries such as Algeria, Morocco and Tunisia were colonised by the French, the government made concerted efforts to flood markets with specific French material, promoting, for instance, 'French over Arabic in education and the institutions of the state' (Suleiman 2019: 11). While some of this material was of good quality, much of it contained manipulative content that subtly endeavoured to undermine the prominence and relevance of Arabic content and identities (Asseraf 2019; Suleiman 2019). Beyond mere content manipulation, the French attempted to ban Arabic publications, and those who ventured to read such publications often found themselves under surveillance (Asseraf 2019). The French government rigorously controlled any information that opposed or questioned their official viewpoint (Stanton and Banham 1996). Opposition to imperialism was met with censorship, both within the colonies and back in metropolitan France, ensuring the perpetuation of a narrative that benefited the colonisers (Asseraf 2019). French censorship was an instrument deftly used to mould, if not outright enforce, a particular worldview and guide discourse production. This systematic suppression of Arabic perspectives and Arab identities was so thorough that speaking, reading and writing in French eventually became a mark of elite status, further alienating native peoples' voices and identities and marginalising their cultures and languages. We will investigate this issue deeper and reflect upon it critically later in this chapter (see the sections '*Core Issues*' and '*Future Directions*').

1.1.3 Mechanisms of Censorship in Translation

That censorship in translation impacts how cultural products are selected, translated, produced, published, circulated and received in different cultural contexts is indubitable. Wolf (2002) distinguishes between *institutional* and *preventive* censorship. While the former is premeditated and involves an official apparatus, the latter is tied closely to self-censorship and centred on the individual (e.g., translator, reviser, editor or publisher). Wolf emphasises that deeply ingrained preventive censorship obviates the need for institutional censorship.

Similarly, Merkle (2002) identifies two primary forms of censorship: *prior censorship*, which requires pre-publication vetting and approval, and *post-censorship*, which is reactive and punitive to already published material. Common in several Arab countries, prior censorship can manifest as what Stephen Greenblatt describes as 'cultural blockage', a form of censorship deemed essential for a culture to maintain its identity, affecting choices on what texts to translate and governing how they are produced and circulated (Greenblatt, as cited in Wolf 2002). Prior censorship extends to preventive measures and self-censorship. Before texts reach the public, they may undergo changes to adhere to specific norms, initiated by translators (or other translatorial agents like publishers or editors) to address personal reservations or anticipate potential issues, externally imposed by other (f)actors in the publication process. Conversely, post-censorship can lead to actions like boycotts, bans, or punitive consequences, such as fines, imprisonment or the threat thereof. For example, Madbouly Books, a prominent Cairo-based bookstore owned by Muhammad Madbouly, has a long-standing reputation in the Arab world for defying censorship and publishing contentious works (Schwartz 2009). This resulted in punitive actions from the state as Madbouly recalls, 'I was sentenced for eight years in prison for publishing banned books, but I am against censorship and support freedom of expression for all' (Suleiman 2007). While his potential eight-year sentence was averted due to a massive outcry from Arab intellectuals, Egyptian security forces have repeatedly raided Madbouly Books, confiscated titles and threatened its workers with more severe consequences for any future infractions (Schwartz 2009).

Building on existing literature, we propose four key stages of censorship in translation, primarily within the Arab context, but potentially applicable to other cultural settings:

1 **Prior censorship**. At this initial gatekeeping or selection stage, gatekeepers like regulators, publishers and translators decide which cultural products can cross borders. Their choices are usually influenced by cultural or religious compatibility, market demand, regulations, and societal norms. Unsuitable or controversial content is often excluded at this stage.

2 **Preventive censorship**. Once a cultural product gains approval for introduction to a new culture and audience, it may undergo modifications either before or during translation. Translators, publishers, and other intermediaries may adjust the content to fit their beliefs, regulatory guidelines or the target culture's expectations. Beyond mere linguistic translation, this stage encompasses cultural adaptation and potentially involves adjusting narratives, visuals and other elements to resonate with the new audience's cultural expectations. This stage is particularly susceptible to self-censorship by individual translatorial agents.

3 **Pre-release censorship**. After translation, the product undergoes scrutiny by editors, publishers, and regulatory authorities. Adjustments are made to prevent potential controversies and ensure compliance with target cultural and regulatory expectations. Notably, economic censorship might come into play at this stage, resulting from financial constraints. That is, the release, censorship and success of a cultural product in a market are not solely a representation of its cultural value but could also be influenced by economic factors. Economic considerations can sometimes overshadow the cultural significance of a work, leading to decisions that prioritise commercial viability over artistic merit or cultural relevance.

4 **Post-censorship**. After release, reactive measures may be necessitated by factors such as public outcry or regulatory oversight. These measures are not time-bound, reflecting evolving societal norms and their impact on the interpretation of cultural products (e.g., the Dahl example

Translation and Censorship in the Arab World and Its Diasporas

above). Modifications can vary, from minor adjustments to full withdrawal. In this dynamic stage, especially in today's digital age, public and state scrutiny occurs in real-time, often rapidly escalating and occasionally prompting immediate modifications or retractions.

1.2 Historical Perspectives

This section offers a concise yet panoramic overview of translation and censorship examples in, on or from the Arab world. We will begin with insights into literary translation and its associated censorship. This will be followed by an exploration of censorship in children's literature translation. Subsequent discussions will explore censorship within media translation and conclude with instances from audio-visual translation. Across all these genres, the primary aim of censorship is to promote conformity to a specific identity that entities enforcing it, regardless of who they are, seek to preserve, foster or alter.

1.2.1 Literary Translation and Censorship

Censorship of literature, whether translated or original, is a prevalent practice that impacts various cultures and political systems, extending to the Arab world and beyond, commonly driven by political, religious or cultural motivations. The banning of *Satanic Verses* in several Arab and Muslim countries due to its perceived sacrilegious content is widely known (Kabil 2014; Merkle 2018). Tragically, this controversy culminated in the murder of Hitoshi Igarashi, a Japanese scholar of Arabic and Persian literature, and the assault on the Italian translator, Ettore Caprioli, both for their roles in translating Salman Rushdie's novel (Khalifa 2017; Merkle 2018). Another example is the controversial work *Awlād Hāratinā* by the only Arab Novel Prize winner, Naguib Mahfouz (Khalifa 2020). First serialised in the Egyptian newspaper *Al-Ahram* in 1959, it incited outrage among Islamic scholars, mainly from Al-Azhar, who saw parallels between its characters and divine figures, even though Mahfouz never explicitly named them (Khalifa 2020). Considered blasphemous, *Awlād Hāratinā* was banned from book publication in Egypt, although a version was released in Lebanon in 1967 by Dar Al-Adab. Mahfouz's 1988 Nobel Prize reignited controversy surrounding the novel, particularly as it was referenced in the Nobel announcement. Sheikh Omar Abdel-Rahman, a cleric with purported connections to the 1993 World Trade Center bombing, subsequently drew parallels between *Satanic Verses*—published the same year as Mahfouz's Nobel recognition—and *Awlād Hāratinā*. Abdel-Rahman asserted that had Mahfouz been punished for writing *Awlād Hāratinā*, Rushdie would not have dared to write his contentious work (Jacquemond 2008; Khalifa 2020). This connection led Philip Stewart, the English translator of Mahfouz's novel, to withhold his translation rights after the Nobel announcement due to safety concerns for himself, Mahfouz, their respective families and broader Islamic-Western relations (Stewart 2001). This eventually resulted in the novel's retranslation (Khalifa 2020). Only after Mahfouz's passing was the book published in Egypt in 2006 by Dar El-Shorouk. Ironically, the very censorship intended to suppress the book boosted its sales, both in its original Arabic form and in translation.

Saudi author Rajaa Alsanea's debut novel, *Banāt al-Riyād*, exemplifies the reach of censorship and its impact on literary translation in the Arab world. First published in Lebanon in 2005 by Dar Alsaqi, the novel immediately stirred controversy and was banned in Saudi Arabia because it speaks of the love affairs and private challenges of adult life for four upper-class Saudi women and the division between the dominant Sunni faction and the minority Shia in the country (Khalifa 2017). Due to its controversial nature and the censorship it faced, the novel was published in an

English translation by Marilyn Booth titled *Girls of Riyadh* not long after its original Arabic publication. Although the translation itself was not without controversy (see Booth 2007, 2008, 2010), it enjoyed 'phenomenal success' (Johnson 2008), selling approximately three million copies and subsequently being translated into around 40 languages (Wagner 2013). Another contentious novel hailing from Saudi Arabia, which generated equal upheaval, is *al-Ākharūn* by Siba Al-Harez. Notably, Siba Al-Harez is a pseudonym, and the identity of the translator remains undisclosed. Like Alsanea's work, this novel was banned in Saudi Arabia and was initially published in Beirut in 2006 (Larson 2009). Its English translation titled *The Others*, includes an extensive and controversial translator's afterword, again without disclosing the translator's identity (Larson 2009). These instances demonstrate the intricate relationship between literary translation and censorship, revealing how the suppression of original works can inadvertently amplify their national and global resonance and reach through translations.

George Orwell's *Animal Farm* and *1984* provide other notable examples of censorship in the Arab world when literary works are translated into Arabic. Viewed as politically contentious, *Animal Farm* was specifically banned in several Arab countries. In 2002, the UAE banned the novel in schools, with the Emirati Ministry of Education claiming it contained material that 'contradicts Islamic and Arab values'—specifically citing images of alcoholic drinks, pigs and other 'indecent images' (Reed 2002; El-Amrani 2010). That same year, J.K. Rowling's *Harry Potter and the Philosopher's Stone* faced a similar ban for the same reason (Reed 2002). However, Orwell's *1984* has endured even more extensive censorship. It was banned in Kuwait for its political and social themes, as well as sexual content (Nordland 2018). Curiously, one Arabic translation of *1984* was banned while another was allowed for no apparent reason (Nordland 2018). In 2014, an Egyptian university student was allegedly imprisoned for carrying and reading the Arabic translation of *1984*. The Egyptian newspaper *Al-Masry Al-Youm* (Abu Sadira 2014) initially reported this incident, noting that the student had a novel which addressed 'dictator and corrupt military regimes'. This sparked widespread discussions on social media as well as criticisms of the Egyptian government, with many drawing parallels between Orwell's depiction of dictatorship and the contemporary political situation in Egypt (BBC Arabic 2014). Though Egyptian security services later denied that the arrest was due to *1984* (Schaub 2014), the controversy significantly boosted the novel's popularity in the region, making it the most searched term on Google after the arrest (Abdel-Rahim 2014).

The above examples highlight the compound relationship between literary translation and censorship, emphasising the profound impact and unintended consequences of such measures. Rather than stifling discourse and controlling narratives, censorship can inadvertently intensify interest in the restricted content, leading to broader dissemination and discussion. Thus, in attempts to control socio-political narratives, censorship may instead amplify the very voices it seeks to suppress, challenging the perceived power structures and prompting deeper societal introspection.

1.2.2 Children's Literature Translation and Censorship

Translation and censorship in children's literature have long been intertwined, reflecting the broader cultural and political contexts in which they are produced, circulated and received. Censorship of children's literature is not exclusive to the Arab world; even liberal democracies engage in covert censorship, often labelled as 'adaptation' for ideological alignment with 'the best interests of the ideological positioning of a larger socio-political entity' (Merkle 2010: 19; see also Merkle 2002). This resonates with Gambier's (2002) discussion on the certification of mainstream films, suggesting that the difference in censorship between dictatorships and democracies might be in degree, not essence. Mdallel (2020) examines the extensive censorship in Arabic children's literature translations. Genres with non-Islamic religious themes or stories featuring pigs, which are considered unclean in Islam, are entirely omitted. Books addressing taboo subjects such as homosexuality or drug addiction are seldom translated. Classics, like *Black Beauty*, undergo significant alterations, including, when translated and published in Syria, ideological insertions glorifying Arab nationalism or changing the setting to Damascus. Mdallel (2020) also highlights post-2003 US-led invasion censorship efforts in Iraq, where the US purged children's textbooks of influences from Saddam Hussein's regime to suppress potential Sunni rebellion, emphasising how children's literature is instrumental in disseminating ideology. This underscores how controlling children's literature (whether in original or in translation) is seen as key to shaping the ideology of new generations under autocratic systems, whether that was Saddam Hussein projecting Baath party propaganda or the US trying to erase his influence after deposing him. Censorship of cultural products (in translation) is seen here as an exercise in ruling by consent, using children's materials to propagate an approved ideology.

In Arabic translations of content meant for children, censorship often goes beyond moderating offensive language, encompassing alterations to potentially sensitive visual and auditory elements. Zitawi (2008) cites examples of visual censorship, such as the modification of a pig's facial features in *Mickey* intended for Gulf audiences. These alterations range from erasing 'black dots' depicting a 'pig's nostrils' to darkening a 'pig's nose' to resemble 'one big black circle' in *Mickey Weekly Magazine* (Zitawi 2008: 143). The rationale behind this, as Zitawi (2008: 143) explains, is that 'Islam prohibits eating the flesh of pigs, which are considered filthy and unclean animals'. The decision to alter such images may arise from adherence to censorship regulations, but also from a translator's or publisher's discretion, aiming to avoid offending viewers. Interestingly, Zitawi (2008) notes that the 'pig' imagery is left unaltered in Egyptian translations of the same content, potentially due to Egypt's sizable Christian population, who do not adhere to Islamic dietary restrictions. This showcases the varying sensitivities and differing self-censorship practices adopted by translators and publishers across Arab countries.

Additionally, even children's literature (in translation), which may appear innocuous, is not shielded from the repercussions of political conflicts, such as the Palestinian-Israeli situation. In Israel, as Merkle (2018: 246) notes, 'censorship is political and military as well as religious and cultural'. An example involving the Arab world and children's literature in translation is evident in the Israeli government barring publisher Salah Abassi from importing Arabic translations of children's books from Syria and Lebanon (AFP 2008; *The Black Iris* 2008). Speaking to Israeli public radio, Abassi recounted how he was cautioned against importing translated classics like *Pinocchio* and widely acclaimed series such as *Harry Potter* in Arabic, attributing the restriction to a 1939[1] British Mandate-era decree. This decree prohibits importing books from nations in conflict with Israel, including Syria and Lebanon. Abassi emphasised that if these books were 'printed in Jordan or Egypt, which are friendly to Israel, I would lose no time in buying them there. Now the significance is that the Arabic reading public in Israel will not be able to enjoy the best literature' (AFP 2008; *The Black Iris* 2008). Consequently, young Arab-Israeli readers are deprived of major literary works in Arabic (translation) because of the national origins of their publishers. This situation underlines the extent to which even children's literature in translation is influenced by political conflict, government censorship and/or state-imposed restrictions. Abassi's sentiments convey a grim reality: owing to political divides, young Arabic speakers in Israel keen to read literary treasures in their native language are potentially relegated to foreign language alternatives (either Hebrew or English), all hinging on an archaic directive and ongoing political animosities.

1.2.3 Translation and Media Censorship

In the Arab world, translation and media censorship emerge especially pronounced in nations deeply anchored in oppressive regimes, or theocratic or monarchical systems. Saudi Arabia stands out as an absolute monarchy, governed by Sharia law, where the king assumes dual roles as the head of State and government. Governance decisions often emerge from consultations between senior royal princes and, until recently, the religious establishment, with the Quran as the country's constitution. Censorship in Saudi media is a pivotal component, especially in the realm of translation. As highlighted by Basalamah (2010), in a nation where media is inherently multilingual, censors from the Ministry of Information meticulously choose intermediaries who are staunchly aligned with the nation's political and religious tenets. Basalamah (2010) provides an in-depth account of his experiences in the French radio section of the Saudi Ministry of Information, describing the meticulous process of excising 'indecent' or religiously inappropriate lyrics during French to Arabic song translations (171–72). He recalls how radio hosts underwent rigorous pre-screening, with the Ministry only approving those who mirrored the nation's stringent moral and religious criteria. Drawing from his work in the foreign language TV station, Basalamah (2010: 175) states, 'the operation was therefore twofold: on the one hand resisting censorship by treating a delicate subject and on the other hand, resisting self-censorship by criticising dominant discourses'. Basalamah (2010) posits that translation within Saudi state media oscillates between resistance against censorship and inherent self-censorship, reflecting postcolonial resistance in a context of censorship where a certain form of emancipation, parenthetically clothed, is attempted. This dual stance underscores the intricacies and contradictions translation faces, situated between the polarities of suppression and the pursuit of freedom.

Additionally, Boéri and Abdel Fattah's (2020) article examines the nuanced manipulation of news translation, suggesting an underlying form of covert censorship, purposed for propaganda amid the turbulent atmosphere of the Gulf crisis, which emerged as a major diplomatic confrontation among the Gulf Cooperation Council countries primarily targeting Qatar. Beginning in June 2017, this crisis saw Qatar subjected to a diplomatic and economic embargo by Saudi Arabia, the UAE, Bahrain and Egypt, stemming from long-standing political disagreements and accusations about Qatar's alleged support for terrorism (see Ulrichsen 2020). Drawing its data from *Al-Ittihad*, a UAE-owned Arabic daily newspaper, Boéri and Abdel Fattah's (2020) article harnesses the synergy of narrative theory and the appraisal framework to demystify how journalistic translation can be weaponised ideologically through manipulation and covert censorship for political gains. For instance, the article underscores the deliberate alteration of the Qatari Foreign Minister's statements during his European Parliament appearance in September 2017. While the Minister stoutly defended Qatar and accused the 'blockading countries' of 'inciting violence', the Arabic translation censored the direct attribution to the minister, diluted direct references, encapsulating his sentiments as '[Qatar] claims it has an unwavering stance on fighting terrorism' (Boéri and Abdel Fattah 2020: 92). This oblique representation, according to the authors, conferred undue neutrality to what was inherently a charged declaration, 'priming the reader to construe the Qatari FM's stance against terrorism as mendacious' (Boéri and Abdel Fattah 2020: 92). Additionally, the research highlights the trans-editing of references to foreign entities to bolster credibility. An anecdote relates to the Arabic reporting of a statement by the Qatari Foreign Minister to *Le Point* (a French weekly political and news magazine), which was misleadingly attributed to 'the widely circulated magazine' (Boéri and Abdel Fattah 2020: 82), despite the absence of any verifiable source. Boéri and Abdel Fattah's thorough analysis of *Al-Ittihad*'s reporting on the Gulf crisis illuminates how, under the guise of neutrality, translation was used as a tool to strategically distort narratives and sources to cast a disparaging light on Qatar, exemplifying multifaceted dynamics of media censorship in translation.

1.2.4   Audio-visual Translation and Censorship

Much of the existing research on translation and censorship in the Arab world focuses on audio-visual (AVT) translation. This focus can be attributed to several factors. Firstly, the edutainment nature of AVT makes it more appealing for researchers. Moreover, the entertainment nature of this genre might make it less vulnerable to political scrutiny. While this does not imply that AVT is immune to censorship, it does suggest that once an AVT material clears censorship, it is generally viewed as pre-approved entertainment. This argument is underscored by Al-Qudah's (2022) observation that research into AVT and censorship in the Arab world has often overlooked discussing the overarching censorial system and the specific laws guiding censors and translators. Another possible reason is that, as Izwaini (2017) argues, any dissemination of audio-visual content in the Arab world often encounters some form of censorship, making AVT a particularly fertile area for research. Given the extensive research on AVT and censorship in the Arab world, this section will be notably longer than others.

While both subtitling and dubbing exist in the Arab world, their context of use varies considerably, with subtitling being more commonly used especially when the source language is English (Al-Qudah 2022), and the genre is not children's films or shows. Audio-visual content from other languages such as Turkish and Persian has tended to be dubbed rather than subtitled. As the primary AVT modes in the region, subtitling and dubbing are where censorship frequently occurs. Izwaini (2017) observes that censorship in AVT in the Arab world often involves religion, sexuality, alcohol, drugs, profanity and other explicit content. For instance, the Arabic-dubbed version of *The Simpsons* underwent significant edits for Arab viewers. Here, Homer Simpson became Omar Shamshoon, alcohol references were replaced with soda, pork became halal beef sausages, and the religious context shifted from Christianity to Islam, to the extent that the American Bart became almost unrecognisable (Tapper 2009; Nassar 2017; Yahiaoui and Abdel Fattah 2020). This religious adjustment led to characters like Moe and any tavern-related scenes being entirely removed (Nassar 2017). Notably, according to *Censorship Wiki* ('The Simpsons' n.d.), this practice of censorship extended to many other countries, including English-speaking ones such as Australia, New Zealand and the UK.

1.2.5   Subtitling and Censorship

The evolution of AVT in the Arab world began with the arrival of the first talkies in Egypt during the early 1930s. Though Italian translation companies initially introduced subtitling in the region with these early films, subtitling was established as a prominent translation mode largely due to Anis Ebaid (Gamal 2007). Egypt spearheaded the production of AV translations for foreign films, setting a benchmark for theatres across the Arab world (Gamal 2007; Al-Qudah 2022). This granted Egypt the authority to make influential decisions that shaped AVT practices throughout the Arab region (Gamal 2007). One of the most notable areas impacted was censorship. Rigorous regulations 'on dealing with sex, foul language, blasphemy and violence were established' (Gamal 2008: 3). Censors determined which films would undergo subtitling and be introduced to local audiences. This necessitated that subtitling companies maintain tight connections with the censorship office. Consequently, the language of subtitling carved its niche as a distinct genre (Gamal 2008). The vast influx of movies from the US led Egypt's censorship body to prioritise three chief concerns: violence, language and sex. As a result, 'swear words had to be sanitised, sexual references deleted and blasphemous references expunged' (Gamal 2008: 4). Despite the evolution of media and the adoption of no-censorship policies by platforms such as Netflix, this historical approach to censorship remains largely influential today, as we illustrate below.

Thawabteh (2017) examined censorship in the English-Arabic subtitling of three American films: *Face Off* (1997), *Crash* (2004) and *John Tucker Must Die* (2006), broadcast on prominent Arab satellite channels (MBC2, MBC4 and Fox Movies). The research discerned that the Arabic subtitles underwent excessive censorship compared to the original English. Two prevalent translation strategies emerged: omission (coupled with or without condensation), where obscene utterances from the English source text were deleted and/or condensed—a striking example being the transformation of 'mother-fucking pig' into the milder 'Oh, shit!' (Thawabteh 2017: 570)—and rendition, whereby English obscenities were translated into less offensive Arabic terms, such as converting 'their asses [sic] sons of bitches' to 'those two low-life people' (Thawabteh 2017: 566). These censorial practices were attributed to factors like the conservative nature of Arab and Islamic cultures, the need to avoid offending the target audience, regional censorship laws, the distinct cultural values of the West versus the Arab-Muslim world, media company policies, and entrenched translator norms advocating for self-censorship. Thawabteh's study reveals how cultural values, regulations, and translator self-censorship practices together intensify censorship in English-Arabic film subtitling, thereby influencing the viewing experience of Arab audiences.

Chabbak (2019) examines instances of censorship in the translations of voiced-over documentaries into Arabic, targeting Arab but particularly Jordanian audiences (see also Chabbak 2018). She examines how censorship manifests, focusing on cultural-specific references including religious, geopolitical and gender aspects. For instance, in the documentary *Jordan, The Horse Dynasty*, the statement 'Jordan is not blessed by the gods'—referring to the country's severe water shortage—was omitted due to its potential clash with monotheistic beliefs and the risk of offending Jordanians by suggesting that Jordan's water scarcity is a result of it not being a blessed country (Chabbak 2019: 615). Geopolitical concerns led to the replacement of 'Israel' with 'the Middle East' in the documentary, referring to an Azerbaijani singer's concert tour there, to avoid provoking Arab audiences in light of the ongoing Palestinian-Israeli conflict (Chabbak 2019: 615). An example of gender censorship that initially linked a Muslim woman's liberation to 'getting rid' of the head veil was neutralised to resonate with and respect an Arab audience where many women are veiled (Chabbak 2019: 616). Chabbak's work underscores how AVT, due to various cultural and geopolitical pressures, often evolves into a form of censorship.

Subtitling practices on global platforms, such as Netflix, have garnered attention from researchers exploring Arabic AVT practices. For instance, Alsharhan (2020, 2022) investigated the Arabic subtitles on Netflix for content featuring taboo language, with a specific focus on the Kuwaiti context and audience. Alsharhan aimed to understand the influence of Netflix's no-censorship policy on the translation strategies for English taboo language into Arabic. The research findings highlighted an extensive range of translation methods used by translators, including retention, direct translation, substitution, paraphrase, standardisation, generalisation, specification, euphemism and even omission. Despite the platform's no-censorship stance, approximately 45% of the taboo language instances were translated using euphemisms, and an impactful 71.5% displayed a shift in register (Alsharhan 2020). Additionally, informal language referring to sexual body parts was rendered more formally in Arabic, making it more acceptable for an Arab, primarily Kuwaiti, audience. Overall, Alsharhan's research highlights that even in the face of Netflix's no-censorship policy, Netflix subtitlers continue to lean on traditional strategies such as euphemisms and register shifts

Translation and Censorship in the Arab World and Its Diasporas

(2020). Alsharhan's work demonstrates that, notwithstanding existing no-censorship policies, translators, inadvertently or not, often resort to self-censorship to bridge linguistic and cultural gaps and mitigate potential sensitivities.

Building on Alsharhan's findings of the self-censorship tendency in subtitling despite existing no-censorship policies, another Arab country where this phenomenon becomes starkly evident is Saudi Arabia. Despite online platforms offering audiences avenues to access programmes that might be censored via traditional channels, these platforms are not impervious to governmental interventions and socio-political sensitivities. An illustrative example is Saudi Arabia's pressure on Netflix concerning an episode of *Patriot Act* hosted by Hasan Minhaj in which he criticised the kingdom over the murder of journalist Jamal Khashoggi (Griffiths and McKirdy 2019; BBC 2019). Minhaj's criticism was not taken lightly, leading the Saudi government to assert that the episode violated an anti-cybercrime law, which prohibits the 'production, preparation, transmission or storage of material impinging on public order, religious values, public morals and privacy' on the internet (BBC 2019). Reacting to this controversy, Netflix ceded to the Saudi government's demands and the episode was deleted from the platform, stating, 'We strongly support artistic freedom worldwide and only removed this episode in Saudi Arabia after we had received a valid legal request—and to comply with local law' (Griffiths and McKirdy 2019). Nevertheless, the episode's censorship generated heightened interest, with the content spreading to other platforms like YouTube, witnessing a great deal of engagement. This situation underlines the same conclusion drawn from Alsharhan's study: even when platforms proclaim a no-censorship policy, external pressures or the inherent desire to bridge cultural gaps can lead to self-censorship (at both individual and institutional levels) and modified content. Consequently, distinguishing between ensuring cultural appropriateness and preserving artistic integrity becomes muddled in the digital domain, emphasising that self-censorship, whether intentional or inadvertent, remains a dominant factor in content translation, circulation and reception.

1.2.6   Dubbing and Censorship

In 1936, Egypt took its first foray into dubbing with the American film *Mr Deeds Goes to Town* (Gamal 2008). However, as Abu Shadi (2004) recounts, this venture was short-lived, with dubbing being ruled out in favour of subtitling for foreign films. This shift significantly impacted the prevalence of dubbing within the Arab cinematic landscape, making it less common than in regions like Spain, Russia and Italy (Al-Qudah 2022). According to Maluf (2005) and Gamal (2007), Egyptian filmmakers, being the primary source of Arabic films for decades, viewed subtitling as a more benign alternative to dubbing. This choice was believed to somewhat level the playing field against American cinema, which was revered for its technical prowess, advanced cinematography and evolved scriptwriting (Gamal 2008). Additionally, subtitling was perceived by several Arab governments as having an educational value, serving as a literacy tool for large Arabic-speaking populations (Volmar 1950). Moreover, the competition posed by Hollywood cemented the decision against dubbing American films due to the fear of 'killing off the local industry' in the Arab world (Gamal 2009: 2).

Given the popularity of Turkish soap operas dubbed for Arab audiences, it is fitting to explore instances of censorship within this context. Elouardaoui (2014) highlights the ascendancy of Turkish soap operas, or 'diziler', on Arab TV channels like MBC in the late 2000s—a phenomenon that continues to this day. A key factor of this success was dubbing into the Syrian dialect, tapping into the Arab audience's familiarity with Syrian actors' voices which can be traced back to the 1990s Arabic dubbing of Spanish-language telenovelas, shown on several Arab

TV channels (Elouardaoui 2014). Yet, MBC introduced significant censorship to align the content with local cultural and religious norms. Elouardaoui (2014) illustrates how *Aşk-ı Memnu* (Forbidden Love) underwent substantial edits, censoring romantic scenes to prevent potential viewers from switching channels during scenes displaying 'sexual intimacy' (Elouardaoui 2014). Likewise, dialogues about virginity were excluded, reflecting the broader cultural stance where 'premarital sex is not permissible and is highly frowned upon' in Arab societies and Islamic law (Elouardaoui 2014). The series *Fatmagül'ün Suçu Ne?* (What Was Fatmagül's Crime?) saw its unsettling rape scene edited out, obscuring the narrative context, and leading Arab viewers to misinterpret the dialogue's significance. As Elouardaoui (2014) notes, MBC's self-censorship expanded beyond religious or sexual content to political matters, for example, censoring any depictions of 'political issues that could invoke the ire of the Saudi royal family'. The sustained popularity of diziler, despite these changes, indicates that audio-visual materials, when localised through dubbing, can find resonance with the target culture's audience. This scenario underscores the profound influence of socio-political and cultural determinants in shaping how cultural products are produced, circulated and received. Dubbing and the nuances of censorship, thus, become instrumental in navigating these determinants, demonstrating their intertwined impact on global media consumption.

Influenced by socio-political tensions, MBC banned Arabic-dubbed Turkish TV shows in 2018, which Turkey's Culture and Tourism Minister, Numan Kurtulmus, called a 'political move' and 'clear censorship' (Uras 2018). He told *Al-Jazeera*, 'It is not a couple of politicians who are supposed to decide who will watch which movies or shows from their desks' (Uras 2018). The ban, rooted in Turkey's decision to back Qatar during the Gulf crisis, showcased the evolving dynamics of audience agency (for a definition of 'agency', see Khalifa 2014: 13–14). In today's digital world, conventional censorship struggles to navigate the rapidly evolving media landscape. Miriam Berg highlighted Arab audiences' adaptability, stating, 'The audience has started to watch Turkish dramas online with English subtitles or Arabic subtitles [...] most of them visit websites of Turkish channels to watch the content in the original language' (Koçak 2020). This shift to digital platforms underscores how technological advancements have magnified audience agency in the Arab world, empowering audiences to circumvent conventional censorship. The complex relationship between dubbing, censorship and audience choice exemplifies how socio-political and cultural factors shape media reception while highlighting the diminishing efficacy of traditional censorship methods in the face of digital empowerment.

A unique illustration of dubbing and censorship in the Arab world revolves around anime. According to *Dragon Ball Wiki* ('Arabic Dub' n.d.), the history of anime dubbing and censorship in the Arab world traces back to 1976 with the pioneering efforts of director Weam Al-Saidi and the owner of Filmali, the first anime dubbing company in the Middle East, Nicolas Abu Samah, who introduced the Arab world to its first Arabic-dubbed anime, *Arabian Nights: Sinbad's Adventures*, paving the way for future works (see also Abbas 2020; Saber 2021). As anime grew in popularity, with classics like *UFO Robo Grendizer*, it faced varying degrees of censorship. For instance, the 1983 Arabic dub of *Sandybell* underwent some of the first instances of censorship, notably concerning religious imagery and cleavage ('Arabic Dub' n.d.). Additionally, in 2001, the Pokémon franchise faced serious controversy after being erroneously associated with themes of Darwinism, Zionism and Satanism, falsely suggesting that character names like 'Pikachu' and 'Magikarp' had anti-Islamic connotations. This spread rapidly, culminating in fatwas against Pokémon in such Arab countries as Egypt and Palestine prohibiting engagement with its content, significantly impacting the anime's presence in the region (*Al-Ahdath Al-Maghribia* 2001: 9).

The Arabic dubbing of the globally popular *Dragon Ball* series, particularly by SpaceToon (a cartoon and anime TV channel) and Venus Centre (a Syria-based animation dubbing company), underwent extensive censorship to make the content more palatable for Arab audiences ('Arabic Dub' n.d.). One of the most conspicuous changes in the *Dragon Ball* 2002 dubbing was the dissociation of the Dragon Balls from any dragon-related entities, eradicating scenes involving Shenron. This alteration shifted the source of the balls' powers from the dragons to the balls themselves. Moreover, themes of evolution were edited out, with Goku's tail and the Saiyan race's transformation abilities depicted as machine-like rather than biological ('Arabic Dub' n.d.). This was purportedly done to avoid potential conflicts with some Islamic teachings on evolution. Sexual innuendos, prevalent in the original, faced the brunt of censorship too. Scenes showcasing Bulma's Bunny costume and the sometimes-risqué antics of Master Roshi and Oolong were either removed or replaced with unrelated shots ('Arabic Dub' n.d.). Such modifications often compromised the integrity of the original storyline, potentially confusing audiences familiar with the source material. This pattern of content alteration and censorship demonstrates the complexities of introducing international media into new cultures. In essence, the journey of anime through the Arab world showcases not just the globalisation of media but also the inherent challenges and responsibilities that come with cross-cultural dubbing and the nuances of censorship. The influence of self-censorship stems from producers' conscientious effort to respect cultural sensitivities, ensuring dubbed materials resonate positively with the target audience and culture without causing inadvertent offence.

1.3 Core Issues

1.3.1 Social Translation and its Censorship in/of the Arab World

This section aims to present a broader understanding of the relationship between translation and censorship in the Arab world, where various forms of published translations are subject to extensive censorship. The concepts of translation and censorship will be reframed within the notion of 'social translation' (Basalamah 2012, 2022), which models the mutual translation of social groups' frames of reference, socio-political claims and projects stemming from their respective horizons of belief. In this context, censorship of social translation functions as social, political, cultural or religious pressure to hold up the needs or will expressed by certain groups to communicate, understand each other, collaborate or cooperate within a common social project. This form of censorship implies the suspension of a desired or needed social translation that many Arab political regimes and governments do not want to see happening in their respective jurisdictions, potentially leading to the entrenchment of the social status quo, political disengagement and reinforcement of immobilism, authoritarianism and repression.

In the postcolonial context common to most of the twenty-two Arab countries since their respective independences, the continuous existence of non-democratic regimes, although not always an immediate inheritance from the colonial powers, is a consequence of that historical period, whereby empires and nations were reshaped and divided into nation-states as per the 1916 Sykes-Picot Agreement,[2] Social dynamics between various cultural and/or religious groups in any Arab country, when it comes to bridging gaps of mutual understanding and peaceful coexistence, are often jeopardised or methodically undermined by the overarching official political powers in place. One reason can be summed up in a nutshell: divide and conquer. Governments tend to take advantage of their hegemonic position to neutralise potential tensions and violence and maintain a status quo that would not allow any form of alliances and possible collusions against the group in power. The Algerian 'Dark Decade' of the 1990s, where the local Algerian Army, with the discreet support of the French government, halted the election process favouring Islamist political formations and managed to spread terror among the population when they committed massacres but deceitfully claimed that these were perpetrated by violent extremist groups related to the 'Islamist' parties (Burgat 2020; Willis 2022), serves as an extreme example of censorship of social translation, comparable with other dramatic situations in multiple locations of the Arab world.

Another notable case is that of Saudi Arabia, which presents itself as the stronghold of the Sunni-majority tradition in the Muslim world. Despite the absence of a census based on religion or ethnicity, the country is reportedly inhabited by at least three local religious minorities: the Shia minority (approximately 10–15% of the population, mostly in the eastern Hasa province), the Ismailis (estimated at 700,000), and the Zaydis (estimated at 20,000), both located in the southern provinces of Jizan and Najran (US State Department 2016). While the Ismailis and Zaydis have not been significantly involved in any known or major civil unrest, the Shia minority has had a long history of conflicts and uprisings since the 1950s against the discriminatory policies of the Saudi government (Jones 2010). For example, in the aftermath of the 1979 Iranian Islamic Revolution, the Shia minority of Qatif, Al-Awamiyah, Safwa and other neighbouring towns of the Eastern Province felt galvanised and openly commemorated the Day of Ashura, which is typically observed by Shiites in a manner that Sunnis consider unacceptable. This sparked a brutal repression that led to popular demonstrations and angry destructions of government-owned properties lasting until 1983, with approximately 220 people killed by the Saudi National Guard (Jones 2006).

Although the harsh repression never stopped in the region, a second period of unrest was inflamed by the winds of the so-called Arab Spring in 2011. In resonance with the uprisings conducted by the Shia populations of neighbouring Iraq and Bahrain, 'between October 2011 and September 2012, twelve Shi'a — mainly young people — have been shot dead by the security forces, and the funerals of some of them turned into the biggest demonstrations Saudi Arabia had witnessed since an uprising by Saudi Shi'a 1979–1980' (Matthiesen 2012: 630). In August 2017, the entire 400-year-old neighbourhood of Al-Musawara in Al-Awamiyah, a town of 3000 people, was 'flattened' by Saudi military forces following several months of clashes with insurgent gunmen (Qiblawi 2017).

These events were inspired by unmitigated condemnations of Shia religious practices by official Sunni clerics close to the Saudi power, creating a struggle for freedom of worship and against discrimination that Shia citizens, as a minority, encounter in education, administration and employment. The recognition of the Shia minority as a legitimate religious group within the fabric of Saudi society and their peaceful coexistence with the majority Sunni population was not granted because of the religious and political censorship imposed by the two-century-old alliance between the Saudi monarchy and Wahhabi clerics (Bowen 2007). This represents a clear case of censored social translation; that is, the prevention of a minority's will to integrate into the political sphere and be recognised as a legitimate social and religious group by a repressive censoring regime, fearing its sovereignty would be shaken or stolen if the influence of the Islamic Republic of Iran were to infiltrate through the Shia minorities of the kingdom.

Although the Province of Quebec is not located in the Arab world, we argue that the Arab-Muslim diaspora is part of it and that the recent situation to which the Arab and Muslim communities of the Province have been subjected may be considered another form of censorship of social translation directly related to the kind described above in the region (Cohen and Fisher 2019). This is even more so when understood against the backdrop of the democratic principles of the rule of law as formulated in the Quebec Charter of Human Rights and Freedoms, which guarantees all

Translation and Censorship in the Arab World and Its Diasporas

citizens their rights to 'freedom of conscience, freedom of religion, freedom of opinion, [and] freedom of expression' (CQLR c C-12 1975/2023: art. 3).

However, since the early 2000s, Quebec has been increasingly dealing with societal reactions toward the developing visibility of Arab and Muslim immigrant communities. In 2006, the 'reasonable accommodation' crisis stirred a great deal of emotion among Quebecers in response to a few claims for religious accommodation made by Arab Muslims, such as a group of North African Muslims who asked the owners of a sugar shack to serve a traditional Quebecois pea soup without lard and were allowed to perform one of their daily prayers in congregation within the premises (Potvin 2008). Despite the owners' willingness, debates and outcries flooded the media with reports of similar 'incidents' throughout the year (Potvin 2008).

In mid-2007, professors Gérard Bouchard and Charles Taylor were appointed to a commission tasked with touring major cities and towns in Quebec, consulting with the public, and publishing a report with their findings and recommendations (Bouchard and Taylor 2008). Although then-Premier Jean Charest did not enact legislation aligned with these recommendations, subsequent Quebec governments have endeavoured to pass a bill to maintain Quebec society's secular nature, a hard-won separation from the institutional dominance of the Catholic Church achieved during the Quiet Revolution of the 1960s. Governments aimed to curtail what was perceived as a 'return of the religious repressed'—a widespread expression inspired by Freudian terminology—symbolised by the growing presence of Arab Muslim immigrants. These efforts were unsuccessful until the Coalition Avenir Québec government took office.

Under Premier François Legault, Bill 21, entitled 'An Act Respecting the Laicity of the State', was passed in June 2019, banning all civil servants from wearing religious signs in all state facilities, including teachers in public schools. While the ban included the Jewish kippa, the Sikh turban, and the Christian cross, it was clear from news media iconography that the main target was Muslim women's headscarves. Despite protests, demonstrations and legal appeals, no suspension or repeal of the Bill has been obtained. A recent report on a survey conducted by the Association of Canadian Studies noted the 'devastating impact' the Bill has had on religious minorities since its enforcement (Taylor 2022). In an interview with CBC News' Steve Rukavina (2022), lead researcher Miriam Taylor elaborated on the consequences stating, 'We saw severe social stigmatization of Muslim women, marginalization of Muslim women and very disturbing declines in their sense of well-being, their ability to fulfil their aspirations, sense of safety, but also hope for the future.' While proponents argue that the Bill is non-discriminatory because it applies equally to all religious symbols worn by employees in state institutions, the media pictography when reporting about the Bill almost exclusively portrays Muslim women wearing the headscarf (hijāb) or face cover (niqāb).

The situation outlined above, although not taking place in the Arab/Muslim world, constitutes a case of censorship of the ongoing social translation with(in) the Arab-Muslim diaspora communities in Quebec society, directed toward the female representatives of Islam and Arab culture. Social translation can take place passively, through the natural interaction of religious/cultural groups in various domains of the public sphere, or deliberately through 'social translators', who act as trustworthy bidirectional facilitators between the social groups on sensitive issues. In the post-national (Habermas 2001) and post-secular era of Western societies, such as Canada's, these social translators are usually embedded in both secular and religious groups to help 'a postsecular society [adapt] to the fact that religious communities continue to exist in a context of ongoing secularization' (Habermas 2003: 104). Furthermore, this type of social translation is dedicated to engaging in a process of 'institutional translation proviso' that allows the religions of civil society to express their convictions and propositions in a secular language and be channelled toward the political sphere (Habermas 2006: 9–10).

In the absence of such a voluntarist undertaking for social inclusion and intercultural deliberation, but even worse in the event of initiatives—such as Bill 21—that hamper these efforts for more social cohesion, there is a clear justification to consider Quebec's contentious legislation as an act of censorship exerted against the processes of social translation in the Arab-Muslim diaspora, whether they may be instigated by social agents or naturally conducted at the level of interpersonal relationships on the overarching social scale.

1.4 Future Directions

A well-known saying in the Arab world, 'What is forbidden is desirable', echoes Mark Twain's sentiment that 'There is a charm about the forbidden that makes it unspeakably desirable'. Despite attempts at censorship, audiences, whether in the Arab world or beyond, invariably find ways to access censored content. The proliferation of user-generated content and distributors (via platforms such as YouTube) has heightened this phenomenon, indicating that even under censorship and restrictions, audiences can exercise agency, influencing and shaping dominant cultural discourses rather than merely being passive consumers of translated (or original) content.

This chapter explored the complex dynamics of censorship in/and translation in the Arab world, emphasising censorship's ambivalent nature: it cannot be wholly negative or positive. While the existence of censorship is undeniable and its complete elimination implausible, its implementation should remain free from power struggles, governmental influences, or individual biases. Censorship should not be used as a tool to suppress diverse voices; individual perspectives must be respected. Instead of imposing bans, an independent, non-governmental entity that prioritises public interest should oversee the evaluation of cultural products, including translations. This body could introduce systems to empower audiences to discern content for themselves, similar to the existing ratings for audio-visual materials in some Arab countries. However, safeguarding vulnerable groups, such as children, and mitigating extremist content, both in translation and original, remains essential. The challenges of navigating political, ideological and cultural boundaries make clear-cut censorship guidelines elusive, transforming censorship into a consideration not just of imposition of limitations but also of production, reception and circulation. The intricacies of political, ideological and cultural factors in the Arab world undeniably complicate defining concrete censorship protocols for translation, requiring a nuanced understanding of the interplay between language, culture, politics and power, as well as the role of translators and other agents in the process of cultural exchange.

Our evaluation in this chapter of censorship in/and translation across various cultural and media contexts in the Arab world highlights that this field of study is far from exhausted. Numerous avenues for future research exist that can further enrich our understanding of this multifaceted phenomenon. Possible future research directions include investigating the evolving relationship between societal norms and censorship practices on translation, particularly in light of the rapidly changing technological and political landscapes. This could involve examining how digital platforms and social media influence censorship practices in translation and how audiences navigate and respond to censored content across different platforms and regions. Comparative studies across various cultural and political contexts can provide valuable insights into how different Arab societies balance freedom of expression with cultural and ethical norms, offering a more comprehensive understanding of censorship in/and translation in the Arab world.

Translation and Censorship in the Arab World and Its Diasporas

Additionally, future research could focus on the role of translators and other agents in the Arab translation industry, examining their decision-making processes, ethical dilemmas and the impact of external pressures on their work. This could involve exploring self-censorship and how Arab translators navigate censorship in their professional practice, considering the region's diverse political and cultural settings. Investigating the influence of political shifts and upheavals on censorship practices in translation can shed light on how changes in leadership, policies, or societal movements shape censorship norms and practices in the Arab world over time. As technological advancements transform the field of translation, future research could also explore how technologies such as machine translation and AI impact censorship practices in the Arab world, including issues of bias in translation as a form of covert censorship. Furthermore, investigating genre-specific censorship across various types of content translation in the Arab context, such as educational materials, literary works and entertainment media, can provide a more granular understanding of how censorship operates in different contexts within the Arab world.

Moreover, the rapidly evolving political and social environment in the Arab world continually presents new challenges and opportunities for studying censorship in/and translation. Between the time we submitted this chapter and received the reviewers' comments, recent events in Palestine have been rapidly unfolding. These developments have given rise to new censorship issues that we would have wanted to include a dedicated section on in this chapter. However, given the limited time available to address these emerging concerns, their importance and the rapid pace at which events are unfolding, we believe that these issues deserve separate, dedicated studies to do them justice. Potential issues for exploration extend beyond the shadow-banning and censorship of (social) media posts and accounts supporting the Palestinian cause to the realm of translation and the concept of social translation as discussed in this chapter. Other issues include the suppression of news coverage and on-the-ground reporting, often manifested through the targeted and systematic killing of reporters, journalists, citizen journalists and their families, as well as the selective or manipulative translation of available reports and testimonies. The latter is exemplified by the BBC's mistranslation of an ex-Palestinian prisoner interview, which was later corrected after Respond Crisis Translation, an advocacy group for language rights in crisis situations, pointed out the inaccuracy (Alkhunaizi 2023; Brawn 2023). Similarly, Meta briefly mislabelled some Palestinian Instagram users as 'terrorists' in their profiles due to improper Arabic translations, a mistake that was later rectified (McMahon and Tidy 2023). These practices prioritise certain narratives while silencing the full scope of Palestinian voices. Such acts of censorship in translation not only restrict information flow and dominate public discourse but also lead to the entrenchment of the social status quo, political disengagement of Palestinians from the public sphere and reinforcement of social and political immobilism, authoritarianism and repression. The impact of these translation practices on cultural perception and international law, as well as the potential for translation to challenge censorship and promote social translation, are critical areas warranting in-depth research.

On a related matter, although Arabic was added as an official language of the UN following the onset of the Palestinian-Israeli conflict, the UN's official website offers fewer documents related to this conflict in Arabic compared to its other five official languages. For instance, Resolution 181, passed on 29 November 1947, which proposed the partition of Palestine into Arab and Jewish states at the end of the British Mandate, is available in all the UN's working languages except Arabic.[3] While we recognise that Arabic is the most recent addition to the UN's official languages, these documents hold significant relevance for the Arab world. Therefore, such disparities, regardless of the reasons behind them, raise concerns of potential censorship and warrant further investigation. Similar discrepancies in the availability of translated documents in Arabic may exist

The Routledge Handbook of Translation and Censorship

within other international organisations and institutions, calling for a comprehensive examination of translation practices and potential censorship in these contexts.

Other potential areas for future research include the censorship of feminist texts and the role of translation in shaping the reception of feminist ideas in the Arab world. The impact of censorship on the evolution of science fiction in Arabic literature is another promising avenue for exploration. Further investigation into the influence of ideology, power and culture on translation and terminology in conflict contexts, as well as the (self-)censorship of socio-politically sensitive elements in various text types (e.g., international agreements, diplomatic communiqués, institutional and policy documents, academic publications and journalism), could provide a better understanding of the dynamic of censorship in/and translation. The visibility of the translator and the strategies employed in translating cultural references in literary works, particularly those dealing with sensitive topics, also merit deeper examination in the context of censorship and translation in the Arab world.

Notably, there has recently been an uptick in (post-)doctoral research addressing censorship in Arab translation studies, with socio-political analyses, in such areas as feminism, science fiction and AVT (Mnakri 2022; Mehawej 2024; Bakhouni Maksoud 2024; Alhajri 2024). While these contributions are significant and sociologically informed, their analyses do not extend to the scope of social translation as developed in this chapter. Therefore, to emphasise the non-exclusively linguistic breadth of the notion of social translation, we would like to point prospectively toward yet another form of censorship that intervenes, not in the social sphere or at the textual level, but rather within the epistemic discourse in Western scholarship. This highlights another significant avenue for future research in the field. In the overarching domination of the rationalist scientific discourse, whereby only empirically verified and especially materially corroborated facts are taken as reliable truths, we argue that other levels of rationality, which are no less empirical but not necessarily material, have been the object of epistemic censorship in mainstream academia (e.g., philosophical intuition; see Basalamah 2024). As these other unrecognised forms of rationality are marginalised and even outcast from the realm of scientific research, there are nonetheless some attempts to engage in various efforts toward epistemic translation between these different levels of rationality.

Robinson (2001) explores an analogical model of the scope of translator subjectivities, taking a diachronic perspective with rationalism as a point of reference, which 'constitutes a kind of ideological operating system for the West, the internalized programming that provides norms and values for virtually every aspect of psychosocial life' (2001: 12). Robinson's mapping covers the 'pre-rationalist' subjectivity ('the possession of channels by discarnate spirits'), the 'rationalist' subjectivity ('the possession of the translator by the source author'), and the 'post-rationalist' subjectivity, which Robinson embraces ('the possession of ideological subjects by collective forces') (2001: 12–13). This tripartite modelisation sets the stage for acknowledging the existence of more than one form of rationality, leading us to argue that rationalism as the privileged hegemonic epistemic model of Western modernity is not the only one to be accounted for (Dussel 1985; Mignolo 2000). This means that, in the presence of a wider spectrum of episteme, there should be a form of translation between the various existing rationalities (Santos 2016), similar to the translation that takes place among disciplines (Strober 2011).

To illustrate the extension of the connection between translation and censorship in relation to the Arab world, it is remarkable that theories and epistemologies prevalent in Western scholarship are often translated and appropriated as they are by Arab scholars, sometimes even borrowed without translation into Arabic. As a result, these scholars find themselves self-censoring their intellectual work from their own cultural imagination to align with expected epistemological preferences in

Translation and Censorship in the Arab World and Its Diasporas

the West, foundational among which is the secular character of Western scholarship inherited from the European seventeenth-century rising modernity and eighteenth-century Enlightenment. This statement is not intended to undermine the value of extant scholarship that contributes to a deeper exploration of some aspects of the realities of translation in the Arab world, but rather to lament the lack of original, theoretically and epistemologically inspiring research programmes that seek to ground their respective works in the Arab cultural imagination and scientific patrimony. A case in point is the lack of a body of theorisation originating from the Arab world, so much so that there is no standardised Arabic terminology for translation studies and beyond, only borrowed ones from the West. While censorship is usually conceived of as a wilful undertaking, self-censorship is more often an unconscious and insidious process driven by discursive power relations. Nevertheless, even if this mimetic trend is not entirely deliberate, the responsibility should be borne primarily by those who practise it.

However, there is always an exception to the rule. Taha Abderrahmane (born 1944), a contemporary Moroccan philosopher of language, ethics and logic, not well-known to Western scholarship because none of his books have been translated into European languages, has long advocated for an original, locally inspired philosophy. Translation holds a central position in Abderrahmane's philosophical thought, starting with his *al-Ḥaqq al-ʿArabī fī al-Ikhtilāf al-falsafī* [The Arab Right to Philosophical Difference] (2002), whereby he calls for the localisation of philosophy in the Arab cultural heritage. He emphasises the Arabs' right and necessity to free themselves from mindless imitation and conformity when engaging in philosophy and, by extension, any intellectual activity. Arabs have naively imitated not only the substance of Western philosophy, e.g., the Greek divide or even divorce between reason and faith, but also the exact manner in which Western thought has been introduced into the Arab library. This implies that Arabic philosophy, which dates to medieval thinkers (Abderrahmane 1994), has been faithfully translated without regard to what he refers to as his 'obsession'—that is, originality (Abderrahmane 2006a). While we could have showcased a broader spectrum of original scholarship from the Arab world, time and space constraints restricted our selection. We hope this encourages further exploration in this area.

Despite the impression that translation conceived of along these lines is completely metaphorised and disconnected from its linguistic bedrock, Abderrahmane advocates beginning this indigenisation process of Arab philosophy through its translation, that is, its Arabisation. However, to reach a form of autonomy and originality of Arab philosophy in Arabic, translation needs to be undertaken over three stages, the last one being *al-Tarjma al-ʾIbdāʿiyya* [creative translation] (Abderrahmane 2006a). To translate creatively consists of transposing the main philosophical meanings of the source text in a way that would translate in a mature (*rashīd*), independent (*mustaqil*) manner and connect them to the typical Arabic cultural currency of the reader so that it can get rooted in their psyche and prompt intrinsic forces to flourish from within. Subsequently, when Arab philosophy becomes grounded in both the Arabic language and ethos, and when it reaches a level of philosophical maturity—one of the four constitutive criteria of modernity (Abderrahmane 2006b)—it would then be capable of epistemologically translating its philosophical imagination and cultural knowledge pedigree into the contemporary forms of a poised, original and autonomous Arab scholarship (Basalamah forthcoming). Ultimately, the current epistemological self-censorship as practised in Arab scholarship would fade away and be replaced by a confident and inspiring research ethos among Arab scholars.

In line with the above examples for future directions in research on translation censorship, we believe that these notions in translation studies scholarship will, in the long run, have to move beyond the exclusively linguistic, semiotic and discursive levels of study—without dismissing them—and embrace a wider frame of reference. Within that framework, space would be given to the social, political and epistemological dimensions, among other possible dimensions, of translation—as well as to the various impediments to translation.

Further Reading

Attar, Samar. 2003. 'Translating the exiled self: Reflections on the relationship between translation and censorship', *Translation Review*, 65(1): 35–46.
Provides a unique reflective account that can inspire future studies, illustrating how self-translation can serve as a strategy to assert a voice that has been suppressed by censorship.

Khalil, Joe, Khiabany, Gholam and Guaaybess, Tourya. 2023. *The Handbook of Media and Culture in the Middle East*. Hoboken, NJ: John Wiley & Sons.
Explores various censorship practices across traditional and new media in the Middle East, including the Arab world, with chapters addressing a wide range of topics, offering a rich foundation for further research on the intersections of translation and censorship in Arab media and culture.

Nsouli, Mona and Meho, Lokman. 2006. *Censorship in the Arab World: An Annotated Bibliography*. Plymouth: Scarecrow Press.
Documents numerous cases of censorship, including those related to translation, across the Arab world, offering valuable insights for readers into the diverse forms and contexts of censorship in Arab countries.

Notes

1 Interestingly, the State of Israel, established in 1948, appears to have adopted pre-existing laws from the British Mandate.
2 See: https://tinyurl.com/Sykes-Picot-Agreement
3 See: https://tinyurl.com/UNRes181

References

Abbas, Amin. 2020. 'Wiam Al Saidi: A pioneer in the art of dubbing anime series in the Middle East', *Arab News Japan*: www.arabnews.jp/en/arts-culture/article_29418/
Abdel-Rahim, Said. 2014. 'Yawma taḥwwlat "1984" min riwāya ʾilā jarīma fī Miṣr', *Al-Araby Al-Jadid*: https://tinyurl.com/AlArabyAlJadid1984
Abderrahmane, Taha. 1994. *Tajdid al-manhaj fi taqwim al-turāth*. Casablanca: Al-Markaz Al-Thaqafi Al-Arabi.
Abderrahmane, Taha. 2002. *Al-ḥaq al-ʿarabī fī al-ʾiḵtilāf al-falsafī*. Casablanca: Al-Markaz Al-Thaqafi Al-Arabi.
Abderrahmane, Taha. 2006a. 'Hawas al-tarjama al-ʾibdāʿiyya', *Al-Jazeera* : https://tinyurl.com/TahaJazeeraInterview
Abderrahmane, Taha. 2006b. *Rawḥ al-ḥadāṯha*. Casablanca: Al-Markaz Al-Thaqafi Al-Arabi.
Abu Sadira, Essam. 2014. 'Ḍabṭ ṭālib biḥyāztuhu riwāyat 1984 wa kashkūl yaḥwī ʿibārāt ʾan «al-Khilāfa»', *Al-Masry Al-Youm*: https://tinyurl.com/AlMasryAlYoum1984
Abu Shadi, Ali. 2004. *Waqāʾiʿ al-sīnimā al-miṣrīyah fī al-qarn al-ʿishrīn*. Damascus: Ministry of Culture.
AFP. 2008. 'Arabic version of Harry Potter "banned"', *Arabian Business*: www.arabianbusiness.com/industries/media/arabic-version-of-harry-potter-banned-45269
Al-Ahdath Al-Maghribia. 2001. 'Lā yajūz lil-muslimīn al-taʿāmul maʿa laʿibat al-būkīmūn', *Al-Ahdath Al-Maghribia*, 9: https://tinyurl.com/Al-Ahdath-Al-Maghribia
Alhajri, Ayed. 2024. *The shaping powers in rewriting popular fantasy: The theory of rewriting and* Game of Thrones *in the age of social media*. Unpublished PhD thesis, Cardiff University.
Alkhunaizi, Hind. 2023. 'BBC slammed for mistranslating Arabic interview of released Palestinian prisoner', *Arab News*: www.arabnews.com/node/2416101/amp

Al-Qudah, Isra. 2022. 'Censorship as enabling: Importing, distributing, and translating foreign films in the Arab Middle East', *Heliyon*, 8(8): www.sciencedirect.com/science/article/pii/S2405844022012658

Al-Riqābah. 1999. *Global Arabic Encyclopedia*, Vol. 11. Riyadh: Encyclopedia Works Publishing & Distribution, 262: https://tinyurl.com/GlobalArabicEncyclopediaVol11

Alsharhan, Alanoud. 2020. 'Netflix no-censorship policy in subtitling taboo language from English into Arabic', *Journal of Audiovisual Translation*, 3(1): 7–28.

Alsharhan, Alanoud. 2022. *The effects of the Netflix no-censorship policy on subtitling taboo language from English to Arabic: A case study based on Kuwait*. Unpublished PhD thesis, University College London.

Arabic Dub. n.d. *Dragon Ball Wiki*: https://dragonball.fandom.com/wiki/Arabic_dub

Asseraf, Arthur. 2019. *Electric News in Colonial Algeria*. Oxford: Oxford University Press.

Bakhouni Maksoud, Mariam. 2024. *Le rôle de la traduction dans la mutation du genre science-fictionnel dans l'espace arabe*. Unpublished PhD thesis, Université Sorbonne Nouvelle.

Basalamah, Salah. 2010. 'Censure et subversion dans les médias d'État saoudiens', *TTR*, 23(2): 167–85.

Basalamah, Salah. 2012. 'Social translations: Challenges in the conflict of representations', in J. K. Dick and S. Schwerter (eds.), *Transmissibility and Cultural Transfer: Dimensions of Translation in the Humanities*. Hannover: Ibidem-Verlag, 91–105.

Basalamah, Salah. 2022. 'Translating (political) religious and secularist worldviews in a post-secular age', *Translation in Society*, 1(1): 1–21.

Basalamah, Salah. 2024. *A Bergsonian Approach to Translation and Time: Toward Spiritual Translation Studies*. London-New York: Routledge.

Basalamah, Salah. Forthcoming. 'Abderrahmane Taha's translation of modernity into an Islamic paradigm: Toward an ethical project of liberation', in M. Hashas (ed.), *Contemporary Moroccan Thought*. Leiden: Brill Publishing.

BBC. 2019. 'Netflix removes Hasan Minhaj comedy episode after Saudi demand', *BBC*: www.bbc.com/news/world-middle-east-46732786

BBC Arabic. 2014. 'Mā sirr shaʿbyat Jūrj Ūrwīl fī miṣr al-āan?', *BBC Arabic*: www.bbc.com/arabic/blogs/2014/11/141110_trending_george_orwell_1984

Boéri, Julie and Abdel Fattah, Ashraf. 2020. 'Manipulation of translation in hard news reporting on the Gulf crisis: Combining narrative and appraisal', *Meta*, 65(1): 73–99.

Booth, Marilyn. 2007. 'Letters to the editor: "Girls of Riyadh"', *The Times Literary Supplement*: https://tinyurl.com/Booth-2007

Booth, Marilyn. 2008. 'Translator v. author (2007): Girls of Riyadh go to New York', *Translation Studies*, 1(2): 197–211.

Booth, Marilyn. 2010. '"The Muslim woman" as celebrity author and the politics of translating Arabic: Girls of Riyadh go on the road', *Journal of Middle East Women's Studies*, 6(3): 149–182.

Bouchard, Gérard and Taylor, Charles. 2008. *Building the Future: A Time for Reconciliation*. Report. Québec: Gouvernement du Québec.

Bourdieu, Pierre. 1990. *The Logic of Practice*. Oxford: Blackwell.

Bowen, Wayne. 2007. *The History of Saudi Arabia*. London: Greenwood Publishing.

Brawn, Steph. 2023. 'BBC apologises after "editing errors" in Gaza report', *The National*: www.thenational.scot/news/23951324.bbc-apologises-editing-errors-gaza-report/

Burgat, François. 2020. *Understanding Political Islam*. Manchester: Manchester University Press.

Chabbak, Salma. 2018. *Manipulation of ideological and culture-specific items in the audiovisual translation from French into Arabic of voiced-over documentaries*. Unpublished PhD thesis, Universiti Sains Malaysia.

Chabbak, Salma. 2019. 'Manipulation of ideological items in the audiovisual translation of voiced-over documentaries in the Arab world', *International Journal of Cognitive and Language Sciences*, 13(5): 609–18.

Cohen, Robin and Fischer, Caroline (eds.). 2019. *Routledge Handbook of Diaspora Studies*. London: Routledge

CQLR c C-12. 1975/2023. 'Charter of human rights and freedoms', *Légis Québec*: www.legisquebec.gouv.qc.ca/en/pdf/cs/C-12.pdf

Diaz, Jaclyn. 2023. 'Changes to new editions of Roald Dahl books have readers up in arms', *NPR*: www.npr.org/2023/02/21/1158347261/roald-dahl-books-changed-offensive-words

Dussel, Enrique. 1985. *Philosophy of Liberation*. Maryknoll, NY: Orbis Books.

El-Amrani, Issandr. 2010. 'Fact-checking Hitchens on *Animal Farm*', *The Arabist*: https://arabist.net/blog/2010/4/18/fact-checking-hitchens-on-animal-farm.html

Elouardaoui, Ouidyane. 2014. 'Turkish soap operas, Arab viewers and censorship', *Turkish Review*, 4(4): www.proquest.com/docview/1565544119

Gamal, Muhammad. 2007. 'Audiovisual translation in the Arab world: A changing scene', *Translation Watch Quarterly*, 3(2): 78–95.

Gamal, Muhammad. 2008. 'Egypt's audiovisual translation scene', *Arab Media and Society*, 5: 1–15: www.academia.edu/7450964/Egypts_audiovisual_translation_scene

Gamal, Muhammad. 2009. 'Adding text to image: Challenges of subtitling non-verbal communication', *Journal of Multicultural Communication*, 1: 1–27: http://academicpress.us/journals/4695/download/v1n1-1.pdf

Gambier, Yves. 2002. 'Les censures dans la traduction audiovisuelle', *TTR*, 15(2): 203–21.

Gouanvic, Jean-Marc. 2002. 'John Steinbeck et la censure: le cas de *The Moon is Down* traduit en français pendant la Seconde Guerre mondiale', *TTR*, 15(2): 191–202.

Griffiths, James and McKirdy, Euan. 2019. 'Netflix pulls "Patriot Act" episode in Saudi Arabia after it criticized official account of Khashoggi killing', *CNN*: www.cnn.com/2019/01/01/middleeast/netflix-patriot-act-hasan-minhaj-jamal-khashoggi-intl/index.html

Habermas, Jürgen. 2001. *The Postnational Constellation: Political Essays*. Cambridge, MA: MIT Press.

Habermas, Jürgen. 2003. *TheFuture of Human Nature*. Cambridge: Polity Press.

Habermas, Jürgen. 2006. 'Religion in the public sphere', *European Journal of Philosophy*, 14(1): 1–25.

Izwaini, Sattar. 2017. 'Censorship and manipulation of subtitling in the Arab world', in J. Díaz Cintas and K. Nikoli (eds.), *Fast-Forwarding with Audiovisual Translation*. Bristol: Multilingual Matters, 47–58.

Jacquemond, Richard. 2008. *Conscience of the Nation: Writers, State, and Society in Modern Egypt*. Cairo: AUC Press.

Johnson, Alice. 2008. 'Learning, discussion focus of literary event', *Gulf News*: https://gulfnews.com/news/uae/leisure/learningdiscussion-focus-of-literary-event-1.143127

Jones, Toby. 2006. 'Rebellion on the Saudi periphery: Modernity, marginalization, and the Shi'a uprising of 1979', *International Journal of Middle Eastern Studies*, 38: 213–33.

Jones, Toby. 2010. *Desert Kingdom: How Oil and Water Forged Modern Saudi Arabia*. Cambridge, MA: Harvard University Press.

Kabil, Nada. 2014. 'Censored: Banned books in the Middle East', *Scoop Empire*: https://scoopempire.com/censored-banned-books-middle-east/

Khalifa, Abdel-Wahab. 2014. 'Rethinking agents and agency in translation studies', in A.-W. Khalifa (ed.), *Translators Have Their Say? Translation and the Power of Agency*. Münster: LIT Verlag, 9–17.

Khalifa, Abdel-Wahab. 2017. *The socio-cultural determinants of translating modern Arabic fiction into English: The (re)translations of Naguib Mahfouz's Awlād Hāratinā*. Unpublished PhD thesis, University of Leeds.

Khalifa, Abdel-Wahab. 2020. 'The hidden violence of retranslation: Mahfouz's *Awlād Ḥāratinā* in English', *The Translator*, 26(2): 145–162.

Koçak, Nalan. 2020. 'Ban on Turkish dramas in the Gulf backfires', *Hürriyet Daily News*: www.hurriyetdailynews.com/ban-on-turkish-dramas-in-the-gulf-backfires-researcher-140606

Larson, Richard. 2009. 'Banned and forbidden in Saudi Arabia', *CounterPunch*: www.counterpunch.org/2009/12/11/banned-and-forbidden-in-saudi-arabia/

Maluf, Ramez. 2005. 'A potential untapped? Why dubbing has not caught on in the Arab world', *TBS Journal*, 1. www.arabmediasociety.com/a-potential-untapped-why-dubbing-has-not-caught-on-in-the-arab-world/

Matthiesen, Toby. 2012. 'A 'Saudi Spring?': the Shi'a protest movement in the Eastern Province 2011–2012', *The Middle East Journal*, 66(4): 528–259.

McMahon, Liv and Tidy, Joe. 2023. 'Instagram sorry for adding 'Terrorist' to some Palestinian user bios', *BBC*: www.bbc.com/news/technology-67169228

Mdallel, Sabeur. 2020. 'Translating for children in the Arab world: An exercise in child political socialization', *Translation Matters*, 2(2): 160–171.

Mehawej, Isabelle. 2024. *La traduction et la réception du féminisme beauvoirien dans le monde arabe*. Unpublished PhD thesis, Université Sorbonne Nouvelle.

Merkle, Denise. 2002. 'Presentation', *TTR*, 15(2): 9–18.

Merkle, Denise. 2010. 'Censorship', in Y. Gambier and L. van Doorslaer (eds.), *Handbook of Translation Studies*, Vol. 1. Amsterdam: John Benjamins, 18–21.

Merkle, Denise. 2018. 'Translation and censorship', in F. Fernandez and J. Evans (eds.), *The Routledge Handbook of Translation and Politics*. London: Routledge, 238–53.

Merkle, Denise, O'Sullivan, Carol, van Doorslaer, Luc and Wolf, Michaela. 2010. 'Exploring a neglected century: Translation and censorship in nineteenth-century Europe', in D. Merkle et al. (eds.), *The Power of the Pen: Translation and Censorship in Nineteenth-century Europe*. Münster: Lit Verlag, 7–26.

Meyer, Richard. 2002. *Outlaw Representation: Censorship and Homosexuality in Twentieth-century American Art*. Hong Kong: Beacon Press.

Mignolo, Walter. 2000. *Local Histories/Global Designs: Essays on the Coloniality of Power, Subaltern Knowledges and Border Thinking*. Princeton: Princeton University Press.

Mnakri, Moufida. 2022. *La visibilité du traducteur et la traduction des référents culturels: Traduire «l'Autre», traduire le «Soi» dans la version arabe du roman* Zone de Mathias Énard. Unpublished PhD thesis, Université Sorbonne Nouvelle.

Nassar, Nourhan. 2017. 'Remember when there was an Arabic version of The Simpsons?', *Step Feed*: https://stepfeed.com/remember-when-there-was-an-arabic-version-of-the-simpsons-7422

Nordland, Rod. 2018. 'From Orwell to "Little Mermaid," Kuwait steps up book banning', *The New York Times*: www.nytimes.com/2018/10/01/world/middleeast/kuwait-ban-books.html

Potvin, Maryse. 2008. *Crise des accommodements raisonnables: une fiction médiatique?* Montréal: Athéna éditions.

Qiblawi, Tamara. 2017. 'Why part of a Shia town in Saudi Arabia has been flattened', *CNN*: www.cnn.com/2017/08/12/middleeast/saudi-arabia-awamiya/index.html

Reed, Betsy. 2002. 'Harry Potter expelled from UAE schools', *The Guardian*: www.theguardian.com/books/2002/feb/14/news

Robinson, Douglas. 2001. *Who Translates? Translator Subjectivities Beyond Reason*. Albany, NY: SUNY Press.

Rukavina, Steve. 2022. 'New research shows Bill 21 having "devastating" impact on religious minorities in Quebec', *CBC*: www.cbc.ca/news/canada/montreal/bill-21-impact-religious-minorities-survey-1.6541241

Saber, Indlied. 2021. 'Why anime has such deep roots in the Arab world', *Middle East Eye*: www.middleeasteye.net/discover/anime-arab-world-popularity-middle-east

Saiegh, Marc. 1994. 'L'audiovisuel arabe entre censure et autocensure', *Mediterraneans*, 85(6): 141–148.

Santos, Boaventura. 2016. *Epistemologies of the South: Justice against Epistemicide*. London: Routledge.

Schaub, Michael. 2014. 'Did George Orwell's "1984" prompt an Egyptian student's arrest?', *Los Angeles Times*: www.latimes.com/books/jacketcopy/la-et-jc-did-george-orwell-1984-prompt-egyptian-students-arrest-20141111-story.html

Schwartz, Lowell. 2009. *Barriers to the Broad Dissemination of Creative Works in the Arab World*. Santa Monica, CA: RAND Corporation.

Stanton, Sarah and Banham, Martin. 1996. *Cambridge Paperback Guide to Theatre*. Cambridge: Cambridge University Press.

Stewart, Philip. 2001. Children of Gebelaawi. *A Translator's Tale*: https://sites.google.com/site/granphi618/arabic/massachusetts.doc

Strober, Myra. 2011. *Interdisciplinary Conversations: Challenging Habits of Thought*. Stanford, CA: Stanford University Press.

Suleiman, Khaled. 2007. 'Madbūlī: fī maktabatī kul al-kutub al-maḥdhūr nashrahā', *Al-Sharq Al-Awsat*: https://archive.aawsat.com/details.asp?section=19&article=407305&issueno=10312

Suleiman, Yasir. 2019. *Arabic Language and National Identity: A Study in Ideology*. Edinburgh: Edinburgh University Press.

Tapper, Jake. 2009. '*The Simpsons* in Arabic', *ABC News*: www.youtube.com/watch?v=L7Eyyz-kGzc

Taylor, Derrick. 2023. 'Roald Dahl's books are rewritten to cut potentially offensive language', *The New York Times*: www.nytimes.com/2023/02/20/books/roald-dahl-books-changes.html

Taylor, Miriam. 2022. 'Law 21: discourse, perceptions & impacts', *Association for Canadian Studies*: https://acs-metropolis.ca/wp-content/uploads/2022/08/Report_Survey-Law-21_ACS.pdf

Thawabteh, Mohammad. 2017. 'Censorship in English-Arabic subtitling', *Babel*, 63(4): 556–579.

The Black Iris. 2008. 'The Arabized *Harry Potter* gets banned', *The Black Iris*: http://black-iris.com/2008/08/11/the-arabized-harry-potter-gets-banned/

The Simpsons. n.d. *Censorship Wiki*: https://censorship.fandom.com/wiki/The_Simpsons#Middle_East_censorship

Ulrichsen, Kristian. 2020. *Qatar and the Gulf Crisis*. Oxford: Oxford University Press.

Uras, Umut. 2018. 'Saudi network ban on Turkey TV shows is 'political': minister', *Al-Jazeera*: www.aljazeera.com/news/2018/3/6/saudi-network-ban-on-turkey-tv-shows-is-political-minister

US State Department. 2016. *Saudi Arabia 2016 International Religious Freedom Report. US State Department*: www.state.gov/wp-content/uploads/2019/01/Saudi-Arabia-3.pdf

Volmar, Victor. 1950. 'Foreign versions', *Journal of the Society of Motion Picture and Television Engineers*, 55(5): 536–546: https://archive.org/details/sim_smpte-motion-imaging-journal_1950-11_55_5/

Wagner, Rob. 2013. '"Girls of Riyadh" author honored in US for stem cell research', *Arab News*: www.arabnews.com/news/472696

Willis, Michael. 2022. *Algeria: Politics and Society from the Dark Decade to the Hirak*. London: C. Husrt & Co. Publishers.

Wolf, Michaela. 2002. 'Censorship as cultural blockage: Banned literature in the late Habsburg monarchy', *TTR*, 15(2): 45–61.

Yahiaoui, Rashid and Abdel Fattah, Ashraf. 2020. 'Shifts in transadapting Western socio-cultural references for dubbing into Arabic. A case study of *The Simpsons* and *Al-Shamshoon*', *InTRAlinea*, 22: www.intralinea.org/archive/article/shifts_in_transadapting_western_socio_cultural_references_for_dubbing

Zitawi, Jehan. 2008. 'Contextualizing Disney comics within the Arab culture', *Meta*, 53(1): 139–53.

2

SUPPRESSION AND DEFIANCE

Translation and Censorship in Germany

Elisabeth Gibbels

2.1 Introduction

This chapter sees censorship as any instrument or constellation of instruments that suppresses or excludes discourse, on the one hand, or favours and empowers it, on the other. Following Bunn (2015), censorship is understood as:

> a phenomenon in which a host of actors (including impersonal, structural conditions) function as effective censors. These 'structural' forms of censorship may be based upon the effects of the market, ingrained cultural languages and grammars, and other forms of impersonal boundaries on acceptable (and indeed intelligible) speech.
>
> (Bunn 2015: 27)

Translation has been studied as an inherently selective process and an act of tacit censorship (Gibbels 2009). This understanding has generated greater interest in the actors in transfer processes. Therefore, when looking at how translation and censorship played out in Germany, I will focus on historical constellations that illustrate how censorship regulations functioned in Germany and how translation was employed both as a means of empowerment and as a means of suppression. The chapter will focus on the time from the Middle Ages to the beginning of the twentieth century. I will first provide a brief overview of censorship regulations in German history. The second section will highlight situations in German history in which translations were at the centre of censorship efforts. I will focus on situations where translators defied censorship or where censorship rules and translations affected access to discursive representation. Finally, I will briefly address instances of structural censorship in the German context.

2.2 Historical Perspectives

Records of punitive measures taken in regard to the censorship of book production in Germany date back to 1475 and 1478. These measures were documented in a note in the margin of a book and in the record of the legal prosecution of a printer (Freund 1971: 7). Shortly after, in 1496, regulations sought to extend censorship to all stages of book production and, with the powerful threat posed by the Reformation movement in Germany, central commissions were installed

DOI: 10.4324/9781003149453-4

to oversee the book trade as well. From 1548, full bibliographical information had to be given regarding all book publications. These attempts were mainly directed at the distribution of heretical ideas. Attempts to suppress knowledge by holding the agents of the book trade accountable were countered by a rise in anonymous publications and fake publishers (Wüst 1998; Creasman 2012). Another strategy was to move publication locations within Germany to more lenient territories (Schütz 1990). Cologne, in particular, became a centre for the publication of banned foreign literature, among them many translations, for example, William Tyndale's English translation of the Bible (1525) and Blaise Pascal's eighteen anti-Jesuit letters (1656) (Raabe 1991). This exploitation of Germany's political situation with its numerous small duchies and territories operating largely autonomously underneath imperial power before German unification in 1871 is evident time and again over the history of censorship and translation in Germany.

A side note in this regard refers to the *Index Librorum Prohibitorum*, arguably the most powerful censorship instrument in the Middle Ages. In Germany, it was found to have been somewhat less influential. First, because it only assessed publications in Latin, French and Italian, all books published in German or translated into German remained outside its reach. Second, the sizeable portion of Germany that had become Protestant did not use it as they had their own secular police regulations (Schütz 1990: 46f.).

The interplay between censorship, efforts to evade it and translation is evident in subsequent centuries, too. Key periods in this regard were 1806, after the French Revolution and during Napoleonic rule; 1848, after the German revolution; 1878 to 1890, following German unification and the fight against social democratic movements; and the years of growing militarism before 1914. These historical constellations will be examined through the lens of suppression and defiance.

2.3   Core Issues and Topics

In the early thirteenth century, it was the classification of a text that determined who would decide whether to ban it or not. If it was classified as philosophy, then the university was responsible; if it was classified as theology, then the church. In the case of the increasing popularity of the writings of Aristotle, it was the university that checked the texts and declared their translations into Latin dangerous. As a consequence, everybody who heard Aristotle's teachings and failed to report it to the authorities within seven days was punished (Löser 2015: 97f.). At the same time, the Dominican monk Meister Eckhart (from around 1260 to around 1328) taught and preached in the German vernacular. Because this was classified as a theological issue, the Archbishop of Cologne was in charge. He had Meister Eckhart's texts translated into Latin, compiled a list of the sentences that he thought should be banned, and submitted them to the Pope (Löser 2015: 104f.). Paradoxically, in both cases, the undesirable parts of the originals had a better chance of surviving because these texts were copied and kept in circulation (90), albeit for censorship purposes.

The situation changed with the invention of print, when censorship had to grapple with the mass distribution of books. In Germany, this coincided with the rise of Protestant thought and so, not surprisingly, by far the most common reason for banning a book was writing against the accepted religion. The bans sought to intercept heterodox texts and were therefore not overly concerned with translated German Bibles, which had been common for some time. This changed, however, with Martin Luther's readable, accessible and hugely popular German translation of the Bible, published in 1522. Despite being immediately banned, it became the most printed book in the German language and, indeed, the use of the German vernacular for religious writings and translations became an act of rebellion in the sixteenth century. The censors reacted and about two thirds of all banned books at that time were books in the German vernacular (Fitos 2000). The use of the vernacular was also the reason for banning texts criticizing dignitaries or against religious authorities, and texts that stirred up 'the common people' or created disunity within the community (Creasman 2012). Still, it proved tricky to ban some publications, especially with new genres like the 'wahrhafte Berichte' (true reports). These were pamphlets that became exceedingly popular during the Thirty Years' War (1618–1648). Quite in contrast to their name, they routinely contained wild, fabricated stories from different regions of the war. Coming from abroad, they were published in translation, for instance, the infamous *Wahrhafter Bericht* (*True Report of the Siege and Conquest of the City of Pilsen*, 1619), which was translated from Bohemian into German. The fantastical nature of the reports resonated with the population and made them difficult to control. In their efforts to suppress them, but without an established reason, the authorities resorted to putting them in the same category as 'apparitions and miracles', so that they ultimately were banned for 'confusing the common people' (Creasman 2012: 190).

At the end of the seventeenth and early eighteenth centuries, another group of texts triggered the suspicion of the censors. These were clandestine writings by Portuguese Jews that discussed heterodox religious ideas and were thought to promote libertine and atheist thinking. They circulated between Amsterdam, where the exiled Portuguese Jewish community lived, Berlin and London (Mulsow 2007). Because it was dangerous to be caught in possession of such texts, they were swapped and the names of previous owners were withheld. The translations were produced for affluent book collectors across Europe. Librarian Samuel Engel, for example, copied the best known of these texts, *De tribus impostoribus* published anonymously in 1688, and then ordered three translations into Latin and French for his clients (Mulsow 2012: 25f.).

The translation history of *Judaeus Lusitanus*, published anonymously in 1699, illustrates the difficulties a translator had to face (Mulsow 2015). Mathurin Veyssière La Croze (1661–1739), librarian to the Prussian King, received the manuscript around 1700 and was unsure whether to translate it; after all, friends of his had been incarcerated for such translations. His love of knowledge overrode his concerns and he sought the advice of Alphonse des Vignoles (1649–1744), a fellow Huguenot intellectual. Vignoles entreated him to translate the text but suggested he take precautions. First, he recommended that La Croze soften blasphemous terms (Vignoles' letter includes detailed and very concrete instructions) and, second, that he add a preface explaining why he did not write a theological refutation (lack of time and insufficient competence). Nevertheless, it took La Croze more than 20 years to finally publish his translation in 1726. The Portuguese original was also kept in circulation and inspired new translations, so that, by the 1730s, *Judaeus Lusitanus* was known across Europe, from Copenhagen to Geneva.

Towards the end of the eighteenth century, another genre of clandestine literature was introduced to the German reading public through translation (Mulsow 2007). Wilhelm Heinse (1746–1803) had written erotic or, as some hold, pornographic verse and tried to establish the genre by way of literary journals. However, it was his approach to translating these erotic books that made inroads, 'sounding out the tolerance limits of the literary system' ('die Toleranzgrenzen des Literatursystems … auszuloten', Mayer 2011: 283). Arguably Heinse's most successful decision was to radically adapt the texts to German culture and make them blend with German readers' horizons of experience. This worked so well that they were widely reviewed, which increased their reach and helped establish the genre of erotic writing in German eighteenth century reading culture (Mayer 2011).

In the Enlightenment period, calendars, almanacs and encyclopaedias became the main mediums through which to spread and consolidate knowledge. These products catered to a semi-literate audience and must be considered a significant factor in the educational agenda of the German Enlightenment movement of the early nineteenth century. As affordable and accessible reading material, calendars in particular shaped German thinking about their national identity and their perception of other nations (Greilich and Mix 2006). Statistics illustrate the scope of their influence: sources list 600 calendar titles for the late eighteenth and early nineteenth centuries (Lanckoronska 1954). Their popularity attracted the attention of the censors, who tried to maintain some sort of control over their contents (Zalar 2018). In Baden-Württemberg, authorities tried to forbid calendars altogether. The calendars were predominantly based on English and French publications, largely relying on translations, of which there were five forms: (1) complete or partial translation; (2) translation of selected features, such as captions or headings; (3) foreign language passages with comments and translation; (4) translation of intertextual elements like oral sayings; and (5) some few transfers from German into other languages (e.g., *Der Hinkende Bote* [limping messenger] (Lüsebrink 2006: 262–77).

Almanacs were equally popular reading matter and were also distributed cross-nationally through translation. Benjamin Franklin's *Poor Richard's Almanack* (1739–1758) serves as a good example of how content was disseminated. Franklin's almanac, a bestseller in the American colonies, was translated into many languages, including German. The German translation worked with a censored version for which Franklin himself had removed all remarks on the Catholic Church, in addition to other passages to which the censors had objected (Lüsebrink 2006: 275). As in the case of Denis Diderot (1713–1784) (see below), German readers were exposed to a much milder version of Franklin's writings. How much the author was distorted in the translation becomes obvious with a later work by Franklin, *Way to Wealth* (1757). Here the text was so radically changed in the German translation (1777) that it became unrecognisable and was translated back into English as somebody else's text (Carpenter 2016). Similarly, the German Diderot is much tamer than the French version. When Diderot could not be published in his native France, publication moved abroad, often to Germany. At that time, one in three distributors of French books and periodicals are thought to have operated from Germany (Lüsebrink 2007: 147), often printing books that had been banned in France. These publications were commonly accompanied by a German translation. It was Diderot's novels that were first published in German translation, making him better known in Germany than in France. However, what kind of Diderot did German readers encounter? The translations aimed to soften all radical or explicit expressions, and the perception of Diderot as a novelist rather than a philosopher persists in Germany to this day (Saada 2003; Lüsebrink 2007). Thus, in Diderot's case, the defiant act of printing a censored author was partly undermined by the mitigation of his radical ideas.

In addition to the calendars and almanacs, encyclopaedias were a major source of public knowledge (Greilich and Mix 2006). The most famous one was Diderot's *Encyclopédie*, likewise banned in France and published abroad, in what is now Switzerland. Encyclopaedias typically were transnational undertakings, with contributors from many different countries. Like the calendars and almanacs, they were comprised of secondary information and translations. To publish one was a risky enterprise, resulting in constant struggles with the censors in many countries. In Germany, Sebastian Münster's *Cosmographia* (1544) was an early successful encyclopaedia. It was published for 84 years, saw 55 editions and was translated into five languages (Hantzsch 1898 contains a complete list of contributors and contributions). During this time, it was repeatedly banned by the Inquisition and various European princes; its publisher, Münster, was banned from entering Italy and Spain, and two of its contributors were burned at the stake. However, it could not be suppressed completely so that there were censored and uncensored editions in circulation at the same time (McLean 2007: 156–63; Jenny 1973).

Suppression and Defiance: Translation and Censorship in Germany

The entries in encyclopaedias often displayed startling, dehumanizing depictions of colonial peoples. Johann Christian Daniel Schreber, for example, included 'peoples of the Pacific' in his history of mammals (*Beschreibung der Säugethiere* 1774) (Dietz 2013: 717f.). Schreber's book relied on a German translation of a French version of an original English book by Thomas Astley (716). Encyclopaedia entries in translation were also found to focus on the physical features of African people or on their economic value in slave trade transactions (Fendler and Greilich 2006). This contrasts with informative first-hand articles, which also described religious practices and forms of government of African peoples. One such careful entry was Hiob Ludolf's article 'Abessinien' [Abyssinia] for the Zedler's *Grosses Universallexicon* (1732–1751). His source was Abba Gregorius, an Ethiopian living in Germany (Fendler and Greilich 2006). Similarly, Christian Georg Andreas Oldendorp interviewed slaves for his *Historie der caribischen Inseln* (1774) (Stein 2006: 179ff.). He also included a systematic description of Creole languages, treating them as linguistic systems in their own right rather than gibberish. When an edition in 1777 eliminated his passages on the history, cultures and languages of slaves and softened the sections on colonialist brutality, Oldendorp protested (Stein 2006: 188). The influential French *De la Littérature des Nègres* (Henri Grégoire 1808) included literary works by slaves, contrary to the purported view that black slave literature was non-existent or worthless (Lüsebrink 2006: 14ff.). The German edition reinforced Grégoire's anti-colonialist message in its own paratexts, retaining the tolerant epigram (whatever their tints may be, their souls are still the same) and using a subtitle that classified the work as scientific (*Beitrag zur Staats- und Menschenkunde*—a contribution to political and civic science).

The late eighteenth and early nineteenth centuries were marked by increased tensions linked to the emergence of a German national identity. In the absence of political unity, Germany relied on language and culture to forge a national identity. Part of this effort involved the wholesale importation of foreign literature, and almost every German author also translated (Kortländer and Singh 2011). Achieving national cohesion relied on the construction of a 'them', often a colonial or minority *Other*. Censorship in this context may not involve an active ban on texts but rather the repression of minority voices and non-colonialist images through non-translation or distorted translation. By contrast, producing respectful translations and using authentic, first-hand sources would make the voice of the *Other* heard and amount to an act of defying hegemonic perceptions.

The effort to promote the national identity by suppressing culturally *Other* voices can be observed in many ways. First, works from some cultures were more frequently selected for translation than others. This is demonstrated by the fact that works from 'prestigious' cultures, such as China, Persia and the Ottoman Empire, were widely translated and read (Lüsebrink 2006), whereas works from African cultures tended to be ignored and stereotyped (Fendler and Greilich 2006). Second, translations of Indigenous voices entered German culture with delay or not at all. For example, *Commentarios Reales* by Garcilaso de la Vega, a sixteenth century Indigenous writer from Peru, had to wait 200 years to be translated (*Geschichte der Ynkas, Könige von Peru*, 1787) (Röben 2006: 371–87). Third, and on a larger scale, colonial cultures were stereotypically presented to German readers when translators worked with a colonial source text that was in fact a pivot translation (Fendler and Greilich 2006; Lüsebrink 2006). The difference between the use of authentic, first-hand sources as opposed to secondary sources will be illustrated in the following sections with examples from popular cultural media of the time.

The field of literature, too, helped to set the tone for how foreign cultures were perceived in the eighteenth century. The so-called reading fever or reading mania produced a huge demand for translated reading material. Authorities, however, were worried that novels would foster immoral and promiscuous behaviour. Censorship here took the form of regulating access and separating desirable titles, which were to be promoted, from undesirable titles, which were to be suppressed. This selection was largely performed through catalogues and periodicals (Nicoli 2013). However, reviews, too, influenced whether translations and the views contained in them gained traction. This is evident with an influential text that came to represent for German readers a 'mystical' paternalistic India. George Forster (1754–1794) translated an old Sanskrit play based on the Indian epic *Mahabaratha*, working with the English translation by William Jones (1789). The figure of Sakuntala, the female heroine, became very popular and launched an Oriental craze in Germany. However, the elements presenting Sakuntala as assertive were eliminated or mitigated in the translation. Subsequent reviews and essays in German journals reinforced the image of docile, submissive Indian women, one that is still very much alive in Germany today (Esleben 2003, 2006).

Cultural *Others* were controlled and, if deemed dangerous, suppressed. Here, translations played a role both as a means of censorship and as a means of assimilation and resistance. The two most significant minorities in Germany were the Jewish German population and the Polish minority.

The Jewish religion and translation have a long history in Germany. The first translated Jewish texts were rabbinic writings, translated by Christians from the tenth century on (Schütz 1990; Burnett 1998). Jewish literature includes Biblical and rabbinic literature, literature written in the Jewish languages of Aramaic, Hebrew and Yiddish, and literature produced by and about Jewish authors. This rich tradition of translation came to an end with the massive persecution of Jews in German territories in the Middle Ages, which culminated in 1510, when emperor Maximilian I issued not only a ban on Jewish books but ordered their physical destruction. Johannes Reuchlin (1455–1522), a Christian scholar, was one of the few to resist the book burning. He wrote the *Augenspiegel* (1511) that defended the translation of Jewish scholarship: 'Verbrennt nicht, was ihr nicht kennt!' [Do not burn what you do not know!], arguing that the development of philosophy and theology needed the exchange with the Jewish tradition and the translation of Jewish texts (O'Callaghan 2013; Breuer 1982: 25). Reuchlin's book was banned by the Pope in 1520, after which the cultural acceptance of Jewish literature devolved into pervasive anti-Semitism.

The Jewish community also used translations to fight exclusion and anti-Semitism and to promote assimilation. Between 1780 and 1783, Moses Mendelssohn (1729–1786) produced a modern German translation of the Pentateuch in Hebrew letters to facilitate access to the Torah for a contemporary German-Jewish readership. His translation was based on a banned book, Johann Lorenz Schmidt's so-called Wertheimer Bible (1735), a translation for a contemporary German-Christian readership. Schmidt was later interrogated and incarcerated for his translation, so Mendelssohn's possession and use of Schmidt's book was an act of assimilation and defiance at the same time. Translation was also used to make Yiddish culture and literature better known in Germany. To pick just one example, Bertha von Pappenheim (1859–1936) translated a women's Talmud, the *Ma'assebuch* (1929), as well as the Yiddish memoirs of a Jewish businesswoman from the Middle Ages (*Erinnerungen der Glikl bas Judah Leib*, 1910). Pappenheim's translations were self-commissioned and are considered her individual effort to make Jewish history visible and to contribute to the empowerment of Jewish women. Such attempts to counter ostracization and exclusion were met with hostility from both sides, though to very different degrees. While toward the end of the nineteenth century Jewish authorities banned translated children's readers from their schools because they did not approve of their secular content (Nagel 1999), anti-Semitism had reached such a degree by the beginning of the twentieth century that the label 'Jewish' had become a category for the censors, and a Berlin theatre, Franz Mehring's *Freie Volksbühne*, was closed on the grounds that it was a 'Jewish-progressive organ' (Stark 2009: 127).

Suppression and Defiance: Translation and Censorship in Germany

The situation of the Polish minority was different in many respects. First, at 2.5 million people, it was a considerably larger community. Second, the community was geographically concentrated mostly in East Prussia and Silesia. Third, due to its history, the Polish community had a fierce desire for national independence and a strong sense of national pride. In addition, the Polish were Catholic in a Protestant part of Germany. These factors made them a threat to the German unification project and, when Germany introduced the Anti-Socialist laws in 1878 to suppress the rising social democratic movement, Polish publications came under a blanket ban too. Two of the four volumes of banned titles were dedicated to 'Polish literature' (Birett 1996). Actually, 'Polish literature' included everything from church hymns to post cards. In 1911, long after the Anti-Socialist laws had been repealed, the censorship office listed 409 literary titles, 244 songs, 35 theatre plays, 43 poems, 318 picture postcards, letter heads, pictures, flags, signs and badges together with half a dozen newspapers and more than 200 non-periodical publications under banned Polish literature (Kobuch 1988). Such oversight required an immense translation effort. Offices were established to compile weekly press reviews (*Gesamtüberblick über die polnische Tagesliteratur* [general overview of Polish daily publications]), and translators in the police headquarters in Berlin were mandated to submit texts in translation. In particular, all theatre plays had to be translated and presented to the authorities for approval (Gibbels 2009; Stark 2009; Rajch 2012). Despite these general bans and anti-Polish sentiments, translations of Polish literature flourished, defying the hegemonic resentment and efforts at total suppression (Joachimsthaler 2014).

The anti-Socialist laws mentioned above were an interesting example of suppression and defiance. The law prescribed an immediate ban on all Social Democratic publications to stop the rise of social democratic forces in Germany, ultimately without success. There was a considerable effort to translate on both sides. While the censors employed agents and spies abroad as well as special translators in their headquarters, the social democrats tried to get around the ban by publishing their works in exile (Gibbels 2009). The party newspaper *Vorwärts* [forward] maintained its influence by being published in London and then smuggled into Germany, with large sections consisting of translated articles, for example, by Eleanor Marx-Aveling (1855–1898) and Nathalie Liebknecht (1835–1909) (Gibbels 2010). This worked so well that, despite the domestic suppression of their publications, the Social Democratic Party managed to increase its share of votes in elections, a success that led to the discontinuation of the laws in 1890 and that was, at least partly, attributable to the constant influx of socialist and anarchist ideas through translations.

The following period, until World War I, was characterised by growing militarism and strict censorship of critical voices. Defiant authors not only faced a ban but were prosecuted under military law. A case with repercussions beyond Germany came from the Alsace-Lorraine region. Author Oswald Bilse was court-martialled for his play *Aus einer kleinen Garnison* [Life in a Garrison Town] because it contained lightly veiled allusions to military figures. When Bilse was given a sentence of six months in prison, the German emperor Wilhelm II personally intervened because he thought the sentence was too lenient. Shortly after its publication (and ban) in 1903, Bilse's play was translated into French and English (both 1904) and later into other languages, and his name became synonymous with literary freedom. One hundred years later, a court case regarding the German author Maxim Biller still referenced Bilse.

2.4 Recent Concepts of Censorship and the Role of Translation

The chapter has so far outlined core issues in the interplay between censorship and translation with the aim of suppressing, restricting and regulating access to information and cultural representations, on the one hand, and of evading, undermining and rebelling against repression, on

The Routledge Handbook of Translation and Censorship

the other. In the process, religions, minorities and political groups have been discussed. The final section will touch upon exclusion from discursive agency and limitation of access to knowledge in Germany through social and economic mechanisms.

One aspect of this structural censorship (Bunn 2015) was cost, whereby the price of a book controlled access to it (Nicoli 2013). Censors considered the:

> price, the number of copies printed, the type of illustrations or dust jacket it had, the way it was advertised, whether it was sold by reputable bookstores or peddled by colporteurs, even the general reputation of the publishing house [...] to determine if a work was a legitimate artistic or scholarly creation intended for serious readers, or a thinly disguised attempt to capitalize on the prurient interests of a broader public.
>
> (Stark 2009: 193)

In general, limited, highly priced editions were permitted, but cheap popular editions were banned (193). This effectively denied access to everyone who could not afford the costlier editions, which was a class-based form of censorship similar to Victorian Britain (Merkle 2006, 2009). In the case of translations, this led to awkward discrepancies. Some translations were banned, whereas the original French versions were considered harmless because they were intended for 'better circles' (e.g., Emile Zola's *Nana* and *Pot Bouille*). At other times, only a particular translation was banned, but other translations were not (Zola's *L'Argent*, *Debacle*, *Le docteur Pascal*).

The practice of exclusion through price setting, that is, economic censorship, was less a concern when it came to women's participation in discourse. Here it can be argued that structural censorship was a social mechanism that effectively kept women out of the marketplace of ideas by silencing them. A key factor in such exclusion was education. It has been shown that women relied on translation to promote female education and access to knowledge (Gibbels 2018). Starting in the early Middle Ages, women in Germany translated with the explicit aim of circumventing exclusion. They also translated texts that were banned or otherwise deemed undesirable. A few examples from the thirteenth to the nineteenth centuries illustrate this. Gertrud von Helfta (1256–1301) was one of many nuns in German cloisters who translated with the explicit aim of spreading knowledge. She translated the teachings of French mystic Marguerite Porète, a banned author, from Latin into German. Likewise, Olympia Fulvia Morata (1526–1555) held public lectures; she also translated excerpts from Giovanni Boccaccio's banned *Decameron*. Noble women, such as Anna Sophie von Anhalt-Bernburg (1604–1640), formed learned societies for women and translated the *Cento novelle antiche* [One hundred ancient tales] with a group of women. She even translated tales that her translator brother thought too risky. Maria Cunitz (1610–1644) translated her own astronomical treatise *Urania Propitia* into German to make her text accessible for women who did not read Latin and, in the process, advancing the use of German in science. To put her achievement into perspective: over one hundred years later, in 1723, the law faculty of the University of Leipzig banned a dissertation by a woman because it was written in German (Kobuch 1988, 251f.). Margarete von Bouwinghausen (1629–after 1679) also considered her translation work to be part of her mission to spread knowledge. She translated philosophical literature, including Pierre Charron's *De la sagesse*, which had been placed on the *Index* in 1605. Barbara Kopsch (1650–1705) was the first German woman to make it her task to promote the oeuvre of another woman, Madame de Scudery, in the German speaking world by translating her work into German. During the early modern period and the Enlightenment, numerous women used their own education to enlighten other women. One of the most industrious of these was Luise Gottsched (1713–1762), who translated the English journal the *Spectator* [Der Zuschauer], edited by her husband. In addition, with the explicit aim of expanding the horizons of female readers, she took on the project of the translation of the liberal journal *Der Freydenker* [the Free-Thinker], which was banned after eight editions. Dorothea (Meta) Forkel-Liebeskind (1765–1853) translated works of natural and political science and, when Forster refused to translate Thomas Paine's *The Rights of Men* because he considered it too dangerous, she translated it and fought for the translation to be published (all examples from Gibbels 2018). These examples of early women translators in Germany illustrate how important translation was in overcoming structural censorship.

2.5 Summary

Because Germany was made up of hundreds of small duchies and estates, censorship was a heterogeneous affair; regulations adopted by the emperor and the courts were subject to political manoeuvring and evasion in the territories. This allowed for books to be published in some parts of Germany while being forbidden in others. Another factor that was specific to the history of censorship in Germany was the division of the country into Catholic and Protestant regions, which made the *Index Librorum Prohibitorum* only relevant in some areas. Much of German book publishing was dedicated to translations, and the main source of knowledge for much of the German population was translations, for example, of encyclopaedias in the sixteenth and seventeenth centuries. A recurring issue in German censorship regulations concerned minorities, as a result of the German quest to establish its national identity, which, in the absence of a unified state before 1871, relied on language and culture.

2.6 Outlook and New Debates

Censorship and translation are increasingly seen as fundamental to identity construction, heritage formation and cultural production. Translation as a culturally relevant transmission process has opened itself up to sociological and agent-focused perspectives and the transfer of knowledge. As a result, questions of cultural citizenship and censorship through restricted access to education and social institutions have come into greater focus. Recent research has also considered censorship within the frameworks of contested heritage formations and collective identity. Censorship, as a perspective on heritage constructions, thus offers the possibility of looking at what is established as heritage or identity, on the one hand, and what is held to be negative or undesirable, on the other. Future research into the history of censorship and translation in Germany may have to take such viewpoints into even greater consideration.

Further Reading

Mix, York-Gothart (ed.). 2014. *Kunstfreiheit und Zensur in der Bundesrepublik Deutschland* [*Artistic freedom and censorship in the Federal Republic of Germany*]. Berlin: de Gruyter.
This volume offers an overview of censorship in Germany after 1949. It includes perspectives on cultural memory and systemic forms of censorship. It does not, however, specifically address translation.

Van Doorslaer, Luc, Flynn, Peter and Leerssen, Joep T, (eds.). 2015. *Interconnecting translation studies and imagology*. Amsterdam: Benjamins.
This volume expands the view of translation to address issues of identity formation. Censorship is touched upon, mainly in discussions of blockage and exclusion. German issues are presented in Emer O'Sullivan's 'Englishness in German translations of *Alice in Wonderland*' and in Pieter Boulogne's 'Champion of the humiliated and insulted or xenophobic satirist? Dostoevsky's mockery of Germans in early translation.'

The Routledge Handbook of Translation and Censorship

References

Birett, Herbert. 1996. *Verbotene Druckschriften in Deutschland* [Banned print publications in Germany]. Liechtenstein: Topos.

Breuer, Dieter. 1982. *Geschichte der literarischen Zensur in Deutschland* [History of literary censorship in Germany]. Heidelberg: Quelle & Meyer.

Bunn, Matthew. 2015. 'Reimagining repression: New censorship theory and after', *History and Theory*, 54(1): 25–44. Available from: www.jstor.org/stable/24543076. [Accessed 5 April 2023].

Burnett, Stephen. 1998. 'The Regulation of Hebrew Printing in Germany, 1555–1630: Confessional Politics and the Limits of Jewish Toleration', in M. Reinhart and T. Robisheaux (eds.), *Boundaries: Order, Disorder, and reorder in early modern German culture*. Sixteenth Century Essays and Studies, No. 40: Sixteenth Century Journal Publishers, 329–48. Available from: *Faculty Publications*, Classics and Religious Studies Department, 49 https://digitalcommons.unl.edu/classicsfacpub/49 [Accessed 6 July 2021].

Carpenter, Kenneth. 2016. 'Translating Benjamin Franklin's *Way to wealth* into German ... and then back into English', *Harvard Library Bulletin*, 25(3), fall 2016: 55–71.

Creasman, Allyson. 2012. *Censorship and civic order in reformation Germany, 1517–1648*. London and New York: Routledge.

Dietz, Bettina. 2013. 'Natural History as Compilation. Travel accounts in the epistemic process of an empirical discipline', in A. Holenstein (ed.), *Scholars in Action: The Practice of knowledge and the figure of the savant in the 18th century*, vol. 1 and 2. Leiden: Brill, 703–19.

Esleben, Jörg. 2003. ' "Indisch lessen": Conceptions of intercultural communication in Georg Forster's and Johann Gottfried Herder's Reception of Kālidāsa's *Śakuntalā*', *Monatshefte*, 95(2): 217–29. Available from: www.jstor.org/stable/30154102 [Accessed 22 July 2021].

Esleben, Jörg. 2006. 'Konstruktionen indischer Sichtweisen in der Rezeption von Kalidasas Sakuntala im Deutschland des späten 18. Jahrhunderts' [Constructions of Indian perspectives in the German reception of Kalidasa's Sakuntala in late 18th century], in H.-J. Lüsebrink (ed.), *Das Europa der Aufklärung und die außereuropäische koloniale Welt* [Enlightenment Europe and the non-European colonial world]. Göttingen: Wallstein, 388–406.

Fendler, Ute and Greilich, Susanne. 2006. 'Afrika in deutschen und französischen Enzyklopädien' [Africa in German and French encyclopaedias], in H.-J. Lüsebrink (ed.), *Das Europa der Aufklärung und die außereuropäische koloniale Welt* [Enlightenment Europe and the non-European colonial world]. Göttingen: Wallstein, 113–37.

Fitos, Stephan. 2000. *Zensur als Misserfolg. Die Verbreitung indizierter deutscher Druckschriften in der zweiten Hälfte des 16. Jahrhunderts* [Censorship as a failure. The distribution of banned German print publications in the second half of the 16th century]. Frankfurt/Main: Lang.

Freund, Hilger. 1971. *Die Bücher- und Pressezensur im Kurfürstentum Mainz von 1486–1797* [Book and press censorship in the electorate of Mainz between 1486 and 1797]. Karlsruhe: Müller.

Gibbels, Elisabeth. 2009. 'Translators, the tacit censors', in E. Chuilleanain, C. Ó Cuilleanain and D. Parris (eds.), *Translation and censorship*. Dublin: Four Courts Press, 57–75.

Gibbels, Elisabeth. 2010. 'Zensur und Translation in Deutschland zwischen 1878 und 1890' [Censorship and translation in Germany between 1878 and 1890], in D. Merkle, C. O'Sullivan, L. van Doorslaer and M. Wolf (eds.), *The power of the pen*. Vienna: LIT, 143–68.

Gibbels, Elisabeth. 2018. *Lexikon der deutschen Übersetzerinnen 1200–1850* [Lexicon of German Women Translators]. Berlin: Frank & Timme.

Greilich, Susanne and Mix, York-Gothart (eds.). 2006. *Populäre Kalender im vorindustriellen Europa: Der 'Hinkende Bote', 'Messager boiteux': kulturwissenschaftliche Analysen und bibliographisches Repertorium; ein Handbuch* [Popular calendars in pre-industrial Europe: The limping messenger]. Berlin: de Gruyter.

Hantzsch, Viktor. 1898. *Sebastian Münster: Leben, Werk, wissenschaftliche Bedeutung* [Sebastian Münster: Life, work, scientific impact] (reprint 1965). Niewkoop: de Graaf.

Jenny, Beat Rudolf. 1973. 'Sancta Pax Basiliensis: neue Quellen und Hinweise zu Sebastian Münster und seiner Kosmographie, insbesondere zu den Beiträgern Hans David und Sigismund Acquer' [Sancta Pax Basiliensis: New sources and information on Sebastian Münster and his cosmographia, in particular on the contributors Hans David and Sigismund Acquer], *Basler Zeitschrift für Geschichte und Altertumskunde* [Basel Journal for History and Archaeology], 73: 37–70. Available from: http://edoc.unibas.ch/dok/A687 345 [Accessed 2 July 2021].

Suppression and Defiance: Translation and Censorship in Germany

Joachimsthaler, Jürgen. 2014. 'Das Übersetzerlexikon—Was kann, was soll es enthalten?' [A translators' lexicon—What can and should it include?], in A. Kelletat and A. Tashinsky (eds.), *Übersetzer als Entdecker* [*Translators as explorers*]. Berlin: Frank & Timme, 83–104.

Kobuch, Agatha. 1988. *Zensur und Aufklärung in Kursachsen. 1697–1763* [*Censorship and enlightenment in the electorate of Saxony*]. Weimar: Böhlau.

Kortländer, Bernd and Singh, Sikander (eds.). 2011. *Das Fremde im Eigensten. Die Funktion von Übersetzungen im Prozess der deutschen Nationenbildung* [*The foreign within the true self. The Function of translation for German Nation Building*]. Tübingen: Narr.

Lanckoronska, Maria and Rümann, Arthur. 1954. *Geschichte der deutschen Taschenbücher und Almanache aus der klassisch-romantischen Zeit* [*History of German paperbacks and almanacs from the Classicist and Romanticist periods*]. München: Heimeran.

Löser, Freimut. 2015. 'Resisting censorship: Cases of the early 14th century', in J. Hartmann and H. Zapf (eds.), *Censorship and exile*. Göttingen: v&r, 97–111.

Lüsebrink, Hans-Jürgen (ed.). 2006. *Das Europa der Aufklärung und die außereuropäische koloniale Welt* [*Enlightenment Europe and the non-European colonial world*]. Göttingen: Wallstein.

Lüsebrink, Hans-Jürgen. 2007. 'Zensur, Exil und Autoridentität (Diderot, Raynal)' [Censorship, exile and the identity as an author (Diderot, Raynal)], in W. Haefs (ed.), *Zensur im Jahrhundert der Aufklärung: Geschichte - Theorie – Praxis* [*Censorship in the century of the Enlightenment: History, theory, practice*]. Göttingen: Wallstein, 145–56.

Mayer, Franziska. 2011. 'Adaptierte Erotik. Wilhelm Heinse als Übersetzer von Petron und Dorat' [Adapted eroticism: Wilhelm Heinse as the translator of Petron and Dorat], in C. Haug, F. Mayer and W. Schröder (eds.), *Geheimliteratur und Geheimbuchhandel in Europa im 18. Jahrhundert* [*Clandestine literature and Book Trade in Europe in the 18th century*]. Wiesbaden: Harrassowitz, 257–83.

McLean, Matthew. 2007. *The Cosmographia of Sebastian Münster: Describing the world in the reformation.* Aldershot: Ashgate.

Merkle, Denise. 2006. 'Towards a Sociology of Censorship: Translation in the Late-Victorian Publishing Field', in M. Wolf (ed.), *Übersetzen – Translating -- Traduire: Towards a 'Social Turn'?* Vienna and Berlin: LIT, 35–44.

Merkle, Denise. 2009. 'Vizetelly & Company as (ex)change agent: Towards the modernization of the British publishing industry', in J. Milton and P. Bandia (eds.), *Agents of translation.* Amsterdam and Philadelphia: Benjamins Publishing, 85–106.

Mulsow, Martin. 2007. *Die unanständige Gelehrtenrepublik: Wissen, Libertinage und Kommunikation in der Frühen Neuzeit* [*The indecent republic of letters: Knowledge, libertinage and communication in the Early Modern Period*]. Stuttgart: Metzler.

Mulsow, Martin. 2012. *Prekäres Wissen* [*Precarious knowledge*]. Berlin: Suhrkamp.

Mulsow, Martin. 2015. *Enlightenment underground: Radical Germany, 1680–1720.* [Transl. H.C. Erik Midelfort]. Charlottesville: University of Virginia Press.

Nagel, Michael. 1999. 'The beginnings of Jewish children's literature in high German: Three schoolbooks from Berlin (1779), Prague (1781) and Dessau (1782)', *Yearbook of the Leo Baeck Institute*, 44, 39–54.

Nicoli, Miriam. 2013. 'Faced with the flood: Scholarly working practices and editorial transformations at the highpoint of scientific publications', in A. Holenstein (ed.), *Scholars in Action: The Practice of knowledge and the figure of the savant in the 18th century*, vol 1 and 2. Leiden: Brill, 609–29.

O'Callaghan, Daniel. 2013. *The preservation of Jewish Religious books in sixteenth-century Germany: Johannes Reuchlin's Augenspiegel.* Leiden: Brill.

Raabe, Paul (ed.). 1991. *Der Zensur zum Trotz* [*Defying censorship*]. Wolfenbüttel: Herzog August Library.

Rajch, Marek. 2012. 'Polnisches Schrifttum und die preußische Zensur 1848–1918. Kriterien, Methoden, Mittel und Techniken' [Polish writing and Prussian censorship 1848–1918. Criteria, methods and techniques], in B. Kortländer and E. Stahl (eds.), *Zensur im 19. Jahrhundert* [*Censorship in the 19th century*]. Bielefeld: Aisthesis, 231–53.

Röben de Alencar Xavier, Wiebke. 2006. 'Tomás Antonio Gonzagas *Cartas Chilenas*: eine satirische Kritik der kolonialen Verhältnisse im brasilianischen Minas Gerais vor dem Hintergrund europäischen Aufklärungsdenkens' [Tomás Antonio Gonzagas *Cartas Chilenas*: A satirical critique of colonialism in Brazilian Minas Gerais against the backdrop of European enlightened thought], in H.-J. Lüsebrink. (ed.), *Das Europa der Aufklärung und die außereuropäische koloniale Welt* [*Enlightenment Europe and the non-European colonial world*]. Göttingen: Wallstein, 317–87.

Saada, Anne. 2003. *Inventer Diderot: les constructions d'un auteur dans l'Allemagne des Lumières* [*Inventing Diderot: The construction of an author in enlightenment Germany*]. Paris: CNRS Éditions.

Schütz, Hans J. 1990. *Verbotene Bücher* [*Banned books*]. München: Beck.

Stark, Gary D. 2009. *Banned in Berlin: Literary censorship in imperial Germany, 1871–1918.* Oxford: Berghahn.

Stein, Peter. 2006. 'Christian Georg Andreas Oldendorps Historie der caribischen Inseln Sanct Thomas, Sanct Crux und Sanct Jan, insbesondere der dasigen Neger und der Mission der evangelischen Brüder unter denselben als Enzyklopädie einer Sklavengesellschaft in der Karibik' [History of the mission of the Evangelical Brethren on the Virgin Islands], in H.-J. Lüsebrink (ed.), *Das Europa der Aufklärung und die außereuropäische koloniale Welt* [*Enlightenment Europe and the non-European colonial world*]. Göttingen: Wallstein, 175–92.

Wüst, Wolfgang (ed.). 1998. *Censur als Stütze von Staat und Kirche. Vergleich von Augsburg, Bayern, Kurmainz und Württemberg* [*Censorship as a pillar for state and church. A comparison of Augsburg, Bavaria, the electorate of Mainz and Württemberg*]. München: Vogel.

Zalar, Jeffrey T. 2018. *Reading and Rebellion in Catholic Germany, 1770–1914.* Cambridge: Cambridge University Press. Available from: doi: 10.1017/9781108561648. [Accessed 20 July 2021].

3

CENSORSHIP IN MODERN IRAN

Arezou Dadvar

3.1 Core Issues

3.1.1 Introduction

According to Reporters Without Borders,[1] Iran is ranked 177 among 180 countries in the 2023 world press freedom index. Censorship in Iran's cultural and artistic fields makes it difficult for the public to access quality subversive works in their entirety and deprives intellectuals and artists of freedom of expression. This type of intervention dates back to before the 1979 revolution, and the fields that are censored and monitored are not limited to literature and the press. The two most recurrent types of censorship—preventive and repressive—have been present in the Iranian cultural field for a long time, but post-release seizure is less common.

Censorship, especially in publishing and film, has become increasingly restrictive since the 1979 revolution, especially since President Ahmadinejad's first term in office in 2005, when the situation for Iranian intellectuals hardly changed with the arrival of social networks because the latter were blocked and monitored. It is now possible to publish artistic creations online anonymously, or to set up groups of artists and intellectuals, again anonymously, to share with the public forbidden content. As soon as virtual content is signed, its authors risk the same penalties as those for non-virtual works. Nevertheless, publishing and cinema remain areas that are rigorously controlled by official censorship institutions and unofficial 'bodies' such as the *Basij*.

The rules controlling translation in Iran are applied in a like manner to all translation products. All translations must be filed with the Ministry of Guidance, and they are evaluated, modified or forbidden. The changes requested by the ministry often concern sentences or words deemed contrary to Islam. Translators correct their translation by replacing the word, sentence or idea with which the ministry has taken issue with similar, less controversial words. Deleting problematic passages is also a way for translators to avoid a total ban on publication. Since the books to be translated are often chosen by the translator, translation orders from institutions or publishing houses are rare, except in the case of collections of a particular author or literary movement. A renowned translator's decision to translate a book is delicate because, after submitting the translation to a publishing house, the latter may reject it if it is considered too risky to publish (for example, the themes are contrary to religion, or the work contains passages of a sexual nature,

DOI: 10.4324/9781003149453-5

deals with feminism or incites revolt, etc.). Thus, once the translator chooses a book, their actions may be subjected first to self-censorship, then to censorship by the publisher and finally to censorship by the Ministry of Guidance.

According to Abiz (2021: 143–4), censorship creates a 'lack of trust' in translation in Iran because, as specified by Abiz (2021: 143–4), even though readers are cognizant of censorship norms, they are unable to recognise an authentic translation. Moreover, the arbitrary censorship standards result in numerous retranslations of foreign books, which are already available on the market. Because the retranslations 'may have been approved by different censors' (Abiz 2021: 144), their content inevitably varies.

3.1.2 Definitions

The following definitions are specific to the Iranian context.

* *Pahlavi*. The last imperial dynasty in Iran was founded in 1925 by Reza Shah; it ended following the revolution of 1979. Mohammad Reza Shah, referred to as 'the Shah', the founder's son, was the last Iranian emperor; he reigned between 1941 and 1979, left Tehran in 1979 and died in Cairo in 1980.
* *Savak*. The 'National Intelligence and Security Organization', founded in 1957, allowed the rulers and the Shah to direct their authority brutally and outside the legal framework against opponents, especially intellectuals, until 1979.
* *Basij*. A paramilitary militia made up of young volunteers, founded in 1979 and now attached to the Revolutionary Guard Corps. The *Basij* defends the interests of the Islamic Republic inside and outside the country by all means and in all fields, including culture and art.

3.2 Historical Perspectives: Publishing, Literature, Translation

Some consider the Constitutional Revolution of 1906 to be the start of the twentieth century in Iran (Digard et al. 2007: 23). But the most important event, the one that upended both Iran's political system and the daily lives of Iranians, was Reza Shah's seizure of power in October 1925.

Although officially 'the young writers' works were not censored by the censorship authority until around 1935 (Dehdarian 2014: 240), during Reza Shah's reign (1925–1941) several entities took charge of controlling all publications mostly according to the personal interpretation of the censors: the Court Ministry (Vezarat-e Nazmiyeh), the Police Office (Edare-ye Shahrbani), the Office of Orientation of Writing (Edare-ye Rahnama-ye Namehnegari), the Office of Publication (Edare-ye Nashr) and, finally, the Organization for Mind Cultivation (Sazman-e Parvaresh-e Afkar) whose aim was to orient the Iranian public, through cultural productions, towards the nationalist values sought by Reza Shah.

In the 1940s, during the years immediately following Mohammad Reza Shah's accession to the throne, no organization had been officially tasked with pre-publication censorship. It was not until the 1953 coup d'état that the Ministry of Culture and Arts became officially responsible for carrying out pre-publication censorship (Akbariyani 2019: 32). After the 1979 revolution, the popular uprising against the monarchy which resulted in the establishment of an Islamic state, the Ministry of Culture and Arts was renamed the Ministry of Culture and Higher Education. However, it was not until 1981 that it finally took its current form and became the Ministry of Culture and Islamic Guidance. It was also at this time that the 'Compilation and Translation Office' joined this ministry.[2] By law, the officers of these two ministries are mandated to monitor the content and form of cultural productions before they are released to the Iranian public. By contrast, the seizure of cultural products after distribution, among other repressive measures, was and still is carried out by agencies whose work was originally unrelated to the cultural field. For example, prior to 1979, the *Savak* tended to intervene in the seizure of books or films that had already been released and was involved in the 'political censorship' of publications (Rajabzadeh 2002: 27). Since the Iran-Iraq war, however, the *Basij* has taken over this kind of intervention, with or without the direct involvement of the Ministry of Islamic Guidance.

3.2.1 *Pahlavi Dynasty*

During Reza Shah's reign, virtually all the main public organizations were involved in censoring publications and the press. Despite a clear-cut law on the subject, it was the censors' personal interpretations that applied to every kind of publication. They could force Sadeq Hedayat to officially agree never to publish his writings again (Katouzian 2023: 31), as well as check the written press on a daily basis, and sanction, arrest and even condemn to exile those who decide to contradict the discourse of the emperor (Mo'taqedi 2002: 108).

Despite the general openness enjoyed by intellectuals under the Shah when he first came to power in 1941, beginning in 1945 it became increasingly difficult for opponents to speak out, except in certain strategic cases, mainly to calm protests. During the 1950s and 1960s, the Shah and his state hold on the people, and especially on the intelligentsia, rarely allowed any exceptions to censorship. This had an impact on the themes and 'the dominant mood vested in literary works' which 'turned from one of forceful resistance to one of pessimistic despair' (Karimi-Hakkak 2019: 30).

Khosravi (1999: 181) classifies censored topics in Iran into five categories: socio-political, religious, moral, scientific and editorial. Although the subjects most likely to be censored at that time were religious (Khosravi 1999: 178), socio-political issues attracted the most attention from *Savak* censors. The rate of political censorship of original books and translations increased from 14 per cent in 1962 to 57 per cent in 1979 (Khosravi 1999: 182). The *Savak*'s repressive interventions in the cultural field involved the arrest, torture and execution of committed intellectuals and writers, often accused of being Marxists because of their writings or public statements. According to Matin-Asgari (2006: 700–1), 'when the International Red Cross visited Iranian jails in 1977, it found about 3000 inmates.' However, as stated by Matin-Asgari (2006: 701), even during the Shah's most repressive period, in the 1970s, there were far fewer political executions than between 1981 and 1985 under the Islamic republic.

The methods undertaken during the reign of the Shah to monitor content in all cultural products as well as to control the market and the public are varied but can be classified under three general categories: prevention, bans on dissemination and seizure.

- **Prevention**. The Office of Censorship or the 'Compilation bureau' of the Ministry of Culture and Arts was officially responsible, 'since 1966' (Khorrami and Ghanoonparvar 2007: 75) until 1979, for verifying any publication, be it a book or press, before it reached the Iranian market. This verification only concerned religious and cultural elements, with the *Savak* taking care of the political passages (Rajabzadeh 2002: 27).

Thus, works dealing with socio-political events against the Shah or encouraging protests were attacked before they were even published. Words banned in publications, cinema and songs included 'winter, night' (Karimi-Hakkak 2019: 66), which evoked the dark situation of society; 'tulip' (Karimi-Hakkak 2019: 66), a flower representing the opponent-martyrs, 'forest (because of its association with the guerrilla movement in the forests of northern Iran)' Karimi-Hakkak 2019: 66); as well as 'comrades and the police' (Rajabzadeh 2002: 30). The list of banned words and another of names of banned writers were regularly sent to publishers and publishing houses (Rajabzadeh 2002: 30).

- **Banning dissemination**. This method applied to particular works that had already been published but not yet disseminated. Since 1966 the speech of opponents has been the target of banning. Beginning in 1977, during the *Spring of Freedom*, when the Shah granted some freedom of expression to intellectuals and because of the chaos that followed the revolution, the literary world enjoyed an unlikely opening thanks to the copies stored in publishers' warehouses (Khorrami and Ghanoonparvar 2007: 76).

- **Seizure**. With this kind of intervention, the *Savak* appeared as an absolute force in the cultural and literary fields. Books published and distributed before 1966 that did not respect the Shah's current policies or opposed them were seized and reprinting was prohibited. A new list of banned books was sent regularly to booksellers who had to return copies of the blacklisted books to the Censorship Bureau (Rajabzadeh 2002: 27). In 1971, the intelligence service launched a program of 'annual checks of public and school libraries' to collect all books that might encourage questioning of the regime (Karimi-Hakkak 2019: 66).

Works by such popular figures in contemporary Persian literature as Hedayat, 'Alavi, Al-e Ahmad, Sa'edi, Akhavan and Behrangi were placed on a long list of banned books sent to elementary and secondary schools and other educational institutions with instructions to remove them from the libraries and send them to the Security Office of the Ministry of Education. As a result, the annual number of publications dropped from '4000 in 1966 to 1300 in 1969' (Rajabzadeh 2002: 27) and then to '700 in 1976' (Karimi-Hakkak 2019: 66).

The founding of the Iranian branch of the American publishing house Franklin in Teheran in 1953 was a decisive event in the field of literary translation in Iran. This publishing house was the first to establish rules governing translation and publishing in Iran. The rules dealt with copyright, the basic salary of translators, the selection of translators according to their profile and the proofreading of translations before publication: 'no more translations go directly from the translator's house to the printing press' (Navabi 2010: 91). Although these policies helped to professionalise the translation profession, the choice of works translated and published followed the US policies at the time, which were applied to the Iranian publishing context.

During this period, when the work of Iranian writers was carefully monitored, translation offered a means of expression with less oversight. As a result, the number of translations increased. This situation did not impact only a few European languages but rather 'no less than forty different cultures' (Navabi 2010: 67) and their respective languages. Consequently, Iranian writers and poets, as well as experienced translators, were able to translate works that fell within their respective socio-political scope of expertise.

Censorship was omnipresent in the literary field under the Shah, allowing him to monitor the discourse to which the public had access and ensure that it conformed to his policies, goals and ambitions. Opposing discourse, whether disseminated in the press or as another form of cultural product, was often suppressed before it could be distributed by the remaining parties and associations that had produced it. When necessary, the *Savak*'s political police intervened after the distribution of any controversial material that had fallen through the cracks. This censorship system ended as soon as the Shah and his supporters left Iran, to be replaced by a new system with different norms and values.

3.2.2   *Under the Islamic Republic*

During the brief period of freedom of expression enjoyed by intellectuals following the revolution, publications multiplied. Censorship did not appear immediately because the political field, which had been shaken by the revolution and had become unstable, needed to be consolidated once again before it could intervene in the management of other fields. Instead, other forms of oppression against intellectuals and writers were applied: arrest, imprisonment, a series of organised murders of intellectuals and even the execution of writers and some leftist members of the Writers' Association.

The Ministry of Culture and Arts changed its name to the Ministry of Culture and Islamic Guidance after the revolution. All these formal changes, however, barely altered the operations and types of government interventions in the literary field. In the process, the Ministry resumed the same 'policies and methods' that the former Censorship Office had adopted (Khorrami and Ghanoonparvar 2007: 77).

By strengthening the government, the Islamic Republic of Iran was gradually taking over supervision of the cultural field, almost returning it to state in which the Shah had left it:

> But soon with the establishment of the government of the Islamic Republic and the imposition of rules and regulations in regard to what was and what was not permissible to appear in print under the Islamic rule, the game of government coercion and artistic subterfuge resumed and even took on new dimensions.
>
> (Khorrami and Ghanoonparvar 2007: 77)

These increasingly restrictive policies created a 'war'-like atmosphere and targeted the 'intellectual and ideological' aspects of opponents' speeches, sometimes endangering the lives of their authors (Khorrami and Ghanoonparvar 2007: 111).

Concerning original or translated literary publications, the ministry initially identified the specific norms of censorship in 1988 in its *Compendium of Laws and Rules of the Ministry of Culture and Islamic Guidance*. However, they were later amended and clarified by then-President Mahmūd Ahmadinejad in 2010. Indeed, the public dissemination of these laws and their accessibility online can also be seen as a form of indirect pressure on authors and translators to self-censor before their writings even reached the ministry for review.

It is worth mentioning that among the 28 prohibited subjects listed in the amendment, 17 are related to religion, culture and language. The rest concern socio-political issues, such as insulting or defaming the Ayatollah Khomeini, the Supreme Leader or political and religious authorities, inciting people to revolt against the Islamic Republic and so on. Table 3.1 presents some of the prohibited cultural or religious topics identified in this amendment.

According to Rajabzadeh (2002: 82), Iranian censors are very sensitive to words that refer to 'women, girls, music, etc.' Therefore, he initially assumed that foreign novels and writings

Table 3.1 Some prohibited cultural or religious topics

Amendment 'Objectives, Policies and Criteria for the Publication of books,' April 13, 2010	
Religion and morals	Promoting superstition
	Detail about sexual relations, obscene words used in a way that encourages prostitution.
	Images that may promote prostitution (dancing, drinking and immoral gatherings).
Culture and public law	Promotion of anarchy and libertinism.
	Propaganda against the family by undermining its value and status.
	Promoting feelings of hopelessness, frustration, emptiness, futility, as well as negative attitudes in society and increasing public distrust.

Source: Official Website of Ministry of Culture and Islamic Guidance. Book Publishing Objectives, Policies and Rules. https://ketab.farhang.gov.ir/fa/principles/bookprinciples67. Accessed 04 Sep 2024.

translated into Persian would be more likely modified, even banned, due to more problematic references to these subjects in the source texts. However, his analysis of books published in 1996 revealed that, in fact, original Persian works were more often banned than were translations (Rajabzadeh 2002: 101).

Apart from the criteria presented in the table above, which are sometimes considered abstract and too general, and which are applied either by the authors (self-censorship) or subsequently by the Ministry, the latter has additional means of intervening in the process of publication and dissemination of literary works. For example, the approval to republish an already published work can be refused, as is the case with Sadeq Hedayat, an Iranian novelist and writer, whose works have been deemed hostile to Islam by the Ministry. Under Ahmadinejad, Persian translations of 'masterworks of world literature, such as Dostoevsky's *The Gambler*, Faulkner's *As I Lay Dying* and García Márquez's *Memories of My Melancholy Whores*' (Atwood 2012: 39) were also banned and removed from bookstores. Censorship is applied not only to primary references but also to critical works that focus on the writings of authors such as Hedayat (Rajabzadeh 2002: 237) or Houshang Golshiri (Rajabzadeh 2002: 118).

Concerning censored translations, Rajabzadeh (2002: 118) refers to Sartre's *L'Engrenage,* which was banned because, according to the censor, the text denounces 'the vicious circle of a popular revolution' (Rajabzadeh 2002: 158). Censoring authorities feared that the scenario could be interpreted as referring to the 1979 revolution against the Shah, which risked awakening dormant memories in Iranian readers and arousing in the public feelings of hopelessness and frustration.

As with Iranian writers, writings about the lives and works of problematic foreign writers are also often censored: ten sentences from the book *Albert Camus* by Khashayar Deyhimi were cut (Rajabzadeh 2002: 258) because 'Sentences dealing with such immoral subjects, according to Islamic traditions, as alcohol, friendship with women, the beauty of women, kissing, brothels, incest, spending the night together and so on must be deleted' (Rajabzadeh 2002: 259).

It is obvious that the censors' subjective interpretation of Islamic law is very often the only justification for this kind of censorship, given that the ministry's guidelines are not precise. According to Salagi (2016), only publishers have the legal recourse to appeal the ministry's decisions and to explain themselves: authors and translators must even negotiate in some cases to convince publishers to take their side and appeal a decision on their behalf, given that the appeal process is long and difficult. Consequently, publishers would often rather refuse a book than defend it before several committees and juries (i.e., 'Appeal Committee, Book Council, Specialised Committee of the Supervisory Board') (Salagi 2016). These committees are made up, according to Salagi (2016), who was director of the Book Development and Reading Bureau of the Ministry of Culture and Islamic Guidance under Rohani's presidency, of 'Devout staff and supporters of the revolution' as well as 'clerics'.

The ultimate way for the government to control what is published is, according to Karimi-Hakkak (2019: 88), to limit access to publication materials:

It exercises control not only through the print and publication processes and procedures but also has, for the first time in the history of the country, openly used state monopolies over the production and importation of paper and other essentials of the printing process to control public access to potentially subversive materials.

Once the books are produced and ready for distribution, another form of censorship may emerge, in response to economic rather than political imperatives: both before and after the revolution booksellers had and continue to have a say in the selection of books presented to the public. Thus, market demand and agents of the book trade can decide the fate of a book that has been lucky enough to slip through the cracks of control. According to Khosravi (1999: 112–7), censorship can extend its reach beyond the familiar forms and into libraries. For example, not all books that are purchased and processed by librarians will be lent out to readers because librarians can also exercise censorship behind the scenes.

3.3   New Debates

3.3.1   How to Subvert Censorship in Iran

The result of all of these censorial interventions is a marked decrease in Iranian publishing, while 'pirated and unauthorised editions' are becoming increasingly numerous (Khosravi 1999: 182).

Publishing abroad has long been used to avoid government surveillance. For example, long before the Shah's reign, Mohammad Ali Jamalzadeh published his short story *Yikī būd, Yikī nabūd* [Once upon a time] (1921) in Germany and Hedayat published his novel *Būf-i kūr* [The Blind Owl] (1936) in India. Publishing abroad continues to this day. In fact, Iranian publishing houses are multiplying abroad; they organise book fairs for the Iranian diaspora, and give banned writers living in Iran the opportunity to have their works published. They publish under a pseudonym and abroad to be able to communicate with readers: 'many remained anonymous for years, and some (such as Sayeh, A. Bamdad and Omid) were known only by their pseudonyms. When exposed, many of these writers were persecuted' (Talattof 2000: 70).

Nevertheless, the Iranian literary field manages to find other ways to subvert the censorial system. For example, writers publish anonymously through 'white cover publications' (پشت‌جلد سفید), which are books published without any indication of the author, title, publishing information or image on the cover. This subversion strategy was obviously illegal before the revolution.

According to Ghanoonparvar (2007: 76), some authors produced 'enigmatic works' by, for example, changing the time and place in which their narratives took place. *Asrār-i ganj-i dari-yi jinī* [The Mysteries of the Treasure of the Valley of Djinns] (1973) by Ebrahim Golestan is a prime example of changing the setting to convey a politically engaged message. The author had set his main character in a small village, but the twists and turns throughout the book enabled the reader to find similarities between the villager and the Shah. This comparison led the *Savak* to confiscate the few remaining copies in bookshops the following year (Milani 2015).

Other authors or poets adopted different approaches; for example, some of them had recourse to folklore or wrote children's literature to describe the bleak situation and express their despair over the socio-political context. For example, Ahmad Shamlu has written several tales, all of which bear indirect witness to the desperate context of life in Iran and the desire for change: *Ghisih-yi Pariâ* [Fairy Tale] (1953), *Mardī kī lab nadāsht* [The Man Who Had No Lip] (1959), *Dukhtarā-ye nani daryā* [The Daughters of Nanih Daryā] (1959), all of which are part of Iranian folklore and have socially engaged themes.

In *Māhī sīāh-i kūchūlū* [The Little Black Fish] (1968), Samad Behrangi uses the genre of children's literature to convey a message that many interpret as anti-establishment and thus against the Pahlavi regime (Hillmann 1989). The story focuses on the life of a small black fish who decides to take the opposite path to other fish and return to the sea in order to discover the world outside the lifeworld that has been imposed on him. The story, aimed not only at the young but also indirectly at the less young, shows the courage and resistance of the black fish in the face of his compatriots' refusal to accept his decision.

The Routledge Handbook of Translation and Censorship

But the method most frequently adopted by authors and translators, which is still very present in the literary field today, is the use of allegory. For example, according to Feuillebois-Pierunek (2011: 23), 'the flight of the last Sassanid in the face of the Arab conquest' in Bahram Beyzai *Marg-i Yazdgird* [The Death of Yazdgird] (1979) is just a metaphorical way of talking about the Shah's departure. Because of the difficulties and issues with which the agents of the literary field are forced to deal, the image of the rulers is quite negative in literary works: the more arbitrary and severe the censorship becomes before and after the revolution, the more respective rulers are associated with historical tyrants portrayed using dark images and metaphors.

There is another element that should be noted because of its importance in the resistance or attempted resistance of Iranian intellectuals: the Writers' Association of Iran (کانون نویسندگان ایران) founded in 1968, which is 'a unique experience in Iranian intellectual history' (Karimi-Hakkak 2019: 53). This association is not only responsible for connecting writers, poets, playwrights and translators but is also the voice of intellectuals in socio-political events. The Association constantly fought against the Shah's intrusive operations through the *Savak* in the literary field. According to Seyed-Gohrab, 'one of the main aims of the Writers' Association was to fight censorship, but the Pahlavi regime did not leave room for any fight. Censorship had a deep impact on intellectual life in Iran' (cited in Karimi-Hakkak 2019: 16) .

The representatives of the Association were very influential among the people and played a significant role during the demonstrations that preceded the revolution. In addition, some canonical literary figures in the world at the time, such as 'Jean-Paul Sartre, Louis Aragon, Simone de Beauvoir and Arthur Miller,' supported the Iranian writers (Karimi-Hakkak 2019: 72). The association continued to exist after the revolution, but its activity was greatly reduced because its interventions were very closely monitored and several of its members were arrested or even murdered.

Although the precise role played by politically engaged literature, whether translated or not, censored or not, is difficult to determine insofar as everything depends on the reader's interpretation, the works, especially left-leaning works, chosen by authors and translators undoubtedly had an impact on the events that led to the revolution. Indeed, the agents of the literary field saw in the revolution a considerable motivation and a unique opportunity to access freedom of expression.

Ayatollah Khomeini's speech was to become the absolute speech of the Islamic Republic, something that was made clear during the first meeting of 21 members of the Writers' Association on 18 February 1979. (Information on the speech can be found on the website of the Internal Affairs Department, The Institute for Compilation and Publication of Imam Khomeini's Works.[3]) In response to the request of Association representatives for the Ayatollah's support against censorship and oppression, the latter insisted on one of his fundamental concepts, that of 'the unification of the speech'. In Persian the Ayatollah said: وحدت کلمه. This expression could also be interpreted as 'the singularity of speech', that is, an ideal Islamic situation, in which everyone agrees, everyone thinks alike and, therefore, everyone says the same thing. Consequently, there is no longer any opposing discourse. Specifically, he said:

> Now you, the writers, have to assume a very important responsibility. Before [the revolution], they broke your pen, now you are free to write. You must use this pen for the freedom of the people and the Islamic instruction [...]. We must now be independent: neither on the right nor on the left; on the contrary, all of us must come together under the banner of independent Islam.[4] (author's translation)

Authors, translators and the government all reacted differently to this atmosphere of mutual distrust following the revolution. In the early years after the revolution, many writers left the country

Censorship in Modern Iran

to write freely. The writings of these self-exiled ex-pat authors were often marked by 'feelings of frustration and hatred' (Daneshvar 2018: 199) toward the revolution as well as by 'melancholy and a sense of failure' since their identities had been 'weakened' (Daneshvar 2018: 199). In addition to the authors, several bilingual self-translators used the language of their host country to make their works known and educate non-Persian speakers about the Iranian sociopolitical context.

Some writers who stayed in Iran chose total silence. For some time after the revolution, readers and authors were united in this silence, which in itself was significant (Karimi-Hakkak 2019: 7). Some of them resumed writing and translating. While they continued to oppose the dominant discourse, they did so in a less politically engaged form and, according to Seyed-Gohrab (cited in Karimi-Hakkak 2019: 19), wrote 'for the sake of art itself'.

Others chose not to oppose the dominant discourse and created instead a kind of 'Islamic fiction': 'Muhammad Nurizad (*Mard va Karbala*) [The Man and Karbala], Nussrat Allah Mahmudzadih (*Marsiah Halabchih*) [Requiem for Halabja], Muhsin Makhmalbaf (*Mara Bibus*) [Kiss me], (*Bagh-I Bulur*) [The crystal garden]' (Talattof 2000: 6), to name but a few.

In addition to author and translator negative reactions to censorship, publishers may also object to bans imposed by the ministry; for example, publishers may decide to publish books without making the changes demanded by the censors. As for banned reprints, they sometimes republish them with the notation 'first edition' (Salagi 2016). Nevertheless, these books may remain in circulation because the government cannot verify the origin or authenticity of all publications on the market. Despite this, photocopied copies of these uncensored works are often available at street booksellers in Tehran and are usually accessible online.

3.3.2   *Cultural and Artistic Activities: Film*

Films are another area particularly prone to censorship, which is as blatant as it is in literature. With a 'classless audience' (Rahbaran 2016: 113), cinema targets a much broader audience than other art forms, which are often aimed at a literate and educated audience. The universality of film makes Iranian cinema more accessible to Iranian and foreign viewers than literature or other art media.

Iranian cinema emerged in the 1960s and 1970s (Tapper 2002: 1), i.e., before the Islamic revolution, and has been received with undeniable success at Western film festivals since the 1990s. There are two distinct forms of Iranian cinema: commercial, entertaining cinema versus auteur cinema, and their access to Iranian and foreign audiences is not the same. While Western festivals favour auteur cinema, Iranian cinemas prioritise profitability and, thus, commercial cinema. Since the 1979 revolution, Iranian auteur cinema has been more successful abroad, but it was not the revolution that gave rise to this type of film production. In an interview on the subject of censorship in the cinema, Bahram Beyzai, one of the greatest and most renowned Iranian directors, confirmed the appropriation of the cinema after the revolution by the Islamic Republic for the purpose of Islamizing the field, which finally did not succeed:

> Fanatical administrators could not stop our cinema, so in the end they came to the conclusion that they could expropriate it and promote their own creation. That was much more profitable for them.
>
> (Beyzai, cited in Rahbaran 2016: 32)

Different censorship norms were applied to Iranian cinema before and after the revolution, and the methods used by filmmakers to subvert censorship also varied.

57

3.3.3 Iranian Cinema Before the Revolution

During the Pahlavi Dynasty, Iranian cinema faced inequitable resource distribution between *Film Farsi*, which quickly produced commercial films geared toward entertaining a large audience, and auteur cinema, which was not funded (Framanara, in Rahbaran 2016: 103) and often refused by cinema owners. Before the revolution, *Film Farsi* and Hollywood productions were as problematic as censorial norms, because they restricted a motivated and often educated audience access to auteur cinema. Under the Shah's rule and to defy censorship and various kinds of pressure (material, certification, distribution, etc.), some Iranian filmmakers took an interest in surreal and even mystical productions, as did writers and translators. Cinema's departure from reality was, in a way, a consequence of Reza Shah's 'paternalistic' (Sadr 2006: 13) approach to cinema. In 1950, the Ministry of the Interior established a strict set of regulations concerning the production and broadcasting of films. Productions on the following subjects, among others, were prohibited: questioning Islam and Shi'ism, challenging the Shah and his family, inciting the people to revolt against the regime, opposing the traditions and customs of the Iranian people, showing scenes of sexual acts and so on (Sadr 2006: 65–6). This regulation was further codified and additional prohibited subjects were added in 1965: challenges to religious and ethnic minorities and the military and politicians (Sadr 2006: 108–9).

Before the revolution, apart from the arson attack on Abadan's Cinema Rex by Islamic protesters in 1978, the clergy 'had either rejected cinema or ignored it' (Tapper 2002: 5). Following the attack, the clergy sought to eradicate all references to the West from artistic products.

3.3.4 Iranian Cinema After the Revolution

During the postrevolutionary period, in the cinema, as in all aspects of daily life, women's freedoms and progress have been significantly curtailed. Compulsory veiling in public spaces has been the Islamic Republic's main hold on Iranian society, even though women and feminist activists had been organizing demonstrations since the early years of the revolution. As a result,

> [A] film must [...] represent "Islamically correct" images, have been shot under strict control of morals and must also be received within this framework. It is a question of eliminating any physical link between the film and the spectator, any impulse, any relation of intimacy.
>
> (Devictor 2006: 117)

Postrevolutionary cinema saw only one way to escape the new censorial norms: pure and absolute realism to avoid ambiguity that could result in prohibition. For example, since actresses must wear the veil even in indoor scenes and in an even more radical way than in social spaces, subversive directors will abstain from these scenes as much as possible (Mehrjui, cited in Rahbaran 2016: 92) to avoid a negative reaction from the audience, should the audience find such scenes absurd. Indeed, 'since 1983, when all political forces other than Islamist were eliminated from the political spectrum' (Devictor 2006: 119), political subjects attract less censorship attention than subjects dealing with Islam and morality.

Filmmakers thus make such realistic films that fiction has almost disappeared from film production (Rahbaran 2016: 17). The only result of this absolute realism has been to transform filmmakers into committed activists, each one acting in line with their personal socio-political interests and commitments: the filmmakers supported by the Islamic Republic take on the responsibility of defending the regime's interests, while other more subversive filmmakers stage only social problems and crises in a heteronomous and independent approach. It is indeed this subversive and rebellious cinema, although within the limits of what is possible in Iran, which is warmly welcomed by Western festivals and audiences.

Despite the severe censorship norms applied to cinema, the seventh art has finally managed to escape the Islamization policies of the Islamic Republic. Since the criteria for censorship are not precise, as in the case of literary publications, it is the censors and associations attached to the Ministry of Culture and Islamic Guidance who, in keeping with their taste and interests and based on a document dating from 1986–1987 entitled the *Law on the Objectives and Responsibilities of the Ministry of Culture and Islamic Guidance*, embark on the evaluation of film productions. A given filmmaker may meet an alternative fate at the hands of a different censor. Filmmakers deal with:

> refusing applications for making and screening films, withdrawing previously approved screening licenses for films, and abusing many filmmakers publicly as 'counterrevolutionaries', 'agents of the decadent West', 'a danger to national security' and 'agitators of public opinion'.
>
> (Rahbaran 2016: Viii)

Filmmakers thus labelled by the control authorities are either silenced and banned from working, or exiled like Bahram Beyzai and Bahman Ghobadi. Their political stance has landed some of them, such as Mohammad Rasulof and Jafar Panahi, in prison. Over the years, Iranian artists, actors and directors have even organised campaigns for the release of their imprisoned colleagues.

Another tactic censors use to avoid any coincidence between the production and screening of a film and socio-political events is the extension of the evaluation time by a few months or even years. The decrease in the number of movie theatres is also a censorship measure, directly aimed at reducing the number of film productions and releases per year.

According to Bahman Farmanara during an interview with Rahbaran, what differentiates film censorship before and after the revolution is not only the subjects to be avoided. He explains:

> [...] the difference between censorship before the revolution and censorship after was formerly, you were not allowed to touch four themes: the royal family, the constitution, Holy Islam, and the military. [...] What happened after the revolution was that the government not only told us what not to show but also what we should show.
>
> (Rahbaran 2016: 106)

The ultimate means of revolt among Iranian filmmakers and other intellectuals producing artistic or cultural works is the refusal to submit their productions to the censorship authorities. The message of this form of resistance is clear: if the rules of the game do not change, then the Iranian intelligentsia will stop playing the game, even at the risk of endangering the survival of their respective cultural fields.

3.3.5   Theatre and Music in Modern-day Iran

As far as theatre is concerned, the subject is more complicated: the text itself is submitted to the same publication process to which any other literary work is submitted. By contrast, for the stage production, the rules are stricter. According to some researchers, such as

Karimi-Hakkak (2019: 101–2), there are particular procedures to follow. As he states, the Ministry of Islamic Guidance wants dramatic artists to try to 'Islamize the theatre' like all other areas of Iranian life:

> According to the minister's logic, because the Islamic theatre, like the Islamic Revolution itself, must be exported to the rest of the world, every theatrical enactment viewed by the public must [include] three basic character types: namely, a revolutionary protagonist, a counterrevolutionary (or an infidel, or, [better yet], a hypocrite, a term referring to a member of the Islamic Socialist Organization named the Mujahidin) antagonist, and a repentant (*tavvab*) or reformed former counterrevolutionary who would mend his ways as a result of the guidance administrated by "the brothers", meaning the followers of Ayatollah Khomeini.
>
> (Karimi-Hakkak 2019: 101–2)

Since 1982, in honor of the victory date of the revolution, namely 11 February 1979, the Fajr Theatre Festival has held an annual event that lasts ten days. This festival allows the theatre field to create and impose its standards, rewarding the plays already validated by the Evaluation Council of the festival under the watchful eye of the Ministry of Islamic Guidance.

One of the particularities of post-revolution theatre is the place of women, who were sidelined until the 1990s only to find a new place within the religious limits imposed on dramatic writing and performances. However, the arrival of foreign plays written by women, as well as the internationalization of the Fajr Festival in 1998, allowed them to at least attempt to assert themselves in the theatrical field: 'among these young artists – especially in the field of playwriting and directing as the two main pillars of any play – are Chista Yasrebi, Anahita Eghbalnejad, Shabnam Tolui, Naghmeh Samini, Afruz Foruzand, Rima Raminfar, etc.' (Radman 2009).

With the return of so-called reformist presidents, the theatre has been granted a little more freedom, as have other arts, such as film and literature. However, unlike other cultural fields, the theatre benefits from very little public funding and relies largely on the private sector; sometimes the directors pay for the cost of the performance out of pocket. According to Radman (2009), the problems faced by artists in the theatrical field include: 'A lack of theatrical facilities such as rehearsal and performance halls, and the budget allocated to the theatre (it does not change proportionally with the increase in the number of artists) as well as other shortcomings.' As for the publication of plays, publishers are not particularly interested in publishing them, despite the commercial success of some theatrical productions in the Iranian market. The plays are often translations and usually classics.

As for music, the prohibition against women singing has continued to characterise this artistic field since the revolution. As of June 1980, following a speech by Ayatollah Khomeini, women singing in front of a male audience is prohibited.

> However, the legislation did not consider it morally reprehensible for women to listen to men singing because, unlike the female voice, which is supposed to arouse a man's carnal desire, the male voice, which is hoarse and less gentle, has no risk of touching a woman and arousing her desire.
>
> (Niane 2021: 188, our translation)

Before the revolution, women played an important role in the development of Iranian music. They still play an important role today in singing, composing, writing song lyrics and playing various instruments; however, some of these activities, as well as dancing, are practised in secret, at private parties or more freely in the Iranian diaspora.

3.4 Potential Research Avenues

Censorship is still a sensitive topic in Iran. As a result, the research done within the country is rare, and it is often difficult to mention the studies done abroad for fear of reprisals. At the same time, it is difficult to undertake a study of the Iranian cultural field without taking into consideration this omnipresent phenomenon that impacts the creation process of creation of all cultural goods in Iran. It is therefore clear that a number of questions and avenues in the field of censorship are yet to be explored and answered. These questions and avenues are awaiting further studies that will be conducted when the fear of violent consequences will no longer hinder scientific and academic analyses. The following are just a few research questions that are awaiting exploration in Iran because the bodies that control publishing are very closed and opaque:

- How can freedom of expression be achieved in today's Iran, a country whose history has rarely known the true meaning of freedom of speech?
- What are the most appropriate methods to ensure public access to non-censored cultural materials within the country?
- Who are the agents working in the control bodies?
- What are the rules of the game within the institutions responsible for censorship?

Further Reading

Mostyn, Trevor. 2002. *Censorship in Islamic Societies*. London: Saqi.
In this book, Mostyn presents the impacts of Islamic policies of some societies on the literary field through direct or indirect interventions, by explaining the radical case of the fatwa against Salman Rushdie.

Khorrami, Mohammad Mehdi. 2014. *Literary Subterfuge and Contemporary Persian Fiction: Who Writes Iran?* London and New York: Routledge.
Khorrami's work is an example of a study on Iranian literature in which the researcher looks at the culturo-political context of a book's production, as well as the text and its aesthetic and stylistic aspects. The originality of this major work lies in the study of the censorship and subversive approaches retained by the writers. The books themselves and concrete examples are examined.

Fouladvind, Leyla. 2014. *Les mots et les enjeux: le défi des romancières iraniennes*. [*Words and Issues: The Challenge of Iranian Women Novelists*]. Paris: L'Harmattan.
By referencing a corpus from the 1990s and examining the works of several Iranian women novelists, Fouladvind tries to show the differences between the status of women in private and public spaces. The work highlights how female power could fight censorship and, thus, any kind of pressure and obligation imposed on women.

Nazmjou, Tinoush (ed.). 2018. *Non-Censuré, Uncensored, Issue Zero*. Paris: Naakojaa.
In a non-academic register, this journal issue gathers several accounts of authors and translators censored in Iran, who provide concrete examples in French, Persian and English. The absurdity of the current censorship norms in all cultural and sports fields in Iran is highlighted. Furthermore, this issue joins the few books in Persian, all published abroad, which give a voice to censored writers and artists who are able to clarify the impact of censorship, which would remain blurred and obscure without these publications.

Notes

1 Reporters Without Borders, 2024 Press Freedom Index, https://rsf.org/fr/classement. Accessed 04 Sep 2024.
2 Official Website of Ministry of Culture and Islamic Guidance. History Page. www.farhang.gov.ir/fa/intro/history. Accessed 04 Sep 2024.
3 Official Website of Imam Khomeini. Imam's Meeting with the Iranian Writers Association. www.imam-khomeini.ir/fa/n21915/. Accessed 04 Sep 2024.
4 Official Website of Imam Khomeini. Imam's Meeting with the Iranian Writers Association. www.imam-khomeini.ir/fa/n21915/. Accessed 04 Sep 2024.

References

Abiz, Alireza. 2021. *Censorship of Literature in Post-revolutionary Iran: Politics and Culture Since 1979*. London: Bloomsbury Publishing.

Akbariyani, Mohammad Hashem. 2019. *Tārīkh-i shafāhī-yi nashr-i muāsir-i Iran: Kitābfurūshī* [*The Oral History of Contemporary Iranian Publishing: Bookstores*]. Tehran: Khānih-yi Kitāb.

Atwood, Blake. 2012. 'Sense and Censorship in the Islamic Republic of Iran', *World Literature Today*, 86(3), 38–41. Available at: https://doi.org/10.7588/worllitetoda.86.3.0038. (Accessed: 01/11/2023).

Daneshvar, Esfaindyar. 2018. *La littérature transculturelle franco-persane: Une évolution littéraire depuis les années 80*. [*Transcultural Franco-Persian Literature: Literary Evolution Since the 1980s*] Leiden: Brill | Rodopi.

Dehdarian, Roja. 2014. 'Newly hatched chickens', in B. Devos and C. Werner (eds.), *Culture and Cultural Politics under Reza Shah: The Pahlavi State, New Bourgeoisie and the Creation of a Modern Society in Iran*. London and New York: Routledge, 234–48.

Devictor, Agnès. 2006. 'Corps codés, corps filmés: Le contrôle du corps des femmes dans le cinéma de la République islamique d'Iran' [Coded bodies, filmed bodies: The control of women's bodies in the cinema of the Islamic Republic of Iran], *Culture & Musées*, 7(1), 117–134. Available at: https://doi.org/10.3406/pumus.2006.1388. (Accessed: 01/11/2023).

Digard, Jean-Pierre, Hourcade, Bernard and Richard, Yann. 2007. *L'Iran au XXᵉ siècle: Entre nationalisme, islam et mondialisation* (revised and expanded edition). [*Iran in the 20th Century: Between Nationalism, Islam and Globalization*]. Paris: Fayard

Feuillebois-Pierunek, Eve. 2011. *Theaters of Persia and Iran: An overview*. Available at: https://hal.archives-ouvertes.fr/hal-00652101. (Accessed: 01/11/2023).

Ghanoonparvar, Mohammad. 2007. 'The Game of Coercion and Subterfuge', in M. M. Khorrami and M. Ghanoonparvar (eds.), *Critical Encounters: Essays on Persian Literature and Culture in Honor of Peter J. Chelkowski*. Costa Mesa, California: Mazda Publishers, 74–85.

Hillmann, Michael G. 1989. 'Behrangi, Samad', in *Encyclopædia Iranica* (Online). Available at: www.iranicaonline.org/articles/behrangi-samad-teacher. (Accessed: 01/11/2023).

Karimi-Hakkak, Ahmad. 2019. *A Fire of Lilies: Perspectives on Literature and Politics in Modern Iran*. Leiden: Leiden University Press.

Katouzian, Homa. 2003. 'Riza Shah's Political Legitimacy and Social Base, 1921–1941', in S. Cronin (ed.), *The Making of Modern Iran: State and Society under Riza Shah 1921–1941*. London: Routledge, 15–36.

Khorrami, Mohammad Mehdi and Ghanoonparvar, Mohammad (eds.). 2007. *Critical Encounters: Essays on Persian Literature and Culture in Honor of Peter J. Chelkowski*. Costa Mesa, California: Mazda Publishers.

Khosravi, Fariborz. 1999. *Tahlīlī bar sānsūr-i kitāb dar durih-yi duvum-i Pahlavi* [*Analysis of the Censorship of Books during the Second Pahlavi*]. Tehran: Muasisih-yi farhangi pazhūhishī-yi chāp va nashr-i Nazar.

Matin-Asgari, Afshin. 2006. 'Twentieth century Iran's political prisoners', *Middle Eastern Studies*, 42(5), 689–707. Available at: https://doi.org/10.1080/00263200600826323. (Accessed: 01/11/2023).

Milani, Abbas. 2015. 'Asrār-i Asrār-i ganj-i darih-yi jinī, rivāyat-hāī mutafāvit az tughīf-i yik film' [The mysteries of the film *The Mysteries of the Treasure of the Valley of Djinns*: different stories about the banning of a film], in BBC News Persian [online]. Available at: www.bbc.com/persian/arts/2015/09/150916_l41_cinema_gang_milani_comment. (Accessed: 01/11/2023).

Mo'taqedi, Robabeh. 2002. 'Censor dar matbūāt-i asr-i Pahlavi-yi avval' [Press censorship under the first Pahlavi], *Ganjīnih Asnād*, 44. Available at: https://ensani.ir/fa/article/179264. (Accessed: 01/11/2023).

Navabi, Davoud. 2010. *Tārīkhchih-yi tarjumih az farānsih bih fārsī dar Iran az āghāz tā kunūn* [*History of Translation from French into Persian in Iran from the Beginning to the Present Day*]. Kerman: University of Shahid Bahonar.

Niane, Ballé. 2021. *La musique iranienne au féminin: De l'Antiquité jusqu'à la fin de la période Pahlavi* [*Women in Iranian music: From Antiquity to the End of the Pahlavi Period*]. Paris: L'Harmattan.

Radman, Saba. 2009. 'Nigāhī bi tārīkhchih-yi huzūr-i zanān dar theatr-i Iran' [Overview of the history of women's presence in Iranian theater (Part 2)]. Official website of Iran Theater [News about theater in Iran]. Available at: https://theater.ir/fa/16709. (Accessed: 01/11/2023).

Rahbaran, Shiva. 2016. *Iranian Cinema Uncensored: Contemporary Filmmakers Since the Islamic Revolution.* London: I.B. Tauris.

Rajabzadeh, Ahmad. 2002. *Mumayyizī-i kitāb: Pazhūhishī dar 1400 sanad-i mumayyizī-i kitāb dar sāl-i 1375* [*Book Censorship: Research on 1400 Documents on Book Censorship in 1996*]. Tehran: Kavīr.

Sadr, Hamid-Reza. 2006. *Iranian Cinema: A Political History*. London and New York: I.B. Tauris in association with Prince Claus Fund Library.

Salagi, Mohammad. 2016. 'Mamnū'īat-i istifādih az kalamih-yi *sharāb* dar kitāb-hā' [Prohibition to use the word 'wine' in books]. *AftabNews* [News website]. Available at: http://aftabnews.ir/fa/news/343397. (Accessed: 01/11/2023).

Talattof, Kamran. 2000. *The Politics of Writing in Iran: A History of Modern Persian Literature*. Syracuse: Syracuse University Press.

Tapper, Richard (ed.). 2002. *The New Iranian Cinema: Politics, Representation, and Identity*. London and New York: I.B. Tauris Publishers

4

CENSORSHIP IN RUSSIA

Tsarist, Soviet and Post-Soviet Contexts

Natalia Kamovnikova

4.1 Core Issues

Defining culture, Juri Lotman and Boris Uspenskii spoke of 'nonheritable collective memory, which expresses itself in a concrete system of bans and prescriptions' (Lotman and Uspenskii 1977: 3). The difference of Russian culture from neighbouring cultures, in Lotman and Uspenskii's view, consists in its dichotomous nature, with a clear demarcation line between good and evil, devoid of axiological neutrality (Lotman and Uspenskii 1977: 4). From the point of view of culture, the past does not disappear, but embodies itself in the collective memory, contributing to the further production of texts and events (Lotman and Uspenskii 1977: 36). In a remarkable manner, this definition is applicable to the history of Russian censorship in general and the history of translation and censorship in particular. Approaches to bans and prohibitions evolved over the course of Russian history, and the lack of a middle ground between good and evil expressed itself in the radicalism, with which official institutions approached the control of literary texts. It also manifests itself in incessant attempts by Russian intellectuals to find ways of bypassing bans in line with the popular Russian saying 'What is not forbidden is allowed.'

In line with the semiotic definition by Lotman and Uspenskii, recent Russian studies on the history of censorship have been calling for revisionist approaches. Censorship, as Mikhail Zelenov defines it, cannot be studied purely as an activity, a product of such activity, an institution, or a feature of human relationships, but as a feature of human psychology, unconsciously 'sewn into human perception of reality', which pushes out anything unconventional from the personal and collective world picture (Zelenov 2015: 16, 18–19). Perception of foreign literature in Russia was also constructed on the principles of duality; literature was imported, translated, published, acquired, banned and destroyed with mixed feelings of triumph and dread. For centuries, censorship in Russia developed to protect the country's national identity, even though that identity underwent multiple transformations over the course of Russian history.

4.2 The Tsarist Period

The rule of Iaroslav the Wise, the Grand Prince of Kievan Rus' in the eleventh century, created favourable conditions for active translations of books from Greek. The language spoken in Kievan

64

DOI: 10.4324/9781003149453-6

Rus' in the eleventh century was called Slavic; it functioned as a lingua franca of the Orthodox Eastern European area through the Middle Ages (Nandris 1969: 2). The supradialect form of Slavic was later adopted for the documentation turnover by Vladimir-Suzdal and Moscow Principalities, thus gradually becoming associated with them (Zalizniak 2004: 6). The translations under Iaroslav the Wise's rule included sermons, religious canons and liturgies, hagiographic writings like 'Life of Vasilii the New', as well as secular works like *The Chronography* by Georgios Synkellos and *The Jewish War* by Flavius Josephus (Likhachev 2004: 300). Official censorship of literary works and translations first came about in the sixteenth century, during the period of active consolidation of the Russian lands around the Moscow Principality. Unyoked from Mongol rule in 1480 and leaving centuries of turmoil and feudal fragmentation behind, Russia underwent an active process of the so-called gathering of Russian lands. By the middle of the sixteenth century, Russia had also conquered the Kazan and Astrakhan khanates and took control over the entire Volga. The idea of Moscow as the Third Rome was becoming at this time a powerful myth: according to it, the autocratic and autocephalous Russian state was destined to inherit power over the Orthodox world from Byzantium (Likhachev 2004: 189). Official control over literature and, most importantly, of spiritual writings, was an important means of strengthening the Russian autocracy.

The first document legalizing censorship was produced during the rule of Tsar Ivan IV (the Terrible) in 1551. Summoned by the Tsar, a council of one hundred Russian bishops (hence its name, *Stoglav,* or 'one hundred heads') made 100 decisions, which were listed in the volume under the same name. The decisions mainly concerned issues of religion and monarchy, but also treated the role of the Tsar and the Russian Orthodox Church in the secular world. Among other things, *Stoglav* called for the revision of all existing religious books in order to ascertain the degree of their correspondence to the sacred originals. It also entitled religious authorities to select and confiscate manuscripts proposed for publication. In other words, *Stoglav* introduced censorship at all stages of book production, from preliminary censorship to control of book circulation (Zhirkov 2001: 8–9).

The introduction of the printing press in Russia contributed to the implementation of the Stoglav council's regulations. Religious books, which were rewritten by hand and so contained unavoidable mistakes, were labelled blasphemous. Once purged of all sacrilegious texts, libraries needed to be replenished with carefully selected and edited books of sacred content. The provision of sanctioned literature on the scale necessary was only possible with a printing press; the first Russian printed book was *Apostol* in 1564. Despite initially enjoying the Tsar's favour, the Russian pioneer printer Ivan Fedorov soon fell from grace for his 'dangerous thinking' and had to flee to Lithuania (Barenbaum 1984: 26–31).

The use and storage of foreign-published literature in private homes was persecuted in the sixteenth and seventeenth centuries. This concerned not only Catholic religious literature, or any religious literature on doctrines other than Eastern Orthodoxy, but also foreign-printed literature in Slavic languages and even Greek Orthodox religious books printed abroad. In 1678, theologian, poet and translator Simeon of Polotsk organised, with the Tsar's permission, a printing house outside the control of the church. His student Sil'vestr Medvedev soon joined him and took charge of the secular printing house after Simeon's death in 1680. Between 1678 and 1688, Medvedev prepared over 150 book editions, which included both Russian originals and Russian translations on educational subjects, as well as religious didactic literature, literary prose and poetry (Pakhomov 2019; Zhirkov 2001: 14). Medvedev also developed a translation method. His activities were opposed by Patriarch Ioakim, whom Medvedev blatantly disregarded as ignorant. Supported by Patriarch Dositheos II of Jerusalem, Patriarch Ioakim accused Simeon of Polotsk and Medvedev of 'Latin heresy' and called for the burning of their books at the stake. However,

The Routledge Handbook of Translation and Censorship

Dositheos and Ioakim succeeded only in closing the printing-house and the school organised by Simeon of Polotsk. Medvedev's subsequent engagement in theological disputes and his support and mentorship of Tsarina Sofia, whose regency infringed upon the rights of the future emperor Peter I (the Great), gave the clerics substantial evidence to accuse Medvedev of plotting against the young Tsar (Pakhomov). Medvedev was arrested, tortured and beheaded in Red Square; his correspondence in different languages and the more than one thousand books and manuscripts belonging to him were destroyed (Zhirkov 2001: 14).

The monopoly of the Russian Orthodox Church on print and publishing was very soon undermined by the regulations of Peter I. After the death of Patriarch Adrian, the Tsar arranged for the patriarchal see to remain unoccupied; he also proclaimed the freedom of Christian worship in 1702. The active reforms of Peter I, including those related to education and culture, required the expansion of existing libraries to include secular literature and therefore the importation of books from abroad. Translations of foreign literature, especially on scientific and technical subjects, were encouraged by the monarch. At the same time, all printed literature was personally controlled by the emperor; Peter I even engaged in issuing recommendations on matters of style and terminology in translations of scientific and technical literature, insisting that the 'unnecessary parts, which do nothing but waste the readers' time and interest' be cut (Zhirkov 2001: 17). The Tsar was also concerned about all editions that could potentially be used as Swedish propaganda during the Great Northern War.

Therefore, during the rule of Peter I censorship focused primarily on secular matters, with religious books remaining under the control of the Russian Orthodox Church. The church, however, continued to claim its rights to control secular literature throughout the eighteenth century. Thus, for instance, in 1756, the Holy Synod interfered with the publication of the translation of the philosophical poem by Alexander Pope, *An Essay on Man*, made by Moscow university professor Nikolai Popovskii. The Synod noted that the essay mentioned heliocentrism and the plurality of worlds, which contradicted the Holy Scripture. By the end of 1756, the Synod had prepared a special report for Empress Elisabeth on the harm posed by heliocentric views to the Orthodox faith. It also suggested the confiscation of the recently published book by Bernard de Fontenelle, *Conversations on the Plurality of Worlds*, in the translation by the famous Russian poet and translator Antioch Kantemir (Zhirkov 2001: 21). The dispute was put to an end when Mikhail Lomonosov, the leading Russian scientist of the eighteenth century, intervened. His epigram, *An Anthem to the Beard*, which mocked the ignorance of church hierarchs, was widely read and quoted across the Russian Empire.

The relatively loose requirements for publishing were done away with during the rule of Catherine II (the Great), who was the first of the Romanov monarchs to embark upon a consistent policy of information control. In 1762, a year after her ascension to the throne, Catherine II instructed the Academy of Sciences to increase its control over imported books, which were 'against the law, good nature, us ourselves, and the Russian nation', naming Jean-Jacques Rousseau's *Emile* as one such book (Zhirkov 2001: 23). Quite notably, Catherine II was very keen on Denis Diderot and Voltaire, with whom she maintained a correspondence. Their ideas, however exciting to her personal taste, were not in line with her pro-nobility policies. A couple of months before her death, Catherine II, gripped by the specter of the French Revolution, issued a decree on censorship covering all published literature written or translated in the Russian Empire. The decree required church and secular censors to work together and defined censors as state officials. Therefore, it was in 1796 that the censor became an official profession in Russia (Zhirkov 2001: 30–1).

The successors of Catherine II continued to develop institutions and practices of censorship. Access to foreign books was limited, especially during the five-year reign of Catherine's son, Paul

I, whose aversion to foreign literature was such that he banned the importation of all foreign-published books into Russia regardless of their content (Blium 1994: 193). Although this absolute ban was soon lifted, censorship in Russia was becoming better regulated. The first censorship statute was signed by Tsar Alexander I on 9 June 1804. The statute established censorship over all materials published in the Russian Empire and designated the Central Administration of Schools of the Ministry of National Education as the central censorship agency of the Russian state (Zhirkov 2001: 42). Yet with the start of the military engagement of Russia in the Napoleonic campaigns, military censorship became more important than the censorship of foreign literature. The Ministry of Police, which was organised in the course of the reforms undertaken in 1811, closely watched booksellers and publishers and was empowered to make censorship decisions, thus making the Ministry of National Education redundant as a censoring organ. The new reform of the Ministry of Education in 1814 tightened the censorship requirements in the country and resulted in the total censorship of university study materials and mass dismissals of university professors in 1821, with their books simultaneously removed from university libraries (Zhirkov 2001: 48–9).

It should furthermore be noted that, in the face of constant warfare, discussions of censorship in tsarist Russia were also quite often subjected to censorship. This was particularly evident in the case of postal censorship, which became widespread in the middle of the eighteenth century under the rule of Empress Elizabeth, when postal officials in St. Petersburg were charged with the duty to open and copy all foreign correspondence of foreign ambassadors; the regulation also affected the treatment private letters. Perlustration increased during the reign of Catherine II; in 1779, the Empress ordered secretly opened correspondence to be delivered to her from the St Petersburg post office. Perlustration was seen as a preventive political measure, which is why the state openly denied its existence and considered it one of the most important state secrets. In December 1813, the Minister of Internal Affairs Osip Kozodavlev in a secret relation to the chief of the Moscow post office, instructed him on the importance of secrecy in perlustration: 'It is necessary that no one should be afraid to communicate his thoughts frankly through the post, so that otherwise the post is not deprived of its credibility, and the government—of this well-tried means of finding out secrets.' Kozodavlev reminded his subordinate of the necessity to destroy all copies and reports on the delayed letters after use, 'so that no traces of these cases would remain' (Izmozik 2000).

The consolidation of statehood and its bureaucratic apparatus reached its peak during the rule of Nicholas I, whose ascent to the Russian throne in December of 1825 began with the suppression of the Decembrist uprising, which targeted constitutional changes. The leaders of the uprising were exiled; five of them were hanged despite their noble status. This tragic start to his reign convinced Nicholas I of the necessity of greater political control over the country. Regulations on censorship and control of published literature were entrusted to Minister of Spiritual Affairs and Public Education Aleksandr Shishkov, who embarked upon his duties with tremendous zeal. It was under Shishkov that the new censorship statute of 10 June 1826 came about. It was nicknamed 'the cast-iron statute' for its comprehensive nature. Consisting of 19 chapters and 230 paragraphs, the statute regulated censorship activities in such excruciating detail that it created much confusion. Within the Ministry of National Education, the administrative of censorship was moved from the Central Administration of Schools to the Central Administration of Censorship.

The cast-iron statute proved itself impracticable within a year and was revised and considerably abridged in 1827–1828. The continued development of the system of censorship and the increase in the number of censors resulted in the creation of various censorial committees. The Committee of Foreign Censorship (Komitet Tsensury Inostrannoi) was founded in April 1828 in order to control all foreign-published literature imported into Russia. Foreign editions banned from circulation could not be considered for translation. The reasons behind bans on imported literature were multiple and were not limited to the contents of the banned books. Minister of Education Count Sergei Uvarov, in his pursuit of a strict censorship policy, declared orthodoxy, autocracy and national spirit to be the three pillars of education. As a censor, Uvarov was particularly apprehensive of French literature, translations of which enjoyed wide popularity in Russia. Uvarov accused French novelists of 'false virtuousness', declaring them unable to provide useful reading material for the Russian nation (Zhirkov 2001: 73). The haste with which novels were translated into Russian and published for the Russian readership indicated, in Uvarov's view, the growing demand for reading about 'human weaknesses, moral disgrace, untamed passions, strong vices and crimes', which harmed the morals and religious feelings of Russian readers and therefore had to be stopped (Zhirkov 2001: 74).

In 1847, Uvarov issued a special regulation, which prevented journals from printing only translations (Zhirkov 2001: 78). In 1848, the Committee of Foreign Censorship was authorised to permit or forbid translations of foreign literature into the Russian language; however, this power was taken away from the committee in 1871 as a result of a conflict in which the committee was accused of incompetence in this regard (Choldin 1985: 30). The instructions prepared for censors in 1848 required that they pay attention to the historical period in which the revised books were written, as well as to the purpose of these books. The language of the original was also considered of prime importance: 'A censor must be stricter with French writings than with German ones and stricter with German than with Italian and English works of the same type' (Patrusheva 2019: 489). This differential approach toward original languages mirrored the existing political and cultural relationships of Russia with France and Germany and the associations that French and German literatures evoked in the minds of the Russian readership. Whereas French works were perceived as potentially fomenting political unrest in light of the French Revolution and its aftermath, the apprehension of German authors was caused by close ties between Russia and Germany and the scope of publications imported to Russia from Germany. While French remained the favourite foreign language of the Russian nobility in the nineteenth century, German was increasingly favoured by Russian intellectuals. For example, over 6000 issues of German newspapers and periodicals were received on subscription in Russia in 1869, which was more than in any other foreign language (Choldin 1985: 8).

The Imperial Public Library in St. Petersburg, currently known as the Russian National Library, received lists of banned and partially allowed foreign literature on a monthly basis. These lists provide detailed information and statistics on banned literature in languages other than Russian and allow us to visualise the degree of influence the Committee of Foreign Censorship had in the nineteenth century. Thus, in the year 1850, the Committee banned 320 foreign titles unconditionally and allowed 113 titles with deletions of selected passages, which meant that banned excerpts were to be removed by the library before the books could be lent to the readers. One of the most banned foreign authors of the year 1850 was Alexandre Dumas, whose *Regency* (published in Brussels, 1849), *The Queen's Necklace* (Brussels, 1849), *France and Europe before, during and after February 24* (in German, Leipzig, 1848), *Memoirs of a Physician* (Brussels, 1848), *One Thousand and One Ghosts* (Brussels, 1850), *The Vicomte of Bragelonne* (Brussels, 1848), and a German edition entitled *A Historic Novel* were 'forbidden unconditionally for the public' in different months. Dumas' *Louis XV* was permitted with omissions in March in the Brussels 1849 edition, but then its Brussels 1850 edition was forbidden unconditionally in November. Among other foreign books listed as banned in 1850 were *Cousin Bette* by Honoré de Balzac, *André Chénier* by Jules Barbier, *Memoirs from beyond the Grave* by François-René de Chateaubriand and *Lucrezia Borgia* by Victor Hugo. *Le roman d'une femme, Les quatre restaurations,* and *Trois hommes forts* by Alexandre Dumas fils were allowed with omissions. Notably, censorship also applied to books in the various languages of the Russian Empire. In the same year, 1850, censors banned eleven books in Yiddish and required omissions in twenty-eight other books in Yiddish and one in Armenian (Delo upravleniia 1850).

Aided by informants, censorship in Russia tightened in reaction to the revolutionary events in Europe in 1830–1831 and 1848. The reforms of Tsar Alexander II, mostly known for the liberation of the serfs in 1861, also included censorship reform, which delegated the responsibility for censorship to the Ministry of Internal Affairs in January 1863. This transfer of responsibilities meant that censorship was officially perceived as a defense measure, maintained to safeguard the interests of the Russian Empire. The danger of revolutionary movements, the risk of terrorist attacks and the active liberation movement in Poland increased the desire of the Russian government to control public discourse in the country.

The approval of a book in a foreign language for circulation did not automatically grant permission for its translation (Patrusheva 2013: 65, 152). Like other publications in the Russian language, translations were revised by the Committee of Secular Censorship. Beginning in 1865, however, translated volumes of over 20 printers' sheets and from all periodical editions were relieved of preliminary approvals (Patrusheva 2013: 152; Zhirkov 2001: 145).

The reasons for the banning of translations in the Russian Empire in the second half of the nineteenth century can be conventionally classified into several categories. First, bans were imposed on the translation of foreign books containing liberal ideas and a potential threat to the monarchy. This concerned social and political writings as well as belles-lettres. For example, in 1872, censors banned the translation of Ferdinand Lassalle's works in two volumes, as well as the translation of the memoirs of Malwida von Meysenbug. In the following year, the translation of Arthur John Booth's biography of Robert Owen was banned and its printed copies were confiscated and destroyed, as well as the translation of William Lecky's *History of European Morals from Augustus to Charlemagne* and *History of the Rise and Influence of the Spirit of Rationalism in Europe* (Dobrovol'skii 1962: 70–3, 81, 98–101).

Censors paid special attention to books on any of the French revolutions of the eighteenth and nineteenth centuries. In 1872, censors banned the Russian translation of the book *Oeuvres de J. P. Marat: L'Ami du Peuple*, compiled by Auguste Vermorel, with 2020 copies burned as a result of the ban, and *The History of the French Social Movements* by Lorenz von Stein, with 1975 copied destroyed (Dobrovol'skii 1962: 74–6, 95–6). The same happened in 1888 to the volume of lectures by the Copenhagen university professor Georg Brandes entitled *Main Currents in the Literature of the Nineteenth Century*, which caused a stir in Europe. The Minister of Internal Affairs, Count Dmitrii Tolstoi, described Brandes's work as extremely pro-revolutionary and 'devoid of any scholarly merit' (Dobrovol'skii 1962: 170).

Socialist ideas were also under tight control of censorship bodies as they presented a threat to Russia's contemporary way of life. The official regulation of 14 January 1884 banned all reproductions of Karl Marx's works, which affected books that contained or referred to Marx's ideas even without mentioning him directly (Dobrovol'skii 1962: 210). This regulation affected, for example, the 1899 volume of translations of the works by Herbert Spencer, John Stuart Mill, Alfred Russel Wallace, Charles Wicksteed and Michael Flürscheim. The last book was found 'especially harmful', and the decision of the Minister of Internal Affairs stated that the book 'tends to shake and topple one of the main foundations of the existing order, namely, the institution of private property' (Dobrovol'skii 1962: 217–8).

In literary works, ideas of revolution and liberalism were equally unwelcome as dangerous to the monarchy. In 1870, the second volume of Hugo's *Les Misérables,* containing the translation of the second and third parts of the original, was banned, while the first volume remained in circulation. In 1880, *Les Misérables* was published with cutouts in a journal, and in 1882—in a

The Routledge Handbook of Translation and Censorship

different translation—also with cutouts. However, *Les Misérables* was banned again in 1891 in the complete translation by Ernest Watson published by M.O. Wolff publishing house. The publisher was invited to introduce changes and remove controversial excerpts, but he refused, and the book remained under a ban for several years (Dobrovol'skii 1962: 69–70, 185–7). The translation of another work by Hugo on the topic of social injustice—*Claude Gueux*—was also banned. Quite notably, this publication was initially approved by preliminary censorship in January 1867, but it was banned and removed from circulation eight years later, in April 1875, with all 421 remaining copies destroyed. The edition continued to be illegally circulated by revolutionary-minded readers and was confiscated by police in the course of house searches (Dobrovol'skii 1962: 61–2). In 1898, the edition of *Reds of the South* by Félix Gras was banned despite having been published in a journal version a year earlier (Dobrovol'skii 1962: 214–5).

Second, translations were banned for undermining Christian faith and morality. One such ban was imposed on the translation of *Leviathan* by Thomas Hobbes in the beginning of the 1870s. Secular censors focused their attention on the third and the fourth parts of the book, where Hobbes speaks about the Christian state. The censors found the work 'harmless', yet it contained erroneous passages 'adverse to the spirit of the Orthodox church'. Censors of the Holy Synod, however, found these passages full of 'insolent blasphemy', which is why the book was banned and destroyed in February 1874 (cited in Dobrovol'skii 1962: 65–6). The same fate befell *The Philosophy of History* by Voltaire in 1872; after an examination by the Committee of Spiritual Censorship, it was found to be extremely harmful. Minister of Internal Affairs Aleksandr Timashev wrote that the book contained 'sarcastic ridicule of the subjects of Christian faith [...] which would deeply wound the virtuous feelings of a believer [...]. In questions of faith, the weapon of mockery, which Voltaire used with such disastrous success, is much more dangerous than serious studies and objections; the latter can be denied, whereas mockery and ridicule, even when denied, destroy the virtue and authority of objects considered sacred and sacrosanct' (cited in Dobrovol'skii 1962: 66–7). The translation of a book of lectures on Voltaire by the German theologian David Friedrich Strauss was also banned and destroyed in 1872; permission for publication was granted to a different publisher only in 1899 (Dobrovol'skii 1962: 76).

The Committee of Spiritual Censorship was not the only institution that banned literary works for religious reasons; the Committee of Secular Censorship was as active and rigorous in detecting blasphemy and threats to morality in works of different genres. In 1873, the St. Petersburg censorial committee banned and ordered the destruction of a translated collection of works by Diderot containing *Jacques the Fatalist and His Master, This Is Not a Story, The White Bird* and other stories. *Jacques the Fatalist* and *The White Bird* were found particularly harmful, and the entire book was characterised as antireligious and cynical (Dobrovol'skii 1962: 99–100). Secular censors also looked with disfavour on Émile Zola, whose novel *The Kill*, translated into Russian, was banned and destroyed in 1874 for being written so realistically that it was 'capable of evoking adverse passions rather than disgust toward them' (Dobrovol'skii 1962: 115). In 1880, the already published translation of *The Temptation of St. Antoine* (translated as 'The Temptation of a Hermit') by Gustave Flaubert was banned for 'mocking Christianity and the Christian church' despite the fact that the original had been approved for circulation 'in its entirety' five years earlier. The book was described as 'not devoid of talent', which was why it was 'bound to find here numerous readers, especially among the unsettled youth of both sexes, and, no doubt, it will produce the most harmful impact on them' (Dobrovol'skii 1962: 139). In 1903, both Moscow and St. Petersburg editions of Zola's *Vérité* were banned for advocating the idea of separation of church and state, and especially church and schools (Dobrovol'skii 1962: 236–7).

Finally, censors also paid close attention to translations of works on natural history and the origin of humankind. The translation of Ernst Haeckel's *History of Creation* was banned and destroyed in 1873, the translation of his *General Morphology of Organisms* was banned and destroyed in 1880, and the translation of *On Our Current Understanding of the Origin of Man* was banned in 1899. The translation of Haeckel's *Riddle of the Universe* was banned twice: first in 1902, then, after being published again, it was banned in 1906 (Dobrovol'skii 1962: 94–5, 138–9, 216–7, 232).

The translation of the Bible into the contemporary Russian language also faced difficulties throughout the nineteenth century. The Russian Biblical Society first attempted to translate the Holy Scriptures in the 1820s, for which it had secured the approval of Alexander I. The Russian Orthodox hierarchs, however, were so opposed to the idea of the translation of sacred texts that several hundred thousand copies were burned almost immediately upon printing. The Holy Synod granted its permission for a complete translation of the Holy Scriptures only in 1859. The translation of the New Testament was published in 1862, and the complete translation of the Bible—the so-called Russian Synodal Bible—followed in 1876 (Miller 2000: 101–3).

In the beginning of the twentieth century, bans were imposed on the translation of works as diverse as *The Bad Shepherds* by Octave Mirbeau (1900), *The Origin of the Idea of Good* by Paul Lafargue (1900), *Woman in the Past, Present, and Future* by August Bebel (1901), *History of the French Revolution* by Louis Blanc (1902), and *Social Problems* by Henry George (1904) (see Dobrovol'skii 1962: 220–221, 223–225, 231–232, 239–240).

4.3   The Soviet Period

The February Revolution of 1917 and the abdication of the Russian monarch created new conditions for further transformations of the censorial apparatus. On 9 March 1917, the Provisional Government officially liquidated the Main Committee for the Press, which was the main censoring organ at that time; the entire publishing community greeted the decision with great joy, happy to bid farewell to unremitting censorship. Newspapers published obituaries to censorship, poems about censors killing themselves with their own red pencil and caricatures of unemployed censors trading in cigarettes on the street (Sonina 2019: 249, 251, 260, 262). The closure of the main controlling body did not, however, neutralise censorship as an activity, especially in the context of Russia's military engagements. The third Russian revolution followed half a year later. On 25 October 1917, the Provisional Government was overthrown and replaced by the Bolshevik government. One of the first decrees issued by the new Soviet state, alongside the Decree on Peace and the Decree on Land, was the Decree on the Press. This decree called for closing all publishing organizations that '1) call[ed] for open resistance or insubordination to the government of Workers and Peasants; 2) cri[ed] havoc by apparently slanderous distortion of facts; 3) call[ed] for apparently criminal, that is penal, actions' (Obichkin 1957: 24–5). In the wake of the Decree on the Press, all private publishing houses were nationalised. Beginning with the introduction of official control of the press, the Soviet state steadily tightened its grip on publishing and literature.

The year 1922 was marked by the emergence of a new institution under the name *Main Administration for Literary and Publishing Affairs (Glavlit) at the RSFSR People's Commissariat of Education*. Throughout the 69 years of its existence, the institution regularly changed its name, eventually becoming the *Agency for the Protection of State Secrets in the Mass Media under the Ministry of Information and Press of the USSR*; it was, however, at all times universally known as *Glavlit*. The main purpose of Glavlit was to control all information undergoing publication and to compile lists of banned literature. Glavlit gradually developed a well-coordinated vertical network consisting of the central office of Glavlit of the USSR at the top, Glavlits of the Soviet Socialist

The Routledge Handbook of Translation and Censorship

republics of the Soviet Union at a lower level, followed by Glavlits of the autonomous republics of the Soviet Union and regional Glavlits (Pribytkov 2014: 46).

Glavlit was primarily engaged in tightly controlling literature and publishing in order to detect any ideologically harmful, politically suspicious or dangerous texts, subjects or authors, even though the existence of censorship in the country was denied by the Soviet government, At the same time, the Bolshevik approach denied the political neutrality of the arts. Such terms as 'party literature' and 'party press' were already used by Lenin, who called for bringing literary and publishing activities in line with Soviet policy. Thus, Glavlit was becoming much more than a censorship body. With its prescriptive, controlling, and preventive functions, it originated as a progressive phenomenon of its time, which aimed at changing the thinking of the citizens of the new state (Shomrakova and Barenbaum 2005: 208). Decisions made by the censorship organs were not limited to bans—they had a prescriptive and 'optimistic' character, dictating to authors the form and content of their writings, thus interfering with the creative process. With the adoption of socialist realism as the main aesthetic policy of Soviet arts and literature and the organization of the Union of Soviet Writers in 1934, non-compliance with the prescribed poetics became the reason for rejecting or removing from general access many literary works on neutral and politic-ally unbiased subjects.

Designed to control information, Glavlit often kept writers and publishers in suspense. The absence of clearly formulated norms and requirements for literary works made writers, translators and publishers feel insecure, while the censors had a sense of impunity. Any work could be declared ideologically harmful on the grounds of personal taste or nepotism (Goriaeva 2009: 146–7, 152–3).

The Catalogue of the Department of Special Storage and Reference Card Index preserved in the archive of the Russian National Library contains data on the editions forbidden in the Soviet Union, making it possible to trace the censorship trends during the first decades of the Soviet state. The main reason for banning books, including those containing translations, was the rapid change in political attitudes and affiliations. Any author, editor or translator could become polit-ically undesirable at a certain point in history. Thus, for instance, the 1932 Russian edition of *The Praise of Folly* by Erasmus of Rotterdam was listed among banned books several years later; the catalogue card reads, 'Remove the introduction' (Katalog Otdela, Box 55). The introduction to the 1932 edition of Erasmus was written by Ivar Smilga, an influential communist official who was arrested and shot for Trotskiist counterrevolutionary activity in 1937. The same reason lay behind the ban on the 1925 Russian edition of *Robinson Crusoe* by Daniel Defoe and the 1935 collection of works by Diderot in ten volumes—in both cases, the editors had fallen into disfavour. This is clearly seen from the handwritten notes on the restricted storage section index cards. In the case of Defoe, the card reads, 'Criminality off (Z. Lilina)', which means that editor Zlata Lilina was at a certain point no longer considered an undesirable person. Lilina was the second wife of Grigorii Zinoviev, who outlived her by seven years and was tried and shot as a leader of the Trotskiist-Zinovievite terrorist center. After the execution of Zinoviev, Lilina's works were removed from libraries. As for the 1935 Diderot collection, it was edited by Ivan Luppol, who was arrested for counterrevolutionary activity in 1940. The index card contains instructions for each volume, for example, 'Remove pages 9–86, keep the illustrations', 'Cross out Luppol's name on the front page' (Katalog Otdela, Box 14).

The contents of books, however, were equally important in decision-making. For example, all editions of *Ten Days That Shook the World* by John Reed up to 1956 remained in the restricted area collection until December 1987 (Katalog Otdela, Box 42). The reason for restricting the cir-culation of this book about the Russian Revolution written by an eyewitness, who was also one of only three Americans buried at the Kremlin Wall Necropolis, was the book's focus on Lev Trotskii, whom Reed portrayed as a central leader of the revolution alongside Vladimir Lenin, whereas Iosif Stalin was barely mentioned. Stalin criticised the book as early as 1924 and accused it of fantasies and exaggerations (Maksimenkov 2005: 93–5). The editions of 1957 and subsequent years, however, enjoyed free circulation.

In the period between the two world wars, special attention was given to the control of literature for children and youth. Children were supposed to be raised as fighters and builders of the new Soviet reality. Three times in the 1920s, public libraries were purged of 'ideologically alien literature', namely, in 1923, 1926 and 1929. In the course of these purges, a considerable number of translated works by Jules Verne, Robert Louis Stevenson, Louis Boussenard and other writers were removed from the libraries (Blium 1994: 256–8).

By the middle of the twentieth century, the Soviet censorship pyramid had become firmly established in Soviet literary life. The elaborate system of approval required of every publication included over ten stages, which could vary depending on the location of the publisher and the type of the literary project. The lack of regulations, fuzzy requirements and the official denial of censorship, which everyone, however, knew to exist, gave rise to self-censorship. In relation to translation, self-censorship was expressed primarily in the selection of original literary works (Kamovnikova 2019: 57–60). In general, the fate of each publication depended greatly on the human factor, because editors and publishers involved in the decision-making process demonstrated different degrees of courage and assumed different degrees of responsibility. Reasons for rejecting texts for translation were numerous and unpredictable. Selected subjects, casual observations, images employed in the literary work—anything could become the critical factor resulting in a ban on publication. The mere mention of Lev Trotsky, for example, was sufficient for a book to be withdrawn (Blium 2009: 137). With time, Glavlit began to issue its *Reports of Important Cross-Outs and Confiscations*, which were revised every five to six years and had to be used by all the censors in the Soviet Union (Blium 2005: 34–5).

The reasons for rejecting works of foreign literature for translation and publication were multiple. First, a book could be rejected because of its author. This concerned foreign writers who expressed disapproval of Soviet politics and lifestyle, like Rudyard Kipling, as well as those who welcomed socialism and so initially appealed to the Soviet authorities, but later changed their attitude and thus fell into disfavour, like André Gide. In light of his initial enthusiasm for the Soviet Union, Gide's books were widely translated into Russian and broadly circulated in the 1920s and 1930s. A five-volume edition of Gide's works was planned for publication in 1935–1936; however, the fourth volume was the last one printed. The reason for the sudden change in attitude toward Gide was his book *Retour de l'URSS,* which he wrote and published in 1936 after his trip to the USSR, in which he expressed his complete disillusionment with communism. This was sufficient reason for banishing Gide from the Soviet literary stage; existing works by Gide were moved to restricted-access collections of libraries and new publications were banned (Blium 2009: 133). Other tabooed authors included Aldous Huxley, Henry James, Ezra Pound and Jean-Paul Sartre (Kamovnikova 2019: 155).

The personal biography of an author was not the sole factor determining the fate of translated literature in the Soviet Union. The requirements for the selection of original authors also applied to translators. The translator's reputation was supposed to be free of any anti-communist activities and affiliations. This requirement naturally precluded émigrés and former political prisoners from taking part in literary activities. This presented a serious complication for editors and publishing houses because many high-quality literary translations were produced by politically undesirable persons. The most difficult period in this regard was the Purge of the 1930s, when repressed translators could not be mentioned and their translations were thus published as anonymous. Despite the incremental improvement in the situation during the Thaw period following Stalin's death, many highly qualified translators remained banished from Soviet literary life. Their active search for publication opportunities was not a search for literary fame; sneaking translations into print was a means of survival for those who had served time in labour camps and undergone public condemnation. In such situations, a translator would assume a pen name or even request that other people publish his/her translations under their name, so that they could receive the payment for the publication and pass the money over to its actual translator. Thus, after having served five years in a strict-regime labour camp for publishing his works abroad, writer and translator Iulii Daniel' was banned from publication. However, Daniel' was a veteran of World War II, during which he had been seriously wounded, which is why the literary officials allowed him to use a prescribed pen name, *Iu. Petrov* (Pann 2016), 'Petrov' being a very common Russian last name. However, after engaging in open conflict in the French press in the defense of Russian writers under Soviet political pressure, Daniel' was officially stripped of his pseudonym. Having lost his pen name, Daniel had to resort to borrowing his friends' names to publish his translations. After his death, poet and songwriter Bulat Okudzhava openly acknowledged that the volume of Daniel' Varuzhan's poetry for which he was listed as a translator was, in fact, translated by Daniel' (Timokhina, n.d.).

The political affiliation of authors and literary translators was sometimes considered a much more important factor in the decision-making process regarding the publication of their works than the content of the works themselves. Some writers were approved due to their communist activity or friendship with famous communist activists, despite the controversial subjects or styles of their works. For example, the communist leanings of many Latin American writers in the 1960s and 1970s resulted in a Latin American literary boom in the Soviet Union. Latin American novels, however, were usually first published in Russian with considerable cutouts, as happened, for instance, with *One Hundred Years of Solitude* by Gabriel García Márquez in 1970. Special attention was also paid to the publication of post-war German literature from the GDR. The emigration of an author from East Germany to West Germany, however, inalterably resulted in bans of his/her publications in the Soviet Union, which happened with the German poet Wolf Biermann.

Apart from the personal biographies and political preferences of the authors and their translators, the controlling institutions paid close attention to the content of each particular literary work. Literature was monitored for infringements on morality, national achievements and social values. Politically undesirable subjects included but were not restricted to sex, religion, anti-communist statements, unconventional discussions of national issues and comparisons of the Soviet Union with other countries. Thus, it took twenty years for the translation of *For Whom the Bell Tolls* by Ernest Hemingway to be published in the Soviet Union despite the fact that translations of other works by Hemingway had made their way into print unhindered. Among the reasons for the repeated rejection of the novel were its unflattering descriptions of the French communist and Political Commissar of the International Brigades during the Spanish Civil War André Marty and the leader of the Spanish Civil War and General Secretary of the Communist Party of Spain Dolores Ibárruri (Blium 2000: 226; Kuznetsova 2012).

Another subject that was considered undesirable in art and literature and that evoked almost automatic rejection was sexuality. Undisguised sexuality in the arts was a taboo, and candid scenes and descriptions of sex were either abridged or removed from translations. Abridgements and removals were also applied to texts relating to religious topics, which impeded publications of literary translations, especially in the light of the recurrent waves of state propaganda promoting atheism. That being said, the research has shown that the censorship of literary works permitted for publication was often more porous, negotiated and unpredictable than previously assumed (see

Sherry 2015; Kamovnikova 2019), and individual translators found ways to translate and circulate works outside official channels (Rossi 2023) or to give a particular spin to officially approved authors (Baer 2011).

4.4 The Post-Soviet Period

The collapse of the Soviet Union triggered the rapid evolution of public freedoms in Russia, including freedom of speech. The period from the end of the 1980s to the beginning of the 1990s was marked by an unprecedented level of information transparency; while dealing with/enduring difficult economic conditions, together with the rest of the country, publishers were free to choose authors, topics and publication formats. The restricted access list shrank considerably. Libraries, however, required that researchers provide official letters from their organisations in order to get access to books containing national-socialist propaganda.

Since 2002, the main Russian law regulating the circulation of literature is the Federal Law on Countering Extremist Activities (Federal'nyi zakon 'O protivodeistvii', n.d.), which enables regional courts to declare published materials extremist. Among extremist activities, the Law lists any forcible change in the foundations of the constitutional order and violation of the territorial integrity of the Russian Federation; public justification of terrorism; incitement of social, racial, national or religious hatred; use of Nazi symbols and attributes and symbols of extremist organizations; and several others (Federal'nyi zakon 'O protivodeistvii', n.d. Chapter 1.). All materials deemed extremist are included in the Federal List of Extremist Materials (Ekstremistskie materialy, n.d.). In February 2021, the list included 5153 items. Another law regulating literary activity in the country is the Federal Law 'On the Protection of Children from Information Harmful to Their Health and Development' (Federal Law 'On the Protection of Children', n.d.). The Law forbids the circulation among children of books including information that encourages children to commit acts posing a threat to their life and health and to the life and health of other persons; is capable of causing children to use narcotic drugs, psychotropic substances, tobacco and alcohol; substantiates or justifies violence and cruelty; contains images or descriptions of sexual violence; denies family values and promotes non-traditional sexual relations; contains obscene language; contains information of a pornographic nature, among others (Federal Law 'On the Protection of Children', n.d.). Publishers admit that the Law inclines them towards censorship and self-censorship, as publishers fear both the interpretation of the law by the authorities and by critically minded readers. Thus, when 'Samokat' publishers published the Russian translation of *Fruitloops and Dipsticks* by the Swedish children's writer Ulf Stark, they decided to cut out a scene they feared would be found too candid; the excerpt was removed with the author's and the translator's permission (Balyko 2018). It also happens that bookstores refuse to sell publications that may potentially draw complaints from readers. This happened, for example, with the third volume of Stephen Fry's autobiography, when one of the biggest Russian booksellers decided against publishing the book, which was considered a potential best-seller. This was done for fear of negative reaction from Russian readers and of violating the law on the promotion of drug use: Fry's volume contained episodes about sex, cocaine addiction and homosexuality (Balyko 2018). The Israeli historian Yuval Noah Harari allowed omissions and amendments in the Russian edition of his third book, *21 Lessons for the 21st Century*, softening his remarks about local authorities and substituting some examples with others. Harari spoke about his decision in the following way, 'Should I replace these few examples with other examples, and publish the book in Russia—or should I change nothing, and publish nothing. I preferred publishing, because Russia is a leading global power and it seemed to me important that the book's ideas should reach readers in Russia.

The Routledge Handbook of Translation and Censorship

[...] The Russian translation still warns readers about the dangers of dictatorship, corruption, homophobia and nationalist extremism' (Prof. Yuval Noah Harari, 2019). In his interview with the BBC, Harari admitted to having performed an act of self-censorship (Pisatel' Iuval Harari, 2019).

4.5 Future Directions

The geographical location of Russia and the distance that separates it from Europe had a significant impact on its internal and external policy. The ideas of Moscow as the Third Rome, of the national glory and the Russian special mission, of the liberating state destined to bring freedom to the new world were self-alienating in their essence. Censorship in general and censorship of translations in particular were well rooted in the traditional self-perception of the Russian nation as a lone fighter charged with a special mission. Consequently, ideas arriving from abroad were vigilantly controlled and perceived as potentially adverse. Suspicion completed the vicious circle: censors performed their tasks by banning books and removing excerpts, thus creating an information void, which, in its turn, contributed to a further rise in suspicion. Occasional periods of latitude encouraged the active rapprochement of Russia with the outside world, and the stiffening that followed met with overt and covert resistance on the part of publishers, editors, translators and all those who persevered in finding ways to bring foreign literature to the Russian readership. The effect the current geopolitical situation is having on literature and translation remains to be investigated in a systematic way; further data collection and analysis will be required to assess the damage, as well as the scale of resistance of those currently engaged in translation.

Further Reading

Blium, Arlen. 2005. *Kak eto delalos' v Leningrade: Tsenzura v gody ottepeli, zastoia i perestroiki. 1953–1991* [*The way it was done in Leningrad: Censorship in the years of thaw, stagnation, and perestroika. 1953–1991*]. St. Petersburg: Akademicheskii proekt.
The monograph by one of the most influential Russian scholars on censorship and totalitarianism describes the mechanisms of thought and freedom suppression in Soviet literature and art in the 1950s–1980s. The book makes a special focus on the KGB activities directed against the literature of the Leningrad underground. The example of the Leningrad censorship is seen as a striking, but nevertheless private, case study of the activities of literature and art controlling bodies throughout the entire Soviet Union.

Choldin, Marianna T. 1985. *A Fence around the Empire. Russian censorship of Western ideas under the Tsars.* Durham: Duke University Press.
The first monograph by Marianna Tax Choldin has become a classic study in the history of censorship in the Russian Empire, especially of the activities of the Committee of Foreign Censorship founded to screen all publications imported for Russian bookstores and libraries. Special attention is paid to the figure of the censor as both a governmental official and a person pursuing individual goals.

Goriaeva, Tat'iana. 2009. *Politicheskaia tsenzura v SSSR. 19171991 gg.* [*Political censorship in the USSR. 1917–1991*]. Moscow: ROSSPEN.
The book studies Soviet political censorship as a system that was designed to control all spheres of public and cultural life. The study covers the entire Soviet period, dwelling on the forms Soviet censorship took under different social and political conditions. The author contrasts the suppressive censorship activities to the facts of literary opposition and resistance to political pressure.

Sherry, Samantha. 2015. *Discourses of regulation and resistance: Censoring translation in the Stalin and Khrushchev era Soviet Union.* Edinburgh: University of Edinburgh Press.
The book is a detailed study of the censorship of translated literature in the Soviet Union. It examines in detail the development of literary translation censorship practices between the 1930s and the 1960s. Speaking about different types and purposes of censorship, it also dwells on the importance of literary translations for the

Censorship in Russia: Tsarist, Soviet and Post-Soviet Contexts

Soviet readership and for the lives and careers of individual translators. The monograph also features detailed case studies and archival material analysis.

Zhirkov, Gennadii. 2001. *Istoriia tsenzury v Rossii XIX –XX vv.* [*History of censorship in Russia, 19–20 c.*]. Moscow: Aspekt press.
The comprehensive study reveals the continuity of censorship practices in tsarist Russia and the Soviet Union. It dwells on the relations between censoring organs and centralised power in different periods of Russian history. The book is brilliantly illustrated by archival materials, including state documents, memoirs, and private correspondence.

References

Baer, Brian James. 2011. 'Translating Queer Texts in Soviet Russia: A Case Study in Productive Censorship', *Translation Studies*, 4(1): 21–40.

Balyko, Anastasiia. 2018. 'Perevodnaia literatura i (samo)tsenzura' [Translated literature and (self-)censorship]. Last modified 02 March 2018. https://godliteratury.ru/articles/2018/03/02/perevodnaya-literatura-i-samocenzura

Barenbaum, Iosif. 1984. *Istoriia knigi* [*History of the book*]. Moscow: Kniga.

Blium, Arlen. 1994. *Za kulisami ,Ministerstva pravdy.'Tainaia istoriia sovetskoi tsensury 1917–1929* [*In the backstage of the 'Ministry of truth.' The secret history of the Soviet censorship 1917–1929*]. St. Petersburg: Akademicheskii proekt.

Blium, Arlen. 2000. *Sovetskaia tsenzura v epokhu total'nogo terrora. 1929–1953* [*Soviet censorship in the epoch of total terror. 1929–1953*]. St. Petersburg: Akademicheskii proekt, 2000.

Blium, Arlen. 2005. *Kak eto delalos'v Leningrade: Tsenzura v gody ottepeli, zastoia i perestroiki. 1953–1991* [*The way it was done in Leningrad: Censorship in the years of thaw, stagnation, and perestroika. 1953–1991*]. St. Petersburg: Akademicheskii proekt.

Blium, Arlen. 2009. 'Zarubezhnaia literatura v spetskhrane' [Foreign Literature in Spetskhran], *Inostrannaia Literatura,*12: 131–46.

Choldin, Marianna T. 1985. *A Fence around the Empire. Russian Censorship of Western Ideas under the Tsars.* Durham: Duke University Press.

Delo upravleniia Imperatorskoi Publichnoi Biblioteki o dostavliaemykh v onuiu iz Komiteta Inostrannoi Tsensury vedomostei o zapreshchennykh knigakh [File of the administration of the Imperial Public Library on the delivery of lists of forbidden books from the Committee of Foreign Censorship]. 1850. The Russian National Library Archive, F.1, Op, 1, d. 15.

Dobrovol'skii, Lev. 1962. *Zapreshcennaia kniga v Rossii 1825–1904* [*The banned book in Russia 1825–1904*]. Moscow: Izdatel'stvo Vsesoiuznoi knizhnoi palaty.

'Extremist Materials' [Ekstremistskie materialy]. *Official Website of the Ministry of Justice of the Russian Federation*, n.d. Accessed 13 February 2021. https://minjust.gov.ru/ru/extremist-materials/

Federal'nyi zakon 'O zashchite detei ot informatsii, prichiniaiushchei vred ikh zdorov'iu I razvitiiu' (s izmeneniiami na 31.07.2020) [Federal Law 'On the Protection of Children from Information Harmful to Their Health and Development' of 29.12.2010 N 436–FZ (with amendments of 31.07.2020)]. n.d. Accessed 13 February 2021.

Federal'nyi zakon 'O protivodeistvii ekstremistskoi deiatel'nosti' ot 25.07.2002 N 114-FZ (s izmeneniiami na 8.12.2020) [Federal Law 'On Countering Extremist Activities' of 25.07.2002 N 114-FZ (with amendments of 8.12.2020)], n.d. Accessed 13 February 2021. https://fzrf.su/zakon/o-protivodejstvii-ehkstremistskoj-deyatelnosti-114-fz/

Goriaeva, Tat'iana. 2009. *Politicheskaia tsenzura v SSSR. 1917–1991 gg.* [*Political censorship in the USSR. 1917–1991*]. Moscow: ROSSPEN.

Izmozik, Vladlen, 2000. 'Chernyi kabinet' [Black Cabinet], *Rodina*, 10. Accessed 13 May 2024. http://vivov oco.astronet.ru/VV/THEME/STOP/PERL.HTM

Kamovnikova, Natalia. 2019. *Made under pressure: Literary translation in the Soviet Union, 1960–1991.* Amherst and Boston: University of Massachusetts Press.

Katalog Otdela spetsial'nogo khraneniia i spravochnoi kartoteki, Rossiiskaia natsional'naia biblioteka [Catalogue of the Department of special storage and reference card index, Russian National Library], Box 14.

Katalog Otdela spetsial'nogo khraneniia i spravochnoi kartoteki, Rossiiskaia natsional'naia biblioteka [Catalogue of the Department of special storage and reference card index, Russian National Library], Box 42.

Katalog Otdela spetsial'nogo khraneniia i spravochnoi kartoteki, Rossiiskaia natsional'naia biblioteka [Catalogue of the Department of special storage and reference card index, Russian National Library], Box 55.

Kuznetsova, Ekaterina. 2012. 'Sposoby ideologicheskoi adaptatsii perevodnogo teksta: O perevode romana E. Khemingueia "Po kom zvonit kolokol"' [Means of Ideological Adaptation of the Translated Text: Towards the Translation of the Novel of E. Hemingway 'For Whom the Bell Tolls'], *Logos*, 3: 153–71.

Likhachev, Dmitrii. 2004. *Vvedenie k chteniiu pamiatnikov drevnerusskoi literatury* [*Introduction to the reading of the Old Russian literature monuments*], edited by Sigurd Shmidt. Moscow: Russkii put'.

Lotman, Iurii, and Boris Uspenskii. 1977. 'Rol' dualnykh modelei v dinamike russkoi kul'tury (do kontsa XVIII veka)' [The role of dual models in the dynamics of Russian culture (untill the end of the XVIII century)], in *Trudy po russkoi i slavianskou filologii. XXVIII. Literaturovedenie*. Tartu: Tartu State University, 3–36.

Maksimenkov, Leonid (ed). 2005. *Bol'shaia tsenzura. Pisateli i zhurnalisty v strane sovetov 1917–1956* [*Big censorship. Writers and journalists in the country of Soviets. 1917–1956*]. Moscow: MFD Materik.

Miller, Aleksei. 2000. *'Ukrainskii vopros' v politike vlastei i russkom obshchestvennom mnenii (vtoraia polovina XIX veka)* [*The 'Ukrainian question' in the state policy and in the Russian public opinion (second half of the XIX Century)*]. St. Petersburg: Aleteiia.

Nandris, Grigore. 1969. *Old Church Slavonic Grammar.* Part II. London: University of London, The Athlone Press.

Obichkin, Gennadii, editor. 1957. *Dekrety Sovetskoi vlasti. T. I* [*Decrees of the Soviet power. Vol. I*]. Moscow: Gosudarstvennoe izdatel'stvo politicheskoi literatury.

Pakhomov, Nikolai. 2019. 'Russkaia Golgofa. Sil'vestr Medvedev (1641–1691)' [Russian Golgotha. Sil'vestr Medvedev (1641–1691)]. Accessed 03 November 2020. https://proza.ru/2019/10/02/448

Pann, Lilia. 2016. 'Iulii Daniel': "Vol'noi voli zapovednye puti"' [Iulii Daniel': "The Secret Paths of Freewill"]. *Interpoeziia*, 1. Accessed 03 May 2024. https://magazines.gorky.media/interpoezia/2016/1/yulij-daniel-volnoj-voli-zapovednye-puti.html

Patrusheva, Natalia. 2013. *Tsenzurnoe vedomstvo v gosudarstvennoi sisteme Rossiiskoi imperii vo vtoroi polovine XIX – nachale XX veka* [*Censorship administration in the State System of the Russian Empire in the Second Half of the XIX – beginning of the XX century*]. St. Petersburg: Severnaia zvezda.

Patrusheva, Natalia. 2019. 'Proekt Nakaza tsenzoram (1848)' [Outline of a Nakaz for censors (1848)], in M. Konashev (ed.), *Tsenzura v Rossii: istroiia i sovremennost'*. Collected papers. Issue 9. St. Petersburg: Rossiiskaia natsional'naia biblioteka, 445–96.

'Pisatel' Iuval' Harari o tsenzure v Rossii: "Ia ne vybiraiu mir, v kotorom zhivu"' [Writer Yuval Harari of censorship in Russia: "I do not choose the world I live in"]. *BBC News Russian Service*, 26 July 2019. www.bbc.com/russian/features-49130145

Pribytkov, Viktor. 2014. *Glavlit i tsenzura: Zapiski zamestitelia nachal'nika Glavnogo upravleniia po okhrane gosudarstvennykh tain v pechati pri Sovete ministrov SSSR* [*Glavlit and censorship: Notes of Deputy Chief of the Main administration for the protection of State Secrets in the press under the USSR Council of ministers*]. Moscow: Molodaia gvardiia.

'Prof. Yuval Noah Harari Responds to Censoring Russian Translation of His Book', *Haaretz*, 26 July 2019. www.haaretz.com/israel-news/yuval-noah-harari-responds-to-backlash-after-he-let-russia-censor-his-book-1.7576761

Rossi, Miriam. 2023. *"Les traducteurs sont die Post Pferde of the Enlightenment": Poet-translators in the Leningrad Samizdat of the Eighties.* Unpublished doctoral dissertation, University of Tallinn.

Sherry, Samantha. 2015. *Discourses of Regulation and Resistance: Censoring Translation in the Stalin and Khrushchev Era Soviet Union.* Edinburgh: University of Edinburgh Press.

Shomrakova, Inga and Iosif Barenbaum. 2005. *Vseobshchaia istoriia knigi* [*The World History of the book*]. St. Petersburg: Professiia.

Sonina, Elena. 2019. 'Proshchanie s tsenzuroi: satiricheskaia grafika 1917 goda o tsenzure i tsenzorakh' [A farewell to censorship: 1917 satirical graphic arts on censorship and censors], in M. Konashev (ed.), *Tsenzura v Rossii: istroiia i sovremennost'*. Collected papers. Issue 9. St. Petersburg: Rossiiskaia natsional'naia biblioteka, 244–63.

Timokhina, M.V. n.d. '"V zhivykh, perepletennykh kozhei sud'bakh, ego literaturnaia sud'ba…": K 70-letiiu Viktora Solomonovicha Serbskogo' ["In living, skin-bound destinies abides his own literary destiny…": On the 70th anniversary of Viktor Solomonovich Serbskii]. Accessed 03 May 2024. https://web.archive.org/web/20111117061927/http://abratsk.ru/lib/serbsky/serbsky_.htm

Zalizniak, Andrei. 2004. *Drevnenovgorodskii dialect* [*The old Novgorod dialect*]. Moscow: Iazyki slavianskoi kul'tury.

Zelenov, Mikhail. 2015. 'Tsenzura kak svoistvo psikhiki i forma ekspozitsii soznaniia' [Censorship as a psychic setup feature and a mentality exposition form], in M. Zelenov (ed.), *Istoriia knigi i tsenzury v Rossii. Tret'i Bliumovskie chteniia: materialy III mezhdunarodnoi nauchnoi konferentsii, posviasjchennoi pamiati A.V. Bliuma, 27–28 maiia 2014*. St. Petersburg: LGU im. Pushkina, 13–22.

Zhirkov, Gennadii. 2001. *Istoriia tsenzury v Rossii XIX–XX vv.* [*History of censorship in Russia, 19–20 c.*]. Moscow: Aspekt press.

5

CENSORSHIP OF TRANSLATED BOOKS IN TURKEY

An Overview

İrem Konca

5.1 Introduction

A brief survey of censorship cases in the Turkish context indicates that censorship has been indiscriminately practised throughout Turkish intellectual and political history on both indigenous and translated books, regardless of the specific government in place. However, a deeper analysis, one that places more emphasis on the political context, indicates that in times when it was apparently more convenient for 'agents' (Milton and Bandia 2019) to further their respective ideological agendas through translation, censorship was predominantly directed against translated books, and translators and publishers involved in the process were targeted with legal prosecution on the basis of Article 2 of the Turkish Press Law, which regards the translators as owners of the work and holds them liable in cases where the source author is not a Turkish citizen residing in Turkey. Focusing on the specific times when the practice of censorship was most prevalent since the late Ottoman empire and delineating the legal grounds for it, this chapter aims to provide an overview of the censorship of translations as it pertains to the Turkish context.

5.2 Historical Perspectives

The beginning of censorship in Ottoman history is generally traced back to the rule of Sultan Abdulhamid II (1876–1908). In fact, the earlier legal regulations of Matbuat Nizamnâmesi (Press Law) and Kararname-i Alî (The High Decree), put into effect in 1864 and 1867, respectively, constituted the legal grounds for exerting oversight on the press. The institutionalisation of the practice of censorship, however, occurred during the oppressive Hamidian regime of Sultan Abdulhamid II. Although the first Press Law enforced in the Ottoman Empire dated back to 1857, it specifically applied to the rules to be followed when opening a printing house and censorship on published material was not within its scope (Alkan 2018). The Press Law of 1864, by contrast, is the first law that formed the basis for exerting censorship on material published in journals and newspapers and targeted opposition voiced by the press. Within the context of this Law, which remained in effect until 1909, it was forbidden to publish a newspaper without the permission of the government. Likewise, it was strictly forbidden to publish articles threatening public peace or against moral values of society, or criticising the Sultan and denigrating the leaders of states with which the Empire had amicable relations (Alkan 2018). What constituted 'a threat to public peace' or 'a violation of moral values' remained ambiguous and was left entirely to the discretion of the censor. As the sanctions imposed by this Law were deemed to be insufficient, the Kararname-i Alî (The High Decree) was enforced on 17 March 1867. The Decree provided the legal grounds for the closing down of newspapers and journals, prosecuting, punishing and exiling members of the press. The culmination and concentration of censorship measures were prompted by the High Decree.

Sultan Abdulhamid II acceded to the Ottoman throne with the promise of establishing Meclis-i Mebûsan, the first Ottoman parliament, following the dethronement of Sultan Abdulaziz in 1876. His rule lasted until the proclamation in 1908 of the Second Constitutional Monarchy (II. Meşrutiyet) (though he remained as the Sultan until 27 April 1909) and is referred to as İstibdâd Dönemi (The Hamidian Regime of Despotism). Works on the rule of Sultan Abdulhamid II represent two opposing poles, viewing the Sultan as Kızıl Sultan (The Red Sultan / 'Le Sultan Rouge') and Ulu Hakan (The Great Sultan) (see, for example, Karakışla 2002: 10). The French historian Albert Vandal was the first to use the term 'Le Sultan Rouge' to refer to Abdulhamid II. The term 'Kızıl Sultan' was employed to indicate his bloody repression of the Armenian revolts in East Anatolia in 1895. Despite the two contrasting viewpoints, there is a general consensus among researchers that extreme pressure was exerted on the press under the Hamidian regime, during which time newspapers publishing news and articles critical of the Sultan were closed down, native and foreign journalists were bribed to prevent criticism and opposition and, finally, both indigenous and translated works were banned and even burnt (Kabacalı 1990; İrtem 1999; Topuz 2003; Demirel 2007). The institution in charge of controlling the press was the Matbaalar İdaresi (Directorate of the Press), which reported directly to the Ministry of Internal Affairs. Censorship under the despotic regime was institutionalised by means of the various agencies of the Office of Indigenous and Translated Works (Telif ve Tercüme Dairesi), which was founded by the state in 1879 within the Ministry of Education and renamed the Encümen-i Teftiş ve Muayene (The Commission of Inspection and Examination) upon its merger with the Directorate of the Press in 1881. Several other governmental bodies, such as Tedkik-i Müellefat Komisyonu (The Commission for the Inspection of Literary Works) and Kütüb-i Diniye ve Şer'iyye Tedkik Heyeti (The Council for the Inspection of Books on Religion and the She'ria) were founded later (in 1892 and 1902, respectively) in the Ottoman capital to reinforce the practice of censorship as the regime became more established. The laws regulating the activities of these institutions stipulated that any and all books to be published within the Ottoman territory should be ratified by these censorship bodies. During the Hamidian regime, works by such well-known European intellectuals and literary figures as Victor Hugo, Jules Verne, Jean Jacques Rousseau, Dante and Emile Zola were banned; the works of native writers like Namık Kemal, Ziya Paşa, Ahmet Mithad Efendi, Şinasi and Halid Ziya were censored; and the attempt by Şemseddin Sami to translate the Quran into Turkish was blocked (İrtem 1999: 262). Halid Ziya Uşaklıgil's translations of short stories from French, collected under the title *Nakil* in 1894, were another example of censored translations (Uşaklıgil 1969: 299–300).

Shakespeare was also one of the censored poets and playwrights. In fact, his plays were not translated and published in full before 1908. Although *Hamlet* and *King Lear* were staged in 1881, their performance was banned in 1889, and *The Merchant of Venice* and *Othello* were staged instead (Paker 1991: 28). The unsystematic and arbitrary nature of censorship caused certain works that were not suppressed or banned in the early years of the Hamidian regime to be censored in the later years. The thousands of reports issued by the Commission of Inspection and Examination indicate that the official rationale for censorship ranged from being an 'irrational work' to 'failure to benefit Ottoman values and morals' (Kabacalı 1990: 65).

Another significant work banned under the rule of Abdulhamid II was *Hulâsa-i Hümâyunnâme* ['Summary of the Book for the Emperor'], Ahmet Midhat's translation of *Kelile and Dimne*, a book on ethics and politics originally written in Sanskrit (Toska 2015: 73). Ahmed Midhat was commissioned by the Sultan himself to translate this book, which provided guidance to rulers, but 'it never saw the light of day' for reasons unclear in the documentary evidence (Toska 2015: 74).

The confiscation and burning of 30,302 books in the Çemberlitaş Public Bath in 1902 represent the culmination of the implementation of censorship under the Hamidian regime (Demirel 2007: 103). This incident is surely the most severe demonstration of the overall extent of censorship, particularly towards the end of the Hamidian regime (Demirel 2007: 104). Among the books burned were Namık Kemal's *Osmanlı Tarihi* [Ottoman History], *İntibah* [Renaissance], *Vatan yahud Silistre* [Homeland or Silistra]; Abdülhak Hamit Tarhan's *Ölü* [Deceased], *Makber* [Grave], *Nazife*; Ahmed Midhat's *Süleyman Musuli, Henüz Onyedi Yaşında* [Only Seventeen], *Hüseyin Fellah*; and Fuzuli's *Leyla ile Mecnun*. The translations were fewer in number and included Fenelon's *Les Aventures de Télémaque*, translated by Yusuf Kamil Pasha as *Terceme-i Telemak* [Translation of *Télémaque*], and Molière's *Tartuffe*, translated by Ziya Pasha as *Riyânın Encamı* [The End of Hypocrisy] (Demirel 2007).

Despite harsh censorship measures during the Hamidian regime, the 'irrevocable' effect on literature of the processes of Westernisation and modernisation, which had started with the Tanzimat [The Reorganisation] (1839), persisted and had a marked impact on the later production of indigenous works (Paker 1991: 18). In other words, censorship measures were ineffective in totally eliminating the transformative role of translations. The proclamation of the Second Constitutional Monarchy by the Sultan on 24 July 1908 was met with pleasant surprise among the Ottoman intelligentsia. One of the first responses was the refusal to continue to send daily newspapers to the chief censor's office for approval. This was a very important step in resisting censorship, leading to the closure of the Commission of Inspection and Examination as well as the Commission for the Inspection of Literary Works. Also, the provision that 'it cannot, therefore, be subjected to pre-publication inspection and control' was added to the article in the Kanun-i Esasi, the Ottoman Constitution, the original content of which was: 'The press is free within the confines of the law'. Indeed, ever since then, July 24 has been celebrated as Basın Bayramı [Press Day] in Turkey.

Soon after the proclamation of the Second Constitutional Monarchy, there was an influx of indigenous and translated works most of which had probably been translated earlier and were awaiting the opportune moment to be published. With the proclamation of the constitutional monarchy, translation began to play a significant role in introducing constitutional values and various ideological movements to the Ottoman public, which quickly influenced public opinion. In 1906, even before the proclamation of the constitutional monarchy, Prince Sabahaddin, one of the major political opponents of the Hamidian regime, expressed the primary objective of the newspaper *Terakki*, as follows: 'Ensuring that works of social science which teach personal liberty and social welfare are translated so that they can be read by the public' (Arabacı 2010: 87). This was a trend that also manifested itself in the Republican period, as a response to which various forms of censorship were employed.

Abdulhamid II remained the Ottoman Sultan until 1909, when he was dethroned as a result of the uprising known as the:

31 Mart Vakası [31 March Incident], which took place on 13 April 1909 (31 March on the Rumi calendar), a few days after the assassination of Hasan Fehmi, the editor-in-chief of the newspaper *Serbesti* which was known to oppose the policies of the CUP. The assassination

led to demonstrations of protest headed by the students of Darülfünun. The uprising instigated by the killing of an opponent journalist was stoked by Derviş Vahdeti, who wrote for *Volkan*, which strongly opposed the CUP press. The 31 March Incident was a countercoup *per se* organized by conservative reactionaries who demanded 'İnkılâb-ı Şer' (Islamic Revolution). The uprising was crushed by Mahmud Şevket Pasha in command of the Army in Action (Hareket Ordusu), the Sultan was deposed and Mehmet V acceded to the throne.

(Konca 2022: 77)

The Hamidian regime was succeeded by the rule of İttihat ve Terakki Cemiyeti [Committee of Union and Progress], the largest Young Turk organisation leading the opposition against Abdulhamid II. The CUP followed a strategy similar to that of Abdulhamid II by using the press to further its interests and attain its political goals of introducing and propagating the benefits of the constitutional regime. Thus, the CUP initially lifted the barriers to freedom of the press and decided to pass a new press law (Konca 2022: 72). However, fearing that the oppressive regime might regain power, the press objected to the enforcement of a new press law. Public demonstrations joined by thousands of people were organised to protest against the enactment of the press law. The Law was put into effect on 29 July 1909. Although it granted more freedom to the press than ever before, the 31 March incident as well as the arrest and the assassination of journalists resulted in martial law, which superseded the press law. Actually, the press law never fully went into effect and harsh censorship measures against the press were implemented (Konca 2022: 77).

5.3 Core Issues and Topics

As discussed in the previous section, in late nineteenth-century Ottoman society, translation was instrumental not only in fostering new literary genres but also in exposing Turks to various ideological movements. Translation maintained that dual function in the early Republican period, which began in 1923. As Tahir Gürçağlar notes, 'an interesting aspect of the trajectory followed by translation in Turkey concerns the way it has conspicuously allied itself with political and ideological agendas, such as westernisation, Marxism and Islamism, to mention a few' (Tahir Gürçağlar 2009: 37). Depending on the political and social conjuncture of the time, the imposition of censorship was, thus, based on different factors.

5.3.1 Censorship on the Grounds of Communist Propaganda

Censorship imposed on Marxist/socialist works on the grounds of propagating communism constitutes an important chapter in the history of censorship under the Republican regime. Within this context, certain publishers and translators, such as Sabiha Sertel, Suphi Nuri İleri, Kerim Sadi, Hikmet Kıvılcımlı and Haydar Rifat, acted as self-appointed agents taking an active role in the formation of a Turkish leftist discourse. In the 1920s, the early years of the Republic, and again during the later years, censorship operated on two levels: (a) pre-censorship, i.e., the banning of certain publications to prevent their entry into the country by decrees issued by the Council of Ministers and (b) post-censorship, in the form of legal action brought against writers, translators and publishers, pursuant to the related articles of the Turkish Penal Code. While the total number of publications banned for propagating communism between 1923 and 1938 was ten, this number rose to 36 during the next decade (1938–1950) (Yılmaz and Doğaner 2007: 14–5).

The 1930s were marked by a concerted effort on the part of agents instrumentalising translation for the dissemination of leftist ideas. This was partly thanks to the principle of statism

The Routledge Handbook of Translation and Censorship

(Étatisme), adopted by the government, as well as good relations with the USSR, which secured the support of the new Soviet state in the Turkish War of Independence (Konca 2022: 100). Statism (in Turkey) refers to the movement toward state-controlled economic development; a shortage of skilled labour and entrepreneurs (caused largely by the reduction of the Greek and Armenian communities, which in 1914 had controlled four-fifths of Ottoman finance, industry, and commerce), a lack of capital, and an intense nationalist desire for industrial self-sufficiency that would banish foreign influence all stimulated the movement in the 1930s toward state ownership or control. While translation proved to be a practical means of ideology transfer in the 1930s, the Turkish leftist movement's lack of theoretical insight in its early stages, for which it has been criticised, can also be attributed to the fact that in the beginning, the movement was dependent on 'imported' texts, which had been created in and for different contexts. As stated above, Suphi Nuri İleri (1887–1945), Hikmet Kıvılcımlı (1902–1971), Haydar Rifat (1877–1942) and Kerim Sadi (Nevzat Cerrahoğlu) (1900–1977) were all prominent agents active in the importation of Marxist literature and the dissemination of socialist ideology through their translations. İleri founded the İleri Bibliyoteği (The İleri Library), which published a series of translated works of Marxism, and Kıvılcımlı translated works for his Marxist Library (Marksist Bibliyoteği) (The Marxist Library) and Library of Labourers (Emekçi Kütüphanesi) (Konca 2022: 112). Kıvılcımlı recounts the struggles he encountered when he founded his Library of Marxism. He states that even if a book with socialist content could be published after having been rescued from censorship and seizure at the hands of the secret police, this only meant that the writer or the translator of the book would suffer 'at the hands of Justice' (Kıvılcımlı 1978: 260). Kıvılcımlı's incomplete translation of Marx's *Das Kapital* is the first version translated into Turkish from the German original, and Kıvılcımlı, like most of the agents involved in the translation and transfer of Marxist/socialist literature, assumed the role of an 'ideologue translator', committing himself to the task as if it were a mission. Kıvılcımlı was prosecuted twice for his translations of Marxist literature, in 1929 and 1935. 'Ideologue translators' took it upon themselves to build a Marxist/socialist repertoire in the Turkish political field through their translations (Konca 2022: 20).

Sabiha Sertel (1895–1968) was another translator of Marxist literature who was brought to court in the 1930s. In addition, she was the co-owner, with her husband Zekeriya Sertel, of the monthly magazine *Resimli Ay*, which ran from 1924 to 1931, during which time it was transformed from a popular magazine into a leftist literary periodical focusing on social issues and challenging single-party rule. Sabiha Sertel was prosecuted in January 1930 for having translated and published an article dealing with leadership psychology from an American magazine. In her defence, she stated that the article was a translation of a scientific article published in an American magazine and that scientific and academic articles were written to inform rather than for the purpose of influencing public opinion (Sertel 1969: 153). Her prosecution was indicative of the state's response to the importation via translations of an ideology that would conflict with the dominant ideology of the state.

The year 1945 marks the beginning of multi-party rule in Turkey with the establishment of the Democrat Party, which came to power in 1950 and soon began implementing changes in the established social, financial and legal systems. The year 1950 saw the adoption of the new Press Law, which was the major legislative instrument for regulating freedom of expression, together with the Law on Intellectual and Artistic Works, 'superseding the Press Law of 1931 that had authorised the government to close down newspapers temporarily if they were deemed to publish articles against the general policy of the state' (Konca 2022: 120). I have argued elsewhere that the liberalisation of the Press Law that occurred in 1950 might be attributed to the fact that some members of the new party in power were journalists, who had suffered under the single-party rule as a result of restrictions on freedom of expression (Konca 2022: 120). However, the relative liberalisation provided by the new law was short-lived as the government favoured those press outlets that supported its ideology while repressing any opposition that might arise from counter-ideologies. Amendments made to the Press Law resulted in an enlargement of the scope of press crimes and a subsequent increase in the number of penalties to be inflicted. These new restrictions on freedom of the press had implications for the legal status of translators as well. A basic amendment concerning translators was made to Article 2 of the Press Law, which now included the translator in its definition of the owners of the work. The underlying motivation was to have someone to blame, prosecute and punish in place of authors who lived outside or beyond Turkish jurisdiction. To this day, censorship cases against translators have been initiated on the basis of this specific article of the Turkish Press Law.

The 1960 military coup took place against a political backdrop of mounting pressure on personal liberties and freedom of expression. Thanks to the promulgation of the 1961 Constitution, which granted more individual liberties than during the previous period, the 1960 military coup presented very favourable conditions for self-appointed agents to pursue their goals. 'Acts 6334 and 6732 on the "felonies to be committed through printed press or the radio broadcasting" as well as the anti-democratic provisions of the Press Law were annulled on October 12, 1960 even before the promulgation of the new constitution' (Konca 2022: 123). For the first time after many long years of suppression, the 'doxa,' to put it in Bourdieu's terms, was conducive to translating and publishing activity promoting leftist ideologies. Nevertheless, this period of relative freedom also turned out to be short-lived as cases were brought against translators throughout the 1960s.

The cases against the translators of the writings of the French revolutionary journalist François-Noël Babeuf and of the Communist Manifesto received high media coverage and aroused great public interest. In both cases, the agents were by no means invisible; on the contrary, they acted as self-appointed cultural (and sociopolitical) agents who took it upon themselves to raise public awareness of current political issues. Sabahattin Eyüboğlu and Vedat Günyol, the co-translators of G. and C. Willard's selection of Babeuf's writings (*Devrim Yazıları* in Turkish), were charged in 1965 with having promoted communist propaganda, which are identified as crimes under articles 141 and 142 of the Turkish Penal Code. In their preface to the translation, Eyüboğlu and Günyol drew parallels between the French Revolution and the 1960 military intervention, expressing strong political opinions regarding contemporary social and political affairs in Turkey (Konca 2022: 134). Günyol and Eyüboğlu also commented on the timing of their publication, stating that the translation had been completed earlier but that they intentionally delayed its publication until 1964, when the political atmosphere was more conducive to a positive reception of the ideas conveyed. They argued that Babeuf, who they presented as representing the left-wing of the French Revolution, could guide Turkish society, which had itself recently experienced a revolution, stating that both revolutions were carried out against a minority who abused the public under the guise of working for its benefit (Eyüboğlu and Günyol 1974: 9–10). The Babeuf case also provides significant insights into the phenomenon of retranslation: the whole work was retranslated as part of the court's ruling in order to determine the 'textual manipulations' alleged by the prosecutor and to support the charge that it was communist propaganda. In the indictment, the mere fact that the original title of the book had been changed and the newly coined Turkish term for 'devrim' [revolution] was used instead of 'ihtilâl' (the old Ottoman term for revolution) was presented as an indication of Günyol and Eyüboğlu's 'hidden agenda' in translating the book (Konca 2022: 143). Although not explicitly indicated in the case records, it might be suggested that 'devrim', which is actually the modern Turkish word for 'ihtilâl', references the Russian Revolution, as it has consistently been the preferred translation of leftist activists and writers. Also alleged in the indictment was that Günyol and Eyüboğlu had deliberately translated the term 'communism' as 'sosyalizm' (socialism), thereby covering up their true aims. However, they defended themselves by arguing that Babeuf's use of the term 'communism' had to be evaluated in its historical context, with the meaning of 'communal living', since communism, in the sense that Marxist ideology employs the term, did not exist at that time (Konca 2022: 147–48).

The Communist Manifesto case, initiated against the translator and publisher Süleyman Ege in 1968, constitutes another significant example of censorship on the grounds of communist propaganda. The *Communist Manifesto* had been translated into Turkish earlier by Mustafa Suphi, Şefik Hüsnü and Kerim Sadi, in 1921, 1922 and 1936, respectively, and various retranslations followed in the later years. Ege was the only defendant in this case as the translator(s)' identity was disguised under the pseudonym 'Gaybiköylü' as a precaution against possible prosecution of those individuals. Indeed, the names of the other translators were revealed only after the ban on the retranslation expired in 1976 (Konca 2022: 168). According to Ege, the complete translation was the product of the joint efforts of himself, Mihri Belli, Erdoğan Berktay, Pertev Naili Boratav and Korkut Boratav (Ege 2009: 189). Ege defended himself by emphasising his mission of educating the public about socialist ideology which is a *sine qua non* for the formation of a social state. The case ended with the acquittal of Ege in 1970, after which a revised version of the translation was published along with documents pertaining to the court case. However, as a consequence of the military coup that soon followed on 12 March 1971, the Court of Appeals annulled the verdict of acquittal and Ege was convicted again. He was sentenced to 30 years in prison and declared the 'world's top "thought criminal"' by Amnesty International that year. Ege was released 37 months later after being pardoned by the state (Konca 2022: 177).

The suppression of translated books continued in the 1970s, culminating in the aftermath of the military coup of 12 March 1971. Not only were translators and publishers taken to court, but also books were seized from bookstores and public libraries in response to governmental decrees. The 1980 military intervention imposed an even higher degree of repression on intellectual production. The seizure and burning of 133,607 books published by Bilim ve Sosyalizm Yayınları [Scientific Socialism Publishing] in 1982 under the military rule and the ensuing legal proceedings against the publisher represent the culmination of censorship. Süleyman Ege provides a detailed account of the incident in his *Kitabın Ateşle Dansı* [*The Dance of the Book with Fire*], published in 1992.

5.3.2   Censorship on the Grounds of Obscenity

Censorship cases against translators and publishers on the grounds of communist propaganda were the most prevalent but not unique. The Turkish Prime Ministry Council for the Protection of Minors from Harmful Publications (abbreviated to 'Muzır Kurulu' [Council against Obscenity]) acted as the main government institution in charge of enforcing censorship on the grounds of obscenity, with the members of this institution serving as expert witnesses in censorship cases. The Council was established in 1927 with the aim of 'protecting from harmful publications minors who were not developed physically and mentally'. It gained more power in the 1980s, when it was empowered to distinguish between 'legitimate literature' and 'sheer pornography' (Üstünsöz [Konca] 2015: 226).

A censorship case that attracted a great deal of interest in the late 1930s was the so-called *Afrodit* case, in which Pierre Louÿs' *Aphrodite: moeurs antiques* (1896) was prosecuted for obscenity. In terms of translated works, obscenity appears to be the second most common basis for prosecution. Indeed, most of the recent cases of censorship brought against translated fiction have been initiated on grounds of obscenity. The legal proceedings against *Afrodit: Eski Adetler*, the Turkish translation of Pierre Louÿs' *Aphrodite: moeurs antiques* (1896), were initiated in 1939. The doctrine of 'joint and several liability' as it pertains to Turkish Press Law means that when a charge is brought against an author, a translator or a journalist on the basis of a published work, the Law holds liable not only the author, the translator or the journalist but also the publisher, the editor-in-chief and even the owner of the printing press. Incidentally, 1939 is the same year the First Publishing Congress convened, at which it was decided to launch a wide-ranging state-sponsored translation project under the auspices of the Ministry of Education. The purpose of the project was to support the modernisation of the young Republic; translation was seen as key to achieving the goal of modernisation and Westernisation.

The translator of *Afrodit: Eski Adetler*, Nasuhi Baydar, was not prosecuted thanks to his legal immunity arising from his position as a member of parliament. Consequently, charges were brought against the publisher Semih Lütfi Erciyas and Kenan Dinçman, the owner of Kenan Basımevi (Printing Press) on the basis of the principle of joint and several liability under the Turkish Press Law. The case generated enormous public and media interest, causing some columnists who advocated for the book to be taken to court 'for attempting to manipulate the legal process through their articles' (Üstünsöz (Konca) 2015: 223). The censorship of this book acquired symbolic significance, being 'evaluated as an attack on the modernisation ideals of the Republic' (Üstünsöz (Konca) 2015: 223). The case ended in the acquittal of the defendants, which had repercussions for the publication of translations of similar works of literature. The translator of the 1944 Turkish retranslation of D.H. Lawrence's *Lady Chatterley's Lover* refers to the *Afrodit* case in his preface, stating that it served as a motivating factor.

The case against the Turkish translation of Henry Miller's *Tropic of Capricorn* [*Oğlak Dönencesi*] is another example of a censorship case on the grounds of obscenity. The case was initiated in 1986, about half a century after the *Afrodit* case. As a result of the two-year prosecution, the Turkish translation of Henry Miller's *Tropic of Capricorn* [*Oğlak Dönencesi*] was banned, all of its published copies were seized and destroyed in line with the court ruling. The expert witness report on which the verdict was based stated that the book questioned common moral values since it aroused and abused 'sexual desires' and thus, fell within the scope of Article 426 of the Turkish Penal Code. The case records and the expert witness report were annexed to the second edition of the translated book published by thirty-nine publishing houses as a protest against the court decision. Indeed, the expert witnesses acted as a literary authority, who claimed that Henry Miller was not a prominent writer and that *Tropic of Capricorn* had no literary value whatsoever. This is clearly indicative of the fact that the Turkish literary field had failed to gain autonomy as the power to determine the literary value of the work was vested in the judicial authorities. As Gouanvic states, to the extent that the literary field achieves autonomy, reactions against censorship imposed by the judiciary become more influential, resulting at times in the withdrawal of a case. He presents the example of the legal proceedings brought against Miller's two translated *Tropics*, which were withdrawn in France in 1946 in response to the reaction of the literary field (Gouanvic 2005: 153). Despite the lack of autonomy of the Turkish literary field, there was still a collective movement protesting the court ruling, and thirty-nine publishing houses in Turkey republished the expurgated book and managed to include the censored parts in their version by including the case records and the expert witness report.

The significance of the two cases emerges from the sharp contrast between the respective court rulings. Following the adoption of the so-called 'Turkish-Islamic synthesis' policy in the 1980s, translations no longer played the transformative role they had assumed in the early years of the

Republic (Üstünsöz (Konca) 2015: 228). That being said, similar censorship cases on the grounds of obscenity can be observed in recent years. Books included in the series 'Books on Sex' published by Sel Yayıncılık are a case in point. The Turkish translations of books by Guillaume Apolliniare, William S. Burrough and Chuck Palahniuk have also been subject to legal proceedings. Ilgın Aktener's research on censorship and literary translation reveals that although the publishers and translators who were charged with obscenity continued publishing and translating books containing obscene content, their 'subsequent publication/translation behaviours changed to some degree' (Aktener 2019: 347).

5.3.3 Censorship on Other Grounds

Along with communist propaganda and obscenity, ethnicity and religion formed the grounds on which censorship cases were based. Starting with the Early Republic (1923), both indigenous and translated publications allegedly propagating Kurdism and Armenian and Greek nationalism were suppressed and banned. The early years of the Republic were a time of tremendous socio-cultural transformation under the leadership of Mustafa Kemal Atatürk. The closing of the sharia courts in 1924 was followed by the adoption in 1926 of legal codes borrowed and translated from various European countries. Normative regulations concerning freedom of the press during the Republican period were characterised by ups and downs in the degree of restriction following a relatively emancipatory attitude (Özek 1978: 18). By contrast, the Law for the Maintenance of Order (Takrir-i Sükun Kanunu) (1925) and the Law for Punishing High Treason (Hıyanet-i Vataniyye Kanunu) (1920) allowed for banning publications and for ruling that certain publications were treasonous (Özek 1978: 18). Besides legal reforms carried out in line with the doctrine of Westernisation, secularising reforms in other fields also paved the way for major revolutionary changes. However, the new Republican regime also had to face opposition and attempts at counter-revolution, reaching a climax with the Kurdish rebellion led by Şeyh Said in 1925 in Eastern Anatolia, which was not supported by the Alevi Kurds, who favoured the secular Republic (Findley 2010: 250). In a vigorous response to the revolt, the government declared martial law in the east and enforced the Law for the Maintenance of Order ('Takrir-i Sükun'), authorising the executive power to ban publications or organisations transgressing the law. In order to punish those who had violated the law, it set up special 'Tribunals of Independence' ('İstiklal Mahkemeleri').

As an example of censorship on the basis of the official ideology of the state, Maksudyan's study compares Turkish translations of several history books with their originals, concluding that 'the contradictory position of the Armenian massacres of 1915–1916 vis-à-vis the official ideology of political power and "national history writing" in Turkey leads to processes of self-censorship by translators, editors and publishers, who strive to abide by social and contextual norms and not to conflict with predominant ideas' (Maksudyan 2009: 635).

Yet another legal ground for the prosecution of translators is 'denigrating Turkishness' and a specific example of this can be observed in the *Baba ve Piç* case. Despite the fact that the book was written by the Turkish author Elif Shafak, it was regarded as a translation since the text was written by Shafak in English under the title *The Bastard of İstanbul*. Soon after the publication of the novel in March 2006, charges of insulting Turkishness were directed against Elif Shafak, the translator Aslı Biçen, and the publisher Semih Gökmen on the basis of Article 301 of the Turkish Penal Code, entitled 'Insulting Turkishness, the Republic and the Institutions and Bodies of the State'. The charges against the translator and the publisher were dismissed because of Article 2 of the Press Law, which does not hold the translator liable when the author is a Turkish citizen residing in Turkey. The charges against Shafak, on the contrary, were based on the statements uttered by some of the Armenian characters in her novel. After the trial, the case was dropped as it was deemed unjustifiable and there were no grounds for an indictment. However, a group of ultranationalist lawyers referring to themselves as the Unity of Jurists took the case to an upper court. Elif Shafak and the publisher Semih Gökmen were acquitted. Meanwhile, the case triggered a heated debate among translation scholars and practising translators about the legal status of the translator in Turkish Press Law. Both the case and the debate following the trial attracted media attention and were given wide news coverage. In their declaration entitled 'Tercümana Zeval Olmaz' [Do not Shoot the Translator], ÇEVBİR, The Association of Book Translators asserted that the translator should not be 'shot', or prosecuted as s/he has the sole responsibility to translate the message (a text or a speech) from one language into another, in line with the properties of both languages and cultures, in a faithful, accurate and impartial manner.[1] Apart from defining the task and responsibility of the translator as such, ÇEVBİR also made a call to start a campaign for having Article 2 of the Turkish Press Law amended by the Turkish Grand National Assembly.

An example of a prosecution initiated for insulting Islamic values is the case against the Turkish translation of Richard Dawkins' *The God Delusion* (2006) [*Tanrı Yanılgısı*]. Following the book's publication in Turkey in June 2007, a complainant petitioned the court, claiming the book was offensive and insulting to the Muslim majority living in Turkey since it denigrated Islamic values, rejected God's existence and incited hatred among members of the public. Legal proceedings were initiated against Erol Karaaslan, who was the editor and publisher of *Tanrı Yanılgısı,* and, apparently, the translator as well. Despite the expert witness report stating that the book did not seek to insult religious values, but rather to pursue a search for truth, the prosecutor countered that the book was a general criticism directed against all theistic thought and that it advocated atheism. The defendant Erol Karaaslan emphasised in his testimony that he was merely the translator, not the writer of the book, and stated that the author of the book was a prestigious scholar. The court verdict of acquittal included a reference to Article 10 of the European Court of Human Rights. An interesting detail about this book is that its first edition was actually roughly translated by a team of four translators, who preferred to disguise their names with a pseudonym. Karaaslan was the proofreader, editor and publisher of this first edition. In response to the negative criticism of the quality of this edition, Tunç Tuncay Bilgin was hired to proofread the translation in preparation of the second edition. He had not been one of the defendants of the penal case, however, as the indictment was based on the first edition. What motivated the translators to disguise their identities certainly had to do with the legal status of translators under Turkish law, as mentioned above.

Translations of children's literature were not exempt from censorship (Kansu Yetkiner 2016). On the basis of historical records, Kansu-Yetkiner states that '(a)nalysis of Turkish politics regarding censorship policies for children in curricula and literature reveals a continuum from state-centered public censorship policies of the early republican period to Islamist structural censorship policies in more recent times.' She also argues that children's books have assumed a critical role as 'didactic political instruments, which are banned, covered in plastic bags, hidden, and stigmatised on the grounds that they constituted harm to minors' (Kansu Yetkiner 2016: 101).

Research on film translations also reveals that there existed 'a close relationship between film translation, state patronage and ideology in early republican Turkey' (Özmen 2019: 292). On the basis of the reports of Central Film Commission prepared between 1939 and 1950, Özmen argues that 'imported films were appropriated to the ideological and political dispositions of the era by means of translation' (Özmen 2019: 292). In other words, Central Film Commissions representing state patronage shaped the poetics of film translation in Turkey exerting censorship on the content as they deemed fit (Özmen 2019: 317).

5.4 New Debates

Until the fall of the Berlin Wall (1989) and during the subsequent disintegration of the Soviet Union in 1991, most of the censorship cases brought against translated books that propagated Communism invoked Articles 141 and 142 of the Turkish Penal Code. In 1991, both articles were annulled, only to be superseded by Terörle Mücadele Kanunu [The Law on the Fight against Terrorism], which made matters even worse by enlarging the scope of charges that could be brought before the courts.

Not surprisingly, communism is no longer regarded as a taboo subject. However, there have been no amendments to the definition of the legal status of translators in the Turkish Press Law, thereby causing subsequent cases to be initiated against them. One notable change is that ever since the involvement of ÇEVBİR (The Association of Book Translators) in 2006 in defence of translators, no translator or publisher has been convicted (for further information, see the interview made with the former head of ÇEVBİR and Süha Sertabiboğlu, one of the translators facing prosecution: www.siddethikayeleri.com/portfolio/cevirmenler-muzir-ve-301-tehdidi-altinda/ #.YRzDnhQzbIU, last accessed: August 2021/ no longer valid) . Yet, such cases, which last for an average of two years, have continued to be a source of distress for both publishers and translators, prompting publishing houses to refrain from publishing translated books with 'thorny' subjects and probably motivating translators to practise self-censorship. The extent to which ÇEVBİR's involvement has contributed to the acquittal of defendants in such cases is open to discussion, but it has certainly had a positive impact.

Censorship cases on the grounds of obscenity, on the contrary, continue to be brought before the courts. The most recent case is the one against Burcu Uğuz, the translator who produced the Turkish translations of Elisabeth Brami's *La Déclaration des droits des filles* [*Kız Çocuk Hakları Bildirgesi*] and *La Déclaration des droits des garçons* [*Erkek Çocuk Hakları Bildirgesi*] and both of these books were published in 2017 by Yapı Kredi Yayınları, one of the most prestigious publishing houses in Turkey. Along with ÇEVBİR, the Turkish Publishers Association ('Türkiye Yayıncılar Birliği'), the Turkish Writers Union ('Türkiye Yazarlar Sendikası') and PEN, Turkey issued a joint declaration in support of the translator and the publishing house stating that such cases constituted a violation of freedom of expression, which is the bedrock principle of democratic states. They added that violations of self-expression prompted self-censorship.

5.5 New Perspectives for Research

The topic of censorship in translated books can be further investigated through textual analysis to determine the extent to which self-censorship prevailed and still prevails. The practice of censorship on the productions of the non-Muslim groups publishing in different languages and alphabets during the Ottoman Period would also provide further insights into the history of censorship.

Further Reading

Erkazancı, Hilal. 2008. 'Language Planning in Turkey: a Source of Censorship on Translations', in T. Seruya and M. L. Moniz (eds.), *Translation and Censorship in Different Times and Landscapes*. City: Cambridge Publishing Scholars: 241–251.
This article analyses the inextricable link between the ideologies of language planning and discourses on language, aiming to reveal how the discourses on purism and standardisation impose censorship on the Turkish translators.

Censorship of Translated Books in Turkey: An Overview

Sariz Bilge, İnci. 2019. *Translator Agency in Turkey under Censorial Constraints: 1990s to the Present.* Unpublished PhD thesis. University of Massachusetts. Amherst, Massachusetts.
This study explores agency in translation under an emerging authoritarian regime in Turkey from the 1990s placing specific emphasis on institutional, structural, and self-imposed forms of censorship and reviewing a variety of translation cases that have triggered legal, academic, and public debate.

Yosmaoğlu, İpek. K. 2003. 'Chasing the Printed Word: Press Censorship in the Ottoman Empire, 1876–1913', *The Turkish Studies Association Journal*, 27(1–2).
This article presents an analysis of censorship as a mechanism of political control on the press delineating continuities and contrasts in terms of the exertion of censorship in the reign of Abdülhamid II and the rule of the Committee of Union and Progress.

Note

1 Please see ÜSTÜNSÖZ (KONCA), İrem (2011). *The Legal Status and the Self-Images of Translators in Turkey.* Lambert Academic Publishing Germany.

References

Alkan, Mehmet. 2018. Ömür biter, baskı ve sansür bitmez. [Life comes to an end, censorship does not]. Available at: www.platform24.org/yazarlar/3350/omur-biter--baski-ve-sansur-bitmez). (Accessed: October 2023)
Aktener, Ilgın. 2019. 'Censorship and Literary Translation in Turkey: Translating Obscenity after *The Soft Machine* and *Snuff* Court Cases', *Neohelicon*, 46: 347–67. Available at: https://doi.org/10.1007/s11059-019-00475-4. (Accessed: October 2023)
Arabacı, Caner. 2010. 'İttihat ve Terakki Basını' [Press of Union and Progress], in H. Aydın (ed.), *İkinci Meşrutiyet Devrinde Basın ve Siyaset* (*Press and Politics during the Second Constitutional Monarchy*). Konya: Palet, 73–171.
Dawkins, Richard. 2006. *The God Delusion.* London: Bantam Press Transworld Publishers.
Dawkins, Richard. 2007. *Tanrı Yanılgısı.* Translated by Kalisto (pseudonym). Kuzey: İstanbul.
Demirel, Fatmagül. 2007. *Abdülhamid Döneminde Sansür* [*Censorship during the Reign of Abdulhamid II*]. İstanbul: Bağlam.
Ege, Süleyman. 1992. *Kitabın Ateşle Dansı* [*Dance of the Book with Fire*]. Ankara: Bilim ve Sosyalizm.
Ege, Süleyman. 2009. *Komünist Manifesto ve Türkiye'deki Öyküsü.* ("The Communist Manifesto and its Story in Turkey"). Ankara: Bilim ve Sosyalizm Yayınları.
Eyüboğlu, Sabahattin and Günyol, Vedat. 1974. *Devrim Yazıları / Babeuf Dosyası.* (Writings on the Revolution / The File on Babeuf). Istanbul: Sosyal.
Findley, Carter Vaughn. 2010. *Turkey, Islam, Nationalism and Modernity: A History, 1789–2007.* New Haven and London: Yale University Press.
Gouanvic, Jean-Marc. 2005. 'A Bourdieusian Theory of Translation, or the Coincidence of Practical Instances' (translated by Jessica Moore), *The Translator*, 11(2): 147–66.
İrtem, Süleyman Kani. 1999. *Abdülhamid Devrinde Hafiyelik ve Sansür.* İstanbul: Temel.
Kabacalı, Alpay. 1990. *Başlangıçtan Günümüze Türkiye'de Basın Sansürü.* İstanbul: Gazeteciler Cemiyeti Yayınları.
Kansu Yetkiner, Neslihan. 2016. 'Banned, Bagged, Bowdlerized: a Diachronic Analysis of Censorship Practices in Children's Literature of Turkey', *History of Education & Children's Literature*, XI(2): 101–20.
Karakışla, Yavuz Selim. 2002. II. 'Abdülhamid'in Saltanatı (1876–1909): Kızıl Sultan mı? Ulu Hakan mı ' [The Reign of Abdulhamid II (1876–1909) Sultan Rouge? The Great Sultan?], *Toplumsal Tarih*, XVII(103): 10–19.
Kıvılcımlı, Hikmet. 1978. *1935 Marksizm Bibliyoteği Serisi: I (Telif ve Tercümeler)* (Marxism Bibliotheque Series: I (Indigenous Works/ Translations). İstanbul: Çağrı.
Konca, İrem. 2022. *State Censorship and Ideologue Translators: A History of Translation and Transfer of Marxist / Socialist Texts in the Turkish Legal Field (1908–1970).* Unpublished PhD thesis. KU Leuven, Belgium.

Maksudyan, Nazan. 2009. 'Walls of Silence: Translating the Armenian Genocide into Turkish and Self - Censorship', *Critique: Journal of Socialist Theory*, 37(4): 635–49.

Millton, John and Bandia, Paul (eds.). 2009. *Agents of Translation*. Amsterdam: John Benjamins.

Özek, Çetin. 1978. *Türk Basın Hukuku (Turkish Press Law)*. İstanbul Üniversitesi Yayınları.

Özmen, Ceyda. 2019. 'Mücadele, Müdahale ve Temsil Alanı Olarak Film Çevirisi: Film Kontrol Komisyonları, Dublaj, Sansür ve Ulus İnşası (1939–1950)' [Film Translation as a Site of Struggle, Intervention and Representation: Film EControl Commissions, Dubbing, Censorship and Nation Building], in D. Eylül (ed.), *Üniversitesi Edebiyat Fakültesi Dergisi*, 6(1): 300–28.

Paker, Saliha. 1991. 'Turkey: The Age of Modernization and Adaptation', in R. Ostle (ed.), *Modern Literature in the Near and Middle East 1850–1970*. London and New York: Routledge, 17–32.

Şafak, Elif. 2006. *Baba ve Piç*. Translated by Biçen, Aslı. Beyoğlu, İstanbul: Metis.

Sertel, Sabiha. 1969. *Roman Gibi [ust like a Novel]*. İstanbul: Ant Yayınları.

Shafak, Elif. 2007. *The Bastard of Istanbul*. England: Penguin Books.

Tahir Gürçağlar, Şehnaz. 2009. 'Translation Presumed Innocent: Translation and Ideology in Turkey', *The Translator*, 15(1): 37–64.

Topuz, H. (2003). *II. Mahmut'tan holdinglere Türk basın tarihi. [Turkish Press History: From the Rule of Mahmut II to Holding Companies]*. İstanbul: Remzi.

Toska, Zehra. 2015. 'Ahmed Midhat's *Hulâsa-i Hümâyunnâme:* A Curious Case of Politics of Translation, "Renewal", Imperial Patronage and Censorship', in S. Tahir-Gürçağlar, S. Paker and J. Milton (eds.), *Tension, Tradition and Translation in Turkey*. Amsterdam and Philadelphia: John Benjamins, 73–86.

Uşaklıgil, Halid Ziya.1969. *Kırk Yıl [Forty Years]*. İstanbul: İnkılâp ve Aka.

Üstünsöz (Konca), İrem. 2011. *The Legal Status and the Self-Images of Translators in Turkey*. Saarbrucken: Lambert Academic Publishing.

Üstünsöz (Konca), İrem. 2015. 'Censorship of "Obscene" Literary Translations in Turkey: An Analysis of Two Specific Cases', in S. Tahir-Gürçağlar, S. Paker and J. Milton (eds.), *Tension, Tradition and Translation in Turkey*. Amsterdam and Philadelphia: John Benjamins, 219–32.

Yılmaz, Mustafa and Doğaner, Yasemin. 2007. *Cumhuriyet Döneminde Sansür (19231973) [Censorship during the Republican Period (1923–1973)]*. Ankara: Siyasal Kitabevi.

PART II

Colonial and Postcolonial Contexts

6

COLD WAR POLITICS IN EAST AFRICA

Between Translation and Censorship

Alamin Mazrui

6.1   Core Issues and Topics

The Cold War has been generally regarded as an ideological battle on a global scale in which books were often seen as cultural arsenals. To that extent, the Cold War played out in many different ways in several regions throughout the world. One of these regions was East Africa, encompassing mainly the countries of Kenya, Tanzania and Uganda as they gained their independence from British colonial rule in the 1960s. The impact of the cultural politics of the Cold War on the interplay between translation and censorship in this region of Africa in the post-colonial period is the primary focus of this chapter.

Historically speaking, censorship in East Africa has manifested itself in various ways, including censorship as an agentive product of the translator, a collective action of the community at large in response to the moral authority of its elite, as well as the repressive intervention of a political regime. For most of this essay, the focus will be on censorship by the state, guided primarily by Pierre Bourdieu's notion of the 'habitus' (1980), those socialised norms and tendencies that guide behaviour and thought. A sufficiently consolidated and stable socio-political situation tends to produce practices and reinforce experiences that promote conformity. In this context, the 'field'—the network, structure or set of relationships—is what controls and directs discourse without the need for some repressive legal intervention. It is when the socio-political situation is in a state of flux, when the discourse of the ruling class is yet to become hegemonic, that the exercise of censorship becomes necessary as a way of consolidating the position of those in power.

The Cold War coincided precisely with that moment of political flux in post-colonial East African nations. Having just emerged from the throes of British colonial rule, all three countries had to contend with competing ideological orientations and interests that had been masked by the strategic unity that had been forged in the struggle for independence. They were now all caught in a quest for self-definition while seeking to establish and maintain governing institutions and institutional legitimacy. The immediate need to create a nation prompted 'a policy of trying to avoid dissension between groups and protect the legitimacy of the government from the dangers of public criticism' (Mazrui 1969: 268). Under these circumstances, the promulgation of repressive legalistic instruments became an appealing option for the control of discourse and with the aim of establishing a discourse of the 'ruling class' as the dominant narrative. As laid out below, some

DOI: 10.4324/9781003149453-9

95

6.2 Censorship in East Africa: an Overview

Censorship has sometimes been regarded as a phenomenon of societies with literacy traditions based on the written word. In the opinion of Piotr Kuhiwezak, for example: 'It would not be an exaggeration to claim that censorship is a phenomenon universal in cultures based on literacy and on the dissemination of knowledge in written or printed form' (2011: 359). However, if we take 'censorship' in its widest sense as the suppression of a text, of any kind or length, that may be considered offensive on religious, moral, political, cultural or other grounds, then the phenomenon could very well exist in oral cultures as much as in cultures of written expression.

In East Africa, inter-ethnic communication and, in the case of the East African coast, trans-national communication between leaders and traders were often mediated by *wakalimani,* interpreters, who employed one form of censorship or another as part of the process of negotiation, often to avoid offending the sensibilities of their interlocutors, or for self-serving reasons. During the European colonial period these African interpreters, usually appointed by the colonial government, were essential in brokering communication between the coloniser and the colonised. Playing a crucial role in the construction of the colonial state itself (Lawrence et al. 2015), the *wakalimani* became active agents in determining what was or was not to be conveyed, sometimes in order to further the interests of colonialism, sometimes to protect the interests of African communities and nationalists, and sometimes to advance the interests of the interpreters themselves. The degree and kind of censorship that took place in these contexts often depended on what was at stake. The stakes were invariably higher in moments of nationalist struggles for freedom, for example, than in moments of relative political calm.

At the same time, the European colonisers were themselves distrustful of some oral productions. The African oral tradition sometimes employed the medium of song to 'talk back' in opposition to colonialism. In some of these cases, the British response was censorious (Salinas 2001: 1326). These instances of censorship were often a direct product of translation or interpretation of African language texts into English by the African interpreters in the service of the colonial administration.

It was during the European colonial period that one begins to see censorship of printed materials as well. In what was then German East Africa, including modern-day Tanzania, Rwanda and Burundi—*Al-Najah*, a local Swahili anti-colonial periodical written in the Arabic-derived Ajami script, was banned. Then in 1954, when Tanganyika—the mainland part of Tanzania before its 1964 merger with Zanzibar—was now under British rule, colonial laws against sedition were invoked to ban the Swahili paper *Mwafrika* (The African), an organ of the nationalist party, the Tanganyika African National Union (TANU), allegedly for referring to the European colonisers as *wanyonyaji damu* (blood suckers) (Scotton 1978: 16).

In colonial Uganda too there were sedition laws, which were part of the penal code as early as 1900. Writers could be imprisoned for up to seven years if found guilty of sedition and false news (Ott 2001: 2488). While there is no evidence of widespread application of these sedition laws during the colonial period, their very existence may have resulted in significant self-censorship among newspaper writers and reporters. In addition, the pressure on the colonial government to make use of the sedition laws intensified as the political struggle for independence reached its peak in the 1950s. In 1956, for example, the '*Uganda Express* and *Uganda Post* were banned by the British colonial authorities for alleged sedition, and the publisher, J.W. (Jolly 'Joe') Kiwanuka, was jailed' (Tabaire 2007: 195). These same laws were carried over and applied more extensively under different post-colonial regimes.

Similar censorship measures were employed in Kenya under British colonial rule. Unlike Tanzania (then Tanganyika) and Uganda, Kenya was a settler colony with a significant population of British colonists who made Kenya their permanent home. Laws were implemented not only to further the colonial agenda but also to protect the interests of the European settlers. As a result, Kenya had a more draconian history of colonial censorship than its neighbouring countries of Tanzania and Uganda.

The first victim of British colonial sedition laws in Kenya was *Muiguithania* (The Reconciler), a publication of the Kikuyu Central Association. Banned at the beginning of World War II, the paper was issued sporadically in the 1920s and 1930, invariably agitating against colonial rule (Scotton 1974: 7). Later, based on translations of several Gikuyu language periodicals into English by the colonial Central Intelligence Department (CID), several 'subversive' African periodicals were marked for potential censorship. Between 1945 and 1952, the Attorney General of Kenya Colony used the sedition law at least nine times to ban local newspapers (Scotton 1974: 22).

In the meantime, as much as the British wanted to convert Africans to Christianity and engaged in concerted attempts to translate the Bible into Swahili and other local languages for that purpose, they sought to limit this mission to what they regarded as 'mainstream' Christianity. As a result, in some of its overseas colonies it banned the Watchtower literature of the Jehovah's Witnesses coming out of the USA, and in 1943, 'the US Government helped by undertaking to forbid mailing to British dependencies from the Watchtower press in Brooklyn' (Read 1967: 32). At the same time, the British enforced what they regarded as Christian morality in their colonies. In 1951, for example, the British colonial government in Kenya banned 'any publication dealing with sex or the psychological or the medical aspects of sex or birth control' (Read 1967: 39). This same religious morality in independent Kenya led to the banning of the adult magazines *Adam*, *Cavalier* and *Men Only* in 1967 (Kenya Government 2009: 175).

Between 1952 and 1960, Kenya Colony was under a State of Emergency due to the outbreak of the armed anti-colonial resistance known as Mau Mau. During this period, the British colonial government moved to ban a number of books by African and African Diaspora writers that had the aim or potential of promoting the struggle against colonial rule. These included Geoge Padmore's *Gold Coast Revolution* and Montagu Slater's *Trial of Jomo Kenyatta* (Read 1967: 32) as well as *Africa, The Lion Awakes* by Jack Woddies, *Land of Sunshine* by Muga Gicaru, *Doctrine of Passive Resistance* by Shri Aurobinds, and *People of Kenya Speak for Themselves* by Mbiyu Koinange (Colony 1962: 855–856).

The European colonial period also intensified contact between people from various parts of the world and in the process facilitated the transfer of texts and the need for translation. Of particular note here are two Swahili translations of the Qur'an from its Arabic 'original', both of which became subject to communal East African Muslim censorship. One was the 1923 translation by Canon Godfrey Dale of the Universities Mission to Central Africa, which essentially amounted to a distorted, Christian perspective of the Muslim Holy Book. The other was the 1953 translation by the Ahmadiyya, widely considered a heretical Muslim sect that originated in India in the late nineteenth century. Under the sway of leading East African Muslim clergy, both these translations were boycotted by East African Muslims of the majority, mainstream Sunni sect of Islam.

The first couple of years of post-colonial East Africa were extremely open, with hardly any instances of government censorship except in the arena of film and sometimes stage plays. Virtually immediately after independence, each of the three nations established government boards

The Routledge Handbook of Translation and Censorship

responsible for the rating and censorship of films, supposedly to ensure that whatever is screened is in conformity with 'African cultures and moral values'. These are institutions that are still in existence and continue to censor films to this day. Outside the film industry, however, censorship was virtually absent at the beginning of independent rule.

Within a couple of years of their independence, however, all three East African countries had become arenas of Cold War contestation between the USA and its Western allies and the Communist bloc. Yet, depending on their own ideological orientations and the local political dynamics, the three East African nations responded differently to translated works into English and Swahili from the Soviet Union and the People's Republic of China. It is these differences in the interplay between translation and censorship that will be addressed below.

6.3 Translation and Censorship During the Cold War Period

On the eve of independence from British colonial rule, a member of Kenya's Legislative Council, Mr. Fritz De Souza, challenged the colonial decision to ban certain publications. He moved that the list of books banned by the colonial government be reviewed and revised accordingly. Mr. Budoh, also a member of the Legislative Council, supported De Souza's motion but went on to add that 'I would be the first to oppose any literature to come from countries like Russia or other Communist countries, because I know that those will only come here for indoctrination purposes, will only be here to foment dissatisfaction and to create more trouble in our country' (Colony 1962: 855–856). This conversation at the legislative forum sent a clear message that independent Kenya was poised to become a capitalist nation and a potential Cold War ally of the USA. Indeed, the main reason William Attwood's book, *The Reds and the Blacks*, was banned in independent Kenya was that it revealed some embarrassing details of the American hold on the then first president of the country, President Jomo Kenyatta, through its Ambassador William Attwood precisely in regard to blocking Communist influence in Kenya.

In spite of the concerted US-supported efforts to keep Communism at bay in Kenyan politics, an ideological confrontation was brewing within the then ruling party, the Kenya African National Union (KANU). This conflict ultimately led to a complete split in the KANU party and the formation of a left-leaning political opposition, the Kenya People's Union (KPU) in 1966. Unlike KANU, KPU advocated a socialist agenda and its leader, Jaramogi Oginga Odinga, proceeded to cultivate a special relationship with both the Soviet Union and the People's Republic of China. In 1969, KPU was officially banned, reaffirming once more the Kenyan government's commitment to a capitalist path of development.

It was against this backdrop that in 1967, the Kenyan government moved to ban, in addition to other quasi-socialist materials, Chinese publications translated into English and Swahili—the two trans-ethnic national languages of the country—and released by the Peking Foreign Language Press. These included *Cheche Moja Yaweza Kuanzisha Moto Mbugani*, a Swahili translation of Mao's *A Single Spark Can Start a Prairie Fire*, and the so-called *Little Red Book* of Mao's quotations, which was available in both English and Swahili translations (Lal 2014: 97). Suspicious of the entire Foreign Language Press's project, the Kenya Government proceeded to place a ban on 'the importation of all past and future publications purporting to be published by the Foreign Languages Press, Peking…' (Colony 1962: 174). This ban remained in place until the beginning of the political reform movement in Kenya, which led to the new 2010 Constitution of Kenya.

By contrast, in spite of its seeming aversion towards Communism, the Kenya government did not ban any publications from Progress Publishers, a Soviet venture with similar aims as the Chinese Foreign Language Press. In fact, while not in wide circulation in Kenya, English and

Cold War Politics in East Africa

Swahili translated works by Lenin, Marx and other writers released by Progress Publishers were readily available at the Wanyee Bookshop in Nairobi, Kenya. How then does one explain Kenya's selective censorship of translated books from the Communist world? Why was the importation and possession of publications from one Communist country, the People's Republic of China, prohibited in spite of the fact that China was then a marginal player on the African political scene, while those from the Soviet Union, the key Communist player in the global Cold War, were not?

Part of the explanation lies in the fact that Jaramogi Oginga Odinga, leader of the socialist-inclined politicians who constituted themselves into the opposition KPU, had made overtures to China—to strengthen his own position in Kenyan politics (Sun 2020) as well as Kenya's bargaining power in regard to aid from Britain and the Western bloc countries (Cullen 2018). Increasingly then, the government of Jomo Kenyatta began to see China as an adversary, leading to a weakening of diplomatic relations between the two countries. By this time, Jaramogi Oginga Odinga had already published his book *Not Yet Uhuru* (Odinga 1968), essentially suggesting that Kenya needed to undergo yet another revolution, a socialist revolution, if the aspirations of its struggle for independence were to be realised. Odinga saw China as a potential ally in his quest for the 'genuine liberation' of Kenya. By reducing communication and cultural contacts with China and therefore China's capacity to engage with Kenya and the Kenyan people, Jomo Kenyatta also hoped to weaken his own political rival, Jaramogi Oginga Odinga. This latter objective would seem to support the position of New Censorship Theory, which regards 'state censors as actors internal to communication networks, and not as external, accidental features' (Bunn 2015: 25).

Social class also helps to explain the difference in Kenya's response to translated materials from China, on the one hand, and those from the Soviet Union, on the other. China's socialist revolution was based on the peasantry while that of the Soviet Union drew primarily from the industrial working class. Like China, Kenya was a country that relied heavily on a rural economy built around peasant producers, which represented the largest demographic constituency. Even the Mau Mau, Kenya's armed movement against British colonialism that had concluded less than a decade earlier, was based primarily on the peasantry rather than on the working class. Under these circumstances, it was the Chinese rather than the Soviet model that was seen as the more relevant and therefore more likely to inspire a revolution in Kenya. This revolutionary, peasant-class basis of the Mau Mau made the post-colonial government of Kenya particularly hostile to positive appraisals of the movement and it often sought to erase that aspect of the Mau Mau's history where possible (Lewis 2001: 1330). Similarly, prohibiting the importation and possession of publications from China was of more pressing concern than censoring publications from the Soviet Union.

As indicated earlier, Kenya banned not only politically oriented literature but all publications from Peking's Foreign Language Press. The irony of this course of action, of course, was that it insulated the Kenyan population from Chinese thought of any kind, political or not. Kenyans could learn from the USA, Europe, India or Russia, but not from China. Reading an English or Swahili translation of a Chinese book on rocks and minerals published by the Foreign Language Press, for example, could earn the reader up to three years of imprisonment. For example, in 1978 Dickson Otieno, a teacher at Nyandarua High School in Kenya, was imprisoned for eighteen months for being in possession of three books—one on the geography of China, another on archeological findings in China, and a third on economics, dealing with wages, prices and profits—all published by the Foreign Language Press (Mwaura 2011).

Cold War politics also took center stage in Kenya in the 1980s with the formation of leftist, quasi-Marxist underground organisations like the December Twelve Movement and Mwakenya, all resulting from the state of extreme political repression in the country. These organisations resorted to clandestine leafleteering and pamphleteering in English, Swahili and other local languages to reach as wide an audience of Kenyans as possible. In many cases, the Swahili leaflets were translated versions of the English ones. Irrespective of their content, these publications were considered by the state to have seditious intent, and their production and consumption became a criminal offense. A number of individuals were arrested and imprisoned for several years for possession of 'subversive' literature (Salinas 2001: 1327).

The culture of silence and fear that continued to evolve in Kenya as a result of state repression also led to censorship by publishing houses. Publishers were particularly cautious of printing books or sections of books of radical, especially Marxist, political orientation, and bookstores were wary of stocking them for fear of government reprisals. This was a recurrent phenomenon especially during the presidency of Daniel Arap Moi (1978–2002), the second president of the country.

Unlike Kenya, Uganda was not affected significantly by Cold War politics. Having achieved its independence in 1962 under the leadership of Milton Obote, its first president, Uganda remained for a while relatively untouched by superpower competition. Because of the political tensions arising from ethno-religious rivalries, Obote's government established a censorship board in 1964; it screened newspapers and required that plays for the stage and television receive clearance before they were performed or transmitted (Ott 2001: 2488). In 1969, Obote released his controversial 'Common Man's Charter: First Steps for Uganda to Move to the Left'. Naturally, this development attracted the attention of the USA. Two years later, in 1971, the government of Uganda was toppled, and a military dictatorship was ushered in, with General Idi Amin Dada as its head. There is some evidence to suggest that this coup was supported by the USA, Israel and Britain (Mamdani 1983), and that the proposed 'move to the left' was its primary trigger. Whatever the case, until 1986 when Yoweri Museveni and his National Resistance Army came to power, Uganda experienced years of instability, conflict and multiple forms of repression. These were years when intellectual and artistic productivity, in local languages, in English and in translation, came to a virtual standstill. Under Yoweri Museveni, freedom of expression greatly expanded, although some censorship, especially of newspapers and journalists, continued (Ott 2001: 2489).

The East African country that stands in marked contrast to Kenya in terms of the politics of the Cold War is Tanzania. This Cold War dimension of the Tanzanian experience was apparent soon after the nation of Zanzibar attained its independence from British colonial rule in December 1963 but before it merged with Tanganyika in 1964 to become the Federal Republic of Tanzania. Within three months of achieving independence, Zanzibar, a predominantly Muslim country, underwent a violent revolution, the aim of which—given the central role of the Marxist-led Umma Party as its architect—was seen by many, especially by the US government, as essentially communist. It was even feared that Zanzibar would become an African Cuba of a sort, poised to influence the rest of the East African region (Wilson 1989). Indeed, some of the 'comrades' of the Umma Party even received military training in Cuba. As a result of this politico-economic development, the Zanzibar government became increasingly intolerant of criticism of its communist ideology and socialist policies and began to crack down on its critics and impose a ban on some publications. One of those banned publications was *Utawala wa Kristo au Utumwa wa Komyunisti*, a Swahili translation of Peter G. Bostock's *The Kingdom of Christ and the Slavery of Communism* (Read 1967: 40). Ironically, pro-Islamic and pro-communist sentiments combined in this island nation of East Africa to make its government particularly suspicious of Christian publications critical of communism.

The Federal Republic of Tanzania that arose out of the merger of Zanzibar and Tanganyika quickly distinguished itself as a socialist-oriented country, contrasting itself in particular with the 'man-eat-man' capitalism of Kenya. But in spite of the Cuba connection in the Zanzibar revolution, the federated nation ended up taking its socialist inspiration from China rather than from the Soviet Union. And while literature from China was banned in Kenya, it was welcomed and readily available in Tanzania. As Priya Lal observes, Chinese publications, 'ranging from technical manuals to *China Pictorial* magazine', became readily available in Tanganyika Bookshop in the capital city of Dar es Salaam. 'Chief among these publications was Mao's *Quotations,* which was also sold in smaller towns throughout Tanzania, and remained widely available by mail order in Swahili and English' (Lal 2014: 107). Kenyans interested in reading Chinese literature that was banned in Kenya could easily access it in English and Swahili translation by crossing the border to Tanzania.

On the whole, Tanzania experienced little censorship when compared with both Kenya and Uganda. One primary reason for this difference might have been the figure of Julius Nyerere, the first president of Tanzania. Nyerere was widely regarded as a kind of philosopher-king, a man who was fascinated by ideas and valued intellectual exchange. He is said to have been 'the most intellectual of all English-speaking Heads of States. He had commanded the same admiration among Anglo-American intellectuals that Leopold Senghor [the first President of Senegal] used to command among French ones. Westerners sometimes saw in the two men an incarnation of their own cultural achievement' (Mazrui 2002: 12). As a political leader, Nyerere was much more tolerant of differences of opinion, and of criticism of his ideology and policies than many other African leaders of his time and seems to have successfully resisted the temptation to censor those with dissenting ideas.

Perhaps no less important in explaining the virtual absence of censorship in Tanzania under Nyerere was his love of literature and the arts. He was particularly fond of Shakespeare and was the first to translate Shakespeare's plays into the Swahili language. He translated *Julius Caesar* into Swahili in 1963 (revising it as *Juliasi Kaizari* in 1969). The translation was praised as 'a remarkable translation done by a remarkable man' and 'a brilliant transformation of Shakespeare's play' (Lindfords 1965: 266). Then in 1969, Nyerere published the Swahili translation of the *Merchant of Venice* as *Mabepari wa Venisi,* a rendering of Shakespeare that became particularly popular in East Africa. It is significant that the title of Nyerere's translation pluralises the term 'merchant' with *mabepari*, meaning merchants or capitalists. In this way he sought to downplay the Jewish-Christian divide and probably the anti-Semitism that was an attribute of the Elizabethan and Jacobean culture and, in line with his socialist convictions, to portray both Antonio and Shylock as members of the same class of the rich who maintained their wealth through the exploitation of others.

In spite of this history of relative openness, and to Swahili and English translations of communist literature and other texts in particular, Tanzania seemed less willing to accept the translation of texts that could be interpreted as critical of its socialist ideology and policies. As indicated earlier, Zanzibar, the island part of the Tanzanian federation, had once banned translations of Christian publications critical of communism. Several years later, as we explain below, there was a similar reaction to the Swahili translation of George Orwell's *Animal Farm* even before its publication.

Orwell intended *Animal Farm* (1945) to be an exposé and critique of the dangers of the Soviet totalitarian government under Joseph Stalin. The story is a satirical fable ostensibly about a group of animals who, through conspiracy, launch an armed revolution to oust their human owners from the farm on which they live. They then run the farm themselves on the agreed revolutionary principles of 'Animalism' that distinguish them from humans and human rule. Within a short period, however, animal rule degenerates into a brutal tyranny, erected on the deliberate erasure of the history of the revolution, muzzling of political dissent, a growing personality cult, corruption and ruthless exploitation. The revolution is betrayed.

The Routledge Handbook of Translation and Censorship

In his brilliant book *Archives of Authority: Empire, Culture and the Cold War* (Rubin 2012), Andrew N. Rubin demonstrates how the USA, during the Cold War period, patronised the arts in a way that aimed to reinforce its ideological attacks against the Soviet Union. An important American initiative of this time was the state sponsorship of the translation of George Orwell's *Animal Farm* into various languages, especially those of the Global South, as a propaganda tool against perceived communist incursions (Rubin 2012: 24–46). One of those US-sponsored translations became *Shamba la Wanyama*, the Swahili rendering of *Animal Farm* by a Tanzanian national, Fortunatus Kawegere. According to the University of Kansas Libraries Exhibit, the Swahili translation was 'underwritten by United States Information Service' (KU Libraries Exhibits 2015), even though there seems to have been a general agreement that these US-sponsored translations should 'contain no references to the Information Department of the Embassy or the United States Information Exchange' (Rubin 2012: 38).

Events in post-colonial Tanzania provided the immediate political context for the translation of *Animal Farm*. As Venuti points out, the inscription of local target-community interests in the process of translation 'begins with the very choice of a text for translation, always a very selective, densely motivated choice' (Venuti 2000: 486). In this case, however, it was not the betrayal of a revolution that had already taken place but the fear of an impending (socialist) revolution that became the driving force behind *Shamba la Wanyama* as part of an anti-communist offensive during the Cold War.

It is true that the socialism of Ujamaa was never formally launched, and the ruling Tanganyika African National Union (TANU) did not become Chama cha Mapinduzi (Revolutionary Party) until 1967, precisely the year that the Swahili translation of *Animal Farm* appeared. But the idea of a quasi-socialist state had certainly been in gestation since at least 1962, when then President Julius Nyerere, released his pamphlet entitled *Ujamaa: The Basis of African Socialism*. America's fears of a socialist turn in Tanganyika were further reinforced when on 26 April 1964, the country merged with the independent island state of Zanzibar to form the United Republic of Tanzania soon after Zanzibar's communist-inspired revolution. A Swahili translation of *Animal Farm* took on particular urgency in the context of the unfolding tensions between pro-socialist and pro-capitalist political camps throughout the East African region.

Critics generally agree that Kawegere's translation leans towards domestication. It is not clear whether the decision to domesticate the text was made independently by Kawegere himself or, as happened in some other parts of the world, was a product of US influence given the fact that the translation itself was sponsored by the United States Information Service. In their attempts to construct their authority of the 'Third World', Rubin notes, both the American and British governments favoured the adaptation of *Animal Farm* to local contexts and conditions:

> In Malaya, where the British fought its longest postwar conflict, there was an effort to produce a less 'English' version of *Animal Farm*. In Egypt, too, where British authority faced mounting anticolonial challenges to King Farouk, the IRD [Information Research Department, a secret unit of the British Foreign Office] viewed *Animal Farm* as particularly 'relevant' to conditions there. Reducing the Arabic language to Islam, Ernest Main wrote Ralph Murray that translating *Animal Farm* is 'particularly good for Arabic in view of the fact that both pigs and dogs are unclean animals to Muslims'.
>
> (Rubin 2012: 38)

Domestication, in other words, was seen as adding to the anti-communist propaganda value of translations and adaptations of *Animal Farm*. Whether or not Kawegere's mode of translation was influenced by the US sponsors, there is no doubt that the domestication of the text was in conformity with the wider imperial agenda to render the translations of *Animal Farm* as germane to their respective local contexts as possible. In the process, Orwell's aim to have *Animal Farm* serve as a critique of Stalinist totalitarianism became virtually ignored in the reading of *Shamba la Wanyama*.

The fact that *Shamba la Wanyama* could be read as a critique of Tanzania's politico-economic shift towards socialism certainly did not endear it to the country's political establishment of the time. As a result, according to Ida Hadjivayanis (2011: 11–12), the book was banned in the country. In an interview with the online SwahiliHub, Kawegere also refers to a visit by Tanzanian intelligence officers soon after the release of his translation and to the possibility that 'viongozi wengi serikalini hawakuipenda' (many government leaders did not like it [my translation]) (Gikambi 2013). Appearing as it did on the eve of Tanzania's Arusha Declaration, declaring its move to the socialist left, the Swahili translation of *Animal Farm* seems to have rubbed the political establishment the wrong way, and its censorship became a fait accompli.

While Kawegere produced *Shamba la Wanyama* for his own compatriots in socialist-leaning Tanzania, it was in capitalist Kenya that the translation achieved its greatest success. The translation quickly found a publisher in Kenya, and once published it was widely available in bookstores in Nairobi and elsewhere. More significantly, the book was adopted by the Swahili Committee of the Kenya Institute of Education as a required text for the Swahili literature paper in the national high school examination. The popular understanding that *Animal Farm* was essentially a reflection on the Russian Revolution of 1917 and a critique of its Stalinist aftermath made its Swahili translation, *Shamba la Wanyama*, readily acceptable to the Kenyan state that had long been entangled in an ideological competition with neighbouring socialist Tanzania.

For as long as *Shamba la Wanyama* was read primarily in educational contexts, in the country's high schools in particular, its presence in Kenya was not seen as threatening. However, when a local theatre group adopted it and put on a play by the same name, alarm bells began to ring. As was the practice then, the group had received a government license to stage the play. But after a few performances, and as the troupe was preparing to perform the play in Kangemi, one of Nairobi's slums, the state intervened quickly and revoked the license (Henry 1991). Similarly, when Nyahururu Secondary School decided to compete in the National School Drama Festival, which was open to the general public, by staging a dramatised version of *Shamba la Wanyama*, it was immediately censured and the play banned (Mazrui 2007: 141). So, how does one explain this Kenyan state's sudden change of heart towards *Shamba la Wanyama*?

The play *Shamba la Wanyama* mostly targeted adult audiences in the country. In the process, it quickly became obvious that many adult members of the society who had the opportunity to see the play left with a more nuanced reading of the text. They related it to the local political history and conditions more intimately than had been done before. For example, many of the adult viewers saw in the totalitarian autocracy and the cult of personality, which Orwell intended as a critique of Stalinist Russia, as aspects of their own lived political reality in Kenya.

The Kenyan revolutionary movement that can be compared most closely with that of *Animal Farm* is perhaps the Mau Mau movement against British settler colonial rule. Under oppressive colonial conditions, Mau Mau became precisely the kind of revolutionary movement that partly inspired Orwell to write *Animal Farm* (Ingle 1993: 75–76). It was a violent, conspiratorial revolution with a popular following. And while Mau Mau's military leaders may not have been known to be power-hungry, those who claimed its political mantle and leadership, and eventually assumed the reins of power when the country became independent in 1963 obviously were. In other words, like Orwell's characterisation of the Russian revolution, the Mau Mau too was a revolution that quickly opened the gates to its own betrayal, as Oginga Odinga, Kenya's first vice-president, came to argue in his controversial book *Not Yet Uhuru* (1968).

A central theme of *Animal Farm* is the rewriting of history to distort the objectives of the revolution in general, and the role of Snowball, a selfless intellectual in the struggle for animal liberation, in particular. This political exercise as it relates to the history of the Mau Mau came to be the hallmark of successive Kenyan regimes in the post-colonial era. Until recently, the silent policy was 'Speak no Mau Mau; Hear no Mau Mau', by which Kenyans were led to develop a culture of amnesia about the movement and its leaders. On 20 October 2001, for example, over 70 Kenyans were arrested and charged with unlawful assembly. The party had apparently angered the government by celebrating October 20th not as Kenyatta Day—as officially named to mark the arrest of Jomo Kenyatta by colonial authorities—but as Mau Mau Day in honour of Kenya's freedom fighters. Similarly, the Kimathi Cultural Centre was denied permission to hold celebrations in honour of Dedan Kimathi, the military leader of the Mau Mau, on February 18th, the day of his execution by the British colonial government (Nation 2006: 4).

In sum, then, even though *Animal Farm* was written as a critique of the 'socialist revolution' of the Soviet Union and was translated into Swahili ostensibly to forewarn Tanzanians against an impending 'socialist revolution', the reverberations of its political message were just as strongly in the staunchly capitalist nation of Kenya. And that message became the primary reason for banning the play, *Shamba la Wanyama*.

6.4 New Debates

As suggested so far, for three decades or so after East African countries gained their independence from British colonial rule, national politics tended to be framed in terms of the Cold War split, often pitting 'the left' and the 'right', especially in Kenya and Tanzania. The end of the Cold War essentially freed local politics from this super-power rivalry and brought to end laws of censorship dictated by the politics of the Cold War. The political gaze now turned inwards, exposing tensions and contradictions that had long been masked by the Cold War dispensation and bringing to visibility social, ethnic and regional contestations that called for the nation-state to be reconfigured anew to better mediate between hitherto hidden conflicting interests. And the best expression of the newly imagined (post-Cold War) nation-state—widely propagated in Kenya in the popular call for 'Kenya tuitakayo' (the Kenya we want)—was regarded to be a revised Constitution, putting in place a legal framework for a new order. Expectedly, then, the dynamics and counter-dynamics of the interplay between translation and censorship soon shifted to the arena of constitution making.

At independence, the constitutions of all the three East African countries existed exclusively in the English language, a language in which only a minority of citizens was and continues to be proficient. The need thus arose for having the constitutions of East African nations available in some of the local languages, especially in Swahili as the East African lingua franca. In spite of the clear and urgent demand for translating the constitution, however, it was not a project that all the states in the region addressed with enthusiasm, which raised the fear that non-translation of the constitution was maintained as a form of censorship to prevent the majority of citizens from knowing the full range of their legally provided rights and freedoms.

Cold War Politics in East Africa

In Tanzania, with its rigorous Swahilization policy and programs and the open-minded disposition of its first president, the constitution was successfully translated into Swahili within a few years after the country's move to the left and its adoption of Ujamaa in 1967—though many other laws of the country continued to be in English. In this way, Tanzanians who did not know English were now able to learn about their constitutional rights and responsibilities as citizens through the Swahili constitution. In Kenya and Uganda, on the contrary, the constitution continued to be an English document decades after independence, inaccessible to majority of citizens who had no competence in the ex-colonial language.

Hope for change in Uganda came in 1995 when the nation adopted a new constitution which, in Article 4, explicitly required the constitution to be translated from English into some of the local languages of the country. For several years, however, the Uganda government seemed to be dragging its feet in implementing the provisions of Article 4. This reluctance on the part of the state led to mounting pressure from civil society and ended up in a civil suit in the High Court, which sought to compel the Attorney General to have the constitution translated into local languages. Finally, in 1999, the country's Ministry of Justice and Constitutional Affairs, in partnership with the United Nations Development Program, produced translations of the constitution in six local languages.

In Kenya, the period from the 1990s to the 2000s was marked by major national protests and civil society actions demanding a new political order, reflected in a new constitution. As a result, the very process of drafting the new constitution became people-centered, requiring popular participation. This pressure ensured that proposed draft constitutions were available in Swahili and accessible to the public. Opportunities were also created for citizens from all walks of life to contribute their views and opinions about various sections of the different versions of the proposed constitutions. By the time the country agreed on the final draft of the new proposed constitution, there was already a complete Swahili version of it that was intended to be published at the same time as the English version. Over a decade after a new government came to power under the new constitution, however, the already translated Swahili version of the constitution is yet to be published and released to the public.

For many in the country, the silence of the state regarding the fate of the Swahili translation of the constitution has meant only one thing: that it is an act of censorship meant to limit public knowledge of the provisions of the constitution. As a result, some language activists considered the possibility of engaging in public interest litigation to compel the state to release the Swahili translation of the Constitution of Kenya. However, wary of antagonising the government, they decided to pursue a more strategic path linked to the requirements of the East African Community (EAC) of which Kenya is a member. According to the protocol to establish a Swahili division of the EAC, the East African Kiswahili Commission, each member-state is obligated to create its own Swahili council which, among other things, would serve as the lead agency for the promotion of the language nationally and implementation of government policies relating to its use in public and other spheres of society. These language activists, including Kimani Njogu and Clara Momanyi, eventually succeeded in galvanising the support of many members of Parliament in drafting a bill, The National Kiswahili Council of Kenya Bill, 2023, which they anticipate would pass into law.[1] If successful, the language activists hope to use the powers of this agency to finally make the publication of a Swahili translation of the Constitution of Kenya possible. In spite of this development, however, the irony remains that the document that once enabled state censorship has now itself become the subject of debate about the interplay between translation and censorship.

6.5 Conclusion

This chapter has attempted to show how the end of colonialism in the East African countries of Kenya, Tanzania and Uganda, intersected with the global politics of the Cold War to create conditions that made the newly independent nations prone to censorship. The quest for nationhood presumed that national cohesion required the muzzling of dissent. The Cold War sought allegiance to one ideology as against the other. The intersection of these two trajectories sometimes led to censorship that was partly determined by a nation's ideological leaning in the Cold War polarisation. And because each of the Cold War super-powers sought to influence other nations and peoples throughout the world with different languages and cultures, translation naturally became implicated.

Each of the three East African countries discussed here had its own peculiar manifestation of the censorship of translated works linked to Cold War politics. However, partly because Kenya and Tanzania were on opposite ends of the Cold War divide more-or-less, with Kenya committed to capitalism and Tanzania tending towards socialism, the two countries present the greatest contrast in terms of their responses to translated literature of the Cold War expression. The reception of the Swahili translation of George Orwell's *Animal Farm* in Kenya and Tanzania provides a good example of this divergence between the two countries on Cold War translation and censorship.

Expectedly, the end of the Cold War also signaled the end of censorship pegged to translations of the Cold War period. Censorship of dissension was now related more to internal politics of the individual nations than to the proxy war of the super-powers of that time. However, because the popular post-Cold War mood was strongly anti-censorship, the state was forced to find extra-legal mechanisms of censorship, like the non-translation of the newly revised 2010 Constitution of Kenya seemingly to limit public awareness and understanding of the new powers invested in 'the people'. For activists in the country then, the earlier struggle to eliminate censorship provisions in the Constitution had now turned into a struggle to save the constitution itself from being the object of state censorship, with non-translation as one of the extra-legal means of preventing potential dissent.

Further Reading

Frederiksen, Bodil Folke. 2020. 'Censorship as Negotiation: The State and Non-European Newspapers in Kenya, 1930–1954'. *Itinerario*, 44(2): 391–411.
This article is concerned with the colonial state in Kenya as a producer, and consumer, and regulator of print. In this context censorship is demonstrated to be an interactive negotiated process—one whose successful management was in the interest of both the censoring agents and those censored.

Mazrui, Alamin. 2017, 'Cold War Translation in the East African Context: Reception and Responses', in Kobus Marais and Ilse Feinauer (eds.), *Translation Studies Beyond the Postcolony*. Newcastle upon Tyne UK: Cambridge Scholars Publishing, 73–93.
The article shows how the Cold War affected the Swahili translation of George Orwell's *Animal Farm*, on the one hand, and Maxim Gorky's *Mother*, on the other. This international political context had a direct impact on which of the two texts was censored where and how.

Talento, Serena. 2017. 'The Discourse (and Silence) on Literary Translation into Swahili during British Rule: Translation as Deconsecration', in Kobus Marais and Ilse Feinauer (eds.), *Translation Studies Beyond the Postcolony*. Newcastle upon Tyne UK: Cambridge Scholars Publishing, 33–72.
The author explores the import of literary texts under British rule in Tanganyika. It shows how translation was conceptualised, and sheds light on the logics underlying the literary exchanges.

Note

1 Personal conversation with Kimani Njogu, September 11, 2023.

References

Bourdieu, Pierre. 1980. *The Logic of Practice*. Translated by Richard Nice. Stanford: Stanford University Press.

Bunn, Matthew. 2015. 'Reimagining Repression: New Censorship Theory and After', *History and Theory*, 54: 25–44.

Colony and Protectorate of Kenya. 1962. *Legislative Council Debates: Official Report, May 8-July 27, 1962*, Vol. 89. Second Sess. Nairobi: Government Press.

Cullen, Poppy. 2018. 'Playing Cold War Politics: The Cold War in Anglo-Kenyan Relations in the 1960s', *Cold War History*, 18(1): 37–54.

Gikambi, Hezekiel. 2013. 'Kutana na Mwandishi Aliyetafsiri Shamba la Wanyama'. Available at: www.swa hilihub.com/habari/MAKALA/-/1310220 /1979574/-/qhupnd/-/index.html. (Accessed: 29 May 2015).

Hadjivayanis, Ida. 2011. *Norms of Swahili Translations in Tanzania: An Analysis of Selected Translated Prose*. PhD diss., School of Oriental and African Studies, University of London.

Henry, Neil. 1991. 'In Kenya, "Animal Farm" Corralled', *The Washington Post*, 13 February 1991.

Ingle, Stephen. 1993. *George Orwell: A Political Life*. Manchester: Manchester University Press.

Kenya Government. 2009. *Laws of Kenya: Penal Code, Chapter 63* (Subsidiary Legislations Orders under Section 52). Nairobi: Government Printers.

KU Libraries Exhibits. 2015. *Shamba la Wanyama* [*Animal Farm*]. Available at: http://exhibits.lib.ku.edu/ items/show/6039. (Accessed: 19 December 2015).

Kuhiwezak, Piotr. 2011. 'Translation and Censorship', *Translation Studies*, 4(3): 358–373.

Lal, Priya. 2014. 'Maoism in Tanzania: Material Connections and Shared Imaginaries', in Alexander C. Cook (ed.), *Mao's Little Red Book: A Global History*. Cambridge, UK: Cambridge University Press, 96–126.

Lawrence, Benjamin N., Osborne, Emily Lynn and Roberts, Richard L. 2015. *Intermediaries, Interpreters, and Clerks: African Employees and the Making of Colonial Africa*. Madison: University of Wisconsin Press.

Lewis, Joanna. 2001. 'Kenya: Mau Mau', in Derek Jones (ed.), *Censorship: A World Encyclopedia*. London: Fitzroy Dearborn Publishers, 1329–1330.

Lindfords, Berth. 1965. 'Review of William Shakespeare, Julius *Caezar* by Julius Nyerere', *Shakespeare Quarterly*, 16(2): 266–267.

Mamdani, Mahmood. 1983. *Imperialism and Fascism in Uganda*. London: Heinemann.

Mazrui, Alamin. 2007. *Swahili Beyond the Boundaries: Literature, Language and Identity*. Athens: Ohio University Press.

Mazrui, Ali A. 1969. *Violence and Thought*. New York: Humanities Press.

Mazrui, Ali A. 2002. *The Titan of Tanzania: Julius K. Nyerere's Legacy*. Binghamton: Institute of Global Cultural Studies, Binghamton University.

Mwaura, Peter. 2011. 'Kenya: Time Was When One Could Be Jailed for Having a Book on Chinese Geography', *Daily Nation*, 25 November 2011.

Nation Correspondent. 2006. 'Kimathi Fete Cancelled As Police Refuse to License It', *Sunday Nation*, 19 February 2006.

Odinga, Jaramogi. O. 1968. *Not Yet Uhuru*. London: Heinemann.

Ott, Dana. 2001. 'Uganda', in Derek Jones (ed.), *Censorship: A World Encyclopedia*. London: Fitzroy Dearborn Publishers, 2488–2489.

Read, James S. 1967. 'Censored'. *Transition*, 32: 37–41.

Rubin, Andrew. N. 2012. *Archives of Authority: Empire, Culture and the Cold War*. Princeton: Princeton University Press.

Salinas, Ann O'Toole. 2001. 'Kenya', in Derek Jones (ed.), *Censorship: A World Encyclopedia*. London: Fitzroy Dearborn Publishers, 1326–1329.

Scotton, James F. 1974. 'Kenya's Maligned African Press: A Reassessment'. Paper Presented at the Annual Meeting of the Association for Education in Journalism, 18-21 August 1974, San Diego, California.

Scotton, James F. 1978. 'Tanganyika's African Press, 1937–1960: A Nearly Forgotten Pre-Independence Forum', *African Studies Review*, 21(1): 1–18.

Sun, Jodie Yuzhou. 2020. 'Now the Cry Was Communism: The Cold War and Kenya's Relations with China, 1964–70', *Cold War History*, 20(1): 39–58.

Tabaire, Bernard. 2007. 'The Press and Political Repression in Uganda: Back to the Future?', *Journal of Eastern African Studies*, 1(2): 193–211.

Venuti, Lawrence. 2000. 'Translation, Community, Utopia', in Lawrence Venuti (ed.), *Rethinking Translation: Discourse, Subjectivity, Ideology*. London: Routledge, 1–17.

Wilson, Amrit. 1989. *US Foreign Policy and Revolution: The Creation of Zanzibar*. London: Pluto Press.

7

TRANSLATION AND CENSORSHIP IN THE HISTORY OF ESTONIA

Multilingualism, Linguistic Hierarchies and Centres of Power

Daniele Monticelli

7.1 Introduction

In 1991 the USSR collapsed and Estonia regained the independence it had lost fifty years earlier. In the same year cultural historian Malle Salupere complained about the absence of chapters on censorship in Estonian literary histories, defining the history of censorship in Estonia as *terra incognita* (Salupere 1991). This is not a mere coincidence, as Salupere directly relates this absence to the recently concluded Soviet experience, when the authorities did not tolerate any reference to the existence of censorship in Soviet Estonia ande were upset at historical references that might generate unwanted comparisons with Soviet reality.

Since Salupere's remarks, several monographs (Veskimägi 1996; Priidel 2010; Tammer 2014) on the censorship of books in Estonia have appeared, all of which focus exclusively on the Soviet period. This is telling of how the history of censorship, like any history, reconstructs a more or less distant past starting from the exigencies of the present, its cultural and political concerns and agenda. It is thus no surprise that post-Soviet Estonia represents the Soviet era as *the* censorship era, while the study of censorship in other periods of Estonian history is limited to individual sections of essays, book chapters and dissertations.

When we bring translation into the picture, we encounter an additional problem. The few studies on the history of Estonian censorship focus mainly on the press, which was a privileged target of the censors, and on original Estonian literature. The only existing studies of censorship with a focus on translation concern the Bible and, once again, during the Soviet period. There is of course a lot of unstudied and possibly relevant material in Estonian archives, but this could not be included in the present overview, which spans five centuries of Estonian history.

As for the use of the notion of censorship in this chapter, the examples considered will cover the following: 1) primary or external censorship, which is the official system of censorship established by ruling authorities through explicit legislation or official decrees; 2) secondary or 'internal' (Sherry 2012: 72) censorship involving institutions such as publishing houses or editorial boards who are expected to comply with the expectations of the authorities and the ruling ideology; and 3) self-censorship, which is practised by translators themselves. The last two are examples of what

DOI: 10.4324/9781003149453-10

Pierre Bourdieu (1986) has called 'structural censorship', which is the function of a *habitus*, or an internalised adherence to the rules within the field in which publishers, editors, translators, and so on, operate. While Billiani defines censorship as 'a form of manipulative rewriting of discourses by one agent or structure over another agent or structure, aiming at filtering the stream of information from one source to another' (2007: 3), we will also consider here bans on foreign authors or books, which prohibit their translation *in toto*. In Toury's terms (1995), one could say that censorship affects both preliminary (the choice of the texts to be translated) and operative norms (how they are translated). To this we should add reception norms, as translations are often prohibited or amended *post-factum*, i.e., after they have been published and circulated, due to changes in ruling ideology and morality.

7.2   Historical Perspectives

The Estonian history of censorship and translation dates back to 1535 when the first known text in the Estonian language was printed. The sections that follow will provide an overview of the censorship systems and their effect on translation from 1535 to the end of the Soviet period in 1991. Over the course of these five centuries of Estonian history the country has been independent only between 1918 and 1940, otherwise being ruled by different foreign powers and belonging to various supranational states (Kasekamp 2010). At the beginning of the sixteenth century, the present territory of Estonia was ruled by the Livonian branch of the Teutonic Order. As a consequence of the Livonian War (1558–1583), the order dissolved and Estonia passed under Swedish rule. The defeat of Sweden in the Great Northern War at the beginning of the eighteenth century delivered the country to Peter I, who turned it into a province of the Russian Empire, which it remained until the Russian Revolution, when the independent Estonian Republic was proclaimed in 1918. While this may seem a very discontinuous story, there is an important constant that was of fundamental importance to the development of the Estonian language, literature and culture. Across the centuries the real, local power belonged to the Baltic German landlords, who were also the cultural elite of the country, while the vast majority of Estonians were peasants until the very end of the nineteenth century. It was the local Germans who were the first to become interested in the study of the Estonian language and culture in the early nineteenth century. In the second half of the century, this interest was taken over by the first generation of highly educated Estonians who headed the national movement, which led to the independence of the country. In this period translation of German writers as well as the adaptation of the German national-romantic agenda to Estonian circumstances constituted the grounds for the formation of Estonian national and cultural identity. Estonian independence ended in 1940 when the country was annexed to the Soviet Union, which, with the exception of the period of German occupation (1941–1944), ruled the country until 1991. My overview of censorship and translation in Estonia generally follows this periodization of Estonian political history, although I will sometimes merge or split the above mentioned periods of Estonian history when this is required by the logic of the censorship system.

7.3   1535–1710: Linguistico-theological Bans

The first period to be considered starts with the first conserved written texts in the Estonian language at the beginning of the sixteenth century and ends with the Russian conquest of the country. The multilingualism that will characterise the country in the following centuries is already in place at this point. Estonian was the spoken language of the local peasantry, which constituted the vast majority of the population. German and Swedish were the languages of

Translation and Censorship in the History of Estonia

the tiny economic and cultural elite, of education and of the vast majority of printed works, to which Latin must be added. Given the economic and cultural dominance of local Germans, the Protestant Reformation spread to Estonia as early as the 1520s, provoking the need for Estonian translations of religious texts to be read by German pastors to illiterate Estonian peasants. Initially, works in Estonian were printed in Germany and in the free imperial city of Riga, during which time censorship was not institutionalised and books were prohibited by administrative organs, such as the Tribunal of the Tallinn City Council. The Estonian translations of the Lutheran catechism were by far the most printed translations in the early modern period (Lotman 2016), while the end of the seventeenth century was dominated by controversies over the translation of the Bible. The translators were almost exclusively Baltic Germans, and in their translations they used both of the two written varieties of the Estonian language: North Estonian and South Estonian (see Raag 1999).

The first (known) written text in Estonian is the translation of a Lutheran catechism printed in Wittenberg in 1535 by the same typographer who had printed Luther's translation of the Bible. This is also the first (known) case of censorship of an Estonian translation. The catechism presented, on the right side, the original text in Low German by Simon Wanradt, pastor of the Niguliste Church in Tallinn, and, on the left side, the Estonian translation by Johann Koell, pastor of the Church of the Holy Spirit in the same town (Ehasalu et al. 1997: 30–1). Fifteen hundred copies of the book were printed, but the translation was prohibited in 1537 by the Tallinn City Council Tribunal and all copies destroyed (Weiss and Johansen 1956). The reasons for the decision are not clear given that the tribunal's record only alludes to 'important mistakes' without further explanation. Given the historical context of the struggle between Lutheranism and the Catholic Church and the subsequent need to uphold Lutheran orthodoxy, scholars tend to interpret these 'mistakes' as theological divergences of the original or the translation from the canonical Lutheran catechism. Another interesting hypothesis refers to a notice added by the translator himself that justifies the linguistic variety chosen for the translation. As Estonian was at the time an almost exclusively oral language with different local varieties, translation became from the very beginning a site of linguistic experimentation, where the struggle for the establishment of a written standard was carried out (Saareste 1930). The decision to censor might therefore refer to linguistic rather than theological 'mistakes', i.e., Koell's choice of a variety of written Estonian that did not suit the hegemonic ambition of the Tallinn City Council.

While the Reformation opened the way for the use of a written Estonian language in translation, Swedish rulers, who dominated Estonia from the mid-sixteenth century to the early eighteenth century, were responsible for the institution of higher education in the country. This went along with the establishment of the first local printing presses at the University of Tartu (1632) and the Tallinn Gymnasium (i.e., high school) (1634), which brought about the institutionalisation of censorship in the country. In Tartu, two professors were appointed by the university as inspectors with the duty of checking all printed books before distribution. The case of Tallinn is more complicated and illustrates the power struggle in the city under Swedish rule. While printing was under the jurisdiction of the city council, and the person responsible for censorship should have been the rector of the gymnasium, Tallinn's Lutheran consistory and bishop claimed the right to censor religious texts (Aarma 1995: 8–27). In 1631, Swedish rulers attempted to centralise censorship, instituting pre- and post-print censorship in all the provinces of the Kingdom, requiring that all printed books be submitted to the royal chancellery for permission to distribute. Even if this did not really change the reality of censorship practices at the local level, it increased the role of the Lutheran church, which now had a more solid basis for bringing local disputes to the attention of the Stockholm royal authorities.

The translation of the New Testament into Estonian in the last two decades of the seventeenth century, during which more cases of censorship arose than during all the preceding periods taken together (Aarma 1995: 34), has to be framed in the context of the competition between different local powers and the struggle for support from the central authorities in Stockholm. This was the country's major translation project, although it differed from earlier state-sponsored enterprises in other Protestant countries, such as the Netherlands and England, where canonic versions were invested with a nation-building function. In the case of Estonia, translation was carried out collaboratively by German experts following explicit rules. Estonian ethnolinguistic identity was not an issue for them, as they were more interested in the struggle for theological and political hegemony in the country. Interestingly, this struggle took the form of translation and linguistic disputes fought through the censors' decrees. Let us briefly reconstruct this history, which more than any other characterises the relations between translation, power and censorship during the Swedish domination of the country, when Estonian slowly turned, through translation, into a written language (Ross 2007; Tafenau 2011).

The Baltic dominions of the Kingdom of Sweden were divided into two provinces with their separate Lutheran consistories: Estonia, which included the northern part of the country, ruled from Tallinn, and Livonia, which included southern Estonia and parts of what is modern Latvia, ruled from Riga. The two main varieties of written Estonian that emerged at the time—Southern and Northern Estonian—roughly coincided with the boundaries of the provinces and the consistories; books in Northern Estonian were printed in Tallinn and books in Southern Estonian were printed in Riga. While only the Livonian Consistory was responsible for the translation of the Bible in Southern Estonian, with the New Testament printed in 1686 (Paul 1999: 325–54), for reasons that have remained obscure but are probably related to the ambitions of the new Superintendent of the Livonian Lutheran Church, Johann Fisher, permission was granted in 1682 by the king of Sweden to both the Estonian and the Livonian Consistory for the translation of the New Testament into Northern Estonian. This generated a struggle that lasted a decade, slowing the translation process and provoking repeated interventions by the Swedish censors.

When the competition began, a lot of work had already been done in Tallinn. However, the special commission appointed to assess the translation mandated that major revisions be made before publication in 1685 due to the 'poorness' of the Northern Estonian language. Fisher successfully used the Estonian Consistory's impasse to gain the support of the king to move the responsibility for the revision from Tallinn to Riga, which could already claim a successful translation of the Bible into Latvian. It is at this point that the power struggle between the two consistories becomes linguistico-theological, with Tallinn defending the orthographic tradition established by Baltic German pastor Heinrich Stahl and the authority of Luther's German translation of the New Testament as the only model for the translators, and Riga supporting the orthographic reform advanced by Estonian-born Swedish educator Bengt Gottfried Forselius and the need to consult the Swedish translations and to check the Greek original in the revision of the translation. While a resolution from the king settled the theological dispute in favour of the Estonian Consistory, establishing Luther's German translation as the only authority for the Northern Estonian translation, the linguistic issue remained open, with the two sides agreeing only that the prevailing translation would set the standard of written Estonian. Two conferences where held, in 1686 and 1687, with delegates from both Riga and Tallinn, resulting in an apparently consensual translation of the New Testament, which was a radical revision of the initial manuscript produced by the Estonian Consistory and which applied the principle of orthographic reform. However, the struggle reignited as explosively as ever when Riga claimed the right to print the revised manuscript, given that it was mostly the work of Livonian translators (Paul 1999: 355–76).

Translation and Censorship in the History of Estonia

A new turn in this struggle was brought about by the further centralisation of censorship in the Kingdom of Sweden with the institution of the *censor librorum* in 1688 (Aarma 1995: 45). The Estonian Consistory immediately appealed to the censor who banned books in Northern Estonian published in Livonia due to the 'big mistakes' they contained, advocating the need to adhere to the old orthographic norm as a guarantee of the orthodoxy of the translations. The result was a royal resolution dated January 1689 prohibiting the printing of the translation in Riga as well as Tallinn until a correct version was produced. The Swedish secretary of state (Aarma 1995: 51) intervened in 1691 to blame J. Fischer for printing the New Testament despite the king's prohibition; he asked the governor of the Livonian province to prohibit the circulation of the book. However, the printing of the translation was probably false information, spread by the Estonian Consistory to discredit its Livonian counterpart. Given the impossibility of sequestering the yet to be printed New Testament in Northern Estonian, the zealous governor ordered the sequestering of the printed New Testament in Southern Estonian, which had been circulating without restriction since 1686 (Salu 1965: 45). While the publication of the New Testament remained blocked, in the following years a whole series of religious translations in Northern Estonian were published both in Riga and Tallinn, accompanied by critical reactions, complaints and new censorial interventions until Fisher eventually left Livonia to avoid incarceration. Nevertheless, the Northern Estonian translation of the New Testament was published in 1715 as a revision of the version prepared under the coordination of Fisher with its reformed orthography, while the first Northern Estonian translation of the whole Bible was printed in 1739. The reformed Northern Estonian of these translations would later prevail over Southern Estonian to become standard written Estonian.

This analysis of translation and censorship under Swedish rule reveals a number of important translational, cultural and political aspects of sixteenth- and seventeenth-century Estonia. The first is the pivotal role of the translation of religious texts in the formation of standard written Estonian. In a fluid linguistic environment, translations were caught up in a series of theologico-linguistic struggles that reflected political struggles and were often fought using censorship as a weapon. The rather decentralised censorship system, at least until the institution of the Kingdom's *censor librorum*, facilitated its instrumental use by the different parties. While in the sixteenth century the struggle for a monopoly on censorship placed the religious power of the Lutheran consistories in opposition to the secular power of the city councils, as was the case with Wanradt-Koell's catechism, in the seventeenth century, the rivalry between the Estonian and the Livonian Consistories turned into tit-for-tat censorship of respective Bible translations, which was only exacerbated by the repeated intervention of the Swedish central power. It is remarkable that what superintendent Fisher called a 'war on letters' [*Buchstabenkrieg*], rather than on theological issues, was at the core of the censorship interventions. These cases reveal post-print (the catechism) as well as pre-print (the New Testament) bans on translations.

7.4   1710–1918: Tsarist Censorship and the Birth of Literary Estonian through Translation

The Lutheran translation of the New Testament and of the entire Bible was finally published under the new Orthodox ruler of the country, the Russian Tsar Peter I. This is only an apparently paradox. In fact, administratively, the tsarist era did not represent a rupture with Swedish times, as the Baltic provinces of the Russian Empire maintained a 'special status' and the Baltic German nobility preserved its rights and privileges, continuing to rule Estonia in exchange for loyalty to the Tsar. In the eighteenth and first half of the nineteenth centuries this also included the cultural field: lectures at the University of Tartu were still delivered in German, which was the language of the educated elite. Publications in Estonian remained a marginal phenomenon in that period, even if Catherine the Great's decree of 1783 ended the state monopoly on the publishing industry, which allowed for the establishment of private printing presses. The 1800 catalogue of Dienes, one of Tallinn's biggest bookshops, reported a total of 742 books, of which only 12 were in Estonian, mainly religious works, cookbooks and first aid books (Reimo 2001: 305).

Although the special status of the Baltic provinces did not extend to censorship and the printing industry, which were regulated by the same laws throughout the Russian empire, at the beginning of Russian domination the Swedish system remained in place *de facto*: the censorship of secular books was entrusted to the rector of the Gymnasium in Tallinn and to university professors in Tartu, while religious texts were censored by the Lutheran Consistories of Estonia and Livonia, thus perpetuating the unending struggle between city and religious authorities (Reimo 2001: 291–2). Tsarist censorship had no interest in Lutheran orthodoxy and Estonian orthography, provided the primacy of the official Russian Orthodox Church was not put into question. For instance, in 1743 the Russian translations of two German Lutheran books were prohibited in order to make them inaccessible to Russian readers, while the German originals continued to circulate freely in the Baltic provinces of the empire (Reimo 2001: 294).

This situation is well illustrated by an incident that occurred a century later, following the establishment of the Estonian Learned Society [*Gelehrte Estnische Gesellschaft*] at the University of Tartu in 1839, whose aim was to study Estonian history, language and literature. The Society, made up of Baltic Germans as well as the first generation of educated Estonians, was very active in improving the education of Estonian peasants through a series of publications, the most popular of which was the annually published *Peasant's Calender* [*Ma-Rahwa Kalender*] which included didactic stories and suggestions in the field of agriculture, economy, and so on. Until 1843 the calendars translated the German word *Reformation* with the Estonian expression *Lutheruse õige usu ülesvõtmine*, which literary means 'the adoption of the Lutheran true religion'. In the 1843 and 1844 editions of the calendars the word *õige* 'true' disappeared and we find only the 'adoption of the Lutheran faith'. That this is a case of censorship is revealed in a letter from the tsarist censor G. F. E. von Sahmen to the director of the Estonian Learned Society Friedrich Robert Faehlmann dated 1844, in which the censor explains that it is prohibited to translate the word *Reformation* as the 'true religion' (est. *õige usk*) because the term must be exclusively used for the ruling Orthodox Church. Faehlmann immediately wrote to the Consistory of the Lutheran Church, complaining about the interference and asking the Consistory to stand up for the established Estonian translation, so as to prevent Russian censorship from contesting its use in literature for peasants. The same day, the censor informed Faehlmann that the censorship committee had decided in favour of the established translation, i.e., *Lutheruse õige usu ülesvõtmine*. The following editions of the *Peasant's Calendar* indeed reverted to this translation with Lutheranism becoming once again the 'true religion' for Estonians (Metse 2016).

After the French Revolution, Russian rulers panicked, resulting in the strengthening and centralisation of censorship, a task that was assigned to the police and specially created censorship boards in St. Petersburg, Moscow, Riga and Odessa. Censorship concentrated at that time on political issues. All French newspapers and journals were forbidden, and foreign books were rigorously checked in the ports of the empire (Tallinn included). Lists of forbidden authors were compiled, including French Enlightenment writers, such as Voltaire and Mirabeau. In addition, individual works by Kant, Goethe, Schiller and Swift, among other authors, were confiscated in Riga before they could circulate and eventually be translated into the languages of the empire. While at the beginning all books to be printed in Estonia had to receive permission from Riga and St. Petersburg, an

Translation and Censorship in the History of Estonia

office of the censor was created in 1799 at the Governorate of the Estonian Province, with censors in the major Estonian cities (Reimo 2001). Pre-print and post-print censorship were applied to all books printed within the empire, alternating between stricter and more liberal periods until 1905.

An interesting example that once again brings to the fore the complexity of the multilingual situation in tsarist Estonia is the publication of the German translation of Russian diplomat and playwright Alexander Griboyedov's comedy *Woe from Wit* [*Gore ot uma*] published in Tallinn in 1831 in the *Russische Bibliothek für Deutsche* series. Written in 1823 as a satire of post-Napoleonic Moscow, the comedy was blocked by Russian censorship and was not published in full until 1861. In order to obtain permission to print, the preface to the German translation misled the censors, claiming that the comedy was known by heart by all educated Russians. When the ruse was discovered, it provoked a scandal and the series was closed after only three publications (Salupere 1991: 12). The publication of Griboyedov's translation shows, on the one hand, that a Russian original prohibited at the centre of the empire could in some cases be published at the imperial periphery in translation. On the other hand, the repressive reaction when the ruse was discovered shows that tsarist authorities had become aware that translated works in languages other than Russian could also be dangerous.

The second half of the nineteenth century is characterised by the rise of Estonian national self-awareness. The first generation of the Estonian intelligentsia, to which Faelhmann belonged, was mainly of peasant origin, although its members were educated in German and started actively to use and develop the Estonian language in many different genres, not only in the abovementioned *Peasant's Calendars*, but also in works of poetry and prose, which gradually became more popular than religious literature. During this period, the ratio of German to Estonian in local book production was still 2:1, but the print runs of works in Estonian were much higher than those of works in German as literacy was already very high among the Estonian peasantry.

However, books were not the principal reading material among Estonians in the second half of the nineteenth century. While the first newspaper for Estonian peasants, *Tarto Marahwa Näddali-Leht,* was shut down in 1806 due to censorship violations and on the initiative of local Baltic German landlords (Issakov 1983: 60–75), the subsequent newspapers *Postimees* (est. 1859) and *Sakala* (est. 1878) took leading roles in the Estonian national movement. Another milestone of nation building, the epic poem *Kalevipoeg*, was written in 1861 by Faehlmann and Friedrich Reinhold Kreutzwald, another protagonist of the national movement. While tsarist authorities initially saw the Estonian national awakening [*rahvuslik ärkamine*] as a means by which to undermine the power of Baltic German landlords, the attention of tsarist censorship shifted very quickly to works published in Estonian (Jansen 2000).

In 1865 the Censorship Board of the Russian Empire was reorganised into the Main Administration for Publishing Affairs, which was the primary organ of Russian censorship until the October Revolution of 1917 (Jansen 2000: 8–9). In 1869 the censorship of all printed texts in Estonian was once again moved to Riga, with the aim of strengthening control over the Estonian press and literature, while decreasing the German influence on censorship by prohibiting Germans and Lutherans from being nominated as censors (Paatsi 2014, 2015). The first editor-in-chief of *Postimees*, Johann Woldemar Jannsen, described his publishing activity at that time as permanently 'walking on eggshells' (Jannsen 1862).

An episode characteristic of the complex relations between translation, the emerging Estonian literature, national self-awareness and tsarist power took place in the second half of the nineteenth century. It involved poetess, writer and playwright Lydia Koidula (1843–1886), who is considered one of the central ideologues of the national movement and a founding figure of Estonian literature. As with most Estonian literature until the end of the nineteenth century, the majority of

Koidula's 'original' works were actually more or less adapted translations of German literary works and motifs, through which she developed the Estonian literary language and national agenda (Monticelli 2019). Her short novel *Martiniiko ja Korsika* (1869/1874) was an undeclared, free and manipulative translation of the popular German author Luise Mühlbach's novel *Kaiserin Josephine: ein Napoleonisches Lebensbild* (1861). The story of the relationship between Josephine and Napoleon is told by Mühlbach as a sentimental journey, while Koidula shifts the focus to the historical background of the French Revolution, its causes and effects, transforming the story into a reflection on the formation of a national people and its actions in revolutionary times. It is exactly this aspect that provoked the intervention of censorship. When Koidula sent her manuscript to Riga in 1869, the censor and Orthodox priest Mihhail Suigussar replied that the publication of the work must be prohibited because 'at this time republicans and democrats are very scary, particularly the ones among the Estonians' (cited in Salupere 2016: 37). Only in 1873 and in response to the author's insistent letters did the censor finally allow the publication of the work, on the condition, however, that the passages relating to the demands of the people and the immoral life of the rulers be significantly shortened and toned down. The edition of the book published in 1874 contains only the first part of Mühlbach's novel; the story ends on the second day of the revolution before Napoleon and Josephine have even met. The manuscript is lost, so it is impossible to ascertain how much of the published text was censored. However Koidula's letters indicate that quite a lot was deleted. Moreover, the entire second part of the novel, which she had also completed, remained unpublished (Monticelli et al. 2018). This is a good example of how the incipient Estonian literature and press, together with the Estonian literary language, cultural and national identity they helped to develop, were shaped through creative translation. It also highlights the constant negotiation between the agenda of Estonian author-translators and the constraints of tsarist censorship, confirmed by the correspondence between Koidula and Suigusaar. While the censor had the last word, author-translators were certainly not passive subjects in the negotiations.

In the 1880s tsarist power changed its attitude toward the special status of the Estonian and Livonian provinces, starting a process of Russification aimed at weakening Baltic German hegemony and assimilating the local peasantry, which was encouraged to convert to the Orthodox Church in exchange for agricultural land. Russian was introduced as the language of education in schools and at the University of Tartu, and Baltic German provincial governors were replaced with Russian ones. This did not, however, produce the expected results as the 1905 revolutionary uprising, which targeted the Baltic German nobility as well as tsarist power, clearly showed. Political demands were radicalised and socialist ideas spread among Estonian intellectuals and workers. The revolution forced the tsarist government to renounce pre-print censorship, while printed volumes still required the approval of the censors before distribution. However, negative censorship decisions now had to be confirmed by a district court, which represented a guarantee against the arbitrary judgement of censors. The main attention of censorship focused henceforth on the socialist press and its publications. For instance, Estonian translations of the works of Karl Kautsky (*Vene revolutsiooni edasiviivad jõud ja tuleviku tee* [The progressive forces and the future of the Russian revolution] 1907), Georgii Plekhanov (*Usk* [Religion] 1910) and Karl Marx (*Palgatöö ja Kapital* [Wage Labor and Capital] 1916), but also journalist Vladimir Korolenko's writings against the death penalty (*Igapäewane nähtus. Ajakirjaniku märkused surmanuhtluse üle* [An everyday occurrence. A journalist's notes on capital punishment] 1911) and Leo Tolstoy's critical pamphlet (*Kas tõeste nii olema peab?* [Must it really be like this?] 1911) were sequestered and destroyed by the censors (Depman 1927; Möldre 2005b).

On the cultural and literary front, the period between the 1905 revolution and the revolutions of 1917 saw the emergence of the Young Estonia (*Noor-Eesti*) movement, a group of young Estonian

Translation and Censorship in the History of Estonia

intellectuals who, inspired by contemporary European modernism, aspired to bring about a profound renewal of Estonian language, literature and culture. This was done through an instrumental use of translation, which shifted attention from German to French, Italian, Anglo-American and Scandinavian literatures. The movement had its own journals and publishing house through which highly experimental (linguistically as well as stylistically) translations of modernist authors, such as Baudelaire, Bourget, D'Annunzio, Maeterlinck, Poe, Rimbaud, Verlaine and Wilde, were promoted. It is interesting to observe that even though some of the members of the movement actively participated in the revolutionary events of 1905 and suffered imprisonment and exile, tsarist censorship was mostly indifferent to the primarily aesthetic, rather than political, agenda of the movement, and its publications were allowed to circulate freely. It was rather the older generation of Estonian intellectuals who publicly censured the literary and linguistic experiments of the Young Estonians, along with the moral laxity introduced by the authors they translated. This might have had some restraining effect on the radicality of the translations. A telling example is the 1913 Estonian translation of Gabriele D'Annunzio's *L'innocente* by Young Estonia movement poet and translator Vilem Grünthal Ridala. The linguistic boldness of the translation provoked a scandal in the Estonian cultural field and the novel's decadent theme was considered immoral (Monticelli 2016b). However, a close analysis of the translation (D'Annunzio 1913) shows that Ridala systematically omitted all of D'Annunzio's references to the protagonist's incestuous desires and his most explicit sexual fantasies. Though the law banned obscene content and censors paid attention to moral issues, this is most probably a case of structural self-censorship, which reflects the limits of the sayable (Bourdieu 1986) in Estonian society of the time even for experimentally daring and innovative Young Estonia intellectuals.

The offices of the censor throughout the territory of the former tsarist empire were abolished after the February Revolution of 1917.

7.5   1918–1940: the Republic of Estonia

The proclamation of the Independent Republic of Estonia on 24 February 1918 made Estonian the official state language, i.e., the language of elementary as well as higher education, thus boosting book production—of both original works and translations—in Estonian.

The 13th paragraph of the new Estonian Constitution of 1920 declared that 'There is no censorship in Estonia' (Eesti Vabariigi Põhiseadus 1934: 5), while prescribing limits on freedom of speech when public security and morality were at stake. This meant that until the beginning of the 1930s there was no separate censorship apparatus, although copies of printed books had to be sent to the police for post-print permission and printed books could be sequestered by order of a Tribunal. After the failed communist insurrection in 1924, state censorship focused on political issues: most of the 12 works prohibited and sequestered between 1919 and 1933 were accused of spreading communist ideas and conspiring against the Republic (Möldre 2019: 149). The only case of a ban caused by offense against public morality in this period was the poetic collection *27*, which included the first five translations of Mayakovsky's poems in Estonian and 22 original poems by Estonian poet and translator Ralf Rond, who simultaneously attempted with his volume to introduce Mayakovsky's poetry in Estonian and to produce new Estonian originals on the model of Mayakovsky's style and themes. The book was withdrawn from shops in 1923 by order of Narva's Tribunal because Mayakovsky's/Rond's crude use of language offended public morality. When the central figures of Estonian literature, such as the novelist Friedebert Tuglas, were called to testify as experts in front of the Tribunal, they defended Rond's work not for its intrinsic quality, but for its merit in introducing Mayakovsky into the Estonian literary system

(Kruus 1962: 577–82). While the Tribunal ordered the destruction of all copies of the book, Rond later published, at his own expense, an entire collection of translations of Mayakovsky's poems.

Things changed quite drastically after the *coup d'état* of 1934, through which the President Konstantin Päts brought about an authoritarian turn similar to what was happening at that time in many other European countries. This final period in the history of the first Estonian Republic is known as 'the silent era' in Estonian historiography, since the new regime exercised strict control over the press and all publishing activities coordinated by the newly created Office for State Propaganda (1935–1940). The new law on publishing of 1938 specified the institutions that could not be criticised and prohibited all topics that might foment social discord, the representation of crimes, such as rape and suicide, and other acts that offended public morality.

The attention of the censors now focused on the press and the rising cinematographic industry; there was no pre-print censorship of books and the censors very seldom intervened when it came to works of fiction. The authoritarian turn in the cultural policies of Päts' regime did not have much of an impact on the percentage of translations among published books, which remained at approximately fifty percent of the total (Möldre 2012a: 95). Almost half of the 55 books prohibited in the period from 1934 to 1940 were Estonian translations of the Watchtower Bible and Tract Society booklets printed in Switzerland, which were considered harmful to Estonia's international relations, disrespectful of other religions and psychologically harmful to the people because of their apocalyptic prophecies about the imminent end of the world. Among the remaining banned books, translations can be counted on one hand; for example, *Elu võõraslaps* [*Ulle der Zwerg*] by Austrian writer Vicki Baum and the memoirs of Casanova were considered by the censors to contain 'vulgar expressions, which harm people's sense of decorum' (Parts 2003: 77, 87). An interesting case is the translation of Romanian writer Panaït Istrati's novel *Uncle Anghel* (Estonian *Onu Angel*, 1935), which was prohibited for the same reasons. The translator Jaan Kangilaski wrote to the minister of the interior on behalf of the *Loodus* publishing house, asking for clear explanations and concrete examples of the kinds of expression that should be avoided in printed books. The minister answered that publishers were intelligent people and should themselves know what was moral and what was not, thus implying that in such cases internal self-censorship should do the job without requiring the intervention of the censors (Möldre 2012b: 29).

Against such a backdrop and despite the fact that the Estonian communist party was an illegal, underground organisation, it may seem surprising that the left-wing cooperative publishing house *Sõprus* legally published Estonian translations of the first volume of Marx's *Capital,* three volumes of Marx and Engels' complete works in the 1936–1939 period, as well as a 1936 translation of the novel *Mother* by leading Soviet writer Maxim Gorky. Whether this can be explained by the progressive rapprochement of Päts' regime with the Soviet Union, which culminated in the Soviet–Estonian Mutual Assistance Treaty in 1939, is an interesting question that points to the role of translation and censorship in the development of international relations.

7.6   1940–1991: the Soviet Period

In 1940 Estonia was annexed to the Soviet Union. With the exception of the period of German occupation (1941–1944), Estonia was a republic of the USSR until 1990. One of the first acts of the new government was the extension of the Soviet censorship system to the newly acquired republic. The Estonian branch of the Main Administration for Literary and Publishing Affairs (known by its Russian abbreviation *Glavlit*) was made responsible for the censorship of all printed works in Soviet Estonia, directly reflecting the control exerted by the Communist Party on publishing activities. Soviet censorship operated at all the levels described in the introduction to this chapter.

Translation and Censorship in the History of Estonia

All existing publications, translations included, were divided into the categories of forbidden and permitted. New translations of permitted books were subjected to pre-print censorship so that ideological manipulation in accordance with current party policy could be enforced. Only after a book had been stamped as suitable for publication (with or without censorial modifications) could it be printed by the few remaining, nationalised publishing houses. In addition to pre-print censorship, all printed books were subject to post-print censorship in order to receive permission for distribution. In addition to *Glavlit*, the Communist Party guided and controlled book production by means of the five-year plan: the party organizations had to sanction thematic and financial plans and print runs. Quotas were established for different categories of translated literature; Russian literature enjoyed the lion's share, followed by the literatures of the 'other Soviet peoples', the socialist countries, and finally capitalist literatures in which case the works of communist or 'progressive' authors sympathizing with the USSR were recommended (Veskimägi 1996; Möldre 2005a).

While this system of extensive control and censorship over printed books persisted unchanged until the collapse of the Soviet Union and the restoration of Estonia's independence in 1991, its application varied considerably according to the general dynamics of Soviet power, which in the case of Soviet Estonia can be divided into four periods: Stalinism (1944–1956); the Khrushchev thaw (1956–1968); Brezhnev stagnation (1969–1987); and perestroika (1987–1991) (see Monticelli and Lange 2014). The Stalinist period coincides with the early Sovietisation of the country, which provoked a fundamental discontinuity in Estonian culture. The percentage of translations among printed books suddenly increased, while Russian dominated the source languages and literatures of translation. As the principles of Marxism-Leninism and Socialist Realism were implanted into the Estonian political, social and cultural fields through translations from Russian, they began to function as a model for imitation by local Estonian authors (Monticelli 2016a). This was accompanied by an unprecedented series of extensive bans on existing translations and foreign authors. The first list of proscribed works, which was issued in 1940, focused on translated popular literature, including adventure and detective fiction, such as E. R. Borroughs' Tarzan novels, Arthur Conan Doyle's works, Disney's Mickey Mouse, Dumas's *The Count of Monte Cristo* and, of course, the translations of religious and spiritual literature, all of which Soviet censors considered as inappropriate for Soviet Estonia's citizens (Priidel 2010: 73). Ten years later, in 1950, the lists of banned books focused on twentieth-century foreign authors whose works were considered ideologically harmful, such as Albert Camus, John Dewey, Bertrand Russell, André Gide, Aldous Huxley and André Malraux, alongside the political figures Charles de Gaulle, Dwight Eisenhower and Winston Churchill (Tammer 2014: 249–309). Existing translations of banned authors were destroyed or moved to special library departments and made inaccessible to readers; new translations were forbidden. Following a general pattern in the Soviet Union, persecuted Estonian authors often earned a living as translators, anonymous in most cases. The works of translators who had been repressed in Estonia or who lived in exile were removed from circulation or the name of the translators were erased from the translations.

Considering this background, it is not surprising that one of the major consequences of the process of destalinisation initiated by Khrushchev in 1956 was an explosive increase in translations from foreign, particularly Western, literatures. A very significant event in this respect was the establishment of various translation series, the most influential of which was *Loomingu Raamatukogu* (The Library of Creation). Established in 1957, the series rapidly became a major literary venue of the time, publishing translations of previously forbidden and ideologically problematic authors such as Jorge Luis Borges, Heinrich Böll, Albert Camus, Joseph Conrad, Franz Kafka, André Maurois and Alexander Solzhenitsyn. The memoirs of the editors of the book series (e.g., Hiedel 2006) show a shift from the repressive external censorship of the Stalinist period to the rather

The Routledge Handbook of Translation and Censorship

accommodating internal censorship of the Thaw period, which gave publishers, editors and translators greater leeway for negotiation with the censors (Monticelli 2020).

After the repression of the Prague Spring by Soviet tanks in 1968, the cultural atmosphere changed, and in 1973 communist authorities removed the entire editorial board of *Loomingu Raamatukogu*. The publication plan for that year had included the translation of John Milton's famous essay *Areopagitica* in defence of freedom of speech, but printing the translation was now blocked by the censors. Communist Party concern over the flood of translations of foreign literature brought back stricter quotas, returning translations from Russian and the other languages of the Soviet Republics to the lead once again. Only with perestroika did the possibility once again arise of publishing books that had been previously banned, such as the abovementioned translation of Milton's *Areopagitica,* which was published in 1987 and, a year later, the first translation of George Orwell's *Animal Farm* in the Soviet Union. Censorship was finally abolished in 1990 by a decree of the self-proclaimed autonomous Estonian government, one year before the official restoration of the independent republic.

As mentioned above, Estonia was occupied by Germany from 1941 to 1944, when the country became a part of the Eastern province (*Ostlandi*) of the *Reich*, ruled by occupation authorities and a local puppet government. Similarly to the Soviets, Nazi occupation authorities immediately compiled a list of banned books that included translations of Soviet and classical Russian literature, Jewish literature, French and English literature after 1933 and Estonian authors who had supported Soviet power in 1940. Whereas the Soviets nationalised publishing houses, the Nazis tolerated private initiatives, although they closely monitored publishing activities. Preprint censorship was doubled as manuscripts had to be sent to the censorship office of the local Estonian government as well as to the German *Amt für Verlagswesen*, which in the case of translations also required that the original texts be provided. An analysis of censorship reviews and decisions show that even if the censors often required changes to the manuscripts that clearly diverged from Nazi worldview and aesthetic values, censorship under German occupation was overall less intrusive than Soviet censorship in the post-war Stalinist period (Möldre 2005a: 70–1).

7.7 Core Issues and Topics

As this historical reconstruction has shown, a core topic in the discussion of translation and censorship in Estonia is the multilingual setting of the country, and the interrelations between linguistic hierarchies and centres of power over the centuries. This was particularly evident in the early modern period, when different forces were engaged in a struggle for hegemony fought through reciprocal censorship of religious texts. Within the Swedish state, German-speaking Church officials reclaimed their right to translate the Bible into Estonian, making the different versions of the translation into tools for censorial intervention. Estonian peasants are absent from this constellation until the second half of the nineteenth century when the children of some of those peasants, having received their education in German, formed the vanguard of the Estonian national movement, producing highly manipulative translations of the works and the national-romantic culture of their landlords and colonisers with the aim of turning Estonian into a literary language and developing a national agenda. Tsarist censorship and policies of Russification were at this point caught in the crosshairs of the powerful Baltic German landlords and the increasing national and political self-awareness of Estonians. In Soviet censorship the relations between power and linguistic-cultural hierarchies were finally formalised through a policy of quotas for translated literature. A related issue here is the plurality and variety of instances of censorship that characterised Estonia until the end of the tsarist period. Only in the last years of the interwar Estonian Republic,

120

Translation and Censorship in the History of Estonia

and more intensely during the Soviet period, do we see evidence of a thorough centralisation of censorship under the full control of the state or party.

Another important issue that emerges from this historical overview is how to define translation broadly enough to include material of particular interest for the study of censorship, while maintaining its specificity in comparison with other writing practices. Contrary to Toury's idea that historical research should consider as a translation whatever texts are considered as such by the target culture (1985: 80), this chapter has adopted in some cases, such as that of nineteenth-century Estonian writers, an anachronistic view, considering as translations texts that were presented and read as originals at the time of their production. This allowed us to draw interesting conclusions on the strategies of adaptation and appropriation of foreign texts, their effect on censorship, and the space of negotiation between the author-translator and the censor.

Another issue that has emerged in this historical overview is the complexity of the notion of agency when dealing with translation and censorship. As Toury has observed, 'even in the case of the most prestigious translators [...] one can never be sure just how many hands were involved in the establishment of translation as we have it and who did what' (1995: 215). In other words, the agency of censorship in shaping a given translation product is often very difficult to determine. Censorship, more often than not, leaves no traces, as in the case of the Soviet censors who mainly communicated their decisions orally. Even in the presence of translation manuscripts with deletions and changes, we cannot in most cases tell who did what. Comparing translations with their source texts allows us to locate manipulations (omissions, changes, additions), but once again, this does not reveal who was responsible. The memoirs of people involved, correspondence between translators, editors and the censors, as well as recorded censorship decisions, when available, are the only sources that can assist researchers in reconstructing the specific contribution of the different agents involved in the translation process, although even these sources are not always completely trustworthy.

A final question here is whether the grip of censorship is looser on translations, which are a more peripheral part of the literary and cultural system, than on original literature, which occupies a more central and therefore influential position. The answer is that it is impossible to generalise. The translation of the Bible has been in Estonia, as in many other countries, a very important literary enterprise and the privileged target of censorship until the establishment of a canonical version; after the French Revolution, the tsarist state, frightened by the role foreign texts could play in the spread of dangerous ideas, developed a profound cultural xenophobia. In contrast, translation in the Soviet sixties became a less strictly censored, more liberal sphere, where translators could experiment with ideas and forms that only later entered original production.

7.8 New Debates

Recent debates on the role of censorship in translation have been inspired by the general critique of strongly dichotomous approaches (Tymoczko 2007) to the study of the relations between power and translation. It is not simply an issue of 'official culture vs counter-culture' and 'compliance vs resistance', given that the relations between coercive power and the different kinds of agency it shapes and influences are more complex than binary oppositions suggest (Monticelli and Lange 2014: 99).

Particularly in studies on the Soviet period (Baer 2015; Sherry 2012; Monticelli 2016a), this questioning of dichotomous approaches has shifted the attention of scholars from the destructive to the productive effect of censorship on translation practices and translated literature. In the case of Estonia, we have, on the one hand, the explicitly dissident activity of exiled translators, who sometimes translated books, for example Boris Pasternak's *Doctor Zhivago* in 1960, because they knew the translations would be banned in the Soviet Union, and then tried to smuggle them into Soviet Estonia. On the other hand, we have a whole series of accommo-dating practices which are, at the same time, a direct product of censorship and offer ways to circumvent it. A very well-known example is Aesopian language (Loseff 1984; Baer 2010), an allusive mode of expression that conceals under apparent conformism critical meanings and for which translations, with their constitutive 'double-voice', are particularly apt. Estonian scholar Peeter Torop (2012) has employed more broadly the concept of 'dissimilation in assimilation' to describe all the situations where apparent compliance with the requirements of censorship actu-ally allow translators and editors to develop their own agendas. For instance, in the mid-1970s Estonian literary scholars planned a series of translations of theoretical texts in order to advance literary studies. The initial plan was to begin with translations of Yuri Lotman, but given that he was officially a *persona non grata*, the first volume in the series was to be a collection of articles by Mikhail Bakhtin, who was a bit more acceptable because he did not live in Estonia. But even the Bakhtin collection could only be published after two books from ideologically orthodox Soviet literary scholars of little intellectual value, but included in the compulsory plan, had been translated. The desired publication of the translation of Lotman's work was finally achieved through a series of detours that can be considered the direct result of censor-ship. Another form of 'dissimilation in assimilation' was obtaining printing permission for the translation of problematic authors by framing them with forewords that established the 'correct' ideological interpretation of the translated work. While such productive understandings of the relationship between censorship and translation have recently been elaborated in the study of Soviet phenomena, they could be fruitfully extended to the study of other historical periods and cultural spaces.

Acknowledgements

This work was supported by the Estonian Research Council's grant PRG1206: 'Translation in History, Estonia 1850–2010: Texts, Agents, Institutions and Practices'.

Further Reading

Paatsi, Vello and Metste, Kristi (eds.). 2016. *Kas keelata või lubada. Tsensuur Rootsi ajast Eesti taasiseseisvumiseni* [*To Allow or to Prohibit? Censorship from the Swedish Times to the Regained Independence of Estonia (1991)*]. Tartu: Eesti Kirjandusmuuseum.
A series of essays on censorship in different periods of Estonian history with no specific focus on translation, but including some examples of censored translations.

Monticelli, Daniele and Lange, Anne. 2014. 'Translation and totalitarianism. The case of Soviet Estonia', *The Translator* 20(1): 95–111.
An overview of the relations between translation and power through the history of Soviet Estonia.

Monticelli, Daniele. 2016. 'Reconfiguring the Sensible through Translation: Patterns of "Deauthorisation" in Postwar Soviet Estonia', *Translation and Interpreting Studies*, 11(3): 416–35.
An analysis of the repressive and productive role of translation and censorship in the Sovietization of postwar Estonia.

Uno Liivaku and Meriste, Henno. 1975. *Kuidas seda tõlkida. Järeltormatusest eestinduseni* [*How to Translate. From Hasty Imitation to Proper Translation*]. Tallinn: Valgus.
A comprehensive though extremely synthetic history of translation in Estonia from the beginning of the six-teenth century to the 1970s.

References

Aarma, Liivi. 1995. 'Tsensuur ja kirjasõna Eestis 16.-17. Sajandil' [Censorship and Literature in Sixteenth-Seventeenth Century Estonia], in P. Lotman (ed.), *Uurimusi tsensuurist*. Tallinn: Eesti Rahvusraamatukogu, 8–64.

Baer, Brian J. 2010. 'Literary Translation in the Age of the Decembrists: The Birth of Productive Censorship in Russia', in D. Merkle, C. O'Sullivan, L. van Doorslaer and M. Wolf (eds.), *The Power of the Pen: Translation and Censorship in Nineteenth-Century Europe*. Vienna: LIT Verlag, 213–42.

Baer, Brian J. 2015. *Translation and the Making of the Modern Russian Literature*. London: Bloomsbury Academic.

Billiani, Francesca. 2007. 'Assessing Boundaries – Censorship and Translation. An Introduction', in F. Billiani (ed.), *Modes of Censorship of Translation. National Contexts and Diverse Media*. London and New York: Routledge, 1–26.

Bourdieu, Pierre. 1986. 'The Forms of Capital', in J. Richardson (ed.), *Handbook of Theory and Research for the Sociology of Education*. Westport: Greenwood, 241–58.

D'Annunzio, Gabriele. 1913. *Süütu* [*The Innocent*]. Translated by Villem Grünthal-Ridala. Tartu: Noor-Eesti Kirjastus.

Depman, Jaan (ed.). 1927. *Tagakiusamise aastatel. 1907–1916* [*Years of Persecution. 1907–1906*]. Leningrad: Eesti Kirjanduseloo ained Wene Isevalitsuse Ahiiwides.

Eesti Vabariigi Põhiseadus [*Constitution of the Estonian Republic*]. 1934. Tallinn: J. Ploompuu Krijastus.

Ehasalu, Epp, Habicht, Külli, Kingisepp, Valve-Liivi and Peebo, Jaak (eds.). 1997. *Eesti keele vanimad tekstid ja sõnastik* [*The Earliest Texts and Vocabularies in the Estonian Languages*]. Tartu: TÜ eesti keele õppetooli toimetised 6.

Hiedel, Lembe. 2006. 'Loomingu' Raamatukogu alaeast. Märkmeid ja meenutusi aastaist 1957–1973' [The Coming of Age of the Library of 'Looming'. Notes and Memoirs from the Years 1957–1973], in T. Kuusik and A. Saluäär (eds.), *Loomingu raamatukogu 50 aastat*. Tallinn: Kultuurileht, 159–203.

Issakov, Sergei. 1983. *Arhiivide peidikuist*. [Out of the hiding places of the archives] Tallinn: Eesti Raamat.

Jannsen, Johann Woldemar. 1862. 'Kirjawastused' [Answers to the letters of the readers], *Perno Postimees*, 58, 26 September 1862: 304.

Jansen, Ea. 2000. 'Tsaristlik tsensuur ja eesti ajakirjandus venestamisajal (1880–1890. aastad)' [Tsarist censorship and Estonian press in the period of Russification [1880s and 1990s], *Tuna*, 2: 42–60.

Kasekamp, Andres. 2010. *A History of the Baltic States*. London and New York: Palgrave Macmillan.

Kruus, Oskar. 1962. 'Kuidas tuli Majakovski Eestisse. Mõningad seoses olevaid kirjandusloolisi üksikküsimusi' [How did Mayakovski come to Estonia? Some related issues for literary history], *Keel ja Kirjandus*, 10: 577–90.

Loseff, Lev. 1984. *On the Beneficence of Censorship: Aesopian Language in Modern Russian Literature*. Munich: Otto Sagner.

Lotman, Piret. 2016. 'Varauusaegsete eestikeelsete luterlike katekismuste tsenseerimisest' [On the censorship of early modern Lutheran catechisms in Estonian], in V. Paatsi and K. Metste (eds.), *Kas keelata või lubada. Tsensuur Rootsi ajast Eesti taasiseseisvumiseni*. Tartu: Eesti Kirjandusmuuseum, 11–16.

Metste, Kristi. 2016. 'Õpetatud Eesti Selts hädas tsensor G. F. E. von Sahmeniga. F. R. Faehlmanni kaks kirja Liivimaa Provintsiaalkonsistooriumile' [The Estonian Learned Society in trouble with the censor G.F.E. Von Sahmen. Two letters by F.R. Faehlmann to the Provincial Consistory of Livonia], in V. Paatsi and K. Metste (eds.), *Kas keelata või lubada. Tsensuur Rootsi ajast Eesti taasiseseisvumiseni*. Tartu: Eesti Kirjandusmuuseum, 23–8.

Möldre, Aile. 2005a. *Kirjastustegevus ja raamatulevi Eestis aastail 1940–2000* [*Publishing Houses and Marketing of Books in Estonia from 1940 to 2000*]. Tallinn: TLÜ Kirjastus.

Möldre, Aile 2005b. 'Political Publications in Estonia during the Revolution of 1905–1907', in A. Maulina (ed.), *Starptautiska konference "Informācija, revolūcija, reakcija: 1905–2005*. Rīga: Latvijas Nacionālā bibliotēka, 51–8.

Möldre, Aile. 2012a. 'Ilukirjanduse tõlked 20. sajandi esimese poole Eesti ja Soome raamatutoodangus (1900–1940)' [Literary translations in Estonia and Finland in the first half of the twentieth century], *Methis. Studia humaniora Estonica*, 9/10: 88–101.

Möldre, Aile. 2012b. 'Kirjastamine ja raamatutoodang Eesti Vabariigis 1918–1940' [Publishing and Book Production in the Estonian Republic 1918–1940], in A. Ainz, *et al.* (eds.), *Eestikeelne raamat 1918–1940. I*. Tallinn: Eesti Rahvusraamatukogu, 27–41.

Möldre, Aile. 2019. 'Publishing Houses and Book Production in Estonia, 1918–1940', *Proceedings of the National Library of Latvia*, 24/4: 144–63.

The Routledge Handbook of Translation and Censorship

Monticelli, Daniele. 2016a. 'Reconfiguring the Sensible through Translation: Patterns of "Deauthorisation" in Postwar Soviet Estonia', *Translation and Interpreting Studies*, 11/3: 416–35.

Monticelli, Daniele. 2016b. '(Trans)forming National Images in Translation. The Case of the "Young Estonia" Movement', in P. Flynn, J. Leerssen and L. van Doorslaer (eds.), *Interconnecting Translation Studies and Imagology*. Amsterdam/Philadelphia: John Benjamins, 277–97.

Monticelli, Daniele. 2019. 'Born Translating: The Transn/lational Roots of Estonian National Identity', in L. Harmon and D. Osuchowska (eds.), *National Identity in Translation*. Bern: Peter Lang, 225–40.

Monticelli, Daniele. 2020. 'Translating the Soviet Thaw in the Estonian context: entangled perspectives on the book series *Loomingu Raamatukogu*', *Journal of Baltic Studies*, 51/3: 407–28.

Monticelli, Daniele and Lange, Anne. 2014. 'Translation and Totalitarianism. The Case of Soviet Estonia', *The Translator*, 20/1: 95–111.

Monticelli, Daniele, Peiker, Piret and Mits, Krista. 2018. 'Jamaicast Pariiisi ning sealt Tartusse tagasi. Lydia Koidula maailmavaatest ja mugandamisstrateegiatest tema saksa eeskujude valguses' [From Jamaica to Paris and back to Tartu. Lydia Koidula's worldview and adaptation strategies in the light of her German models], *Keel ja Kirjandus*, 12: 915–41.

Parts, Margit. 2003. *Tsensuur ja infopoliitika esimese eesti vabariigi ajal* [*Censorship and Information Policy in the first Estonian Republic*]. Diplomitöö. Tallinn: Tallinna Pedagoogika Ülikool.

Paatsi, Vello. 2014. 'Kui Liivimaa ajakirjandus tsenseeriti Riias' [When the Livonian press was censored in Riga], *Keel ja Kirjandus*, 4: 284–90.

Paatsi, Vello. 2015. 'Miks eestikeelsete trükiste tsensuur kolis 1869. aastal Riiga?' [Why did the censorship of Estonian literature move to Riga in 1869], *Keel ja Kirjandus*, 7: 497–99.

Paul, Toomas. 1999. *Eesti piiblitõlke ajalugu. Esimestest katsetest kuni 1999. aastani* [*The History of the Translation of the Bible into Estonian. From the First Attempts to 1999*]. Tallinn: Emakeele Selts.

Priidel, Endel. 2010. *Vägikaikavedu ehk vaim ja võim (1940–1990)* [*The Struggle between Power and Culture (1940–1990)*]. Tallinn: Eesti Keele Sihtasutus.

Raag, Raimo. 1999. 'One plus one equals one: the forging of Standard Estonian', *International Journal of the Sociology of Language*, 139: 17–38.

Reimo, Tiiu. 2001. *Raamatukultuur Tallinnas 18. sajandi teisel poolel* [*Book Culture in Tallinn in the Second Half of the Nineteenth Century*]. Tallinn: TPÜ Kirjastus.

Ross, Kristiina (ed.). 2007. *Põhjaeestikeelsed Uue Testamendi tõlked 1680–1705* [*The Northern-Estonian Translations of the New Testament 1680–1705*]. Tallinn: Eesti Keele Sihtasutus.

Saareste, Andrus. 1930. 'Wandfadt-Kõlli katekismuse keelest' [On the Wandfadt-Kõlli's catechism], *Äratrükk Eesti Keelest*, 4-5: 1–24.

Salu, Herbert. 1965. *Tuul üle mere ja muid lühiuurimusi eesti kirjandusest* [*The Wind from across the Sea and Other Essays on Estonian Literature*]. Stockholm: Kirjastus Vaba Eesti.

Salupere, Malle. 1991. 'Pudemeid tsensuurikorraldusest vene tsaaririigi päevil' [Fragments on censorship at the times of the Russian Empire], in P. Lotman (ed.), *Eesti Rahvusraamatukogu toimetised* 2. Tallinn: Eesti Rahvusraamatukogu, 8–22.

Salupere, Malle. 2016. 'Vene tsensuuriseadustest ja tsensoritest ning eesti (aja)kirjandusest Jannseni(te) ja Jakobsoni päevil' [On Russian censorship and censors and the Estonian press at the times of Jannsen and Jakobson], in V. Paatsi and K. Metste (eds.), *Kas keelata või lubada. Tsensuur Rootsi ajast Eesti taasiseseisvumiseni*. Tartu: Eesti Kirjandusmuuseum, 35–39.

Sherry, Samantha. 2012. *Censorship in Translation in the Soviet Union in the Stalin and Khrushchev Eras*. PhD diss., University of Edinburgh.

Tafenau, Kai. 2011. *Uue Testamendi tõlkimisest Rootsi ajal: käsikirjad, tõlkijad ja eesti kirjakeel* [*On the translation of the New Testament during the Swedish Period: Manuscripts, Translators and the Estonian Written Language*]. Tartu: Tartu Ülikooli Kirjastus.

Tammer, Enno. 2014. *Punatsensuur mälestuses, tegelikkuses, reeglites* [*Red Censorship in Memoirs, Reality and Regulations*]. Tallinn: Tammeraamat.

Torop, Peeter. 2012. 'Dissimilation in Assimilation', in *Translating Power, Empowering Translation: Itineraries in Translation History (Abstracts of the Conference Held in May 24–26, Tallinn)*. Tallinn: Tallinn University Press.

Toury, Gideon. 1985. 'A Rationale for Descriptive Translation Studies', in T. Hermans (ed.), *The Manipulation of Culture. Studies in Literary Translation*. London and Sydney: Croom Helm, 16–41.

Toury, Gideon. 1995. *Descriptive Translation Studies and Beyond*. Amsterdam/Philadelphia: John Benjamins.

Tymoczko, Maria. 2007. *Enlarging Translation, Empowering Translators*. Manchester: St. Jerome Publishing.

Veskimägi, Kaljo-Olev. 1996. *Nõukogude unelaadne elu. Tsensuur Eesti NSV-s ja tema peremehed* [*The Sleepy Life of the Soviets. Censorship and Its Masters in the Soviet Socialist Republic of Estonia*]. Tallinn: Raamatutrükikoda.

Weiss, Hellmuth and Johansen, Paul. 1956. *Esimene eesti raamat anno 1535. Wanradt-Koell'i katekismus 1535. aastal* [*The first Estonian Book. The Wanradt-Koell's Catechism from the Year 1535*]. New York: The Guinn Company.

8

CENSORSHIP AND TRANSLATION IN HISPANIC SOUTH AMERICA

The First Translation of the Declaration of the Rights of Man and of the Citizen

Álvaro Echeverri

8.1 Introduction

The political and social ideas associated with the Enlightenment filtered furtively throughout the Spanish Empire during the eighteenth century. Although they did not circulate as freely in the Spanish territories as they did in Europe or in North America, the liberal ideologies that had already transformed the political and social landscape in Europe were certainly present in Spain. Among them was the will to reconsider the principle of a social contract in which the people accept the rules imposed by monarchs in exchange for security and welfare. In England, the failure of monarchs to fulfill their part of the contract and the arbitrary nature of the social organization were denounced by philosophers such as John Locke. In France, the need for a new social contract was actively disseminated by, among others, Montesquieu, but mostly by Rousseau. The new political organization was based on the need to protect the natural rights of people and on the acceptance that human beings are basically motivated by self-interest. In Spain, political and religious censorship prevented the free circulation of books written by authors associated with ideas that inspired the English Reformation and the French Revolution. Nevertheless, these books were read by influential members of the Spanish political and religious elites. Their contents were discussed at social gatherings as they made their way into periodical publications, on many occasions in the form of reported speech. As novel textual products, periodicals were able for some time to avoid the controlling censorial power of the Inquisition and Spanish civil authorities.

In the Spanish American colonies, the new class of merchants and landowning *Criollos* (people of European descent born in the Americas), whose descendants were to change the political fate of the continent in the first half of the nineteenth century, had become familiar with Enlightenment ideas. Censorship was instrumental in slowing, but not stopping, the free circulation of the economic, political and philosophical ideas that had fueled the independence movement in the United States and the French Revolution. At the core of these two major historical events was the need to promote and protect the natural rights of citizens. It is not a coincidence that both historical events were supported by the drafting of a declaration of rights: the Virginia Declaration of the Rights

126

DOI: 10.4324/9781003149453-11

of Man (1776) in the United States and the French Declaration of the Rights of Man and of the Citizen (1789) in France.

8.2 Historical Perspectives: Historiography as Rewriting

The writing of history and translation represent forms of rewriting and, as such, are influenced by the cultural systems in which the historians and translators evolve. Putting aside cultural determinism, human beings are exposed in their lifetime to the narratives and discourses promoted by the culture in which they are immersed:

> [...] culture consists of whatever it is one has to know or believe in order to operate in a manner acceptable to its members, and to do so in any role that they accept for any one of themselves.
>
> (Goodenough 1964: 36; cited by Nord 2018: 32)

This definition of culture is linked to the idea of a 'complex system of systems' (Levefere 2016: 11). Education, economy, religion, politics, literature, translation and history could be seen as subsystems of that culture. The interaction among the subsystems is determined by the 'logic of the culture' to which they belong (Lefevere 2016: 11). In other words, the subsystems of a culture are related. For example, it should be possible to observe how the religious systems influence artistic values and practices. The educational system could also be affected by the political choices made by the members of the culture. Likewise, translation practices and ideas about translation are likely to be affected by the cultural system in which they are produced. In line with Lefevere's work, this chapter refers to the concept of system to explore how the locus of control of the Spanish Empire influenced the social practices related to the dissemination of knowledge by means of translation and historiography as modes of rewriting. In the translation of political and philosophical texts during the last decades of Spanish rule in Hispanic America, the locus of system control was both internal and external. Typically, the professionals within the system represent the internal locus of control. In South America the professionals were politicians, administrative authorities, editors, political philosophers and members of the clergy, who, based on their expertise, decided which political ideas and text genres corresponded to the shared values of the professionals' community. Members of the *criollo* elite made up an important part of this group of professionals who exerted control over the system. The second locus of control is external and refers to the people and to the institutions that have the power to promote or to forbid the free circulation of ideas, practices and texts. In the case of colonial Spain, this power was held both by the Government and by the Spanish Inquisition and was applied in both the European and Hispanic American territories. Censorship practices in the first years of Spanish colonization focused on destroying everything that was different to Spanish culture. The Aztecs and the Mayas had sophisticated systems of written communication in the form of pictograms drawn either on Aztec paper, called *amatle,* made from the inner bark of a certain tree, or drawn on animal skins. In these texts, called *codices*, the Indigenous peoples recorded their history, their wars and the lives of some members of their ruling classes. Just as Islamic manuscripts were burned in Granada by Cardinal Francisco de Cisneros in 1499, Aztec books and idols were burned in Texcoco in 1530 by order of the first bishop of Mexico, Juan de Zumárraga. In 1562, Diego de Landa did the same with Mayan books in Maní, in the Yucatán Peninsula (Báez 2004). The same kind of censorship befell artistic forms such as theatre in the time of the Aztecs. Hence, the Spanish censorship strategy during the first two centuries of colonization aimed mainly at the superposition of Spanish culture over the

Indigenous culture, rather than on the censorship of religious or artistic manifestations that were contrary to the Catholic faith. The best example of this strategy was the construction in the sixteenth century of the City of Mexico over the ruins of the ancient Aztec capital (Báez 2004). In doing so, the Spanish not only took over the land, but they also erased the history of the Indigenous peoples. Writing the history of translation has unwittingly adopted chronologies that cover this epistemicide (or the destruction of a knowledge system) (Santos 2015: 149). According to those chronologies, the history of translation in America started in 1492. However, we know that many of the Indigenous peoples that inhabited and transformed the continent before the arrival of the Europeans did not live in isolation. Rather, they interacted for commercial and other reasons, and did not share the same language. As a result, they would have necessarily had recourse to different forms of translation (Valdeón 2014: 18). The object of censorship varied in the first centuries of the colony. From the beginning of the sixteenth century, the Spanish religious authorities had the double task of converting the Indigenous populations in the new territories to the Catholic faith and keeping a watchful eye on the influence of Protestantism. The Reformation coincided with the invention of the printing press and Protestants had always made good use of printed materials to circulate their message. According to Henry Kamen (2014: 118),

> [...] the diffusion of the printing press in Europe at the end of the fifteenth century revolutionized the art of communication, made it cheaper and easier to produce and distribute works, and facilitated the spread of both news and ideas.

During the so-called Age of Enlightenment, Spanish religious zealots expelled Muslims and Jews from Castile, burned the written history of the indigenous peoples of Hispanic America and worked to keep the Protestant faith outside the Spanish realm. The 'Age of Revolution (1760–1850)' (Uribe-Urán 2000: 426) was a time of scientific, economic, social, political and cultural changes that had important repercussions in the Spanish territories in America. The Spanish colony, like Spain itself, was not as prolific as some European countries in their contributions to the scientific advances that made possible, for example, the industrial revolution that took place in England. Nor had they undergone through the political and social changes that transformed France into a republic in the last quarter of the eighteenth century. Outwardly, Spain was rather closed to the scientific advancements made by its European neighbours. Those who wanted to learn about the developments of their contemporaries had to find a way to import the knowledge without arousing the ire of the religious zealots. They did by travelling and reading books which contents they later imported into Spain in the form of comments and reported speech. That was one of the strategies to which Spanish translators most frequently resorted to avoid censorship. And, as we will see in the next section, that was also a strategy used by translators in Hispanic America as their readership had to be convinced that there was nothing contrary to the Catholic faith in the translations.

8.3   Core Issues and Topics

8.3.1   Political Censorship: the Spanish Monarchy

In Spain, the first pragmatic sanction drafted by the King and Queen of Castile was issued in 1502 (Kamen 2014: 118). From that moment on, all of those who wished to print or to import books into the realm had to obtain a license from the regional religious authorities. However, after learning about the presence of Protestants in Castile, in 1558, a decree was issued to prohibit the printing of books outside of Spain. The printed materials were to be censored before and after publication.

Any infringement of this ruling was to be punished with death and confiscation. However, no one was executed as punishment for reading, possessing or trading foreign printed materials (Kamen 2014: 120). In fact, as Kamen demonstrates in his study, the legislation drafted to control the circulation of printed documents was of little help in preventing books from entering Spain. Those who wanted to obtain books about astrology, alchemy and the sciences could do so without much difficulty or risk thanks to the impossibility of fully controlling all ports and border crossings. At that time, those who could read were also the ones who could travel between countries or who could have books brought to them by travelling acquaintances.

8.3.2   Religious Censorship: the Inquisition

The Inquisition is a recurring topic in historical studies of censorship in the Spanish context. The goal of the Inquisition was to protect the Catholic community from the 'malicious' forces presented by other religious manifestations. Threats changed with the passing of time and with the cultural and scientific advances of societies. Thus, in the first years of its inception in Spain, the Inquisition served the religious authorities by persecuting, prosecuting and converting Jews and Muslims in Europe, as well as expelling them. The Inquisition's task was fundamental to converting new subjects to the Catholic faith, as well as bolstering the economic might of the Spanish empire and its alliance with the Vatican. In 1493, Pope Alexander VI issued the Papal Bull '*Inter Caetera*' giving exclusive rights to Spain over the territories discovered by Christopher Columbus. The Bull stated explicitly that any land that was not occupied by Christians was to be claimed and exploited, and that the non-Christians should be converted to the Catholic faith. Also known as the 'Doctrine of Discovery', this is the same principle invoked by other 'civilized' European monarchies to dispossess Indigenous peoples in Africa, America and Asia of their ancestral lands. The Monroe doctrine, which followed in the Expansion of the United States of America to the West in the nineteenth century, also invoked the 'Doctrine of Discovery'.

8.3.3   Circulation of Non-literary Texts in Imperial Spain and its American Colony

As historian Richard Herr points out, the Benedictine monk Benito Gerónimo Feijóo (1676–1764): '[…] almost single-handedly kindled the flame that was to arouse Spain from the intellectual slumber into which it had fallen at the end of the seventeenth century' (Herr 1958: 37). Feijóo defended the idea that Spain did not need any more books on religion because it had already produced some of the best works on that matter in the world. He also argued that modern science was not necessarily contrary to religion. Taking such a stand, Feijóo knew he risked prosecution from his fellow clergyman and, as insurance, he obtained the support of King Fernando VI in the form of a royal order prohibiting refutations to his writings. The case of this Benedictine monk is relevant to the history of translation censorship because his works are proof of the translation practices that were being applied at a time when many of the works of authors associated either with contemporary political and scientific revolutions were banned in Spain. An examination of his writings reveals that Feijóo had firsthand knowledge of Descartes' philosophical ideas, which Feijóo opposes to scholasticism, declaring that the former should take the place of the latter in the education of young Spaniards. Whereas the works of the French philosophers Montesquieu, Voltaire and Rousseau, among others, were closely monitored by Spanish censors, Feijóo was proposing that instead of Latin, young Spaniards should be learning French. Lafarga and Garrosa

García's (2004) analysis found that many of the documents used as documentary sources by Feijóo had French as the source language. Among Feijóo's main works were *Teatro crítico universal* and *Discursos varios en todo género de materias para desengaño de errores communes* [Critical Universal Theatre Various Discourses in all Kinds of Subjects, to Disillusion Common Errors]; the first of its eight volumes was published in 1726 and the last one in 1739. Feijóo's intellectual activity extended to conducting scientific research. He was a recognised expert on Francis Bacon's empiricist epistemology, and he insisted that controlled experimentation and observation should be implemented, particularly in medical research. Inspired by Bacon's ideas on how to do science, he sought a way to overcome '[…] exaggerated devotion to the saints and false religious miracles, and he especially belaboured superstitions' (Herr 1958: 39). The reception of Feijoo's *Teatro Crítico* and his other major work, *Cartas eruditas,* was very positive and his writings were reprinted several times. By 1786, his works had been reprinted fifteen times. The only work that was more popular than Feijoo's at the time was *Don Quixote* (Herr 1958: 40). The Benedictine monk was a noteworthy and interesting agent of translation. First, he practised a kind of indirect translation in which he, the 'translator', read the texts of Descartes in French or Bacon in English. He then rewrote the ideas he took from the source texts in the form of explanations and commentaries. He essentially took the ideas from the source texts that supported his own arguments. Second, as shown by Lafarga and García Garrosa (2004) in their anthology about the discourse on translation in the eighteenth century, Feijóo translated passages, but he does not appear to have translated a complete book. He always took what he considered worth translating from source texts because of the knowledge they contained. Third, like other translators, Feijóo wrote introductions, prefaces, dedications, translator notes, translator warnings, and other paratext, in which he proclaimed that his motivation to translate was to serve his country and countrymen; Lafarga and García Garrosa (2004: 60) collected 139 paratexts authored by Feijóo. Like other translators, Feijóo was motivated by a desire to inform and, in most cases, to educate. Fourth, Feijóo, like many other eighteenth-century Spanish translators, was aware of the prohibition to own, to trade and, of course, to translate the works of those authors who were considered responsible for the philosophical thought that set the stage for the French Revolution. A case in point is Diderot's *Encyclopedia,* which was banned by the Inquisition in 1759. In 1775 Pedro Martinez de Campomanes y Pérez, an important member of the government under King Charles III, recommended the translation of some articles of the *Encyclopedia* provided that passages contrary to Spanish values be censored (Herr 1958: 53). Many of the ideas of the 'Age of Revolution' in relation to science, economy and philosophy circulated rather freely, initially, among those who had access to books, who could either discuss the contents of those texts in social gatherings (*tertulias*) or read extracts taken from them in the growing number of journals that started to circulate in Spain at the time. *El Diario de Madrid* and *El Correo de Madrid* were two periodicals, among others, that circulated scientific information. Other periodicals informed their readers about progress in science, political economy and philosophy in other parts of Europe. In 1787, the weekly *Correo literario de la Europa*, a journal printed by the Royal press, was replaced by the journal *Espíritu de los mejores diarios literarios que se publican en Europa,* a privately edited journal. These periodicals were used as a 'Trojan horse' to publish extracts taken from banned books. The journals as such were not prohibited. Herr establishes that the main European economic theories of the time, i.e., mercantilism, liberalism and the principles of the physiocrats (who advocated for an increase in exports and in tax imports), were circulating in Spanish translation among the nobility. He quotes an article published in the *Espíritu de los mejores diarios que se publican en Europa* in which a contributor claims:

Censorship and Translation in Hispanic South America

[...] to have been at a *tertulia* or evening social gathering at the home of 'Marqués de N' where there occurred what evidently presents a typical Spanish discussion of economics. The names of Ulloa, Ustariz, Campomanes, and other Spanish economists were bandied about with those of the French mercantilists Colbert, the Marquis de Vauban, and 'Neker' (Jacques Necker), the physiocrats Mirabeau and 'La Riviere,' and the enemies of both groups, The Abbé Raynal et Simon Linguet.

(Herr 1958: 56)

Concerning political economy, the circulation in Spain of the ideas espoused by Adam Smith in his *An Inquiry into the Nature of the Wealth of Nations* (1776) in the last quarter of the eighteenth century is of the upmost importance for the discussion because *The Wealth of Nations* can rightly be considered the 'bible of capitalism'. The most elemental principles in Smith's theory are that the search for personal profit motivates every person to contribute to the wealth of the nation, that there is an invisible hand that regulates the market, and that the basic role of the government is to create and protect an environment that will lead to the country's prosperity. It is well documented that Spaniards on both sides of the Atlantic were familiar with the *Wealth of Nations* in its original version in English or its French translations. The first Spanish translation of Smith's book was the work of José Alonso Ortiz; it was published in 1794 (Smith 1957: 105). The founding principle of Adam Smith's ideas is that the state must protect the right to property and to accumulate capital, and that it is the role of the courts to protect the rights of the citizens. These were the kinds of ideas that were discussed at the social gatherings of the Spanish nobility and published in the journals of the time. The circulation of prohibited books and the ideas they conveyed was confirmed in cases brought before the Inquisition. In 1778, the Spanish inquisition condemned Pablo de Olavide y Jauregui, a prominent lawyer and politician of Peruvian origin for reading prohibited books, for corresponding with Voltaire and Rousseau, and for embracing the philosophy of Diderot's *Encyclopedia*. Herr (1958: 78) reports the following:

A royal councilor who witnessed the reading of Olavide's sentence was so impressed by the ceremony that he confessed to the Inquisition to having read Voltaire, Rousseau, Hobbes, Spinoza, D'Alembert, Diderot, and other prohibited authors. In order to obtain absolution, he was forced to name all other persons he knew who were also reading such works. He gave a detailed list including Aranda, Campomanes, Floridablanca, Almódovar, and other government officials too prominent for the Inquisition to risk troubling.

Issues of *El Diario de Madrid*, *El Correo de Madrid* and *Espíritu de los mejores diarios que se publican en Europa* found their way into the Spanish colonies in America where a similar kind of intellectual effervescence was also taking shape with the emergence of a public sphere. As was the case in Spain, *tertulias* were also popular in the colonies.

The first journal to be printed in the Spanish colonies in America was the *Gazeta de Mexico* in 1722. Many more journals were created in cities like Guatemala, The Habana, Santa Fe de Bogotá, Lima, Buenos Aires before the end of the eighteenth century. The main objective of these journals was to spread new practical knowledge on health, education, technology, industry and agriculture. However, the periodical publications also informed their readers about history, philosophy and literature. Works of literature were translated and presented in many cases in abridged or synthetised form (Rodríguez 1998: 54). The first journals, such as the *Gazeta de Mexico,* were created by representatives of the church, who were able to work under relative freedom of the

The Routledge Handbook of Translation and Censorship

press. Censorship was certainly applied but only sporadically and in a rather inconsistent way. As happens with new inventions and technologies, the novelty of periodicals allowed them to circulate rather freely because no legislation had yet been drafted to control them. Printers, however, had to be very careful not to publish any content that was contrary to the Catholic faith. As in Spain, many writings that could be considered revolutionary found their way into the pages of the journals either as summaries, as quotes, or as paraphrased material.

Until the eighteenth century, most of the population was illiterate, and so the transfer of political, cultural and religious knowledge was done mostly via the spoken word. Social gatherings, the *tertulias*, among friends and family of the upper layers of society offered a possibility to discuss current news despite state control; concepts like freedom of religion and freedom of speech were difficult to put into practice. Even personal privacy was controlled by the authorities (Uribe-Urán 2000: 428). The *tertulias*, as with the case of the printing press, became a source of concern for the colonial authorities who witnessed a growing number of uprisings in the different regions of the colony led by heterogenous segments of the population: Indigenous peoples, slaves and even members of the upper class. In 1794, in Santa Fe de Bogotá, a group of young men belonging to the *Criollo* aristocracy, most of them lawyers-to-be, were accused of organizing secret meetings to conspire against the authorities, posting subversive posters in public places, and translating the *Declaration of the Rights of Man and of the Citizen*.

By the late seventeenth century, the most important advances in science, economics, philosophy and politics were being made by the English and the Dutch, and their books were quickly brought to the attention of the Inquisition; by this time, however, the institution had already lost most of its power to deter. Therefore, even though the scientific revolution associated with the Age of Reason and the Enlightenment threatened the Catholic faith and Spanish cultural values, any condemnation emanating from the authorities risked being considered as an arbitrary act. Foreign books had been entering the realm on both sides of the Atlantic, and the ideas and knowledge they conveyed had been discussed in public gatherings giving rise to a public sphere. Of course, it was translators who provided access to these foreign works through their translations.

A highly significant text for eighteenth century Hispanic America was the Declaration of the Rights of Man and of the Citizen (17 articles), drafted on 26 August 1789, by the General Assembly of the French Revolution. On December 13 of that year, the Tribunal of the Inquisition of Cartagena promulgated an edict banning the circulation of the document in the colony. By 1790, in the aftermath of the French Revolution, this edict enabled Spanish authorities to tighten their control over printed materials originating in France.

8.3.4 The First Translation into Spanish of the Declaration of the Rights of Man and of the Citizen

Nevertheless, a translation was made in Santa Fe de Bogotá, Colombia, on 15 December 1793. At that time, the colony was going through a social transformation triggered by the emergence of a public sphere (Uribe-Urán 2000), that is, the emergence of social practices that moved discussions from private residences into public spaces. This social displacement was provoked by the circulation of periodicals and the spread of *tertulias*, public social gatherings. In these two forms of communication, the literate (*letrados*) segment of society found a space to share and discuss literary texts, news, and other kinds of information from both the metropolis and foreign countries. In the *tertulias* and through hearsay, many of the ideas of the time trickled down from the people who had access to the sources of information (i.e., periodicals and books) and could read and travel, to those who were unable to read or travel. It was in this context that the *Declaration of the Rights of Man and of the Citizen* drafted by French revolutionaries fell into the hands of the *Criollo* Antonio Nariño. The translator had found the original text in the third volume of *Histoire de la Révolution de 1789, et de l'établissement d'une constitution en France. Précédée de l'exposé rapide des administrations successives qui ont déterminé cette révolution mémorable. Par deux amis de la liberté* [History of the Revolution of 1789, and of the Establishment of a Constitution in France. Preceded by a Brief Exposition of the successive Administrations that Determined this Memorable Revolution]. The book was published in Paris in 1790 and its authors were F.M. de Kerversau and G. Clavelin.

Antonio Nariño was the son of an official accountant born in Galicia, Spain. His mother was the daughter of a former professor at the University of Salamanca, who was also an *Oidor*, an ordinary judge in civil cases at the time of the colony. As a child, Nariño did not enjoy good health. Consequently, he was mostly educated by private tutors at home. Biographers of Nariño often highlight that he spent most of his childhood at home immersed in his father's books. At sixteen, he enrolled in the Spanish army organised to thwart the *Comuneros* insurrection, which was the most important popular uprising against the Spanish government in Nueva Granada before the wars of independence. The execution of some of the leaders of this insurrection was deeply felt by Nariño and he asked to be discharged from the army. Thanks to his family's social standing, he was able to occupy several intermediate positions in the government. He was adjunct mayor (*alcalde de Segundo voto*) and interim treasurer of the tithes *(tesorero de diezmos)* of the Viceroyalty of Nueva Granada, a position that was directly controlled by the political authorities. Nariño was appointed to the position by the Viceroy. After the death of his father, he became a prosperous merchant of, among other things, quinine, tobacco and leather. He later became a book trader and printer. He is now considered a pioneer of journalism in Colombia. In 1791, Nariño imported a printing press and two years later he founded the second printing company, which he called '*The Patriótica*' [The Patriotic]. It was here that he printed, in December 1793, the first Spanish translation of the *Declaration of the Rights of Man and of the Citizen*. On 19 and 20 August 1794, a set of subversive posters was hung in Bogotá. The act was harshly punished by the authorities. Nariño was associated with this seditious act and was prosecuted specifically for having translated the *Declaration of the Rights of Man and of the Citizen*. Nariño was found guilty and sentenced. All his possessions and properties were confiscated. The list of his books drawn up by the authorities included, among Greek, Latin and Spanish classics, Feijóo's *Teatro crítico universal*, books on economics and philosophy, and many books on practical knowledge related to chemistry, geography, medicine, mineralogy and physics. In addition, a set of 'seditious' books was confiscated from the Capuchin monastery in Santa Fe de Bogotá. According to the authorities, the books belonged to Nariño, who used to lend them to a member of the religious community. They were written by authors such as Baron d'Holbach, Montaigne, Montesquieu, the Abbot Raynal, George Robertson, and Voltaire. In 1795, he was sent to prison in Spain. He managed to escape and, like many of his fellow *Criollos* before and after him, traveled throughout Europe to Madrid, Paris and London in order to garner support for colonial independence. In 1796, he returned to New Granada and was incarcerated until 1803 when he was freed because of health issues. In 1808, Napoleon invaded Spain and appointed his brother Joseph as the new king. In opposition to the French invader, an insurrection formed and the revolutionaries created what was called *Juntas de gobierno* (a group of individuals who take control of the government for the administration of a community, in this case, provincial governments). Emissaries were sent to the Latin American provinces. In 1809, the Spanish authorities in Quito (Ecuador) were ousted and a *Junta de gobierno* was created. Fearing a similar fate, the authorities in Santa fe de Bogotá decided to imprison Nariño again in Cartagena de Indias because he had been seen in the company of an emissary sent from Spain. On 20 July 1810, the viceroy in Santa fe de Bogotá was overthrown and the declaration of independence from Spain, and the French invaders, was promulgated. Six months later, Nariño returned to the capital and was named secretary of the new congress. Opposed to the federalist principles of the congress, he decided to express his political ideas in his own periodical *The Bagatela* (1811–1812). His argument won the day and he became the president of the province of Cundinamarca. Nariño became a general in the patriotic army and played a key a role in the war of independence. The image of Nariño is omnipresent in Colombian numismatics, philately and toponymy. The official residency of the Colombian president in Bogotá is called La Casa de Nariño (Nariño's House), which epitomises the place of Antonio Nariño in the history of Colombia. The case of Nariño, the translator, and his prosecution are very particular. Not a single original copy of his translation has survived. The translation was reproduced by Nariño in 1811 and attached to a request for financial compensation from the government of Santa Fe de Bogota. The accessible digitalised translation is housed in the Colombian National Library.[1] No other important translations to his credit have been identified. He was brought to justice by the Real Audiencia for the crime of clandestine translation, publication and the dissemination of a paper entitled: 'Derechos del Hombre y del Ciudadano'. Even his prosecutors at the time were unable to find a single copy of the text because the translator admitted to having burned all the copies he had printed. In his defense, Nariño and his lawyer produced a text of 124 maxims, which was more than forty pages long. The accused admitted that he had translated the text because in his opinion nothing in it was contrary to the Catholic religion or the Spanish government '[…] traté de hacer ver que mi intención, cuando imprimí el papel del que se me hace cargo, no era criminal' [I tried to demonstrate that there was nothing criminal in my intention to print the paper in question] (Guerrero and Wiesner 2015: 177). The translator argued that the principles exposed in the Declaration were of common knowledge and very well-known to the public since they had already been published in the journals that were imported from Spain. In other words, there was nothing illegal in the translation.

The document that Nariño and his lawyer produced for the trial was considered by the authorities to be more inflammatory than the translation itself. In his argument, Nariño tried to explain that the translator is not to blame for the content of the source text. He was trying to dissociate himself from any responsibility for the ideas conveyed in the translation by arguing that the fault was to be found in the source text. In order words, the translator was merely reporting what the source text said.

> […] si el papel que imprimí es tan malo como yo no pensé jamás, si es seductor, si es execrable, se examine su malicia por él mismo, pues existe el original, […]
> [...] I never thought that the paper I printed was pernicious, if it is tempting, if it is execrable, its malice can be examined in the text itself, for the original exists [...].
>
> (Guerrero and Wiesner 2015: 183)

In his trial, the accused translator argued that the form in which the source text was written and its title cleared him of any crime. The paper was written in the form of precepts, the title was *'Los Derechos del hombre'* [The Rights of Man], and was published by the French National Assembly. In his defense, the translator argued:

> todo hombre que sea capaz de leerlo, sabe que la Asamblea Nacional de Francia no tiene derechos ni facultad de imponer preceptos a las demás naciones, por consiguiente cualquiera que lea el papel, suponiéndolo lleno de errores, no ve en él otra cosa que los errores que la Asamblea Nacional de Francia ha preceptuado a la nación de Francia, […]
>
> (Guerrero and Wiesner 2015: 184)

Censorship and Translation in Hispanic South America

[Those who can read it know that the French National Assembly does not have any right or power to impose its precepts on other nations. Consequently, anyone who reads the paper and assumes that it is full of mistakes, will see only the mistakes that the French General Assembly has imposed on the French nation].

Clearly, the translator is attempting to distance himself from the content of the text by declaring that, because it was explicitly written by the French General Assembly and addressed to the French people, any of the principles it contained applied only to the French nation. According to him, any good reader could see and understand this. The translator also contended that the principles published in the declaration were circulating freely in Spain so the French document could not be judged pernicious. He added that if he had a copy of the Declaration to which to refer, he could trace all its principles in books that were available in the colony. To prove that the precepts included in the Declaration were already known to all Spaniards on both sides of the Atlantic, he quoted *El Espíritu de los mejores diarios*.

Teniendo que citar autores latinos o extranjeros, que anden en manos de todos, para no interrumpir el discurso con relatos de otra lengua, los pondré traducidos. *El Espíritu de los mejores diarios*, obra publicada en Madrid, y que aquí anda en manos hasta de los niños y las mujeres, trae pasajes que no solo comprenden los principios del papel, sino otros de mayor entidad, teniendo al frente entre sus suscriptores, a nuestros augustos monarcas y principales ministros de la Nación.

(Guerrero and Wiesner 2015: 186)

[As I must quote Latin and foreign authors whose writings are available to everyone, and to avoid interrupting my speech with quotations from other languages, I will translate them. *El Espíritu de los mejores diarios*, a periodical published in Madrid, is available even to women and children and includes passages of greater value than those contained in the Declaration. Among its subscribers are our monarchs and the nation's most important ministers.]

He then acknowledged having burned the copies of the translated text.

aún no sé si he cometido un delito en imprimirle. Pero en quemarle si hice acto de virtud, y di una prueba relevante de mis buenos sentimientos y de mi amor al Rey, al gobierno y a la patria.

(Guerrero and Wiesner 2015: 206)

[I still do not know if I committed a crime by printing it. But by burning it I acted virtuously, and I proved my good feelings for and love of the King, the government and the country.]

The severity of the sentence he and his alleged co-conspirators received became a turning point in the relations between the *Criollo* elite and the Spanish authorities in the colonies because of the blatant discriminatory treatment to which the *Criollos* had been subjected. The alleged misconduct would not have been punished, it was believed, had the 'culprits' been influential European Spaniards. Just as Feijóo and other Spanish translators had tried to separate political and religious values in Spain, research into the history of translation at the time of independence reveals that

Hispanic American translators also tried to separate political and religious values. In one of the most influential translations of the time, Manuel García de Sena's *La independencia de la Costa Firme justificada por Thomas Paine treinta años há. Extracto de sus obras traducido del inglés al español por D. Manuel Garcia de Sena* [The Independence of Costa Firme as Justified by Thomas Paine Thirty Years Ago. Selections from his Works Translated from English into Spanish by Mr. Manuel García de Sena] (1811), the translator explicitly states in a letter addressed to his brother and attached to the translation that not a single word contrary to the Catholic religion can be found in his text. In Argentina, Mariano Moreno used a similar strategy in his translation of Jean-Jacques Rousseau's *Social Contract* when he omitted chapter VIII of book IV about civil religion. The translator considered that Rousseau's position on religion was contrary to the Catholic faith and censured the chapter (Eiris 2014: 109).

8.4 New Debates

The historiography of translation provides an opportunity to contribute to changing the misconception that the history of Hispanic America started in 1492 with the arrival of Christopher Columbus (see, for example, Bastin and Echeverri 2004; Bastin et al. 2004, 2010). In addition, digitalised documents have expanded the documentary corpus to provide new research material on censorship and translation.

The study of censorship and translation reveals the influential role of journals printed in Spain, such as *El Espíritu de los Mejores Diarios que se publican en Europa,* on the people who led the emancipation movement in Hispanic America. For example, Nariño not only referred to the periodical, he also added that it was available to everyone, including government officials. The presence of Feijóo's works in Nariño's library is telling because it confirms that the internal influences coming directly from Spain on the independence of the Spanish colony in America have been underestimated in previous research.

Much has been written about the roots and causes of the emancipation of the Spanish colony in Hispanic America. There is no doubt that the Independence of the United States and the French Revolution played a crucial role in the Hispanic American view on independence. These external influences have been abundantly discussed and documented (Bastin and Echeverri 2004; Rodríguez 1998). By contrast, this chapter has highlighted that the liberal ideas of the time were also imported directly from Spain, like almost everything that entered the continent. It underscores that while translation censorship played a role in the emancipation of the Spanish colony, internal influences may have played a much larger role in translation practices and that these practices may have been more influenced by metropolitan translation practices than previously thought.

8.5 Conclusion

Looking at the first translation in Hispanic America of the *Declaration of the Rights of Man and of the Citizen* through the lens of censorship has permitted the exploration of the mechanisms used by the Spanish authorities to exert control on printed materials. At the same time, it has brought to light the strategies used by authors and translators in the Metropolis to import the ideas of the Enlightenment first into Spain and from there to the colonies in America thanks to *tertulias* and periodicals. Prior to independence, periodicals published in the colony were a new type of text that managed to escape the control of the religious authorities and were instrumental in the creation of a public sphere and public opinion. Most importantly, the censorship perspective makes it possible to explore the role translation played in importing directly from Spain and into the colony the liberal ideas that dramatically changed the political landscapes of the Western world in the last three decades of the eighteenth century and the first half of the nineteenth century.

Further Reading

Navarro, Aura. 2018. *Traducción y prensa temprana. El proceso emancipador en la Gaceta de Caracas 1808–1822*. Valladolid: Ediciones de la Universidad de Valladolid.
In her work, Navarro explores the role played by the press in introducing political ideas into the Spanish colonies based on a corpus of translations published in the *Gaceta de Caracas* from 1808 to 1822. During this period, the journal was, at times, controlled by monarchists, and at other times, by independentists. Depending on who was in control of the journal, the texts related to the liberal ideologies of the time might find their way into the pages of the journal through translation or they might be censored.

Valdeón, R. and Calafat, C. (eds.). 2020. 'The Politics of Translation and the Translation of Politics', Special issue of *Translation & Interpreting*, 12(2).
The set of articles published in this special issue of *Translation & Interpreting* start the premise that translation is a political act independently of the time and the place under study. Some of the articles revisit censorship under Franco's dictatorship and its control over textual productions in other Iberian languages. Other articles deal with the fact that people from different political affiliations (monarchist, independentists, communist, socialists, conservatives and liberals) have always seen the power of translation as a political weapon.

Sosa, Pedro. 2008. 'Persecución inquisitorial de los libros prohibidos en la Venezuela colonial', *Revista de Historia de América*, 139: 39–60.
Censorship as a subject of scholarly research finds in the history of the Spanish-speaking countries material for case studies proper to each country on either side of the Atlantic Ocean. Besides Franco's dictatorship, the other main historical issue that has most attracted researchers' attention is the Inquisition. Concerning the latter, limiting the research to one country ensures its feasibility and allows the researcher to look for detailed data about censorship practices in that country. Sosa has done such a study in the case of Venezuela by offering a view into the censorial practices, the texts and the people involved in censorship cases in the country in colonial times.

Note

1 ('Escrito presentado por don Antonio Nariño al tribunal de gobierno de Santa fe de Bogotá, 17 de abril de 1811', Catálogo en line Biblioteca Nacional de Colombia. Accessed 29 March 2023. https://catalogoenlinea.bibliotecanacional.gov.co/client/es_ES/search/asset/68703/0)

References

Báez, Fernando. 2004. *Historia universal de la destrucción de libros: De las tablillas sumerias a la guerra de Irak.* Barcelona: Ediciones Destino.
Bastin, Georges and Echeverri, Álvaro. 2004. 'Traduction et révolution à l'époque de l'indépendance hispano-américaine'[Translation and Revolution at the Time of Independence in Hispanic-America], *Meta*, 49(3): 562–75. https://doi.org/10.7202/009379ar.
Bastin, Georges, Echeverri, Álvaro and Campo, Ángela. 2004. 'La traducción en América Latina: Propria y Apropriada' [Translation in Latin America: Local and Appropriated], *Estudios de Investigaciones Literarias y Culturales*, 24: 69–94.
Bastin, Georges, Echeverri, Álvaro and Campo, Ángela. 2010. 'Translation and theEmancipation of Hispanic America,' in M. Tymoczko (ed.), *Translation, Resistance, Activism*. Amherst and Boston: University of Massachusetts Press, 42–64.
Eiris, Ariel. 2014. 'Mariano Moreno y la construcción del discurso legitimador de la Revolución de Mayo a través de la Gazeta de Buenos Ayres' [Mariano Moreno and the Construction of the Ligitimizing Discourse

The Routledge Handbook of Translation and Censorship

of May's Revolution in the Buenos Ayres Gazete], *Temas de historia Argentina y Americana*, 103–33. https://repositorio.uca.edu.ar/bitstream/123456789/7074/1/mariano-moreno-construccion-discurso.pdf

García De Sena, Manuel. 1811. *La independencia de la Costa Firme justificada por Thomas Paine treinta años há. Extracto de sus obras traducido del ingles al español por D. Manuel Garcia de Sena* [*The Independence of Costa Firme as Justified by Thomas Paine Thirty Years Ago. Selections from his Works Translated from English into Spanish by Mr. Manuel García de Sena*]. Philadelphia: Thomas and George Palmer.

Goodenough, Ward. 1964. 'Cultural Anthropology and Linguistics', in D. Hymes (ed.), *Language in Culture and Society. A Reader in Linguistics and Anthropology.* New York: Harper & Row, 34–40.

Guerrero, Javier. and Wiesner, Luis (eds.). 2015. *Antonio Nariño: Revolucionario y Ciudadano de Todos los Tiempos* [*Antonio Nariño: Revolutionary and Citizen of All Times*]. Bogotá: Universidad Pedagógica y Tecnológica de Colombia.

Herr, Richard. 1958. *The Eighteenth-Century Revolution in Spain.* Princeton: Princeton University Press. www.jstor.org/stable/j.ctt183q2kq (Accessed: 14 May 20024).

Kamen, Henry. 2014. *Spanish Inquisition: A Historical Revision.* New Heaven: Yale University Press.

Kerversau de, François-Marie and Clavelin, Guillaume. 1790. *Histoire de la Révolution de 1789, et de l'établissement d'une constitution en France. Précédée de l'exposé rapide des administrations successives qui ont déterminé cette révolution mémorable. Par deux amis de la liberté* [*History of the Revolution of 1789, and of the Establishment of a Constitution in France. Preceded by a Brief Exposition of the Succeeding Administrations that Determined this Memorable Revolution*]. Paris: Clevelin.

Lafarga, Francisco and Garrosa García, María-Jesús. 2004. *El discurso sobre la traducción en la España del siglo XVIII* [*Discourse about Translation in XVIII Century Spain*]. Kassel: Edición Reichenberguer.

Lefevere, André. 2016. *Translation, Rewriting and the Manipulation of Literary Fame.* Abingdon, Oxon: Routledge.

Nord, Christiane. 2018. *Translating as a Purposeful Activity: Functionalist Approaches Explained.* Abingdon/New York: Routledge. ProQuest Ebook Central. https://ebookcentral.proquest.com (Accessed: 14 May 2024).

Rodríguez, Jaime. 1998. *La independencia de la América Española* [*The Independence of Spanish America*]. México: Fondo de Cultura Económica.

Santos, Bonaventura de Sousa. 2015. *Epistemologies of the South: Justice against Epistemicide.* Abingdon/Oxon: Routledge. https://doi.org/10.4324/9781315634876. (Accessed: 14 May 2024).

Smith, Robert. 1957. 'The Wealth of Nations in Spain and Hispanic America', *Journal of Political Economy*, 65(2), 104–25.

Uribe-Urán, Victor. 2000. 'The Birth of a Public Sphere in Latin America During the Age of Revolution', *Comparative Studies in Society and History*, 42(2), 425–57.

Valdeón, Roberto. 2014. *Translation and the Spanish Empire in the Americas.* Amsterdam and Philadelphia: John Benjamins.

9
CENSORSHIP OF TRANSLATIONS IN LATVIA
A Historical Perspective

Andrejs Veisbergs

9.1 Core Topics

Latvia experienced various regimes of censorship over the turbulent course of the twentieth century and, given the prominent place of translations in the Latvian literary polysystem, provides an especially interesting example of the interface between translation and censorship. The Latvian literary and translation scene has always been characterized by a 'defective stance' (see Robyns 1994: 60 and Veisbergs 2016) towards the alien, tending to absorb from foreign literary systems what is missing. Accordingly, translated literature was subject to the full spectrum of censorship.

In some instances, translation was fully governed by state censorship, whereas in others, censorship was a discrete outside force, as acting, for example, through the market, which occasionally affected some translations. In the first case **all** agents of translation throughout the translation process had to reckon with the presence of censorship, which also resulted in a regime of self-censorship. Notwithstanding the risk of losing the opportunity to publish or even one's life, some agents tried to circumvent the rules.

In tsarist times, censors often acted in a subjective manner. While hunting for subversive information, they could be careless or superficial. They often entered into a cat-and-mouse game with the translators and publishers. By contrast, the post-censorship of the independence period could only limit the dissemination of 'unwelcome' translations. As a result, the translation process was broad and determined by translators, publishers, public interest and market forces.

9.2 Historical Perspectives

Latvia entered the twentieth century as part of the Russian Empire but with a highly developed written culture in Latvian and a diverse translation history (Veisbergs 2012). Latvia gained independence after the First World War and had 20 years to develop independently with very limited censorship. This was followed by the first Soviet occupation, which immediately imposed comprehensive Soviet-style censorship. Then came four years of German occupation followed by another Soviet reoccupation that lasted 50 years. Soviet censorship gradually grew more sophisticated and intricate, finally imploding at the end of the Soviet period before Latvia regained independence in

DOI: 10.4324/9781003149453-12

The Routledge Handbook of Translation and Censorship

1991. Thus, for two thirds of the twentieth century Latvia lived under various regimes of externally imposed censorship.

9.2.1 Tsarist Censorship

Censorship was at its most severe at the beginning of the twentieth century and it included translations. The 1890 law 'On the Press and Censorship'[1] envisaged a system of pre-censorship: texts were scrutinised before printing, and decisions depended on the censor's personal views (Veinberga 2018: 162). 'A mood close to panic prevailed in Latvian literary circles' as more was banned than allowed (Limane 2004: 36). At the turn of the century censors were particularly on the lookout for Marxist and anarchist ideas, often detecting them even in texts where they did not exist (Apīnis 2004: 35), e.g., in works by Tolstoy, Goethe and Ibsen. However, there were ways of circumventing censorship, such as changing the names of the authors, avoiding taboo terms like 'socialism' or 'the agrarian question', or publishing outside Latvia. It was also well-known that the Latvian censor in St. Petersburg was much more liberal than the Riga man. Censorship was not limited to banning publications. Repressive measures often followed: translators and publishers were exiled, imprisoned and even shot.

Among the moderate concessions in the 1905 *October Manifesto*, post-censorship was instituted instead of the pre-censorship that had previously been applied. Periodicals were established in the more liberal atmosphere, and a number of them offered a broad range of translations. Statistics show that 96 Latvian books were banned in the period between 1906 and 1913 (Apīnis 2004: 42). After the February democratic revolution in 1917, a brief period followed, marked by a virtual absence of censorship; during the turbulent period of World War I, however, when the German-Russian front crossed Latvia, hardly anything substantial was translated and published.

9.2.2 Independence

Once *de facto* independence was established and warfare ceased, publishing picked up gradually. For a time, censors worked according to a medley of tsarist, pre-revolutionary Russian laws and Latvian Defence Ministry regulations. In 1921 the Minister of the Interior issued a regulation banning pornographic works thus setting a precedent for censorship. Political control was lax and only the Communist press, which was hostile to the idea of independence, was regularly banned, though imported Soviet editions were freely available in Latvian shops (Zelmenis 2012: 81). In the 1920s and 30s Nazi literature was also banned; however, in 1935 an exception was made for the German edition of *Mein Kampf,* no doubt as a diplomatic gesture of good will towards Nazi Germany. This decision was not made public, however, so people generally believed the book was still forbidden.

In 1925 Latvia ratified the *Geneva Convention for the Suppression of the Circulation of and Traffic in Obscene Publications.* A decision-making commission of state and public representatives was formed, given that there was no clear definition of obscenity. Until 1934, 221 books had been deemed obscene. They were mostly pulp editions with sexual or criminal content, and predominantly translations. The publishing of pulp literature diminished, and the commission took this to be a result of its activities. The day after the 15 May 1934 coup d'état, the authoritarian government introduced pre-censorship of periodicals, but after six months it was abolished. In 1938 a new less liberal and more extensive Press Law was adopted; it focused mostly on periodicals and military secrets. Latvia joined the Berne Convention in May 1938.

Censorship of Translations in Latvia: A Historical Perspective

Throughout the 20-year independence period, the translation industry grew substantially, especially as a result of the novelty of cheap subscription books. The average number of titles in Latvian fluctuated from around 1500 to 1800 annually with about 20% of them being translations. In the category of novels, 80% were translations. The number of source languages also grew considerably, and the traditional source language of German was gradually surpassed by English.

Censorial interference in the sphere of translation was minimal. A notable exception is D.H. Lawrence's *Lady Chatterley's Lover*, which was banned in 1934. The book had been translated into Latvian from Russian in 1934 by Augusts Mežsēts, who prudently identified himself only by his initials. This practice often protected the translator from bad publicity and was frequently used with translations of pulp literature. We do not know whether the sex scenes or the international reputation of the novel contributed to the censor's decision. Demands for legal action against the publisher were thrown out in court.

When a major publisher was about to publish the Latvian translation of E.M. Remarque's *Three Friends* in 1937, the Latvian Foreign Ministry wanted to block it, since the German Ambassador had protested, arguing that the book was unwelcome in Germany. A compromise was reached whereby the book could be published, but the publisher had to refrain from advertising it in newspapers (Rudzītis 1997: 117). The Latvian translation and the German original, published in Amsterdam, appeared in print almost simultaneously.

9.2.3 First Soviet Occupation

In 1940 the Soviet army invaded and occupied the Baltic States, after which the Soviet Union organised fake elections resulting in their annexation. The transfer of power was swift; step by step Soviet norms were introduced into all walks of life. The establishment of Soviet Latvia was proclaimed on 21 July 1940 and the nationalisation of publishers the next day. On 5 August Latvia was incorporated into the USSR, and on the following day a single publisher, VAPP *(State publishing and polygraphic enterprises authority)*, was set up, making publishing a state monopoly. A total of 134 publishers were nationalised (Zelmenis 2007: 21). On 10 August LGLP, a Latvian version of the Soviet censor *Glavlit,* was established, followed by the introduction of pre-censorship on 3 September (Strods 2010: 11). There was repressive censorship at three levels: manuscript, typesetting and release for sale. Around 90 publishers, authors and translators were deported to Siberia, killed (Unāms 1969: 22) or chose to commit suicide.

The proscription and destruction of ideologically unacceptable books began. Religious books were removed from public and school libraries, as were books deemed bourgeois or those dealing with the history and politics of the Republic of Latvia. Altogether, it is estimated that half a million to one and a half million books were withdrawn and destroyed (Zelmenis 2007: 33–4), including many innocuous titles that were withdrawn by overzealous, often semi-illiterate overachievers, who considered, for example, Dante's *Divine Comedy* to be religious enough to warrant a ban (Latviešu 1941).

Latvians had to be moulded into good Soviet citizens. To this end, the proportion of ideological literature grew exponentially. One third of all books fell under the category of political or socio-economic (Zanders 2013: 341), and were translations from Russian. Print runs for political literature were huge: the *History of the Communist Party*[2] ran to 50,000 copies.

All in all, the Russian year (mid-1940 to mid-1941) saw approximately 1100 titles published, about two-thirds of the previous annual level. The proportion of translated books grew fast, eventually constituting more than half of the total, with Russian immediately becoming the dominant source language (Karulis 1999: 109). Soviet literature turned into the mainstay of fiction

The Routledge Handbook of Translation and Censorship

translation: five books by Gorky, three by Mayakovsky, two by Fadeyev and Sholokhov's *And Quiet Flows the Don* had large print runs. Political literature was translated from Russian as were plays for the theatre. The translation of Russian classics also experienced a boom. Like in Estonia, Russian suddenly occupied the centre of the literary polysystem and provided a matrix for new, original socialist literature (Monticelli 2011: 191). German was almost completely banished. This is interesting given that Nazi Germany and the Soviet Union were nominally allies at this time. Other languages were minimised: Western literature was reduced to a few 'progressive' authors only. The transition to new schoolbooks, surprisingly even those for foreign languages, started with translations from Russian.

The Soviets repealed the copyright system for foreign writers. Fees were occasionally paid to pro-Soviet ones. This system remained in force until the seventies. Translator visibility disappeared, especially in non-fiction and political books. For example, a guide for Soviet writers, i.e., a compilation of Gorky's essays and speeches, was translated by the anonymous 'translators collective of the Latvian SSR Writers Union.'

It is interesting that translation occasionally became the refuge of politically unreliable people who accepted freelance jobs translating from Russian. Amazingly many prominent Latvian writers, out of fear or necessity, took to translating propagandistic works and literary trash. Nevertheless, the new leader of the Soviet literary scene, Jānis Niedre (the first head of *Glavlit*), declared that 'the social moment is paramount in translation. Every translator, whether consciously or not, will show his class view' (Niedre 1940: 11). This was a clear reference to the Soviet premise that the translator is an ideological worker.

9.2.4 German Occupation

The Nazi occupation in 1941 came swiftly; within a week the Germans had captured Riga, capital of Latvia, and a week later the army had gone beyond the Latvian borders, deep into Russia. Latvia was experiencing terror, a holocaust against its Jewish population and the repression of Communist sympathizers at the hands of the Nazis. Yet, initially, the German occupation was nevertheless seen as less brutal than the first Soviet occupation and certainly more predictable and civilised than the Soviets' Year of Terror. However, early aspirations and hopes for renewed independence were quickly quashed, resulting in disillusionment; the wartime scarcity of resources caused hardship and the German authorities' arrogant behaviour provoked resentment.

The various Nazi organisations produced many different plans for the future of the Baltic peoples, and for the Latvians in particular, none of which bode well. However, the *Ostministerium*, or Ministry for the Occupied Eastern Territories, was so notorious for its internal divisions related to its Baltic policies that it became known as *Chaostministerium*. In addition to the German authorities, there was a semiautonomous Latvian self-administration that dealt with cultural matters. This self-administration both collaborated with the Nazis and resisted them. The Latvian self-administration soon learned to play the German agencies off against one another (Unāms 1969: 72). The German authorities themselves recognised that 'in Latvia more than elsewhere in *Ostland*, the *Generalkommissariat* had largely lost control to the semiautonomous Latvian self-administration' (Bassler 2003: 82). The first detailed instructions for the *Reichskommissar* contained not a single line on cultural policies (Instruktion 1947). It was suggested that petty squabbles and sanctions on language-related issues be avoided 'since they could negatively affect the situation' (Strods 1991). The spoken guidelines stated that 'books should not spoil the good relationship between Germans and Latvians, should not contradict Germany's war aims and should not discredit the German

Censorship of Translations in Latvia: A Historical Perspective

people' (Unāms 1969: 130). The cultural sphere was very much ruled by consensus, by imitating German practices, or by spontaneous decisions and oral directives from local agents.

Like the Soviet authorities, the German regime started purging the libraries of unwelcome books. These included first and foremost books that had been banned in Germany itself: those by Jewish authors, Communist literature, Western left-wing literature (apart from the classics), as well as works of Latvian nationalism. The lists were drawn up as early as September 1941 and sent to libraries and bookshops (Liste 1941). In time, some titles were added, while others were reclassified as harmless. Specific pages were torn out of some books (Zellis 2012: 134). Around 750,000 books were destroyed. Schoolbooks had to be rewritten to replace Soviet-era books. However, those new books were written by Latvians. In some cases, a few comments on Germans or Germany were added; for example, the traditional Latvian geography schoolbook (1941) added the subtitle 'with information on Greater Germany and general geography' to acknowledge the addition of a couple of pages describing Germany.

In many cultural fields there was relative freedom compared with the year of Soviet rule. The Germans did not interfere in the theatre: among the imported plays, the proportion of German ones rose, but works of Shakespeare, Molière, Ibsen, G.B. Shaw and even Russian classics were regularly staged. Thus there was a 'relatively tolerant cultural policy' (Lumans 2006: 201).

Soon after occupying the region, the Germans set about denationalising Soviet nationalised enterprises and publishers. As in Nazi Germany, censorship was implemented or attempted by a whole range of agents and was neither fully formalised nor very coherent (Sturge 2002). Nominal pre-censorship was performed by the censors of the *Generalkommisariat*, who mostly focused on original Latvian writing. Censorship, however, found nothing wrong with the translations, possibly because the source texts had been judiciously chosen. Nazi officials actually suggested dropping censorship of translations from German in 1943, yet the Latvian self-administration could not agree on political, technical and linguistic issues (Unāms 1975: 175). The authorities relied on editors and publishers to know what was good and acceptable. No confiscations of translations were reported. Latvian publishing returned to a relatively tolerant and bearable state, which fell in line with the cultural normality that the Germans seemed to have felt in Germany (Schäfer 1981).

The percentage of translations was broadly the same as in the independence period (around 20 percent), and print runs initially rose from 2000 to 5000, and occasionally to 10,000 or more. Another reorientation occurred, with German literature now providing around 70 percent of the source texts. This may be viewed as an ideological imperative or a convenience (for example, copyright issues, which were strictly observed, must have been problematic in wartime). Most other source texts were Nordic and Estonian, including the works of Frans Eemil Sillanpää who was banned in Germany after an ideological misstep in 1939. Translations from other languages were scarce. Only a couple of translations from Russian were published during the German period, and a few from English: Archibald Joseph Cronin's *The Stars Look Down* came out in July 1944, shortly before the Russians returned. Cronin was considered anti-capitalist and was published in Germany even in wartime. Incidentally the same translation was republished a few months later by the Soviets who must have missed the fact that the translator had fled to the West.

Most translated literature was clearly apolitical. However, anti-British and anti-American views were propagated by a couple of books. These were published because most Latvians hoped that, after the war ended, things might go back to the way they had been after the First World War. John Amery (the son of a senior British MP) published an anti-Bolshevik monograph called *L'Angleterre et l'Europe* (*England and Europe*) in Paris in 1943. His book was translated into Latvian and had two editions. Similarly, Eric Linklater's *Juan in Amerika* (1931) was published in Latvian in 1943 and 1944. The book grew in popularity and saw many reprints in Germany after

The Routledge Handbook of Translation and Censorship

the Nazi Propaganda minister Josef Goebbels read it and decided it was worth paying the copyright fee in order to have access to such a blatant exposition of American corruption.

As for the general range of topics, there was a strikingly high proportion of books on German composers, considered a safe subject for all concerned. Biographies of German inventors, scientists, musicians, sportsmen, as well as travel books were popular as well. This can also be seen as a practice of soft propaganda (Solberg 2020).

Translators were clearly named both in fiction and nonfiction publications, usually on the title page. Translations were precise, in keeping with the German tradition of fidelity to the original and the Latvian norm for the translation of serious literature.

9.2.5 Second Soviet Occupation: the Stalin Years

The Soviet army reconquered Riga in October 1944, though part of Latvia remained under German rule until the end of the war. Unlimited Sovietisation resumed, enveloping all spheres of life including translation. Within a short period 16 million books were destroyed (Strods 2010: 180), and five million unwelcome books were removed from Riga libraries in 1946 alone. The basic principle was to eliminate anything printed under fascism. Long lists of books to be removed from circulation were published regularly. The books to be destroyed were euphemistically called dated or unwelcome. The first list, published as early as November or December 1944, was the longest, with 3573 titles. Ten lists of forbidden books were published between 1944 and 1961, in addition to separate decrees and rulings (Dreimane 2004: 38). They focused mostly on Latvian authors but included many translations, some of which could hardly be characterised as anti-Soviet. The selection was affected by the political trends of the moment; for example, the 1951 list contained a recently published book by Soviet Jewish author Isak Mintz about the Great Patriotic War in the Soviet Union (Apvienotais 1951). Most likely the author's ethnicity was viewed as unacceptable in view of the anti-Zionist campaign then under way.

It is interesting to note that 'all forewords and introductions by [translators] Z. Mauriņa and K. Raudive [were] to be removed from all books' (No 1948), including translations of works by Miguel Unamuno, Cervantes and others. These two intellectual Latvians, living abroad, were considered obviously anti-Soviet, and their views on any topic therefore had to be expunged. The withdrawn books were generally burned or pulped, or sometimes the unwelcome pages or introductions were simply torn out. Two or three copies were left in a special archive with access restricted to politically reliable comrades. We thus see the 'erasure' (Monticelli 2011: 191) of a large part of Latvian written culture.

The publishers and printing houses were renationalised immediately after the Soviet reoccupation of Riga. The monopoly publisher VAPP was reinstated, and the Soviet model of censorship was reintroduced to Latvia. Apart from military secrets, censorship mostly focused on ideological issues. Its aim was to 'protect' the Soviet population from dangerous foreign ideologies. Rather than provide a window giving unimpeded access to the West, translations of foreign literature were required to portray the West according to the Kremlin's skewed image. The early stages of censorship occurred in the post or customs office where the text could be confiscated, after which came the editorial decision on whether the work could be published. Only later came translation, editing and the final decision to publish. Latvian censorship generally copied Moscow's agenda, which is well described by Sherry (2015), although it was occasionally more zealous and suspicious. Censorship was carried out by a network of agents of translation: the censors themselves; the KGB; party organs who followed the current decrees and directives; editors; and translators who self-censored. Censorship had to adapt quickly to constant changes in the party line in regard to new priorities, taboo issues and unmentionable facts and personalities. There seems to have been a lapse by censors in 1946 when the 'inappropriate' translation of E.T.A. Hoffmann's *Devil's Elixirs* was published. The translation had been done during the German occupation and the book, while printed, had been waiting for illustrations. The Soviets changed the title page information on the publisher and ingeniously added a second reliable Soviet translator's name. Nevertheless, it must have been considered an ideological breach given that the book was never commented upon by Soviet critics.

Translations accounted for more than half of the titles published, and the source language of 97 per cent of them was Russian. The number of Western translations was minimal. Translations of Marx, Engels, Lenin and Stalin until the ideological thaw of the mid-1950s alone constituted around 250 titles. The dominant approach was not to publish anything that did not suit the ideological dogmas. The translated texts were purged of their dangerous or unwelcome elements without consulting any living author (Friedberg 1997: 139). Items purged might be religious elements (even linguistic, such as references to God in idioms), critical remarks about socialism or the USSR, or suggestions that life was good under capitalism. Translations were supplied with ideologically tinted introductions or postscripts, which instructed the reader on how to interpret the work. Finally, some well-known works were rewritten in Russian and then disseminated throughout the Soviet empire and its satellites. Even though Defoe's *Robinson Crusoe* had been translated into Latvian (a two-volume edition) during the independence period, two Latvian editions from the Russian translation were published in 1946 and 1949. The Russian translation was done by Korney Chukovsky in the USSR in the 1920s. Chukovsky was a well-known Soviet Russian children's author, a good translator and translation theoretician. However, his translation of *Robinson Crusoe* fundamentally changed the tonality of the novel: it was purged of religious and Christian references, as well as the hero's philosophical musings, which were deemed unsuitable for Soviet citizens (Clark 2000: 46). It became a canonical work of the socialist camp and was retranslated in Eastern Europe (Pokorn 2012: 125). The 'real' *Robinson Crusoe* was not available to the Latvian reader until 1966, and even then only the first part, with a truncated ending referring to the second volume. Such 'rewriting' was a regular occurrence in the USSR. Consequently, in 1936 Alexey Tolstoy transformed Carlo Collodi's *Pinocchio* into *Buratino,* which was more acceptable to Soviet dogma, while A. Volkov reconfigured L. Frank Baum's *The Wizard of Oz* into the Soviet *The Wizard of the Emerald City.* These Russian rewrites were in turn translated into Latvian: while *Pinocchio* had been translated during Latvian independence, *Buratino* was published in 1952. Volkov's rewrite was published in 1962, whereas Baum's original story had to wait until Latvia regained independence in 1991.

Extreme ideologisation pervaded all mass media (Hoyer et al. 1993: 189). The Writers' Union of the Latvian SSR (which had a Translators' Section) issued ideological edicts to the literary world. The party line was announced to everybody by the few official newspapers and magazines that manifestly demonstrated the new content and style of literature required by the Soviets for publication, such as works from Russia or the 'brotherly nations', as well as the occasional foreign piece or classic to celebrate a jubilee or anniversary.

Apart from everyday ideologisation, there were several huge campaigns aimed at the total ideological and cultural subjugation of the Latvian people to the Communist party spirit. Cultural workers, or so-called 'engineers of human souls,' who did not understand the new system had to be re-educated. The first great campaign that would affect the cultural media for a long time was initiated by the Central Committee decision of 14 August 1946 entitled 'On the Journals *Zvezda* and *Leningrad*', which introduced rigid norms for literature. This decision and Zhdanov's report were hastily republished in Latvian newspapers followed by an anonymous local counterpart of

The Routledge Handbook of Translation and Censorship

the same style (Par 1946: 840–9). Translation criticism was always entangled with the campaigns of the moment: there was an interminable battle with 'Latvian bourgeois nationalists', Orwellian fulmination against Endzelinists (followers of Jānis Endzelīns's linguistic theories), followed a short while later by another against their opponents, the Marrists (followers of Soviet academician Nikolai Marr), as well as a campaign against 'cosmopolitans' (Zionists). Ideologisation was particularly directed towards the young condemning the enduring interest of the youth in the bourgeois novel and calling on readers to read only Soviet writings (Avote 1945: 3).

Foreign texts were arbitrarily shortened and transformed in the process of translation. Not only were things deleted, but they were also added at will. For example, Jekabs Mentsendorf's Russian translation of a story by the Latvian writer Arvīds Grigulis turned the main character into 'a conscientious revolutionary' and had him participate in the revolutionary movement, of which there was not a word in the original. Even the ideologically die-hard overseer of literature Niedre (1945: 933) had to concede that 'the Russian translation [was] a creation very far removed from Grigulis' story.'

9.2.6 Second Soviet Occupation: the Thaw

After Stalin's death in 1953 and Khrushchev's liberalisation (Friedberg 1997), the situation in the USSR changed considerably. The basic tenets of the Soviets remained in effect, but there was some opening up to the world, some modernisation and a certain rehabilitation of Latvia's pre-Soviet heritage. The new policies 'encouraged more variety in the assessment of Western culture than the vocabulary of degeneration and decadence used before' (Talvoja 2018: 337). Works by contemporary foreign writers were published if they corresponded to the tenets of progressive literature, and books were increasingly translated from the originals. The new guidelines determined by the Resolution of the Central Committee of the Communist Party of 4 June 1957 stated that Western translations should include long introductions and annotations to help Soviet readers understand the difference between right and wrong. Passages without scientific and practical value were to be deleted. This policy, as well as the unwritten rule that books to be translated into Latvian needed to have been translated in Moscow first, remained in effect until the collapse of the Soviet regime. Latvian translators and editors would then be provided with a sample of what should be omitted or transformed.

Ignoring the principle resulted in punishment. For example, when Latvian poet and translator Māris Čaklais compiled an anthology of Estonian poetry in the 1970s and the censors found he had included poems as yet untranslated into Russian, the printed books were destroyed. A similar thing happened with an anthology of French poetry that contained poems untranslated into Russian. However, the censors were too late to destroy the books before distribution, and so Čaklais was fired from the publishing house and his own poetry banned (Adamaite 2020: 9).

The proportion of translations from Russian fell rapidly from the 97 percent of the Stalinist period to two thirds as a new phenomenon emerged: the reprinting of pre-war translations without the permission of authors, translators or publishers. Thus, the reprint of Remarque's *Three Friends* (translated before the war by Valdemārs Kārkliņš who was now in the USA) did not mention the translator. It was, however, supplied with a postscript that criticized Remarque for his limited humanism and ignorance of communist ideas. But Cronin's *The Stars Look Down* was republished twice with a less overtly propagandistic postscript, and even named the translator, Kārkliņš.

9.2.7 Second Soviet Occupation: Stagnation

In the Brezhnev period (1964–1982) censorship, which was exercised by *Glavlit*, the KBG and the relevant Communist party departments, became more sophisticated. Censorship went beyond written texts and libraries to include radio and TV, music, painting, photos, postal services science, museums, personal correspondence and telephone conversations, all of which were subjected to various forms of censorship from the jamming of foreign radio stations to the confiscation of foreign books. The latter could rarely be bought or sent by post.

Though Russian dominated in all fields of translation, literature of the 'brotherly' nations (Soviet and Eastern bloc) and the rest of the world was extensively translated. Preference was clearly given to the classics or works by Marxist, socialist or realist writers that criticized capitalism (e.g., Hemingway, Dreiser, Steinbeck, Brecht, Priestley, Rolland), in addition to numerous second-rate writers. A considerable number of retranslations were done, mostly of the classics, making them more accurate and modernizing the language.

Works that were ostensibly too modern, like Joyce's *Ulysses* (translated into Latvian abroad), were taboo. However, many of the 'untranslatable' authors were regularly criticized in the press: Ezra Pound, Sigmund Freud, Ian Fleming, Alexander Solzhenitsyn, Boris Pasternak. The authors' political views and especially their attitude towards the Soviet Union were decisive factors. If they were positive, their writings could be translated, perhaps with some omissions. But favourite ones, like André Gide and Alan Sillitoe, could fall from glory after making ideological mistakes. Klienes' memoirs of a translator (1979) had to be reworked since she mentioned various 'dangerous' authors and spoke favourably of Knut Hamsun (Strods 2010: 245). Or a translated book about games had to be reworked as it failed to emphasize that the Kuril Islands were part of the USSR. Censorship was even applied to Latvian translations of Soviet Russian works. For example, censors found that undue attention had been paid to some Russian authors such as Marina Tsvetaeva, Anna Akhmatova, Yevgenii Yevtushenko and Boris Pasternak in a poetry anthology.

The following story illustrates the meticulousness of censorship at this time. The Latvian *Glavlit* boss Valentin Agafonov (LVA 1964) informed the First Secretary of the Latvian Communist Party in 1964 of an ideological breach in the magazine *Woman of Soviet Latvia.* An article written by Anna Sakse (a stalwart Communist writer and translator) had in passing praised Lofting's *Doctor Dolittle.* However, the latter had not been published in Latvian during Soviet times; it had been published in 1937.

Interpenetration of translation and censorship is well illustrated by the incredible publishing history of Hemingway's *For Whom the Bell Tolls* (Kuznetsova 2017). The novel was subjected to nearly 30 years of editing before the Russian translation was finally published in the USSR in 1968. For its part, the translation underwent a plethora of manipulations, including cuts, changes, the introduction of Soviet clichés, deletions of even slightly erotic passages, softening and highlighting of political statements by changing their place in the narrative. Naturally, the book would not be translated into Latvian until 1971 when it was equally manipulated according to the Russian example.

While censors, literary editors and proof-readers ensured the linguistic quality of the final product through multiple re-readings of the target text, the translations did not faithfully render the modern originals either linguistically or in terms of content. Ambiguity, wordplay, in addition to unusual and creative use of language were often reduced, simplified or paraphrased. Unwelcome statements or facts were deleted or changed (Zauberga 2001; Lange 2012). To ensure publication, publishers and translators had to accept these distortions.

The translation of Vonnegut's *Cat's Cradle* (1963) into Latvian in 1973 was so extensively amended politically, ideologically and linguistically that it was retranslated by the same translator in 2002 and published with a statement on the cover, which clarified that the new version was in no way censored. But many Soviet period translations have been republished in their censored variants thus affecting the new generations.

Translations of Western literature were generally prefaced by introductions by editors and experts, who provided the correct interpretation of ambiguous or unwelcome information. For example, the translation of Alistair MacLean's *The Guns of Navarone* stated that the translation was 'slightly abridged'. However, a relatively long postface was added; it minimised the importance of the British war effort, while praising the Soviet army, though the latter is not mentioned in the book, which deals with the conflict in the Mediterranean.

A Finnish book on matrimonial life was published in Latvian, even though it had not been first translated into Russian, which attracted extra scrutiny. The publishers were thus obliged to apply various safeguards: abridgement (which was stated), an introduction by a Latvian psychotherapist and another by an Estonian psychotherapist, both explaining that human sexuality was a normal phenomenon that 'should not be exaggerated' (Paloheimo 1976: 10). Apart from that, there were numerous footnotes by the editors rigorously explaining differing official Soviet positions on issues, such as homosexuality and drinking. There must have been serious discussions on what to abridge, delete and retain with the explanations of the correct Soviet viewpoint.

Though politics ultimately determined what could be translated and how, the resulting product sometimes undermined communist goals despite censorship. A fine-tuned system of ambiguous subtexts and undercurrents developed behind the monolithic official façade. Soviet citizens often cultivated an incredible ability to read between the lines, and complicity between translators and readers often went undetected by the censors.

Translation occasionally became the refuge for disgraced dissident Latvian writers. For example, the poet Vizma Belševica was attacked by Communist authorities, who branded her as an extremely dangerous element for cunningly drawing parallels in her poetry between the Teutonic invasion of the Baltic region and the Soviet incursion into Czechoslovakia, parallels that were 'liable to create utter ideological chaos among politically inexperienced readers' (Latvijas 1969: 2). As a result, Belševica's work was withdrawn from circulation, and she was subsequently watched by the KGB. Since proscribed writers were occasionally allowed to translate, she devoted her time almost exclusively to translating, mainly from English. The result was many brilliant translations.

9.2.8 Second Soviet Occupation: the Late Soviet and Post-Soviet Periods

Under perestroika and glasnost, Gorbachev acknowledged the existence of censorship in 1986. Accordingly, in September, *Glavlit* adopted decree Nr. 29 which asked the censors to focus on issues connected with protecting state and military secrets in the press and to inform the Communist party only about essential breaches of ideological issues. Consequently, censorship started gradually losing force from 1987 onwards. This was criticised by the Central Committee of the Latvian Communist party that desperately tried to retain its grip (Briedis 2010: 165–6). In 1986 and 1987 reported breaches by censorship actually increased (Strods 2010: 253). A new liberal magazine *Avots* published Orwell's *Animal Farm* in Latvian translation in 1988. The translation in book form appeared in 1990 together with a translation of Orwell's *1984*, that had been published abroad already in 1951. By 1989 publishing a book by Nabokov was possible. On 10 August 1990

Censorship of Translations in Latvia: A Historical Perspective

the new reformist Latvian government, while still part of the USSR, adopted a decision forbidding censorship. Until then the Latvian *Glavlit* continued to report to Moscow (Millers 2013).

After Latvia regained de facto independence in August 1991, Latvian was re-established as the sole official language of the state in 1992. This led to enormous growth in the volume of translated information in Latvian as well to a rapid linguistic reorientation, since most information now came via English. Within ten years the source language pattern changed radically: if in 1985 the proportion of books translated from Russian and English was 15 to 1, in 1994 the proportion was 1 to 6. It has remained unchanged since 1994.

The transition to normality was incredibly fast, though some Soviet traditions lingered. For example, the translation of *Lady Chatterley's Lover* was finally published in 1991 with the translator's name in full on the second page, but also with a postface by a well-known Latvian sex therapist, who explained that the book was perfectly acceptable, and in the parlance in vogue at the time that only 'Stalinists [would] see anything bad in literature like this' (Lorenss 1991: 283).

While there was no censorship, the authorities felt at a loss when Hitler's *Mein Kampf* was translated and published with the interesting subtitle: *authorized exposition*. This occurred a short time before Latvia again acceded to the copyright convention in 1995. The publication did not mention the translator(s) and the preface offered the text to Latvian readers for them to judge for themselves. However, the authorities finally withdrew the book from shops and charged the editor with publishing a work that propagated violence and cruelty. The clumsy trial ended with the confiscation and destruction of up to 3500 copies. However, more copies had been printed, so they are in unofficial circulation and can be read in libraries. This seems to be the only case of translation censorship in the 30 years of Latvia's renewed independence.

9.3   New Debates

One of the challenges of researching censorship is related to its (in)visibility. In tsarist Russia, for example, pre-censorship was visible and, arguably, the most transparent: the title page would have an inscription in Russian, 'allowed by the censors', with the date and occasionally also the place of censorship. At other periods censorship was not transparent. Soviet authorities did not use the term 'censorship' per se in books, including translations. However, the end of the book included a 'passport', which documented the entire approval and publishing process: the dates and decisions of text composition and permit to print, as well as the names of the translators, editors, technical editors and proof-readers. In the 1980s this information was published in Russian and Latvian. While an average reader would pay no attention to this 'passport' information, an initiated reader could see, for example, whether months or years had passed since the beginning of the process.

Another interesting debate relates to the success of Soviet censorship. While ideological literature was unpopular and often remained unread on the bookshelves, the rare Western works were bought immediately and avidly devoured. Since there was practically no access to the originals, the extent of textual manipulations remained unknown and the general reader read the doctored texts uncritically. Yet, Soviet citizens often cultivated an ability to read between the lines. An invisible link established between the translator and the reader sometimes bypassed the numerous censors' eyes (Baer 2010). Furthermore, clandestine underground (samizdat) translations circulated: in the Latvian case, emigre translations, which in Stalin's time far surpassed Soviet production in terms of volume and quality, were a good source. They could occasionally be purchased on the black market and were shared by close acquaintances. Personal libraries as well as second-hand bookshops had numerous pre-war publications; bookshops, however, did not accept banned books for sale. Two libraries with a special fund provided access to a select group of people of originals and translations that were banned: this select group was composed of vetted researchers and party ideologists. Despite these loopholes, the ideological stranglehold on the system was tight and distorted the average citizen's picture of the world in translation.

While there is no censorship today one can, of course, ponder the issue of translator's self-censorship in light of political correctness as regards the use of certain terms referring to race, nationality, illnesses and similar issues that are occasionally discussed in media.

9.4 Directions for Future Research

While censorship has been well researched, the issue of ideology requires further study (Merkle 2010: 20). By comparing the approaches to translation censorship of the different totalitarian regimes in Latvia one can see some similarities and many differences. Similarities are seen in the regime of pre-censorship and certain taboos: Jewish and communist literature for the Germans; anti-Soviet, liberal, modernist, erotic literature for the Soviets.

The Nazi system was disorganised and often subjected to institutional and personal infighting. It mostly practised a soft power approach (similar to the practice in Estonia, Norway, etc.). Germans amazingly offered the Latvian Self-Administration the possibility to forego censorship of texts from Germany (no doubt those published after 1933). German censorship, therefore, largely relied on translators' and publishers' self-censorship. The regime did, however, orient the translation industry towards German as a source language, and German and European culture and civilization in the interpretation of the Third Reich. But it did not delve into details. A relatively free choice of titles and access to them was offered. This is in line with Rundle's observations (2011: 36–7) that translated literature under fascism in Italy and Germany was not restricted or repressed institutionally.

In contrast, Soviet censorship was all-encompassing, centralized, suspicious and nit-picking. As a result, despite the vaunted mantra of internationalism, the Stalinist system actually practised an almost total iron-curtain policy coupled with blatant ideologisation and a distinct Russification tendency. Translations had to borrow, copy, imitate and replicate patterns of Soviet Russian culture while remaining closed to the rest of the world. The isolation was gradually reduced and approaches became more nuanced. Since the Soviet period was longer, one can also see both ideological zigzags and a general evolution. Under the Soviet system censors and other agents were not free parties, but only cogs in a mighty and intricate ideological machine under their communist party masters. Censorship reacting to a magazine reference to an innocuous children's book translation done before Latvia's occupation serves as a good example of the Orwellian erasure of anything even remotely alien to the regime.

Provided a book was deemed appropriate, the translator could do a loyal and precise translation. However, revisers, editors and other 'competent authorities' often changed the manuscript beyond recognition, and the translator was unable to protest. We thus see a blending of censorship with editorial work. The very end of the Soviet period started to resemble the tsarist give-and-take policies.

Further Reading

Sherry, Samantha. 2015. *Discourses of Regulation and Resistance*. Edinburgh: Edinburgh University Press. This is a study of the censorship of translated literature in the Soviet Union during the Stalin and Khrushchev eras. The book focuses on the rather abrupt change that occurred after Stalin's death when the Party loosened

Censorship of Translations in Latvia: A Historical Perspective

ideological constraints while attempting to control thought using more nuanced and malleable means. It concentrates on two major Soviet journals that published foreign literature and presents carefully analyzed archival material on the whole process of translation, notes and correspondence between the agents involved in censorship.

Strods, Heinrihs. 2010. *PSRS politiskā cenzūra Latvijā 1940–1990* [Political Censorship of the USSR in Latvia 1940–1990]. Rīga: Jumava.
This comprehensive monograph on Soviet censorship in Latvia describes the structure of the mechanism, its main organisations and their activities with respect to libraries, fiction and scientific literature, press, radio, museums, cinema, correspondence and so on. Based on archival information, it provides a comprehensive overview of censorship activities and their impact. Translation censorship is not specifically addressed.

Veisbergs, Andrejs. 2020. *Latvian Translation Scene in the 20th Century*. Berlin: Lambert Academic Publishing.
A monograph covering the Latvian translation scene with its zigzags imposed by the frequent change of power. It shows how the political masters could manipulate, to a large extent, the translation scene to advance their interests since translated literature was for the most part at the centre of the Latvian polysystem.

Notes

1 All translations from the Latvian are the author's, unless otherwise noted.
2 Only the English translation of foreign book titles are provided, unless otherwise noted.

References

Adamaite, Undīne. 2020, 30 July. Šampinjons zem asfalta. *Kultūras diena,* [Mushroom under the asphalt], 8–10.
Apīnis, Aleksejs. 2004. Latviešu grāmatniecība un cenzūra līdz 1918. gadam. L. Limane, A. Apīnis (red.) *Cenzūra un cenzori latviešu grāmatniecībā līdz 1918. gadam.* Latvijas Nacionālā bibliotēka. Reto grām. un rokr. nod [Latvian publishing and censorship until 1918.]. Rīga: Latvijas Nacionālā bibliotēka, 11–54.
Apvienotais novecojušo izdevumu saraksts (1-7) un Novecojušo izdevumu saraksts No.8. 1951. [The joint list of dated publications (1-7) and Dated publications Nr.8.]. Rīga: Latvijas PSR Ministru padomes literatūras un izdevniecību galvenās pārvaldes izdevums.
Avote, L. 1945, 15 November. Ko tu lasi? *Padomju jaunatne,* [What do you read?] 3.
Baer, Brian. 2010. 'Literary Translation in the Age of the Decembrists: The Birth of Productive Censorship in Russia'. In D. Merkle, C. O'Sullivan, L. van Doorslaer and M. Wolf (eds.), *The Power of the Pen: Translation and Censorship in Nineteenth-century Europe.* Vienna and Münster: Lit Verlag, 213–39.
Bassler, Gerhard. 2003. 'The collaborationist agenda in Latvia 1941–1943'. Thematic Issue: '*The Baltic Countries under Occupation, Soviet and Nazi Rule 1939–1991*', *Acta Universitatis Stockholmiensis, Studia Baltica Stockholmiensia*, 23. Stockholm: Stockholm University, 77–84.
Briedis, Raimonds. 2010. *Teksta cenzūras īsais kurss: prozas teksts un cenzūra padomju gados Latvijā.* [The short course of text censorship: prose text and censorship in the years of soviet Latvia]. Rīga: LU Literatūras, folkloras un mākslas institūts.
Clark, Katerina. 2000. *The Soviet Novel: History as Ritual.* Indiana: Indiana University Press.
Dreimane, Jana. 2004. *Latvijas bibliotēkas otrās padomju okupācijas gados.* Promocijas darbs filoloģijas doktora darba iegūšanai komunikāciju zinātnes nozarē bibliotēkzinātnes apakšnozarē. [Latvian libraries in the years of second soviet occupation]. Rīga: Latvijas Universitāte.
Friedberg, Maurice. 1997. *Literary Translation in Russia: A Cultural History.* Pennsylvania: The Pennsylvania State University Press.
Hoyer, Svennik, Lauk, Epp and Vihalemm, Peeter (eds.). 1993. *Towards a Civic Society. The Baltic Media's Long Road to Freedom.* Tartu: Baltic association for Media Research/Nota Baltica Ltd.
Instruktion für einen Reichskommissar im Ostland. 8.5.1941 (1947). [Instruction for Reich's Commissioner in Ostland]. *IMG XXVI.* Nürnberg. 1947, 573–76.
Karulis, Konstantīns. 1999. 'Grāmata pirmajā padomju okupācijas gadā: atmiņas un skaitļi' *Bibliotēka, Grāmatniecība, Ideoloģija Otrā Pasaules kara laikā (1939–1945) Starptautiskā konference. Materiālu*

krājums. [Books in the first soviet occupation year: memories and numbers]. Rīga: Latvijas Nacionālā bibliotēka, 99–110.

Kuznetsova, Ekaterina. 2017. 'Hemingway's Transformations in Soviet Russia: On the Translation of *For Whom the Bell Tolls* by Natalia Volzhina and Evgeniia Kalashnikova', in B. J. Baer and S. Witt (eds.), *Translation in Russian Contexts: Culture, Politics, Identity*. London/New York: Routledge, 159–73.

Lange, Anne. 2012. 'Performative Translation Options Under the Soviet Regime', *Journal of Baltic Studies*, 3(43): 401–20.

"Latviešu literātūras moku gads [The year of torture of Latviand literature]." 1941, 24 July. *Tēvija*.

Latvijas Komunistiskās partijas CK plēnums. 1969, 17 June. *Cīņa*. [The plenum of the CC of Latvian Communist party].

Limane, Lilija. 2004. *Cenzūra un cenzori latviešu grāmatniecībā līdz 1918. gadam*. Rīgā: Latvijas Nacionālā bibliotēka, Reto grāmatu un rokrakstu nodaļa. [Censors and censorship in Latvian publishing until 1918.].

Liste des aus den lettischen Volksbuechereien un Antiquariaten zurueckstellenden Schrifttums.[List of books shelved from Latvian public libraries and second-hand bookshops]. 1941. Sast.: Mākslas un kultūras lietu direkcijas Bibliotēku nodaļa. Rīga.

Lorenss, Dāvids Herberts. 1991. *Lēdijas Čaterlejas mīļākais [Lady Chatterley's Lover]*. Rīga: Avots.

Lumans, Valdis. 2006. *Latvia in World War II*. New York: Fordham University Press.

LVA. 1964. P 101.f., 27. April, 88.l., 5. -10.

Merkle, Denise. 2010. 'Censorship'. In Y, Gambier and L. Van Doorslaer (eds.), *Handbook of Translation Studies*. Amsterdam/Philadelphia: John Benjamins, 18–21.

Millers, Juris. 2013. *Galvenās literatūras pārvaldes darbība Latvijā. 1985–1990*. [Activities of the Main literature Directorate in Latvia, 1985–1990] Promocijas darbs. Rīga: LU.

Monticelli, Daniele. 2011. '"Totalitarian translation" as a means of forced cultural change: the case of postwar soviet Estonia', in A. Chalvin, A. Lange, D. Monticelli (eds.), *Between Cultures and Texts. Itineraries in Translation History*. Frankfurt am Main: Peter Lang, 187–200.

Niedre Jānis. 1940, 15 August. Tulkojumu technika. *Padomju Latvija*. [Translations technique]: 11.

Niedre, Jānis. 1945. 'Literārā tulkojuma problēma', *Karogs* 9-10 [The problem of literary translation]: 930–935.

No apgrozības izņemamo grāmatu un brošuru saraksts Nr.6. [List Nr. 6. of books and brochures to be withdrawn from circulation]. 1948. Rīga.

Paloheimo, Martti; Rouhunkoski, Mauri; Rutanena Mirja. 1976. *Atklāti par laulības dzīvi [Openly about Matrimonial Life]*. Rīga: Zvaigzne.

'Par idejiski augstvērtīgu latviešu padomju literaturu' [About Ideologically High Quality Latvian Soviet Literature]. 1946. *Karogs*, 9: 840–49.

Pokorn, Nike K. 2012. *Post-Socialist Translation Practices: Ideological struggle in children's literature*. Amsterdam and Philadelphia: John Benjamins.

Robyns, Clem. 1994. 'Translation and Discursive Analysis', in C. Robyns (ed.), *Translation and (Re) Production of Culture*. Leuven: CETRA, 57–77.

Rudzītis, Helmars. 1997. *Manas dzīves dēkas [Adventures of My Life]*. Rīga: Zinātne.

Rundle, Christopher. 2011. 'History through a translation perspective', in A. Chalvin, A. Lange and D. Monticelli (eds.), *Between Cultures and Texts. Itineraries in Translation History*. Frankfurt am Main: Peter Lang, 33–43.

Schäfer, Hans Dieter. 1981. *Das gespaltene Bewußtsein. Deutsche Kultur und Lebenswirklichkeit1933–1945*. [*The Split Consciousness, German Culture and Reality of Life*]. Munich/Vienna: Carl Hanser.

Sherry, Samantha. 2015. *Discourses of Regulation and Resistance*. Edinburgh University Press.

Solberg, Ida Hove. 2020. 'Translated literature as soft propaganda: Examples from occupied Norway (1940–1945)', *Translation Matters*, 2(2): 144–59.

Strods, Heinrihs. 1991. Oficiālā (vācu) un vietējā (latviešu) valoda. *Dabas un Vēstures kalendārs 1992. gadam*. [*Official (German) and Local (Latvian) Language*]. Rīga: Zinātne, 276–77.

Strods, Heinrihs. 2010. *PSRS politiskā cenzūra Latvijā 1940–1990 [Political Censorship of the USSR in Latvia 1940–1990]*. Rīga: Jumava.

Sturge, Kate. 2002. 'Censorship of translated fiction in Nazi Germany', *TTR*, XV(2): 153–69.

Talvoja, Kädi. 2018. 'The official art of the Khrushchev Thaw: The Severe Style as an ambassador of the Estonian national school at Baltic art exhibitions in Moscow', *Journal of Baltic Studies*, 49(3): 333–50.

Unāms, Žanis. 1969. *Karogs vējā*. Latvju grāmata [The flag in the wind]. Latvju Grāmata,

Unāms, Žanis. 1975. *Zem Barbarosas šķēpa [Under the Spear of Barbarossa]*. Michigan: Apgādi Aka un Gauja.

Veinberga, Sandra. 2018. 'Publicistikas attīstība līdz Latvijas valsts neatkarības iegūšanai (1918)', *Aktuālas problēmas literatūras un kultūras pētniecībā*, 23 [*Development of Journalism Until Gaining of Latvian Independence (1918)*]. Liepāja: LiePA, 154–73.

Veisbergs, Andrejs. 2012. 'The Latvian translation scene: Paradigms, change and centrality', *Translation Quarterly*, 66: 31–57.

Veisbergs, Andrejs. 2016. 'Defensive and defective stance in translation and translation criticism in Latvia between the wars (1918–1940)', *Procedia - Social and Behavioral Sciences*, 231: 11–18.

Zanders, Viesturs. 2013. 'Nacionālā grāmatniecība gadsimtu ritumā'. J. Stradiņš (red.) *Latvieši un Latvija*, 4. sēj [*National Publishing over the Centuries*]. Rīga: LZA, 331–54.

Zauberga, Ieva. 2001. 'Ideological Dimension in Translation', in A. Veisbergs (ed.), *Contrastive and Applied Linguistics. X*. Riga: University of Latvia, 113–22.

Zellis, Kaspars. 2012. *Ilūziju un baiļu mašinērija* [*Machinery of Illusions and Fears*]. Rīga: Mansards.

Zelmenis, Gints. 2007. 'Kultūras pārraudzība un cenzūra Latvijā padomju okupācijas apstākļos 1940–1941. gadā'. *Latvijas vēsture 20. gadsimta 40.-90. gados. Latvijas vēsturnieku komisijas raksti*, 21. sēj [*Culture Supervision and Censorship in the Conditions of Latvian Soviet Occupation 1940–1941*]. Rīga: Latvijas vēstures institūta apgāds, 15–44.

Zelmenis, Gints. 2012. 'Cenzūra un to reglamentējošā likumdošana Latvijā (1918–1934)' [Censorship and legislation regulating it in Latvia (1918–1934)], *Latvijas Vēstures institūta žurnāls*, 4: 79–104.

10

CENSORSHIP AND TRANSLATION OF SLOVENE TEXTS IN THE HABSBURG MONARCHY AND THE KINGDOM OF YUGOSLAVIA

Nike K. Pokorn

10.1 Introduction

In the sixth century, a Slavonic tribe, the Slovenes, settled in the Eastern Alps. After two brief periods of autonomy in the seventh and ninth century, they became subjects of the Frankish empire in the tenth century. From the end of the thirteenth century and up to the end of the First World War in 1918, the ethnic Slovene territory came under the rule of the House of Habsburg. The Slovene population lived in the so-called lands of 'Inner Austria' (encompassing the historical provinces of Carniola, Carinthia, Styria, and the lands of the Austrian Littoral, cf. Gow and Carmichael 2000: 10–13), and were subject to Austrian legislation, including regulations concerning censorship. After the dissolution of Austria-Hungary in 1918, the majority of the ethnic Slovene territory became part of the Kingdom of Serb, Croats and Slovenes (from 1929 called the Kingdom of Yugoslavia), and remained a part of this state until the Second World War.

If we understand translation censorship as any kind of prohibition or rewriting of the translated text by any of the agents involved in the production of the target text, such as the authors, translators, editors, publishers, revisers or censors, in line with a particular, usually dominant ideology, worldview, political position, or with social standards and norms or poetics, then the history of censorship of translations into and from the Slovene language in imperial contexts is intricate and complex. This is especially true since, until the middle of the twentieth century, translations into Slovene were subject to several systems of censorship that changed under different monarchical forms of government.

The first instances of censorial control imposed upon Slovene translations were linked to particular periods in the Habsburg monarchy, where at different historical periods different aims were pursued: censorial mechanisms during the post-Reformation period of the sixteenth and seventeenth centuries differed considerably from those practised during the Enlightened Absolutism of Maria Theresa and her son Joseph II in the eighteenth century, and those introduced in the

154

DOI: 10.4324/9781003149453-13

aftermath of the March Revolution of 1848. After the collapse of Austria-Hungary in 1918 when most of the ethnic Slovene territory was incorporated into the Kingdom of Serbs, Croats and Slovenes (renamed to the Kingdom of Yugoslavia in 1929), state censorship survived, albeit again in a slightly different form. With the change of monarchs and monarchies, the form of censorship also changed: over the course of history Slovene translations were subject to implicit, but also to preliminary and retroactive explicit censorship, and very often both systems functioned side by side.

10.2   Historical Perspectives

While the first written document in the Slovene language (a collection of translated confessions and sermons called the *Freising Fragments*) dates from the end of the tenth century, the first recorded instances of translation censorship took place at the end of the sixteenth and the beginning of the seventeenth centuries, when ethnic Slovene territory had already been a part of Habsburg's empire for a few centuries.

The Habsburg royal family was one of the most important and powerful Catholic dynasties in Europe, which in the sixteenth century was challenged by the growing Reformation movement and ensuing religious conflicts. While the Habsburgs remained staunchly Catholic, they sometimes assumed a softer approach towards the growing popularity of Lutheranism in their lands. This duality was also felt in the lands inhabited by the Slovene speaking population, which were from 1521 onward ruled by Ferdinand I (1503–1564). The Habsburg lands in Central Europe were consigned to Ferdinand by his older brother, Holy Roman Emperor Charles V (1500–1558), before Ferdinand's marriage to Anna Jagiellon, the sister of the future king of Bohemia and Hungary, in order to satisfy the Hungarian Estates which insisted on accepting only ruling princes as possible grooms for the heiress of the Jagiello dynasty. It was Ferdinand I, who introduced in 1523 the 'first genuinely Austrian censorship measure' (Bachleitner 2017: 42) by prohibiting the reproduction and the sale of Luther's writings and those of his followers. After Ferdinand's death, his lands were divided among his three sons, and Inner Austria, which encompassed the majority of the ethnic Slovene territory, was assigned to his youngest son, Charles II (1540–1590).

Although the court of Charles II in Graz remained Catholic throughout his reign, it is estimated that in the second half of the sixteenth century more than 70% of the population in this area, including nobility, espoused Protestantism. This relative religious freedom was made possible because Charles II had to obtain the consent of the Estates to levy taxes, which he desperately needed to protect the lands against Turkish incursions. In 1572, for example, Archduke Charles granted the nobility an 'edict of pacification' in which he proclaimed his attachment to Catholicism but also granted lords and knights freedom of worship, which was extended to their family, servants and peasants. Two years later, in 1574, in order to obtain additional financial support for defence against the Ottoman Empire, the archduke even allowed Lutheran preachers in the towns of Graz, Klagenfurt and Ljubljana (the last two situated within the ethnic Slovene territory), and granted confessional liberty to the burghers as well. Thus, in the second part of the sixteenth century the constant threat from the Ottoman Empire led Archduke of Inner Austria to a considerable religious tolerance. Consequently, in the period between 1550 and 1595 around 50 Slovene Protestant books were published (mostly in the German towns of Tübingen, Wittenberg, and in Ljubljana, the capital of Carniola), including the first Slovene translation of the Bible (1555–1584), and the first Slovene grammar (1584) (Ahačič 2007), which also served as a basis of the Slovene written language.

However, under the influence of his pious Catholic wife, especially after inviting the Jesuit order to Graz, Archduke Charles's tolerance abated. When Archduke died and his son Ferdinand II (1578–1637) came of age and became the ruler of Inner Austria, the monarchy's tilt toward militant Catholicism became further pronounced. Ferdinand II, who will in 1619 reunite Inner Austria with Danubian Austria and become the head of the Austrian line of the Habsburg family, soon set on the course of re-Catholicizing his dominions. Inner Austria entered a period of fierce Counter-Reformation: Ferdinand's subjects were given the choice of either converting to Catholicism or going into exile. As a result, numerous Protestants were banished, and their original and translated publications were made illegal (see, e.g., Bérenger 1994: 232–3, Winkelbauer 2003).

10.2.1 Counter-Reformation

At the beginning of the seventeenth century, the Catholic Church, backed by the Habsburg court, initiated the Counter-Reformation. When in 1628 Archduke Ferdinand II forbade Protestant worship and teaching in Inner Austria (Sutter Fichtner 2014), this act was also reflected in the retroactive censorship of Protestant works: all Slovene translations of the Bible by the Protestant theologian Jurij Dalmatin (1547–1589) and translations of biblical texts by the Lutheran cleric Primož Trubar (1508–1586) were listed in the *Index librorum prohibitorum* from the time of Pope Paul IV (1559) to Pope Benedict XIV (1758). These two Slovene Protestant authors were listed among 'authors of the first class', which meant that all of their works, including translations, were banned in their entirety (Ditmajer 2020).

During this period what was acceptable or unacceptable in print was defined by the Catholic Church. Although it was the monarch, who, in principle, regulated printing and bookselling in the Habsburg empire, censorship was relegated by the Catholic ecclesiastical authorities (Dović and Vidmar 2021: 23–4). In fact, locally in Habsburg lands, censorship was in the hands of Jesuit colleges and bishops, who, when needed, informed the secular authorities and the inquisition in Rome of any transgressions. In general, the interests of the Catholic Church were in line with those of the Habsburg monarchy, which meant that censorship was directed mainly against the presence of anti-Catholic and non-Catholic publications. For example, Catholic Bishop Janez Tavčar (also Tautscher) informed Charles II that the Protestant printer Mandelc was attempting to print the Slovene translation of the Bible by the Protestant preacher Jurij Dalmatin in Ljubljana, and the Archduke in his letter of 1581 instructed the authorities to prevent the printing of this and any other Protestant work in Carniola and to banish Mandelc from Inner Austria (Reisp 1993: 510). The authorities swiftly responded, and Mandelc left Carniola in 1582. Additionally, at the end of the sixteenth and the beginning of the seventeenth centuries, during the reign of Archduke Ferdinand, retroactive censorship was practiced by special committees under the leadership of local bishops. In the town of Maribor in Styria, and in the towns of Kranj, Škofja Loka and Ljubljana in Carniola in 1600 and 1601, Protestant books were publicly burned—in Ljubljana, for example, in 1600 a pile of around 2000 confiscated Lutheran books was burned in front of the town hall (including, most probably, also Slovene Protestant translations) (Dović and Vidmar 2021: 25).

During this period censorship was thus carried out by local bishops and Jesuit colleges, working hand in hand with secular authorities. In addition to being instrumental in the dominant practice of retroactive censorship, the Catholic church also orchestrated preliminary censorship, manifested in the control of print shops.

Censorship and Translation of Slovene Texts

10.2.2 *Enlightened Despotism (1751–1848)*

In the eighteenth century, control of all written works, including translations, gradually passed from the hands of the Catholic Church to the offices of the Habsburg court. In the second half of the eighteenth century, during the reign of Maria Theresa (1740–1780), censorship was institutionalised, centralised, and bureaucratised. For example, a committee on book censorship (est. in 1751) and a special office for theatre censorship (est. in 1770) were founded (Bachleitner 2017: 239–58; Dović 2020: 244); they operated according to the principles of moderate enlightenment and secularism. This moderation meant that despite the court's upholding of Enlightenment ideas, publications were not allowed to openly support atheism and free thought or attack religion and conventional morality. On the other hand, this transfer of censorial control resulted in the censorship of some Catholic works. For example, the court's *Catalogus librorum a commissione aulica prohibitorum* of 1758 (the catalogue was subsequently amended and expanded several times) contained not only works that were considered morally questionable and some radical French Enlightenment writings but also selected works of Baroque devotional literature, which were accused of spreading superstition. This meant that in monasteries, devotional literature continued to be translated into Slovene (for example, the works of the German Capuchin Friar Martin of Cochem, 1634–1712) but was denied publication and so remained in manuscript form (Ogrin 2020: 119–50).

After Maria Theresa's death, her son Joseph II (1741–1790), who had criticised the severity of censorial control in the monarchy already during the reign of his mother, reformed censorship practices, which brought about liberalization in the field of literary production, printing, and public debate. Although censorship control was lightened, it was not abolished. The Catholic Church continued to practise censorial interventions. For example, in 1781 Johann Karl von Herbertein, the Bishop of Ljubljana, refused to give his formal support to the Slovene translation of the first five books of the Old Testament by the Augustinian friar Marko Pohlin (1735–1801), choosing instead a circle of priests connected to Jansenism to carry out this translational task (Dović and Vidmar 2021: 34–5). Despite such instances of preventive censorship, the period is marked by increasing use of the written Slovene language, culminating toward the end of the eighteenth century in the appearance of a Slovene Roman Catholic translation of the Bible (1784–1802) and the first Slovene secular theatrical texts, by Anton Tomaž Linhart (1756–1795). The first two examples of Slovene secular plays were, in fact, translations from German and French: a translation of the German play *Die Feldmühle*, by Joseph Richter, and that of Pierre-Augustin Caron de Beaumarchais' *La Folle Journée, ou Le Mariage de Figaro*. While both translations must have received print permission since they were printed together in Ljubljana in 1790, problems most probably arose when Linhart applied for a license to perform the plays. There is, however, no extant documentation that would allow us to reconstruct the events. Linhart's translation of the first play by Richter was staged in 1789, while the second one premiered in 1848, more than 50 years after Linhart'death, which allows us to speculate that the performance of the Slovene adaptation of Beaumarchais' play was not permitted due to its attack on aristocratic privilege (Dović 2020: 250; Jurak 2009: 3).

Josephinian relaxation of censorship led to the liberalization of the press, which occasionally allowed the publication of critical voices directed against government policies. This in turn led to the tightening of censorial control toward the end of Joseph's reign, which intensified throughout the reign of his descendants to the throne, Leopold II (1747–1792) and Francis I (1768–1835). The latter, in 1801, formally linked censorship to the police with the establishment of the Court Police and Censorship Office [*Polizei- und Zensurhofsstelle*] (Cvirn 2010: 15). In this period,

The Routledge Handbook of Translation and Censorship

and particularly when the Austrian monarchy was largely governed by Chancellor Klemens von Metternich (who held office between 1809 and 1848), censorship was entirely carried out by the police. A sophisticated system of control ensured that nothing critical of the imperial household and the political system was published. The Court Police and Censorship Office in Vienna, which was presided over by Count Josef Sedlnitzky (1778–1855), Metternich's chief of police, censored everything that could be understood as lèse-majesté or an attack on the government or any foreign monarchs or heads of state, any public abuse of religion, as well as any text, performance, picture or even pottery, fabric and monumental inscriptions that were seen as defamatory or as endangering public morality (cf. Vidmar 2020b: 9; Juvan 2020: 216; Wolf 2015: 134–5; Cvirn 2010).

At the beginning of the nineteenth century, the first Slovene scholarly grammar was published (1808), which initiated the standardisation and codification of the Slovene language. The author of this grammar, Jernej Kopitar (1780–1844), worked in Vienna as the first curator at the Vienna Court Library, and between 1810 and 1844 served as the imperial censor for books written in Slavic languages and Modern Greek (later also in Romanian) (Juvan 2020: 226). As the imperial censor he became embroiled in several disputes with some of the most prominent Slovene literary figures of the time, among them, the national Romantic poet France Prešeren (1800–1849). However, Kopitar did not act on his own, for he could not monitor everything that was published in Slovene: literary production at the time was generally controlled by local censorial offices that were connected to the police, and only more complex cases or complaints were transferred to Vienna (Juvan 2020: 219). Similarly to other parts of the empire, the local censors tended to rely on reports provided by trusted locals who knew the language and the subject matter, which meant that some of the most prominent scholars and intellectuals of the period provided expertise in such censorial matters (Juvan 2020: 221).

The beginning of the century also saw the ethnic Slovene territory briefly occupied by Napoleon (1809–1813), whose administration promised the Slovene population the use of the Slovene language in administration and schools. After the defeat of Napoleon's army, the territory was again incorporated into the Austrian Empire. However, the Slovene language continued to develop, and its public use expanded with the appearance of the first newspaper in the Slovene language in Ljubljana in 1843. In the first half of the nineteenth century, Slovene publications appear to have largely avoided the official prohibition of the Habsburg censors, since in the period between 1792 and 1848 only one Slovene book was listed in the catalogue of prohibited books: an anonymous religious tract *Shivlenje svetiga Joshta* [The Life of Saint Judoc] (Pastar 2020: 167).

10.2.3   *March Revolution of 1848 and its Aftermath (1848–1914)*

In the early 1840s, when approximately one fifth of books were banned in the pre-publishing stage in Austria, a series of complaints and petitions were made by journalists and artists against state censorship. In March 1848 revolution broke out in Vienna, Metternich was overthrown, serfdom was abolished, a constitution was adopted, and freedom of the press was introduced. In fact, on 15 March 1848, Emperor Ferdinand I (who reigned from 1835 to 1848) abolished press censorship altogether, which led to a publishing frenzy (Cvirn 2010: 19). However, this total liberalization was short-lived. In 1851 preventive censorship targeting primarily the press was reinstated: every printed work had to be submitted for inspection three days before publication, and every periodical one hour before it went to print. That did not last long either. In 1862 the new press law effectively abolished pre-publication censorship and introduced post-publication censorship, which was soon in full swing: already in the three years following the introduction of the law, 389 works were

Censorship and Translation of Slovene Texts

banned (Wolf 2015: 135). Censorship was directed against the same social elements that were found problematic in the Metternich Era (Cvirn 2010: 20). Through a network of prosecutors and courts, the government often seized print runs, prosecuted the press, and imposed heavy fines on authors, editors, publishers and printers, which drove some of them to imprisonment or bankruptcy (Dović 2020: 262; Cvirn 2010: 18–31).

During the revolutionary movement in 1848 the Slovene intelligentsia unsuccessfully demanded a unified Slovene province within the Austrian Empire. Despite the rejection of their demand, they were not discouraged. In 1851 the first Slovene publishing house was established, and by the end of the century several political parties were formed that continued to fight for national recognition (Pokorn 2012: 17).

At the turn of the century, literary production in Slovene soared. Writers belonging to the so-called Slovene *Moderna*, a literary movement that combined the influences of Decadence, Realism, Impressionism, Symbolism and Expressionism, created some of their most renowned works. Most of the copies of *Erotika* (Erotics 1899), the first collection of poems by Ivan Cankar (1876–1918), the most prominent author among the Moderna group, were bought and burned by the Ljubljana Catholic bishop Anton B. Jeglič. This incident was a visible reflection of the deep rift within the society of the time between a left-wing liberal position and a right-wing 'clerical' political position. The latter retained close links with the Roman Catholic Church and defined much of Slovene politics before the end of the Second World War. While the burning incident was not backed by the repressive mechanism of the state, the banning of Cankar's socially critical play *Hlapci* [Servants] was. The play was banned in 1909 by the official state censorship office and was staged for the first time only in 1919, a year after the death of its author (Dović 2020: 275–8). Not only original works but also translations were subject to censorship: in 1909 the Slovene translation of the French play *Florette et Patapon* by Maurice Hennequin and Pierre Veber did not receive a license to be performed because the censors found the play to be too 'lascivious' (Dović 2020: 278).

10.2.4 Between the First and Second World Wars (1914–1945)

The First World War, during which Austrian censorship was directed against everything that might impede the war effort (Svoljšek 2010), ended with the dissolution of Austria-Hungary. One third of the Slovene population was left in Italy and Austria, outside the borders of the new State of Slovenes, Croats and Serbs, which only a month after its inception joined the newly formed Kingdom of Serb, Croats and Slovenes (from 1929 called the Kingdom of Yugoslavia). The lands inhabited by Slovenes remained a part of this state from 1918 until the beginning of the Second World War in 1941. Although the new Kingdom favored the Serbs, the Slovenes continued using the Slovene language in official settings. In reality, however, its use was increasingly relegated to the cultural sphere.

Soon after the formation of the Kingdom of Serbs, Croats and Slovenes, large-scale emigration took place, mainly among radical Croatian nationalists called *ustaši* and communists (Drnovšek 2010: 67). From 1921 onward, the Communist Party was considered a terrorist organization, and its members, if caught, were imprisoned for a period of two years. As a result, many of them went abroad and continued their activity there, in part, through publications and pamphlets, which were then smuggled back into the Kingdom. During this period the authorities exercised retroactive censorship and mainly focused on border checks and post offices (Drnovšek 2010).

When in 1929 King Alexander Karadjordjevic declared a dictatorship and renamed the kingdom as the Kingdom of Yugoslavia, he founded the Central Press Bureau in Belgrade (Serbia). This bureau would send censorship instructions to State Prosecutor's offices throughout the kingdom, including Slovenia or 'Dravska banovina' [the Drava Banate], as it was called at that time. Since after 1932 only publications supporting the regime were allowed, the bureau's censorship activities focused mainly on the press (however, radio and film were not exempt) (Studen 2010). In Slovenia, the newspaper *Slovenec* [Slovene], the publication of the forbidden oppositional Slovene People's Party, was targeted (Gašparič 2010). In addition to the press, other writings were subjected to censorial control. For example, in 1932 performances of two translated texts were prohibited: *The Merry Vineyard* by the German dramatist Carl Zuckermayer was branded immoral, while the play by the Soviet playwright Valentin Petrovich Kataev *Million Troubles* was considered too communist in tone. A similar fate befell the Slovene translation of the Soviet play *Alien Child* by Vasiliy Shkvarkin, which was removed from the repertoire in the 1935–1936 season (Gabrič 2010: 174–5). From 1938 onward, all plays selected by theatres for the next season were scrutinised by the censors, who purged the texts of any references that were thought to oppose traditional Catholic morality; any negative representations of Catholic priests were omitted, all plays that were considered revolutionary or critical of the kingdom or the monarchy were banned, and all negative references to Italians and Germans were rewritten or omitted (Gabrič 2010: 177–9).

The Slovenes, who were left out of the new state after the dissolution of Austria-Hungary (the peninsula of Istria with Trieste and the former Princely County of Gorizia and Gradisca were ceded to Italy), faced a far more radical censorship. In his speech in the Istrian town of Pula in 1920 Benito Mussolini described the Slavic race as inferior and barbaric. In line with this position, fascists carried out intense Italianization of the Slovene minority and censored all Slovene printed works, translations included. This was particularly hurtful, since some of the most important Slovene cultural centers and institutions were situated in this area, in particular in Trieste and Gorizia. To name just a few: in the second half of the nineteenth century several Slovene newspapers, among them *Slavjanski rodoljub* (est.1849), *Jadranski Slavjan* (est. 1850), *Edinost* (est. 1876), *Primorski list* (est. 1893), the first Slovene women's literary magazine *Slovenka* (est. 1897), appeared in Trieste, regularly publishing literary translations. Various Slovene publishing houses in Trieste published original and translated Slovene literature, and in 1905 the Slovene theatre started performing at the new building of the Slovene cultural centre in Trieste. The situation was similar in Gorizia, where the Slovene published house Goriška tiskarna (Gorizia Publishing [est. 1893]), led by Andrej Gabršček between 1983 and 1915, published ten newspapers and 167 Slovene literary translations in various book series dedicated to translated literature (Mikolič Južnič 2023).

After the First World War this cultural flowering was brought to an abrupt end: the Slovene cultural center in Trieste was burned down by the fascists in 1920, and the Slovene newspapers and publishing houses were abolished and closed down. In Gorizia two Slovene publishing houses (Goriška matica [est. 1919] and Goriška Mohorjeva družba [est. 1924]), which were established in order to cater to the cultural needs of Slovenes cut off from the Slovenes in the Kingdom of Serbs, Croats and Slovenes, which published, among other things, Slovene literary translations (Mikolič Južnič 2023, 480–3), were first subjected to censorial control, and then closed down. After 1934, all Slovene publications in the province of Venezia Giulia (Italy) were completely forbidden (Bajc 2010).

10.3   Core Issues and Topics

While very few works focus explicitly and uniquely on the censorship of Slovene translations, translations tend to be mentioned in research focusing on censorship as such or on censorship of literary works. In what follows, not only works explicitly focusing on censorship of translations, but also those that only implicitly discuss translation practices within the system of censorship will be mentioned.

In Slovenia there exist two publications dedicated exclusively to censorship in imperial contexts: the collected volume edited by Luka Vidmar (2020a), which focuses on censorship in Slovenia from the sixteenth to the mid-nineteenth century, and the special issue of the journal *Slavica Tergestina*, titled *Habsburg Censorship and Literature in the Slovenian Lands* (2021), which provides, in addition to some new articles, English translations of partially amended chapters already published in the collected volume of 2020.

The collected volume and the special issue of the journal bring together interesting contributions on various forms of censorship of literary works; however, the fact that censored works are often translations is not singled out. For example, the extensive introduction to the special issue of the journal provides a very instructive outline of the history of censorship in the ethnic Slovene territory but refers to translation only in some instances. There are, however, contributions in both outlets that deal specifically with translated works: for example, Nina Ditmajer (2020) focuses on the prohibited books kept in monastic libraries in Styria in the sixteenth and seventeenth centuries, which were very often Protestant translations of religious texts; Matija Ogrin (2020) discusses Slovene manuscript translations of baroque devotional literature that were not allowed to be printed, and Marijan Dović (2020) reconstructs possible censorial interference with the first productions of Linhart's translated plays at the end of the eighteenth century. None of these authors pays particular attention to the fact that in all these instances it was translations and not original works that were subjected to censorship.

Translations are also briefly mentioned in another collected volume focusing on censorship from the nineteenth to the twenty-first centuries published in 2010 (Režek 2010). Although none of the individual contributions focuses solely on censorship in translation, two chapters might be interesting for translation studies scholars. The first one is written by Janez Cvrin (2010) and focuses on censorship of the press—Cvirn does not mention translation, but nevertheless provides a very detailed overview of the legal framework of the Habsburg system of censorship between 1848 and 1914. The second chapter is by Aleš Gabrič (2010), in which he compares theatre censorship in the time of the Kingdom of Yugoslavia to that of socialist Yugoslavia and also discusses cases of preventive and retroactive censorship of translated plays.

There do exist, however, works that deal explicitly with the censorship of translations. Michaela Wolf's monograph *The Habsburg Monarchy's Many-Languaged Soul* (2012: 134–5) provides a very good introduction to translation censorship in the Habsburg monarchy, although not explicitly singling out translations into Slovene. The chapter on translation activity in the nineteenth century in *Zgodovina slovenskega literarnega prevoda* [History of Slovene literary translation] briefly discusses censorship of Slovene literary translations in the nineteenth century (Pokorn 2023: 255–7).

10.4   New Debates

Departing from the discussion of censorship as a purely negative social phenomenon, some recent publications attempt to outline the importance of censors for the development of the Slovene literary field. For example, Marko Juvan (2020) argues that in the 'pre-March' period, before the revolutions of 1848, Habsburg censors, such as Jernej Kopitar, used their symbolic capital to promote their aesthetic judgments. Consequently, they could be compared to contemporary literary critics. Marijan Dović (2020) takes this argument even further and posits that the preventive pre-March censorship also functioned as an important means of quality control. Censors are thus no longer necessarily seen as a negative force, hampering the development of literature, but may be considered important actors in the literary field, promoting literary development and profoundly influencing the literary taste of the period.

Acknowledgements

Nike K. Pokorn acknowledges the financial support from the Slovenian Research and Innovation Agency (research core funding No. P6-0446).

Further Reading

Vidmar, Luka (ed.). 2020. *Cenzura na Slovenskem od protireformacije do predmarčne dobe* [Censorship in Slovenia from the Counter Reformation to the Pre-March Period]. Ljubljana: ZRC SAZU, Inštitut za slovensko literaturo in literarne vede.
Special issue of *Slavica tergestina: European Slavic Studies Journal* 2001, 26(1).

A collective volume with chapters in Slovene and a special issue of *Slavica tergestina* (in which slightly amended chapters from the collective volume are published in English) provide insight into different forms of censorship before the 1848 March Revolution. Chapters by Ditmajer and Ogrin discuss censored translations from the Protestant and Baroque periods.

Wolf, Michaela. 2015 [2012]. *The Habsburg Monarchy's Many-Languaged Soul: Translating and interpreting, 1848–1918*. Amsterdam, Philadelphia: John Benjamins.
A very thoroughly researched work that outlines translation policy in the Habsburg Monarchy. A chapter dedicated to censorship provides a very good introduction to studying the censorship of Slovene books in this period.

References

Ahačič, Kozma. 2007. *Zgodovina misli o jeziku in književnosti na Slovenskem: protestantizem*. [*History of Thought on Language and Literature in Slovene Lands: Protestantism.*] Ljubljana: Založba ZRC, ZRC SAZU. (Linguistica et philologica, 18).
Bachleitner, Norbert. 2017. *Die literarische Zensur in Österreich von 1751 bis 1848*. [*Literary Censorship in Austria from 1751 to 1848.*] Wien, Köln, Weimar: Böhlau.
Bajc, Gorazd. 2010. 'Značilnosti fašističnih cenzurnih posegov med obema vojnama' [Characteristics of fascist censorship interventions in between the two wars.], in M. Režek (ed.), *Cenzurirano: Zgodovina cenzure na Slovenskem od 19. stoletja do danes* [*Censored: History of Censorship in Slovenia from the 19th Century to Today*]. Ljubljana: Nova Revija (Zbirka Razprave 2), 113–28.
Bérenger, Jean. 1994. *A History of the Habsburg Empire 1273–1700*. London, New York: Routledge.
Cvirn, Janez. 2010. 'Naj se vrne cenzura, ljubša bi nam bila: Avstrijsko tiskovno pravo in slovensko časopisje (1848–1914)' ['Let censorship return, we preferred it': Austrian print law and Slovene newspapers (1848–1914)], in M. Režek (ed.), *Cenzurirano: Zgodovine cenzure na Slovenskem od 19. stoletja do danes* [*Censored: History of Censorship in Slovenia from the 19th Century to Today*]. Ljubljana: Nova revija (Razprave 2), 13–44.
Ditmajer, Nina. 2020. 'Prepovedane knjiga v samostanskih knjižnicah na Štajerskem v zgodnjem novem veku' [Banned Books in the Libraries of the Styrian Monasteries in the Early Modern Period.], in L. Vidmar (ed.), *Cenzura na Slovenskem od protireformacije do predmarčne dobe* [*Censorship in Slovenia from the Counter Reformation to the Pre-March Period*]. Ljubljana: ZRC SAZU, Inštitut za slovensko literaturo in literarne vede, 11–37.
Dović, Marijan. 2020. 'Slovenski literati in cesarska cenzura: izbrani primeri iz dolgega 19. Stoletja' [Slovene Writers and Imperial Censorship: Selected Cases from the Long Nineteenth Century.], in L. Vidmar (ed.), *Cenzura na Slovenskem od protireformacije do predmarčne dobe* [*Censorship in Slovenia from the Counter Reformation to the Pre-March Period*]. Ljubljana: ZRC SAZU, Inštitut za slovensko literaturo in literarne vede, 243–86.

Dović, Marijan and Luka Vidmar (eds.). 2021. 'Habsburg Censorship and Literature in the Slovenian Lands', Special Issue of *Slavica tergestina: European Slavic Studies Journal*, 26(1).

Drnovšek, Marjan. 2010. 'Nadzor med komunisti-emigranti in cenzura' [Control over émigré Communists and censorship.], in M. Režek (ed.), *Cenzurirano: Zgodovina cenzure na Slovenskem od 19. stoletja do danes* [*Censored: History of Censorship in Slovenia from the 19th Century to Today*]. Ljubljana: Nova Revija (Zbirka Razprave 2), 67–88.

Gabrič, Aleš. 2010. 'Cenzura gledališkega repertoarja v prvi in drugi Jugoslaviji' [Censorship of Theatre Repertoire in the First and Second Yugoslavia.], in M. Režek (ed.), *Cenzurirano: Zgodovina cenzure na Slovenskem od 19. stoletja do danes* [*Censored: History of Censorship in Slovenia from the 19th Century to Today*]. Ljubljana: Nova Revija (Zbirka Razprave 2), 171–88.

Gašparič, Jure. 2010. 'Cenzura v času diktature kralja Aleksandra' [Censorship in the time of King's Alexander dictatorship, in M. Režek (ed.), *Cenzurirano: Zgodovina cenzure na Slovenskem od 19. stoletja do danes* [*Censored: History of Censorship in Slovenia from the 19th Century to Today*]. Ljubljana: Nova Revija (Zbirka Razprave 2), 89–98.

Gow, James and Cathie Carmicheal. 2000. *Slovenia and the Slovenes: A Small State and the New Europe*. London: Hurst & Company.

Jurak, Mirko. 2009. 'William Shakespeare and Slovene dramatists (I): A. T. Linhart's Miss Jenny Love', *Acta Neophilologica*, 42(1/2): 3–34.

Juvan, Marko. 2020. 'Cenzor in literarno polje: Kopitar, Čop in *Kranjska čbelica*' [The Censor and the Literary Field: Kopitar, Čop and *Kranjska čbelica*], in L. Vidmar (ed.), *Cenzura na Slovenskem od protireformacije do predmarčne dobe* [*Censorship in Slovenia from the Counter Reformation to the Pre-March Period*]. Ljubljana: ZRC SAZU, Inštitut za slovensko literaturo in literarne vede, 211–42.

Mikolič Južnič, Tamara. 2023. 'Prevajanje v Italiji in zamejske založbe' [Translating in Italy and Slovene minority publishing houses], in N. K. Pokorn, R. Grošelj and T. Mikolič Južnič (eds.), *Zgodovina slovenskega literarnega prevoda* [*History of Slovene Literary Translation*]. Ljubljana: Ljubljana University Press, Faculty of Arts and Cankarjeva založba Press, 479–94.

Ogrin, Matija. 2020. 'Poznobaročni slovenski rokopisi – literarna tradicija v spoprijemu z razsvetljensko cenzuro' [Slovenian Manuscripts of the Baroque Period: The Encounter of the Literary Tradition and Enlightenment Censorship.], in L. Vidmar (ed.), *Cenzura na Slovenskem od protireformacije do predmarčne dobe* [*Censorship in Slovenia from the Counter Reformation to the Pre-March Period*]. Ljubljana: ZRC SAZU, Inštitut za slovensko literaturo in literarne vede, 119–50.

Pastar, Andrej. 2020. 'Cenzura na Kranjskem pod Jožefom II' [Censorship in Carniola under Joseph II], in L. Vidmar (ed.), *Censorship in Slovenia from the Counter Reformation to the Pre-March Period*. Ljubljana: ZRC SAZU, Inštitut za slovensko literaturo in literarne vede, 151–80.

Pokorn, Nike K. 2012. *Post-Socialist Translation Practices: Ideological Struggle in Children's Literature*. Amsterdam, Philadelphia: John Benjamins.

Pokorn, Nike K. 2023. 'Prevajanje v devetnajstem stoletju' [Translation in the 19th century], in N. K. Pokorn, R. Grošelj and T. Mikolič Južnič (eds.), *Zgodovina slovenskega literarnega prevoda* [*History of Slovene Literary Translation*]. Ljubljana: Ljubljana University Press, Faculty of Arts and Cankarjeva založba Press, 253–60.

Reisp, Branko. 1993. 'Prvi (protestantski) tiskar na Slovenskem' [The first (Protestant) printer in Slovene lands], *Zgodovinski časopis*, 47(4): 509–14.

Režek, Mateja (ed.). 2010. *Cenzurirano: Zgodovina cenzure na Slovenskem od 19. stoletja do danes* [*Censored: History of Censorship in Slovenia from the 19th Century to Today*]. Ljubljana: Nova Revija (Zbirka Razprave 2).

Studen, Andrej. 2010. 'Ukrepi cenzure na Štajerskem neposredno po objavi Koroščevih punktacij' [Censorship measures in Styria immediately after the publication of Korošec's *Slovenian Declaration*], in M. Režek (ed.), *Cenzurirano: Zgodovina cenzure na Slovenskem od 19. stoletja do danes* [*Censored: History of Censorship in Slovenia from the 19th Century to Today*]. Ljubljana: Nova Revija (Zbirka Razprave 2), 99–112.

Sutter Fichtner, Paula. 2014. *The Habsburgs: Dynasty, Culture and Politics*. London: Reaction Books.

Svoljšek, Petra. 2010. '"Zapleni vse, česar ne razumeš, utegnilo bi škoditi vojevanju." Delovanje avstrijske censure med veliko vojno' [Confiscate everything you do not understand, since it may harm the war effort: Austrian Censorship between the Great War], in M. Režek (ed.), *Cenzurirano: Zgodovina cenzure na Slovenskem od 19. stoletja do danes* [*Censored: History of Censorship in Slovenia from the 19th Century to Today*]. Ljubljana: Nova Revija (Zbirka Razprave 2), 55–65.

The Routledge Handbook of Translation and Censorship

Vidmar, Luka (ed.). 2020a. *Cenzura na Slovenskem od protireformacije do predmarčne dobe* [*Censorship in Slovenia from the Counter Reformation to the Pre-March Period*]. Ljubljana: ZRC SAZU, Inštitut za slovensko literaturo in literarne vede.

Vidmar, Luka. 2020b. 'Uvod' [Introduction.], in L. Vidmar (ed.), *Cenzura na Slovenskem od protireformacije do predmarčne dobe* [*Censorship in Slovenia from the Counter Reformation to the Pre-March Period*]. Ljubljana: ZRC SAZU, Inštitut za slovensko literaturo in literarne vede, 7–10.

Winkelbauer, Thomas. 2003. *Ständefreiheit und Fürstenmacht. Länder und Untertanen des Hauses Habsburg im konfessionellen Zeitalter* (= Österreichische Geschichte 1522–1699, ed. by Herwig Wolfram), vol. 2. [*Freedom of the Estates and Princely Power. Lands and Subjects of the House of Habsburg in the confessional age = History of Austria 1522–1699*]. Wien: Carl Ueberreuter Verlag.

Wolf, Michaela. 2015 [2012]. *The Habsburg Monarchy's Many-Languaged Soul: Translating and Interpreting, 1848–1918*. Amsterdam and Philadelphia: John Benjamins.

11

TRANSLATION AND CENSORSHIP IN UKRAINE UNDER RUSSIAN AND AUSTRIAN RULE, 1800–1917

Oleksandr Kalnychenko and Lada Kolomiyets

11.1 Historical Perspectives

The Ukrainian translation tradition began soon after the adoption of Christianity in 988 and accelerated when the Grand Prince of Kyivan Rus' Yaroslav the Wise 'brought together' in 1037 in the Cathedral of St. Sophia in Kyiv 'many scribes, who translated [from Greek] into the [Old] Slavic language', as written in the earliest East Slavic chronicle *The Tale of Bygone Years* (Povĕstĭ vremęnĭnyxŭ lĕtŭ) (see, e.g., Moskalenko 1995). This chapter will discuss translation only into the modern, vernacular-based Ukrainian language, established in literature with the publication in 1798 of Ivan Kotliarevsky's poem *Eneida na malorossiiskyi iazyk perelytsiovannaia* [The *Aeneid* 'dressed' in the Ukrainian language], a travesty of Virgil's *Aeneid*. Further developed by Ukrainian writers, that language acquired the status of a literary language in the second half of the nineteenth century (see, e.g., Danylenko and Naienko 2019).

Starting from the early 1800s Ukrainian translation developed side by side with the new Ukrainian literature, both of which were marked by Ukraine's status as a colony of the Russian empire, which instituted prohibitions and restrictions on the use of the Ukrainian language. By its formal status, Ukraine was not a colony, as some of the Ukrainian provinces belonged to the empire proper, while the Right Bank, as a former part of the Polish-Lithuanian Commonwealth, had some specific administrative arrangements. But in fact, all of Ukraine under Russian rule was treated by the Russian government as a colony. The Russian government fiercely oppressed Ukrainians (and Belarusians) as an ethnic group, although Ukrainians were at the same time much less discriminated against as individuals as they were officially regarded as Russians and so were, in principle, open to any career, provided they spoke Russian (Kappeler 2003: 73). In the absence of 'separatist' intentions, they could reach the highest levels of the imperial hierarchy (without abandoning their regional attachments, such as songs, cuisine and historical relics, in the case of the families of the left-bank nobility). In order to do this, however, they had to recognise themselves unconditionally as part of the 'triune Russian nation', for which regional peculiarities did not supercede state and spiritual unity (Strikha 2020: 56). The aim and the result of such a policy was the Russification of Ukrainian urban areas and the reduction of Ukraine to a peasant nation.[1] The Ukrainian language in the Austrian Empire and, after 1867, in the Austro-Hungarian Empire, did not fare much better: the language bills of 1866 and 1869 made Polish the

DOI: 10.4324/9781003149453-14

165

lingua franca in lieu of German in the province of Galicia (Ukr *Halychyna*), which drastically reduced the sociolinguistic status of Ukrainian (Danylenko 2010: 21), though one could freely publish there in Ukrainian, and Ukrainian was used in education, however, mainly at the elementary level. Contrasting the situation in the Austrian-ruled part of Ukraine to the Russian-ruled part, although Austria-Hungary was hardly a paragon of freedom of speech, it offered the possibility of publishing Ukrainian-language materials, including translations, during the periods of bans and repressions on the Russian side.

Ukraine under Russian rule was a quintessential case of translation impacting censorship and censorship impacting translation, especially during the repressions and prohibitions of Ukrainian publications from 1863 to1905. A unique phenomenon of the 1800s, which makes the case of Ukrainian translation very different from that of neighbouring Russia or Poland, is the outright prohibition on the Ukrainian language in print and the total ban on the publication of any translations into Ukrainian. Consequently, the readers of translations into Ukrainian comprised a narrow stratum of national, mostly multilingual, intellectuals (Fylypovych 1930). Translation, therefore, was not merely a source of information; it served the function of nation-building (Strikha 2006). Although translations were for the most part restricted to belles-lettres, they nonetheless became a major factor in shaping the national identity of Ukrainians. From the beginning of the nineteenth century through the Soviet era, translation into Ukrainian, especially of literary works, was a part of the resistance to colonial domination (Strikha 2006). It was also the means by which vocabulary was introduced into the Ukrainian language in fields where it did not exist due to a dearth of Ukrainian-speakers among the upper classes, army, administrators, scientists and clergy (Strikha 2006).

Beginning in the late 1840s, Ukrainian literature and culture became the object of particularly severe persecution by the Russian government. Hryhorii Kvitka-Osnovianenko's *A Short Sacred History* [Biblical stories for common people] became one of the many victims of censorship. It could not be printed for the sole reason that it was written in Ukrainian (Krevetsky 1904: 133; Fabrikant 2017: 156).

The tsarist police tracked down and arrested the Ukrainophile intelligentsia of the time and exposed secret societies of historians, ethnographers and writers, such as The Brotherhood of Saints Cyril and Methodius in Kyiv (1845–1847), who were influenced by the ideas of the Ukrainian renaissance of the first half of the nineteenth century as well as by European Romanticism. The members of the Brotherhood believed in a federation of Slavic peoples and advocated for the distinct nationality of Ukrainians (Sokhan et al. 1990).

Putting forth the idea of the liberation of Ukraine, the Brotherhood proved to be a milestone in the history of Ukrainian Romanticism and 'the first modern Ukrainian political platform' (Luckyj 1991: 1). Among its members, whose number may have amounted to a hundred people, one should mention the names of its organisers Mykola Hulak (1821–1899), Mykola Kostomarov (1817–1885) and Vasyl Bilozersky (1825–1899) (Sokhan et al. 1990). After the Brotherhood was denounced in March 1847, many of its members were arrested, imprisoned and exiled without trial, including the poet Taras Shevchenko (1814–1861) (for more details, see Kolomiyets 2016). Panteleimon Kulish (1819–1897) and Taras Shevchenko were prosecuted and convicted for their literary works, which, in the opinion of political police officials, had the greatest influence on the formation of 'Ukrainophile' feelings. The short-lived Brotherhood of Saints Cyril and Methodius has been regarded as 'first, the birthplace of modern Ukrainian identity; second, an early center of federalist thought in the Russian Empire; and third, a secret society of religious-minded intellectuals' (Luckyj 1991: 3). This movement of Ukrainian youth was in line with the pan-European movement for the rights of enslaved peoples against reactionary autocracy, which manifested itself in the revolutionary uprising of Italians, Germans, Hungarians and Poles in 1848 during the 'Spring of Nations' (Procyk 2019).

During the revolutionary movement in the western Ukrainian lands in 1848, national political programs were formulated, and the first Ukrainian newspaper, *Zorya Halytska* [The Galician Star], a weekly published in Lviv, was set up. It published a manifesto declaring the ethnic unity of Ukrainians in the Austrian and Russian Empires and their right to develop their own culture. Moreover, that same year the University of Lviv began teaching Ukrainian language and literature (Isaievych 2002: 398).

Although the first known example of a translation of the canonical text of the Scriptures— the Peresopnytsia Gospel—into Middle Ukrainian dates from the sixteenth century (1561), the Russian ecclesiastical authorities for centuries resisted the translation of the Holy Scriptures even into Russian; the complete Russian New Testament was published only in 1862. At that time, the Ukrainian translation of the Gospels, completed by Pylyp Morachevsky (1806–1879) in 1861, received a favourable review from academics (Danylenko 2010). The prospect of publishing the Holy Scriptures in vernacular Ukrainian ('Little Russian') appeared to be among the immediate reasons behind the issuance of the secret instructions of 1863 by Russia's Minister of Internal Affairs, Pyotr Valuev, to the censorship committees of Kyiv, Moscow and St. Petersburg. These instructions imposed restrictions on Ukrainian-language publications in the Russian Empire. The Censorship Administration 'could license for publication in this language only such books that belonged to the realm of fine literature; at the same time, the authorisation of books in Little Russian with either spiritual content or intended generally for primary mass reading should be ceased' (in Miller 2003: 264). The 1863 Valuev Circular announced, in essence, that '[T]here has never been, is not, and cannot be any separate Little Russian language, and that [the] dialect, spoken by the common people, is the selfsame Russian language, only spoiled by the influence of Poland' (in Fabricant 2017). And therefore, the possibility of printing 'the Little Russian Gospel' was withdrawn from the agenda and Morachevsky's translation of the Gospels was published only in 1906 after the First Russian Revolution of 1905 (for a more detailed account, see Strikha 2006: 101–6; Danylenko 2010).

It was a translation, again, that triggered an even more rigorous ban on the Ukrainian language and culture, namely, the secret decree, known as the 'Ems Ukase', signed by Tsar Aleksandr II on 30 May 1876, in the German town of Bad Ems. The translation in question was the first Ukrainian translation to be published in the Russian Empire of the historical novella *Taras Bulba*, authored by the Ukrainian-born writer Nikolai Gogol (Hohol 1874) and translated by Mykhailo Lobodovsky (1841–1919). Incidentally, the clearance of this publication by the censor lasted only a year—until Mikhail Yuzefovich, an instigator of the Ukase, referred to this translation in his 1875 Memorandum *On the So-called Ukrainophylic Movement,* pointing out the faults of the translation, including the deletion of the words *Russia* and *Russian land* from Gogol's text and the 'arrogant' substitution of them with the words *Ukraine* and *Ukrainian land*, and so forth. Yuzefovich also accused the translator of prophesizing 'the arrival of the future Ukrainian Tsar' (Miyakovsky 1919: 1820; in Kalnychenko and Kalnychenko 2019: 73).

The Yuzefovich Memorandum resulted in the establishment of an imperial commission, the recommendations of which laid the foundation for the repressive Ems Ukase which (with minor amendments) remained in force until the Revolution of 1905. The Ukase declared: '[N]o books or pamphlets published in the Little Russian dialect are to be permitted to be imported into the borders of the Empire without special permission from the Chief Administration for Press Affairs' and 'the printing and publishing in the Empire of original works and translations in the said dialect' was banned, with the sole exception of historical documents and works of *belles-lettres*, provided that 'in works of belles-lettres no deviations from the accepted Russian orthography are permitted' (Savchenko 1930: 374; in Fabrikant 2017: 161). But the prohibition spread beyond the written word. In accordance with the Ukase '[v]arious theatrical presentations and readings in the Little Russian dialect are also to be forbidden, as is the printing in it of texts to music' (Savchenko 1930: 374; Boriak 2015: 139–40; in Fabrikant 2017: 161). Moreover, in 1892, the Chief Administration for Press Affairs unconditionally banned any translations of Russian-language works into Ukrainian (Boriak 2015: 247).

Still, the Ems Ukase and Valuev Directives were never passed into law; they were never published for the public but were distributed as departmental acts within the Ministry of Internal Affairs, which characterises the Russian state as an autocratic empire engaged in illegal coercion, which did not even require the legalization of its actions (Shandra 2015).

Translations of books recognised as 'harmful' in their content were prohibited at various times across the world, but in Russian-ruled Ukraine the period of 1876–1905 (for details about the period 1906–1914 see Danylenko 2017) was a time when the translation of anything at all could be prohibited, even the most innocent *Tale about a Fisherman and a Fish* by the outstanding Russian poet Alexander Pushkin on the eve of the Pushkin Jubilee of 1899 (Beletskii 1929). Pavlo Fylypovych (1891–1937) (1927/1930: XLVII–XLVIII) reported on an interesting correspondence about Pushkin's fairy tale that took place between the Odesa censor and the Chief Administration for Press Affairs. In response to the censor's request, the Chief Administration replied briefly: 'translations are not allowed' (Fylypovych 1927/1930: XLVIII). The translator Mykhailo Slastin, however, was not satisfied with the reply and sent his manuscript to the Kharkiv censor. Again, correspondence with the Chief Administration took place, followed by another ban, with the explanation that one should use 'every opportunity to reduce publications in the Little Russian dialect' (Fylypovych 1927/1930: XLVIII).[2]

In 1898, composer Mykola Lysenko (1842–1912) applied to the St. Petersburg Censorship Office for permission to publish the text for his musical interpretation of Adam Mickiewicz's poem *Moja pieszczotka* [My darling] in Russian, Polish and Ukrainian (*Moya mylovanka* in Starytsky's Ukrainian translation). The Chief Administration for Press Affairs passed the following resolution: '... the printing of the Polish text and the Russian translation is permitted' (Boriak 2015: 281). Although the ban on musical publications in Ukrainian was lifted in 1881 (see Boriak 2015: 190), the ban on publishing translations remained in place, and between 1876 and 1881 even folk songs were forbidden for public performance in Ukrainian—they could only be performed in translation into French, Russian or Czech.

In Western Ukraine under the comparatively liberal government of Austria-Hungary, the printing of books in Ukrainian was permitted, although censorship restrictions were placed on the content: 'the paragraphs of the Criminal Code considered relevant to publishing' range from 'disturbing the peace, sedition, endangering public morality and defamation up to lèse-majesté and high treason' (Wolf 2015: 135). Consequently, to circumvent the bans of the tsarist government, translators and original writers in Russian-ruled Ukraine looked for ways to publish their work in Western Ukraine. For example, Panteleimon Kulish, the first professional Ukrainian writer and a versatile translator, who introduced a new Ukrainian orthography (the Kulishivka script), which was banned in the Ems Ukase of 1876, published most of his works in the Habsburg Empire under pen-names, thus eluding the draconian constraints on Ukrainian-language publications in the Russian Empire (for a more detailed account, see Danylenko 2016).

Translation and Censorship in Ukraine, 1800–1917

In cooperation with Ivan Puliui (Puluj) (1845–1918), a Ukrainian-born physicist and electrical engineer at the University of Vienna and the Prague Polytechnic Institute, Kulish published a translation of the Gospels in 1871 (in Vienna) and of the entire New Testament in 1880 (in Lviv). In 1881, Ivan Puliui petitioned (via the Russian embassy) the Chief Administration for Press Affairs to permit a Ukrainian translation of the New Testament to be imported into Ukraine. The request was denied. After Kulish's death, a full translation of the Bible was completed by Puliui and Ivan Nechui-Levytskyi (1838–1918) and appeared in 1903 under the auspices of the British and Foreign Bible Society. Puliui again took measures to legally admit it into Russia. But again, he received a resolute refusal (Studynsky 1931: XXXV; Strikha 2020: 114), while several copies were smuggled across the border.

Kulish, who intended to translate all of Shakespeare's works into Ukrainian and who provided the first secular variant of Ukrainian high style in his translations of Shakespeare, went to Lviv in 1881 to publish his translations of *Othello, Troilus and Cressida*, and *Comedy of Errors* (1882), which preserved the playwright's vulgarisms and bawdy jokes (for details, see Hordynsky 1928). His attempts to publish translations of Shakespeare in Russian-ruled Ukraine failed because the Chief Administration for Press Affairs banned their publication in 1883 (Boriak 2015: 199), while admitting that the permission of 1881 to publish his translation of *Hamlet*, provided the necessary orthographic changes were made (Boriak 2015: 195), '[had been] issued by mistake' (Boriak 2015: 199). Given that Russian translations of Shakespeare were permitted, the decision was based on the language of Kulish's translations, not the contents. All in all, Kulish translated 13 of Shakespeare's plays, but managed to publish only the three mentioned above. The manuscripts of his translations of ten other dramas by Shakespeare remained unpublished for about twenty years; they saw the light of day only in 1899–1902 in Lviv (Halychyna), after Kulish's death (1897). All other attempts to publish Shakespeare in Ukrainian in the Russian Empire were doomed (for details see Danylenko 2020; Luchuk 2018). When Kulish's widow Hanna Barvinok (1828–1911) applied for permission from the censorship office to publish his translation of Shakespeare's tragedy *Romeo and Juliet*, she received a response from the censor Sokolov that 'the emperor allows the publication of belles-lettres in Little Russian, but the rules for translations remain the same' (Kochur 2008: 710).

In that same year, 1882, Mykhailo Starytsky (1839–1904) published his translation of Shakespeare's *Hamlet* (translated in 1877) as a separate book in Kyiv (i.e., in the Russian Empire), and in 1883 his second volume of *From an Old Notebook*, comprised mostly of translations of Russian poets, was published. The writer's daughter Liudmyla Starytska-Cherniakhivska admitted in a letter to Ivan Franko (16 December 1901) that the Ems ban had been circumvented with the help of a hundred-ruble bribe to the Kyiv censor Leimitz (Dotsenko 2013: 426).

Petro Nishchynsky (1832–1896), who was the first to translate Sophocles' *Antigone* and Homer's *Odyssey* from the original Greek into modern Ukrainian, was permitted to publish *Antigone* in Odesa in 1883 but was forbidden to publish the translation of *The Odyssey* even though translations of classical works did not require preliminary censorship in the Russian Empire (Krevetsky 1904: 156). So, *The Odyssey* had to be published in Halychyna and then secretly imported into Russia (Shevelov 1994), as were the translations of Homer's *Iliad* by Stepan Rudansky (1834–1873), of Dante's *Divine Comedy* and Molière's *Tartuffe* by Volodymyr Samiilenko (1864–1925), of Schiller's *Maria Stuart* and *Wilhelm Tell* by Borys Hrinchenko (1863–1910), of Heinrich Heine's poetry by Lesia Ukrainka (1871–1913) and Maksym Slavinsky (1868–1945), among others (Krevetsky 1904: 152). Translators in Russian-ruled Ukraine, such as Pavlo Hrabovsky (1864–1902) (exiled to Siberia), Olena Pchilka (1849–1930), Ivan Nechui-Levytskyi, Ivan Steshenko (1873–1918), Maria Zahirna (1863–1928), Lesia Ukrainka, Maksym

The Routledge Handbook of Translation and Censorship

Slavinsky, Yevhen Tymchenko (1866–1948) and many others published their works in Austrian-ruled Halychyna and Bukovyna.

In 1896 when his translation of Schiller's tragedy *Maria Stuart* was being published in the Lviv journal *Zoria*, Hrinchenko also submitted it to the Russian censor in Odessa, who did not allow its publication. The translator complained to the Chief Administration for Press Affairs, to the Minister of Internal Affairs and, finally, to the Senate, receiving repeated refusals. Only in 1911 did he obtain permission to publish the translation in Kyiv (Khoptiar 2012: 199). To increase the likelihood of obtaining permission to publish in Russia, translators would occasionally send several versions of their translated texts under different names and pseudonyms to different censorship committees at the same time (Rudnytska 2021).

In 1895, the Shevchenko Scientific Society in Lviv published, at long last, the Ukrainian translation (made by Oleksand Konysky (1838–1900) in Russian-ruled Ukraine) of Taras Shevchenko's *Journal*, his daily diary written in Russian in 1857–1858. This edition restored the numerous passages that had been censored or removed on ethical grounds in the first publication in the journal *Osnova* [Foundation] in 1861–1862 because they were written in the original manuscript. But the Halychyna edition also contained signs of censorship, on this occasion for moral reasons, as the great national poet had no right to a mere mortal's vices (just as he had no right to compose 'the Muscovy poems', which were also deleted) (Strikha 2020: 137).

The persistent prohibition on publishing translations in Ukrainian served as a crucial obstacle to the structural, expressive and stylistic development of the Ukrainian language. The ban was also applied to translations from the Russian language, which, naturally, would emphasise the contrast between these structurally close and at the same time distinct languages (Hrytsenko 2015). In 1892, the Chief Administration for Press Affairs gave orders to the Kyiv censor to reduce the number of Ukrainian publications 'as much as possible on the grounds of the slightest excuses' and unconditionally ban any translations of Russian language works in Ukrainian (Boriak 2015: 247). Three years later a ban on children's literature was added (Boriak 2015: 294–5, 301–2, 310–11).

A strategy to circumvent censorship involved the publication of translations of foreign works as original works of Ukrainian literature. To do so, translators often had to rehash or adapt their source texts and conceal the translated authors' names. For instance, Borys Hrinchenko (1863–1910) turned Leo Tolstoy's novella *The Prisoner in the Caucasus* into the story *The Black Sea Men in Captivity* (Raliv 1929: 24). In 1884, he used the same strategy to circumvent the ban on the publication of his Ukrainian translation of Daniel Defoe's *Robinson Crusoe*, submitting the translation to the censorship office as his own story *Vasyl Hayda. The Story by V. Chaichenko on the Topic of Robinson*. Although he was at first turned down, the text was allowed to be published in 1886 in the 'Supplements' section of the journal *Batkivshchyna* and in 1891 the adaptation was published in Kyiv as a separate book under the title *Robinson. The Story of How One Man Traveled to Foreign Lands and How He Lived all Alone on an Island in the Middle of the Sea. Written by V. Chaichenko*. The latter version underwent several reprints in Kyiv (1892, 1894), as well as in Halychyna (Khoptiar 2012: 72).

In 1883, Panas Myrny (1849–1920) retold in Ukrainian the *Tale of Igor's Campaign* (*Слово о пълкоу Игоревъ*), an old epic in the Old East Slavic language (aka Old Ukrainian). After several attempts to get this work published, Myrny received the response that the work 'is a translation of the famous *Tale of Igor's Campaign* and, as a non-original work, on the basis of the Directive of the Chief Administration for Press Affairs dated January 8, 1892, No. 96, cannot be allowed to be published' (Boriak 2015: 300). Thus, intra-lingual translations were also prohibited. Eventually, Myrny's retelling of the tale saw the light of day 13 years later, while his translation of *The Tragedy of King Lear* remained unpublished until 1970.

Translation and Censorship in Ukraine, 1800–1917

Ukrainian theatre was also under the vigilant control of Russian imperial censorship. There were 'limitations on the depiction of certain topics (no satire or history, no plays about middle-class life, no romantic verse drama), and language use (the middle- and upper-class characters were supposed to speak Russian)' (Makaryk 2004: 10). It was permitted to show a Ukrainian play on the same night as a Russian one, only if it followed the Russian play and contained the same number of acts.

The restrictions remained on the books until 1905 but were formally abolished only in 1907. Although in 1905 censorship was loosened and the language ban was no longer applied, in 1907, for example, 'the tsarist censors still refused permission to stage *Hamlet* because, they argued, a Ukrainian production might evoke laughter by its presumption of treating a world classic in a "peasant" language' (Makaryk 2004: 10). A period of leniency after 1905 was followed by another strict ban in 1914, which also affected Russian-occupied Halychyna.

Consequently, in order to circumvent the outright prohibition of the Ukrainian language in print Ukrainians from the Russian Empire had to publish their translations abroad (e.g., in Austrian-ruled Ukraine), adapt the source texts and hide the names of the translated authors, or pay a bribe to the censor.

11.2 Core Issues and Topics

Ukrainian political theorist Mykhailo Drahomanov (1841–1895) initiated an investigation into the bans and restrictions on the Ukrainian language carried out by the Russian imperial censors. He resolutely condemned the secret Ems Ukase at the International Literary Congress in Paris in 1878 and defended the Ukrainian language in his pamphlet about how Ukrainian literature was proscribed by the Russian government (Dragomanov 1878). The first history of Russian censorship of Ukrainian cultural products, ranging from book publishing to theatre performances, however, was written by Krevetsky (1883–1940) (1904). This well-researched work, which is still of considerable relevance today, appeared in the leading Ukrainian journal of the time, *Literaturno-naukovyi vistnyk*, published in Halychyna. The Russian translation of Krevetsky's article 'There Has Not Been, Is Not, and Cannot Be!' was published under the pseudonym Nik. Fabrikant (1905) in the Russian liberal journal *Russkaia mysl'*. The English translation of the Russian translation of this article appeared in 2017.

Several scholarly articles on the cultural activities of Ukrainian intellectuals of the 1820s through the 1870s and on tsarist censorship were published by the Ukrainian researcher Miyakovsky (1888–1972), who began the work of cataloguing the censored writings contained in the archives of the Chief Administration for Press Affairs, which were declassified after the February Revolution of 1917. He managed to make some of them public in the late 1910s and 1920s, when some freedom of the press was allowed (Miyakovsky 1919, 1984). The only book on the policies of the tsarist authorities regarding the suppression of the Ukrainian language in 1876 was written in the late 1920s by Ukrainian historian Savchenko (1892–sometime after 1938); it was published in 1930 and reprinted in 1970 in Munich. It includes a large number of documents, most published for the first time.

Literary scholar and translator Fylypovych in 'Pushkin in Ukrainian Literature' (1927, reprinted in 1930), his voluminous foreword to an anthology of Ukrainian translations of Pushkin, starting from 1830, analyses the changes in translation methods, readers' reception and linguistic resources, and documents censorial bans on certain Ukrainian translations of Pushkin. In his outline of translation history in Ukraine from the mid-1800s to 1928, Biletsky (1884–1961) (Beletsky 1929)[3] surveys the bans on Ukrainian translation in the Russian Empire, as well as the hesitancy of Ukrainian intellectuals in the case of translating world masterpieces, and objects to Russian 'public opinion' regarding the 'needlessness' of translations into Ukrainian.

Russian historian Miller's monograph (2000; English translation 2003), which draws on extensive archival research, aims to reconstruct the process by which administrative decisions were adopted by the Russian tsarist government on the 'Ukrainian question'. Miller analyses Russian-Ukrainian relations as a conflict between the Ukrainian nation-building project and the project of forming the 'great Russian nation', which sought to include Russians, Ukrainians and Belarusians.

As ruthless prohibitive censorship was an integral part of state policy in both the Russian Empire and later in the Soviet Union, scholars of Ukrainian translation history are bound to place particular emphasis on the impact of censorship on translation, as demonstrated in a series of essays on Ukrainian translation history covering the period from its very beginning up to the early 1900s and published in *Vsesvit* monthly by Mykhailo Moskalenko (1948–2006) from 1993 to 2006. Strikha's monumental monograph (2006), the first complete history of the Ukrainian translation tradition, critically summarised in English by Chernetsky (2011), traces the development of Ukrainian translation in the 1800s and 1900s as the implementation of a conscious project of anti-colonial resistance and of nation-, language- and literature-making under conditions of persistent imperial and Soviet bans and restrictions.

11.3   New Debates

The recent decade has witnessed the publication of new collections of documents facilitating research on the topic of translation and censorship. First and foremost among them is Boriak's edited volume (2015), which, at more than 800 pages, offers an excellent collection of almost 300 documents found in approximately forty archives in Ukraine and Russia that deal with Russian imperial efforts to prevent the development of the Ukrainian language within the time span of 1847–1914. The book by Remy (2016), also based on a rich array of archival sources, investigates Ukrainian national activism and its relationship to Russia and Russian and the imperial policies on the Ukrainian question.

The 2017 issue of *EAST/WEST: Journal of Ukrainian Studies* (vol. IV, issue 2) features a special thematic section titled 'Banning a Language "That Does Not Exist": The Valuev Directive of 1863 and the History of the Ukrainian Language.' Edited by Michael Moser, the section includes five articles and Krevetsky's 1904 'A Brief Outline of the History of the Treatment of Ukrainian Literature by Russian Censorship Laws', with an introduction. As Moser demonstrates in his essay (2017), the Valuev Circular did not outlaw the Ukrainian language as such, but rather prevented its standardization and dissemination in the early 1860s as well as its development into a standard language in the contemporary sense of the word. Remy (2007), by contrast, investigates books that were published in Ukrainian despite the imperial bans on the Ukrainian language.

The reasons and effects of the Valuev Circular and Ems Ukase are also discussed in a monograph by Vulpius (2005b), essays by Vulpius (2005a), Dibrova (2017), Danylenko (2010), Reyent (2012), Shandra (2015, 2017) and others. Danylenko's monograph (2016) offers a detailed investigation into Panteleimon Kulish's translation projects and practices under permanent bans and restrictions and demonstrates Kulish's key role in the process of the formation of the written Ukrainian language.

In her monograph, Dzera (2017) examines Ukrainian Bible translations, emphasizing ideological differences and the influence of censorship on their publication and distribution in Ukraine. The study reveals that official bans, silence surrounding these translations, and gaps in reception shed light on translation policies within colonial religious and cultural contexts. Dzera and Shmiher (2023) compiled a chronology of Ukrainian biblical and liturgical translation, containing numerous facts of prohibitions in this area.

Translation and Censorship in Ukraine, 1800–1917

Rudnytska's monograph (2021) researches the impact of censorship on translation as an integral part of the study of ideological aspects of translation in Ukraine from the mid-1800s to the present day, highlighting the methods, channels, mechanisms, and agents of ideological impact on the praxis of literary translation.

Strikha's seminal work (2020) is a political history of Ukraine told through the lens of primarily literary translation, with biographical profiles of the most prominent Ukrainian translators.

Further Reading

Chernetsky, Vitaly. 2011. 'Nation and Translation: Literary Translation and the Shaping of Modern Ukrainian Culture', in B. J. Baer (ed.), *Contexts, Subtexts and Pretexts: Literary Translation in Eastern Europe and Russia*. Amsterdam and Philadelphia: Benjamins, 33–53.

Partly a critical summary in English of Maksym Strikha's seminal book *Ukrainskyi khudozhnii pereklad: Mizh literaturoiu i natsiietvorenniam* [Ukrainian Literary Translation: Between Literature and Nation-Making] (2006), this book chapter explores how Ukrainian translation aided anti-colonial resistance and national identity formation; the other half of the chapter discusses translation's role in nation-building processes in other parts of the globe.

Danylenko, Andrii. 2016. *From the Bible to Shakespeare: Pantelejmon Kuliš (1819–1897) and the Formation of Literary Ukrainian*. Brighton: Academic Studies Press.

The monograph discusses the language program of the prominent Ukrainian writer and public figure Panteleimon Kulish whose translations of the Bible and Shakespeare proved ground-breaking in the formation of Ukrainian literature and of the national self-consciousness of Ukrainians against the background of language policies in the Russian Empire and Austria-Hungary.

Fabrikant, Nikolai. 2017. 'A Brief Outline of the History of the Treatment of Ukrainian Literature by the Russian Censorship Laws', translated from Russian by R. Hantula, *East/West: Journal of Ukrainian Studies*, 4(2): 155–72.

This is an English translation of a polemical article on the Russian censorship of Ukrainian literature 'Kratkii ocherk iz istorii otnoshenii russkikh tsenzurnykh zakonov k ukrainskoi literature' published under the pseudonym Nik. Fabrikant in 1905 in the Russian liberal periodical *Russkaja mysl* which was a revision of the Ivan Krevetskyi's Ukrainian-language article 'Ne bylo, net i byt' ne mozhet!' ('There Has Not Been, Is Not, and Cannot Be!') published in 1904 in the prime Ukrainian journal *Literaturno-naukovyi visnyk* (Literary Scientific Herald).

Flier, Michael S. and Graziosi, Andrea (eds.) 2017. *The Battle for Ukrainian: A Comparative Perspective*. Cambridge, Massachusetts: Ukrainian Research Institute.

An interdisciplinary study of the treatment of the Ukrainian language in the Russian Empire and Soviet Union that documents and illuminates the tortuous path of the Ukrainian language in tsarist, Soviet and post-Soviet history.

Wolf, Michaela. 2015. *The Habsburg Monarchy's Many-Languaged Soul. Translating and interpreting, 1848–1918*. Amsterdam and Philadelphia: Benjamins.

Based on a close reading of administrative, judicial, and diplomatic documents, the book investigates translation practices in both private and official contexts, multilingualism and language policies in the Habsburg Monarchy, with a very detailed overview of the role of different types of translation and interpreting across different Habsburg crownlands.

Notes

1   In 1627, Moscow Church authorities prohibited Ukrainian books; with the only printing house under its complete control, Muscovy was deeply mistrustful of private Ukrainian print shops, which existed in the annexed part of Ukraine, in Kyiv and Chernihiv. For the first time Muscovite Russia established censorship that mainly affected Ukraine (Danylenko 2010). Under Peter I the so-called 'special dialect', i.e., the

The Routledge Handbook of Translation and Censorship

Ukrainian language, as well as literature, would become primary targets for censorship and Synod's decrees. Thus, in 1720, an edit issued by Peter I banned the printing of books in Ukraine in the local idiom with the purpose (stated in the edict) to Russify the people there. As a result, throughout the 1700s no Ukrainian book was published in the Russian Empire; during the 1700s the only language of instruction in schools in Ukraine became Russian with an absolute ban on teaching in Ukrainian issued in 1782 by Catherine II.

2   All direct quotations from the texts written in Ukrainian and Russian languages in this article are the authors' translations into English.

3   The differences in the spelling of Oleksandr Biletsky's name are explained by the fact that his name was transcribed from Ukrainian, and in the reference to the article, since the article was published in Russian, is from Russian.

References

Beletskii, Aleksandr. 1929. 'Perevodnaia literatura na Ukraine' [Translated Literature in Ukraine], *Krasnoe Slovo*, 2: 87–96. Reprint in O. A. Kalnychenko and Y. Y. Poliakova (eds.), 2011. *Ukrainska perekladoznavcha dumka 1920-kh – pochatku 1930-kh rokiv: Khrestomatiia* [*Ukrainian Translation Studies of the 1920s – Early 1930s: A Textbook*]. Vinnytsia: Nova knyha, 376–91.

Boriak, Hennadii (ed.). 2015. *Ukrainska identychnist i movne pytannia v Rosiiskii imperii: Sproba derzhavnoho rehuliuvannia (1847–1914). Zbirnyk dokumentiv i materialiv.* [*Ukrainian Identity and Language Question in the Russian Empire: An Attempt of State Regulation (1847–1914). A Collection of Documents and Writings*]. Kyiv: Klio.

Chernetsky, Vitaly. 2011. 'Nation and Translation: Literary Translation and the Shaping of Modern Ukrainian Culture', in B. J. Baer (ed.), *Contexts, Subtexts and Pretexts: Literary Translation in Eastern Europe and Russia*. Amsterdam and Philadelphia: Benjamins, 33–53.

Danylenko, Andrii. 2010. 'The Ukrainian Bible and the Valuev circular of 18 July 1863', *Acta Slavica Iaponica*, 28(1): 1–21.

Danylenko, Andrii. 2016. *From the Bible to Shakespeare: Pantelejmon Kuliš (1819–1897) and the Formation of Literary Ukrainian*. Brighton: Academic Studies Press.

Danylenko, Andrii. 2017. 'The "Doubling of Hallelujah" for the "Bastard Tongue." The Ukrainian Language Question in Russian Ukraine in the Years 1905–1916', in M. S. Flier and A. Graziosi (eds.), *The Battle for Ukrainian. A Comparative Perspective. Harvard Ukrainian Studies*, 35(1–4), 59–86.

Danylenko, Andrii. 2020. 'Kulish yak perekladach Shekspira' ['Kulish as a Translator of Shakespeare'], in O. Fedoruk (ed.), *Panteleimon Kulish. Povne zibrannia tvoriv. Pereklady ta perespivy. Tom I. Shekspirovi tvory. Tom I.* [*Panteleimon Kulish. Complete Collection of Works. Translations and Versions. Volume I. Shakespeare's Works*]. Kyiv: Krytyka, 327–50.

Danylenko, Andrii and Naienko, Halyna. 2019. 'Linguistic Russification in Russian Ukraine: Languages, Imperial Models, and Policies', *Russian Linguistics*, 43(1): 19–39.

Dibrova, Volodymyr. 2017. 'The Valuev Circular and the End of Little Russian Literature', *Kyiv-Mohyla Humanities Journal*, 4, 123–38.

Dotsenko, Rostyslav. 2013. 'Sto rokiv tomu, na zori ukrainskoho Shekspira' [A Hundred Years Ago, at the Dawn of Ukrainian Shakespeare], in R. Dotsenko (ed.), *Krytyka. Literaturoznavstvo. Vybrane* [*Criticism. Study of Literature. Selected*]. Ternopil: Bohdan, 426–32.

Dragomanov, Michel. 1878. *La littérature oukrainienne proscrite par le gouvernement russe*. Rapport présenté au congrès littéraire de Paris. Genève: Georg.

Dzera, Oksana. 2017. *Bibliina intertekstualnist i pereklad: anhlo-ukrainskyi kontekst* [*Biblical Intertextuality And Translation: The Anglo-Ukrainian Context*]. Lviv: Ivan Franko National University of Lviv.

Dzera, Oksana and Shmiher, Taras. 2023. *Khronolohiia bibliinoho ta liturhiinoho perekladu v Ukraini* [*A Chronology of Ukrainian Biblical and Liturgical Translation*]. Lviv: Ivan Franko National University of Lviv; Shevchenko Scientific Society.

Fabrikant, Nikolai. 1905. 'Kratkiy ocherk iz istorii otnoshenii russkih cenzurnyh zakonov v ukrainskoi litera-ture' [A Brief Outline of the History of the Treatment of Ukrainian Literature by the Russian Censorship Laws]. *Russkaja mysl* [Russian Thought], Book 3: 128–46.

Fabrikant, Nikolai. 2017. 'A Brief Outline of the History of the Treatment of Ukrainian Literature by the Russian Censorship Laws', translated from Russian by R. Hantula, *East/West: Journal of Ukrainian Studies*, IV(2): 155–72.

Fylypovych, Pavlo. 1927/1930. 'Pushkin v ukrayinskii literaturi' [Pushkin in Ukrainian Literature], in P. Fylypovych (ed.), *Pushkin A. Vybrani tvory*. Kharkiv–Kyiv: Knyhospilka, v–lx.

Fylypovych, Pavlo. 1930. 'Sotsiyalne oblychchia ukrainskoho chytacha 30–40 rokiv XIX viku' [The Social Face of the Ukrainian Reader of the 1830s1840s], *Zhyttia i revoliutsiia*, 1: 155–72.

Hohol, Mykola. 1874. *Taras Bulba: Vyklad Hoholiv*. Translated by M. Loboda. Kiev: Typography of M.P. Fritz.

Hordynsky, Yaroslav. 1928. 'Kulishevi pereklady dram Shekspira' [Kulish's Translations of Shakespeare's Dramas], *Zapysky naukovoho tovarystva im. Shevchenka* [*Annals of the Shevchenko Scientific Society*], 138: 55–164.

Hrytsenko, Pavlo. 2015. 'Ukrainska mova v Rosii XIX – pochatku XX st.: shliakhy utverdzhennia' [The Ukrainian Language in Russia of the 19thearly 20th c.: Ways of Strengthening], in H. Boriak (ed.). *Ukrainska identychnist i movne pytannia v Rosiiskii imperii: Sproba derzhavnoho rehuliuvannia (1847–1914). Zbirnyk dokumentiv i materialiv* [*Ukrainian Identity and Language Question in the Russian Empire: An Attempt of State Regulation (1847–1914). A Collection of Documents and Writings*], XXXIX – LII. Kyiv: Klio.

Isaievych, Yaroslav. 2002. *Ukrainske knyhovydannia: vytoky, rozvytok, problemy* [*Ukrainian Book Publishing: Origins, Development, Problems*]. Lviv: Ivan Krypiakevych Institute of Ukrainian Studies of the National Academy of Sciences of Ukraine.

Kalnychenko, Oleksandr and Nataliia Kalnychenko. 2019. 'Taras Bulba in Ukrainian Garb: National Self-Image in Translation', in L. Barcinsky (ed.), *National Identity in Literary Translation*. Berlin: Peter Lang, 71–80.

Kappeler, Andreas. 2003. '*Mazepintsy, Malorossy, Khokhly*: Ukrainians in the Ethnic Hierarchy of the Russian Empire', in A. Kappeler et al. (eds.), *Culture, Nation, and Identity. The Ukrainian-Russian Encounter (1600–1945)*. Edmonton, Toronto: Canadian Institute of Ukrainian Studies Press.

Khoptiar, Alla. 2012. *Perekladatska diialnist Borysa Hrinchenka ta yii rol v ukrainskomu literaturnomu protsesi kintsia XIX – pochatku XX st.* [Borys Hrinchenkoes translation activity and its role in the Ukrainian literary process of the late 1800s – early 1900s]. Thesis for the degree of Candidate of Philological Sciences. Ivano-Frankivsk.

Kochur, Hryhorii. 2008. 'Shekspir na Ukraine' [Shakespeare in Ukraine], in *Hryhorii Kochur, Literatura ta pereklad: Doslidzhennia. Retsenzii. Literaturni portrety. Interv'iu* [Literature and Translation: Research. Reviews. Literary Portraits. Interview]. Edited by A. Kochur and M. Kochur; Introduction by I. Dzyuba, R. Zorivchak. Kyiv: Smoloskyp, vol. 2, 704–29.

Kolomiyets, Lada. 2016. 'Ukrainian Romanticism and the Modern Ukrainian Psyche', *The Ukrainian Quarterly: A Journal of Ukrainian and International Affairs*, LXXII(1–4): 8–36.

Krevetsky, Ivan. 1904. 'Ne bylo, net i byt ne mozhet' [There Has Never Been, Is Not, and Cannot Be], *Literaturno-naukovyi vistnyk*, XXVI: 129–58; XXVII: 1–18.

Luchuk, Olha. 2018. *Panteleimon Kulish i Mykola Lukash: perekhresni stezhky perekladachiv. Shekspirova drama "Troil i Kressyda" v konteksti ukrainskoi kultury* [*Panteleimon Kulish and Mykola Lukash: Cross Paths of Translators. Shakespeare's Drama Troilus and Cressida in the Context of Ukrainian Culture*]. Kharkiv: Akta.

Luckyj, George S.N. 1991. *Young Ukraine: The Brotherhood of Saints Cyril and Methodius in Kiev, 1845–1847. The Constantine Bida Lectures, 1986*. Ottawa: University of Ottawa Press.

Makaryk, Irena. 2004. *Shakespeare in the Undiscovered Bourn: Les Kurbas, Ukrainian Modernism and Early Soviet Cultural Politics*. Toronto: University of Toronto Press.

Miller, Alexei. 2003. *'The Ukrainian Question': The Russian Empire and Nationalism in the Nineteenth Century*. Translated by Olga Poato. Budapest: Central European University Press.

Miyakovsky, Volodymyr. 1919. 'Z istorii ukrainskoi knyzhky. Tsenzurni umovy' [From the History of Ukrainian Book. Censorship Conditions], *Knyhar*, (27): 1819–28.

Miyakovsky, Volodymyr. 1984. *Unpublished and Forgotten Writings: Political and Intellectual Trends of the Nineteenth Century Modern Ukrainian Literature (Sources of Modern History of the Ukraine)* New York: Ukrainian Academy of Arts and Sciences in the U.S.

Moser, Michael. 2017. '*Osnova* and the Origins of the Valuev Directive', *East/West: Journal of Ukrainian Studies,* IV(2): 39–95.

Moskalenko, Mykhailo. 1995. 'Tysiacholittia: Pereklad u derzhavi slova. Peredmova' [Millennium: Translation in the State of Word. A Foreword], in M. Moskalenko (ed.), *Tysiacholittia: Poetychnyi pereklad Ukrainy-Rusi* [*Millennium: Poetic translation of Ukraine-Rus*]. Kyiv: Dnipro, 5–38.

Procyk, Anna. 2019. *Giuseppe Mazzini's Young Europe and the Birth of Modern Nationalism in the Slavic World*. Toronto: University of Toronto Press

Raliv, M. 1929. 'Lev Tolstoi v ukrainskykh perekladakh' [Leo Tolstoy in Ukrainian translations], *Zapysky Odeskoho naukovoho tovarystva*, 2(92): 24–34.

Remy, Johannes. 2007. 'The Valuev Circular and Censorship of Ukrainian Publications in the Russian Empire (1863-76): Intention and Practice', *Canadian Slavonic Papers*, 49(1–2): 87–110.

Remy, Johannes. 2016. *Brothers or Enemies: The Ukrainian National Movement and Russia from the 1840s to the 1870s*. Toronto, ON, Buffalo, NY, and London: University of Toronto Press.

Reyent, Oleksandr. 2012. 'Ukrainskyi natsionalnyi rukh u Rosiiskii imperii ta polityka derzhavnoi vlady z "ukrainskoho pytannia" v modernu dobu' [The Ukrainian National Movement in the Russian Empire and the State Policy on the "Ukrainian Question" in the Modern Era]. *Problemy istorii Ukrainy XIX – pochatku XX st.* [Problems of the History of Ukraine in the Nineteenth and Early Twentieth Centuries], 20(2012): 6–37.

Rudnytska, Nataliia. 2021. *Pereklad i ideolohiia (vid kintsia XIX stolittya do siohodennia)* [*Translation and Ideology (From the End of the 19th Century to the Present)*]. Vinnytsia: Nova knyha.

Savchenko, Fedir. 1930. *Zaborona ukrainstva 1876 roku* [*The Suppression of the Ukrainian Activities in 1876*]. Kharkiv and Kyiv: DVU.

Shandra, Valentyna. 2015. 'Mova yak zasib formuvannia natsionalnoi identychnosti' [Language as a Means of National Identity Shaping], in H. Boriak (ed.), *Ukrainska identychnist i movne pytannia v Rosiiskii imperii: Sproba derzhavnoho rehuliuvannia (1847–1914). Zbirnyk dokumentiv i materialiv.* [*Ukrainian Identity and Language Question in the Russian Empire: An Attempt of State Regulation (1847–1914). A Collection of Documents and Writings*]. Kyiv: Klio, VII-XXXVII.

Shandra, Valentyna. 2017. 'Kyiv's Intellectual Environment on the Eve of the Valuev Directive', *East/West: Journal of Ukrainian Studies*, IV(2): 97–112.

Shevelov, George Y. 1994. 'Homer's Arbitration in a Ukrainian Linguistic Controversy: Alexander Potebnja and Peter Niscinskyj', *Ukrainian Philology and Linguistics*, 18(1–2): 104–116. Harvard Ukrainian Studies.

Sokhan, Pavlo et al. (eds.). 1990. *Kyrylo-Mefodiivske tovarystvo* [*Cyril and Methodius Society*], 3 vols. Kyiv: Naukova dumka.

Strikha, Maksym. 2006. *Ukrainskyi khudozhnii pereklad: Mizh literaturoiu i natsiietvorenniam* [*Ukrainian Literary Translation: Between Literature and Nation-Building*]. Kyiv: Fakt.

Strikha, Maksym. 2020. *Ukrainskyi pereklad i perekladachi: mizh literaturoiu i natsiietvorenniam* [*Ukrainian translation and translators: between literature and nation-building*]. Kyiv: Dukh i litera.

Studynsky, Kyrylo (ed.). 1931. *Halychyna i Ukraina v lystuvanni 1862-84 rokiv. Materiialy do istorii ukrainskoi kultury v Halychyni ta yii zviazkiv z Ukrainoiu.* [*Halychyna and Ukraine in Correspondence of 1862–1874. Materials on the history of Ukrainian culture in Galicia and its relations with Ukraine*]. Kharkiv: Proletar.

Vulpius, Ricarda. 2005a. 'Jazykovaja politika v Rossijskoj imperii i ukrainskij perevod Biblii (1860–1906)' [Language Policy in the Russian Empire and the Ukrainian Translation of the Bible (1860–1906)], *Ab Imperio*, 2: 191–224.

Vulpius, Ricarda. 2005b. *Nationalisierung der Religion. Russiizierungspolitik und ukrainische Nationsbildung 1860–1920* [*The Nationalization of Religion: Russification Policy and Ukrainian Nation-Building, 1860–1920*]. Wisbaden: Harrasowitz Verlag.

Wolf, Michaela. 2015. *The Habsburg Monarchy's Many-Languaged Soul. Translating and Interpreting, 1848–1918.* Amsterdam and Philadelphia: Benjamins.

PART III

Communist/Socialist Contexts

12

CENSORSHIP AND TRANSLATION IN CHINA

Tan Zaixi

12.1 Introduction

The basic view of this chapter is that censorship is ubiquitous in human society, and the author wishes to clearly state it from the outset. Therefore, it is natural to believe that the mechanisms underpinning translation censorship are lawfully based in all countries in the world. In the Chinese context, its mechanisms were unleashed and empowered by the country's constitution and lawful regulations. This, then, constitutes an important issue for discussion in the chapter. Other issues, topics and debates concerning how translation and censorship operate in China, also covered in the chapter, include an attempt to distinguish various major periods of development of the country's censorial policies and practices in the contemporary times, the conceptualisation of a tripartite typology of how translations may be affected by censorship, and a discussion, amid other issues, of how translational self-censorship functions, sometimes quite forcefully, over the Chinese translator's act. To illustrate the author's points of view, examples of censorship-related translations are presented from various sources. But before discussing these issues and points, an overview is in order of the historical backdrop against which Chinese censorial policies and practices may be more meaningfully examined.

12.2 Historical Perspectives

State censorship in China can be traced back to as early as the times of Qin the First Emperor (259 BCE–210 BCE). Beginning in 213 BCE, the 33rd year of his reign, at the instigation of his prime minister, Li Si, and to suppress unfavourable attempts by Confucian scholars to compare his reign with those of former dynasties, Qin ordered existing scholarly books, except those on agriculture, astrology, medicine and the history of the State of Qin, to be burned. Such classical works as the *Book of Songs* and the *Chronicles of the Eastern Zhou Kingdoms* were banned and those who tried to keep and read them were to be severely punished. According to the *Historical Records*—the first general biographical history of China written between 104 BCE–91 BCE by Sima Qian the Grand Historian—some 460 Confucian scholars and other types of learned men were purged and buried alive for owning the forbidden books. Since Qin's times, the country has, in a sense, had an unbroken line of censorship, differing from dynasty to dynasty, or from

DOI: 10.4324/9781003149453-16

179

time to time, only in the kind of literature that was allowed or forbidden, and in the scale on which censorship was exercised. A few telling examples that readily come to mind include 'the massive banning movement of books' in the Song Dynasty (960–1279), which came next in scale to that of the aforesaid Qin Dynasty, though not quite as violent (Wu 1986); and the harsh literary inquisitions of both the early Qing Dynasty (1636–1912; Jin 1989) and part of the Republican Period (1912–1949; Wang and Zhu 2007). This historical, unbroken line has apparently run right up to the modern and contemporary times. Since its founding in 1949, the People's Republic of China (PRC) has also endured various modes of censorship, many of them bearing directly or indirectly on the activity of translation. The following sections, then, will focus on this area of present-day Chinese culture and cultural politics, and will, more specifically speaking, investigate how government and non-government censorship in the PRC has affected the enterprise of translation, and how underlying Chinese politics, ideology and cultural values have functioned during the transfer or non-transfer of foreign information and ideas.

From the perspective of the censorial practices since 1949, it is possible to distinguish three major periods of their development: 1) 1949–1966; 2) 1966–1976; and 3) 1976 to present. First, during the pre-Cultural Revolution period (1949–1966), especially in the early years of the PRC, the translation of foreign literature was quite heavily censored. This was due, on the one hand, to the influence of 'fraternal' ties with the Soviet Union (at least before close Sino-Soviet ties began to weaken towards the end of the 1950s), and, on the other, to a political, ideological and moral need for the new-born socialist state to survive and develop against the backdrop of a rather unfriendly if not hostile international environment, mostly created by the major anti-communist powers of the West. To a large extent, what was allowed at the time was the translation of Soviet Russian literature and literature from East European socialist countries. As the political and ideological line upheld by the Chinese government was a line of 'the proletariat', anything that conflicted with this proletarian line was banned, which prevented its importation and translation.

The Soviet influence in the early years of the PRC was embodied in three ways. First, the translation of Soviet Russian literature was prioritised as the most valued. According to statistics provided by Chen (2009), from 1949 to 1959, a total of more than 3500 literary works from the Soviet Union were translated and published with a circulation of more than 82 million copies, amounting to over 60% of the total amount of translated foreign literature across the country. Second, the translation of literature from other socialist countries, as well as weaker nations and those oppressed by capitalism in other parts of the world, was also prioritised because that was the line taken by the socialist-communist model of the Soviet Union. Third, Chinese literary criticism and, by extension translation criticism, followed the Soviet model, that of a Marxist-Leninist materialist realism aimed at eradicating the bad influence of Western bourgeois works and 'making translated foreign literature serve the needs of the Chinese people' (Chen 2009: 14). In order to enable the newly-established socialist state to progress through the unstable first few years that any new system must face, tight government control was imposed in its superstructure of society, including tight control over the press and publishing.

In contrast with the strong Soviet influence, Western (mainly Anglo-American) literature was confined to a rather limited scope. Throughout the 17 years from 1949 to 1966, a mere 460 Anglo-American works of literature were translated. According to Sun (1996: 3–6), 245 of these were translations of British texts and 215 American. They mainly consisted of works by such British authors as Chaucer, Shakespeare, Dryden, Milton, Defoe, Swift, Fielding, Scott, Austin, Byron, Shelley, Keats, Dickens, Thackeray, the (Barret) Brownings, the Brontë sisters, Eliot, Hardy, Conrad, H. G. Wells and Galsworthy; and by such American authors as Allen Poe, Mark Twain, Jack London, Dreiser, Faulkner, Hemingway, Steinbeck and so on. Typical

Censorship and Translation in China

examples of censored and forbidden books during the period included Pearl Buck's *The Good Earth* (forbidden on political grounds for arguably vilifying the Chinese people, especially the Chinese peasants), George Orwell's *Animal Farm* and *1984* (forbidden on ideological grounds because they satirised communism), D. H. Lawrence's *Lady Chatterley's Lover* and Vladimir Nabokov's *Lolita* (both forbidden on moral grounds because they were considered licentious or obscene).

Second, during the Cultural Revolution period (1966–1976), events that took place were even more revealing in terms of how cultural politics, through Party-led censorship, affected the importation and translation of foreign literature into the Chinese language. This socio-political movement, launched by Party Chairman Mao Zedong with its stated goal being to remove capitalist, seditious and anti-proletarian, as well as conservative traditional elements from Chinese society, in order to consolidate and strengthen socialism, was marked by ultra-leftist upheaval in almost all walks of life, bringing about serious damage to the country, not only socio-politically and economically, but also, and perhaps most seriously of all, educa-tionally and culturally. As part of this ultra-leftist upheaval, an almost xenophobic resent-ment against the capitalist West and the revisionist Soviet Union (the Sino-Soviet ideological split had in the early 1960s turned the two countries from friends into foes) re-enforced the country's guard against 'subversive', 'alien' cultures. During the first few years of the Cultural Revolution, the Red Guards were so belligerently backed by the central political line of the Party, and political and ideological censorship became so severe, that the translation of any-thing alien and perceived as anti-socialist was totally out of the question. In fact, the publica-tion of foreign material almost came to a complete standstill. Very often, even talking about it publicly was taboo and doing so could get people into political trouble.

Third, the post-Cultural Revolution period (1976–present) started when the Cultural Revolution ended in October 1976, about a month after Chairman Mao's death. The period may be further sub-divided. For example, many scholars divide the translation of Anglo-American literature into three sub-periods: the 'Defreezing' (1976–1978), 'Revival' (1978–1989) and 'Flourishing' (1990–present) periods (Sun et al. 2009; SHISU 2010). However, despite such possible differentiations, events in China since the end of the Cultural Revolution can nonetheless be broadly described as constituting a continuum. Everything that has happened since the end of the Cultural Revolution, especially since late December 1978 when the Chinese government officially abandoned the country's former 'closed-door' policies, is but part of one and the same movement, i.e., that of reform and opening up to the outside world. What differentiates the possible sub-stages of this 'post-Cultural Revolution' period is not the characteristics of the stages, but rather the develop-mental pace.

One of the most important features of the post-Cultural Revolution period in the field of trans-lation has been the gradual loosening of the country's restrictions on the import of foreign literary works, which began at the end of 1978 and was followed in the early 1990s by an even more lib-eral government position on what would have been strictly forbidden foreign literature in previous years. For example, the previous ban on such works as Buck's *The Big Earth*, Orwell's *Animal Farm*, Lawrence's *Lady Chatterley's Lover* and Nabokov's *Lolita*, among other works that had been categorised as 'forbidden literature', was lifted and the translations now all found their way into the Chinese book market.

However, it is also arguably true that the end of the Cultural Revolution did not put an end to translational censorship in the absolute sense. Despite the big changes over the past 40 and more years, the PRC maintains to this day its system of literary and translational censorship, at least insofar as sensitive subject areas are concerned. Given that these subject areas are identified and defined under Chinese law, hence not to be treated lightly, they will be discussed separately and their underlying censoring mechanisms explained in the section below.

12.3   Core Issues and Topics

On the understanding that censorship is a general feature of human culture and society, it is natural that the mechanisms underlying it are lawfully and legally based in all countries in the world. In the Chinese context, as pointed out above, such mechanisms were unleashed and empowered by the country's constitution and regulations. Going back to the very early years of the PRC, actual censorship was first put into effect by the setting up of a Publishing Committee in February 1949 under the Publicity Department of the Central Government, which was renamed the Central People's Government's General Administration of Publishing in November of that same year and then replaced in 1954 by a new organization, the Publication Bureau under the Ministry of Culture. As the country's top administrative body for publishing, it not only took charge of the planning and organization of the country's publishing activities but also, and most importantly, it was the advisory and censorial body of all major publication projects, including translation projects. For example, in 1952, the General Administration of Publishing followed the Soviet model in issuing 'Guidelines for Implementing *The Regulations on Editorial Boards and Working Systems of State-Run Publishing Houses*.' These guidelines required, among other things, that all publishing houses submit their publication plans to the authorities for official scrutiny and approval in order to ensure that before publication, every book or translation manuscript went through a process of initial review by a copy-editor, double review by a senior editor and third review by the editor-in-chief before being submitted for final approval to the publishing house director (Ni 2011: 41).

In the early years, these guidelines and regulations were normally issued through the 'internal' channels of the publishing houses and were not made known to the general public—partly because the relevant policies were not considered of everyday importance and partly because the government did not want to appear as if it was encroaching on people's rights, given that freedom of speech and freedom of the press have always been professed to be the constitutional rights of Chinese citizens. However, today, after more than 40 years of the country's opening up to the outside world, and with the development of modern science and technology, many changes to the handling of censorship have been introduced by the government. Though it has not completely lifted its censorial restrictions on translation and publication, it has clearly become more open-minded and more transparent. Instead of shying away from admitting that a censorship system exists in the country, the government now makes its position publicly known by documenting, in print and online, all decisions on translation and publication (laws, policies, regulations, guidelines, etc.).

This change of attitude first began in 1997. On 1 February, an ordinance, entitled *Regulations on the Administration of Publication*, the first of its kind, was adopted and promulgated by the State Council of China through the media to make it known to the general public. On 25 December 2001, an expanded version was decreed by the State Council. On 19 March 2011 a newly revised version was adopted and decreed. On 29 July 2014 a third amendment was made and then on 6 February 2016 a fourth. It is the 2016 Chinese-language version and its 2014 English-language translation of the ordinance that are now found on the Policies and Regulations page of the website of the General Administration of Press and Publication (GAPP) of the People's Republic of China. Of the 73 articles listed in the 2016 version (GAPP n.d.), the two most important concerning publication (and by extension, translation) are Articles 26 and 27, which provide concrete guidelines for the imposition of censorship.

Censorship and Translation in China

In the spirit of these articles, it is possible to conceptualise a tripartite typology of translations under Chinese censorship: First, at one extreme of censorship, there is the prohibition of a given foreign literary work, meaning that its translation is categorically prohibited. I call this 'non-translation' in English and '缺席翻译' or '缺译' in Chinese (meaning literally: 'absented/absent translation'). Non-translation can fall into two sub-categories:

1. Translations that have not or not yet been made but whose absence is significant because such non-translations are the result of government censorship and/or the translator's (or publisher's or editor's) self-censorship, on various grounds, whether they be political, ideological, religious, moral or ethical, socio-cultural, and even stylistic or linguistic. In the context of the PRC, non-translations that fall under this category are often considered anti-China, anti-Communist, anti-Chinese constitution, politically subversive, ideologically reactionary/seditious, morally unhealthy, ethnically separatist, harmful to national security, obscene, instigating violence or instigating an anti-harmonious society, and so forth. Typical examples include works that are considered unfriendly and unwelcome or even hostile to top-Chinese leadership and that deal with such sensitive and topical issues as the Tiananmen Square events of 1989, the government-banned 'Falungong' Cult, and Taiwan, Hong Kong, Tibetan or Xinjiang (Uygur) independence, to name but a few.

2. Translations that were made at an earlier time, but are later banned, usually under changed censorship conditions, so that the earlier translations become non-translations, i.e., 'suppressed or absented translations' as I would alternatively call them under such circumstances. Later again, as the result of a subsequent change of conditions, the non-translations, i.e., suppressed or absented translations, become permissible or restituted translations. The best illustration of the phenomenon is the shifting status between the translation and non-translation of Lawrence's *Lady Chatterley's Lover*, a point to which I shall return further below.

The second general category of the tripartite typology involves what could be called partial translations. Partial translations can be defined as 'translations that contain omissions, shifts of meaning or modulation of overall author-tone that necessarily change the intentions (however partially) of the author' (Tan 2014b: 197). These omissions, shifts and modulations, as well as additions, are sometimes made in order to comply with overt government censorial requirements. By contrast they sometimes result from the translator's, editor's or publisher's self-censorship in an attempt to conform to the country's dominant ideology as well as social conventions so that potential conflict with government censors can be avoided and the translational products can be safely published and marketed. Translations that fall into this category include those whose source texts have passed the scrutiny of government censors and are considered 'translatable' in principle; nevertheless, translational modulations must be made where the ST content is regarded as 'sensitive' and 'unacceptable' to the target culture. Among the more recent examples of such 'partly (self-)censored Chinese translations' are those of Hillary Clinton's *Living History* (English original in 2003, PRC version in 2003); Henry Kissinger's *On China* (English original in 2011, PRC version in 2012) and Ezra F. Vogel's *Deng Xiaoping and the Transformation of China* (English original in 2011, PRC version in 2013). In all of these cases, censorship- and/or self-censorship-driven additions, omissions, shifts or modulations are abundant.

The third category, called full/near-full translations, covers translations that result from full or almost full translatorial commitment to the source text, in the sense that everything in the source text can be, and often is, faithfully transferred to the target text. With full/near-full translations, the material being translated is considered completely 'translatable' and fits in harmoniously with

The Routledge Handbook of Translation and Censorship

Chinese laws, or so to speak. Under such circumstances, the translator is not primarily concerned with the ideology or the political orientation of the work being translated, but with translation strategies and techniques on an operational level. In other words, additions, omissions and modulations are made to ensure that the target text is linguistically or stylistically understandable, readable and acceptable. Most Western classics, including present-day classics, fall into this broad category.

In sum, in the current Chinese context, whose constitution allows for the exercise of overt translation censorship, the translation act is bound to involve the three broad types of translatorial commitment, leading to three types of translations: 'non-', 'partial' or 'full/near-full' translation. It is important to note at this point that, although [translational] censorship is an obvious phenomenon under state laws and regulations that impact publishing, including the publishing of translations, discrepancies may arise in their interpretation and implementation, especially in areas that may be considered fuzzy or have changed over time.

Take, for example, the changing status from translation to non-translation and then back to translation of Lawrence's *Lady Chatterley's Lover*. Its first Chinese version was published in 1936, at a time when the English original was itself a banned work in its native England, as well as in much of the Western world. However, the status of non-translation (in the sense of suppressed translation) of *Lady Chatterley's Lover* came into being with the founding of the PRC in 1949, because it was considered an 'obscene' and 'decadent' work of literature. This non-translation status was maintained until the post-Cultural Revolution period, when in 1986, inspired by the country's increasingly more liberal policies and the publisher's commercially-motivated ambitions, the Hunan People's Publishing House published a new translation (which was essentially a republication of the original translation made by Rao Shuyi [饶述一], which had been published in Shanghai in 1936). This 'new publication' immediately converted a non-translation into a translation. However, for essentially the same reason as that used to justify the initial ban, which had transformed the first translation into a non-translation in the aftermath of the 1949 revolution, hardly two weeks had passed before a strict ban was once again placed on the circulation of this new publication. With as many as possible of the few sold copies recalled, and the more than 300,000 printed but unsold copies either reduced to pulp or sealed and locked up in the publisher's storerooms, the new translation was turned yet again into a new non-translation. Furthermore, the publishing house, the translation's general editor and a few other major figures behind the project were subjected to a harsh penalty, including the removal of the general editor from his post and the issuing of severe letters of warning to the others by the authorities. *Lady Chatterley's Lover*'s non-translation status remained in effect until 2004, 55 years after its first translation was made a non-translation in the PRC and 18 years after its dramatic change of status from non-translation to translation and then back from translation to non-translation. In 2004, a new translation was made by Zhao Susu [赵苏苏] and published by the People's Literature Publishing House in Beijing. Founded in 1951 and hitherto the largest publisher of literary works in China, this state-owned publishing house often functions as a weathervane of the kind of literature that may be branded as politically correct under the country's censorship system. Therefore, the publication of Zhao's new translation by this publisher was broadly regarded as the lifting of the ban on foreign literary works, including *Lady Chatterley's Lover*, that had been censored because they were deemed 'not-translatable' and unpublishable for reasons of obscenity or decadence. Consequently, an outcome of the evolution of attitudes towards morality and obscenity in China, which resulted in the loosening of post-censorship, was to change the status from suppressed translation or non-translation to full translation.

By contrast, it is also important to note that there are still subject areas in the Chinese context of today to which translation censorship restrictions are applied as much as before, if not more so.

According to the *Regulations on the Administration of Publication* (Articles 26 and 27) mentioned earlier, typical targeted texts have content that 'endanger[s] the unification, sovereignty and territorial integrity of the State', 'incite[s] national hatred or discrimination, undermine[s] the solidarity of the nation, or infringe[s] upon national customs and habits', or 'propagate[s] obscenity, gambling, violence or instigate[s] crimes'. Of course, it is important to keep in mind that all countries are sensitive to issues surrounding national unity, sovereignty and territorial integrity, and set limits on what can be said in public and published online or in print. In this regard, China is no exception.

12.4   New Debates

When Holman and Boase-Beier (1999) equated translators with censors in the sense that they are both 'gatekeepers, standing at crucial points of control, monitoring what comes in and what stays outside any given cultural or linguistic territory' (cited in Merkle 2002: 9; also in Merkle et al. 2010: 12), they were actually equating the translator's censorial role to that of a self-censor. The reason is simple: in their role as gatekeepers 'monitoring what comes in and what stays outside', translators very often regulate or censor their own work, for example, by making additions, omissions and modulations or other changes to the translation. Even when the translators' role as gatekeeper involves selecting or not selecting a given author's work, the act of selecting or not-selecting may still be of a self-regulatory nature, at least in part. For although such an act may be undertaken under the coercion of a 'true' censor, it is nonetheless in the main an act that translators inflict upon themselves.

Clearly, the very fact that a translator's self-censorial behaviour can be of both a willing and a coerced nature would seem to support my main argument, i.e., that, at least insofar as the Chinese context is concerned, not only does self-censorship go hand in hand with censorship of translations but also, with the translator's internalization of the gatekeeping mechanism, there is often no distinct dividing line between what is the result of censorship and what is the result of self-censorship. Between the two, there is often a rather fuzzy interface with no clear boundaries. In other words, under the coercive ideological, political, social, ethical/moral, religious, economic/commercial and other constraints of their time and location, translators establish a coping system, consciously or subconsciously. This premise leads to two potential outcomes: on the one hand, translators could make a different translational choice for a given ST when subjected to external censorship; on the other hand, they may still stick to the same choice whether or not external censorial restrictions are imposed on them.

In reality, however, and especially in the Chinese context where censorial operations are more formally enforced than in some other contexts, there may be situations where 'translators must prioritise and pick a strategy to deal with [the potentially] oppressive or coercive cultural constraints' that characterise their time and location by exercising 'some self-censorship for a greater good' (Tymoczko 2009: 36), whether this 'greater good' means introducing a new or pioneering school of thought into the target culture or making some potentially dangerous facts known to target readers at the cost of losing, or omitting, certain details. Of course, such sacrifices in the form of translational omissions or modulations are sometimes made merely for economic or commercial reasons, such as to get the books into the local market or to appeal to the taste of target readers.

In contrast, translators who do what they want to do, irrespective of external, censorial constraints, have a tendency to conform, or not to conform, to norms, a tendency that is cultivated as part of their life experience. On a philosophical note, it may be argued that behind all such translatorial self-censorship there lies the invisible hand of the censor, nevertheless. In other words, if censorship did not exist and there were no norms of any kind to which translators must conform, there would be no (or no call for) self-censorship of any kind; it would be a society of 'absolute freedom', which, in reality, does not exist. Therefore, with censorship of translations being a common feature of all cultures, translators easily become active collaborators. In fact, the more powerful the external constraints, the more collaborative the translators may become. Also, the anticipatory anxiety or fear of possible penalty for translatorial violations of government-imposed restrictions produces 'much harsher acts of self-censorship' on the part of the translator 'than any censor would have expected to exercise' (Kuhiwczak 2009: 55).

Interestingly, in the Chinese context, translators, publishers or patrons of translation projects may consciously or subconsciously avoid selecting certain types of material for translation, or avoid faithfully translating certain 'sensitive' parts of a chosen text. Often, it is not because the material is of an overtly prohibitive nature in the political, ideological or religious sense, but because there is a wish (on the part of the translator) to conform to the expectations of a moral, ethical or cultural tradition, or a wish to make economic gains out of the translated work. For example, back in the late 1990s, when scholar Zhu Jiarong (竺家荣) was asked to translate the Japanese novel 失楽园 [A Lost Paradise] by Junichi Watanabe (渡边淳一) into Chinese, she refused unless the publisher agreed to her omission of the original work's explicit sexual content. The portrayal of the extra-marital affair of two middle-aged people and their desperate passion for each other despite worldly prejudices had become an immediate bestseller in Japan and the Asia region after it was first published in 1997. But to the Zhu of the 1990s, the use of explicit sex language in her translation was out of the question. This was because '[a]s a college teacher,' Zhu said in an interview many years later during which she explained how she had felt when first invited to undertake the project, 'translating a novel full of erotic content would be my last choice. I would feel so embarrassed [in the sense of losing face] to see my students in class' (Zhu, cited in Du 2010). The publisher agreed to her conditions and she went ahead with the project, producing a heavily 'translator self-censored' version of Watanabe's work which was published in 1998. But with the passing of time accompanied by a change of the general social aura in China as a result of people becoming more liberal-minded towards representations of extra-marital relationships and descriptions of sexual acts, Zhu's stance on Watanabe changed. In 2010, some 12 years after she made her first, translator-abridged version of Watanabe, she came out with a full, uncensored second version. In this new version, all explicit sexual descriptions in the original that had been omitted from her first translation were now restored and faithfully reproduced. This resulted in an increase of some 30,000 Chinese characters/words spread throughout the book (amounting to more than 40 pages in total) as compared with the older version of 1998.

In the case of the translation of some, if not all, politically- or ideologically-loaded texts, self-censorial acts are also often carried out. Examples that readily come to mind are the translations of Kissinger's *On China* and Vogel's *Deng Xiaoping*. The two authors are friendly international figures in the eyes of the Chinese government and highly regarded by the Chinese reading public, so there is virtually no fear of censorship of their books, at least not in any explicit government sense. However, in spite of the overall welcoming attitude of the Chinese government towards them, their translations were nevertheless subjected to translational modulations or abridgements of content, likely the result of the editor's/publisher's or the translator's own censorship of politically or ideologically sensitive issues.

A few observations can be made in this connection. First, when we compare the translations of the two above-mentioned books with the translations of other books such as Lawrence's *Lady*

Chatterley's Lover, Buck's *The Big Earth*, Orwell's *Animal Farm* and Nabokov's *Lolita*, we discover the following distribution pattern with regard to the various translatorial interventions: a) in the translation of *On China*, everything concerning the issue of the 1989 Tiananmen events was either completely deleted or drastically altered (e.g., in Chapter 15 alone there were some 25 omissions and more than 30 modulations or changes, ranging from single words to phrases and sentences to whole paragraphs); b) in the translation of *Deng Xiaoping*, 294 omissions, seven additions and 39 modulations were made, all concerning the central figure of the book, Deng Xiaoping, or events associated with him; and c) the more recent translations of *Lady Chatterley's Lover*, *The Big Earth*, *Animal Farm* and *Lolita*, in particular, tend to be more complete, or 'fully' made, or, to put it differently, there are less purposeful omissions and changes. These examples demonstrate that translatorial interventions tend to occur, sometimes quite heavily, in works that deal with the political and ideological situation of present-day China, whether it be the country's general socio-political and ideological development or the development of its socio-political system or top leadership, but decreasingly less so in literary works that do not deal with contemporary political matters. This apparently confirms that a graded structure of (self-)censorship exists where materials with politically and/or ideologically hostile, unfriendly, or simply sensitive content directed against the Chinese government or the political system as well as top Chinese leadership are at the top of the 'to-be-strictly-censored' list.

Under the country's increasingly more relaxed censorship system since the 1980s, such formerly censored and 'not-translatable' works as *Lady Chatterley's Lover* and *Lolita* are now seen as more of a literary masterpiece than as books of 'obscene' and 'decadent' content. As for *Animal Farm*, although it is widely recognised as a work of bitter political and ideological sarcasm directed at socialism and communism, it is now no longer regarded by the Chinese government as seriously harmful to the Chinese brand of socialism and communism, especially after the Chinese Communist Party adopted a resolution at its congress in July 1981 to view the country as having entered only the 'primary', rather than 'advanced', stage of socialism. It is therefore understood that the exercise of self-censorship by the translator, the editor or the publisher is something to be taken for granted and 'is probably almost always judicious in a charged cultural interface' (Tymoczko 2009: 42). The question is perhaps where and how to draw the line between what may have been specifically demanded by the censor and what may have been simply self-initiated by the translator, a question that is worth researching further, especially because, as Tymoczko (2009: 42) cautions, there is always 'the temptation to compromise in translation, to self-censor more than is needful'.

Translation censorship in the Chinese context, like elsewhere in the world, functions as a form of government and non-government control of how foreign information and ideas circulate or do not circulate in the country. Its underlying dynamics is determined by the fact that the ways in which given censorial policies operate tend to change, both with the times and with the evolution of the socio-political system that impacts them. The translator is under the constant influence of censorial forces, both visible and invisible. While the visible forces, i.e., those which relate primarily to overt government censorship, determine the general direction of the dynamic movement between non- and partial and full/near-full translations, it is the invisible forces, i.e., those that inhabit the translators themselves, which orient how the general censorial policies are implemented.

Before the translation process begins, self-aware translators will have already established a 'safe zone' of their own, presumably in compliance with the censorship policies of the socio-political system in which they translate. In China, like in other countries, translators have the constitutional right to freedom of speech, and by extension, the freedom to translate. However, such freedoms must be understood in relative rather than absolute terms. In other words, translators can only act 'freely' within the boundaries of political, ideological, moral and cultural 'translatability'. These boundaries are a combination of what is placed on them by the external forces of institutional (such as government) censorship and those forces internalised as a result of externally imposed censorship, as well as the translators' past experiences of translation and publication failure.

With regard to research publications on translation censorship in China, a rather small number of articles have been published. The first two are by Chang Num Fung (2008) and Red Chan (2007) respectively, both authors in China's Special Administrative Region of Hong Kong. A general study of 'censorship in translation and translation studies in present-day China', Chang's paper cites examples from the translations of Hillary Clinton's *Living History*, Mandla Langa's short story *A Gathering of Bald Men*, Vladimir Nabokov's *Lolita* and David Lodge's *Small World* with which to describe how governmental censorship operates in China. Chang also discusses other questions such as the degree of censorship acknowledged by the government, different pressures, censorial or otherwise, to which publishers are subjected, and which may end up pressuring or constraining individual translators, such as requirements related to translational accuracy and faithfulness, the market norms of competition, and pressure from the dominant ideology and the power of the state.

Published one year earlier than Chang's, Red Chan's paper discusses the 'one nation, two translations' issue by focusing on how 'self-censorship' imposed by the publisher, rather than overt censorship and political pressure imposed by the government, was at work in the publication of the PRC version of Hillary Clinton's *Living History*. Instead of inviting the translators of the original Chinese edition published in Taipei to make changes, the Chinese Mainland publisher Yilin Press, who had purchased the rights to publish the same translation in the Chinese Mainland, cut a number of passages and changed the tone of the memoir to avoid potential political and ideological confrontation within the context of the Mainland. According to the Reading Guide published in the aftermath of the publication of the Chinese version on the home page of Clinton's American publisher Simon and Schuster's website (Simon and Schuster n.d.), such omissions and changes were found on some ten pages. Apparently, those omissions and changes were the result of censorship, or rather the translator's and/or publisher's self-censorship, and the various actors had different hidden agendas.

Hillary Clinton was reportedly quite upset about her book being censored, but nonetheless the 'censored' version was published and over 600,000 copies were said to have been sold, 200,000 of them in the book's first month of sale. In Chan's view, this is a case of censorship taking more than just a political or ideological form as would have conventionally been thought of. 'Now the market can be used as an excuse, or a gateway, to bypass political agendas. It has become difficult to discern whether an act of censorship is made on political grounds or mere commercial convenience.' (Chan 2007: 128)

Two things need commenting on. First, Chan's 'act of censorship' in the above quote must be understood to refer to an act of the translator/publisher's self-censorship because their purpose for undertaking the translation project was to have the translation successfully published without backlash from the authorities. Their pre-emptive self-censorship is thus both politically and economically-driven, in the sense that they deleted politically 'offensive' passages in the Mainland version in order to suit the target context and that the huge sales of the translation made the project quite lucrative to both Yilin the Chinese press and the American publisher of the original work. Second, that 'commercial' considerations often prevail over political considerations in translation censorial practices can also be proven by this fact: In spite of the rows over the omissions and changes made to the Chinese text of Hillary Clinton's *Living History*, 'Yilin Press was still granted the rights to translate Bill Clinton's memoir, *My Life*' (Chan 2007: 128). Though Robert Barnett, the lawyer in charge of Clinton's work, insisted that 'Yilin Press sign an agreement which entitled him to examine and return any problematic Chinese translations. [...] a hard fact remains: whether it is the Chinese press or the American publisher, it is money, not politics that dictate the world of publishing' (Chan 2007: 128) .

A third paper, authored by Tan (2014a), was on a different, yet closely related topic. Entitled '变化中的翻译禁忌：辩证视角下的探索' [Changing Taboos on Translation: Explorations from a Dialectical Perspective] and published in the most influential translation studies journal in China, i.e., *Chinese Translators Journal*, the paper posited that translation taboos are a socio- and culturo-political phenomenon at once universal and particular. Their universality lies in their existence in all cultures and societies and their particularity lies in the fact that some translation taboos exist in some cultures and societies but do not in others, as well as in their tendency to change with time and socio- and culturo-political conditions. In translation, efforts are made not only to facilitate cross-societal/cultural exchanges, but also to curb and inhibit the very same exchanges because the given texts considered to be carrying positive values in the source language-culture may be considered unacceptable in the target culture and society. Any attempt to translate such texts would involve breaking a taboo. While conventional taboos often respond to superstitious beliefs, such as believing in ghosts, translation taboos are based in reality because breaking or trying to break them could have real consequences for the translator, including penalties and punishment. For those of the Islamic faith, one taboo was the translation of Salman Rushdie's *The Satanic Verses* (1988). The novel became the focus of controversy when the Islamic world accused it of blasphemy. Publishing and purchasing the book thus became illegal in most Islamic countries, as was its translation. Though the author of the book was not physically harmed when this chapter was first drafted, despite a *fatwa* calling for his death, other people including translators fell victims to violence: a Japanese translator was stabbed to death; an Italian translator was seriously injured in an assassination attempt; and a Turkish translator managed to escape an angry mob that set fire to his hotel, killing 35 people. Moreover, on 12 August 2022, Salman Rushdie was attacked during a talk in the U.S. state of New York and was left seriously injured in the neck and stomach. Against this background, and also presumably out of deference to the sensibilities of Muslims, including those (some 30 million strong) in China, no Chinese individuals or collectives have ever attempted to translate and publish the novel in Chinese. Clearly a translation taboo on Rushdie's novel is at work here.

This example of translation taboo resulted essentially from censorship. Therefore, Tan's paper on 'changing taboos on translation [in China]' was indeed a discussion of the country's censorship of translation. In this connection, it may be regarded as the first and thus far the only paper yet published in a major Chinese-language TS journal on the rather 'sensitive' issue of translational censorship in the Chinese Mainland. The paper based its argument on the view that translational censorship in China operates under the mandate of the country's constitutional laws. It calls for the adoption of an open and dialectical attitude towards translation taboo studies, arguing that such an attitude would ensure a better understanding of translation as not only a linguistic but also a socio-/culturo-political act (Tan 2014a: 26). The author's stance was accepted by the editorial board, and the article published without having to make changes to content. It is therefore assumed that research into translation censorship is after all not as formidable a topic for scholarly work in China as researchers may fear.

The same argument also holds true for the English-language papers that the author has subsequently published in international journals. All include the terms 'censorship' and/or 'self-censorship' in their titles, whilst the discussed Chinese-language essay avoided using them. The papers investigated many issues concerning translation and censorship in China, including the impact of '(self-)censorship on the translator-author relationship' (Tan 2014b: 192); 'how censorship functions in affecting translation activities in China' (Tan 2015: 313); the 'dynamics of translational censorship' that results in the production of 'non-, partial and full/near-full translations' in China's translated literature (Tan 2017: 45); and the 'fuzzy interface between translational censorship and self-censorship in the Chinese context' (Tan 2019: 39). This chapter can be seen as an attempt to pull together, as much as possible, the research presented in those English articles, together with the research analysed in the Chinese article on 'translational taboos'.

Further Reading

Shei, Chris and Gao, Zhao-Ming (eds.). 2018. *The Routledge Handbook of Chinese Translation*. London and New York: Routledge.
This handbook offers a comprehensive overview of contemporary research on key issues in Chinese translation. Some of the topics covered, such as those on 'the general practice of censorship and translation in [the] Mainland [of] China', 'the identity and ideology of Chinese translators' and 'the norms of source-initiated translation in China and national auto-image', are of particular interest to students of censorship and translation in the Chinese context.

Koskinen, Kaisa and Pokorn, Nike K. (eds.). 2021. *The Routledge Handbook of Translation and Ethics*. Abingdon, Oxon and New York: Routledge.
This volume provides discussions on various issues surrounding the moral and ethical aspects of translating and interpreting. Though not bearing directly on censorship in translation, the philosophical and theoretical underpinnings of moral and ethical thinking in TS research are of relevance to studies of the culturo-political and ideological dimensions of translation, hence the dimension of translation censorship, however indirectly. Of particular interest in this connection are discussions in the chapters of Part I on 'translation ethics in the Chinese tradition', 'ethics in socialist translation theories', 'the ethics of postcolonial translation' and 'feminist translation ethics'.

Billiani, Francesca (ed.). 2007. *Modes of Censorship and Translation: National Contexts and Diverse Media*. Manchester, UK: St. Jerome Publishing.
This collection of papers presents case studies on censorship in translation in different contexts in Europe. Along with other works such as those edited by Salama-Carr (2007), Seruya and Moniz (2008), and Ni Chuilleanáin et al. (2009), as well as the special journal issues guest-edited by Merkle (2002, 2010), Billiani's volume makes an important contribution to how the issue of censorship and conflict in translating and interpreting can be addressed in various national, historical and media settings, and what socio-cultural, political, ideological and aesthetic implications are to be found in the study of censorship in translation.

References

Chan, Red. 2007. 'One Nation, Two Translations: China's Censorship of Hillary Clinton's *Memoir*', in M. Salama-Carr (ed.), *Translating and Interpreting Conflict*. Amsterdam and New York: Rodopi, 119–31.
Chang, Nam Fung. 2008. 'Censorship in Translation and Translation Studies in Present-day China', in T. Seruya and M. L. Moniz (eds.), *Translation and Censorship in Different Times and Landscapes*. Newcastle, UK: Cambridge Scholars Publishing, 229–40.
Chen, Zhongyi. 2009. 'Looking Back and Rethinking the 60 Years of Translation and Study of Foreign Literature in the PRC' [回顾与反思外国文学翻译与研究六十年], *Chinese Translators Journal [中国翻译]*, 30(6): 13–19.
Du, Guodong. 2010. 'The Return of a Paradise Lost in Translation'. Available at: www.chinadaily.com.cn/cndy/2010-05/31/content_9909650.htm. (Accessed: 28 Feb. 2021.)
GAPP. n.d. *Regulations on the Administration of Publication* (Chinese version). Available at: www.gov.cn/gongbao/content/2016/content_5139389.htm. (Accessed: 12 Jan. 2021.)

Holman, Michael and Boase-Beier, Jean. 1999. 'Introduction', in J. Boase-Beier and M. Holman (eds.), *The Practices of Literary Translation: Constraints and Creativity*. Manchester, U.K.: St Jerome Publishing, 1–17.

Jin, Xingrao. 1989. *Literary Inquisitions in the Qing Dynasty [清代笔祸录]*. Hong Kong: Chung Hwa Books Co.

Kuhiwczak, Piotr. 2009. 'Censorship as a Collaborative Project: A Systemic Approach', in E. Ní Chuilleanáin, C. Ó Cuilleanáin and D. Parris (eds.), *Translation and Censorship: Patterns of Communication and Interference*. Dublin and Portland: Four Courts Press Ltd., 46–56.

Merkle, Denise. 2002. 'Presentation', *TTR: Traduction, Terminologie, Redaction: Censorship and Translation in the Western World*, 15(2): 9–18.

Merkle, Denise. 2010. 'Presentation', *TTR: Traduction, Terminologie, Redaction*: Censorship and Translation *Within and Beyond the Western World*, 23(2): 11–21.

Merkle, Denise, O'Sullivan, Carol, van Doorslaer, Luc, and Wolf, Michaela (eds.). 2010. *The Power of the Pen. Translation and Censorship in Nineteenth-Century Europe. Representation – Transformation 4*. Vienna: LIT Verlag.

Ní Chuilleanáin, Eiléan, Ó Cuilleanáin, Cormac, and Parris, David (eds.). 2009. *Translation and Censorship: Patterns of Communication and Interference*. Dublin and Portland: Four Courts.

Ni, Xiuhua. 2011. 'Imagined China: A Study of English Translations of Chinese Literature in the PRC (1949–1966)' [想象的中国:中国文学英译研究 (1949–1966)]. PhD Dissertation, Hong Kong Baptist University.

Salama-Carr, Myriam (ed.). 2007. *Translating and Interpreting Conflict*. Amsterdam and New York: Rodopi.

Seruya, Teresa and Moniz, Maria Lin (eds.). 2008. *Translation and Censorship in Different Times and Landscapes*. Newcastle, UK: Cambridge Scholars Publishing.

SHISU. 2010. 'Introduction to the Translation of English-American Literature in the New Era' [新时期英美文学翻译概述]. Available at: http://research.shisu.edu.cn/s/20/t/30/a/2002/info.jspy. (Accessed: 20 Jan. 2021.)

Simon and Schuster. n.d. 'Untitled document on Simon & Schuster Website Announcing the Availability of Chinese Translations of Deleted Parts in the Simplified Chinese Version'. Available at: www.simonsays.com/extras/html/LivingHistory/LivingHistoryPressRelease.htm. (Accessed: 10 Dec. 2020.)

Sun, Zhili. 1996. *On Translating British and American Literature in China: 1949–1966 [我国英美文学翻译概论: 1949–1966]*. Nanjing: Yilin Press.

Sun, Zhili *et al.* 2009. *Chinese Translations of British and American Literature: 1949–2008 [中国的英美文学翻译: 1949–2008]*. Nanjing: Yilin Press.

Tan, Zaixi. 2014a. 'Changing Taboos on Translation: Explorations from a Dialectic Perspective' [变化中的翻译禁忌: 辩证视角下的探索], *Chinese Translators Journal [中国翻译]*, 35(1): 23–28, 126.

Tan, Zaixi. 2014b. '(Self-)censorship and the Translator-author Relationship: The Case of Full Translation, Partial Translation, and Non-translation in the Chinese Context', *Asia Pacific Translation & Intercultural Studies*, 1(3): 192–209.

Tan, Zaixi. 2015. 'Censorship in Translation: The Case of the People's Republic of China', *Neohelicon*, 42(1): 313–39.

Tan, Zaixi. 2017. 'Censorship in Translation: The Dynamics of Non-, Partial and Full Translations in the Chinese Context', *Meta*, 62(1): 45–68.

Tan, Zaixi. 2019. 'The Fuzzy Interface between Censorship and Self-censorship in Translation', *Translation and Interpreting Studies*, 14(1): 39–60.

Tymoczko, Maria. 2009. 'Censorship and Self-censorship in Translation: Ethics and Ideology, Resistance and Collusion', in E. Ní Chuilleanáin, C. Ó Cuilleanáin and D. Parris (eds.), *Translation and Censorship: Patterns of Communication and Interference*. Dublin and Portland: Four Courts Press Ltd., 24–45.

Wang, Xuhua and Zhu, Yibing (eds.). 2007. *Sourcebook on Banned Books in China: 1927–1949 [1927–1949年禁书(刊)史料汇编]*. Beijing: Beijing Library Press.

Wu, Xi. 1986. 'Why Was There Massive Banning of Books in the Northern and Sothern Song Dynasties? [两宋为什么大肆禁书], *Chinese Literature and History [文史知识]*, 3: 105–8.

13

CENSORSHIP IN DISGUISE

The Multiple Layers of Censorship of Literary Works in the GDR

Hanna Blum

13.1 Introduction

When the German Democratic Republic (GDR) was officially founded in October 1949, it was by no means an isolated state. Its founding rather reflected the global political situation at the time in a striking way. With the GDR, an East German state was created as the successor to the Soviet Occupation Zone (SBZ) created after World War II; the resulting division of Germany into two parts manifested the global division into East and West at the beginning of the Cold War. The GDR was strongly tied to the Soviet Union, especially at the beginning of its existence, but it also had intensive exchanges with other satellite states. This embedding in world political events made an exchange with other nations inevitable, which is why translational activities played a central role in the maintenance of the socialist state. Not only was political and ideological exchange made possible through translation, but also a socialist literary canon including not only newly written East German literature but also world literature, which was strongly shaped by the Soviet literary canon, of course, was established in the newly founded state, as well as international exchange in the fields of economics and science.

Being a newly founded country that was part of the East during the Cold War but used to be deeply embedded in the Western world, the GDR government felt the need to protect its ideological beliefs, which were mainly based on Marxism-Leninism, from negative influences. Cultural products were considered a particularly important means of educating the East German people. Literature, for example, was seen as key to the formation of the 'new man', as head of state Walter Ulbricht phrased it in 1950 (Ulbricht 1950: 149). The desire to enforce ideological beliefs, combined with the recognition of the potential for cultural products to influence the people made it necessary for the government to control the content of these products, notably translations, as they brought in foreign ideas. Yet, censorship was forbidden in the GDR by its constitution, which granted freedom of opinion and speech to all citizens of East Germany:

> Every citizen of the German Democratic Republic has the right, in accordance with the spirit and aims of this Constitution, to express his opinion freely and publicly. This right is not limited by any service or employment relationship. Nobody may be placed at a disadvantage for exercising this right.
>
> (Constitution of the GDR 1968, article 27, translated by Hanna Blum)

The addition of a subclause stating that the right to freedom of opinion and speech had to be exerted in accordance with the constitution, in fact, allowed the government to legally justify any intervention. Still, censorship was a taboo word in official discourse; if mentioned at all, such government intervention was construed as guidance for readers (Jäger 1993: 21) or as a necessary tool in the fight against 'imperialistic barbarism' (Breuer 1982: 242). For this reason, censorship of translations, and of any other cultural product, had to take place in a more covert way.

Before providing an overview of the research on covert censorship of translation in the GDR, an important distinction needs to be made. While literary translations were considered part of the literary canon, they were subjected to the same rules and regulations, including those concerning censorship, as literature written in East Germany. The situation was different for specialised translation and interpreting, however; while academic texts had to adhere to the same regulations as literary texts (Peiter 2006), all other forms of translation and interpreting did not fall into this category and were, consequently, regulated in a different way. The regulations regarding censorship for both translatorial fields will be discussed in the following section. The analysis is based on research from literary and book studies, which will be complemented with findings from translation studies in order to highlight the peculiarities of translation censorship.

13.2 Historical Perspectives

Research on the literary system in the GDR had already been carried out in both East and West Germany prior to German reunification, but a critical examination of the cultural and literary policies and the institutionalised censorship system of the GDR only became possible after the fall of the Berlin Wall and the opening of archives, which allowed scholars to revisit and also re-evaluate GDR history in the years that followed. Works published in the West about the GDR before 1990 did not have access to extensive information and often focused on the negative aspects of East German literary life, whereas those published in the GDR completely ignored the print permit process as an unofficial censorship procedure, thus leaving out an important aspect of German literary life. However, not only did the material that had become available for study greatly expand after reunification, but scholarly interest also shifted after 1990, allowing for more objective research based on the documentation of actual practices. It is interesting to note that previous publications on censorship in the GDR primarily examined censorship during the Ulbricht era (1949–1971) (see, e.g., Barck, Langermann and Lokatis 1997), neglecting the period under the rule of Erich Honecker (1971–1989). This may be due to the fact that at the beginning of the GDR, cultural policy and thus the censorship apparatus had to be established, and both were much more restrictive in that time period than in the 1970s and 1980s, which makes it easier to provide clear evidence of censorship activities as well as document and describe them in research.

The research published after 1990 on the GDR's literary system and literary translation have mainly focused on various aspects of censorship in the form of the so-called *Druckgenehmigungsverfahren* [print permit process], the institutionalised, albeit unofficial, censorship process in the GDR.[1] If a publishing house wanted to publish a book in the GDR, be it fiction, non-fiction or specialised literature, it had to apply for a publisher's printing permit at the *Hauptverwaltung Verlage und Buchhandel* (HV) [central office for publishing houses and the book trade] of the *Ministerium für Kultur* [ministry of cultural affairs], the unofficial 'censorship office' of the GDR. The application had to contain a standardised form including information such as the author, title and language of the original book, but also the name of the translator. It also had to indicate the number of copies planned and, when it was not the first edition, the number of copies already printed. After all, the number of copies printed was one way to control the circulation of works that did not fully align with the ideological prerequisites of the state. Additionally, it was necessary to indicate the number of pages as well as the amount of paper required for the requested print run. In the case of translation, another important detail that had to be included was the amount of foreign currency needed to pay for any copyright or licenses. When the manuscript included a foreword or an afterword highlighting the significance and educational value of the book, a print permit for this kind of paratext had to be granted by the HV as well. The publisher also had to include a report by the editor and at least one expert opinion with the manuscript and the application document. The report and expert opinion were supposed to underscore the value of the publication and explain any ideological problems noted in the manuscript. Usually, the publishing house asked a well-known academic to write the foreword or afterword and the expert opinion in order to enhance the credibility of the proposal.

Applications for print permits were reviewed by the HV, which was divided into various areas, namely fiction, humanities and natural science (Barck, Langermann, and Lokatis 1997: 186–187). The area 'fiction, art and music literature' included the subject areas cultural heritage, GDR contemporary literature, foreign literature, youth and children's literature, literary studies, art and music (Lokatis 1999: 1265). The staff members responsible for these subject areas were assigned to the respective publishing houses where they were responsible for supervising the planned publication and reviewing the submitted manuscripts. If reviewers were uncertain about their assessment, they consulted colleagues at the HV, the editors or, in some cases, the authors themselves. In general, very few titles were denied print permits. Statistically speaking, the rate of rejected books was less than one percent (Lokatis 1999: 1276). Some printing permits were issued with restrictions or amendment requirements, which reduced outright rejection to very few cases.

13.3   Core Issues and Topics

The GDR censorship process has been investigated from several different angles in translation studies as well as book and literary studies. In translation studies, the mechanisms of this process have been documented in relation to children's literature (Thomson-Wohlgemuth 2009), fairy tales (Thomson-Wohlgemuth 2007a) and poetry translation (Owen 2011), among others. Several publications have investigated the transfer of literature from the Soviet Union (Reichardt 2014) and other socialist or communist countries (e.g., Yang 2020 for China) to the GDR through translation. Others have looked at the censorship files of translations of works from Western countries, such as the United States of America (Giovanopoulos 2000), Great Britain (Korte et al. 2008, Owen 2008), Norway (Jager 2014) or Latin America (Kirsten 2004). All of these publications discuss government influence on translation through censorship on one or more levels. These levels will be discussed in the following section.

13.3.1   Further Censorship Mechanisms

The censorial actions of the state constituted a highly complex system, which is why it is impossible to speak of censorship in the GDR, although the GDR's censorship system is often equated with the print permit process. Research on the censorship of literary translations has, in fact, shown not only that these texts were restricted through the print permit process, but also that the government had many other ways of censoring cultural products, some of which took place much earlier in the publishing process. The publication of literature was controlled just as much by filling positions with ideologically loyal people, distributing resources such as paper and supervising thematic plans as by the general cultural policy of the state (Blum 2022). In the following section, the various layers of this complex system will be outlined.

13.3.1.1 Centralisation

Although, or precisely because, a multitude of institutions were involved in this multi-layered censorship apparatus, one of the most important overriding principles of state control of the literary establishment was the centralisation of the publication process (Lokatis 1999: 1250). Centralisation was mainly achieved through monopolisation and the organisation of the state government. In the GDR, the highest organ of state power was the *Volkskammer* [parliament]. According to the constitution of the GDR (1968, article 48), it was the 'supreme state organ of power' and also elected the members of the *Staatsrat* [state council] (article 50), which was the collective head of state. However, in fact, both state organs possessed little importance because of the absolute claim to power of the state party, the *Sozialistische Einheitspartei Deutschlands* SED [socialist unity party]. The SED presided over the *Volkskammer* and all other institutions. The highest organ of the SED was the *Parteitag* [party congress], which elected a *Zentralkomitee* (ZK) [central committee] every five years. The *Zentralkomitee* in turn elected the *Politbüro* [politburo] and the *Sekretariat* [secretariat] of the ZK with the *Generalsekretär* [general secretary], later called *Erster Sekretär* [first secretary], of the ZK (Löffler 2011: 62–71), who was, in fact, the most powerful man in the GDR. The SED, in its capacity as the most powerful legislative institution, influenced the *Volkskammer* and all organisational structures subordinate to it, such as the *Ministerrat* [council of ministers], which was composed of the GDR's ministers and headed by a prime minister. The individual ministries, such as the ministry of cultural affairs, which included the HV, were responsible for implementing the decisions of the SED leadership in their respective areas (Darnton 2014: 181).

Centralisation as an instrument of control thus meant not only a centralised organisational structure of the state and party system but also the centralisation of the institutions and organisations involved in the publication process. For example, the printing office *VOB Zentrag* was managed by the ZK of the SED, which meant that the entire printing business was not only under the direct control of the party but also had to pay a considerable portion of its revenues to the party (Löffler 2011: 37). Another important organisation in the publishing process was the so-called paper commission of the ZK, which was responsible for paper distribution. The allocation of the paper quota available to each publisher was generally one of the most effective means of promoting or hindering a publisher's work (Thomson-Wohlgemuth 2007b: 103). However, the allocation of paper was based not only on ideological factors, which were reflected in the amount of paper distributed to the different publishers but also on economic factors related to the absolute quantity of paper available in the GDR (Thomson-Wohlgemuth 2007b: 169–177). Another organisation that was in party hands was the largest distribution organ of literature in the GDR, the *Leipziger Kommissions- und Großbuchhandel* (LKG), which meant that the most important production organ and the most important distribution organ in the GDR were both under the direct control of the SED.

13.3.1.2 Planning

The next step in the publication process was the planning of titles to be published. This was a long and time-consuming process. Publishers had to submit to the ministry of cultural affairs lists of planned titles, so-called *Perspektivpläne* [prospective plans] and *Themenpläne* [thematic plans].

The Routledge Handbook of Translation and Censorship

These plans fulfilled both censorial and economic functions (Lokatis 1999: 1251) since they had to specify the print runs, the paper quota required for them, expected profits and possibly needed licenses or copyright permissions. These lists were reviewed by the HV, whereupon individual titles were deleted or the plan was approved. While it was unnecessary at this point to provide detailed information for the prospective plan, which covered a five-year period, it had to be provided in the thematic plan, which represented the annual plan for the following calendar year (Thomson-Wohlgemuth 2007b: 100–102). In both the broader prospective plans and the detailed thematic plans, publishers were expected to establish a certain focus coinciding with their publishing profile (*Verlagsprofilierung*); such plans reflected the necessity of all publishing houses in the GDR to distinguish their publishing programs from one another (Löffler 2011: 159). Specialising in different domains prevented the publication of the same title by more than one publishing house. One reason was surely monetary, but a competitive relationship among publishing houses, as in the capitalist West, was completely undesirable. Another important reason was that the distinction of the publishing houses made it easier for the HV to control publications by having a better overview of the titles planned (Löffler 2011: 159).

During the title acceptance process publishing houses decided which titles would be included in their respective thematic plans (Lokatis 1999: 1251). Of course, the political and ideological content of the works was crucial, and the publishing houses tried to avoid controversial titles that would not survive the subsequent print permit process. This decision rested with the publishing house editors, who either directly supervised authors or were responsible for certain foreign literatures. The censorial responsibility, if one can and wants to speak of such a responsibility, thus lay primarily with the publishing house editors, who themselves decided which titles to include in the plans, effectively censoring themselves. However, individual factors also played a role in deciding which titles to include in the plans, such as the size of the publishing house and thus the range of possible publications (Reichardt 2014: 74).

In the case of foreign titles, the foreign exchange situation, as well as the general cultural-political situation, were particularly decisive in determining whether to include them in the plans (Thomson-Wohlgemuth 2009: 86–87). For some translations, licenses for the publishing rights had to be purchased in Western currency. A lack of access to that foreign currency often prevented a book from being published in the GDR. Until 1956, each publisher had its own foreign currency account (DR 1/1395), after which publishers had to apply to the office for licensing contracts if foreign currency was needed. If it was often an actual lack of foreign currency that blocked publication, this additional step in book production also offered the possibility of preventing the publication of an undesirable work. Conversely, it was much easier to publish foreign classical works, since they no longer fell under copyright law and their publication was thus possible without raising funds in the GDR. In return, however, translations produced in the GDR represented a potential source of income as they could be sold to Western countries in the form of licenses, as the sporadic cooperation with publishers, primarily from Switzerland and Austria, shows (Blum 2021).

For publishers, such long-term planning proved to be particularly difficult for several reasons. Due to the constantly changing cultural policy line of the SED (Bathrick 1995), it was difficult to estimate which titles would meet the cultural policy goal in five years' time. Because of this, but also in order to have the ability to react to the developing literary landscape at home as well as abroad, an attempt was made to include as many vacant titles as possible in the prospective plan. Vacant titles, which amounted to about ten percent of the total number of titles (Löffler 2011: 181), were titles that the publishers could leave open in the respective plan and fill much later with works they wanted to publish. This, for example, allowed the publishing houses to include titles

Censorship in Disguise: Literary Works in the GDR

that would have been deleted from any prospective plan right away. Quick reactions to political, but also to literary developments were difficult because the translation publication process took an average of 18 months (DR 1/1255).

13.3.2 Distribution and Circulation

Once a literary text had been published, publishers did not usually allow it to circulate freely; its distribution was controlled by government organisations. The motto to bring 'the right book to the right man at the right time' (Böhm 1951: 628) meant not only limiting the books to be published but also controlling the circulation of those books, both in bookstores and libraries.

13.3.2.1 Book Trade

Already in the SBZ and later in the GDR, private bookstores and libraries were closed as part of the denazification process and new government-owned bookstores were set up that were used to distribute ideologically appropriate literature (Löffler 2011: 211). It was argued that the distribution of literature should not be for profit, but should pursue socio-political and cultural-political goals, which is why bookstores needed to be Communised (Brilla 1956: 689). The Soviet military administration and later the SED introduced numerous obstacles to limit the influence of privately-owned bookstores, such as a special tax, the so-called 'capitalist tax', which was placed on private businesses whose profits exceeded a certain threshold, and a relicensing procedure initiated in the 1960s, as a result of which many private bookstores were no longer granted a license (Löffler 2002: 10). These restrictive measures fulfilled their purpose. Statistics show that the number of private bookstores steadily decreased over the years and that, by 1962, three-quarters of private businesses had already closed (Löffler 2002.: 10–11).

At the same time, a strong expansion of the *Volksbuchhandlung* [public bookseller] network took place; in the 1970s, about 85 percent of the book trade was handled by *Volksbuchhandlungen* (Rumland 1993: 78). The individual bookstores were in turn structured according to their function (Börner and Härtner 2012). For example, there were 'houses of books', which stocked the entire catalogue of the GDR. City bookstores, as the smallest organisational form, were supposed to cover the 'needs of the individual buyers of the territory to be served' (N.N. 1976: 33), while company bookstores supplied their workers with literature (Börner and Härtner 2012). The state also sought to diversify the locations of bookstores, which is why people's bookstores were founded in more remote areas. The goal was to establish a bookstore in every community with more than 5000 inhabitants (Löffler 2011: 227). This restructuring of the book trade was intended to create a centrally controlled system that determined the distribution of literature (Börner and Härtner 2012). The bookstores as well as the publishers reported to the HV.

13.3.2.2 Libraries

From the beginning of the 1950s, the network of libraries in the GDR was expanded at about the same time as the book trade, and an attempt was made to establish a library in every community with more than 1000 inhabitants (Löffler 2011: 252). Through this dense network of libraries, it was possible to determine which books reached which part of the population at what time. Private libraries were seen by the socialist government as a threat to this endeavour, especially if their catalogue included literature that did not align with the official aesthetics of Socialist

Realism. Therefore, in the early 1950s, there was an uptick in reporting such libraries, which were accused of continuing to circulate National Socialist literature (Löffler 2011.: 212–213). This led to the closure of most of these libraries. Denazification measures were implemented in all libraries, which involved removing all books with fascist or anti-socialist ideas before the libraries could be reopened. The choice of books to be removed was based on a list of banned books (Marks 1983: 8). Both private and state libraries had to adhere to this list.

Unlike the publishing houses and the book trade, the public library system was not headed by the HV, but rather, from 1950, by the *Zentralinstitut für Bibliothekswesen* [central institute for libraries], which in turn was assigned to the ministry of cultural affairs beginning in 1954. Thus, the entire literary system, from planning to production and distribution, was in the hands of the party.

13.3.3 Censorship Criteria

An important aspect of researching censorship involves not only uncovering the mechanisms behind it but also the various motivations for it, as reflected in the censorship criteria that were applied to both literary works written by East German authors as well as translations of foreign works produced in East Germany.

There were two pivotal censorship criteria in the GDR: anti-fascism and the guiding principles of Socialist Realism. Both were emphasised in the official discourse on literature and also in the paratexts of literary works (Blum 2021). The GDR was founded as an anti-fascist state, which is why the banning of fascist literature was one of the key guidelines from the beginning of the SBZ to the end of the GDR. The second most important censorship criterion was Socialist Realism, considered the only admissible form of art by government officials. Socialist Realism had four leading principles (Schubbe 1972: 40–1): the truthful and realistic representation of reality in its revolutionary development, that is, reality with a socialist worldview; the creation of art for the masses by cultivating a close connection between art and life; the depiction of typical people whose features are exaggerated to reflect a desirable ideal; and the conveying of social optimism through the positive development of the hero or heroine. In Socialist Realism, the central precepts are progress and the positive development of life, the sustained development of the hero or heroine concludes a work (Schubbe 1972: 40–1). Thus, a key element of any work of fiction should be to depict reality in a positive light. Naturalistic and especially formalistic elements were rejected outright. Considering form as an important aspect of a work of art was dismissed as an expression of Western imperialism, making formalism another important justification for censorship.

The demand for Socialist Realism and the categorical rejection of formalism were fundamentally political decisions taken in reaction/response to negative or pessimistic images of socialist society. The main aim of censorship, after all, was to keep the SED in power. As a result, criticism of the political system and its institutions was not tolerated. For example, foreign authors who openly criticised communism or socialism were not published in more politically doctrinaire times, such as when the Berlin Wall was being built (see, e.g., Jager 2014), nor were depictions of revolt and resistance (Thomson-Wohlgemuth 2007a). Thus, socialism was not only to be portrayed in a generally positive light, but its merits were also to be highlighted at the expense of imperialist and capitalist societies, first and foremost the United States. The counterpart to this was the USSR and the fraternal states of the socialist bloc; friendship with these states was to be emphasised. For example, a briefing on the procurement of foreign and West German literature stated:

Censorship in Disguise: Literary Works in the GDR

The procurement of literature directed against the GDR as a state of workers and peasants and its allies, and which incites racial and ethnic hatred, colonial oppression, war and moral brutalisation, as well as fascist, militarist and anti-communist literature is prohibited.

(DR 3/173, translated by H. Blum)

This quotation illustrates the politically and ideologically motivated selection criteria, which also affected the field of translation in the sense that publishing houses were aware of the criteria and tried to adhere to them in their publication plans. Further censorship criteria, which were often mentioned in print permit files, concerned religious utterances and the call for humanist content (Thomson-Wohlgemuth 2009: 155–96).

13.3.4   *Importance of Paratexts*

A significant number of publications on the censorship of (translated) literary texts in the GDR have analysed documents related to the print permit process, namely the application files, the reports written by the publishing houses and experts as well as the reports by the HV (not) granting publication rights. In other words, studies published in the discipline of translation studies, among others, have mainly concentrated on the investigation of the paratexts accompanying a literary work (see, e.g., Giovanopoulos 2000, Korte et al . 2008, Thomson-Wohlgemuth 2009, Yang 2020). This emphasises the importance of these texts and the role they played in the censorship process.

The discursive work in the paratexts submitted by the publishing houses, which was intended to show publications in the right ideological light, took on greater importance than interventions in the text itself when it came to censorship (Blum 2019). As an instrument used by publishing houses to support a publication (Kirsten 2004: 105–107), paratexts played a performative role as they discursively fulfilled the criteria necessary to avoid censorship. They either emphasised the authors' political loyalty or explained their possible political non-conformity; they emphasised the realistic character of a work or excused its formalistic aspects; they emphasised a novel's educational value or called out its lack of educational value as an imperfection (Thomson-Wohlgemuth 2006). Both the editors and the experts writing the reports thus played a decisive role in whether a publication was successful or not (Giovanopoulos 2000: 380). By resorting to these strategies to avoid censorship, the vast majority of requests for permission to print were approved by the HV. Consciously acknowledging the ideological imperfections of a work and explaining them allowed the authors of the paratexts to then emphasise ideologically positive aspects of the work, which ended up carrying more discursive weight. To sum it up, it can be said that censorship in the GDR mostly took place on a discursive level rather than a textual level in the sense of textual alterations.

The paratexts produced by the HV, namely the reports that either granted or denied permission to print, support these assumptions about the instrumental role of publishers' paratexts in the censorship process. Analyses of such paratexts reveal that the reports of the HV can be seen as replies to publishers' reports and forewords or afterwords (Blum 2021). The latter two types of texts laid the argumentative foundation for the HV's appraisals and attempted to anticipate problematic passages in a novel. Therefore, it is not surprising that the same or at least similar strands of discourse can be found in these reports as in the publishers' paratexts, i.e., the ideological positioning of the authors and their work in favour of socialism and against fascism, formalism and capitalism.

13.4 New Debates

The multi-layered censorship apparatus for literary texts, which includes translations, has been extensively researched in literary and book studies; however, translation studies has contributed to a more targeted examination of the specificities involved in the censorship of literary translation. The latter discipline still has much to reveal and will undoubtedly ignite new debates surrounding the censorship of translations in the GDR.

13.4.1 Investigation of Actors

Previous research has, for the most part, analysed (para)textual sources in order to investigate which authors and texts were translated and how they were translated in the GDR, along with which censorship mechanisms restricted these publications. This initial focus on textual analysis is based on the fact that hardly any research on translation and its censorship in the GDR was available after 1990, and so this field had to be explored from scratch. Another reason for this focus was that the print permit files are now accessible in the Federal Archives of Germany, some of which are available online. This offers a rich well of valuable data for research. After the fall of the Berlin Wall, it became possible for researchers, including those working in translation studies, to investigate these files in detail, which explains the vast number of case studies looking into the publication of translations by certain authors or from different languages or countries. Additional material, such as minutes of meetings of the writers' union of the GDR, is available in the Academy Archives, which allows for an even more thorough investigation of the professional life of literary translators, including their experiences with censorship. In recent years, however, and in line with the rising importance of sociological approaches in translation studies, the role of the actors involved has become the focus of research on censorship in the GDR.

Apart from the translators themselves, editors also played a pivotal role in the censorship of translations. In the field of literature in the GDR, editors were prominent figures who had to meet certain ideological criteria to even be considered for such a position, which was ensured mainly/ primarily through ideological training. As a result, most editors conformed to the ideological expectations and requirements of the state, even though some might have had a more liberal way of thinking prior to their indoctrination. They were aware that they had to internalise the censorship criteria and try to adhere to them as much as possible when planning the publications for the next period, whether they did this out of their own political beliefs or out of fear of repression (Giovanopoulos 2000: 367–378). This meant that they had to perform self-censorship by selecting texts for their planning lists for which they could expect little or no resistance from the HV, or they deliberately tried to 'push through' controversial texts (Owen 2011: 135). They had to choose wisely how to present critical texts by accompanying them with appropriate paratexts, i.e., forewords or afterwords and the reports that were submitted with the application for a print permit. As mentioned above, censorship was avoided mainly on a discursive level by emphasising the convenient aspects of a novel and trying to excuse any deviations from socialist or communist ideology.

The same held true for translators. Interestingly, hardly any of the studies published so far have dealt with the work of translators and the translation process itself, focusing instead on the processes surrounding it. Although evidence shows that the translations themselves were not heavily censored, which is probably the reason for the lack of research, translators have confirmed

Censorship in Disguise: Literary Works in the GDR

that they were aware of the way they were supposed to translate in order for a novel to be published (Blum 2021). It was seldom asked of them or of their editors to delete entire passages, but they knew that one word could be translated in different ways and that they were expected to select the option that best suited the political and ideological circumstances in the GDR.

Some research studies have used interviews with editors and translators in the field as sources or to support their findings from other sources (see, e.g., Thomson-Wohlgemuth 2009, Rotroff 2020). Since censorship in the GDR happened mainly on a discursive level, as indicated by the important role played by paratexts in framing texts has shown, rather than on a textual level in the sense of alterations in the text, further research is needed on the personal experiences of actors involved, such as translators, editors, etc., which will shed light on aspects of the censorship process that are still hidden or only vaguely known. Such research could, for example, clarify the impression that most of the censorship work had been outsourced by the HV to the publishers through the various steps preceding the final publication, meaning that self-censorship was a crucial part of the editors' job.

13.4.2 Cadre Politics

Closely related to the topic of the investigation of actors involved in the process of censoring translations is the topic of cadre politics, meaning the ideological training of people who hold important positions and who are supposed to adhere to and spread socialist ideology through their professional activities. Cadre politics were practised in important organisations and institutions (Lokatis 1999: 1272), which meant that, following the Soviet model, ideologically trained individuals were placed at all levels of the publication process to enforce and implement the decrees issued by the ZK of the SED. Cadre politics primarily affected publishing houses, where party-compliant editors were generally employed. The party expected ideologically trained editors to avoid ideological 'mishaps' by every means possible (Barck, Langermann, and Lokatis 1997: 436). This development intensified in the mid-1950s after a short-term thaw period (Lokatis 2009: 113). One example of cadre politics was the appointment of Klaus Gysi, later Minister of Culture, as head of the publishing house Aufbau-Verlag in 1957, after the former head, Walter Janka, and publishing editor, Wolfgang Harich, were sentenced to prison terms for 'forming a counterrevolutionary group' according to Walter Ulbricht, as they had attempted to publish progressive literature in their publishing house (Bundesstiftung Aufarbeitung 2019a). Gysi had also worked as an informant for the Stasi (Bundesstiftung Aufarbeitung 2019b). The editor Joachim Schreck supported Gysi in bringing the Aufbau-Verlag back to the party line (Wurm 2002: 37). Giving a louder voice to people in such positions in research will create the opportunity to explore another layer of translation censorship in the GDR. Other sections have made reference to self-censorship in the form of the internalisation of censorship criteria. This is an important aspect of censorship, which was enforced through ideological training in cadre politics, among other things.

13.4.3 Specialised Translation and Interpreting

Although the censorship of literary works and translations in particular is a well-researched field, hardly anything is known about the censorship of specialised translation and interpreting. The reasons for this have already been mentioned and are mainly methodological in nature. While many archival documents are available in the field of literary translation, no such archival documents are yet available in the fields of specialised translation and interpreting. This is why the necessary information needs to be gathered from other sources, such as from interviews with people working as translators and interpreters in the GDR, and this needs to be done urgently as long as the actors involved are still alive to tell their stories. For interpreting in particular, it is essential to find alternative methodological tools to archival documents in order to investigate this field, since no written documents describe this professional practice in detail. Other reasons for the tendency to concentrate on literary translation in translation studies in general is the prestige and public interest in this area of the translatorial field, even though it represents only one small part of translation activity (Olohan/Salama-Carr 2011: 179) and in particular for the GDR, since it allows researchers to draw conclusions about GDR cultural policy. Moreover, literary translation in the GDR reproduced the image of the East German state as a dictatorial regime, a view that is predominant both in society at large and among scholars.

The first research steps are currently being taken to close the knowledge gap between censorship of literary translations on the one hand and of specialised translation and interpreting on the other hand (Blum 2019, Blum/Hofeneder 2020, Blum 2021). These studies have shown that in the field of specialised translation and interpreting, cadre politics were even more important than in literary translation. The work produced by translators and interpreters employed as language mediators [*Sprachmittler*] for businesses, private individuals or journals did not have to go through the print permit process. In order to ensure ideological conformity in this field, government officials had to make sure that the respective positions, namely those of translators and interpreters, were held by people who were ideologically trained and compliant (Blum/Hofeneder 2020).

13.4.4   Ideological Training

Closely linked to the subject of specialised translation and interpreting versus literary translation as well as cadre politics is the issue of education and the role of the ideological training of translators and interpreters in the GDR. In the vast majority of cases, literary translators studied philology and had not completed any translational training before being employed by publishers. In contrast, technical translators and interpreters studied *Sprachmittlung* [language mediation]. This university program consisted of linguistic and translational training in at least two languages (see Neubert 1986, Salevsky and Schmitz 1986). Marxism-Leninism as the leading state ideology was also taught in these programs, although professional translator organisations, namely the *Vereinigung für Sprachmittler* VdS [union of language mediators], was a more prominent place for ideological training. For their part, literary translators received ideological indoctrination in the section for literary translators of the *Schriftstellerverband der DDR* [writers' union of the GDR]. These organisations were not only used by translators and interpreters to discuss work-related problems, but they also offered educational courses that included ideological training. Language mediators were expected to be 'partisan', meaning that they had to actively promote the cause of socialism in their work, since no foreign text was written for the population of the GDR. The terms partisanship and partisan translation were understood as acting responsibly toward the readers, the authors and the text (SV 777, SV 779). Attending these courses was especially important for specialised translators and interpreters since it gave them access to jobs. In fact, the government used the courses to monitor who was supposedly loyal to the state ideology (Blum 2019, Blum 2021).

13.5 Conclusion

The censorship of literary translations in the GDR was a complex system that comprised many more steps than the actual print permit process itself. It started with the centralisation of the entire publishing industry, which was controlled by the SED, allowing the party to place ideologically loyal people in important positions, such as those held by editors and translators. In the planning process, these politically conscious people aimed to apply censorship criteria to their publication plans so that the latter would be accepted by governmental institutions. Once accepted, manuscripts were translated by literary translators who were also aware of the expected criteria and adapted the text, so that it would pass the print permit process. After the successful issuance of a print permit, the distribution of literary texts was controlled by bookstores and libraries. The multiple layers of the censorship process underscore how important certain self-censoring actors were. Once further research sheds more light on those actors, knowledge about translation censorship in the GDR will be greatly expanded.

Other research gaps that still need to be filled concern the mechanisms of censorship in the fields of specialised translation and interpreting about which hardly anything is known. In order to address these gaps, more diverse methodological approaches need to be developed, such as interviews with the people involved, as well as new archival documents. Learning more about the professional realities of specialised translators and interpreters in the GDR will contribute to correcting the overemphasis on literary translation that still exists in translation studies today.

Further Reading

Barck, Simone, Langermann, Martina and Lokatis, Siegfried (eds.). 1997. *'Jedes Buch ein Abenteuer'. Zensursystem und literarische Öffentlichkeit in der DDR bis Ende der sechziger Jahre.* Berlin: Akademie-Verlag.
This volume offers a comprehensive collection of essays that shed light on crucial organisations and events that were relevant for the censorship of literary works in the GDR.

Löffler, Dietrich. 2011. *Buch und Lesen in der DDR: ein literatursoziologischer Rückblick.* Berlin: Ch. Links Verlag.
This book summarises important aspects of the literary field of the GDR such as planning, ideological control as well as the production and distribution of literature, focusing on the sociology of literature in the GDR.

Lokatis, Siegfried and Sonntag, Ingrid (eds.). 2008. *Heimliche Leser in der DDR. Kontrolle und Verbreitung unerlaubter Literatur.* Berlin: Ch. Links Verlag.
This volume includes several interesting articles on the circulation of forbidden literature among the people of the GDR.

Thomson-Wohlgemuth, Gabriele. 2009. *Translation under State Control. Books for Young People in the German Democratic Republic.* New York/London: Routledge (Children's Literature and Culture 63).
In this book, Thomson-Wohlgemuth provides an overview of the literary field of the GDR controlled by the state, including an in-depth analyses of print permit files of translated children's literature from English-speaking countries.

Note

1 For a detailed description of this censorship process for literary texts in general, see, e.g., Barck, Langermann, and Lokatis 1997, Lokatis 1999 and Löffler 2011, and for translations in particular, see, e.g., Thomson-Wohlgemuth 2006 and 2009.

References

Archive Documents and Political Documents

Bundesarchiv

DR 1/1255
DR 1/1395
DR 3/173

Archiv der Akademie der Künste

SV 777
SV 779
Böhm, Karl. 1951. 'Ein verheißungsvoller Anfang', *Börsenblatt für den Deutschen Buchhandel*, 118(48): 627–29.
Brilla, Fritz. 1956. 'Es ging um die Arbeit des Volksbuchhandels', *Börsenblatt für den Deutschen Buchhandel*, 123(44): 689–92.
N.N. 1968. *Verfassung der DDR 1968*. Available at: www.verfassungen.de/ddr/verf68-i.htm (Accessed: 10 October 2023).
N.N. 1976. *Ordnung für den Literaturvertrieb. 2. Fassung*.
Ulbricht, Walter. 1950. 'Welches sind die Hauptaufgaben auf dem Gebiet der Kultur?', in E. Schubbe (ed.), *Dokumente zur Kunst-, Literatur- und Kulturpolitik der SED*. Stuttgart: Seewald Verlag: 149–51.

Secondary Sources

Barck, Simone, Langermann, Martina and Lokatis, Siegfried (eds.). 1997. *'Jedes Buch ein Abenteuer'. Zensursystem und literarische Öffentlichkeit in der DDR bis Ende der sechziger Jahre*. Berlin: Akademie-Verlag.
Bathrick, David. 1995. *The Powers of Speech: The Politics of Culture in the GDR*. Lincoln: University of Nebraska Press.
Blum, Hanna. 2019. 'Paratexts as Patronage: The Case of John Desmond Bernal and the Social Function of Science in the GDR', in R. Y. Schögler (ed.), *Circulation of Academic Thought. Rethinking Translation in the Academic Field*. Berlin: Peter Lang, 125–41.
Blum, Hanna. 2021. '"Der Übersetzer ist weniger als der Schriftsteller, und der Übersetzer ist mehr als der Schriftsteller": Translationskultur und Zensur in der ehemaligen DDR'. PhD, University of Graz.
Blum, Hanna. 2022. 'The Impact of the Cultural Policy of the GDR on the Work of Translators', in C. Rundle, A. Lange and D. Monticelli (eds.), *Translation Under Communism*. London: Palgrave Macmillan, 281–314.
Blum, Hanna and Hofeneder, Philipp. 2020. 'Specialized Translators in the GDR: A Case-Study of the Journal "Sowjetwissenschaft"', *Translation and Interpreting Studies*, 15(3) (special issue on translation and the cultural Cold War): 333–53.
Börner, Hein and Härtner, Bernd. 2012. *Im Leseland: Die Geschichte des Volksbuchhandels*. Berlin: Das Neue Berlin.
Breuer, Dieter. 1982. *Geschichte der literarischen Zensur in Deutschland*. Heidelberg: Quelle & Meyer (Uni-Taschenbücher, 1208).
Bundesstiftung zur Aufarbeitung der SED-Diktatur. 2019a. 'Klaus Gysi', in *Wer war wer in der DDR? Ein Lexikon ostdeutscher Biographien*. Available at: www.bundesstiftung-aufarbeitung.de/de/recherche/katal oge-datenbanken/biographische-datenbanken/klaus-gysi?ID=1186 (Accessed: 10 October 2023).
Bundesstiftung zur Aufarbeitung der SED-Diktatur. 2019b. 'Walter Janka', in *Wer war wer in der DDR? Ein Lexikon ostdeutscher Biographien*. Available at: www.bundesstiftung-aufarbeitung.de/de/recherche/katal oge-datenbanken/biographische-datenbanken/walter-janka?ID=1566 (Accessed: 10 October 2023).
Darnton, Robert. 2014. *Censors at Work: How States Shaped Literature*. New York: W. W. Norton.
Giovanopoulos, Anna-Christina. 2000. *Die Amerikanische Literatur in der DDR: Die Institutionalisierung von Sinn zwischen Affirmation und Subversion*. Essen: Blaue Eule.

Jager, Benedikt. 2014. 'Vorbilder und Renegaten. Probleme mit der norwegischen Literatur in der DDR', in S. Lokatis, T. Rost and G. Steuer (eds.), *Vom Autor zur Zensurakte. Abenteuer im Leseland DDR*. Halle: Mitteldeutscher Verlag, 224–44.

Jäger, Manfred. 1993. 'Das Wechselspiel von Selbstzensur und Literaturlenkung in der DDR', in E. Wichner and H. Wiesner (eds.), *«Literaturentwicklungsprozesse». Die Zensur der Literatur in der DDR*. Frankfurt on the Main: Suhrkamp (Texte aus dem Literaturhaus Berlin, Bd. 8), 18–49.

Kirsten, Jens. 2004. *Lateinamerikanische Literatur in der DDR. Publikations- und Wirkungsgeschichte*. Berlin: Ch. Links Verlag.

Korte, Barbara, Schaur, Sandra and Welz, Stefan (eds.). 2008. *Britische Literatur in der DDR*. Würzburg: Königshausen und Neumann.

Löffler, Dietrich. 2002. 'Zwischen Literaturvertrieb und Buchmarkt. Der Buchmarkt der DDR seit den siebziger Jahre', *HALMA*, 5(13): 1–40.

Löffler, Dietrich. 2011. *Buch und Lesen in der DDR: ein literatursoziologischer Rückblick*. Berlin: Ch. Links Verlag.

Lokatis, Siegfried. 1999. 'Die Zensur- und Publikationspraxis in der DDR', *Materialien der Enquete-Kommission "Überwindung der Folgen der SED-Diktatur im Prozeß der deutschen Einheit" (13. Wahlperiode des Deutschen Bundestages)*, 4(2): 1248–304.

Lokatis, Siegfried. 2009. 'Zensur', in M. Sabrow (ed.), *Erinnerungsorte der DDR*. München: C. H. Beck, 109–17.

Lokatis, Siegfried and Sonntag, Ingrid (eds.). 2008. *Heimliche Leser in der DDR. Kontrolle und Verbreitung unerlaubter Literatur*. Berlin: Ch. Links Verlag.

Marks, Erwin. 1983. 'Die staatliche Neuorganisation der Bibliotheksarbeit in der sowjetischen Besatzungszone von 1945 bis 1949', *Studien zum Buch- und Bibliothekswesen*, 3: 5–14.

Neubert, Gunter. 1986. 'Die Ausbildung von Fachübersetzern in der DDR', *Babel*, 32(2): 124–25.

Olohan, Maeva and Salama-Carr, Myriam. 2011. 'Translating Science', *The Translator*, 17(2): 179–88.

Owen, Ruth J. 2008. 'British Poets in the GDR Poesiealbum', *Angermion: Yearbook for Anglo-German Literary Criticism, Intellectual History and Cultural Transfers / Jahrbuch für britisch-deutsche Kulturbeziehungen*, 1: 157–72.

Owen, Ruth J. 2011. 'Freedoms of Expression: Poetry Translations in the East Berlin Poesiealbum', *Translation Studies*, 4(2): 133–48.

Peiter, Hermann. 2006. *Wissenschaft im Würgegriff von SED und DDR-Zensur. Ein nicht nur persönlicher Rückblick eines theologischen Schleiermacher-Forschers auf die Zeit des Prager Frühlings*. Berlin: LIT Verlag.

Reichardt, Ann-Kathrin. 2014. *Von der Sowjetunion lernen? Die Zensur sowjetischer belletristischer Literatur in der DDR in den 1970er und 1980er Jahren*. Münster: LIT Verlag.

Rotroff, Heidi. 2020. 'Interview mit der Übersetzerin Elga Abramowitz', in A. Tashinskiy, J. Boguna and A. Kelletat (eds.), *Übersetzer und Übersetzen in der DDR: Translationshistorische Studien*. Berlin: Frank & Timme, 151–64.

Rumland, Marie-Kristin. 1993. *Veränderungen in Verlagswesen und Buchhandel der ehemaligen DDR 1989–1991*. Wiesbaden: Harrasowitz Verlag.

Salevsky, Heidemarie and Schmitz, Manfred. 1986. 'Zur Sprachmittlerausbildung in der Deutschen Demokratischen Republik', *Babel*, 32(2): 118–24.

Schubbe, Elimar. 1972. 'Einführung in die Dokumentation', in E. Schubbe (ed.), *Dokumente zur Kunst-, Literatur- und Kulturpolitik der SED. Dokumente zur Kunst-, Literatur- und Kulturpolitik der SED. 1946–1970*. Stuttgart: Seewald Verlag, 37–54.

Thomson-Wohlgemuth, Gabriele. 2006. 'Translation from the Point of View of the East German Censorship Files', in A. Pym, Z. Jettmarová and M. Shlesinger (eds.), *Sociocultural Aspects of Translating and Interpreting (Benjamins Translation Library 67)*. Amsterdam and Philadelphia: John Benjamins, 61–72.

Thomson-Wohlgemuth, Gabriele. 2007a. '... and He Flew Out of the Window on a Wooden Spoon', *Meta*, 52(2): 173–93.

Thomson-Wohlgemuth, Gabriele. 2007b. 'On the Other Side of the Wall. Book Production, Censorship and Translation in East Germany', in F. Billiani (ed.), *Modes of Censorship and Translation. National Contexts and Diverse Media*. Manchester and Kinderhook: St. Jerome, 93–116.

Thomson-Wohlgemuth, Gabriele. 2009. *Translation under State Control. Books for Young People in the German Democratic Republic (Children's Literature and Culture 63)*. New York and London: Routledge.

Wurm, Carsten. 2002. 'Saison für Lyrik. Kulturpolitische Störfälle im Aufbau-Verlag am Ende der sechziger Jahre', *Horch und Guck. Zeitschrift zur kritischen Aufarbeitung der DDR-Literatur*, 37 (Konflikte in der DDR 1958–1968): 37–40.

Yang, Luo. 2020. 'Chinesische Literatur im Verlag Volk und Welt 1980–1990. Was verraten die Gutachten?', in A. Tashinskiy, J. Boguna and A. Kelletat (eds.), *Übersetzer und Übersetzen in der DDR: Translationshistorische Studien*. Berlin: Frank & Timme, 107–28.

14

COMMUNIST CENSORSHIP IN HUNGARY AND BEYOND[1]

Zsófia Gombár

14.1 Introduction

The present chapter provides an overview of censorship practices with respect to literary translation in Socialist Hungary. It brings together and examines the available published documentation in Hungarian and English, and also incorporates new findings and perspectives on the subject. Although the scope of this study is principally confined to the analysis of literary translations published in book form in Hungary under Communist rule, the section 'Historical perspectives' offers broader insights into the historical background of censorship in order to better contextualise Hungary's long dictatorial past and the place of censorship within its society. Emphasis has been put on analysing the inner workings of censorship during the Communist era and, in addition to external institutions and methods of censorship, internal constraints have been studied in more detail and in greater depth.

14.2 Core Issues and Topics

Long-standing foreign oppression, along with the lack of national independence and unity, is part of Hungary's historical experience and has left its mark on the formation of the nation. Before Communist rule was implanted in Hungary, democratic traditions were not well established and freedom of expression was routinely violated. Hungarian society's tacit and passive acceptance of Soviet control can in part be attributed to the country's long history of repression, and also to the fact that, at the end of the war, Hungary fell under the full control of the Soviet military administration. The country's powerless and defenceless position is also well demonstrated by the tragic fate of the Revolution of 1956. When the Hungarian people finally revolted against their puppet government—in the absence of military intervention by Western Powers—the uprising, together with the hope of a democratic Hungary, was quickly crushed by Soviet tanks.

Mátyás Rákosi, the Stalinist leader of Hungary between 1948 and 1956, wished to emulate the Soviet totalitarian model and apply it to the Hungarian political and social system forcefully. The new regime's major function was to eliminate the remaining bourgeois roots from Hungarian society and remould the latter completely according to the Stalinist ideal of the USSR. From that point forward state and cultural policies alike were based on the simplified binary of friend or foe. Those who refused to conform to the Communist ideological or aesthetical standards of Socialist realism immediately became enemies of the state. Writers, for instance, who did not wish to toe

DOI: 10.4324/9781003149453-18

the official party line, had two choices, either to emigrate or to write for their desk-drawer. The same rule applied to artistic products. Literary works, including translations, that did not fit into the Socialist ideal could be easily withdrawn from bookstores and library shelves and locked up in sealed departments, or simply destroyed. It is estimated that in the course of Hungarian history, never had so many books been destroyed as during the Stalinist years (see Gombár 2011).

Hungarian literary culture and its institutions were rapidly remodelled on the Soviet model. The eight-part pattern appears to be quite similar in every satellite country of the Soviet Bloc. (1) Publishing houses along with bookstores and printshops were nationalised and brought under strict ideological control; (2) former cultural institutions, such as writers' organisations or literary journals were suppressed and new ones were created in keeping with the Soviet model; (3) the doctrine of Socialist realism as well as the Stalinist ideological perspective was introduced and enforced in the field of literature; (4) all publications were subject to strict control and ideological censorship; (5) Soviet-controlled Eastern Bloc countries became more and more isolated from Western culture; (6) Soviet literature inundated the book market; (7) literature taught in secondary schools and universities adopted Marxist-Leninist principles; (8) all these processes were accompanied by wide-spread political arrests and show trials and the accused included many writers (Neubauer 2007: 36).

Like Rákosi, General Secretary János Kádár (1956–1988) also rose to power with the help of the Soviet army. After the reprisals and mass executions following the 1956 Revolution, the new post-Stalinist government gradually modified its stance from outright totalitarianism to authoritarianism. The pragmatic compromise offered by Kádár to the Hungarian people is summed up well in the much-quoted slogan: Who is not against us is with us! in which Kádár aptly reversed Rákosi's former catchphrase: He who is not for us is against us. In exchange for the population agreeing to cooperate willingly with the implantation of Socialism, instead of undermining it and revolting against it, Kádár guaranteed greater individual freedom in private life and a reasonable standard of living.

As far as national and translated literature is concerned, Kádár's new cultural administration no longer insisted on imposing the dogma of Socialist realism on an obligatory basis. Writers and publishers were allowed more leeway for creativity and artistic innovation. Publishing houses could broaden their palette of foreign authors, even including works which might not be in perfect conformity with the formal and ideological demands of Socialist realism as long as they did not convey an overtly adverse political message to the public. The previous strict binary division of the cultural sphere between friend and foe was replaced by a far more flexible ternary system, also known as the three Ts policy (in Hungarian: 'tilt' [prohibit], 'tűr' [tolerate] and 'támogat' [promote]) (Gombár 2011: 112–3).

Literary works that openly criticised the USSR, its satellite states or the one-party system remained prohibited essentially throughout the era, and included Arthur Koestler's *Darkness at Noon*, George Orwell's *Animal Farm* and Aleksandr Solzhenitsyn's *The Gulag Archipelago*. Pornographic and erotic literature, such as John Cleland's *Fanny Hill* or the majority of Henry Miller's works, were likewise forbidden. Tolerated works, for example, the allegedly subversive and pessimistic writings by Françoise Sagan, J.D. Salinger and Norman Mailer or innovative fiction by Marcel Proust, James Joyce and André Gide, did not necessarily support Marxist ideology or contribute to the building of Socialism, but were considered of higher literary merit. In contrast to high literature, popular literature, e. g., detective and science fiction novels, was not enthusiastically welcomed by the cultural establishment either. However, the rules of what works should be tolerated or prohibited were not fixed, and were in a constant state of flux. The

Communist Censorship in Hungary and Beyond

publication of certain translations that were previously banned could be authorised later on and vice versa.

14.2.1 Withdrawal Lists (1949–1950)

Prior to the Communist political takeover, Hungary had a rich tradition of translating Western literature. The appearance of the left-leaning journal *Nyugat* [West] in 1908 marked a significant milestone in the reception of foreign literatures in Hungary. The journal, true to its emblematic title, aimed to become a harbinger of all European national literatures in the country. Many poets and liberal-minded thinkers belonging to the *Nyugat* generation, such as Mihály Babits, Antal Szerb and Lőrinc Szabó, translated works by classic and modern Western authors, and wrote critical reviews and essays endorsing the artistic significance of these writings. Apart from *Nyugat*, other literary journals and even newspapers published translated foreign fiction on their pages and within their book series, contributing to a vibrant culture of translated Western literature in Hungary from the 1910s onwards (Szili 2007).

In 1948, however, when Rákosi assumed full political power, a cultural purge was launched against all forms of literature that were perceived as diverging from the official party doctrine. The primary aim of this cleansing crusade was to eliminate the bourgeoise cultural heritage of the past, which notably encompassed the prevailing influence inspired by the journal *Nyugat*. This marked a drastic shift, as all translations of literary works by authors residing or having lived in Western capitalist countries were viewed with the utmost suspicion.

Between 1949 and 1950, the new government issued several withdrawal lists with the objective of identifying and removing all printed materials considered politically unreliable from public libraries and bookstores. The withdrawal campaign reached its peak in 1950, when the entire process came under the full control of the Communist cultural authorities. The Ministry of Culture published two official withdrawal lists for village and work-trade libraries, but due to certain bureaucratic miscommunications, these lists were also applied to bookshops and second-hand bookshops. Numerous bookstores throughout Hungary lost countless invaluable items from their collections. In Budapest alone, over 120,000 books were destroyed at that period (Kövér 1998: 204–5).

The first catalogue consisted of 1848 titles, encompassing writings by Erich Kästner, Marcel Proust, Albert Camus, Jean Cocteau, D.H. Lawrence, Virginia Woolf, E.M. Forster, Edith Wharton, Ernest Hemingway, Arnold Bennett, Frances Hodgson Burnett, Herman Melville, Ferdynand Antoni Ossendowski and Pitigrilli. The second catalogue was significantly larger, listing 6552 titles. It included works by Alexandre Dumas, Alphonse Daudet, Antoine de Saint-Exupéry, André Gide, Wilkie Collins Thomas De Quincey, Robert Southey, Rudyard Kipling, John Priestley, Upton Sinclair, Aldous Huxley, Lewis Carroll, Willa Cather, Sinclair Lewis and Henryk Sienkiewicz. It is worth noting that the exact number of titles is unclear, as the two lists marked the complete oeuvre of 426 authors for destruction (Népkönyvtári Központ 1950).

The true reasons behind the Hungarian Communist regime's decision to destroy these books remain unclear, since every piece of archival material related to the book destruction campaign was systematically eliminated shortly after. The book destruction campaign sparked a great international scandal, with the French being the first to criticise the Hungarian government for considering Dumas and Daudet as dispensable. *The Times* also published a full-page editorial titled 'The Blimps of Buda' on 7 December 1950, condemning the purge campaign. Amid the international outcry, József Révai, the powerful cultural potentate of the Hungarian Stalinist regime,

The Routledge Handbook of Translation and Censorship

openly distanced himself from the biblioclastic activities, even going so far as to identify and reprimand those he labeled as 'culture destroyers', insinuating as if they had acted independently of his directives (Sipos 2007: 702). The lists were, in part, withdrawn, and the individuals purportedly responsible were impeached. It is believed that the quick destruction of archival evidence was an attempt to conceal the identity of the real culprits as well as the consequences of the purge. The full extent of the cultural loss and its long-term effects on Hungarian literature and intellectual life are, therefore, almost impossible to assess.

Upon examining the book lists, it becomes quite evident though that the main reason for discarding the selected books was that they seemingly failed to serve an essential function as reliable political tools. They were either considered to be non-educational mass literature, for example, works by Edgar Rice Burroughs, Agatha Christie or P.G. Wodehouse, or because their content or the authors themselves seemed to conflict with the official political standpoint. For instance, George Orwell and André Gide were seen as anti-Communists, while Rudyard Kipling was regarded as an imperialist ideologue. Novels by Aldous Huxley, D.H. Lawrence and André Gide were condemned for their pessimistic individualism. Intriguingly, however, the majority of these books were withdrawn not because of their politically or ideologically objectionable message, but on the grounds of containing forewords or afterwords written by politically undesirable figures like Sándor Márai, or because they were published by an allegedly reactionary publishing house such as Athenaeum, as was the case with the Hungarian translation of *Winnie-the-Pooh* by A.A. Milne (Gombár 2011: 108–10).

14.2.2 The Mechanisms and Institutions of Censorship

Piotr Kuhiwczak, in his study on social collaboration and censorship, challenges the common misconception that the blame for censorship should fall solely on a powerful minority of politicians and censors. Dictatorial regimes could, in fact, not endure for long periods of time without the tacit acceptance and collaboration of the masses (Kuhiwczak 2009: 47). Intellectuals are subjected to the same external constraints as the rest of the population, and, as a result, often willingly or unwillingly internalise the norms and ideology of the dominant political culture, and write and act accordingly. Therefore, in autocratic regimes, the distinction between external and internal coercion is normally 'blurred in the extreme' (Tymoczko 2009: 27). According to Maria Tymoczko, 'institutionalised censorship will induce self-censorship in translators, publishers, booksellers and even readers, all of whom will be disposed to avoid the penalties associated with the regulations and mechanisms of censorship' (Tymoczko 2009: 39).

To complicate matters further, censorship rules were never clearly defined by the ruling regimes, nor were they publicly discussed in the Soviet Union or in its satellite states. Indeed, censorship was never formally instituted in Hungary either. In theory, the Hungarian National Constitution of 1949 guaranteed many of the fundamental rights, such as the freedom of speech, press and assembly, that are now guaranteed in the constitution of 2011 (cf. Hungarian Const. of 1949 and of 2011). However, scholars agree that the existence of constitutional provisions for fundamental rights does not necessarily ensure that those rights will be protected (see Meydani 2014 and Fournier 2019). In Communist Hungary, the discrepancy between constitutional rhetoric and de facto practice was too glaring to be ignored.

Furthermore, the authorities meticulously avoided written communication concerning censorship issues, opting instead for telephone or in-person conversations with authors and publishers behind closed doors in order not to leave evidence that censorship actually existed in the People's Republic of Hungary. In contrast to other dictatorial regimes, such as Salazar's Portugal or

Franco's Spain, institutions functioning as organs of censorship never included the word 'censorship' in their names.

The *Országos Könyvhivatal* [National Book Publishing Office], for instance, was established in 1948 in order to monitor and coordinate the activities of the then still private publishing houses and printing offices. In fact, no books were allowed to be published without the Book Publishing Office's consent. After the nationalisation of the remaining publishing sector in 1949, the Office ceased to exist, and was subsumed into the Ministry of Education. The book industry was subsequently supervised by the *Irodalmi Főosztály* [Literary Department]. Then again in 1953, it changed its name to *Kiadói Tanács* [Publishing Committee] and in 1954, to *Kiadói Főigazgatóság* [Publishers' Directorate] (Varga 1985: 123, 147, 266–8 and 307–13). This exemplifies the opaque structure of State-Socialist Hungary: the state and its highest-ranking leaders concealed themselves in a complicated and constantly changing system whose inner hierarchy and interconnections were almost impossible for ordinary citizens to understand (Oikari 2000: 138).

Publishers, editors-in-chief and managing editors were all politically trusted functionaries who were also expected to be well informed on the current party line as well as the current political sentiments of the leadership. They received their indirect orders by telephone, and as a rule no written instructions followed. They were expected to fully understand the party language and follow orders to the letter. All publishers were required to send their annual publishing plans, that is, the list of books they intended to publish the following year, to the incumbent book department for inspection. The list was later double-checked by another book committee. Finally, it was Rákosi himself and Révai, who had the final word on what should be translated and published, or not (Mihályi 1993: 52–3).

After the 1956 Revolution, not only did Kádár replace Rákosi, but György Aczél, another omnipotent leader in the cultural sphere, replaced Révai. Most importantly, the new publishing and translation industry was based exclusively on self-censorship. The external censorship institutions of the Rákosi regime lost their absolute authority over publishing houses, which paved the way for a more indirect censorship mechanism, namely self-censorship practised by the publishers themselves. Although the Publishers' Directorate did not cease to exist in the Kádár era and annual publishing plans still had to be submitted to the Directorate for approval, the Directorate rarely used its power to prohibit a publication (Bart 2000: 12–4).

Unlike other Socialist satellite countries, such as the German Democratic Republic, Poland or Romania, Hungary's Kádár-regime had no official censorship board. However, this does not mean that pre-publication censorship did not exist and thrive in the post-Stalinist years. If a publisher intended to translate and publish a foreign book, at least three positive reader reports were necessary. Besides giving a brief summary and critical assessment of the work in question, the reviewer had to report even the slightest political or moral threat the proposed translation might pose to the Hungarian Socialist reader. The artistic merit of the work along with its potential ideological pitfalls were further discussed in a closed editorial meeting, and if the general manager also consented to its publication, the literary work was included in the annual list (Géher 1989: 9; Sohár 2022: 246).[2] In reality, no direct external intervention was needed, given that the censoring and filtering process had already been carried out by the aforementioned publishing experts.

Nevertheless, it would be erroneous to define these professionals as mere censors, since their function and position were far more complex than that. Many of them were silenced intellectuals, such as political theoretician István Bibó, journalist Miklós Vásárhelyi and literary translator and later president of the Hungarian Republic Árpád Göncz, who had all been imprisoned in the aftermath of the 1956 Revolution. After their release, they found themselves without a means of subsistence, and became publishers' readers or translators out of necessity. They were highly

The Routledge Handbook of Translation and Censorship

knowledgeable and reliable readers, whose nonconformist and dissident attitudes were widely known. Their impartial and uncompromising reports were greatly appreciated by publishers, because they gave brief, but very clear indications of any potentially problematic aspects of the book, which could cause troubles for the publishing house.

Based on the reader's reports, the editors in charge were able to decide whether it was worth fighting for the publication of the work under consideration or not. They would also take into account factors, such as potential political and moral dangers, translatability, copyright and foreign currency issues, and most importantly, the estimated aesthetic value of the literary piece. The editors or general manager might also request minor textual changes in the translation. For example, a passage describing a cannibalistic act committed by starving Soviet prisoners-of-war in Curzio Malaparte's *Kaputt* (Lator 2002: 73–4) or twenty lines referring to the crimes carried out by the Soviet Liberation Army in Danzig in Günther Grass' *Die Blechtrommel* [The Tin Drum] were eliminated from the Hungarian translations (Takács 2002: 78). A scene of nudity was bowdlerised in Alberto Moravia's *Gli indifferenti* [The Time of Indifference] in order to diminish the sexual explicitness of the text (Lator 2002: 74).

Publishing professionals were undeniably part of the censoring process. Their collective and even individual, responsibility is a very complex issue and needs to be addressed with the utmost care. What Tymoczko defines as translators' 'strategic self-censorship' might easily be applied to other publishing professionals as well:

> In most circumstances translators accept and buy into some cultural norms and restrictions, but oppose and challenge others. Moreover, in many situations where translators must prioritise and pick a strategy to deal with oppressive or coercive cultural constraints, they undertake some self-censorship for a greater good: in order to strategically pursue resistance for particular ideological ends or their larger purposes for translation, translators acquiesce in certain other aspects of social decorum.
>
> (Tymoczko 2009: 36–7)

Thus, censorship in Kádár-regime Hungary should not be defined simply as a restrictive and oppressive process, but more of a continuous process of negotiation between professionals and the authorities. In other words, editors and first readers repeatedly tried to obtain more publishing freedom and kept testing the boundaries imposed by the regime (Takács 2002: 77).

Although editors and readers were supposed to be politically trustworthy individuals and represent the state ideology of the regime unfailingly in their work, in practice this was seldom the case (Czigányik 2011: 224). They indeed often attempted to mislead their superiors in their reviews and recommendations, particularly in the case of works they regarded as culturally or artistically relevant. If not for their insistence, hundreds of politically risky works would never have been translated and published (Schandl 2011: 268). In that sense, publishers should be regarded as active members of the intellectual resistance rather than as passive collaborators of the state.

All in all, the publishing industry's self-censorship apparatus proved to be a very effective and reliable instrument in the pre-selection process. As a result, translations were rarely subjected to punitive or post-publication censorship. One of the few exceptions was the scandal over Milan Kundera's *Žert* [The Joke]. The novel was banned due to the author's involvement in the Prague Spring in 1968, despite the fact that the Hungarian translation had recently been published. Three thousand three hundred bound volumes were immediately withdrawn from the market, most of which were destroyed and pulped (Murányi 2004: 268).

Other bizarre examples of post-censorship interventions were the cases of *Rue du Havre* [Le Havre Street] by Paul Guimard and *The White Deer* by James Thurber. The authorities had thousands of copies of their respective translations blue-pencilled. The translation of the former novel contained the phrase 'összeesküvő oroszok' [conspiring Russians], albeit in an absolutely innocent context. It was widely feared, however, that the expression might offend the Soviet occupying forces in Hungary, so the text was corrected to 'összeesküvő orvosok' [conspiring doctors] (Lator 2016: 72–74). The latter novel was translated by Pál Békés, who changed the original English names 'Tarcomed' and 'Nacilbuper' (in reverse writing: Democrat and Republican) in the short story to 'Trápa' and 'Tnorfpén' (a Párt = the Party; Népfront = Popular Front), the names of the governing bodies in Hungary the translator must have heard on a daily basis (Békés 2002: 72).

14.2.3 *Some Literatures are more Equal than Others*

The Rákosi administration's takeover in 1948 almost completely isolated Hungary from the Western cultural sphere. The number of literary translations from Western European languages, such as French, English and German, diminished dramatically, while translations of literature from the USSR and its client states made up two-thirds of all literary translation production between 1945 and 1955 (cf. Bak 1956 and Varga 1975). Also, Soviet literary works had to be given far longer print-runs, regardless of their artistic quality. Although the proportion of Russian translations considerably decreased under the Kádár regime, the order of priorities basically remained the same. These prevailing political preferences are also reflected in the so-called *ív-ár* [sheet price] system, which was introduced in 1968.

According to the system, the book price was established based on the number of pages, and the value of a page was tied to its content. The cheapest were the literature pages from preferential countries, such as Hungary, the USSR and other contemporary People's Democracies (0.70 HUF/ sheet). Next on the list came classic works from the aforementioned countries (0.80 HUF/sheet); then contemporary literature from other foreign countries, such as France, the UK and the USA (1.0 HUF/sheet); followed by other foreign classics and light literature, such as entertainment literature, biographies, romance and history novels (1.2 HUF/sheet); finally, detective and adventure stories (1.8 HUF/sheet). In short, an American whodunit, for example, would cost almost double the price of a contemporary Soviet Social Realist novel (Bart 2000: 29–30). However, since book retail prices were kept extremely low throughout the era, it is very unlikely that the somewhat higher retail price of Western books would have affected the customers' reading habits.

The primary aim of the sheet price system was to discourage the expansion of commercial bestseller literature in the Socialist book market, which was openly despised by both Hungarian regimes. Their overtly hostile attitude was founded on the belief that this type of literature was deemed to have no educational value and was therefore harmful to the Socialist reader. Publishing houses were also obliged to pay a so-called *kulturális járulék* [cultural contribution], popularly known as the *giccsadó* [kitsch tax revenue], if they intended to publish highly profitable popular literature (Sohár 2022: 248). The financial gains were then transferred to a shared fund created to subsidise commercially less successful publications, such as scholarly works, high literature or unsellable contemporary Socialist realist novels.

Even a cursory comparison of popular literature published in State-Socialist Hungary and in other Western European countries reveals the notable absence of such emblematic authors as Margaret Mitchell, John Buchan, Ian Fleming or H.P. Lovecraft. Although the absence of cold-war spy novels by Fleming and John le Carré might not come as a surprise, the near absence of romance novels, such as *Gone with the Wind*, is somewhat perplexing. The novel was not authorised to be published in Hungary until 1986 on aesthetic and political grounds, despite the fact that the novel had already been published in Hungary in 1946, shortly before Rákosi came to power, and in Poland in 1957 (Tóth 1992: 401).

Sohár argues that popular genres, such as science fiction, detective fiction or family sagas challenged the totalitarian way of thinking by showing alternatives, favouring individualism and private life (Sohár 2022: 243–4). 'For instance, romance, focusing on private life, love and family affairs in particular, counters the communist principle that the individual is "expendable material", is of no importance, and that only society, the community, matters' (Sohár 1999: 34–5).

Intriguingly, science fiction enjoyed relatively high status among popular literature genres. This might be attributed to the fact that in the USSR, a great number of Soviet authors dedicated themselves to science fiction writing, inspired by the country's pioneering space programme from the 1950s on. The genre was also very popular in other satellite countries, such as Czechoslovakia and Poland (Gombár 2013: 265). Nevertheless, the same censorship rules applied to science fiction literature as to other genres. Any possible offensive references to or unfavourable fictional portrayal of the USSR or its client states were not tolerated. Nor were intensely violent scenes, abusive language or graphic descriptions of sexual organs and acts (cf. Sohár 2022). Horror and erotic fiction was equally prohibited in Communist Hungary.

Popular literature was not the only victim of the unshakeable official conviction that art should always have a social function. *L'art pour l'art* literature had no place in the Socialist literary canon. Nor was any room left for experimental or self-reflective texts (Scholz 2009: 208). Even if during the Stalinist era it would have been unthinkable to publish works by such soi-disant navel-gazing novelists as James Joyce, Samuel Beckett, Virginia Woolf or Aldous Huxley, access to these authors continued to be rather limited under the Kádár administration as well. László Scholz also calls attention to the intentional absence of Latin American avant-garde authors, for example, José Lezama Lima, Felisberto Hernández, Macedonio Fernández and Pablo Palacio, in the Hungarian canon (Scholz 2009: 212–3).

It is noteworthy that the Hungarian authorities relied on the strategy of simply putting problematic works aside. For instance, John Updike's *Rabbit, Run*, James Baldwin's *Giovanni's Room*, Hubert Selby Jr's *Last Exit to Brooklyn* and Christopher Isherwood's *Goodbye to Berlin* had to wait decades before being published in Hungary. The advantage of this delaying technique was twofold: publishers could wait for a politically more favourable atmosphere to publish the book, and they could wait and see whether the work in question stood the test of time and received critical acclaim or not (Gombár 2017: 151). By not promoting writers whose critical reception was still in doubt, publishers avoided potentially wasting foreign currency on copyright fees. In fact, the shortage of foreign currency constituted a constant problem in Socialist Hungary (Révész 1997: 346–50).

Insistence on classic literary works and canonical literature was also very characteristic of Socialist publishing policies. Thomson-Wohlgemuth (2003: 245) asserts that one of the reasons for classic literature's dominance in the Socialist book market lies in the fact that the copyright of these time-honoured literary works had already expired, and so no royalties had to be paid in foreign currency by the publishers. Setting aside the economic factor, the principal motive of Communist regimes was the idealistic conviction of the didactic potential of classic literature. According to Scholz, 'The classics offer authority, continuity, legitimacy, and education for the people, and, above all, they efficiently restrict the notion of progress' (Scholz 2009: 208). Importantly, he also notes that 'the publication of the classics flourished at the expense of more contemporary and innovative texts' in State-Socialist Hungary (Scholz 2009: 208).

Apparently, tried-and-true classics were regarded as a far more reliable political tool for mass education and indoctrination than politically unsafe lesser-known modern literature. The deader the better policy was, therefore, also a distinctive feature of the Hungarian publishing industry, since it prevented the publishing houses from bringing to market translations which might raise the objections of cultural leaders, given that the ideological approval rating of dead authors had already been well established, while the ideological positions of contemporary writers might still be doubtful or in flux (Gombár 2013: 270–1).

14.3 Historical Perspective

Censorship has existed in Hungary in almost all periods of its history. The first official censorship document dates back to 1524, when King Louis II decreed in a royal letter that Martin Luther's writings should be sought out and burnt (Keul 2009: 47). Two years later, in 1526, the young king died childless in the battle of Mohács. Soon after, the country was split into three parts by the Austrian Habsburgs, the Ottomans and Hungarian princes in Transylvania, in addition to being divided religiously between Catholics and Protestants. At that stage in the country's history, censorship was predominantly religious and its primary function was to prevent the spread of heretical beliefs in the Catholic-controlled regions. With the promulgation of the *Index Librorum Prohibitorum* in 1559, censorship practices became far more systematic and oppressive (Gömöri 2015: 1120). Censorship, in fact, was and remained solely in the hands of the clergy until 1730 (Pruzsinszky 2014: 37).

Eventually, it was Maria Theresa's and Joseph II's enlightened absolutism that brought political reforms and a relaxation of censorship to Hungary. However, the outbreak of the French Revolution of 1789 had far-reaching consequences for contemporary Europe as well as for the internal politics of the Habsburg Empire. The subsequent era was marked by far greater conservatism and reactionary tendencies. As for censorship, a new round of restrictive legislation was decreed. Any foreign or national literary works, periodical and non-periodical publications, theatrical plays or other activities that might cause public unrest or reduce obedience to the emperor were considered suspicious and could be prohibited. Translations of foreign books were also drastically curtailed. Book imports from abroad along with private correspondence were systematically monitored by customs officers at the borders of the Empire.

In place of the written Protestant doctrines of schismatic theologians, such as Luther and Calvin, now works by Enlightenment thinkers became the principal target of censorship. French proponents of the Enlightenment, including Voltaire, Rousseau and Helvetius were regarded as ideological instigators of the French Revolution and hence strictly prohibited (cf. Sashegyi 1938). Moreover, citizens of the Empire who overtly sympathised with revolutionary France could easily face severe punishment, including the death penalty or lengthy incarceration. For example, the renowned Hungarian poet and linguist Ferenc Verseghy was imprisoned for nine years for translating 'La Marseillaise' and for participating in the Hungarian Jacobin Movement. Another celebrated Hungarian translator and man of letters Ferenc Kazinczy was likewise sentenced to a lengthy term of imprisonment for his support of the movement, while the Hungarian poet János Batsányi was interned in Linz for the remaining 30 years of his life for translating Napoleon's proclamation to the Hungarians (Czigány 1986: 93–105).

Censorship was first abolished in Hungary by the short-lived Revolution of 1848. After the defeat of the Revolution in 1849 with the help of the Russian army, savage reprisals followed, and the country was again subject to absolutist control and suppression. It was only after the

The Routledge Handbook of Translation and Censorship

Austro-Hungarian Compromise of 1867 that the Hungarian press laws of 1848 were restored, and pre-publication censorship was eventually withdrawn. A relatively small number of political and censorship controversies notwithstanding, the period of the Austro-Hungarian Dual Monarchy is commonly remembered as a golden age of peace and justice (see Cieger 1999; Freifeld 2002; Kemény 1982; and Pruzsinszky 2014: 144–50).

In 1914, a more restrictive piece of press legislation was issued, which, it was generally feared, would decisively restrict the freedom and autonomy of the press. Besides the author, his or her editor and publisher could be punished for press offences. In the same year, Austria-Hungary declared war on Serbia, which ultimately led to the outbreak of the First World War. Subsequently, no news coverage, including translated materials, that could allegedly jeopardise the course of the war or hinder victory was allowed publication (see Scheer 2018).

After the collapse of the Austro-Hungarian Monarchy, followed by the downfall of the First Hungarian Republic and the subsequent Hungarian Soviet Republic, a counter-revolutionary government and militias took control of the country. Admiral Miklós Horthy, the leading figure of the counter-revolutionary armed forces, was elected as regent and provisional head of state. Under his regency, Hungary shifted markedly to the far right and adopted anti-Semitic, reactionary nationalistic and irredentist policies that eventually would lead to Hungary's participation in the Second World War on the side of Nazi Germany.

Regarding censorship legislation, the first list of prohibited books was published as early as September 1919. Apart from revolutionary publications by prominent Hungarian political and literary figures, the list contained translations of works by Karl Marx, Friedrich Engels, Lenin, Leon Trotsky, the Belgian Socialist politician Emile Vandervelde and the future British Labour MP Morgan Philips Price (Kelemen 2018: 103–7).

Dissident writers were often under surveillance by the state police and police informers in Hungary, and the investigative materials were annually published in so-called *Vörös Könyvek* [Red Books] for internal use. Aside from prominent Hungarian authors, the *Könyvek* contained information on problematic foreign authors, including Bertrand Russell, Henri Barbusse, Lion Feuchtwanger, Stefan Zweig and Theodore Dreiser (Markovits 1985: 30–1, 155). While foreign nationals could not be punished for political incitement under Hungarian law, their Hungarian translators and publishers could be.

The most notorious lawsuits of the period were brought against, among others, the following writers for having translated subversive literary texts: Tibor Déry, who was sentenced to two months incarceration for translating André Gide's *Retour de l'URSS* in 1938 (Roszkowski and Kofman 2016: 195); Lajos Kassák, who was sentenced to two months in prison for publishing the translation of an ancient Chinese pacifist poem in 1939 (Markovits 1967: 376); and Andor Tiszay, who was sentenced to one month incarceration for translating Franz Carl Weiskopf's revolutionary poem 'Die Reise nach Kanton' in 1931 (Markovits 1985: 101). It should be noted that as a consequence of the 1914 press law, the translator or author was always taken to court with his or her publisher and charged with disrupting public order.

For instance, Attila József, along with the printer Lajos Müller, was prosecuted for obscenity for the translation of the poem 'Ballade de Villon et de la Grosse Margot' [Ballad about the Plump Margot] by François Villon (Lehotay 2018: 186). Although the obscenity charges against the poet and the printer were eventually dropped, the Hungarian translators (and publishers) of Joris-Karl Huysmans's *Là-Bas* [The Damned], Octave Mirbeau's *Le Jardin des supplices* [The Torture Garden], Arthur Schnitzler's *La Ronde* [Circle of Love] were not so fortunate. All of these works were banned in Hungary, as were *Jahrgang 1902* [Class of 1902] by Ernst Glaeser, *Švejk* by Jaroslav Hašek and *Chocolate* by Alexander Tarasov-Rodionov (Markovits 1985: 168).

After Horthy's failed attempt to negotiate a separate peace with the Allies, Hungary was occupied by Nazi Germany in 1944. Along with the ghettoisation and deportation of the Hungarian Jewish population, anti-Jewish book campaigns were launched. Two consecutive official lists were published in great haste, according to which 243 Hungarian and 45 foreign Jewish authors' works were to be pulled immediately from public libraries, publishing houses and bookstores to be destroyed in pulp mills. The lists of foreign authors included Sigmund Freud, Tristan Bernard, Henri Bernstein, Alfred Döblin, Jean-Richard Bloch, Max Brod, Lion Feuchtwanger, Arthur Schnitzler, Stefan Zweig, Verona de Guido, Heinrich Heine and Marcel Proust.

14.4 New Debates

More than thirty years have passed since the change of the regime in 1989. Yet literary censorship under Communism, especially the censorship of translated literature, continues to be relatively unexplored in Hungary. One of the most obvious explanations for this apparent lack of interest is the absence of written evidence of the existence of censorship in Communist-ruled Hungary. The lack of tangible proof seems to have discouraged researchers from engaging in serious study of the subject. Another possible explanation for scholarly reluctance to investigate censorship as well as, for instance, former political agents from the period could be that the Communist past may continue to haunt certain individuals and their surviving family members.

Despite this unpromising context, in 2009, several senior and early-career researchers, including Gabriella Hartvig, Géza Maráczi, Judit Acsády, Márta Goldmann, Veronika Schandl and Zsófia Gombár decided to launch the project 'English-Language Literature and Censorship in Hungary (19451989)', which was housed at the University of West Hungary. The research primarily relied on reader's reports commissioned by the *Európa Könyvkiadó*, a Hungarian publishing house specialising in world literature. Some of the research findings were published in English (see, for example, Schandl 2011, Cziganyik 2011, Hartvig 2013, Maráczi 2013 and Gombár 2017). In 2018, just a month before the political scandal erupted surrounding the Museum and the forced replacement of its managing director, the reader's reports were relocated from the Petőfi Irodalmi Múzeum to a remote provincial storehouse of the *Európa Könyvkiadó*. As a result, the research project came to a standstill.

Although a great number of the reports had been digitalised and analysed within the framework of the project, it was quite clear from the beginning of the research, as Looby also notes with reference to the Polish Communist translation industry, that even with archival evidence, it is often impossible to fully understand the censorial rationale for the decision to censor a given book (Looby 2015: 14). Even if it was not possible to draw overall conclusions in the end, the archival material of the *Európa Könyvkiadó* and other publishing houses could help to reconstruct several individual cases as well as to detect overall patterns in the censorship of thematic literature, e.g., homosexual-themed fiction (Gombár 2017: 2018).

As a case in point, the latter research uncovered that, from the early 1980s, homosexual-themed literary translations were officially promoted to encourage AIDS awareness among readers (Gombár 2017: 151–2). Moreover, the first overtly LGBTQ+ young adult novel *I'll Get There. It Better Be Worth the Trip* by John Donovan, was published by a juvenile and children's publishing house *Móra* in Hungary as early as 1987. This clearly suggests that the publicly dictatorial Kádár regime appears to have been far more progressive and tolerant regarding LGBTQ+ education than, for instance, the current prime minister Viktor Orbán's self-proclaimed illiberal democratic government, which more than thirty years later, in 2021, passed a law banning the portrayal of homosexuality in books addressed to minors.

14.5 Conclusion

As has been shown, Hungary has no deeply rooted democratic traditions. Censorship and information control have been a dominant element of everyday Hungarian life for centuries. The country also has a long history of being overrun and conquered by outside powers, from the Ottoman Empire and the Habsburgs, to Nazi Germany and the USSR. Therefore, the institution of censorship has, as a general rule, been has been imposed by foreign invaders throughout Hungary's history. After the Communist seizure of power in 1948, the Hungarian political and administrative structure, including the system of censorship and control of the print media, was dramatically reshaped in keeping with the Soviet totalitarian model.

The Kádár administration's political relaxation brought certain reforms and gave a sort of country-specific feature to the system by placing more responsibility on the publishers, who became fully accountable for their publication choices and decisions. Literary publications were first and foremost filtered through self-censorship exercised by publishing professionals whose work was, nevertheless, constantly monitored by a definite set of controlling institutions. Besides the publishers' pre-selection system, other direct and indirect methods were used to control the translation production of the era, such as (1) national quotas of foreign literature; (2) the sheet-price system; (3) insistence on the classics; and (4) delaying technique.

Even though the number of scholarly publications on translation and censorship, along with knowledge on constraints on the Communist publishing industry have grown over the years, far more comprehensive studies are needed to better comprehend the impact and repercussions of censorship on translation production then as well as now. Conservative elitism, the unabashed obsession with canonical literature or the belief that state-funded art should always reflect the incumbent government's political agenda are only a few issues whose roots date back to the Communist era.

Evidently, it is impossible to undo the long history of dictatorial rule in Hungary, and certain attitudes, such as those involving culture and literature are unlikely to change within just one or two generations. Nonetheless, one can still try to deconstruct the different parts of its legacy, since if the country's democratic institutions fail, the country's long-term historical patterns of authoritarianism will definitely reappear. Thus, it is essential to face the past, identify its legacy and make serious attempts to eradicate the shameful after-effects.

Further Reading

Bart, István. 2000. *Világirodalom és könyvkiadás a Kádár-korszakban* [World Literature and Book Publishing under the Kádár Regime]. Budapest: Scholastica.
It is a relatively short monograph in Hungarian on the post-war and post-revolutionary translation industry in Socialist Hungary.

Miklós, Vajda (ed.). 2002. *Hungarian Quarterly*, 43(165): 64–75 http://real-j.mtak.hu/12049/1/Hungaria nQuarterly_165_2002.pdf (accessed 17 May 2024).
The volume contains three articles in English by László Lator, Pál Békés and Ferenc Takács, respectively, which contain relevant information on translation practices from the Communist era.

Notes

1 This work has been funded by national funds through the Portuguese funding agency FCT – Fundação para a Ciência e a Tecnologia, I. P. within the framework of the projects UIDB/00114/2020 and UIDP/00114/2020.
2 I would like to thank Anikó Sohár for allowing me to consult her study prior to publication.

References

Bak, János. 1956. *Az új magyar könyvkiadás tíz éve, 1945–1955* [The First Decade of Hungarian Book Publishing, 1945–1955]. Budapest: Kiadói Főigazgatóság.

Bart, István. 2000. *Világirodalom és könyvkiadás a Kádár-korszakban*. Budapest: Scholastica.

Békés, Pál. 2002. 'Trápa and Tnorfpén', *Hungarian Quarterly*, 43(165): 72–3. http://real-j.mtak.hu/12049/1/HungarianQuarterly_165_2002.pdf (accessed 17 May 2024).

Cieger, András. 1999. 'Kormány a mérlegen a múlt században. A kormány helye és szerepe a dualizmus politikai rendszerében, 1867–1875' [Government on the Scales in the Last Century. The Place and Role of the Government in the Political System of Dualism, 1867–1875], *Századvég*, 14(4): 79–107.

Czigány, Lóránt. 1986. *The Oxford History of Hungarian Literature*. Oxford: Clarendon Press.

Czigányik, Zsolt. 2011. 'Reader's Responsibility: Literature and Censorship in the Kádár Era in Hungary', in B. Gárdos, Á. Péter, N. Pikli and M. Vince (eds.), *Confrontations and Interactions. Essays on Cultural Memory*. Budapest: L'Harmattan, 223–34.

Fournier, Théo. 2019. 'From Rhetoric to Action, A Constitutional Analysis of Populism', *German Law Journal*, 20(3): 362–81.

Freifeld, Alice. 2002. 'Kossuth: The Hermit and the Crowd', *Hungarian Studies*, 16(2): 205–14.

Géher, István. 1989. *Mesterségünk címere* [The Coat of Arms of Our Craft]. Budapest: Szépirodalmi.

Gombár, Zsófia. 2011. 'Dictatorial Regimes and the Reception of English-Language Authors in Hungary and Portugal', in A. Lázaro Laufente and C. O'Leary (eds.), *Censorship Across Borders: The Censorship of English Literature in Twentieth-Century Europe*. Newcastle upon Tyne: Cambridge Scholars Publishing, 105–28.

Gombár, Zsófia. 2013. 'Translation Anthologies and British Literature in Portugal and Hungary Between 1949 and 1974', in T. Seruya, L. D'Hulst, A. Assis Rosa and M. L. Moniz (eds.), *Translation in Anthologies and Collections (19th and 20th Centuries)*. Amsterdam and Philadelphia: John Benjamins, 259–74.

Gombár, Zsófia. 2017. 'Literary Censorship and Homosexuality in Kádár-Regime Hungary and Estado Novo Portugal', in B. Baer and K. Kaindl (eds.), *Queering Translation – Translating the Queer. Theory, Practice, Activism*. London and New York: Routledge, 144–56.

Gombár, Zsófia. 2018. 'A Comparison: Translated Homosexual-Themed Novels in *Estado Novo* Portugal and State-Socialist Hungary', *Via Atlântica*, 1(33): 187–205. www.revistas.usp.br/viaatlantica/issue/view/10270 (accessed 17 May 2024).

Gömöri, George. 2015. 'Hungary', in D. Jones (ed.), *Censorship. A World Encyclopedia*. London: Routledge, 1119–6.

Hartvig, Gabriella. 2013. 'Hungarian Swift Scholarship in the Period of Censorship', in H. J. Real, K. Juhas and S. Simon (eds.), *Reading Swift. Papers from The Sixth Münster Symposium on Jonathan Swift*. München: Wilhelm Fink, 633–45.

Hungarian Constitution of 1949, art. 55. § 1. https://net.jogtar.hu/getpdf?docid=94900020.TV&targetdate=ffffff4&printTitle=1949.+%C3%A9vi+XX.+t%C3%B6rv%C3%A9ny&referer=http%3A//net.jogtar.hu/jr/gen/hjegy_doc.cgi%3Fdocid%3D00000001.TXT (accessed 17 May 2024).

Hungarian Constitution of 2011, art. 8 art §, 1. 9 § 1 and 1. 9 § 2. https://net.jogtar.hu/jogszabaly?docid=a1100425.atv (accessed 17 May 2024).

Kelemen, Roland. 2018. *Sajtójogi források a kivételes hatalom árnyékában. A magyar sajtójog a hatalmi/legitimációs kivételes állapotok időszakában (1918–1922)* [Press Law Sources in the Shadow of the Exceptional Power: Hungarian Press Law in the Period of Exceptional State of Power/Legitimacy (1918–1922)]. Budapest: Magyar Katonai Jogi és Hadijogi Társaság.

Kemény, G. Gábor. 1982. 'A demokratikus szabadságjogok védelmezői. Böszörményi László és Irányi Dániel pályaképéhez' [The Defenders of Democratic Freedoms. László Böszörményi and Dániel Irányi.], *Tiszatáj*, 36(6): 39–46.

Keul, István. 2009. *Early Modern Religious Communities in East-Central Europe. Ethnic Diversity, Denominational Plurality, and Corporative Politics in the Principality of Transylvania (1526–1691)*. Leiden: Brill.

Kövér, György. 1998. *Losonczy Géza 1917–1957*. Budapest: 1956-os Intézet.

Kuhiwczak, Piotr. 2009. 'Censorship as a Collaborative Project: A Systematic Approach', in E. Ní Chuilleanáin, C. O Cuilleanáin and D. Parris (eds.), *Translation and Censorship: Patterns of Communication and Interference*. Dublin: Four Courts, 46–56.

The Routledge Handbook of Translation and Censorship

Lator, László. 2002. 'My Life as Editor', *The Hungarian Quarterly*, 43(165): 64–74. http://real-j.mtak.hu/12049/1/HungarianQuarterly_165_2002.pdf (accessed 17 May 2024).

Lator, László. 2016. *A megmaradt világ. Emlékezések* [Remaining World. Memories]. Budapest: Petőfi Irodalmi Múzeum Digitális Irodalmi Akadémia https://reader.dia.hu/document/Lator_Laszlo-A_megmaradt_vilag-16089 (accessed 17 May 2024).

Lehotay, Veronika. 2018. '... ha ügyész fizet a verseimért. Költőperek a Horthy-korszakban [If a Prosecutor Pays for My Poems: Poet Trials in the Horthy Era]', in S. Pál (ed.), *Híres történelmi perek* [Famous Historical Trials]. Miskolc: Miskolci Egyetemi Kiadó, 181–200.

Looby, Robert. 2015. *Censorship, Translation and English Language Fiction in People's Poland*. Leiden: Brill Rodopi.

Maráczi, Géza. 2013. 'Dickens in Hungary', in M. Hollington (ed.), *The Reception of Dickens in Europe*. London: Bloomsbury, 560–71.

Markovits, Györgyi. 1967. 'Kassák Lajos az osztálybíróság előtt [Lajos Kassák Before the Court]', *Magyar Könyvszemle*, 4(83): 371–6. www.epa.hu/00000/00021/00269/pdf/MKSZ_EPA00021_1967_83_04_371-376.pdf (accessed 17 May 2024).

Markovits, Györgyi. 1985. *A magyar írók harca a cenzúra ellen (1919–1944)* [Hungarian Writers' Struggle Against Censorship (1919–1944)]. Budapest: Akadémiai Kiadó.

Meydani, Assaf. 2014. *The Anatomy of Human Rights in Israel. Constitutional Rhetoric and State Practice*. New York: Cambridge University Press.

Mihályi, Gábor. 1993. 'The Dual Nature of Censorship in Hungary, 1945–1991', in I. Peleg (ed.), *Patterns of Censorship Around the World*. Boulder: Westview Press, 49–63.

Murányi Gábor. 2004. *A múlt szövedéke. Históriák a megbicsaklott 20. Századból* [The Fabric of the Past: Stories from the Faltering 20th Century]. Budapest: Noran.

Népkönyvtári Központ. 1950. *Útmutató üzemi és falusi könyvtárak rendezéséhez* [Guide to Organizing Work-Trade and Village Libraries]. 2 vols. Budapest: Népkönyvtári Központ.

Neubauer, John. 2007. 'General Introduction', in M. Cornis-Pope and J. Neubauer (eds.), *History of the Literary Cultures of East-Central Europe. Junctures and Disjunctures in the 19th and 20th Centuries*. Amsterdam and Philadelphia: John Benjamins, 1–61.

Oikari, Raija. 2000. 'Discursive Use of Power in Hungarian Cultural Policy During the Kádár Era', *Hungarologische Beiträge*, 14(2): 133–62. http://epa.oszk.hu/01300/01368/00001/pdf/08oikari.pdf (accessed 17 May 2024).

Pruzsinszky, Sándor. 2014. *Halhatatlan cenzúra* [Immortal Censorship]. Budapest: Médiatudományi Intézet.

Révész, Sándor. 1997. *Aczél és korunk* [Aczél and His Era]. Budapest: Noran.

Roszkowski, Wojciech and Kofman, Jan. 2016. *Biographical Dictionary of Central and Eastern Europe in the Twentieth Century*. London and New York: Routledge.

Sashegyi, Oszkár. 1938. *Német felvilágosodás és magyar cenzúra* [The German Enlightenment and the Hungarian Censorship]. Budapest: Minerva.

Schandl, Veronika. 2011. 'Where Public is Private: Reading Practices in Socialist Hungary', *Primerjalna književnost*, 34(2): 111–9. www.google.com/url?sa=t&source=web&rct=j&opi=89978449&url=https://ojs-gr.zrc-sazu.si/primerjalna_knjizevnost/article/download/5466/5122&ved=2ahUKEwiL5Lm2x5WGAxUdExAIHXxjCbkQFnoECBQQAQ&usg=AOvVaw0Njymwlw2iywkaS4azsSC9 (accessed 17 May 2024).

Scheer, Tamara. 2018. 'War Surveillance Office (Austria-Hungary)' (Version 1.1), in U. Daniel, P. Gatrell, O. Janz, H. Jones, J. Keene, A. Kramer and B. Nasson (eds.),1914–1918. *International Encyclopedia of the First World War*. Berlin: Freie Universität Berlin. DOI: 10.15463/ie1418.10203/1.1. https://encyclopedia.1914-1918-online.net/article/war_surveillance_office_austria-hungary (accessed 17 May 2024).

Scholz, László. 2009. 'Squandered Opportunities. On the Uniformity of Literary Translations in Postwar Hungary', in B. J. Baer (ed.), *Contexts, Subtexts, Pretexts: Literary Translation in Eastern Europe and Russia*. Amsterdam and Philadelphia: John Benjamins, 205–18.

Sipos, Anna Magdolna. 2007. 'Könyvek kivonásával és megsemmisítésével a politika szolgálatában: Könyvindexek 1949–1950 [Serving Politics by Withdrawing and Destroying Books: Book Indexes 1949–1950]', *Könyvtári Figyelő*, 53(4): 684–712. https://epa.oszk.hu/00100/00143/00065/82.htm (accessed 17 May 2024).

Sohár, Anikó. 1999. *The Cultural Transfer of Science Fiction and Fantasy*. Frankfurt am Main: Peter Lang.

Sohár, Anikó. 2022. 'Anyone Who isn't Against Us is for Us. Science Fiction Translated from English in the Kádár Era', in C. Rundle, D. Monticelli and A. Lange (eds.), *Translation Under Communism*. London: Palgrave Macmillan, 241–79.

Szili, József. 2007. 'Uncompromising Standards of Nyugat (1908–1941)', in M. Cornis-Pope and J. Neubauer (eds.), *History of the Literary Cultures of East-Central Europe: Junctures and Disjunctures in the 19th and 20th Centuries*. Vol. 3: *The Making and Remaking of Literary Institutions*. Amsterdam: John Benjamins, 70–9.

Takács, Ferenc. 2002. 'The Unbought Grace', *The Hungarian Quarterly*, 43(165): 75–8. http://real-j.mtak.hu/12049/1/HungarianQuarterly_165_2002.pdf (accessed 17 May 2024).

Tomson-Wohlgemuth, Gaby. 2003. 'Children's Literature and Translation Under the East German Regime', *Meta*, 48(1–2): 241–9.

Tóth, Gyula. 1992. *Írók Pórázon: A Kiadói Főigazgatóság irataiból, 1961–1970* [Writers on a Leash: From the Documents of the Publishers' Directorate]. Budapest: MTA Irodtudományi Intézet.

Tymoczko, Maria. 2009. 'Censorship and Self-Censorship in Translation: Ethics and Ideology, Resistance and Collusion', in E. Ní Chuilleanáin, C. O Cuilleanáin and D. Parris (eds.), *Translation and Censorship: Patterns of Communication and Interference.*. Dublin: Four Courts, 24–45.

Varga, Alajosné. 1975. *A magyar könyvkiadás 30 éve, 1945–1974* [The Thirty Years of Hungarian Book Publishing, 1945–1974]. Budapest: Magyar Könyvkiadók és Könyvterjesztôk Egyesülése.

Varga, Sándor. 1985. *A magyar könyvkiadás és könyvkereskedelem története 1957-ig* [The History of Hungarian Book Publishing and Bookselling Until 1957]. Budapest: Gondolat.

15
INSTITUTIONAL CENSORSHIP AND LITERARY TRANSLATION IN COMMUNIST POLAND, 1945–1958

Kamila Budrowska and Beata Piecychna

15.1 Introduction

The chapter discusses institutional censorship practices affecting literary translation in post-war Poland. The main focus is on the activities of the Main Office for Control of the Press, Publications and Public Performances (*Główny Urząd Kontroli Prasy, Publikacji i Widowisk, GUKPPiW*)—an institution established to oversee publications—while the practices of other controlling bodies are only briefly mentioned to complement the discussion and stimulate further research. The chapter examines manipulative techniques applied in literary translation and possible ideologisation of the translated text, which are analysed mainly from a macro perspective, i.e., a big-picture view on the socio-historical context. The case studies consider examples of censorship in Polish translations of fictional works written in Russian, English, German and French. The material was chosen based on two criteria: a work's outstanding artistic value resulting in its positive reception and, possibly, a tradition of translation, and the fact that it represents a characteristic example of censorial activities. All archival materials available at the GUKPPiW that refer to book censorship from 1945–1958 have been thoroughly analysed. That being said, analysis of documents generated by totalitarian regimes must be carried out with a great deal of caution. Therefore, the following assumptions were adopted: 1) the sources were read critically and approached with a low level of trust, and 2) we harboured no illusion of uncovering an unfiltered past.

Research on communist censorship and literary censorship is being conducted simultaneously in many countries and approached from different angles. In the ground-breaking chapter 'Censorship and Cultural Regulations. Mapping of Territory' (Müller 2004: 1–25), Müller states that the topic has become very popular and is producing significant scholarly outcomes; the increased interest, as is the case with 'general' research on communism has been fostered by the collapse of the Soviet bloc, the opening of state archives and the broadening of the concept of censorship. The contemporary theoretical foundations of research on censorship in the broad sense are based on such classics of sociology as Bourdieu's works on symbolic violence (Bourdieu 1990, 1991, 2005) and Foucault's critical analysis of social institutions (Foucault 1998, 2010). These scholars understand censorship as social control and underscore its structural presence in all forms of interpersonal communication. However, as rightly observed by Müller, a broad understanding of the term 'censorship' and the failure to differentiate it from other forms of regulation is not conducive to research on the control

222

DOI: 10.4324/9781003149453-19

Institutional Censorship in Communist Poland, 1945–1958

of publications in totalitarian states. Instead, the scope of this term should be clearly confined to *authoritarian intervention by a third party in an act of communication between the sender and the receiver* because censorship 1) is always based on official regulation, 2) has an extensive organisational and administrative structure, and 3) has a tendency towards bureaucratisation (Müller 2004: 12–13). This is the understanding of censorship that will be used in the chapter. A distinction between 'institutional' and 'institutionalised' censorship will also be made.

Institutionalised censorship in the Polish People's Republic was an important tool of repression used by the authorities. Censors were subservient to the Communist Party and represented its interests. Censorship was therefore 1) ubiquitous and 2) preventive, which means that all communications in the public sphere were controlled before they were published (Nałęcz 1994; Pawlicki 2001; Bates 2000, 2002; Budrowska 2009).

The methodology used is based on the hermeneutic approach. In this context, the censorship of foreign literature is seen as a way of building a propagandistic vision of the world, which legitimises the new authorities. Furthermore, the censorship of literary translation can also be considered as the embodiment of Gadamer's (1989) notion of *effective history* given that all those who prepare a text for publication, translate or edit it, or write a foreword or an afterword can be seen as *historical creatures*, i.e., related to history understood as a series of chronological events, but also as those who will influence future events linked to (para)translation activities, such as the reception of translations or the shape of subsequent translations in a given series. Finally, a micro perspective requires the study of textual changes and the comparison of different translations.

The chapter will demonstrate that the censorship of translation in Poland from 1945 to 1958 can be isolated from the general system of censoring literary fiction. Although the system operated in the same way in relation to both original Polish works and translations, the oversight practices were different. Censors very rarely proposed detailed changes to texts fearing that they might be easily spotted by those readers who knew the original or its pre-war translation. After all, the very existence of censorship was kept secret. This is why the GUKPPiW officials preferred to suggest adding a paratext or holding up publication.

15.2 Historical Perspectives

The system of state censorship created after World War II was modelled on the USSR model and lasted, in a slightly modified version, until 1990. Its establishment was supervised by political officers and workers of the Main Administration for Literary and Publishing Affairs (*Głavnoje Uprawlienije po Dziełam Litieratury i Izdatiel'stw- Głavlitu*) (Romek 2010; Kamińska-Chełminiak 2019). At first, censorship was exercised by the employees of the Ministry of Public Security from July 1944 until July 1946, and on 5 July 1946, a separate institution was established especially for this purpose—the GUKPPiW, which was not a part of any ministry. Officially, the GUKPPiW (Nałęcz 1994) was the only government agency charged with dealing with publishing houses and authors and the responsibility for all public communication but, in fact, the system had a much more complicated structure because there were many other entities that officially or unofficially contributed to the control of publications: ministries, publishers, editors, reviewers and even authors themselves (self-censorship) and translators (censorship and self-censorship). The censorship office was not an independent institution: All recommendations and final decisions were made by party authorities, in particular by the Propaganda Department of the Polish United Workers' Party (*PZPR*) and by the Culture Division of *PZPR*, which took place before the unification congress of the party in December 1948, when the *PZPR* was established by the Polish Workers' Party (PPR) (Pawlicki 2001; Bates 2000, 2002; Romek 2010).

The Routledge Handbook of Translation and Censorship

Institutional censorship was introduced in Poland by means of a regulation (Nałęcz 1994) that was illegal because the constitution guaranteed citizens the right to freedom of speech and expression. Therefore, its existence and operations were kept secret: censorship itself became a 'censored' topic (Woźniak-Łabieniec 2013: 89–97). The main task of censorship was to eliminate from the public sphere any communication the communist regime considered a threat to their interests (political censorship) or to people's morality (moral censorship). In regard to Polish and foreign fiction, much attention was devoted to the artistic value of printed works (aesthetic censorship) (Budrowska 2009: 37).

Not only was the literary work itself controlled but so too were the paratexts and such external factors as the choice of periodical or publishing house where the text would be published, the print run, the choice of editor, the foreword's author and, in the case of translation, the translator. Control activities were also undertaken after the work had appeared in print, i.e., repressive censorship: allowing or forbidding reissues, approval by or exclusion from libraries, allowing or forbidding the publication of newspaper reviews or research papers concerning a particular book.

The strictness of censorship practices changed with the political situation. In the period under study one can differentiate three sub-periods: 1) from 1945 until mid-1948, when censorship was relatively mild as the authorities were just starting to build and strengthen their institutions and private publishing houses were still operating (the possibility of conducting primary research during this period is very limited due to the lack of archival sources and the necessity to interpret the scarce material that is available), 2) from mid-1948 until 1955, when censorship was very restrictive, which was connected with the Stalinisation of social life and the enforcement of socialist realism, and 3) in 1956–1957, when censorship was very mild, which was related to the culmination of liberalisation from October 1956 to October 1957 (Eisler 1993) as a result of the Hungarian Revolution that shook the whole eastern bloc and of events in Poland, such as workers' strikes, the stepping down of current communist leaders and the return to power, under public pressure, of Wladyslaw Gomulka, an ideational communist, formerly imprisoned by the regime. The year 1958 can be seen as 'transitional': On the one hand, due to the length of the publication process, works were subjected to initial control in the most liberal period while, on the other, the first signs of increased oversight appeared with the end of the political changes mentioned above.

All communications were subjected to censorship. Particular attention was devoted to daily newspapers due to their treatment of contemporary events, their large-scale circulation and their mass readership. Literary fiction was also closely scrutinised because of the physical durability of books (they could be read multiple times over a number of years) and their cultural and educational role. The control of belles lettres was usually assigned to well-educated censors but, when censorship bodies were understaffed, as was the case just after the war or in culturally neglected regions, the task was given to uneducated officials, which resulted in numerous bizarre opinions or decisions. Censorship practices affected both new publications and reissues of Polish as well as foreign literature, including literary classics and children's literature.

The censors belonged to the same cultural community as the readers. They knew very well the language as well as the historical and contemporary cultural contexts. Because of that, to smuggle subversive messages authors and translators used 'Aesopian language', i.e., a system of linguistic and artistic devices created and used when Poland had no independent existence (1795–1918). In many cases in the nineteenth and the twentieth centuries, however, censors were able to recognise this strategy and thwart such efforts (Budrowska 2009).

It must be emphasised that despite prolonged efforts to develop and reform the system of institutional censorship in People's Poland, it was never as tight and as oppressive as the 'all-encompassing Soviet censorship' (a term proposed by Choudin, after Goriajeva 1997: 7). The key reason for this was that the most severe punishments, such as imprisonment, deportation to a labour camp or the death penalty, were not meted out to authors in response to their work, and the censorship organs were not directly linked to the political police (except for the first months after the war).

15.3 Critical Issues and Topics

Reporting on the state of knowledge about translation censorship is not an easy task due to the comprehensive character of the term 'censorship' and, consequently, the comprehensive nature of such research. This review section covers only those studies that consider censorship mainly as institutional interference on the part of the state (see, for example, Rajch 2015; Matkowska 2017; Ślarzyńska 2017).

There is a relatively high number of published studies describing the role of censorship in the translation of children's literature, where such censorship is somehow institutionally motivated (e.g., Pollak 1973; Frycie 1977; Adamczyk-Garbowska 1988; Staniów 2000, 2006; Żurawlew 2005; Dymel-Trzebiatowska 2007, 2010; Manasterska-Wiącek 2015; Woźniak 2009; Biały 2012; Rogoż 2013; Bednarczyk 2015; Looby 2015; Zarych 2016). While most articles on translation censorship focus on fiction, some attempts have been made to explore this issue from the perspective of other genres. For instance, several studies have analysed the censorship of translated press articles in communist Poland (Źrałka 2016, 2017a, 2017b, 2018, 2019a, 2019b), and one article has studied censorship in Polish cinema from the point of view of a film translator (Paszkowska-Wilk 2016). The relationship between censorship and translation is discussed briefly by those literary scholars who explore the general issue of censorship in Polish literature (e.g., Budrowska 2009; Gardocki 2019). In this context, Budnik (2014) presents an interesting case of what might be called intralingual translation of 81 books adapted to the needs of the illiterate during the Stalinist era/period.

Over the last decade, much of Polish research in TS has focused on the influence of power, manipulation, rewriting and ideology (indirectly connected to censorship) on the shape of translation as both product and process (Adamowicz-Pośpiech 2013; Truskolaska-Kopeć 2014; Rozwadowska 2018), in addition to post-colonialism applied to Poland (Kuhiwczak 2008, 2011). There have been a number of publications about the influence of different entities (e.g., publishers, proof-readers, editors) on translation (Małczak 2018; Winiarska-Górska 2018). It must be emphasised that although research on literary censorship in People's Poland is abundant, the number of studies focusing specifically/precisely on the censorship of translations is relatively small (e.g., Brzezińska 1995; Bates 2004, 2011, 2014; Bystydzieńska 2007; Looby 2008, 2015; Rajch 2015; Mojsak 2016). These researchers tend to concentrate on similar aspects of censorship and translation, and describe mainly translations from English (Bates 2004, 2011, 2014; Bystydzieńska 2007; Looby 2008, 2015) and, less frequently, from German (Brzezińska 1995; Rajch 2015).

A ground-breaking often cited study is Looby's (2015) *Censorship, Translation and English Language Fiction in People's Poland*, which explores issues related to censorship of translated English-language literature and offers a particularly well-targeted and multilevel analysis. Looby looks at censorship from two main points of view: ideology-oriented (a macro perspective) and text-oriented (a micro perspective). The first refers to the socio-historical context of censorship, e.g., the drafting of reviews of translated books, while the second perspective focuses on a more detailed analysis of the translator's linguistic choices. The key conclusions drawn by Looby are that censors in the Stalinist period 'were trying to break and [...] make the habits of the Polish reading public' (Looby 2015: 30), and that they shaped readers' tastes in line with the dominant ideology and political thought. Efforts were made to promote books considered to be politically correct and preference was given to the translations of Soviet literature as well as to those authors who took the correct ideological position. More freedom came in 1956, after the political 'thaw', when 'censorship in general [was] less harsh' (Looby 2015: 90) while 'reviews [were] shorter, fewer and show[ed] less ideological zeal after 1956' (Looby 2015: 92). This was also a time when a greater number of translations from English were allowed, as well as translations of the works of authors who in the Stalinist period had been considered non-progressive (Looby 2015: 89).

Looby revisits the topic of translation censorship in an article (2008), where he focuses, among other things, on the Polish translations of Sean O'Casey's plays. The article includes a much-needed discussion on how censorship affects translation in terms of changes introduced to the source text. Looby quite rightly underscores the impossibility of establishing who, in fact, is responsible for such changes: the censor, the editor or perhaps the translator. He also notes that it is impossible to predict the associations that readers will make with passages in the translation because associations 'will depend on the [readers'] political sympathies and their distance from the everyday life of communist Poland' (Looby 2008: 58). The topic of censorship in the Stalinist period is also discussed by Bates (2000, 2004, 2011). The researcher draws our attention to how the GUKPPiW operated, one of his most important contributions being a list of books 'where interventions had to be made', which was presented by a censor, Laskowska, in February 1949 during a briefing organised for the heads of the censorship offices (Bates 2000: 100). It is evident that the censor was obliged to assess the political correctness as well as the ideological and social impact that a given work could have on a potential reader. Published books were supposed to address a general public rather than just educated individuals (Bates 2004: 101). Bates (2011) analyses the influence of censorship on the Polish book market from 1948 to 1967, with a particular focus on literary translations from English. The author analyses not only censors' reviews of certain works but also the status of translations in the Stalinist period and the role played by forewords in framing the 'correct' reader interpretation of the message transmitted by the author of the source text. Similarly to Looby, Bates concludes that the domination of Russian literature as the main choice for translation adversely affected the cultural development of Poland: 'Literature, including translation, would be organised according to the rules of socialist planning' (Bates 2011: 62).

The issue of censorship in the Stalinist period is also touched upon by Bystydzieńska (2007), who studies the reception of Jane Austin's works in Poland. She gives the example of the first post-WWII translation of *Pride and Prejudice* by Anna Przedpełska-Trzeciakowska, which was published in 1956, during the 'thaw'. Bystydzieńska believes that the novel was not translated earlier because it deals with the life of the landed gentry and includes a love story, which 'was not popular [...] compared to serious ideological issues' (Bystydzieńska 2007:325). Like Looby and Bates, Bystydzieńska emphasises that the authorities preferred those authors who were inclined to take a realist approach, which conformed to party preferences. Such authors included: 'H.E. Aldridge, Defoe, Dickens, Fielding, Galsworthy, Shaw, Swift and Wilde' (Bystydzieńska 2007: 325). By contrast, there were authors who were 'definitely unapprovable,' such as 'Joyce, Virginia Woolf, Yeats and T.S. Eliot, Huxley, Lawrence' (Bystydzieńska 2007: 325). Looby's and Bates' findings are reflected, at least to a certain degree, in the conclusions drawn by Rajch (2015) and Brzezińska (1995) regarding translations from German, which may indicate the existence of some general rules governing translation censorship. Some cases have been described by Rajch in his seminal

'Unsere andersartige Kulturpolitik' Zensur und Literatur in der DDR und in der Volksrepublik Polen (2015). The author describes in detail the particular stages of controlling non-periodical publications, text censoring methods, and the criteria (political and ideological merits, socio-educational value, artistic quality) applied by the censors when deciding whether to permit the publication of a given book (Rajch 2015: 159). Like Looby, Bates and Brzezińska, Rajch notes a two-stage assessment/evaluation/reviewing procedure of translated books (2015: 159–62). Interestingly, censors were rarely well-prepared for their job; they typically lacked familiarity with literary fiction or literary expertise, which often resulted in opinions that erred on the side of caution (Rajch 2015: 163). Censors often disagreed on whether a certain translation should be released. That was the case with *Green Olives and Bare Mountains* by Eduard Claudius (Rajch 2015: 165), which was not published until the 'thaw' (Rajch 2015: 165). Furthermore, the censors' recommendations, or lack thereof, were not always supported by the heads or directors of relevant departments (see Rajch 2015: 175–6). Rajch, like Looby and Bates, noted the importance of paratextual elements, which were supposed to 'guide' the reader towards a certain interpretation (Rajch 2015: 176).

Rajch differentiated six categories of translations from German: 1) literary texts that did not raise concern from the censor; 2) literary texts allowed for publication but criticised; 3) literary texts that required substantial changes; 4) literary texts conditionally approved for publication; 5) literary texts that were highly controversial (so-called problematic); and 6) literary texts that were forbidden (Rajch 2015: 163). This classification is, certainly, a general one and, what is more, the same text could be classified in more than one category (Rajch 2015: 166).

The authors who were usually almost automatically recommended for publication (category 1) due to the 'correct' ideological message of their books were, for instance, Anna Seghers, Friedrich Wolf and Alex Wedding. Classical writers were also treated with reverence, although it was not until 1955 that a larger number of such works were published (Rajch 2015: 166). The second category included, among others, *Synowie* [*Sons*] by Willi Bredel, published by the State Publishing Institute (*Państwowy Instytut Wydawniczy, PIW*). The censors criticised 'the narrator's political immaturity' and the lack of references to the beginnings of the revolutionary movement in German (Rajch 2015: 168). Similar criticism was directed at the novel *Buddenbrooks* by Thomas Mann, who was reproached for his inadequate representation of the working class (Rajch 2015: 168). According to Rajch, the third category includes, among others, *The Path through February* by Anna Seghers (an example of an author who can be placed in two categories), *Paradise Amerika* by Egon Erwin Kisch or *Berlin Alexanderplatz* by Alexander Döblin. In the last case, the censor recommended that the translation be published subject to the modification of statements made by 'an unemployed anarchist, who opposed Communists' (Rajch 2015: 174–5). Category four includes works that had to be properly interpreted in a special foreword or afterword (Rajch 2015: 177). That was the case of the novel *Pablo, der Indio* by Karl Bruckner, published originally in 1949 and then translated in 1951, where an 'instructional' afterword had to be added. Interestingly, paratexts were also subjected to censorial control. Some of them, such as the afterword to *Schach von Wuthenow* by Theodor Fontane, written by Marcel Ranicki, were praised, while others were criticised, e.g., Andrzej Wirth's paratexts to Wolfgang Borchert's short stories, *The Man Outside* (Rajch 2015: 181–2). The fifth category of problematic cases included books by authors who did not follow the party line (Heinrich Mann and Lion Feuchtwanger) and works of little artistic value written by East German communist authors. Sometimes, the problematic nature of a book was interpreted by censors in a very broad and multifaceted way. An example is Hans Marchwitz's *Die Kumiaks*, which was

The Routledge Handbook of Translation and Censorship

negatively assessed for its inappropriate ideological and political message, which jeopardised the development of Polish-German relations, for the excessive 'naturalism' of descriptions and for the author's poor language and style (Rajch 2015: 189). The sixth and last category includes forbidden texts (Rajch 2015: 190), some of which were eventually published despite initial objections, whereas others were rejected as unacceptable (Rajch 2015: 190). The first sub-category includes 'problematic' texts that required censorial intervention, while the second one includes only two books: *Zielone oliwki i nagie skały* [*Green Olives and Bare Mountains*] by Edward Claudius and *Sharks and Little Fish* by Wolfgang Ott (Rajch 2015: 191). The first was printed in 1958 while the second one was published by Bellona Publishing House only in 2004. These books were not initially approved for publication not only because they deviated from the ideological and political line promoted by the party but also because they contained vulgar, naturalistic and immoral descriptions, which, according to the censors, could deprave society. For her part, Brzezińska examines the issue of publication control by looking at works written nearly exclusively by authors from the German Democratic Republic (Rajch 2015: 107), emphasising that censors paid special attention to a given book's political correctness, didactic potential and its author's ideological position. For his part, Mojsak (2016: 187–222) devotes a chapter to the censorship of Polish translations of western literature in a later historical period (1956–1965), in which he presents numerous interesting findings regarding the 'thaw'. For example, a wave of translations from western languages was a sign of political liberalisation along with the fact that censorial interventions were only occasional or non-existent and rather cosmetic in nature (Mojsak 2016: 186). In order to make translated authors ideologically acceptable and their books publishable, censors categorised them as 'progressive humanists.' In addition, the GUKPPiW preferred a more optimistic outlook and, in particular, favoured anti-fascist works (Mojsak 2016: 199–200). The scholar notes that after 1956 a great deal of US literature was published, introducing it to a much wider public in Poland (Mojsak 2016: 203–4). He also agrees with other scholars (Szkup Jerzy, 1972), who assert that decisions regarding the publication of prominent writers such as Sartre, Beckett and Kafka were made by more highly ranked officials than those in the censorship office (Mojsak 2016: 230).

15.4 New Debates

A broad analysis of archival sources, including materials related to translations from languages other than English and German, confirms many of the findings made by other researchers. It also allows researchers to propose a preliminary taxonomy as well as new research topics. The most important type of censorial documents, which permit the study of the scope and methods of censoring translations from all languages into Polish, is the descriptive reports of the Publishing Control Division, which were drafted in the GUKPPiW and contained a synthetic presentation of data on all publications that were published and censored in a given month, with a breakdown by 1) publisher, 2) type of publication: belles lettres, scientific literature, textbooks, children's literature, 3) new publications or reissues, 4) publications authorised or books rejected by the censor, and 5) Polish books or translations (from whatever language). Not all materials from the period under study have survived (or have been found), but the existing documents from 1949 to 1951 make it possible to draw conclusions on how translations of belles lettres were censored in the 1940s and 1950s. These findings can be verified and complemented thanks to other materials generated in the GUKPPiW from earlier and later years.

Institutional Censorship in Communist Poland, 1945–1958

15.4.1 General Methods of Censoring Translations

15.4.1.1 Procedure

In principle, the censorship methods applied by the GUKPPiW to translations of foreign literary fiction did not differ much from those applied to local Polish literature. The rules of conducting the oversight process were the same and so were instructions regarding substance, which were published in documents drafted by the party, the, so-called 'Books of notes and recommendations' (Romek 2015: 9–27).

A book translated from a foreign language was censored twice: during an initial evaluation before the text was permitted for publication and during a follow-up evaluation, which was conducted after the book had been printed in order to establish whether a reissue could be allowed and to evaluate the work done by the censors during the initial oversight. At each stage, two independent opinions were issued, and in the case of a disagreement, a third opinion, or even more, could be ordered (in extreme cases more than a dozen evaluations were prepared over several months!). The oversight covered both the main text and the paratexts: the introduction, the translator's note, the editor's note and the footnotes. Censors tended to suppress in translated literature the same elements that were forbidden in Polish literature, targeting, in particular, criticism of the USSR, criticism of communism, praise of capitalism and the "bourgeois' lifestyle, religious themes or motifs and immorality in the text. Furthermore, stories that attracted great popularity were not allowed, which was a major blow to adventure fiction, romance novels and children's literature. It was believed that absorbing plots could distract readers' attention from important problems of the contemporary world.

All publications, whether first issues or reissues, had to pass through the same censorial sieve and were subjected to the same rules. The employees of the GUKPPiW read the Polish language version but better educated censors could also read the original, especially if a book was a world 'classic'. In addition, they could read texts in Russian since it was a very widely-spoken language. The popularity of the Russian language was the effect of: 1) the period of Partitions, when Russian was the official language and the language of instruction in the Kingdom of Poland, 2) the Soviet occupation (1939–1941) of the eastern part of Poland, and 3) the post-war period when Russian was informally the official language and, from 1949, a compulsory course in Polish schools course (Figarski 2008: 90). It did happen, then, that censors referred to the original work or to earlier translations. A distinctive feature of translation censorship was the text's 'starting point'. All works, both those originally written in Polish and those translated into Polish, were submitted for oversight by publishing houses, who usually ordered the translation and signed a contract with a translator. The translation process, which was time-consuming and costly, forced editors to think twice before accepting a book: the latter had to be unobjectionable and publishable. Virtually no initial costs were involved in the publication of a Polish text, other than the first editing of the text (in the first years after the war censors would even read unedited manuscripts). When it came to a translated text, a rejection incurred serious financial losses (for private publishers) or a tainted image (for government publishers). Such situations, therefore, had to be avoided. According to Looby, no censor would ever change the text as much as its translator, who during his or her work had to make 'thousand[s]' of decisions (Looby 2015: 7). After 1945, to protect their reputation and their careers, translators had to, first of all, choose a book they would translate very wisely and, second, interpret it in line with the dominant ideology.

During the lengthy translation process, especially in the case of voluminous novels or multi-volume works, there was the risk that the evaluation criteria could change. Such situations were quite common when censorship was increasingly tightened during the Stalinist period. Many translations begun just after the war or during WWII got 'held up' for years, waiting for political change and the attendant modifications of censorial decisions. Such translations would fall into the category of forbidden works (Budrowska 2013).

Therefore, due to the dominant role of the editor and the translator in preliminary text selection as well as the length of the translation process, it can be hypothesised that the outright rejection of a literary text by the GUKPPiW was the most frequent decision.

15.4.1.2 Text Selection

During the period under study, the most eagerly published translations were those of nineteenth century classics and books with themes that were consistent with communist ideology, works written in the eastern bloc countries (a selection criterion based on the language family), texts by authors sympathising with the communist movement (author-based selection) and texts translated by translators with a 'correct' political attitude (translator-based selection).

In the early post-war period, publishers relied mostly on pre-war translations and successively commissioned translations of contemporary texts (predominantly works of socialist realism) and new translations of classics adapted to the socio-political doctrine (translation manipulation). Many pre-war translations were re-issued with an indoctrinating foreword and footnotes, which were easier and faster to prepare than ordering a new translation. Such new editions were an attempt to reconcile the expectations of the authorities with what the publishers could produce. However, the result was unsatisfactory because it often occurred that the message of the paratext did not conform to the message of the translation, which readers would find confusing. An example is the 1950 reader's edition of *Wuthering Heights* by Emily Brönte, in which the anonymous foreword criticises the novel's incompatibility with the contemporary political climate (Bates 2014: 232). Looby, by contrast, points to the positive side of adding an indoctrinating foreword or other paratexts; it was the only way for the book to make it into print, and for the existing translation to be read (Looby 2015: 64–5). It was also the only way to avoid the book's rejection by the GUKPPiW.

Reissues of books translated and published before WWII stopped at the end of 1948, when the authorities adopted a stricter cultural policy. The first measures were taken by the authorities at the end of 1947 (Kondek 1993); private publishing houses in Poland began to disappear a year later, and with them the last, partially independent source of translated foreign literature, mainly popular fiction and children's literature (Kondek 1999). The source languages of literary translations can be divided into three groups: 1) translations from Russian, 2) translations from other eastern bloc languages, and 3) translations from 'western' languages. Translations from Russian were greatly overrepresented under Stalinism during the 1949–1955 period (Kondek 1993, 1999; Smulski 2004a; Smulski 2004b; Looby 2015; Bates 2004, 2011, 2014). As a result of the USSR's political expansion and the consequent expansion of the Russian language and Soviet culture, an attempt was made to completely replace the canon of Polish children's literature with new Soviet literature (Looby 2015: 159). Moreover, a few carefully selected elements of old Russian culture were present in those books. As a result, given that socialist realism in the arts had been mandatory in the USSR since 1934, a large number of Polish-language versions of socialist realist books appeared, as well as new translations or reissues of Russian classics. For example, during the first three months of 1950, three volumes of translated poetry were published: one was from Spanish—Federico Garcia Lorca's *Wybór, wierszy*, translated by W. Słobodnik, and two from Russian—Vladimir Mayakovsky's *Wiersze i poematy*, translated by A. Ważyk, and a collection of

Institutional Censorship in Communist Poland, 1945–1958

poems and stories about the Soviet Army written by different authors. As far as prose is concerned during this period, 33 literary works translated from Russian were published and, more or less, the same number of translations from all other languages combined: twelve from English, several (an exact number was not provided) from French and 16 translations from other languages (including German). It is evident that the number of translations from Russian is higher than or equal to the total number of translations from all other languages (AAN, GUKPPiW, 77, file 4/2a: 21–2). At the National Council of Heads of Provincial Offices for Control of the Press, Publications and Public Performances (*Wojewódzki Urząd Kontroli Prasy Publikacji i Widowisk, WUKPPiW*) held on 11 December 1949, it was openly stated that Soviet literature is exemplary and should be used as a model for new Polish literature (AAN, GUKPPiW, 421, file 4). Russian-language literature was treated with reverence, and consequently was censored very mildly, if at all. Rather, censors were lavish in their praise and emphasised the high ideological and artistic value of those texts. A large number of translations from Russian can be seen as an element of the USSR's colonial policy. Domańska, who believes Poland to be both colonising (under the First and the Second Republics) and colonised (during the Partitions, the occupation during WWII, and the post-war period), underscores that postcolonial theory puts the communist past of the country in a certain context and allows for formulating new questions (Domańska 2008: 167–86), the most important of which is: To what extent did the translations of Soviet and Russian literature convince Poles of the dominant role played by the USSR on the world stage, and how successful were the Polish state's censorial efforts in concealing Soviet Russia's aggressive policy and its activities targeting, Polish society, both during and after the war? According to postcolonial translation theory, a translation act is imbedded in the intricacies of power relations and, as a result, it can reflect the domination of a stronger culture (Gaszyńska-Magiera 2011: 20). It is clear that the Russian and Soviet culture was officially recognised as stronger than Polish culture, hence, the belief in the unequal value of texts, which was expressed in theory and in practice through censorial practices.

Translations from the languages of other communist countries constitute the majority of all translations from 1945–1958 (Smulski 2004a: 230–4). For instance, in the first quarter of 1950, there were four new translations and three re-editions of Czech novels (AAN, GUKPPiW, 77, file 4/2a: 22). Translations from Czech, Slovak, Bulgarian, Romanian, Hungarian, Albanian, the languages of Soviet republics and even Chinese and Korean were supposed to make the Polish reader more familiar with the contemporary life of 'brotherly nations' and show the achievements of communism. That is why, as in the case of Russian literature, the works chosen for translation were usually contemporary or, less often, carefully selected classics, such as the *Laughter Chronicle* by Jaroslav Hašek, translated by Stefan Krysiak (AAN, GUKPPiW, 77, file 4/2a: 22).

While the censorship of literature from other communist countries was stricter than in the case of Soviet literature, the controlling body's willingness to permit publication occurs through a careful pre-selection of texts to be translated. Interestingly, GUKPPiW officials very often criticised such works in follow-up post-publication reviews. This may be because of the long translation process during which the source text's message may have become inconsistent with the current party line.

German literary translations occupy a unique position because, after the formation of the DDR in1949, they were treated as translations from the eastern bloc, while those published earlier were seen as translations of western literature (Brzezińska 1995; Rajch 2015). This is reflected in the censor reports, which always contain an indication of whether the text came from East Germany or the Federal Republic of Germany. The strictness of censorial control was adjusted accordingly.

The censorship of translated literature from 'people's democracies' requires further research. However, it can be affirmed that from 1945 to 1958 many more translations from Russian and other eastern bloc languages were produced, which changed the traditional emphasis in Poland,

The Routledge Handbook of Translation and Censorship

characterised by a high percentage of translations from western languages. It is also worth adding that these translations, while certainly serving as propaganda, also contributed to familiarising Polish readers with little-known cultures.

The censorship of translations of western literature, especially from English, but also from German, has been extensively researched; however, more research is required on different historical periods and on the censorship of other western languages. Of particular interest is the institutional control of translations from French, given Polish Francophilia: the pre-war elite spoke French and read French literature. Interestingly, in the Stalinist period, one of the most frequently published translations of French literature was *The Human Comedy*, as Balzac's prose was treated as a model example of realist literature (Smulski 2004b: 236). Yet, censors' reports warn against too frequent reissues of such books as 'they can easily cause unwanted longings and desires in inexperienced readers' (AAN, GUKPPiW, 375, file 31/35). The approach to translation and censorship of western literature was quite different during the 'thaw' (1956–1957), when many works that had previously been refused publication found their way into print as reissues or first translations. Among the books published were the greatest contemporary works translated from English, French, German and other languages, including those written by Nobel Prize winners as well as novels by great American modernist writers (Bates 2011; Looby 2015; Mojsak 2016). In the years 1956–1957, the GUKPPiW permitted the publication of numerous books that expressed a humanist perspective, named 'progressive humanism', to satisfy the needs of Marxist criticism (Mojsak 2016: 196).

During political liberalisation, avant-garde culture flourished and translations as well as foreign-language culture magazines that made their way into Poland and, just like the opening of the borders and greater freedom to travel, they played the role of a 'transmission conduit' for new standards and patterns coming from the West (Leder 2013: 191–2).

In late 1957, reforms ended and censorship was tightened again but for the next several months local literature and translations that did not conform to the party line still found their way into print (Budrowska 2009). A major change came in 1959, when a new publishing policy was adopted by the party, which aimed to disseminate works that promoted progress and socialism (Mojsak 2016: 188).

15.4.2 Author-based Censorship

Authors of controlled publications—classic authors who were usually dead or contemporary authors—were prime targets for institutionalised censorship. According to Bates, Enlightenment or Realist authors such as Dickens, Galsworthy, Defoe, Swift and Fielding were acceptable. Bystydzieńska adds more names to this list: H.E. Aldridge, Shaw and Wilde [Bystydzieńska 2007: 325]. By contrast, Rajch believes that German classics had to be published with utmost care, especially after 1955 (Rajch 2015: 166). The greatest realist novels and texts from other literatures were also published on a regular basis (Smulski 2004a: 231). An additional example from Russian literature, the 1952 edition of Tolstoy's *Anna Karenina*, is worth noting.

Decisive factors in determining whether a literary classic was publishable were its realist content and its positive critical reception, while in the case of nineteenth century novels other factors were the author's biography and his or her political views. There was a strong preference for communist authors from the USSR and other eastern bloc countries as well as western proponents of communism. Such authors were mentioned in the censors' reports and their correct ideological position often made up for a work's artistic shortcomings and became an argument in favour of its publication.

Much has been written about the work of Howard Fast, who became a symbol of an American writer with 'correct' political views (Smulski 2004b: 235; Bates 2011; Looby 2015: 27, 29, 31). Other interesting examples include Antonio Gramsci, an Italian communist and the author of *Letters from Prison*, Jean Laffitte, a French Communist Party activist, the author of *The Silent Masts* (AAN, GUKPPiW, 77, file 4/2a: 22), Martin Andersen Nexø, a Dutch author of the novel *Morten the Red*, published in Polish translation in September 1949 with an impressive print run of 100,000 copies.

15.4.3 Censorship Because of the Translator

The political views of the translator as well as their pre- and post-war life choices played a key role in determining whether the publication of a particular book would be authorised. No censor ever changed a text as much as its translator (Looby 2015: 7), who essentially determined whether the Polish version of a book would be approved or not. The translator was chosen by the publisher, but the GUKPPiW commented on the choice.

An example is the censorship office's refusal to allow a reissue of Jack London's translated collection of short stories *Wisdom of the Trail*. The first Polish edition published in 1921 was translated by Stanisława Kuszelewska, who in the 1920s translated several volumes of London's prose. Kuszelewska was an anti-communist, a member of the Home Army, a Warsaw insurgent and, in her private life, the wife of General Ludomił Rayski, with whom she moved to the United Kingdom after the end of the war. The censor's report laconically notes that a reissue cannot be allowed because of the translator (AAN, GUKPPiW, 77, file 2a).

After WWII, a new group of translators appeared in Poland. The group was politically 'less reliable,' but educated and cultured, and composed of pre-war intellectual elites, expropriated landowners, soldiers and refugees returning from the West and from the East. During the Stalinist period, the group included professors expelled from universities for their non-communist views as well as blacklisted writers, for whom translation was the only job they could get, in addition to being an important element of building their lives in the new socio-political system. Bronisław Zieliński, for example, was a former army officer and an excellent translator of American literature who translated until his retirement. Other translators, such as Kazimiera Iłłakowiczówna, a poet who worked as Marshall Józef Piłsudski's secretary, spent many years translating literary masterpieces before returning to writing. Her most important translations were Goethe's *Egmont. Tragedia*, Schiller's *Don Carlos* and Tolstoy's *Anna Karenina*.

15.4.4 Interventions and Rejections

Censors' interventions in texts translated from English have been described by Looby (2015), who identifies changes to lexical elements, such as vulgarity, swear words and vocabulary related to human sexual and bodily functions. Thus, the alterations made were not significant but rather aimed at toning down the style and language of the translation. Rajch comes to similar conclusions through his analysis of translations from German (2015). He underscores the fact that censors did not often change texts but instead required publishers to add ideological paratexts. As far as classics are concerned, the researchers agree that modifications were suggested only in the case of less popular authors or works. Our research to date (more detailed research is required) confirms those findings with reference to translations from other languages: the GUKPPiW rarely proposed textual changes, instead making interventions that were external to the text, i.e., holding up the publication, reducing print runs or adding paratexts.

The Routledge Handbook of Translation and Censorship

The rejection of a translation by the censorship office is another method of oversight. The 'Descriptive Reports for 1949–1951' confirm that until April 1949 no text was rejected in full and then, following the tightening of censorship rules, as many as 25 books (Polish and translated ones) were refused authorisation in the second quarter of 1950 alone (AAN, GUKPPiW, 77). The peak of rejections was reached in 1950, and the number stabilised in 1951.

As for translations from foreign languages, few titles are given in the reports. One of them is *The Incredulity of Father Brown*, a Gilbert Keith Chesterton novel about a priest-detective. A request made by Catholic publisher Księgarnia Św. Wojciecha to reissue this 1929 novel was denied in 1950 (AAN, GUKPPiW, 77, f. 4/2a: 92) because publishers did not submit the most objectionable works to the GUKPPiW.

15.4.5   Interventions and Detentions

A test of the methods of controlling translations may also be the recall of those that had not been fully approved for printing by the office. The 'Descriptive Reports for the Years 1949–1951' reveals that until April 1949 no text was retained in its entirety, and then, due to the tightening of censoship rules, in the second quarter of 1950 alone, as many as 25 items were not allowed to be printed (a total of Polish and translated works) [AAN, GUKPPiW, 77]. The peak of detentions was in 1950, and in 1951 the number of detentions stabilised.

When it comes to translations from foreign languages, reports provide few specific titles; for example: Graham Chesterton's novel about the priest-detective *Father Brown's Unbelief*, submitted as a proposal to reissue the 1929 title by the Catholic publishing house Saint's Bookstore. Wojciech, was not approved for printing in 1950 [AAN, GUKPPiW, 77, vol. 4/2a:92]. It seems that this is due to the fact that most obscene works did not reach the censorship stage at GUKPPiW as they were not reported by publishing houses. The exception was the period of tightening control from mid-1948, when publishing houses (mainly private ones) did not react in time and sent works that did not fit the assumptions of the new cultural policy (Budrowska 2013). In the Stalinist period, the censorship office did not receive works by 'definitely uncensorable' writers, such as 'Joyce, Virginia Woolf, Yeats and T.S. Eliot, Huxley, Lawrence', avant-garde (Mojsak 2016), or, what may come as somewhat of a surprise, Fyodor Dostoyevsky.

15.5   Case Studies

15.5.1   Russian

In 1950, the Czytelnik publishing house submitted to the censorship office a new translation of a comedy by Aleksander Griboyedov *Woe from Wit* [*Gorie ot yma*]. The censor, Fleszarowa, permitted publication, noting, 'An exquisite translation by Tuwim! – may I be forgiven for starting with the translation but the quality of almost all translations is such that the one done by Tuwim feels like a heavenly oasis' (AAN, GUKPPiW, 145, file 31/26). Griboyedov's famous comedy was first published in the original version in 1825 after it had been abridged by tsarist censorship (the work was not published in full until 1862). In the nineteenth century, three Polish translations were made and the first full Polish edition, translated by Józef Lewant-Lewiński, *Biada temu, kto ma rozum* [*Woe to him who has reason*], was published by Wyd. H. Natanson in 1857 (Roszkowska 1994). Lewiński's translation included some fragments that had been deleted by the tsarist censor, which may mean that the Polish translator used Griboyedov's manuscripts

(Roszkowska 1994: 205–6). Thus, the edition of the comedy published by the Czytelnik in spring 1951 as *Mądremu biada. Komedia wierszem w 4 aktach* [*Woe to the wise. A verse comedy in 4 acts*] was a new, contemporary translation made by one of the greatest Polish poets, who was also an excellent translator from Russian, specialising in Pushkin and Russian symbolist poetry. In *On the Art of Translation,* the proceedings of a translation conference organised by the Polish branch of PEN-Club, Seweryn Pollak proclaims Tuwim to be the founder of the modern Polish school of translation (Pollak 1955: 341–2), and declares his translation of Griboyedov's comedy to be a masterpiece (Pollak 1955: 341–2). Julian Tuwim's translation does not show any signs of political indoctrination. Most probably, what helped the translator avoid the requirement of adding a contemporary political touch to the work was the fact that it was written in the distant past and that it sharply satirises the landed gentry and high-ranking civil servants in tsarist Russia. The 1951 edition is not accompanied by any paratexts and the few footnotes provided by the translator consist of politically neutral linguistic comments and translations of French phases. Since then, this excellent translation has been reissued in several editions. A positive censor's review turned out to be consistent both with the sentiment of both experts and readers.

15.5.2   German

The first Polish edition of *The Magic Mountain* by Thomas Mann was published in 1930. The first volume was translated by Józef Kramsztyk and the second one by Kazimierz Czachowski and Juliusz Feldhorn. The book was reissued after the war with a fresh translation of the second volume since the original one had been considered poor (Dwutygodnik.com, access 2021). The new translation was done by blacklisted professor Władysław Tatarkiewicz (under the pseudonym Jan Łukowski), a great philosopher who had been banned from the university for six years. However, according to the copyright page of the Czytelnik 1953 edition, it was based on the translation from 1929, which does not give credit to the retranslation and in fact conceals it.

Submitted to the GUKPPiW in 1952, when restrictions were at their peak, the Polish translation proved to be a very difficult 'case' for censors due to its semantic and artistic complexity as well as its ideological message. Judging from a non-standard document found in the GUKPPiW archives, the decision to allow a reissue must have been made by high party officials since such reports were only written in controversial cases (Budrowska 2009). An extensive, undated 'Censor's note on a novel by Thomas Mann: *The Magic Mountain*' was drafted by censor Kazimierz Dobrzyński (AAN, GUKPPiW, 375, f. 31/28: 458–60), who criticises the novel for its representation of 'decadent individualism', openly stating that 'The opinions on political, social, philosophical and worldview issues expressed by the novel's characters **are today not only hostile but also harmful to us** if the book appears in print' (AAN, GUKPPiW, 375, f. 31/28: 458, in bold in censor's note). However, he adds that 'The only way to diminish the potentially negative impact of this reissue is to limit the print run of what is, in fact, nothing but an elitist psychological novel' (AAN, GUKPPiW, 375, f. 31/28: 458). Thus, his verdict is not categorically negative. The book was eventually published in 1953. The copyright page states that 10,160 copies were printed, a smaller print run than the usual 20,000 copies. Apparently, the censor Dobrzyński's suggestion was followed. Typesetting started in August 1952 and in September 1953 the book was finally printed. Its journey through the GUKPPiW was long, lasting over a year. Furthermore, the issue was falsely marked as the first edition in order to discourage potential readers from looking for the pre-war edition. It included an

The Routledge Handbook of Translation and Censorship

indoctrinating foreword, which was in direct conflict with the ideas expressed in Mann's book. Its author, Roman Karst, a literary critic, German literature expert and translator of Franz Kafka, uses language that is typical for the period, e.g., 'a vicious circle of bourgeois problems', 'a crowd of thoughtless, inert and idle residents of Berghof sanatorium' (Karst 1953: 4). He concludes, however, by defending Mann's ideological position stating that he was an anti-fascist: 'All of Thomas Mann's works, regardless of any reservations we may have, are the fruit of the self-critique of a German who bears on his shoulders the burden of co-responsibility for the plight of his nation. *The Magic Mountain* is a prologue to this self-critique' (Karst 1953: 7).

It is worth emphasising that the publication of a German novel not written in East Germany and that was translated from German just a couple of years after the end of WWII required a great deal of effort from all agencies engaged in the process. Also, it had to be accompanied by a specific commentary that 'defended' the German author against possible allegations of supporting Nazi ideology. Before 1956, a revisionist and neo-fascist view of Western German literature, including works written before WWII, developed in Poland (Eberharter 2014: 119) because of the long-standing mistrust of and aversion toward German literature on the part of the Polish reader. Therefore, in the case of German literature, the censorial activities conducted by the GUKPPiW just after the war were in many aspects consistent with general public opinion (Bates 2002: 79–92).

15.5.3 English

In early 1956, PIW (State Publishing Institute) submitted a short novel by Ernest Hemingway, *The Old Man and the Sea,* to the authorities for approval and received a positive review. The censor wrote that the story had a valuable message: 'an optimistic belief that life wins' (AAN, GUKPPiW, 386). The book was released in February and printed in April 1956, which was fast and may indicate that higher-ups considered the book publishable. This confirms the findings of other researchers regarding an evident relaxing of censorial restrictions (Bates 2000; Looby 2015: 30 and 89; Mojsak 2016). The first English edition appeared in 1952 and, two years later, the author received the Nobel Prize, which might have also contributed to speeding up the decision of the Polish authorities to immediately commission the translation.

The translation is preceded by a foreword with a surprising title: *Hemingway's Fairy Tale.* The author, Andrzej Kijowski, tries to demonstrate that great American Realist writers (e.g., Hemingway and Steinbeck), 'who have been increasingly burdened with obligations imposed by realism', introduce into their works fantastic elements and fairy-tale morality. The ideas expressed in Kijowski's paratext oppose the meaning conveyed by the main text in order to make the book publishable.

However, the most interesting aspect of censorial control of Hemingway's short story is related to its translator, Bronisław Zieliński (1914–1985), who was a highly controversial figure from the communist authorities' point of view. He was a Polish officer, a member of the Home Army and the Government Delegation for Poland (an agency of the Polish Government in Exile during WWII) and a participant in the Warsaw Uprising, who was imprisoned from 1947 to 1950. Zieliński started his career as a translator after the war but he managed to introduce Polish readers to a number of important English literary works such as *Moby Dick* by Herman Melville and the works of John Steinbeck and Truman Capote. He is best known, however, as Hemingway's translator; his very accomplished translation of *The Old Man and the Sea* was his first achievement in this field. His name is not mentioned in the censor's report, which may indicate that censorship in general was less harsh or that the translator had not been identified by lower rank officials of the GUKPPiW.

15.5.4   French

Another example of translation censorship that is worth noting involved the translation of Albert Camus' *L'Étranger* [*The Stranger*]. Czytelnik publishers reported their intention to publish the work in January 1948, which was very early considering that the original had been published in 1942. The text had been translated by Maria Zenowicz, the author of numerous translations from French, including other works by Camus. The refusal drafted by a GUKPPiW official includes a very meaningful summary: 'It is not just the entire book but the whole philosophical system together with its founders that should be deleted' (AAN, GUKPPiW, 145, file 31/22). It is worth emphasising that the censor's categorical view was expressed several months before the famous speech condemning existentialism delivered by Zhdanov at the World Congress of Intellectuals in Defense of Peace in Wrocław in 1948 (Smulski 2009: 144). There might be several reasons behind the decision not to publish the translation: The screws were being gradually tightened (a very early sign of the Stalinist offensive), Camus' pessimistic view of the human condition had to be 'eradicated', or the censors were not happy with the translation, which was not ideologised. The novel by Camus was eventually published by PIW in January 1958, ten years later during the 'thaw', when Camus was counted among the representatives of 'progressive humanism' (Mojsak 2016: 197). The translation was not accompanied by politicised paratexts; there was just a short author's biography.

The censorship of the Polish translation of *The Stranger* is a good example of the most serious intervention, i.e., banning publication for many years. Although the novel did finally appear in print, the ten-year delay had a negative impact on the Polish reception of Camus' works (*La Peste* [*The Plague*], translated by Joanna Guze, was published only in 1957) and deprived Polish society of a serious debate on the human condition during the crisis of values, which the book stirred in the post-war years in other European cultures.

15.6   Potential Research Avenues

An interesting topic for further research is the working conditions and career choices of translators, which were closely correlated with tragic historical circumstances. In particular, it is worth verifying whether Looby's thesis that 'one does not find in this period any serious attempt at passive resistance to communism on the part of translators' (Looby 2015: 64) applies only to translators of English or to other languages as well. We agree that 'the refusal to improve on source texts [...] could in itself be seen as an act of resistance' (Looby 2015: 65) and would like to take a closer look at other possible resistance strategies.

Further research might also go beyond the adopted time frame (and include, for instance, the censorship of translated Jewish texts in 1968 or the 1980s and the erosion of the system) or focus on in-depth analyses of translations from one language only. It could also be important to investigate how key dissident writings published in the illegal 'second circulation', such as *Nineteen Eighty-Four* by George Orwell, *The Gulag Archipelago* by Aleksandr Solzhenitsyn, *The Captive Mind* by Czesław Miłosz, *The Master and Margarita* by Mikhail Bulgakov, were received in the eastern bloc countries and in Western Europe.

The Routledge Handbook of Translation and Censorship

Another interesting issue to be explored is the censorship of translated Polish fiction and its reception in other communist countries; an intriguing case study would be the prose of Stanisław Lem, a Polish science-fiction giant, immensely popular in the USSR in the late 1950s and 1960s.

Further Reading

Budrowska, Kamila. 2020. *Writers, Literature and Censorship in Poland. 1948–1958.* Bern: Peter Lang GmbH.
The book, based on an analysis of archival materials, describes in detail the system of censorship of fiction in People's Poland in the years 1948–1958. Among the numerous descriptions of examples of the impact of censorship on literary texts is a consideration of the censorship of translations into Polish, with particular emphasis on literary classics and children's literature.

Looby, Robert. 2015. *Censorship, Translation and English Language Fiction in People's Poland.* Leiden and Boston: Brill Rodopi.
The book is the most serious scientific achievement in the field of the problem of censorship of translated fiction in People's Poland. It brings a systematized knowledge of the theory of censorship of literary translation p and an analysis of numerous cases of censorship of fiction translated into Polish from English.

Krystyna Wieszczek de Oliveira. 2024. *George Orwell and Communist Poland: Émigré, Official and Clandestine Receptions.* London-New York, Routledge.
Krystyna Wieszczek de Oliveira's book is a pioneering attempt to present the Polish post-war reception of George Orwell's works from three complementary angles: official reception, i.e., subject to the supervision of institutional censorship, émigré reception and clandestine reception (samizdat). It opens a new current of comparative research: on the history of editing, translation and censorship of the most outstanding works of world literature, including English-language literature, in Poland of 1944–1989.

The above monographs are concise, state-of-the-art publications depicting the history and specificity of censorship in post-war Poland, including literary translations. Authors of the monography are eminent, outstanding scholars specialising in censorship of Polish literature and literary translations within the period of communist Poland.

References

Primary (Archival Materials)

Published

Nałęcz, Daria. 1994. *Dokumenty do dziejów PRL. Główny Urząd Kontroli Prasy, no. 6.* Warszawa: Instytut Studiów Politycznych PAN.

Unpublished

AAN, GUKPPiW.

Secondary

Literature Pertaining to General Censorship

Bourdieu, Pierre. 1990. *Reprodukcja. Elementy teorii systemu nauczania.* Translated by E. Neyman. Warszawa: PWN.
Bourdieu, Pierre. 1991. *Language and Symbolic Power.* Translated by G. Raymond and M. Adamson. Cambridge: Harvard University Press.

Institutional Censorship in Communist Poland, 1945–1958

Bourdieu, Pierre. 2005. *Dystynkcja. Społeczna krytyka władzy sądzenia*. Translated by P. Biłos. Warszawa: Scholar.

Foucault, Michel. 1998. *Nadzorować i karać. Narodziny więzienia*. Translated by T. Komendant. Warszawa: Aletheia.

Foucault, Michel. 2010. *Historia seksualności*. Translated by B. Banasiak, T. Komendant and K. Matuszewski. Gdańsk: słowo/obraz/terytoria

Müller, Beate. 2004. 'Censorship and Cultural Regulations. Mapping of Territory', in B. Müller (ed.), *Censorship and Cultural Regulation in the Modern Age*, Amsterdam and New York: Rodopi, 1–25.

Literature Pertaining to Censorship in People's Poland

Bates, John M. 2000. 'Cenzura w epoce stalinowskiej', *Teksty Drugie*, 1–2: 95–120.

Bates, John M. 2002. 'Cenzura wobec problemu niemieckiego w Polsce (1948–1955)', in D. Dąbrowska and P. Michałowski (eds.), *Presja i ekspresja. Zjazd szczeciński i socrealizm*. Szczecin: Wydawnictwo Naukowe Uniwersytetu Szczecińskiego, 79–92.

Bates, John M. 2004. 'From State Monopoly to the Free Market of Ideas? Censorship in Poland, 1976–1989', in B. Müller (ed.), *Censorship and Cultural Regulation in the Modern Age*. Amsterdam/New York: Rodopi, 141–67.

Budrowska, Kamila. 2009. *Literatura i pisarze wobec cenzury PRL. 1948–1958*. Białystok: Wydawnictwo Uniwersytetu w Białymstoku.

Budrowska, Kamila. 2013. *Zatrzymane przez cenzurę. Inedita z połowy wieku XX*. Warszawa: IBL PAN.

Gardocki, Wiktor. 2019. *Cenzura wobec literatury polskiej w latach osiemdziesiątych XX wieku*. Warszawa: IBL PAN.

Kamińska-Chełminiak, Kamila. 2019. *Cenzura w Polsce 1944–1960. Organizacja –kadry – metody pracy*. Warszawa: Wydawnictwo Uniwersytetu Warszawskiego.

Kondek, Stanisław Adam. 1999. *Papierowa rewolucja. Oficjalny obieg książek w Polsce w latach 1948–1955*. Warszawa: Biblioteka Narodowa.

Mojsak, Kajetan. 2016. *Cenzura wobec prozy nowoczesnej, 1956–1965*. Warszawa: IBL PAN.

Pawlicki, Aleksander. 2001. *Kompletna szarość. Cenzura w latach 1965–1972. Instytucja i ludzie*. Warszawa: Trio.

Romek, Zbigniew. 2010. *Cenzura a nauka historyczna w Polsce. 1944–1970*. Warszawa: INH PAN.

Woźniak-Łabieniec, Marzena. 2013. 'Cenzura w okresie odwilży jako temat tabu', *Acta Universitatis Lodziensis*, 1: 89–97.

Literature Pertaining to Censorship in Communist Poland and Translation

Adamczyk-Garbowska, Monika. 1988. *Polskie tłumaczenia angielskiej literatury dziecięcej. Problemy krytyki przekładu*. Wrocław: Ossolineum.

Adamowicz-Pośpiech, Agnieszka. 2013. *Seria w przekładzie. Polskie warianty prozy Josepha Conrada*. Katowice: Wydawnictwo Uniwersytetu Śląskiego.

Bates, John M. 2011. 'Censoring English Literature in People's Poland, 1948–1967', in C. O'Leary and A. Lázaro (eds.), *Censorship Across Borders: The Reception of English Literature in Twentieth-Century Europe*. Newcastle, UK: Cambridge Scholars, 59–72.

Bates, John M. 2014. 'Cenzura literatury angielskiej w Polsce. 1948–1967', in K. Budrowska, E. Dąbrowicz and M. Lul (eds.), *Literatura w granicach prawa (XIX–XX w.)*. Warszawa: IBL PAN, 225–42.

Bednarczyk, Anna. 2015. 'Soviet Literature in Primary Schools in the People's Republic of Poland: Arkady Gaidar's *Timur and His Squad* as an Example of Political School Readings', in E. Skibińska, M. Heydel and N. Paprocka (eds.), *La voix du traducteur à l'école = The Translator's Voice at School, vol. 2: Praxis*. Montréal: Éditions québécoises de l'œuvre, 1–31.

Biały, Paulina. 2012. 'Cultural Adaptations in Translation of English Children's Literature into Polish: The Case of Mary Poppins', *Linguistica Silesiana*, 33: 105–25.

Brzezińska, Bogna. 1995. 'Polens zentrale Zensurbehörde und die deutschsprachige Literatur 1945–1956', *Studia Germanica Posnaniensia*, XXII: 107–23.

The Routledge Handbook of Translation and Censorship

Budnik, Magdalena. 2014. *Książka Nowego Czytelnika: Literatura dla byłych analfabetów przeszkolonych w Polsce w latach 1948–1951.* Białystok: Alter Studio.

Bystydzieńska, Grażyna. 2007. 'Jane Austen in Poland', in A. Mandal and B. Southam (eds.), *Jane Austen in Europe.* London and New York: Thoemmes Continuum, 319–33, 390–3.

Dymel-Trzebiatowska, Hanna. 2007. 'Znikający Bóg. Ideologizacja w przekładach baśni Hansa Christiana Andersena', in A. Szczęsny NS and K. Hejwowski (eds.), *Językowy obraz świata w oryginale i przekładzie.* Warszawa: ILS UW, 319–25.

Dymel-Trzebiatowska, Hanna. 2010. 'Utemperowane urwisy. Puryfikacja i dydaktyzacja w przekładach prozy Astrid Lindgren na język polski', in A. Małgorzewicz (ed.), *Translation: Theorie – Praxis – Didaktik.* Dresden and Wrocław: Neisse Verlag, 485–94.

Eberharter, Markus. 2014. 'Socjologiczne spojrzenie na rolę tłumaczy literatury. Na przykładzie Wandy Kragen i recepcji literatury niemieckojęzycznych w Polsce po roku 1945', *Rocznik Przekładoznawczy:* 115–28.

Frycie, Stanisław. 1977. 'Przekłady z literatury dla dzieci i młodzieży w latach 1945–1956', *Polonistyka,* 1: 17–22; 2: 99–104.

Kuhiwczak, Piotr. 2008. 'Censorship as a Collaborative Project: A Systemic Approach', in E. Ní Chuilleanáin, C. Ó Cuilleanáin and D. Parris (eds.), *Translation and Censorship: Patters of Communication and Interference.* Dublin: Four Courts Press, 46–56.

Kuhiwczak, Piotr. 2011. 'Translation and Censorship', *Translation Studies,* 4(3): 358–66.

Looby, Robert. 2008. 'Looking for the Censor in the Works of Sean O'Casey (and Others) in Polish Translation', *Translation and Literature,* 17(1): 47–64.

Looby, Robert. 2015. *Censorship, Translation and English Language Fiction in People's Poland.* Leiden and Boston: Brill–Rodopi.

Małczak, Leszek. 2018. 'Przekład jako akt subwersji, czyli o pewnym polskim tłumaczeniu tragedii historycznej Theodora Körnera pt.', *Zriny. Przekłady Literatur Słowiańskich,* 9: 299–319.

Manasterska-Wiącek, Edyta. 2015. *Dyfuzja i paradyfuzja w przekładach literatury dla dzieci.* Lublin: Wydawnictwo UMCS.

Matkowska, Ewa. 2017. 'Cenzura i recepcja literatury polskiej w NRD', in Z. Romek and K. Kamińska-Chełminiak (eds.), *Cenzura w PRL. Analiza zjawiska.* Warszawa: Oficyna Wydawnicza ASPRA-JR, 29–38.

Paszkowska-Wilk, Anna. 2016. 'Cenzura a przekład', in J. Lubocha-Kruglik and O. Małysa (eds.), *Przestrzenie przekładu.* Katowice: Wydawnictwo Uniwersytetu Śląskiego, 39–46.

Pollak, Seweryn. 1973. 'Rosyjska poezja dla dzieci w przekładach polskich', in H. Skrobiszewska (ed.), *Poezja i dziecko. Materiały sesji literacko-naukowej.* Poznań: Wydział Kultury Prezydium Rady Naukowej m. Poznania, Wielkopolskie Towarzystwo Przyjaciół Książki, 89–104.

Rajch, Marek. 2015. *'Unsere andersartige Kulturpolitik'. Zensur und Literatur in der DDR und in der Volksrepublik Polen.* Poznań: Wydawnictwo UAM.

Rogoż, Michał. 2013. 'Przekłady zagranicznej literatury dla dzieci i młodzieży w okowach polskiej cenzury. Ocena książek skierowanych do wydania w latach 1948–1956', in G. Gzella and J. Gzella (eds.), *Nie należy dopuszczać do publikacji. Cenzura w PRL.* Toruń: Wydawnictwo Naukowe UMK, 99–122.

Rozwadowska, Kinga. 2018. *Przekład i władza. Polskie tłumaczenia* Braci Karamazow *Fiodora Dostojewskiego.* Kraków: Wydawnictwo Uniwersytetu Jagiellońskiego.

Ślarzyńska, Małgorzata. 2017. 'Polskie przekłady wybranych fragmentów prozy włoskiej w świetle uwarunkowań kulturowych i historycznych recepcji literatury obcej w PRL', *Między Oryginałem a Przekładem,* 37: 47–67.

Smulski, Jerzy. 2004a. 'Przekłady z literatury krajów socjalistycznych', in Z. Łapiński and W. Tomasik (eds.), Kraków: Universitas, 230–4.

Smulski, Jerzy. 2004b. 'Przekłady z literatury zachodnie', in Z. Łapiński and W. Tomasik (eds.), Kraków: Universitas, 234–7.

Smulski, Jerzy. 2009. '"Przedodwilżowe" dyskusje na temat polityki przekładowej w latach stalinizmu', in J. Smulski (ed.), *Przewietrzyć zatęchłą atmosferę uniwersytetów. Wokół literaturoznawczej polonistyki doby stalinizmu.* Toruń: Wydawnictwo Uniwersytetu Mikołaja Kopernika, 143–56.

Staniów, Bogumiła. 2000. *Książka amerykańska dla dzieci i młodzieży w Polsce w latach 1944–1989. Produkcja i recepcja.* Wrocław: Wydawnictwo Uniwersytetu Wrocławskiego.

Staniów, Bogumiła. 2006. *Z uśmiechem przez wszystkie granice. Recepcja wydawnicza przekładów polskiej książki dla dzieci i młodzieży w latach 1945–1989.* Wrocław: Wydawnictwo Uniwersytetu Wrocławskiego.

Institutional Censorship in Communist Poland, 1945–1958

Truskolaska-Kopeć, Emilia. 2014. *Problematyka ideologiczna w twórczości George'a Orwella i jej polskich przekładach*. Unpublished Doctoral Thesis. Warszawa: Uniwersytet Warszawski.

Winiarska-Górska, Izabela. 2018. 'Ideologia unitariańska a strategie translatorskie i styl przekładu *Nowego Testamentu* Marcina Czechowica (1577)', *Poznańskie Studia Polonistyczne. Seria Językoznawcza*, 25(45): 2, 277–313.

Woźniak, Monika. 2009. 'Czym jest "poprawność polityczna" w przekładach literatury dziecięcej?', in K. Hejwowski, A. Szczęsny and U. Topczewska (eds.), *50 lat polskiej translatoryki*. Warszawa: ILS UW, 505–12.

Zarych, Elżbieta. 2016. 'Przekład literatury dla dzieci i młodzieży – między tekstem a oczekiwaniami wydawcy i czytelnika', *Teksty Drugie*, 1: 206–27.

Źrałka, Edyta. 2016. *Manipulation in the Translation of British and American Press Articles into Polish in the Communist Era: The Case of Forum Magazine 1965–89*. Katowice: Wydawnictwo Uniwersytetu Śląskiego.

Źrałka, Edyta. 2017a. 'The Translator's Intentions – The Same or Different from the Author's? Cases of Manipulation in Polish Translations of British Press Articles in 1965–1989', in A. Piskorska and E. Wałaszewska (eds.), *Applications of Relevance Theory. From Discourse to Morphemes*. Newcastle upon Tyne: Cambridge Scholars Publishing, 132–50.

Źrałka, Edyta. 2017b. 'Principles of "Newspeak" in Polish translations of British and American Press Articles Under Communist Rule', *Research in Language (RiL)*, 15(1): 97–118.

Źrałka, Edyta. 2018. 'Cenzura w tłumaczeniu anglojęzycznych artykułów prasowych przed upadkiem komunizmu i po nim – stara i nowa rzeczywistość polityczna a wolność słowa', in Z. Romek and K. Kamińska-Chełminiak (eds.), *Cenzuro wróć? Mechanizmy ograniczania wolności słowa w Polsce po 1990 roku*. Warszawa: Oficyna Wydawnicza ASPRA-JR, 205–22.

Źrałka, Edyta. 2019a. 'The Image of the People's Republic of Poland in Translations of British and American Press Articles into Polish Under Preventive Censorship', in L. Harmon and D. Osuchowska (eds.), *National Identity in Translation*. Berlin: Peter Lang, 167–178.

Źrałka, Edyta. 2019b. *Manipulation in translating British and American press articles in the People's Republic of Poland*. Newcastle upon Tyne: Cambridge Scholars Publishing.

Żurawlew, Tomasz. 2005. 'Wpływ światopoglądu katolickiego na przekład wybranych tekstów baśniowych braci Grimm na język polski', in K. Hejwowski (ed.), *Kulturowe i językowe źródła nieprzekładalności*. Olecko: Wszechnica Mazurska, 113–25.

Others

Domańska, Ewa. 2008. 'Obrazy PRL w perspektywie postkolonialnej. Studium przypadku', in K. Brzechczyn (ed.), *Obrazy PRL. O konceptualizacji realnego socjalizmu w Polsce*. Poznań: IPN, 167–86.

Eisler Jerzy. 1993. *List 34*. Warszawa: PWN.

Figarski, Władysław. 2008. 'Język rosyjski w Polsce – Fakty i myty', *Przegląd Rusycystyczny*, 1(121): 84–97.

Gadamer, Hans-Georg. 1989. *Truth and Method*. Translated by J. Weinsheimer and D. G. Marshall. New York: Seabury Press.

Gaszyńska-Magiera, Małgorzata. 2011. *Recepcja przekładów literatury iberoamerykańskiej w Polsce w latach 1945–2000 z perspektywy komunikacji międzykulturowej*. Kraków: Wydawnictwo Uniwersytetu Jagiellońskiego.

Goriajeva, Tamara M. 1997. *Priedislov'e, in: Istorija sovietskoj politiczeskoj cenzury. Dokumenty i komentari*. Moskva: ROSSPEN.

Karst, Roman. 1953. *Przedmowa*, in T. Mann, *Czarodziejska góra*, t. 1. Translated by J. Kramsztyk. Warszawa: Czytelnik, s. 3–16.

Kondek, Stanisław A. 1993. *Władza i wydawcy. Polityczne uwarunkowania produkcji książek w Polsce w latach 1944–1949*. Warszawa: Biblioteka Narodowa.

Leder, Andrzej. 2013. *Prześniona rewolucja. Ćwiczenie z logiki historycznej*. Warszawa: Wydawnictwo Krytyki Politycznej.

Pollak, Seweryn. 1955. 'Uwagi o poezji rosyjskiej w Polsce', in M. Rusinek (ed.), *O sztuce tłumaczenia. Materiały ze Studium Przekładowego zorganizowanego przez PEN Club Polska w latach 1950–1953*. Warszawa: Wydawnictwo Czytelnik, vol. 1, 341–42.

Roszkowska, Anna. 1994. '"Mądremu biada" Aleksandra Gribojedowa w interpretacji polskich tłumaczy XIX wieku', *Roczniki Humanistyczne*, 7: 201–31.

Online resources

Dwutygodnik.com www.dwutygodnik.com/artykul/963-alfabet-czarodziejskiej-gory-l-jak-jan-lukowski.html (last accessed April 10, 2021).

16

TRANSLATION AND CENSORSHIP IN SOVIET AND INDEPENDENT UKRAINE

Lada Kolomiyets and Oleksandr Kalnychenko

16.1 Historical Perspectives

This chapter discusses censoring literary translation only in the former Russia-ruled part of Ukraine, excluding Galicia, Bukovyna and Transcarpathia, since otherwise four other states (namely, Poland, Romania, Czechoslovakia and Hungary) and their censorship rules would have to be discussed. For religious (Biblical) translations, which were a primary focus of censorial prohibition in the Soviet Union, see Kolomiyets 2019; Dzera and Shmiher 2023; and Shmiher 2024. The practice of administrative, scientific and technical, military and journalistic translation, as well as interpreting, where one can find many interesting examples of censorship, require a separate investigation as the use of Ukrainian in them was continuously reduced in the Ukrainian SSR.

16.1.1 Translation and Censorship in Soviet Ukraine between the World Wars (1922–1939)

After defeat in the War of Independence (1917–1921), Eastern and Central Ukraine, or the so-called 'Ukrainian heartland', had to join the USSR, becoming a Soviet Socialist Republic (SSR), as proclaimed in 1922. In that same year the central censorship agency of the Ukrainian SSR, Holovne Upravlinnia v spravach literatury i vydavnytstv [Main Department for Literature and Publishing], abbreviated as *Holovlit,* began to function and continued to do so until 1991. It was a replica of the Main Administration for Literary and Publishing Affairs under the People's Commissariat of Education of the Russian Federation. The Communist Party of the Soviet Union (CPSU) introduced an elaborate system of censorship over the cultural resources of its various peoples. The Soviet state apparatus applied the practice of dual control over all publications, moving from the bottom up in a hierarchical fashion: pre-censorship in the preparation for the publication stage (the author's 'self- censorship', editorial control in publishing houses and print media, preliminary control by the authorities from *Holovlit*) and post-publication censorship for almost the entire duration of the book's existence in public use (control over the layout and further control by Soviet secret police agencies at the level of published works[1]), as well as control by ideological departments of the Central Committee and regional committees of the Party, which could exercise both types of control. The top-down Soviet censorship policy, on ideological and

DOI: 10.4324/9781003149453-20

The Routledge Handbook of Translation and Censorship

linguistic levels, needs to be studied in its various forms: institutional, structural and self-imposed (for a detailed study of the influence of ideology on translation, see Rudnytska 2021). From the early days of the Soviet Union, the Russian language played the exclusive role of language-mediator in the field of journalism, and for translations of political, military and scholarly literature it became a compulsory mediator in the late 1920s and early 1930s.

In the 1920s, the Ukrainian translation of literary prose, non-fiction, scientific and technical texts became widespread, and Ukrainian lexicography was standardised. Also, poetry translation into Ukrainian of the classics of world literature, including works by the ancient Greeks and Romans, developed at a rapid pace (see Kolomiyets 2015: 13–121). Dozens of special terminological dictionaries in particular, dictionaries of business, legal and military terminology, were published in various fields of science and the humanities (see Pylypchuk 2020). Introduced in 1923, Ukrainianisation—the local form of the Soviet policy of indigenisation (*korenizatsiia*) decreed by the ruling Communist Party of the Soviet Union—effectively lasted from 1925 to 1929 but formally lasted until the late 1930s. Through the Ukrainianisation of the administrative apparatus and of major state-financed institutions of the Ukrainian SSR (schools, universities, the press, etc.), Bolsheviks sought to strengthen their power in Ukraine. During the period of Ukrainianisation, translated books were published in rather large print runs (three to five thousand copies).

Numerous state and cooperative publishing houses paid translators, which enabled the emergence of professional translators of fiction into Ukrainian. One of the finest professional translators of fiction was Mykola Ivanov (b. in the 1890s – d. unknown), and in the field of fiction and philosophical literature, Valerian Pidmohylny (1901–1937). In the 1920s, there was increased demand for Ukrainian translations of world classics as readers opted to read these works in Ukrainian. This decade entered the history of Ukrainian culture as the Ukrainian National Renaissance.

At the end of the 1920s, mass repressions began against Ukrainian intellectuals. They can be divided into three stages: 1) the arrest of older Ukrainian literati and scholars on the charge of belonging to the Union for the Liberation of Ukraine, which was an organisation fabricated by the Soviet secret police; arrests started in the autumn of 1929 and culminated in the show trials staged in Kharkiv from 9 March to 19 April 1930, which targeted the leading Ukrainian linguists, who were accused of trying to separate the Ukrainian language from 'the fraternal Russian' language. This was a devastating blow to the old Ukrainian intelligentsia who had cooperated with the new government; 2) mass executions of the new Soviet intelligentsia in late 1934; and, finally, 3) the Stalinist terror of 1937–1938, which struck indiscriminately. As Ukrainian poet-translator and translation historian Strikha argues, the fate of Ukrainianisation was finally decided when Stalin proclaimed in 1934, at the Seventeenth Congress of the CPSU, that the main danger at the present stage was no longer 'Great Russian chauvinism' but 'local nationalism' (Strikha 2020:180). The Great Terror dealt an irreparable blow to the cultural landscape of Ukraine. Not only were people exiled and killed, but unlike in the 1920s when the works of writers shot by the Bolsheviks continued to appear in print, in the 1930s arrest and sentencing meant the automatic banning of a writer's books in all languages, including translations. The principles of Soviet censorship in such cases have been analysed in detail by historian Bilokin (1999: 65–74).

As early as 1931, the private translation market ceased to exist in Soviet Ukraine as all co-operative publishers (the *Knyhospilka* cooperative union was the largest) and private publishing enterprises (such as the *Rukh* publishing house and the *Chas* literary circle in Kyiv) were either banned or merged and converted into the State Publishing House of Ukraine (*Derzhavne Vydavnytstvo Ukrainy, DVU*), a mega-enterprise centred in Kharkiv, and from 1934, in Kyiv. The department of children's literature (*Dytlitvydav*) had branches in several large cities, in particular in Odesa. With the centralisation of Ukrainian publishing houses, a centralised 'state commission' (*derzhavne zamovlennia*) was introduced, which involved the formation of unified lists of authors and titles of foreign works for translation approved by the censor, including recommended circulations for various translated publications. In the late 1930s, long lists of banned publications were compiled. Forty-seven of the lists of repressed literature, which were approved in the Ukrainian SSR in 1938–1939, were preserved and have recently been published (see Bilokin 2018). Prohibition lists primarily concerned Ukrainian writers arrested and shot as directed by the authorities of the Communist Party (Bolsheviks) of Ukraine (CP(b)U), which meant that their works, including translations, could not be legally published; the writer's name was automatically banned, and all his/her works in any language were removed from libraries and bookstores.

In the 1930s, a Soviet canon of classical and contemporary Russian literature was formed, and a canonic list of foreign classics to be translated began to take shape (see Kolomiyets 2021: 7–12), which included only texts deemed 'useful' in promoting a Soviet outlook; all other Western authors were considered either unnecessary or harmful. Translation played a very active role in these processes. The censorship of translations was carried out in order to present the originals in the 'correct' light and to bring their authors closer to the ideological paradigm of a 'Soviet writer'. A series of Western writers from the late nineteenth to mid-twentieth century were 'Sovietised' through translation into Russian, such as Ethel Lilian Voynich, Jack London and Theodore Dreiser. Ukrainian (re)translations of many of Western European and American authors in the 1930s and 1940s were modeled on their 'canonical' Russian translations and showed a tendency to Russification of the Ukrainian language (Kolomiyets 2020). In 1932, the Union of Soviet Writers was founded, and in 1934 the Writers' Union of Ukraine began to operate. Conceived as a monolithic ideological and political support for the CPSU, it was granted complete control over literary output.

To bring the Ukrainian language closer to Russian, the first Soviet orthography of the Ukrainian language, which had been approved in 1928, was reformed in April–June of 1933. The 1928 Orthography, known as the Kharkiv Orthography (*Kharkivskyi pravopys*), which was a synthesis of both the Eastern-Central and Western Ukrainian (*Halychyna*) vernacular traditions, united those traditions for the first time in the history of Ukrainian language. Worked out by prominent Ukrainian linguists and writers, most of whom were later repressed, this Orthography was soon labeled as 'nationalist' by the Bolsheviks. After the resolution of the Central Committee of the CPSU(b) of 3 April 1932 'On the Suppression of Nationalism in Ukraine', a policy of de-Ukrainianisation began (aligning the Ukrainian language with Russian and excluding it from political, economic, administrative, military, journalistic, scientific and technical spheres). A total of 126 amendments were made to the new version of the orthography, and the spelling of words of foreign origin was brought into line with the Russian. The purpose of the work was generally defined as the elimination of 'nationalist spelling rules that oriented the Ukrainian language to Polish and Czech bourgeois cultures' (in Kubaichuk 2004: 86).[2] Andrii Khvylia, chairman of the Orthographic Commission of the People's Commissariat of Education, established in 1933, claimed that the previous orthography inhibited the mastery of literacy by the broad working masses and placed a barrier between the Ukrainian and Russian languages (Khvylia 1933).

A turning-point was the article by Kahanovych 'Nationalistic Distortions in the Ukrainian Translations of the Works of Lenin'. Ordered by the Communist Party, the article appeared in the academic journal *Movoznavstvo* [Language Science] in 1934, triggering a wave of publications accusing 'nationalistic translators' of semantic distortions. The article unleashed a campaign against 'nationalistic wrecking'[3] in translation. Kahanovych wrote that the meaning of Lenin's works had been falsified in the first edition of the Ukrainian translation and that the 'nationalistic translators' had pursued a course of action aimed at the 'artificial delimitation' of the Ukrainian language and its separation from Russian (Kahanovych 1934: 11).

Similar charges were then brought against most of the translators into Ukrainian in a series of articles that labeled them as 'nationalistic' or 'counter-revolutionary wreckers' and counted them among the enemies of the Party, the working class, and the working masses of Soviet Ukraine. It was a large-scale, top-down campaign. Not only were translations of works by Lenin accused of 'nationalistic wrecking' but so too were translations of ideologically inflected texts of modern Russian literature, primarily the works of Maxim Gorky and Mikhail Sholokhov (for a more detailed account, see Kalnychenko and Kalnychenko 2020). The accusations were followed by the rewriting of existing translations, not only those from Russian literature, but also from Western European and North American literatures. The new translations were purged of so-called 'archaic' elements, that is, specific Ukrainian vocabulary and phraseology, which were declared 'nationalist', and were replaced by 'internationalisms,' or, simply put, Russianisms. Eventually, on the basis of a critical article published in the newspaper *Pravda* on 4 October 1937, the Politburo of the Central Committee of the CP(b)U adopted a resolution on the need to bring the Ukrainian language and its vocabulary closer to Russian by removing words 'common with the Polish language', as well as other 'foreign words' that denote new concepts for which Russian words already exist (in Cherkaska 2013).

16.1.2   Translation and Censorship in Soviet Ukraine from WWII to the Collapse of the USSR

During the Second World War, the regime significantly relaxed censorship restrictions and exploited heroic events of national history in every possible way to spark a wave of patriotism among the Ukrainian people. Shortly after WWII, in 1948, a large-scale campaign against 'nationalist perversions' was launched, accusing the acclaimed Soviet writers Maksym Rylsky (1895–1964), Ivan Senchenko (1901–1975) and Yuri Yanovsky (1902–1954) of the offense. Shortly thereafter, the persecution of 'rootless cosmopolitans', personified by the Ukrainian poets and translators of Jewish descent Leonid Pervomaisky (1908–1973) and Sava Holovanivsky (1910–1989), gained momentum. In 1952, several members of the Jewish Anti-Fascist Committee, which had been created during WWII on the instructions of the CPSU authorities themselves, were shot dead on charges of aiding 'world imperialism and Zionism' (Strikha 2020: 255). Among those killed were the noted Jewish poets David Hofstein (1889–1952) and Lev (Leib) Kvitko (1890–1952).

Edited translations of repressed translators were republished anonymously or under the editor's name. Take, for example, translations of Nikolai Gogol's writings: No translator was mentioned in the third volume of Gogol's *Works* published in 1952, in which the translation of *Mertvi dushi* (*Dead Souls*) by Hryhorii Kosynka (1899–1934) was reprinted, and only the name of the volume editor, Ivan Senchenko, was provided on the title page. All translations that had appeared in print in the 1920s–early 1930s underwent later editing, altering them almost beyond recognition. Even the writers and translators who survived the Great Terror and managed to demonstrate their devotion to the Soviet government, as Maksym Rylsky did, could not avoid periodic accusations of 'bourgeois nationalism'. Notably, at the plenum of the board of the Writers' Union of the Ukrainian SSR, held on 15–20 September 1947, Rylsky was accused of sympathising with nationalist ideas.[4] His translations could be published in the 1930s–40s only after redaction and mostly anonymously. For example, in the 1948 edition of *Mykola Hohol. Vybrani tvory* [*Mykola Hohol. Selected Works*], Rylsky's translation of *Povist pro te, yak posvarylysia Ivan Ivanovych z Ivanom Nykyforovychem* [*The Tale of How Ivan Ivanovich Quarreled with Ivan Nikiforovich*] was published under the name of its editor, Antin Khutorian (1892–1955). Rylsky's name as the translator of this work in the late 1920s surfaced again only in the aforementioned 1952 edition.

Translations published in the Ukrainian SSR from the late 1930s on were mainly of Russian classics and works of the literatures of the peoples of the USSR. Among foreign classics and contemporary authors, only so-called 'progressive' and 'revolutionary' writers could be chosen for translation. Moreover, the tradition of translating European classics from Russian translation was established at this time. According to Strikha's apt observation, '[t]he time of a truly "Soviet" translation had come, the main purpose of which was no longer to assert the value of Ukrainian literature, but to fit it into a rigidly defined hierarchy of literatures of "fraternal peoples"' (2020: 247).

After the Second World War, in addition to translations of works 'from the fraternal literatures of the peoples of the USSR', translations from literatures of the 'socialist camp', 'people's democracies' and 'peoples struggling for liberation from colonial oppression', all typical clichés from the Soviet newspapers of the time, were officially encouraged. Such translations were made and printed en masse. Works of Russian classics in Ukrainian translations were most widely published in the first half of the 1950s (a one-volume edition of Lermontov, a three-volume edition of Gogol, four volumes of Tolstoy's novel *War and Peace*, a four-volume edition of Pushkin, and a three-volume edition of Chekhov), as well as mass publications of so-called 'proletarian' writers, primarily the works of Gorky, who had been canonised and promoted by Soviet literary scholarship. Many publishers resorted to translations done by repressed and banned writers of the mid-1920s–early 1930s, albeit unrecognisably distorted by 'corrective' redactions.

Although the repressions of the 1930s and early 1940s created an intellectual desert in the Ukrainian literary and translation fields, a new generation of professional translators was reaching maturity in the 1950s, exemplified by the appearance in Kyiv in 1955 of a highly artistic translation of Goethe's *Faust* by the brilliant young translator Mykola Lukash (1919–1988), with an introductory article by Oleksandr Biletsky (1884–1961). Lukash convincingly showed, as Strikha argues, that a 'Ukrainian translator, even referring to texts of the highest complexity, can do without the Russian "colonial mirror"' (Strikha 2020: 285). In February 1956, at a conference of the Union of Soviet Writers of Ukraine on translation, Lukash gave a report under the ideologically 'correct' title 'Progressive Western European Literature in Ukrainian Translations' (US literature was also included in the review). In his almost four-hour speech, Lukash made a detailed and in-depth analysis of 210 books by Western authors published in Ukrainian in the decade after the war. He dared to criticise the practice of translating not from the originals, but from Russian translations, openly discussing the impoverished, artificial and leveled language of the translations, as well as the negligence and low professional level of many translators. Banned, Lukash's report was not published in the proceedings of the conference, which appeared in print the following year. It was first published long after the translator's death in 1988, in honor of his 90th birthday (Lukash 2009).

The inauguration in 1958 of the literary translation journal *Vsesvit* [The Universe], which was initiated by the Writers' Union of Ukraine, marks a change in the status of literary translation into Ukrainian. There were political guidelines imposed by Soviet censorship that could not be circumvented: the works of writers of the socialist camp (then called 'people's democracies') were to make up half of the publications, and works from the 'capitalist world' had to critique the capitalist system. According to Oleh Mykytenko (1928–2020), the journal's Editor-in-Chief from 1986–2012, '[i]n addition to the usual, poetic censorship,[5] there was also the Department of Culture of the Central Committee of the Party, which further controlled the journal. In addition, there was the State Committee (*derzhkomitet*), or Head Publisher (*holovvydav*),[6] whose employees exercised a certain control over the planning of the journal as well. These were the 'shackles' for *Vsesvit*' (Mykytenko 2010). The journal also undertook to publish translations of modern 'progressive' foreign writers who had not yet been published in the USSR, as works already published in Russian could not be published in Ukrainian translation. This restriction prompted the editorial board to compete fiercely for authors and translators, and on numerous occasions the journal managed to be the first in the USSR to publish works by Nobel laureates Hermann Hesse, Albert Camus, Gabriel Garcia Marquez, William Golding, Saint-John Perce, Salvatore Quasimodo, as well as the bestselling novel *The Godfather* by Mario Puzo. It is important to note that *Vsesvit* achieved such success and popularity among readers not because Kyiv-based censorship was less stringent than Moscow-based censorship (on the contrary, censors were more diligent in Kyiv than in Moscow), but primarily due to the dedicated work of the journal's editorial board and its skillful translators (Oleksandr Terekh [1928–2013], Volodymyr Mytrofanov [1929–1998], Ivan Bilyk [1930–2012], Mar Pinchevsky [1930–1984] and many others) who raised the prestige of the Ukrainian language through their quality translations.

In the 1960s, translation into Ukrainian again played a decisive role in the process of national revival. Translations from multivolume editions of Western classics published at the turn of the 1920s and 1930s were reprinted in edited form at the turn of the 1960s and 1970s. Such editions include the 12–volume *Works* of Jack London, and the eight-volume *Works* of Guy de Maupassant (both collections published in 1969–1972). However, unlike the 1920s, when many highly educated, talented writers participated in the translation process, in the 1960s there were no more than a dozen. Although they were few, they were unique translators, each of whom translated from a dozen or more languages without cribs. Literary critics often use the word 'phenomenon' when referring to the key players in the Ukrainian translation field during the Khrushchev and Brezhnev eras (e.g., 'the phenomena' of Mykola Lukash, Hryhorii Kochur [1908–1994], Vasyl Mysyk [1907–1983], Borys Ten [1897–1983]).

Hryhorii Kochur, a close friend of Lukash, became the informal leader of the resurrected school of Ukrainian translation. In 1943, Kochur and his wife were convicted as 'enemies of the people' and sent to the Inta Corrective Labour Camp (*Intalag*) of the Gulag, which was located near the town of Inta in the Komi Autonomous SSR. Soon after his rehabilitation during the Khrushchev thaw, Kochur joined those protesting against further arrests of members of the Ukrainian intelligentsia. A polyglot translator and a powerful symbol of the resistance movement of the 1960s–1980s, Kochur had the reputation of being an 'unwavering translator'.

In the suffocating cultural atmosphere of the time, the school of literary translation headed by Kochur, which opposed the model of Ukrainian culture based on primitive folk humor and dancing, did not represent the mainstream. Moreover, public criticism of Kochur started in the early 1970s, when a new wave of arrests began and the Ukrainian school of translation was declared erroneous, fictional, polluting the language of translation, and hindering the development of 'language culture, logic of thinking and aesthetic tastes' (Bilodid 1979: 4). In 1974, the official newspaper of the Writers' Union *Literaturna Ukraina* [Literary Ukraine] declared victory over the 'Kochur-Lukash tandem', who were accused of using forbidden dictionaries and distancing the Ukrainian language from Russian (Cherniakov 2019: 190).

From then until the end of the 1970s, the names of Kochur and Lukash were totally banned. Not only were they no longer mentioned, even their students, especially Anatol Perepadia (1935–2008), began to be criticised. For example, in the 1978 anthology of Renaissance poetry *Svitanok* [*Dawn*], two sonnets by Petrarch in Kochur's translation were published under the name of Dmytro Palamarchuk (1914–1998), a close friend since the time of their imprisonment in the Inta labour camp. For Kochur, this was the only way to have his translations published. A talented poet, Palamarchuk became an outstanding poet-translator in his own right. He is the author of the first complete Ukrainian translation of Shakespeare's sonnets in the Soviet Union (published in 1966).

Even after the political climate began to soften in 1979, the ban on Kochur was completely lifted only in 1987, and in 1989 he was awarded the Maksym Rylsky Literary Prize for his achievements in the field of literary translation. The second, expanded edition of his anthology of world poetry, *Druhe vidlunnia* [*The Second Echo*], was published in 1991, and his most complete collection of translated poetry representing 33 national literatures, *Tretie vidlunnia* [*The Third Echo*], which embraces more than 130 authors and translations from 28 languages, appeared in print in the year 2000.

The 1960s were very fruitful years for Lukash as well. Boccaccio's *Decameron*, translated by Lukash and published in 1964 (reprinted with illustrations in 1968), is noteworthy. In attempting to reconstruct the stylistic richness of the Ukrainian language, the translator created a synthesis of the vernacular and the 'bookish' Ukrainian language of the Baroque period, with its specific literary and rhetorical characteristics, Latin expressions, and vocabulary taken from religious, polemical, and philosophical treatises. This language had been almost completely destroyed during the years of Russian imperial domination over Ukraine. In the words of literary critic Maryna Novykova (b. 1944), Lukash managed to reconstruct the cornucopia of Ukrainian language in 'thin layers'—as seeds of its versatile stylistic potential (Novykova 1995: 62).

On 23 March 1973, Lukash sent a letter to the heads of the legislative and judicial branches of the Ukrainian government protesting the arrest of literary scholar Ivan Dziuba, by offering to serve Dziuba's sentence himself and justifying his decision by the lack of any fundamental difference between his 'freedom' as a citizen of the Ukrainian SSR and the life of a prisoner. Specifically, he wrote: 'in this period (the end of which neither You, nor I can predict even approximately), for me personally living in any mode [either out of prison, or in prison] seems almost equivalent, therefore more or less inconsequential' (published by Cherevatenko 2002: 730). For this courageous act, Lukash was expelled from the Writers' Union of Ukraine, dismissed from the editorial board of the journal *Vsesvit*, and virtually deprived of all means of subsistence.

The ban on publishing translations by Kochur and Lukash (note: only translations, and not articles or other literary-critical materials) was lifted after the dismissal of Valentyn Malanchuk, the secretary for ideology of the Central Committee of the Communist Party of Ukraine (CPU). Malanchuk, a zealous fighter against 'nationalist activity' in Ukrainian SSR, had held this position from October 1972 to April 1979. During his first six months in office alone, he blocked the publication of more than 600 proofs of ready-to-print Ukrainian books. Malanchuk's predecessor as secretary of ideology, Fedir Ovcharenko, recalls that Moscow demanded that they 'keep in focus and intensify the struggle against Ukrainian bourgeois nationalism and accelerate the assimilation of the Ukrainian nation in every possible way' (in Radyk 2011).

Compared to the Stalin era, the political climate in Khrushchev and Brezhnev's time was somewhat less oppressive, i.e., translators were no longer persecuted or murdered for 'wrecking', or sabotage, and counter-revolution. However, the accusation of 'Ukrainian bourgeois nationalism' became new grounds for imprisonment. Until the collapse of the Soviet Union, every editor-in-chief of a publishing house or periodical received a list of undesirable Ukrainian words that could not be used. Moreover, each editor-in-chief had a list of banned names, which could not be mentioned under any circumstances. This practice lasted to varying degrees of severity until the beginning of Gorbachev's perestroika (Strikha 2020: 289). Ukrainian translation was forced to exist within the framework of Soviet colonialism until the fall of Soviet censorship and the emergence of the independent Ukrainian state in 1991.

Only a handful of Ukrainian writers, who also proved to be talented translators during the Ukrainianisation period during the 1920s and early 1930s, managed not only to survive physically during the Great Terror, but also to create strategies of coexistence with the Bolshevik regime

The Routledge Handbook of Translation and Censorship

that helped them become living classics of Soviet Ukrainian literature, such as Maksym Rylsky, Pavlo Tychyna (1891–1967) and Mykola Bazhan (1904–1983). Interestingly, these authors as well as their translations did not lose readership in the early post-Soviet period when the attention of Ukrainian readers was focused mainly on repressed and diasporic writers. This fact testifies to the high literary quality of their texts, despite the propagandistic discourse woven into them.

The system of censorship in the 1970s and 1980s, according to Ukrainian translator, historian and theorist of translation Mykhailo Moskalenko (1948–2006), who worked in several editorial offices at the time, was as follows: before the layout of a book was submitted by the publishing house to *Holovlit*, the book's editor had to write on the first page: 'Personalities checked. There are no unwanted names or characteristics', then sign and date the statement. If *Holovlit* crossed out an opinion, name, or description, the editor was obliged to inform the author that this change was the editor's own decision as it was strictly forbidden to talk about the very existence of *Holovlit*. Over the years, all cases of *Holovlit*'s interference in texts were carefully recorded by *Holovlit* itself. If the editor's 'liberalism' was noted, then in cases where such 'mistakes' were repeated, the editor was removed from the publishing house for one reason or another and was prevented from getting another so-called 'ideological job' (Moskalenko 2011: 440). That said, an average editor might not even be fully acquainted with the 'forbidden' lists, which were stored in safes.

The Soviet translation project involved blurring the distinction between the style of this or that canonical Western author and that of a mediocre Soviet writer whose works, written according to the requirements of 'socialist realism', were mostly devoid of artistic value. The regime considered all Ukrainian translators with literary talent to be their hidden opponents, even those who showed political loyalty, much like Maksym Rylsky (who in 1950 was awarded the Stalin Prize for his translation of the poem *Pan Tadeusz, czyli ostatni zajazd na Litwie* [*Pan Tadeusz, or the Last Foray in Lithuania*] by Polish poet Adam Mickiewicz) and Mykola Bazhan (a recipient in 1939 of the Order of Lenin for his translation of the epic poem *Vepkhist'q'aosani* [*The Knight in the Panther Skin*] by the medieval Georgian poet Shota Rustaveli). After all, thanks to talented translations of world classics, the Ukrainian literary language had been established and continued to develop even after the purges of the 1930s and 1940s, despite the fact that Kremlin ideology forced it into a state of maximum lexical and grammatical duplication of the Russian language, in an attempt to turn it into a superfluous, redundant language. Its disappearance in the communist future seemed obvious and predictable, insofar as the Ukrainian language was not used at all in key areas of public life, such as defense, government, industry, statistical reporting, health, transportation and communications, all of which were controlled by the All-Union ministries.

Translation was of particular importance to Ukrainian political prisoners and dissidents during the 1960s, 1970s and 1980s as the only opportunity for artistic self-expression. Among prominent Ukrainian writers who occupied themselves with translation during their Soviet imprisonment were Valerian Pidmohylny and Mykola Zerov (1890–1937) in the mid-1930s, Hryhorii Kochur and Dmytro Palamarchuk in the 1940s and 1950s, and Ivan Svitlychny (1929–1992) and Vasyl Stus (1938–1985) in the 1970s and 1980s. The Soviet government was careful to minimise contact between political prisoners and the world outside the prison, including close relatives and friends. Prisoners were secretly, but strictly, forbidden from literary activities (unless, of course, it was propaganda for the glory of the Communist Party); however, local administrators and censors of the prisoners' private correspondence tolerated literary translation. Therefore, there were cases when imprisoned poets disguised their original works as translations in letters sent to their relatives and friends, hoping to save them from destruction. At the same time, true translations were also sent to the outside world in this way; however, they, too, aroused suspicion and were quite often

Translation and Censorship in Soviet and Independent Ukraine

censored. Notably, Ukrainian poet and dissident Ivan Svitlychny copied some of his own poems and the poems of his fellow prisoners, disguised as translations, in several private letters to his wife (Svitlychny 2001).

Translations of Rilke and Goethe by the noted Ukrainian dissident poet Stus turned into a series of dramatic episodes in the history of translation. Stus began to translate his favorite poets in the Kyiv remand prison, where he received permission to obtain Goethe's originals together with a dictionary of the German language. He continued his translation work while imprisoned in the Mordovian (1972–1977) and Ural (1981–1985) labour camps. Translations from Goethe became an organic part of his collection *Chas tvorchosti / Dichtenszeit* (1972). In his first letter from the Mordovian camp (dated 17 December 1972), Stus asked his wife to hand-copy Rilke's poems for him in her letters (Stus 1997: 11). To prevent any possible loss during the various inspections Soviet prisoners were subjected to, Stus wrote out the German originals in a separate notebook because private letters were not only censored but were also frequently confiscated, together with translations. Once Stus asked his friend Mykhailyna Kotsiubynska (1931–2011) to send him a metric scheme of the elegiac distich. The censors suspected cryptography, or so-called 'conventions' in the text, in the standard metrical signs for alternation of long and short syllables (in Stus 1997: 30–1). Under this pretext, the letter was confiscated. It is obvious that the confiscation of translations, as well as private letters containing handwritten originals and/or translations, was not provoked by the censors' suspicion of the foreign author since only permitted authors were chosen for translation. An unmotivated confiscation was an act of intellectual and psychological violence against Soviet prisoners of conscience and had a punitive goal—to demonstrate the complete worthlessness of a 'non-Soviet' person to the Soviet political system.

The Ukrainian school of literary translation, which was developed by Zerov, Rylsky and Pidmohylny, as well as dozens of other talented writers of the national revival period of the 1920s, who had been executed or psychologically broken by the system in the 1930s, was revived in the 1950s and 1960s by such powerful figures as Lukash, Kochur, Mysyk and Borys Ten. Moreover, a new generation of highly skilled translators, like Perepadia and Moskalenko, was nurtured. Despite the political reaction of the 1970s, these translators carried on the nation-building function of literary translation until the period of independence, preparing Ukrainian society for the tectonic shifts that took place in the late 1980s and early 1990s.

16.1.3   *Translation and Censorship in Independent Ukraine*

As Mykytenko noted, since the fall of censorship in 1988, 'the widest horizons of world literature have opened' up to Ukrainian readers, and previously banned names of Western thinkers have begun to appear (Mykytenko 2010). It is noteworthy that in 1989, two years before the proclamation of Ukraine's independence, the Communist Party leadership of the Ukrainian SSR decided to honor the demands of the nationally-oriented intelligentsia by making Ukrainian the official language. Deputies of the Verkhovna Rada of the 11th convocation, under pressure from CPU Secretary Volodymyr Ivashko and Verkhovna Rada Presidium Chairman Valentyna Shevchenko, passed, almost unanimously, the Law 'On Languages in the Ukrainian SSR' and an amendment to the Constitution of the Ukrainian SSR, which proclaimed Ukrainian the only state language in the republic.

At the turn of the millennium, the Ukrainian school of literary translation continued to develop through the translations of Anatolii Onyshko (1940–2006), Maksym Strikha (b. 1961), Yurii Andrukhovych (b. 1960), and other intellectuals, whose individual writing styles had been formed during the Soviet era. Since the 2000s, many new translators have appeared who have no direct connection to the Soviet era. Their numbers increased especially in the second half of the 2010s, a period described by Strikha as a 'boom' time in the field of translation (2020: 444). The tendency established by Soviet censorship of using a Russian translation either as a model for imitation, or even in place of the original had become a 'bad habit' among some publishers in post-Soviet Ukraine, who tolerated indirect translations from Russian instead of commissioning direct translations from the source language (for a more detailed account, see Kolomiyets 2019). Concurrently, during the first two decades of the post-Soviet period, translations of modern Russian prose were extremely rare and mainly in the field of children's literature. The publication of a Ukrainian translation of the novel *Zhizn' i neobychainye priklyucheniya soldata Ivana Chonkina* [*The Life and Unusual Adventures of Soldier Ivan Chonkin*], by Russian dissident writer Vladimir Voinovich in 1992 (before a separate Russian edition) is a rather happy exception to the rule. According to the UNESCO *Index Translationum*, only a few adult books by Russian authors, such as Boris Akunin and Viktor Suvorov, were translated into Ukrainian from 1992 to 2010. Among the classics, Ukrainians have shown interest mostly in Gogol, but predominantly as a Ukrainian-born writer.

Translations of Gogol's works from the late 1920s and early 1930s were reprinted in the 2000s and branded as classics (Hohol 2009). In the 2010s, a new multicultural dialogue emerged in the field of Ukrainian literary translation, based on translations of works by contemporary authors from the former Soviet republics who write in Russian (such as Svetlana Alexievich, Oleg Panfilov and Maryam Petrosyan). During that same period, only those contemporary Russian writers who openly condemned the Kremlin's policy toward Ukraine (e.g., Lyudmila Ulitskaya) or who parodied Putin's regime (e.g., Vladimir Sorokin) have been translated (for a more detailed account, see Kolomiyets and Kalnychenko 2024).

The book market is not only a component of the country's market economy, but also a part of its humanitarian security system. With the beginning of Russia's hybrid war in Ukraine in 2014, and in the wake of the rising patriotic sentiment in Ukraine caused by this war, there was a growing demand for books in the Ukrainian language, including translated editions. In December 2016, the Verkhovna Rada of Ukraine adopted the Law 'On Amendments to Certain Laws of Ukraine Concerning Restrictions on Access to the Ukrainian Market of Foreign Printed Products of Anti-Ukrainian Content'. This Law provides for the introduction of a permission procedure for the importation of publications from Russia into Ukraine. From 1 January 2017, when the Law came into effect, the products of Russian publishing houses could legally enter Ukraine only after passing an assessment by the expert council of the State Committee for Television and Radio Broadcasting. This made it difficult to import Russian books, including translations into Russian published in the aggressor country. In March 2021, the Verkhovna Rada of Ukraine adopted a resolution on the escalation of the Russo-Ukrainian armed conflict, which officially recognised that Ukraine was at war with the Russian Federation.[7]

The role of translation as a guardian of the Ukrainian language and identity has been extremely important in the transition of Ukrainian society as a whole and its cultural products from a post-colonial to a decolonised state of development, which has been taking place for more than three decades, accelerating since 2014 with Russia's open war on Ukraine, aimed at the destruction of Ukrainian statehood and everything Ukrainian, which on 24 February 2022, turned into the brazen genocide of the Ukrainian people.

Censorship measures aimed at limiting Russian influence in Ukraine were recently strengthened with the help of a number of resolutions and laws, in particular the Law of Ukraine 'On the

Prohibition of Propaganda of the Russian Nazi Totalitarian Regime, the Armed Aggression of the Russian Federation as a Terrorist State against Ukraine, Symbols of the Military Invasion of the Russian Nazi Totalitarian Regime in Ukraine', which was signed by the President of Ukraine on 22 May 2022 (No. 2265-IX) and the Law of Ukraine 'On the Condemnation and Prohibition of Propaganda of Russian Imperial Policy in Ukraine and Decolonisation of Toponymy', signed by the President of Ukraine on 21 March 2023 (No. 3005-IX).

Therefore, in independent Ukraine, political censorship was introduced gradually after the Russian Federation annexed Crimea and began sponsoring a proxy war in Donbas in 2014, and from February 2022 with the expansion of Russia's war against Ukraine, several laws were adopted prohibiting propaganda of Russian imperial policy in Ukraine.

16.2   Core Issues and Topics

The publishing process in the USSR was the institutional basis of multi-layered and scattered censorship in the broadest sense. In the vast majority of cases, the work of the censors was performed by the authors and editors themselves using self-censorship. Therefore, the figure of the editor appears as a key cultural and ideological mediator and agent of mass Russification. Censorship became so widespread that after World War II and later into the era of late socialism, it coexisted almost 'peacefully' with interpretive communities that tried to circumvent it by finding ways to read 'between the lines' and learning to ignore the interference of the translator, editor and censor. At the institutional level, Russification was inexorably successful, because it was carried out not only with the help of censorship but also by such broad means as language policy, education policy and demographic policy, which included movement of the workforce within the USSR, forced migrations and deportations. The systematic suppression of key Ukrainian linguists, lexicographers, writers, teachers, translators, public and cultural figures also significantly contributed to the implementation of Russification.

However, during the decade of the 'Ukrainian Renaissance' and particularly in the late 1920s and early 1930s, public debates arose regarding the inadmissibility or, vice versa, the appropriateness of Soviet censorship in translations, especially of works from the capitalist world. Volodymyr Derzhavyn (1899–1964), for instance, condemns the Soviet ideological censorship of translations when passages directed against the French Revolution were expunged from the classic works of Victor Hugo, and the very fact of their excision was concealed (1929: 140). Ivan Kulyk (1897–1937), the compiler and translator of *Antolohiia amerykanskoi poezii. 1855–1925* [*The Anthology of American Poetry. 1855–1925*] and a member of the Central Committee of the All-Union Communist Party of Bolsheviks, on the contrary, insists in his foreword that the ideological substratum of the translation process justifies deviations from the source texts, arguing that 'the verses of American poets, if translated accurately, would have had one sense in New York and another in Kharkiv' (Kulyk 1928/2011: 486).

Since the early 1930s, when the essence of culture became identified with ideology, the ideological aspect of translation (due to the general ideological bias of Soviet scholarship) has occupied an important place in Soviet translation research: all other aspects of translation were treated from an ideological perspective, and literary translation was recognised as an important instrument of ideological struggle. As a result, the selection of works to be translated and the method of translation were considered effective tools of ideological control (Rudnytska 2021: 17). Despite that fact, the topic 'translation and censorship' was not discussed, with the exception of occasional publications in diaspora. Thus, Oswald Burghardt (1891–1947), the general editor of the complete 27-volume Ukrainian collection of the works of Jack London (1928–1932), who had emigrated by that time, condemned the censorship of translation in Soviet Ukraine as a means of preserving the antihuman regime (1939).

The period from 1933 to 1935 witnessed numerous publications in the press (by N. Kahanovych, A. Shevchenko, Ye. Kasianenko, A. Paniv) condemning 'nationalistic wrecking' in translation—of both political and fictional texts—accusing the translators of nationalistic distortion and counter-revolutionary actions aimed at separating the Ukrainian language from Russian (Kalnychenko and Kalnychenko 2020). The campaign triggered the censorship policy of revising and rewriting formerly published translations to make them as close as possible to Russian; it also resulted in a flow of retranslations and relay translations from Russian.

The rejection of Russification through translation took the shape of opposition to slavish literalism and indirect translations, expressed by several translators at the All-Ukrainian confer-ence of literary translators in February 1956 (Mykola Lukash, Oleksa Kundzich [1904–1964], Stepan Kovhaniuk [1902–1982] and others) (see, e.g., Kovhaniuk 1957; Lukash 2009). It was Ivan Dziuba (1931–2022) who, using Marxist phraseology, openly opposed Russification in his book *Internatsionalizm chy rusyfikatsiia? [Internationalism or Russification?]* written in 1965 and spread via *samvydav (samizdat)*. The book analyses Soviet national and cultural policy in Ukraine, arguing that during Stalin's rule the CPSU had moved to a position of Russian chauvinism; Dziuba convincingly demonstrated the hypocrisy of the Soviet system with its slogans proclaiming 'the friendship of Soviet nations' and the actual reality of the Ukrainian nation being ruthlessly destroyed. The bans and restrictions on the Ukrainian language during Ukraine's membership in the USSR have been documented by Dziuba (1965), Shevelov (1989), Masenko (2005) and others—as the continuation of restrictions on the Ukrainian language in Russian-ruled Ukraine before 1917, though in updated forms and with different consequences. Nahaylo and Swoboda (1990), in particular, investigated Soviet nationality policy, including translation and censorship.

After the collapse of the USSR, scholars gained access to the secret KGB archives in Ukraine. Consequently, the book by Bilokin (1999; expanded edition 2017), a result of scrupulous arch-ival research into the means and mechanisms of Bolshevik terror, contains a special chapter titled 'An outline of Soviet censorship', covering the period from 1917 to 1941. It tells the story of the uneven and tragic confrontation of Ukrainian intellectual elites and representatives of the Soviet state with the ruling party, who sought to subdue or destroy everything they could not control.

The impact of censorship on translation and via translation was an integral part of state policy in the Soviet Union. In addition to this dark side of translation, however, there was also a bright side, documented by historians of translations in the USSR. For instance, Zorivchak (1934–2018) rightly asserts that the modern history of Ukraine has witnessed translations playing a compen-satory role for the country's own literature, which was being purposefully and systematically destroyed (Zorivchak 2001). In his historiography of the Ukrainian translation tradition, Strikha (2006) maintains that, for the most part, Ukrainian translation has been a conscious project of anti-colonial resistance and nation building under pressure from the Russian imperial centre. The first book-length history of Ukrainian translation studies by Shmiher (2009) also contains many pages about personal censorship and deals with the complete exclusion from the scholarly literature of an entire generation of translation scholars of the 1920s and 1930s, namely, Derzhavyn, Zerov, Hryhorii Maifet (1903–1975), Burghardt, Fylypovych (1891–1937), Kulyk and others.

The 1996 democratic Constitution of Ukraine prohibits censorship (Article 15) and protects the right to freedom of thought and speech, as well as the free expression of one's views and beliefs (Article 34) (Ukraine's Constitution of 1996 with Amendments through 2016). Concurrently, print media has shown a tendency toward self-censorship in matters believed to be sensitive to their

Translation and Censorship in Soviet and Independent Ukraine

readership, as Olshanskaya (2008) demonstrates in her case study of articles on the Iraq war in Ukraine's most influential newspaper *Weekly Mirror*, published in Ukrainian, Russian and English. Olshanskaya's study reveals that information transfer to the East and to the West underwent different forms of censorship: translations packaged for an Eastern readership were accompanied by different illustrations than those packaged for Western audiences; English translations were more circumscribed than translations into Russian; moreover, half of the articles were removed from the English edition.

The optimal combination of state regulation and the free market in the development of Ukrainian book publishing and translation has become one of the main topics for discussion in independent, post-colonial Ukraine. Since August 1991, the de-Russification of the Ukrainian language has been taking place slowly but surely through the revision of existing translations of world classics as well as bi-lingual and special dictionaries with the aim of returning to the best lexicographic sources and artistic translations from the period of the national renaissance, which had been either directly prohibited, or considered undesirable in the Soviet era, by promoting their creative assimilation and the further development of the Ukrainian school of translation. Strategies of decolonising Ukrainian language, literature, translation, and lexicography while resisting and subverting Russia's neo-colonising efforts have been among the most burning issues since the early 1990s (Motyl 1993; Kobets 2001).

The Security Service of Ukraine opened the archives of the Ukrainian branch of the former State Security Committee of the Soviet Union for public access. Many secret materials were made public, in particular, regarding the persecution of translator-dissidents in Soviet Ukraine (see, for example, Ovsiienko 2013).

At first glance, the censorial issues of translating from Ukrainian, especially into world languages, turned out to be less urgent, but in the long run, no less important for the formation and perception of Ukraine's image in the world, given Russia's powerful and multisectoral information war against Ukraine (Smyth 2009).

16.3   New Debates

New scholarship on translation and censorship in Ukraine have appeared over the past decade. The period of the Ukrainian Renaissance, which developed in Soviet Ukraine during the decade of the 1920s–early1930s, is particularly attractive to modern researchers as a phenomenon of large-scale Ukrainian linguistic and cultural revival under conditions of Russia's weakening colonial grip. Following the Bolshevik takeover in 1917, the short-lived Ukrainian People's Republic (1917–1921), established in the former Russian Ukraine, gave birth to a brief flowering of Ukrainian language, literature, and culture. The Bolshevik nationalities policy of 'indigenisation' was terminated in the early 1930s, having degenerated into Russian national Bolshevism (Brandenberger 2002) with Stalin's and later Brezhnev's campaigns against 'bourgeois nationalism' in the Union republics.

Bilokin's collection of documents (2018) contains lists of books published in Soviet Ukraine in the 1920s and 1930s, which were to be removed from libraries and destroyed. The lists were prepared by *Holovlit* and, in line with the needs of librarians and censors of that time, they were divided according to theme and the 'degree' of a text's link to 'public enemies' (books by 'public enemies' (including translations), books with prefaces by 'public enemies' (translated books usually contained a foreword), books that mention 'public enemies' and so on).

Kolomiyets' monograph (2015) is a scrupulous and detailed bio-bibliographic presentation of literary translation into the Ukrainian language in the 1920s and 1930s, with portraits of 55 translators of the generation of the 'Executed Renaissance'.[8] Kolomiyets' recent publications deal with the assimilatory influence on translation of the ideologies of Sovietisation, Proletarianisation, and Russification in Soviet Ukraine from the 1930s through the 1950s, implemented by all agents in the translation process via retranslations and revised translations (Kolomiyets 2020), and the Soviet regime's use of indirect translation as techniques and tactics of domination (Kolomiyets 2019, 2023).

Noteworthy are the monographs of individual dissident translators. The book by Savchyn (2014) examines the work of Mykola Lukash, a leading Ukrainian twentieth-century translator, whose case exemplifies the clash between the individual translator's agency and institutionalised agency, which in a totalitarian society was used as a means of state control, power, and coercion. The monograph by Hrytsiv (2017) presents a holistic picture of the polyglot translator Vasyl Mysyk, an important intellectual in the context of twentieth-century Ukrainian culture.

The recently published monograph by Rudnytska (2021) is an especially valuable work of research on the influence of state ideology on the censorship of artistic translations, including censorial powers, agents, channels and mechanisms. Rudnytska's 2023 article considers de-Sovietisation as an important issue on the post-Soviet Ukrainian agenda; the research material provided includes data on the translated texts published in contemporary Ukraine in the state bibliographical index and the catalogues of the leading Ukrainian publishers of foreign literature as well as para- and metatexts (translators and editors' commentaries, interviews and publications in media).

Strikha's new historiographic research on Ukrainian literary translation and translators (2020) is a great source of information in the field of genre translation. In this regard, of particular interest is chapter six, 'A case study: Maksym Rylsky as a Translator of Opera Librettos (the Literary, Artistic, and Nation-building Dimensions)' (2020: 347–426), which is essentially a history of Ukrainian opera translation. The chapter dwells on the 1930s through the 1970s, when translated operas in particular suffered not only from the intrusion of censors who demanded that 'nationalistic' lexical items be avoided but also from the intrusion of the singers themselves, many of whom insisted on wording that was phonetically similar to the Russian originals or to Russian translations of Western operas.

Dzera's monograph (2017) offers an overview of Ukrainian translations of the Bible, highlighting their ideological divergencies and the impact of censorship on the publication and distribution of these translations in Ukraine. The author demonstrates that official bans, silence surrounding Ukrainian Bible translations and gaps in its reception by the targeted receiver have become fundamental in revealing the translation policy in the colonial religious and cultural contexts. In their chronology of Ukrainian biblical and liturgical translation, Dzera and Shmiher (2023) applied the principles of compilation which are quite easy to extrapolate to other branches of Ukrainian translation.

If historically Russian-Ukrainian translation has often been a 'channel of colonisation', to use Robinson's phrase (1997), after 24 February 2022, this channel of colonisation is likely to be forgotten in Ukraine for many years. It has been destroyed by the Russian armed aggression and genocidal crimes. After 'the Bucha massacre'[9] and other similar war crimes committed by Russia, the attitudes of Ukrainian citizens have changed not only toward Russia as a state, but also toward 'classic' Russian literature, which Ukrainian intellectual leaders directly accuse of fostering a sense of superiority, xenophobia and militarism, as well as spreading imperialist myths (Zabuzhko 2022).

Further Reading

Dziuba, Ivan. 1968. *Internationalism or Russification? A Study in the Soviet Nationalities Problem.* London: Weidenfeld & Nicolson.

The famous Ukrainian literary critic and dissident convincingly demonstrates that the Communist Party authorities chose the chauvinistic strategy of elaborate censorship of the cultural reserves of indigenous peoples as one of their principal belligerent campaigns, purposefully increasing the pace and scope of Russification of the Ukrainian and other non-Russian nationalities of the Soviet Union.

Kalnychenko, Oleksandr and Kolomiyets, Lada. 2022. 'Translation in Ukraine during the Stalinist Period: Literary Translation Policies and Practices', in C. Rundle, A. Lange and D. Monticelli (eds.), *Translation under Communism.* Basingstoke: Palgrave Macmillan, 141–72.

The chapter offers a general overview of the field of literary translation of Western and Russian authors in Soviet Ukraine since the early 1920s until the mid-1950s and shows how the Stalinist regime attempted to openly regulate literary expression in translated books, including not only textual choices and source language, but also translation methods.

Kalnychenko, Oleksandr and Kalnychenko, Nataliia. 2020. 'Campaigning against the "Nationalistic Wrecking" in Translation in Ukraine in the mid-1930s', in L. Harmon and D. Osuchowska (eds.), *Translation and Power.* Peter Lang Gmbh, Internationaler Verlag Der Wissenschaften, 53–60.

The chapter describes the Stalinist campaign against translators, which is unique in the world history of censorship, during which the 'translator-wreckers' were blamed for 'nationalistic distortions' of the works of Vladimir Lenin and other 'classics' of Marxism-Leninism, together with Russian writers of the nineteenth century and Soviet authors.

Kolomiyets, Lada. 2023. 'The Politics of Literal Translation in Soviet Ukraine: The Case of Gogol's "The Tale of How Ivan Ivanovich Quarreled with Ivan Nikiforovich"', *Translation and Interpreting Studies: The Journal of the American Translation and Interpreting Studies Association,* 18(3): 325–59.

The article discusses the dynamics of translation—from creative stylisation to awkward literalism—during the period from the late 1920s to the early 1950s. The study reveals a tension between Ukrainian national idealism and the Soviet regime's pragmatic use of language as a means of political propaganda.

Kolomiyets, Lada and Kalnychenko, Oleksandr. 2024. 'Translating Russian Literature in Soviet and Post-Soviet Ukraine', in M. Maguire and C. McAteer (eds.), *Translating Russian Literature in the Global Context.* Cambridge: Open Book Publishers, 295–320.

The chapter describes Russian-Ukrainian literary translation from the early 1920s to the early 2020s within the so-called 'common cultural space'. The study distinguishes nine stages in Russian-Ukrainian translation, which has both bright and dark sides: on the one hand, it allowed Ukrainian writers to absorb the experience of Russian culture, its literary forms and ideas, thereby contributing to the advancement of Ukrainian literature, and on the other hand, through the Russian language and translations from Russian, the Soviet cultural space was established, which was deliberately isolated from the world cultural space and was supposed to replace it, contributing to the Russification of the Ukrainian language and the provincialisation of Ukrainian literature.

Notes

1. These agencies had different names (and abbreviations) throughout the history of the Soviet Union: GPU (1922–23), OGPU (1923–34), NKVD (1934–46), MGB (1946–53), KGB (1954–91).
2. All direct quotations from the texts written in Ukrainian are translated in this article by the authors.
3. This term meant the distancing of the Ukrainian language from Russian at the grammatical, lexical and syntactic levels; 'wrecking' in translation was equated to 'wrecking' in any other sphere of Stalin's national economy.
4. In early October 1947, the newspaper *Radianska Ukraina* published an article on his nationalist mistakes. Having been accused of 'bourgeois objectivism', the lack of Bolshevik ideology, and dependence on the influence of 'bourgeois-nationalist' worldview, Rylsky was forced to repent publicly. On 11 December 1947, the newspaper *Literaturna gazeta* published his 'penitent' article 'On Nationalist Mistakes in My Literary Work'.

The Routledge Handbook of Translation and Censorship

5 'Poetic censorship' refers to the manipulation with the aesthetics of a literary work, i.e., its expressive means, and through them, the manipulation with the most important function of the literary language, namely the poetic function, which relates to the writer's intent to influence the reader and evoke certain feelings of beauty and creativity using linguo-stylistic forms and resources.
6 Main Department of Publishing and Printing Industry of the Ministry of Culture of the Ukrainian SSR.
7 'Resolution on the Escalation of the Russo-Ukrainian Armed Conflict' (adopted by the Verkhovna Rada of Ukraine on 30 March 2021), https://zakon.rada.gov.ua/laws/show/1356-20#Text.
8 The term denotes the extinction of the Ukrainian intellectual elite, starting from the early 1930s and especially during the Great Terror of 1937–1938, which effectively destroyed the newly established infrastructure of Ukrainian culture and conditioned its maldevelopment for decades to come.
9 The atrocities perpetrated by the Russian troops in Bucha in March 2022 have become an indelible part of the global lexicon.

References

Bilodid, Ivan. 1979. 'Pro kryterii yakosti perekladu' [On the Quality Criteria of Translation], *Teoriia i praktyka perekladu* [Theory and Practice of Translation] 1: 3–4. Kyiv: Vyshcha shkola.

Bilokin, Serhii. 1999. *Masovyi teror yak zasib derzhavnoho upravlinnia v SRSR* (1917–1941 rr.): Dzhereloznavche doslidzhennia [Mass Terror as a Means of Public Administration in the USSR (1917–1941 Years): Source Research], vol. 1. Kyiv: The Petro Mohyla Kyiv Scientific Society.

Bilokin, Serhii. 2018. *Spysok represovanoi literatury* [List of Repressed Literature]. Kyiv: Ukrainski propilei.

Brandenberger, David. 2002. *National Bolshevism: Stalinist Mass Culture and the Formation of Modern Russian National Identity, 1931–1956*, vol. 93. Russian Research Center Studies. Harvard University Press.

Burghardt, Oswald. 1939. 'Bolshevytska spadshchyna' [The Bolsheviks' Legacy], *Vistnyk* 1(2): 94–99.

Cherevatenko, Leonid. 2002. 'Spodivaius, nikhto ne skazhe, shcho ya ne znaiu ukrainskoi movy' (pisliamova) ['I Hope No One will Say That I Do Not Know the Ukrainian Language' (Afterword)], in O. I. Skopnenko and T. V. Tsymbalyuk (eds.), *Frazeolohiia perekladiv Mykoly Lukasha: slovnyk-dovidnyk* [Phraseology of Translations by Mykola Lukash: A Dictionary-Reference Book]. Kyiv: Dovira, 711–34.

Cherkaska, Hanna. 2013. 'Mova – derzhavy osnova' [Language as the Foundation of the State], *Ukrainskyi pohliad*, 4 September 2013. http://ukrpohliad.org/national-memory/mova-derzhavy-osnova.html

Cherniakov, Borys Ivanovych. 2019. 'Mykola Lukash na storinkakh perekladoznavchoi krytyky i v pryzhyttievykh publikatsiiakh' [Mykola Lukash on the Pages of Translation Criticism and in Lifetime Publications], in L. M. Chernovatyi and V. I. Karaban (eds.), *Mykola Lukash – Mozart ukrainskoho perekladu: biohrafichno- bibliohrafichnyi ta mystetskyi narys* [Mykola Lukash – Mozart of Ukrainian Translation: Biographical-Bibliographic and Artistic Essay], 2nd ed. Vinnytsia: Nova Knyha, 100–216.

Derzhavyn, Volodymyr. 1929. [Retsenziia na kn.:] [Review of the Book:] Hugo, V. Bug-Jargal. *Krytyka*, 2: 239–142. Reprint in O.A. Kalnychenko and Yu.Yu. Poliakova 2015 (eds.), *Volodymyr Mykolayovych Derzhavyn. Pro mystetstvo perekladu: Statti ta retsenzii 1927–1931 rokiv* [On the Art of Translation: Essays and Reviews of 1927–1931 Years]. Vinnytsia: Nova Knyha, 138–142.

Dzera, Oksana. 2017. *Bibliina intertekstualnist i pereklad: anhlo-ukrainskyi kontekst* [Biblical Intertextuality and Translation: The Anglo-Ukrainian Context]. Lviv: Ivan Franko National University of Lviv.

Dzera, Oksana and Shmiher, Taras. 2023. *Khronolohiia bibliinoho ta liturhiinoho perekladu v Ukraini* [A Chronology of Ukrainian Biblical and Liturgical Translation]. Lviv: Ivan Franko National University of Lviv; Shevchenko Scientific Society.

Dziuba, Ivan. 1965. *Internatsionalizm chy rusyfikatsiia?* [Internationalism or Russification?]. Samvydav (Samizdat).

Hohol, Mykola. 2009. *Povisti Hoholia. Naikrashchi ukrainski pereklady u dvokh tomakh. Za redaktsiieiu Ivana Malkovycha* [Stories of Hohol. The best Ukrainian translations in two volumes. Edited by Ivan Malkovych]. Kyiv: A-BA-BA-HA-LA-MA-HA.

Hrytsiv, Nataliia. 2017. *Vasyl Mysyk. Riznohrannyi diamant ukrainskoho khudozhnioho perekladu* [Vasyl Mysyk. A Multifaceted Diamond of Ukrainian Literary Translation]. Vinnytsia: Nova Knyha.

Kahanovych, Naum. 1934. 'Natsionalistychni perekruchennia v ukrainskykh perekladakh tvoriv Lenina' [Nationalistic Distortions in Ukrainian Translations of the Works of Lenin], *Movoznavstvo* 2: 9–24.

Kalnychenko, Oleksandr and Kalnychenko, Nataliia. 2020. 'Campaigning Against the "Nationalistic Wrecking" in Translation in Ukraine in the Mid-1930s', in L. Harmon and D. Osuchowska (eds.), *Translation and Power*. Peter Lang Gmbh, Internationaler Verlag Der Wissenschaften.

Kalnychenko, Oleksandr and Kolomiyets, Lada. 2022. 'Translation in Ukraine During the Stalinist Period: Literary Translation Policies and Practices', in C. Rundle, A. Lange and D. Monticelli (eds.), *Translation Under Communism*. Basingstoke: Palgrave Macmillan, 141–72.

Khvylia, Andrii. 1933. 'Vykorinyty, znyshchyty natsionalistychne korinnia na movnomu frontì' [Eradicate, Destroy Nationalist Roots on the Language Front], *Bilshovyk Ukrainy*: *Partvydav* [published by the Central Committee of the CP(b)U], 7: 42–56.

Kobets, Svitlana. 2001. 'Ukraine', in D. Jones (ed.), *Censorship: A World Encyclopedia*. London: Fitzitroy Dearborn Publishers, 2492–5.

Kolomiyets, Lada. 2015. *Ukrainskyi khudozhnii pereklad ta perekladachi 1920-30-kh rokiv: Materialy do kursu 'Istoriia perekladu'* [Ukrainian Literary Translation and Translators in the 1920s–1930s: 'History of Translation' Course Materials]. Vinnytsia: Nova Knyha.

Kolomiyets, Lada. 2019. 'The Psycholinguistic Factors of Indirect Translation in Ukrainian Literary and Religious Contexts', *East European Journal of Psycholinguistics*, 6(2): 32– 49.

Kolomiyets, Lada. 2020. 'Translation as an Instrument of Russification in Soviet Ukraine', in L. Harmon and D. Osuchowska (eds.), *Translation and Power*. Peter Lang Gmbh, Internationaler Verlag Der Wissenschaften, 29–43.

Kolomiyets, Lada. 2021. 'Pershodruk materialiv Mykoly Zerova z arkhivu Hryhoriya Kochura' [First Publication of the Materials of Mykola Zerov from the Archive of Hryhoriy Kochur: "A List of Works of Foreign Literature That Should be Translated in the First Place" and "Course Syllabus *Methods of Translation*"], *Bulletin of Taras Shevchenko National University of Kyiv: Foreign Philology*, 1(53): 5–15.

Kolomiyets, Lada. 2023. 'The Politics of Literal Translation in Soviet Ukraine: The Case of Gogol's "The Tale of How Ivan Ivanovich Quarreled with Ivan Nikiforovich"', *Translation and Interpreting Studies: The Journal of the American Translation and Interpreting Studies Association*, 18(3): 325–59.

Kolomiyets, Lada and Kalnychenko, Oleksandr. 2024. 'Translating Russian Literature in Soviet and Post-Soviet Ukraine', in M. Maguire and C. McAteer (eds.), *Translating Russian Literature in the Global Context*. Cambridge: Open Book Publishers, 281–305.

Kovhaniuk, Stepan (ed.). 1957. *Pytannia perekladu: z materialiv respublikanskoi narady perekladachiv (liutyi 1956)* [Issues of Translations: Proceedings of the All-Ukrainian Meeting of Translators (February 1956)]. Kyiv: Derzhlitvydav.

Kubaichuk, Victor. 2004. *Khronolohiia movnykh podiy v Ukraini (zovnishnia istoriia ukrainskoi movy)* [Chronology of Language Events in Ukraine (External History of the Ukrainian Language)]. Kyiv: K.I.S.

Kulyk, Ivan 1928. 'Suchasna poeziia Pivnichnoi Ameryky: Peredmova' [Modern Poetry of the North America. Foreword], in I. Kulyk (comp.). *Antolohiia amerykanskoi poezii 1855– 1925*. Kharkiv: DVU, 9–38. Reprint in *Kalnychenko & Poliakova* 2011, 483–6.

Lukash, Mykola. 2009. 'Prohresyvna zakhidnoievropeiska literatura v perekladakh na ukrainsku movu (Dopovid na naradi Spilky Radianskykh Pysmennykiv Ukrainy v spravi khudozhnikh perekladiv 16– 18 liutoho 1956 roku) – vidnovleno B. I. Chernyakovym' [Progressive Western European Literature in Translations into Ukrainian (Report at the Meeting of the Union of Soviet Writers of Ukraine on Literary Translations on February 16–18, 1956) – Restored by B. I. Cherniakov], in L. M. Chernovaty and V. I. Karaban (eds.), *Mykola Lukash – Mozart ukrainskoho perekladu* [Mykola Lukash – Mozart of Ukrainian Translation]. Vinnytsia: Nova Knyha, 190–232.

Masenko, Larysa (ed.). 2005. *Ukrainska mova u XX storichchi: Istoriia linhvotsydu. Dokumenty i materialy* [The Ukrainian Language in the XX century: History of Linguicide. Documents and Materials]. Kyiv: Vydavnychyi dim "Kyievo-Mohylianska akademiia".

Moskalenko, Mykhailo. 2011. 'Notatky na berehakh rukopysu (cherven – lypen 2005 roku)' [Notes on the Margins of the Manuscript (June–July 2005)], in M. Labinskyi (ed.), *Statti. Publitsystyka. Spohady pro Mykhaila Moskalenka* [Articles. Journalism. Memories of Mykhailo Moskalenko]. Kyiv: Solomiia Pavlychko Publishing House Osnovy, 438–40.

Motyl, Alexander J. 1993. *Dilemmas of Independence: Ukraine After Totalitarianism*. New York: Council of Foreign Relations Press.

Mykytenko, Oleh. 2010. 'Storinkamy istorii "Vsesvitu": iz vystupu O. I. Mykytenka, holovnoho redaktora chasopysu inozemnoii literatury "Vsesvit" u Lvivskomu natsionalnomu universyteti imeni Ivana Franka 20 lystopada 2007 roku' [Pages of the History of *Vsesvit*: From the Speech of O. I. Mykytenka, Editor-in-Chief of the Journal of Foreign Literature *Vsesvit* in the Ivan Franko National University of Lviv on 20 November 2007]. Visnyk Lvivskoho Universytetu. Seriia inozemni movy (Bulletin of Lviv University. Foreign languages series). No. 17 (2010). http://publications.lnu.edu.ua/bulletins/index.php/lingua/article/view/2446.

Nahaylo, Bohdan and Swoboda, Victor. 1990. *Soviet Disunion: A History of the Nationalities Problem in the USSR.* London: Hamish Hamilton.

Novykova, Maryna. 1995. 'Ukrainska "Bozhestvenna komediia"' [Ukrainian *Divine Comedy*], *Suchasnist* 5: 62–64.

Olshanskaya, Nataliya. 2008. 'Ukraine: Translating the Wars," in T. Seruya and M. L. Moniz (eds.), *Translation and Censorship in Different Times and Landscapes.* Newcastle: Cambridge Scholars Publishing.

Ovsiienko, Vasyl. 2013. 'Dva dokumenty z HDA SBU (pro vydavnytstvo *Dnipro*, Rostyslava Dotsenka, Yuriia Lytvyna)' [Two Documents from the State Administration Archive of the SBU (About the Publishing House *Dnipro*, Rostyslav Dotsenko, Yurii Lytvyn)], *Virtual museum "The Dissident Movement in Ukraine".* 5March 2013. https://museum.khpg.org/1367604869

Pylypchuk, Dmytro (ed.). 2020. *Slovnyky ukrainskoi movy: 1596–2018: bibliohrafichnyi pokazhchyk* [Dictionaries of the Ukrainian Language: 1596–2018: Bibliographic Index]. Kyiv: Prosvita.

Radyk, Oleh. 2011. 'Ulenshpihel z Proskurova' [Uhlenspiegel from Proskuriv]. *Novyi Pohlyad*, 22 April 2011. https://web.archive.org/web/20160922181230/ http://www.pohlyad.com/zhyttya/n/3814

Robinson, Douglas. 1997. *Translation and Empire: Postcolonial Theories Explained.* Manchester: St. Jerome Publishing.

Rudnytska, Nataliia. 2021. *Pereklad i ideolohiia (vid kintsia XIX stolittya do sohodennia)* [Translation and Ideology (From the End of the 19th century to the Present)]. Vinnytsia: Nova Knyha.

Rudnytska, Nataliia. 2023. 'Literary Translation and Elimination of the Soviet Ideology in Contemporary Ukraine', *Academic Journal of Modern Philology* 19: 283–92.

Savchyn, Valentyna. 2014. *Mykola Lukash – podvyzhnyk ukrainskoho khudozhnioho perekladu* [Mykola Lukash, A Devotee of Ukrainian Literary Translation]. Lviv: Litopys.

Shevelov, George Y. 1989. *The Ukrainian Language in the First Half of the Twentieth Century (1900–1941). Its State and Status.* Cambridge, Massachusetts: Harvard University Press.

Shmiher, Taras. 2009. *Istoriia Ukrayins'koho perekladoznavstva* [History of Ukrainian translation scholarship]. Kyiv: Smoloskyp.

Shmiher, Taras. 2024. *Liturhiinyi pereklad Ukrainy ta Polshchi: komparatyvnyi pidkhid do tekstu, relihii ta kultury.* [Liturgical Translation in Ukraine and Poland: A Comparative Approach to Text, Religion and Culture]. Lviv: Ivan Franko National University of Lviv.

Smyth, Sarah. 2009. '"Razom nas bahato, nas ne podolati": Remixes of the Orange Revolution Anthem', in E. Ní Chuilleanáin, C. Ó Cuilleanáin and D. Parris (eds.), *Translation and Censorship: Patterns of Communication and Interference.* Portland: Four Courts Press, 205–20.

Strikha, Maksym. 2006. *Ukrainskyi khudozhnii pereklad: Mizh literaturoiu i natsiietvorenniam* [Ukrainian Literary Translation: Between Literature and Nation-Building]. Kyiv: Fakt.

Strikha, Maksym. 2020. *Ukrainskyi pereklad i perekladachi: mizh literaturoiu i natsiietvorenniam* [Ukrainian Translation and Translators: Between Literature and Nation-Building]. Kyiv: Dukh i Litera.

Stus, Vasyl. 1997. *Tvory.* vol. 6 (additional), Book 1. *Lysty do ridnykh* [Letters to Relatives], compiled by Mykhailyna Kotsiubynska. Lviv: Prosvita.

Svitlychny, Ivan. 2001. *Holos doby. Kn. 1: Lysty z "Parnasu"* [The Voice of the Day. Book 1: Letters from 'Parnassus'], arranged by Leonida Svitlychna. Kyiv: Sfera.

Zabuzhko, Oksana. 2022. 'No Guilty People in the world? Reading Russian Literature After the Bucha Massacre', *Times Literary Supplement*, 22 April 2022. www.the-tls.co.uk/articles/russian-literature-bucha-massacre-essay-oksana-zabuzhko/

Zorivchak, Roksolana. 2001. 'Khudozhniy pereklad v Ukraini i buttia natsii' [Literary Translation in Ukraine and the Being of the Nation]. *Zapysky perekladatskoi maisterni. 2000–2001*, vol. 1. Lviv: Prostir-M, 9–17.

17

TRANSLATION AND CENSORSHIP IN ROMANIA

Rodica Dimitriu

17.1 Introduction

In the last decades, discourse on translation and censorship has constantly developed, from a topic of interest to 'the Manipulation School', to an independent area of research, which has known its own evolution, constantly broadening its scope and gaining in flexibility and complexity. Romanian censorship serves as a good illustration of the ways in which translation control and manipulation have served political and socio-cultural planning, its history offering a wide range of instances in which censorship took both dramatic and milder forms, from cultural amputation, to something to learn and even benefit from.

17.2 Historical Perspectives

17.2.1 Beginnings of Modern Censorship (Late Sixteenth to the Nineteenth Centuries)

As in many other European countries, the first form of censorship in the three Romanian historical regions (the principalities of Moldavia and Wallachia, as well as Transylvania) was church censorship, which strove to preserve the religious status quo. In Habsburg Transylvania, Catholic control was exerted over Reformist and Orthodox writings, whereas (mainly) Orthodox Moldavia and Wallachia regarded all the religious doctrines from the West as an attack on the Orthodox faith. A first restrictive document in this respect, which was issued in Moldavia at the end of the sixteenth century, forbade any 'importation' of Calvinist texts (Petcu 1999: 81). Nevertheless, translations of such texts crossed the borders from one region to another, and contributed to the development of the Romanian literary language (Kohn 2009: 511). It is also throughout the seventeenth and eighteenth centuries that lists and catalogues of banned and prohibited books were elaborated in Wallachia and in Habsburg Transylvania, where the *Cathalogus librorum prohibitorum* included, for instance, Anton Friedrich Büsching and Johannes Cocceius. In 1784 Prince Mihai Şuţu, ruler of Moldavia, set up royal censorship and informed the Metropolitan bishop of Moldavia that nothing could be printed and disseminated without royal approval, along with that of the church (Petcu 1999: 86).

DOI: 10.4324/9781003149453-21

261

The Routledge Handbook of Translation and Censorship

However, despite church control, censorship was gradually secularised in all three Romanian regions starting in the eighteenth century, and many translations and adaptations (mainly from French literature) circulated rather freely across borders, propagating 'the spirit of the Enlightenment'. Moreover, in many Transylvanian schools, subjects such as logic, ethics or metaphysics were taught using translations of Greek textbooks (Kohn 2009: 512). These relatively relaxed forms of censorship continued to be practised at the beginning of the nineteenth century and, little by little, in Moldavia and Wallachia other printing houses, in addition to the ones owned by the Orthodox Metropolitanate, were granted the privilege of printing books. However, all this ended in May 1828, when the two Romanian provinces succumbed to Russian occupation during the Russian-Turkish war, and the censorship system was considerably tightened. From this point, control over the publication and circulation of books and newspapers was exerted by both Russian and Romanian officials, and political censorship was carried out according to strict regulations adopted in 1833 (Petcu 1999: 88). Theatrical performances were also subjected to preventive censorship. Even if in Moldavia, it was allowed, for instance, for Romanian and French plays to be staged in both languages, the texts underwent prior censorship to suppress any criticism levelled at the Moldavian prince or the current state of affairs. In Transylvania, *The Transylvania Gazette*, the first Romanian-language political newspaper, founded in 1838, was drastically censured by the representative of the imperial Habsburg chancellery, but, even before it reached that level, it underwent censorship review by the local authorities and then by a Hungarian government official.

All in all, in the first half of the nineteenth century there were mainly political reasons for justifying censorial activity: preserving Habsburg and Hungarian repression in Transylvania and Russian domination in the Romanian principalities. Even so, a great deal of translated foreign literature was published and theatre texts performed. The main cultural model was the French one, but there were also translations from Italian, German, American and British literature—albeit the books in English came out mainly via indirect translations of French and German sources. Besides the moral value of these writings, some ideas present in these literary texts (e.g., Byron's poems and Shakespeare's plays) were sources of inspiration for significant political events such as the 1848 revolution or the Unification of the Romanian principalities in 1859. In Transylvania, the translation of Jules Verne's *Carpathian Castle* in 1897, subtitled by its translator as *A Novel on the Life of the Romanian People Living in Transylvania*, helped Romanians from that region prepare themselves mentally for the 'Great Union' with Romania in 1918 (Neț 2021: 73). Another inspiring book that escaped censorship was Harriet Beecher Stowe's *Uncle Tom's Cabin*, published in 1852 in the U.S. and translated into Romanian only one year later in Iași, Moldavia (1853), followed by Bucharest, Wallachia (1854). Interestingly enough, the Romanian readers did not associate the book with the abolition of slavery, but rather applied the theme to their own concerns: emancipation of the Roma, a democratic idea shared by the intellectuals of the time (Kohn 2009: 514).

During the 1848 revolutions in Transylvania and in the Romanian principalities, the abolition of censorship and freedom of the press were among the revolutionaries' main objectives, explicitly expressed in their proclamations. After the repression of the three revolutions, censorship became harsher yet again, with censored topics including criticism directed at the ruler, official religion, foreign sovereigns and their representatives, political life, laws, public morality. In Moldavia, the Russian influence over censorship was still very strong, so much so that in 1849 theatrical performances that alluded to the tsar's family, such as the French vaudeville play *Madame Peterhoff* (Petcu 1999: 108), were forbidden.

The Unification of Moldavia and Wallachia in 1859 paved the way for a series of democratic reforms that included the abolition of censorship. A few years later, the Constitution promulgated by the future king of Romania, Carol I, also guaranteed freedom of publication and freedom of the press. Meanwhile, in Transylvania, which was incorporated into the Hungarian part of the Austro-Hungarian Empire in 1867, Hungarian control over Romanian newspapers became stricter than ever; publications in this language were suspended, and the editors fined and/or sent to prison according to the seriousness of the offenses (Petcu 1999: 116).

However, both in Transylvania and Romania censorship mainly targeted political publications (books and articles) rather than literary texts, with the notable exception of occasional satires and pamphlets. Thus, a lot of translated foreign literature was published without being censored, particularly in the second half of the nineteenth century. The prevailing cultural model continued to be the French one, but there were also many texts from what is today known as Germany, as well as from British, American, Russian, Italian and Spanish literatures. The main selection criterion for books to be translated was positive source-culture reader reception; however, a second criterion was genuine literary merit, which was frequently discussed by the cultural figures of the time (Neţ 2021). The co-existence of translated 'popular fiction', side by side with literary masterpieces, confirmed the functioning of the law of supply and demand in the literary field (Cornea 1970) and was, ultimately, a form of economic censorship exercised by the publishers themselves, and not imposed by the state.

17.2.2   *The Twentieth Century: Democracy between the Two World Wars*

Whereas the first decade of the twentieth century was still a period of uninhibited translational activity of literary texts, making it clear that both readers and publishers wanted to stay attuned to the latest trends in Western literature, the outbreak of WWI brought yet another dramatic twist to the country's political scene. Political censorship was now exerted at the level of more elaborate state structures such as, starting in 1915, the Service of News Surveillance, which included a press department responsible for controlling the information that had to be disseminated to the population. When German troops occupied Bucharest in November 1916, all national publications, as well as theatrical performances and films were banned; the newly created Imperial German Government of the City of Bucharest, with its own justice and press system, immediately issued an ordinance regarding the establishment of military and political censorship (Petcu 1999: 127). The latter's function was not to preserve the 'old ideology' of Romanian national political and cultural values, but to impose a new one. During the German occupation, the only theatrical performances permitted were either those of Romanian plays not tinged by nationalism, or translations of German plays and those of neutral countries. These strict measures were enacted through an equally drastic government decree (1918) stipulating that it was the Presidency of the Minsters' Council that exercised censorial control over all publications, as well as theatrical performances and cinema viewings.

After WWI, with Romania on the winning side, there followed a (short) period of democracy and unprecedented economic development, and the promulgation of a new democratic constitution (1923) that guaranteed freedom of the press. However, control continued to be exerted over political parties and political groups whose ideology ran counter to the official policy. One such 'group' was the (insignificant at the time) Communist Party, which was eventually outlawed in 1926.

During the 20 years of political relaxation between the two world wars, translations were generally unaffected by political censorship and their popularity exploded on the Romanian book market. Most of them were from French literature, as French culture had retained its 'power and prestige' (Bassnett and Lefevere 1998: 8) in Romanian society; however, there were also outstanding works from other 'great' foreign literatures (British, German, American, Spanish, Italian,

The Routledge Handbook of Translation and Censorship

Russian), or from more 'peripheral' ones (Portuguese, Belgian, Swiss, Polish, etc.), as well as from more exotic spaces (Latin America, India, Japan, etc.). From the third decade of the twentieth century, British and American literary texts were translated directly from English rather than through indirect translations, French. The criteria for publication were similar to those of the nineteenth century with the sole distinction that the book market had considerably developed. The randomly selected books for translation were a combination of works of high literary merit—by both classical and contemporary authors—and highly successful works of popular fiction (Dimitriu 2000).

The only institutions exerting preliminary censorship over what was to be published were the private publishing houses, which were more interested in book sales than in translation quality. The limitations imposed by the publishers included book length—no longer than 120 pages so as not to bore the readers—and literary genre, with the short story being the most popular. These usually shortened translations were published in book form, but also in newspapers and magazines or in collections such as *Floarea literaturilor străine* ('Best Foreign Short Stories') with suggestively illustrated covers, so as to immediately attract readers' attention (Dimitriu 2000: 182). The profit-driven censorship exercised by publishers had the undesirable effect of excluding from translation a relatively high number of canonical literary works. Furthermore, when it came to great authors, their reception was not only incomplete, but also somewhat distorted by the random selection of their works to be translated. However, unlike in other countries where censorship went as far as burning D.H. Lawrence's *Lady Chatterley's Lover*, in Romania the British modernist's work was not censored in translation, and Lawrence became quite popular (Eliade 1943). Thus, even if moral concerns were constantly present in the editors-as-censors' minds, there were instances when they turned a blind eye to such issues if the work promised to be profitable.

The short period of democracy came to an end in 1938 when, after a series of political crises, King Carol II instituted a royal dictatorship and the press was subordinated to the state. The old constitution was replaced by a new one, and freedom of expression was limited after the General Directorate of the Press and Propaganda was established, with the king himself playing an important part in censorial activity (Petcu 1999: 144). The outbreak of WWII, with Romania supporting the Axis Powers (Nazi Germany and Italy) and the military dictatorship that was established between 1941 and 1944 meant the imposition of an extreme right-wing ideology with many restrictions targeting Jews (e.g., Jewish theatres were forbidden to stage plays by Romanian authors, the Jewish population was no longer authorised to own cinema halls, books by Jewish authors were removed from libraries, etc.). Furthermore, in 1940 Northern Transylvania was relinquished to Horthyst Hungary with obvious consequences for the censoring of articles published by Romanians; at the same time, books in the Romanian language were no longer available in bookshops. In Bessarabia, a Romanian territory occupied by Russia in 1940, the Romanian language spoken in that area was turned into a so-called Moldovan language and artificially separated from the former: its alphabet was changed from Latin to Cyrillic, and Romanian literary texts were regarded as 'fascist' and removed from bookshops and libraries.

The association of Romania with the Allies and against Germany toward the end of WWII, and the armistice signed between Romania and the governments of the United Nations in September 1944 resulted in a change in the country's political regime. Among many other specific changes, one censorship system was replaced by another, the harshest Romania had known in its history: communist censorship.

Translation and Censorship in Romania

17.2.3   The Communist Period (1945–1989)

17.2.3.1   Beginnings of Communism (1945–1958)

In Communist Romania, 23 August 1944 was celebrated as the 'Liberation from Fascist Occupation Day'. In reality, what Romanians were celebrating on their 'National Day' was the beginning of an oppressive political regime, initiated under the complete control of the Soviet Union. From a cultural and literary perspective, what distinguishes the new communist regime from the previous historical periods is the fact that culture in general and (translated) literature in particular played a key role in substantiating and promoting its political discourse. As a repressive regime, communism constantly resorted to various forms of censorship to block capitalist ideology and impose the new one.

According to historian Nițescu, the communist years witnessed the 'politicisation of literature and fictionalisation of politics' (1995: 142). 'Politicisation of literature' refers to 'the undifferentiated, coarse and paralysing invasion of literature by political and ideological slogans, whereas the 'fictionalisation of politics' relates to 'expressing political] slogans in a less violent manner […], in a language that is closer to literature' (1995: 142, my translation). In his 'study of the minor' [Romania] that covers the Soviet period, Sean Cotter aptly notes that 'translators knew that their work participated in a terribly unbalanced power dynamic, in which the state's discourse was seconded by extralinguistic coercive power' (2014: 27).

However, a periodisation of Romanian communism shows significant fluctuations in the country's policies from one phase to another, and hence in the number of (translated) publications and the functioning of censorship. During the first (Stalinist) phase (1945–1958), Romania, a traditionally Western-oriented country, with an insignificant Communist Party, was transformed, almost overnight, into a Soviet satellite led by a single Party modelled on its Soviet counterpart, and a censorship apparatus that replicated the Soviet Glavlit. As the objective of the communist regime was the creation of a New Man [sic], Romanian culture in general and (translated) literature in particular played a key role in validating and promoting this ideal. Thus, one of the main tasks of the newly established system of control was to eliminate all the (translated literary) works that were regarded as detrimental to the process of mass education. A climactic year in this respect was 1948, with the new regime replacing previous lists of forbidden books with a 534-page catalogue of about 10,000 banned books written by outstanding Romanian writers and literary critics as well as by canonical foreign authors and philosophers (e.g., Plato, Kant, Dante, Schopenhauer, Heidegger, Poe, Baudelaire, Rilke, Benedetto Croce), who had all been purged on 'decadent', 'reactionary' and 'racist' grounds (Denize 2009: 43). Some of their (translated) works could, nevertheless, be read by 'reliable' specialists and researchers who were granted access to the so-called 'special [secret] fund' that had been set up in every important library of the country (Corobca 2020: 260). The cultural and literary gaps resulting from these far-reaching bans were compensated for, particularly since 1948, by massive translations from Russian and Soviet literature, most of which illustrated 'socialist realism', the newly imposed literary aesthetic that all writers had to adopt, or, at least, take into consideration, if they wished to build a literary career. In addition, there were also translations from French literature (mainly nineteenth-century novels), which had 'managed to maintain its dominance' (Baghiu 2016:10) not only in view of the long tradition that linked it to Romanian culture, but also because it best illustrated if not socialist realism, then at least 'critical realism', by adopting a critical attitude toward bourgeois realities. Finally, there were translations from literatures from more remote geographical spaces with ideological affinities, such as Asia (over fifty Asian novels during the first communist decade, from

The Routledge Handbook of Translation and Censorship

which half were Chinese) and Latin America (around thirty novels between 1947 to 1960, before the 'international literary boom of the 1960s') (Baghiu 2016: 17).

The General Directorate of Press and Printing (Direcția Generală a Presei și Tipăriturilor – DGPT), a complex censorship institution modelled on Soviet Glavit, was set up in 1949. It was directly subordinated to the Council of Ministers and was in charge of, among other things, every publication in the country (newspapers, magazines, books, etc.), as well as of the export or import of similar materials. It also authorised the circulation of films and set the operating conditions for bookshops and public libraries (Denize 2009: 43). For almost three decades, the DGPT kept under strict control the circulation of any kind of (factual or fictional) information throughout the country. As for translated literature, the criteria for pre-selection censorship were general and vague with such interchangeable justifications as 'formalist', 'decadent' or 'cosmopolitan' (Corobca 2020: 266). Initially the DGPT was in charge of all three forms of censorship: 1) pre-selection, 2) preventive censorship (which required that a text be stamped as 'good for print') and 3) post-control. Subsequently, pre-selection was taken over by publishers, whereas post-control was (also) exercised by institutions and agents other than the DGPT (members of various structures of the Communist Party, critics, even members of the much-feared *Securitate*) (Corobca 2020: 267).

The strange and uneasy association between censorial activity and the state-orchestrated promotion of translation once again inspired by the Soviet Union, was, no doubt, one of the paradoxes of communist translation shaped, as it was, 'by the tension between xenophobia and internationalism' (Baer 2011: 9). This happened because the book industry had always enjoyed state protection and investment (not just censorship and control), given the communist system's interest in encouraging a 'mass cult of literature' above all other forms of entertainment (Corobca 2020).

17.2.3.2 First Signs of Political Emancipation (1958–1965)

During the second phase of the communist period, after Stalin's death in 1953, there was a distancing from previous Stalinist ideology both in the Soviet Union and in Romania. After Soviet troops ultimately withdrew from the country in 1958, Gheorghe Gheorghiu-Dej, General Secretary of the Communist party, initiated a gradual policy of emancipation from Moscow and increased trade relations with the West. Meanwhile, despite this political turn, censorship inside Romania developed to include the banning of more recent collections of newspapers and magazines from the Stalinist years, whose ideology was no longer acceptable (Rad 2005: 70). As to source text pre-selection, in keeping with the mainstream cultural discourse of the time, censors encouraged the translation of novels from neighbouring (socialist) countries (Czechoslovakia, Hungary, Yugoslavia, Bulgaria), as well as from Latin American and African countries that shared common political ideals and aspirations. At the same time, translations from Russian classics (Chekhov, Pushkin, Gogol, Tolstoy) continued to be produced together with (mostly canonical) Western literature. Publishers implemented coherent, carefully planned translation policies, which made it easier for censors to exert stringent oversight of everything that was published (Dimitriu 1999; Baghiu 2020).

17.2.3.3 (Relative) Liberalisation (1965–1974)

The anti-Soviet foreign policy of emancipation, consisting not only of tightening links with the West but also with China, was pursued and developed more intensively by Ceaușescu during the third phase of the communist period. The 1965–1974 phase was one of relative political relaxation—the highest reached by the communist regime—and economic growth. Those years also saw a higher number of published translations than ever before, as a result of what was regarded at the time as 'logical, conscious and mature coordination' (Ionescu 1981: 37), leading to 'the setting up of a group of professional translators and critics of foreign literature that could best meet the needs for competence and analysis [...] of the translation phenomenon' (Ionescu 1981: 37, my translation). The print runs were also quite large as translated foreign literature was always in great demand (e.g., in 1966 *Jane Eyre* by Charlotte Bronte, 100,160 copies; *The Adventures of Tom Sawyer* by Mark Twain, 127,160 copies, etc.) (Macrea Toma 2009: 164). In terms of source text origin, this was also a period of 'Western hegemony'—with French and English novels dominating the scene, and American literature standing as vivid proof of 'political relaxation' (Baghiu 2020: 108), even if many of the selected authors were leftists (e.g., Steinbeck, Faulkner, Hemingway). This wide selection of translated books should not, however, be misinterpreted. During this phase, like the previous ones, even if pre-selection had become increasingly permissive, careful textual censorship continued to operate, the result of which was frequently mutilated literary texts. Obviously, the eliminated passages, phrases and words all violated, in one way or another, ideological acceptability: religious passages (e. g., various editions of Defoe's *Robinson Crusoe*), references to socialism in negative contexts (e.g., Aldous Huxley's *Eyeless in Gaza*), erotic scenes (e. g., D.H. Lawrence's, *Women in Love*), and so on. Apart from the radical strategy of deletion, censors, or frequently translators themselves through (self)censorship, also resorted to attenuation, flattening, substitution and shifts of meaning (Dimitriu 2007), as well as other techniques, thus replacing adequacy, i.e., faithfulness to the source text (Toury's initial norm, 1995) with ideological acceptability. However, neither censors nor translators displayed highly 'systematic behaviour' with regard to problematic textual instances so that, on rare occasions, morally questionable sequences or lewd language surprisingly survived the censors' merciless pen (Ionescu 2010; Pâcleanu 2018; Vrinceanu 2022).

17.2.3.4 The Last Years of Communist Dictatorship (1975–1989)

On a political level, this brief period of relative liberalisation came to an end in 1975, after Ceaușescu's visits to China and North Korea, which marked a shift in the country's politics toward nationalism and Ceaușescu's personality cult. The elaboration, in 1971, of the so-called 'July theses' heralded a new (mini)cultural revolution, during which both culture and literature resumed their mainly propagandistic function. The fourth—and last—phase of Romanian communism was, in fact, a period of harsh dictatorship, the end of which coincided with the end of the regime itself. However, from a literary viewpoint, the translation field continued to be relatively dynamic until 1975 (Dimitriu 1999; Baghiu 2020). Tentative explanations for this state of affairs could be the editorial planning elaborated by publishers during the previous, more relaxed phase, which needed to be completed; the apparent 'freedom' of the members of the Writers' Union to express their (critical) opinions with regard to book publications and a certain ideological inertia, given that this political turn occurred quite abruptly in comparison with the previous phase. The last communist decade was clearly one of economic decline, actual paper shortages being a reason invoked by political institutions to reinforce strict control over publishing activity both in terms of (constantly dwindling) numbers of published (translated) books and the content of what got published. For example, author photos were censored from the book covers; only the images of classic, long deceased writers (Shakespeare, Balzac, Tolstoy, etc.) were allowed, so as not to distract people's attention from the dictator's ubiquitous portrait (Avramescu 2005: 426). Ironically, all this happened at the time when censorship was officially abolished. In 1977 the General Directorate of Press and Printing was dismantled and the censors were transferred to the

Council of Socialist Culture and Education (CCES); this new institution was now also in charge of guiding and coordinating censorship activities in a more discrete manner. The communist government had thus replaced censorship by a subtler system of 'diluted responsibilities', which were transferred to publishing houses and editorial committees (Corobca 2020: 273).

In the mid-eighties, a new structure was created, the Reading Service, affiliated with the CCES. Far from being diminished, censorship was, on the contrary, enhanced, through the self-censorship practised by authors and translators themselves, followed by the editors' censorship and, finally, by the control exerted by the newly established CCES (Manea in Corobca 2020: 274).

17.2.4 Post-communism

The beginning of the post-communist period coincides with the beginning of the last decade of the twentieth century. The 1990s witnessed the unprecedented development of mass media, the rapid establishment of new private publishing houses, which co-existed (for a short while) with state-owned ones; the latter were privatised and some of them ultimately disappeared. The decade was also a time when formerly forbidden texts, such as George Orwell's *1984* (translated in 1991) and Aldous Huxley's *Brave New World* (translated in 1997), among many other texts deemed unacceptable, which had been blocked by the communists, were now translated and published.

The publishers' increasing permissiveness with regard to what got published and translated, the regular appearance of new periodicals, books and reviews as well as the restoration of links with the pre-communist past were all obvious signs of a new democratic system. Both historical and literary texts were interpreted from a primarily anti-communist viewpoint, but this 'new language' was, sometimes, strangely similar to the communist jargon. At the same time, an unprecedented plurality of voices ushered in the post-modern age in Romanian society, after a overly long period of dogmatic 'truths' (Dimitriu 1999). However, even if, in 1991, a new Constitution was adopted that forbade censorship of any kind and, consequently, the suppression of any publication, censorship continued to survive, albeit under different forms. Economic censorship was manifest, for example, through the government's monopoly over the paper factories (Petcu 1999: 185). Today, corporate censorship is still imposed on the press, which is frequently manipulated by so called 'private initiatives' (Pierrat in Corobca 2020: 278). Moreover, the press is subjected to the owners' political commitments.

Political censorship of translations has been replaced, to a great extent, by market censorship. Thus, in the last decades, the selection of books for translation has been a hybrid process: on the one hand, some private publishers (e.g., Polirom and Humanitas) have built their reputation on publishing only high quality (literary and non-literary) translations; others have preferred to be guided by the market laws. For example, Editura Miron (Miron publishing house) has so far published over 6000 books, the overwhelming majority of which are highly successful works of popular fiction (love stories) (Sâsâiac 2021: 204). At the same time, the random selection of books, according to the principle that 'anything goes' as long as it sells well, and the lack of any aesthetic or ethical control have led to an oversupply of translations, with potentially negative consequences on reader education and personal development. Moreover, for economic reasons, in order to avoid paying for copyright permissions, old, low-quality translations of the pre-communist period were republished, particularly in the 1990s; in other cases and for similar reasons, high quality communist translations, mutilated by the censors, were recycled without any revision; there are also cases of overlapping target texts, i.e., translations of the same book issued by different publishers and produced by different translators appearing within a very short time frame for no apparent reason. Finally, the lack of revision that negatively impacted censored communist translations is also responsible for the poor quality of some recent translations issued by profit and money-driven publishing houses.

17.3 Core Issues and Topics

Although links between censorship and cultural production exist in all political regimes, in Romania, the Eastern European state that was subjected to the harshest form of communist dictatorship, it is censorship under communism that has captured the greatest researcher interest, triggering a series of interdisciplinary studies published in Romanian in the form of monographs, collected volumes and articles. However, in some of these publications, mainly those that are historical in nature, the study of censored translated literature is limited to a part of a section or chapter devoted to cultural products in general or to censored original literature, rather than translated texts. Still, in addition to (re)writing the history of communism, these studies describe the successive transformations of (communist) censorship, the agents and mechanisms involved, as well as the process of gradual de-centralisation of the censorial apparatus.

Romanian literature on censorship also comprises first-hand testimonials of agents (editors, writers, translators, and censors), who in essays, memoirs and interviews reveal their interactions with this intricate—whether strict, or, occasionally, unexpectedly permissive—system of guidance and control.

17.3.1 'Paradoxes' of Communist Censorship

17.3.1.1   Cultural Isolation?

In recent decades, Romanian researchers have sought to demonstrate, through various studies, that 'the severe censorship designed to strengthen the new regime was often more permeable than originally thought' (Merkle 2018: 245).

A first 'paradox' regards the initial pre-selection of books for translation, by editors and censors alike (with the former frequently filling both roles), that made possible the publication, despite the vigilance of the official censor and the mainstream ideology of the time, of thousands of translations of Western literary texts that had nothing in common with socialist realism and clearly did not meet the 'official' communist criteria on moral, aesthetic or religious grounds. This was the case for the Romanian translation of anglophone works, such as Thomas de Quincey's, *Confessions of an English Opium-Eater* (1971), D.H. Lawrence's *Sons and Lovers* (1971), Saul Bellow's *Humboldt's Gift* (1979), Edward Bulwer-Lytton's *The Last Day of Pompeii* (1989) (cf. Macrea-Toma 2009), among so many others. Actually, the many exceptions of this kind made it possible for Romanian readers to have access to high quality world literature and for Romanian writers to constantly keep pace with the latest literary trends. These statistically-documented facts (see Ionescu G. 1981; Dimitriu 1999; Macrea-Toma 2009; Baghiu 2020) contradict the generally accepted reports in the Romanian media that excessively invoke cultural isolation. Ralian (2005), one of the outstanding Romanian literary translators of both the communist and post-communist periods, points out during an interview that 'until 1989 almost all major works from classic world literature as well as a great amount of contemporary literature had been translated', whereas archival and censorship files show that

> despite firm ideological control and limited access to direct information, Romanian theatres were not totally divorced from contemporary reality. Moreover, the presence of some [...]

authors who definitely did not fit the prescribed profile proves that state control was not completely ubiquitous and that the text selection policies were not *only* politically motivated. (Antochi 2012: 46, author's italics)

The publishers' (occasionally) questionable book selections in terms of ideological acceptability—which, nevertheless received the censors' approval—were not limited to literature. During the 1970s and (bleak) 1980s, Univers Publishing House, one of the most important translation-oriented publishing houses in communist Romania, also published works of literary theory and criticism; consequently, works written by highly important contemporary critics and theorists, leftist or not, were released, something that was impossible to achieve in other less repressive communist regimes. Slovakian professor of Romanian language and culture, Libuša Vajdová (2021), explains that she and her colleagues specialising in Romanian language and literature used to buy the Romanian translations of the great contemporary literary critics and theorists in order to get acquainted with the most recent developments in these fields. Translations of this kind were forbidden in the former Czechoslovakia. In Vajdova's opinion, 'despite the fact that Romania's situation was so difficult, these editors and translators managed to keep Romanian culture attuned to the great values worldwide' (Vajdová 2021: 599–600, my translation).

17.3.1.2   Editorial Censorship: Vigilance and Collusion

The paradox of cultural attunement to the world despite physical and 'ideological blockage' (Wolf 2002) could also be explained by another anomaly in an otherwise hierarchical and highly bureaucratic censorship system, related, this time, to the relationships between the agents involved: translators, authors, editors, censors, publishers and so on. According to Comănescu, editor in-chief at Univers publishing house for many years (1978–2007), during the last communist decade, the censorship hierarchy operated on four levels:

the editor himself was supposed to be the first censor, yet he actually fought censorship the most in order to see the book out. He was sometimes sacked or reassigned to a menial job for doing it, which was a radical price to pay. The next step was censorship proper. All manuscripts were directed to the inferior level of censorship, known as the Editorial Central House. [...] When the manuscript had been approved by this department of the Ministry of Culture, it went to the superior body of censors of the same Ministry, who were the strictest and the most official. These people working for censorship were all graduates of some university, even remarkably good in their own field, translators and even writers, some of them. They knew all the codes of censorship, what could be allowed to be printed and what was definitely forbidden, *but they were human, after all:* some would negotiate, others could even close an eye, but most of them were actually afraid of losing their jobs. (Comănescu 1998: 230, my emphasis)

As for translation policies, Comănescu notes that 'Univers *was privileged with flexible censors.* Consequently [...], we could publish updated criticism, theory, and philosophy of culture' (1998: 230, my emphasis); moreover, the censorship of translated literature was more flexible than the censorship of original creations. Macrea-Toma makes a similar observation, finding the 'freedom' enjoyed by foreign translations all the more surprising given that it took place at a time when the regime was becoming increasingly authoritarian (2009: 241).

Translation and Censorship in Romania

Ultimately, first-hand testimonials of the people directly involved and studies dealing with such 'paradoxes' reveal 'internal contradictions', 'structural deficiencies' (Popa 2018: 428), 'sinuosities, whims, and inconsistencies' (Rad 2011: 321) in the censorship system, while rejecting, at the same time, a linear, strictly causal and thus simplistic interpretation of such discontinuities.

17.3.1.3   Productive Censorship

Some studies and accounts go so far as to say that communist censorship was even beneficial (e.g., Augustin-Doinaş, Macrea-Toma, Rad). By imposing socialist realism and purging all direct attacks against the communist political system, it paradoxically not only supported the development of an alternative subversive, elusive, even cryptic literature, which encompassed all genres, but it also sharpened the readers' attention, mind and aesthetic sense in a more sophisticated direction.

In critic Negoiţescu's words, 'Just like Henry de Montherlant during the war, I believe that censorship can sharpen the writer's/critic's mind by making him strive to cheat it. With an allusive style, you can sometimes make the public see it. You can "expose" it, while winning the approval of the readers who know what it is all about' (1998: 19). In the period of relative political relaxation, Romanian poetry connected to Western poetry, becoming increasingly difficult and cryptical (Rad 2005: 272). Poet Ştefan Augustin-Doinaş also speaks of the 'Aesopian language of poetry' in order to escape the 'vigilant, killing eye of censorship' (1992: 37). Similar things were happening to (translated) literary prose as well.

17.3.2   Textual Censorship

If source-text preselection ultimately led to the translation and publication of most canonical works and literary masterpieces, the price to pay for this initial permissiveness was textual censorship, exercised on ideologically problematic passages (with)in the accepted books. In other words, some of the otherwise high-quality translations had been submitted to various (from insignificant to major) degrees of mutilation in order to be stamped as 'ready for publication'. In the absence of the censors' notes and reports as well as of the annotated manuscripts, most of which were destroyed by the censorial authority itself (Avramescu 2005: 20), research on this topic has had to be carried out through the minute comparison of the originals and their translations. This archeological enterprise, mainly built around case studies, has unearthed how translators actually coped with 'forbidden topics' of communist discourse (e.g., religion, morally offensive passages and negative references to communism), and how they negotiated the ideological obstacles using different strategies, including, ultimately, self-censorship.

Some of these highly contextualised case studies correlate censorship operations with a distorted reception of the literary works. Modernist authors serve as good examples in this respect, as their rebellious spirit frequently tended to contest the limits of socio-political acceptability. Censored sexuality led to a systematic 'un-sexing' operation when translating Joyce's *Ulysses* during the communist period (1984), but, even so, 'it must have been one of the most tolerated books by the Romanian censorship' as it remained 'still laden with explicit sexual talk and allusions' (Ionescu 2010: 242). Similarly, the erotic passages from D.H. Lawrence's *Women in Love* were either omitted or attenuated in the novel's 1978 translation, even if sexuality, in Lawrence's case, is part of a more complex existential theory and thus of paramount importance to the understanding of the author's 'life philosophy' (Pâcleanu 2021: 121).

At the same time, (self)censorship deprived a very large number of novels of their spiritual dimension, through strategies of elimination of religious passages, or their replacement by more general counterparts, the rephrasing of intensely religious scenes, and so on. The translator of the pre-communist edition of *Robinson Crusoe* (1943) was asked to delete from the communist editions of the book all the religious passages in which the character was praying to God for salvation and support; as a result, Crusoe was turned into an atheist whose personality was shaped so as to correspond to the communist ideal of the New Man (Dimitriu 2006). Likewise, in communist translations of novels such as D.H. Lawrence's *The Plumed Serpent* (1989) and Somerset Maugham's *The Painted Veil* (1972), religious and mystical terms were replaced or omitted, preserved only in negative contexts (Pâcleanu 2021). George Volceanov, a contemporary translator of Shakespeare's plays, notes his predecessors' tendency to bowdlerise Shakespeare's language during the communist period, thereby contributing to 'the invention of a "Shakespeare for the people" in the light of Marxist-Leninist ideology' (Volceanov 2021: 142–3).

However, the most sensitive issue that resulted in (self)censorship was criticism of the communist political system (from straightforward indictment to mere allusions) in the source texts. In fact, it was the main criterion for blocking entire literary works that were perceived to pose a real threat to the political order. Whereas during the first communist decade the number of dangerous books was very high, consisting of both banned volumes and books deemed unacceptable for translation, figures decreased significantly starting from the 1960s when partial textual censorship was already regarded as preferable to non-translation. For instance, Aldous Huxley's *Eyeless in Gaza*, a novel on existential choices that promoted an ideology hardly compatible with the communist one, was, nevertheless, translated into Romanian and published in 1974. That being said, the surprising publication of this text was the result of drastic textual censorship practised at all levels, mainly through the (radical) strategy of deletion: from the elimination of words such as 'socialism', 'communism' and 'Russian', to sentences, paragraphs, subchapters and even to the amputation of a whole chapter (Chapter 35), which leaves the Romanian translation with 53 chapters instead of the 54 of the original (Dimitriu 2007). Such critical passages were eliminated *en masse* from translated literature in the communist years (Comănescu 1998; Ralian 2005), which negatively impacted the reception of the authors' work. Detecting translator self-censorship is a difficult operation unless there is clear documentary evidence (e.g., translator testimonials and manuscripts, 'official' documents) that separates institutional from individual intervention. However, even if relatively rare, such studies do exist, throwing new light on processes of self-censorship, sometimes in association with self-translation (e.g., Volceanov 2005; Rădulescu 2010).

17.3.3 Censorship, Manipulation and Imagology

Perhaps one of the most revealing instances of the manipulative power of textual censorship is its role in shaping (ethnic, auctorial, etc.) images in the direction intended by a particular regime. Studies have shown how, depending on particular configurations of power relations, ethnic clichés can be carefully negotiated by translators, who blocked or reshaped the ethnic images present in the source texts (Dimitriu 2016). Defoe's ethnic stereotypes in *Robinson Crusoe* were treated differently by the (same) Romanian translator, during and after WWII. For instance, references to the Spanish colonisers stigmatised as extremely cruel in the source text were completely deleted from the 1943 (pre-communist) translation of the book, probably because Spain was, at the time, a strong nationalist dictatorship, and it would have been undiplomatic for the still capitalist Romania to perpetuate negative stereotypes of Spain. On the contrary, in the aftermath of WWII, with the

Translation and Censorship in Romania

rise of communist ideology, the sharp criticism of any form of human exploitation became a hot topic in political discourse. Thus, for political reasons (the different political configuration of the Cold War years), as well as for reasons of professional integrity, the translator reinserted the negative stereotyping of the Spanish colonisers in the many communist (revised) editions of the book (Dimitriu 2016: 207).

By contrast, censorship and propaganda were extremely effective in exporting ethnic images through translated literary texts, i.e., in practising so-called 'translation by imposition' (Dollerup 1997: 46). According to the Soviet model, such exported images were regarded as instrumental in promoting international solidarity among communist countries as well as in enhancing the quality of Romania's diplomatic relations during the Cold War. For instance, during the Stalinist period (1954), in a collection of short stories inspired by the Romanian war of independence written in 1905, the author, the canonical Romanian writer Mihail Sadoveanu, in collusion with the unknown translator, (self)censored, then distorted the Russians' ethnic stereotypes from negative in the original text, into strongly positive ones in the propagandistic translation. Thus, through such radical strategies as deletion, replacement and attenuation, the exported translation changed the Russians' image from the subject of the Romanian soldiers' disparaging jokes to true brothers-in-arms, who enthusiastically join forces for the noble cause of Romania's independence from the Ottoman empire (Dimitriu 2016: 205).

17.3.4 *Censorship and Theatre Repertoire*

In all countries that have been subjected to totalitarian political regimes, there is a long history of various types of censorial activities exerted on (translated) theatre texts, performances and repertoires. Moreover, in view of their huge educational and propagandistic potential, plays have always been the centre of attention in autocratic political systems. In 'Behind the Scene: Text Selection Policies' in Communist Romania' (2012), Antochi applies Toury's concept of 'culture planning' (Toury 2003) to explain the functioning of censorship in totalitarian regimes, given that it implies guidance, limitation and control of cultural products for the purpose of mass indoctrination. Even if the author is mainly interested in text selection for the purpose of building theatre repertoires, which, from a censorship perspective, means, among other things, 'to block the entry of supposedly pernicious elements, in the form of pre-censorship procedures' (Antochi 2012: 38), she also refers to other aspects of performance-related control. These aspects concern the ways in which 'the accepted plays were performed and delivered to the audience, by means of post-censorship forms of control—the so called "pre-premieres" in the case of the theatre' (Antochi 2012: 38). Even at the level of compiling repertoires for various national and state theatres, censorship is shown to have been particularly elaborate. Thus, a given list searched for approval from various agents, from the 'Workers' Committee' of the theatre to the Regional Committee for Culture, after which it was read at 'a meeting between the members of this Committee, theatre representatives and the regional Party secretary' (Runcan 2006: 307). The next step was the Regional Committee of the Party, whereas the final performance screening took place at the Theatre Board in Bucharest, which 'eventually contacted the theatre to confirm the final list with the plays' (Runcan 2006: 307). Censorship control was further exerted at the performance level, through pre-premieres, the first one organised for the Workers' Committee and the second for the ideological Commission. Antochi's article also provides the justification for the selection of playwrights as well as an analysis of the Spanish and Latin-American plays performed between 1945 and 1989 .

The Routledge Handbook of Translation and Censorship

17.3.5   The 'distant reading' Perspective

A useful theoretical direction and methodological tool in investigating translation policies and censorship activities at the macro level in different political contexts is 'distant reading', which consists in the application of computational methods to literary data, followed by subsequent analyses and 'interpretive hypotheses' (Rambsy 2021). Such quantitative-plus-qualitative investigations were undertaken, among others, by Baghiu in his studies on communist translations (e.g., 2016, 2019, 2020), which led him to interesting conclusions with regard to the intricate links between Russian/Soviet and French literatures and their interplay with the translation policies imposed on Romania during the Stalinist period:

> [I]n the 19th century, tsarist Russia's administration brought the French culture to the Romanian territories, as Russia was also fascinated by the French, and in order to counteract the Ottoman influence. After World War II, Soviet domination in Eastern Europe brought along with it French literature as a legitimiser of socialist realism. Later on, during the 1960s, French literature was used to overcome proletarian and socialist realist trends, and Soviet literature in general. (Baghiu 2019: 84–5)

This assessment of translation dynamics also made it possible for the author to suggest a periodisation of translation and censorship in communist Romania in terms of prevailing Eastern-Western orientations of translation selection during the different phases of the communist period from 1945 to 1989 (Baghiu 2020).

17.4   New Debates and Future Pathways

The more we advance into the twenty-first century, perspectives on censorship—as theoretical discourse and a significant aspect of an 'ongoing reality'—have gained sophistication. On the one hand, recent research has revealed increasing awareness that there has always been more to this concept than its (mere) association with severe political control, and strictly deterministic investigations may deprive it of its nuanced meanings. On the other hand, the complexity of globalisation has multiplied the number of contexts in which 'new censorships' may be asserted, thereby inviting a plurality of (sometimes interrelated) interpretations of censorship-related phenomena. Moreover, so-called 'digital capitalism' already displays a clearly noticeable 'tendency for surveillance' (Copilaș 2022: 201), signalling new intricate forms of censorship in democratic societies. Even the notion of 'political correctness' and its relation to censorship, despite occasional claims to the contrary, requires more refined investigations.

17.4.1   Revisiting (Post)-communist Censorship

In the general context briefly outlined above, Romanian research on translation and censorship has its own agenda. The previously mentioned distant reading method is regarded as a promising direction for further research that will assign more precision, depth and complexity to the study of communist censorship in a country that is still very much haunted by its communist past (Pop 2022: 209).

Another censorship-related issue that has kept researcher interest alive focuses on the translators themselves, more precisely on *self-censorship*, drawing on archival materials and, increasingly, on the interviews, journals and (auto)biographies (Doinaș 1992; Vianu 1998; Ralian 2005) that writers

Translation and Censorship in Romania

and translators, active in the communist period, have published in the post-communist years. Such studies highlight the translators' personal experiences and their outstanding role as agents contributing 'willingly or unwillingly, to shaping the target culture's understanding of foreign languages and cultures in conformity with the vision dictated by those in power' (Merkle 2018: 247). There is also an obvious ethical dimension to this topic, as critic Negoițescu (1998: 19) observes:

> Self-censorship is even more dangerous than censorship itself, because it can break/struggle free from the writer's critical mind and act subconsciously, falsifying the message. For example, under the pressure of censorship you avoid treating certain topics, certain authors, while being positive [sic] (no hypocrisy implied) that these topics and authors are of no interest to you, when, in fact, you are afraid of censorship and try to avoid facing it.

Quantitative approaches have also provided necessary evidence for studies dealing with translations published during the post-communist period, when communist censorship was abruptly replaced by market censorship which imposes popular taste as a significant criterion in order to ensure the prosperity and, sometimes, survival of the 229 publishing houses that were set up in the 1990s. However, selecting books on the basis of their literary value has never been eliminated from the equation. It is also (ideologically) significant that, after half a century of communist dictatorship, during the country's first decade of democracy (1990–2000) the number of translations from American literature exceeded by far translations from other literatures, both classical texts and best-sellers (Sâsâiac 2021: 199–200). Speaking of an *invisible*, still very much present censorship in democratic states, Corobca (2020: 279), citing Durand's (2006) classification of censorship (material/technical, economic and cultural), argues that it applies to post-communist societies as well.

17.5 Conclusion

Censorship exerted on (translated) literary texts has been a topic of considerable interest in post-communist Romania in view of the anti-communist stance of a significant segment of Romanian society after the downfall of communism in 1989. Even if censorship was present during different periods of the country's history, it is during communism that, following the Soviet model, it reached a high level of elaboration at both political and administrative levels, leaving indelible marks on the subsequent development of Romanian literature and culture. The repressive side of censorship left untranslated or mutilated a series of literary works the ideology of which departed from the official discourse of the period. On the whole, the most frequent translation strategies applied to literary works were intervention, adjustment, attenuation and deletion of ideologically problematic passages. They were the preferred options to leaving untranslated important texts that were part of the world literary canon. Censorship-dictated textual interventions inevitably led to distorsions affecting the overall image of the source culture, of the source text in its entirety, of the author, the characters and plot, and, ultimately, they had an undesirable impact on the reception of the text as a whole by the target readers.

Nevertheless, setting aside these undeniable negative impacts, it must be recalled that censors were 'human beings' (Comănescu 1998), particularly those operating on the lower levels, hence the possibility of negotiation (e.g., preserving an otherwise unacceptable word, phrase, even an idea) and, occasionaly, of collusion between censors and their 'victims'.

On the productive side, in Romania, censorship led to the creation of alternative, encoded, allusive, 'magic' (translated) discourses, which created paradigm shifts in literary theory and criticism,

The Routledge Handbook of Translation and Censorship

and taught readers and audiences to read between the lines and refine their interpretations of literary texts, whether performed on the stage or written on the page.

Globalisation has imposed different, ubiquitous and de-centralised forms of more discrete censorship. In democratic Romania as elsewhere, consistent research needs to be undertaken to observe and describe, in a more accurate manner, the functioning of the new forms of censorship, including market censorship and media-related types of censorship. These invisible forms of surveillance and control are linked to digital censorship; they may or may not involve translation, and it may be difficult to ascertain whose interests they serve. However, their presence in propaganda, mass manipulation and education is significant, and the future New Person targeted by mediatic shaping that includes censorship is more difficult to grasp than the communist New Man of the twentieth century.

Further reading

Baer, Brian James (ed.). 2011. *Contexts, Subtexts and Pretexts.* Amsterdam and Philadelphia: John Benjamins Publishing.
This volume, and the editor's introduction in particular, offers an in-depth perspective on the Eastern European countries and Russia, broaching issues of identity and self-perception while also revealing the workings of censorship in a geopolitical area in which translation has always held a privileged position.

Macrea-Toma, Ioana. 2009. *Privilighentia. Instituţii literare în comunismul românesc* [Privileged Intelligentsia. Literary Institutions in Communist Romania]. Cluj-Napoca: Casa Cărţii de Ştiinţă.
Although this book mainly focuses on a particular category of Romanian intellectuals under the communist regime, it includes analyses of the modes of operation of communist censorship in relation to the cultural and literary institutions of the time, through an approach that is both sociological and literary.

Popa, Ioana. 2013. 'Communism and Translation Studies', in Y. Gambier and L. van Doorslaer (eds.), *Handbook of Translation Studies*, Vol. 4. Amsterdam and Philadelphia: John Bejamins Publishing, 25–30.
This chapter offers a broader and absolutely necessary contextualisation and integration of the research on censorship with investigations of the internationalist communist ideology, translation flows and the translators' status during various communist regimes in Eastern Europe.

References

Antochi, Roxana-Mihaela. 2012. 'Behind the scene: Text selection policies in communist Romania. A preliminary study on Spanish and Latin-American Drama', in B. Fischer and M. Nisbeth Jensen (eds.), *Translation and the Reconfiguration of Power Relations. Revisiting Role and Context of Translation and Interpreting.* Graz: LIT-VERLAG, 35–52.
Avramescu, Tiberiu. 2005. 'Cenzura în edituri', in M. Petcu (ed.), *Cenzura în spaţiul cultural românesc* [Censorship in the Romanian Cultural Space]. Bucureşti: Editura Comunicare.ro, 417–29.
Baer, Brian James. 2011. 'Introduction. Cultures of translation', in B. Baer (ed.), *Contexts, Subtexts and Pretexts.* Amsterdam and Philadelphia: John Benjamins Publishing, 1–18.
Baghiu, Ştefan. 2016. 'Translating novels in Romania: The age of socialist realism. From an ideological center to geographical margins', *Studia UBB Philologia*, LXI(1): 5–18.
Baghiu, Ştefan. 2019. 'The French novel in translation. A distant reading for Romania during communism (1944–1989)', *Transylvanian Review*, XXVIII(1): 83–98.
Baghiu, Ştefan. 2020. 'O periodizare a traducerilor de roman în perioada comunistă' [A periodisation of novel translation in the communist period], *Vatra*, 8–9: 107–14.
Bassnett, Susan and Lefevere, André (eds). 1998. *Constructing Cultures: Essays on Literary Translation.* Bristol: Multilingual Matters.
Comănescu, Denisa. 1998. '*Our Father* only at home', in L. Vianu, *Censorship in Romania*. Budapest: Central European University Press, 219–21.

Copilaș, Emanuel. 2022. 'Capitalismul românesc. Tendințe oligarhice, tehnocratice și digitale' [Romanian capitalism. Ologarchic, technocratic and digital tendencies], in L. Corobca (ed.), *Panorama postcomunismului în România* [A Survey of the Romanian Post-Communism]. Iași: Polirom, 194–203.

Cornea, Paul (ed.). 1970. 'Cerere și ofertă în determinarea profilului traducerilor de la jumătatea veacului trecut' [Supply and demand in determining translation profile in the latter half of the 19th century], in *Probleme de literatură comparată și sociologie literară* [Problems of Contemporary Literature and Literary Sociology]. București: Editura Academiei Republicii Socialiste România, 109–15.

Corobca, Liliana (ed.). 2020. *Panorama comunismului în România* [A Survey of the Romanian Communism]. Iași: Polirom.

Corobca, Liliana. 2020. 'Cenzura în comunism: instituții, atribuții, practici' [Censorship under communism: institutions, functions and practices], in L. Corobca (ed.), *Panorama comunismului în România* [A Survey of the Romanian Communism]. Iași: Polirom, 254–80.

Cotter, Sean. 2014. *Literary Translation and the Idea of a Minor Romania.* Rochester: University of Rochester Press.

Denize, Eugen. 2009. *Propaganda comunistă în România (19481953).* Târgoviște: Cetatea de Scaun.

Dimitriu, Rodica. 1999. *Aldous Huxley in Romania.* Iași: Editura Timpul.

Dimitriu, Rodica. 2000. 'Translation policies in pre-communist and communist Romania', *Across Languages and Cultures*, 1(2): 179–92.

Dimitriu, Rodica. 2006. 'From Robinson Crusoe to Robinson in Wallachia. The intricacies of the reception process', in M. Shlesinger, Z. Jettmarowa and A. Pym (eds.), *Sociocultural Aspects of Translation and Interpreting.* Amsterdam and Philadelphia: John Benjamins Publishing, 73–82.

Dimitriu, Rodica. 2007. 'Ideological clashes in translation', in *Mapping the Future: Permanence and Change.* Iași: Universitas, 343–52.

Dimitriu Rodica. 2016. 'Translation as blockage, propagation and recreation of ethnic images', in P. Flynn, J. Leerssen and L. van Doorslaer (eds.), *Interconnecting Translation Studies, and Imagology.* Amsterdam and Philadelphia: John Benjamins Publishing, 201–15.

Dollerup, Cay. 1997. 'Translation as imposition vs. translation as requisition', in M. Snell-Hornby, Z. Jettmarová and K. Kaindl (eds.), *Translation as Intercultural Communication*, Amsterdam and Philadelphia: John Benjamins Publishing, 45–56.

Doinaș, Ștefan Augustin. 1992. 'Cenzura a viciat conștiințele' [Censorship did alter moral values], *Agora*, V(1): 34–40.

Durand, Pascal. 2006. *La censure invisible.* Arles and Paris: Actes Sud.

Eliade, Mircea. 1943. 'Aldous Huxley', in M. Eliade, *Insula lui Euthanasius* [The Island of Euthanasius]. București: Fundația Regală pentru Literatură și Artă, 232–51.

Ionescu, Arleen. 2010. 'Un-Sexing *Ulysses*: The Romanian translation "under" communism', *Scientia Traductionis*, 8: 237–52.

Ionescu, Gelu. 1981. *Orizontul traducerii* [The Horizon of Translation]. București: Univers.

Kohn, Janos. 2009. 'Romanian tradition', in M. Baker and G. Saldanha (eds.), *Routledge Encyclopedia of Translation Studies.* London and New York: Routledge, 510–17.

Macrea-Toma, Ioana. 2009. *Privilighentia. Instituții literare în comunismul românesc* [Privileged intelligentsia. Literary institutions in communist Romania]. Cluj-Napoca: Casa Cărții de Știință.

Merkle, Denise. 2018. 'Translation and censorship', in F. Fernández and J. Evans (eds.), *The Routledge Handbook of Translation and Politics.* London and New York: Routledge, 238–53.

Negoițescu, Ion. 1998. 'The freedom of expression is the salt of culture', in L. Vianu (ed.),*Censorship in Romania.* Budapest: Central European University Press, 19–24.

Neț, Mariana. 2021. 'Sfârșit și început de secol (1895–1905)'[Late 19th and early 20th century (1895–1905)], in M. Constantinescu, T. Vîlceanu and D. Dejică (eds.), *O istorie a traducerilor în limba română din secolul al XX-lea* [A 20th Century History of Translation into the Romanian Language], Vol. 1. București: Editura Academiei Române, 71–5.

Nițescu, Marin. 1995. *Sub zodia proletcultismului. Dialectica puterii* [Under the Sign of Proletkult. The Dialectic of Power]. București: Humanitas.

Pâcleanu, Ana-Maria. 2018. *Not Only Taboo: Translating the Controversial Before, During and After Communism.* Cluj Napoca: Casa Cărții de Știință.

Pâcleanu, Ana-Maria. 2021. 'Traducerea literaturii engleze sub cenzura comunistă' [The translation of English literature under communism], in M. Constantinescu, T. Vîlceanu and D. Dejică (eds.), *O istorie a traducerilor în limba română din secolul al XX-lea* [A 20th Century History of Translation into the Romanian Language], Vol. 1. București: Editura Academiei Române, 113–21.

Petcu, Marian. 1999. *Puterea și cultura. O istorie a cenzurii* [Culture and Power. A History of Censorship]. Iași: Polirom.

Pop, Doru. 2022. 'Ideile care ne sucesc și ne răsucesc mințile' [Ideas that twist and warp our minds], in M. Corobca (ed.), *Panorama postcomunismului în România* [A Survey of the Romanian Post-Communism]. Iași: Polirom, 204–18.

Popa, Ioana. 2018. 'Translation and communism in Eastern Europe', in F. Fernández and J. Evans (eds.), *The Routledge Handbook of Translation and Politics*. London and New York: Routledge, 424–41.

Rad, Ilie. 2005. 'Aspecte ale cenzurii literare' [Aspects of literary censorship], in M. Petcu (ed.), *Cenzura în spațiul cultural românesc* [Censorship in the Romanian Cultural Space]. București: Editura Comunicare. ro, 267–78.

Rad, Ilie (ed.). 2011. *Cenzura în România* [Censorship in Romania]. Cluj-Napoca: Tribuna.

Rădulescu, Anda. 2010. 'Entre censure et autocensure littéraire en Roumanie. L'odyssée d'un journal intime à l'époque communiste', *TTR*, 23(2): 23–52.

Ralian, Antoaneta. 2005. 'Toată literatura lumii este una pregnant erotică' [All world literature is predominantly erotic], O. Șimonca (interviewer), *Observator cultural*, 800. Available at: www.observatorcultural. ro/articol/toata-literatura-lumii-este-una-pregnant-erotica-interviu-cu-antoaneta-ralian-realizat-in-2005/ (Accessed: 16 June 2023).

Rambsy, Kenton. 2021. 'What is distant reading', in P. Ossom-Williamson and K. Rambsy, *The Data Notebook*. Mavs Open Press. Available at: 1.4 What is Distant Reading? – The Data Notebook (pressbooks.pub) (Accessed: 5 April 2024).

Runcan, Miruna. 2006. 'Mecanisme și instituții ale cenzurii în teatru' [Mechanisms and institutions of theatre censorship], in L. Malița (ed.), *Viața teatrală în și după comunism* [Theatre Life During and After Communism]. Cluj: Eefes, 299–312.

Sâsâiac, Andi. 2021. 'Traducerea romanului britanic și american: o abordare cantitativă' [The translation of the British and American novel: a quantitative approach], in M. Constantinescu, T. Vîlceanu and D. Dejică (eds.), *O istorie a traducerilor în limba română din secolul al XX-lea* [A 20th Century History of Translation into the Romanian Language], Vol. 1. București: Editura Academiei Române, 198–209.

Toury, Gideon. 1995. *Descriptive Translation Studies and Beyond*. Amsterdam and Philadelphia: John Benjamins Publishing.

Toury, Gideon. 2003. 'Culture planning and translation', in S. Petrilli (ed.), *Translation Translation*. Amsterdam and New York: Rodopi, 399–412.

Vajdová, Libusa. 2021. 'Traduceri de teorie și critică literară în România comunistă: o perspectivă cehoslovacă' [Translations of literary theory and criticism in communist Romania: A Czechoslovakian perspective], in M. Constantinescu, T. Vîlceanu and D. Dejică (eds.), *O istorie a traducerilor înlimba română din secolul al XX-lea* [A 20th Century History of Translation into the Romanian Language], Vol. 1. București: Editura Academiei Române, 595–602.

Vianu, Lidia. 1998. *Censorship in Romania*. Budapest: Central European University Press.

Volceanov, George. 2005. 'Bowdlerizing Shakespeare: Here, there, and everywhere', *BAS*, 11: 117–30.

Volceanov, George. 2021. *Un Shakespeare pentru mileniul trei: istoria unei ediții* [A Shakespeare for the Third Millenium: The History of an Edition]. București: Tracus Arte.

Vrînceanu, Alexandra. 2022. 'Muriel Spark: Domnișoara Brodie în floarea vîrstei (1975, 2007) / Cei mai frumoși ani (2006)' [Muriel Spark's The Prime of Miss Jean Brodie in Romanian translations], in M. Constantinescu, T. Vîlceanu and D. Dejică (eds.), *O istorie a traducerilor în limba română din secolul al XX-lea* [A 20th Century History of Translation into the Romanian Language], Vol. 2. București: Editura Academiei Române, 66–71.

Wolf, Michaela. 2002. 'Censorship as cultural blockage: Banned literature in the Late Habsburg Monarchy', *TTR*, 15(2): 45–62.

18

CENSORSHIP UNDER COMMUNISM IN SOCIALIST SLOVENIA

Nike K. Pokorn

18.1 Introduction

At the end of the 1930s the ethnic Slovene territory belonged to three different states: the Kingdom of Yugoslavia, Italy and Austria, however, the borders changed again at the beginning of the Second World War, when these lands were divided into German, Italian and Hungarian occupation zones, and after the war, when they became a part of a republic in the socialist Yugoslavia. During the Second World War, the Italian and German occupying forces introduced their form of censorial control, and in the socialist period (between 1945 and 1991), when the Federal Republic of Slovenia was a constituent part of the Socialist Federal Republic of Yugoslavia, the dominant ideology also imposed certain censorial pressures on translators. Censorship in socialist times was, contrary to the practice in the Habsburg empire and in the Kingdom of Yugoslavia, hidden and denied by the ruling party. This meant that translators had to resort to different strategies: some of them practised self-censorship by displacing, omitting or rewriting passages that the ruling political party or ideology found problematic, others witnessed their translations being adapted by other agents in the publishing process, and still others saw their translations denied publication or public performance, or taken out of print and removed from public libraries.

18.2 Historical Perspectives

18.2.1 The Second World War

At the beginning of the Second World War in 1941, the Kingdom of Yugoslavia surrendered to Axis forces, and consequently, the ethnic Slovene territory was divided between Germany, Italy and Hungary, with the Italians controlling the capital city of Ljubljana and the lands to the west; the northern part of the Kingdom was annexed by the German Reich while Hungary occupied the easternmost territory of Prekmurje. In the territory where the Slovenes were the majority population, the Italians, in principle, granted the Slovenes ethnic and cultural autonomy, a cooperative role in administration and bilingualism (Godeša 2010: 129). Despite this fairly liberal position, which was in stark contrast to the genocidal policy in place in the German-occupied territory of Slovenia, the Italian occupiers nevertheless established the Press and Censorship Bureau [*Ufficio Stampa e Censura*], which practised preventive censorship of periodicals. In addition, numerous

DOI: 10.4324/9781003149453-22

literary works that had already been prepared for publication were not sent to the printers (in some cases, the authors themselves withdrew their publications). The Press and Censorship Bureau also drafted a list of more than 500 Slovene, Croatian and German books that were to be taken out of public libraries. Among them were also the Slovene translations of works by the French authors André Maurois, André Gide, and the communist Henri Barbusse, the Austrian Jewish writer Stefan Zweig, the philosopher Otto Weininger, the politician Richard Coudenhove-Kalergi, the journalist and historian Max Beer, the philosopher Karl Kautsky and the Social Democrat Otto Bauer, as well as the German anti-fascist writer Heinrich Mann, the American novelist Ernest Hemingway, the Czech writer Jaroslav Hašek, the communist Croatian writer Miroslav Krleža and the Soviet author Mikhail Aleksandrovich Sholokhov. Translations were not only removed because the occupying forces found their authors problematic; some of them were prohibited because of the problematic paratexts accompanying the translations. For example, the Slovene translation of Machiavelli's *The Prince* was banned because of the introduction, which negatively portrayed Italians (Godeša 2010: 137–8).

After the capitulation of Italy in 1943, German troops occupied the territory that had previously been under the control of fascist Italy and renamed it the 'Operational Zone of the Adriatic Littoral'. With the help of local collaborators, the province of Ljubljana retained some cultural and political autonomy; however, it was carefully monitored by the Ljubljana censorship office, which was subordinate to the second department of Nazi High Commissariat in Trieste called 'Propaganda, Press, Culture' [*Propaganda, Presse, Kultur*]. In addition to the German bureau in Ljubljana, there existed another press bureau that was run by the local collaborating forces and that was also subordinate to the German bureau. Both Ljubljana bureaus controlled primarily periodicals, however, they also monitored original and translated literature (Mlakar 2010: 150).

In addition to the censor's offices of the occupying forces and collaborators, the Slovene resistance exercised control over its publications. The Slovene resistance movement, called the Liberation Front, was founded soon after the occupation in April 1941 by representatives of different left-wing movements. This coalition fell under the exclusive leadership of the Slovene Communist Party in 1943 (Repe 2008: 45) and kept close ties with Tito's Partisans, so that Slovene representatives of the Liberation Front were present in Bosnia when the Federal Republic of Yugoslavia was proclaimed. All the publications of the Liberation Front were controlled by the Communist party, in particular, by its Agitprop committee (i.e., Committee for Agitation and Propaganda), so that very few instances of retroactive censorship were needed (Deželak Barič 2010).

18.2.2 The Socialist Federal Republic of Slovenia (1941991)

18.2.2.1   The Early Years of Total Control (19451952)

The Second World War ended in Slovenia in May 1945 when the communist-led Liberation Front and partisan forces took control of the territory that had belonged to the Kingdom of Yugoslavia and of the territories inhabited by Slovenes in Italy and Austria after the dissolution of Austria-Hungary. A new Federal People's Republic of Yugoslavia (later renamed the Socialist Federal Republic of Yugoslavia) was formed consisting of six federal republics, among them, the Socialist Federal Republic of Slovenia. Slovene became one of the three official languages of Yugoslavia (besides Serbo-Croat and Macedonian), and the primary official and administrative language in the Republic of Slovenia (in bilingual border areas Italian and Hungarian were also used as co-official languages).

In the first years after the war, Yugoslav communists assumed all important positions in society and closely followed the Soviet model, which included the swift elimination of all political

Censorship under Communism in Socialist Slovenia

opponents, total control of cultural life and a negative attitude toward organised religion, which in Slovenia's case, was directed toward the Catholic church, in particular. Religion was, on the one hand, rejected philosophically: it was seen as a superstition, a historical phenomenon that hampers people's emancipation and their embrace of their true selves. On the other hand, the Catholic church was pushed to the margins of society because of its involvement in daily politics during the interwar period and its role in supporting anti-communist movements during the war, notably, in the Ljubljana province (Pokorn 2022).

The new socialist government, similar to other socialist states, claimed that censorship did not exist. However, the state carried out very efficient control of everything that was published, exhibited, included in cinema or theatre repertoires or said in public, and practised both preventive and retroactive censorship. The mechanisms of censorship, however, differed according to the historical period, with the strictest control being imposed in the first years after the war.

Immediately after the war, the new government destroyed or took out of public libraries and bookshops all publications that were considered propagandistic literature of the defeated side, for example, all books and leaflets that were published by the Italian and German occupying forces or by Slovene collaborators. The Agitprop Committee, which, following the Soviet model, operated in the shadows, appointed a special commission to examine the existing stocks in bookshops and decide which books and pamphlets should be withdrawn from the market. If the decision was similar to that taken in West European states during the post-war period, the fact that the list of banned literature included numerous works of literature not directly connected to the occupying forces was not. Agitprop banned the originals and translations of authors who had either supported the defeated side (e.g., Knut Hamsun) or whose works were, according to the ruling communist party, 'contrary to our views on the fundamental issues of life'[1] (AS2 231, a.u. 37, 3159/2–45; Gabrič 2008: 65), which meant all works that explicitly expressed a religious worldview. These works were not destroyed but were kept in libraries under restricted access. For example, the third amended list of prohibited books issued by the Ministry of Education in November 1945 contained the titles of Nazi, Fascist and Home Guard works of propaganda, works by Slovene authors who emigrated after the war or were prosecuted in the post-war period, as well as a considerable number of translated literary works by Serbo-Croat, Italian, French and German authors, including the translations of works by authors who were critical of the Soviet Union, such as the Romanian author Panait Istrati, the French writer André Gide, and Irish novelist Liam O'Flaherty. The purge of Slovene bookshops and public libraries continued throughout the next three years and was completed in 1948 (Gabrič 2008: 66).

Agitprop also monitored theatre productions. In 1946 Ben Jonson's *Volpone* was prohibited from the repertoire, and the translation of the Soviet play *Family Happiness* (*Семейное счастье*, 1945) by Mikhail Vasilyevich Vodopyanov and J. Laptev closed after only two performances. The reasons for these prohibitions were not given. Archival material reveals that the censorship of theatre productions continued into the early 1950s and was mainly exercised through informal instructions via telephone. For example, in 1951 the director of the national theatre in Ljubljana was instructed over the phone to replace in the next season's repertoire Shaw's *Pygmalion* with his *Caesar and Cleopatra*, and, surprisingly, existential Marxist Sartre with politically ambiguous Anouilh (Gabrič 2010: 182, 185).

During the period, translations also featured in trials. In 1947, in one of the communist show trials against a group of more liberal, pro-Western resistance fighters in Ljubljana, the dean of the law faculty, Boris Furlan (1894–1957), was, among others, accused of possessing and attempting to translate Orwell's *Animal Farm*. Furlan admitted only to reading the book but was nevertheless found guilty and consequently stripped of all political rights for three years and sentenced to seven years of forced labour (Puhar 2001: 253–4).

In addition to retroactive censorship, preventive censorship was carried out. After the war, out of 26 existing publishing houses, only three were allowed to continue their activities: Slovenska matica (Slovene society, est. 1864) and the publishing house of the Academy of Arts and Sciences (est. 1938), which were taken over by the new ideological elite, and Mohorjeva družba (the society of St Hermagoras, est. 1851), which remained in the hands of the Catholic Church and retained some degree of independence due to its influence on the Slovene minority in Austrian Carinthia (Žnideršič 1995: 119–36; Pokorn 2012). All other publishing houses were nationalised and their equipment confiscated. Parallel to that, the new government established new publishing houses that had to submit their publishing programs to Agitprop for examination. Gabrič (2010: 67) reports on how Agitprop commented on one such program in 1948: without any explanation, orders were given to cease the planned translations of John Steinbeck's *Of Mice and Men* and Tolstoy's *Polikushka,* orders that were promptly carried out by the publishers. Times, however, were changing quickly. Tolstoy's translation was published only two years later in 1950, while the Slovene translation of Steinbeck's novel appeared in 1952, the same year Agitprop committees were abolished.

18.2.2.2   From 1952 to 1990

In 1952 the Yugoslav Communist Party changed its name to the League of Communists. With this act the Yugoslav party indicated its complete rupture with the Soviet model of government, which had already started in 1948 with the Tito-Stalin split. Despite this symbolic gesture, the Yugoslav communists did not relinquish control over publishing activity. On the one hand, the production of the state publishing houses continued to be monitored by various committees of the newly established Socialist Alliance of the Working People (SAWP), an all-inclusive organisation led by the communists, and by different committees of the League of Communists functioning behind the scenes. On the other hand, publishing houses were governed by communist general managers, and additional control was carried out by so-called publishing councils. In 1955 the Yugoslav Assembly passed a new law on publishing activity that obliged all publishing houses in Yugoslavia to introduce a publishing council whose main function was to approve the yearly publishing program of a publishing house, and whose members were selected by the republic SAWP's print committees. As a result, these publishing councils were led by trustworthy communists (Žnideršič 1995: 129; Gabrič 1995: 23). Therefore, in order to avoid problems, the editors tended not to include those works in their yearly programs that they thought might be rejected by the publishing councils, and also selected translators who were either staunch communists or who were prepared to modify translations to put them in line with the ruling ideology. The control of publishing activity through the managerial structure of publishing houses functioned so well that no official censor's office was needed.

Yugoslav and Slovene socialist translation censorship was also practised on the textual level and was carried out by editors or translators themselves, mainly when children's literature was concerned. There is evidence of editors occasionally influencing translators by giving them instructions on how to translate and what to omit from their translations (Pokorn 2012: 151), of editors changing the target text without the knowledge of the translators (Pokorn 2018), and of translators willingly changing the text to align it with the dominant ideology (Pokorn 2012: 152). Children's classics, such as fairy tales by the Brothers Grimm and by Hans Christian Andersen, were retranslated in the first decade after the war, and references to religion were either omitted or replaced by passages in line with dialectical materialism (Pokorn 2012: 51–73). Other disturbing elements for the dominant ideology were any criticism of socialist revolution or overly positive descriptions of Germans as found, for example, in Karl May's work, but also anything that was considered of low quality (for example, some imported picture books were branded as kitsch). (Self-)censorship of literature for adult readers was rarely practised. Only a few isolated instances of censorship of religious passages were found in retranslations of literature for the masses, such as in retranslations of Jules Verne's work (Pokorn 2012: 125–8), and in translated Slovene literature into English printed in Slovenia and targeting readers abroad (Pokorn 2000).

The anti-religious fervour of the Communist Party gradually abated, and in 1971 the president of Yugoslavia, Josip Broz Tito, was the first communist leader to be received by the pope. The liberalisation continued throughout the 1980s and was most pronounced in the Republic of Slovenia; for example, between 1981 and 1987 'only' 19 Slovene citizens were prosecuted for the defamation of the state compared to 172 Croats and 81 Serbs (Pokorn 2012: 30). Finally, in 1983, the Committee of the Presidency of the Central Committee of the League of Communists of Slovenia for Information and Propaganda condemned and rescinded the practice of censoring translations—a practice that had never been officially introduced (AS 1589, a.u. 697; Pokorn 2012: 147).

In the 1980s the official list of banned books published in the Official Gazette was reduced to only 11 titles; however, many more publications were unofficially prohibited. For example, there existed a special reserve in the national library in Ljubljana, the so-called 'D-Reserve' (the director's reserve), which by the 1980s contained more than 700 works, written mostly by Slovene political émigrés; however, the hidden works also included pornographic literature—at one point even D.H. Lawrence's *Lady Chatterley's Lover*. The D-Reserve was not available to the general public, nor was it included in the public catalogue (Švent 2010: 251; Gabrič 2008: 74).

In 1980 Josip Broz Tito died and Yugoslavia entered an economic, social, political and institutional crisis, which ended with the first Yugoslav multiparty elections in Slovenia in May 1990 and Slovenia's separation from Yugoslavia in 1991, which marked the beginning of the end of the common state.

18.2.2.3   The Post-Socialist Period after 1991

In the post-socialist period censorial practices in literature in the Republic of Slovenia are mainly associated with libel and defamation law. Two cases earned a great deal of public attention: the prohibition of two Slovene novels. In both cases some individuals recognised themselves in fictional characters and managed to have the books legally banned (Pikalo 2008; Smolnikar 2008). Children's literature continues to be adapted to changing social norms and standards: passages describing cruel and vindictive acts are often deleted from classic fairy tales, and sometimes passages describing racial prejudice or traditional gender roles that are today considered politically incorrect are rewritten, usually by the editors of the books. As far as translations are concerned, reprints of translations of children's literature that were censored during socialist times are amended by editors, who occasionally re-introduce elements that were removed in the socialist period (Pokorn 2018).

18.3   Core Issues and Topics

Few publications are dedicated exclusively to the censorship of Slovene translations, more of them focus on censorship in general in the period after the Second World War, among them a special issue of the journal *Primerjalna književnost* [Comparative literature] published in 2008 (Dović 2008), and a collected volume focusing on censorship from the nineteenth to the twenty-first centuries published in 2010 (Režek 2010). None of the individual contributions in these two publications focuses solely on censorship in translation, however, many of them mention censorial control of translated texts. The special issue of the journal *Comparative Literature,* for example, contains an important article by the historian Gabrič (2008), in which he describes the main characteristics of censorial practices in socialist Slovenia. Although Gabrič does not explicitly focus on translations, he dedicates a paragraph to this issue, in which he mentions that translations were ideologically altered during this period (Gabrič 2008: 75). In the collected volume edited by Režek on the history of censorship in Slovenia from the nineteenth century onward, Godeša (2010) in his description of censorial practices during the Italian occupation between 1941 and 1943 also mentions some censored translated works, and Mlakar (2010: 150) describes different positions taken by the Slovene and German censorship office during the German occupation, also regarding translated literature. And finally, Gabrič (2010), in his comparison of theatre censorship in the time of the Kingdom of Yugoslavia and that of socialist Yugoslavia, discusses cases of preventive and retroactive censorship of translated plays.

There do exist, however, works that deal explicitly with the censorship of translations, for example a monograph dealing with socialist censorship in children's translations (Pokorn 2012). In this work, Pokorn analyses 96 retranslations of children's classics made in the Socialist Federal Republic of Yugoslavia, such as Grimms' 'Cinderella' and Hans Christian Andersen's 'The Little Mermaid'. Textual analyses are supplemented with archival research and interviews with editors from the period. The results show that eighty per cent of selected retranslations published in the socialist period omitted or rewrote passages referring to Christian religion with an attempt to indoctrinate new generations by promoting dialectical materialism and atheism.

The fact that Yugoslav communists, in particular in the first decades after the war, focused intensely on influencing the minds of the young people was reflected in original and translated children's literature. On the one hand, several authors of Slovene children's literature self-censored their work for the post-war editions, mainly omitting or replacing positive references to Christian religions (Svetina 2011), while, on the other hand, ideological changes were introduced into translated and retranslated children's literature. Consequently, this topic has been researched by various scholars. Smolik (1995), for example, was one of the first authors to draw attention to textually manipulated translations of children's classics by Karl May, publishing a partial textual analysis in the Catholic weekly *Družina*. Orel Kos in her article also mentions transformations and omissions in the socialist translation of Hans Christian Andersen's fairy tale 'The Wild Swans' (Orel Kos 2001). Several articles written by Pokorn focus on retranslations of Johanna Spyri's *Heidi* and Felix Salten's *Bambi* (Pokorn 2005, 2010, see also 2012).

In addition to the socialist rejection of a religious worldview, the socialist attitude toward racist discourse has been studied, focusing on Slovene translations of American classics such as *Adventures of Huckleberry Finn* (Trupej 2012), *Uncle Tom's Cabin, Gone with the Wind* and *Of Mice and Men* (Trupej 2015). In his article on Slovene translations of Sienkiewicz's novel *In Desert and Wilderness*, Snoj compares socialist attitudes toward racism and religion, concluding that, surprisingly, socialist translations show greater lenience toward racism than toward religion (Snoj 2020). And finally, the circulation of censored books in post-socialist times has been researched (Pokorn 2018). The results showed that in 2015, 43% of accredited primary school textbooks and primers still contained passages taken from ideologically manipulated translations in the socialist period, although ideologically unaltered versions were available on the market. Moreover, when choosing a particular translated passage for their textbook, the authors of the textbooks and primers, predominantly unaware of the ideological changes, mainly focused on the stylistic aspects of the translation, preferring a more fluid style, and introduced into their textbooks

Censorship under Communism in Socialist Slovenia

passages from those translations that were available in the public libraries, which mainly stock translations from the socialist period.

18.4   New Debates

New debates depart from purely textual comparative analysis to focus more on deciphering the mechanisms of censorial control. For example, the complexity of the system of control in place in socialist publishing houses has recently been researched in regard to Mladinska knjiga, the leading publishing house for juvenile fiction in Yugoslavia (Pokorn 2022). There is a need to supplement this with research focusing on Slovene exchanges with languages other than central European languages and on periods prior to socialism that remain understudied. In addition to that, the role of socialist cultural arbiters in different party committees, who fought against what they termed 'kitsch' in literature, also deserves some scholarly attention in the context of a general reappraisal of censorship not only as a repressive but also as, what Billiani (2007: 4) calls, a productive tool in the literary field.

Acknowledgements

Nike K. Pokorn acknowledges the financial support from the Slovenian Research and Innovation Agency (research core funding No. P6-0446).

Further Reading

Dović, Marijan (ed.). 2008. *Primerjalna književnost*, 31 (Special issue) Literatura in cenzura: Kdo se boji resnice literature? [Literature and Censorship: Who is Afraid of the Truth of Literature?].
This special edition of the most eminent Slovene literary theory journal was the first collective volume entirely dedicated to censorship in Slovenia. Besides providing a theoretical framework for the discussion of censorship in literature, the volume also includes the article by Aleš Gabrič on censorship in socialist Slovenia, which explicitly mentions translations.

Pokorn, Nike K. 2012. *Post-Socialist Translation Practices: Ideological Struggle in Children's Literature*. Amsterdam and Philadelphia: John Benjamins.
This volume attempts to describe socialist translation practice through the study of retranslations of children's classics in socialist Yugoslavia, paying particular attention to the Slovene situation. Textual analysis is accompanied by archival research on the Communist Party of Slovenia and the Socialist Alliance of the Working People, interviews with the editors, as well as research on the circulation of socialist translations at the beginning of the twenty-first century.

Režek, Mateja (ed.). 2010. *Cenzurirano: Zgodovina cenzure na Slovenskem od 19. stoletja do danes* [Censored: History of Censorship in Slovenia from the 19th Century to Today]. Ljubljana: Nova Revija (Zbirka Razprave 2).
A collected volume mainly written by historians systematically describes censorial practices in Slovene lands from the March Revolution of 1848, through WWI, the interwar period, WWII, and from the socialist period to post-socialist times.

Notes

1   Translated into English by the author of the chapter.
2   Archival records. The in-text citations to the archival material from the Archives of the Republic of Slovenia (National Archives): a) the name of institution: Archives of the Republic of Slovenia (AS), b) the serial number of the fund or the collection (AS 1589), c) the document reference, i.e., number of the archival unit which contains the archival records (AS 1589, a. u. 697).

The Routledge Handbook of Translation and Censorship

References

Billiani, Francesca. 2007. 'Assessing boundaries – Censorship and Translation', in F. Billiani (ed.), *Modes of Censorship and Translation: National Contexts and Diverse Media*. London, New York: Routledge, 1– 25.

Deželak Barič, Vida. 2010. 'Cenzura v slovenskem odporništvu med drugo svetovno vojno' [Censorship in Slovenian resistance during World War II.], in M. Režek (ed.), *Cenzurirano: Zgodovina cenzure na Slovenskem od 19. stoletja do danes* [Censored: History of Censorship in Slovenia from the 19th Century to Today]. Ljubljana: Nova Revija (Zbirka Razprave 2), 153–70.

Dović, Marijan (ed.). 2008. *Primerjalna književnost* 31 (Special issue Literatura in cenzura: Kdo se boji resnice literature? [Literature and Censorship: Who is afraid of the truth of literature?].

Gabrič, Aleš. 1995. *Socialistična kulturna revolucija: slovenska kulturna politika: 1953–1962*. [Socialist cultural revolution: Slovene cultural politics: 1953–1962] Ljubljana: Cankarjeva založba.

Gabrič, Aleš. 2008. 'Cenzura v Sloveniji po drugi svetovni vojni: od komunističnega *Index librorum prohibitorum* do ukinitve "verbalnega delicta"' [Censorship in Slovenia after World War II: From the communist *Index Librorum Prohibitorum* to abolition of the 'verbal offence'], *Primerjalna književnost* (Special issue ed. by Marjan Dović): Literatura in cenzura: Kdo se boji resnice literature? [Literature and Censorship: Who is Afraid of the Truth of Literature?], 31: 63–78.

Gabrič, Aleš. 2010. 'Cenzura gledališkega repertoarja v prvi in drugi Jugoslaviji' [Censorship of theatre repertoire in the First and Second Yugoslavia], in M. Režek (ed.), *Cenzurirano: Zgodovina cenzure na Slovenskem od 19. stoletja do danes* [Censored: History of Censorship in Slovenia from the 19th century to Today]. Ljubljana: Nova Revija (Zbirka Razprave 2), 171–88.

Godeša, Bojan. 2010. 'Italijanska cenzura v Ljubljanski pokrajini' [The Italian censorship in the Province of Ljubljana (1941–1943)], in M. Režek (ed.), Cenzurirano: Zgodovina cenzure na Slovenskem od 19. stoletja do danes [Censored: History of Censorship in Slovenia from the 19th Century to Today]. Ljubljana: Nova Revija (Zbirka Razprave 2), 129–40.

Mlakar, Boris. 2010. 'Primeri delovanja nemške in slovenske cenzure v Rupnikovi Ljubljanski pokrajini' [Examples of German and Slovenian censorship in Rupnik's Province of Ljubljana (1943–1945)], in M. Režek (ed.), *Cenzurirano: Zgodovina cenzure na Slovenskem od 19. stoletja do danes* [Censored: History of Censorship in Slovenia from the 19th Century to Today]. Ljubljana: Nova Revija (Zbirka Razprave 2), 141–52.

Orel Kos, Silvana. 2001. 'Let divjih labodov med nebesi in peklom' [The flight of wild swans between heaven and hell], in M. Ožbot (ed.), *Prevajanje Prešerena, prevajanje pravljic*, 289–309. Ljubljana: Društvo slovenskih književnih prevajalcev.

Pikalo, Matjaž. 2008. 'Kdo se boji resnice literature?' [Who's afraid of the truth of literature?], *Primerjalna književnost*, 31 (Special issue ed. by M. Dović): Literatura in cenzura: Kdo se boji resnice literature? [Literature and Censorship: Who is Afraid of the Truth of Literature?]: 149–50.

Pokorn, N. K. 2005. 'Ste brali Heidi? Primer (post)socialistične cenzure prevodov' [Have you read Heidi? An example of (post)socialist translation censorship], in N. Kocijančič Pokorn, E. Prunč, and A. Riccardi (eds.), *Beyond Equivalence* [Graz Translation Studies 9]. Graz: Institut für Theoretische und Angewandte Translationswisenschaft, 57–72.

Pokorn, Nike K. 2000. 'Prevod kot interpretacija: Leemingova *Hiša Marije Pomočnice*' [Translation as interpretation: Leeming's *Ward of Our Lady of Mercy*], *Primerjalna književnost*, 23/2: 109–23. URN:NBN:SI:doc-E4EFZVJ3 from www.dlib.si

Pokorn, Nike K. 2010. 'A world without God: Slovene *Bambi*', in D. Gile, G. Hansen, and N. K. Pokorn (eds.), *Why TS Matters*. Amsterdam and Philadelphia: John Benjamins, 57–68.

Pokorn, Nike K. 2012. *Post-Socialist Translation Practices: Ideological Struggle in Children's Literature*. Amsterdam and Philadelphia: John Benjamins.

Pokorn, Nike K. 2018. 'Who are the real guardians of translated texts? Translators, editors and others', *Hieronymus*, 5: 1–25. www.ffzg.unizg.hr/hieronymus/wp-content/uploads/2019/01/H5-2018_1_Pok orn.pdf

Pokorn, Nike K. 2022. 'Ideological control in a Slovene socialist state publishing house: Conformity and dissent', in C. Rundle, A. Lange, and D. Monticelli (eds.), *Translation Under Communism*. London, New York: Palgrave Macmillan, 207–40.

Puhar, Alenka. 2001. 'Orwellovo tihotapljenje na Kranjsko', in G. Orwel, *Živalska farma/Izbrani eseji* [Animal Farm/Selected Essays]. Ljubljana: Mladinska knjiga, 253–62.

Repe, Božo. 2008. 'The liberation front of the Slovene people', in J. Pirjevec and B. Repe (eds.), *Resistance, Suffering, Hope: The Slovene Partisan Movement 1941–1945.* Trieste: Založništvo tržaškega tiska, 36–47.

Režek, Mateja. 2010. 'Predgovor' [Introduction], in M. Režek (ed.), *Cenzurirano: Zgodovina cenzure na Slovenskem od 19. stoletja do danes* [Censored: History of Censorship in Slovenia from the 19th Century to Today]. Ljubljana: Nova Revija (Zbirka Razprave 2), 9–11.

Smolik, Marijan. 1995. 'Razkristjanjeni Karl May – 1–4', *Družina*, 7: 29–32; 13: 34–7 and 39–42; 38: 21.

Smolnikar, Breda. 2008. 'Sanjski snežno beli prtič na košari slovenske literature' [A dream napkin white as snow on the basket of Slovenian literature], *Primerjalna književnost*, 31 (Special issue ed. by M. Dović: Literatura in cenzura: Kdo se boji resnice literature? [Literature and Censorship: Who is Afraid of the Truth of Literature?]: 151–3.

Snoj, Janž. 2020. 'Translating ideology with ideology: The case of Sienkiewicz's novel *In Desert and Wilderness* and its Slovenian translations', in A. Ketola, T. Mikolič Južnič, and O. Paloposki (eds.), *New Horizons in Translation Research and Education 5.* Tampere: Tampere University, 101–23.

Švent, Rozina. 2010. 'Narodna in univerzitetna knjižnica – ujetost med veljavno zakonodajo in narodnim poslanstvom' [National and University Library – trapped in between legislation and the national mission], in M. Režek (ed.), *Cenzurirano: Zgodovina cenzure na Slovenskem od 19. stoletja do danes* [Censored: History of Censorship in Slovenia from the 19th Century to Today]. Ljubljana: Nova Revija (Zbirka Razprave 2), 247–56.

Svetina, Peter. 2011. 'Pionirji na promenadi: slovenska mladinska književnost med obema vojnama in oblikovanje literarnega kanona po drugi svetovni vojni', in P. Svetina (ed.), *Pionirji na promenadi* [Pioneers on a Promenade]. Ljubljana: Mladinska knjiga. 551–98.

Trupej, Janko. 2012. 'Translating racist discourse in Slovenia during the socialist period: Mark Twain's Adventures of Huckleberry Finn', in B. Fischer and M. Nisbeth Jensen (eds.), *Translation and the Reconfiguration of Power Relations: Revisiting Role and Context of Translation and Interpreting.* Wien/ Berlin: LIT Verlag, 91–107.

Trupej, Janko. 2015. 'The reception of four American novels and their Slovenian translations in the context of racist ideology / Recepcija štirih ameriških romanov in njihovih slovenskih prevodov v luči ideologije rasizma', *Primerjalna književnost* 38(2): 213–35.

Žnideršič, Martin. 1995. 'Pregled razvoja založništva in knjigotrštva v Sloveniji od začetkov do danes' [The overview of the development of publishing and bookselling in Slovenia from their beginnings to present day], in M. Orožen (ed.), *Informativni kulturološki zbornik* [Informative Culturological Collected Volume]. Ljubljana, Seminar slovenskega jezika, literature in kulture pri Oddelku za slovanske jezike in književnosti Filozofske fakultete, 119–36.

PART IV

Democratic Capitalist Contexts

19

CENSORSHIP AND IDEOLOGICAL MANIPULATION IN INTRALINGUAL LITERARY TRANSLATION

Manuel Moreno Tovar

19.1 Intralingual Translation: A Cultural, Historical and Political Endeavour

Intralingual translation has come a long way since Jakobson's oft-quoted tripartite division of translation (1959/2021: 157). In describing intralingual translation as '*rewording*' and 'an interpretation of verbal signs by means of other signs of the same language', Jakobson appeared to be referring to standard, national languages. Today, the notion of intralingual translation is used to conceptualise a wide variety of phenomena of textual transfer occurring within the 'same language', and translation scholars are increasingly aware of the challenges of establishing clear-cut distinctions between languages, chronolects, dialects, sociolects and so on. Despite this considerable progress, numerous concepts and approaches rooted in (interlingual) translation studies, with censorship as a case in point, have yet to be applied to intralingual translation with any depth or systematicity.

Some of the rewritings that are being examined under the umbrella term of intralingual translation have been conceptualised as adaptations in the framework of adaptation studies. Rather than categorically identifying said rewritings as translations and not adaptations, this study operates under the assumption that the difference between translation and adaptation is 'never an essential […] one' (van Doorslaer and Raw 2016: 200), but rather, 'a matter of degree' (Chan 2020: 87). The underlying idea is that both adaptation and translation are characterised by change. By building on the concepts and methods developed in translation research, this chapter seeks to contribute to a maturing corpus of studies working with a more open definition of translation.

As a term, intralingual translation allows for different conceptualisations. From a linguistic approach, it can be seen as an attempt to find equivalents for lexical or discursive items (Penas Ibáñez 2015); alternatively, it can be conceptualised as a 'cultural, historical, and political endeavor, going beyond the attempt to find equivalents for words' (Berk Albachten 2014: 583). It is true that the increasingly complex practices studied as instances of intralingual translation remain, in essence, different forms of 'rewording'. Nevertheless, there is a growing emphasis on the non-linguistic aspects of intralingual translation. Brems (2017) discussed how intralingual translation was used by stakeholders in the construction of alterity in the Dutch language area, e.g., by means of the intralingual subtitling of Dutch and Flemish TV series in Flanders and the

DOI: 10.4324/9781003149453-24

Netherlands, respectively. She proposed adding a fifth parameter, 'cultural politics', to the four main factors influencing intralingual translation that Zethsen (2009) had earlier identified: knowledge, time, culture and space.

The parameter of cultural politics can help to explain changes in social values that occur over time, as well as help to address the existence of conflicts and power structures among and within communities who use the 'same language'. Intralingual practices that are likely to be influenced by cultural, historical and political motivations may include the revision of dated expressions in books for children, the production of cultural rewritings in a postcolonial context and the updating of the language used in literary texts to make them accessible for new generations of readers. These three types of intralingual translation are described in more detail by Berk Albachten (2014), who also discusses the phenomenon of censorship. For instance, some intralingual translations of pre-mid-twentieth century literature produced in the aftermath of the Turkish language reform have been found to contain 'major omissions, additions, or other changes at a textual level' (Berk Albachten 2014: 580), including excisions of information about their historical context and passages on religion; in other words, they were (self-)censored (Özalp 2011, as summarised in Berk Albachten 2014). The three practices could be considered instances of intralingual literary translation (IlT), a term that will be used in this chapter to analyse how censorship and ideological manipulation operate across various interfaces of textual and paratextual production at the crossroads of 'intralingual translation' and 'literary translation'.

19.2 Core Issues and Methodology

19.2.1 Defining Intralingual Literary Translation

In this chapter, 'intralingual literary translation' (IlT) refers to any process of textual derivation that is based upon a literary work and results in another text in what is generally regarded as the same language. The lower-case 'l' in the acronym is meant to emphasise that the product resulting from such an intralingual process is not necessarily considered a form of 'literature' in the conventional sense of the term. Graded readers, described by Extensive Reading (ER) scholars as 'language learner literature'—understood by Day and Bamford (1998) as analogous to 'young adult literature' and 'children's literature'—are an illustrative example. The conceptual move from Literature to literature has an even longer history for English language teaching scholars and practitioners. Over three decades ago, McRae made a case against the 'institutionalising capital' of literature in the context of second language learning and teaching, favouring an approach that sees literature 'in the widest possible sense of the word' (1991: vii). McRae stipulated two criteria for establishing that a text (a term that he also understood in the widest possible sense) is 'literature with a small "l"' (1991: vii): first, that it go beyond the 'purely referential' (the aim of conveying information); and second, that it stimulate a reaction in the receiver.

By contrast, a more recent account questions the validity of graded readers as a form of literature. Skopečková describes these books as a 'somewhat marginal and controversial phenomenon in the field of literary translation' (2013: 243) and argues that the very essence of literature resides in its aesthetic function, which allows readers to 'establish completely novel and unprecedented relations' (2013: 245). This condition appears to align with McRae's idea of literature with a small 'l', but Skopečková contends that graded readers do not in fact meet that condition because their receivers 'hardly enjoy the process of searching for and discovering of [sic] new relations and meanings' (2013: 248). Graded readers, she concludes, constitute a product that 'beyond all doubt fails to correspond to the definition of literature' (2013: 250). Skopečková's objection to

Censorship in Intralingual Literary Translation

graded readers as a form of literature is based on the assertion that they fail to transfer the literary effect of the source text. This is a restrictive view of graded readers—one which ignores the variability in the extent to which these are simplified—as well as a restrictive view of literature, which capitalises it, even if inadvertently. By conditioning the 'success' of a graded reader on the extent to which it retains the literary effect of its source text, Skopečková subordinates graded readers to their original texts. Such a hierarchy does not align with the pragmatic-functional nature of many forms of IIT.

In looking at lower-case literature, the purpose is not to obliterate the differences between graded readers and texts more commonly understood as Literature. In fact, it is precisely the prestige of Literature that inspires publishing houses to engage in IIT. The aim, rather, is to shift the focus from the centre of the literary field to its periphery, where many products of IIT are situated. That being said, IIT is meant as an inclusive term that stretches far beyond graded readers and covers all types of literature, simplified or not.

19.2.2 Examining Intralingual Censorship and Ideological Manipulation

The adjacency of translation and censorship has long been debated among translation scholars, as showcased by the exchange published on the *Translation Studies* Forum (TSF) in 2011. Although the exchange adopted a predominantly interlingual approach to translation, Kuhiwczak did address the concept of 'intralingual censorship' and contrasted it with its interlingual counterpart:

> The difference between intralingual and interlingual censorship is only one of access. When a text is censored within the same language, such intervention eventually comes to light. It is visible, conspicuous and in a majority of cases it causes indignation. If undertaken across language barriers, however, the act of censorship remains largely invisible. (Kuhiwczak 2011: 363)

Although Kuhiwczak did not provide any concrete examples, we can assume that he had the literary context in mind, given the strong literary focus of his account. It is less clear whether he was considering instances of intralingual rewriting or mere occurrences of censorship in a monolingual setting, as he does not explicitly refer to intralingual translation. In any case, his affirmations raise some questions: is the difference between interlingual and intralingual censorship *only* one of access? Does intralingual censorship *always* become visible and conspicuous to readers? Are there types of intralingual censorship that tend to cause more indignation than others? This chapter will attempt to shed light on these questions by exploring various types of IIT, namely, parallel-text editions updating the language used in an old literary work, simplified versions of a literary classic for targeted groups of readers, including language learners, and a US version of a British novel.

Several scholars on the TSF critiqued Kuhiwczak's remarks as Eurocentric, and though this is valid, it is methodologically essential to restrict one's focus. Following this logic, as well as Kuhiwczak's claim that children's literature constitutes a genre in which translation is a 'censoring mechanism that operates within the field of cultural production' (2011: 363), the corpus of texts retained for this study is limited to the literature of the UK and the US and to IITs that are generally, although not exclusively, aimed at and read by young audiences. In order to be temporally inclusive, literary works from three different centuries (late sixteenth, early nineteenth and late twentieth) have been selected. The corpus contains two IITs of William Shakespeare's *Romeo and Juliet*, three of Mary Shelley's *Frankenstein; or, The Modern Prometheus* and one of Philip Pullman's *The Amber Spyglass*.

The Routledge Handbook of Translation and Censorship

The methodology applied to the three case studies of various types of IIT is inspired by a recent contribution to ideology-informed perspectives on intralingual translation (Leonardi 2020). In that monograph, Leonardi investigates the phenomenon of ideological manipulation in children's literature through three case studies on intralingual translations. There are three major differences between the present study and Leonardi's. First, the corpus used in the present investigation does not include examples that are unmistakeably influenced by cultural politics, such as feminist retellings. Second, the retained IITs do not diverge radically from their source text nor are they presented as sequels to it, as in one of the rewritings of *Pinocchio* analysed by Leonardi, since this becomes a major hindrance to conducting contrastive analysis at the sentence-level. Lastly, the corpus is limited to literature that was originally written in English. To do otherwise would complicate the identification of source texts and add a layer of interlingual transfer to the analysis.

Omission will be a major focus in this chapter, as the term 'censorship' will be understood to refer to the modification of a cultural product through attenuation or cutting, in the words of Merkle, Sullivan, van Doorslaer and Wolf (2010: 14). As these scholars point out, not all deletions (and for that matter, not all attenuations) may necessarily be considered instances of censorship; for instance, some might occur to meet target reader expectations or for cultural or stylistic reasons. This observation holds especially true for graded readers, where omission is a prevalent strategy, but possibly also for other forms of IIT.

Beyond the study of omissions and other textual modifications, such as lexical substitutions, the analysis of paratextual additions will help to identify broader tendencies of ideological manipulation in IIT. Indeed, readers' access to a text is mediated through its paratexts and multimodal elements, such as supplementing illustrations. Paratexts accompanying IITs may include biographical information about the author, character descriptions, discussion questions and activities (pre-reading, reading and post-reading), glossaries, introductions, summaries, and side notes, among other elements. The study of discussion questions in particular, which have the potential of activating or neutralising particular readings of a text, represents an original contribution to translation studies, since they are yet to be meaningfully discussed in the literature on paratexts.

19.3   Case Studies

19.3.1   *Modernising Language in William Shakespeare's* Romeo and Juliet

William Shakespeare's works seem like an obvious choice for a case study on censorship, a term that is sometimes used interchangeably with 'bowdlerisation' or 'bowdlerism', especially in the British context. *Romeo and Juliet* was one of the plays included in *The Family Shakespeare* anthology, edited by Thomas Bowdler two centuries after the world-famous tragedy was first printed in a quarto version (1597). A product of ideological manipulation rather than diachronic updating, this version of Shakespeare's texts, which omitted words and expressions that 'cannot with propriety be read in a family' (Bowdler in Shakespeare 1853/2009: original cover) has become a symbol of editorial censorship.

Among the textual elements that Bowdler and his sister Henrietta considered unsuitable are the puns about genitalia and sex uttered by Mercutio, Romeo's close friend. Delabastita conceptualises 'pun' as an umbrella term covering 'the various discursive phenomena in which certain features [...] are mobilised to produce a communicatively significant, near-simultaneous confrontation of at least two linguistic units with more or less dissimilar meanings and more or less similar forms' (2011: 140). To study puns, Delabastita argues that we need to contextualise them carefully, adopt a historical approach and address the historicity of our interpretations. Our contemporary

Censorship in Intralingual Literary Translation

Table 19.1 Romeo and Juliet, *Act 2, Scene 1*

NFS	OTD
O Romeo, that she were! Oh, that she were An open arse, and thou a poperin pear. (Shakespeare [Crowther, trans.] 2003: 76).	O, Romeo, that she were, O that she were An open et cetera and thou a pop'rin pear! (Shakespeare [Snodgrass, trans.] 2006: 70).

interpretative strategies do not merely enable us to find wordplay in Shakespeare: 'they can also become [...] discursive strategies that *generate* the puns within the essential context of the *critic*'s writing' (2011: 161–2). More recently, Delabastita (2017) analysed over a dozen intralingually modernised versions of *Romeo and Juliet*, though he did not focus on sexual puns. This case study draws from two parallel-text editions of his corpus, *No Fear Shakespeare* (2003) and *Shakespeare on the Double!* (2006), henceforth referred to as *NFS* (2003) and *OTD* (2006). These two rewritings were described by Delabastita (2017: 16) as 'self-study aids' and contain extra features aimed at helping learners. Each IIT uses a different source text, as can be seen in Table 19.1.

The glosses of the 2012 Arden Shakespeare edition of *Romeo and Juliet* (Shakespeare 2012: 184) explain that 'open Et caetera' was a euphemistic phrasing used in *The First Quarto*. In some later versions of the play, this expression appeared as 'open, or' and 'open-arse' (a slang term for the medlar, which is a fruit that Mercutio mentions in the same utterance). This example speaks to the immense variability of *Romeo and Juliet*; there are multiple 'originals' from which editors can choose.

Table 19.2 shows how an extended version of the excerpt in Table 19.1 was handled in intralingual translation. In this and the subsequent example, Weis's edition of *Romeo and Juliet* (2012) is shown as a reference source text for convenience, but traces of manipulation are detected taking into account the respective 'originals' as featured in the parallel-text editions. The text in italics reproduces the full content of explanatory side notes that appear in *NFS* (2003).

In addition to the stark contrast between the overt sexualisation of *NFS* (2003) and the seemingly more bowdlerising approach adopted by *OTD* (2006: 70–71) ('et cetera' becomes 'unmentionable', 71), it is interesting to note the interpretive possibilities of the passage, which, it has been argued, may refer to anal sex (Wells 2010: 157). In the case of *NFS* (2003: 77), there is a dissonance between the explanations of the look of the medlar at a textual level ('one of those fruits that look like female genitalia') and at a paratextual one ('considered to look like a vulva or an anus'). Given the in-text choice, *NFS* (2003) arguably favours a vulval interpretation of this pun, which is advocated by scholars such as Partridge (1947/2005: 129). Contrastingly, *OTD* (2006: 71) opts for a different pun for the fruit ('the kind of apple that girls call "meddlers" when there is no one to hear them'). The term 'meddler' is neither deprived of sexual connotations nor foreign to Shakespeare's plays; in fact, its related verb '"meddle (with)' has been suggested to mean 'to be intimate (with)' in *Coriolanus* (Partridge 1947/2005: 190)". Admittedly, readers of *OTD* (2006) who are not familiar with the punning use of 'meddler' may not easily understand what the text alludes to and therefore miss out on the interpretive possibilities of the passage.

The excerpt in Table 19.2 offers at least two further examples of potential sexual puns, one considerably more obvious than the other: the 'Poperin pear' and the 'hitting of the mark'. The former is addressed (one could say manipulated) textually and paratextually in *NFS* (2003), where the formal closeness between the term 'Popperin' and the sexual phrase 'pop her in' is made explicit in the same line of the text. However, unlike in the case of the medlar, there is no direct mention

The Routledge Handbook of Translation and Censorship

Table 19.2 Romeo and Juliet, *Act 2, Scene 1*

Reference source text	NFS	OTD
If love be blind, love cannot hit the mark. Now will he sit under a medlar tree, And wish his mistress were that kind of fruit As maids call medlars when they laugh alone. O Romeo, that she were, O, that she were An open-arse, thou a poperin pear! (Shakespeare 2012: 183–4).	If love is blind, it can't hit the target. Now he'll sit under a medlar tree and wish his mistress were one of those fruits that look like female genitalia. Oh Romeo, I wish she *were* an open-arse, and you a Popperin pear to 'pop her in'. *The medlar is a tree whose fruit was considered to look like a vulva or an anus. The fruits were often called 'open-arses'. Popperins are Belgian pears; Mercutio uses the name in an obscene double entrendre.* (Shakespeare [Crowther, trans.] 2003: 77).	If love is blind, then Cupid can't hit the target with his arrow. Now he will sit under a medlar tree and wish his lover were the kind of apple that girls call 'meddlers' when there is no one to hear them. Oh, Romeo, if she were only an open unmentionable and you were a Belgian pear! (Shakespeare [Snodgrass, trans.] 2006: 71).

of this fruit's physical resemblance to genitalia (penis and scrotum, according to Partridge 1947/ 2005: 129). The paratextual explanation does not touch upon the shape of the pear either; it merely refers to an 'obscene double entrendre [sic]' in relation to its name. By contrast, *OTD* (2006) replaces 'Poperin' with the more indirect term 'Belgian pear', which erases the verbal resemblance to 'pop her in'.

As concerns the 'hitting of the mark', both editions use the phrase 'hit the target', which does not clearly ascribe any sexual connotation to the phrase but preserves the confrontation of meanings that characterises puns. Indeed, Partridge describes 'hit' as a pun for attaining 'the sexual target of the pudend' (1947/2005: 155). The addition of Cupid and his arrow in *OTD* (2006), far from desexualising the dialogue, introduces a potential phallic pun. This reference to Cupid's arrow as a phallic symbol appears at another point of the 'original' play (in Table 19.3), where it seems clearer that Romeo is referring to coitus.

Here, again, we observe a dissonance between both IlTs. While *NFS* (2003) alludes to chastity (textually) and to Diana being the goddess of virginity (paratextually), it couples the allusion with a less sexual interpretation of Cupid's shooting of arrows: that they make humans fall in love. This is not the case of *OTD* (2006), which explicitly rewords the source text and loses any reference to 'love'.

Table 19.3 Romeo and Juliet, *Act 1, Scene 1*

Reference source text	NFS	OTD
She'll not be hit With Cupid's arrow. She hath Dian's wit, And in strong proof of chastity well armed From love's weak childish bow she lives uncharmed. (Shakespeare 2012: 139).	She refuses to be hit by Cupid's arrow. She's as clever as Diana, and shielded by the armor of chastity. She can't be touched by the weak and childish arrows of love. *Cupid, the Roman god of love, shoots arrows at humans that make them fall in love. Diana is the Roman goddess of virginity and hunting.* (Shakespeare [Crowther, trans.] 2003: 25).	She dodges Cupid's arrow. She is as witty as Diana, the goddess of chastity. She protects her virginity. (Shakespeare [Snodgrass, trans.] 2006: 29).

Censorship in Intralingual Literary Translation

In the two examples previously discussed, considered to be particularly illustrative, a pattern seems to emerge: *NFS* (2003) tends to be sexually blunt—in fact, it was the subject of complaints by schoolchildren's parents in South Carolina due to its explicit descriptions of genitalia and sex (American Library Association 2012). However, it also tells readers where to see a pun, and in so doing, it may discourage them from seeking new meanings or generating their own puns, as Delabastita notes. By contrast, *OTD* (2006: 71) mobilises Shakespearean punny terms from other parts of the play or even from other works (Cupid's 'arrow', 'meddlers'), but it paraphrases more freely and refrains from making explicit anatomical allusions. It is not obvious that one of these IITs should be considered more censored than the other: both versions include manipulations of the source text, which seem to inevitably occur in the production of modern-day versions of a sixteenth-century classic, and both limit the interpretive possibilities of the readers to a greater or lesser extent. One thing is clear: given the absence of a definitive version of *Romeo and Juliet*, it is questionable to present any source text edition as the 'original' without accounting for the play's great variability. Moreover, today's readers may be unaware that the source text they are faced with in the parallel-text editions does not correspond exactly to Shakespeare's writing.

19.3.2 Rewriting Mary Shelley's Frankenstein; or, The Modern Prometheus for Young Readers

The Gothic classic *Frankenstein* was first published anonymously in 1818. Mary Shelley's story is known to have undergone significant intralingual editing, most famously in the form of her husband's contributions to the manuscript and the revision that the author herself introduced to the third edition in 1831, a revision that was studied by translation scholars Süren and Uras Yılmaz (2020) as a form of ideological rewriting. Regardless of the version, the tale of Victor Frankenstein and his creature has proven to be a productive source of adaptations, many of which are marketed for children and young adults. The present case study concerns two forms of IIT for young audiences: one adaptation from The Pacemaker Classics (1986) and two graded reader versions, Oxford Bookworms (1989) and Oxford Dominoes (2016). The first is aimed at targeted groups of US students (according to the Pacemaker Classics website, these include struggling learners, students at risk and students in differentiated education, among others), and the latter two are for learners of English. All three are based on the 1831 edition; consequently, the passages from the source text in the following tables have been taken from that edition.

When graded reader publishers, among other agents, are confronted with issues that they deem too controversial for their young readers, such as violence or death, they may resort to omission 'as a means of censorship and ideological manipulation' (Moreno Tovar 2020: 62). This hypothesis will be explored in a more nuanced way through the comparison of the two above-mentioned forms of IIT. Let us begin with the excerpt in Table 19.4, which corresponds to Victor Frankenstein's collection of materials.

In terms of textual deletion, it is worth noting the omission of animal torture in the target texts, as well as the absence of references to charnel-houses and slaughterhouses from all three IITs. The graded readers are the most succinct: they omit Victor's tormented feelings about the horrors of his actions and fail to mention grave robbing. However, this activity is transferred intersemiotically by means of an illustration in the Bookworms edition, which depicts Victor unearthing human remains from a grave (1989/2000: 10). Based on a strictly textual analysis, one could argue that this graded reader attempts to manipulate and even moralise the story, as Victor is said to have bought some of the body pieces. A paratextual analysis complicates the vision of graded readers being indisputably prone to censorship: in the after-reading activities, young readers are asked to critically engage

Table 19.4 Frankenstein, *Volume I, Chapter 4*

Source text	Pacemaker Classics	Oxford Bookworms	Oxford Dominoes
Who shall conceive the horrors of my secret toil, as I dabbled among the unhallowed damps of the grave, or tortured the living animal to animate the lifeless clay? [...] I collected bones from charnel houses; and disturbed, with profane fingers, the tremendous secrets of the human frame. [...] The dissecting room and the slaughter-house furnished many of my materials; and often did my human nature turn with loathing from my occupation, whilst, still urged on by an eagerness which perpetually increased, I brought my work near to a conclusion. (Shelley 1818/2009).	I shake when I think of the things I did. I robbed graves and cut up the dead bodies. I can still see all those staring, dead eyes. I stole bones and organs. The horror of it stays with me, even today. (Shelley [Bethancourt, trans.] 1986: 22).	I bought or stole all the pieces of human body that I needed, and slowly and carefully, I put them all together. (Shelley [Nobes, trans.] 1989/2000: 10).	After that, in my rooms in town I began to make a creature from parts of dead bodies. I worked day and night. (Shelley [Bowler, trans.] 2016: 4).

with the question of whether doctors, scientists and artists should re-use parts of people's dead bodies (1989/2000: 67). This contrasts with the Dominoes edition, in which a message of warning is conveyed: 'new ideas in science can be dangerous' (2016: 42). Let us now delve into the description of the first murder perpetrated by the creature: that of Victor Frankenstein's younger brother, William.

The example in Table 19.5 illustrates how the adaptation for US students is more censored than the graded readers. The translation of the excerpt in Pacemaker Classics is, in fact, longer than its source counterpart; such expansions are possible in the process of adapting key parts of the narrative. The omission here is limited in scope but crucial in content: the sentence 'You shall be my first victim' in the source text shows that the killing of William is not involuntary. Omission is not used in isolation, but together with an attenuating paraphrase ('I have sworn eternal revenge', 1818/2009 becomes 'I promised myself I would get even with Frankenstein', 1986: 49) as well as with addition ('But I am so strong, and the child was so small...'; 'At first, I felt bad', 1986: 49). The intention seems to align with a trend in *Frankenstein* adaptations for young audiences: that the creature is a victim with whom the reader should sympathise (Coats and Norris Sands 2016). Unlike the Pacemaker Classics edition, both graded reader versions use the intentional verb 'to strangle' (textually in Dominoes, as showed in Table 19.5, and also paratextually in Bookworms, both in a while-reading activity and in the glossary). This is an explicit and violent wording that could cause strong reactions, especially since the reference is made to strangling a child.

Table 19.6 provides one last example of death, this time, that of the creature. Once again, we observe how the story in Pacemaker Classics is clearly sanitised. However, against expectations of censorship, the graded readers do not shy away from the creature's chosen way of committing suicide, neither textually nor paratextually: Bookworms asks its readership 'How did the monster plan to die?' (1989/2000: 63), and Dominoes includes two graphic illustrations that are not even part of the original story, merely for the sake of inviting learners to guess what happens in the last chapter. In one, Victor sets the creature on fire and, in the other, the creature strangles Victor in his sleep (2016: 31). Given the time interval between the two Oxford editions, is it possible that the ideological norms of graded reader production have shifted, meaning that producers are

Censorship in Intralingual Literary Translation

Table 19.5 Frankenstein, *Volume II, Chapter 16*

Source text	Pacemaker Classics	Oxford Bookworms	Oxford Dominoes
'Hideous monster! let me go; My papa is a Syndic—he is M. Frankenstein—he will punish you. You dare not keep me.' 'Frankenstein! you belong then to my enemy—to him towards whom I have sworn eternal revenge; you shall be my first victim.' The child still struggled, and loaded me with epithets which carried despair to my heart; I grasped his throat to silence him, and in a moment he lay dead at my feet. I gazed on my victim, and my heart swelled with exultation and hellish triumph: clapping my hands, I exclaimed, 'I, too, can create desolation; my enemy is not invulnerable; this death will carry despair to him, and a thousand other miseries shall torment and destroy him.' (Shelley 1818/2009).	'Let me go, you monster!' [...] 'Let me go, or my papa will take care of you. He's an important man. He's Mr. Frankenstein. Don't you dare hurt me!' As soon as I heard the name, I became angry. 'Frankenstein!' I cried. 'You belong to him? I promised myself I would get even with Frankenstein. And I will start with you!' The child began to scream even more. I tried to quiet him. I grabbed his throat. But I am so strong, and the child was so small... in a moment, he was dead. At first, I felt bad. Then I was filled with joy. I even clapped my hands in hellish joy. This child belonged to your family. I would show you. I would bring as much sadness to you as you had to me! (Shelley [Bethancourt, trans.] 1986: 49).	'Let me go, you monster,' the child shouted. 'Let me go, or I will tell my father, Mr. Frankenstein. He will call the police, and they'll punish you.' 'Frankenstein!' I shouted. 'You belong to my enemy, the man that I want to hurt.' The child fought and screamed, and I put my hand round his neck to stop him shouting. In a moment, the child lay dead at my feet. I looked down at his body, and was pleased with what I had done. I knew that the death of this child would hurt you, Victor Frankenstein, my creator. (Shelley [Nobes, trans.] 1989/2000: 31).	There, at Plainpalais, I met a young boy. He was not afraid of me. 'Do you know Alphonse Frankenstein's house in Geneva?' I asked him. 'Yes,' he answered. 'Alphonse Frankenstein's my father.' I was suddenly very angry. I took the boy in my hands and strangled him. (Shelley [Bowler, trans.] 2016: 22).

Table 19.6 Frankenstein, *Volume III, Walton,* in continuation

Source text	Pacemaker Classics	Oxford Bookworms	Oxford Dominoes
I shall quit your vessel on the ice-raft which brought me thither, and shall seek the most northern extremity of the globe; I shall collect my funeral pile, and consume to ashes this miserable frame, that its remains may afford no light to any curious and unhallowed wretch, who would create such another as I have been. (Shelley 1818/2009).	'I came to the ship on a floating piece of ice. It is still by the side of your ship. I will float away to the land of ice and snow. Without food, even I shall die. I shall die as I lived: alone, without love, and hated by all.' (Shelley [Bethancourt, trans.] 1986: 74).	I shall leave this ship and go north, across the ice. I shall build a great fire, and lie down on it to die. (Shelley [Nobes, trans.] 1989/2000: 54).	'I'm going to travel north now on my sled.' He said. 'And when I come to the coldest part of this cold land, I'm going to make a big fire and finish my sad life in it. [...]' (Shelley [Bowler, trans.] 2016: 37).

less afraid to expose young readers to violence? A larger corpus of graded readers—one which includes paratextual and multimodal elements, particularly activities and illustrations—would be necessary to answer this question. As regards the remaining IIT, one preliminary conclusion can be reached: it seems that the portrayal of *explicit* violence in the US (the killing of a child, burning someone alive) is—or at least used to be—more censurable than the portrayal of *implied* violence (the profaning of graves).

19.3.3 *A US Version of a British Novel: Philip Pullman's* The Amber Spyglass

Philip Pullman is known internationally for his fantasy trilogy *His Dark Materials*, published between 1995 and 2000. Like other fantasy novels for young readers, this trilogy aroused censorial controversy in the US on the basis of its being 'anti-Christian'. In an article in *The Guardian*, Pullman stated that he reacted with 'glee' when *The Golden Compass*, released in the UK under the title *Northern Lights*, appeared among the top five on the American Library Association's list of 2007's Most Challenged Books: first, because he had 'obviously annoyed a lot of censorious people' and second, because this increased the sales of the book (Pullman 2008, in Bird, Danielson and Sieruta 2014: 106).

In a 2019 interview for *The New Yorker* (Schwartz 2019), the topic of censorship was raised again, this time regarding some textual modifications concerning sexuality in the US version of the third novel, *The Amber Spyglass*. The interviewer, Alexandra Schwartz, referred to the importance of Pullman's books to her own early adolescence, particularly the love story between the two young protagonists at the end of *The Amber Spyglass*; Pullman expressed surprise that it was 'that much altered', since the UK version is not 'much raunchier' than the US one (Pullman in Schwartz 2019). He mentioned two possible reasons behind the US editors' decisions to expurgate: the trilogy 'was published by a children's publisher' and the US adult public is more easily offended than its European counterpart:

> [A]s it happened, *His Dark Materials* was published by a children's publisher, or by a children's division of an adult publisher. And that meant various things. It meant that it was put on bookshelves in different parts of bookshops. It was sold into bookstores and wholesalers by people who knew children's lists, and not really by adult representatives. So it had a big children's readership, and I think that might have governed what my American editors thought ought to be done to the text.
>
> I don't think very much was done, but, then, as we from this side of the Atlantic have had occasion to observe, you on that side—I mean the great big 'you' of the American public—are much more easily offended. Even, dare I say, *eager* to be offended. (Pullman in Schwartz 2019)

In 2014, Ersland analysed the translational shifts (i.e., changes occurring in the translation process) at play in the production of a US edition of *The Amber Spyglass*. She categorised the above-mentioned changes as macro-structural deletions of content relating to emotion or sexuality. Unlike other deletions that were determined to be the result of obligatory shifts (for example, those concerning lexical and structural differences between British English and American English), Ersland identified those changes as resulting from optional shifts, that is, those occurring for stylistic, ideological or cultural reasons. Ersland concluded that her findings confirm what other studies had already suggested: the norm that dictates content in children's and young adults' literature is stricter in the US than in the UK.

Censorship in Intralingual Literary Translation

In a more recent monograph, Pillière (2021) studied the Americanisation of British novels with a corpus of over 80 works (none of which were from *His Dark Materials*). Pillière mentioned ideological modifications but did not use the concept of censorship; she found the omissions in her corpus to be motivated by cultural reasons (e.g., explanations of cultural terms that are already comprehensible to the US readers). In her conclusions, she stressed the difficulty of separating dialectal changes from stylistic changes traditionally labelled as editing: 'It is not always clear whether the preference for a linguistic form should be labelled dialectal or not, and the same sentence can include both dialectal and editing procedures. Separating the two is often an impossible task' (2021: 205).

Pillière's conclusion casts doubts as to which deletions can be considered ideologically-motivated shifts, and ultimately, instances of censorship. To shed light on that question, this case study contextualises the intralingual deletions related to emotion or sexuality in the retained IIT, as identified by Ersland. It does so by referring to Llompart Pons's work (2021) on the use of metaphor in fantasy literature as a filter that mediates the portrayal of topics such as non-heteronormative desire and sexual abuse. According to Llompart Pons, fantasy constitutes 'a clever strategy to elude censorship *and* a form of censorship in itself at the same time': it mediates taboo issues around sexuality, but it also reinforces the notion that 'only through fantasy can this topic be discussed in children's fiction' (2021: 26). In this context, the protagonists' sexual awakening can be read as 'a reaction against the absence of sexuality in children's fiction, even though Pullman himself is sometimes unable to tackle this subject without resorting to metaphors and other censorial filters' (Llompart Pons 2021: 16). Bearing this in mind, let us examine the first excerpt.

In the scene at hand, the adult Mary has just told two children, Lyra and Will, a story about a romantic encounter. The story prefigures the climax of the trilogy, in which the protagonists re-enact original sin. Llompart Pons (2021: 25) posits that storytelling has a metalinguistic function here, as it allows for commentary on its own power and on the genre of children's literature itself, from which children's sexuality is often absent. As can be seen in Table 19.7, Lyra's reaction is significantly shortened in the Random House edition.

In the excerpt in Table 19.8, Pullman draws and then subverts an allegory: Mary has taken the part of the serpent in Genesis, and Lyra is Eve. Nevertheless, the new forbidden knowledge

Table 19.7 The Amber Spyglass, *Chapter 33*

Scholastic (UK)	*Random House (US)*
As Mary said that, Lyra felt something strange happen to her body. She felt a stirring at the roots of her hair: she found herself breathing faster. She had never been on a roller-coaster or anything like one, but if she had, she would have recognized the sensations in her breast: they were exciting and frightening at the same time, and she had not the slightest idea why. The sensation continued and deepened, and changed, as most parts of her body found themselves affected too. She felt as if she had been handed the key to a great house she hadn't known was there, a house that was somehow inside her, and as she turned the key, deep in the darkness of the building she felt other doors opening too, and lights coming on. She sat trembling, hugging her knees, hardly daring to breathe, as Mary went on: […]. (Pullman 2000/2001: 467–8).	As Mary said that, Lyra felt something strange happen to her body. She felt as if she had been handed the key to a great house she hadn't known was there, a house that was somehow inside her, and as she turned the key, she felt the other doors opening deep in the darkness, and lights coming on. She sat trembling as Mary went on: […]. (Pullman 2000/2003: 444).

301

The Routledge Handbook of Translation and Censorship

Table 19.8 The Amber Spyglass, *Chapter 33*

Scholastic (UK)	Random House (US)
As for Lyra, she hadn't moved a muscle since that strange thing had happened, and she held the memory of those sensations inside her like a fragile vessel brim-full of new knowledge, which she hardly dared touch for fear of spilling it. She didn't know what it was, or what it meant, or where it had come from: so she sat still, hugging her knees, and tried to stop herself trembling with excitement. Soon, she thought, soon I'll know. I'll know very soon. (Pullman 2000/2001: 471).	As for Lyra she hadn't moved a muscle since that strange thing had happened, and she held the memory of the sensation inside her. She didn't know what it was, or what it meant, or where it had come from; so she sat hugging her knees, and tried to stop herself from trembling. Soon, she thought, soon I'll know. (Pullman 2000/2003: 447).

Table 19.9 The Amber Spyglass, *Chapter 34*

Scholastic (UK)	Random House (US)
A quick glance at Will's warm cheeks showed that he knew just as well as she did. She couldn't tell whether he also felt that half-frightened, half-excited feeling, as she did, the one that had come over her the night before: here it was again. (Pullman 2000/2001: 482).	A quick glance at Will's warm cheeks showed that he knew just as well as she did. (Pullman 2000/2003: 457).

Table 19.10 The Amber Spyglass, *Chapter 35*

Scholastic (UK)	Random House (US)
And there it was: the dark-blonde movement that was the girl's hair. He moved a little closer, and took out the rifle. There was a telescopic sight: low-powered, but beautifully made, so that looking through it was to feel your vision clarified as well as enlarged. Yes, there she was, and she paused and looked back so that he saw the expression on her face, and he could not understand how anyone so steeped in evil could look so radiant with hope and happiness. His bewilderment at that made him hesitate, and then the moment was gone, and both children had walked in among the trees and out of sight. Well, they wouldn't go far. He followed them down the stream, moving at a crouch, holding the rifle in one hand, balancing with the other. (Pullman 2000/2001: 489).	He watched them go in among the trees. They hadn't looked back once since coming over the top of the ridge, but he still kept low, moving down the stream at a crouch, holding the rifle in one hand, balancing the other. (Pullman 2000/2003: 464).

with which Mary has tempted Lyra is neither a disgrace nor a curse, but rather a turning point. In the Scholastic version of the text, Pullman uses a language that openly celebrates preadolescent sexual awakening, which is toned down intralingually in the IIT. The excerpt in Table 19.9 further touches upon Lyra's emotions of fear and excitement, which are again manipulated in the process of Americanisation.

Censorship in Intralingual Literary Translation

Table 19.11 The Amber Spyglass, *Chapter 35*

Scholastic (UK)	Random House (US)
Lyra's heart was beating so fast she felt the pulse in her throat. She and Will looked at each other, a curiously formal and serious look, before setting off to follow the stream. (Pullman 2000/2001: 488).	They looked at each other, a curiously formal and serious look, before setting off to follow the stream. (Pullman 2000/2003: 463).

The story ends as Lyra and Will mature intellectually and morally, but also sexually. By dissociating sexuality from shame and evil, Pullman may have been aware that he would give offense to religious conservatives. In the excerpt in Table 19.10, Father Gomez chases the children in the conviction that they are walking into mortal sin.

The excerpts described above contain all of Ersland's examples of content deletions relating to emotion or sexuality, but she mentions having identified a total of eight instances. It is conceivable that the excerpt in Table 19.11 could also be classified as such a deletion, although it is not as unequivocally related to sexuality as the rest. Indeed, Lyra's rapid heartbeat could be explained by the excitement of the imminent reunion with her dæmon (in the books, humans have animal-shaped companions called dæmons).

In conclusion, while most of the passages discussed in this case study leave no doubt about the fact that Pullman's novel was 'cleansed' for young US audiences, it seems that at a micro-textual level it is not always easy to clearly distinguish sexual excitement from other emotions, or an ideological change from a stylistic one, or an act of censorship from a deletion that does not entail a moral judgement. This challenge, however, should not deter us from investigating the expurgations that may occur in IIT.

19.4 Future Debates

The three case studies presented in this chapter shed light on the presence of censorship and ideological manipulation in intralingual literary translation (IIT). Clearly, scholars working with IIT—perhaps even more so than those working with interlingual translation—should tread carefully when identifying acts of censorship and establishing the motivation behind omissions, for that motivation might not be specifically ideological. Regarding the questions that arise from Kuhiwczak's affirmations (2011), it seems impossible to ascertain how censorship in intralingual translation differs from censorship in interlingual translation without conducting a large-scale comparative study. Nonetheless, this chapter provides some starting points for future debates.

As illustrated by the case studies, not all types of 'manipulated' intralingual translation offer the same degree of access to the 'uncensored' original. Parallel-text editions make it easier for the reader to notice omissions, but agents of IIT may still resort to other questionable strategies, such as failing to contextualise the choice of the source text. It is also safe to assume that if readers opt for a simplified version of a literary work, they will not always be able to access the full interpretive possibilities of the original, let alone identify instances of censorship. When a case of censorship does become known to readers, as in *The Amber Spyglass*, it may well cause indignation. However, had those changes been made in a graded reader version of the novel, they may not have stirred up controversy or have even been noticed. This may be explained by different expectations concerning the use of omission in this genre, as well as by the marginal status of 'language learner literature'. Intralingual subtitling and surtitling, oral reformulation, whether literary or not, and essentially all sorts of intralingual translation of non-literary texts are material for future research. Intralingual literary and non-literary translation in languages other than English also require study, in addition to intralingual intersemiotic products, such as graphic novel adaptations). The study of cultural, historical, political and, indeed, ideological factors influencing intralingual translation offers vast potential for translation research. Future contributions, particularly non-Eurocentric ones, will undoubtedly expand its horizons.

Further reading

Dam, Helle V., Brøgger, Maltide Nisbeth and Zethsen, Karen Korning (eds.). 2019. *Moving Boundaries in Translation Studies*. New York and London: Routledge.
Available through Open Access, this edited volume on the conceptual borders of translation studies contains multiple references to oral and written intralingual translational processes, both literary and non-literary. In chapter ten, Berk Albachten analyses two cases of intralingual translation from the nineteenth-century Ottoman literary context.

Pillière, Linda and Berk Albachten, Özlem (eds.). 2024. *The Routledge Handbook of Intralingual Translation*. New York: Routledge.
Authored by a range of scholars with an interest in rewriting as a translational practice, this handbook provides the first comprehensive overview of intralingual translation. It covers theoretical, political and ideological aspects, as well as various forms of intralingual literary translation, including graded readers.

Sydorenko, Sergiy. 2019. 'A victim of prudishness: Chaucer's *Miller's Tale* retold over the centuries', *Babel*, 65(2): 200–21.
In this article, Sydorenko examines the diachronic intralingual translations of 'The Miller's Tale', one of Geoffrey Chaucer's *Canterbury Tales*. The scholar conducts a study on twentieth-century and early twenty-first century modernisations of the tale and reaches conclusions about the use of censorious practices by the modernisers in response to its alleged vulgarity.

References

Primary sources

Pullman, Philip. 2000/2001. *The Amber Spyglass*. London: Scholastic.
Pullman, Philip. 2000/2003. *The Amber Spyglass*. New York: Random House.
Shakespeare, William. 2003. *No Fear Shakespeare. Romeo and Juliet*. Translated by J. Crowther. New York: Spark Publishing.
Shakespeare, William. 2006. *Shakespeare on the Double! Romeo and Juliet*. Translated by M.E. Snodgrass. Hoboken, New Jersey: Wiley Publishing.
Shakespeare, William. 2012. *Romeo and Juliet (The Arden Shakespeare Third Series)* (R. Weis, ed.). London: Bloomsbury.
Shelley, Mary. 1986. *Frankenstein*. Translated by T.E. Bethancourt. Belmont, California: David S. Lake Publishers.
Shelley, Mary. 1989/2000. *Frankenstein*. Translated by P. Nobes. Hong Kong: Oxford University Press.
Shelley, Mary. 2016. *Frankenstein*. Translated by B. Bowler. Oxford: Oxford University Press.
Shelley, Mary Wollstonecraft. 1818/2009. *Frankenstein. A Romantic Circles Electronic Edition* (S. Curran, ed.). https://romantic-circles.org/editions/frankenstein/editions.2009.frankenstein (Accessed: 7 March 2024).

Secondary sources

American Library Association, Intellectual Freedom Committee. 2012. *Newsletter on Intellectual Freedom*, 61(3). https://journals.ala.org/index.php/nif/issue/viewFile/437/244 (Accessed: 7 March 2024).
Berk Albachten, Özlem. 2014. 'Intralingual Translation: Discussions Within Translation Studies and the Case of Turkey', in S. Bermann and C. Porter (eds.), *A Companion to Translation Studies*. Chichester: John Wiley & Sons, 573–85.

Bird, Betsy, Danielson, Julie and Sieruta, Peter D. 2014. *Wild Things! Acts of Mischief in Children's Literature.* Sommerville, Massachusetts: Candlewick Press.

Brems, Elke. 2017. 'Separated by the Same Language: Intralingual Translation Between Dutch and Dutch', *Perspectives*, 26(4): 509–25.

Chan, Leo Tak-hung. 2020. *Western Theory in East Asian Contexts Translation and Transtextual Rewriting.* New York: Bloomsbury Academic.

Coats, Karen and Norris Sands, Farran. 2016. 'Growing up Frankenstein: Adaptations for Young Readers', in A. Smith (ed.), *The Cambridge Companion to Frankenstein.* Cambridge: Cambridge University Press, 241–55.

Day, Richard R. and Bamford, Julian. 1998. *Extensive Reading in the Second Language Classroom.* Cambridge: Cambridge University Press.

Delabastita, Dirk. 2011. 'Wholes and Holes in the Study of Shakespeare's Wordplay', in M. Ravassat and J. Culpeper (eds.), *Stylistics and Shakespeare's Language: Transdisciplinary Approaches.* London and New York: Continuum, 139–64.

Delabastita, Dirk. 2017. '"He shall Signify from Time to Time". *Romeo and Juliet* in Modern English', *Perspectives*, 25(2): 189–213.

Ersland, Anlaug. 2014. *Is Change Necessary? A Study of Norms and Translation Universals in Intralingual Translation.* Master's Thesis. University of Bergen.

Jakobson, Roman. 1959/2021. 'On Linguistic Aspects of Translation', in L. Venuti (ed.), *The Translation Studies Reader.* London and New York: Routledge, 156–61.

Kuhiwczak, Piotr. 2011. '*Translation Studies* Forum: Translation and Censorship', *Translation Studies*, 4(3): 358–73.

Leonardi, Vanessa. 2020. *Ideological Manipulation of Children's Literature Through Translation and Rewriting: Travelling Across Times and Places.* Cham, Switzerland: Palgrave Macmillan.

Llompart Pons, Auba. 2021. '"Just a Little Cut": Censorship and Preadolescent Sexuality in Philip Pullman's *His Dark Materials*', in P. Venzo and K. Moruzi (eds.), *Sexuality in Literature for Children and Young Adults.* New York and London: Routledge, 15–28.

McRae, John. 1991. *Literature with a Small 'l'.* London: Macmillan.

Merkle, D., O'Sullivan, C., van Doorslaer, L. and Wolf, M. 2010. 'Exploring a Neglected Century: Translation and Censorship in Nineteenth-Century Europe', in D. Merkle, C. O'Sullivan, L. van Doorslaer and M. Wolf (eds.), *The Power of the Pen. Translation & Censorship in Nineteenth-Century Europe.* Vienna and Berlin: LIT Verlag, 7–26.

Moreno Tovar, Manuel. 2020. '(A)bridging the Gap – A Study of the Norms and Laws in the Intralingual Translation of the Novel *And Then There Were None* by Agatha Christie', *Revista de lenguas para fines específicos*, 26(1): 51–68.

Özalp, N. Ahmet. 2011. *Refik Halid Karay: oklar kırılmış kirpi.* Istanbul: Kapı Yayınları.

Partridge, Eric. 1947/2005. *Shakespeare's Bawdy.* London and New York: Routledge.

Penas Ibáñez, María Azucena. 2015. 'La traducción intralingüística', in M.A. Penas Ibáñez (ed.), *La traducción: nuevos planteamientos teórico-metodológicos.* Madrid: Síntesis, 75–103.

Pillière, Linda. 2021. *Intralingual Translation of British Novels: A Multimodal Stylistic Perspective.* London: Bloomsbury Academic.

Schwartz, Alexandra. 2019. 'The Fallen Worlds of Philip Pullman', *The New Yorker.* www.newyorker.com/culture/the-new-yorker-interview/the-fallen-worlds-of-philip-pullman (Accessed: 7 March 2024).

Shakespeare, William. 1853/2009. *The Bowdler Shakespeare. Volume 6* (T. Bowdler, ed.). Cambridge: Cambridge University Press.

Skopečková, Eva. 2013. 'A Marginal Phenomenon in the Field of Literary Translation: The (Im)possibility of "Translating" Literature into a "Simplified" Version', in J. Zehnalová, O. Molnár and M. Kubánek (eds.), *Tradition and Trends in Trans-Language Communication.* Olomouc: Palacký University, 243–51.

Süren, Merve Sevtap and Uras Yılmaz, Arsun. 2020. 'Bir yeniden yazım örneği olarak *Frankenstein*', *İstanbul Üniversitesi Çeviribilim Dergisi – Istanbul University Journal of Translation Studies*, 12: 29–52.

van Doorslaer, Luc and Raw, Laurence. 2016. 'Adaptation Studies and Translation Studies: Very Interactive Yet Distinct', in Y. Gambier and L. van Doorslaer (eds.), *Border Crossings: Translation Studies and Other Disciplines.* Amsterdam/Philadelphia: John Benjamins, 189–204.

Wells, Stanley. 2010. *Shakespeare, Sex, and Love.* New York: Oxford University Press.

Zethsen, Karen Korning. 2009. 'Intralingual Translation: An Attempt at Description', *Meta*, 54(4): 795–812.

20

CENSORSHIP AND LANGUAGE POLICY

The Case of Canada and Québec

Denise Merkle

20.1 Definitions

In 2001, Mark Cohen proposed the following definition of censorship in *Censorship in Canadian Literature*: 'the exclusion of some discourse as a result of a judgment by an authoritative agent based on some ideological predisposition' (p. 8). Although Cohen does not discuss translation, his definition will be used in this chapter as it is sufficiently broad to account for various types of control over interlinguistic discourse in the officially bilingual (English-French) Canadian and (unilingual French) Québec contexts, since the arrival of the first settlers at the beginning of the seventeenth century until the twenty-first century. Censorship legislation covering obscenity and sedition falls generally under the purview of the Criminal Code of Canada but also specifically under the War Measures Act during wartime (see Chapter 22), although the most prevalent form of control over discourse in Canada may be silencing by withdrawing the right to use one's language and by the refusal to translate (or interpret). 'Discourse' will encompass languages—primarily Indigenous and French, their relationship, as well as the relationship of both language groups to English. A 'judgment by an authoritative agent' can be a decision taken by the Church, in particular the Catholic Church, especially in Québec, the Canadian government—e.g., Parliament, Canada Border Services, Canadian courts, the military during times of war—as well as community groups, publishers or translators. Their decisions may result in censorship or self-censorship. The decision to exclude a given discourse is based on an overt or internalised 'ideological predisposition'. When that ideological predisposition is direct, overt and intentional, it can be identified, as with the work of the Catholic Church, the Canadian government, community groups and certain publishers and translators. However, a 'subtle, systemic discursive process [also] shapes the very boundaries of what can be said' (Cohen 2001: 13), and that process, along with the ideological predisposition underpinning it, can be harder to identify. This subtle and systemic discursive process falls under a broader, socio-discursive understanding of censorship, which is not limited to repressed versus free utterances but includes receivable versus unreceivable discourse (or sayable versus unsayable), in other words what is considered legitimate discourse versus what is considered illegitimate. This socio-discursive understanding is what Pierre Bourdieu has labelled 'structural censorship' (1991: 138). The present chapter will take Cohen's (2001) broad view of control over discourse as a starting point to examine censorship activities and their impact on (self-)translation in Canada.

306

DOI: 10.4324/9781003149453-25

20.2 Core Issues and Topics

It may come as a surprise that, in a country as interested in translation as is officially bilingual Canada, no studies dealing specifically with translation and censorship exist. This observation harkens back to Cohen's observation: 'While there has been much written on censorship, from John Milton to Stanley Fish, almost none of it has focused on Canadian literature' (2001: 20). His 2001 *Censorship in Canadian Literature* was in fact the first to do so. Only relatively recently have Canadian and Québec scholars begun to take a serious interest in censorship activities in their respective geo-sociopolitical spaces, with several studies appearing in the last decade of the twentieth century, after Canada patriated its Constitution from the UK in 1982, to which it added the Charter of Rights and Freedoms (CRF). For example, Petersen and Hutchinson's edited collection *Interpreting Censorship in Canada* (1999) explores various mechanisms that contributed to controlling discourse and maintaining social order in the country, ranging from legislation to customs officials, social groups and publishers. For his part, Pierre Hébert has published alone or in collaboration a number of volumes and articles on censorship since the late 1990s, notably the seminal *Dictionnaire de la censure au Québec: Littérature et cinéma* (2006), a 716-page overview of censorship of literary and cinematographic works in the province. Both Canada and Québec clearly have a tradition of censorship; yet, translation is rarely explicitly discussed in the literature, although mention may be made, for instance, of control of the public through language manipulation (e.g., Petersen and Hutchinson 1999: 393–4). Consequently, this chapter will offer an introductory overview of censorship and translation in Canada and Québec.

20.2.1 Federal Versus Provincial Jurisdiction

The control of discourse in Canada is complicated by the fact that the country is a (con)federation that has delegated many, but not all, powers to the relatively sovereign provinces. While the provinces have jurisdiction over libraries, education and film boards, among other portfolios, the federal government adopts Criminal Code legislation and controls cross-border importing (border services) and customs. A telling example of provincial jurisdiction over film censorship is the province of Ontario Board of Cinema Censors, which was often stricter than elsewhere in the Western world.

Prior to the 1980s the existence of the board and its decisions were secret; cuts became known to audiences only if they were discussed in the media, and decisions could not be appealed (Letterboxd n.d.). The Ontario Censorship Board banned the Academy Award-winning German film *The Tin Drum* in 1980. As Tremonti (2004) comments, 'The adaptation of the novel by Gunter Grass was first cut, then banned as child pornography.' Furthermore, it banned the French films *Stepfather* in 1981 (Boyd 1985: 56) and *Rape Me* in 2000 (Poirier 2000). On the other hand, the West German film *Nekromantik* (1987) was banned in Iceland, Finland (1993–2001) and New Zealand, in addition to other countries, but was banned in Canada only in the provinces of Nova Scotia and Ontario (Parents Guide n.d.). The renamed Ontario Film Review Board ceased operation in October 2019. Adult films have since been cleared for screening in Ontario upon approval elsewhere in Canada, and ratings are no longer required (Ontario 2021).

20.2.2 Canada and Québec: Different Legal Traditions

It is imperative to distinguish the Canadian and Québec traditions because Canada was first colonised by the French who had a civil law system and then by the British who had a common law system. While the British parts of the colony have always fallen exclusively under common law, since the Conquest of 1759–1763 Québec has institutionalised bijuralism, with a system of civil law (property, inheritance, etc.) and common law (criminal law).

The French colonisers were traditionally Catholic and the British primarily Protestant, although Catholic English-speakers have always resided in Canada. It should be noted that not only French-speaking Catholics but also English-speaking Catholics have been denied many of the rights afforded to Protestants (e.g,, the right to vote until the 1830s), not to mention the fundamental rights denied to Black Canadians, immigrant groups (Chinese, Germans, Japanese, Ukrainians, etc.) and the various Indigenous populations throughout the country's history. The denial of rights was and is tantamount to silencing these groups in the public domain.

20.2.3 Criminal Code of Canada

The Criminal Code regulates what is publishable domestically and

> makes it an offence to mail 'obscene, indecent, immoral or scurrilous' matter [...], and the Post Office Act provides for interruption of such service. Similarly, the Customs Tariff Act prohibits the importation of 'treasonable, seditious, immoral or indecent' literature. [...] Material which promotes hatred against identifiable groups can also be halted at the border, while the Canadian Human Rights Act permits the filing of a court order to cease and desist using the telephone to communicate hate messages (see *Canada (HRC) v Taylor*[, 1990]).
>
> (Tarnopolosky and Schneiderman 2006b)

An active policy of domestic censorship has been generally restricted by Canadian governments to times of war and crisis, when national security is at stake, i.e., when the war measures act is invoked (see Chapter 22).

By contrast, during peace time, obscenity is the most frequent justification for censorship in Canada. It had first become an offence in Britain in 1663 when Sir Charles Sedley, a minor libertine poet and dramatist, was fined, jailed for a week and 'bound over *to keep the peace* [our emphasis] because (in the legal French reintroduced at the Restoration)'

> 'il monstre son nude Corps in un Balcony in Covent Garde', in addition, according to another report, to 'throwing down bottles (pist in) ... contra pacem, and to the Scandal of the Government'. His counsel argued that since the abolition of Star Chamber by the Long Parliament in 1641, there had been no court of public morals. On the contrary, the judges said, counsel should know that the court of King's Bench *was* the guardian of public morals—'de touts les Subjects le [sic] Roy'.
>
> (Sedley 2022, the author's emphasis)

The case of Charles Sedley was invoked to prosecute, in 1727, the pioneering publisher of erotic works Edmund Curll (1675–1747), who had published two pornographic translations: 1) in 1723, Johann Heinrich Meibomius' *Treatise of the Use of Flogging in Venereal Affairs,* which had been translated from Latin into English by a physician; and 2) in 1724, *Venus in the Cloister or the Nun in her Smock (Vénus dans le cloître, ou la Religieuse en chemise)* (1683) by Jean Barrin or François de Chavigny de La Bretonnière. The publisher was convicted under the common law offence of

Censorship and Language Policy: The Case of Canada and Québec

disturbing the peace, which was associated with obscenity. His was the first conviction for obscenity in the United Kingdom and the case established the crime of obscene libel (Colligan 2002: 4).

The Obscene Publications Act of 1857 (England), with its definition of obscenity, was applied in 1868 in Regina *v.* Hicklin. To uphold an order for the destruction of the Hicklin publication, Lord Chief Justice Alexander Cockburn, who presided over the case, supplied a broad definition of obscenity based on the following test: 'And I think that the test of obscenity is this, whether the tendency of the matter charged as obscenity is to deprave and corrupt those whose minds are open to such immoral influences, and into whose hands a publication of this sort may fall' (cited by Mackay 1958: 4, note 4).

Since its enactment in 1892, the Criminal Code of Canada has included as an offence the publication of material that could corrupt morals. Such material is judged obscene. However, a definition of obscene matter was not provided since the test applied was that of the British Hicklin case.

It should also be noted that Canada is a signatory to two international treaties on censorship to which the Supreme Court may refer: 1) Agreement for the Suppression of the Circulation of Obscene Publications (original title: Agreement for the Repression of Obscene Publications), which is a multi-lateral anti-pornography treaty that was initially signed in Paris in 1910 and amended by a 1949 Protocol. The treaty has 57 signatories, including Canada. Member states agree to designate a government authority tasked with tracing and suppressing 'obscene writings, designs, pictures or objects' in order to share information on censored works as well as on current and new obscenity legislation with other member states (United Nations 1949: 1); and 2) Convention for the Suppression of the Circulation of and Traffic in Obscene Publications, a 1923 League of Nations anti-pornography treaty signed in Geneva, which was intended to supplement the 1910 Agreement for the Suppression of the Circulation of Obscene Publications. It was amended by a 1947 Protocol. Member states agree to criminalise '[the making or producing] or hav[ing] in possession [for purposes of or by way of trade or for distribution or public exhibition] obscene writings, drawings, prints, paintings, printed matter, pictures, posters, emblems, photographs, cinematograph films or any other obscene objects' (United Nations 1923: Article 1). Given that the treaties deal with obscene materials that may cross international borders, translations are necessarily included in the definition of obscene materials.

20.2.4   *Canadian Definitions of Obscene Material*

Edmund Davie Fulton's 1960 amendment (s. 159.8) to the obscenity law (1959) replaced Hicklin's test with the following: 'Does the publication complained of deal with sex, or sex and one or more of the other subjects named [crime, horror, cruelty and violence]? If so, is this the dominant characteristic? Again, if so, does it exploit these subjects in an undue manner?' (Charles 1966: 254). In 1985 the Supreme Court of Canada, added that 'material which exploits sex in a "degrading and dehumanising manner" will fail the community standards test as it places women in positions of subordination, servile submission or humiliation which, if available, is likely to cause harm to society' (Tarnopolosky and Schneiderman 2006a). Community standards of acceptance are '[s]omething approaching a general average of community thinking and feeling [...]. Community standards must be contemporary. [...] we must determine what is obscene by Canadian standards, regardless of attitudes which may prevail elsewhere, be they more liberal or less so' (Mr Justice Freedman cited by Marsh 1999: 1691). In 1992, the Supreme Court's *Regina v Butler*

> tied the community standards test to the harm caused to women (and sometimes men) by the proliferation of pornography. The greater the likelihood of harm, the more likely the material

will offend the community standard of tolerance. Even if material is found to unduly exploit sex, the 'internal necessities' test, also known as the defence of 'artistic merit', is available for material which advances a literary or artistic theme that is internally necessary to the work itself and is not merely 'dirt for dirt's sake'.

(Tarnopolosky and Schneiderman 2006a)

More recently, under s. 163 of the Criminal Code, obscenity as defined in Canada 'involves creating, distributing, or possessing obscene material like photos, videos or audio recordings. This includes anything that unreasonably exploits sex, crime, horror, cruelty and violence' (CCH 2021-2022). No reference is made to books.

20.2.5   First Nations, Métis and Inuit

Both of Canada's colonising groups have actively participated in the forced assimilation of First Nations, Métis and Inuit peoples through the intentional silencing of their voices (for socio-cultural censorship of Native and Black Canadian voices, see Cohen 2001: 199–249). Prior to the residential school system promulgated by the federal government in 1883, various religious groups had created their own (residential) schools aimed at converting Indigenous children and adults to their respective Christian sects, whereas the federal government conceived the reserve and treaty system, which physically excluded Indigenous peoples from 'the places which allow one to speak with authority' (Bourdieu 1991: 138). While the Evangelisation process and reserves negatively impacted Indigenous self-image, culture and traditional way of life, languages were nonetheless preserved, and religious texts were often translated into Indigenous languages by missionaries. For example, James Evans created a syllabic writing system for Cree, and a variation of his system would be adopted by the Inuit to write in Inuktitut. On the contrary, the mission of federal residential schools was to assimilate Indigenous children into 'European' culture because Indigenous languages, cultures and traditions were no longer considered legitimate in the Canadian context.

The 'education' dispensed in residential schools taught marginalised Indigenous children the official—legitimate—languages of the country (Bourdieu 1991: 48–9), which in the process contributed to the delegitimisation of their languages. This is a flagrant example of traditional nation-state linguistic unification through socio-cultural censorship. According to First Nations Board Member of the Rainbow District School Board (Sudbury, Ontario), Linda Debassige:

> [R]esidential schools were established with one purpose in mind, not to educate, not to protect, not to preserve, but to intentionally and systematically assimilate Indigenous children and adolescents into European culture, 'to take the Indian out of child' and to remove and isolate children from their [sic] influence of their home, families, traditions, languages and culture, all based on racist assumptions that First Nations cultures were inferior.

(Quoted in Sasvari 2021)

This violent act of censorial silencing aimed at destroying Indigenous cultures was termed cultural genocide in the 2015 Truth and Reconciliation Commission Report and acknowledged publicly in 2019 by Prime Minister Justin Trudeau (Canadian Encyclopedia 2020).

Three notable Indigenous writers, who through sheer strength of character and creativity refused to let their mother tongue be silenced by the dominant culture, have poignantly shared the impact of the residential school experience on their first language and (self-)translation: Rita Joe (Mi'kmaq), Joséphine Bacon (Innu) and Tompson Highway (Cree). Joe (1932–2007) eloquently expressed the pain of maternal language loss in her poem 'I lost my talk' (1978), written when she

Censorship and Language Policy: The Case of Canada and Québec

was in her mid-forties. One of the purposes of Shubenacadie Residential School in Nova Scotia, like all of Canada's residential schools, was to forcibly replace the mother tongue of Mi'kmaq children, with the coloniser's more powerful language, in this case English, even though, as Rita Joe writes: 'I think like you / I create like you' (CCA 2021). She concludes by gently asking that she be allowed to rediscover her maternal language so that 'I can teach you [the dominant culture] about me' (CCA 2021). After leaving residential school, she relearned her native language, which enabled her to write poems not only in English but also in Mi'kmaq. Her deeply personal poems written in simple language reflect on Indigenous identity, Mi'kmaq beliefs and traditions, and racism in Canadian society.

Bacon (1947–) attended residential school at the Maliotenam reserve, or Mani-utenam (literally 'city of Mary' in Innu-Aimun), where she was forced to learn the dominant language of Québec, French. She nevertheless refused to abandon her mother tongue and has published since 2009, when she turned 62, four bilingual—Innu and French—collections of poetry, the most recent of which was published in 2023, with progressive Montréal publisher Mémoire d'encrier, founded in 2003 by writer Rodney Saint-Éloi (Bacon n.d.). She insists that she creates her poetry, which nostalgically recalls her authentic Innu nomadic life in the tundra as a child, in her native language Innu and creates it again in French, rather than translating it from one language into the other. However, she has translated for Québec anthropologists Rémi Savard, Sylvie Vincent and José Mailhot as well as for members of the Innu community (Bertrand and Henzi 2018).

After many years of self-censorship by translating into the settler language, Highway (1951–) reverted to writing in his mother tongue, Cree, which he had spoken, along with Dene, until age six. At residential school, he was forced to learn English. Consequently, English was the language of his first dramatic works, despite his conflicted relationship with the language. In his mid-50s, the dramatist started writing in Cree, explaining: 'the characters speak in Cree in [my] head but the words often come out in English or French' (Highway 2010). He has published: an opera libretto, *Pimooteewin* (*The Journey*), in Cree (2008); the Cree originals of the plays *The Rez Sisters* and *Dry Lips Oughta Move to Kapuskasing* (2010), which had been performed in English since the mid-1980s; his libretto for *The (Post) Mistress* (2011) in French and Cree. Highway explains that 'the Cree versions […] are actually the original versions. As it turns out, the […] ones that came out 20 years ago were the translation […]. The language that I'm most familiar with—that I'm closest to, emotionally and otherwise—is Cree, which is my native tongue […]' (Highway 2010).

Subsequent to the censoring of their respective mother tongues in residential school, Joe, Bacon and Highway each wrote in one of the nation's official languages, recognised as 'more powerful' (CCA 2021), which granted them access to the country's 'cultural gatekeepers' (Cohen 2001: 124–9). Writing and publishing first in a European language, particularly in the cases of Highway and Joe, opened the door to writing and publishing in their heretofore censored mother tongues. While they have certainly contributed positively to raising awareness of non-Indigenous Canadians and changing attitudes toward censorial assimilation, the legacy of residential schools, which is inseparable from the silencing and violence endured by Indigenous children, continues to haunt many of Canada's Indigenous peoples.

20.2.6 *Canada's and Québec's Young Publishing Industry*

A factor that has certainly impacted publishing censorship throughout the country, and which Cohen discusses with respect to literary censorship in Canada, is the country's relatively young publishing industry. Until the 1980s most books were published outside Canada and Québec and imported, allowing any problematic material to be confiscated and destroyed at the border before entering the country. However, the country now has a greater number of publishers, and more international publishers have opened offices in Canada, primarily in Toronto and Montréal, which has reduced reliance on publishing Canadian books outside the country.

20.3 Historical Perspectives

20.3.1 Federal and Provincial Language Politics and Policies

The 1867 Constitution recognises English and French as the country's two official languages at the federal level, as well as in Québec. It requires that all bills be printed in English and French before they are adopted into law and guarantees legal proceedings in both official languages. It has never extended to the public service. More often than not, English public servants are unilingual and French public servants bilingual because of English-speaker refusal to learn French. In other words, French-speakers are forced to (self-)translate. As the dominant population, English-speakers tend to have decision-making power over what gets translated into the other official language. Québec cofounded the confederation as the only bilingual province in 1867. The other cofounding provinces, Ontario, New Brunswick and Nova Scotia, were unilingually English. A condition of Québec membership in the confederation was bilingualism at the federal and provincial level in the legislature and the courts, and provincial responsibility over denominational education. It became the only unilingual French province when Robert Bourassa's Liberal government passed the *Loi sur la langue officielle* (The Official Language Act) in 1974. Translation is today a dynamic industry in Québec.

Although Parliament has in theory been bilingual since confederation, in practice French-speaking members of Parliament had to speak English if they wished to be understood by the majority of Parliamentarians who did not, or refused to, speak and understand French. Consequently, until simultaneous interpretation was introduced in the House of Commons in 1959, the only sayable language of Parliament was English, despite the equal status of French. French-speaking members of Parliament spoke in their native language when the message was directed to members of their socio-linguistic communities. In other words, French-speakers had to be bilingual, whereas English-speakers did not. Another problem was the length of time it took to translate the Parliamentary debates and other official documents into French. While this is not typically classified as censorship, not making legislative material readily available to the French-speaking population, who until post-WWII often did not speak or understand English, was tantamount to censoring the material, if only temporarily.

Since the means to achieve official bilingualism, i.e., translation, were not specified in federal legislation in 1867 and are not specified still today, there is a disconnect between the notion of official bilingualism and how to accomplish it. In fact, the publication of official records and their translation was not foreseen in the early years of Confederation. Prior to 1875, journalists' condensed versions of debates were published in English primarily in the *Ottawa Times* and *Toronto Globe*. Although not the result of any government censorship policy or legislation, the non-existence of French versions amounted to de facto censorship.

One of the rare cases of political censorship in Canada involved a Parliamentary translator Rémi Tremblay (1880–1887), who translated primarily into French, but also into English when required. He was a passionate defender of the French language throughout his career and a political activist at a time of marked political corruption. When Parliament was prorogued and he

Censorship and Language Policy: The Case of Canada and Québec

was unpaid by the government, he worked as a French-language journalist in Québec's Eastern Township or in neighbouring Massachusetts. Because the Northwest Rebellion of 1885, led by Louis Riel, enflamed anti-French sentiment among the English-speaking population in the country, Prime Minister John A. MacDonald and his Conservative party—including twenty-five French-Canadian members of Parliament—were not inclined to ease the concerns of French-speaking nationalists. Rather, Macdonald decided to charge Riel with high treason, based on an obscure British law dating to the year 1342. This law carried the death penalty whereas Canada's treason law did not. The hanging of Riel in November 1885 served to reinforce French-Canadian nation-alism and harden the linguistic position of the MacDonald government, along with that of certain provincial governments, including Manitoba (Merkle 2015).

On 15 January 1887, Parliament was dissolved and a federal election was called for 22 February. In his introduction to *Aux chevaliers du nœud coulant: poèmes et chansons* [To the Knights of the Noose: Poems and Songs], Levasseur (2007, cited by Hébert, Lever and Landry 2006: 59–60) explains that former Conservative Tremblay, supported by two translator colleagues hoped that a Liberal government led by Wilfrid Laurier would be elected. To that end, Tremblay mobilised Eastern Township support for Liberal James Naismith Greenshields, who had advised Louis Riel during his trial. He also publicly declared his support for the Métis leader and his opposition to those who had supported the death sentence. The Conservative candidate William Bullock Ives managed to get reelected with a reduced majority, as did the Conservative Party. Four days after the election, Tremblay completed his controversial poem 'Aux chevaliers du nœud coulant' in which he lambasted the French-Canadian MPs who had supported MacDonald. The poem was published in Québec newspapers, after which federal authorities launched an enquiry to determine the guilt of the translators, who had voiced their opposition to the Conservative government that employed them. The report, however, found that the translators had broken no laws. Nevertheless, the three Parliamentary translators were let go in 1888. A lengthy public debate in Québec newspapers on the legitimacy of the dismissals was unable to sway Prime Minister MacDonald. The censored poem was read into the Parliamentary Debates by the Liberal leader of the Opposition Wilfrid Laurier and translated into English by none other than the three translators, prior to their dismissal (Hébert, Lever and Landry 2006: 59–60).

Manitoba joined the confederation in 1870 as a bilingual province thanks to the negotiation efforts of Louis Riel who had led the Red River uprising. However, in 1890 the provincial gov-ernment illegally adopted the Official Language Act that suppressed French language rights in an attempt to delegitimise the French language and assimilate Francophones. In 1912, the govern-ment of Ontario adopted regulation 17, which proscribed the teaching of French beyond grade two in all Catholic (i.e., French) schools. These laws were designed to silence French voices in Manitoba and Ontario, and they were largely successful, particularly in Manitoba (Merkle 2015).

20.3.2   The Criminal Code and Customs

Customs regulations fall under the Border Services Agency Tariff item 9899.00.00 (Government of Canada 2020). Prior to confederation, the importation of books, both originals and translations, and drawings of an immoral or indecent nature was prohibited by the 1847 Customs Act of the province of Canada. In 1859 the definition was expanded to include paintings and prints (Ryder 1999: 139). The session of Parliament of the Government of Canada in 1867 adopted the same legislation. According to the Criminal Code enacted in 1892, customs agents determined which books, newspapers or journals could enter the country, and from 1895 to 1958 they could refer to a list of proscribed publications.

20.3.3 1868–1959 The Hicklin Test, Communist and Socialist Writings and Crime Comics

Literature in Canada is banned primarily for reasons of obscenity, but also for reasons of sedition. In the aftermath of World War I, out of fear of sedition, censorship was still enforced under the war measures act, which resulted in the censorship of socialist and communist writings. Karl Marx's *Das Kapital* (American translation by Ernest Untermann, commissioned by editor Charles H. Kerr) was banned by Canada Customs in 1919 along with other Communist texts. Decades later, in 1948, during the early years of the Cold War, Trotsky's *Chapters from My Diary* (1918, anonymous translator) was included in the Canada Customs list of prohibited books because the author was a Russian Communist.

Nevertheless, obscenity was the primary reason behind censorship. Balzac's *Droll Stories* (imported from the UK; anonymous translator), along with other French books in translation, such as de Maupassant's short stories, had already been banned by the Vancouver Public Library in 1905 before being banned by Canada Customs in 1914 (Thomas 2011: 1). Balzac meant his *Droll Stories* to be humorous, but the work's sexual themes were considered highly inappropriate.

In English Canada the number of translations has historically been lower since many books read by the public are British, American or English-Canadian literature. The list of books banned for obscenity resembles that of banned translations in non-English-speaking countries, and the authors are recognisable: Aldous Huxley, Arthur Miller, James Joyce, D.H. Lawrence, Henry Miller, among others. However, the French versions of two of the most notorious works by these authors, the French version of D.H. Lawrence's *Lady Chatterley's Lover*, and James Joyce's *Ulysses*, were also banned. *Ulysses* was banned for 26 years starting in 1923, and its French translation, *Ulysse,* translated by Auguste Morel in 1929, could not enter the country. Unlike Sir Richard Burton's eroticised translations of Sanskrit and Arabic texts, the 16–volume *The Book of the Thousand Nights and a Night*, Aubert's *Ulysse* was removed from the list in 1949. Until 1955 the University of Toronto allowed students who had certified that they were free from 'mental problems' to read the works of the Marquis de Sade, among those of other writers sequestered in the 'Art Room', after which the books were moved to the public stacks or to the rare books room (Bernstein 1997: 2).

Violence may be equated with indecency and obscenity as the following case demonstrates. In 1948, two preadolescents killed a driver while playing with a rifle. In response, MP Davie Fulton (BC), who would propose the Fulton test of obscenity eleven years later as Minister of Justice, noted that the children were avid readers of crime comic books, such as *Batman* and *Wonder Woman*. His bill, according to which it was 'illegal to corrupt morals' by 'produc[ing], printing, publishing, distributing, selling or having in one's possession for the purpose of publishing, distributing or disseminating an illustrated crime story', was adopted in 1949. The law was part of the Criminal Code, until it was repealed in 2018 (Canada 2024). This legislation, however, would not have a significant impact in Canada given that most popular crime comics, such as *Batman* and *Wonder Woman*, were imported from the US and allowed to enter the country.

20.3.4 1959–1992 The Fulton Test

The French translation of *Lady Chatterley's Lover* by Frédéric Roger-Cornaz was banned from entry in 1932. In November 1959, five copies of the English-language novel were seized at a Montréal bookstore. The copies of the book had somehow evaded confiscation by Canada Customs. In 1960, the Crown prosecuted the work, or rather isolated passages deemed to contravene the law, with reference to the new Fulton Obscenity Law (1959), applying the Fulton test. However, the

Censorship and Language Policy: The Case of Canada and Québec

Supreme Court of Canada ruled five to four in favour of the bookstore, reversing the decision of the lower courts, including the 1961 appeal. Marc Allégret's 1955 French-language film adaptation of the novel was also banned in Québec.

Fulton's crime comics censorship law was last cited in a legal case in 1987, when a Calgary-based comic retailer faced charges for the books they carried. Nevertheless, censorship of comics is ongoing. For example, Vittorio Giardino's *Little Ego* (anonymous translation), a parody for adults of the dreams of *Little Nemo*, which won the US Harvey Award and the Italian Attilio Micheluzzi Award, was seized twice by customs, in 1994 and 1996, for bestiality, and again six years later in 2002, for its troubling depiction of sexual relations; however, it was ultimately allowed to enter the country.

20.3.5 *1992 Regina v Butler: Limits of Freedom of Expression*

In 1987 Donald Butler, the owner of a store that sold hard-core pornographic videos and sexual paraphernalia in Winnipeg, Manitoba, 'was charged under the *Criminal Code*'s obscenity provision for selling, possessing and publicly exposing obscene material. He argued this violated his freedom of expression under s. 2(b) of the *Charter*' (WLEAF n.d.), and '[t]he trial judge agreed that [the sale] of obscene material could […] be protected under s. 2(b)' provided the materials did not depict 'violence or cruelty mixed with sexual activity', did not show 'lack of consent to sexual activity' and did not contain 'dehumanising material'. Consequently, Butler was convicted of only eight counts of distribution of eight films, and was acquitted on the remaining charges (69 counts). However, the Manitoba Court of Appeal determined that the seized materials unduly exploited and degraded human sexuality and convicted Butler on all counts. Mr. Butler appealed to the Supreme Court of Canada, where the Women's Legal Education and Action Fund argued that pornography amounted to sex discrimination against women. The regulation of pornography could be constitutionally justified by focusing on 'the actual harms done by and through pornography' as a 'violent' or 'discriminating form of expression', 'with harm meaning that people become predisposed to act in an anti-social manner' (WLEAF n.d.).

Subsequent to the conviction of Butler, violent and degrading pornography, in particular Japanese adult manga, anime and DVDs, has been targeted by Border Services. For example, in 2015 Canada Customs prohibited the DVD *Nightmare Campus 4* (original title *Gedou Gakuen*, directed by Koji Yoshakawa and translated/licensed by The Right Stuf International in 2003) (Mann 2015). The decision, however, also generated debates about 'the discourses of anti-pornography feminism [that] have continued to make inroads into legal frameworks, most recently in Canada' (Segal 1998: 43) and its implications for alternative sexualities and 'subversive expressions of women's sexual agency' (Segal 1998: 43).

20.3.6 *Québec In Peacetime*

Pierre Hébert (Biblioassnat 2021) has identified three phases of censorship in Québec: casual censorship (1625–1840); Church censorship (1840–1960); and legal censorship (1960–2000). The French colony did not have a printing press until 1764 when it was introduced by the British shortly after the Conquest, so all books were imported, primarily from France. Reading was essentially limited to the educated population composed of the religious and seigneurial elites, since the early economy was based on the fur trade and peasant farming. Imported books were not always screened before they were sent to the colony, so the Catholic Church consigned problematic, i.e., obscene, heretical, non-Catholic, publications to the *Enfer* (literally 'Hell') of the Québec

Seminary, which is a collection of thousands of books listed on the Vatican's Index identified by the Sacred Congregation of the Index. These varied writings were locked away and only a small number of people were authorised to consult them. Lafond in *Promenade en Enfer* (2019: 64, 84–5) explains that unauthorised French translations of the Bible, including two editions of the *Nouveau Testament de Nostre seigneur Jésus-Christ traduit en francois selon la Vulgate,* were sent there. The translator was Emeritus Professor Charles Huré, a Jansenist, who himself was placed on the Index in 1717, the same year the book was deposited in the Library of Reverand Récollet Fathers of Québec. The 1702 edition of the translation contains the censor's handwritten comments, referencing an ideological quarrel about norms for translating Holy writings, and sits next to the 1711 edition in the *Enfer*. The Index, which targeted print literature, was abolished in June 1966.

The Québec Board of Censors for Moving Pictures had been very active since the early years of the twentieth century. The minutes of the Censorship Bureau were in English until 1923, after which they were bilingual (Lever 2008: 69). In 1926, US distributors threatened to boycott Canada because the Board of Censors was blocking the entry of too many of their films, deemed a corrupting influence on Québec youth. The industry made $1.4 million in Québec that year, while the cost of subtitling into French was only $60,000 (Lever 2008: 72). On 4 April 1931, the Québec Board of Censors adopted its translation of the Hollywood Production Code written by two well-known US Catholics, to which it added criteria from the 1921 Québec censorship code (Lever 2008: 97–104). During the 1930s, censors examined 3500 films a year, 600 of which were feature films (Lever 2008: 118). One 1932 example is Howard Hawk's *Scarface* deemed 'Unfit for showing in the province of Québec' and again censured in 1943 for 'Gangsterism. Immoral, as too many details are given in the preparation and execution of crimes'. The film was finally authorised in September 1947 after cuts had been made (Hébert, Lever and Landry 2006: 606).

Before 1944, almost no US films were dubbed into French (Lever 2008: 118). However, one film, *I Confess* (1952, released in 1953), was (*La loi du silence* 1955). This is a particularly interesting example of a motion picture shot in Québec by none other than Alfred Hitchcock, himself a Catholic, who found the Catholic atmosphere of the city most appropriate to the mood of the film, but perhaps more importantly because he wished to contribute to the Canadian Cooperation Project (1948–1958) (Hébert, Lever and Landry 2006: 325). The latter was 'an initiative of the Motion Picture Association of America (MPAA) [...] designed to ensure that the government did not block the flow of film-rental revenues (estimated to be worth about $17 million annually at the time) to the American studios, nor stimulate feature film production in Canada. In return, the MPAA agreed that Hollywood producers would film some of their features on location in Canada' (Morris n.d.). *I Confess* is based on a 1902 French play by Paul Anthelme titled *Nos deux consciences* (Our Two Consciences), which Hitchcock saw in the 1930s. The Québec technical consultant was Abbé Paul La Couline, whose role was to remove from the script everything that did not conform to a Catholic view on religious reality and that might displease local authorities. The director had to accept those censorial constraints in order to film inside Québec city churches, especially St. Zéphirin's. He cut, for example, the scene where the Abbé Michael Logan explains to the police that he cannot talk because of the standard of secrecy protecting a confession, as well as a passionate scene between Logan and his former girlfriend Ruth upon his return from the war and before becoming a priest. The 'official' film was 95 minutes, but the version brought to censorship was 90 minutes, from which another 2.5 minutes were cut before the film was approved by the censors in February 1953. Hitchcock viewed the 90-minute version at the screening. He was so angry that he cancelled his appointment with Archbishop Maurice Roy and said that the Québécois would be the only public to view a mutilated version of his film, unlike the rest of the world. The censors quickly backtracked and approved the 95-minute version of the film with only the initial cuts of 26 February. The same scenes were cut in the dubbed version and the film was rated 'Pour tous' (general audience) (Hébert, Lever and Landry 2006: 325–7).

During the 1960s, French films were dubbed in English, but it remained difficult to have English-language films dubbed or subtitled into French (Lever 2008: 211) due to a lack of funding, which can be considered a form of market censorship (Jansen 1998).

In 1950, the Québec Legislative Assembly passed a law banning any illustration that evoked real or fictional scenes of crime or the everyday life of criminals, or obscene or morbid situations or attitudes, which could corrupt young people and deprave morals. Two types of publication were targeted by the legislation: crime comic books and highly sexualised yellow journalism (see Namaste 2017). The mandate of the Québec Board of Censors (QBC), initially responsible for film censorship, was expanded to include written publications. The QBC was responsible for enforcing the law. In practice, however, the law was ineffective because it targeted illustrations and only crown attorneys could submit censorship recommendations to the Bureau, who did not consider written publications a priority and provided editors with no clear criteria (Biblioassnat 2021). Interestingly, despite comic books being illegal and thus censured in the province since 1950, except for a few short Superman and Batman adventures, from 1968 until the beginning of the 1990s, Québec published uncensored French translations of US superhero comic books despite the provincial and federal ban (Rioux 2022). The translations of *Batman* and *Spiderman*, among other crime comics, enjoyed tremendous and unfettered popularity in the province from 1968 until the advent of video games (Houdassine 2022).

20.4   Current Debates

This broad overview has barely scratched the surface of translation and censorship in Canada. In addition to researching in more detail the various issues addressed in the chapter, the following institutions and questions merit particular attention: the CBC/Radio-Canada; the NFB/ONF; community standards and the role of the public in determining what should be censored (from legislated censorship to public decision-making); the censorship of LGBTQ2S+ cultural products; hate and terrorism; market censorship; the role of the Agreement for the Suppression of the Circulation of Obscene Publications (original title: Agreement for the Repression of Obscene Publications) 1910/1949 and the Convention for the Suppression of the Circulation of and Traffic in Obscene Publications (1923) on censorship in Canada, along with other signatory parties.

Further Readings

Cohen, Mark. 2001. *Censorship in Canadian Literature.* Montréal: McGill-Queen's.
The author makes an innovative argument in favour of 'just censorship' given that censorship is inevitable in democratic market societies.

Hébert, Pierre, Lever, Yves and Landry, Kenneth (eds.). 2006. *Dictionnaire de la censure au Québec.* Montréal: Fides.
Even though the encyclopedic dictionary, available in French only, does not deal explicitly with translation, given Québec's legislated bilingualism prior to 1974 and French unilingualism since then, issues of translation, adaptation, dubbing and subtitling inevitably come into play in a book devoted to the censorship of literature and film in the province.

References

Bacon, Joséphine. n.d. 'Joséphine Bacon'. *Mémoire d'encrier*. Joséphine Bacon (memoiredencrier.com).

Bernstein, Karen. 1997. *A Chronicle of Freedom of Expression in Canada*. www.efc.ca/pages/chronicle/chronicle.html

Bertrand, Karine and Henzi, Sarah. 2018. Table-ronde avec Joséphine Bacon, Sonia Bonspille Boileau and Fernand de Varennes [Round Table with Joséphine Bacon, Sonia Bonspille Boileau and Fernard de Varennes]. *Colloque: La traduction transculturelle et interlinguistique*. [Conference: Transcultrural and Interlinguistic Translation]. Available at: Table ronde – Colloque: La traduction transculturelle et interlinguistique – YouTube (Accessed 20 March 2024).

Biblioassnat. 2021, 15 December. 'À l'Index! Regards sur la censure littéraire au Québec: lumière sur un pan méconnu de l'histoire parlementaire québécoise' [Relegated to the Index! Perspectives on Literary Censorship in Québec: Shedding Light on a Little Known Period of Québec Parliamentary History] *Bibliothèque Assemblée nationale du Québec* [Québec National Assembly Library]. Available at: À l'Index! Regards sur la censure littéraire au Québec: lumière sur un pan méconnu de l'histoire parlementaire québécoise – PREMIÈRE LECTURE (assnat.qc.ca) (Accessed 20 March 2024).

Bourdieu, Pierre. 1991. *Language and Symbolic Power*, ed. and intro J. B. Thompson. Translated by G. Raymond and M. Adamson. Cambridge, MA: Harvard University Press.

Boyd, Neil. 1985. 'Censorship and Obscenity: Jurisdiction and the Boundaries of Free Expression', *Osgoode Hall Law Journal*, 23(1): 37–66. Available at: Censorship and Obscenity: Jurisdiction and the Boundaries of Free Expression (yorku.ca) (Accessed 20 March 2024).

Canada. 2024, 15 March. 'Criminal Code: Version of Section 163 from 2018-12-13 to 2024-03-06'. *Justice Laws Website*. ARCHIVED – Criminal Code (justice.gc.ca).

Canada Council for the Arts (CCA). 2021. 'I Lost My Talk. Rita Joe', *Poetry in Voice/Les voix de la poésie*. Available at: www.poetryinvoice.com/poems/i-lost-my-talk (Accessed 20 March 2024).

Canadian Encyclopedia, The. 2020. 'Genocide and Indigenous Peoples in Canada', in *The Canadian Encyclopedia*. Available at: Genocide and Indigenous Peoples in Canada | The Canadian Encyclopedia (Accessed 20 March 2024).

Charles, William H. 1966. 'Obscene Literature and the Legal Process in Canada', *Canadian Bar Review*, 44(2): 243–92. https://canlii.ca/t/t66f

Cohen, Mark. 2001. *Censorship in Canadian Literature*. Montréal: McGill-Queen's.

Colligan, Collette. 2002. *Obscenity and Empire: England's Obscene Print Culture in the Nineteenth Century*. Unpublished Dissertation. Queen's University.

Criminal Code Help (CCH). 2021–2022. 'Obscenity Laws in Canada'. Available at: Obscenity Offence Laws in Canada | Criminal Code Help (Accessed 20 March 2024).

Government of Canada, Canada Border Services Agency. 2020. 'Chapter 98. Special Classification Provisions – Non Commercial'. *Customs Tariff – Schedule*. Available at: Microsoft Word – cn98Eng.docx (cbsa-asfc.gc.ca) (Accessed 20 March 2024).

Hébert, Pierre, Lever, Yves and Landry, Kenneth. 2006. *Dictionnaire de la censure au Québec* [Dictionary of Québec Censorship]. Montréal: Fides.

Highway, Tomson. 2010, 8 November. 'Tomson Highway Releases Plays in Cree'. *CBC News Ottawa*. cbc.ca/news/canada/ottawa/tomson-highway-releases-plays-in-cree-1.895683?ref=rss

Houdassine, Ismaël. 2022, 28 December. 'Les superhéros dans la BD au Québec', *Le Devoir*. [Superhéros in Québec Comics, *Le Devoir*]. Available at: [Coup d'essai] Les superhéros dans la BD au Québec | Le Devoir (Accessed 20 March 2024).

Jansen, Sue C. 1998. *Censorship: The Knot That Binds Power and Knowledge*. New York: Oxford University Press.

Lafond, Pierrette. 2019. *Promenade en Enfer. Les livres à l'Index de la bibliothèque historique du Séminaire de Québec* [A Walk Through Hell: Books on the Index in the Historical Library of the Québec Seminary]. Québec: Septentrion.

Letterboxd. n.d. *Cut, Banned and Censored in Ontario*. Available at: Cut, Banned and Censored in Ontario, A List of Films by P S • Letterboxd (Accessed 20 March 2024).

Levasseur, Jean. 2007. *Aux chevaliers du nœud coulant: poèmes et chansons* [To the Knights of the Noose: Poems and Songs]. Québec: Presses de l'Université Laval.

Lever, Yves. 2008. *Anastasie ou la censure du cinéma au Québe* [Anastasia or film censorship in Québec]. Sillery (Québec): Septentrion.

Mackay, Robert Simson. 1958. 'The Hicklin Rule and Judicial Censorship', *The Canadian Bar Review*, 36(1): 1–24.

Mann, Bryan K. 2015. 'Witchcraft', *Quarterly List of Prohibited Materials*. Available at: Quarterly List of Prohibited Materials: Banned Comics in Canada Update – Sequential (sequentialpulp.ca) (Accessed 20 March 2024).

Marsh, James H. (ed.). 1999. 'Obscenity', in *The Canadian Encyclopedia*. Toronto: McLelland and Stewart, 1690–1.

Merkle, Denise. 2015. 'L'exécution de Louis David Riel (16 novembre 1885) et les enjeux de la traduction au Canada' [The Exécution of Louis David Riel (16 November 1885) and the Stakes of Translation in Canada], in L. Arnoux-Farnoux, Y. Chevrel and S. Humbert-Mougin (eds.), *L'Appel de l'étranger* [The Call of the Foreign]. Tours: Presses universitaires François-Rabelais, 301–15.

Morris, Peter. n.d. 'Canadian Cooperation Project (1948–1958)', in *Canadian Film Encyclopedia*. TIFF. Available at: Canadian Film Encyclopedia – Canadian Cooperation Project (1948–1958) (tiff.net) (Accessed 17 March 2024).

Namaste, Viviane. 2017. *Imprimés interdits. La censure des journaux jaunes au Québec, 1955–1975* [Banned Printed Material. The Censorship of Yellow Journalism in Québec]. Québec: Septentrion.

Ontario. 2021, 8 June. Updated 15 May 2023. 'Film Content Information in Ontario'. Available at: Film Content Information in Ontario | ontario.ca (Accessed 20 March 2024).

Parents Guide. n.d. *Nekromantik.* Available at: Nekromantik (1988) – Parents Guide – IMDb (Accessed 20 March 2024).

Petersen, Klaus and Hutchinson, Allen C. (eds.). 1999. *Interpreting Censorship in Canada*. Toronto: University of Toronto Press.

Poirier, Agnes. 2000, 21 November. 'Ontario Upholds Ban on *Baise-moi*', *Screendaily*. Available at: Ontario Upholds Ban on Baise-moi | News | Screen (screendaily.com) (Accessed 20 March 2024).

Rioux, Philippe. 2022. *Alter ego: Le genre superhéroïque dans la BD au Québec (1968–1995)* [Alter Ego: The Superhero Genre in Québec Comics (1968–1995)]. Montréal: Presses de l'Université de Montréal.

Ryder, Bruce. 1999. 'The Regulation of Publications in Canada', in K. Petersen and A. C. Hutchinson (eds.), *Interpreting Censorship in Canada*. Toronto: University of Toronto Press, 129–56.

Sasvari, Tom. 2021, 16 June. 'Residential Schools Were Established to Take the "Indian Out of the Child", says Rainbow Board Trustee', *The Manitoulin Expositor*. Available at: Residential schools Were Established to Take the 'Indian Out of the Child', says Rainbow Board Trustee – The Manitoulin Expositor (Accessed 20 March 2024).

Sedley, Stephen. 2022, 10 March. 'Keep the Baby Safe', *The London Review of Books,* 44(5). Available at: Stephen Sedley · Keep the baby safe: Corrupt and Deprave (lrb.co.uk) (Accessed 20 March 2024).

Segal, Lynne. 1998. 'Only the Literal: The Contradictions of Anti-Pornography Feminism', *Sexualities*, 1(1): 43–62.

Tarnopolosky, Walter S. and Schneiderman, David. 2006a. 'Obscenity', in James H. Marsh (ed.), *The Canadian Encyclopedia.* Available at: Obscenity | The Canadian Encyclopedia (Accessed 20 March 2024).

Tarnopolosky, Walter S. and Schneiderman, David. 2006b. 'Censorship', in James H. Marsh (ed.), *The Canadian Encyclopedia.* Available at: Censorship | The Canadian Encyclopedia (Accessed 20 March 2024).

Thomas, Deb. 2011. 'A Century of Censorship Challenges in BC: Presented by Dr. Ann Curry', *BCLA [British Columbia Library Association] Browser: Linking the Library Landscape*, 3(3): 1–2.

Tremonti, Anna Maria. 2004, 19 April. The Current: Whole Show Blow by Blow. *CBC Radio.* Available at: CBC Radio | The Current | Whole Show Blow-by-Blow (archive.org) (Accessed 20 March 2024).

United Nations. 1923. International Convention for the Suppression of the Circulation of and Traffic in Obscene Publications. Available at: Ch_VIII_03p.pdf (un.org) (Accessed 18 March 2024).

United Nations. 1949. Agreement for the Suppression of the Circulation of Obscene Publications. Available at: Ch_VIII_05p.pdf (un.org) (Accessed 18 March 2024).

Women's Legal Education and Action Fund (WLEAF). n.d. 'Case Summary: R v. Butler (1992)'. Available at: R. v. Butler (1992) – LEAF (Accessed 16 March 2024).

21

MARKET CENSORSHIP AND TRANSLATION

Michelle Woods

21.1 Introduction

In 1969, Milan Kundera's first novel, *Žert*, was published in translation in England as *The Joke*. When he received a copy, Kundera realised that the novel had been abridged and the structure had been substantially altered. He wrote an open letter, published in the *Times Literary Supplement*, decrying the alterations: 'Individual chapters have been shortened, rewritten, simplified, some of them omitted. [...] The whole text has been cut up into pieces and put together in a daring "montage" so as to form a completely different book' (Kundera 1969: 1259). What was especially galling about these alterations (made without his knowledge or permission) is that his novel had spent two years held up in the Czech censor's office (1965–1967), as Kundera and the Czech censors negotiated what could be published in a novel that exposed, in part, the illusions about and disillusions with the Czechoslovak communist post-WW II experiment. Kundera, 'a difficult customer' (Hamšík 1971: 87), ultimately refused to change a word and the censors acquiesced; the novel was a huge bestseller in Czechoslovakia upon publication in 1967. That the novel was tampered with in translation in the democratic West led Kundera to accuse his English publisher, Macdonald, of being worse than the 'Moscow censors' even if their motivation was different. 'I do not doubt', Kundera wrote, 'that the English publisher has broken up my book in good faith that this would improve the sales' (Kundera 1969: 1259).

'Some of the most dramatic testaments against market censorship', Curry Jansen writes, 'have paradoxically come from writers seeking refuge in the West from oppressive censorship regimes' (Jansen 2010: 19). Emerging from societies that had stringent conditions of state censorship, a writer like Aleksandr Herzen 'experience[d] profound disillusionment later as he discovered the extremely narrow limits imposed on freedom of expression by market constraints in the West' and, over a century later, Aleksandr Solzhenitsyn 'repeated the cycle, escaping Soviet censorship only to be demoralised by what he condemned as the commercialism, sensationalism and moral bankruptcy of Western materialism' (Jansen 2010: 19). Writers banned in and/or exiled from their homelands are often dependent on translation as a means of survival, but translations are 'financially risky' and carry only a 'tenuous economic value' in the larger English-speaking publishing world (Venuti 1998: 124). They—like Kundera (who emigrated to France in 1975, having been banned from publishing in his home country in 1970, after the Soviet invasion of

320

DOI: 10.4324/9781003149453-26

Market Censorship and Translation

Czechoslovakia)—come face to face with idealistic, and ingrained, notions of free speech and self-expression in societies that have their own constraints based on market worth.

This chapter first theorises the notion of market censorship and relates it to current thinking in translation studies on covert censorship, networks of censorship agents in the translation process, patronage and the effect of non-translation. The chapter then focuses on four cases: the first two concern the market censorship of Czech literature, in the cases of Milan Kundera's first novel, *Žert* [The Joke], published in 1967 and first translated into French in 1968 and English in 1969, and Václav Havel's 1978 play, *Protest* [Protest], first performed in English translation in 1980. Both translations, written under strict censorship in Czechoslovakia, were heavily edited in English translation in order to make the works more marketable and acceptable for an English-speaking readership and audience. The third case focuses on pre-translation censorship, namely of Hollywood movies in the current era being readied—and censored—for the Chinese market (now the largest box office in the world). Finally, the chapter focuses on the potential of consumer censorship in the market, analysing whether the case of the translations of Amanda Gorman's poem, 'The Hill We Climb', might suggest agency on the part of the consumer in the neoliberal marketplace.

21.2   Core Issues and Topics

Market censorship, according to Jansen, delineates 'practices that routinely filter or restrict the production and distribution of selected ideas [...] based upon their anticipated profits and/or support for corporate values and consumerism' (Jansen 2010: 13). Furthermore, she argues, these 'practices are reified, naturalised and integrated' into public discourse, 'and re-presented to the public as outcomes of consumer choices within a rational market system rather than as the result of calculated managerial responses to profit imperatives' (Jansen 2010: 13). '[M]arket censors decide what ideas will gain entry into "the marketplace of ideas" and what ideas will not [...] *they decide what cultural products are likely to ensure a healthy profit margin*' (Jansen 1991: 16, her italics). The 'oligopoly' of multinational corporations and the 'Consciousness Industry—press, advertising, public relations, mass entertainment, and organised leisure'—serve as gatekeepers for knowledge, which is not free but a commodity to be sold (Jansen 1991: 164, 136). As a result, 'some ideas get extensive exposure in multiple media outlets, while others are marginalised [...] because they are deemed too controversial, risky or commercially unviable. In short, market censorship refers to the conditions of production and consumption that produce cultural hegemony' (Jansen 2010: 14).

John Keane similarly argues that 'Market competition produces market censorship' but warns that this market censorship 'is not an underhanded conspiracy to swindle or brainwash gullible publics for the sake of profit [...] It results from the fact that commercial publishers of opinion are little interested in the non-market preferences of readers, listeners and viewers' (Keane 1991: 91). Media corporations and publishers provide choice, but this kind of free-market choice is presented 'always within the framework of *commercially viable* alternatives' (91, his italics). The problem, too, is constituted in the structure of market capitalism in which there is a 'privileging of corporate speech' which becomes 'an apology for the power of king-sized business to organise and determine and therefore to *censor* individuals' choices concerning what they listen to or read and watch' (Keane 1991: 89–90, his italics).

With the 'emergence of modern corporate capitalism in the late 19th and early 20th century, control over the production and distribution of ideas and cultural artefacts was industrialised, and commodified and concentrated within private hands' (Jansen 2010: 19). While, particularly in America and through the self-presentation of American ideals in Europe and beyond, a post-Enlightenment ideal of 'freedom of expression' reigned, it was 'largely contingent on decisions made by private producers' who 'now possess the kind of power over "what we know" and "how we know it" that was once the exclusive purview of popes, kings, commissars and inquisitors' (Jansen 2010: 19–20). More invidious though, Jansen argues, is the opaque structure of censorship parading as free market choice; it is a censorship 'frequently free of easily traceable human fingerprints' and 'all but invisible', ready even to coopt and absorb 'critical challenges' (Jansen 2010: 18). Jansen was among several critics writing at the end of the Cold War questioning the triumphant idea of the global victory of free speech when there were still obvious examples of the 'chilling-effect' of censorship in the West (Lamarche 1991: 56), and a reaction in the US to Reagan-era ideological censorship packaged as moral censorship, what critics felt was a 'new censorship' (Burt 1994: xi).

In terms of translation, the invisibility of fingerprints can mean, for instance, what Jaroslav Špirk calls 'non-translation' (Špirk 2014: 156), i.e., choosing not to translate texts at all, or a deliberate reframing or rewriting of texts to make the eventual product more commercially viable or to absorb their threat or even their critiques of the very truthfulness of idealised notions of freedom of expression. André Lefevere noted the relationship between rewriting and patronage; how, throughout history, patrons have altered texts to suit their own ends. They are 'the powers (persons, institutions) that can further or hinder the reading, writing, and rewriting of literature' (Lefevere 1992: 14–5). Patrons act as a 'constraint on the choice and development of both form and subject matter' (Lefevere 1992: 16). For Lefevere, this patronage works alongside a network of agents who apply 'control factors' on literature; in the case of translation, a series of literary professionals, 'critics, reviewers, teachers, translators' (Lefevere 1992: 14). These agents, 'will occasionally repress certain works of literature that are all too blatantly opposed to the dominant concept of what literature should (be allowed to) be—its poetics—and of what society should (be allowed to) be—ideology. But they will much more frequently rewrite works of literature until they are deemed acceptable to the poetics and the ideology of a certain time and place' (Lefevere 1992: 14).

Billiani reads this form of acceptability, through Pierre Bourdieu and Michel Foucault, as being constructed through the ideological structures of taste. 'Censorship of foreign texts cannot help but act according to the wide national patterns of taste, or in other words to what is perceived as the sought after national textuality' (Billiani 2007: 6). These 'patterns of taste' usually fall into four broad categories: political, moral, religious, aesthetic and translations, coming from outside a given habitus, often highlight the borders of what is acceptable. Translations are chosen, or manipulated, for their ability to uphold the given norms of a culture at a given time. Because translations, as a product, hold a 'tenuous economic value', publishers tend to choose foreign bestsellers; their approach is 'primarily commercial, even imperialistic, an exploitation governed by an estimate of the market at home' (Venuti 1998: 124). Literature, particularly postcolonial and world literature, has increasingly become a 'commodified artifact' (Huggan 2001: 158). The 'text or writer accumulates symbolic capital—recognition, prestige and, occasionally, celebrity—through a cumulative process of legitimation', by domestic cultural gatekeepers (Huggan 2001: 212). Such 'covert censorship' in the act and marketing of translation, as Merkle suggests, should be studied (Merkle 2002: 10). Contemporary Anglo-American taste tends to produce a conservative form of aesthetics, Venuti argues, a 'realism typical of the popular aesthetic' that might produce 'the illusory effect of transparency' (Venuti 1998: 126), a strange and unthreatening sense of non-translation, seen in the recent translation successes of writers like Karl Ove Knausgaard and Elena Ferrante. The hegemony of realist forms and the *Bildungsroman* reinforce Western conceptions of identity formation. As we will see, works coming from abroad often face reframing and reediting during the translation process to subscribe to marketable aesthetic norms.

21.3 Historical Perspectives

21.3.1 The Joke

Žert [The Joke], Milan Kundera's first novel, centres around the voices of four characters: Ludvík, Helena, Jaroslav and Kostka, who converge on a Moravian town for a folk celebration, The Ride of the Kings. Twenty years earlier Ludvík had been thrown out of university by his fellow students, led by the charismatic Pavel Zemánek, for a joke written on a postcard. Ludvík intends to sleep with Pavel's wife, Helena, to enact revenge. Unbeknownst to him, Pavel and Helena are long separated; the joke is on him. The deeper metaphysical joke is that all four characters were true believers and now, the reader at least, can see the hollowness in those beliefs: Ludvík and Helena in the early years of communism; Jaroslav is a true believer in Moravian folk culture and music; Kostka is intensely religious (a dangerous choice in communist Czechoslovakia). Each character, in multiple intertwined monologues, tells their story. Only the reader gets to see their respective blindnesses, the parts of their intersecting stories they will never know themselves, and so only the reader will come to a full understanding of the profound tragedy in each characters' ignorance.

Jaroslav is interested in musical polyphony, and how the sophisticated thread of classical music finds its way into folk tunes; he speaks at length about the idea.[1] Kundera, an accomplished musician was the son of a music professor; his father was a student of the great Czech modernist composer, Leoš Janáček. Not only does Jaroslav focus on the idea of polyphony in the musical tradition he is obsessed by, but Kundera the novelist, attempts to integrate the polyphonic tradition into the architectonics of the novel—it is, as Květoslav Chvatík wrote, 'fundamentally *polyphonic*' (1994: 46, my translation, italics in the original) in the multiple interweaving voices of the four characters, and the absolute silence of one, Lucie, with whom Ludvík was madly in love and whom he never understood: her silence—the silence of a gang rape survivor—devastatingly rings through the novel. As Le Grand writes, 'none of the four narrators knows anything of the discourse of the three others', thus, the truth is only 'one fragment in a vast mosaic of relative truths and knowledge, which polyphony in fact puts together' (Le Grand 1999: 68–9).

The form and content are inseparable and were urgent especially in the time that Kundera— himself a disillusioned believer in communism—wrote, when Czechoslovaks were gaining some freedom to publicly discuss what had gone wrong with the utopian society many of his generation believed they had been building. The thaw of the 1960s, the Prague Spring, allowed writers to push at the limits of monovocal authoritarian truth (thus giving an urgency to the idea of multiple truths), but works still had to be approved by the central censor's office. Kundera's strategy was to refuse 'even to acknowledge the existence of the Central Publications Board, and with fastidious perseverance he had avoided any meetings or dealings with its staff. As a result, his manuscripts for the most part failed to get published' (Hamšík 1971: 86–7). Even when asked 'for minor changes [...] Kundera would refuse [...] he would rather take his copy back and once more forego publication' (Hamšík 1971: 87). He was 'a difficult customer', Hamšík wrote, but his absolute refusal and his 'rather eccentric consistency bore surprising fruit' (Hamšík 1971:86–87). The censors 'would often turn a blind eye [...] In this way Kundera procured for himself, albeit at a high price, slightly more dignified treatment than was normal' (Hamšík 1971: 87). The back and forth over *Žert*, a novel so openly critical about communism, lasted two years. Hamšík noted that Kundera, a notorious rewriter of his own texts, in some ways enjoyed the parry; Kundera would add revisions alongside the sentences crossed out by the censor, thus producing 'fresh [sentences], then these [were] in turn crossed out until, word by word, the author returned by devious routes to his original version' (Hamšík 1971: 91). *Žert* was published in 1967 without a single censored alteration.

When Kundera received his copy of the British translation of the novel, published by Macdonald in 1969, he discovered that over 300 sentences had been omitted and that the carefully arranged and polyphonically composed chapters had been spliced and rearranged without his permission. In an open letter to the *Times Literary Supplement*, he tried to contextualise why these major edits in the English translation were so upsetting. He wrote that he 'had to witness with rage how whole paragraphs were disappearing' in the Czech censor's office but had refused absolutely to agree to any of their changes to his novel. He was not 'willing to accept the slightest intervention in my texts, even if this should mean that they will not be published owing to my attitude' (Kundera 1969: 1259). Following the Soviet invasion of Czechoslovakia in August 1968, all of Kundera's books would be banned. In his letter to the *TLS*, he compares the British publisher to the 'Moscow censors', who had altered his novel for overt ideological reasons; he accuses his British publisher of doing so with the market in mind. The British edition of *The Joke* was 'broken up [...] in good faith that this would improve the sales' (Kundera 1969: 1259). He would later argue that the British publishers had ideological reasons for altering the book: they wanted a novel pared down to what they perceived as its anti-communist message. It became a 'political fantasy' he wrote in his preface to the first revised translation (Kundera 1982: x). A decade later, in his preface to a second revised translation, he described their desire for a 'political pamphlet' (Kundera 1991: 325). It should be noted that while all 300 missing sentences were reinstated for the 1970 British paperback edition of *The Joke*, Kundera had already omitted a sentence or two of these from his second Czech edition in 1968, and then removed some more of them in his first and second revised English editions (Woods 2006: 77–8).

What was marketable in 1969 was Czechoslovakia itself because of the world's reaction to the Soviet invasion the previous year. This novel, that in part critiqued communism, fed into a Cold War narrative that implicitly buoyed up a Western self-image as the place of freedom and free debate. Czech writing, sparsely translated, saw a short boom as a result, at least any writing seen as overtly critical of the communist regime. The problem was with any material seen as extraneous to this message, even within the novel itself. One of the translators, Oliver Stallybrass, defended his editing in two open letters also published in the *Times Literary Supplement*; yet, it is clear from his defense that he saw the omitted and altered material as irrelevant and confusing to English readers because, one can surmise, they desired a novel that not only conformed to target literary norms but also to their horizon of expectations as to the content of a Czech novel published when the Soviet invasion was still very much in the news. The substantial edits changed the experimental structure of the novel (which moves back and forward in time, and which presents the story through the eyes of different characters) and highlighted the political disillusion in the novel to make it more marketable to a general British readership.

'My enormous admiration for *The Joke*', Stallybrass wrote, 'was only slightly qualified by my agreement with the publisher that it could benefit *artistically* from some tightening up' (1969a: 1339, Stallybrass's italics). Stallybrass clarified that part of his job was to edit the novel; he had been employed 'as a professional translator and editor, to go through the faithful and literal version provided by Mr. David Hamblyn (who is blameless in all this) making it freer and more idiomatic wherever this seemed appropriate' (1969b: 1283). As Kuhiwczak noted, the translators believed that Kundera's narrative structure was peculiarly Czech, distinguished by its 'lack of strict chronology' (1990: 125), and thus inferior, a choice that reflected the 'translators' and publisher's untested assumptions about Eastern Europe' (Kuhiwczak 1990: 124), underpinned by a sense of British cultural superiority.

Market Censorship and Translation

Stallybrass cut most of Jaroslav's reflections on polyphony in music (a reflection key to revealing the structure of the polyphonic novel itself) because 'the vast majority of English readers, as opposed to Czechoslovakian readers with their different cultural traditions, would surely find the chapter on Moravian folk music (with musical examples), if not tedious, at least "abstruse"' (1969a: 1339). In fact, what the character does in this chapter is to connect and compare a local form of music (Moravian folk music) with a wider European tradition of polyphony; Jaroslav attempts to contextualise the tradition transnationally. More importantly, however, Jaroslav is reflecting not so much on Moravian folk music but on the idea and structure of polyphony: in reflecting on it, he is providing the reader with knowledge of how it works. Stallybrass defended his removal of over 300 sentences with the following analogy: 'A Moravian reader would doubtless react in much the same way to a chapter, in an English novel, devoted entirely to one of the characters' reflections on, let us say, the county cricket championship, complete with averages, and I would hardly feel he was being defrauded if the Prague publisher of such a novel quietly omitted the chapter in question' (Stallybrass 1969a: 1339).

Stallybrass assumes that the material is extraneous because it seems unrelated and irrelevant to the anti-communist message in the novel. 'The whole text has been cut up in pieces and put together in a daring "montage" so as to form a completely different book', Kundera wrote. 'The publisher (Macdonald)', who was focused solely on selling an anti-communist book that spoke to the historical zeitgeist, 'has merely considered my text as a free basis for bizarre inventions of manipulators' (Kundera 1969: 1259). The first US edition (using the Stallybrass translation), published in 1969, omitted even more material and added a subtitle that reveals the market framing of the novel: *The Joke: A Novel about Life in Czechoslovakia Today*.

Ironically, one of the main intertexts of Kundera's novel is an anchor of the English canon, *Paradise Lost* (1667), by a writer, John Milton, famous for his *Areopagitica* (1644), a pamphlet decrying censorship. Ludvík, thrown out of the communist idyll as a young man, returns for revenge; he is a deeply Miltonic figure, echoing Milton's Satan intent on wrecking Paradise but caught in his own hell. One of *Žert*'s key words, repeated through the novel, and sometimes repeated euphonically through a paragraph is 'zást' [rancor], a Czech word invented by Josef Jungmann in his 1811 Czech translation of *Paradise Lost, Ztracený ráj*.[2] Jungmann compiled the first Czech dictionary as a means to revive the Czech language; he also used translations of canonical works to invent Czech words for the modern era. In Kundera's famous 1967 speech against censorship (and for translation as a means to challenge it), he invokes Jungmann whose 'celebrated translation of Milton is a foundation-stone of Revivalist Czech [...] it was the practice of translation' he added, 'which enabled Czech to mould and perfect itself as a language on a par with other European languages' and which gave rise to original works in Czech, and 'it was in the form of translations that Czechs had been making their own, Czech-language, contribution to European literature' (Hamšík 1971: 170–1). What Kundera would find, within a year of making this brave speech, was that Czech contributions in translation would likely be edited to conform to Western political—rather than intercultural, intertextual, transnational—readings of Czech writers' works. For the main material worth they held, the reason they seemed marketable, was in their relevance to Cold War anti-communist discourse.

21.3.2 Protest

The late 1960s saw some interest in, and a handful of English-language productions of, the plays of Václav Havel, at least in New York. Havel, and his plays, were at the forefront of the Prague Spring; after the 1968 Soviet invasion he would be banned, harassed, interrogated, and imprisoned by the communist regime. One of the co-founders of Charter 77, he became known worldwide as a dissident (though he firmly rejected the label); and he led the Civic Forum movement during the 1989 Velvet Revolution, becoming the first post-communist President of Czechoslovakia. In a 2003 *New Yorker* profile of Havel, David Remnick noted that Havel's plays were 'emblems of the Prague Spring' that 'were all understood by their audiences as implicit critiques of the regime', but, as such, in the post-communist era, the plays were now redundant. 'Far more ambitious, and more lasting, were Havel's dissident essays' (Remnick 2006: 147)—even, one assumes, his most famous one, 'The Power of the Powerless', in which he explicitly rejects the title 'dissident' as one serving the reductive interests of both the regime and the West.

Havel found a champion in New York in Joe Papp, who ran the downtown Public Theatre, which produced his play *The Memorandum* in 1968. Not everyone was supportive. 'For a couple of years', one magazine wrote in a 1969 review of Havel's next play, *The Increased Difficulty of Concentration*, the 'Public Theatre harangued its audiences with post-Kafka satires of bureaucracy in the totalitarian state' (*Women's Wear Daily*, VBA 9:3, 12/5/69). Luckily, 'Joseph Papp's theatre finally rid itself of these naïve, middle European anti-conformity plays' and moved on to 'more original projects. But like cockroaches, which move into the bedroom when you spray the kitchen, these plays just turned around and marched uptown to Lincoln Centre [...] it may be wisest to head the roaches off at the pass' (*Women's Wear Daily*, VBA 9:3, 12/5/69). The production was dull and predictable as an anti-communist satire, the reviewer concluded: 'Now to spray the bedroom' (*Women's Wear Daily*, VBA 9:3, 12/5/69).

The shocking xenophobia of the review carries within it a kernel of Remnick's dismissal of Havel's plays as simply being read 'as implicit critiques of the regime': uptown interest in Havel was predicated in the newsworthiness of the Prague Spring and the Soviet invasion, and his plays were read entirely through the lens of political oppression and upheaval: 'these naïve, middle European anti-conformity plays' (*Women's Wear Daily*, VBA 9:3, 12/5/69) were reductively read since they were produced and marketed as such. 'We know!' another reviewer cried in exasperation at the prolixity of Havel's dialogue (*Newsday*, VBA 9:3, 12/5/69); the audience got the point before they even entered the auditorium that this was a political satire of 'a thinly-disguised Czechoslovakia' (VBA 9:3, 12/5/69). Once entering the theatre, visual cues often reinforced this reading. A 1983 Public Theatre production of Havel's one-act plays, *Audience*, *Private View*, and *Protest*, physically framed the action through an anti-communist lens: 'the proscenium framing the action is covered with slogans in Cyrillic' one reviewer wrote, adding: 'This constantly reminds us that everything we see is taking place within a communist regime in which all lives serve the state' (*New York Tribune*, VBA 6:2, 11/24/83); it was 'a marvelous piece of agitprop, which puts the whole thing in perspective' (*Women's Wear Daily*, VBA 6:2, 11/22/83). It should be noted, of course, that the Czech language does not use the Cyrillic alphabet.

At the heart of Havel's plays is a dialogue with language itself —a lesson certainly learned from the warped uses of propagandistic language, but one that was also universal, not least in a market-oriented culture. Language, according to his translator, Vera Blackwell, was 'really not only a character [in the plays] but its protagonist, its "Villain"' (VBA 1:1, 4/16/64). Havel's verbose, prolix style showed characters trying to master and use language as a way to gain power and mold reality; in the end, they inevitably get entrapped by it, by these semantic fireworks, and we see the ensuant linguistic delusions untethered from reality. Havel's main English-language translator exhaustively tried for years to interest producers and directors in his work—after 1969, there were no professional productions in English until 1980 (Havel's work was entirely banned in Czechoslovakia through this period; he was financially dependent on translations)—but the common complaint was this very aesthetic, the interminable language that seemed to cloud the obvious (to US and English producers and audiences) political message. The style of the plays did not suit a market ready for realistic plays or experimental absurdist plays predicated on a dearth of language, such as the work of Samuel Beckett or Harold Pinter.

It was not until Havel became politically newsworthy again that any interest was shown in his plays. Havel co-founded the Charter 77 petition, calling for free speech, and was imprisoned. Before going to jail, he wrote three one-act plays, semi-autobiographical, about a self-effacing, non-judgmental resistor interacting with characters who quietly go along with the regime for an easy life. One of these, *Protest*, was chosen to be part of the English National Theatre's 'Havel Afternoon' in 1980, an event produced to shed light on the now imprisoned Havel: Harold Pinter also read Havel's open letter to the Czechoslovak president, Gustav Husák, and there was a staged version of Havel's Charter 77 trial. *Protest*, already a short one-act play, was further shortened as a result of heavy editing. Blackwell, its translator, was horrified at what she felt was a tone-deaf attempt to strip the play down to a reductive political message of the good dissident, Vaněk, and his interlocutor, Staněk, as a laughable, pathetic collaborator. 'The complex picture of the dissidents' situation becomes a dull, straightforward statement', Blackwell complained (VBA 7:1, May 1980).

Particularly edited down was a pages-long speech by Staněk, when he debates with himself whether or not he should sign a petition and talks himself out of it; it's a tour de force representation of how we all sometimes talk ourselves out of actions that we know to be moral or ethical.[3] Blackwell wrote at length to the director, Michael Kustow, to explain why the whole speech was integral to the play and its ruminations on language and the self (rather than anti-communist politics):

It reveals, strips bare his hang-ups, his pathetic wangles, his regrets, indeed his real sufferings, his painful swayings between the man he would like to be (a man living in truth) and the man he actually is (a man accepting the ever-present lie), the man as seen by his own children and the man as he'd dearly love to be seen by them, the man as he's seen by the dissidents and the man he almost begs the dissidents to see, the shrewd man who manages to swim with the tide and the man Staněk can't help seeing in the bathroom mirror every morning as he shaves (VBA 7:1, May 1980).

In order to produce the effect of this moral vacillation, she argued that Havel 'skillfully and strategically deployed clauses and subclauses, concepts and words which not only mirror each other, but in fact shift (sometimes slightly, sometimes radically) the previously reflected picture' (VBA 7:1, May 1980). The semantic effect 'can be likened to the tragic wandering of a man through a "laughing gallery", "lined with misshapen mirrors" but: "All this has been rubbed out, flattened both by the massive cuts and by the pedestrian alterations in the remaining lines given to Staněk by Kustow [...] Staněk becomes just a mildly amusing bastard"' (VBA 7:1, May 1980).

Vaněk, the 'dissident' figure, is comically inarticulate, his speech defined by pauses and hesitations, shown in the playtext by dashes after two- or three-word sentences. His relative silence is integral, though, to both his lack of judgment regarding Staněk and to the trap language has become for Staněk who has to fill the silence in order to drown out his own complicity. As such, the playtext is full of noises of hesitation and em-dashes finishing incomplete often one-word sentences. Some of these were struck out, or exclamation points were added, subtly changing Vaněk's compassionate silences and hesitations as he refuses to condemn a man he understands. In the edited English translation, however, Staněk is to be condemned as a lackey of the regime; Vaněk begins to embody the judgement of the audience through these small rhythmic changes to the text. Havel's work, then, effectively underwent a double censorship: first, at home because of his courageous stance against the totalitarian regime; but, then once again, in a more subtle form, once it faced British and American audiences.

21.3.3 Self-censorship and the Market

'Christ, I miss the Cold War,' M., played by Judi Dench, says in the film *Casino Royale* (2006), annoyed as she is by James Bond's stupidity; back then, a feckless spy could be persuaded to defect. Dench was asked to re-dub this line for the Chinese market, perhaps indicating that this movie, filmed in post-communist Czechia, faced a market in which the wager of the Cold War might actually not have been won. 'God, I miss the old times,' she says instead to a Chinese audience (PEN 2020). According to a coruscating 2020 PEN report on China's censorship of Hollywood movies, these post-production changes are among the least intrusive forms of censorship required to enter the huge Chinese market. Although the film industry, since its inception in the twentieth century, has been an inherently commercial enterprise (more so, in the past at least, than literary fiction) with a network of agents requiring changes for various—both commercial and ideological reasons—the extent of Chinese influence (it is now the largest box-office in the world) on US films is only now becoming apparent, as is the US film industry's acquiescence for purely monetary gain.

Demands by the Chinese Central Propaganda Department begin even before scripts are written; there is a Chinese presence on some film sets advising Hollywood productions on what might or might not be acceptable; some American actors and directors are blacklisted, and films associated with them are likely never to reach a Chinese audience. 'The big story is not what's getting changed', Michael Berry says in the report, 'but what is not ever even getting greenlit' in Hollywood because of Chinese pressure (PEN 2020). 'A culture of acquiescing to Beijing's censors is now the norm and there is little sign of it changing' runs the sub-headline of Shirley Li's recent article headlined 'How Hollywood Sold out to China' (Li 2021). 'China's interest in the American film industry' Erich Schwartzel writes, connecting commerce to power, 'revealed itself to be a complement to its political ascendence, one that is rewriting the global order of the new century' (2022: xiv).

'As the Chinese box office grew', Schwartzel adds, 'then, parts of movies started to disappear' (Schwartzel 2022: 104). China overtook North America as the largest movie market in 2020 and thus 'can effectively wield its economic clout in order to compel substantial cooperation from Hollywood studios' (PEN 2020), who see the Chinese market as necessary to the economic success of their movies. Unlike other illiberal regimes which might censor foreign films *a posteriori*, because of the size of the Chinese market, the 'Chinese government can insist that Hollywood studios do their dirty work for them, producing edits and alterations that more effectively hide the fact that the movie had been censored' (PEN 2020); what Erich Schwartzel names as 'anticipatory censorship' (2022: 135). Certain subjects are off-limits, for instance 'the "Three T's" – Tiananmen, Tibet and Taiwan' (Olesen 2015: 8) or Xinjiang, and actors, directors or studios who voice comments on these subjects are likely to be blacklisted. Recent films by the Chinese-born director Chloé Zhao have not been shown in China because of critical comments made almost a decade ago in an interview (Li 2021). When he was the Disney CEO, Michael Eisner apologised to the Chinese government for the 1997 Martin Scorsese film *Kundun* (about the 14th Dalai Lama), a film he told them that 'insults our friends'; 'in the future we should prevent this sort of thing' he said, adding, 'The bad news is that the film was made; the good news is that nobody watched it' (PEN 2020).

China uses the market—investing in Hollywood movies, keeping a strict quota on foreign films, refusing to let certain films open in multiple theatres, or controlling the advertising and play a movie gets once it's released, releasing movies at deliberately inopportune times, and delaying releases, which opens the door to pirating—to further ideological ends and to control 'anything that

Market Censorship and Translation

casts doubt on the CCP's right to rule China' (PEN 2020), including an understood (in Hollywood) aversion to time-travel plots that might suggest a mechanism for any alternative, non-deterministic political reality in the country. The manifestation of censorship is deliberately ambiguous, leaving US 'filmmakers uncertain as to what content is permitted and what is prohibited' (PEN 2020). 'There's no document, no checklist', a Hollywood producer told PEN. 'You'll hear through the grapevine, or someone hears from a contact [. . .] it's so mercurial and constantly shifting', leading producers and directors 'to anticipate and preempt Beijing's objections' and self-censor projects from the start. 'This is, of course, exactly how censorship succeeds', PEN (2020) notes; filmmakers 'internalise it to the point where the censor actually has to do very little. Over time, writers and creators don't even conceive of ideas, stories, or characters that would flout the rules, because there is no point in doing so. The orthodoxies press down imperceptibly, and the parameters of the imagination are permanently circumscribed' (PEN 2020). Rather than censoring films specifically for the Chinese market—like Judi Dench's re-dubbed lines—'one Sony executive made it clear that it was better for them to alter the master version of the film in order to better hide the extent of their self-censorship' (PEN 2020). We know this executive's thoughts—not wanting 'bloggers [to] invariably compare the versions and realise we changed the China setting just to pacify that market'—because of the huge cyberattack on Sony, seen as a retaliation by North Korea for the portrayal of its leader in the Sony produced film *The Interview*. This is yet another way to instill fear and self-censorship (PEN 2020).

Further, there is pressure on US studios to do what 'Hollywood insiders commonly describe as "pandering"—deliberately orienting specific scenes, characters, sets, or themes in order to better appeal to Beijing', which, under President Xi, has emphasised the importance of 'discourse power' (PEN 2020), cementing, in narratives, the presentation of China as a 'good actor' on the geopolitical world stage. Erich Schwartzel describes this as 'a kind of reverse censorship', in which, for 'the first time since Hollywood's founding, creative decisions [...] were being made with China, not America, first in mind' (2022: 145). '[I]t is now commonly accepted that there will be no Chinese villains in any Hollywood film in the years to come', PEN (2020) notes, but the report also mentions a positive side-effect of these constraints: the increased casting of Asian and Asian-American actors in high-profile films and the positive—and non-racist—portrayal of Asian and Asian-American characters.

It should first be said that Chinese audiences find some of these attempted non-stereotyped portrayals an 'obvious' form of 'pandering'—as Chinese audiences call it, 'getting soy sauced' (Schwartzel 2022: 151)—especially when Asian and Asian-American actors are given slight roles—these mealy-mouthed inclusions have their own name: 'hua ping' or 'flower vases', i.e., actors included to decorate the set for market reasons. In recent months, there has been a backlash to Marvel's first movie starring an Asian superhero, *Shang-Chi* (Young et al. 2021), and suggestions that it won't be allowed access to the mainland Chinese market because of the racist origins of the comic book, especially of its main character, Fu Manchu. 'How can Chinese people be insulted like this' the Party-controlled *Global Times* asked, 'while at the same time we let you take our money?' (Young et al. 2021).

It should be noted that Hollywood has removed Asian characters in deference to Chinese censorship; for instance, turning the Tibetan mentor of the hero of another Marvel film, *Dr. Strange* (2016), into an amorphous 'Celtic' one, played by Tilda Swinton. The film's writer, C. Robert Cargill, was candid about the decision; if he kept her character 'Tibetan, you risk alienating one billion people who think that that's bullshit and risk the Chinese government going, 'Hey, you know one of the biggest film-watching countries in the world? We're not going to show your movie because you decided to get political' (PEN 2020). The decision was also, however, read in the US and elsewhere as 'the "whitewashing" of Asians in American films' (Addley 2016). AAPI actor Margaret Cho wrote to Swinton that 'there's a frustrated population of Asian Americans who feel the role should have gone to a person of Asian descent [...] Our stories are told by white actors over and over again and we feel at a loss to know how to cope with it' (Addley 2016). The awareness of both the Chinese box-office and a Chinese audience has fundamentally altered US moviemaking at once placing deleterious overseas ideological controls on it, but also changing the awareness of a global world of customers with their own tastes and preferences.[4]

21.3.4 Consumer Censorship

If a movie like *Shang-Chi* may have been greenlit with a Chinese and East Asian audience in mind (and it has in fact made huge box office returns outside of the Chinese mainland), is there a positive or productive end-result to the constraints imposed by market censorship? *Shang-Chi*'s AAPI screenwriter, David Callaham, noted that he and the AAPI director, Destin Daniel Cretton, drew 'up a list of Hollywood stereotypes about Asians that they hoped to dispel', including the over-sexualisation of Asian women (Ito 2021). They cast Hong Kong superstar, Tony Leung, to play the father figure (Fu Manchu in the comic books—a character 'problematic for a billion reasons'), partly as 'a signal to just about everybody that Fu Manchu wouldn't be in the movie, in any form' (Ito 2021). Callaham added that he has in the past been 'hired to write a movie-star role' that's 'usually a beautiful white man named Chris', meaning that 'I've always had to put myself in a position of imagining what it would be like to be somebody else. This was the first time in my life I've been able to sit back and not have to imagine it anymore' (Ito 2021). A Chinese film producer, Jin Yang, also noted that the film is largely in Mandarin rather than in English. 'It's amusing', she said, 'that it's Americans' turn to read subtitles in a Marvel film' (Young et al. 2021). After the animated film, *Kung Fu Panda*, was a commercial hit in China, the animators went further with movie dubbing; in its third installment, *Kung Fu Panda 3*, they 'reanimated the mouths of Po and others in 60 percent of the shots so their cartoon lip movements matched the Mandarin being spoken' (Schwartzel 2022: 165) because it was commercially worthwhile doing so. The movie was 'the highest-grossing animated movie in Chinese box-office history' (Schwartzel 2022: 165). The inclusion of 'more Chinese actors and content represents a step forward, rather than a step back', the PEN report notes but warns that this shouldn't hide the repressive pressures that come with it (PEN 2020). For instance, the report details the Chinese government's repression of other identities, including LGBTQ characters or representations of queer identity. Schwartzel, too, underlines the explicit censorship of LGBTQ identity (and not only in China, but in Africa also, where the Chinese now have a powerful satellite industry): 'Gay people stay in the closet or off-screen' (Schwartzel 2022: 105).

However, is there a kernel here, or suggestion, of the power of readerships and audiences *as consumers* to challenge the status quo of identity representation in translated works? A case in point might be the controversy surrounding the Dutch translation of Amanda Gorman's poem, 'The Hill We Climb', a poem Gorman, a Black spoken-word poet, recited at the inauguration of US President Joe Biden in January 2021. Dutch publisher Meulenhoff hired a nonbinary poet, Marieke Lucas Rijneveld, to translate the poem immediately after Gorman's celebrated and widely-broadcast performance. The choice of a white poet—who had never translated before—led to a public uproar. 'Isn't it—to say the least—a missed opportunity', Janice Deul wrote in protest, pointing out that Meulenhoff could have chosen a 'spoken-word artist, young, female and unapologetically Black' to translate Gorman's poem (Flood 2021). Translators, newspapers, and Twitter furiously argued whether a work should innately be translated by a translator of the same identity as the author. The social media firestorm led to Rijneveld's resignation; 'For translators', Allison Braden wrote in *Asymptote*, the world literature translation website, 'the episode speaks to a foundational question: Who gets to translate whom?' (Braden 2021).

For some writers of colour—for instance Jhumpa Lahiri and John McWhorter—the incident smacked of cancel culture, our contemporary form of ultra-speedy market censorship, through the ostracisation, boycotting or shunning of Rijneveld and Meulenhoff for having acted inappropriately. But translators, translation scholars and professional organisations pointed out what fault lines were exposed by reader-initiated questioning of so-called colour-blind hiring. 'The question raised by Deul', Haidee Kotze wrote, 'is not principally about who "may" (who has permission) or even "can" (is able to) write or translate particular experiences. The question is who is, institutionally, given the space to articulate this experience, to participate, to be visible' (Braden 2021). The American Literary Translators' Association similarly argued that the 'question of whether identity should be the deciding factor in who is allowed to translate whom is a false framing' of the issues; that the choice of who is chosen to translate is 'based on a complex network of factors' but that the real issue at hand 'is the scarcity of Black translators and other translators of colour', a situation revealed by the controversy (ALTA 2021). 'This is not about who can translate', Deul told the *New York Times* that 'it's about who gets opportunities to translate' (Marshall 2021). Social media amplified—though, perhaps, simplified—the debate, but the reaction of readers, translators, and the media produced 'a translation controversy [...] taking the world by storm', Black translator Aaron Robertson said, adding, 'This feels like something of a watershed moment' (Marshall 2021).

The *New York Times'* journalist, Alex Marshall, frames the controversy as giving an illuminating visibility as it 'shone a light on the often unexamined world of literary translation and its lack of racial diversity', which is suggestive indeed of the structural racism of the publishing and translation world and the paucity of translators of colour, a state of affairs being challenged by readers now made aware of the translator-figure through social media. Indeed, some publishers interviewed by Marshall, were using market forces to promote the translations by employing Black translators who are celebrities in their own right: a Swedish rapper, Timbuktu, translated it into Swedish and a Belgian-Congolese-Rwandan singer and rapper Marie-Pierra Kakoma (performing as Lous and the Yakuza) into French. 'The world is watching', Braden ends her article in *Asymptote*, 'and the translator is no longer invisible' (Braden 2021).

21.4   New Debates

Curry Jansen, the leading theorist of market censorship, noted that the 'increased frequency of use of the term "market censorship" and its synonyms is correlated with the end of the Cold War and the rise of neoliberalism' (Jansen 2010: 24). For Jansen, the perceived victory of the neoliberalist market over communism and the resultant globalisation of the market led to an increased awareness and critique of its overreach and its institutional and socio-political power. Theorising market censorship was thus 'a critical response to changing historical conditions'— a historical moment, in the defeat of Soviet-styled communism, of exultant 'market fundamentalism' (Jansen 2010: 24). Jansen's hope was for a sort of historical correction, 'that the conditions of cultural production change in ways that make the concept and practices of market censorship less central to discussions of cultural production. It may be that the excesses of the immediate Cold War era will prove transitory' and, thus, that 'the concept of market censorship has a short life' (Jansen 2010: 27). She optimistically notes that the internet may be mobilised to challenge market censorship, creating "some significant space for organised resistance" Jansen 2010: 27).

The Routledge Handbook of Translation and Censorship

Certainly, 'the permeability created by improved communication technologies nowadays tends to drive [translation censorship] out into the open' (Ní Chuilleanáin et al. 2009: 13–4). For instance, Hillary Clinton's memoir, *Living History*, was published in China in 2004 with various elisions made by the translator and/or editors of material about Tiananmen, but her publisher, Simon & Schuster published the censored material from *Living History* online in Chinese (Tan 2015: 327; Olesen 2015: 19). The internet has also opened up the market for translations and translators, with an increasing number of translation or translation-friendly literary sites (*Words Without Borders*, *Asymptote*, *LitHub*, etc.), and platforms that have given translators a more visible voice (podcasts and social media, for instance). New printing technologies (POD, or print on demand), alongside such sites and platforms, have opened up a niche market for new independent publishers who focus on translated works (in stark contradistinction to the increased mergers of big-name publishers and market monopoly).

The internet promised a free marketplace of ideas, but, as Jansen argues, even that very concept —the free marketplace of ideas—grew out of Cold War ideological positioning; the phrase itself 'gaining traction only in the 1950s and apparently reaching peak usage in the 1980s' as it provided a distinction between the free West and the lack of discursive choices behind the Iron Curtain (Jansen 2010: 17). The new version of this neoliberal phraseology, the libertarian language of Big Tech, has found accommodation with both neoliberal and illiberal regimes, leading to worries about the realities of socio-political manipulation and 'techno-authoritarianism' (Kynge and Yu 2021). Much of this is hidden or elided by the language of market choice and might be argued to be a form of '*meta-censorship*, whereby all information about the existence of censorship is censored and removed texts and phrases are not marked as having been censored' (Špirk 2014: 150, his italics), a notion Špirk identifies with authoritarian regimes (Salazar's Portugal and post-war communist Czechoslovakia), but which equally might be applied to market economies (as we see above, with Hollywood).

Covert forms of market censorship, especially of potentially destabilising socio-political critiques of the systemic class, race and gender power asymmetries of the market, include a quiet absorption and marketisation of these critiques. As Jansen notes: 'the "theatre" of consumer capitalism is a remarkably resilient system capable of absorbing, domesticating and even sometimes profiting from critical challenges so that, for example, the advertising and branding industries have demonstrated that they are able to absorb and even apply ideas borrowed from Marx, Barthes, Foucault and other critical social theorists' (Jansen 2010: 18). Estée Lauder, for instance, called Amanda Gorman's agent 'as soon as the poet walked offstage' at the presidential inauguration and had talked to the poet 'within an hour of her appearance' (Friedman 2021). Gorman became a spokesperson for Estée Lauder; within a month of the inauguration, 'she had turned down about $17 million in various promotional opportunities' from other brands (Friedman 2021). Clearly, Gorman was astutely, 'weaponising a big brand with a big platform to her own ends' as an effective way to promote racial and social equity; at the same time Estée Lauder materially and metaphorically profits from the association (Friedman 2021).

Václav Havel sharply elucidated the power of corporations to absorb criticism; he described giving a speech to 'the representatives of the largest multinational corporations, the actual rulers of our current global world', which was 'highly critical of the behavior of global corporations [...] of the omnipresent dictatorship of advertisements, of profit, and so on' (Havel 2007: 36–7). Expecting these corporate titans to boo him or walk out in protest, he was surprised to receive a standing ovation. He dwelt on why; what had motivated them to respond to his sharp critique? He proposed three possible answers: one, they liked him as an 'icon' and the inspirational nature of his 'story' (Havel 2007: 36–7); two, they were 'applauding themselves' and their 'limitless power' alongside their own 'broad-mindedness in hiring such a sharp critic' and, in doing so, 'in the most elegant way imaginable, [they could] undermine his ideas'; or third, they may in fact completely agree with him, but they 'dare not say anything' because 'in doing so they might risk their own livelihoods' (Havel 2007: 36–7). Havel's wry assessment is damning of the capitalist appropriation of free-speech criticism as a performative, brand-led story, one consolidated by the titans' own silence and self-censorship. If they had read his plays as far back as the 1960s, not as two-dimensional critiques of the great market-antagonistic communist regime, but as how we become enslaved to power and its language, however powerful we imagine ourselves to be, one wonders if indeed the world might begin to be changed.

Further Reading

Billiani, Francesca (ed.). 2007. *Modes of Censorship: National Contexts and Diverse Media*. Manchester: St. Jerome.
Billiani provides a seminal introduction to this collection that outlines a Foucauldian and Bourdieusian, approach in translation studies to the discourse and modality of censorship and translation that has become highly influential. The book includes essays on Mussolini's Italy, Franco's Spain, communist East Germany, the Greek military dictatorship (1967–1974), as well as censorship in Restoration and Victorian England. The range of ideologies across places and time in these case studies suggest similar ways of imposing and escaping censorship, and the role of different agents in the process.

Jansen, Sue Curry. 2010. 'Ambiguities and Imperatives of Market Censorship: The Brief History of a Critical Concept', *Westminster Papers in Communication and Culture*, 7(2): 12–30.
Jansen's article is an invaluable history of the critical use of the term 'market censorship' and why there has been resistance to its use. She locates the growth of its use alongside the growth of neoliberal discourse, especially following the end of the Cold War, as a critical response to privatisation and the saturating language of the markets.

Jansen, Sue Curry. 1991. *Censorship: The Knot that Binds Knowledge and Power*. Oxford: OUP.
Jansen's book presents a Foucauldian genealogy of censorship, focusing on how censorship has been entwined in language and its use through state and market controls. She challenges the notion that censorship exists only in totalitarian societies, arguing that it is also an embedded feature of liberal, market-based societies. The book introduces Jansen's theory of market censorship.

Merkle, Denise. 2002. 'Presentation', *TTR: Traduction, Terminologie, Rédaction*, 15(2): 9–18.
Merkle's groundbreaking introduction to a special issue of *TTR* on censorship, 'Censure et traduction dans le monde occidental', importantly established the question of covert censorship in translation. Whereas focus had been on overtly censorious regimes—fascist, communist, etc.—Merkle suggests that non-autocratic regimes also implement forms of covert, less immediately identifiable, censorship, through market conditions or a rejection of texts that do not conform to predominant socio-political ideologies in the target culture. Merkle edited a second special issue of *TTR* in 2010 on 'Censure et traduction en deçà et au-delà du monde occidental'.

Woods, Michelle. 2012. *Censoring Translation: Censorship, Theatre and the Politics of Translation*. New York: Continuum.
A case study of the censorship of the Czech playwright, Václav Havel's plays, this book argues for a reconsideration of how we read censorship both under conditions of totalitarianism and of the market. Using archival material from Havel's translator, Vera Blackwell, the book focuses on the substantial editing and framing of Havel's plays in the West as an example of Cold War and post-Cold War market censorship.

Notes

1   For a fuller discussion of this section see: Woods (2006: 45–48).
2   In the initial French and English translations of *Žert*, the word 'zášt" was inevitably translated variously. For a full discussion, see Woods (2024).

3 For a detailed discussion of this speech, please see Woods (2012: 101–13).
4 Two things should be noted: first, that Hollywood has a system of censorship through its film ratings system, part of a history of film censorship in the US; and, second, that it has pandered to overseas governments before, most notably and devastatingly, as Schwartzel (2022) writes, to the Nazi regime (see 116–21).

References

Addley, Esther. 2016. 'Tilda Swinton Releases Margaret Cho Emails About Film Role Diversity', *The Guardian*, 21 December. Accessed at: www.theguardian.com/world/2016/dec/21/tilda-swinton-releases-margaret-cho-emails-about-film-role-diversity Last accessed: 26 September 2021.

ALTA. 2021. 'ALTA Statement on Racial Equity in Literary Translation', 22 March. Accessed at: https://literarytranslators.wordpress.com/2021/03/22/alta-statement-on-racial-equity-in-literary-translation/ Last accessed: 26 September 2021.

Billiani, Francesca (ed.). 2007. *Modes of Censorship: National Contexts and Diverse Media*. Manchester: St. Jerome.

Braden, Allison. 2021. 'Translators Weigh In on the Amanda Gorman Controversy', *Asymptote*, 17 March. Accessed at: www.asymptotejournal.com/blog/2021/03/17/translators-weigh-in-on-the-amanda-gorman-controversy/ Last accessed: 26 September 2021.

Burt, Richard (ed.). 1994. *Administration of Aesthetics: Censorship, Political Criticism, and the Public Sphere*. Minneapolis and London: University of Minnesota Press.

Chvatík, Květoslav. 1994. *Svět románů Milana Kundery*. Brno: Atlantis.

Flood, Alison. 2021. '"Shocked by the Uproar": Amanda Gorman's White Translator Quits', *The Guardian*, 1 March. Accessed at: www.theguardian.com/books/2021/mar/01/amanda-gorman-white-translator-quits-marieke-lucas-rijneveld Last accessed: 26 September 2021.

Friedman, Vanessa. 2021. 'The Poetic Justice of Amanda Gorman's Estee Lauder Contract', *New York Times*, 2 September. Accessed at: www.nytimes.com/2021/09/02/style/amanda-gorman-estee-lauder.html?searchResultPosition=1 Last accessed: 26 September 2021.

Hamšík, Dušan. 1971. *Writers against Rulers*. Translated by D. Orpington. London: Hutchinson.

Havel, Václav. 2007. *To the Castle and Back*. Translated by Paul Wilson. New York: Knopf.

Huggan, Graham. 2001. *The Postcolonial Exotic. Marketing the Margins*. London and New York: Routledge.

Ito, Robert. 2021. 'How Shang-Chi, Master of Kung Fu, Knocked Down Stereotypes', *New York Times*, 3 September. Accessed at: www.nytimes.com/2021/09/03/movies/shang-chi-marvel.html?action=click&module=Well&pgtype=Homepage&section=Movies Last accessed: 26 September 2021.

Jansen, Sue Curry. 1991. *Censorship: The Knot that Binds Knowledge and Power*. Oxford: OUP.

Jansen, Sue Curry. 2010. 'Ambiguities and Imperatives of Market Censorship: The Brief History of a Critical Concept', *Westminster Papers in Communication and Culture*, 7(2): 12–30.

Keane, John. 1991. *The Media and Democracy*. Cambridge: Polity Press.

Kuhiwczak, Piotr. 1990. 'Translation as Appropriation: The Case of Milan Kundera's *The Joke*', in S. Bassnett and A. Lefevere (eds.), *Translation, History, Culture*. London: Cassell, 118–30.

Kundera, Milan. 1969. 'The Joke', *Times Literary Supplement*, 30 October: 1259.

Kundera, Milan. 1982. *The Joke*. Translated by Michael Henry Heim. Harmondsworth: Penguin.

Kundera, Milan. 1991. *Žert*. Brno: Atlantis.

Kynge, James and Yu, Sun. 2021. 'China and Big Tech: Xi's Blueprint for a Digital Dictatorship', *Financial Times*, 6 September. Accessed at: www.ft.com/content/9ef38be2-9b4d-49a4-a812-97ad6d70ea6f Last accessed: 26 September 2021.

Lamarche, Gara. 1991. 'Some Thoughts on the "Chilling Effect"', *Art Journal*, 50(4): 56–58.

Le Grand, Eva. 1999. *Kundera or the Memory of Desire*. Waterloo: Wilfred Laurier Press.

Lefevere, André. 1992. *Translation, Rewriting and the Manipulation of Literary Fame*. London and New York: Routledge.

Li, Shirley. 2021. 'How Hollywood Sold Out to China', *The Atlantic*, 10 September. Accessed at: www.theatlantic.com/culture/archive/2021/09/how-hollywood-sold-out-to-china/620021/ Last accessed: 26 September 2021.

Marshall, Alex. 2021. 'Amanda Gorman's Poetry United Critics. It's Dividing Translators', *New York Times*, 26 March. Accessed at: www.nytimes.com/2021/03/26/books/amanda-gorman-hill-we-climb-translation.html Last accessed: 26 September 2021.

Merkle, Denise. 2002. 'Presentation', *TTR: Traduction, Terminologie, Rédaction*, 15(2): 9–18.

Ní Chuilleanáin, Eiléan, O Chuilleanáin, Cormac and Parris, David (eds.). 2009. *Translation and Censorship: Patterns of Communication and Interference*. Dublin: Four Courts Press.

Olesen, Alexa. 2015. *Censorship and Conscience. Foreign Authors and the Challenge of Chinese Censorship*. New York: PEN American Center.

PEN America. 2020. 'Made in Hollywood: Censored by Beijing'. Accessed at: https://pen.org/report/made-in-hollywood-censored-by-beijing/ Last accessed 26 September 2021.

Remnick, David. 2006. *Reporting: Writing from The New Yorker*. New York: Vintage.

Schwartzel, Erich. 2022. *Red Carpet. Hollywood, China, and the Global Battle for Cultural Supremacy*. New York: Penguin.

Špirk, Jaroslav. 2014. *Censorship, Indirect Translation and Non-translation: The (Fateful) Adventures of Czech Literature in 20th Century Portugal*. Newcastle: Cambridge Scholars Publishing.

Stallybrass, Oliver. 1969a. 'The Joke', *Times Literary Supplement*, 20 November, 1339.

Stallybrass, Oliver. 1969b. 'The Joke', *Times Literary Supplement*, 6 November, 1282–3.

Tan, Zaixi. 2015. 'Censorship in translation: The case of the People's Republic of China', *Neohelicon*, 42: 313–39.

Venuti, Lawrence. 1998. *The Scandals of Translation. Towards an Ethics of Difference*. London and New York: Routledge.

Vera Blackwell Archive (VBA). n.d. *Bakhmeteff Collection*. Rare Books Archive, Columbia University.

Woods, Michelle. 2006. *Translating Milan Kundera*. Clevedon: Multilingual Matters.

Woods, Michelle. 2012. *Censoring Translation: Censorship, Theatre and the Politics of Translation*. New York: Continuum.

Woods, Michelle. 2024 (Forthcoming). 'Kundera's Sophisticated, Euphonic, and Rhythmic Style in Translation, Language and Reading', in K. von Kunes (ed.), *Milan Kundera Known and Unknown: Multidimensional Analysis of Selected Works*. New York: Bloomsbury.

Young, Jin Yu, Chang Chien, Amy, and Paybarah, Azi. 2021. '"Shang-Chi" Wins a Warm Asia Greeting. Then There's China', *New York Times*, 17 September. Accessed at: www.nytimes.com/2021/09/17/business/shang-chi-china-marvel.html Last accessed 26 September 2021.

22

TRANSLATION AND CENSORSHIP IN WARTIME

The Case of Canada and the United States of America

Denise Merkle and Brian James Baer

22.1 Core Issues and Topics

In liberal democracies, censorship legislation is promulgated for reasons of national defense during wartime and associated with heightened political tensions (Beauregard 1998: 27; McDonough Dolmaya 2014). Such was the case in Canada and the United States of America, along with their Allies, during World War I, World War II and, in Canada, during the October Crisis of 1970.

While the censorship of the press is linked as much to wartime morale as to intelligence, postal censorship of, for example, commercial correspondence, is usually linked to espionage as well as intelligence gathering. Both civilian and military mail, including the mail of service people, could be subjected to censorship in support of economic warfare, security and intelligence, and such censorship work was often carried out by various organisations. The correspondence of prisoners-of-war and internees, who under the Prisoners of War Convention of 1929 had the right to send mail to their loved ones, was also subject to postal censorship, frequently both military and civil, which is permitted under Articles 70 and 71 of the Third Geneva Convention (1929–1949). In Canada, during WWI, 'At its high point 120 postal employees helped the Censor's Office keep an eye out for "unpatriotic" materials. The posties, as they were then called, were empowered to open suspicious letters—generally those not in English or French—and report their contents' (CFPI 2020). Bilingual or multilingual readers of foreign languages were recruited to translate in Canada, often in close collaboration with Great Britain because of the two nations' colonial ties, and in the United States of America (USA).

22.2 Historical Perspectives

22.2.1 Canada

22.2.1.1 World War I

The United Kingdom's declaration of war on Germany on 4 August 1914 automatically brought the Dominion of Canada into the war, given that Canada's foreign policy was decided by the British parliament and Canadians were British subjects (until 1947). However, the same day,

336

DOI: 10.4324/9781003149453-27

Translation and Censorship in Wartime

the Governor General declared war between Canada and Germany. The War Measures Act was passed into law on 22 August 1914, which authorised the censorship, control and suppression of publications, writings and communications, among other documents (Beauregard 1998: 24). When it came to censorship work during the world wars, the British and Canadians, and later the Americans, collaborated closely, along with other Allies.

The War Measures Act of 1914 authorised Prime Minister Robert Borden's government to create a censorship apparatus: 'The government was out to stop any news or talk that would damage the Allied cause, or make [citizens] doubt the war effort' (CWM n.d.). Between 4 August 1914 and 10 June 1915, Lieutenant-Colonel Ernest J. Chambers was the 'cable censor for military authorities' (Keshen 1992: 316).

A June 1915 Order in Council (OIC) established a Chief Press Censor's Office to deal with journalism that was critical of military policy, in addition to supervising 'surveillance of inland telegraphic and telephonic communication' (Keshen 1992: 316). According to Basen (2014, who cites Bourrie), any stories 'assisting or encouraging the enemy, or preventing, embarrassing, or hindering the successful prosecution of the war' were banned. Chambers, a former MI5 operative and former editor of the *Calgary Herald,* was named Chief Press Censor (1915–1919). MI5 developed from the British Secret Service Bureau, founded in 1909. Prior to the outbreak of WWI, the Bureau was split into foreign and home sections, the latter known as the Directorate of Military Intelligence, Section 5 (MI5), the domestic intelligence agency responsible for rooting out foreign spies.

The small Canadian press censorship system initially comprised the Chief Censor, two press censors (one English and one French), an office manager, a German translator who was also an assistant censor, a messenger and freelance translators who worked with 31 languages (Bourrie 2009: 33–4). Until April 1919, in addition to books and films, Chambers 'banned 253 tracts; of these 222 came from the United States [where it had been legal to criticise the war until late 1917 (Bourrie 2018)], 164 appeared in a language other than French or English, and 93 espoused leftist philosophy. [...] An OIC issued in September 1918 allowed him to close down all publications in an "enemy language"' (Keshen 2005). The Chief Censor

> stretched the reach of his small department to the utmost through his method of acquiring translators to examine the multitude of foreign-language newspapers that circulated in Canada. Some he obtained from other government departments, such as Miss E. Mercer, who read German [...], or Mr P. Van Veen, who was fluent in Scandinavian languages [...]. Chambers also recruited individuals he believed were competent [...], such as Professor E. Tartak, who taught Slavonic studies at McGill University, and he paid them for each paper they translated. Others [...] offered their services for some extra money. For instance, M. Sung of Vancouver made $36 for scanning nine days' [sic] worth of Chinese tracts.
>
> (Keshen 1992: 322)

Fearing that an American bank advertising in Regina's *Der Courier* was sending money to Germany—Canada felt threatened by the 'neutral United States containing about fifteen million people of German origin' (Keshen 1992: 322)—'Chambers instructed a translator to gather objectionable articles, explaining that "naturally we are anxious to prevent German papers ... [from] going too far"' (Chambers, in Keshen 1992: 330). The paper's editor, C. Eyeman, 'was required to send the censor a copy of each edition' (Keshen 1992: 330). 'In the last months of the war', notes

Mark Bourrie, 'the censors began poking through record stores and demanded catalogues from the major US record companies. Thirty-four records were banned, all of them foreign language songs' (in CFPI 2020).

In Canada, the war measures act was extended to January 1920 in response to fears of socialism. During the war and until 1920, enemy aliens included immigrants from the German, Austro-Hungarian (among them, Ukrainians) and Ottoman empires and Bulgaria. Their possessions were confiscated, and they were moved to internment camps, where their correspondence was closely monitored. After the war ended and with an expanded mandate, Chambers continued to censor material that had nothing to do with the war. Prime Minister Borden also used censorship to identify German and Slavic subversives and non-conformists. During post-war peace time Borden's censorship was expanded to include Communists and Socialists. During the Winnipeg General Strike in May-June 1919, Chambers banned the multilingual Yiddish, German and Hebrew East European journal *Volksstimme*, which supported the strikers.

22.2.1.2   World War II

As WWII was drawing near, a censorship law (Bill 8) was adopted in 1937 by the government of Maurice Duplessis to protect Québec against communist propaganda. The commonly called Padlock Law made it illegal to print, to publish in any form or to distribute in Québec a newspaper, a magazine, a pamphlet, a flyer, a document or any writing which promoted or intended to promote Communism or Bolshevism (Biblioassnat 2021). The distinction was not made between foreign texts translated into French or English and texts produced in Québec.

In March 1937, the sub-committee of the federal Interdepartmental Committee of Censorship submitted the first version of what was to become the Defence of Canada Regulations of 1939 (Beauregard 1998: 27–30). The adoption of the 1914 War Measures Act on 3 September 1939 divided censorship into three sections: the press and military intelligence, both of which fell under national security; personal communications, and intelligence to ensure that no information of potential use to the enemy left the country. The organisation of censorship was decentralised: the Secretary of State was responsible for press censorship, National Defence for telegraph communications surveillance and censorship (Regulation 13), Department of Transport for radio censorship (Regulation 11) and Postal Service for mail censorship (Regulation 14) (Beauregard 1998: 33). In 1939, Colonel Maurice Pope was the Director of Military Operations and Intelligence in Canada. When he became the Director of Censorship in March 1940, he provided publishers with directives that explained the military need for censorship, which publishers generally accepted (d'Eon 2016: 53, 57). A civilian Directorate of Censorship within the Department of National War Services, formed in July 1940, was responsible for the security of information in newspapers, radio and film, as well as in postal and telegraphic communications. The Wartime Information Board's chief for much of the war was John Grierson, who also headed the National Film Board (NFB). The mandate of the Board and other propaganda organisations was to ensure high morale and patriotic fervour (CWM). Censorship authorities seemed satisfied with these propaganda, surveillance and post-censorship efforts. Consequently, 'during the course of the war [...] the Secretary of State [never did] avail himself of his power under Regulation 15 to order the submission of matter for censorship prior to publication' (Purcell 1947: 251).

The Director of Military Intelligence, Colonel Murray, destroyed thousands of cables, telegrams, radiograms, transcriptions and summaries of telephone conversations, as well as surveillance lists and censorship reports in September 1945 (Beauregard 1998: 159–60). Nevertheless, the availability of the final report on censorship activities as well as Ministry of Foreign Affairs archives

Translation and Censorship in Wartime

enabled Beauregard (1998: 146) to piece together the censorship of personal communication (mail, telephone, telegram). Postal censorship hired 16 censors on 6 September 1939; 721 censors were employed on 31 March 1945.

Censorship of the press in Canada was technically voluntary:

> The censors' club over errant publication was the possibility of fines, imprisonment, suspension of publication. The censors themselves had absolutely no power to impose a penalty. Censorship was an emanation of the Defence of Canada Regulations but no censor was a judge of guilt. That prerogative remained with the courts of law. Canada's powerful and effective censorship therefore was technically voluntary. Newspapers were told what might harm the effort of Canada at war—then they printed what they liked and took their chances with the law.
>
> (Purcell 1947: 250)

In total, '[a] dozen publications were banned during WWII and at least three corporate dailies— *Vancouver Sun, Le Droit* and *Le Soleil*—were fined for breaching censorship regulations. Many books were also banned [...].' (CFPI 2020) On 26 March 1940, the French Montréal daily *Le Devoir* published the article 'Interdiction de l'usage de la poste: Liste noire' [Prohibited from Using the Postal Service: Blacklist] that updated blacklisted publications, businesses and individuals primarily from the USA. Banned foreign-language titles from the USA included *Partiynoye Stroyitel'stvo* [Party Construction], a Russian bimonthly magazine published by the Central Committee of the Communist Party in Moscow, *Volksblatt und Freiheits-Freund* [The Peoples Newspaper and Friend of Freedom], a German daily published by Volksblatt Publishing in Pittsburgh and *Die Abendschule* [Nightschool], a German bimonthly published in St. Louis (CWM).

During WWII the federal translation bureau, created in 1934, was called upon to do technical translation and terminology work from English into French; however, no mention is made of the war censorship effort (Delisle and Otis 2016: 221–4). On the contrary, the Canadian Broadcasting Corporation played an active role in controlling discourse. To counter the sway exercised by pro-Vichy propaganda published in Québec nationalist newspapers, the Undersecretary of External Affairs Norman Robertson relied on the 'word-for-word [French] translations of the English C.B.C. newscasts' that were broadcast by French-Canadian stations (Bourrie 2009: 265) to present the Allied point of view. According to Beauregard (1998: 127), the officers responsible for press censorship had been journalists before entering the army.

In terms of recruiting translators during wartime, it was generally assumed that any bilingual could do the work. Werner von Janowski, for example, was a German spy who, after landing in New Carlisle, Québec, in a Nazi U-boat, was captured in November 1942. He clearly spoke English since he had lived in Canada in the 1930s, where he had worked as a freelance news journalist before fleeing the country (and his wife) (Bourrie 2009: 182–90). One rumour claimed that after the war 'Janowski was back in Europe working as an investigator and translator for Allied war crimes investigators' (Bourrie 2009: 190). However, according to Bourrie (2009: 190), he was '[i]n fact, [...] in a British jail and was released from detention in 1947'.

Censorship was reorganised in 1942 because decentralisation had proven to be inefficient and the USA had just entered the war. Prior to 1942, Canada censored mail not only in Canada but also in Liverpool (England), Hong Kong and Singapore (Beauregard 1998: 152). In May 1942, '[t]he censorship function was shifted to the National War Office, Colonel O[liver] M[owat] Biggar [replaced Maurice Pope as] the director of censorship, and a committee was formed to coordinate and set priorities for censorship activities' (Jensen 2008, in Summary 2024). All branches of censorship would be centralised and co-ordinated under the new director, who would continue to act as joint chairman of the Canada-United States Joint Permanent Defence Board. The new censorship directorate would co-operate with United States censorship authorities. Henceforth the directors of the several existing branches of censorship—press (W. Eggleston and F. Charpentier), postal (F.E. Jolliffe), radio (R. Landry), and the cable and telegraph censor—would act as assistants to Biggar (The Ottawa Journal 1942: 14).

Following this reorganisation, Britain, the USA and Canada would submit their censorship to similar regulations, including the censorship of personal correspondence, and to a common objective (Beauregard 1998: 146–47), and censorship would be coordinated in Washington. The objective of censorship was to intercept all communications to and from foreign nations, especially those able to communicate easily with enemy nations, out of fear that some of the communications could hurt the Allied war effort (Beauregard 1998: 165): 'Off-limits were any discussions of the size and number of armaments, equipment, munitions or troops, any talk of specific military operations or efforts at fortification, any information about the location or numbers of prisoners of war, and any information "which would or might be directly or indirectly useful to the enemy"' (Summary 2024).

Canadian intelligence censors worked with 47 languages in Vancouver, Halifax, Saint John's, Moncton, Québec, Montréal and Toronto, in addition to mail examination centres in 21 Canadian cities. In the Atlantic provinces and on the West Coast, domestic mail was censored as was mail sent outside Canada and foreign mail entering Canada. The mail was sorted based on a list of addresses of individuals and companies whose correspondence the censors wished to read. The mail of Japanese Canadians and prisoners of war, among other groups, was censored without exception (Beauregard 1998: 160). Between 1939 and 1945 postal censorship examined more than 45 million letters and packages; more than 134 million telecommunications were censored and almost 1.5 million copied for intelligence purposes (Beauregard 1998: 161): 'At its high point the Department of National Defence's Directorate of Censorship oversaw nearly 1000 employees who mostly opened mail' (CFPI 2020). Soldiers' letters from abroad, dispatches from war correspondents at the front and all mail from Canadian families to prisoners of war overseas were censored by the Canadian Army for sensitive military information (CWM n.d.).

Canada declared war on Japan shortly after 8 December 1941. In response to fears that anyone of Japanese descent might subvert Canadian war interests, in particular British Columbia coastal fishers, the government seized Japanese Canadian fishing vessels and sold them to mostly white fishers before interning 22,000 Japanese Canadians in 1942, many of whom were born in Canada and had no ties with Japan (McRae 2017).

The Japanese civil rights newspaper *The New Canadian*, edited by Thomas Kunito Shoyama, was targeted for censorship in March 1942 by Colonel Maurice Pope, the Chairman of the Canadian Joint Staff Mission in Washington, head of the Censorship Branch and military staff officer to Prime Minister Mackenzie King. Pope mandated Les Gordon, the local censor, to vet the English material and have the Japanese articles translated, in order to prevent 'the position of the Japanese in Vancouver [from] being misunderstood by any white readers of the paper' (censor John Graham, in Bourrie 2009: 334). Dr. E.C. Hennigar, a member of the Post Office Censorship staff, translated from Japanese into English. However, his translations were not necessarily literal. For example, when Shoyama wrote in Japanese that B.C. fruit growers 'exploited people', Hennigar's English version read that they 'tyrannised people' (Bourrie 2009: 347). Shoyama would later be named an Officer of the Order of Canada (1978), recognised for Outstanding Achievement in the Public Service of Canada (1978) and awarded the Vanier Medal in Public Administration (1982), as well as several honorary degrees, in addition to the Order of the Sacred Treasure (gold and silver star) by the Japanese government in recognition of his contributions to the Japanese-Canadian community (Anonymous 2006).

The Allies recruited second generation Japanese, *Nisei*, as 'translators of Japanese military radio traffic […]. The Canadian military refused to follow the lead of the other Allies and accept internees for service in the Pacific War' (Bourrie 2009: 354). Until late January 1945, censor Graham prohibited *The New Canadian*, and other mainstream publications in Canada, from reporting 'on the recruitment by American and British forces of Japanese-speaking translators from among the internees. […] Military intelligence had upheld the ban on reporting the recruitment of Nisei the previous September, when Graham had queried them in three requests to lift it' (Bourrie 2009: 354). Shoyama enlisted about six weeks before the Pacific War ended, when, in 1945, the *Nisei* were finally allowed to enlist. He served in the S-20 Canadian Army Japanese Language School, part of the Intelligence Corps of the Canadian Army, continuing his work as a translator and rising to the rank of Sergeant before he was discharged in 1946 (Anonymous 2006).

22.2.1.3   The Front de la libération du Québec (FLQ) [Québec Liberation Front] and the October Crisis of 1970

FLQ activist Pierre Vallières wrote a number of works during his four-month incarceration in New York's Manhattan House of Detention for Men in 1967, the most famous of which was *Nègres blancs d'Amérique* (1968), translated into English by US translator Joan Pinkham for Monthly Review Press as *White Niggers of America: Autobiography of a Quebec "Terrorist"* (1971). The book compared the historical situation of French-Canadians to that of Afro-Americans during the civil rights movement. Vallières had escaped arrest in connection with a Montréal robbery on 17 August 1966 by fleeing with Charles Gagnon to the United States, where they conducted a hunger strike at the United Nations headquarters in New York City to protest the plight of the Québecois in Canada. The original French version of his memoir was 'used as evidence to support the federal government's charges of sedition against Vallières and was briefly banned around the time of the October Crisis' (McDonough Dolmaya 2014: 120). The work was published in French by the leftist Parisian publishing house Maspero in 1969, and quickly translated into German (1969), English (1971) and Spanish (1972). During the October Crisis when the Public Order Temporary Measures Act, which replaced the War Measures Act, was in force until 30 April 1971, 'French copies of the book were banned and being seized in bookstores and libraries in Québec, and yet the English translation was being made available to Canadians who spoke little or no French' (McDonough Dolmaya 2014: 121). McDonough Dolmaya (2014: 127 note 7) explains that copies of the original continued to circulate in Québec despite the ban: 'One example can be found in Reynolds ("Les bibliothèques de McGill"), who includes an account by a McGill librarian who denied being able to locate the library's copy of *Nègres blancs* when the police came to seize it'. This is an interesting case of a translation subverting the censorship of a source text, notably the English translation produced in the USA by Monthly Review Press with Vallière's blessing. The Canadian edition of the translation published by McClelland and Stewart did not include paratextual material and was accused by left-wing Canadians of having been censored (McDonough Dolmaya 2014: 125).

The National Film Board (NFB) of Canada can edit, even ban, films. Denys Arcand's film *On est au coton* [*Cotton Mill, Treadmill*] (1970) was completed after the War Measures Act had been imposed at the height of the crisis. Encouraged by Dominion Textile president and general director Mr. King, among other industry executives, NFB Chairman Sydney Newman blocked the release of the film, considering 'The general tone […] a slashing attack on the English-controlled textile industry' (Bradburn 2009: 5). Newman's successor, André Lamy, who as Assistant Film Commissioner had informed Newman about the problematic content of the film in 1970 (two [FLQ] members call for armed revolution in the film), decided to release an edited version in 1976 rather than take legal action as political violence had subsided and the Québec Film Council had decided to distribute an unlicensed copy of the film.

According to Denys Arcand:

> At the time I had [...] a [...] record of all the interviews I did with Mr. King [...] to show him [...]. [W]e brought that copy to the Cinémathèque Québécois in Montreal who kept it for thirty years hidden in their vaults. After that [...] even the cut version [...] was eventually censored by the NFB and placed on the shelf for four or five years until they discretely made it available for those who wanted to study it (but in its edited version, without the Mr. King footage). [...] the NFB decided to contact Mr. King's son [...] to show him the complete version of the film, with the footage of his father in it, and [...] he came to the conclusion that [...] the film was pretty sympathetic to his father [who] came across as intelligent and honest [...].

(In Morissette 2005)

The film was not released in its original, uncensored form until 2004. Since Newman was a unilingual English-speaker, he had to rely on the accuracy of his 'interpreters', i.e., on André Lamy, who would have acted more generally as an interpreter between the NFB's two official language communities, and on bilingual textile industry executives. Newman also blocked the release of Gilles Groulx's *24 heures ou plus* (a Marxist critique of capitalism) and Michel Brault's *Ordres* (a docufiction on the trauma of innocent people caught up in the October Crisis). After winning numerous awards, the latter film is still considered a masterpiece of Canadian cinema. The NFB produces English versions (usually subtitled or dubbed) of French films.

22.2.2   The US Context

In democratic societies with strong freedom of speech protections, like the United States, where freedom of speech is enshrined in Article 1 of the Constitution, as well as in state constitutions and various federal and state laws, overt government censorship is typically sanctioned and acknowledged under two conditions—to protect vulnerable citizens, mostly women and children, from obscenity and in times of war. As Byron Price, director of the US Office of Censorship during World War II, comments, 'Even the most vociferous critics of the principle of censorship agree that in wartime some form and amount of censorship is a necessity' (Price 1942: 837). Indeed, war-time censorship has been a reality in the United States since its founding. Nonetheless, it is also widely acknowledged that, 'freedom of speech often suffers during times of war. Patriotism at times devolves into jingoism and civil liberties take a backseat to security and order' (Hudson 2024). Price (1945: 1) puts it more categorically: 'Everything the censor does is contrary to the fundamentals of liberty'.

Wartime censorship in so-called open societies, or societies with strong free speech provisions and traditions, is often described as temporary or anomalous, unlike in more closed societies where it represents a tightening of already existing structures and procedures. As Skipton and Michalove (1989: A6) note in regard to censorship in tsarist Russia during World War I: 'Insofar as military censorship was concerned, its structure had been in place for quite some time. Nicholas' decree of 20 July 1914 had as its legal basis an article that had been on the books for years, its most recent review having come in 1906'. It is also more likely in such societies for wartime censorship to remain in place long after the cessation of hostilities, as was the case in the Soviet Union.

Nevertheless, even in more open societies, 'wartime' censorship has been instituted under a perceived threat of conflict, that is, before the outbreak of hostilities, and censorship restrictions passed in wartime have often remained in place long after military conflict has ceased. In other words, war can also serve as a pretext for censorial interventions, as was arguably the case with the first official government censorship acts, the Alien and Sedition Acts of 1798, which made it a federal crime 'to speak, write, or print criticisms of the government that were false, scandalous, or malicious'. Although President Adams sought to justify the acts on the basis of increasing tensions with France, Thomas Jefferson would describe them as authorising 'witch hunts' and repealed the acts upon assuming the presidency. It was also the case before the US entry into World War II that 'Snooping into the private affairs of resident aliens through their mail was one of many means by which U.S. intelligence agencies collected information on potential enemy aliens *prior to the war*' (Fiset 2001; emphasis added).

That being said, in societies with strong freedom of speech protections and traditions, it is more likely that censorship will not go unnoticed but be covered by the media, as evident in the following headlines from major US newspapers in early 1942, only months after the US entered World War II in December of 1941 and the Office of War Information (OWI) issued its 'Code of Wartime Practices for the American Press' on 15 January 1942, providing strict instructions on the proper handling of news: 'In the Nation: The Ever-Tightening Grip on Censorship', *The New York Times* (13 March 1942, p. 18), and 'Censorship Rules Clarified on Trade with Enemy Firms', *Wall Street Journal* (19 March 1942, p. 6), among others. In countries without such protections, referencing the existence of censorship was typically forbidden. In regard to Imperial Russia, for example, Skipton and Michalove (1989: 143) note, 'It was not until 22 September 1855 that the Post could even put up notices about postal schedules without censorship'. The censoring of censorship also held true in the Soviet Union, which included in its *Index of Information Not to Be Covered in the Open Press*: 'Mention of *Glavlit* organs and the jamming of foreign radio broadcasts' (Vladimirov 1972: 39).

22.2.2.1   World War I

While censorship restrictions were put in place during the US Civil War and intensified during the Spanish-American War (see Brown 1965), most scholars agree that World War I represents an important moment in the history of censorship in democratic countries. As Davidson (2014) notes,

> The war was more than a conflict of armies, it was seen as a conflict of societies, and failure on the home front could lead to defeat on the battlefront. Public opinion gained a new significance. At the same time, advances in technology and the development of a centralised postal service meant controlling communications could be achieved relatively easily. This saw the censorship of all forms of communication, restrictions placed on movement (the modern passport was born in 1916), and a myriad of war regulations controlling what could or couldn't be expressed.

The US Congress took swift action, passing the Espionage Act of 1917 just two months after the US entered World War I, and extending the government's censorship authority one year later with the Sedition Act of 1918. The Espionage Act was very broadly written, and prohibited

Uttering, printing, writing, or publishing any disloyal, profane, scurrilous, or abusive language intended to cause contempt, scorn [...] as regards the form of government of the United States or Constitution, or the flag or the uniform of the Army or Navy [...] urging any curtailment of the war with intent to hinder its prosecution; advocating, teaching, defending, or acts supporting or favouring the cause of any country at war with the United States, or opposing the cause of the United States.

(Hudson 2024)

The US Army took its own initiatives in regard to censorship, establishing the MI-10 Censorship Section within the War Department's Military Intelligence Division in July of 1918. It included 15 subsections dedicated to censorship of, among other things, mail, publications, telegraph, radio, and photographs (Tagg 2018). With the establishment of MI-10, 'the press censorship system was formalised and extended, according to the Army's official history, to include anything that might "injure morale in our forces here, or at home, or among our Allies", or "embarrass the United States or her Allies in neutral countries"' (Tagg 2018).

Three Supreme Court cases of this time largely affirmed the government's expansive censorship authority during wartime: *Debs v United States* (1919); *Schenk v United States* (1919); and *Frohwerk v United States* (1919). The first two involved attempts to interfere with the recruiting and enlisting of soldiers. Another case, *Abrams v United States* (1919) upheld the conviction of several individuals for distributing pamphlets against US intervention in Russia. Although the pamphlets had nothing to do with the war with Germany, they were seen by the justices as undermining the war effort. This case is also noteworthy for the dissent written by Justice Oliver Wendall Holmes, who put forward the concept of a free society as a 'marketplace of ideas'.

From the point of view of translation and censorship, *Frohwerk v United States* (1919) is especially interesting as it involved the publication of material deemed anti-war in the Missouri-based, German-language newspaper *Staats Zeitung*. One of the major concerns of censorship authorities at this time was the many foreign-language newspapers printed in the US following the massive waves of non-English-speaking immigrants that entered the country in the late nineteenth century, incentivised by the US government to settle newly acquired lands in the West (Homestead Act of 1862) and to build up the country's population, which had been decimated in the Civil War. One of the results of these waves of immigration was 'the hundreds, even thousands of small papers and magazines [in nineteenth-century America], all publishing in multiple languages, and translating both from the "foreign" English language into their own and translating their own stories for publication in English journals' (Gentzler 2008: 27).

During wartime, those 'hundreds, even thousands of small papers and magazines' were seen as a threat to national security. As a result, on 6 October 1917, Congress passed the Trading with the Enemy Act, which enlarged the censorship powers of the Postmaster General by requiring all foreign-language newspapers to obtain prior approval before mailing translated material related to the war (Stone 2004). The enforcement of the law appears to have been somewhat haphazard. It may have been directed initially at German-language newspapers, as suggested by the Frohwerk case, mentioned above, as well as the conviction of the publishers of *Tageblatt,* a Philadelphia-based German-language daily under the 1917 Act. Incidentally, that wartime conviction was upheld by the US Supreme Court in 1920 in the case *Schaefer v United States*, in which the 'the [Supreme] Court affirmed the convictions of three men associated with the Philadelphia *Tageblatt*, a German-language newspaper, for the offense of translating several articles from English-language newspapers in such a way as to reflect pro-German bias' (Stone 2004: 210). According to the ruling,

In a prosecution under the Espionage Act for willfully making and conveying false reports and statements with intent to promote the success of Germany and obstruct the recruiting and enlistment service of the United States to the injury of the United States in the war with Germany, where there was evidence that persons conducting a German language newspaper systematically took news despatches from other papers and published them with omissions, additions, and changes, *held* that the falsity of such publications, within the meaning of the statute, depended on the fact and purpose of the alterations and the resulting tendency of the article to weaken zeal and patriotism, and thus hamper the United States in raising armies and conducting the war, that the determination of such falsity, the evidence being sufficient, was clearly for the jury and not for the court, and that the court rightly allowed the jury to have recourse to their general knowledge of the war and war conditions in making such determination.

(Schaefer v United States 1920)

Other immigrant newspapers, however, fell under the 1917 Act *after* the war had ended. The Russian emigré newspaper *Novoe Russkoe Slovo,* for example, announced that it had been placed under censorship only in February of 1921:

'Novoe Russkoe Slovo' placed under censorship
    The Postal Department in Washington has informed the publisher of 'Novoe Russkoe Slovo' that it has deprived it of the privilege of publishing the newspaper without submitting translations into English. This restriction, which had been placed on all radical newspapers, is now entering into effect for 'Novoe Russkoe Slovo' as of today.
                    (*Novoe Russkoe Slovo*. 1921. "*Novoe Russkoe Slovo* vziato pod tsenzuru."
                                    11 Feb 1921:1; translated by Brian Baer)

At that time, *Novoe Russkoe Slovo* was, if not radical, then at least left leaning, but subsequent waves of emigration to New York over the course of the twentieth century would make it increasingly conservative. Henceforward, all articles printed from the foreign press included the note in English: 'True translation filed with the Postmaster of New York on [date] as required by the act of October 6, 1917'. It is not entirely clear when this requirement was lifted, how vigorously it was enforced, or to what extent the translations were vetted.

While the post-war period saw the continuation of government efforts to surveille the immigrant press alongside new attempts to control the influx of immigrants, criticism of those efforts also appeared. In what may be the first scholarly study of the immigrant press in the U.S., *The Immigrant Press and Its Control* (1922), Park argues against strict government control of immigrant periodicals. After mentioning a proposal to require an intra-linear translation of all foreign-language newspapers, he argues against such 'coercive Americanisation', which, he alleges, does not work; instead the press should be used 'in a cooperative manner' (448–9).

Given the federal government's reluctance to engage productively with immigrant communities at this time, non-government agencies were left to fill the void, the most striking example of which is, arguably, the Foreign Language Information Service (FLIS). Under the direction of Josephine Roche, this former government agency now a voluntary organisation took a very positive approach to immigrant newspapers, seeing them as 'an important venue for the dissemination of useful information and for the promotion of civic engagement' (Baer and Pokorn 2018: 150–1). FLIS 'routinely translated press releases from federal agencies and sent them to 850 newspapers and 67,000 foreign language organisations and their branches' (Muncy 2015: 98). Only in the

The Routledge Handbook of Translation and Censorship

1930s, under the Roosevelt administration, did the US government develop a more positive relationship with immigrant newspapers, producing and distributing translations to them.

22.2.2.2 *World War II*

US involvement in the Second World War resulted in unprecedented censorship restrictions, directed not only at citizens but also at military personnel. Even reporters for the official newspaper of the US Army, *The Stars and Stripes*, were required to submit their stories to military authorities for approval. On 15 January 1942, the Office of War Information (OWI) issued its 'Code of Wartime Practices for the American Press' providing strict instructions on how to handle news. Although the immigrant press was monitored during the war (Hayashi 2008: 93), it is interesting to note that, despite calls for the suppression of Japanese immigrant newspapers after the bombing of Pearl Harbor, the US government decided against it, 'meaning that the Japanese-language press would be immune from total suppression or censorship throughout the war' (Mizuno 2004).

The First War Powers Act, passed on 18 December 1941, included a provision on censorship, which allowed the president to censor mail between the United States and foreign countries. As Fox (2000) points out: 'Many members of the armed forces were immigrants or the children of immigrants and they were more comfortable communicating at home in their native language. A letter written in Polish or Italian usually wasn't delivered because the typical censor didn't know what it said'. To meet the demand, the Office of Censorship began intensive recruitment efforts. As Price (1945: 19) explains:

> Recruiting of civilian personnel had scarcely been started and had to be stepped up a hundredfold. From a wide range of applicants the Civil Service Commission provided housewives, school teachers, retired business men—anyone with good general intelligence or some specialised knowledge who could be entrusted to act on his own judgment, plus general regulations and consultation with supervisors. It was particularly important to obtain translators in some 100 principal languages, for it would have been impractical to require that all letters be written in English.

Special attention was given to letters sent from and into the mass internment camps created to sequester and surveille resident aliens and US citizens of German, Italian and Japanese ancestry. The initial proclamation of 8 December 1941, declaring that 'an invasion has been perpetuated upon the territory of the United States by the Empire of Japan', also included the provision that all resident Japanese nationals over the age of fourteen residing in the United States and its possessions were immediately 'liable to restraint, or to give security, or to remove and depart from the United States' (Fiset 2001). This was followed by Executive Order 9066, issued by Franklin Roosevelt on 19 February 1942, calling for the internment of 'all Americans of Japanese ancestry', focusing on those living in the San Francisco Bay Area. Already by the end of 1941, 2405 enemy aliens were in INS custody. Fort Missoula, in Montana, housed 633 Japanese Americans and 28 Italian nationals, along with nearly 1000 Italian seamen and World's Fair workers. At Fort Lincoln, in North Dakota, 104 German resident aliens resided alongside 300 German seamen. As Fiset (2001) points out, 'The growing numbers placed multiple strains on INS personnel, not the least of whom included a cadre of Japanese, German, Italian, and Spanish language censors who were under orders to examine 100 percent of the detainees' incoming and outgoing mail'.

While US citizens were forbidden to send mail to Germany, Italy or Japan during the war, internees were allowed to do so, in line with the relevant war conventions. The surveilling of

346

Translation and Censorship in Wartime

such correspondence offered the possibility of garnering valuable intelligence, but it also posed the difficulty of finding qualified translators, as many of the children and grandchildren of the Japanese immigrants could not read and write in Japanese. The other problem involved finding 'politically reliable' translators, which the government addressed by turning to Japanese-speaking Koreans—that is, Koreans who had learned Japanese as a result of Japan's colonial occupation of the Korean peninsula (see Ahn 1995). As Fiset (2001) notes, 'The Korean populace had been required to learn Japanese under duress by their occupiers, who had been suppressing Korean culture since 1905'. That being said, given the pressing needs of the US military during the war, some Japanese internees were offered rather well-paid positions in the Army's Map Service. As Hayashi (2008: 158) explains: '[Government workers] looked over records of internees and contacted prospective candidates directly, and made offers to those having the personal knowledge to read and translate the Chinese characters of a given location'.

To aid with the increasing backlog of internee correspondence, INS administrators, with help from the Office of Censorship, drafted a set of guidelines for both letter writers and censors: 'Each of the detention stations received copies, and key portions relevant to letter writers were translated into Japanese and Italian and posted on bulletin boards' (Fiset 2001). In mid-1942 a form letter for detainees was created and sent to the various camps to facilitate letter writing and censorship. The other way to deal with the problem of volume was to restrict the use of languages other than English:

> Initially, detainees were allowed to send two letters a week, one of which had to be in English. In addition, camp officials allowed four postcards if written in English, or two in a language other than English. The length of letters was limited to twenty-four lines, postcards to seven. These restrictions, which changed from time to time, were imposed to buffer censors from overwhelming volumes of outgoing mail.
>
> (Fiset 2001)

The censor-translators were terminated in 1946, several months after the official end of the war in the Pacific, and 'all subsequent foreign-language mail was forwarded to the Ellis Island immigration station' (Fiset 2001).

It should be noted that other immigrant communities not subject to internment were also placed under heightened surveillance during the war. Rosas, for example, has documented US government surveillance of Mexican works in the Bracero program, which was a US government-sponsored initiative that imported farm and railroad workers from Mexico. The program began in 1942, shortly after the US entry into World War II, and continued to 1964. The correspondence between the so-called *braceros* and their family members in Mexico was subjected to censorship, with letters often entirely blocked. The purpose of the censorship, Rosas argues, was 'to prevent reunification in the United States with relatives and friends who did not have program contracts. It was also intended to demonstrate the wide and effective reach of the US government's border enforcement' (Rosas 2014: 86). Such censorship was kept secret in the name of national security during wartime.

22.3 Current Debates

While it is tempting to contrast censorship in so-called open societies to censorship in more closed societies, important distinctions can and should be made within these categories. For example, whereas freedom of speech is enshrined in Article 1 of the US Constitution and has been affirmed by numerous court decisions, free speech was vulnerable to attack in Canada until the promulgation of the Canadian Charter of Rights and Freedoms (CCRF) in 1982. Moreover, 'Canadian defense regulations [were] not referable to Parliament and [were in effect] for the duration of the war' rather than renewable on a yearly basis like in the United Kingdom (Swindler 1942: 444). And because Canada had no explicit guarantee of press freedom until the adoption of the CCRF, provinces, such as Alberta, did not hesitate to restrict civil liberties in the form of, for example, the 'press gag law', invalidated nevertheless in 1938 by the Supreme Court of Canada, which argued: 'Any attempt to abrogate this right of public debate or to suppress the traditional forms of the exercise of the right (in public meeting and through the press) would be incompetent to the Legislatures of the provinces [...] as repugnant to the B.N.A. (British North America Act)' (Swindler 445 and note 7). This may explain why 'Dominion [of Canada] censorship restrictions [were] considerably more stringent than those of the British Isles at the supreme moment of London's peril' (Swindler 1942: 444)

Another direction for future research involves transnational censorship efforts. Censorship in wartime has typically been treated within individual countries, but efforts were made, especially during World War II, to coordinate censorship among allied nations. As Canada Declassified comments:

> The Americans also pursued international coordination of the censorship efforts. Price initiated conversations with British censorship in early 1941, and a tripartite censorship agreement between the United States, United Kingdom, and Canada was signed in January 1942. [...] The three nations agreed to 'a complete exchange of information between the three Censorships, and that insofar as possible the work would be divided to avoid duplication'.[...] The groundwork had been laid for a cooperative relationship.
>
> (Summary 2024)

Whether translations done by allied nations were simply accepted or subjected to vetting is also worth investigating.

Finally, more attention might be paid to the deleterious effects of censorship, not only in the sense expressed by Bourrie (2018), who convincingly argues that extensive censorship during WWI cost lives, but also in alienating non-English speaking citizens whose speech and communications were most heavily surveilled and censored during the war.

Further Reading

Baker, Mona. 2006. *Translation and Conflict.* London and New York: Routledge.
The book shows that translators and interpreters can actively participate in the circulation and the resistance of narratives linked to violent conflict, such as war, which has resulted in situations and accusations of divided loyalties.

Footitt, Hilary and Kelly, Michael. 2018. 'Translation and war', in F. Fernández and J. Evans (eds.), *The Routledge Handbook of Translation and Politics*. London and New York: Routledge, 162–76.
The chapter examines the broad role played by language mediation as well as the shifting roles, skills and status of translators and interpreters called upon during wartime throughout history.

Salama-Carr, Myriam (ed.) 2007. *Translating and Interpreting Conflict*. Amsterdam: Rodopi.
This interdisciplinary volume brings together case studies on the involvement of translators and interpreters in military and ideological conflict, and theoretical reflections on mediation and neutrality, ethical involvement and responsibility, and the implications for translator and interpreter training.

Sturge, Kate. 1999. 'A Danger and a Veiled Attack. Translating into Nazi Germany', in J. Boase-Beier and M. Holman (eds.), *The Practices of Literary Translation. Constraints and Creativity*. Manchester: St Jerome Publishing, 135–46.

Translation and Censorship in Wartime

The chapter demonstrates that a constrained porous form of translation was active in Nazi Germany and that official censorial intervention was marked by contradictory attitudes to translation. While literary policymakers generally attacked foreign literature, certain politically acceptable forms of the latter were promoted or were translated and made accessible to the public despite official disapproval.

References

Ahn, Hyung-Ju. 1995. *Korean Interpreters at Japanese Alien Detention Centers during World War II: An Oral History Analysis.* Unpublished Masters Thesis, California State University at Fullerton.

Anonymous. 2006. 'Thomas Shoyama Obituary', *The Globe and Mail.* Available at: THOMAS SHOYAMA Obituary (2006) – The Globe and Mail (legacy.com) (Accessed 13 March 2024).

Baer, Brian James and Pokorn, Nike. 2018. 'Translation as a Distinct Site of Transnational Activity: The Case of US Immigrant Newspapers, 1918–1942', *TTR*, 31(2): 141–65.

Basen, Ira. 2014. Why Canadian media embraced censorship during WWI. CBC News.

Beauregard, Claude. 1998. *Guerre et censure au Canada 19391945* [*War and Censorship in Canada 19391945*]. Sillery (Québec): Septentrion.

Biblioassnat. 2021, 15 December. 'À l'Index! Regards sur la censure littéraire au Québec: lumière sur un pan méconnu de l'histoire parlementaire québécoise' [Relegated to the Index! Perspectives on literary censorship in Québec: shedding light on a little-known period of Québec parliamentary history], *Bibliothèque Assemblée nationale du Québec* [Québec National Assembly Library]. Available at: À l'Index! Regards sur la censure littéraire au Québec: lumière sur un pan méconnu de l'histoire parlementaire québécoise – PREMIÈRE LECTURE (assnat.qc.ca) (Accessed 13 March 2024).

Bourrie, Mark. 2009. *Between Friends: Censorship of Canada's Media in World War II.* Unpublished PhD Dissertation, University of Ottawa.

Bourrie, Mark. 2018. 'How censorship became deadline during the First World War', *Maclean's.* Available at: How censorship became deadly during the First World War – Macleans.ca (Accessed 13 March 2024).

Bradburn, Jamie. 2009, 11 July. 'Historicist: The Adventures of Sydney Newman', *Torontoist*, 7. Available at: https://torontoist.com/2009/07/historicist_the_adventures_of_sydney_newman_1/ (Accessed 13 March 2024).

Brown, Charles H. 1965. 'Press Censorship in the Spanish-American War', *Journalism Quarterly*, 42(4): 581–90.

Canadian Foreign Policy Institute (CFPI). 2020. 'Wartime Censorship'. Available at: Wartime Censorship — Canadian Foreign Policy Institute (Accessed 13 March 2024).

Canadian War Museum (CWM). n.d. 'Introduction: Information, Propaganda, Censorship and the Newspapers. Democracy at War: Canadian Newspapers and the Second World War'. Available at: WarMuseum.ca – Democracy at War – Information, Propaganda, Censorship and the Newspapers (Accessed 13 March 2024).

Davidson, Jared. 2014. 'The History of Censorship and State Control during the First World War'. Available at: https://ww100.govt.nz/censorship-state-control (Accessed 15 April 2024).

Delisle, Jean and Otis, Alain. 2016. *Les Douaniers des langues.* Québec: Université Laval.

d'Eon, Ryan Alan. 2016. *Morale of Canadian Censors During the Second World War.* Unpublished B.A. Thesis, Acadia University. Available at: Ryan d'Eon.pdf (acadiau.ca) (Accessed 13 March 2024).

Fiset, Louis. 2001. 'Return to Sender: U.S. Censorship of Enemy Alien Mail in World War II', *Prologue Magazine*, 33(1 Spring). Available at: www.archives.gov/publications/prologue/2001/spring/mail-censorship-in-world-war-two-1 (Accessed 15 April 2024).

Fox, Myron. 2000. 'Censorship!'. Available at: www.pbs.org/wgbh/americanexperience/features/warletters-censorship/ (Accessed 20 April 2024).

Gentzler, Edwin. 2008. *Translation and Identity in the Americas: New Directions in Translation Theory.* London: Routledge.

Hayashi, Brian Masaru. 2008. *Democratizing the Enemy: The Japanese American Internment.* Princeton: Princeton University Press.

Hudson, David L. 2024. 'Free Speech during Wartime'. Available at: https://firstamendment.mtsu.edu/article/free-speech-during-wartime/ (Accessed 15 April 2024).

Keshen, Jeff. 1992. 'All the News That Was Fit to Print: Ernest J. Chambers and Information Control in Canada, 1914–19', *Canadian Historical Review*, LXXIII(3): 315–43.

Keshen, Jeffrey A. 2005. 'Chambers, Ernest John', in *Dictionary of Canadian Biography.* Available at: Biography – CHAMBERS, ERNEST JOHN – Volume XV (1921–1930) – Dictionary of Canadian Biography (biographi.ca) (Accessed 13 March 2024).

McDonough Dolmaya, Julie. 2014. '1971: Pierre Vallières Comes to English Canada via the United States', in K. Mezei, S. Simon and L. von Flotow (eds.), *Translation Effects. The Shaping of Modern Canadian Culture.* Montréal: McGill-Queen's, 119–30.

McRae, Matthew. 2017, May 19. 'Japanese Canadian Internment and the Struggle for Redress', in *Canadian Museum for Human Rights.* Available at: https://humanrights.ca/story/japanese-canadian-internment-and-struggle-redress (Accessed 13 March 2024).

Mizuno, Takeya. 2004. 'To Suppress or not to Suppress, That is the Question: Pros and Cons over the Suppression of the Japanese-language Press from Pearl Harbor to Mass Evacuation'. Paper Presented at the *Association for Education in Journalism and Mass Communication*, Toronto, CA, August 2004.

Morissette, Isabelle. 2005. 'An Interview with Denys Arcand. The Documentary Worlds of Denys Arcand', *Off Screen*, 9(5). Available at: An Interview with Denys Arcand – Offscreen. (Accessed 13 March 2024).

Muncy, Robyn. 2015. *Relentless Reformer: Josephine Roche and Progressivism in Twentieth-century America.* Princeton and Oxford: Princeton University Press.

The Ottawa Journal. 1942, May 5. 14. Available at: The Ottawa Journal from Ottawa, Ontario, Canada – Newspapers.com™ (Accessed 13 March 2024).

Park, Robert E. 1922. *The Immigrant Press and Its Control.* New York: Harper and Brothers.

Price, Byron. 1942. 'Governmental Censorship in War-Time', *The American Political Science Review*, 36(5): 837–49.

Price, Byron. 1945. *A Report on the Office of Censorship.* Washington, D.C.: United States Government Printing Office.

Purcell, Gillis. 1947. 'Wartime Press Censorship in Canada', *International Journal*, 2(3): 250–61.

Rosas, Ana Elizabeth. 2014. *Embracing the Spirit/Abrazando El Espíritu.* Berkeley: University of California Press.

Schaefer v United States, 251 U.S. 466 (US Supreme Court, 1920).

Skipton, David M. and Michalove, Peter A. 1989. *Postal Censorship in Imperial Russia.* Volume I. Urbana, Illinois: John H. Otten.

Stone, Geoffrey R. 2004. *Perilous Times: Free Speech in Wartime from the Sedition Act of 1798 to the War on Terrorism.* New York: Norton.

Summary. 2024. *Canada Declassified.* Available at: https://declassified.library.utoronto.ca/exhibits/show/---reasonable-censorship-privi/summary (Accessed 13 March 2024).

Swindler, William. 1942. 'Wartime News Control in Canada', *The Public Opinion Quarterly*, 6(3): 444–9.

Tagg, Lori. 2018. 'U.S. Army, Press Censorship in World War I'. Available at: www.army.mil/article/199675/u_s_army_press_censorship_in_world_war_i (Accessed 3 September 2024).

Vladimirov, Leonid. 1972. '*Glavlit*: How the Soviet Censor Works', *Index*, 1(3/4): 31–43.

PART V

Fascist Contexts

23

TRANSLATING THE ENEMY IN FASCIST ITALY

The Anthology *Americana*

Christopher Rundle

23.1   Core Issues

One of the most notorious cases of Fascist censorship was that of the anthology of American literature edited by the writer and translator Elio Vittorini and published by Valentino Bompiani, entitled *Americana*, which was blocked as soon as it came out in May 1941, before it had been distributed, and was eventually authorised in late 1942, but with a new critical apparatus. Despite being famous as an instance of Fascist censorship and of Fascist anti-American hostility, I will argue that in allowing *Americana* to be published at all, the regime showed remarkable flexibility, considering that Italy and the United States were at war when the volume came out, and that, after years of inaction as far as translated books were concerned, the regime had recently adopted a much more hostile stance towards translations and instituted the first restrictive measures against them.[1]

This case study will also be an opportunity to reflect on two key issues concerning research into the censorship of translation. The first is the importance of distinguishing between policies and decisions that affect both translations and domestic production, and those that actually target translations because they are translations. There is a significant difference, in my opinion, between a translated novel that was censored or restricted because of it fell foul of mores and values that were being imposed on all books, regardless of their origin (by touching upon taboo subjects or being too sexually explicit, for example), and one that was censored *simply because it was a translation*, irrespective of its content—the more so if it was censored because it was translated from a specific source language. The second key issue is the difficulty of interpreting archival evidence and arriving at a clear picture of the policies that were put in place and the decisions that were made. As I shall show in reference to *Americana*, the evidence can lend itself to quite different and contradictory interpretations.

23.2   Fascist Policy on Translations

23.2.1   *The Invasion of Translations*

In September 1929 the publisher Arnoldo Mondadori published the first four novels of a new crime series called *I libri gialli* [the Yellow Books], so called because of their yellow covers. The four

DOI: 10.4324/9781003149453-29

353

The Routledge Handbook of Translation and Censorship

novels, by Edgar Wallace, S.S. Van Dine, Anna Katharine Green and Robert Louis Stevenson, which were distributed in cheap magazine-format editions, sold 50,000 copies in the first month—a staggering number by the standards of the day (Decleva 1993: 152). In the years that followed, up to the start of the Second World War in 1939 and the collapse of the regime in 1943, translated popular novels were to have a profound impact both on the Italian publishing industry and on the cultural establishment. As the demand for popular novels grew, Italian publishers hastened to meet it; and such was the extent of the demand that the only way to keep pace with it was to turn to foreign novels, which could be translated and published quickly, cheaply and frequently, and with profit margins that were significantly higher than those possible with domestic novels. By way of illustration, over 5,000,000 copies of the *gialli* series were sold up to 1942, with an average print run of 26,000 per title (Tranfaglia and Vittoria 2000: 312). There were a few Italian bestselling popular authors, the most successful being Guido da Verona (who was Jewish) and Pitigrilli (real name Dino Segre, who collaborated with the Italian secret police, known as the OVRA); but the output of these domestic best-selling authors was not enough to feed the demands of the market.

Even before the first *Libri gialli* were published, there had already been talk of an 'invasion of translations'. Writers who felt threatened by the increasing success of translated fiction, and intellectuals with a more nationalist or protectionist view of culture, all complained that these translations were corrupting the Italian readership: the novels were of low literary quality, they were badly translated in ungrammatical Italian, and they were published in cheap, low-quality editions. According to them, the main culprits for this invasion were the publishers, who were putting their own profits ahead of their loyalty to their national culture (Rundle 2010: 69–78).

This accusation continued to be levelled at the publishers during two campaigns against translations: the first in 1929–1934, and the second in 1936–1938. The first campaign focused principally on the perceived invasion of translations, and reference was frequently made to the statistics on translations that had become available since the launch of the *Index Translationum* in 1932, a journal published by the Institute for Cultural Cooperation in Paris that collected information on translations from different national libraries (see Roig-Sanz 2021: 453–6). It was clear from these statistics that Italy was publishing more translations than any other country for whom figures were available, closely followed by Germany and France. Many within the Italian cultural and literary establishment felt threatened by the impact of translated popular novels, which were transforming the market and making it much less receptive to their own work (Rundle 2010: 96–111). Furthermore, Italy was particularly unsuccessful in exporting its own culture in the form of translations from Italian. This negative 'cultural trade balance' (*bilancia culturale*), as it was called at the time, was unfavourably compared with the very positive balance enjoyed by Germany, and was seen as an embarrassing indicator of the excessive receptiveness of Italy and its inability to expand its cultural influence abroad (Rundle 2010: 55–9).

On 3 October 1935 Italy invaded Ethiopia with the intention of founding its own empire in Africa and of joining the elite club of imperial powers. It did not take long for the international community to react, however, and within a month the League of Nations had imposed a series of economic sanctions on Italy. These sanctions are generally considered to have been ineffective because they were not sufficiently severe (cf. Ristuccia 2000), but they did serve as a means for the regime to mobilise Italian public opinion, especially with the regime's campaign for economic autarky.

In this context of heightened nationalism and xenophobia (especially against Britain, frequently referred to as 'perfidious Albion'), and as Italy declared the founding of its Empire in East Africa in 1936, a second campaign against translations was launched, led by the Authors and Writers Union and its president, the futurist poet F.T. Marinetti. Invoking a principle of cultural autarky,

Translating the Enemy in Fascist Italy: The Anthology Americana

and exploiting the xenophobic political climate, the authors called for a series of measures to be implemented to stem the flow of translations. These included a ministerial commission to monitor the quality of proposed translations and apply a principle of reciprocity, meaning, for example, that a translation from English into Italian would be authorised only if an Italian work was translated into English. Their main target was the Publishers Federation who they accused of unpatriotically favouring foreign products over domestic ones, an accusation that was very difficult for the publishers to refute in the prevailing ideological climate (see Rundle 2010: 114–42).

23.2.2 The Reaction of the Regime

What, then, was the reaction of the regime to this perceived invasion and to the two campaigns against translations? According to current research, the Ministry for Popular Culture, the state censor, took no specific action concerning translations until 1937–38, as we shall see.[2]

Until then, translations had been subject to the same censorship procedures as domestic books. Books were not preventively checked by the regime, but permission was needed for a book to be distributed. Furthermore, an informal system evolved whereby publishers could ask the Ministry for a preventive opinion if they had doubts about a particular text. This would be done at the proofing stage in order to minimise the cost of any cuts that might be imposed. The system was relatively unsystematic and relied on the occasional exemplary intervention by the Ministry and on the publishers pre-emptively self-censoring their publications in order to avoid trouble. The archives of the Mondadori publishing house, the most important publisher of translations in the 1930s, contain a collection of 'readers' reports' (*pareri di lettura*) on possible books for translation. These reports were mostly written by translators in the employ of the publisher, and their task was to judge whether a book was suitable for translation or not. Their recommendations often included suggestions as to which sections might need to be cut. When the cuts were significant and the text was by an important author, Mondadori would ask the author for their permission. The readers clearly had a good understanding of what was acceptable or not to the Ministry, and the aim was to avoid the economic damage of a ban (Albonetti 1994 has collected a number of these reports).

23.2.2.1 Preventive Censorship of Books

In 1934 a change was made to the system due to a book by the Italian author Mura (pen name of Maria Volpi) entitled *Sambadù amore negro*, the story of an ill-fated love affair between an Italian woman and an African man. The cover of the book carried the image of an elegantly dressed black man holding an adoring white woman in his arms. The cover came to the attention of Mussolini who was incensed that this image should be published just as Italy was preparing a colonial expedition in Africa, an enterprise that was premised on the racial superiority of the Italians. To ensure that such a mistake could not happen again, Mussolini instituted a system of preventive censorship, which involved the publishers being obliged to send three copies of each book to the local prefecture before it was distributed or sold. This did not mean that the books were necessarily read by the authorities, but it did serve to place additional pressure on the publishers. These new instructions were communicated via a circular letter and were never officially publicised or made law.[3]

Interestingly, the regime maintained that its system of censorship could not be called censorship because it was not preventive, as we can observe in this speech given to the Senate by the then Minister for Popular Culture Dino Alfieri, in May 1937:

The Ministry has so far limited itself to checking periodicals and books after publication, a system which therefore cannot be called censorship but which is applied by sequestering [post-publication] any publication which offends public decency or is politically incompatible.[4]

None of these measures were specific to translations, however, and there is no evidence of translations being subject to a specific set of rules. So, on the one hand, it is clear that although not subject to systematic preventive censorship, all books published in Fascist Italy, including translations, were routinely censored, either by the publishers and their translators to pre-emptively avoid trouble, or by the Ministry when a particular publication came to its attention. On the other hand, although translated books were naturally affected by these procedures, we cannot, in my opinion, describe them as a form of censorship of translations. *It was censorship that included translations but did not target them specifically.*

That being said, translations probably did offer publishers greater scope for pre-emptive self-censorship, given that it was easier to make preventive cuts and changes to a translated text than to a text written in Italian.[5]

23.2.2.2 First Measures Targeting Translations

The first action taken by the Fascist regime that specifically targeted translations, was a circular sent out in January 1937 informing publishers that henceforth they were to give the Ministry prior notice every time they decided to translate a text. This first step was followed a year later, in January 1938, by a much more ominous one. The Ministry sent out a telegram to all publishers requesting that they submit, 'with the utmost urgency', a complete list of all the translations they had published to date and those they intended to publish that year. The report that the publisher Arnoldo Mondadori submitted in response to this telegram is very revealing and confirms that he felt threatened by the regime's new concern with translations. Mondadori declared that he had published 269 translations since his publishing house was founded and that he planned to publish 29 in 1938. In fact, he had published 716 and would go on to publish 91. Mondadori achieved this sleight of hand by excluding from his report the *Libri gialli* and *Romanzi della palma* book series, because they were, as he put it, 'ephemeral periodical publications'—a reference to the fact that these series were sold in magazine format in railway stations and news kiosks. As these were series with a high proportion of translations, this excision succeeded in significantly reducing the number of translations he appeared to be publishing.[6]

Then in March 1938, just two months later, the Ministry sent out a circular instructing publishers that they were now required to seek prior permission before distributing a translation.[7] Different interpretations have been given concerning this measure. According to Billiani (2020: 138–9) and Fabre (2018: 295) it increased the severity with which translations were being treated; but, in fact, prior authorisation was already required for all books, so it does not seem to me that this measure involved any significant procedural changes. What it must have done is increase the sense that translations were being closely monitored and that the previously detached and neutral attitude of the regime towards translations was coming to an end.

It is important to note that 1938 was the year that Italy would become an officially racist country, with anti-Semitic legislation introduced in November. So, Fabre may well be right when he suggests that the March circular was an anticipation of the anti-Semitic purge that would begin later in the year (Fabre 2007: 32–3).

Translating the Enemy in Fascist Italy: The Anthology Americana

23.2.2.3 The Commission for the Purging of Books

A couple of months before anti-Semitism became law in Italy, the then Minister for Popular Culture, Dino Alfieri, decided to form a Commission for the Purging of Books (*Commissione per la bonifica libraria*) whose purpose was to:

> establish precise criteria and determine the most suitable and efficient methods to achieve a complete review of Italian book production and that of foreign books translated into Italian. This review has become all the more necessary in view of the racial directions from above.[8]

What is significant about this statement is that Alfieri treats the anti-Semitic purge of the Italian book market (the 'complete review of Italian book production') and a closer monitoring of translations as part of the same initiative. There is a certain logic to this: once the regime had decided to abandon its former strategy of leaving the publishers to operate relatively freely (despite the frequent and aggressive calls by the Authors and Writers Union for action against the 'invasion' of translations) and launch a purge of all Jewish authors, which was going to inflict a major upheaval on them, there was no longer any point in holding back as far as translations were concerned.

However, in practice, the Commission did not intervene against translations and devoted its energies to eliminating Jewish and other 'undesirable' authors from circulation. Realising that any resistance was futile, and despite being excluded from much of the work of the Commission, the Publishers Federation did their best to collaborate by announcing that the publishers had voluntarily removed 900 books from their catalogues due to their being 'an anachronistic residue within Fascist culture'. The Commission continued to meet until February 1940, when it held its sixth and final meeting. Overall, it would ban over 900 mostly Jewish authors, making an exception only for those works that were considered classics and part of the patrimony of world culture.[9]

23.2.2.4 A Translation Quota

In October 1939 Alessandro Pavolini took over from Alfieri as Minister for Popular Culture. He will be an important figure in the case study we shall be looking at below. As the anti-Semitic purge of the Commission drew to a close, Pavolini started to turn his attention to the 'problem of translations'. In September 1940, representatives of the Publishers Federation were informed that it was the Minister's intention to impose a quota on translations of 10%—meaning that translations could not exceed 10% of the production of each publisher. This was a very drastic cut if we consider that translations made up around 40–50% of the production of a publisher like Mondadori. That Mondadori was one of the targets of this measure is clear in a letter, dated 23 September 1940, which he received from the President of the Publishers Federation, Attilio Vallecchi, who had just been to a meeting at the Ministry, and in which Vallecchi says: 'I have already done everything that in all conscience I felt I could do for you; unfortunately the decision allows for no option other that what you've been told (10%)'.[10]

A meeting was called in Rome on 3 October 1940 between representatives of the Publishers Federation and the Minister, during which Pavolini explained that he wanted to reduce the number of translations by imposing a quota and by promoting Italian works. The publishers responded by explaining how damaging such a policy would be for them, and by arguing that the low royalties paid on translations (5%) allowed publishers to pay much higher royalties to Italian authors (15–20%), so that translations were actually beneficial to Italian authors. Furthermore, translations

The Routledge Handbook of Translation and Censorship

provided important employment for writers and teachers. They also cited the principle of reciprocity, only in reverse, saying that they could not be expected to export Italian works in foreign translation (a declared objective of the Ministry) if they were not permitted to publish translations into Italian.[11]

Pavolini seems to have been at least partially convinced by these arguments because no further steps were taken on the question of the translation quota until 1942. On 3 January of that year, Pavolini held another meeting with the publishers on the problem of translations and asked them to draw up some proposals that might satisfy his objective of limiting them, first by favouring translations of foreign works of high artistic value, and secondly by applying a principle of reciprocity in order to promote the translation of Italian works abroad. The publishers duly prepared a proposal, and in May 1942 the Ministry announced the application of a much less severe quota of 25%. The quota included: 'literary, political and philosophical works – both classical and non' but did not include scientific, technical or legal works.[12]

This quota is significant for a number of reasons. On the basis of my own and current research on translation under fascism, it appears that this is the only instance of a blanket policy restricting translations *merely because they were translations*, regardless of the author or the source language, and regardless of the canonical status of some of the works. In Nazi Germany, Francoist Spain and Salazarist Portugal, there was no comparable policy, although Germany did introduce a blanket ban against 'enemy' nations (not the language); but this did not include authors who were seen as ideologically aligned with Nazism or works that were no longer under copyright, so its purpose seems to have been to protect the wartime economy by ensuring that valuable foreign currency was not used in favour of enemy countries and hostile authors (cf. Rundle and Sturge 2010; Rundle 2018). What is significant is that the main purpose of Pavolini's blanket policy was simply to reduce the numbers. In other words, the Minister's main concern was not the content that was being transmitted by translations, or even their impact on the economy, but Italy's image as an overly receptive culture that was signally unsuccessful in exporting its products abroad, as the statistics on translations showed so irrefutably.

23.2.2.5 Policy Towards Translations of Anglo-American Literature

Given the success and impact of translated Anglo-American popular fiction and considering that the United States and Great Britain were seen by Mussolini as political antagonists after their refusal to recognise Italy's colonial conquest of Ethiopia, one might have expected some form of restriction to be placed on translations from English. But there is no evidence of the regime applying any systematic ban against English, or any other source language for that matter.

There are three exceptions to this general rule. The first was the culture-specific nature of the restrictions that were placed on children's literature, and especially comics. Comics were seen as an American import, from a morally corrupt and decadent society, like crime novels. The harm they might potentially cause Italy's young people, who were the future of the Fascist regime and were seen as even more vulnerable than the masses, meant that the regime overcame its usual hesitancy and imposed much more rigid restrictions, with all American comics being banned in November 1938 with the exception of Walt Disney's Micky Mouse, known as *Topolino* in Italian. It is said that Mussolini made an exception for *Topolino* because it was a favourite of his son Romano (Dunnett 2015: 348), although Romano Mussolini himself told the story slightly differently: apparently, he said to a functionary of the Ministry, Ferdinando Mezzasoma, 'Look Ferdinando, there are two things which seem absurd to me: that we can't listen to Jazz and that we can't read comics as we did before' (from an interview given in 1995 and quoted in Gadducci et al.

Translating the Enemy in Fascist Italy: The Anthology Americana

2020: 199–200). Despite this 'complete ban on all imported foreign material, with the exception of the creations of Walt Disney', American comics continued to be published, fitfully and often disguised as Italian creations.[13]

The second exception is the principle of reciprocity touched upon above, an idea that was aggressively promoted by the Authors and Writers Union. Technically speaking, this was a form of language-specific restriction on translations. And although it potentially affected all languages, there can be little doubt that translations from English would have been among those most affected, given how few translations were being made at the time from Italian into English. However, it was never formally adopted as a policy by the regime, although the instances in which publishers paid lip service to it would imply that at an informal level the authors had succeeded in giving this principle a degree of currency. In practice, publishers would boast of their success in placing contracts with foreign publishers for translations of Italian works as a way of acquiring political credit to cover them for when they would publish a translation into Italian, without the target languages of the translated Italian books necessarily matching the source languages of the Italian translations. We shall see an example of this in the following section with the publisher Bompiani. Mondadori also frequently invoked the principle of reciprocity to cover his many translations into Italian (Rundle 2010: 152–7).

The third exception is the evidence that Francesca Nottola (2010) has found of one particular publisher, Giulio Einaudi, being systematically denied permission to translate 'enemy' (i.e., Anglo-American) books—even as authorisation was being given to other publishers, such as Mondadori and Bompiani. Einaudi was the son of Luigi Einaudi, an eminent economist and future first President of the Italian Republic, who was also actively involved in the activities of the publishing house. Giulio Einaudi was part of an extended group of dissident intellectuals and writers who were more or less directly involved with the anti-Fascist organisation Justice and Freedom (*Giustizia e libertà*) and who suffered variously at the hands of the regime. Einaudi and a group of his associates were arrested in May 1935, but, thanks to the status of his father, he was eventually acquitted with a warning and he managed to re-establish a working relationship with the regime (Tranfaglia and Vittoria 2000: 380–1). When the United States declared war on Italy in December 1941, the Ministry started to apply a 'semi-informal' ban on Einaudi publishing British and American authors. It is clear from the reaction of some of the translators who worked for Einaudi that he was being subjected to a particularly harsh set of criteria: while he was being denied permission to translate English classics such as Thomas Hardy, Bompiani was publishing contemporary American authors (Nottola 2010: 182). Bonsaver (2007: 223–4) has noted that Bompiani also faced difficulties in obtaining permission for some translations from English. But this did not amount to the more systematic refusal that Einaudi faced and is in line with the Ministry's general policy of adopting a rather unpredictable and arbitrary approach towards the publishers, as we shall see. In trying to understand why Einaudi should be treated differently, we should keep in mind his past record as a political dissident. While there is no way of proving this, it seems possible that applying an anti-Anglo-American ban allowed the regime to harass Einaudi in a way that was impossible to challenge politically, given the fact that Britain and the United States were officially enemy nations. The evidence is in any case contradictory: Petrillo recounts that in 1943 the Ministry authorised a translation of Hemingway's *Farewell to Arms,* which Einaudi wanted to publish. So not only was Einaudi given permission in this instance to publish an American novel, but it was one that had been banned for years because of its unflattering account of the battle of Caporetto during WWI, when the Italian army suffered a humiliating defeat. The translation was blocked later that year when the Germans searched the Einaudi offices and found the contract between Einaudi and the translator Fernanda Pivano, and she was briefly arrested (Petrillo 2020). Einaudi also published another famous translation of American literature, one which would acquire mythical status in Italy, Edgar

Lee Master's *Spoon River Anthology*. The collection was translated by the same Fernanda Pivano and published in 1943 with the title *Antologia di Spoon River*. The (widely cited) apocryphal story goes that in order to obtain authorisation, Cesare Pavese, who was working for Einaudi and who had originally given Pivano a copy of *Spoon River*, applied for permission to publish a book entitled *Antologia di S. River*, disguising its American origin and implying that it was a tract by a 'Saint River' (preface to Lee Masters 1993: vii, xvii).

23.3   The Anthology *Americana*

We come now to the notorious case of the anthology *Americana*, one that encapsulates the unpredictable and sometimes contradictory nature of Fascist censorship policy towards translations and that highlights the difficulties of interpreting archival evidence, given that it is possible to read this case either as an instance of Fascist censorship or as an instance of Fascist flexibility. It is also a case that brings together all the key issues surrounding Fascist policy towards translations and its attitudes towards Anglo-American literature.

Americana was an anthology of excerpts from American literature, ranging from the early 1800s to the 1930s, translated by Italian writers, poets and intellectuals. It was edited by Elio Vittorini and would be published by Valentino Bompiani. It included translations of Edgar Allen Poe, Nathaniel Hawthorne, Herman Melville and Mark Twain, as well as more contemporary authors such as Willa Cather, Sherwood Anderson, F. Scott Fitzgerald, William Faulkner, Ernest Hemingway and John Steinbeck. The translators included the poet Eugenio Montale who would win the Nobel prize in 1975, the novelist Alberto Moravia, who was Jewish and would become one of Italy's most prominent post-war writers, Cesare Pavese, who would also become a very prominent post-war writer, and Vittorini himself.

Together with the *Spoon River Anthology*, *Americana* became a key text in what would be widely known as the 'myth of America' (*il mito dell'America*), a passion for contemporary American literature and culture that began to grow in the late 1930s and 1940s and would become thoroughly established after the war. It is the post-war popularity of a certain American literature that could be viewed as a kind of counterculture, as well as the post-war status of writer-translators like Pavese and Vittorini, that lent their pre-war translations such a retrospective (and perhaps exaggerated) fascination and status. This 'legendary' status is important because, as shall be argued later, it affects the way the archival evidence concerning *Americana* has generally been interpreted.[14]

23.3.1   First Edition v.1 (Vittorini 1941): with Introductory Notes by Vittorini

Americana was intended by Bompiani and Vittorini as the inaugural volume of a new series called Pantheon. As its name suggests, this was to be a series of anthologies showcasing masterpieces of world literature. The series would continue until 1969 and would include twenty literary anthologies and seven anthologies of theatrical texts (Pavese 2009: 140 n.1). Work began in the spring of 1940 with the intention of bringing the first volume out in time for Christmas (Pavese 2009: 141).

At the beginning of November 1940, Bompiani sent the galley proofs to the Ministry for its approval, as required by Circular No. 1135 of 26 March 1938 (see n.7). These were the proofs of what I shall call the First edition v.1 (Vittorini 1941), which would include the translations and introductory notes by Vittorini placed before each group of authors (called *corsivi* in Italian because they are less formal than a preface and are printed in italics like a blurb). That Bompiani was confident of the Ministry's approval is apparent from the fact that the anthology was announced in the publisher's publicity in December (Pavese 2009: 143), and an announcement also appeared in the *Giornale della libreria*, issues 47 (23 November) and 48–49 (7 December).

Translating the Enemy in Fascist Italy: The Anthology Americana

Contrary to expectations, however, the Ministry informed Bompiani that Pavolini had blocked the distribution of the volume 'for reasons of general disposition' (*per ragioni di indole generale*), after Bompiani had already printed 'three quarters' of the volume. Bompiani wrote to Pavolini on 30 November 1940 and tried to argue his case by saying that this was to be the first of a long series of anthologies of classic literature, including four volumes of Italian works, one of German classics, one of Hungarian classics and one of Scandinavian classics. Furthermore, invoking the principle of reciprocity, Bompiani underlined that these anthologies of foreign literature would be 'balanced' by similar publications in the countries whose literature he was translating, on the basis of 'planned and existing agreements'. To strengthen his credentials as a successful exporter of Italian literature, Bompiani wrote again to Pavolini on 16 December and listed 30 Italian books published by Bompiani that had been sold abroad for translation in 1940, including one into English. Pavolini replied on 20 December saying that he was very pleased and congratulated Bompiani on this 'very useful work of penetration' (*utilissima opera di penetrazione*).[15]

At the beginning of December, Vittorini went to Rome to talk to Pavolini, but the Minister's decision remained unchanged. Pavolini told Vittorini that he would be prepared to authorise the American volume once an Italian volume had been published in the series, as well as one of translations from a 'friendly' nation (Vittorini 2008: 164, in Pavese 2018: 17). The first volume of the series did come out around Christmas, a collection entitled *Lettere d'amore degli scrittori italiani* [Love letters of Italian writers].

On 7 January 1941, Pavolini wrote again to Bompiani in reply to his letter of 30 November 1940. It is clear that Pavolini had now had the chance to examine the proofs of *Americana*. The anthology is admirable, he says in the letter, as is its presentation (a significant comment given his later objection to Vittorini's notes), but in his opinion this is not a time to be performing 'acts of courtesy' towards the Americans, who are 'a potential enemy of ours'. Having said this, however, he adds that if a similar anthology of Italian literature were to be published in America, then he would see no difficulty in giving his approval. Here too, the principle of reciprocity was evoked, with Pavolini not wanting to be seen to perform 'acts of courtesy' unless a similar courtesy were extended by the Americans. Bompiani replied on 6 February that he agreed with the Minister and would wait for his permission once some other volumes had come out in the series. He added that the intention of *Americana* was to 'put readers on their guard' and 'throw water on any excessive enthusiasm for recent American literature'—a statement that could hardly have fooled Pavolini.

There is a further exchange between Bompiani and Pavolini in this sequence. On 6 March 1941, Pavolini wrote to deny the compensation Bompiani had requested in February when informed that *Americana* would not be authorised, but Pavolini promised that the Ministry would buy a certain number of future anthologies in the series. Bompiani then replied on 10 March saying that the anthology on Spanish theatre had come out, and those on Spanish and German narrative, Italian lyrical poetry and medieval chronicles would be published soon.

These apparently minor details are significant because they may help us to understand how it was that the First edition v.1 of *Americana* was published in May, just three months later—or, at least, prepared for publication. The records at the Bompiani archives state that they finished printing the volume on 30 April 1941, and that the first edition came out on 31 May but was 'sequestered by the Fascist censor'—which meant that, while it could not be distributed, no copies were actually impounded or destroyed.[16] As no records have survived covering the gap between the exchange in March, when it was still clear that the volume was not authorised, and the recorded date for the first edition in May, it is hard to understand why Bompiani completed the printing and went ahead with preparing the volume for publication. Either there are some documents missing, or it is possible, but this is mere supposition, that having published the other volumes in the series

361

The Routledge Handbook of Translation and Censorship

(as announced on 10 March), Bompiani now felt authorised to proceed with *Americana*, in line with what Pavolini had told Vittorini in December 1940 (see letter of 18 December 1940 above).

That this was a fullyfledged edition, not an unbound print, would appear to be confirmed by the Bompiani catalogue (Bompiani 1998: 117) and by Esposito (2009: 2) who cites two surviving copies that have the date 30 April 1941 in the colophon. In her notes to Vittorini (2008), Rodondi suggests that it was 'by no means a virtual edition' (in Esposito 2009: 2). Vittorini also refers to a first edition of 1941 in his book *Diario in pubblico* [Public Diary], explaining that it was blocked by the censor because of his introductory notes and 'never put on sale' (1957: 108). However, both Esposito (2009: 6) and Marquette (2018: 19, 23 n.14) have confirmed that the two surviving copies do not include the illustrations that had been prepared for the volume, which would seem to imply that these were provisional or private copies not intended for distribution; though some copies must have been circulated to the authorities for the book to have incurred a ban.

Marquette (2018: ch.4, 64) offers an interesting analysis of the illustrations, arguing that their impact was in line with the critical stance of Cecchi's preface and gave 'a strong sense of the more problematic aspects of American culture'. Perhaps for this reason, no mention was made of them by the Ministry at any point during the negotiations over the anthology.

23.3.2   First Edition v.2 (Vittorini 1942a): with a Preface by Cecchi and Introductory Notes by Vittorini

With the First edition v.1 printed but blocked by the censor, Bompiani needed to find a way to publish the book and avoid severe financial loss. The solution he came up with was the addition of a preface by the eminent scholar and member of the Royal Academy of Italy, Emilio Cecchi. Although an admirer of Anglo-American culture, Cecchi was very critical of American modernity and had recently published a book of essays with the eloquent title of *America amara* [Bitter America] (Cecchi 1939).

The idea was to frame the anthology in a more critical light so as to 'throw water on any excessive enthusiasm' for American modernity (as Bompiani had claimed was the purpose of the volume in his letter to Pavolini of 6 February 1941), and so that it would no longer seem such an inappropriate act of courtesy to the enemy. The gambit appeared to work as Pavolini wrote to Bompiani on 2 October 1941 saying that he was willing to reconsider his decision concerning *Americana* once he had had the opportunity to read Cecchi's preface (Bompiani 1988: 40, in Pavese 2018: 23). After this exchange, however, the situation dragged on without any further progress while Bompiani waited for Cecchi to finish.

Finally, Cecchi completed his preface in March 1942, almost nine months after it was first agreed. On 5 March, Cecchi wrote to Bompiani saying that he had delivered a copy to Pavolini that same day. On 30 March, Bompiani received Pavolini's verdict on this new version of the anthology (Vittorini 1942a). While Cecchi's preface was acceptable, casting the anthology in an appropriately critical light (much of it was adapted from *America Amara*, see Marquette 2018: 21), Vittorini's introductory notes to each section were not:

> The preface by Emilio Cecchi is excellent and should make it possible to authorise the publication of the anthology of American writers: but it is necessary, for obvious reasons of consistency, that the volume be reviewed given the essentially negative light cast by Cecchi's preface. In particular, the notes [by Vittorini] which precede each group of writers must be removed as they are not only ill-advised in the current state of affairs, unilateral and critically questionable, but they wholly contradict the interpretation that the preface gives of the volume.

> Also, a phrase should be chosen from the preface and printed on the publicity strip. For example, the following: 'Thirty years ago we succumbed to the ineffable of the Slav soul,

362

Translating the Enemy in Fascist Italy: The Anthology Americana

and now we were succumbing to the ineffable of the American soul. And so a new literary bacchanal began'.[17]

23.3.3 First Edition v.3 (Vittorini 1942b): with a Preface and Introductory Notes Compiled by Cecchi

The First edition v.2 (Vittorini 1942a), then, was also blocked and could not be distributed; the only thing left to do was to remove Vittorini's notes. However, this was not a straightforward operation: it needed to be carried out in such a way as to save as many pages as possible of the original print run (the volume is over 1000 pages long). The key was to replace Vittorini's notes with texts that were of the same length so that only those pages needed to be reprinted. As it would take too long to write them from scratch, the idea was for Cecchi to prepare a selection of extracts from existing literary criticism, adjusted to fit the pages correctly.[18] Bompiani wrote to Pavolini on 14 April 1942 to obtain his approval for this solution; and Pavolini replied on 22 April that he agreed with the idea but still wanted to check the texts that Cecchi chose (Bompiani 1988: 44–5, cit. Pavese 2018: 32).

Once again, progress was slow. Cecchi started work on the new notes in April and did not complete them until sometime in September 1942. Interestingly, a number of these notes were those written originally by Vittorini himself, reformatted and indicated as extracts from a non-existent volume entitled *Breve storia della letteratura Americana* [A short history of American literature] (Esposito 2009: 5; Marquette 2018: 29), though Esposito suggests that they were 'certainly not the most significant' (2009: 5). In a letter that Bompiani had written to Cecchi on 28 March 1942, he had suggested that Cecchi 'look at those points that the Minister has marked and that could cause problems and tone them down or change them'; so the intention seems to have been to change only what was absolutely necessary and disguise the rest.[19] It is also interesting to note that, after Vittorini and D. H. Lawrence, the most frequently anthologised critic in the notes compiled by Cecchi was the Jewish American Ludwig Lewishon (Marquette 2018: 29, 32). Bompiani and Cecchi exchanged letters over Lewishon's writings; Bompiani suggested that some be cut, to which Cecchi replied on 30 September 1942: 'one piece more or less by Lewishon is not going to do any harm; after all, critical and historical works by Jews continue to survive undisturbed [in Italy]' (Vittorini 1985: 226, in Marquette 2018: 32 n19).

The reprint of the pages containing Cecchi's notes was completed on 27 October 1942 and they were sent to the binder's to be inserted into the existing copies (Bompiani 1988: 134, in Pavese 2018: 39). When the binding was complete the book (Vittorini 1942b) was finally published— at the end of November according to Pavese (2018: 39), at the end of December according to Bonsaver (2007: 229). A copy was sent to Mussolini (Bonsaver 2013: 122); and one was sent to Pavolini who wrote and thanked Bompiani in January 1943.[20]

23.3.4 The Final Act

For a few months *Americana* appears to have circulated without any problems; Bonsaver (2013: 122) says that it was reviewed in newspapers without any serious issues being raised, although in his review of May 1943, Ezra Pound complained that the anthology was inspired by the ideas of 'the Jew' Lewishon (Pound 1943: 1, in Esposito 2009: 6). That the anthology was a success is clear from the fact that it went through two reprints within six months: according to records in the Bompiani archive, a first reprint of *Americana* was published on 11 February 1943 and a second on 18 June 1943. The situation changed, however, in late June 1943. It was a period

The Routledge Handbook of Translation and Censorship

in which the Allies were preparing to open a second front by invading Italy from the south and they were engaged in a bombing campaign over Italy.

On 26 June 1943 an unsigned note was sent to Gaetano Polverelli, who had replaced Pavolini as Minister for Popular Culture in February. It reads as follows:

> In the days of the massacres at Grosseto, in Sardinia and in Sicily, the editor Bompiani has the gall to publish a 'lump' entitled 'AMERICANA', an anthology of little value with a preface by an academic and translations by Vittorini; an anthology modelled on that Jew Lewis. And the same Bompiani continues to publish and republish Cronin, Steinbeck and others – out and out Bolsheviks, and in any case extremely pernicious. Mondadori too, having for years helped to 'educate' our youth to appreciate American immorality and frivolousness with the series 'La Palma' and the crime series, today continues to publish English and American authors.
>
> [In red type, the Minister has added] I agree entirely. I have given instructions that a strict ban be applied and that the titles mentioned above be taken out of circulation.
>
> [In blue pencil, Mussolini has written] Yes. It's time this was stopped![21]

The question, then, is whether *Americana* was actually banned or whether Polverelli was merely showing an appropriate level of severity for the benefit of Mussolini? The evidence is not clear. Both Jane Dunnett (2015: 368) and Giorgio Fabre (1998: 294 n.1, 2007: 44) suggest that Polverelli issued a sequestration order against *Americana* the same day that the note was received, but they provide no sources to back this up, other than the unsigned note itself. Bonsaver (2013: 123) argues that a sequestration order was given but that it was never carried out due to the chaos that enveloped the regime just a month later when Mussolini was overthrown on 25 July 1943.

Catherine Marquette has found a document in the Bompiani archives which would seem to indicate that the book was not banned outright but rather that all further reprints were forbidden. A typewritten report of a phone conversation with the Bompiani representative in Rome, Cosimo Cherubini, dated 2 July 1943, reads: 'AMERICANA – stop the reprint'.[22] This version of the facts is in line with evidence that the anthology continued to circulate and be publicised in the months that followed.

We should keep in mind that on 8 September 1943, the Italian government, under the leadership of General Badoglio, signed an armistice with the Allies, effectively changing sides in the war overnight. The country was split in two: a southern part which was under the control of the Allies, who were pushing northwards, and the rest of Italy which came under the control of the Germans and the puppet regime they had installed called the Repubblica sociale italiana [Italian social republic], also known as Repubblica di Salò because its administrative capital was in the town of Salò. So, in the chaotic situation which prevailed from the armistice onwards, it is unclear what influence the regime could realistically exert over those publishers who were operating in the new Republic.

Bonsaver (2013: 123) has found advertisements for *Americana* on the dust jackets of books that were published by Bompiani in the autumn of 1943, when Milan was under the control of the regime (though these dust jackets could well have been printed earlier); while Pavese (2018: 71–3) has found copies of *Americana* with dust jackets that advertise products we know were published in 1944. These small pieces of evidence appear to indicate that *Americana* continued to circulate after June 1943. It is possible that despite the ban on further reprints, Bompiani was tacitly allowed

Translating the Enemy in Fascist Italy: The Anthology Americana

to sell remaining stocks (which must have been considerable given that there had been a new reprint on 18 June). Or it is possible that in such a fluid situation, Bompiani was able to continue quietly selling the book without provoking a reaction on the part of the regime.

23.4 Conclusions

This chapter began by suggesting that there are two key issues that need to be considered in any research on the censorship of translation: first, the distinction between policies or acts of censorship that merely include translations within a broader brief and those that specifically target translations; second, the difficulty we face in interpreting the archival evidence.

Concerning the first issue and how it applies to Fascist Italy, we saw how until 1937, there was no policy that specifically targeted translations. So, although books were subject to censorship, and although translations were caught up in this system, mainly due to the self-censorship carried out by publishers, they were not being censored *because they were translations*. From 1938 onwards, by contrast, the regime increasingly targeted translations, in the wake of the anti-Semitic purge, until a blanket quota was applied to translations in 1942. In my opinion, there is a qualitative difference between the Circular (No. 442/9532, see note 3) with which Mussolini introduced a system of preventive monitoring of books and the quota that Pavolini imposed on translations: the former is not an example of translation censorship, while the latter clearly is. How many other cases that are presented as instances of translation censorship are, in fact, just instances of censorship that happened to affect a translation?

With this in mind, there is little doubt that *Americana* was censored because it was a translation and because it was an anthology of American literature. This brings us to the second issue. Although there is a considerable amount of archival evidence about this case, it is still open to quite different interpretations:

A. The predominant interpretation is that because Vittorini's critical commentary was cut from the anthology, this is a book that was censored—even if it was published eventually, without any significant cuts or changes being imposed on the actual translations themselves.[23] In line with this interpretation, we could argue, along with Cesare Pavese, that Vittorini's commentary was important and offered a significant new interpretation of modern American literature, and that without it the anthology lost some of its literary value and capacity to innovate the Italian literary field: 'all the meaning and value of *Americana* is derived from your notes. In ten years of reading about that literature I have never found such an appropriate and illuminating summary' (Cesare Pavese 1966: 634, in Pavese 2018: 33).

B. An alternative interpretation would be to consider that, rather than simply block the anthology and tell Vittorini and Bompiani to wait until the war ended, Pavolini went to some trouble to find a way to allow them to publish it, without he or the Ministry losing face. In the circumstances, we could focus on what Pavolini allowed to remain (the translations of an 'enemy' literature) and argue that it was more significant than what he had removed (Vittorini's 'over-enthusiastic' critical commentary). To strengthen this argument, we could suggest that very few readers were taken in by the 'discursive camouflage' of Cecchi's critical introduction, however sincerely written on his part, or by the phrase that Pavolini picked out for the publicity strip (on the notion of discursive camouflage, see Tyšš 2017, 2022). As Billiani (2020: 160) puts it:

Cecchi [was] aware that his preface would not change the opinion of either type of reader: an 'informed' reader would not be led astray by the conflicting positions of [himself and Vittorini] and would still be able to form an independent opinion, whilst an 'ordinary' lay reader would only be interested in the text itself, rather than the accompanying critical interpretations'

Finally, we could add that, regardless of the tenor of the accompanying paratexts, the translations had a profound impact on the Italian readership and contributed to the myth of America that developed after the war.

Both these arguments fit the available evidence; what distinguishes them are their different perspectives. Within the broader history of Fascist cultural policy, I am more persuaded by the second argument. It seems significant to me that Pavolini approved the volume, even if he did impose some face-saving changes to the critical apparatus. But for scholars whose primary perspective is the 'myth' of America and the idea that translating American literature during the Fascist period was an act of courage and cultural subversion, and that the translators were 'literary partisans' (a phrase used by Van Wagenen 2019: 682 in reference to Pavese and Pivano and intended to cast them in the role of cultural resistance fighters), a narrative where Vittorini and his anthology were victims of an act of censorship by the regime is more in line with their point of view. And there is no question that this has been the dominant interpretation among cultural historians so far.[24]

Acknowledgements

I would like to thank Catherine Marquette for her very useful feedback and for sharing some of her archival research with me.

Further Reading

Fabre, Giorgio.1998. *L'elenco. Censura fascista, editoria e autori ebrei*. Torino: Silvano Zamorani editore.
This is one of the best and most detailed accounts of the Fascist censorship system and it reconstructs the anti-Semitic purge of the publishing sector. Unfortunately, the book is not available in English.

Billiani, Francesca. 2020. *National Cultures and Foreign Narratives in Italy, 1903–1943*. Translated by Georgia Wall. Cham, Switzerland: Palgrave Macmillan.
A translation of a book that originally appeared in Italian in 2007. More than other studies available in English, this reconstruction of the role of foreign literature in Italy takes into account the literary and aesthetic debates of the period.

Bonsaver, Guido. 2007. *Censorship and Literature in Fascist Italy*. Toronto: University of Toronto Press.
A detailed reconstruction of Fascist censorship of literature which includes a chapter on translations.

Rundle, Christopher. 2010. *Publishing Translations in Fascist Italy*. Oxford: Peter Lang.
This book reconstructs the ideological debate the developed around translations and their perceived invasion of the Italian book market, as well as the regime's reaction. Includes detailed statistics on the translation industry.

Archival Sources

ACS: Archivio centrale dello stato, Roma
AME: Archivio Storico Arnoldo Mondadori Editore, Fondazione Arnoldo e Alberto Mondadori, Milano
ASMi: Archivio di stato, Milano
BOM: Archive of the Bompiani publishing house, Milano

Translating the Enemy in Fascist Italy: The Anthology Americana

DAGR: Divisione afari generali e riservati
DGPS: Direzione generale pubblica sicurezza
MCP: Ministero della cultura popolare
MI: Ministero degli interni
PMG I: Prefettura di Milano, Gabinetto – I serie
SAM: Sezione Arnoldo Mondadori

Notes

1 There was another notorious instance of Fascist censorship involving Vittorini, though as a writer this time. His novel *Il garofano rosso*, which was being serialised in the journal *Solaria* in 1933–1934, was banned for obscenity. See Greco (1983) for more details.

2 For simplicity's sake, I am referring to the state censor by its final name, the Ministry of Popular Culture. The first office to take on the role of censor was the Prime Minister's Press Office in 1923. In August 1933, Mussolini's son-in-law, Galeazzo Ciano, became head of the Press Office and under his initiative it was upgraded in September 1934 to State Under Secretariat for the Press and Propaganda. In June 1935, the office was upgraded again and it became the Ministry for the Press and Propaganda, with Ciano as Minister. Finally, in May 1937 the name of the ministry was changed to Ministry of Popular Culture, Ciano having been replaced as Minister by Dino Alfieri in 1936.

3 The instructions are contained in Circular No. 442/9532, dated 3 April 1934. The circular was first discovered by Giorgio Fabre (1998: 22–8). A copy can be found in ACS, MI, DGPS, DAGR, Massime, b. S4 (provv.), f. S4 A 1/1. 'Disciplina delle pubblicazioni. Circolari.'

4 The copy of the speech is undated but would appear to be the one given by Dino Alieri at the Senate on 21 May 1937. In ACS, MCP, b.105 'Dino Alieri'. All translations from the Italian are mine.

5 The Spanish research group TRACE (https://trace.unileon.es/en/) have carried out very detailed and systematic research on translations into Spanish during the Franco regime, and have tried to measure both the extent of the censorship that took place during the translation process (or it might be better to call it self-censorship) and the type of content that was being censored. So, although there was no specific censorship policy in Francoist Spain which targeted translation, translations were clearly subjected to a significant amount of self-censorship on the part of publishers and translators. We should keep in mind, however, that our perception of the censorship which took place is conditioned by the fact that it is much easier to find evidence of changes that might constitute a form of self-censorship when looking at translations, than it is when looking at domestic products. Merino and Rabadan (2002) provide a useful introduction to the work of the group; see Vandaele (2010) for an overview of translation under the Franco regime; see also Rundle (2018) for a comparison of the censorship policies in Fascist Italy, Nazi Germany, Francoist Spain and Salazarist Portugal.

6 The 1937 circular, dated 30 January, can be found in ASMi, PMG I, b.716 'Rassegna Bibliograica. Elenco delle pubblicazioni'. A copy of the 1938 telegram, dated 15 January, can be found in AME, SAM, 'Ministro della Cultura Popolare'. A copy of Mondadori's report, dated 18 January 1938, can be found in AME, SAM, 'Minstero Cultura Popolare', Busta 65–6. The 'correct' figures were compiled by the author using the Mondadori catalogue; see Rundle (2010: 224–6) for more details.

7 Circular No. 1135, 26 March 1938. ACS, MI, DGPS, DAGR, Massime, b. S4 103 A (provv.), f. S4 B5, 'Traduzione e difusione nel Regno di opere di autori Stranieri'. Quoted in Fabre (1998: 32).

8 From a letter written by Alfieri to Mussolini on 13 September 1938, the day before the first meeting of the Commission. ACS, MCP, b. 56, 'Produzione libraria italiana e straniera tradotta in italiano. Revisione totale'.

9 The quote is from the sector journal of the Publishers Federation, *Giornale della libreria* LII/6 (11 February 1939): 42. For details of the work of the Commission, see a report by Gherardo Casini, who was head of the Books Division at the Ministry of Popular Culture, to the Minister Alessando Pavolini, dated 9 February 1940; in ACS, MCP, b.56, 'Produzione libraria italiana e straniera tradotta in italiano. Revisione totale'. For a very detailed reconstruction of the regime's (mainly anti-Semitic) blacklist of authors, see Fabre (1998).

10 From a letter from Vallecchi to Mondadori, dated 23 September 1940; found in AME, SAM, 'Federazione Nazionale Fascista degli Industriali Editori', Busta 42.

The Routledge Handbook of Translation and Censorship

11 A detailed but imcomplete report on this meeting can be found at AME, SAM, 'Federazione nazionale fascista degli editori'.

12 An account of the meeting on 3 January was published in the *Giornale della libreria* LV/8–9 (28 February 1942): 29–31. The announcement of the quota was published in *Giornale della libreria* LV/19 (20 May 1942): 77–8.

13 The ban was announced in the *Giornale della libreria* LI/47 (19 November 1938): 327. For more details see Dunnet (2015: 343–53); Sinibaldi (2013, 2016); and especially Gadducci et al. (2020).

14 The Italian word 'mito' is difficult to translate adequately into English because it's primary sense when used metaphorically is rather different; while in English myth is primarily used metaphorically to describe something that is fictitious or even erroneous, in Italian its primary metaphoric sense is that of something or somebody that has acquired an exhalted, legendary status. For more details on the myth of America and its birth under Fascism, see Dunnett (2015); and for its importance as a reaction against Fascism after the war, see Billiani (2020: 180). For an example of how translating American literature under Fascism is interpreted as an act of subversion or resitance, see Ferme (2002).

15 All the letters are in ACS, MCP, b.116 'Valentino Bompiani (Editore)'.

16 Publisher's file on *Americana* in BOM.

17 Letter from Pavolini to Bompiani, dated 30 March 1942. In ACS, MCP, b.116 'Valentino Bompiani (Editore)'.

18 See letters from Bompiani to Cecchi, dated 3 and 7 April 1942. In BOM, 'Carteggio Emilio Cecchi'.

19 The letter can be found in BOM, 'Carteggio Emilio Cecchi'.

20 Letter from Pavolini to Bompiani, dated 7 January 1943. In ACS, MCP, b.116 'Valentino Bompiani (Editore)'.

21 Unsigned note to the Minister Gaetano Polverelli, dated 26 June 1943. In ACS, MCP, b.116, 'Bompiani Valentino (Editore)'. A photograph of the note can be found in Bonsaver (2007: 231). Pavese (2018: 20) attributes the two phrases added to the note differently: he describes the first in red type as an unsigned note and attributes the second in blue pencil to Polverelli.

22 The document can be found in BOM, Area 2. Area Amministrativa, Serie 1. Amministrazione e gestione, Sottoserie 1. Casa editrice Valentino Bompiani % C., 2.1.1.2 Censura fascista: Ministero della cultura popolare. Segnatura 1369ACEB. 01/01/1934 – 31/12/1942. As well as an outright ban, the regime would often adopt less restrictive measures when it wanted to censor a publication. The Ministry might indicate simply that there should be no further reprints; it might also limit distribution to bookshops, rather than itinerant booksellers so as to make it more difficult for the masses to access a book. See, for example, Pavolini's report on the ongoing purge of the book market to the Chamber of Fasces and Corporations in April 1940 which provides a clear summary of the different types of restriction applied: '425 works have been confiscated; 40 have been withdrawn from circulation; 45 cannot be reprinted; 74 cannot be sold by itinerant booksellers and 4 have been allowed to be reprinted with modiications'. Quoted in *Giornale della libreria* LIII/18 (4 May 1940): 70.

23 Marquette (2018: Appendices 7–9) has made a close analysis of some of the translations and the changes that were made to the text. Only a few details can be attributed unequivocably to a form of self-censorship and she confirms that no changes were imposed on the translations by the Ministry (2018: 66).

24 In addition to the scholars already cited, other examples of this dominant interpretation of the censorship of *Americana* are D'Ina and Zaccaria (1988: 38–46) and Manacorda (1973). An exception is Marquette (2018: 20) who also underlines the 'flexibility' of Pavolini in authorising the book.

References

Albonetti, Pietro. 1994. *Non c'è tutto nei romanzi: Leggere romanzi stranieri in una casa editrice negli anni Trenta [Not Everything Is in Novels. Reading Foreign Novels in a 1930s Publishing House]*. Milano: Fondazione Arnoldo e Alberto Mondadori.

Billiani, Francesca. 2020. *National Cultures and Foreign Narratives in Italy, 1903–1943*. Translated by Georgia Wall. Cham, Switzerland: Palgrave Macmillan.

Bompiani [Publishing house]. 1998. *Catalogo Generale Bompiani 1929–1999 [Bompiani General Catalogue 1929–1999]*. Milano: RCS Libri.

Bompiani, Valentino. 1988. *Caro Bompiani. Lettere con l'editore [Dear Bompiani. Letters with the Publisher]*. Milano: Bompiani.

Translating the Enemy in Fascist Italy: The Anthology Americana

Bonsaver, Guido. 2007. *Censorship and Literature in Fascist Italy*. Toronto: University of Toronto Press.

Bonsaver, Guido. 2013. *Mussolini censore. Storie di letteratura, dissenso e ipocrisia* [*Mussolini Censor. Stories of Literature, Dissent and Hypocrisy*]. Roma and Bari: Laterza.

Cecchi, Emilio. 1939. *America amara* [*Bitter America*]. Firenze: G. C. Sansoni.

Decleva, Enrico. 1993. *Arnoldo Mondadori*. Torino: UTET.

D'Ina, Gabriella and Zaccaria, Giuseppe (eds.). 1988. *Caro Bompiani. Lettere con l'editore* [*Dear Bompiani. Letters with the Publisher*]. Milano: Bompiani.

Dunnett, Jane. 2015. *The 'Mito Americano' and Italian Literary Culture Under Fascism*. Roma: Aracne editrice.

Esposito, Edoardo. 2009. 'Per La Storia Di "Americana"' [For the history of Americana], in E. Esposito (ed.), *Il Dèmone dell'anticipazione. Cultura, letteratura, editoria in Elio Vittorini* [*The Demon of Anticipation. Culture, Literature, Publishing in Elio Vittorini*]. Milano: Il Saggiatore, 31–44.

Fabre, Giorgio. 1998. *L'elenco: censura fascista, editoria e autori ebrei* [*The List: Fascist Censorship, Publishing and Jewish Authors*]. Torino: Silvano Zamorani editore.

Fabre, Giorgio. 2007. 'Fascism, Censorship and Translation', in F. Billiani (ed.), *Modes of Censorship and Translation: National Contexts and Diverse Media*. Manchester: St. Jerome, 27–59.

Fabre, Giorgio. 2018. *Il Censore e l'editore. Mussolini, i libri, Mondadori* [*The Censor and the Publisher. Mussolini, Books, Mondadori*]. Milano: Fondazione Arnoldo e Alberto Mondadori.

Ferme, Valerio. 2002. *Tradurre è tradire: la traduzione come sovversione culturale sotto il fascismo* [*To Translate Is to Betray: Translation as Cultural Subversion under Fascism*]. Ravenna: Longo.

Gadducci, Fabio, Gori, Leonardo and Lama, Sergio. 2020. *Eccetto Topolino. Lo scontro culturale tra fascismo e fumettiì* [*Except Topolino. The Cultural Battle between Fascism and Comics*]. Rome: Nicola Pesce Editore.

Greco, Lorenzo. 1983. *Censura e scrittura. Vittorini, lo pseudo-Malaparte, Gadda* [*Censorship and Writing. Vittorini, the Pseudo-Malaparte, Gadda*]. Milano: Il Saggiatore.

Lee Masters, Edgar. 1993. *Antologia di Spoon River. A cura di Fernanda Pivano. Con tre scritti di Cesare Pavese* [*Spoon River Antholog. Edited by Fernanda Pivano. With Three Pieces by Cesare Pavese*]. Translated by Fernanda Pivano. Torino: Einaudi.

Manacorda, Giuliano. 1973. 'Storia minore ma non troppo. Come fu pubblicata Americana' [Not Such a Minor Story. How Americana Was Published], *Rapporti*, (dicembre): 21–6.

Marquette, Catherine. 2018. *Americana (1942): An Analysis of Its Paratext and Translations*. Unpublished dissertation. School of Languages and Area Studies, University of Portsmouth.

Merino, Raquel and Rabadan, Rosa. 2002. 'Censored Translations in Franco's Spain: The TRACE Project. Theatre and Fiction (English-Spanish)', *TTR: Traduction, Terminologie, Rédaction*, 15(2): 125–52.

Nottola, Francesca. 2010. 'The Einaudi Publishing House and Fascist Policy on Translations', in C. Rundle and K. Sturge (eds.), *Translation under Fascism*. Basingstoke: Palgrave Macmillan, 178–200.

Pavese, Cesare. 1966. *Cesare Pavese. Lettere 1924‑1944* [*Cesare Pavese. Letters 1924–1944*]. Torino: Einaudi.

Pavese, Claudio. 2009. 'L'avventura di *Americana*' [The adventure of Americana], *Bibliologia. An International Journal of Bibliography, Library Science, History of Typography and the Book*, 4: 139–78.

Pavese, Claudio. 2018. *L'avventura di Americana. Elio Vittorini e la storia travagliata di una mitica antologia* [*The Adventure of Americana. Elio Vittorini and the Difficult History of a Legendary Anthology*]. Milano: Edizioni Unicopli.

Petrillo, Gianfranco. 2020. 'Che ti dice la Patria? / 3 (Segue)' [What Does Your Country Tell You? Part 3 (Continued)], *Tradurre – Pratiche, Teorie, Strumenti*, (18). https://rivistatradurre.it/che-ti-dice-la-patria-3-segue/

Pound, Ezra. 1943. 'Scrittori e zavorra' [Writers and Dead Weight], *Meridiano di Roma* 18, 2 May: 1.

Ristuccia, Cristiano Andrea. 2000. 'The 1935 Sanctions against Italy: Would Coal and Oil Have Made a Difference?', *European Review of Economic History*, 4(1): 85–110.

Roig-Sanz, Diana. 2021. 'The International Institute of Intellectual Cooperation: Translation Policies in the Interwar Period (1925–1946)', in C. Rundle (ed.), *The Routledge Handbook of Translation History*. London and New York: Routledge, 452–68.

Rundle, Christopher. 2010. *Publishing Translations in Fascist Italy*. Oxford: Peter Lang.

Rundle, Christopher. 2018. 'Translation and Fascism', in F. Fernández and J. Evans (eds.), *The Routledge Handbook of Translation and Politics*. London and New York: Routledge, 29–47.

Rundle, Christopher and Sturge, Kate (eds.). 2010. *Translation under Fascism*. Basingstoke: Palgrave Macmillan.

Sinibaldi, Caterina. 2013. 'Dangerous Children and Children in Danger. Reading American Comics Under the Italian Fascist Regime', in C. Kelen and B. Sundmark (eds.), *The Nation in Children's Literature: Nations of Childhood*. London and New York: Routledge, 53–68.

Sinibaldi, Caterina. 2016. 'Between Censorship and Innovation: The Translation of American Comics during Italian Fascism', *New Readings*, 16: 1–21.

Tranfaglia, Nicola and Vittoria, Albertina. 2000. *Storia degli editori italiani. Dall'unità alla fine degli anni Sessanta* [*The History of Italian Publishing. From Unification to the End of the 1960s*]. Roma; Bari: Laterza.

Tyšš, Igor. 2017. 'Discourse Camouflage in the Representation of American Literature in the Literary Magazine "Mladá tvorba"', *World Literature Studies*, 9(2): 73–85.

Tyšš, Igor. 2022. 'The Allen Ginsberg "Case" and Translation (in) History: How Czechoslovakia Elected and Then Expelled the King of May', in C. Rundle, A. Lange and D. Monticelli (eds.), *Translation Under Communism*. Cham, Switzerland: Springer International Publishing, 315–49.

Van Wagenen, Julianne. 2019. 'Masters vs. Lee Masters: The Legacy of the Spoon River Author Between Illinois and Italy', *Forum Italicum*, 53(3): 679–98.

Vandaele, Jeroen. 2010. 'It Was What It Wasn't: Translation and Francoism', in C. Rundle and K. Sturge (eds.), *Translation under Fascism*. Basingstoke: Palgrave Macmillan, 84–116.

Vittorini, Elio (ed.). 1941. *Americana. Raccolta di narratori. Dalle origini ai nostri giorni* [*Americana. A Collection of Narrators. From the Origins to Current Times*]. Milano: Valentino Bompiani & C. [Version 1 with notes by Vittorini: never distributed].

Vittorini, Elio (ed.). 1942a. *Americana. Raccolta di narratori. Dalle origini ai nostri giorni* [*Americana. A Collection of Narrators. From the Origins to Current Times*]. Milano: Valentino Bompiani & C. [Version 2 with preface by Cecchi and notes by Vittorini: never distributed].

Vittorini, Elio (ed.). 1942b. *Americana. Raccolta di narratori. Dalle origini ai nostri giorni* [*Americana. A Collection of Narrators. From the Origins to Current Times*]. Milano: Valentino Bompiani & C. [Version 3 with preface by Cecchi and notes compiled by Cecchi: published in Nov-Dec 1942].

Vittorini, Elio. 1957. *Diario in pubblico* [*Public Diary*]. Milano: Bompiani.

Vittorini, Elio. 1985. *I libri, la città, il mondo: lettere 1933–1943* [*Books, the City, the World: Letters 1933–1943*]. Torino: Einaudi.

Vittorini, Elio. 2008. *Letteratura arte società. Articoli e interventi 1926–1937* [*Literature, Art, Society. Articles and speeches 1926–1937*]. Torino: Einaudi.

24

THE CENSORSHIP OF TRANSLATIONS AND FOREIGN BOOKS DURING THE PORTUGUESE DICTATORSHIP (1934–1974)

Teresa Seruya

24.1 Core Issues and Topics

24.1.1 The Institutions of Censorship (1934–1974)

24.1.1.1 The Estado Novo

The Portuguese First Republic (1910–1926) was overthrown in 1926 by a coup d'état that established a military dictatorship, followed by what became known as the Estado Novo (New State) in 1933, after the ratification of a new Constitution. The Estado Novo lasted until 1974, with the advent of the Carnation Revolution, which ended the longest dictatorship in Western Europe. It is generally agreed that this was an authoritarian, corporatist, anti-parliamentary, anti-democratic and anti-liberal regime that endured through violent means, both preventative and punitive, through the deployment of a political police force and through censorship, control by the Armed Forces, an effective corporatist configuration, a relative social consensus regarding colonialism, and an efficient propaganda apparatus in the areas of education and labour (cf. Rosas 2020: 47–62). The regime's central figure was António de Oliveira Salazar (1889–1970), head of Government ('President of the Council') between 1933 and 1968, followed by Marcelo Caetano (1906–1980), from 1968 to 1974.

24.1.1.2 Legislation

Censorship was institutionalised as early as 1933 (Decree-Law no. 22469/1933), although the legislation was largely a continuation of the (prior) censorship of the press that had begun with the military dictatorship. Although the 1933 Constitution guaranteed 'freedom of expression under any and all circumstances', the aforementioned Decree-Law, curiously issued on the same day (11 April), stated that censorship served the purpose of 'preventing the perversion of public opinion given its [censorship's] function as a social force' and would be carried out in such a way as to nullify 'all factors' likely to 'direct' Portuguese public opinion 'against truth, justice, morals, good

DOI: 10.4324/9781003149453-30

The Routledge Handbook of Translation and Censorship

governance and the common good' (in Ó 1996: 140). These 'factors' were plainly linked to the media (press and radio), entertainment (theatre and film), periodical publications and lastly, books. In fact, between 1926 and 1933, censorship only targeted periodicals, posters and pamphlets with political and social content. However, as early as 1933, Oliveira Salazar, by then head of government, showed great concern over the matter of books, and requested a report on the subject from the director of Censorship Services, Major Álvaro Salvação Barreto (between 1932 and 1944). This document, entitled 'Immoral Readings, Political and Social Propaganda against the Estado Novo and their Suppression', would become the basis of the Censorship's[1] practices in relation to non-periodical publications. The 1933 Decree-Law was reinforced three years later by Decree-Law no. 26589/1936, published alongside the *Censorship Services Regulations* issued by the Presidency of the Council, which forbade 'the distribution and sale in Portugal of newspapers, magazines and any other foreign publications dealing with proscribed topics, which were destined for the national market' (Rodrigues 1980: 71).

As for books (whether Portuguese, foreign or translations), the Censorship began its activities in 1934. Unlike periodical publications, theatre and films, books (whether Portuguese or foreign) were not subject to prior censorship, so they made their way to the censorship services through post-publication seizures in bookshops, interception of postal correspondence (in the case of private book orders) or, if considered dangerous, when found in the possession of private individuals (for example, during luggage checks). It was the responsibility of various institutions to forward these books to the censors. Their closest partner was the political police, PIDE/DGS (who 'paid visits' to bookshops, for example), followed by the Post Office (CTT), Customs and, sporadically, the regular police force (PSP). Occasionally, editors and (Portuguese) authors submitted draft manuscripts to the Censorship Commission, more or less of their own accord, so as to avoid future confiscation and loss of revenue.

In 1944, the Censorship became an official training and political propaganda agency when it was incorporated into the SPN (National Propaganda Secretariat), later rechristened SNI (National Information Secretariat), which in turn reported directly to Salazar (Decree-Law no. 33545). The final major change in legislation came after Salazar's death in 1968, when Marcelo Caetano became his successor. Despite the hopes placed on the 'Primavera Marcelista' (Marcelist Spring), Decree-Law no. 150/72 of 5 May 1968, while abolishing the main Censorship agency (the Directorate-General for Censorship Services), nonetheless upheld the ethos of the social role of censorship—'the need to defend the highest interests of the nation'—as set out in 1933 (Azevedo 1999: 463ff.). In the early 1970s, the array of books that were the subject of reports and the respective workflow changed. Reports were now issued by the Directorate-General for Information, the agency that replaced the National Propaganda Secretariat, subsequently renamed the State Secretariat for Information and Tourism. This agency reported to the head of Government, namely Caetano, after 1968. Essentially, a report was requested from this organisation's Office of Studies. Next, information was sought by or provided to the Judicial Police or to the Directorate-General of Security (formerly PIDE) so that these agencies could proceed with the confiscation of banned books and respective 'criminal proceedings' or, should the books be cleared, their return to the publishers. Banned foreign books were returned to the importers. The Directorate-General for Information had final say in all decisions.

24.1.1.3 The Agents: the Censors ('Readers' and 'Decision-makers')

The agents of the Censorship (around 85 in number) were, for the most part (80%), army officers, ranging in rank from Ensign to Colonel. They were, on occasion, promoted over the course of their service as censors. In effect, we should emphasise the importance of the military component in the machinery of censorship during the military dictatorship and the Estado Novo, which was only demilitarised gradually, and to a minimal degree (cf. Gomes 2006: 97). This is, in fact, a defining feature of Portuguese censorship, when compared with Italian fascism, National Socialism and even Francoist Spain. Only long after World War II did a few civilians join the censors' unit (Gomes 2006: 12).

24.1.1.4 Procedures

On arrival at the Censorship via the channels described above, books were then distributed among readers, who would number (until 1971) and date each report, generally issuing one of three recommendations: 'authorised', 'authorised with cuts', or 'banned'. Uncertainty was rare, but some reports do exist where no decision was reached. Then, on the same day, or a few days later, the director of the service rubber-stamped these reports, either ratifying the recommendation (almost always) or occasionally opposing it, with or without comments.

The censors prepared these reports based on specific legal requirements. The reasoning behind each recommendation detailed what specific contents threatened the stability and preservation of the regime, and took into account not only legal directives, but also prevalent governmental political practice, press censorship, and so on. As trusted readers of 'suspect' materials, the censors were not meant to issue subjective judgments or to apply personal criteria. In effect, in the 1970s (until 1974) the reports invariably included the legislation on which the censors based their decisions. As a consequence, despite some minor stylistic differences, they adopted, for the most part, a fairly uniform discourse.

Regarding the criteria for assessing books (as well as pamphlets and brochures), it should be noted that no author or topic was ever summarily rejected *a priori,* that is, each case was reviewed on its merits. For example, different works by D.H. Lawrence, Jean-Paul Sartre and Bertolt Brecht were either banned and authorised, depending on the work in question. In addition to the primary goal of not undermining the foundations of the regime, the potential damage of censorship to the regime's international reputation was also considered. This was the case of Colette's *Chéri,* whose translation in Portugal by José Saramago (1960), included a note by a censor (R4484/64)[2] to the effect that even the French government had honoured the author, and that it might not be judicious to ban the work. Nevertheless, it was banned.

The fact that some topics were already covered in the press; that a film based on a particular book had already been released in Portugal (see R6942/61 on *Spartacus* by Howard Fast, or R6991/62 on *A Ciocara* by Alberto Moravia); that its author was a renowned 'canonical' writer, such as Hemingway or Gorky, or a famous individual such as Einstein could also lead to the grudging approval of a book. In the 1960s, the latter argument would also apply to authors such as Albert Camus, Bertrand Russell and G.B. Shaw. In the 1970s, particularly after 1972, a significant change in the censors' decisions regarding some authors and subjects is noticeable—towards Marxism, for example, which was treated with less ideological stringency.

24.1.2 *General Perceptions of Translation during the Estado Novo*

Regarding translators, while it is true that there are many who, to this day, have not been identified, others belonged to the cultural elites of the time, namely writers, philosophers and visual artists. Even so, translation was held in little esteem, since the ability to read the works in the original language was viewed as a sign of cultural superiority. An eloquent example of this was the monthly magazine *Ocidente,* which published in 1943 a scathing denunciation of what it described as an 'epidemic of translations' and decried the 'denationalising impulses' and 'mental lethargy' revealed in the high number of translations (quoted in *Livros de Portugal*,1943, No. 15/16, p. 2). This resulted in a 'Statute of translations', issued by Portuguese publishers and booksellers (*Livros de Portugal*, 1943, No. 17/18, p.5), but which did little to change things. In 1960, in the same magazine, the same agents reported on the extent to which the translation of literature was considered 'astonishingly' unfaithful to the original (*Livros de Portugal*, 1943 No. 19, p.1–2). This was attributed to the linguistic incompetence of translators who, as well as writing in often incorrect Portuguese, did not shy away from adding, omitting or interpreting the original texts at will. Testimonies from the end of the decade continue in much the same vein.

24.1.3 Corpus and Methodology

The starting point for the study of book censorship in Portugal is the analysis of the set of reports prepared by censors for each particular book. These reports were numbered and dated by the censors, from the inception of the agency's activity on 16 April 1934 (Report no. 1) until the eve of the Carnation Revolution on 25 April (report dated 22 April 1974). They are, for the most part, housed in the Torre do Tombo National Archives (ANTT). The organisation of this documentation does not allow us to ascertain the exact number of reports. The latest number is close to 10,000, a figure that includes the reports missing from ANTT (equivalent to 22.8%). Although some of these have been cited in works published on censorship in Portugal, and a few others (close to 30) have been traced back to private archives, it has not been possible, so far, to determine the whereabouts of the majority (they are likely lost or remain in private hands). As such, a total of 7646 reports was examined. Of these, the percentage of Portuguese-language authors (Portuguese, Brazilian and unidentified Portuguese language) is 30.6%. In turn, of the reports examined, 30.7% involve translations. Of these, 60.1% were approved and 35.1% were banned. As for foreign volumes, some of which were considered for translation, these make up 37.9% of the total of reports examined. Of these foreign volumes, 41.9% were authorised and 55.7% were banned.

We shall present the concrete results of our analysis, which is necessarily selective, while nonetheless representative, of the reports referring to translations and foreign books, both literary and non literary, organised by decade, which enabled us to detect dominant trends at the political level, to which institutional Censorship is inevitably linked. Thus, the 1930s, beginning in 1934, were dominated by the Spanish Civil War (1936–1939) and the beginning of World War II; the 1940s, by World War II and its impact on the dictatorship; and the 1950s, by a certain greyness, devoid of major political upheavals. Conversely, the 1960s witnessed the beginning of the African Colonial War (1961) and the death of Oliveira Salazar, accompanied by expectations of a loosening of repression, which remained largely unmet until 1974, with the military coup and the ensuing Carnation Revolution. The major topics that raised suspicion were, not suprisingly, closely related with the foundations of the regime, from a political, social and religious point of view. There are thus recurring topics during the 40 years of the Censorship, the difference being one of emphasis, depending on the times: first and foremost, politics and ideology, followed by sexuality and morality and, to a lesser extent, religion and colonialism.

24.1.4 The Fear of Translation: Ideas Regarding Translation in the Censorship

Although censors were not be expected to develop a theory of translation, it is possible to glean from their analysis of foreign books (whether originals or translations) a view of translation that, incidentally, would remain largely unchanged over four decades. Censors were interested in translation neither as a process nor a product, but only as a function, that is, in its effect on its audience. In short, translation gave a variety of readers access to foreign texts, which is why it was considered a 'social peril' (as described in R374/1937).

Essentially, readers were divided into two categories: the 'masses' and the 'elites'. The latter category of 'educated people' included foreign language readers, on the one hand, and, on the other, the professional classes who read technical, scientific or apolitical books. When it was determined that a book would interest only the elites, it would be approved, even if its topic might otherwise merit censorship, due to the small number of target readers. In addition, it was argued that elites had already formed an opinion on controversial issues, so a ban would prove ineffective. The justification for the approval of *Études socialistes* [*Socialist Studies*] by Jean Jaurès, published at the end of the 19th century, is a case in point: 'A book on socialist doctrine whose availability for purchase shall not become an issue; the majority will not be able to read it, and the small number who will is limited, and it [...] will not alter their beliefs in the least' (R520/1938). Conversely, the rationale for banning *Révolutionnaires, où allez-vous?* [*Revolutionaries, Where Are You Going?*], by Jove and Jean Nocher (1935), a volume explicitly intended for translation, is predicated on its being aimed 'at the uneducated', with its plain language and 'easily grasped' examples. The conclusion is that 'a translation into Portuguese would be exceedingly inconvenient' (R667/1938).

Furthermore, the danger of translation outweighed the literary quality of the work. For example, Colette's *Chéri*, translated by José Saramago (see above), despite being considered 'a literary masterpiece', was deemed 'one of the works [...] the least worthy of publicity. Not to mention that the Portuguese translation [would] facilitate the dissemination and assimilation of the work's intrinsic evil' (R8567/1969). In short, one might speak of a fear of translation. In 1960, shortly before the beginning of the Colonial War, censors described the novellas by African-American writer Richard Wright collected in *Uncle Tom's Children* (1938), as 'an apologetic testimonial of black racism'. The Portuguese translation of 'the passionate work written by an African American' was judged to wield great political power because 'once disseminated among us (namely in our Overseas African provinces), [it] would be like adding fuel to the already blazing fire that threatens our national integrity' (R6636/1960).

24.2 Historical Perspectives: General Trends by Decade

The Spanish Civil War was the first major external challenge to the new regime in the 1930s although Salazar's support for the Francoist regime was unequivocal and tangible, and could indeed be said to have contributed to General Franco's victory. It is not surprising, therefore, that any publication issuing from Spain or dealing with events or political actors during the Civil War underwent rigorous examination. It was only to be expected that some readers would attempt to counterbalance the one-sided war reports: since radio and the press were both subject to prior censorship, books were seen as a likely source of information, provided they eluded interception and seizure of correspondence. Of the nearly 1300 titles that were submitted to the Censorship between 1934 and 1939, 66 dealt with the Spanish Civil War. Of these, 39 were banned (half of the total number of banned titles). It is not surprising that the number of banned titles (favourable to the Republican side of the conflict) during the Spanish Civil War always exceeded the number of authorised ones (cf. Seruya 2018a: 236–255).

Several books on the conflict arrived in Portugal in the same year they were published. This was the case for the fictional autobiography by Ramón J. Sender, *Contraataque* (1937) [*The War in Spain*], and the French translation of Anton Sieberer's *Spanien gegen Spanien* [*Spain against Spain*], published in Geneva in 1937.

The Routledge Handbook of Translation and Censorship

Books authored by women constituted a substantial group (see Seruya 2018b). All of them were sympathetic to the Republican cause: Clara Campoamor (*La révolution espagnole vue par une républicaine,* R444/1937), Marguerite Jouve (*Vu, en Espagne,* R485/1937), Sofia Blasco (*Peuple d'Espagne,* R604/1938), Geneviève Tabouis (*Chantage à la guerre,* R665/1938), Katharine Stewart-Murray, Duchess of Atholl (*Searchlight on Spain,* R690/1938), Pilar Fidalgo (*Une jeune mère dans les prisons de Franco,* R725/1938), and Dolores Ibarruri (*Pour la victoire,* R962/1939).[3] These were all banned, with the exception of Clara Campoamor's volume. This clearance is surprising, since the author was a Republican politician and a women's rights activist who promoted the feminist movement in Spain and was forced into exile at the beginning of the Civil War. She lived in exile in Argentina and France, and died in Lausanne (1972); Francoist Spain never authorised her return.

As for fiction, two cases stand out. One is the novel *Les grands cimetières sous la lune* (1938) [*Great Cemeteries under the Moon*], by Georges Bernanos. Bernanos was a French writer and journalist working in Spain during the Civil War. He belonged to a group of writers who reported on the conflict without directly participating in it (Hurcombe 2011, see Chapters 1 and 7). Bernanos, like François Mauriac, initially sympathised with the Nationalist cause but subsequently rejected the terror it visited upon the civilian population. The ban on this book (R638/1938) was particularly effective, since it was only after the Carnation Revolution that its first translation into Portuguese was published (in 1988). It should be noted, however, that translations of other works by this author were in circulation during the Estado Novo. Another prominent author is Sender, an outspoken opponent of Franco who was forced into exile after the end of the Civil War. In Spain he is considered one of the greatest novelists of his generation, but he was not read in Portuguese until 1974. Three of his political works of fiction ended up at the Censorship, and all were banned: *A Love letter from Moscow* (1936), *Madrid-Moscow* (1936) and *The War in Spain* (1937).

The presence of texts from the Basque Country is surprising. The French translation of Spanish priest Iñaki de Aberrigoyen's *Seven Months and Seven Days in Franco's Spain* (1938) arrived at the Censorship via the Post Office, which may signify that it was originally a private book order that, for whatever reason (perhaps its title), raised suspicion. The censor's assessment was harsh: '[a]n inept and violent attack on Spanish Nationalism, accusing Franco's supporters of the barbarities committed by the Communists' (R707/1938). Three banned Basque works are worth mentioning: *The Basque Problem* (R736/1938) by Dr de Azpilikoeta [sic] (1938); *Basque Clergy*, unidentified author (R732/1938) and *The Case of Basque Catholics* by J. de Hiriartia (R731/1938). For the Catholic Salazar and his regime, which received the support of the Catholic Church, Basque nationalism was somehow more questionable than solidarity with the Catholic victims of Republican persecution. Finally, it should be mentioned that the topic of 'Guernica' (the bombings that took place in April 1937) also reached the Censorship. Unsurprisingly, *Clamor de Euzkadi ante la destrucción de Gernika* [*The Basque Country's Outcry over the Destruction of Guernica*] was banned, as it was deemed a 'mouthpiece for Spanish Marxists' (R473/1937).

There were, of course, books on the Spanish Civil War that were approved. The clearance, in 1940, of Robert Brasillach and Maurice Bardèche's *History of the Spanish War* (R1165/1940) is not surprising, considering that Brasillach collaborated intellectually with National Socialism, and was a racist and anti-Semitic supporter of the Vichy regime. He was executed for treason in 1945. The speedily translated book was published in 1939 (2nd ed., 1940), which means that the translation had been completed by the time the original was assessed by the censors. This history book was virtually without competitors in Portugal over the next two decades, despite the fact that it was not republished during the period. Only in 1961 did the Spanish translation of *The Spanish Civil War* by Hugh Thomas introduce a more balanced point of view (see Loff 2006). As for Jérôme and

376

Jean Tharaud, two French pro-Francoist writers, when their book *Cruelle Espagne [Cruel Spain]* (1938) was approved (R653/1938), the two brothers were well known to the Portuguese authorities. It was in fact the practice of the SNI to invite foreign personalities to Portugal to take them on a selective tour of the country, as a way out of its financial straits. Jérôme Tharaud, together with Gabriela Mistral, François Mauriac, Ramiro de Maetzu, Maurice Maeterlinck, and Miguel de Unamuno, among others, were part of a 'cultural embassy' that visited Portugal in June 1935 (see Medina 1996: 89f.) But the fact that one of the brothers had been an official guest of the country did not in any way guarantee the automatic approval of their book.

The most significant reports of the first half of the 1940s refer to propaganda material originating from Germany and Great Britain (rarely from France or Italy). This sub-corpus deserves special attention, since these translations were made in Germany and Great Britain, or in their respective embassies in Lisbon, with the addition of texts originally produced in Portuguese. Salazar's foreign policy was defined, as early as 1939, as one of 'geometric neutrality' in relation to the warring countries and was later replaced by a 'collaborative neutrality' (with the Allies) (Ferreira 1996: 666ff.). This stance was clearly mirrored in the censorship of the above-mentioned materials. However, it must be recalled that during this period Lisbon was a privileged espionage hub for both sides of the conflict (Telo 1990; Pimentel 2018).

While it is true that there was a current within the regime that sympathised with National Socialism (youth organisations such as Portuguese Youth and workers' associations such as the National Foundation for Joy at Work, for example, were openly inspired by their Nazi counterparts), the censors tried to comply with Salazar's guidelines, maintaining equal distance from Great Britain and Germany: each faction could defend and praise its own policies but never attack or defame the enemy (see R1528/42). Hitler, 'the head of the German state' (R992/1940), could not be the object of mockery in British books (see R1192/40, on a forbidden translation of a book on Hitler by Hermann Rauschning), but the Germans similarly could not ridicule Britain or Churchill (R2324/43; R2336/43). Occasionally, the German Embassy expressed its opposition to the Commission's assessments, and the Commission would acquiesce (R1217/40; R2319/43).

It is clear that the Commission was unable to conceal both its preference for the German regime and its distrust of democracy: the Portuguese translation of Emil Ludwig's *Die neue heilige Allianz* (1938) [*The New Sacred Alliance*] was banned for being 'an attack on all regimens [sic] of authority and an exaltation of democracies' (R771/39). Moreover, words such as 'anti-fascism' or 'pacifism' had a negative connotation, since both were viewed as 'communist propaganda'. Antisemitism was not an integral part of the regime's ideology, but it does surface sporadically. For example, information on the persecution of Jews by the Nazis was banned, namely in Victor Gollancz's book *Let my People Go* (R2295/43). Another example can be found in the report on Louis-Ferdinand Céline's *Bagatelles pour un massacre [Trifles for a Massacre]*, a clearly anti-Semitic book that was approved for the following reasons: 'Using humorous language, it presents the decline of the world under the influence of the Jews. It is a book that can be promoted and disseminated without any drawbacks. On the contrary, it could prove quite beneficial' (R569/1938).

The 1950s became known in Portugal as the 'Leaden Years' (1950–1958) (see Seruya and Moniz 2008: 3–20). The expression refers to the seeming political lull that started in 1949, when Marshal António O. F. Carmona, the regime-backed candidate, won the presidential elections, and succeeded in restoring 'order' in the 'streets' and 'peace in the souls', after relentless police action (Rosas 1994, 408). There was a vigorous resurgence of 'anti-communist, corporatist, Catholic, nationalist and ultramontane' discourses, as expressed in the regime's jargon (Rosas 1994.).

As for the topics monitored by the Censorship, the ideological climate of the 'Leaden Years' led to some abatement in the targeting of political and ideological works, while there was a significant increase in the targeting of literary and cultural works. However, the difference in the variety of works banned in each of these fields is not significant. The number of books about sexuality and morality also decreased, but their prohibition rate remained high.

Among the arguments in support of a ban, the labelling of a book as 'propaganda' (generally, Marxist) was perhaps the hardest to justify, not only because this label implicitly conceded the existence of 'good' propaganda, but also because censors themselves could not ignore that they worked for a propaganda agency (see above, the SPN). Bans on the grounds of propaganda applied to books related to Marxism-Leninism, the USSR or China, and works of fiction by leftist writers such as Paul Éluard (R5215/54) or Pablo Neruda (R5273/55). Conversely, anti-communist propaganda was fully embraced. As such, the French translation of *Murder in Mexico. The Assassination of Leon Trotsky* by Leandro A. S. Salazar and Julian Gorkin was authorised for circulation, because it revealed 'the fierce persecution to which Stalin's enemies [were] subjected abroad', turning this into 'an anti-communist propaganda book of sorts' (R4322/1950).

In the field of politics, it is necessary to emphasise the censors' discomfort with issues related to the defeat of Nazi Germany, democracy and war. This underscores the continuities with the 1940s and indicates that the allied victory over National Socialism was never entirely accepted by the majority of the members of the Censorship Commission. As such, the novel *Kaputt* by Curzio Malaparte, a 'staunch anti-fascist' author, was considered inappropriate by the censors because it did not seem 'apposite to unearth facts that the current dictates of international politics find advisable to leave behind' (R5481/1955). Similarly, pacifism and humanism were unwelcome topics: the first pages of *L'Enseigne de Gersaint* [*Gersaint's Sign*] by Louis Aragon were deemed 'an apology of the concept of humanity, which [took] precedence over, or worse, overshadowed the concepts of Fatherland and Nationality'. For the censors, the book also conveyed a 'morbid defeatism and many anti-militarist and pacifist ideas of a reddish persuasion' (R5208/1954).

As in the 1940s, the ban on literature considered pornographic and, in general, offensive to Christian morality, continued throughout the 1950s, supported by the claim that it was tantamount to a doctrine of 'social dissolution'. Two frequently banned authors were Louis-Charles Royer and Dino Segre (Pitigrilli). The Portuguese translation of the latter's *Painted Faces* prompted the censor to write: 'it is full of entirely corrupting thoughts and narratives, especially for the young' (R4613/51).

Another stigmatising word often applied to literature was that of 'realism'. Works by Busch, Lawrence and Dos Passos, among others, were banned due to their descriptions of how 'things really are', according to the censors. The association of realism with immorality was intended to create a fantasist and alienated image of the world. This association played an important role in the political agenda of the Portuguese authoritarian regime. In fact, the manipulation of the words 'propaganda' and 'realism' is a recurring and striking feature of the censors' reports.

The early 1960s inaugurated a new historical phase, marked by the beginning of the Colonial War in Angola in 1961 (the regime's 'Overseas war'). Thus, criticism of colonialism emerged as a new issue for the Censorship. In most cases, anti-colonial books referring to Cuba or the Algerian revolution, for example, were considered 'communist propaganda', defamation of the Portuguese administration and, above all, a 'threat to territorial integrity'. As for what was considered propaganda, some censors differentiated, for example, between propaganda and history, when justifying their decision to ban. As such, the French translation of Joel Carmichael's *A Short History of the Russian Revolution* was banned because, were it 'History' it would have been 'an objective and impartial record'. Rather, it revealed itself to be a 'incomplete, biased and propagandistic record of inconvenient partiality' (R7828/1966). Clearly, in Salazar's Portugal, those who assessed the books were never 'partial' since they invariably believed that they possessed the correct interpretation on the 'facts'. Dizzying heights of irony were reached when Lucien Goldmann's *Introduction to Kant's Philosophy* was approved with the following argument: 'The right to culture and thought justifies the free circulation of this book' (R8375/69).

In the 1960s, 'realism' remained, as in the 1950s, a stigmatising label, given its association with immorality. It was now applied to Italian neorealism. The books in question dealt with poverty, were 'anti-social in nature' and revealed 'immorality' (cf. R6621/60, regarding *Il Sempione strizza l'occhio al Frejus [The Twilight of the Elephant]* by Elio Vittorini, the Portuguese translation of which was banned). Political issues in neorealist novels were the object of the censors' most vehement disapproval, of which the Portuguese translation of Vasco Pratolini's *A Hero of Our Time* (1947) is a prime example (R7806/66). The report reveals the censor's persistent discomfort with Italian Fascism, National Socialism and World War II, over twenty years after their conclusion, while applying the negative label of 'speculation' to issues of sexuality considered too liberal, or to political positions sympathetic to communism.

But the censors' language also included subtle distinctions, such as that between 'sexuality' and 'sexualism'. Books with the word 'sexuality' in the title were considered scientific and serious and, as such, were not condemned; for example, *La sexualité [Sexuality]* by Dr. Willy and C. Jamont is described as 'a comprehensive study on sexuality, conceived and carried out in a purely scientific way', devoid therefore of 'any trace of sexualism' (R8349/69). On the contrary, 'sexualism' acquired an immoral, even pornographic, connotation. Yet, *Nymphomania* by American authors Albert Ellie and Edward Sagarin, which 'deals with issues of sexualism, was approved because it appeared before the Censorship Commission as a German translation. This 'put […] it out of reach of the majority of the Portuguese public' (R8368/69). In fact, we can observe a certain liberalisation of the Censorship in this area – as indicated, for example, in the approval of *The Function of the Orgasm* (R8477/69) by Wilhelm Reich.

In the years leading up to the April 1974 Revolution, there was a significant increase in the number of titles that reached the Censorship, considering that less than half a decade had elapsed (1970–1973 and, in 1974, only four months). In fact, a total of 1080 titles were reviewed, compared to around 1630 from 1960 to 1969. The specific case of translations is also illustrative. While the total number of translations among the titles reviewed in the 1960s was around 530, from 1970 to 1974 this number increased to almost 560. The ratio between authorised and banned translations is also significant. In the 1960s, 225 titles were authorised and 297 banned, while in the early 1970s, 363 were authorised and 180 banned. In other words, there was a sharp decrease in the number of banned titles. This ratio is seen again for foreign titles. In the 1960s, well over half of foreign titles were banned, compared with less than half in the early 1970s. This trend is reflected in the approval of key texts of Marxism-Leninism and related works of history and sociology, which previously would have been unlikely to receive such approval.

Marcelo Caetano's rule (1968–1974) following the death of Salazar did not, as a whole, bring about significant changes. This period is now considered a 'failed transition' (Rosas and Oliveira 2004). It is useful to remember that the new legislation on Censorship (1968, see above) while seemingly abolishing the department containing this designation, maintained and in fact strengthened not only the control over books but also the 'punishment' of those responsible for their arrival in the country (in the case of foreign books) or their circulation (Portuguese publishers). These agents were now literally criminalised. The censors' discourse became increasingly legalistic, as reflected in the practice of referencing the laws under which a particular book was banned. This new approach gave the censors' verdicts an air of objectivity, which was, in reality, nothing more than compliance with the law. It should be added that the Censorship functioned with unabated rigour until the eve of the Carnation Revolution (25 April), despite some signs pointing to the

The Routledge Handbook of Translation and Censorship

imminent demise of the regime. A case in point is General António de Spínola's *Portugal e o Futuro* [*Portugal and the Future*] (February 1974), which defended a political solution to the problem of the colonies, as well as the conspiracies of the Captains' Movement between the summer of 1973 and April 1974, aimed at overthrowing the Caetano government. It is nonetheless surprising that, in a State service linked to the head of Government and to the political police, and in which the military abounded, there appeared to have been no inkling of what lay ahead, as neither the activity nor the discourse of the censors seems to have been affected (at least in the reports found to date). As before, important essays on politics, ideology, and sexuality, as well as literature, continued to be the preferred targets of surveillance.

The relative abatement of censorship in this final phase was based on the distinction, now essential for the approval or banning of a book, between ideology and politics. While the former was now acceptable, the latter remained inherently dangerous. If a book, even a Marxist treatise, was deemed to have no 'political impact' because it remained 'theoretical and scientific', 'there [wa]s no need to interfere with its circulation', as noted in numerous reports. Lucien Goldmann's *Marxism and the Humanities* was approved in 1973 because it was 'an ideological work, without practical political implications' (PT-TT-SNI-DSC-13-7_m0737).[4] The Brazilian translation of André Piettre's *Marxismo* was approved in 1972 based on another argument that was common over the decades, namely that it was a 'didactic work aimed at scholars', as evident in the 'aridity of the questions addressed' (PT-TT-SNI-DSC-13-7_m0747). Conversely, the Portuguese translation of Adam Schaff's *Marxism and the Individual* was banned in 1972, with an explanation that illustrates the great demand enjoyed by Marxism-Leninism in those years: '[i]t might be considered a simple exploration of a doctrine that has already been much analysed, if it were not for the fact that the infiltration of a large quantity of works of a Marxist nature may appear to stoke movements of social unrest' (PT-TT-SNI-DSC-13-7_m=757). If a work was considered to be merely of a 'historical nature', it would be approved, as was the case of *Marx-Engels* by Jean Bruhat in 1973 (PT-TT-SNI-DSC-13-7_m0731). By contrast, a book bearing a title such as Solomon Losovski's *Marx and the Trade Unions* would be banned.

This distinction applied, in fact, to all thematic groups, including sexuality. While there may have been scientific theories and ideas about sexuality, accounts of sexual practices were categorised as 'immoral' and classified under 'pornography'. Thus, the Brazilian translation of Irving Wallace's *A Compelling Novel of One Man's Intimate Problem* was banned in 1974 for 'the crime of outrage to public morality' (PT-TT-SNI-DSC-13-7_m0297). Furthermore, the Portuguese translation of Trudy Baker and Rachel Jones's *Coffee, Tea or Me?* (PT-TT-SNI-DSC-13-7_m0591) was also banned in 1974 for the crime of 'incit[ement] to extra-marital relations'.

Scarcely two weeks before the Revolution, the emancipation of women was still considered a threat to the social order. The Portuguese translation of the novel by Claudie Broyelle, *La moitié du ciel* [*Half of Heaven*], was banned because emancipation (in China) was associated with the abolition of capitalism; it thereby constituted incitement to 'political struggle through violence' (PT-TT-SNI-DSC-13-7 _m0028). However, the *New Dictionary of Sexology* (by Hugo Beigel) despite dealing with topics considered 'shocking', was deemed to 'help demystify and even popularise some issues that should not remain hidden' (PT-TT-SNI-DSC-13-7_m0617) according to one censor. This is a somewhat surprising assertion under the circumstances, perhaps explained by his perception that the Censorship was absurd. Another possible explanation, in keeping with the final justification found in several reports, is that the book was approved to avoid generating the publicity invariably produced by a ban.

The distinction between ideology and politics was also applied to the field of religion. Any 'book on theology', 'based on the study of biblical texts', was guaranteed approval (such as the

Portuguese translation of Ernst Käsemann's *Jesus Means Freedom* in April 1973) (PT-TT-SNI-DSC-13-7_m0800). However, in response to a Portuguese translation of a German volume by Paulus Gesellschaft, *Christians and Marxists in a Changing World*, one censor commented, 'the arguments presented by the Communists seem to me to be too incisive', so the translated text was banned (R8726/1971). Admittedly, the censor does not identify any politics in Cardinal Maurice Roy's reflection on Pope John XXIII's encyclical, published in April 1963, which suggests that the translation was edited by the translator himself, Mário S. Barbosa. The censor writes in his report that 'there is nothing positive in the book, only moral principles. It may, however, be employed speculatively'. It was probably the use of the last adverb that led the final decision-maker to ban the work (PT-TT-SNI-DSC-13-8_m0034). What was definitely considered to belong to the realm of objectionable politics was any critical stance towards the Vatican (Holy See) or the Church as an institution. This is the case of Carlos Simões Coelho's translation of Nino Lo Bello's *The Vatican Empire*, in which 'progressives' present the Vatican as 'an emporium of unprecedented wealth, implicating the Pope in shady businesses, commercial scandals and injustices' (R8762/1970).

Conscientious objectors and racism are two themes linked, respectively, to the Colonial War and colonialism. They resulted in contradictory assessments. The translation of a volume on conscientious objectors was banned (1973), due to squeamishness surrounding 'a country [...] at war' (PT-TT-SNI-DSC-13-7_m0836). By contrast, racism could be discussed freely, as exemplified by the Portuguese translation (1973) of *A Rap on Race* by Margaret Mead and James Baldwin. The topic, which has become very controversial in recent years in Portugal, was judged at that time to be 'a problem entirely foreign to Portuguese society, and which [...] in no way affects it' (PT-TT-SNI-DSC-13-8_m0004). Brazilian Gilberto Freyre's 'lusotropicalism' (*Casa Grande e Sanzala*, 1933) contributed greatly to the establishment of a pervasive image of Portuguese colonisation as being quite different from British or Belgian colonisation, given the supposedly good relations with the local populations. Until the 1974 Revolution, there was no mention of colonialism in history lessons, much less of a slave-trading or racist past. In recent years, some sectors of society have vociferously contested this view.

24.3 New Debates

The first desideratum to investigate the present corpus is to find the missing reports, which will finally enable a truly systematic analysis of the documentation. For the time being, we are faced with two main tasks: first, a sociological study of the censors as members of the military, through biographical research and finer textual analysis of their respective discourses, with a view to a possible differentiation, and, secondly, to develop and complete the study on the effectiveness of the Censorship. While the former has never been done, the latter has been partially undertaken (Seruya and Moniz 2018: 306–27). The topic is in no way intended to whitewash the role of censorship as a 'coercive and forceful act that blocks, manipulates, and controls cross-cultural interaction in various ways' (Billiani 2009: 28), but simply to analyse, with maximum objectivity, the effects of a particular kind of agency of the dictatorial State. The truth is that the censors themselves reveal, in their reports, an awareness of the limits of their role, so numerous were the escape routes within the system: 1) first and foremost, the lack of prior censorship; 2) the clear impossibility of monitoring the entire publishing market (the actual confiscation of books might occur long after they were banned, which is why, in the meantime, they were able to circulate, despite being proscribed, as was the case of the novel *Gretta* by Erskine Caldwell, or the French translation of *Cell 2455. Death Row* by the American Caryl Chessmann); 3) the complicity between booksellers, bookshops, and private customers, who were given access to prohibited volumes;

4) the considerable ease of movement of books across borders (as in the case of several volumes by Simone de Beauvoir, brought over from France), and so on.

Moreover, it is certainly relevant to research the fate of the censored translations, as has already been done for Francoist Spain (Gómez Castro 2008; Ortega Sáez 2013) and was recently initiated for Portugal by M. Lin Moniz (Moniz 2022). After the 1974 Revolution, was there any desire and willingness to translate what had previously been proscribed? Were the censored translations reprinted, this time without cuts, or bearing the same excisions? Is there enough evidence to research cases of self-censorship in uncensored translations? What was the effect of these prohibitions on Portuguese culture?

Further Reading

Billiani, Francesca (ed.). 2007. *Modes of Censorship and Translation. National Contexts and Diverse Media.* Manchester, UK: St Jerome Publishing; USA, NY: Kinderhook.
A good introduction to translation and censorship. It covers different media and includes case studies from different cultures and historical periods.

Rundle, Christopher and Sturge, Kate (eds.). 2010. *Translation under Fascism.* Palgrave Macmillan
This book discusses the role of translation in the history of fascism, followed by solid, detailed overviews of the four European fascisms (Italy, Germany, Spain, and Portugal). The third section presents case studies focusing on literary exchanges, translation policies, WWII poetry anthologies and the staging of Shakespeare in Portugal during the Estado Novo.

Barros, Júlia Leitão de. 2022. *Censura. A Construção de uma Arma Política do Estado Novo.* Lisboa: Tinta-da-China
A critical rereading of different theoretical, political and sociological aspects of official censorship during the Estado Novo, focusing mainly on the press. This research with new insights makes clear how it functioned as a political weapon in the hands of the dictatorial government over four decades (1934–1974).

Notes

1 Censorship with a capital "C" refers to the official services that performed this function. Among the general population, this was the term by which they became known. In fact, the censors would call themselves 'The Censorship' in their own reports.
2 Reports will be identified with an R followed by the respective number and year.
3 Reports up to 1971 are, in effect, identified with an R, followed by an identification number and the respective date. Book titles have been reproduced as shown in the reports. Accessed at http://antt.dglab. gov.pt/pesquisar-na-torre-do-tombo/ between January-April 2021.
4 Between 1972 and 1974 the reports' identification system changed, in line with the alterations described above (1.1.2). I reproduce the reference number contained in each digitised unit.

References

Azevedo, Cândido de. 1999. *A Censura de Salazar e Marcelo Caetano*. Lisboa: Editorial Caminho.
Billiani, Francesca. 2009. 'Censorship', in M. Baker and G. Saldanha (eds.), *Routledge Encyclopaedia of Translation Studies*. 2nd ed. Abingdon: Routledge, 28–31.
Ferreira, José Medeiros. 1996. 'Neutralidade', in F. Rosas and J. M. Brandão de Brito (eds.), *Dicionário de História do Estado Novo*, vol. 2. Lisboa: Círculo de Leitores, 666–667.
Gomes, Joaquim Cardoso. 2006. *Os Militares e a Censura. A Censura à Imprensa na Ditadura Militar e Estado Novo (1926–1945)*. Lisboa: Livros Horizonte.
Goméz Castro, Cristina. 2008. 'The Francoist Censorship Casts a Long Shadow: Translations from the Period of the Dictatorship on Sale Nowadays', in T. Seruya, Teresa and M. Lin Moniz (eds.), *Translation and Censorship in Different Times and Landscapes*. Newcastle: Cambridge Scholars Publishing, 184–195.

Hurcombe, Martin. 2011. *France and the Spanish Civil War. Cultural Representations of the War Next Door, 1936–1945.* London: Routledge.

Livros de Portugal. 1943. Órgão Mensal de Informações Bibliográficas do Grémio Nacional dos Editores e Livreiros (1940ss). Dir António Maria Pereira. Lisboa: Imp. Soc., Ind. de Tipografia.

Loff, Manuel. 2006. "A memória da Guerra de Espanha em Portugal através da historiografia portuguesa", *Ler História*, 51 (2006): 77–131.

Medina, João (ed.). 1996. *História de Portugal,* Vol. XIII, *O Estado Novo – II: Opressão e Resistência.* Madrid: n.n.

Moniz, Maria Lin. 2022. 'A Revolução e os livros censurados no Estado Novo', in A. Lopes and M. Lin Moniz (eds.), *Mudam-se os tempos, mudam-se as traduções? Reflexões sobre os vínculos entre Revolução e tradução.* Lisboa: Universidade Católica Editora, 109–125.

Ó, Jorge Ramos do. 1996. 'Censura', in F. Rosas and J. M. Brandão de Brito (eds.), *Dicionário de História do Estado Novo,* vol. 1. Lisboa: Círculo de Leitores, 139–141.

Ortega Sáez, Marta. 2013. *Traducciones del franquismo en el mercado literario español contemporáneo. El caso de* Jane Eyre *de Juan G. de Luaces.* Tesis doctoral como requisito para la obtención del título de Doctora en Filología Inglesa, Universitat de Barcelona

Pimentel, Irene Flunser. 2018. *Espiões em Portugal durante a II Guerra Mundial.* 2nd ed. Lisboa: A Esfera dos Livros.

Rodrigues, Graça Almeida. 1980. *Breve História da Censura Literária em Portugal.* Lisboa: Instituto de Língua e Cultura Portuguesa.

Rosas, Fernando. 1994. *O Estado Novo (História de Portugal),* vol. 7, edited by José Mattoso. Lisboa: Editorial Estampa.

Rosas, Fernando. 2020. *O Século XX Português. Política, Economia, Sociedade, Cultura, Império .* Lisboa: Tinta-da-China, 17–115.

Rosas, Fernando and Oliveira, Pedro Aires. 2004. *A Transição Falhada. O Marcelismo e o fim do Estadodo Estado Novo (1968–1974).* Lisboa: Ed. Notícias.

Seruya, Teresa. 2018a. 'A Espanha e a Guerra Civil no Filtro da Censura em Portugal (1934–1940)', in *Misérias e Esplendores da Tradução no Portugal do Estado Novo.* Lisboa: Universidade Católica Editora, 236–255.

Seruya, Teresa. 2018b. 'Women and the Spanish Civil War in the Portuguese Censorship Commission 1936–1939', in G. Zaragoza Ninet, J. J. Martínez Sierra, B. Cerezo Merchán and M. Richart Marset (eds.), *Traducción, género y censura en la literatura y en los medios de comunicación.* Granada: Comares, 39–48.

Seruya, Teresa and Lin Moniz, Maria. 2008. 'Foreign Books in Portugal and the Discourse of Censorship in the 1950s', in T. Seruya and M. Lin Moniz (eds.), *Translation and Censorship in Different Times and Landscapes.* Newcastle: Cambridge Scholars Publishing, 3–20.

Seruya, Teresa and Lin Moniz, Maria. 2018. 'A eficácia da Censura ao livro no Estado Novo', in *Misérias e Esplendores da Tradução no Portugal do Estado Novo.* Lisboa: Universidade Católica Editora, 306–27.

Telo, António José. 1990. *Propaganda e Guerra Secreta em Portugal 1939–1945.* Lisboa: Perspectivas & Realidades.

25

CENSORSHIP AND PERFORMED TRANSLATED DRAMA IN PORTUGAL DURING THE *ESTADO NOVO* (1950–1970)

Manuela Carvalho

25.1 Core Issues and Topics

What role did theatre translation play on the cultural scene in *Estado Novo* (1933–1970) Portugal, and how did it contribute to cultural change, theatre creation and practice? In addition to the preceding questions, the chapter addresses questions such as which plays were translated and licensed to be performed, who translated them, and how the plays were circulated, as well as briefly describing how theatre censorship operated during the 1950–1970 period in Portugal.

25.1.1 Theatre, Theatre Translation and Censorship during the Estado Novo in Portugal

Located at the crossroads between literature and performance, as well as between the pluralities of textual production and reproduction in which the text is but one of the signs to be considered, theatre translation has witnessed increased academic interest in the last decades (Brodie 2022; Marinetti 2013; Aaltonen 2000). In the case of translated performed theatre, one must also contemplate the reconfigured text in the receiving culture and its networks of transmission and reception—the social dimension of translation and theatre. Certain scholars have even called attention to the role of the spectator in this context, the co-creative action that is inherent in live performance (Marinetti 2013; Johnston 2004). Thus, the context of production, dissemination and reception become paramount for understanding the rewriting of theatre across languages and cultures.

According to in-depth studies on censorship and theatre during the Portuguese fascist regime (Cabrera 2013; Santos 2004: 2006), performed theatre was the most repressed and controlled artistic practice. The censorship authorities closely scrutinised theatre through a dual intervention: first, the play script was submitted to the General Inspection Office (Inspecção Geral dos Espectáculos), which was part of the SNI (Secretariado Nacional de Informação—National Secretariat of Information). The play could be approved, approved with cuts or rejected. If cuts were substantial, the play had to be rewritten and submitted again to the censors for approval (Santos 2006:13). After that, the play had to be approved for the second time by the same censors,

384

DOI: 10.4324/9781003149453-31

who read the revised version of the play while they attended the general rehearsal in order to confirm that the cuts and changes had been implemented, supervise stage sets, props and costumes, and identify whether any innuendo had been added during the staging process (Cabrera 2013: 31). Even posters and playbills had to undergo inspection for approval. Actors described how censors, during general rehearsal, followed the text of the plays with torchlights in order to confirm that the text voiced by the actors corresponded to the revised play they were reading (Dolores 1984; Santos 2004: 273). The censorship authority restricted any attack on the Church, military or civil institutions, as well as references to social, moral, and political issues, particularly communist ideology. According to Santos (2006:13), this complex mechanism of repression had material and financial effects, and it could take a rather long time to obtain full approval for a play to be performed. Censorship, therefore, represented a clear constraint on theatre performance, which affected the life of theatre companies and programs at various venues (Santos 2004).

The relationship between censorship and theatre changed over the course of the *Estado Novo* regime, however, oscillating between more and less repressive periods. Censorship was influenced by national and international events as well as by changes at the level of the political structure and ministerial positions. It is noteworthy that by the end of 1950s, there was a consensus within the censorship commission that the manner in which censorship was being exercised was restricting the growth if not the very existence of Portuguese theatre. Consequently, a decree authorising a certain number of censored Portuguese and translated plays was approved in 1956. The dispatch also stated that, in the future, plays would only be censored on the following grounds: 'Immorality as the ultimate purpose. Covert or open propaganda of the communist doctrine'[1] (Censorship files: book 8, 1956. SNI-IGE/ANTT, in Cabrera 2013: 47). The social and political movements of the 1960s and the underlying events—such as the colonial war in Africa (begun in 1961), student riots or massive waves of emigration to Europe—combined with innovative theatrical and artistic practices that were taking place outside Portugal, such as the Living Theatre, *happenings* or Grotowsky's theories—gave rise to the introduction of new theatrical aesthetics and repertoires in Portugal, which attempted to react to all of these changes and discontents. Most of these reactions were expressed in translation.

Translated theatre has, for some reason, been neglected in studies on censorship and translation and censorship and theatre in Portugal, except for the odd article on specific translations. However, the work undertaken under the aegis of the TETRA[2] project clearly shows not only that translation was a major part of theatre repertoires in *Estado Novo*, but that it played a crucial role in the renewal of theatrical practices. Since the source cultures were located outside Portugal, they were seen as something far from the national reality and, therefore, more acceptable in the eyes of the censors (Carvalho 2015).

When one examines performed theatre during the *Estado Novo*, it is evident that the majority of performances occurred in state-controlled commercial theatre venues and were performed by state-controlled theatre companies. Two types of theatre prevailed: music hall style theatre (*teatro de revista*), on the one hand, and comedies and vaudeville-type plays or naturalistic plays, with well-known actors/actresses in the leading roles, on the other. The latter were mounted in 'commercial' theatre venues, located mainly in Lisbon. The commercial performances and theatre venues were governed by old-fashioned and repetitive theatrical formulas, and repertoires were filled mostly with translated plays, predominantly comedies imported from Spain and France. The task of translating theatre was not valued, for it was assumed that anyone could do it, even secretaries or assistants to theatre managers.

From the late 1950s onwards, groups of independent, amateur, experimental and university companies began proliferating in the main urban areas. These groups were marginal in the Portuguese

The Routledge Handbook of Translation and Censorship

cultural sphere, but they had an impact on the younger generations and were pivotal agents for change and for the creation of new forms of drama written in Portuguese. Translation was not only a vehicle for aesthetic and theatrical innovation but also the impulse behind the relative euphoria that prevailed in theatre circles after the Revolution (from 1974 on). A few of these experimental and amateur groups continued their work until recently (such as Teatro Experimental do Porto, TEP), and new ones were created in the post-revolution period, benefiting from the legacy of the earlier ones. It is important to recall that members of this generation had also lived abroad, many in exile, where they had had the opportunity to experience cultural and theatrical performances they hoped to bring back to Portugal. Importantly, the ambiguous status of the translated text, prone to manipulation by translators, provided a certain degree of productive freedom for performed translated drama, which incorporated new staging and performing techniques—even when performing classical, traditional or canonical plays; it also dealt with themes and issues that domestic plays simply could not deal with or stage. Thus, theatre translators—often playwrights, writers and practitioners—were theatre creators and practitioners who were promoting cultural renewal while bringing ideological and political issues to the stage. Furthermore, the repertoires of theatre companies reveal the potential to avoid censorship restrictions, underscoring the dysfunction of the latter. The examples that are presented in the following sections challenge the notion of the (in)accessibility of culture in an overtly ideological and repressive context like that of the *Estado Novo*.

25.2 Historical Perspectives

25.2.1 Translated Theatre in Experimental Theatre Companies and University Theatre Groups Repertoires

Numerous scholars have dedicated studies to the role of experimental theatre companies (Santos 2004; Rebello 1977) and university companies (Barata 2009) during the Salazar regime, particularly from the late 1950s on; however, the place of translation and the mechanisms of censorship can bring a fresh perspective on the impact and work of these performing groups.

Table 25.1 presents the most influential, prolific and audacious experimental companies at the time, but there are several others that survived only one or two years and performed only a few plays. With a few exceptions, they were concentrated in Lisbon and its outskirts. The majority of the plays in the repertoire of these companies were translated plays, with, exceptionally, a few Portuguese ones. In the selection of playwrights and plays, there were no clear criteria. Although a few theatre companies claimed the didactic purpose of bringing contemporary aesthetics and plays to the Portuguese stage, others stated the grander ambition of revitalising the national theatre. Nevertheless, there were playwrights and plays that spanned all the repertoires: a combination of avant-garde, absurdist theatrical experiments and canonical and classical plays, often modernised and adapted to please a contemporary Portuguese audience. Theatre companies and directors manifestly wished to capitalise on the success enjoyed by certain contemporary foreign playwrights, but they also continued to stage classical plays, adapting them to current aesthetic and ideological debates. Authors such as Harold Pinter, Samuel Beckett, August Strindberg, John Arden, Arnold Wesker, Fernando Arrabal, Eugène Inoesco, Friedrich Durrenmat, Max Frisch, Luigi Pirandello and Molière are represented in all the repertoires. The closer one gets to the late 60s and early 70s, however, the more daring the performances are in terms of text selection as well as staging and acting choices, and the more professional these companies become. This group of intellectuals looked to writers and artists abroad for inspiration. Simultaneously, these intellectuals were creating new opportunities for autochthonous creation. The constraints

Censorship of Translated Drama in Portugal, 1950–1970

Table 25.1 List of the ten main experimental theatre companies, between 1946 and 1974

Theatre company	Director(s) and/or founders	Dates and number of performances
Teatro – Estúdio do Salitre	Gino Saviotti, Luiz Francisco Rebello, Vasco Mendonça Alves	1946–1950 (17 performances)
Teatro Experimental de Lisboa	Pedro Bom	1951–1960 (6 performances)
Círculo de Cultura Teatral – Teatro Experimental do Porto (TEP)	António Pedro	1953– (101 performances until 1974)
Teatro d'Arte de Lisboa	Orlando Vitorino	1955–1970 (13 performances)
Círculo Experimental de Teatro de Aveiro (CETA) (www.cetateatro.pt/ceta.aspx)	Cândido Ferreira	1959– (8 performances until 1974)
Teatro Moderno de Lisboa – Sociedade de Actores	Armando Cortez, Fernando Gusmão, Carmen Dolores, Costa Ferreira, Rogério Paula, Armando Caldas, Ruy de Carvalho	1961–1965 (8 performances)
Casa da Comédia	Fernando Amado	1962–1991 (43 performances until 1974)
Teatro Estúdio de Lisboa (TEL)	Helena Félix, Luzia Maria Martins	1964–1989 (26 plays until 1974)
Teatro Experimental de Cascais	Carlos Avilez	1965– (27 performances until 1974)
Grupo 4: Sociedade de Actores	Irene Cruz, João Lourenço, Morais e Castro, Rui Mendes	1967–1981 (5 performances until 1974)

Source: CET-Base (http://ww3.fl.ul.pt/CETbase/).

on producing original plays on particular subjects gave rise to the introduction of foreign voices of dissent and avant-garde aesthetics. In the words of Luzia Maria Martins, a theatre director and translator at the time,

> If censorship was severe with foreign authors, it was extremely severe with Portuguese authors, at least from what I have witnessed in this activity. [...] I cannot be certain of how many national authors have been forbidden to me. And I am not counting those texts that have not been proposed for obvious reasons. This approach is terrible. This year, for instance, we have not yet staged a single Portuguese original, because what we had proposed was forbidden.
>
> (Interview of Luzia Maria Martins, in *Cinéfilo* Magazine, 4 May 1974; quoted in Figueiredo 2023: 105n)

25.2.2 *Under the Wing of Pirandello*

Teatro – Estúdio do Salitre was the first post-World War II experimental theatre company in Portugal. It was co-founded by Luiz Francisco Rebello (1924–2011), playwright, translator, theatre historian and critic, Gino Saviotti (1891–1980), who was the Director of the Italian Institute in Lisbon at the time, and Vasco Mendonça Alves (1883–1962), writer and playwright. Luiz Francisco Rebello played a crucial role in the renovation of theatrical languages and practices. He is considered one of the main introducers of Brecht's theatrical aesthetic in Portugal, which he accomplished by publishing articles on Brechtian drama, translations and versions of the plays (published in anthologies) (Rebello 1957) and by introducing this aesthetic in his translation, playwriting and theatrical practice (Delille 1991). The company's intentions were 'to develop a taste for theatre as literary and performing invention, intellectual culture, artistic sense and capacity of creating poetry and dramatic thought' (Rebello 2004: 79).

Plays were performed in a small theatre room in the Italian Cultural Institute in Lisbon. Although this group lasted only four years, it staged 17 productions and marked a turning point in the Portuguese theatre scene, not so much for the audience but in terms of staging and innovation in theatrical language. They called their repertoire 'essentialist' theatre, inspired by their essentialist drama manifesto, an anti-naturalism movement. The group intended to explore contemporary aesthetic possibilities and to bring theatre back to its original spontaneity, which was closer to the audience. To this end, it refused elaborate stage settings, hierarchical relations and fixed ideas about theatre. Apart from the eclectic selection of texts, dominated by Portuguese plays, the social concern of their essentialist manifesto was made evident by the staging techniques used, the close relationship between actors and audience, and the meta-theatrical resource of alienating realism (influenced by Pirandello's anti-bourgeois drama). Most of the actors were non-professional, and many of them were young theatre students (Sousa 2013: 56). Each of the 17 performances comprised three or four play texts by different authors, predominantly Portuguese and translated Italian plays, totalling approximately 45 texts. One of the criteria for text selection was undoubtedly socio-political, since the company had an agenda that was both artistic and political, particularly in the early years of its existence. Their first show was preceded by the reading of the company's 'Essentialist Theatre Manifesto', followed by the performance of a combination of four plays. The first one was Pirandello's *l'Uomo dal fiore in bocca* (1923) directed by Saviotti; the other three plays were Portuguese: politically charged plays by the Portuguese neo-realist writers Alves Redol (1911–1969), D. João da Câmara (1852–1908) and Vasco Mendonça Alves. Pirandello was staged again, in addition to other Italian playwrights, such as Vittorio Alfieri and Roberto Zerboni (both for political reasons). Moreover, plays by Chekhov, by modernist movement Portuguese playwrights like José de Almada Negreiros (1893–1970), and by other contemporary playwrights were performed for the first time in Portugal. Pirandello's drama set the tone for these performances. In other words, there was an attempt to provide social critique and psychological analysis while conveying a political message. Furthermore, staging techniques involved an empty stage and the removal of the so-called fourth wall, which created distance between the audience and the pseudo-realism of the play. Freeing the stage of all artifice also enabled the creation of the desired level of ambiguity (Fadda 2006: 279). The ambiguity was in part the reason for a less repressed theatrical experience.

This short-lived theatrical experiment, often reviewed negatively by the press, was the catalyst for other experimental and ground-breaking experiences in Portuguese theatre. The experimental companies that followed exhibited a more international influence. Thereby, they also contributed to a considerable change in Portuguese theatrical language.

25.2.3 The Avant-garde, Absurdism and Brecht's Influence

The late 1950s and early 1960s was a period marked by the professionalisation and artistic autonomy of many of the theatre companies that were being created. There are three singular cases that represent, first, a gendered voice in the case of Teatro Estúdio de Lisboa (TEL), co-founded by Luzia Maria Martins (1927–2000) and Helena Félix (1920–1991), and, second, a geographical shift with Teatro Experimental do Porto (TEP), founded by António Pedro in Porto, which was the first experimental theatre company created outside Lisbon. One of the founders of the Portuguese Surrealist Group, António Pedro was a poet and painter friend of Portuguese modernists, and attempted a few innovative theatre experiments before moving to Porto. The third case, Teatro Moderno de Lisboa (TML), was founded by a group of well-known actors of the time. These companies had a repertoire dominated by foreign plays and bear witness to the influence of censorship both in the selection and manipulation of play texts.

As Luzia Maria Martins put it in a 1972 interview with the magazine *Rádio e Televisão*, 'I believe that the audience in Portugal has missed a number of plays that I consider fundamental for their knowledge of a world dramaturgy' (*Rádio e Televisão*, 8 January 1972). One of Martins' intentions was to train her theatre company and educate the audience through the presentation of 'fundamental' plays. Apart from these theatrical and didactic purposes, Martins also claims an implicit social dimension for her theatre. In the same interview, she declared her intended audience to be Portuguese youth: 'We want to reach out to a young audience more than anyone else. The youngsters are our hope of a better and more enlightened audience than my generation was, lost and dormant with their acquired tastes.' Like the majority of directors of experimental companies, she rejected the star system and worked mostly with amateur actors.

Martins was the stage director, translator, author and dramaturg of most of the plays performed by the TEL, usually in the Teatro da Feira Popular, managed by Vasco Santana, a well-known theatre manager at the time. There was a European, mainly British, influence on text selection, but most of the translations that Martins authored (18 in total) were adaptations and free versions of works focusing on questions of gender and social inequality. The first play staged by the TEL, Maxwell Anderson's *Joan of Lorraine* performed in 1964 (the play was originally written in 1946) is noteworthy. It is a play about a theatre company that stages a play about Joan of Arc and the effect that this story has on the actors. Again, in her interview with *Rádio e Televisão* magazine, she explains that she chose this play to inaugurate the TEL because it defined both her ideology and that of the company: 'In terms of the form, it was a rehearsal that allowed actors to find themselves as human beings' (*Rádio e Televisão*, 8 January 1972). She translated Ted Willis's *Hot Summer Night* (1968), which addressed the theme of racism and discrimination; Robert Bolt's *A Man for All Seasons* (1960) and plays by Peter Shaffer, Arnold Wesker, Terence Rattigan, John Osborne, David Storey, August Strindberg, Vaclav Havel, Chekhov and Shakespeare.

Her free adaptation of Shakespeare's *Romeo and Juliette* into, literally, *Anatomy of a Love Story* is an interesting case of manipulation, highlighting the translator's relationship with censorship. In fact, her translation inaugurates a strategy that would be commonly used by these companies: obtaining approval for plays by relying on the different points of view of the eight censors who assessed the rewritings. Plays were re-submitted when refused or when cuts were so severe that they would compromise the play's unity. Occasionally, after a few attempts, the plays were finally approved.

Martins's free adaptation of Shakespeare's play was a pioneering inter-arts expressionist performance that mixed film and dance. The play began with the screening of a short film on the 1968 student riots in Paris. The film was banned during the general rehearsal. The company managed to get it approved subsequently, however, after making cuts (deleting those parts considered subversive or biased). The final editing of the film was the responsibility of the censors themselves. About this adaptation Martins states that both the text and the *mise-en-scene* attempt to express a

The Routledge Handbook of Translation and Censorship

position, but an implicit one. The love story served merely as a pretext to address social conflicts and inequalities.

In 1968, the group submitted a translation of Arnold Wesker's *The Kitchen* translated by Valentina Trigo de Sousa (another close collaborator of the TEL) to the censorship commission. The play was initially forbidden because of its subversive intention. While some of the censors who assessed the play considered it performable to an adult audience after cuts had been made, the majority did not. As two of the censors wrote: 'the play has a motivation and intention that warrant disapproval. I do not see any possibility of solving that problem with cuts, since it would be necessary to cut the end of the play [...], I disapprove' and 'It is in my opinion a play with clear subversive intentions. I disapprove' (Censorship file: 18715 SNI DGE: ANTT). In 1969, the TEL asked for a reversal of the decision. Again, censors reassessed the play, and this time, the majority approved it with cuts:

> It is a comedy that criticises the current industrial society, in which a man living under constant pressure cannot fulfil himself totally. The dialogue's language is realistic, sometimes touching on sensitive subjects, but I do not consider them enough to prevent its public performance. I approve the play for adults after the cuts have been made.
>
> (Censorship file: 18715 SNI DGE: ANTT)

Cabrera (2006) claims that this change in the decision, one year after the initial ban in 1969, is the result of a less repressive period in Portuguese history, marked by social discontent, student revolts and the replacement of Salazar by Marcello Caetano as prime minister in 1968. However, what stands out in the justification for the play's approval is the analysis of the subversive message and potential to influence the audience. The play's symbolic aspects, its unrealistic depiction and non-specific location, as well as its unclear message—oscillating between resignation and a fatalistic stance toward revolt—somehow contributed to lifting the ban on the play. Moreover, the justification shows that several censors understood the play and its symbolic potential. Certain censors were of the option that only a small percentage of the play's audience would grasp its implicit and ambiguous message.

In the report on the general rehearsal (which took place in 1971), the TEL was asked to cut certain words, such as 'war', 'sabotage' and the employees' acts of revolt, such as throwing their hats to the floor or playing with knives (Censorship file: 18715 SNI DGE: ANTT). Thus, all actions that could inspire revolt or contestation, or that referred to something that was politically sensitive at this time in Portugal had to be cut. The rewriting of the play's script was substantial, but live performance allowed for compensation strategies and inventive solutions. The company fully realised that words often mattered more to the censors than visuals and actions.

Like the other groups described above, António Pedro's TEP struck a balance between theatrical breakthroughs and censorial restrictions until 1974 (Porto 1997). The choice of repertoire represents a compromise between the two poles of innovation and control, by introducing new voices while carefully selecting texts that could be potentially approved by the censorship committee. Apart from the innovative stage sets, acting practices and choice of repertoire, the TEP created an acting school, thereby adding an extra educational dimension to the project.

Again, translated drama represented a significant component of the TEP's repertoire. Two general strands can be discerned in the process of theatre importation. The first one follows an absurdist tradition, with the importation and translation of the works of European playwrights such as Cocteau, Ionesco, Max Frisch, Ibsen and John Osborne. Ionesco's *Rhinocéros*, translated by António Pedro himself, was the first absurdist play performed by the TEP in 1960, just one year after the play's publication (1959). According to Carlos Porto, despite the interest of Pedro and his collaborators in the Theatre of the Absurd, they were reluctant to include it in their repertoire, in part because they feared censorship (Porto 1997). However, after staging Ionesco's *Rhinocéros* (which was performed after cuts and changes had been made), the TEP staged other Ionesco plays, such as *Le Nouveau locataire* in 1967 and *Victimes du devoir* in 1973. Beckett's *Endgame* was performed in 1970, with a translation by the Portuguese actor Curado Ribeiro (1919–1995).

North America represents the second strand of imported plays. Prominent contemporary American playwrights on the list include Arthur Miller, William Faulkner and Eugene O'Neill. The number of these plays is noteworthy. In fact, some of the US plays had had recent successful runs or were still having success on Broadway when they were performed in Portugal. Some of the plays were also known to the Portuguese audience through film adaptations. The TEP attempted to capitalise on their success. Arthur Miller's *Death of a Salesman* was performed in 1954, five years after its Broadway premiere. The play had an enormous impact on the Portuguese audience, partially due to the criticism of American capitalism but also due to the minimalist stage set that Pedro and his collaborators created. In 1964, the TEP performed another of Miller's plays, *All My Sons*, which explores the themes of guilt and denial provoked by war (the comparison with the Portuguese colonial war was inevitable in this context). In 1958, O'Neill's *Long Day's Journey into Night* was staged (the original play was first performed in 1957); that year also saw a production of Faulkner's *Requiem for a Nun*, written in 1951. Finally, Clifford Odets's *Awake and Sing!*, an example of agitprop theatre, was performed by the TEP in 1965. Originated from the combination of the words 'agitation' and 'propaganda', agitprop theatre developed in Russia and Germany in the 1920's; it is a form of committed and 'political combative' theatre (Filewod 2017). Along with aesthetic innovation, political thematics were also central in the selection of plays. For obvious reasons, all of the above-mentioned plays, particularly Odets's *Awake and Sing!*, were subjected to severe adaptation and cuts before they could be staged (Porto 1997: 152).

The translators selected for the task of adaptating and translating the plays were Portuguese writers, such as José Cardoso Pires (1925–1998), novelist and playwright, known for his political stance, who is also known as the author of the Brechtian-inspired play *O render dos heróis* (1960) about the popular historical revolt known as Maria da Fonte, which occurred in 1846 (this was the last play performed by Teatro Moderno de Lisboa); Jorge de Sena (1919–1978), poet, novelist, playwright, translator, critic and academic (his strong criticism of Salazar's regime eventually led to his exile in Brazil from 1959 until 1965, when he moved to the US, where he lived until his death); and Egito Gonçalves (1920–2001), who was a surrealist poet and translator and one of the founders of TEP. They were all members of an intellectual elite in Portugal known for its critical stance towards the Regime. These translations gave them the opportunity to write for performance as well as to experiment with aesthetic language while addressing social themes that would be otherwise forbidden in original Portuguese works. Moreover, a few of their translations have remained in circulation, even after 1974. For example, Sena's translation of O'Neill's play was adopted by other theatre companies over the decades and also found its way into the publishing system. It is the only translation of the play that has been published in Portugal since the 1970s. The latest edition of this translation is from 1999 (Eugene O'Neill, *Jornada para a noite*, translated by Jorge de Sena, Lisbon: Cotovia, 1999).

Finally, a number of translated plays submitted for censorship review were never approved and so belong to an archive of never performed plays. Some of them ended up being published, but they never found their way onto the stage. John Osborne's *Look Back in Anger*, translated by the writer and translator José Palla e Carmo (1923–1995), was submitted to the censorship commission for a performance license in 1960, but refused on the grounds that, although it was of great literary value, 'the play was not proper for a general audience. [...] It is filled with improper concepts for our way of living and it is very far from our dearest moral values' (Censorship file: 6096 SNI DGGS). In 1966, after the play had been approved for performance in a commercial theatre in Lisbon, the TEP applied again for a performance license for the play in the same translation, which in the meantime had been published in the theatre series *Teatro* by Minotauro publisher (a small-scale publishing house) with a slightly different title, literally translated as *Time and Anger*. This time, the play was granted a license but with substantial cuts, including the deletion of a few speeches. The general rehearsal was approved in 1967. In 1968, the same translation was performed by the Experimental Theatre of Cascais (TEC) (www.tecascais.com/o-tempo-e-a-ira/).

The last company that will be considered is the TML, which lasted four years and performed eight plays; it represents a unique case of a company created by well-known actors, which contributed to a renewal of theatre plays. There are several studies dedicated to this company. Those studies alongside the memoirs of actors and practitioners linked to it help to portray the work and contribution of the company. The small number of plays performed was due to the rejection of several plays the TML had submitted to the censorship commission (Lívio 2009: 58).

The TML advocated similar principles to those advocated by other experimental theatre companies: art for art's sake (with no commercial purpose) and engaged theatre, which called for freedom. They wanted to build a repertoire comprised of unknown authors and to generate a new relationship with the audience, particularly the younger generation (Lívio 2009: 28).

Their first performance, *El tintero* by Carlos Moñiz, translated by António José Forjaz, was a huge success in Lisbon; the play also toured Portugal. It was licensed to be performed with severe cuts. Despite the fact that the censored play was more ambiguous than the original, the character Crock nevertheless remained an employee who is completely destroyed by a bureaucratic system and dies of hunger. He is not only the victim of society and oppressive power structures but is also unable to adapt to a dehumanised society (he migrated from the countryside to the city in search of work). The play represents rebellion against political power and the bourgeoisie. According to other fellow actors who witnessed the play, the play was controversial in the cultural milieu of the time. The actor Armando Caldas described the impact of the play in the following manner: 'The success this play enjoyed put the political power at the time on high alert. In its aftermath, we noticed the relentlessness censorship of the plays that we sent for licensing' (Lívio 2009: 177). Alarmed by the widespread favourable reception of the company's plays, the censorship committee scrutinised TML's productions more closely.

The last translated play performed by TML is Luiz Francisco Rebello's free translation of Shakespeare's *Measure for Measure*, the Portuguese title of which is literally translated as *tooth for a tooth* (1964). It is clearly influenced by the techniques of Brechtian epic drama. The play was produced in order to celebrate the four hundredth anniversary of Shakespeare's birth and to modernise Shakespeare's classic. According to Fran Rayner, Rebello's desire to make the play modern in order for it to be understood by a contemporary audience and, simultaneously, the need for a translation that would be approved by the censors was the basis of the translation strategies that were adopted. The strategies included nine songs created to deal with contemporary political topics, with music by António Vitorino de Almeida, a well-known Portuguese music conductor (Rayner 2008: 66). In the words of Rayner, 'if the songs have a clear political purpose and theatrical reference point, they also form part of Rebello's strategy to make the play performable, for the sections of the text that the songs replace would have meant little to a contemporary audience for the play' (Rayner 2008: 66). Furthermore, several scenes were suppressed, and names that

Censorship of Translated Drama in Portugal, 1950–1970

were difficult to pronounce were changed. Temporal ambiguity was created to establish an implicit parallel with contemporary Portugal. Moreover, this example confirms the tendency to modernise classic texts occasionally as a strategy to introduce specific aesthetic devices and social topics, particularly under conditions of censorship. This was a strategy also employed by university theatre groups, as discussed below.

25.2.4 *University Theatre Groups*

If experimental theatre companies were targeted by severe censorship, university groups were even more closely scrutinised. Particularly during the 1960s (until the late 1950s, there were only a few university theatre groups and they were politically conservative; it is only in the late 1950s that new groups exploring more controversial ideas began to proliferate). According to Barata:

> University theatre, in particular from the late 1950s onwards, was subject to closer surveillance, a direct consequence of the growing political commitment and effort that repertoires revealed. Groups started to send to the censorship committee plays that were already included on the list of forbidden texts. They gambled on the possibility that censors might be 'momentarily distracted', which would make it feasible to perform fundamental texts from national and international dramaturgy.
>
> (Barata 2009: 321)

This strategy described by Barata intended not only to provoke the censors but also to confront them with the incoherence of their decisions, since occasionally a few plays on the list of banned works would be approved.

The theatre groups were based at Portugal's three main universities, in Lisbon, Porto and Coimbra. These groups were associated with specific faculties or student guilds (Barata 2009: 325–8). To a greater degree than the experimental companies, the university groups resorted to classical plays as the remoteness of their temporal and cultural references made it easier to obtain a performance license for them, although the adaptations of the plays often included implicit references to the current political situation. The strategy was eventually detected by the censors, who realised that the rewritten plays were not entirely innocent. Often, the censors could not agree on whether to grant a performance license based only on implicit references to sensitive topics such as war, revolt and communism. For example, one of the University of Coimbra theatre groups—named the Circle of Theatre Initiation of Coimbra Academy (CITAC)—applied for a licence in 1966 to perform Aristophanes' *Peace*. The proposal incited different opinions among the censors (Barata 2009: 322). It was regarded by some as dangerous because of the reference to war (associated with the theatre group's political affiliation), whereas others believed that the audience would not understand a plot based on mythology. Still others approved the play since they believed that the language would make it difficult for a general audience to understand and the situation portrayed in the play was not, in any manner, equivalent to the Portuguese one. The censorship committee nevertheless asked that the staging of the play be carefully scrutinised. It was eventually approved, despite the divergent opinions and positions of censors (Censorship report: 18119 SNI DGE/ ANTT, Barata 2009: 322–3). Again, the censors considered carefully the audience—and how much of the symbolic message that audience would be likely to grasp. As long as the target audience was limited to intellectuals, there was a greater chance of approval despite the hidden messages. Nevertheless, university theatre was considered dangerous not only because of its clear political stance, but also because its audience was young adults. Moreover, as mentioned before, live performance presented the opportunity to add meanings that were not present or were less evident in the play texts. In fact, it is well-known that during the general rehearsal attended by censors, these groups would say the text without any intonation and interpretation, thereby hiding the multiple meanings that the staging and performance could give to the text; they would add appropriate intonations only during the live performance.

In addition, numerous plays—both Portuguese or those translated into Portuguese—that were forbidden on Portuguese stages ended up being performed on European stages by exiled Portuguese intellectuals and students (Rebello 1977: 133–6). For example, Peter Weiss', Brecht's and Sartre's texts were strictly forbidden on Portuguese stages. A few forbidden authors were indeed performed clandestinely, without the scrutiny of censorship, or as part of certain cultural events where they could pass unnoticed. A very interesting example is Peter Weiss' (1916–1982) anti-colonial play *Lusitanian Bogeyman* (1967) performed clandestinely in the canteen of the University of Lisbon in 1971 and analysed by Madeira (2017) and Delille (1996). These performances were only available to a small audience and were not reviewed by the national press; as a result, they had little to no influence on public opinion although they inspired numerous writers and theatre practitioners.

25.3 New Debates

As stated elsewhere (Carvalho 2015), at the level of published drama, there was a tendency in Portugal to publish series or anthologies of different plays and playwrights with the intention of introducing new theatrical aesthetics, forms and structures, including a few plays by Portuguese playwrights, which would become more difficult to control or scrutinise in a multi-author series or anthology. One noteworthy practice during this period was the partnership between experimental companies and university theatre groups and small-scale publishing houses—such as Minotauro, Prelo, Contraponto, A Antologia, and Barca Solar—which would publish the performed translated or original plays in a dedicated series. These paperback books were intended to follow and complement the performance of plays and the theatre scene in Portugal at the time in keeping with these groups' didactic purpose of recording an ephemeral performance or serving to register a memory of a banned performance. Their didactic purpose was also achieved through prefaces and introductions explaining the plays' impact on the source culture, its aesthetic language and its innovations. Artistic manifestos, such as translations of the work of the European theorists Grotowsky, Brook, Craig and Appia, to name but a few, were also published. Most of these series were not sold in bookshops but circulated and were sold in alternative networks, such as at the entrance of theatre venues. These series supported the intended renewal of theatre repertoires and language.

In 2012, the Portuguese playwright, theatre director and practitioner Tiago Rodrigues presented his play *Three Fingers below the Knee* for the first time in Portugal. This performance, which used censored material as well as quotations from censorship reports, is striking not only for portraying the reality of censorship on the Portuguese stage but also for revealing the number of translated plays performed or forbidden at the time. In fact, it gives a clear picture of how much Portuguese theatre repertoires were then dominated by translated texts.

For different reasons, Portuguese theatre repertoires were and continue to be dominated by foreign models and translated plays. This is particularly evident during the period of the *Estado Novo*, particularly from 1950 onwards, which was marked by prolific translation for the stage and for publication, subject to looser control by the Regime and characterised by a movement for aesthetic renewal, which was promoted and implemented by experimental and university theatre companies (Santos 2004: 313). In contrast with other genres, theatre was the channel through which the most provocative, challenging and politically motivated authors and their writings entered the Portuguese cultural system, despite the fact that it was closely scrutinised by the censors—more so than any other art form, even cinema. The number of translated plays also stands in contrast to very few Portuguese plays performed during this period. According to Santos, Portugal was the country where the percentage of national plays performed was the lowest in the world (Santos 2006: 66). This constraint on Portuguese playwrighting had lasting effects even after the dictatorship's demise in 1974.

Overall, one can discern that Portuguese alternative theatre was dominated by European avant-garde aesthetics, often through the work of Portuguese intellectuals and students who had lived in other European cities. Summarised below are several strategies adopted to by-pass censorship:

- staging techniques and actors' inflection of expressions and words
- free adaptation of classics and classical plays in order to resonate with a contemporary audience; in these and other cases, translators would use parables, historical metaphors and absurdism in order to obtain a performance licence. Translators and theatre practitioners were aware that censors would pay more attention to sensitive words than to the situations portrayed; thus, a certain level of self-censorship was practised
- the publication of banned theatre texts in dedicated theatre series served the general educational purpose of these groups (formation of taste) while also creating a memory of a banned performance
- repeated submission of banned texts was intended not only to be provocative but also to draw out possible divergent and contradictory opinions of censors regarding the potential danger of implicit and symbolic messages; there was also awareness of the oscillation in restrictive measures over the years.

A few translations were so influential that they are still the only ones on the Portuguese market and have inspired the creation of original plays in Portuguese.

Through the examples presented, one can argue that censorship was, in fact, both a repressive and a creative force (Billiani 2007: 10), and it could, in fact, be characterised as 'productive censorship' (Baer 2011: 22). The censors considered the intended audience very carefully because the potential impact of a live performance was proof of the productive power of reception.

Theatrical language, including revolutionary stage language, enabled the questioning of 'internalised dominant social norms' (Woods 2012: 5), especially in regard to translated drama, particularly published texts. It was the performance, the performing venues, and the relationship between audience and practitioners that shook up established social and political ideas. Theatre practitioners and playwrights recognised that the only means to enhance Portuguese theatre was through translation and the importation of theatrical theories, staging and acting techniques that were influencing and shaping the European and international theatrical scene. Staging and props could compensate for the constraint in translating certain situations and characters. In a way, the alterations brought about through translation have always been more acceptable in theatre than in other literary forms, thus providing a certain degree of freedom to manipulate what could be potentially censored.

Coming back to Tiago Rodrigues' play, it signals the living and creative force of theatre that was recognised by the censors themselves. In their words, cited in Rodrigues' play:

At the limit, we allow the publication of the book, but not the performance of the play, because the censor anticipates and takes very seriously the subversive consequences of

The Routledge Handbook of Translation and Censorship

face-to-face communication in theatre: reading in silence is different from reading out loud.

(Rodrigues 2013: 25)

The title of Rodrigues' play already hints at the dual potential of the message conveyed by theatre, which was not only verbal but also visual. 'Three fingers below the knee' is a recommendation left by one censor regarding the skirt of an actress, implying that the length of the skirt must finish at least three fingers below the knee. This play, which was published in 2013, uses the same words that silenced theatre during the *Estado Novo*, thereby symbolising the force of performed theatre, which even when constrained, can thrive and become a creative force.

Further Reading

Santos, Graça dos. 2004. *O espectáculo desvirtuado. O teatro português sob o reinado de Salazar.* Lisbon: Caminho.
This book is the first comprehensive survey and study of theatre and censorship during the *Estado Novo*. It is a well-documented portrait of the constrains in which theatre was produced during the Salazar regime.

Seruya, Teresa and Moniz, Maria Lin (eds.). 2008. *Translation and Censorship in Different Times and Landscapes*. Newcastle upon Tyne: Cambridge Scholars Publishing.
This volume of essays offers a view on the mechanisms of censorship on translation with a particular emphasis on the *Estado Novo*. Some articles are dedicated to theatre translation.

Barata, José de Oliveira. 2009. *Máscaras da Utopia. História do Teatro Universitário em Portugal 193874.* Lisbon: Fundação Calouste Gulbenkian.
This book presents a fascinating history and study of university theater in Portugal between 1938 and 1974. It is the first comprehensive study of university theatre in Portugal and it contains numerous archival photographs and documentation.

Notes

1   All translations from the Portuguese in this chapter are the author's.
2   The TETRA project was funded by the Portuguese Research Funding Agency (FCT) and was implemented at the Centre for Comparative Studies, University of Lisbon, between 2009 and 2012. The project set out to examine the meaning, relevance, and reception of theatre translation in different historical and social contexts in Portugal (Carvalho and Di Pasquale 2012).

References

Aaltonen, Sirkku. 2000. *Time-Sharing on Stage: Drama Translation in Theatre and Society.* Clevedon: Multilingual Matters.
Baer, Brian James. 2011. 'Translating Queer Texts in Soviet Russia', *Translation Studies*, 4(1): 21–40.
Barata, José de Oliveira. 2009. *Máscaras da Utopia. História do Teatro Universitário em Portugal 193874* [*Masks of Utopia: The History of University Theatre in Portugal 193874*]. Lisbon: Fundação Calouste Gulbenkian.
Billiani, Francesca. 2007. 'Assessing Boundaries—Censorship and Translation. An Introduction', in F. Billiani (ed.), *Modes of Censorship and Translation. National Contexts and Diverse Media*. London and New York: Routledge, 1–25.
Brodie, Geraldine. 2022. 'Translating for the Theatre', in K. Malmkjaer (ed.), *The Cambridge Handbook of Translation*. Cambridge: Cambridge University Press, 424–39.

Cabrera, Ana. 2013. 'Censura e estratégias censurantes na sociedade contemporânea' [Censorship and Censorship Strategies in Contemporary Society], in A. Cabrera (ed.), *Censura nunca mais! A censura ao teatro e ao cinema no Estado Novo [No More Censorship! Theatre and Cinema Censorship in the Estado Novo]*. Lisbon: Alétheia Editores, 17–75.

Carvalho, Manuela. 2015. 'The TETRA Project: Preliminary Results and Perspective', in R. Bueno Maia, M. Pacheco Pinto and S. Ramos Pinto (eds.), *How Peripheral is the Periphery? Translating Portugal Back and Forth. Essays in Honour of João Ferreira Duarte*. Newcastle upon Tyne: Cambridge Scholars Publishing, 45–61.

Carvalho, Manuela and Di Pasquale, Daniela (eds). 2012. *Depois do Labirinto: Teatro e Tradução [After the Labyrinth: Theatre and Translation]*. Lisbon: Nova Vega.

Delille Maria Manuela Gouveia. 1996. 'A recepção portuguesa do drama Gesang Vom Lusitanischen Popanz de Peter Weiss' [The Portuguese Reception of Peter Weiss' Play Gesang Vom Lusitanischen Popanz], in M.A.H. de Oliveira (ed.), *Portugal – Alemanha – África do imperialismo colonial ao imperialismo político. Actas do IV encontro Luso-Alemão [Portugal – Germany – Africa: From Colonial Imperialism to Political Imperialism: Proceedings of the 4th Luso-German Conference]*. Lisbon: Colibri.

Delille Maria Manuela Gouveia. 1991. *Do Pobre B.B. em Portugal—Aspectos da Recepção de Bertolt Brecht antes e depois do 25 de abril de 1974 [Poor BB in Portugal – Aspects of Bertolt Brecht's Reception before and after 25 April 1974]*. Aveiro: Estante, 215–25.

Dolores, Carmen. 1984. *Retrato inacabado: memórias [Unfinished Portrait: Memories]*. Lisbon: O Jornal.

Fadda, Sebastiana. 2006. 'A dramaturgia de Luiz Francisco Rebello: do Teatro Estúdio do Salitre às significações do palco', [Luiz Francisco Rebello's Dramaturgy: From Teatro Estúdio do Salitre to Meanings of the Stage] *Estudos Italianos em Portugal*, n.1: 261–91.

Figueiredo, Marta Ribeiro. 2023. "Teatro Portugués en el 25 de abril: Procesos de censura (1973–1974)", *InvestigARTES*, 9: 99–107.

Filewod, Alan. 2016. 'Agitprop Theatre', in *The Routledge Encyclopedia of Modernism*. www.rem.routledge. com/articles/agitprop-theatre. doi:10.4324/9781135000356-REM1672-1.

Johnston, David. 2004. 'Securing the Performability of the Text', in S. Coelsch-Foisner and Holger Klein (eds.), *Drama Translation and Theatre Practice*. Frankfurt: Peter Lang, 24–43.

Livio, Tito. 2009. *Teatro Moderno de Lisboa (19611965): um marco na história do teatro português [Teatro Moderno de Lisboa (19611965): A Milestone in the History of Portuguese Theatre]*. Alfragide: Caminho.

Madeira, Cláudia. 2017. 'A peça *Canto do Papão Lusitano* de Peter Weiss—retrato e discurso crítico sobre o colonialismo português' [Peter Weiss' play *Canto do Papão Lusitano* – A Portrait and Critical Discourse of Portuguese Colonialism], *Comunicação Pública. Fotografia e Propaganda no Estado Novo Português*, 12(23): 1–26.

Marinetti, Cristina. 2013. 'Transnational, Multilingual and Post-dramatic: The Location of Translation in Contemporary Theatre', in S. Bigliazzi, P. Ambrosi and P. Kofler. (eds.), *Theatre Translation in Performance*. London and New York: Routledge, 27–38.

Porto, Carlos. 1997. *O TEP e o teatro em Portugal: histórias e imagens [TEP and Theatre in Portugal: Stories and Images]*. Porto: Fundação Eng. António de Almeida.

Rayner, Fran. 2008. 'Shakespeare and the Censors: Translation and Performance Strategies under the Portuguese Dictatorship', in T. Seruya and M. L.in Moniz (eds.), *Translation and Censorship in Different Times and Landscapes*. Newcastle: Cambridge Scholars Publishing, 61–73.

Rebello, Luiz Francisco. 1977. *Combate por um teatro de combate [Fighting for a Theatre of Combat]*. Lisbon: Seara Nova.

Rebello, Luiz Francisco. 2004. *O passado na minha frente: memórias [The Past in Front of Me: Memories]*. Lisbon: Parceria A.M. Pereira.

Rodrigues, Tiago. 2013. *Três dedos abaixo do joelho. Tristeza e alegria na vida das girafas. Coro dos amantes [Three Fingers Below the Knee. Sadness and Joy in the Life of Giraffes. Plays]*. Coimbra: Imprensa da Universidade de Coimbra.

Santos, Graça dos. 2006. 'La scène sous surveillance', [Surveilled Stage], *Ethnologie française*, 36(1): 11–17.

Santos, Graça dos. 2004. *O espectáculo desvirtuado. O teatro português sob o reinado de Salazar [The Distorted Spectacle: Portuguese Theatre under Salazar's Reign]*. Lisbon: Caminho.

Sousa, Alexandre Barros de. 2013. *Teatro Estúdio do Salitre, um teatro improvável entre a arte e a política* [*Teatro Estúdio do Salitre: An Improbable Theatre Venue between Art and Politics*]. MA Thesis in Contemporary History. Lisbon: Faculdade de Ciências Sociais e Humanas, Universidade Nova de Lisboa.

Woods, Michelle. 2012. *Censoring Translation. Censorship, Theatre, and the Politics of Translation.* London and New York: Continuum.

Documentation

CETbase – Teatro em Portugal. http://cetbase.pt/search/client/searchFS.htm. Last accessed 13/6/2023.

National Archive Torre do Tombo, SNI, DGE. File numbers: 16096, 18119, 18715, 6096. *Rádio & Televisão* (8 January 1972) – Magazine.

26
TRANSLATION AND CENSORSHIP IN SPAIN
Focus on Francoism

Maria del Carmen Camus Camus and Cristina Gómez Castro

26.1   Conceptualising Translation and Censorship in Franco's Spain

Spain was under the rule of general Francisco Franco for a period of almost forty years (1939–1975), and even after the disappearance of the dictator the country did not approve a constitution that guaranteed freedom of expression until three years later (1978). During this period, censorship is best described as 'an administrative and institutionalised restriction of freedom of speech as a means of preventing the diversification of political, moral or religious discourses' (Larraz 2014: 22). The means used to achieve the desired restriction of freedom of speech were complex. It is therefore necessary to make a distinction between what can be called 'external censorship' and 'internal censorship' (Pegenaute 1999: 90) in this context.

- **External censorship** refers to restrictions imposed by the Spanish state through different laws and decrees and applied to translation as a finished product. Pegenaute (1999: 88) subdivides this type of censorship into *prepublication* and *postpublication* censorship. The severity of the former was in keeping with the adopted legislation, whereas the latter was mainly enforced through confiscation of the material once published.
- **Internal censorship** refers to the constraints imposed on translators during the rewriting process. The translator as rewriter follows norms before and during the translation process in order to adapt foreign works to the official ideology of the target culture. This is known as self-censorship, a stratagem that was openly acknowledged by Spanish writers working at the time, which led to the attenuation of certain expressions or their replacement with more neutral ones (Gómez Castro 2012).

In strong nationalist contexts, as in Spain under Franco, foreign products tended to be received with some suspicion. In such cases, censorship acts as a modifying force that changes the translated text to make it acceptable to the receiving culture (Gómez Castro 2009). Aware of the potential danger of foreign works for the Spanish public, the years of the Franco regime instituted a system of prepublication censorship that considered some content taboo (Abellán 1980: 88), namely:

- sexual morals: particularly targeted by a publication ban were any references to abortion, homosexuality, divorce and extramarital relationships

DOI: 10.4324/9781003149453-32

- political beliefs: opposition to the regime was not tolerated
- language use: indecorous or provocative language, as well as language that was incongruous with the good manners that governed the behaviour of decent people, were targeted
- religion: attacks on religion and the Church as institutions and as hierarchies were prohibited.

Thus, censorship created a negative environment for translation activity, corroborating what Boase-Beier and Holman (1999: 10–11) have already pointed out: when translation is done from a less restrictive to a more restrictive context, censorship becomes a constraint on the act of translation. Different measures were mobilised depending on the cultural product to be adapted.

26.2 Historical Perspectives

26.2.1 Contextual Framework: Spain in the 1939–1975 Period

The temporal framework of the censorial restrictions imposed by the Franco dictatorship can be divided into three periods characterised by shifting relationships between the Catholic Church and Franco's regime, which had a direct influence on the forging of the censorial apparatus, as well as the enactment of laws and policies. The first period extends from 1939, the year Franco declared victory, to 1952, when the XXXV Eucharistic Congress was held in Barcelona. In the Franco era, 'Spain was isolated from the rest of the world, with an economy devastated by the civil war and suffering the consequences of World War II' (Camus 2010: 41). Thus, this first period represents the years of the emergence of the new regime, characterised by isolation, internal power struggles among the different sectors that had promoted Franco's victory (the Church, the Military and the Falange), and eventually, the cutting of ties with the Falange. The second period runs from 1952 until 1962, when the regime was consolidated and it gradually became accepted by democratic governments throughout the Western world. Spain and the United States signed the 1953 Covenant, which granted the dictatorship financial and military support, and both countries agreed to a shared commitment to promoting anticommunism. This alliance brought about the end of financial autarchy and inaugurated the transition from a rural to an emerging industrial economy. Also in 1953, the Catholic Church and the regime endorsed the Concordat, an agreement that granted the Church substantial benefits and, on the censorship front, strengthened the Church's role in the enforcement of censorship restrictions. The third and final stage, from 1963 to 1975, corresponds to the slow disintegration of the Franco dictatorship. During this period, the prolonged dictatorship was now undermined by increasing social unrest. In the religious realm, strong reactions against the dictatorship began to appear, and at the Second Vatican Council (1962–1965) the ecclesiastical hierarchy clearly articulated its disagreement with the policies pursued by the Spanish government. To appease the growing demand for social change that threatened to end the dictatorship, the government conceded, passing important new legislation respecting socio-cultural norms, such as the 1963 Film Censorship Norms, the 1966 Press Law, the 1975 Book Law and the 1975 Film Censorship Norms.

26.2.2 Official Censorship

The consolidation of the dictatorship required the support of a stable censorship apparatus, and, as Franco's troops gained control over different parts of Spain, the insurgent government was swift to pass legislation aimed at controlling the publication and dissemination of all information and cultural products. In view of the substantial amount of legislation concerning freedom of expression passed over the 40 years of censorship in Spain, this section briefly reviews the legislation that had the most significant impact and represented a turn of the screw. The initially limited censorship apparatus underwent sustained development, eventually growing into a complex and robust censorship network of colossal proportions that controlled every minute instance of 'freedom'. Even before the end of the Civil War, the 1938 Press and Publications Law (BOE 23/04/1938) represented the first move toward forging a solid censorship structure to control the press and news media, or 'the fourth estate'. It was drafted to ensure the formation of a unifying structure to support the principles of the dictatorship. Initially intended as a tool of war to control enemy disinformation, this law remained in force for 28 years. A few days after the Press and Publications Law was adopted, the Ministry of the Interior (BOE 30/04/1938) issued a ministerial order that established a procedure for the publication and sale of books, both national and imported. Then, in November of that year, a ministerial order was passed addressing film censorship (BOE 05/11/1938). The following year—four months after the end of the war with Franco's victory on 1 April 1939—saw the creation of a censorship bureau under the National Propaganda Service, later integrated within the so-called Vice-Secretariat of Popular Education (BOE 22/05/ 1941), which aimed at unifying criteria and co-ordinating censorship activities (BOE 30/07/1939). However, the wording of the ministerial order on film hampered the establishment of clear and meaningful censorship criteria because it did not state explicitly what guidelines censors should follow when performing their task. This did not occur until 1963 when the Film Censorship Norms were approved (BOE 08/03/1963). However, the arbitrary interpretation and application of the much-awaited film censorship norms fuelled serious discontent and resulted in the rejection of the recently passed film censorship bill. The increasingly strained relationship between public administration and social agents (e.g., the press, news media and publishers) continued for more than a decade until a new film censorship code was passed in 1975 (BOE 19/02/1975), a year that also saw the promulgation of the Book Law (BOE 14/03/1975), which sought to put the brakes on the avalanche of demands by publishers, which threatened the dictatorship. Franco's dictatorship ended with the dictator's death in November 1975. However, censorship regulations remained in force until the Law on Freedom of Public Expression (BOE 12/04/1977) revoked the 1966 Press Law and a new bill was passed to regulate film activities (BOE 11/11/1977), both of which were a prelude to the definitive end to over 40 years of censorship with the 1978 Spanish Constitution.

26.2.3   The Franco Dictatorship and the Church

In Spain, the involvement of the Catholic Church in censorship goes back to 1502 when, with the arrival of the printing press, the Catholic monarchs, Ferdinand and Isabella, taking heed of Pope Alexander VI's bull *Inter Multiplices*, established the prior censorship of books. The archbishops of Toledo and Seville were appointed to implement the procedure. These appointments preceded innumerable provisions that reveal an ecclesiastic presence or intervention over the course of Spanish literary history (Martínez Bretón 1987: 7).

After General Franco had come to power in a military coup d'état, and institutionalised censorship had become the norm, the Catholic Church 'continued to provide an intense private response to implement moral censorship which had started prior to the military uprising' (Martinez Bretón 1987: 36). Even before the Civil War, the Catholic Church, through guidelines outlined in pontifical documents, informed its followers of the Church's stance on certain moral behaviour.

In the early years of Franco's rule, the Catholic Church played a key role in establishing the dictatorship, by endorsing the regime's beliefs and initiatives. The conservatism promoted by the

The Routledge Handbook of Translation and Censorship

regime fitted well with Catholic morals and dogma. In this section we will review three significant events that worked to strengthen this bond and to construct the censorial apparatus: the XXXV Eucharistic Congress (1952), the Church-State Concordat (1953) and the celebration of the Second Vatican Council (1962–1965).

The Catholic Church was, from the very start, one of the sturdiest pillars of the dictatorship. In the years of the civil war, the ecclesiastic authorities granted their covenant blessings on the politics pursued by Franco's nationalists. The deeply-rooted Catholic tradition in Spanish society ensured that a close relationship between the Church and the State would continue after Franco's victory. The military uprising was justified as a 'Holy war' to free Spain from the endemic evils of liberal democracy, such as communism, atheism and freemasonry. Church and State were so closely integrated that the coalition was referred to as National-Catholicism. Nevertheless, in January 1944, the group called Spanish Catholic Action created a new organisational body, the Secretariado de Orientación Bibliográfica (Secretariat for Bibliographic Guidance), which through their journal *Ecclesia* initiated a process of reviewing contemporary texts approved by the Franco regime. This sometimes resulted in discrepancies and tensions owing to their different perspectives: the one worldly and political and the other moral and spiritual (Peres del Puerto 2021). After more than a decade in power, the autarchic State, which had been isolated from the surrounding democratic governments and was still dealing with a war-torn economy, used the celebration of the XXXV Eucharistic Congress in Barcelona in 1952 to whitewash the negative aspects of its dictatorial rule. The event marked the beginning of a prolonged courtship between the Catholic Church and the Francoist government; their union was sealed the following year when both sides endorsed the 1953 Concordat, which granted the Church manifold concessions and privileges in exchange for its support. The strength of the Church-State union, which came to an end between 1962 and 1965 with the celebration of the Second Vatican Council, varied over the course of the dictatorship.

The 1952 Eucharistic Congress was the first international public display of the Church-State partnership. The congress, which was presented as a symbol of political and religious peace, was used to project a positive image of Spain to the rest of the world. Its motto, 'Eucharist and Peace,' symbolised the need for reconciliation both in the international sphere and in Spain. It represented a significant milestone in consolidating the Church-State union, which would be formalised the following year with the signing of the Concordat (1953). The agreement with the Holy See established a favourable framework for Francoism to consolidate its reputation and to enhance its credibility on the world stage as well as within Spain's borders. The terms of this political partnership granted the Church generous benefits and significant tax exemptions, which became a cornerstone of the system. The imprint of this alliance also served to tighten the censorship apparatus. However, at the end of the fifties, the harmonious State-Church bond began to crumble as divisions began to emerge in the previously monolithic structure of Spanish Catholicism.

At the beginning of the sixties, Spain started to open up to millions of foreign tourists and, as a consequence of this influx, Spain was increasingly exposed to a secularised modern Europe, which had a liberalising effect on younger Spanish Catholics. These new attitudes and behaviours did not comport well with the strict religiosity that had been promoted by the hierarchy of the Spanish Catholic Church. Some political revolts in the north of Spain generated dissenting views in a segment of the clergy. In this context of social unease, the celebration of the Second Vatican Council (1962–1965), which was intended to open a dialogue with the modern world by updating the life of the Church without re-defining any dogmas, made apparent the fissure in the coalition and represented a turning point in Church-State relations. On the censorship front, the chasm materialised in the promulgation of the 1963 Film and Censorship Norms and the 1966 Press Law (BOE 19/03/1966).

Rising public discontent with regard to the arbitrariness of censorship restrictions and incipient social unrest posed a challenge to the regime. In an effort to ease tensions and appease the growing demands for social change, the government passed the 1966 Press Law, which was meant to present a more tolerant face to the world. The law, in theory, represented the end of official censorship for the press and literary production, which had been in force since the 1938 Press Law. However, it soon became clear that this meant 'the institutionalisation of a legal norm of ideological control of culture and information' (Cisquella et al. 1977: 53). The law introduced mechanisms that restricted freedom of the press as much as actual censorship had done. In the new wording, publishers could choose to send their works directly to be published; this so-called 'direct publication', however, risked the confiscation of these works post publication, but could receive 'administrative silence', which tacitly authorised publication. The other option was to send the works, as before, for 'voluntary censorship' (a euphemism for compulsory censorship). To enjoy the benefits of the first option, publishers needed first to have obtained a registration number, which was hardly ever granted. As a consequence, most editors, unwilling to lose their investment, continued to send their works to be censored.

26.3   Core Issues and Topics

This section delves into some aspects of the influence of the dictatorship on the promotion and restriction in fiction and films and the specific measures adopted by the regime towards the translation of narrative, films, theatre and poetry.

26.3.1   Cultural Planning under Franco's Dictatorship: the Turn of the Screw in Narrative Fiction and Film

In an attempt to shield itself from criticism and perpetuate its power, the Francoist regime designed a rather crafty cultural framework aimed at promoting its ideals and values and, at the same time, fending off pernicious foreign attacks. Although censorship affected all aspects of society, the main targets of political intervention were the domains of literature and cinema given that both target a wide spectrum of society. Books and films produced in foreign countries were the object of the most comprehensive regulations, implemented to strengthen the Francoist 'rule of law' and good governance. In this context, language became the target of censorship intervention, and translations, especially in the first years of the dictatorship, were deemed suspicious and a dangerous threat to the monolithic structure of Spanish culture.

A legislative amendment to the 1946 Book Production Law, preserved as an unpaginated internal document found in the AGA archive, which was tabled by Gimenez Caballero, as first signatory, while endorsed by another eight representatives in Franco's parliament, argued:

> As long as translations deal with religious or technical matters, no objection can be made to their publication, although they should be quota-bound to encourage the production of similar Spanish works, if we really want to exert an influence on our [Spanish] Religion, Science and Technology. But when translations deal with politics or fables, then they really become dangerous since through them there could seep into Spanish culture a spirit that is at the very least non-Spanish, and in many cases surreptitiously and venomously anti-Spanish.[1]

Earlier, in 1944, the editor Gustavo Gili Roig had decried the grave danger posed by translations, which jeopardised Spanish book production. He also lamented the lack of political attention directed at the issue. Spain seemed to be mainly concerned with promoting the idea of empire, rather than solving the problem of foreign influences:

> There is talk about Spain's policy of empire building and the need to define its full scope. Such talk aspires to provide a solid foundation for the so-called Hispanic reaffirmation, which considers Spanish Americanism to be one of the fundamental pillars of the new empire [...]. One cannot talk of an imperial policy if one ignores the most effective vehicle for its expansion, and if the book is not considered as the most precious instrument to convey the feelings of Spain to and to share the country's long-standing civilisation with all countries that have inherited the treasure of our language, which is tantamount to saying our soul.
>
> (Gili Roig 1944: 21)

So, in an attempt to preserve the Spanish 'soul' and as a vehicle to promote Francoist principles, the 1946 Book Production Law was passed (BOE 19/12/1946). This law was mainly concerned with State protection of books produced in Spain, but also indirectly 'aimed at putting a brake on the importation of foreign works, and represented a stimulus to publishers to heed the regime's call to promote a truly Spanish book' (Camus 2011: 238). It, therefore, played a pivotal role in the cultural planning of the regime and also in launching the Spanish book industry. As stated in the preamble to the Law:

> On the greatest possible dissemination of Spanish books, both at home and abroad.
> The unfavourable position and lack of protection of Spanish books in foreign markets, together with the selling prices—inaccessible to modest budgets—in the home market, which is clearly detrimental to the dissemination of any type of culture, require immediate and effective action to end this precarious situation and to lay the foundations for the future expansion for which Spanish books are destined, principally in Spanish-America, because of the universality of our language and the Catholicity of our spirit.
>
> (BOE 19/12/1946)

The Law prescribed a number of measures, such as the granting of tax concessions to Spanish publishing companies. At the same time, it introduced initiatives that might curb the entry of foreign works by controlling and promoting the production and launching of truly Spanish books both within and beyond Spain's borders. In other words, 'true' Spanish books were those written in Spanish that reproduced the regime's ideology. They were clearly different from non-Spanish books, i.e., translations, and anti-Spanish books which, though written in Spanish, communicated an ideology that was contrary to that propounded by the regime.

Translations are cultural products used to fill a void in a given culture at a particular time. By contrast, pseudotranslations, as imitations of foreign source culture texts, are produced in the country where such a need has been created (Toury 1995). Because translations were anathema to the regime and publishers sought to promote not only Spanish book production but also narrative models popular among readers, pseudotranslation became the main vehicle employed to bring about the emergence of Spanish popular fiction (Merino and Rabadán 2002). These narratives fitted well with the necessities of both publishing houses and the general public. There was the need to fill the void left by the talented Republican writers that had fled the country during and after the civil war: 'To fill the gap left by the exiled intellectuals, publishers recruited an army of ready-made writers from diverse professions and even employed Republican writers for their new enterprise' (Camus 2010: 44). To screen from the public eye both the lack of writers and the fact that Republicans were producing the works, publishers encouraged writers to sign their works under cover of pseudonyms. While the use of pseudonyms in the popular novel is not restricted to Spain, what is remarkable about the Spanish popular narrative is that the pseudonyms chosen by writers often sounded foreign. Government authorities knew the authors' real names, but by using this stratagem the regime was presented to the general public as being more open to foreign ideas.

Thus, the Spanish book became the agent of the cultural intervention promoted by the new regime through pseudotranslations, the imported narrative models of which ironically inspired Spanish authors whose identities were disguised by foreign-sounding pseudonyms (Camus 2008: 161). Despite the boom in pseudotranslations, there is little evidence that the number of imported narrative works decreased as a result of these measures.

In addition to official film censorship, a Ministerial Directive (Order 23/04/1941) was passed in 1941 making it mandatory to dub foreign films into Spanish in an attempt to control the content of these films even further, to put a brake on the entry of foreign customs and lifestyles, and to preserve the purity of the Spanish language. The same order required the payment of a tax to the Spanish National Performances Department for foreign films to be shown in Spain. The funds raised by this tax acted as an incentive and helped to finance indigenous film production. The protection of Spanish cinematography against the importation of foreign films was subsequently regulated by ministerial orders (28/10/1941 and 28/10/1943). However, compulsory dubbing did not have the desired effect since it inadvertently encouraged the promotion of foreign films and thus had a negative impact on the incipient Spanish film industry. As a result, a new attempt was made to placate the irate Spanish film industry, and dubbing ceased to be mandatory (Order 28/06/1946). This order re-established the freedom to project foreign films in their original language on condition that subtitles be provided. Since subtitles discouraged some viewers, they had an indirect, and unexpected, negative effect on the Spanish film industry because distributors with a modest budget had to invest in films for which they did not foresee making a profit on their investment.

A new order (31/12/1946) granted exclusive authorisation for subtitling or dubbing into Spanish to those Spanish film producers whose films had obtained the approval of the *Junta Superior de Ordenación Cinematográfica* (film censorship board), based on their quality. This measure required that a foreign film first undergo censorship review and obtain approval in the original version. Next, in order to obtain permission for dubbing, the companies had to have already produced Spanish films endorsed by the censorship board. The Spanish producers of first-category films were granted a dubbing quota of three to four films. First-category films were those that represented a considerable advance in any production aspect or which showed sufficient merit or decorum to be considered an object of value and protection (Order 12/06/1947).

However, order 29/07/1948 reduced the dubbing quota to three films for those companies producing Spanish films considered of national interest, and further reduced the quota to only two dubbing authorisations for those companies producing category A films. A new order 19/06/1950 correlated the number of films that were allowed to be dubbed to the length of the films. The granting of dubbing and subtitling permits and licenses continued to be regulated in different ministerial orders, while timelines were modified; for instance, the period of six months for companies to present films to be censored, established in the order of 19/02/1960, was extended to nine months by the order of 05/12/1961. In addition, the taxation on viewing and screen share of foreign films was gradually adjusted.

In 1965 foreign films considered of particular interest could obtain authorisation to be projected in original or subtitled versions in special cinemas (Order 10/02/1965). This marked a significant departure for foreign films for, while film companies still needed to obtain a projection certificate, the censoring procedure had become more relaxed, which opened a new path for regulating special cinemas where original versions of films would be projected. Although censorship may have ended in Spain in 1977, the dubbing of films into Spanish for screening in commercial cinemas continues to be a profitable investment for the Spanish film industry, and original versions of foreign films continue to be projected only in special cinemas catering to a small audience.

A brief analysis of the impact of the censoring mechanism across different genres is presented in the following section.

26.3.2 Translation and Censorship across Genres

Numerous studies have been carried out on the impact of Francoist censorship on translation across genres. Scholars have produced case studies of individual works, focused on specific genres, and analysed different historical periods, thus offering a panoramic view of how the multiple changes in legislation affected translation activity over the course of Francoist rule.[2] Special mention should be made of the coordinated effort of the TRACE Research group. TRACE stands for TRAnslation and CEnsorship and is a research group established in 1997 with the aim of mapping the incidence of censorship on the translations carried out in Spain during the Francoist regime and the transition to democracy (1939–1985).[3]

In what follows a brief review of the main translated genres impacted by censorship during Franco's regime is presented.

26.3.2.1 Narrative Fiction

The 1940s was a period that witnessed the exile of many Republican intellectuals and the 'internal exile' of those who remained in Spain after the Civil War. In this context, foreign authors were added to the lists of publishing houses, although protests soon arose against this 'invasion' composed mostly of authors of Anglo-Saxon origin. Concerning the kind of material received via translation (specifically novels and anthologies of short stories), the main body of that which had been translated to that point belonged to what was considered 'kind literature', i.e., a type of fiction designed to entertain the reading public and at the same time avoid problems with the official system of censorship (Gómez Castro 2009: 360).

The fifties were a decade when Spain's isolation from the rest of the world eased slightly in favour of greater economic and cultural openness. The importation of films 'made in Hollywood' was also an important liberalising factor, since this kind of production typically involved the normalisation of controversial moral topics such as abortion or divorce, which were far from legitimised in the country but which could be accepted if coming from abroad, allowing them to be reflected in written fiction due to the connection between cinema and novels.[4] There was greater tolerance towards foreign literary and cinematic works, and serialised publication made it possible to read the writings of some members of the American 'lost generation'. Authors such as Aldous Huxley, however, did not authorise translation of their works into Spanish for fear they would be mutilated by the censorial apparatus (Hurtley 1986).[5]

As already indicated above, the 1966 Press and Print Law brought about changes in the publishing landscape in response to the greater openness demanded by society and, as a consequence, the red pencil changed hands from those of the censors to those of the publishers, who were making significant readjustments and modernising their projects to adapt to the new needs of the late 1960s (Martínez Martín 2015).

During the seventies, the country's book industry still relied on translations for a substantial portion of its profits. Increasing importance was given to profit margins when selecting material for publication, and publishing houses invested mostly in works of narrative fiction that had previously enjoyed success in North America or worldwide. The introduction of these best sellers had a significant impact on native literary production since they brought a new atmosphere of freedom to the changing Spanish literary scene: themes and topics that would have been categorically forbidden were now permitted mainly because they represented a different culture, while also providing foreign models that Spanish authors could imitate in their narrative fiction. Thus, translations from English can be said to constitute a quantitatively central and qualitatively innovative element in the Spanish polysystem of that time, even if occasionally hindered by the guardians of official morality. The end of the regime was close at hand, and the book control system reflected this in its leniency, which paved the way for negotiations and behind-the-scenes manoeuvering among the different agents involved in the processes of translating, editing and censoring, thus permitting the entry of new ideas and literary forms into the country (Gómez Castro 2009).

26.3.2.2   Cinema[6]

As the most popular form of mass entertainment, cinema was very closely surveilled by the Francoist authorities. As a result, numerous laws were passed to achieve this control over the course of the dictatorship. With regard to translated material, American productions constituted the highest percentage of premieres in Spain, resulting in the gradual introduction of concepts specific to Anglo-American culture, including more liberal morals (Gutiérrez Lanza 2000). Both the Church and the State exerted censorship over cinema, and this had a significant impact on the strictness of the different agents in charge of censoring. It has been shown (Gutiérrez Lanza 2008) that, in the period 1951–1962, the vast majority of film releases were given the lowest moral hazard ratings (1, 2 and 3); however, beginning in 1963, as a result of the imposition of Film Censorship Norms and changes in the age of attendance, there was a considerable increase in the release of films rated as more morally reprehensible (3R and 4) (Gutiérrez Lanza 2008: 216). Although censorship was supposed to be applied equally to national and foreign products, foreign cinema was treated with a greater level of permissiveness in regard to thematics (Gutiérrez Lanza 2000). In line with the political changes taking place in the period 1969–1973, national film production was treated more severely, but that treatment was eventually softened for the sake of economic profits. Official censorship of English-language films swung like a pendulum, depending on the greater or lesser socio-political immobility of the groups that were alternating in power (Gutiérrez Lanza 2000). The primary and ultimate aim of the control apparatus was the same throughout the entire period, i.e., a cinema tailored to the relevant censorship body and current legislation.

26.3.2.3   Theatre

Theatre, as a form of public entertainment, was also zealously scrutinised by the censors. The overview of theatrical productions, translated or published and produced/staged in Spain during the dictatorship, has been created by several scholars in the TRACE network, who have produced studies devoted to specific time periods or specific authors.[7] Translated theatre was a constant on the Spanish stage, especially in the early years of the regime. American theatre was one of the most translated and staged as a result of the popularity of Hollywood cinema, which contributed to the subgenre of crime melodrama (Pérez L. de Heredia 2000: 157). These plays resulted in the emergence of pseudotranslation in the realm of national theatre, similar to the phenomenon discussed above in the realm of narrative fiction.

The attitude of the official censors assigned to monitor these popular dramas was conditioned by the fact that they viewed the plays as useful for the dissemination of the official ideology of the regime.

The real avalanche of American titles began in the late 1950s, and the progressive increase in premieres firmly established American theatre in Spanish culture (Sánchez Reboredo 1988). The effect of censorship on this kind of material was not terribly harsh, with only a small percentage being banned and the rest authorised for an audience over 18 (Sánchez Reboredo 1988: 111). Theatre managers were required to have the certificate of censorship and the printed version of the play authorised by the theatre censorship section to ensure that improvisation, so common in theatre, would be kept to a minimum (Sánchez Reboredo 1988: 164). Nevertheless, in the theatre, as in other genres, internal or self-censorship was common, so that by the time a foreign drama entered the Spanish polysystem, it had already been softened by the translator in anticipation of its compulsory submission to economic and censorial patronage.

Concerning classical theatre, it is worth noting that some of these works were exempt from prior censorship following the order passed on 25 March 1944, the intent of which was to free religious, scientific and technical books from this requirement, as well as songs composed prior to 1900 and Spanish literary works written before 1800 (art. 1). On the whole, foreign literary products were acceptable to the regime as long as they were not updated to offer a new reading of the classical play (Bandín 2007).

26.3.2.4   Poetry[8]

Poetry is a genre that does not typically draw a broad reading public, and this could explain its marginal position in the book market. As with other genres, the situation of Spain at the beginning of the dictatorship was not favourable to the national production of poetry. As a result, translations were an important source of poetic material, especially English-language poetry. Thus, 'the influence of contemporary English-language poetry is also perceived in the poetic output of several leading Spanish poets, who had an interest in translating the poetry of English-speaking authors from previous generations' (Lobejón Santos 2020: 114). Literary magazines specialising in poetic texts were one means of disseminating both national and translated poetry during the Franco regime. However, translated works were most often published in poetry collections, anthologies and, to a lesser extent, newspapers.

As for the impact of censorship on poetry, there seems to have been more permissiveness with this genre than others, possibly due to the indeterminacy of poetic language. However, differences in treatment have been observed. According to Lobejón Santos (2020: 127), 'poetry books written by authors whose liberal ideology was well known and protest books released by left-wing publishing houses came under censorial fire [...] while the opposite often held true for books produced by publishing companies operated by regime advocates or collaborators, which were received more favourably [...].' The regime's intervention was certainly more direct with the works of contemporary authors than with classical verse. It was most strict in its treatment of anti-establishment poets, such as the Beat Generation, who opposed many of the regime's fundamental beliefs (Lobejón Santos 2020).

Internal or self-censorship was a common strategy among poets, who often wrote between the lines and created their own coded vocabulary to deal with polemical issues. In the case of translations, this strategy could also be implemented by both translators and publishers, without being directly attributed to either unless the identity of the agent responsible for the self-censorship had been confirmed. Be that as it may, the Francoist legacy endured after the fall of the regime; for example, several translations of poetry with censored fragments intact were re-published during the democratic period.

26.4 New Debates: 'Franco dies slowly' and Potential Research Avenues

The 1978 Spanish Constitution announced the end of official censorship. Writers were now able to write in a climate of freedom while publishers could worry less about the potentially offensive nature of the material they wanted to put on the market and concentrate more on marketing and sales. This may explain why some translations that circulated during the dictatorship can still be purchased in Spanish bookshops in reprints. In terms of financial gain, it is understandable that publishers might exploit an already existing translation even though it may have been expurgated by order of the censorship boards, because 'it may often be cheaper to recycle an already existing translation than to commission a new translation' (Milton 2000: 177). During the first years of democracy, the phenomenon was more noticeable in cinema as films with cut scenes were being shown without the addition of the censored material. In the case of narrative fiction, the maintenance of censored passages was more difficult to identify, since readers were often not aware that they were reading a translation (the country is so used to them that sometimes this has been internalised by them, in the same way films were always dubbed). Some research has been carried out on the topic (see Gómez Castro 2008; Abellán 1995; Lázaro 2001; Cornellá 2015), but it has yet to be addressed systematically. Cornellá's research has provided useful insights into the impact of translation and censorship on the press and news media, paving the way for deeper and more systematic investigations of press censorship. Spaniards may assume that the publishing industry no longer reprints translations from the Franco period, but new research will reveal the extent to which that assumption is true.

Further Reading

Merino Álvarez, Raquel and Rabadán, Rosa. 2002. 'Censored Translations in Franco´s Spain: The TRACE Project – Theatre and Fiction (English-Spanish)', *TTR—Traduction, Terminologie et Redaction*, XV(2): 125–52. DOI: https://doi.org/10.7202/007481ar
This article deals with the relationship between translation and censorship in the Spanish context under Franco and specifically concerning the genres of theatre and fiction.

Gutiérrez Lanza, Camino. 2000. *Traducción y censura de textos cinematográficos en la España de Franco: doblaje y subtitulado inglés-español (19511975)*. León: Servicio de Publicaciones de la Universidad de León. ISBN: 84-7719-903-5.
Book which tackles the Francoist censorship with a focus on the cinema imported and dubbed at the time, featuring a catalogue of films and their official classification by the censors.

Lobejón Santos, Sergio. 2013. *Traducción y censura de textos poéticos inglés-español en España: TRACEpi (19391983)*. León: Universidad de León. Unpublished PhD dissertation. Available at: https://buleria.unileon.es/handle/10612/6133
Until today, this is the most comprehensive study devoted to the genre of poetry written in English and translated into Spanish during Franco's dictatorship.

Notes

1 Internal document found in the AGA archive, no page references available.
2 See, for example: Franco Aixela and Abio Villarig (2009); Lázaro (2014, 2016, 2019, among many); Linder Molin (2011, 2014); Monzón Rodríguez (2021).
3 Website of the TRACE Research Group. https://trace.unileon.es/es/. (Accessed 4 September 2024).
4 This is what came to be known as 'tie-in', i.e., a close relationship between novels and film scripts which is responsible for the nurturing of the film industry from literature, a very common phenomenon by then and still now.

The Routledge Handbook of Translation and Censorship

5 Nonetheless, many of his books were finally published during Franco's Spain, not without negotiation between the different agents being involved (see, for example, Meseguer Cutillas 2015).
6 For a comprehensive study on translation and cinema during Franco's dictatorship, see Gutiérrez Lanza (2000), Lobejón Santos et al. (2021). Other authors have tackled specific cinema genres, such as the Western (Camus 2009) or specific periods (Serrano Fernández 2003).
7 See, for example, Bandín (2007), Pérez L. de Heredia (2004) or Andaluz Pinedo (2022).
8 For a comprehensive study of the translation of poetry under Franco's Spain see Lobejón Santos (2013).

References

Abellán, Manuel Luis. 1980. *Censura y creación literaria en España (19391976)* [*Censorship and Literary Creation in Spain (1939-1976)*]. Barcelona: Península.
Abellán, Manuel Luis. 1995. 'Algunos determinismos sociales del franquismo y la transición' [Some Social Determinisms of Francoism and the Period of Transition], in F. Bonaddio and D. Harris (eds.), *Siete ensayos sobre la cultura posfranquista* [*Seven Essays on Postfrancoist Culture*]. Aberdeen: Central Services University of Aberdeen, 2–9.
Andaluz Pinedo, Olaia. 2022. *Traducciones teatrales (inglés-español) desde la censura franquista hasta el siglo XXI: análisis del corpus TEATRAD* [*Theatre Translations (English-Spanish) from Franco's Censorship to The 21st Century: An Analysis of the TEATRAD Corpus*] Vitoria. Universidad del Pais Vasco/ /Euskal Herriko Unibertsitate. Unpublished PhD dissertation. http://hdl.handle.net/10810/56092
Bandín, Elena. 2007. *Traducción, recepción y censura de teatro clásico inglés en la España de Franco. Estudio descriptivo–comparativo del Corpus TRACEtci(1939–1985)* [*Translation, Rreception and Ccensorship of Cclassical English Ttheatre in Franco's Spain:A Ddescriptive-comparative Analysis of the Ccorpus TRACEtci (1939-1985)*] León: Universidad de León. Unpublished PhD dissertation. Available at: https://buleria.unileon.es/handle/10612/1885
Boase-Beier, Jean and Holman, Michael (eds.). 1999. *The Practices of Literary Translation: Constraints and Creativity.* Manchester: St. Jerome.
Camus, Carmen. 2008. 'Pseudonyms, Pseudotranslation, and Self-Censorship in the Narrative of the West during the Franco Dictatorship', in T. Seruya and M. L. Moniz (eds.), *Translation and Censorship in Different Times and Landscapes.* Newcastle: Cambridge Scholars Publishing, 147–62.
Camus, Carmen. 2009. *Traducciones censuradas de novelas y películas del oeste en la España de Franco* [*Censored Translations of Western Nnovels and Ffilms in Franco's Spain*]. Vitoria–Gasteiz: Universidad del País Vasco. Unpublished PhD dissertation.
Camus, Carmen. 2010. 'Censorship in the translations and pseudotranslations of the West', in D. Gile, G. Hansen and N. K. Pokorn (eds.), *Why Translation Studies Matter.* Amsterdam: John Benjamins, 41–56.
Camus, Carmen. 2011. 'How Some of the West Was Lost in Translation: The Influence of Franco's Censorship on Spanish Westerns', in D. Río, A. Ibarraran and M. Simonson (eds.), *Beyond the Myth: New Perspectives on Western Texts.* London: Portal Editions, 237256.
Cisquella, Georgina, Erviti, José Luis and Sorolla, José A. 1977. *Diez Años de Represión Cultural. La censura de libros durante la ley de prensa (196676)* [*Ten Years of Cultural Repression. Book Censorship during the Press Law (1966--76)*]. Barcelona: Editorial Anagrama.
Cornellá, Jordi. 2015. "La persistencia de la censura franquista durante el período democrático", *Quimera: Revista de Literatura*, 374: 47–49.
Franco Aixelá, Javier and Abio Villarig, Carlos. 2009. 'Manipulación ideológica y traducción: atenuación e intensificación moral en la traducción de la novela negra norteamericana al español (1933-2001)' [Ideological Manipulation and Translation: Moral Attenuation and Intensification in the Translation of the American Noir Novel into Spanish (1933-2001)], *Hermeneus*, 11: 109–44.
Gili Roig, Gustavo (ed.). 1944. *Bosquejo de una política del libro* [*Outline of a Book Policy*]. Barcelona: Imprenta Hispano Americana.
Gómez Castro, Cristina. 2008. 'The Francoist Censorship Casts a Long Shadow: Translations from the Period of the Dictatorship on Sale Nowadays', in T. Seruya and M. L. Moniz (eds.), *Translation and Censorship in Different Times and Landscapes.* Newcastle: Cambridge Scholars Publishing, 184–95.
Gómez Castro, Cristina. 2009. *Traducción y censura de textos narrativos inglés-español en la España franquista y de transición TRACEni (1970-1978)* [*Translation and Censorship of English-Spanish Narrative Texts in Franco's Spain and ts Aftermath: TRACEni (1970-1978)*]. León: Universidad de León. Unpublished PhD dissertation. Available at: https://buleria.unileon.es/handle/10612/1413

Gómez Castro, Cristina. 2012. 'Traducción y censura de textos narrativos inglés-español durante la España franquista: algunas prácticas traductoras' [Translation and Censorship of English-Spanish Narrative Texts during Franco's Spain: Some Translation Practices'], in A. Muñoz Miquel and J. L. Martí Ferriol (eds.), *Estudios de Traducción e Interpretación: Entornos de especialidad (vol. 2)*. Castellón de la Plana: Universitat Jaume I, 221–29.

Gutiérrez Lanza, Camino. 2000. 'Proteccionismo y censura durante la etapa franquista: cine nacional, cine traducido y control estatal' [Protectionism and Censorship during the Franco Era: National Cinema, Translated Cinema and State Control'], in Rosa Rabadán (ed.), *Traducción y censura Inglés-Español 1939-1985: estudio preliminar [English Spanish Translation and Censorship 1939-1985: A Preliminary Study]*. León: Universidad de León, 23–59.

Gutiérrez Lanza, Camino. 2008. 'Traducción inglés-español y censura de textos cinematográficos: definición, construcción y análisis del Corpus 0/Catálogo TRACEci (1951-1981)' [English-Spanish Translation and Censorship of Cinematographic Texts: Definition, Construction and Analysis of the TRACEci Corpus 0/Catalogue (1951-1981)], in R. Merino Álvarez (ed.), *Traducción y censura en España (1939-1985). Estudios sobre corpus TRACE: cine, narrativa, teatro*. Bilbao: Universidad del País Vasco, 197–242.

Hurtley, Jacqueline. 1986. *Josep Janés, el combat per la cultura [Josep Janés, the Struggle for Culture]*. Barcelona: Curial.

Larraz, Fernando E. 2014. *Letricidio español. Censura y novela durante el franquismo [Spanish Letricide. Censorship and the novel during Franco's regime]*. Gijón: Trea.

Lázaro, Alberto. 2001. 'George Orwell's *Homage to Catalonia*: a Politically Incorrect Story', in A. Lázaro (ed.), *The Road from George Orwell: His Achievement and Legacy*. Bern: Peter Lang, 71–91.

Lázaro, Alberto. 2014. 'The Reception of Doris Lessing's Novels in Franco's Spain', *Atlantis*, 36(2): 97–113.

Lázaro, Alberto. 2016. 'The Reception of Thomas Hardy in Franco's Spain: The Cases of *Tess* and *Jude the Obscure*', *BAS: British and American Studies*, 22: 17–24.

Lázaro, Alberto. 2019. 'The Spanish Version of E. M. Forster's *Maurice*: A Curious Censorship Case', *Perspectives: Studies in Translation Theory and Practice*, 27(6): 785–96.

Linder Molin, Daniel P. 2011 'The Long Goodbye en español: traducciones abreviadas, completas, plagiadas y censuradas' [The Long Goodbye in Spanish: Abridged, Complete, Plagiarised and Censored Translations], in J. Sánchez Zapatero and A. Martín Escribà (eds.), *Género negro para el siglo XXI: Nuevas tendencias y nuevas voces [Film Noir Genre for the 21st Century*. Barcelona: Laertes, 75–86.

Linder Molin, Daniel P. 2014. 'Reusing Existing Translations: Mediated Chandler Novels in French and Spanish', *Jostrans – The Journal of Specialised Translation*, 22: 57–77.

Lobejón Santos, Sergio. 2013. *Traducción y censura de textos poéticos inglés-español en España: TRACEpi (1939-1983 [Translation and Censorship of English-Spanish Poetic Texts in Spain: TRACEpi (1939-1983)]*. León: Universidad de León. Unpublished PhD dissertation. Available at: https://buleria.unileon.es/handle/10612/6133

Lobejón Santos, Sergio. 2020. 'Translations of English-language Poetry in Post-War Spain (1939--1983)', *Translation Matters*, 2(2): 113–30.

Lobejón Santos, Sergio, Gómez Castro, Cristina and Gutiérrez Lanza, Camino. 2021. 'Archival Research in Translation and Censorship: digging into the "True Museum of Francoism"', *Meta: Translators' Journal*, 66(1): 92–114.

Martínez Bretón, Juan Antonio. 1987. *Influencia de la Iglesia católica en la cinematografía española (1951-1962) [Influence of the Catholic Church on Spanish Cinematography (1951-1962)]*. Madrid: Harofarma.

Martínez Martín, Jesús A. 2015. 'El capitalismo de edición moderno. Las empresas editoriales: negocios, política y cultura. Los años sesenta' [Modern Publishing Capitalism. Publishing Companies: Business, Politics and Culture. The 1960s'], in J. A. Martínez Martín (dir.), *Historia de la edición en España, 1939–1975*. Madrid: Marcial Pons, 273–328.

Merino Álvarez, Raquel and Rabadán, Rosa. 2002. 'Censored Translations in Franco's Spain: The TRACE Project – Theatre and Fiction (English-Spanish)', *TTR—Traduction, Terminologie et Redaction*, XV(2): 125–52. DOI: https://doi.org/10.7202/007481ar

Meseguer Cutillas, Purificación. 2015. *Sobre la traducción de libros al servicio del franquismo: sexo, política y religión [On the Translation of Books in the Service of Francoism: Sex, Politics and Religión]*. Berna: Peter Lang.

Milton, John. 2000. 'The translation of mass fiction', in A. Beeby, D. Ensinger and M. Presas (eds.), *Investigating Translation*. Amsterdam and Philadelphia: John Benjamins, 171–79.

Monzón Rodríguez, Sofía. 2021. 'Censoring poetics through translation: the filtered reception of Sylvia Plath in Franco's Spain', *Translation Matters*, 3(1): 110–24.

Pegenaute, Luis. 1999. 'Censoring Translation and Translation as Censorship: Spain under Franco', in J. Vandaele (ed.), *Translation and the (Re)Location of Meaning: Selected Papers of the CETRA Research Seminars in Translation Studies*. Leuven: CETRA, 83–96.

Peres del Puerto, Ángela. 2021. *Reprobada por la moral: La censura católica en la producción literaria durante la posguerra* [*Reproved by Morals: Catholic Censorship in Post-war Literary Production*]. Madrid and Frankfurt-Main: Iberoamericana y Vervuert.

Pérez López de Heredia, María. 2000. 'Traducción y censura en la escena española de posguerra: creación de una nueva identidad cultural' [Translation and Censorship on the Post-War Spanish Stage: the Creation of a New Cultural Identity], in R. Rabadán (ed.), *Traducción y censura, inglés-español 1939 1985: estudio preliminar* [*English Spanish Translation and Censorship 1939-1985: A Preliminary Study*]. León: Universidad de León, 153–89.

Pérez López de Heredia, María. 2004. *Traducciones censuradas de teatro norteamericano en la España de Franco (1939–1963)* [*Censored Translations of American Theatre in Franco's Spain (1939-1963)*]. Bilbao: Universidad del País Vasco. Unpublished PhD dissertation.

Sánchez Reboredo, José. 1988. *Palabras tachadas (Retórica contra censura)* [*Words Crossed out (Rhetoric vs. Censorship)*]. Alicante: Juan Gil-Albert.

Serrano Fernández, Luis. 2003. *Traducción y censuras de textos cinematográficos inglés–español 1970–1985* [*Translation and censorship of English-Spanish cinematographic texts 1970-1985*]. León: Universidad de León. Unpublished Phd dissertation.

Toury, Gideon. 1995. *Descriptive Translation Studies and Beyond*. Amsterdam: John Benjamins.

Main Legislation

All the legislation referenced is published in the Boletín Oficial del Estado, the official Spanish gazette (www. boe.es/).

Specific ministerial orders cited in the text are listed below: all accessed 25/09/2023.

Order 28/06/1946. Available at: www.boe.es/datos/pdfs/BOE//1946/200/A05716-05716.pdf Order 31/ 12/1946. Available at: www.boe.es/datos/pdfs/BOE//1947/025/A00572-00573.pdf Order 12/06/1947. Available at: www.boe.es/datos/pdfs/BOE//1947/166/A03391-03391.pdf Order 10/08/1948. Available at: www.boe.es/datos/pdfs/BOE//1948/223/A03867-03867.pdf Order 19/06/1950. Available at: www. boe.es/datos/pdfs/BOE//1950/176/A02792-02792.pdf Order 19/02/1960. Available at: www.boe.es/boe/ dias/1960/03/19/pdfs/A03465-03465.pdf Order 05/12/1961. Available at: www.boe.es/boe/dias/1961/12/ 18/pdfs/A17756-17757.pdf Order 10/02/1965. Available at: www.boe.es/boe/dias/1965/02/27/pdfs/A03 101-03105.pdf

27

CENSORING SEXUALITY IN TRANSLATION

An Overview of Research on Spain (English–Spanish)

José Santaemilia

27.1 Introduction

Censorship and translation is a topic that has received substantial attention in academic circles in recent years. Indeed, there are countless publications on censorship and translation, as well as dedicated scholars and research groups, special issues of journals and international conferences organised around the topic, which has gained a recognised position in academia in the humanities and social sciences in recent years. Without a doubt, sexuality is one of the main sources of censorship, both in original texts as well as in translations. Texts dealing with sex and sexuality have been written and disseminated since the beginnings of civilisation. The terms used to refer to sex and sexuality in writings, *erotica*, *pornography* and *obscenity*, 'remain heavily theorised and heavily contested' (Sigel 2005: 6) and their frontiers 'are never clear-cut' (Colligan 2006: 2). In spite of this, the specific terms used in different historical periods are highly relevant, as 'the labels have important consequences that continue to affect policy and perceptions' (Sigel 2005: 7); e.g., while *erotica* has kept a certain aura of respectability, *pornography* 'might have a certain risqué ring' (Sigel 2005:7, ineluctably placing the focus on people's desires. Obscenity seems to refer to a wider phenomenon (what cannot be publicly said or represented, not exclusively or necessarily of a sexual nature). For Hunt (1996: 13) obscenity 'has existed just as long as the distinction between private and public behaviour'. 'As a commercial enterprise and a shared concept, obscenity was interleaved in the culture at large, intersecting majority and minority culture, circulating from home to empire, searching out new print and visual media, and readily globalising' (Colligan 2006: 9; for a more extended discussion, see Hunt 1996; Sigel 2005; Colligan 2006).

Erotica, pornography or *obscenity* served to define, and sometimes proscribe, the type of writing found in classics such as the *Kama Sutra*, or in writers such as Sappho, Catullus, Ovid, Boccaccio, Casanova, John Cleland, D.H. Lawrence, and many others. The works of these and other authors have been (and will continue to be) translated into innumerable languages. However, sexuality is not only present in erotic or pornographic writings; it also features increasingly in a

DOI: 10.4324/9781003149453-33

413

variety of literary or audiovisual genres to the point that we may talk about a growing *sexualisation* or *pornification* (Weeks 2011: 200) of all literary or filmic production, and even of cultural life.

Edited collections (Merkle 2002, Billiani 2007b, Seruya and Moniz 2008, Ní Chuillenáin et al. 2009, Merkle et al. 2010, Zaragoza et al. 2018, among others) have attempted to document the cross-discipline of censorship and translation, covering mainly specific well-researched periods, particularly the official state censorship regimes under dictatorships (e.g., Italy and Spain under Fascist dictators Mussolini and Franco, or Nazi Germany under Hitler) or in nineteenth-century Europe. Official state censorship is used throughout this paper to indicate the 'prevention by official government act of the circulation of messages already produced, or a system of direct official constraints on publication' (Merkle 2002: 9). To date, however, sexuality has been studied unevenly and only partially in connection with censorship or self-censorship. Comparatively few publications (Reynolds 2007; O'Sullivan 2009, 2010) deal exclusively with the censoring of sexual matter, sexual(ised) language and sexual representations in translation. This is perhaps due to sexuality being a sensitive topic in almost all societies, even taboo in certain historical periods, and to human beings' resistance to dealing openly with such intimate and sensitive matters.

Studying the censorship of sexuality in translation constitutes a difficult task, as texts related to or dealing with sex and sexuality are 'notoriously difficult to translate for reasons of cultural and generational differences—a *cas limite* that in some ways serves as a test of translation' (von Flotow 2000: 16). When one translates sex-related terms or sexual activities, or deals with the expression of pleasure or sexual taboos, 'the translator's personality, identity, experience, and background will feed into the new texts, also affecting the translated version' (von Flotow 2000: 15). Consequently, providing an overview of the censorship of sexuality in translation offers an excellent opportunity for the person translating to explore both his or her inner self and the period in which the translation was produced, as it is likely to reveal the prejudices, gendered and sexual(ised) configurations, and ethical dispositions of both translator and his/her time.

27.2 Historical Perspectives

This chapter aims to offer an initial overview of the studies on the censoring of sexuality in Spain, in the English–Spanish language combination. Some clarification is required here: I take into account both the production of researchers working in Spain and that of scholars working abroad, who focus on English–Spanish translations and adaptations published or distributed in Spain. For the sake of coherence, research carried out in other Spanish-speaking countries will not be considered here, although embarking on a more comprehensive project of studying the censorship of sexuality in the English–Spanish language pair throughout the Spanish-speaking world would be more than welcome. A focus on translations from Catalan, Basque and Galician would also provide a more comprehensive portrait of the complex plurilinguistic and plurinational reality of today's Spain. Consequently, Table 27.1 aims to be a modest, initial mapping of the main texts and researchers working on the censorship of translated sexuality in Spain, i.e., working on literary and audiovisual texts meant for distribution in Spain. The reason for this focus on the English–Spanish combination is straightforward: a thorough review of the publications has revealed that the vast majority of the academic books and articles published over the last four decades focuses on the translation of English-language literary or audiovisual texts. However, a more rigorous quantitative survey would be needed in order to determine a specific percentage.

Censoring Sexuality in Translation

Most of the growing research in Spain (English–Spanish) is devoted to the period of Francisco Franco's dictatorship (1939–1975), whose censorship machinery nevertheless continued to function beyond the proclamation of the Spanish Constitution of 1978, and was actually dismantled only in 1985 following the opening of the censorship archives (see Rabadán 2000: 9). Two periods are usually identified (Abellán 1980: 1) a 'glorious' period (1939–1965), characterised by strict control of all intellectual production, in the hands of highly-reputed intellectual censors; and 2) a 'trivial' period (1966–1985) of 'supervised openness' (Somacarrera 2017: 85), represented by low-profile, academically-irrelevant censors. Much more limited is the research on the censoring practices of sexual content in the English–Spanish translations of other historical periods, such as the early nineteenth century (Lasa 2015), the late nineteenth century (Campillo Arnaiz 2004, 2005; Franco Aixelá 2008), and post-1975 democratic Spain (Ortega Sáez 2007; Gómez Castro 2008a; Santaemilia 2008a, 2008b, 2018; Gómez Castro and Pérez L. de Heredia 2015; Sanz-Moreno 2017). Table 27.1 is a preliminary attempt at a comprehensive list of English-language texts (literary and non-literary) translated into Peninsular Spanish, and censored on account of their sexual language; in addition, specific reference to the respective researchers is provided.

The bulk of research focusing on the censorship of translated sexuality revolves around literary texts and also—especially since the late 2010s—audiovisual texts. Among the literary texts, we find classic authors such as William Shakespeare (Campillo Arnaiz 2004, 2005; Sullivan and Bandín 2014), William Thackeray (Rodríguez Espinosa 2001, 2004), Mark Twain (Craig 1997), Oscar Wilde (Rojas-Lizana and Hannah 2013) or James Joyce (Sanz Gallego 2013). Twentieth-century popular authors include American writers of hard-boiled detective fiction, such as Dashiell Hammett (Franco Aixelá 2008; Franco Aixelá and Abio Villarig 2009; Linder 2014) and Raymond Chandler (Linder 2004; Franco Aixelá and Abio Villarig 2009), and a fairly long list of twentieth-century authors such as Richmal Crompton (Craig 1997), Elinor Glyn (Riba and Sanmartí 2017), Margaret Mitchell (Williams Camus 2017), Daphne du Maurier (Zaragoza and Cerezo 2019), J.D. Salinger (Gómez Castro 2007; Santaemilia 2018), John Dos Passos (Bautista Cordero 2013), Mary Renault (Meseguer Cutillas 2014; Meseguer Cutillas and Rojo 2014), Margaret Laurence (Somacarrera 2017), Evan Hunter (Gómez Castro 2008a), Kingsley Amis (Meseguer Cutillas 2014; Meseguer Cutillas and Rojo 2014), Thomas Berger (Camus Camus 2012), Irwin Shaw (Gómez Castro 2009, 2017), Erich Segal (Gómez Castro 2009), Mary McCarthy (Godayol 2019), W. Peter Blatty (Gómez Castro 2009), Mario Puzo (Gómez Castro 2009), E.M. Forster (Lázaro Lafuente 2019), Harold Robbins (Gómez Castro 2008b, 2009, 2020), Colleen McCullough (Gómez Castro 2009, 2014), Helen Fielding (Santaemilia 2008a, 2008b) and Annie Proulx (Gómez Castro and Pérez L. de Heredia 2015). Attention in the research literature has also been paid to playwrights such as Tennessee Williams (Merino Álvarez 2016), Robert Anderson (Merino Álvarez 2016), Edward Albee (Merino Álvarez and Rabadán 2002; Merino Álvarez 2016), Graham Greene (Merino Álvarez and Rabadán 2002; Merino Álvarez 2012) and Mart Crowley (Merino Álvarez 2007a, 2012, 2016). Interestingly, overtly erotic or sexualised writings constitute a small number of works by John Cleland, notably *Fanny Hill; or, Memoirs of a Woman of Pleasure,* (Toledano 2002, 2003), Radclyffe Hall (Zaragoza 2018), Henry Miller (Monzón Rodríguez 2020, 2022, 2023) and Djuna Barnes (Monzón Rodríguez 2023). With a few exceptions (Campillo Arnaiz 2004, 2005; Ortega Sáez 2007; Franco Aixelá 2008; Gómez Castro 2008a; Santaemilia 2008a, 2008b, 2018; Linder 2011, 2014; Lasa Álvarez 2015; Sanz-Moreno 2017), most studies in Table 27.1 refer exclusively to the censorious practices of the Francoist dictatorship. In spite of the wide panorama covered by these studies, there are still significant gaps that leave plenty of room for other researchers to map out the workings of censorship in Spain when faced with sexual language or mores.

The research literature on censorship and book translation in the twentieth century has monopolised the field over the last three decades. With the new century, however, and in line with the exponential surge in audiovisual translation (AVT) research, 'seen by many scholars as one of the most thriving branches of Translation Studies' (Díaz-Cintas and Neves 2015: 1) over the last few years, films and TV series figure with increasing frequency in the publications on the censorship of sexuality in translation. Some scholars are starting to locate information on the censorship of films during the Franco dictatorship. Camus Camus (2015) analyses the complex passage of King Vidor's *Duel in the Sun* (1946) through the Spanish Censorship Board. This included a variety of processes, such as self-censorship, suppressions and negotiations between the distribution company and the censors, in order to tame 'the controversial aspects such as the love triangle, the passionate scenes, Pearl's exuberant sexuality and those related to seduction, rape and murder' (Camus Camus 2015: 13). In the Spanish dubbing of Joseph L. Manckiewicz's *The Barefoot Comtessa* (1954), Díaz-Cintas (2019: 197–8) studies how 'Maria's uninhibited, sexy, and promiscuous performance, which to some foreigners symbolises the stereotypical image of the passionate, carefree Spaniard, had to be reined in through changes to the dialogue and twists to the plot'. Zaragoza and Cerezo (2019) document how the combined effect of the American Hays Production Code and the Spanish press laws resulted in a complete deletion of all explicit sexual references in the Spanish production of Alfred Hitchcock's *Rebecca* (1940). Other films analysed include Vincente Minnelli's *Tea and Sympathy* (1956) (Martínez Pleguezuelos and González-Iglesias González 2015), as well as icons of queer cinema, such as Ang Lee's *Brokeback Mountain* (2005) (Gómez Castro and Pérez L. de Heredia 2015; Sanz-Moreno 2017) or comedy films such as *There's Something with Mary* (1998) or *The Hangover I & II* (2009, 2011) (Sanz-Moreno 2017). Gutiérrez Lanza (2023) provides an overview of the state and church legislation on cinema censorship during the Franco dictatorship, with some discussion of the treatment of sexuality-related matters. TV series, in particular, constitute an ideal domain for examining contemporary articulations and representations of freer sexual relationships, more open morality and increasingly liberal sex-related language, and, for the purposes of this chapter, the types of censorship (or absence thereof) they are subjected to via dubbing, subtitling, audio-description and other AVT modalities. To date, however, no significant inroad has been made into this promising territory with regards Spanish audiences.

27.3 Core Issues and Topics

Particularly well researched in the field is censorship in twentieth-century European dictatorships (Italy, Spain and Portugal under fascist dictators Mussolini, Franco and Salazar, or Nazi Germany under Hitler), which imposed tight censorship measures, such as pre-publication or editorial censorship, and favoured systematic self-censorship. Sexual morality, political orthodoxy, religion and racism are among the most frequent targets of censorship (e.g., Merkle 2002; Vega 2004; Gallego Roca 2004; Billiani 2007a; Seruya and Moniz 2008; Ní Chuilleáin et al. 2009; Rundle and Sturge 2010; Bennett 2020). As for the English–Spanish language combination in Spain, the most articulated research project on translation and censorship is that of the TRACE group—a large-scale research programme on censored translations initiated in 1995 by Rosa Rabadán at the Universidad de León, followed by Raquel Merino and her research team at the Universidad del País Vasco in 1997. The initial overarching objective was to map the translating practices (in literature, cinema and theatre) in Spain under the Franco dictatorship. Over time, more scholars from other universities have embraced this ambitious initiative, discovering, cataloguing and analysing censored translations of foreign novels, plays and films during the Francoist dictatorship. Since 2006 the research group has been based at the Universidad de León, and the target time frame of research has been extended beyond the Francoist period, in order to accommodate the (self) censoring practices of translation until today.

Rabadán (2000) is a collected volume on the preliminary factors related to translational activity and the workings of the Francoist censorship system between 1939 and 1975, with regard to cinema, theatre, fiction and history, with contributions from founding members of the TRACE group (Rosa Rabadán, Raquel Merino, José Miguel Santamaría, Eterio Pajares, Marisa Fernández López), followed later by researchers who completed their doctoral projects under their supervision (Camino Gutiérrez Lanza, Carmen Camus Camus, María Pérez López de Heredia, Cristina Gómez Castro and others). Merino Álvarez (2007b) is another key reference; the volume brings together more contributions from members of the TRACE research group and adds interesting insights into topics that had been seldom explored before, such as self-censorship, pseudotranslations and the Francoist censorship of homosexuality. These publications describe the political and religious context of the period, as well as the mechanics of the censoring apparatus, based on a strict observance of morality and an outright rejection of any criticism of the political regime. The targets of the Francoist censoring system included 'mainly sexual morals, political beliefs, the use of improper language and religion' (Gómez Castro 2008b: 65). Sexuality, however, has only occasionally featured as a central object of study in the earliest publications of this group.

Within the TRACE research group, relevant and sustained research has been carried out by Gómez Castro, whose work illustrates the workings of Francoist censorship on the Spanish translations of a variety of key English-language literary works, combining archival research with qualitative linguistic and discursive analysis. Sexuality and censorship feature regularly, albeit not exclusively, in her research. Gómez Castro (2007) examines the first Spanish translation of J.D. Salinger's *The Catcher in the Rye* (1951), a literary phenomenon depicting teenage rebellion in the post-war US, with blasphemous language and sexual references. The Spanish translation was done by Carmen Criado in 1978, a year in which the censorship system had officially disappeared, thus raising the issue of the translator's pre-emptive self-censorship when faced with the censorial machinery of the Franco regime, which advocated strict sexual morality, restrictions on religion and political opinions, and the outlawing of taboo language. Gómez Castro (2013) also studies the Spanish translations of US anthologies of science fiction which were, during the 1970s, closely scrutinised for sexual immorality and sexually-charged language. Her 2014 publication analyses the treatment by the Francoist censors—still at work in spite of the disappearance of the dictatorial system—of a passage from Colleen McCullough's *The Thornbirds* (1977), a novel featuring a priest (Ralph de Bricassart) who falls in love with a woman, and which contains sexual encounters, explicit sexual language, and frequent references to homosexuality and divorce. This example underscores the difficulty of establishing clear time demarcations between dictatorial censorship under Franco and the censorship practised in post-Franco democratic Spain. Another contribution to the study of gender and sexual morality in the late Francoist period is once again Gómez Castro (2017), which describes the passage of Irwin Shaw's novel *Rich Man, Poor Man* (1969) through the Spanish censorship system. Although the book was not prohibited, the censors, working in a progressively weakening system of oversight, expressed their reluctance to give Spanish readers access to the novel's frank and 'insatiable' (Gómez Castro 2017: 100) treatment of sexual relations and divorce in the Spanish translation.

Other TRACE researchers have contributed to our understanding of the workings of censorship as it relates to sex and sexuality in translation (English–Spanish). Merino Álvarez (2007a), for example, focuses on the censoring of homosexuality in Spanish theatre productions since the 1960s, as documented in the Francoist regime's censorship files. Sexual morality, in general, and homosexuality, in particular, constituted conspicuous targets of the Francoist censorial apparatus. In fact, for Merino Álvarez (2007b: 13), sexual morality constituted the main editorial 'filter' through which to evaluate (and censor) the translation of books or the adaptation of foreign dramatic works. Seruya and Moniz (2008) include in their collected volume a number of contributions on both censorship and self-censorship during the Franco dictatorship, including the pseudotranslation of narratives of the West (Camus Camus 2008), and the long shadow cast by the Francoist censorship system beyond the period of the dictatorship, clearly illustrated with the number of censored translations that were on sale in the years of transition towards democracy in Spain (Gómez Castro 2008a) and that are on sale even today.

The initial mission of the TRACE group has been maintained and diversified by an increasing number of other researchers dealing with the workings of the censorship system during the Franco dictatorship. Of special significance is the work carried out by Daniel Linder, who has focused—thoroughly and consistently—on the treatment in Spanish translation of various sex-related aspects in some of the most famous American *noir* novels, such as Raymond Chandler's *The Big Sleep* (Linder 2004), which contains a number of veiled references to male homosexuality and subtle references to female nudity, as well as sexually suggestive dialogues. In 2014, he analyses the translation of both colloquial terms (*queer, fairy*) and specialised slang (*gunsel, the gooseberry lay*) as covert references to depict homosexual characters in American novelist Dashiell Hammett's *The Maltese Falcon* (1930). These terms were clearly attenuated in the harshest period of Francoist censorship (1946 Spanish edition), but were preserved (1968 and 1974 editions) and intensified after the end of the dictatorship (1992 and 2011 editions). In his publications, Linder pays special attention to the moral code imposed by the Spanish Catholic Church during the dictatorship and to the fuzzy boundaries between officially-imposed censorship and translators' own self-censorship.

Franco Aixelá and Abio Villarig (2009) examine the treatment of sexuality and vulgar language in the four Spanish-language translations of Chandler's *Farewell, my lovely* (1940), produced between 1945 and 2001. The authors highlight the impossibility of ideological neutrality in the translated versions of this sensitive source text and ascribe the adaptation of the translations to the dominant poetics at the time of publication. While democratic periods in Spain (e.g., the Spanish Second Republic and the transition towards democracy that began in 1975) are more tolerant of moral and sexual elements, autocratic and repressive periods (e.g., the Francoist dictatorship) sought to attenuate, and often delete, all traces of sexual or erotic language.

With the goal of identifying the main strategies used to censor sexual material, Meseguer Cutillas and Rojo (2014) focus on the Francoist censorship of French and English novels that have sexuality as a central theme, including Mary Renault's *The Last of the Wine* (1956) and Kingsley Amis's *The Anti-Death League* (1967), both of which were quite liberal in depicting sexual scenes. The researchers document a tendency to omit sexual material, unlike the political material in the source texts, which Francoist censors were likely to rewrite even going so far as to add covert propaganda for the regime.

Somacarrera (2017) studies the Spanish translations of Canadian writer Margaret Laurence's novel *A Jest of God* (1966), which revolves around female selfhood and the gender-related constraints imposed by society. A detailed analysis of the Spanish translation (*Raquel, Raquel*), done by Agustín Gil Lasierra in 1969, reveals clear instances of self-censorship. Lázaro Lafuente (2019) focuses on the censorship files of the Spanish translation of E.M. Forster's *Maurice* (1971), which today stands as a classic of gay fiction, although there are 'no very explicit sex scenes in the novel' (Lázaro Lafuente 2019: 787). The Spanish translation was published in 1973 and managed to pass through the homophobic lens of the Francoist censorship system unscathed, although the censors took the opportunity to express their condemnation of homosexuality in their censorship reports (see Lázaro Lafuente 2019: 788).

Although extensively mined, the censorship files at the Spanish General Administration Archive (AGA) in Alcalá de Henares are still an essential source for reconstructing the norms, or at least the logic, of the censorship apparatus established by Franco's dictatorial regime, which attempted to impose a system of political and religious orthodoxy, with a constant focus on sexual morality that would reinforce the tenets of their autocratic systems. Twentieth-century state archives offer immense possibilities for research, as they are 'a faithful reflection of the literary world' (Merino Álvarez and Rabadán 2002: 128) of their time and 'offer a unique vantage point from which to look at the history of translation practices' (Lobejón Santos et al. 2021: 93). The systematic work of an important number of scholars (see Table 27.1) underscores the crucial role of archival work in helping to (re)construct the parameters of authorised cultural production (original and translated), in (dis)confirming official histories of literature or cinema, and unveiling well-entrenched prejudices or taboos, particularly in the areas of politics, religion and sexuality (see Martín Ruano 2018). For an authoritarian regime, state censorship was a first-order ideological instrument for moral indoctrination, and 'controlling information and filtering cultural products were deemed of utmost importance' (Merino Álvarez and Rabadán 2002: 126).

Published research on periods other than the twentieth-century Spanish dictatorship is also included in the database. Lasa Álvarez (2015) documents the 1792 Spanish translation of Frances Sheridan's *Memoirs of Miss Sydney Bidulph* (1761), which was censored by the Holy Office of the Spanish Inquisition in the early eighteenth century. Censorship resulted mainly from disagreements on the interpretation of Catholic dogma and only partially from the novel's adulterous relations and lascivious issues. Campillo Arnaiz (2005) studies the translation of sexual puns in translations of Shakespeare's *Hamlet* (ca. 1600) into Spanish in the nineteenth century, showing how the obscenity of the original play posed 'rather complicated issues for the Spanish translators' (Campillo Arnaiz 2005: 29). Her analysis reveals two opposing trends: 1) bowdlerizing, the strategy adopted by Guillermo Macpherson in 1873, showing his uneasiness with Shakespeare's sexual puns; and 2) maximising; Jaime Clark, in 1874, opted for a literal rendering of sexual references, while occasionally reinforcing the sexual elements, perhaps 'as a reaction against previous censorship of the original' (Campillo Arnaiz 2005: 33). Franco Aixelá and Abio Villarig (2009) analyse the first Spanish translation of Hammett's *The Maltese Falcon* (1930), done by Fermín de Casas Gancedo in 1933, during the period of the Spanish Second Republic (1931–1936). According to the researchers, the translation is 'hotter than the original' (Franco Aixelá 2008: 95), a perspective that would end abruptly with Franco's *coup d'état* in 1936 and the ensuing dictatorship.

Under the Francoist dictatorship, authors such as Fay Weldon, Joanna Trollope, Jeannette Winterson and even Barbara Cartland were not translated. A key feature of this period is the absence of translations of erotic literature; a case in point is John Cleland's *Fanny Hill* (1748–1749). Toledano (2003) is a fine analysis of the reasons why Cleland's erotic novel could not get through the Francoist censorship system and was not published until 1976, most probably on the

The Routledge Handbook of Translation and Censorship

grounds that it advocated natural morality and religion-free sexuality (Toledano 2003: 242). Her contention is that *obscenity* is the most readily identified utterance or act in a text to be targeted by state censorship systems. And what is more, whether there is an official censorship apparatus or not, it seems that '[s]exuality in books and other media—overt or suggested—continues to fuel the fury of would-be censors' (Sova 2006: xi).

Here another phenomenon requires some rethinking. Ortega Sáez (2007) underscores the fact that Spaniards are still reading today the same texts that were heavily censored under the Francoist dictatorship. This is likely a universal phenomenon and begs the question of whether readers care about what is lost in translation—be it sexuality, appeals for democracy or criticism of religious intolerance. In any case, the issue deserves detailed individualised analyses of specific texts and specific reception studies. All in all, censoring texts and films may seem dramatic for some readers and viewers while for others it may be simply irrelevant or even necessary.

A slippery and highly subjective area of research is that of self-censorship. While censorship may be defined as an external constraint that involves 'the suppression or prohibition of speech or writing that is condemned as subversive of the common good' (Allan and Burridge 2006: 13), self-censorship is rather an individual moral/ethical struggle between the individual and society. In many historical circumstances, translators tend to censor themselves—either voluntarily or involuntarily—in order to produce rewritings that are 'acceptable' from both social and personal perspectives. Santaemilia (2008a) focuses on the Spanish and Catalan translations of *fuck*, as a sex-related term, in Helen Fielding's novels *Bridget Jones' Diary* (1996) and *Bridget Jones: The Edge of Reason* (1999). Santaemilia (2008b) presents options for dealing with sensitive and taboo language other than through official censorship—i.e., including self-censorship; individual ethics; and one's attitudes towards religion, sex, impoliteness and indecency. While explicit state censorship can be more easily documented thanks to archival resources, the range of self-censorship phenomena cannot be as easily documented since such sources do not exist. Barrale (2018: 11) suggests that self-censorship is the '"best" form of surveillance'. She adds that '[t]he success of self-censorship is, indeed, the result of a controlling system (surveillance), which can create independent pressures that make the surveillance itself unnecessary' (Barrale 2018: 12).

27.4 New Debates, New Challenges and Future Prospects

A great majority of the earliest research carried out on the censoring of translations of sexuality in Spain was, perhaps implicitly, based on a limited number of assumptions, which can be summarised as follows:

1 censored translations were mainly written books, followed by dubbed films and theatre adaptations;
2 the main censorial modalities were: a) official state censorship; and b) institutionally-induced self-censorship;
3 censorial interventions were necessarily negative, coercive and repressive;
4 the results of censorial interventions were always the total or partial loss or elimination of a significant number of linguistic elements or passages from the original;
5 sexuality may have played a certain role in translation censorship, but it was not the defining role and certainly did not constitute the only theme worthy of censorial attention.

420

Within this broadly defined paradigm, it is not surprising, then, that most scholars have devoted their efforts to researching either the censorial mechanisms of twentieth-century dictatorships or the individual books or publications that seemed to evince the presence of some form of difficult-to-substantiate self-censorship. The basic research lines put forward in CORE ISSUES have been maintained and, gradually, intensified. No radical development can be seen in the field, but more serious and focused studies are being carried out. The confluence of translation, censorship and sexuality needs to affirm itself as a legitimate field of study in order to generate more systematic and comprehensive treatments of a range of textual genres, authors and traditions. These pages are an invitation for future research into the field, which would cover more texts and a wider variety of texts, more language combinations, more cultural landscapes, more countries and, especially, more attention to minority languages and cultural spaces traditionally neglected in mainstream research.

Recent publications show that a wide-ranging interest in the censorship mechanisms of twentieth-century Franco dictatorship continues to be strong. Extensive work has been carried out in the past, but there are still countless state censorship files to be examined, not to mention the 'private archives of publishers, authors, translators, film distributors, and literary agents' (Lobejón Santos et al. 2021: 99) as well. Therefore, hundreds of translated books, adapted plays or dubbed films are still in need of analysis and of comparison with versions in other languages. It is likely that sexuality plays a significant role in the censorship of these materials. Future research will surely continue to unveil blatant targets of state censorship, but will also uncover less obvious cases, e.g., those with minor cuts or suggestions for change imposed by state censorship. The latter texts can offer insights into the artistic canon for most important works of literature, theatre and cinema, as well as editorial production in general during the Francoist authoritarian regime, which are extraordinarily relevant for future developments in the creation and/or translation of literary and audiovisual texts.

Significant research should be devoted to the study of the books, plays and films that were not authorised and have remained untranslated, especially those by female writers. Studying these circuits of banned books and films is likely to provide more insights into the unconscious drives of a dictatorship—its prejudices, fears and phobias—than the list of authorised cultural products, which were sometimes heavily censored without the public's knowledge (see Toledano 2003, discussed above).

Archival material can shed light not only on the products of the censorship policies imposed by Franco's dictatorial regime but also on the interventions of other agents, from the censors themselves (with their own ideologies as well as contradictions) to the publishers, who adopted a variety of positions vis-à-vis the autocratic regime and who, in any case, established a sort of decades-long negotiation with the civil servants in charge of the administration of the censorship apparatus, in order to adjust their translating strategies and make them 'censor-oriented' (Barrale 2018: 863). This negotiation consisted most often in the adoption of a sort of pre-emptive censorship (or self-censorship) in order to secure publication. Both the autocratic regime and the publishers needed each other. While the former needed the publishing industry and the complicity of the intellectual class for furthering their political or religious creed, the latter needed the patronage of the government. In this scenario, figures such as Carles Barral, Pablo del Molino or Josep Janés, to mention just a few, constitute in Spain crucial interlocutors with the Franco dictatorship authorities in determining cultural taste and in negotiating the limits and the timing of the censoring machinery (see Vega 2004; Gallego Roca 2004; Jané-Lligé 2015).

Although the vast body of research documented in this chapter may give the impression that all has been done on the Franco period, some lines of inquiry could be reinforced. For instance, studying the ways in which official state censorship was resisted, circumvented and even avoided, if that was the case. Were there other instances of mediation (apart from the editors) between the censoring apparatus and the cultural or literary world? What were the methods for avoiding or curtailing censorship of sexual material? What is the picture offered by the literary, dramatic or film production authorised by the system?

It would also be interesting to study two interrelated phenomena: first, the fact that a number of editors kept on publishing censored books even after the path towards democracy was restored in 1975 (see Gómez Castro 2008a). This may be attributed to economic reasons, given that editors could continue to make money from a book that did not require a new translation or revision. In the process, they disregard the quality and accuracy of the books they sell. It may be useful to study whether the Francoist censorship system was a successful enterprise, whether cultural consumption today in Spain is highly acritical or even whether there are still traces of the Franco era in the cultural world. Have the authors that were banned/blocked by the Francoist system been recovered today from the depths of oblivion, or are they to be forever censored? What role has sexuality played in all of this?

Second, and closely related to the first phenomenon, is the issue of whether there is some form of censorship in Spain's democracy or, by contrast, whether Spanish democracy overrides the existence of any censoring mechanism directly targeting the expression of sexuality. This issue has yet to be explored in a significant number of literary and non-literary texts, in a multiplicity of written and audiovisual formats. Are there any forms of sexual behaviour, or any sex-related linguistic forms, particularly apt for suppression, toning down, and so on?

As attested in Table 27.1 (Appendix 1), films and TV series dubbed during the Franco regime are increasingly falling under the lens of censorship, translation and sexuality research. A very interesting hypothesis has been recently put forward by Valdeón (2020), positing that contemporary Anglo-American audiovisual products show an increased sexualisation when dubbed into Peninsular Spanish through the exponential rise in the use of sexually suggestive swearwords. This is what Valdeón (2020: 261) terms the 'vulgarization hypothesis', an intriguing idea that needs further testing and confirmation. The study of audiovisual products, with its novelty and urgency and its new modalities, is beginning to cast new perspectives on the censoring of translated sexuality A very interesting development is offered by Sanz-Moreno (2017) on audiodescription, an emergent modality, as she analyses audiodescribed sexual references in English- and French-language films and concludes that around 50% of them have been altered, reduced or omitted in Spanish.

A more critical interrogation of sexuality and sexual identities, which very often involves either some form of censorship or censorial reaction, is another line of research. Gay and queer research takes a unique approach to its critical interrogation of sexuality, through its holistic approach to gender, sexuality, class and race matters. Unlike much research on the translation of sexuality in erotic texts or on censorship processes, gay and queer researchers tend to emphasise the discursive approach to sexuality-related language, and focus significantly on both sexuality and translation as intercultural processes that are of great significance to our bodies, our desires, our pleasures and our discourses (see Epstein and Gillett 2017; Baer and Kaindl 2018; Baer 2011). In stark contrast to much of the research on official censorship systems, censorship can be viewed as productive 'if it gives rise to forms of resistance which develop out of censorship practices' (Drewett 2004: 203). The idea of 'creative' (Billiani 2007a: 10) or 'productive' censorship (Butler 1998; Baer 2011) is especially linked to subordinated sexualities, which may use translation as a liberating force. Inquiring into this productive side of censorship 'relates not only to the generation of individual texts but also to the (re)production of alternative (sub)cultures and of a moral if not overtly political opposition' (Baer 2011: 21), thus explicitly considering the translation of sexuality as a political issue. This view draws heavily both on Foucault's conception of discourse as requiring some form of silencing or discipline and on his idea of censorship as productive and not merely repressive (see Foucault 1978), as well on Bourdieu's notion that censorship may be an unavoidable structural necessity in certain fields of specialisation (Bourdieu 1991: 37). The productive or creative potential of censorship has at times been overlooked in Spain at the expense of its repressive elements. This offers a radical change of perspective, which centres on the experience of being censored and on the opportunities to evade, circumvent, appease, deny, redefine, (re) negotiate or challenge the mechanisms or the effects of the censorious interventions in authoritarian and dictatorial contexts, for example. In this vein, Martínez Pleguezuelos and González-Iglesias González (2015) explore the consequences of acts of censorship on the representation of homosexual identity in the Spanish adaptations of Robert Anderson's *Tea and Sympathy* (1953) and its cinematic adaptation (1956). In the case of gay and queer texts, censorship (through translation) constitutes a traditional strategy of discursive (re-)construction of a type of sexuality for a heterocentric audience.

A phenomenon that has not been dealt with appropriately or extensively in research on English–Spanish translation in Spain is the processes of de-censorship of translated products on sexual grounds, i.e., coming 'to terms with "prohibited" books, or "offensive literature"' (Sutherland 1982: preface). Santaemilia (2018) analyses the heavily self-censored Spanish translation of Salinger's *The Catcher in the Rye* (1951), made by Carmen Criado in 1978. In 2006, however, the translator decided to restore a great deal of the hundreds of expletives and sex-related terms ('hell', 'goddam', 'bastard', 'sex', 'ass' and so on) present in the original book. How can we define such a move? Re-translation, de-censorship, reverse censorship, un-self-censorship? In any case, this type of translation strategy deserves further investigation. The area of retranslations is also gaining ground today (Cadera and Walsh 2017, Albachten and Gürçağlar 2019), dealing increasingly with censorship of sexuality in books by, for example, Federico García Lorca, D.H. Lawrence, Italo Svevo, Octave Mirbeau. But if retranslations are important and essential to the cultural dynamics of a language, lack of retranslations—and, therefore, the continued consumption of censored books—is another significant area that merits exploration. Cornellà-Detrell (2013: 131) warns that '[t]he advent of a new political system [...] did not stop the production and circulation of censored books, which have been able to duly fulfil their role in markedly divergent contexts'.Some of these questions are certainly worth exploring, raising interesting (and controversial) issues of copyright, marketing concerns and literary canon formation, among others.

The study of the censorship of sexuality in translations (English–Spanish) in Spain seems to be making steady progress. It falls under the more general sub-discipline of translation and censorship, which to date has been somewhat monopolised by the study of explicit forms of censorship set up by the Franco dictatorship – pre-emptive or repressive censorship (see Merkle 2018). The future is bright and full of research possibilities for sexuality and translation, given the great number of still uncharted personal and institutional dimensions. An intensification of research, with a specific focus on sexuality, into the Spanish dictatorship censorship files is to be expected, along with a certain degree of standardization of procedures for search and analysis, and more systematic inquiries into public and private archives. Of particular interest are the publishers' archives. Apart from the focus on censored literature, a diversification of texts is to be expected, with more attention paid to plays, films and TV series. The idea of 'censored' texts should probably be broadened so as to include not only partial suppression of textual elements, but also, and more dramatically, the outright exclusion of an English-text from entering a new cultural space (see Wolf 2002 on cultural blockage). A rigorous study of books, films or plays excluded from the Spanish cultural space during the Franco regime might prove a worthwhile transcultural journey of discovery and self-understanding. An area that is likely to grow in the near future is the investigation of the censoring of sexuality in translation in democracy. Here new concepts or notions are needed, with perhaps new types of 'censorship' at work, including post-censorship (Merkle 2018), structural censorship (Bourdieu 1980), market censorship (Woods 2012), political correctness (Assis Rosa 2008) and the ubiquitous self-censorship. Democratic periods generate new phenomena: not only the appearance of new forms of censorship, but also the paradoxical phenomenon that today in Spain people are still reading and viewing some of the books and films censored by the Francoist repressive apparatus; no doubt this deserves textual and sociological analyses. In general, a progressively stronger and more critical articulation of sexuality with translation and censorship studies would be welcome, along the lines of feminist translation studies (Castro and Ergun 2017) and queer translation studies (Epstein and Gillett 2017, Baer and Kaindl 2018). A stronger focus on sexuality will add strength and validity to the two disciplines (censorship and translation) that are most closely associated with the expression of self and our truly intimate struggles.

Further Reading

Albachten, Özlem Berk and Gürçağlar, Şehnaz Tahir (eds). 2019. *Perspectives on Retranslation. Ideology, Paratexts, Methods*. London and New York: Routledge.
Insightful volume that brings together a variety of papers on retranslation from diverse contexts (France, Spain, Greece, Poland, United Kingdom, Turkey, United States, Brazil). An entire section is devoted to censorship and retranslation, focusing mainly on sexual matters. The changing attitudes to sexual taboos (homosexuality, bisexuality, prostitution) are likely to mobilise an unending censorship/retranslation circuit.

Ben-Ari, Nitsa. 2006. *Suppression of the Erotic in Modern Hebrew Literature*. Ottawa: Université d'Ottawa.
A good example of the combined effects of (self-)censorship and sexuality in the formation of a national and cultural identity in Israel, considering both translated and original Hebrew literature. Due to the influence of puritan norms in the representation of sexuality in pre-state Israel, the new Hebrew literature marginalised any form of literature about sex.

Billiani, Francesca (ed). 2007. *Modes of Censorship and Translation. National contexts and diverse media*. Manchester: St. Jerome Publishing.
An edited volume offering a wealth of perspectives on the relationships between censorship and translation in different contexts (Italy, Greece, United Kingdom, Spain, Germany), with a number of papers focusing on sexual morality and the (self-)censorship of sexual references, prostitution, homosexuality or moral issues in different historical periods.

Seruya, Teresa and Moniz, Maria Lin (eds). 2008. *Translation and Censorship in Different Times and Landscapes*. Newcastle: Cambridge Scholars Publishing.
A wide-ranging collection of essays opening up new perspectives on censorship and translation in Portugal, as well as in other European territories (Spain, Czechoslovakia, Turkey, Ukraine, United Kingdom) and beyond (Brazil, China). Questions of sexual morality, sexual violence, sex-related taboos and the translation of feminist essays feature prominently.

Sova, Dawn B. 2006. *Banned Books. Literature Suppressed on Sexual Grounds*. New York: Books on File.
A comprehensive alphabetical list of the books which, across history, were censored in the United States for depicting sexual acts or sexual language. An entry with information on the content of the book, the court cases, and its literary significance is offered for each of the books censored.

References

Abellán, Manuel. 1980. *Censura y creación literaria en España (1939-1976)*. Barcelona: Ediciones Península.

Albachten, Özlem Berk and Gürçağlar, Şehnaz Tahir (eds). 2019. *Perspectives on Retranslation. Ideology, Paratexts, Methods*. London and New York: Routledge.

Allan, Keith and Burridge, Kate. 2006. *Forbidden Words: Taboo and the Censoring of Language*. Cambridge: Cambridge University Press.

Assis Rosa, Alexandra. 2008. 'Who is Holding the Blue Pencil? A Visit to Intralingual Translation in the Portuguese Theme Park "Portugal dos Pequenitos"', in T. Seruya and M. L. Moniz (eds), *Translation and Censorship in Different Times and Landscapes*. Newcastle: Cambridge Scholars Publishing, 84–100.

Baer, Brian James. 2011. 'Translating Queer Texts in Soviet Russia: A Case Study in Productive Censorship', *Translation Studies*, 4(1): 21–40.

Baer, Brian J. and Kaindl, Klaus (eds). 2018. *Queering Translation, Translating the Queer. Theory, Practice, Activism*. New York and London: Routledge.

Barrale, Natascia. 2018. 'Foreign Literature As Poison: (Self-)censorship in the Translation of German Popular Fiction in Italy during the 1930s', *Perspectives*, 26(6): 852–67.

Bautista Cordero, Rosa María. 2013. 'The Spanish translation of *Manhattan Transfer* and Censorship', *Estudios de Traducción*, 3: 149–62.

Bennett, Karen (ed). 2020. Special issue: 'Translation under Dictatorships', *Translation Matters*, 2(2): 1–181.

Billiani, Francesca. 2007a. 'Assessing boundaries –Censorship and Translation: An Introduction', in F. Billiani (ed), *Modes of Censorship and Translation: National Contexts and Diverse Media*. Manchester: St. Jerome, 1–25.

Billiani, Francesca (ed). 2007b. *Modes of Censorship and Translation*. Manchester: St. Jerome.

Bourdieu, Pierre. 1980. *Le sens pratique*. Paris: Minuit.

Bourdieu, Pierre. 1991. *Language and Symbolic Power*. Ed. and intro. by John B. Thompson. Trans. by Gino Raymond and Matthew Adamson. Cambridge: Polity Press.

Butler, Judith. 1998. 'Ruled out: Vocabularies of the censor', in R. C. Post (ed), *Censorship and Silencing. Practices of Cultural Regulation*. Los Angeles: The Getty Research Institute, 247–59.

Cadera, Susanne M. and Walsh, Andrew Samuel (eds). 2017. *Literary Retranslation in Context*. Oxford: Peter Lang.

Campillo Arnaiz, Laura. 2004. 'Translating Measure for Measure in Nineteenth-Century Spain: Republican and Conservative Readings', *Folio, Shakespeare-Genootschap van Nederland en Vlaanderen*, 11(2): 17–30.

Campillo Arnaiz, Laura. 2005. 'Bowdlerizing or Maximizing? Two Strategies to Render Shakespeare's Sexual Puns in Nineteenth-century Spain', *Ilha do Desterro*, 49: 25–36.

Camus Camus, María del Carmen. 2008. 'Pseudonyms, Pseudotranslation and Self-censorship in the Narrative of the West during the Franco dictatorship', in T. Seruya and M. L. Moniz (eds), *Translation and Censorship in Different Times and Landscapes*. Newcastle: Cambridge Scholars Publishing, 147–162.

Camus Camus, María del Carmen. 2012. 'Traducción y censura. El discurso censurado de *Memorias de un Rostro Pálido/Mémoires d'un Visage Pâle/Little Big Man*', in P. Martino and S. Jarilla (eds), *Caleidoscopio de traducción literaria*. Madrid: Dykinaon, 79–93.

Camus Camus, María del Carmen. 2015. 'Negotiation, censorship on translation constraints? A case study of *Duel in the Sun*', in J. Díaz-Cintas and J. Neves (eds), *Audiovisual Translation: Taking Stock*. Newcastle: Cambridge Scholars Publishing, 9–27.

Castro, Olga and Ergun, Emek (eds). 2017. *Feminist Translation Studies: Local and Transnational Perspectives*. London/New York: Routledge.

Colligan, Colette. 2006. *The traffic in obscenity from Byron to Beardsley. Sexuality and exoticism in the nineteenth-century print culture*. Basingstoke and London: Palgrave Macmillan.

Cornellà-Detrell, Jordi. 2013. 'The Afterlife of Francoist Cultural Policies: Censorship and Translation in the Catalan and Spanish Literary Market', *Hispanic Research Journal*, 14(2): 129–43.

Craig, Ian S. 1997. *Children's Classics Translated from English under Franco: The Censorship of the William Books and The Adventures of Tom Sawyer*. PhD dissertation, Queen Mary University of London.

Díaz-Cintas, Jorge. 2019. 'Film Censorship in Franco's Spain: The Transforming Power of Dubbing', *Perspectives*, 27: 182–200.

Díaz-Cintas, Jorge and Neves, Josélia (eds). 2015. *Audiovisual Translation: Taking Stock*. Newcastle: Cambridge Scholars Publishing.

Drewett, Michael. 2004. 'Aesopian Strategies of Textual Resistance in the Struggle to Overcome the Censorship of Popular Music in Apartheid South Africa', in B. Müller (ed), *Censorship and Cultural Regulation in the Modern Age*. Amsterdam and New York: Rodopi, 189–208.

Epstein, B. J. and Gillett, Robert (eds). 2017. *Queer in Translation*. London and New York: Routledge.

Foucault, Michel. 1978. *The History of Sexuality. Vol. 1: Introduction*. Translated by Robert Hurley. New York: Pantheon Books.

Franco Aixelá, Javier. 2008. 'Ideology and Translation. The Strange Case of a Translation Which Was Hotter than the Original: Casas Gancedo and Hammett in *The Falcon of the King of Spain* (1933)', in M. Muñoz Calvo, C. Bueso Gómez and M. Ruiz Moneva (eds), *New Trends in Translation and Cultural Identity*. Newcastle: Cambridge Scholars Publishing, 95–104.

Franco Aixelá, Javier and Abio Villarig, Carlos. 2009. 'Manipulación ideológica y traducción: Atenuación e intensificación moral en la traducción de la novela negra norteamericana al español (1933-2001)', *Hermeneus*, 11: 1–23.

Gallego Roca, Miguel. 2004. 'De las vanguardias a la Guerra Civil', in F. Lafarga and L. Pegenaute (eds), *Historia de la traducción en España*. Salamanca: Editorial Ambos Mundos, 479–526.

Godayol, Pilar. 2019. 'Depicting Censorship under Franco's Dictatorship: Mary McCarthy, a Controversial Figure', in L. Pintado Gutiérrez and A. Castillo Villanueva (eds), *New Approaches to Translation, Conflict and Memory: Narratives of the Spanish Civil War and the Dictatorship*. Basingstoke: Palgrave Macmillan, 91–111.

Gómez Castro, Cristina. 2007. '*El Guardián entre el centeno* o cómo traducir a Salinger sin ofender la moral patria', in P. Cano López (ed), *Actas del VI Congreso General de Santiago de Compostela, 3-7 de mayo de 2004*- Vol. 1 (Métodos y aplicaciones de la lingüística). Madrid: Arco Libros, 655–66.

Gómez Castro, Cristina. 2008a. 'The Francoist Censorship Casts a Long Shadow: Translations from the Period of the Dictatorship on Sale Nowadays', in T. Seruya and M. L. Moniz (eds), *Translation and Censorship in Different Times and Landscapes*. Newcastle: Cambridge Scholars Publishing, 184–95.

Gómez Castro, Cristina. 2008b. 'Translation and Censorship in Franco's Spain: Negotiation as a Pathway for Authorization', in C. O'Sullivan (ed), *Translation and Negotiation: Proceedings of the Seventh Annual Portsmouth Censorship and Translation Conference (10 November 2007)*. Portsmouth: Portsmouth University, 63–76.

Gómez Castro, Cristina. 2009. *Traducción y censura de textos narrativos inglés-español en la España franquista y de transición: TRACE (19701978)*. PhD dissertation, Universidad de León.

Gómez Castro, Cristina. 2013. 'The Reception of Science Fiction and Horror Story Anthologies in the Last Years of Francoist Spain Censoring Aliens and Monsters in Translation', in T. Seruya, L. D'hulst, A. Assis Rosa and M. L. Moniz (eds), *Translation in Anthologies and Collections (19th and 20th Centuries)*. Amsterdam and Philadelphia: John Benjamins, 217–28.

Gómez Castro, Cristina. 2014. 'Thorny Issues in Translation. The Case of *The Thornbirds* in the Spanish Society of the Seventies', *Babel*, 60(3): 281–302.

Gómez Castro, Cristina. 2017. 'Hombre rico, mujer pobre: género y moral sexual en traducción bajo censura', in J. Santaemilia (ed), *Traducir para la igualdad sexual/Translating for Sexual Equality*. Granada: Comares, 95–108.

Gómez Castro, Cristina. 2020. 'Harold Robbins' *The Betsy* and Its Spanish Translation under Dictatorship: A Race against Censorship', *Translation Matters*, 2(2): 97–112.

Gómez Castro, Cristina and Pérez L. de Heredia, María. 2015. 'En terreno vedado: género, traducción y censura. El caso de *Brokeback Mountain*', *Quaderns de Filologia. Estudis Literaris*, 20: 35–52.

Gutiérrez Lanza, Camino. 2023. 'Normativa y legislación de la censura eclesiástica y estatal del cine en la España franquista y su aplicación a las películas traducidas del inglés', *Mutatis Mutandis*, 16(2): 293–314.

Hunt, Lynn (ed). 1996. *The Invention of Pornography: Obscenity and the Origins of Modernity, 15001800*. New York: Zone Books.

Jané-Lligé, Jordi. 2015. 'Traducción, censura y construcción del discurso literario. La labor de los editores J. Janés, C. Barral y J.M. Castellet durante el franquismo', *Quaderns de Filologia. Estudis Literaris*, 20: 73–90.

Lasa Álvarez, Begoña. 2015. 'Novela inglesa y censura inquisitorial durante el reinado de Fernando VII: un expediente de 1815-1816', *Quaderns de Filologia: Estudis Literaris*, 20: 145–161.

Lázaro Lafuente, Alberto. 2019. 'The Spanish version of E. M. Forster's *Maurice*: A Curious Censorship Case', *Perspectives*, 27(6): 785–796.

Linder, Daniel. 2004. 'The Censorship of Sex: A Study of Raymond Chandler's *The Big Sleep* in Franco's Spain', *TTR: Traduction, Terminologie, Rédaction*, 17(1): 155–82.

Linder, Daniel. 2011. '*The Long Goodbye* en español: Traducciones abreviadas, completas, plagiadas y censuradas', in A. Martín Escribà and J. Sánchez Zapatero (eds), *Género negro para el siglo XXI: nuevas tendencias y nuevas voces*. Barcelona: Editorial Laertes, 75–85.

Linder, Daniel. 2014. 'Getting Away with Murder: *The Maltese Falcon*'s Specialization Homosexual Slang Gunned Down in Translation', *Target*, 26(3): 337–60.

Lobejón Santos, Sergio, Gómez Castro, Cristina and Gutiérrez Lanza, Camino. 2021. 'Archival Research in Translation and Censorship: Digging into the "True Museum Of Francoism"', *Meta*, 66(1): 92–114.

Martín Ruano, M. Rosario. 2018. 'Issues in Cultural Translation: Sensitivity, Politeness, Taboo, Censorship', in S.-A. Harding and O. Carbonell (eds), *The Routledge Handbook of Translation and Culture*. London and New York: Routledge, 258–78.

Martínez Pleguezuelos, Antonio and González-Iglesias González, David. 2015. 'La identidad censurada: representación y manipulación de la homosexualidad en la obra *Té y simpatía*', *Quaderns de Filologia. Estudis Literaris*, 20: 53–67.

Merino Álvarez, Raquel. 2005. 'From Catalogue to Corpus in DTS: Translations Censored under Franco. The TRACE project', *Revista Canaria de Estudios Ingleses*, 51: 85–103.

Merino Álvarez, Raquel. 2007a. 'La homosexualidad censurada: estudio sobre corpus de teatro TRACEti inglés–español (desde1960)', in R. Merino Álvarez (ed), *Traducción y censura en España (1939–1985). Estudios sobre corpus TRACE: cine, narrativa, teatro*. Bilbao: Universidad del País Vasco/ Universidad de León, 243–85.

Merino Álvarez, Raquel (ed). 2007b. *Traducción y censura en España (19391985). Estudios sobre corpus TRACE: cine, narrativa, teatro*. Bilbao: Universidad del País Vasco/ Universidad de León.

Merino Álvarez, Raquel. 2012. 'A Historical Approach to Spanish Theatre Translations from Censoring Archives', in I. García-Izquierdo and E. Monzó (eds), *Iberian Studies on Translation and Interpreting*. Oxford: Peter Lang, 123–40.

Merino Álvarez, Raquel. 2016. 'Mapping translated theatre in Spain through censorship archives', in C. O'Leary, D. Santos and Mé Thompson (eds), *Global insights on theatre censorship*. Oxford: Routledge, 176–90.

Merino Álvarez, Raquel and Rabadán, Rosa. 2002. 'Censored Translations in Franco's Spain: The TRACE Project-Theatre and Fiction (English-Spanish)', *TTR—Traduction, Terminologie, Rédaction*, 15(2): 125–52.

Merkle, Denise. 2002. 'Presentation', *TTR—Traduction, Terminologie, Rédaction*, 15(2): 9–18.

Merkle, Denise. 2018. 'Translation and censorship', in Fruela Fernández and Jonathan Evans (eds.), *The Routledge Handbook of Translation and Politics*. London/New York: Routledge, 238–253.

Merkle, Denise, O'Sullivan, Carol, van Doorslaer, Luc and Wolf, Michaela (eds). 2010. *The Power of the Pen: Translation and Censorship in Nineteenth-century Europe*. Berlin and Vienna: Lit Verlag.

Meseguer Cutillas, Purificación. 2014. *La traducción del discurso ideológico en la España de Franco*. PhD dissertation, Universidad de Murcia.

Meseguer Cutillas, Purificación and Ana Rojo. 2014. 'Literatura, sexo y censura. Traducción y recepción de Amis, Daudet y Renault bajo el régimen franquista', *Revista Española de Lingüística Aplicada*, 27(2): 537–58.

Monzón Rodríguez, Sofía. 2020. 'The Struggles of Translating Henry Miller in Franco's Spain (19391975): The Different Versions of *Black Spring* (1936)', *Transletters*, 4: 203–19.

Monzón Rodríguez, Sofía. 2022. 'Traductores, censores y editoriales transatlánticas: la circulación de *Primavera negra* de Henry Miller en España (1964-1978)', *Entreculturas*, 12: 101–11.

Monzón Rodríguez, Sofía. 2023. 'Traducción, afecto y censura desde el mundo hispánico: *Nightwood*, de Djuna Barnes, y *Tropic of Cancer*, de Henry Miller', *Mutatis Mutandis*, 16(2): 429–52. (Special issue on 'Traducción (auto)censurada en los mundos hispánicos').

Ní Chuilleanáin, Eiléan, Ó Cuilleanáin, Cormac and Parris, David (eds). 2009. *Translation and Censorship: Patterns of Communication and Interference*. Dublin: Four Courts Press.

O'Sullivan, Carol. 2009. 'Censoring These "Racy Morsels of the Vernacular": Loss and Gain in the Translation of Apuleius and Catullus', in E. Ní Chuilleanáin, C.Ó Cuilleanáin and D. Parris (eds), *Translation and Censorship: Patterns of Communication and Interference*. Dublin: Four Courts Press, 76–93.

O'Sullivan, Carol. 2010. 'Translation within the Margins: The "Libraries" of Henry Bohn', in J. Milton and P. Bandia (eds), *Agents of Translation*. Philadelphia and Amsterdam: John Benjamins, 107–30.

Ortega Sáez, Marta. 2007. 'Un pasado muy presente: Traducciones del inglés al español en la época contemporánea', in F. Navarro, M.A. Vega Cernuda and J.A. Albaladejo Martínez (eds), *La traducción: balance del pasado y retos del futuro*. Alicante: Aguaclara, 297–309.

Ortega Sáez, Marta. 2011a. 'Censors Also Cry: A Hypothesis on the Translation of Rosamond Lehmann's *The Weather in the Streets* (1945)', in J. Hurtley, M. Kenneally and W. Zach (eds), *Literatures in English: Ethnic, Colonial and Cultural Encounters*. Tübingen: Stauffenburg Verlag, 389–95.

Ortega Sáez, Marta. 2011b. 'The Reception of Rosamond Lehmann in Franco's Spain', in C. O'Leary and A. Lázaro Lafuente (eds), *The Reception of English Literature in Twentieth-century Europe*. Newcastle: Cambridge Scholars Publishing, 171–92.

Rabadán Rosa (ed). 2000. *Traducción y censura inglés- español: 1939-1985. Estudio preliminar*. León: Universidad de León.

Reynolds, Matthew. 2007. 'Semi-censorship in Dryden and Browning', in F. Billiani (ed), *Modes of Censorship and Translation. National contexts and diverse media*. Manchester: St. Jerome Publishing, 187–204.

Riba, Caterina and Sanmartí, Carme. 2017. 'Censura moral en la novela rosa. El caso de Elinor Glyn', *Represura, nueva época*, 1: 40–54.

Rodríguez Espinosa, Marcos. 2001. 'Ideological Constraints and French Mediation in Hispanic Translated Texts: 1860-1930', *TRANS (Revista de Traductología)*, 5: 9–22.

Rodríguez Espinosa, Marcos. 2004. 'El discurso ideológico de la censura franquista y la traducción de textos literarios: *Las aventuras de Barry Lyndon* y la Editorial Destino', in Grupo TLS – Grupo Traducción, Literatura y Sociedad (ed), *Ética y política de la traducción literaria*. Málaga: Miguel Gómez Peña, 219–38.

Rojas-Lizana, Isolda and Hannah, Emily. 2013. 'Manipulación del género gramatical y sexual en la traducción española de un cuento de Oscar Wilde', *Babel*, 59(3): 310–31.

Rundle, Christopher and Sturge, Kate (eds). 2010. *Translation under Fascism*. London and Basingstoke: Palgrave Mzcmillan.

Santaemilia, José. 2008a. 'The Danger(s) of Self-censorship(s): The Translation of 'Fuck' into Spanish and Catalan', in T. Seruya and M. L. Moniz (eds), *Translation and Censorship in Different Times and Landscapes*. Newcastle: Cambridge Scholars Publishing, 163–73.

Santaemilia, José. 2008b. 'The Translation of Sex-related Language: The Danger(s) of Self-censorship(s)', *TTR –Traduction, Terminologie, Rédaction*, 21(2): 221–52.

Santaemilia, José. 2018. 'Carmen Criado, ¿traductora, autocensora, retraductora? A propósito de *El guardián entre el centeno*, de J.D. Salinger', in Gora Zaragoza, J.J. Martínez Sierra, B. Cerezo Merchán and M. Richart Marset (eds), *Traducción, género y censura en la literatura y en los medios de comunicación*. Granada: Comares, 135–48.

Sanz Gallego, Guillermo. 2013. 'Translating Taboo Language in Joyce's *Ulysses*: A Special Edition in Spanish for Franco and Perón', *Atlantis*, 35(2): 137–54.

Sanz-Moreno, Raquel. 2017. 'La (auto)censura en audiodescripción. El sexo silenciado', *Parallèles*, 29(2): 46–63.

Seruya, Teresa and Moniz, Maria Lin (eds). 2008. *Translation and Censorship in Different Times and Landscapes*. Newcastle: Cambridge Scholars Publishing.

Sigel, Lisa Z. (ed). 2005. *International Exposure. Perspectives on Pornography, 18002000*. New Brunswick: Rutgers University Press.

Somacarrera, Pilar. 2017. 'Rewriting and Sexual (self-)censorship in the Translation of a Canadian Novel', in C. Camus Camus, C. Gómez Castro and J. T. Williams Camus (eds), *Translation, Ideology and Gender*. Newcastle: Cambridge Scholars Publishing, 83–101.

Sova, Dawn B. 2006. *Banned Books. Literature Suppressed on Sexual Grounds*. New York: Books on File.

Sullivan, Karen and Bandín, Elena. 2014. 'Censoring Metaphors in Translation: Shakespeare's *Hamlet* under Franco', *Cognitive Linguistics*, 25(2): 177–202.

Sutherland, John. 1982. *Offensive Literature: Decensorship in Britain, 19601982*. London: Junction Books.

Toledano, Carmen. 2002. 'Recepción de *Fanny Hill* en España: Estudio preliminar', *Atlantis*, 2: 215–27.
Toledano, Carmen. 2003. *La traducción de la obscenidad*. Santa Cruz de Tenerife: La Página Ediciones.
Valdeón, Roberto A. 2020, 'Swearing and the Vulgarization Hypothesis in Spanish Audiovisual Translation', *Journal of Pragmatics*, 156: 261–72.
Vega, Miguel Ángel. 2004. 'De la Guerra Civil al pasado inmediato', in F. Lafarga and L. Pegenaute (eds), *Historia de la traducción en España*. Salamanca, Editorial Ambos Mundos, 527–78.
von Flotow, Luise. 2000. 'Translation Effects: How Beauvoir Talks Sex in English', in M. Hawthorne (ed), *Contingent Loves. Simone de Beauvoir and Sexuality*. Richmond: University Press Virginia, 13–33.
Weeks, Jeffrey. 2011. *The Languages of Sexuality*. London and New York: Routledge.
Williams Camus, Julia T. 2017. 'Traducción y autocensura en la obra de Margaret Mitchell: lo que la censura se llevó', in C. Camus Camus and M. Marcos Aldón (eds), *Traducción literaria, otras traducciones especializadas y disciplinas afines a la traducción*. Granada: Comares, 129–40.
Wolf, Michaela. 2002. 'Censorship as Cultural Blockage: Banned Literature in the Late Habsburg Monarchy', *TTR*, 25(2): 45–61.
Woods, Michelle. 2012. *Censoring Translation: Censorship, Theatre, and the Politics of Translation*. London and New York: Continuum.
Zaragoza, Gora. 2018. 'Gender, Translation and Censorship: *The Well of Loneliness* (1928) in Spain as an Example of Translation in Cultural Evolution', in O. I. Seel (ed), *Redefining Translation and Interpretation in Cultural Evolution*. Hershey, PA: IGI Global, 42–66.
Zaragoza, Gora and Cerezo, Beatriz. 2019. 'Rebeca maltratada: Un estudio comparativo de su censura a través de las leyes de prensa españolas y el código Hays estadounidense', *Revista Clepsidra*, 18: 107–27.
Zaragoza, Gora and Llopis, Sara. 2021. '*The Unlit Lamp* (1924): Translation, Reception and Censorship', *Language and Intercultural Communication*, 21(1): 37–54.
Zaragoza, Gora, Martínez Sierra, Juan José, Cerezo Merchán, Beatriz and Richart Marset, Mabel. (eds). 2018. *Traducción, género y censura en la literatura y en los medios de comunicación*. Granada: Comares.

Appendix

Table 27.1 TS Spain database. Censorship of sexuality in translation (English-Spanish): Researchers and works researched (An initial database)

Text type	Texts researched	Researchers
LITERARY TEXTS	William Shakespeare, *Hamlet* (*ca.* 1600)	Campillo 2005, Sullivan and Bandín 2014
	William Shakespeare, *Measure for measure* (*ca.* 1604)	Campillo 2004
	John Cleland, *Fanny Hill* (1748–49)	Toledano 2002, 2003
	Frances Sheridan, *Memoirs of Miss Sydney Bidulph* (1761)	Lasa 2015
	William Thackeray, *Barry Lindon* (1844)	Rodriguez 2004
	Charlotte Brontë, *Jane Eyre* (1847)	Ortega 2007
	William Thackeray, *Vanity Fair* (1848)	Rodríguez 2001
	Mark Twain, *The adventures of Tom Sawyer* (1876)	Craig 1997
	Oscar Wilde, 'The happy prince' (1888)	Rojas/Hannah 2013
	Richmal Crompton, *Just William* stories (from 1919 onwards)	Craig 1997
	James Joyce, *Ulysses* (1922)	Sanz Gallego 2013
	Elinor Glyn, *Six days* (1924)	Riba/Sanmartí 2017
	Radclyffe Hall, *The unlit lamp* (1924)	Zaragoza and Llopis 2021

(*Continued*)

Table 27.1 (Continued)

Text type	Texts researched	Researchers
	John Dos Passos, *Manhattan Transfer* (1925)	Bautista 2013
	Elinor Glyn, *Love's blindness* (1926)	Riba/Sanmartí 2017
	Radclyffe Hall, *The well of loneliness* (1928)	Zaragoza 2018
	Dashiell Hammett, *The Maltese Falcon* (1930)	Franco 2008, Franco and Abio 2009; Linder 2014
	Elinor Glyn, *Glorious flames* (1932)	Riba/Sanmartí 2017
	Margaret Mitchell, *Gone with the wind* (1936)	Williams 2017
	Henry Miller, *Black Spring* (1936)	Monzón 2020, 2022
	Daphne Du Maurier, *Rebecca* (1938)	Zaragoza/Cerezo 2019
	Raymond Chandler, *The big sleep* (1939)	Linder 2004
	Raymond Chandler, *Farewell my lovely* (1940)	Franco and Abio 2009
	Rosamond Lehmann, *The weather in the streets* (1945)	Ortega 2011a, 2011b
	Tennessee Williams, *A streetcar named desire* (1947)	Merino 2016
	J.D. Salinger, *The Catcher in the Rye* (1951)	Gómez 2007, Santaemilia 2018
	Robert Anderson, *Tea and sympathy* (1953)	Merino 2016
	Raymond Chandler, *The long goodbye* (1954)	Linder 2011
	Tennessee Williams, *Cat on a hot tin roof* (1955)	Merino 2016
	Mary Renault, *The last of the wine* (1956)	Meseguer 2014, Meseguer/Rojo 2014
	Edward Albee, *The zoo story* (1958)	Merino and Rabadán 2002; Merino 2005, 2016
	Graham Greene, *The complaisant lover* (1959)	Merino and Rabadán 2002, Merino 2012
	Thomas Berger, *Little Big Man* (1964)	Camus Camus 2012
	Kingsley Amis, *The anti-death league* (1966)	Meseguer 2014, Meseguer and Rojo 2014
	Margaret Laurence, *A Jest of God* (1966)	Somacarrera 2017
	Mart Crowley, *The boys in the band* (1968)	Merino 2007a, 2012, 2016
	Evan Hunter, *Last summer* (1968)	Gómez 2008a
	Mario Puzo, *The Godfather* (1969)	Gómez 2009
	Irwin Shaw, *Rich man, poor man* (1969)	Gómez 2009, 2017
	Erich Segal, *Love story* (1970)	Gómez 2009
	Mary McCarthy, *A charmed life* (1970)	Godayol 2019
	Mary McCarthy, *Birds of America* (1971)	Godayol 2019
	Harold Robbins, *The Betsy* (1971)	Gómez 2008b, 2009, 2020
	W. Peter Blatty, *The exorcist* (1971)	Gómez 2009
	E.M. Forster, *Maurice* (1971)	Lázaro 2019
	Colleen McCullough, *The Thornbirds* (1977)	Gómez 2009, 2014
	Helen Fielding, *Bridget Jones's Diary* (1996)	Santaemilia 2008a, 2008b
	Annie, Proulx, 'Brokeback Mountain' (1997)	Gómez and Pérez 2015
	Helen Fielding, *The Edge of Reason* (1999)	Santaemilia 2008a, 2008b

Censoring Sexuality in Translation

Table 27.1 (Continued)

Text type	Texts researched	Researchers
FILMS/ TV SERIES	*Rebecca* (1940), dir. Alfred Hitchcock	Zaragoza and Cerezo 2019
	Duel in the Sun (1946), dir. King Vidor	Camus Camus 2015
	The barefoot comtessa (1954), dir. Joseph L. Manckiewicz	Díaz-Cintas 2019
	Tea and sympathy (1956), dir. Vincente Minnelli	Martínez/González 2015
	There's something with Mary (1998), dir. Peter/Bobby Farrelli	Sanz-Moreno 2017
	American Beauty (2000), dir. Sam Mendes	Sanz-Moreno 2017
	Brokeback Mountain (2005), dir. Ang Lee	Gómez and Pérez 2015, * Sanz-Moreno 2017
	The hangover 1 (2009), dir. Todd Phillips	Sanz-Moreno 2017
	The hangover 2 (2011), dir. Todd Phillips	Sanz-Moreno 2017

28

CENSORING WOMEN'S WRITING IN TRANSLATION IN FRANCO'S SPAIN

A View from the Archive

Gora Zaragoza Ninet

28.1 Introduction

In recent years, there has been a growing interest in studying the effects of censorship in the translation of texts by foreign women writers of the twentieth century and by feminist writers, especially texts expressing a feminist sensitivity, during the years of the Franco dictatorship, which extended over a great deal of the past century. The intertwining of censorship, translation and women's writing leads to different subareas for study and analysis: studies that focus on censored texts written by women, studies that compare translations in the pre- and post-Franco era, and works that look at the role of publishers in the importation, translation and publication of foreign literature.

Studying censorship is not an easy task. First and foremost censorship in translated literature is silent. Unless it is suspected, tracked and confirmed, firstly by looking into the censorship files and secondly through a thorough intratextual analysis, its effects may go unnoticed. Second, the whole process of researching censorship is complex. Censorship reports must be located and analysed; finding the source and target texts (some almost a century old) can also prove difficult. Third, the study of reception is intricate. In the context of Spain under Franco, this chapter proposes a methodological, theoretical and practical framework for studying censorship of women's fiction titles and essays in Francoist Spain from a feminist perspective. The framework could prove useful to scholars and students working on the censorship of women writers, an area of study that is both highly relevant and necessary. Though mainly focused on the translation and import of twentieth-century British women novelists into Spanish, the methodological approach could easily be adapted to other genres and origins.

A previous study (Zaragoza 2008) showed that 40% of 111 British women novelists from the twentieth century remain untranslated into Spanish, including Enid Bagnold (1889–1981), Brigid Brophy (1929–1995), Annie Bryher (1894–1983), Lettice Cooper (1897–1994), Constance Holme (1980–1955), Willa Muir (1890–1970), Aileen Arnot Robertson (1903–1961) and Stevie Smith (1902–1971). The works of these British novelists were published in Britain at a time when in Spain, a severe censorship apparatus banned works containing ideas that did not comply with the principles

432

DOI: 10.4324/9781003149453-34

of the Francoist regime. The dictatorial regime was set in motion after the Spanish Civil War, lasted from 1939 until the death of the dictator in 1975 and continued until the transition towards a democratic government in the early 1980s. The texts of these untranslated British novelists were at the avant-garde because they portrayed independent women or different ways of loving that did not conform to the ideal of the patriarchal family. While it is difficult to assess the degree of censorship, we seek to determine how many texts by women writers were banned (complete censorship) and remain untranslated, or were partially censored and still circulate in the literary market with cuts.

In order to do so, our goal is to suggest a viable framework for the study of the translation and censorship of women's texts. To accomplish our objective, first, we examine in the core issues and topics section the key concept of censorship, analysing and illustrating the different types of censorship (partial vs total, prior vs post, self-censorship) and justifications for censorship: political, moral (based on sexual tendencies, feminist ideology, etc.) or religious. Second, in the same section, we review the censoring apparatus: the censorship files and agents involved in the process. Third, in the new debates section, we suggest a method to study censored texts, from the analysis of partially censored texts comparing translations before and after dictatorship to the study of reception, by researching the impact of the author in the target cultural, literary and sociopolitical system in book reviews, press clippings, correspondence, the paratext of translations, and so on. We also provide practical information regarding field research in this section.

Finally, we will provide case studies that illustrate research on women, translation and censorship in Francoist Spain, while highlighting how these case studies aim at recovering texts by women writers, (re)writing the historiography of translation in Spain, while in the process contributing to a re-writing of literary history.

28.2 Previous Studies and Methodologies

Studying examples of women's writing that were censored during Francoism is supported by Descriptive Translation Studies, or DTS (Toury 1995), which analyses translation as a product or result of the historical, social, cultural and political developments of the target culture. DTS is interested in identifying and describing the factors and norms that shape translations and that explain a text in its specific cultural and historical context.

Another important theoretical framework is reception studies. Yet reception is difficult to track, especially in the case of old texts. Reception can be researched by analysing the following sources of information: sales figures, print runs, the number of editions and reprintings, press clippings from newspapers, publishing information, translation reviews, correspondence, the paratext of translations, translator comments, literary awards, and so on. The information gathered from the preceding sources will be considered when comparing versions of translations published during the dictatorship and alternative/new versions published in the democratic era.

Toury (1995) suggests situating the translated text in the target culture to analyse its relevance and acceptance. Moreover, he highlights the importance of comparing source and target texts and identifying the relationships between them. In the case of censorship, this textual analysis requires meticulous attention. If translators have traditionally been considered responsible for creating the target image of a foreign text or author, in the case of institutional censorship, such as censorship in Spain during Franco's dictatorship, this needs to be questioned because translators are unable to take free decisions in the process of producing the target text and are thus not themselves entirely responsible for final decisions.

Munday (2014) emphasises focusing on the details, experiences and actions of the actors and institutions that influence the process and reception of translation. In terms of method, he encourages the consultation of primary sources such as archives, manuscripts and personal papers, as well as secondary sources such as memoirs, letters, biographies, interviews, press and criticism in general.

In 1997, Massardier-Kenney compiled feminist translation strategies which she divided into the categories of author-centred and translator-centred. When strategies are aimed at highlighting the authorial figure, in the case, for example, of women authors whose texts have been forgotten in contexts of patriarchy, they are defined as author-centred strategies. These strategies comprise the recovery of marginalised texts and commentary, i.e., the use of metadiscourse to reflect on the author who is being translated (and sometimes even introduced), and resistance, which describes the act of making the work of translation visible through linguistic means. By contrast/On the contrary, if the strategies contribute to a conscious, visible and militant translation labour, they are classified as translator-centred and include commentary (from the point of view of the choices, ethics and responsibility of the—feminist—translating self), parallel texts (parallel women's voices in the cultures involved in the transfer), and collaboration between translators or between author and translator. Recovery is particularly interesting in the context of gender and censorship. Recovery is an author-centred strategy that aims to widen and reshape the canon. The 'canon' is indeed a central yet problematic term: how is the canon defined and construed? Is it ideological and thus related to power, literary movements and the norms imposed by the literary culture and the political context (e.g., Francoism)? Is it a term the meaning of which evolves over time? As Massardier-Kenney suggests: 'One possible way to define what *feminist* means in the context of translation is to take "women's experience as a starting point" […] and contribute through translation to a rethinking of the canon from which women's experience has been excluded' (1997: 59). Godayol advocates for a re-writing of the historiography about women:

> It is essential to go to historiographic sources to study the context in which the translation of a foreign woman author was published (or not) and to reveal the various factors involved in the production and circulation of such a translation. Historiographic excavation of the texts and paratexts of women authors must be carried out and the inherited patriarchal history re-written with the aim of making women visible as an active social group within the history of translation.
>
> (Godayol 2021: 149).

Along similar lines, Massardier-Kenney explains that translating previously ignored authors can shift the outline of a country's literary history (1997: 59) just like Zavala's project (1998) which attempted to rewrite a feminist history of Spanish literature. Godayol (2021: 25) concurs by pointing out that post-Franco work on the translation and censorship of women writers should aim to re-write the Francoist historiography of translation and literature by women. In this context, recovery becomes a key feminist translation strategy which may be applied to texts by women who were previously excluded from the canon. These texts, by women authors who were (or remain) partially or totally censored, may be adapted and recovered via publication of the text in the source or target language. However, this strategy also raises important questions, issues and debates. Is the recovery of censored texts possible? Is the act of recovery legitimate? Should new translations of texts that were fully or partially censored during the Francoist period replace the texts that were published with the cuts imposed by censors and omissions accepted by authors? Or, instead, should the Franco-era texts be allowed to circulate as they were originally published because they reflect the laws, values and norms of the period and circulate together with the new rehabilitated texts for comparative purposes? Panchón and Zaragoza (2023) suggest how to adapt the recovery strategy as defined by Massardier-Kenney to the context of censorship. For instance, passages that were previously erased by censors could be highlighted textually and typographically when they are included for the first time in rehabilitated translations. In addition, the paratext could be used as a place to reflect on both the previous act of censorship and the new recovered text which is now published without deletions.

In Spain, there are a number of pioneering research groups in literary censorship research, especially translated literature research. However, we will only refer to a few groups that deal specifically with the intersection between gender, translation and censorship. One research group is TRACE from the University of León, which has done great work in compiling corpora of translated literature.

The TRACE group has been conducting research on censored translations (English-Spanish) since 1997. TRACE's archives have been of fundamental importance in rebuilding the history of translations in twentieth-century Spain. Databases of censored translations have been compiled mainly from censorship data, and textual corpora of print (narrative, poetry) and audiovisual (cinema, theatre, television) culture have been analysed. However, the group does not concentrate on the intersection between gender, translation and censorship.

Another outstanding contribution to this field of research on translation and censorship is the work of scholars at UVic (Universitat de Vic-Universitat Central de Catalunya). The work of Godayol is essential to understanding the effect of censorship in the translation of key feminist figures into Catalan, as minority languages were often targeted by the censors. Her work on Simone de Beauvoir, Betty Friedan and Mary McCarthy (Godayol 2017) and on feminist essayists Lidia Falcón, Maria Aurèlia Capmany and Amparo Moreno (Godayol 2021) is noteworthy. Godayol has also co-edited the volume *Foreign Women Authors under Fascism and Francoism* (Godayol and Taronna 2018) which establishes connections between two censorship contexts and codes. Teresa Julio's work on Maria Luz Morales is also significant (2018). Likewise, Riba and Sanmartí are responsible for the study of the translation and censorship of writers such as Florence Barclay (2018) and George Eliot (2020). Camus (2011) has explored work on the translation of violence against women in the discourse of the Far West and she has also co-edited the volume *Translation, Ideology and Gender* (2017). Zaragoza has analysed the translation and censorship of writers Winifred Holtby (2012), Daphne du Maurier (2019) and Radclyffe Hall (Zaragoza 2017; Zaragoza and Llopis 2021) and co-edited the volume *Translation, Gender and Censorship in Literature and the Media* (2018). Ortega's work sheds light on the translation and censorship of the work of Vita Sackville-West (2011) and of Charlotte Brontë's *Jane Eyre* (2013), while Hurtley's contribution to the study of writer Rosamond Lehmann (2007) and to the study of translation and censorship is also notable. Llopis (2020) focuses on the translation and censorship of Anglophone lesbian novelists during the Francoist dictatorship.

28.3   Censorship

28.3.1   *Types of Censorship in Francoist Spain*

Censorship is an act that controls and limits freedom of speech. According to Abellán, (1987: 16) censorship is 'the set of actions carried out by the de facto state or formally existing groups able to impose deletions or modifications of any kind on a manuscript or galley proofs of a writer's work—prior to its dissemination—against the author's will or approval'.

In Franco's Spain, a book could be banned entirely (total censorship), or words, paragraphs or pages could be cut or manipulated (partial censorship). In cases of partial censorship, after receiving documents, censors working on behalf of the *Comisión de Propaganda* identified the sentences, whole pages or entire sections that had to be deleted, after which publishers cut the identified material. Publishers had to prove that they had made the required cuts by sending the galley proofs back to the censors. However, in cases of total censorship, the entire work was censored, the work was labelled NOT AUTHORISED, and was simply not published.

In Figure 28.1, the censorship file calls for the deletion of a part of the text in which the female protagonist, Rosamund Stacey, pregnant after her sole sexual encounter, talks about the properties of gin as a method to induce abortion: 'On page 6, however, the section on the method that would be used to cause the abortion should be crossed out' (my translation). The censor's/censorship apparatus forced the publisher to omit a passage dealing with abortion. The galley proofs of the translation, kept at the Archivo General de la Administración (AGA), show how the censor marks the section in red that is to be deleted from the translated text, see Figure 28.2.

Margaret Lane was an English writer and journalist who was one of the pioneers to claim a place in a male-dominated world. She also contributed to the Suffragist Movement through her journalism. Her first novel, *Faith, Hope, no Charity*, published in 1935, won the *Femina Vie Heureuse* prize. In 1941, she published *Walk into My Parlour*. The novel was banned in Spain in 1946, see Figures 28.3 and 28.4.

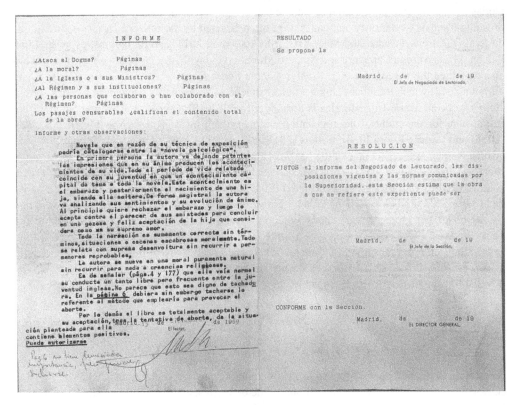

Figure 28.1 Censorship file for Margaret Drabble's *La rueda del molino*, file number 289–70, 12 January 1970.

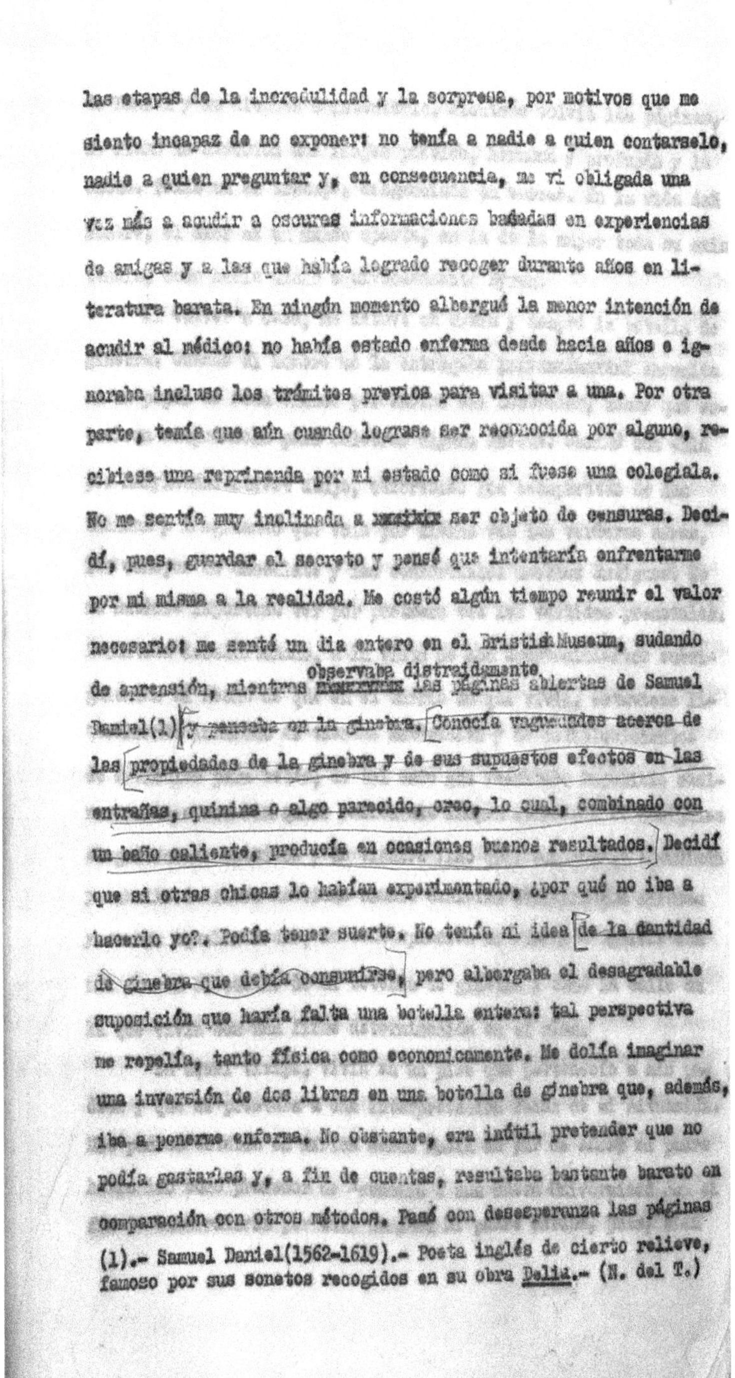

Censoring Women's Writing in Translation in Franco's Spain

las etapas de la incredulidad y la sorpresa, por motivos que me
siento incapaz de no exponer: no tenía a nadie a quien contárselo,
nadie a quien preguntar y, en consecuencia, me vi obligada una
vez más a acudir a oscuras informaciones basadas en experiencias
de amigas y a las que había logrado recoger durante años en literatura barata. En ningún momento albergué la menor intención de
acudir al médico: no había estado enferma desde hacía años e ig-
noraba incluso los trámites previos para visitar a una. Por otra
parte, temía que aún cuando lograse ser reconocida por alguno, re-
cibiese una reprimenda por mi estado como si fuese una colegiala.
No me sentía muy inclinada a ~~existir~~ ser objeto de censuras. Decidí, pues, guardar el secreto y pensé que intentaría enfrentarme
por mí misma a la realidad. Me costó algún tiempo reunir el valor
necesario: me senté un día entero en el British Museum, sudando
de aprensión, mientras ~~miraba~~ *observaba distraídamente* las páginas abiertas de Samuel
Daniel(1) y pensaba en la ginebra. Conocía vagamente acerca de
las propiedades de la ginebra y de sus supuestos efectos en las
entrañas, quinina o algo parecido, creo, lo cual, combinado con
un baño caliente, producía en ocasiones buenos resultados. Decidí
que si otras chicas lo habían experimentado, ¿por qué no iba a
hacerlo yo?. Podía tener suerte. No tenía ni idea de la cantidad
de ginebra que debía consumirse, pero albergaba el desagradable
suposición que haría falta una botella entera: tal perspectiva
me repelía, tanto física como económicamente. Me dolía imaginar
una inversión de dos libras en una botella de ginebra que, además,
iba a ponerme enferma. No obstante, era inútil pretender que no
podía gastarlas y, a fin de cuentas, resultaba bastante barato en
comparación con otros métodos. Pasé con desesperanza las páginas
(1).- Samuel Daniel(1562-1619).- Poeta inglés de cierto relieve,
famoso por sus sonetos recogidos en su obra Delia.- (N. del T.)

Figure 28.2   Galley proofs for *La rueda del molino*, using underlines in red ink to identify the passage that needs to be deleted for the work to be accepted for publication.

The Routledge Handbook of Translation and Censorship

Figure 28.3(a, b)   Censorship file number 3241–46, whereby the translation of *Walk into My Parlour* (1941), *Pase al gabinete* was banned.

Censoring Women's Writing in Translation in Franco's Spain

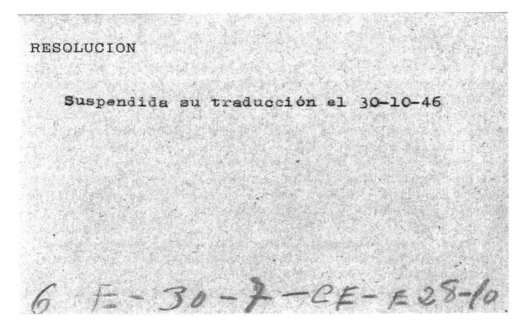

Figure 28.3(a, b)   (Continued)

This example is a case of total censorship. In fact, the novel has not yet been published in Spain. There are no comments in the censorship reports explaining the reasons for the total ban.

Another form of censorship was self-censorship, which occurred when writers and translators omitted or disguised what they feared would be censored in order for their texts to be authorised for publication. Abellán (1982: 169) defines self-censorship as:

> foresight measures that, consciously or unconsciously, a writer adopts with the purpose of evading the possible reaction or repulsion that his text may provoke in all or some of the groups or bodies of the State empowered to impose deletions or modifications with or without their consent (my translation).

Feminist writers and essayists such as Lidia Falcón self-censored, as Godayol (2021: 16) explains with regards to Falcón's work *Mujer y Sociedad*:

> In short, despite the fact that Lidia Falcón was one of the closely watched intellectuals by the censorship apparatus of Franco's regime—as a communist, feminist and anticlerical, after the initial refusal, the Ministry for Information and Tourism (MIT) finally authorised the publication of *Mujer y Sociedad* thanks to the publisher's patience and insistence, as well as the self-censorship that the author imposed on herself before resubmitting the application.

The Routledge Handbook of Translation and Censorship

Montejo Gurruchaga explains that self-censorship in written work can be conscious or unconscious, but it is impossible to assess its consequences (2010: 22). In the case of translations, we can identify and analyse instances of self-censorship by comparing source and target texts and examining the censorship reports. For instance, Marià Manent translated English writer Rosamond Lehmann's *Invitation to the Waltz* (1932) as *Invitación al vals* (1942). According to Hurtley (2007: 70): 'Manent's translation of *Invitation to the Waltz* reveals [...] that the translator, perhaps in anticipation of the response in the Vice-secretary's Office, had already acted as a censor by omitting pieces of the text' (Hurtley 2007: 70). Ortega Sáez (2013) has analysed attenuations due to self-censorship in the rendering of female sexuality and desire in the first Spanish translation of *Jane Eyre* (1943) by Juan G. de Luaces, a very prolific translator of English literature during the Francoist dictatorship. In the example below (Ortega Sáez 2013: 261), Jane's desire in the original text has been translated as haste or impatience, thus nuancing feminine desire:

> I have never heard Mr Rochester's voice or step in the house today; but surely I shall see him before night: I feared the meeting in the morning: now I desire it, because expectation has been so long baffled that it is grown impatient. When dusk actually clased, and when Adèle left me to go and play in the nursery with Sophie, I did most keenly desire it.

> (Brontë 2006: 183)

> [...] y en todo el día no he visot ni oído a Mr. Rochester, Seguramente lo veré antes de la noche. Por la mañana lo temía; pero ahora estoy impaciente por reunirme con él. Mi impaciencia se acrecentó cuando se hizo noche cerrada y Adèle se marcho a jugar con Sophie.

> (Brontë 2011: 181)

As Ortega Sáez further highlights (2013: 192), this is particularly problematic because the novel is one of the first examples of female voice and feminist desire and has been described as a 'cult text of feminism'.

28.3.2 Context

Our study of censorship directed at texts written by women novelists is limited to the particular context of Francoist Spain. We therefore need to present the context (the two Press Laws of 1938 and 1966) and the agents who were responsible for the censorship of translation and who thus shaped the scenario. A key e deserving further investigation is that of the censor: who were the censors? What was the focus of the censorship reports? Which aspects of the translation and the translator were referred to when determining what was to be censored in texts by women? This investigation and future research about why and how texts by women were censored could help identify patterns of behaviour that will, in turn, further contribute to our understanding of how censorship worked and how it dealt with texts by women. While it is true that 'trying to explain such irrational and complex phenomena as The Great Terror, the Holocaust, or the different manifestations of violence unleashed by dictators has always been a difficult task for historians' (Casanova 2015: 13), dissecting the behaviour of this particular cultural system of censorship might provide new insights into this period in the history of Spain, while contributing tangibly to (re)writing the historiography of women's writing and translation.

The first Press Law was the 1938 law, which was the work of Ramón Serrano Suñer, Minister for the Interior. The Law was enacted in the middle of the Civil War to suppress the Republican press, thereby turning the press into an institution at the service of the State, a transmitter of official values, and an instrument of political indoctrination. It established very rigid and effective control mechanisms. The 1938 Press Law instituted prior censorship (*censura previa*), which had the power to approve or prohibit certain literary? material or artistic works before they were made public. Each work had to follow a strict application process to be granted authorisation for publication. In the case of native and foreign literature, as well as in the case of translations, publishers had to initiate the process.

The 1966 Press Law (also called Fraga's Law in reference to Manuel Fraga, the head of the Ministry for Information and Tourism when the 1966 Press Law was passed) eliminated prior censorship and opened the path to voluntary consultation. Article 64.2 of the new Press Law stipulated that judicial authorities were to be involved when the Administration sought to sequester a book. Voluntary consultation was the official term to refer to censorship after the 1966 Press Law was adopted. It meant that consultation was no longer legally required, though the deposit of galley proofs prior to publication was still required. Consultation was strongly advised by the Administration, and publishers could easily be sanctioned for not having sought consultation. Authors and publishers still applied for publication authorisation for fear of future retaliation (Abellán 1978: 38):

> Voluntary consultation was clearly not compulsory, but most writers resorted to it as they were scared of being the victims of imprudence. In addition, this new form of censorship obliged publishers to monitor—but above all to expurgate—manuscripts, since, in the very likely case that an institution of the Regime considered that what had been published had infringed the law in some way, publishers were subsidiarily complicit in the committed offence (my translation).

28.3.3   Bureaucratic Process

The process of censorship started with a request by a publisher to the censorship board for permission to translate a work. The censorship process followed a fixed pattern.

1   The publisher applied for authorisation for publication, a request for importation or to translate the book. This application included important data such as the proposed print runs, number of pages of the work and price.
2   The institution in charge of censorship opened a numbered censorship file and then passed it on to the assigned/censors. At the beginning, the responsibility for censorship fell within the purview of the Delegation of Press and Propaganda. The delegation functioned under the Vice-Secretariat for Popular Education, which would disappear in 1951. Its competences were transferred to the Ministry for Information and Tourism (MIT) from 1951, with Arias Salgado in charge until 1962, when he was replaced by Manuel Fraga.

3 The censors were asked to provide a report in which they answered questions and provided comments. Two or three censors were generally assigned to a file; however, more could be assigned, based on the complexity of the work.
4 The censors wrote a summary, identified controversial passages and issued a verdict: accepted, accepted with cuts or denied.
5 Higher censorship bodies supervised the final decision. If the verdict was negative, the publishing house was allowed to appeal or make a second request. If the proposal was accepted, the procedure would conclude with the obligation of the publishing house to submit six copies of the accepted text to the MIT upon its publication.

Censors worked on three different levels: on the first level, the 'censors' would read the work and write a report that was structured into three sections: a summary, an assessment and a verdict. On the second level, it was the duty of the *dictaminadores* (those who gave the final judgment) to deal and negotiate with publishers. The third level was reserved for decision-makers in charge of censorship policy. To reach this level, writers needed important connections and considerable popularity (Abellán 1980: 115–6).

There was intentional secrecy surrounding/about the work of the censor; even the term 'censor' was avoided and replaced by 'reader'. Readers were assigned a number and often signed their reports with an illegible doodle (Montejo Gurruchaga 2010: 39). In addition, it is often difficult to understand the censors' handwriting. This, together with the absence of a comprehensive catalogue of censors, make it difficult to draw connections between the comments in reports and the profiles of specific censors, despite some valuable work, such as Larraz's (2014) study on censors. The censorship files include documents which are very old, almost a century old in some cases, and the document paper and ink may have degraded over time, which, together with illegible handwriting, make it difficult to track censors' names. Censors comprised members of the Church and the military, scholars or writers, and staff who worked for the Administration. Censors also included women, who were mostly in charge of reading children and young adult fiction (Rojas 2019: 109). The ideological complexity of the text to be translated would determine the type of censor in charge of the censorship report, from a linguistics or literature specialist to a clergyman or priest (Godayol 2021: 11). Another aspect that can make research on censorship reports difficult is the fact that very frequently, the questions regarding the different tenets (morality, regime, Church) have been left unanswered.

Censorship files at the Archivo General de la Administración at Alcalá de Henares (Madrid) include the following information:

- censorship file number
- application form: publisher's name and address, proposed print run, volume pages and price, publishing house (requesting publication in the source or target language)
- censorship report: answers to the questions on tenets, verdict/decision; e.g., if the verdict was 'publish with cuts', the censors had to request, for example, deletions (partial censorship) in their comments (see Figure 28.2)
- translation galley proofs and source texts are worth checking as they often show underlined sections and notes by censors
- blue card with verdict (see Figure 28.4)

Sometimes the publisher would request permission to translate a source text and submitted said text for review. The censors indicated the pages containing passages that should be omitted when producing the translation, as seen in the example below from the 1949 censorship file for Radclyffe Hall's *The Unlit Lamp* (1924) (file number 203–49):

> to translate the referenced work, the edition and sale of the Spanish version are subject to the prior presentation of the galley proofs. The information indicated on pages 160, 166, 188, 189 and 190 has been deleted.
>
> (Zaragoza and Llopis 2021: 32)

When the censorship board decided to fully censor a text, it would conclude by recommending the outright refusal to import or publish, as shown in Figure 28.4.

28.3.4   Criteria

Decisions to censor women's writing in the original or in translation were anchored in Franco's ideological pillars. The basic pillars upon which Francoism was established were the Catholic Church, the Fatherland and the Family, where women played the secondary role of 'los *ángeles del hogar*' (the 'hearth's angels'), Figure 28.5 illustrates the 'ángel del hogar' concept, a metaphor invoking both home and religion, which aptly summarises the position to which women were relegated in Franco's regime:

> The hegemonic representation of women under Francoism institutionalised gender hierarchy and male superiority in the new Spain through a patriarchal value system. It allowed for a single Christian and biological reading of femininity based on compulsory motherhood and sought to impose a hierarchical gender domination that ordered Franco's society.
>
> (Nash 2015: 193)

This new condition for women represented a step backwards for women's rights achieved during the Second Republic, which existed prior to the Civil War and the establishment of the dictatorship: 'According to Franco's ideologues, feminism and the principles of equality and citizenship introduced during the Second Republic attested to the growing corruption of women and the denial of their natural role as mothers' (Nash 2015: 192). *The Well of Loneliness* was banned because it dealt with subject matter that contravened the taboo categories outlined by Hurtley (2007: 66):

> [The novel's subject matter is] symptomatic of issues which constituted taboo subjects in Spain under the Franco regime: the representation of the army and, more particularly, the rank occupied by the dictator in power, of the elements of the Catholic rite and unconventional women.

However, the criteria that guided censors in their report preparation were not limited to their pre-'woman question' ideological stance.

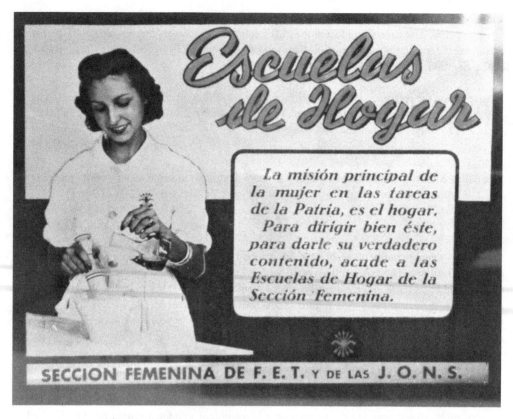

Figure 28.5 The Women's Section of the Spanish Falange (Spanish fascist political organisation active from 1933 to 1934): 'A woman's main purpose in service of the fatherland is caring for her household. Women should attend the Household School of the Women's Section to successfully manage her home' (my translation).

A set of questions guided censors when they wrote their reports (Abellán 1980: 19):

1 Does the book attack dogma? Pages.
2 Does it attack morals? Pages.
3 Does it attack the Church or its ministers? Pages.
4 Does it attack the Regime or its institutions? Pages.
5 Does it attack people who collaborate or have collaborated with the Regime? Pages?
6 Do objectionable passages account for the total content of the work? Pages?

The topics below represent the four main categories upon which the decision to censor was based:

1 inappropriate sexual and moral material, especially material that broke the Sixth Commandment (thou shalt not sin against chastity), as well as references to abortion, homosexuality and divorce
2 expression of political opinions that did not support the Regime
3 unseemly, improper or provocative use of language

Censoring Women's Writing in Translation in Franco's Spain

4 expression of opinions that questioned religion, the Catholic Church as an institution or its place in the Regime's hierarchy (Abellán 1980: 88–9; my translation).

Portrayals of sexual and moral freedom were two of the most censored aspects until democracy (Hurtley 2007; Godayol 2021). An aspect worthy of further investigation is the nature of the censorship reports. Questions to be asked might include: what do these reports handle and judge in terms of women? What was most censored in women's writing? What was the nature of the comments? Were there any comments relating to the literary value of these works?

Considering what is outlined above, it seems crucial for current and future researchers working on women and censorship in translation to suggest possible methods and structures for shaping a framework for the study of the censorship of women's writings.

28.4 Analysis

As briefly outlined earlier, to conduct research on the translated author from the point of view of translation and censorship, it is advisable to obtain relevant biographical data (especially those aspects related to feminism when researching feminist translation) and a bibliography of the author's writings in both the source and target languages. A very useful practice is to draw up a table that lists the author's works in the source and target languages along with all the relevant information, such as the year of publication of all editions, including new editions and reprintings, publishing houses, metatextual information and translators. A table summarises and presents facts simply and clearly. It will reveal, for instance, that a British work, originally published in the 1920s or 1930s, for example, was not published in Spanish until the 1980s, 1990s or even the twenty-first century. The timespan between the original publication date and the Spanish translation will raise the spectre of censorship, especially if the work is a key feminist text or has a feminist theme. Research into censors can shed light on their relationships with books, authors, publishers and the censorship process, and help us discern censorship trends. Another key aspect worth investigating is the work of the translators themselves, who translated the work of women authors whose writings portrayed new types of women, in contradistinction to the archetype of the hearth's angel promoted by the Francoist regime, and new types of love and relationships, in addition to more overtly feminist issues and themes. As noted above, one way to gain some insight into their work and determine the degree of visibility of translators is through an examination of self-censorship: for example, instances where translators would have anticipated the reactions and manoeuvres of the censors by attenuating or suppressing content that contested the regime's principles. It is therefore necessary to uncover certain information in order to reconstruct the whole censorship process:

A major obstacle when commenting on archival material related to censorship is the fact that researchers often have to deal with incomplete documentation. This may include the source and target texts, contemporary and modern accounts from the parties involved in their production and distribution (i.e., translators, film distributors, book publishers and censors) obtained via published materials (e.g., monographs, bibliographic indexes, press articles, reviews and other paratextual materials), personal interviews, and public and private archives.

(Lobejón, Gómez and Gutiérrez 2021: 93–4)

The Routledge Handbook of Translation and Censorship

28.5   Field Research

The Archivo General de la Administración is the main archival source for researching censorship. The most interesting resources for researchers in the areas of censorship, translation and gender are the following:

- The Books Section (050), where all translations are listed.
- The Repository of imported books (052.117): Imported books, including original Spanish and foreign titles, as well as translations, followed the same bureaucratic procedure as works produced in Spain. Import files up to 1965 can be found in the book censorship catalogue and are often categorised by the suffix _EXT (foreign) next to the file number (Lobejón, Gómez-Castro and Gutiérrez-Lanza 2021: 106).
- The Publishing Companies Registry: After 1966 registering the publishing house was a mandatory requirement prior to publication. Companies had to send an update of the company's operations and capital every six months, including their publication plan in which they presented the translations they planned to publish. The administration could intervene, unauthorising the registration or temporarily putting the process on hold (Lobejón, Gómez-Castro and Gutiérrez-Lanza 2021: 107). Anyone with an ID card can access the Archivo General de la Administración, but it is necessary to book an appointment. A maximum number of reports can be requested per day. Once in the main consulting room, the first step is to look for the selected author in a computer database. Author names are listed alphabetically. Once the author has been located, all the works by that author will be listed alphabetically. Note that authors' names are often misspelled. As a result, the same author might be listed under several names, so all the different names will have to be checked in order not to miss any files. In fact, researchers are advised to avoid searching by name and instead to search names in alphabetical order in this colossal database (Book Censorship) while checking whether certain similar names might represent misspellings. This is a significant limitation together with the restriction on the number of boxes that can be ordered per day.

Once the censorship files linked to a specific work have been located, the researcher must write down the number, which is its identification and location number, classified by IDD (*Instrumento de Descripción* or Description Instrument), box and censorship file number. The file also shows the year of the censorship file(s) and the publisher who made the request to publish the translation. As an example, results for the English writer Winifred Holtby (1898–1935) are listed below:

- IDD (03)050.000, box 21/07092, file number 624–43: censorship file for 'Pobre Carolina', author Winifred Holtby (José Janés) – Year 1943 (the year when the application form was submitted and a subsequent file for acceptance or rejection was opened).
- IDD (03)050.000, box 21/07170, file number 3280–43: censorship file for 'Mandoa Mandoa', author Winifred Holtby (José Janés) — Year 1943.
- IDD (03)050.000, box 21/07389, file number 2224–44: censorship file for 'Distrito del sur. Un paisaje inglés', author Winifred Holtby (José Janés) – Years 1944–1947.

Each censorship file is generally found in an envelope, which may also contain the censored work (even translations that have never been published) and the translation's galley proofs. Such was the case of Winifred Holtby's *Mandoa Mandoa* (1933), see Figure 28.6, another example of total censorship.

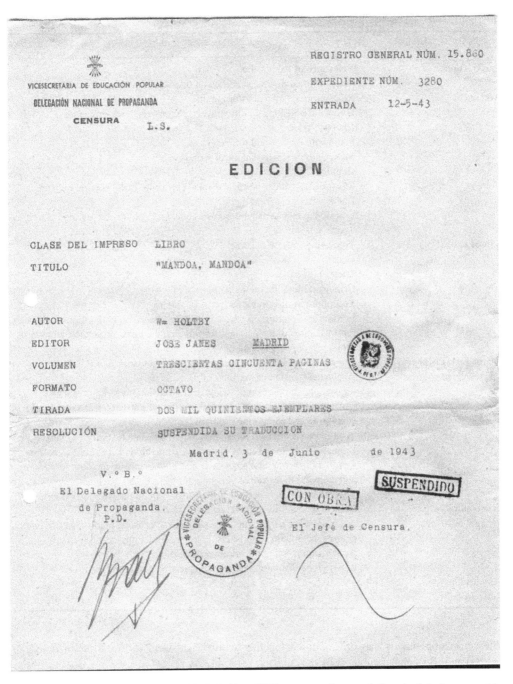

Figure 28.6 Mandoa, Mandoa (Winifred Holtby, 1933): request for translation denied, in censorship number 3280 from 1943.

The Routledge Handbook of Translation and Censorship

Table 28.1 Proposed outline for the study of translation, censorship and gender

SECTION	CONTENT
Introduction	- Relevance of the research. - State of research?/the art, based on previous literature review.
Author	- Relevant biographical information. - Groups, friendships, family, travels, cultural relations, influences. - Literary style. - Feminism: themes and forms. - Status: minor versus canonical writers. - Genres.
Context	- Most relevant socio-political events, especially in connection to women. - Literary trends. - Censorship mechanisms in source and target culture: Press Laws, actors, agents, censors.
Source texts (STs)	- Title - Genres - Themes. - Criticism: literature on the author/specific work. - Reception: awards, reviews, press clippings. - Editions and re-editions (these may suggest success in the source culture); reprints; study of the paratext surrounding the texts (prologues, afterwords, footnotes, drawings, book covers).
Target Texts (TTs)	- Target texts: published translation in the target language. - Analysing translation(s); study of the paratext accompanying the translation; comparison of the different translations. A key issue here is what to focus on when comparing different translations. One way of examining and comparing different translations (key texts are more likely to be retranslated) is to focus on feminist translation strategies (Massardier-Kenney 1997). In the cases of partial censorship (such as Hall's *The Unlit Lamp*) a further textual analysis is needed to compare the original version and the partially censored version after the requested deletions. - Reception: reviews, periodicals, awards, (re)editions, re-translations.
Censorship	- Context: Press Law in force, agents, actors. - Analysis of the censorship files and reports: censors, publishers, translators, censors' comments. Publishers' response. Deletions, self-censorship. Authorisation and publication versus ban. - Research publishing funds involved, letters, publishers' archives.
Conclusions References	

The censorship reports can be examined together with the answers to the different questions (tenets) and additional comments by the censors (see Table 28.1).

28.6 Conclusions

This chapter has proposed a viable framework for the study of texts produced by women that were partially or completely censored during the years of the Francoist dictatorship. A feminist framework could be adapted and applied to the study of censored texts produced by women in other contexts. We have briefly defined the key terms of feminism and censorship, as well as the latter's different manifestations: partial, total and self-censorship. Furthermore, examples of these types of censorship have been analysed. We have also proposed a process for conducting research on censored women authors, which covers both the theoretical basis of the approach and the analysis that the process and approach should include. We have outlined where scholars and students working on censorship under Franco can find further information on the context in which censorship took place and the regulations behind it (the Press Laws of 1938 and 1966), as well as the agents involved in enforcing censorship. In addition, important work on the intersection of women, censorship and translation in the context of Francoist Spain has been highlighted. This literature is fundamental to framing research on the translation of the works of women writers. Finally, the nature and form of the censorship reports have been illustrated, and the location of important information concerning the whole censorship process and the connections between all the agents (publishers, translators, censors (readers), and authors themselves) have been outlined.

For this purpose, we have suggested adapting the feminist translation strategy of recovery to previously censored texts, to rehabilitate, translate in full or translate these texts for the first time. Recovery entails 1) identifying works that do not have a Spanish translation because of censorship; 2) analysing censorship reports (see above); and 3) comparing source texts and partially censored translations to ascertain whether the latter implemented all the corrections/modifications imposed by the censorship board. The outcome of this research may lead to a new phase: rehabilitating or partially restoring censored texts that are still circulating in the literary market, and providing a full translation. This proposal is not devoid of issues or debates, which will inform future research.

Further Reading

García-Domínguez, María J., Díaz-Peralta, Marina and Pinero-Pinero, Gracia. 2016. 'Traducción y censura en la España franquista'. *Bulletin hispanique*, 118(2): 591–610.
The main focus of this article is an examination of the Spanish version of *Claudine à Paris*, by the French writer Colette, which was translated in 1963 by E. Piñas. The authors show how censorship influenced the translation of a famous work by a female writer.

Zaragoza Ninet, Gora, Martínez Sierra, Juan José and Avila-Cabrera, José Javier (eds.). 2015. 'Traducción y Censura: nuevas perspectivas', *Quaderns de Filologia*, 20. Universitat de València.
This monograph includes 13 articles which describe cutting-edge research on translation and censorship by renowned scholars in the field.

Merino Alvarez, Raquel (ed.). 2007. *Traducción y censura en España (1939–1985): estudios sobre corpus TRACE: cine, narrativa, teatro*. Universidad de País Vasco.
This book is the result of years of consolidated research by project members of TRACE (Universidad de León and Euskal Herriko Unibertsitatea). The aim of the project is to examine the reception, translation, and censorship of translated texts during Francoism (1939–1985) in Spain. This work is divided into three sections: narrative, film and drama, and includes a total of six academic articles. It provides enlightening research into the censorship of children's fiction by women and about the translation and censorship of Emily Brontë's *Wuthering Heights*.

References

Abellán, Manuel L. 1978. 'Censura y práctica censoria', *Sistema*, 22: 29–52.
Abellán, Manuel L. 1980. *Censura y creación literaria en España (1939–1976)*. Barcelona, Spain: Península.

Abellán, Manuel L. 1982. 'Censura y autocensura en la producción literaria española', *Nuevo Hispano*, 1: 69–180. Available at: www.represura.es/represura_4_octubre_2007_articulo6.html (Accessed: 23 September 2023).

Abellán, Manuel L. 1987. 'Fenómeno censorio y represión literaria', in *Censura y literaturas peninsulares, Diálogos hispánicos de Amsterdam*, vol. 5. Amsterdam: Rodopi, 5–25.

Brontë, Emily. 2006. *Wuthering Heights*. London: Penguin Classics.

Brontë, Emily. 2011. *Cumbres borrascosas*. Translated by Juan G. de Luaces. Madrid: Espasa Calpe.

Camus Camus, Carmen. 2011. Women, Translation and Censorship in the Franco Regime. *MonTI* 3: 447–470.

Camus Camus, Carmen, Gómez Castro, Cristina and Williams, Julia T. 2017. *Translation, Ideology and Gender*. Newcastle upon Tyne: Cambridge Scholars Publishing.

Casanova, Julián (ed.). 2015. *40 añon con Franco*. Barcelona: Crítica.

Godayol, Pilar 2021. 'Ensayos feministas censurados durante el tardofranquismo: Maria Aurèlia Capmany, Lidia Falcón y Amparo Moreno', *Bulletin of Spanish Studies*, 98(4): 557–82.

Godayol, Pilar and Taronna, Annarita. 2018. *Foreign Women Authors under Fascism and Francoism. Gender, Translation and Censorship*. Cambridge: Cambridge Scholars Publishing.

Julio, Teresa. 2018. 'María Luz Morales y las Lettres portugaises de Mariana Alcoforado', in G. Zaragoza Ninet, J. J. Martínez Sierra, M. Beatriz Cerezo and M. R. Marset (eds.). *Traducción, género y censura en la literatura y en los medios de comunicación*. Granada: Comares, 27–37.

Hurtley, Jacqueline, A. 2007. 'Tailoring the Tale: Inquisitorial Discourses and Resistance in the Early Franco Period (1949–50)', in F. Billiani (ed.), *Modes of Censorship and Translation*. London: Routledge, 51–92.

Larraz, Fernando. 2014. *Letricidio español. Censura y novela durante el franquismo*. Gijón: Ediciones Trea.

Lobejón Santos, Sergio, Gómez Castro, Cristina and Gutiérrez Lanza, Camino. 2021. 'Archival Research in Translation and Censorship: Digging into the "True Museum of Francoism"', *Meta* 66(1): 92–114.

Llopis Mestre, Sara and Zaragoza Ninet, Gora. 2020. 'Censorship and Translation into Spanish of the Lesbian Novel in English: The Case of *Rubyfruit Jungle* (1973)', *TRANS: Revista De Traductología*, 24: 353–74.

Massardier-Kenney, Françoise. 1997. 'Towards a Redefinition of Feminist Translation Practice', *The Translator*, 3(1): 55–69.

Montejo Gurruchaga, Lucia. 2010. *Discurso de autora: género y censura en la narrativa española de posguerra*. Madrid: UNED.

Munday, Jeremy. 2014. 'Using Primary Sources to Produce a Microhistory of Translation and Translators: Theoretical and Methodological Concerns', *The Translator*, 20(1), 64–80.

Nash, Mary. 2015. 'Vencidas, represaliadas y resistentes. Las mujeres bajo el orden patriarcal franquista', in J. Casanova et al. (eds.), *40 años con Franco*. Barcelona: Crítica, 91–227.

Ortega Sáez, Marta. 2011. 'Narrativa y censura de Vita Sackville-West en la España de Franco (1939–1975)', in S. Coll-Vinent, C. Eisner and E. Gallén Miret (coord.), *La traducció i el món editorial de postguerra*. Barcelona: Punctum, 65–80.

Ortega Sáez, Marta. 2013. *Traducciones del Franquismo en el mercado literario español contemporáneo: el caso de Jane Eyre de Juan G. de Luaces*. Universitat de Barcelona, Doctoral Thesis.

Panchón Hidalgo, Marian and Zaragoza Ninet, Gora. 2023. Récupération/Réhabilitation (de textes censurés d'écrivaines) (FR) / Recovery (of censored texts by women writers) (ENG) / Recuperación (de textos censurados de escritoras) (ESP). Dictionnaire du genre en traduction / Dictionary of Gender in Translation / Diccionario del género en traducción. IRN World Gender (CNRS). ISSN: 2967–3623.

Riba Sanmartí, Caterina and Sanmartí Roset, Carme. 2018. 'La traducción de literatura sentimental entre 1920 y 1960: El rosario de Florence Barclay: versiones, adaptaciones y censura', in G. Zaragoza Ninet et al. (eds.), *Traducción, género y censura en la literatura y en los medios de comunicación*. Granada: Comares, 99–111.

Riba Sanmartí, Caterina and Sanmartí Roset, Carme. 2020. 'La recepción de tres novelas de George Sand en España a través de sus ediciones y (re)traducciones', *Çédille: Revista de Estudios Franceses*, 18: 623–47.

Rojas Claros, Francisco. 2019. 'Mujer, censura y disidencia editorial en el segundo franquismo. Una aproximación', *Represura*, 4: 105–82.

Toury, Gideon. 1995. *Descriptive Translation Studies*. Amsterdam: John Benjamins.

Zaragoza Ninet, Gora. 2008. *Censuradas, criticadas, olvidadas: las novelistas inglesas del siglo XX y su traducción al castellano*. València: Publicacions de la Universitat de València.

Zaragoza Ninet, Gora. 2012. 'Winifred Holtby: la lucha de una mujer singular. Las mujeres, la escritura y el poder', *Quaderns de Filologia. Estudis literaris* 17: 125–134.

Zaragoza Ninet, Gora. 2017. 'Gender, Translation, and Censorship: The Well of Loneliness (1928) in Spain as an Example of Translation in Cultural Evolution,' in O. I. Seel (ed.), *Redefining Translation and Interpretation in Cultural Evolution*. Hershey, PA: IGI Global, 42–66.

Zaragoza Ninet, Gora and Llopis Mestre, Sara. 2021. 'The Unlit Lamp (1924): Translation, Reception and Censorship', Language and Intercultural Communication, 21: 37–54. DOI: https://doi.org/10.1080/1470 8477.2020.1852244

Zaragoza Ninet, Gora, Martínez Sierra, Juan José, Merchán, Beatriz Cerezo and Richart Marset, Mabel (eds.). 2018. *Traducción, género y censura en la literatura y en los medios de comunicación*. Granada: Comares.

Zaragoza Ninet, Gora and Merchán, Beatriz Cerezo. 2019. 'Rebeca maltratada: un estudio comparativo de su censura a través de las Leyes de Prensa españolas y el Código Hays estadounidense', *Clepsydra* 18: 107–127.

Zavala, Iris M. (coord.). 1998. *Breve historia feminista de la literatura española (en lengua castellana) V. La literatura escrita por mujer (Del s. XIX a la actualidad)*. Barcelona: Anthropos.

PART VI

Genre- and Mode-specific Contexts

29

RELIGIOUS TEXTS, TRANSLATION, AND CENSORSHIP

Jacobus A. Naudé and Cynthia L. Miller-Naudé

29.1 Introduction

As a complex phenomenon, a religion together with its sacred writings forms an inextricable part of culture. Religion is a central part of human experience, influencing how an individual within a religious tradition perceives and reacts to their environments. Moreover, such an individual may also be engaged in a community of believers or a religious organisation. Religious organisations are influenced and shaped by the social, political and cultural context in which they are situated, but *vice versa* they influence and shape the societies in which they are set. Religious traditions emerge through time with respect to the development of ideas, thoughts and values, on the one hand, and the critical roles they play over time shape religious communities in particular and societies in general, on the other hand. As religions emerge through time, their intertwined oral-written traditions evolve together as realised *inter alia* in religious texts—often translated—through a transmission process that involves the selection of conforming knowledge and the adaptation or suppression of threatening knowledge. In addition, the interpretation of a religious text is restricted by the way its own circle of believing readers understands it. These dimensions form the broad context within which censorship concerning the production of religious texts and their translations is to be situated.

According to Billiani (2007: 3–4; 2020: 56), censorship is a coercive and forceful act by a hegemonic power, largely aimed at imposing a certain ideology through manipulative rewriting of discourses. That rewriting aims to filter (that is, to block, manipulate or control) the stream of information in the complex process of cross-cultural transfer in four broad categories: political, moral, religious and aesthetic. The point of departure is Michel Foucault's view that power is a function of discourse and knowledge—language and literature become avenues to control human communicative behaviour (Foucault 1972; Foss and Gill 1987). As a locus of power, foreign knowledge, which is transferred into a receiving cultural space, will come under scrutiny by those who control access to it in their efforts to maintain social order (Bourdieu 1991; Merkle 2018: 225). Accordingly, the study of censorship involves translations because they expose readers to foreign cultures and ideologies, which represent potential threats. Translations make the borders of acceptance visible and may conform to or evade censorship restriction (Billiani 2020: 59).

DOI: 10.4324/9781003149453-36

The Routledge Handbook of Translation and Censorship

Lefevere (1984: 128) calls the space of censorship, which lies between acceptance and refusal, 'the margin': if you want to be listened to at all, you will have to say it within a certain margin, and any attempt to express oneself outside the margin lays one open to a range of possible negative outcomes. It is more than a border line between the acceptable and the unacceptable but rather a 'liminal zone of operation' within which subversive or unwelcome material after sufficient discretion may be made available to readers. Depending on the nature of a given society, this margin may be broad or narrow and is likely to change over time. Focusing on reception, Merkle (2010: 19) views either the protection of the vulnerable (which may be viewed as positive) or the creation of a political or cultural system, including a religious system (which may be viewed as repressive) as motivation for censorship. Bourdieu (1991: 137–59) states that the compromise act of censorship is the product of strategies of euphemising and consists of two inseparable processes: imposing convention and respecting convention. According to Reynolds (2007: 187–204), Dryden and Browning employed euphemism, innuendo and transliteration as textual strategies in their translations of classical literature to say what 'cannot be said'. In the twenty-first century there is thus a broadening of the understanding of the conventional concept of censorship as a complex phenomenon to include other processes of discourse regulation and control that impact message content such as canon formation (Merkle 2010: 18; 2018: 227). This development is referred to by the term 'new censorship' (Müller 2004: 1). Research in contemporary translation studies focuses on how censorship functions (the process), rather than simply what effects it has (the product) (Woods 2019: 511).

The goal of this chapter is to come to a better understanding of the manifestations of new censorship in the translation of religious texts. We focus on representative religious texts of religions with dominant written traditions, namely the three monotheistic religions—the Jewish religion, Christianity and Islam (55% of the global population as indicated by Pew Research Center Forum 2012)—from the earliest time until the present (see Naudé 2010a, Naudé 2018, Naudé and Miller-Naudé 2018). Religions with a dominant oral tradition and religions with oral tradition and foundational texts do not promote translation of their texts and thus they fall outside the scope of this essay (Naudé 2021). The assumption is that the translations of religious texts exhibit commonalities with the translations of other literary and non-literary texts with respect to the modality of censorship, the mechanisms by which it works, the complex human interactions that support it as well as the role of the translator in supporting and eliding censorship.

Censorship of religious texts and their translations has occurred throughout history. Censorship of religious texts includes restrictions and prohibitions on possessing, reading or using them or their translations. Violators of banned religious literature have been punished by killing, imprisonment, forced labour, banishment, as well as by burning or confiscating the religious texts produced, used or distributed. In this regard the following section provides historical perspectives with a selection of examples.

29.2 Historical Perspectives

Early examples of censorship or gatekeeping of religious texts can be found in the Hebrew Bible/ Old Testament. The cause of censorship was a theological bias of a certain elite exercising control over the scribal production of texts. As an outcome of a textual process of appropriation and translation, censorship involved the assimilation of the polytheistic traditions in ancient Israel into the monotheistic ideology of the Hebrew Bible, that is, the expression of belief in a single deity. This early form of censorship is illustrated by Smith (2008: 187–212) utilising Deuteronomy 32:8–9, the description of how the head god (El Elyon 'God Most High') divided the world into various nations. According to the Dead Sea Scroll version (DSS 4QDeut^j), which is the oldest manuscript copy, the division of the world into nations was done according to the number of divine children, 'the children of El', that is, the various gods of the world. To avoid a picture of polytheism, a deliberate alteration involved the replacement of 'El' with 'Israel' to read 'the children of Israel', that is, the patriarch 'Jacob', in the biblical text, as well as in a number of translations, namely the Samaritan Hebrew Pentateuch, the Aramaic Targum, the Syriac Peshitta, and the Latin Vulgate. Accordingly, the following interpretation was generated: Genesis 10 states that the number of peoples in the world was seventy. The number of persons belonging to Israel (the name given to the patriarch Jacob) was likewise seventy when Jacob went to live in Egypt (Genesis 46:27; Exodus 1:5). Therefore, the borders of the nations were drawn according to the number of the people of Israel (or Jacob), the portion of Yahweh when they settled in Egypt. In the Greek Septuagint, 'the children of El' is translated as 'the angels of God' to avoid a picture of polytheism.

Another example where censorship involved the assimilation of the polytheistic traditions in ancient Israel into the monotheistic ideology of the Hebrew Bible follows in Genesis 14:22, where Israel's deity is referred to with the phrase 'Yahweh, El Elyon' in the Hebrew source text as well as in the Aramaic Targum and the Latin Vulgate. The Samaritan Hebrew version reads 'God El Elyon'. However, in the Greek Septuagint and the Syriac Peshitta, the deity is referred to simply as El Elyon, an epithet meaning 'God Most High', a phrase applied to Yahweh that was also used in a polytheistic context to refer to the chief god of the pantheon. Most biblical scholars view the explicitation of El Elyon as either Yahweh (the personal name of Israel's distinctive deity), the strategy of the Hebrew source text, or as God, the strategy of the Samaritan Hebrew text, as scribal adaptations in order to preclude a polytheistic interpretation and insure that readers understand El Elyon as an epithet of Israel's sole deity.

A Jewish and Christian tradition regarding King Hezekiah as a censor of religious texts was recovered by Mroczek (2021: 481–502), who demonstrates that ancient readers were aware that their texts were a product of human acts and institutional decisions. King Hezekiah reigned in the kingdom of Judah from 715 BCE to the Babylonian exile in 687 BCE. The tradition of King Hezekiah as a censor in Jewish and Christian sources in different languages and genres rests on Hezekiah's portrayal in the Bible as both an anti-idolater (2 Kings 18–20) and as the transmitter of Solomon's proverbs in his court (Proverbs 25:1). These traditions were intertwined to refashion Hezekiah as a curator of public knowledge who distinguished between texts to be transmitted and texts to be suppressed, by which he gradually took on a legendary role as a handler of texts, a censor and a canon maker. The Solomonic oeuvre as described in 1 Kings 5:13–15 (Hebrew; English = 4:32–34) as consisting of three thousand proverbs, one thousand and five songs, and writings about trees ('from the cedar that is found in Lebanon to the marjoram that grows on walls'), as well as about animals, birds, reptiles, and fish, is much larger than what is included in the Hebrew Bible/Old Testament canon. If Solomon had once produced so much, the question is what became of it. The reason for exclusion of the Solomonic corpus of writings on fauna and flora in the Hebrew Bible was not because of authenticity. As a guardian of orthodoxy, Hezekiah rather hid them because of their association as depicted in the Jewish and Christian tradition with foreign medical knowledge, which was thought to be a gateway to idolatry and a threat to proper piety (Mroczek 2021: 491–3).

The public burning of religious texts and their translations for ideological reasons occurred throughout history. An early example from the Hebrew Bible/Old Testament can be found in the description (Jeremiah 36) of the burning of a Hebrew scroll by Jehoiakim, the king who governed Judah from 609 to 598 BCE. The scroll contained the prophecies of Jeremiah that the king of Babylon would destroy the land of Judah (Jeremiah 22:25–27), which could be avoided if the king of Judah changed his political agenda by not casting his lot with Egypt (Jeremiah 2:18, 36) but accepting the suzerainty of Babylon (2 Kings 24:1–2). Jehoiakim censored these oracles of destruction by burning the scroll and then sought to have Jeremiah and his scribe, Baruch, arrested. In Jeremiah 36 the techniques of scribal craft are used to construct an overtly subversive discourse (Moore 2021).

An example of a ban of a religion for political and ideological reasons occurred in the Roman Empire when Emperor Diocletian (245–313 CE) attempted to use state religion, that is, the Imperial Cult, to unify the empire. Because the Christians were a large community that refused to show any allegiance to the gods of the empire, they could no longer be tolerated. In an attempt to wipe out Christianity, he issued an edict in 303 CE ordering the destruction of Christian buildings, the burning of all copies of their religious texts and the reduction of Christians to the lowest status of citizen across the Roman Empire (Freeman 2002: 85–6).

The powerful role of language use to impose a distinct ideology of religious purity as a means of censorship for differentiating acceptable and unacceptable religious knowledge is demonstrated by the Jewish Essene sectarian movement (circa 250 BCE to 68 CE), associated with the Dead Sea Scrolls. The Essenes translated their idea of separation into conscious linguistic choices as is evident from the various terms used to describe language, for example, in the Thanksgiving Psalms (1QH^a 9:29–31): 'You yourself [= God] created spirit in language, and You know its words. You determined the fruit of the lips before they exist. You set the words according to the measuring line/ archetype and the utterance of the breath of the lips by calculation. You bring forth the measuring lines/archetypes according to their mysteries and the utterances of the spirits/the breath according to their calculus.' The primordial pattern or archetype for (pure) language and speech akin to the primordial language of creation was intended to set the speakers of the sectarian movement and their language apart from speakers of (impure) vernacular Hebrew, as well as Aramaic, who were involved with an unacceptable ongoing oral interpretative/intra-translational process of religious texts (Schniedewind 2021: 280–91).

Similarly, the Book of James in the Christian New Testament (Chapter 3:1–12) describes the powerful role of language, especially concerning the responsible speaking/teaching of teachers/ leaders in the church community (James 3:1–2). The disproportionate power of the tongue as a small organ with huge power associated metaphorically with speech production (James 3:5) is compared to bits in the mouth of horses that control them, and the small rudder that steers a ship (James 3:3–4). The destruction caused by irresponsible speech is compared to a small spark that sets a great forest on fire (James 3:5). The tongue metaphor is developed further in James 3:6–9 as a universe in which every sort of unrighteousness exists; everyone must remember the infinite possibilities of evil of which speech is capable. In this way, the writer of James provides advice concerning responsible language use (James 3:10–11), which is controlled by self-censorship: a fig tree does not produce olives; a grapevine produces grapes, not figs (James 3:12); similarly, language use should be consistent with the values of the gospel.

Although the synagogue forms part of the history of both the Jewish religion and Christianity, no one solution to the complex problem of its origins has yet been accepted by the majority of scholars (Runesson 2001: 477–88). Although Nehemiah 8:1–8 (530 BCE) alludes to public reading, translation and interpretation of sacred scriptures on a public square (see below for explanation of event), literary evidence for the synagogue and its practices begins to appear in the first century CE with public reading of the sacred scriptures as a principal activity (Flesher and Chilton 2011: 3). It was generally accompanied by the recitation of a translation, which the rabbis regulated by means of rules aimed at distinguishing the Hebrew text from the Aramaic translation and emphasising the priority of the Hebrew. As regulated by the rabbis, the translation into Aramaic was performed from memory, whereas the Hebrew scripture was read from a written scroll (Smelik 2013: 173–85). Censoring occurred during reading and translating since some passages, which concern matters of sexual impropriety or idolatry, were considered inappropriate for the general Jewish public, especially women and children (Flesher and Chilton 2011: 303). The Mishnah (Megillah 4:10) indicates which passages could be read in Hebrew, but not translated, while others should not even be read. In the former cases, those who knew Hebrew would hear and understand the story, but those who did not would remain uninformed about this sinful behaviour. The passages concerning Amnon's rape of his half-sister (2 Samuel 13) and David's adulterous seduction of Bathsheba (2 Samuel 11) were not to be read in a worship setting, even in Hebrew. In subsequent centuries, this list was reduced because the rabbis had a distaste for censorship, which they practised rarely and with a light hand (Flesher and Chilton 2011, 305).

As a missionary to the Goths, Wulfila (Ulfilas in Greek, 311–382 CE), the son of a Cappadocian father and a Gothic mother, translated the Bible (with the assistance of a translation team) into Gothic following his creation of a writing system for the Gothic language (Noss 2019: 63). He suppressed knowledge by omitting from the translation the four Books of Kings from the Greek Old Testament on the grounds that their content was too warlike and that Gothic readers needed no further encouragement to be warriors (Noss 2019: 63).

As a kind of preventative or prior censorship, early Christianity initiated an innovative way of warding off the heretical threats to Christian doctrine by introducing ecumenical councils (that is, a council of the whole church as a controlling religious authority) at pivotal and critical moments in the life of the church. These councils then formulated definitive religious texts in the form of a statement on doctrine or discipline. Until Vatican II (1962–1965), the Roman Catholic Church recognised twenty-one such ecumenical councils. Core tenets were summarised, sometimes in the form of a creed, to be followed by all insiders, such as the Nicene Creed promulgated by the Council of Nicaea in 325 CE, which condemned Arianism (MacCulloch 2009: 215–22). The creed set the limit of what was considered to be acceptable. To avoid censorship, a Bible translation had to avoid formulations contradictory to the tenets of the creed (see, for example, Arianism as a reason for censorship in the case of Erasmus's Latin translation below).

Ecumenical councils also selected which religious texts were to be regarded as sacred by the community, the so-called canon, setting them apart from other written works. Canonisation implies a fixed or standard version of a specific religious text. Canonical writings express in a definitive way the content of what the community believes and establishes a framework for censorship. An example from about 530 BCE follows from the Ezra and Nehemiah narratives in the Hebrew Bible/Old Testament (Ezra 9–10 and Nehemiah 8–10, 13), which narrate the enforcement of a law code, promulgated as canonical law at a meeting of the faith community, to correct a particularly unacceptable situation, where the Levites had abandoned the temple service to take up farming, people traded on the Sabbath day, the Hebrew language was neglected and intermarriage with non-Israelites was practised. Members who wanted to remain part of the religious community simply had to accept the canonicity of the law read out and explained to them, and to follow the laws in the canon.

As exposed by Al-Azami (2015: 1616–20), censorship is evident in the compilation and canonisation of the Qur'ān (about 650 CE), which is very different from that of the Bible in that the Qur'ān is not the product of numerous authors over a long period of time. The entire Qur'ān was recited in a period of twenty-three years by the prophet Mohammed to his circle of listeners, who wrote (or dictated to scribes) what he had said. Omar, the second Caliph, collected these records. Regional differences over the pronunciation of the Qur'ān resulting from various Muslim groups each with their own dialect caused conflict during the reign of 'Uthman, the third Caliph (644 to

The Routledge Handbook of Translation and Censorship

656 CE). His solution was to provide Muslims with a single version compiled by a commission consisting of Zayd ibn Thābit, ʿAbd Allāh ibn al-Zubayr, Saʿīd ibn al-ʿĀṣ and ʿAbd al-Raḥmān ibn al-Ḥārith ibn Hishām. who worked under his supervision from the numerous fragments of the Qurʾān in public circulation. The last-mentioned three scholars were Qurayshī speakers with the brief that where they disagree with Zayd ibn Thābit on any point, they have to write the Qurʾān in Qurayshī (Al-Azami 2015: 1617). Since all Arabic dialects would be of equal difficulty for non-Arabs who desired to read the Qurʾān, the most favourable choice was the Qurayshī dialect, because that was the dialect in which it was believed the revelation was delivered. After the final intratranslation, editing and compilation were completed, ʿUthman dispatched certified duplicate copies for distribution throughout the provinces of the Islamic state to replace the unofficial private copies, which were to be burnt. ʿUthman's script and spelling became the new standard for centuries to come. This event contributes to the viewpoint that no translation of the Qurʾān into any other language is able to render the linguistic nuances, the words and meanings, the many levels of interpretation and symbolic significance associated with the sound and structure of the words in the sacred Arabic language, chosen by God (Lumbard 2015: 1601–6; see also Naudé 2010b for an example of iconicity featured in the Arabic text of the Qurʾān). Consequently, the official use by Muslims of the Qurʾān in translation is prohibited. Lumbard (2015: 1606) states:

> The only true translation of the Qurʾān possible is of existential order: only those who have assimilated the revelation or immersed themselves in its teachings so thoroughly that its meanings speak through their thoughts, words and deeds.

Within the Catholic Church, the Inquisition, which was initially a judicial procedure and later a powerful institution, played the role of institutional censorship. Over the course of history there have been a number of inquisitions. The papal bull *Ad abolendam* of 1184 CE required bishops to make a judicial inquiry, or inquisition, to combat heretics in their dioceses and to hand them over to the secular authorities for punishment (Bowden 2007: 184–5; MacCulloch 2009: 396–401). This was not very effective with the result that in 1233 Pope Gregory IX appointed full-time inquisitors to root out heretics (Bowden 2007: 202). The Spanish Inquisition was set up in 1478 by Pope Sixtus IV at the request of the Spanish monarchy for the purpose of preserving religious unity and doctrinal orthodoxy throughout Spain and its colonies until its abolition in 1834 (MacCulloch 2009: 584–91). As an agency of both the Roman Catholic Church and the kingdom of Spain, the inquisition dealt primarily with the Jews and Muslims who had not been baptised and then with those who were baptised but still practised the Jewish religion or Islam in private. It was broadened later to include any suspected heretics. In 1542 Pope Paul III instituted the Congregation of the Holy Office, the Roman Inquisition, to supervise local inquisitions; it lives on as the Congregation for the Doctrine of Faith (Bowden 2007: 276; MacCulloch 2009: 640–2, 662–5).

Contrary to the speculation of some scholars (for example, Robinson 1996; 2018), there was no blanket Catholic prohibition against the translation of the Bible into vernaculars. Vernacular translations of the Bible were widespread and popular before the Reformation and were used by clergy and laity without any objection by the ecclesiastical authorities, provided they avoided association with heretical groups. Major European languages had Bibles. For example, Daniell (2003: 108) refers to eight Bibles or Psalters printed in German, five New Testaments or Psalters in French, and three (the Old Testament, most of the New Testament, and the Psalter) in Dutch. From 1466 to 1522, the date of Martin Luther's New Testament, 14 versions were translated into German. In cases of prohibition, the concern was more with the content of the teaching and

Religious Texts, Translation, and Censorship

preaching from the Bible than with the vernacular translations with the result that restrictions were placed on the usage or possession of the Bible and its vernacular translations. The opinions and practices were localised, made in direct response to heresy threats and were not always consistent. For example, in reaction to the opposition to the Roman Catholic Church by the Albigensian anti-sacerdotal party of Toulouse in southern France, the Council of Toulouse decreed in 1229 that lay people may not possess Bibles (Bowden 2007: 201). Five years after the expulsion of the Jews from Spain, the Spanish Inquisition ordered the destruction of all Hebrew books and all vernacular Bibles in 1497 to ensure that former Jews and their descendants who had converted to Christianity did not revert back to Judaism.

Daniell (2003: 108–10) describes a century and a half of the severest institutional censorship in England's history. It began in 1401 with an act of the English Parliament against heresy, *De heretico comburendo*, which decreed death by burning alive for English heretics. This kind of censorship was new in England—before 1401, no one in England had been put to death for reading or hearing the Bible in Old or Middle English—and it had no parallel in the rest of Europe. This act, which was finally repealed in 1559, was in reaction to the Lollards, who were followers of John Wycliffe (1330–1384). Wycliffe was an Oxford University theologian, who was associated with the Wycliffe ('Lollard') Bibles (1380–1388) in vernacular English and who emphasised personal piety, humility and simplicity in his followers' relationship to God (Daniell 2003: 66–95). It was made fully effective by Archbishop Thomas Arundel's Constitutions of Oxford in 1409. Heresy included reading and not just owning a Bible (or part of it) that was not in Latin. The act forbade the future translation of the Bible into English unless the local bishop or a provincial council approved the translation. William Tyndale (14941536), already under suspicion for having criticised certain doctrines and practices of the Roman Catholic Church, applied in 1523 to Cuthbert Tunstall, the Bishop of London, for authorisation to translate the New Testament into English. On being refused, he went to Germany, where he published the first edition of his translation of the New Testament into English in 1525, with revisions in 1526 (reprinted four times) and in 1534. His translation of the first Five Books of the Old Testament was published in 1530 and the Book of Jonah in 1531. His translations aroused fierce opposition in England and smuggled copies were burned in public by Tunstall. While translating the historical books of Joshua to 2 Chronicles from Hebrew with the help of John Rogers, a colleague and friend in Antwerp, Tyndale was betrayed, arrested and imprisoned in May 1535. In his trial Tyndale was accused of the heresy of following Luther. His captors in the Low Countries believed that his destruction would remove heresy from England and would bring glory to them. In 1536 he was executed at Vilvoorde near Antwerp. When Tyndale was arrested, Rogers took Tyndale's translated manuscripts to create a volume attributed on the title page to Thomas Matthew, an invented name, perhaps inspired by two of the disciples in the New Testament (see Naudé 2022: 4–6 for a historical overview of the emergence of English Bible translation during this period). The Matthew's Bible was published in 1537 and licensed by King Henry VIII scarcely a year after the execution of Tyndale (Matthew's Bible, Introduction, ix–x). The publication of Tyndale's translation under a pseudonym after his execution circumvented censorship.

Another attempt at preventive or prior censorship to address the challenges to authority that translation inevitably generates led to the compilation of the *Complutensian Polyglot* (CP), named after the Latin Complutum for the Spanish town Alcalá de Henares, where it was created between 1502 and 1514 (Reynolds 2019: 14–7). It presents the Hebrew Bible/Old Testament in five different languages: the Hebrew on the left, Latin in the middle, Greek (with Latin gloss) on the right and Aramaic with its Latin translation at the bottom. In the New Testament the Greek text and Latin translation are presented side by side. This method did not differentiate variants among

461

the versions, thus preserving the authority of the Latin version at a time when the rediscovery of Hebrew and Greek knowledge drew new interest. The layout of the CP, as well as the metatextual statements in its prologue, reveal that the Latin translation was deemed more authoritative than the Hebrew and Greek texts from which it emerged, because they were associated with the rival beliefs of the Jewish religion and Greek Orthodoxy, respectively. A further aspect of censorship is illustrated by the publishing of the CP. A printed work is considered to be published not when it comes off the press, but when it becomes available for public distribution. Although the CP was already printed in 1514, its publication was delayed until the pope granted his approval in 1522. The censorship process had implications for the Greek New Testament. Although the New Testament for the CP was the first edition of the Greek New Testament ever printed, Erasmus of Rotterdam's *Novum Instrumentum* was the first printed Greek New Testament to be published in 1516, followed by subsequent editions in 1519, 1522, 1527 and 1535.

In contrast to the CP, Desiderius Erasmus of Rotterdam (1467/9–1536) followed a different strategy to rescue the Latin translation, as described by De Jonge (2016: 29–41). Erasmus believed that a new Latin translation of the Bible according to the criteria of classical Latin was necessary. Erasmus's motivation was to correct textual corruption and translation errors and to render the Greek of the source text in a grammatically clearer, purer and more expressive Latin. His new Latin version was accompanied by the Greek text. However, Erasmus's Greek manuscripts lacked the Johannine comma ('comma' means 'clause'), a marginal gloss on 1 John 5:7–8—'There are three who give testimony in heaven: the Father, the Word, and the Holy Spirit; and these three are one'—that is absent from the earliest Latin Bibles, but had found its way into almost all Latin texts by the thirteenth century and did not appear in any Greek manuscript until the fifteenth century CE, when it was used as support for the doctrine of the Trinity (McDonald 2016,:42–55):

> There are three who give testimony in heaven: the Father, the Word, and the Holy Spirit; and these three are one. And there are three that give testimony on earth: the spirit, and the water, and the blood; and these three are one.

> (1 John 5:7–8)

Therefore, Erasmus discarded the gloss in his Latin translation and used the shorter reading of these verses—'There are three that give testimony: the spirit, and the water, and the blood; and these three are one'—leading to the accusation that he was promoting the heresy of Arianism by denying the trinity. This is contrary to the editors of the CP, who kept the Johannine comma. They even back translated it from the Latin and inserted it into the Greek text. The Greek text of Erasmus served as the source text for William Tyndale's English translation and Luther's translation of the New Testament into German in 1522, which were all banned. At the Council of Trent in 1546 the Latin translation of the Bible was officially declared to be the authentic and authoritative Bible of the Roman Catholic Church and given the name 'Vulgate'. In 1589, the Sistine edition of the Vulgate was published to be replaced in 1592 by the Clementine, which was the official text edition of the Roman Catholic Church. They all include the Johannine comma. In 1893 the Roman Catholic Church issued an encyclical on the study of the Bible, *Providentissimus Deus*, to give official guidance to the clergy about the manuscript discoveries and the rise of the field of textual criticism during the nineteenth century. This was followed in 1943 by the encyclical letter *Divino Afflante Spiritu*, which enabled Bible translators to utilise source texts in the original biblical languages. This led to the Nova Vulgate or New Vulgate as the official Latin translation published in 1979 (revised in 1986); it omits the Johannine comma—a case of de-censorship.

The Catholic Church decreed in 1557 that no book could be printed or sold without the permission of the church. A major instrument of the Counter-Reformation (the formal actions taken by the Roman Catholic Church to strengthen Roman Catholicism in response to the criticism of the Protestant Reformation) was the *Index of Prohibited Books*, which refers to a list of books (including various Bible translations) issued by the pope that Roman Catholics were forbidden to print, possess or read. Pope Paul IV ordered the first *Index of Prohibited Books* in 1559. Some religious texts and translations listed are the writings of Erasmus, as well as the Bible translations of Tyndale and Luther. Wherever these measures were applied, they effectively hindered the production and distribution of Bible translations. No Bibles were printed in Italy until 1773 and in Spain until 1793. However, Bible translations in various languages continued to be published in Antwerp, Geneva, Leuven, Paris and Venice. The last *Index of Prohibited Books* was finally abolished in 1966.

Any translation diverging from the accepted interpretation was likely to be deemed heretical. To prevent a translation from being censured or banned, Bible translators often defended themselves and their translations by utilising metatexts or paratexts to (re)frame the translations of sacred texts and to narrate the nature of the specific translation as a means of mediating conflicting theological views. For example, the Aristeas writing served as a metatext for the Greek Septuagint, St. Jerome's letter which he wrote to Pammachius served as a metatext for his Latin Bible translation and Luther's *Sendbrief vom Dolmetschen* (Circular Letter on Translation) of 1530 served as metatext for the Luther Bible translation (Naudé 2009: 281–97; Naudé 2012: 343–334). By keeping silent about contemporary issues and instead focusing on the basic principles of translation, the metatexts of the King James Version (KJV) (1611) shaped the reader's expectations for a translation that diverged from the accepted sectarian interpretations in order to ensure that broader, non-sectarian interpretations would be considered orthodox (Naudé 2013: 157–94). In this respect, the KJV adopted a stance toward both metatext and translation strategy that was diametrically opposed to that of the Geneva Bible (1561), even though much of the specific wording of the KJV was drawn from or agrees with the Geneva Bible. Furthermore, to confer an aura of familiarity, the visual presentation of the KJV was drawn from the history of English Bible presentation, which culminated in the latest version of the Bishops' Bible (1568). The dedication to King James prepared the reader mentally to accept the translation as the version to be used by all English-speaking subjects of King James, regardless of their religious affiliation. By focusing on the basic principles of translation, the second preface entitled 'The Translators to the Reader' prepared the reader to consider the new translation, that is, the KJV, as orthodox. By contrast, the Geneva Bible's metatextual notes served to enhance the reader's mental preparedness to read the translated verses in accordance with Puritan views concerning the king and the monarchy, ecclesiastical structure and Calvinistic theology. Because of their anti-note policy, the KJV translators used metatextual notes in a highly restricted way. Many notes provided alternative renderings of the source text that could support an alternative theological reading, but only a few provided an overt theological or ideological interpretation. More frequently, the KJV translators omitted the ideological notes of the Geneva Bible, thus simultaneously opening up the translated verse to multiple interpretive possibilities while suppressing a distinctively Puritan ideological reading. The metatexts of the KJV, far from being incidental to the ideology and goals of the king who commissioned its translation, are instead a subtle but powerful means of mediation for advancing, achieving and implementing his goals of political unity and theological harmony. Metatexts were removed from Bible translations in the nineteenth century. By removing the metatexts (for example in the KJV and the Dutch Authoritative Translation, the *Statenvertaling*), the translations were presented as originals and the translators were made invisible. Metatexts were reintroduced in many Bible translations of the twenty-first century.

29.3   Core Issues and Topics

29.3.1   Various Forms of Control

Merkle (2018: 225) lists various forms of censorship, which are also applicable to religious text translation, namely the pre-selection of foreign texts or their exclusion from the target culture (cultural blockage); preventive or prior censorship; self-censorship or self-correction (proof that prior censorship has accomplished its purpose); and post-censorship (unsuccessful prior censorship), boycotting or formal banning. Censorship functions overtly and covertly (Woods 2019: 511).

Related to the pre-selection of foreign texts or their exclusion from the target culture (cultural blockage) is the canonisation of religious texts, discussed below.

29.3.1.1   Canonisation of Religious Texts as the Foundation for Censorship

Religious canons are created to prevent, curb or reverse an unacceptable situation of anomie by enhancing or restoring the identity of a group as well as its value system. It is their ability to resolve power struggles not their superior literary quality that leads to the canonisation of some texts over others. In this regard the whole process of canonisation is in itself a process of censorship. The form of the canon, that is the collection of religious texts to be included, as well as the specific form of the texts, are determined by the leaders or elites who decide on behalf of a society in danger of falling apart. Such a process may be an official decision or the development of consensus among members of the most influential section of a particular group. The canon as well as the form of the texts are marked as authoritative and unalterable (for a discussion of the canonisation of the Hebrew Bible/Old Testament, see Barton 1996). Therefore, the choice of what is included in a canon reflects the leadership's view of group identity and orthodoxy and sets the frame for further censorship.

As a canon is static and fixed, canonised religious texts require rational substantiation. Hence various protective fences are built around the canon by theories of divine inspiration, authority and inerrancy. Gatekeepers of the truth entrusted with power, that is, legitimate and authoritative interpreters trained in special interpretive methods (such as typology, allegory, kabala, dogmatic interpretation, etc.) ensure the acceptable interpretation and determine the nature of censorship. In terms of censorship, the canon not only defines the boundaries of the religious group but also its standard of conduct with the result that insiders can identify outsiders, renegades, revolutionaries and heretics and legitimise their oppression, exclusion, ban or persecution accordingly.

The moment a religious canon and the processes surrounding it are questioned, the power base of its initiators is eroded, and the demise of the canon is possible. However, a new generation of gatekeepers, operating in a different paradigm, may gain power and start enforcing the canon's mode of interpretation in the community so that the relevant collection of religious texts may regain its canonical status.

Therefore, censorship can be considered any textual manipulation of religious texts to make their reception acceptable in terms of religious, social or moral norms of the target culture.

29.3.2 Manifestations of Censorship

In all its manifestations, censorship creates conflictual situations in which the dominating person or institution who controls the reception of foreign knowledge is opposed to the dominated, who is subjected to their control (Merkle 2018: 227). In addition to what is called regulatory (repressive), interventionist or institutional censorship, new censorship also encompasses constitutive or structural censorship, which is a set of unwritten rules, and which affects social interaction and communication by discourse regulation of what can be said by whom, to whom, how, and in which context (Müller 2004: 1). As described by Merkle (2018: 225), constitutive or structural censorship takes the form of preventive or prior censorship that can range from cutting passages in the target text to prohibiting its publication, that is, influencing the form of cultural transfer by various forms of rewriting. It entails self-censorship.

Structural or constitutive censorship implies a set of unwritten rules shaped by habits and the symbolic capital of discursive products in the field, though often not consciously acknowledged (Merkle 2010: 18; 2018: 227). Enforced ideological norms result in self-censorship that begins with a translator who understands that certain texts will be acceptable and others not. Translators and editors are aware that certain topics are taboo, which might either preclude an entire translation or lead to proactive editing of a translation in anticipation of censorship.

One of the most controversial situations involving censorship of the translation of sacred texts relates to the problem of divine familial imagery in the New Testament (see Miller-Naudé and Naudé 2016). The descriptions of God as 'father' and Jesus as God's 'son' are central metaphors in the New Testament. Within Christian theology, these metaphors are understood as metaphorical or metaphysical rather than literal, but Muslims understand these Christian metaphors as reflecting literal, biological reality (De Kuyper and Newman 1977; Greer 2012). The view that God is literally either father or son is explicitly prohibited in the Qur'ān: 'Say: He is God, One; God, the eternal; he brought not forth, nor hath he been brought forth; co-equal with him there hath never been any one' (sūra 112). Opposing viewpoints concerning translations of the New Testament within Muslim contexts have emerged, both involving censorship, although the translators involved often do not recognise that censorship is taking place. One viewpoint involves the self-censorship (intended as preventive censorship) by the translators of the offensive metaphors and the substitution of alternative words and phrases that explicate the meaning of the metaphor within the immediate textual context, such as functional equivalents (for example, 'God's beloved' for 'son of God'), a simile rather than a metaphor (for example, 'the Christ whom God loves as a father loves his son'), a modification of the metaphor to avoid implications of biological relationship (for example, 'the son from God' or 'the spiritual son of God'), a transliterated source text phrase as a loanword with the meaning in a paratextual footnote, or a diglot text with a source text interlinear on one page and functional equivalent translation on a facing page, or the addition of metatexts to provide functional equivalents (Naudé and Miller-Naudé 2019b). The purpose of the self-censorship is to provide a translation that will not be offensive to Muslims, especially Muslim followers of ʿIsā (Jesus), but instead will open up the foreign concepts of the New Testament to them through what is called "Muslim-Idiom Bible Translation" (Brown, Penny and Gray 2009). Proponents of this viewpoint see literal translations as suppressing or censoring the Muslim interpretation and understanding of the New Testament through insistence upon a literal and offensive translation of key sacred terminology. The other viewpoint views the Bible as a sacred text whose meaning must be conveyed even when it is offensive to readers, especially the central metaphorical concepts of divine familial images. In addition to some Christian missionary organisations (and the donors who fund them), traditional Christian churches within Muslim majority contexts insist that divine familial terms must be translated literally (Diab 2010; Griffith 2013). Proponents of this viewpoint see Muslim-oriented, i.e., indigenising, translations as promoting religious syncretism, which must be rejected so that the metaphysical nature of Jesus as both human and divine is not compromised. They further see these indigenising translations as suppressing or censoring central tenants of the Christian faith with the result that Muslim readers are denied full access to the theological ideas of the Christian sacred texts (Horrell 2010). Officially condemning the sponsoring churches and withholding funding from the translators was followed by regulatory (repressive), interventionist or institutional post-censorship, which resulted in the boycotting of the 'Muslim-Idiom Bible Translation' project and formally banning the translation. Nonetheless, several translations aimed at Muslim readers were issued, although they have been rejected by traditional Christians.

Therefore, in addition to governmental or societal structures, institutional censorship in Bible translation may involve donors and funding organisations, religious structures and Bible translation organisations. In 2020 the Danish Bible Society published the New Danish Bible Translation, the most significant change to which was the replacement of most of the occurrences of the word 'Israel' with 'the Jews' or 'the Jewish people' (Gerdmar 2021). This prior or preventive censorship was firstly a response to the fear that the modern state Israel might disturb modern Danish readers and secondly, because of the theological presupposition that the Land of Israel is unimportant for Christians in the 'new covenant'. The translation was heavily criticised (and largely boycotted) by the public, both by the affected (Jewish) community and the intended Scandinavian readers— a case of unsuccessful prior censorship. An example of post-censorship where prior censorship was unsuccessful is the case of the *Good News for Modern Man: The New Testament in Today's English Version* (1966) translated by Robert G. Bratcher, a professional Bible translator and translation consultant, who replaced 'blood' with 'death', because he understood the Greek term *haima* to point metonymically to Jesus' violent death and not merely to physical blood (Stine 2018: 343) in passages such as Colossians 1:20: 'God made peace through his Son's death (lit. blood) on the cross.' The loss of figurative language especially involving theologically significant terms such as 'blood' led to severe criticism and even violent reaction in the form of a Bible-burning ceremony which turned in the end into a Bible burial rally in the Concord and Kannapolis areas of North Carolina (Nida 1976: 10–11).

Market censorship involves practices that routinely filter or resist the production and distribution of selected ideas, perspectives, genres or cultural forms based upon their anticipated profits. Publishers tend to publish translations that have the potential to be bestsellers and that appeal to the norms and tastes of the target readership, in other words, translations that will sell (Woods 2019: 518–9). An example is the 2020 Bible translation in Afrikaans, which is ecumenical since all 25 Afrikaans church denominations participated for the first time in a single Bible translation project (see Naudé 2020). All participating churches unanimously supported the project, despite petitions and concerns voiced by individuals. When five church denominations insisted that capital letters must be used for referents in Old Testament contexts that are understood in the New Testament as messianic, the decision was eventually made that in addition to footnotes, which were used to indicate which of the Old Testament texts may be interpreted as messianic, two editions of the translation would be published, one without messianic referents in capital letters for general use and one with messianic referents in capital letters for use in these five denominations. In fact, three products become available for simultaneous circulation in bowdlerised or expurgated and full editions accommodating the needs of all of the Afrikaans denominations, namely *Die Bybel* [The Bible] (without messianic referents in capital letters and without the Deutero-canonical books), *Die Bybel: Hoofletteruitgawe* [The Bible: Capital Letter Edition] (without the Deutero-canonical books) and *Die Bybel met Deuterokanonieke boeke* [The Bible with Deutero-canonical Books] (without messianic referents in capital letters). To accommodate Afrikaans Jewish and Jewish-Messianic readers, the preface provides an explanation of how the order of the Hebrew Bible was accommodated. A list of Hebrew names of God and their translations are also included in the Preface. These strategies succeeded in maximising the ecumenical impact of the project.

To appreciate the complexity of censorial forces, it is necessary to move beyond traditional, and simplistic, binary schemas of creation and oppression, because censorship can promote creativity, the censor can be censored, and censorship can be socially useful, that is productive (Baer 2010; Merkle 2018: 228). Censorship can be a creative power where translators use various means to cir-cumvent censorship: translators include coded language in their translations; adopt translation as their creative voice when banned from writing; use paratexts and metatexts to ideologically legit-imise what might be seen as a subversive translation (for example, prefaces or postscripts that pos-ition the translations in an acceptable way); or utilise fiction that, while considered less threatening (children's literature, science fiction, detective fiction), can still convey a subversive message.

In the history of translation studies, the strategy of pseudotranslation can be a convenient and somewhat safer way for writers to comment on sensitive topics or introduce politically or socio-logically controversial themes. For example, until the end of the nineteenth century Afrikaans was not regarded as a standard (formal) cultural language but as a colloquial (vernacular) language. The church imposed a ban on the use of the Afrikaans language for sermons and Bible translation. Furthermore, the British and Foreign Bible Society refused to allow the Bible to be translated into Afrikaans. The change from a vernacular to a formal written language and from a colloquial to a cultural language requires radical social and linguistic processes. For Afrikaans, this change was facilitated by the first Afrikaans novel, written in 1898 by SJ du Toit precisely for the purpose of demonstrating that written Afrikaans could be used to convey all of the concepts and ideas of the Bible (Naudé 2008; Naudé 2019; Naudé and Miller-Naudé 2019a). The novel concerns the ficti-tious, i.e., fictive, translation (in the sense of translation as product) of a so-called parchment scroll in Classical Hebrew purporting to have been written by Elihoref, Solomon's scribe and consort of the queen of Sheba. The novel also concerns a fictitious, i.e., fictive, translation of the three so-called parchment scrolls discovered beneath Mount Afoer in what was then Rhodesia. In the novel, Du Toit himself as a character in his novel translated the scrolls, which consist mainly of sixteen pseudotranslations. They are in a poetic and biblical style. They tell of paradise on the African plateau, the flood, the diaspora of the nations and finally the establishment of the empire of Sheba. Hatasu, the Queen of Egypt, sent the first fleet of ships to the Land of Gold, anticipating Solomon's enterprise by seven centuries. Thanks to Du Toit's pseudotranslations, Afrikaans was able to play a role similar to that of the dominant languages, English and Dutch, and thereby achieve an identity as a formal written and cultural language. The narrative in the novel is spatially and chronologic-ally remote from the South Africa of Du Toit, but by utilising foreign and ancient cultures in the novel, Du Toit proved that it is possible to write in Afrikaans about any topic, no matter how far removed from the common colloquial language. The biblical connection to the pseudotranslation in the novel is momentous. It afforded Du Toit the opportunity to involve the world of the Bible without infringing on the church-imposed ban on the use of the Afrikaans language for sermons and Bible translation and the refusal by the British and Foreign Bible Society to translate the Bible into Afrikaans. Pseudotranslation thus helped to extend the expressive capacities of a minority 'target' language. However, Afrikaans readers considered the narrative misleading because the so-called discovered scrolls did not really exist. Nevertheless, the influence of the pseudotranslation

The Routledge Handbook of Translation and Censorship

and its role in promoting Afrikaans was considerable, resulting in the translation of the Bible into Afrikaans in 1933 and the eventual acceptance of Afrikaans as one of the official languages of South Africa. The institutional censorship efforts of the British and Foreign Bible society and the self-censorship of the Afrikaans-speaking churches were productively transformed through the pseudotranslation of SJ du Toit.

Meta-censorship refers to the suppression or removal of all information concerning the fact of censorship so that it is impossible to discern that censorship has taken place (Woods 2019: 519–21). Meta-censorship thus censors all traces of censorial activity, that is, it makes the censor invisible while validating the censored text. A recent article by Perry (2021) describes cases of censorship (though he does not use the term) in the *English Standard Version* (ESV), which removed references to slavery and antisemitism in order to protect the Bible from 'damning social interpretations' by outsiders (Perry 2021: 614; for the question of whether instances of socio-cultural adaptation should be considered censorship, see the section on New Debates below). Concerning the translation of words for slave/servant, the initial 2001 edition of the ESV of the Bible (itself a revision of the *Revised Standard Version* [RSV]) employed meta-censorship in translating the Hebrew word *'ebed* by 'servant' (rather than the rendering 'slave' of the RSV) or a circumlocution in twenty occurrences without any explanation in the preface or in footnotes. For the New Testament term *doulos*, the 2001 ESV did not censor the RSV's rendering 'slave' but rather introduced numerous footnotes at key passages to indicate alternative translations such as 'servant' or 'bondservant', which effectively minimise the rendering 'slave'. In the 2011 edition of the ESV, however, important changes were made to further modify the translation. In the New Testament, the 2001 renderings of *doulos* as 'slave' were replaced with the alternative renderings 'servant' or 'bondservant' that were previously in the footnotes. The footnotes were then modified to indicate that the new translation is a 'contextual rendering' (for example, the footnote to 1 Timothy 6:1, see Perry 2021: 629). In addition, the preface was modified to include a discussion of the translation of these terms:

> A particular difficulty is presented when words in biblical Hebrew and Greek refer to ancient practices and institutions that do not correspond directly to those in the modern world. Such is the case in the translation of *'ebed* (Hebrew) and *doulos* (Greek), terms which are often rendered 'slave'. These terms, however, actually cover a range of relationships that require a range of renderings—either 'slave', 'bondservant', or 'servant'—depending upon the context. Further, the word 'slave' currently carries associations with the often brutal and dehumanising institution of slavery in nineteenth century America. For this reason, the ESV translation of the words *'ebed* and *doulos* has been undertaken with particular attention to their meaning in each specific context.

(2011: 21)

As Perry (2021: 631) demonstrates, the specific verses in which there is censorship of the term 'slave' relate to those cases in which the biblical depiction of slavery correlates most closely with antebellum slavery in the American South. In the 2016 edition of the ESV, the censorship of *doulos* (plural *douloi*) became complete with the deletion of alternative rendering 'slave' or 'slaves' from footnotes of key passages such as 1 Timothy 6:1 and Titus 2:9, where the footnote was modified to read (see Perry 2021: 629–30):

*For the contextual rendering of the Greek word *doulos*, see Preface.

As Perry notes, 'readers of the 2016 ESV edition ... are no longer made aware that 'slave(s)' is even an option for translating *doulos/douloi* in these passages' (2021: 631). In other words, the 2016 ESV again employed meta-censorship. Seen as a whole, the censorship of the ESV regarding slavery involves complex and emergent features of censorship. The overall concern for (self-) censoring mentions of slavery in the Bible is to make the Bible palatable in a pluralistic society. The earliest version of the ESV in 2001 involves meta-censorship in that there is no acknowledgement or explanation of the censorship involved, especially with respect to the Hebrew term *'ebed*. The 2011 preface 'packages' the censorship of terms for 'slave' as a 'contextual interpretation', thus allowing the ESV to censor in a way that will not damage the marketability of the version for evangelical readers, for whom the ESV is known as a 'literal' translation that does not shrink from translating gender terminology in ways that are not politically correct. The 2016 ESV again returns to meta-censorship by removing the literal rendering of *doulos* as 'slave' from an alternative rendering in the footnotes, so that the reader is not informed that the rendering 'slave' is even a possibility. The ESV has thus engaged in censorship of various kinds in its various editions with the result that the alterity of the biblical world in which slavery was an accepted institution is obscured in translation. Furthermore, the viewpoint of the ESV editors that slavery is an obsolete institution does not reflect the sad reality that slavery of various kinds remains a plague in various parts of the world today. The more serious question is how the biblical text speaks to contemporary slavery.

Another issue relates to the fact that censorship can subsequently be un-done (de-censorship) and even re-done (re-censorship). Because the Bible is an extensively re-translated text, numerous instances of de-censorship and even re-censorship have occurred as a result of varying theological and ideological viewpoints and cultural contexts. De-censorship after censorship by the Catholic Church occurred in various editions of the RSV. In 1952, the first edition of the RSV was published. To accommodate Catholic theological concerns, a Catholic edition of the RSV was published in 1966 with 67 changes, such as particular renderings of verses, issues of canon (inclusion and order of the Apocryphal books), textual issues (for example, the disputed longer ending of Mark's Gospel [Mark 16:9–20]) and footnotes to provide a Catholic interpretation of the translation. As an example, Matthew 16:18 is a central verse for the Catholic viewpoint concerning the supremacy of Peter. Whereas the 1952 edition uses a footnote to explain the play on words in the Greek (' "Peter" translates the Greek word *petros*, "rock" translates the Greek word *petra*'), the 1966 edition expands the footnote to provide the Catholic interpretation of the verse, which is central to Catholic dogma: 'The name "Peter" comes from the Greek word for "rock"; Jesus makes him the foundation on which the church is to be built. The word "church" means "assembly" or "society" of believers. The Hebrew equivalent is used in the Old Testament to indicate the chosen people. In applying it to the church Jesus shows it to be the Messianic community foretold by the prophets.' The footnote thus censors the translation by providing only the Catholic interpretation of a theologically disputed verse to the reader. In 1973 an ecumenical edition of the RSV, known as the *Common Bible*, acceptable to Protestant, Roman Catholic and Eastern Orthodox churches alike, was issued (Kubo and Specht 1983: 54–8), thus effectively de-censoring the 1966 Catholic edition of the RSV.

An instance of censorship followed by re-censorship relates to gender terminology and can be found in the various versions of the *New International Version* (NIV) of 1984, the *Today's New International Version* (TNIV) of 2005, and the *New International Version* (NIV) of 2011. In Acts 28:14, the Greek uses the term 'brothers' to refer to believers; the term is literally translated in the NIV 1984. In 2005, the TNIV used the word 'believers', thus self-censoring the offensive gender-laden term of the original. However, the backlash from evangelical Christians against the

TNIV resulted in the eventual withdrawal of the translation by the publisher (Zondervan) and the subsequent moderate updating of the NIV. The resultant NIV 2011 used 'brothers and sisters', thus re-censoring the TNIV's 'believers' on the basis of marketability for a phrase that reflects both the Greek original and gender inclusivity.

29.4   New Debates

In light of the broadening of the conventional concept of censorship in the twenty-first century, Merkle (2010: 18; 2018: 226) alludes to the continuous debate concerning what the definition of censorship should encompass. In this regard she asks the question whether children's versions of adult literary works be considered as censored or are they simply adapted. Another question she raises is whether the textual manipulation of literary works to conform to the religious, social or moral norms of the target culture is to be considered a form of censorship. The same questions pertain to the translation of religious texts. As one example, the *New Revised Standard Version Updated Edition* (eBible 2021; hardcopy 2022) contains revisions relating to contemporary sociocultural sensibilities concerning gender (for example, 'magi' rather than 'wise men' in Matthew 2:1), conditions rather than identity (for example, 'an enslaved woman' rather than 'a slave woman' in Galatians 4:22) and religious traditions (for example, the capitalisation of Jewish holy days to show respect, such as 'Passover', 'Sabbath' and the 'Festival of Unleavened Bread') (Miller-Naudé and Naudé 2022: 6–7).

Censorship as (belonging to) 'a set of cultural practices situated within a larger context of the production of media and knowledge' has recently been argued by Smith (2008: 187–242, esp. 190) as applying to the formation, transmission and translation of the Hebrew Bible. In his view, the theological bias of elites, especially those from the priestly class, can be seen in the scribal production of the biblical text, for example, as illustrated in Deuteronomy 32:8–9 and Genesis 14:22 above. Contrary to most biblical scholars who view explicitations as scribal adaptations in order to preclude certain interpretations, Smith views the scribal explicitations as a variety of censorship—by adding explicitations, scribal activity has censored 'the past' and foreclosed previous interpretations (Smith 2008: 212–4). Smith further argues that in the ancient Near East, scribal 'censorship' more regularly involved addition or expansion rather than deletion (Smith 2008: 214). Smith's perspective introduces/leaves open the controversial possibility that any scribal explicitation or gloss occurring in the production, transmission or translation of texts could be seen as censorship in the sense that such additions narrow the interpretive possibilities of a text. This claim needs further investigation.

Complexity theory provides a way to conceptualise translation and various kinds of translation censorship (Marais 2014, 2019, 2023). Translation is dynamic and emergent, involving complex interlocking adaptive systems. Censorship of translation similarly involves complexity. Censorship may involve multiple, interlocking, dynamic forces of control over the translation that interconnect in multi-faceted ways with the translation process and the emergence of the subsequent texts. Complexity also highlights the ethical dimensions and dilemmas of censorship especially with respect to the invisibility of meta-censorship and the portrayal of alterity in the biblical text.

Further Reading

Bourdieu, Pierre. 1991. *Language and Symbolic Power*. Cambridge: Polity Press.
This is an early source of the philosophical underpinnings of language, dealing inter alia with the field of religion (popular and institutionalised), the polysemy of religious language and structural censorship. When Bourdieu speaks of censorship, he is not referring to the explicit activity of religious organisations seeking to suppress or restrict the diffusion of symbolic forms. Based on the philosophical discourse of Heidegger

Religious Texts, Translation, and Censorship

that language is preoccupied with distinctions, allusions and rhetorical effects, that is, euphemised, Bourdieu refers rather to the observance of the forms and formalities of the religious field, where discourse is adapted to fulfil these demands.

Moore, James D. 2021. *Literary Depictions of the Scribal Profession in the Story of Ahiqar and Jeremiah 36*. Berlin: De Gruyter.
This is the first study to compare the allusions to scribal culture found in the Aramaic Story of Ahiqar and the Hebrew Tale of Jeremiah and Baruch's Scroll in Jeremiah 36 to address explicitly the scribal experience in terms of ideology. Moore shows that disguised in the royal propagandistic message of Ahiqar is a sophisticated Aramaic critique on the social practices of Akkadian scribal culture. Jeremiah 36, however, uses the tools of the scribal craft to construct an overtly subversive piece of literature.

Naudé, Jacobus A. and Miller-Naudé, Cynthia L. 2019b. 'Theology and Ideology in the Metatexts of Bible Translations in Muslim Contexts: A Case study', in G. R. Kotzé, C. S. Locatell and J. A. Messarra (eds.), *Ancient Texts and Modern Readers. Studies in Ancient Hebrew Linguistics and Bible Translation*. Leiden: Brill, 280–99.
Metatexts are supplementary materials provided by translators to 'frame' the translation in order to guide readers' interpretation of the texts. Metatexts are especially important for sacred texts which are translated (or published) specifically for individuals who are not members (or not originally members) of the religious group in question. The authors are interested in considering how the alterity ('otherness') of the source text and its theological and ideological distance from Muslim audiences can be bridged. This chapter analyses the metatexts of a UBS New Testament study edition which was prepared 'for those interested in learning about the life and teaching of Jesus the Messiah (*Isa al Masih*) and his followers' to show how key cultural terms are rendered in the translation and explained in their accompanying metatexts to avoid rejection by the readership.

Smelik, Willem F. 2013. *Rabbis, Language and Translation in Late Antiquity*. Cambridge: Cambridge University Press.
The image that emerges from this study is of a movement of religious renewal that self-consciously promotes the Hebrew language as a vehicle but also as an ideological and polemical tool. The rabbis promoted the Hebrew source text as the original and uniquely inspired vehicle of divine revelation. Translations had a role in the study of the Hebrew text, in both liturgical and educational contexts. Therefore, a public performance of translation accompanied by a reading of the Hebrew text is at the heart of synagogue worship. The rabbis regulate translation by means of rules, because they were concerned to assert the authority of the Hebrew scriptures and relegate the Aramaic translations to the rank of oral Torah which made the subordinate authority of translations plain. The status of written Greek translations was problematic, since their use had been specifically permitted, and it sometimes appeared that they could be considered as sacred scripture. A rabbinic insistence on reading from texts written in the square Hebrew or Aramaic characters may be intended to undermine the status of the Greek translation utilising the rounded characters of Greek.

Smith, Mark. 2008. *God in Translation. Deities in Cross-Cultural Discourse in the Biblical World*. Grand Rapids, Michigan: Eerdmans.
The Hebrew Bible has long been understood as condemning foreign deities. While many biblical texts do condemn other deities, many other passages show how early Israelites sometimes accepted the reality of deities worshiped by other peoples. However, at a certain stage Israel expressed its worldview of a single god. As a result, biblical writers and scribes engaged in sophisticated hermeneutics to mediate between the new worldview and older expressions of translatability embedded within its emergent monotheistic expressions in which censorship played a role. The Greco-Roman period witnessed an explosion in the types and genres of cross-cultural discourse about deities, and as a result, Jewish authors and some New Testament sources responded to this sort of discourse, sometimes negatively and at other times quite positively.

References

Al-Azami, Muhammad M. 2015. 'The Islamic View of the Quran', in S. H. Nasr (ed.), *The Study Quran. A New Translation and Commentary*. New York: HarperCollins Publishers, 1607–23.
Baer, Brian. 2010. 'Literary Translation in the Age of the Decembrists: The Birth of Productive Censorship in Russia', in D. Merkle, C. O'Sullivan, L. van Doorslaer and M. Wolf (eds.), *Power of the Pen: Translation and Censorship in the Nineteenth-Century*. Vienna and Münster: Lit Verlag, 213–39.

Barton, John. 1996. 'The Significance of a Fixed Canon of the Hebrew Bible', in M. Sæbo (ed.), *From the Beginnings to the Middle Ages (Until 1300)*, Volume 1 of *Hebrew Bible/Old Testament: The History of Its Interpretation*. Göttingen: Vandenhoeck & Ruprecht, 67–83.

Billiani, Francesca. 2007. 'Assessing Boundaries – Censorship and Translation: An Introduction', in F. Billiani (ed.), *Modes of Censorship and Translation: National Contexts and Diverse Media*. Manchester: St Jerome, 1–25.

Billiani, Francesca. 2020. 'Censorship', in M. Baker and G. Saldanha (eds.), *Routledge Encyclopedia of Translation Studies*. London and New York: Routledge, 56–60.

Bourdieu, Pierre. 1991. *Language and Symbolic Power*. Cambridge: Polity Press.

Bowden, John. 2007. *A Chronology of World Christianity*. London: Continuum.

Brown, Rick, Penny, John and Gray, Leith. 2009. 'Muslim-Idiom Bible Translations: Claims and Facts', *St. Francis Magazine*, 5: 87–105.

Daniell, David. 2003. *The Bible in English: Its History and Influence*. New Haven and London: Yale University Press.

De Jonge, Henk J. 2016. 'Erasmus's Translation of the New Testament: Aim and Method', *The Bible Translator*, 67(1): 29–41.

De Kuyper, Arie and Newman, M. Barclay. 1977. 'Jesus, Son of God – A Translation Problem', *The Bible Translator*, 28: 432–8.

Diab, Issa. 2010. 'Challenges Facing Bible Translation in the Islamic Culture of the Middle East', *The Bible Translator*, 61(2): 71–80.

Flesher, Paul V. M. and Chilton, Bruce. 2011. *The Targums. A Critical Introduction*. Waco, Texas: Baylor University Press.

Foss, Sonja K. and Gill, Ann. 1987. 'Michel Foucault's Theory of Rhetoric as Epistemic', *Western Journal of Speech Communication*, 51(4): 384–401.

Foucault, Michel. 1972. *The Archaeology of Knowledge and the Discourse on Language*. New York: Pantheon Books.

Freeman, Charles. 2002. *The Closing of the Western Mind. The Rise of Faith and the Fall of Reason*. New York: Vintage Books.

Gerdmar, Anders. 2021. Deleting Israel from the New Testament: The New Danish Bible Translation and Its Omission of "Israel". Paper read at Society of Biblical Literature, November 2021.

Greer, Bradford. 2012. 'Revisiting "Son of God" in Translation: Reading Acts, Luke, and Matthew in Historical and Biblical Context', *St. Francis Magazine*, 8: 188–212.

Griffith, Sidney H. 2013. *The Bible in Arabic: The Scriptures of the "People of the Book" in the Language of Islam*. Princeton and Oxford: Princeton University Press.

Horrell, J. Scott. 2010. 'Cautions Regarding "Son of God" in Muslim-Idiom Translations of the Bible: Seeking Sensible Balance', *St. Francis Magazine*, 6: 638–66.

Kubo, Sakae and Walter F. Specht. 1983. *So Many Versions? Twentieth-century English Versions of the Bible. Revised and enlarged edition*. Grand Rapids: Zondervan.

Lefevere, André. 1984. 'Translation and Other Ways in Which One Literature Refracts Another', *Symposium: A Quarterly Journal in Modern Literatures*, 38: 127–42.

Lumbard, Joseph. 2015. 'The Quran in Translation', in S. H. Nasr (ed.), *The Study Quran: A New Translation and Commentary*. New York: HarperCollins Publishers, 1601–6.

MacCulloch, Diarmaid. 2009. *A History of Christianity: The First Three Thousand Years*. London: Penguin.

Marais, Kobus. 2014. *Translation Theory and Development Studies: A Complexity Theory Approach*. Advances in Translation Studies. London: Routledge.

Marais, Kobus. 2019. *A (Bio)Semiotic Theory of Translation: The Emergence of Social-Cultural Reality*. Advances in Translation Studies. London: Routledge.

Marais, Kobus. 2023. *Trajectories of Translation: The Thermodynamics of Semiosis*. Advances in Translation and Interpreting Studies. London: Routledge.

McDonald, Grantley. 2016. 'Erasmus and the Johannine Comma (1 John 5.7-8)', *The Bible Translator* 67(1): 42–55.

Merkle, Denise. 2010. 'Censorship', in Y. Gambier and L. van Doorslaer (eds.), *Handbook of Translation Studies. Volume 1*. Amsterdam: Benjamins, 18–21.

Merkle, Denise. 2018. 'History of Reception: Censorship', in L. D'Hulst and Y. Gambier (eds.), *A History of Modern Translation Knowledge. Sources, Concepts, Effects*. Amsterdam and Philadelphia: John Benjamins Publishing Company, 225–30.

Miller-Naudé, Cynthia and Naudé, Jacobus A. 2016. 'Covert Religious Censorship: Renderings of Divine Familial Imagery in Translations of the New Testament Within Islamic Contexts', *Open Theology*, 2: 818–31.

Miller-Naudé, Cynthia and Naudé, Jacobus A. 2022. 'The *Revised Standard Version* (1952) and Its Revisions as a Linear Emergence of the Tyndale–King James Version Tradition', *HTS Teologiese Studies/Theological Studies*, 78(1), a7647 https://doi.org/10.4102/hts.v78i1.7647

Moore, James D. 2021. *Literary Depictions of the Scribal Profession in the Story of Ahiqar and Jeremiah 36*. Berlin: De Gruyter.

Mroczek, Eva. 2021. 'Hezekiah the Censor and Ancient Theories of Canon Formation', *Journal of Biblical Literature*, 140(3): 481–502.

Müller, Beate. 2004. 'Censorship and Cultural Regulation: Mapping the Territory', in B. Müller (ed.), *Censorship & Cultural Regulation in the Modern Age*. Amsterdam and New York: Rodopi, 1–31.

Naudé, Jacobus A. 2008. 'The Role of Pseudo-Translations in Early Afrikaans Travel Writing', *Southern African Linguistics and Applied Language Studies*, 26(1): 97–106.

Naudé, Jacobus A. 2009. 'The Role of Metatexts in the Translations of Sacred Texts: The Case of the Book of Aristeas and the Septuagint', in J. Cook (ed.), *Septuagint and Reception: Essays Prepared for the Association for the Study of the Septuagint in South Africa*. Leiden: Brill, 281–97.

Naudé, Jacobus A. 2010a. 'Religious Translation', in Y. Gambier and L. van Doorslaer (eds.), *Handbook of Translation Studies. Volume 1*. Amsterdam and Philadelphia: Benjamins, 285–93.

Naudé, Jacobus A. 2010b. 'Iconicity and Developments in Translation Studies', in J. Conradie et al. (eds.), *Signergy*. Iconicity in Language and Literature 9. Amsterdam and Philadelphia: John Benjamins, 387–411.

Naudé, Jacobus A. 2012. 'Metatexts and the Regulation of Reader Responses in the Translation of Sacred Texts', *Folia Orientalia*, 49: 339–55.

Naudé, Jacobus A. 2013. 'The Role of the Metatexts in the King James Version as a Means of Mediating Conflicting Theological Views', in D. G. Burke, J. F. Kutsko and P. H. Towner (eds.), *The King James Version at 400. Assessing Its Genius as Bible Translation and Its Literary Influence*. Atlanta: Society of Biblical Literature, 157–94.

Naudé, Jacobus A. 2018. 'History of Translation Knowledge of Monotheistic Religions with Written Traditions', in L. D'Hulst and Y. Gambier (eds.), *A History of Modern Translation Knowledge. Sources, Concepts, Effects*. Amsterdam and Philadelphia: John Benjamins Publishing Company, 389–95.

Naudé, Jacobus A. 2019. 'Pseudotranslation', in P. A. Noss and C. S. Houser (eds.), *A Guide to Bible Translation. People, Languages, and Topics*. Swindon: United Bible Societies, 676–7.

Naudé, Jacobus A. 2020. 'New and Old Treasures: The 2020 Afrikaans Translation of the Bible as a Retranslation', *Journal of Humanities*, 60(4): 869–91.

Naudé, Jacobus A. 2021. 'Religious Texts and Oral Tradition', in Y. Gambier and L. van Doorslaer (eds.), *Handbook of Translation Studies. Volume 5*. Amsterdam and Philadelphia: Benjamins, 191–8.

Naudé, Jacobus A. 2022. 'Emergence of the Tyndale–King James Version tradition in English Bible Translation', *HTS Teologiese Studies/ Theological Studies*, 78(1), a7649. https://doi.org/10.4102/hts. v78i1.7649

Naudé, Jacobus A. and Miller-Naudé, Cynthia L. 2018. 'Sacred Writings', in K. Washbourne and B. Van Wyke (eds.), *The Routledge Handbook of Literary Translation*. London and New York: Routledge, 181–205.

Naudé, Jacobus A. and Miller-Naudé, Cynthia L. 2019a. 'Rev. Stefanus Jacobus Du Toit', in P. A. Noss and C. S. Houser (eds.), *A Guide to Bible Translation. People, Languages, and Topics*. Swindon: United Bible Societies, 22–4.

Naudé, Jacobus A. and Miller-Naudé, Cynthia L. 2019b. 'Theology and Ideology in the Metatexts of Bible Translations in Muslim Contexts: A Case study', in G. R. Kotzé, C. S. Locatell and J. A. Messarra (eds.), *Ancient Texts and Modern Readers. Studies in Ancient Hebrew Linguistics and Bible Translation*. Leiden: Brill, 280–99.

Nida, Eugene A. 1976. *Good News for Everyone*. Waco: Word Books.

Noss, Philip A. 2019. 'Wulfila', in P. A. Noss and C. S. Houser (eds.), *A Guide to Bible Translation. People, Languages, and Topics*. Swindon: United Bible Societies, 63.

Perry, Samuel L. 2021. 'Whitewashing Evangelical Scripture: The Case of Slavery and Antisemitism in the English Standard Version', *Journal of the American Academy of Religion*, 89(2): 612–43.

Pew Research Center Forum. 2012. *The Global Religious Landscape. A Report on the Size and Distribution of the World's Major Religious Groups as of 2010*. Washington, DC: Pew Research Center.

Reynolds, Matthew. 2007. 'Semi-Censorship in Dryden and Browning', in F. Billiani (ed.), *Modes of Censorship and Translation: National Contexts and Diverse Media*. Manchester: St Jerome, 187–204.

Reynolds, Matthew. 2019. 'Babel: Curse or Blessing?', in D. Duncan, S. Harrison, K. Kohl and M. Reynolds (eds.), *Babel. Adventures in Translation*. Oxford: Bodleian Library, 8–33.

Robinson, Douglas. 1996. *Translation and Taboo*. DeKalb, Illinois: Northern Illinois University Press.

Robinson, Douglas. 2018. 'The Sacred and Taboo', in L. D'Hulst and Y. Gambier (eds.), *A History of Modern Translation Knowledge. Sources, Concepts, Effects*. Amsterdam and Philadelphia: John Benjamins Publishing Company, 57–9.

Runesson, Anders. 2001. *The Origins of the Synagogue. A Socio-Historical Study*. Stockholm: Almqvist & Wikell International.

Schniedewind, William, M. 2021. 'Language and Group Identity in the Dead Sea Scrolls: The Case for an "Essene Hebrew"', in S. E. Fassberg (ed.), *Hebrew Texts and Language of the Second Temple Period*. Leiden: Brill, 280–91.

Smelik, Willem F. 2013. *Rabbis, Language and Translation in Late Antiquity*. Cambridge: Cambridge University Press.

Smith, Mark. 2008. *God in Translation. Deities in Cross-Cultural Discourse in the Biblical World*. Grand Rapids, Michigan: Eerdmans.

Stine, Philip. C. 2018. 'From *Good News for Modern Man* to *Good News Bible*: Origins and Early Issues', *The Bible Translator*, 69(3):335–46.

Woods, Michelle. 2019. 'Censorship', in K. Washbourne and B. Van Wyke (eds.), *The Routledge Handbook of Literary Translation*. London and New York: Routledge, 511–23.

30

ON TRANSLATION AND CENSORSHIP OF CHILDREN'S LITERATURE DURING THE COLD WAR IN EUROPE

Eliisa Pitkäsalo and Riitta Oittinen

30.1 Introduction

Censorship is generally understood as an activity carried out by governmental organs that aim at banning unsuitable books either as originals or translations, at suppressing parts of a work to be published or adding contents that follow the government's censoring policies. This chapter, however, does not deal with political censorship as such. Rather, it deals with how the image of the child has influenced what is chosen for translation and publication within the field of children's literature during the Cold War in Europe. Naturally, this also involves what is written or not written and what is translated or not translated. This chapter examines the external censorship carried out by publishers and the internal censorship carried out by authors, illustrators and translators. Leaving out questionable contents from works for child readers or banning such works altogether involves both the verbal and the visual.

In this chapter, children's literature is defined both as literature read by children and as literature intended for children (Hunt 1990: 1, 60–4). In addition, as Nodelman points out, children's literature is a category built on restrictions. Adults tend to believe that children do not need to have as much knowledge about the world as adults do. On some level, this kind of thinking may lead to children's literature being thought of as less than literature for adults (Nodelman 2015: 33).

The chapter examines children's literature and its translations in Europe after World War II. It begins by depicting the ambience of children's literature in two contexts: Northern Europe and Eastern Europe. It then discusses the societal background of the characters portrayed in children's literature, and in its translations and retranslations, followed by a discussion of how children's literature and its translations reflect the traits and trends of the prevailing political and social systems. Examples from the works of the Swedish-speaking Finnish author Tove Jansson (1914–2001) and the Swedish author Astrid Lindgren (1907–2002) and their translations into German, Polish and Finnish will be referenced to illustrate these traits and trends. The chapter concentrates on how the social changes may be reflected in the literatures published and translated in the era of the Cold War, when the influence of the Soviet Union was great. It also looks at the shadow of Stalinism

DOI: 10.4324/9781003149453-37

that was cast on translation for children in Eastern Europe, as well as on the retranslations made in the post-socialist era.

30.2 Historical Perspectives

Europe after World War II was politically in turmoil. Eastern Europe largely landed under Soviet influence, which drastically altered the political situation in those countries. Towards the end of the 1940s began the period that Thomson-Wohlgemuth (2005) has named, in the East German context, *socialist construction* (1949–1961), or the period during which the 'principles of socialism' were introduced to East German society and were also reflected in literary works. This partly stemmed from the fact that 'the necessary educational and theoretical background knowledge was derived from Soviet experts', as Thomson-Wohlgemuth (2005: 19) states. The mission of literature to shape people's minds and mould them into socialist citizens was similar throughout the Eastern Bloc, and this mission was enforced most rigorously during the period of socialist construction. According to Borodo (2006: 171), executing the mission of socialist construction in Poland and enforcing it in practice, the publishing system was reorganised, and strict censorship was initiated.

The end of Stalinism (1927–1953) laid the foundations for a new, relatively liberal period in Eastern Bloc countries such as Poland and East Germany. Thomson-Wohlgemuth (2005) names this era *the period of consolidation* (1961–1971), which began with the building of the Berlin wall. Although the border to the West was closed, authors were given the opportunity to pursue a new kind of debate (Thomson-Wohlgemuth 2005: 24). In Poland, too, even the publishers were given greater autonomy (Borodo 2006: 174). Yet, this relatively liberal phase only lasted until the mid-1960s, when censorship and the 'monitoring of cultural and media issues' by the state security service increased (Thomson-Wohlgemuth 2005: 25). This led to authors, artists and publishers being disciplined if they did not follow the restrictions imposed upon them (Thomson-Wohlgemuth 2005: 25).

These changes were visible in literature as well. While in the 1960s Eastern European literature—including children's literature—was still realistic, from the mid-1960s on, mythological narrations and adaptations appeared on the literary scene (Thomson-Wohlgemuth 2005: 27). During the period of strict censorship, mythological themes in literature were a way of discussing even sensitive topics in everyday life by embedding them in the lofty realm of myth.

Thomson-Wohlgemuth (2005) calls the last period of Eastern European socialism (1971–1989) a time of liberalisation and developed industrial society. This period brought with it new critical trends and impetuses. It was a time when children's books were seen as a platform to discuss even contentious topics. Because children's literature was considered simply literature for children and therefore not to be taken too seriously (Thomson-Wohlgemuth 2005: 39), the censors turned a blind eye, either intentionally or unintentionally, to, for instance, underlying connotations.

However, the situation in Western Europe, especially in the Nordic countries, was different. Finland's relationship with the Soviet Union was closer than that of the other Nordic countries such as Sweden. For instance, Finland and the Soviet Union signed the Agreement of Friendship, Cooperation and Mutual Assistance of 1948, which influenced all aspects of Finnish political life. Yet, despite the close relationship, Finland was never a socialist country or under Soviet rule. By contrast, it is notable that, among the Nordic countries, only Finland was at war with the Soviet Union during WWII; however, it managed to remain independent. Due to this background, there was a need to walk a fine line with the Soviet Union. This is why the years between 1956–1982 (the era of Urho Kekkonen's presidency) are often called the time of Finlandisation, which later became a general term that does not only concern Finland but other countries in a similar situation.

476

It was the time of self-censorship of public debate and cultural life. Gradually, the end of the era signified freedom from the obligation to insert propaganda and patriotic messages into children's literature, which is especially typical of texts written during wartime.

30.3 Core Issues and Topics

30.3.1 The Image of the Child and Writing for Children

Over time, societies change, which may cause changes in what is considered appropriate literature for children. Whatever we write, illustrate or translate for children is influenced by our image of the child. How adults see children and how children see themselves are dependent on the do's and don'ts of the surrounding adult social and cultural contexts. The image of the child strongly influences which books publishers choose to include or not to include in their catalogues. These images are not set in stone but evolve over time and change in society, for example, during war time.

The child and being a child have been seen from many different angles over time (Ariès 1962: 41–4; Haynes and Murris 2012: 125–41). In the Eastern Bloc countries children were seen as small adults, a view largely shaped by the socialist *Weltanschauung*. While this kind of adultification of children prevailed in the Soviet Union before World War II, in Nordic countries such as Finland, the understanding of children as miniature adults was mainly the heritage of the agricultural lifestyle (for illustrated children's literature under Lenin and Stalin, see Swift 2020). This way of thinking had an impact on the child's position as an extra pair of hands in the family or as a working citizen in society. In other words, in socialist countries, children were seen as having an equal status as that of their elders (Thomson-Wohlgemuth 2003: 242). Over the years, however, it has become more common to understand the child as a 'homo ludens', a playing human being (Huizinga 1984: 10), who needs to be neither useful nor a true socialist hero, i.e., a model child with optimism, energy, courage and a self-sacrificing attitude (Thomson-Wohlgemuth 2003: 242).

Censorship is often a protective response motivated by ideological views. However, censorship can result in misleading or even twisted information. Censored content is typically considered harmful or frightening to children, and the aim of censorship is therefore to edit content that could shape the child's outlook on life in a dangerous or improper way (Tervaharju, Nordling and Ihonen 2017: 2–3). Such censorship is always involved in writing and translating literature. Translation, which is a complex cultural artefact and has been defined in innumerable ways, also involves ideology and power. If translation is rereading and rewriting words and images for different audiences and purposes, in the case of translating for children, the translator translates for an audience that is multilayered and can be depicted as a spectrum of readers (Alvstad 2018: 161).

While translation may be seen as retelling, rewording, and interpretation of words and images, there is another, more authoritarian kind of discourse, transcreation, where the translators use their power by editing and transmuting texts for commercial or other purposes (see Pedersen 2019: 44). We consider this as part of Translation Studies, even though some scholars (Frank 1989; Lal 1996; Pedersen 2014) draw a clear line between the terms. Additionally, at the very core of transcreation are issues such as text design, in the sense of branding. There is not much research on designing texts for ideological purposes in fiction written, illustrated and translated for children, because transcreation seems to be understood as mainly concerning marketing texts. It is both interesting and important, however, to consider the extent to which a story for children might be seen as a conveyor of ideas and ideologies with the intent of educating the child about how to be a good citizen. This kind of branding may be seen as an operative tool, a way of producing texts, for instance, with a persuasive or dictatorial purpose.

The Routledge Handbook of Translation and Censorship

Moreover, the branding of a text is not far removed from the idea of the skopos of a text (Reiss and Vermeer 1984). Both involve the image of the receiver and the surrounding society and culture, which leads to adapting texts for different audiences with different ideologies. The idea of a branded translation or transcreation is about modifying the meanings of texts, with the aim of reaching a desirable persuasive or dictatorial effect wished for by the commissioner of the text (Pedersen 2014: 69).

As for the commissioned translations of children's literature in Eastern Europe after World War II, the main focus was reinforcing the *brand's voice*, that is, the ideology behind transcreations of that time. In other words, it was considered important to present texts in the way desired by those who commissioned the translations. In the socialist countries of the era, stories for children were adapted to fit in the socialist agenda. Children's literature was branded verbally and visually to suit the political purposes of the texts, i.e., to modify children's attitudes and support socialist ideas and values. In this case, a good translation faithfully conformed to the ideals of the socialist agenda, rather than to the concept of a faithful translation, as it is understood in translation studies today. On the contrary, adapting source texts was considered acceptable and suitable for the audiences of children's literature in the socialist countries. In other words, this kind of branding of children's literature meant domesticating the texts to 'conform to dominant cultural values' (Venuti 1995: 18–22). While foreignising texts celebrates the source language and culture, adaptations tend to delete the foreignness of the originals. Yet, when it comes to children's literature, the truth lies somewhere in between: in Liseling-Nilsson's (2006: 212) words, children's 'ability to take in a text that differs from the culture they know is relatively low'. All in all, although translation certainly adds to our ways of understanding the world and the people within it, it is never an 'innocent act' (Oittinen 2006: 34–45; Haynes and Murris 2012: 40–54).

30.3.2   *Mechanisms of Censorship*

In modern times, while adults are responsible for taking care of children, their responsibility may also give them authority over the child, and the often positive power of caregiving may turn negative. This is often seen in repressive pedagogical environments. Miller (1990: 4, 96–102) labels this kind of adult attitude toward children 'black pedagogy' (*schwarze Pädagogik*), which may be harmful, even poisonous for children, who are especially vulnerable due to their affection for and dependence on their parents. In black pedagogy, adults use corporal punishment or emotional manipulation to force their children to submit to order and discipline. In the Bakhtinian sense, this would be authoritative or absolute discourse (see Bakhtin 1990: 227 and the Glossary edited by Holquist in Bakhtin 1990: 424). In authoritarian societies controlled by means of censorship, rewriting and textual manipulation have been used as tools for those in power to discipline what is published, for whom, how and why.

Censorship may be divided into internal and external mechanisms, as Heikkilä-Halttunen (2000: 96–7) points out. Internal censorship includes various associations of authors, illustrators and translators of children's literature and their activities. External censorship is enforced by gatekeepers regulating the status and appreciation of children's literature. These gatekeepers may be publishers, literary award committees and literary critics. Additionally, histories of literature and literary studies play an important role in attributing prestige to authors and books as well as determining their place within the literary canon, although their influence may not be immediately recognised and may only be evident on a long-term basis (Heikkilä-Halttunen 2000: 96–7).

In many socialist countries, there were censoring organs, and even writers' associations, which were regulated by the state and acted as gatekeepers controlling access to the literary field. For example, in East Germany, most translators were members of the Writers' Association, which guaranteed financial and intellectual support in exchange for loyalty to the state and its ideology (Thomson-Wohlgemuth 2003: 24). However, as Pokorn remarks, in Slovenia, a part of the former Socialist Federal Republic of Yugoslavia, there was no direct censorship organ. Instead, there was unofficial censorship and even self-censorship, which created an illusion of non-interference. The gatekeepers, as the owners and presidents of the publishing houses, made the final decisions on what was and was not acceptable for publication. They were all party members who scrupulously monitored the publishing business, as well as authors and translators who showed loyalty to the party and worked 'without any direct intervention being necessary' (Pokorn 2012: 155).

However, as Alvstad (2018: 171) comments, it is not only censorship that determined which books would be chosen for publication; the saleability of books was also an issue. In publishing for children, therefore, it is not only a question of morality but also one of money (Hade, Paul and Mason 2013: 137). According to Thomson-Wohlgemuth (2003: 245), other issues to be dealt with were copyright laws and royalties, in addition to the very real problem of shortages of paper and ink, which influenced the book business in the post-war East Germany.

In addition to the above-mentioned gatekeepers, the translators also have an important role to play in the book publishing business. Translators not only make linguistically-motivated decisions, but also ideologically motivated decision in order to respect the ideological agenda of the state. According to Alvstad (2018: 160), in literary cultures that emphasise education, the translators may play a strong role in steering the process of translation to comply with educational priorities at the expense of the aesthetic. All publishing processes, including authoring and translating, are subjected to issues of power. As Lefevere points out, '[p]atronage is usually more interested in the ideology of literature than in its poetics, and it could be said that the patron "delegates authority" to the professional where poetics is concerned' (Lefevere 1992: 15).

Moreover, translators often participate in the process, for example, by suggesting books to be translated; however, it is the publisher who has the last word on that matter. To some degree, this was also the situation in the post-war socialist countries of Eastern Europe, where the suggestions of trustworthy translators were taken into consideration. In the ideologically-driven socialist state, both internal and external censorship influenced what content would be cut and how the translation would be done. Although external guidance is always present when a translator translates, in highly ideological systems, publishers must modify texts according to governmental requirements. This is evident for example in the German translations of Jansson's and Lindgren's works. In the first German translations of the Moomin stories *Eine drollige Gesellschaft* (1954, orig. *Trollkarlens hatt* 1948) and *Sturm im Muminthal* (1954, orig. *Farlig midsommar* 1954), not only were the contents changed but so too were the illustrations, including the cover images, which were replaced by another illustrator's works. It is noteworthy that the link between Moomin's imaginary world and Finnish reality in the books was obliterated by leaving out the maps originally appearing in Jansson's stories (Jendis 2007: 138).

30.3.3   *The Role of Children's Literature in Eastern and Nordic Europe*

Publishers of children's literature do not automatically have a say as to which books are eventually sold. Rather, it is often the parents, acting as gatekeepers and echoing the customs, values and ideologies of the society, who choose the books for their children. Interestingly, the same parents who deny their children access to books with sensitive themes may present their children with folk tales with frightening or controversial content (Evans 2015: 11). In the long run, it is not clear what children should be protected from. As Fraiberg (1959: 23) points out, human life involves risks, and adult attempts to shield children may often be counterproductive.

No matter the political ideology involved, protecting children from harmful literature was considered essential all over Europe, including the Eastern Bloc and Nordic Europe. In Finland, for instance, parents were encouraged to keep an eye on what their children read because it was understood that literature had a strong influence on its readers (Heikkilä-Halttunen 2000: 87–8). For example, the unconventional role models of Jansson's Moomin books and the independence of her characters challenged the image of the ideal nuclear family and was likely seen as harmful for children's development (see Heikkilä-Halttunen 2000: 286). This may be one of the reasons why the Moomin books were only translated into Finnish beginning in 1955, although in the 1940s the first Moomin books were already published in Finland in Swedish, one of the country's two official languages.

The role of children's literature as a mediator of values and ideologies is especially evident during political and nationalist turning points. For instance, as Lehtonen and Rajalin (1984: 21, 28) explain, as already by the end of the nineteenth century, children's literature in Finland was playing a special role as a mediator of Finnish identity and patriotism. In 1917, towards the end of World War I, Finland gained her independence from the Russian empire, and heroic adventure stories for children were produced to boost confidence in the country's bright future. For similar reasons, this kind of adventure story was also used in East Germany in the period of socialist construction, when the heroes of the stories conveyed a spirit of loyalty toward the regime and transmitted socialist and patriotic values for children. As Thomson-Wohlgemuth writes, children's literature was more progressive than literature for adults, challenging old taboos and stimulating young readers to find out about what happens in real life. In other words, children's literature played the role of social trendsetter (Thomson-Wohlgemuth 2005: 42).

Modernist trends in literature were also visible in writing for children. For example, the line between reality and imagination became hazy, which was reflected in many works of fantasy (Heikkilä-Halttunen 2000: 55). Metaphors in fairy tales facilitated the discussion, even the critique of traditional themes, and fantastic stories provided an escape from reality. In fact, the 1950s in Finland was a rich and productive decade for fairy tales and fantasy, both originals and translations from the English language (Lehtonen and Rajalin 1984: 57–8). For Finland, the 1950s, the decade of modernism, signified opening up into new directions and the beginning of internationalisation (Koskinen and Paloposki 2015: 53). The situation was very different from that of the socialist Eastern European countries where, under the influence of socialist construction, fairy tales were regarded as a dangerous 'bourgeois' influence on good socialist citizens (Thomson-Wohlgemuth 2005: 23). Liseling-Nilsson (2006: 210) explains that in Poland, only realistic books depicting children's everyday life were considered acceptable in the publishing scene. While books served a primarily educational purpose in socialist countries, in Finland, children's literature performed the dual role of entertaining and educating.

Instead of fairy tales, in East Germany during the period of socialist construction, domestic adventure stories with a socialist agenda were offered to children. The aim of this kind of mass literature was to convey ideological values, such as 'courage, determination, stamina and honesty' (Thomson-Wohlgemuth 2005: 23). During socialist construction, in the socialist Eastern Bloc, foreign and domestic literature had the same requirement: it had to comply with the ideological criteria of the state (Thomson-Wohlgemuth 2003: 247). This was achieved by branding.

This also explains why the source texts of translated literature mostly came from other socialist countries. Out of the desire to protect children from 'western propaganda', hardly any western children's literature was published. For instance, while Lindgren's first Pippi book, *Pippi Långstrump* (1945, in English *Pippi Longstocking* 1950), was translated and published in West Germany in 1949, it was published in East Germany only in 1975, which, according to Thomson-Wohlgemuth (2003), already belonged to the period of liberalisation. Although the adventurous main character, Pippi, represented the ideological values of 'courage, determination, stamina and honesty' (Thomson-Wohlgemuth 2005: 23) mentioned above, the rebelliousness of the western child heroine might have been seen as too dangerous. Because Pippi does not respect authorities, such as old ladies and teachers, she did not align with the ideal socialist image of a good child and a model citizen. Rather, she criticises and laughs at authoritarian social structures (Jendis 2001: 144). The same applies to Jansson's Moomin stories: contrary to real children, her characters are allowed to do whatever they feel like doing without having to obey adult norms and conventions (Heikkilä-Halttunen 2000: 275).

Not meeting the expectations of the target culture is one of the reasons why children's literature has been adapted over the years. For instance, the first Polish-language translation of *Pippi Longstocking* (*Fizia Pończoszanka*), which appeared in 1961, was an expurgated adaptation: Pippi was portrayed as more gentle, less rude, less rebellious and less critical of the adult world (Teodorowicz-Hellman 1999: 79–80). At the same time, there were changes in Pippi's manner of speaking: she became less jolly in the Polish adaptation to fit in the pedagogical ideals of this period (Teodorowicz-Hellman 1999: 78). However, the Polish critic Nicpan (in *Nowe Książki* 1986) commented that the Pippi books should have been banned altogether because of Pippi's unrestricted and dangerous freedom (Teodorowicz-Hellman 1999: 61). Adaptations are often used to impose adult values on children, especially in response to radical ideological shifts in society (Alvstad 2018: 163). Rewritings and adaptations were considered to be purifications of not only politically suspicious content and rebellious characters but also morally sensitive content and taboo subjects, such as references to religion, sexuality and adult vices (see Shavit 1986: 29, 43; for translation and adaptation see Oittinen 2000: 98–9). Omitting dubious content was often explained as modernising outdated texts (Alvstad 2018: 167). Certainly, such editorial decisions were also about acting for the good of the child.

Behind this editorial aim was the educational role attributed to children's literature. The task of children's literature was to develop a child's cognitive and emotional capacities and to give the child knowledge of various topics, such as history and sociocultural insights (Alvstad 2018: 163), and teachers acted as important gatekeepers by recommending books for children. For example, in the socialist school system, teachers played an important role by serving "proper" literature to their pupils and educating them to become good socialist citizens. Yet, in the end, it was not clear who decided which books children actually read. In East Germany, there were more abstract motivations, such as fostering a child's curiosity to learn and promoting collectivism and a positive work ethic, which were seen as desirable ideals (Alvstad 2018: 171). Importantly, these motivations also indicated general respect or disrespect for children's culture in a given society. In the context of socialist construction, censorship could, therefore, be negative, neutral or, in some cases, even positive.

30.3.4 Censoring Multimodal Texts

Censoring children's literature involves both words and images. The verbal and the visual appear in many different formats created for children, such as comics and other illustrated stories. One of the main formats of children's literature is the picturebook, which represents a combination of the verbal and the visual. It is also a social, cultural, and historical document, which is commercially produced for the book market and, first and foremost, for the child (Bader 1976: 1). Picturebooks may be seen from different points of view: as art, as a sequence of images, as prompting the turning of pages, and as promoting the active participation of the child reader (Oittinen et al. 2018: 15–22). Picturebooks may provide mainstream reading material with no challenging style or content, or they can be controversial and break boundaries.

Whichever way we define or describe a picturebook, writing, illustrating and translating children's literature take place in a dialogue between the verbal and the visual. As Bakhtin describes the situation, everything can be understood as an interaction, as a part of a greater whole: in every book there is the 'I' and the 'you' meeting in some kind of a context (regarding dialogue and interaction, see Morson and Emerson 1990: 49–52; regarding dialogism, see Holquist in Bakhtin 1990: 426–7; and regarding dialogue and the word, see Oittinen 2000: 29–32). In an illustrated story, words and images interact, in collaboration or opposition. As Kress and van Leeuwen (1996: 183) point out, the entity of an illustrated story depends on what we share and how similar our backgrounds are. It is important to remember that, as Lefevere points out, 'nobody is ever able to escape from the ideology and/or the poetics prevalent in the literary system of his or her time, to which his or her translation will be seen to belong' (Lefevere in Hermans 1985: 239). In other words, we are both individuals as interpreters of texts and also part of the surrounding culture and other circumstances.

Not only is the translation of illustrated texts about translating the words interlingually, from one language into another, but it is also about taking into consideration the interplay between the verbal and the visual modes within the multimodal whole. This is connected to what Jakobson (1959: 238) means by intersemiotic translation, that is, from one semiotic system into another (e.g., from the written mode into the oral). In other words, when translators translate picturebooks, they must contend with the interaction between the verbal and the visual.

Yet similar items may affect the readers, including the translators, in different ways, through congruency and deviation: the verbal and the visual may support each other or they may take different directions. The visual may or may not make the verbal message more believable. Sometimes it may be the very intention of the author, translator or illustrator to accentuate different aspects, which again constitutes the story as a whole. When even the tiniest verbal or visual detail of a text is changed as a result of censorship, and the text appears in a new societal or political environment, the new readers will see the text in new ways. Moreover, the relationship of the verbal and the visual is a construction in the reader's mind, where these differences are combined—and new meanings arise. In the translation process, the translators' understanding of the text is based on the entity combining the verbal and the visual to be translated. In practice, translators of children's literature make decisions concerning the text and the target audience on the basis of their image of the child.

The style and contents of translated children's literature are modified, even censored, in different times for different reasons: on the one hand, the structure of texts may be simplified, or, on the other hand, the style may be elevated not only for educational but also for propagandistic purposes, i.e., the manipulative indoctrination of ideologies (Alvstad 2018: 162). Translating always involves changes, such as additions and omissions, but censoring is about modifying texts intentionally in certain directions to meet the aims of those holding power.

For example, in the illustrations of the German-language translations of Moomin books produced in East Germany, the purpose was apparently to keep the idyllic depictions of everyday life and to omit any threatening or otherwise dubious content (Jendis 2007: 137). The publishing principle was similar to the ideological branding of books for children in the socialist regime: the purpose of choosing books for publishing and translation was to align them with the ideological agenda and to avoid foreignisation. Stolt (1978) has discussed these issues in connection with Astrid Lindgren's Emil books and their different illustrated versions, which are also good examples of a heteroglossic situation: different illustrations and verbal translations open new windows to the original text and highlight their mutual relationship. They also show how texts are adapted to reflect the prevailing values of the surrounding society. For example, in the German translation of *Emil in Lönneberga* (*Michel in der Suppenschüssel* 1971, orig. *Emil i Lönneberga* 1963) the original peasant village with its inhabitants was transformed into a prettified small town, and 'the positively gripping realism into an artificially playful world of appearances' (Stolt 1978: 143–4). The aroma and taste of the Emil books has been altogether 'diluted and oversweetened' (Stolt 1978: 143–4). This is especially discernible in the illustrations.

The same happened in the Polish translations of Lindgren's books, as Liseling-Nilsson (2012: 291) points out. Through the modification of illustrations, using such methods as purification, Polonisation, exoticisation, folklorisation and neutralisation, the Swedish village depicted by the original illustrator Björn Berg was transformed by illustrator Hanna Czajkowska into a Polish town. Even the clothing of the characters was folklorised and thus domesticated (Liseling-Nilsson 2012: 298–9). The changes were also made in order to purify the texts by deleting unsuitable scenes, for instance, the rebellious behaviour of children and contempt towards authorities (Liseling-Nilsson 2012: 300).

30.3.5 *Retranslating and Rewriting*

The different forms of retranslation are also connected with adaptation, branding and rebranding. In its simplest form, according to the retranslation hypothesis, first translations are usually domesticated or adapted to meet with target culture expectations, whereas later translations are closer and more faithful to the source texts (see Venuti 2004). This seems to be the situation in the case of censured children's literature in the Eastern Bloc, but retranslations do not always support the hypothesis as factors different from those envisioned by Venuti (2004) may motivate and structure the translation process, such as time, place, culture and also the image of the child.

Along with time, while original texts seem to stay young forever, their translations are said to age with time and thus become culturally or linguistically outdated. This perception of the influence of time on translations may lead to 'presentism', 'a tendency to impose present-day values and expectations [...] on historical events and artefacts' (Koskinen 2018: 322). In other words, it is the audience and the ambient society and culture that have changed for ideological and ethical reasons, not the translations that have depicted the time of their own. This was the case with Lindgren's *Pippi Longstocking*, which was retranslated in Finland in 2007 by Rikman. It was felt that a retranslation into Finnish was needed due to the use of some sensitive expressions, such as the *n-word*, in earlier translations. At the same time, out-dated vocabulary and style were modernised with the idea that the target audience needed a new version that reflected the present language use as there was a gap of approximately 50 years between the first translation by Järvinen (1946) and the retranslation by Rikman (2007) (Koskinen and Paloposki 2015: 55). This kind of presentism was not required in the German-language retranslations because racism had never been tolerated in East German children's literature; for instance, stereotypical illustrations of indigenous peoples were erased (Alvstad 2018: 163; Thomson-Wohlgemuth 2009: 152).

Although racism was therefore not an issue in East German retranslations of children's literature, there were other problems. For example, texts such as the Moomin stories with a tolerant outlook on life and a broadminded conception of family and gender roles may have aroused debate at their appearance as the first German translations of the Moomin books were adapted and marketed for children to tone down or eliminate those aspects of the stories. In response to twenty-first century changes in the general atmosphere and the image of the child in Europe, the retranslations have restored this diversity. In addition, most of the original illustrations and the map of the Moomin valley drawn by Jansson were added (Jendis 2007: 138). As Jendis (2007: 142) writes, 'Finally, after 50 years, the Moomin books can now be read in the same way in German-speaking countries as they originally appeared in the Nordic lands.' In other words, the Moomin books were rebranded for new times and audiences.

As Liseling-Nilsson (2006: 211) points out, a new culture with a new language always requires new versions that introduce new writings with new meanings. Interestingly, after the era of Finlandisation and the collapse of the Soviet Union, it may have been expected that new, 'more accurate' translations would have been published in Finland, but this was not the case. Perhaps the publishers feared that releasing this kind of literature would have been considered too risky and dangerous (Koskinen and Paloposki 2015: 214). Moreover, it is possible that the status of the translators had an impact on the publishing decisions made. Books are sometimes retranslated because the earlier translations were made by translators who have since become personae non grata (Koskinen and Paloposki 2015: 215; Pokorn 2012: 42–9). This was the case in Slovenia where some works were retranslated because their earlier translators had become politically dubious (Pokorn 2012: 42). By contrast, there is no evidence of a similar motivation for retranslation in Finland (Koskinen and Paloposki 2015: 215).

30.4 New Debates

Some of the most controversial debates related to the censorship of children's literature involve comics, on the one hand, and folk tales, on the other.

30.4.1 Censorship of Comics in Europe

In addition to picturebooks, illustrated children's literature also includes comics. Comics as such cannot be studied in the geopolitical context under the socialist regime because there were hardly any comics produced in the Eastern Bloc after World War II. In fact, comics were considered unsuitable readings for socialist citizens because comics were seen as junk literature. It is also possible that comics were considered morally dubious, even dangerous due to their visuality (Nygård 2017: 211). One way of looking at the censorship of comics would be to examine the ethical questions concerning the visual presentation in illustrated children's literature. As Zanettin argues, in the 1950s, censorship was practised in both dictatorial and democratic governments and, until the 1960s, a general hostility prevailed towards comics. In some countries, attempts were made to enact legislation; even though no laws were ultimately passed, 'the publishers adopted self-imposed codes of ethics' (Zanettin 2018: 877).

In Western Europe, the Code Europress Junior (*Le code moral Europresse junior*) was adopted in 1966. Most of the European publishing houses joined the code Junior with 11 articles (Nygård 2017: 211). It was the equivalent to the Comics Code introduced in the USA. It is remarkable how much this code and the Eastern European censorship rules have in common. According to the Code Europress Junior, there were several requirements concerning social order, moral values and the dignity of human life (Nygård 2017: 212; Pierre 1976: 133–4).

For instance, the Code Europress Junior emphasised that the value of family life and marriage should be respected in comics and that themes such as sexuality, eroticism and debauchery should not be exploited in verbal texts and illustrations (Nygård 2017: 213; Pierre 1976: 133–4). This was also evident in Francoist Spain and Fascist Italy, as Zanettin (2018: 874) points out. As an example, he mentions the case of Flash Gordon, whose lover became his sister in the Italian version. Additionally, the themes of prejudice, intolerance and disputes over political propaganda were banned. Violence and sadism too had to be avoided. Instead, comics were supposed to respect nobility, generosity and the brotherhood of human kind, and stand up for such values as honesty, loyalty, kindness and charity (Nygård 2017: 212–3; Pierre 1976: 133–4). Interestingly, the above ideological values were also shared by the socialist hero. This would certainly be a fruitful topic for further examination.

30.4.2   To censor Folk Tales or Not

As mentioned above, even though parents typically withhold from their children literature with harmful content, they may, even unintentionally, offer their children folktales, which contain controversial or even frightening scenes featuring violence, death and other taboo subjects. On the one hand, protecting the child by censoring unsuitable contents is considered an adult's responsibility. On the other hand, folk tales, especially when read to a child by a parent or guardian, may be a safe way to expose children to new and disturbing emotions, including fear (Bettelheim 1989: 28).

Because children's literature is as a rule created by adults, there is always a shadow text in the background, one that consists of not only what the author avoids saying but also what is between the lines, hidden from the child's eyes (Nodelman 2008: 8). Furthermore, as Bettelheim (1989: 19) emphasises, frightening folk tales, such as the stories of the Brothers Grimm, should not be censored but told in their original form, because of the 'true meaning and the impact' of the folk tale. Finally, the reading situation may be negative, too, as adults often wish for their children to internalise order and discipline, which makes them easier to control (Oittinen 2000: 52–3).

However, it is also important to understand that children are not helpless but rather omnipotent sorcerers in the magical world of their own, where the evil may be undone through magic and laughter. Here again the main factor is the image of the child and the different versions reflecting this image.

Acknowledgements

This chapter was the result of the authors' common work. However, Eliisa Pitkäsalo was particularly responsible for sections 30.1, 30.2, 30.3.2, 30.3.3, 30.4.1 and 30.5 and Riitta Oittinen for sections 30.3.1, 30.3.4 and 30.4.2.

Further Reading

Dybiec-Gajer, Joanna, Oittinen, Riitta and Kodura, Małgorzata (eds.). 2020. *Negotiating Translation and Transcreation of Children's Literature*. New Frontiers in Translation Studies. Singapore Pte Ltd. Singapore: Springer Nature.
The book contains fresh and critical insights into translation and transcreation of children's literature. The chapters balance text-related problems and genre conventions with readers' expectations, canonical translations and publishers' demands. The book investigates phenomena where transcreation is at play in children's literature. The methodologies cover cognitive linguistics and ethnolinguistic semiotics as well as autoethnographic approaches. The book is essential reading for students and researchers of translation and transcreation for children.

Oittinen, Riitta, Ketola, Anne and Garavini, Melissa. 2018. *Translating Picturebooks. Revoicing the Verbal, the Visual, and the Aural for a Child Audience.* New York and London: Routledge.
The book offers its reader a wide overview of picturebooks and their translation. It examines the topic from several theoretical and analytical viewpoints. It discusses ideology and translator's child image, adult influences, foreignising and domesticating policies and different types of picturebooks as well as the interaction and performance of words and images. The book also contains discussions on intertextuality and intervisuality, reading strategies of the verbal and the visual and pedagogical implications.

Pokorn, Nike K. 2012. *Post-Socialist Translation Practices. Ideological Struggle in Children's Literature.* Amsterdam and Philadelphia: John Benjamins Publishing Company.
Pokorn discusses translation practices during the time of communism in the Socialist Federal Republic of Yugoslavia. The author contemplates the hegemonic pressure on translations through purging texts to follow the guidelines regulated by the regime. The book offers perceptive insights into censorship and self-censorship and takes a look at translations and retranslations of classical fairy tales and bestsellers for children.

Thomson-Wohlgemuth, Gaby. 2009. *Translation Under State Control: Books for Young People in the German Democratic Republic.* London and New York: Routledge.
Thomson-Wohlgemuth explores the effects of ideology on children's literature under the socialist regime of the GDR. She presents ideological literary policies in Eastern German censorship machinery and the publishers' self-censoring practices. The book is genuinely interesting reading and provides a thorough survey of the historical context of children's literature in the GDR and translating processes of literature for the young under the state control.

References

Alvstad, Cecilia. 2018. 'Children's literature', in K. Washbourne and B. Van Wyke (eds.), *Routledge Handbook of Literary Translation.* London and New York: Routledge, 159–80.
Ariès, Philippe. 1962. *Centuries of Childhood: A Social History of Family Life.* Translated by R. Baldick. New York: Knopf.
Bader, Barbara. 1976. *American Picturebooks from Noah's Arc to the Beast Within.* New York: Macmillan Publishing Co.
Bakhtin, Mikhail M. 1990. *The Dialogic Imagination. Four Essays.* Translated by C. Emerson and M. Holquist. Glossary by Holquist. Austin: University of Texas Press.
Bettelheim, Bruno. 1989. *The Uses of Enchantment. The Meaning and Importance of Fairy Tales.* New York: Vintage Books.
Borodo, Michal. 2006. 'Children's literature translation in Poland during the 1950s and the 1990s', in V. Joosen and K. Vloeberghs (eds.), *Changing Concepts of Childhood and Children's Literature.* Newcastle: Cambridge Scolars Press, 169–82.
Evans, Janet. 2015. 'Picturebooks as strange, challenging and controversial texts', in J. Evans (ed.), *Challenging and Controversial Picturebooks. Creative and Critical Responses to Visual Texts.* London and New York: Routledge, 3–32.
Fraiberg, Selma. 1959. *The Magic Years: Understanding and Handling the Problems of Early Childhood.* New York: Charles Scriber's Sons.
Frank, Armin Paul. 1989. 'Translation as system'. *New Comparison* 8: 85–98.
Hade, Daniel, Paul, Lissa and Mason, John. 2013. 'Are children's book publishers changing the way children read? A panel discussion', *Children's Literature Association Quaterly*, 28(3): 137–43.
Haynes, Joanna and Murris, Karin. 2012. *Picturebooks, Pedagogy and Philosophy.* New York, London: Routledge.
Heikkilä-Halttunen, Päivi. 2000. *Kuokkavieraasta oman talon haltijaksi. Suomalaisen lasten- ja nuortenkirjallisuuden institutionalisoituminen ja kanonisoituminen 1940–1950-luvulla.* Helsinki: SKS.
Huizinga, Jan. 1984. *Leikkivä ihminen. Yritys kulttuurin leikkiaineksen määrittelemiseksi.* Transl. Sirkka Salomaa. Helsinki: WSOY.
Hunt, Peter. 1990. *Children's Literature: The Development of Criticism.* London: Routledge.
Jakobson, Roman. 1959. 'On linguistic aspects of translation', in R. A. Brower (ed.), *On Translation. Harvard Studies in Comparative Literature.* Cambridge: Harvard University Press, 232–239.

Jendis, Mareike. 2001. *Mumins Wundersame Deutschlandabenteure: Zur Rezeption von Tove Janssons Muminbüchern*. Umeå: Umeå University.

Jendis, Mareike. 2007. 'Moomin's adventures in the German-speaking countries', in K. McLoughlin and M. Lidström Brock (eds.), *Tove Jansson Rediscovered*. Cambridge: Cambridge Scholars Publishing, 131–45.

Koskinen, Kaisa. 2018. 'Revising and retranslating', in K. Washbourne and B. Van Wyke (eds.), *Routledge Handbook of Literary Translation*. New York and London: Routledge, 315–24.

Koskinen, Kaisa and Paloposki, Outi. 2015. *Sata kirjaa, tuhat suomennosta. Kaunokirjallisuuden uudelleenkääntäminen*. SKS: Helsinki.

Kress, Gunther and van Leeuwen, Theo. 1996. *Reading Images: A Grammar of Visual Design*. London and New York: Routledge.

Lal, Purushottama. 1996. *Transcreation*. Writers Workshop: Calcutta 1996.

Lefevere, André. 1985. 'Why waste our time on rewrites? The trouble with interpretation and the role of rewriting in an alternative paradigm', in Hermans, Theo (ed.), *The Manipulation of Literature. Studies in Literary Translation*. London: Croom Helm, 215–44.

Lefevere, André. 1992. *Translation, Rewriting, & the Manipulation of Literary Fame*. New York and London: Routledge.

Lehtonen, Maija and Rajalin, Marita (eds.). 1984. Barnboken i Finland förr och nu. Stockholm: Rabén & Sjögren.

Liseling-Nilsson, Sylvia. 2006. 'Translating the already seen', in V. Joosen and K. Vloeberghs (eds.), *Changing Concepts of Childhood and Children's Literature*. Newcastle: Cambridge Scholars Press, 209–19.

Liseling-Nilsson, Sylvia. 2012. *Kod kulturowy a przekład: Na podstawie wybranych utworów Astrid Lindgren i ich polskich przekładów / The Cultural Code and Translation: The Case of Selected Works by Astrid Lindgren into Polish*. Acta Universitatis Stockholmiensis. Stockholm Slavic Studies 41.

Miller, Alice. 1990. *For Your Own Good. Hidden Cruelty in Child-Rearing and the Roots of Violence*. USA: The Noonday Press.

Morson, Gary Saul and Emerson, Caryl. 1990. *Mikhail Bakhtin. Creation of a Prosaics*. Stanford, California: Stanford University Press.

Nodelman, Perry. 2008. *The Hidden Adult. Defining Children's Literature*. Baltimore: The John Hopkins University Press.

Nodelman, Perry. 2015. 'The scandal of the commonplace. The strangeness of best-selling picturebooks', in J. Evans (eds.), *Challenging and Controversial Picturebooks. Creative and Critical Responses to Visual Texts*. London and New York: Routledge, 33–48.

Nygård, Severi. 2017. *Sarjakuvasensuuri*. Helsinki: Jalava.

Oittinen, Riitta. 2000. *Translating for Children*. New York and London: Garland Publishing Inc.

Oittinen, Riitta. 2006. 'No innocent act: On the ethics of translating for children', in J. Van Coillie and W. P. Verschueren (eds.), *Children's Literature in Translation: Challengies and Strategies*. Manchester: St Jerome Publishing, 35–45.

Oittinen, Riitta, Ketola, Anne and Garavini, Melissa. 2018. *Translating Picturebooks. Revoicing the Verbal, the Visual, and the Aural for a Child Audience*. New York and London: Routledge.

Pedersen, Daniel. 2014. 'Exploring the concept of transcreation – Transcreation as more than translation'? *Cultus*, 7: 57–71.

Pedersen, Daniel. 2019. 'Managing transcreation projects: An ethnographic study', in H. Risku, R. Rogl and J. Milosevic (eds.), Special Issue: *Translation Practice in the Field. Current Research on Socio-Cognitive Processes, Translation Spaces*. 6(1): 44–61.

Pierre, Michel. 1976. *La Bande Dessinée. Idéologies et sociétés*. Paris: Librairie Larousse.

Pokorn, Nike K. 2012. *Post-Socialist Translation Practices. Ideological Struggle in Children's Literature*. Amsterdam and Philadelphia: John Benjamins Publishing Company.

Reiss, Katharina and Vermeer, Hans J. 1984. *Grundlegung einer allgemeinen Translationstheorie*. Tübingen: Niemeyer.

Shavit, Zohar. 1986. *Poetics of Children's Literature*. Athens: University of Georgia Press.

Stolt, Birgit. 1978. 'How Emil Becomes Michel – On the translation of children's books', in G. Klingberg, M. Ørvig and S. Amor (eds.), *Children's Books in Translation. The Situation and the Problems*. Stockholm: Almqvist & Wiksell International, 130–46.

Swift, Megan. 2020. *Picturing the Page. Illustrated Children's Literature and Reading Under Lenin and Stalin*. Toronto: University of Toronto Press.

Teodorowicz-Hellman, Ewa. 1999. *Svensk – polska litterära möten. Tema: Barnlitteratur.* Stockholm: Svenska institutet.

Tervaharju, Minttu, Nordling, Päivi and Ihonen, Maria. 2017. *Tätä en lapselleni lue! Sensuuritapauksia ja paheksuttuja lastenkirjoja.* Tampere: Lastenkirjainstituutti.

Thomson-Wohlgemuth, Gaby. 2003. 'Children's literature and translation under the east German regime', *Meta*, 48(1–2): 241–9. https://doi.org/10.7202/006971ar

Thomson-Wohlgemuth, Gaby. 2005. 'Parallels in east German adult and children's literature between 1949 and 1989', in J. Webb and M. Müürsepp (eds.), *Sunny Side of Darkness: Children's Literature in Totalitarian and Post-Totalitarian Eastern Europe.* Tallinn: TLÜ Kirjastus, 15–46.

Thomson-Wohlgemuth, Gaby. 2009. *Translation Under State Control. Books for Young People in the German Democratic Republic.* London and New York: Routledge.

Venuti, Lawrence. 1995. *The Translator's Invisibility: A History of Translation.* London and New York: Routledge, 1995.

Venuti, Lawrence. 2004. 'Retranslations: The creation of value', *Bucknell Review*, XLVII(1): 25–38.

Zanettin, Federico. 2018. 'Translation, censorship and the development of European comic cultures', *Perspectives*, 26(6): 868–84.

31

THE CENSORSHIP OF COMICS IN TRANSLATION

The Case of Disney Comics

Federico Zanettin

31.1 Introduction

Translation has played a fundamental role in the development of comics cultures and industries around the world (Zanettin 2018), and the interconnections between comics, translation and censorship are part of a long history of struggle for control of social discourse (Merkle 2018). Since the end of the nineteenth century comics have been a frequent target of censorship, regardless of their translation status. The Yellow Kid, the iconic character of early American comics, had his yellow nightgown extended to his ankles after letters were sent to the editor accusing the character of corrupting the youth, and in 1912, after a two-year-long campaign by women's groups and religious organisations to remove comics from newspapers, supported by women's magazines, press syndicates 'forbade references to divorce, race, and religion and outright banned the discussion of politics' (Sergi 2012) in comics. The newly formed syndicates, such as King Features and United Features distributed the most popular strips, several of which were also translated overseas from the 1930s. In Europe US comics acted as a model for indigenous comics, spurring the development of national comics industries and cultures, but were also banned in Nazi Germany and in Fascist Italy (although with notable differences, see below), as well as in Communist countries. After the war and throughout the 1950s a general hostility against comics also characterised cultural politics in liberal democracies. Several countries, including France, the UK, Germany, Portugal and Spain passed laws and instituted boards and committees against comics, while in other countries publishers adopted self-imposed codes of ethics (Patrick 2011; Moor 2012; Green and Karolides 2005). Notably, in the USA, after decency crusades promoted in the 1940s by organisations such as the National Office for Decent Literature (sponsored by the Catholic Church), a campaign against comics was launched in the 1950s drawing on the ideas of the neuropsychiatrist Fredric Wertham, who in his book *Seduction of the Innocent* (1954) suggested a relationship between the reading of comic books and juvenile delinquency. Ultimately, the federal government did not legislate against the comics industry (though bills against comic books were later passed in various states and municipalities), but the publicity surrounding the issue put the publishers on the defensive and convinced them to adopt, in1954, a self-regulation code (see Comics Magazine Association of America 1955) detailing the strict guidelines that had to be followed in order to

DOI: 10.4324/9781003149453-38

489

obtain the Comics Code Authority's seal of approval, which guaranteed mass distribution (Green and Karolides 2005).

Censorship has often been presented as a way to protect readers from representations of objectionable behaviour on ethical, political, religious as well as aesthetic grounds, and censorship of foreign comics has been portrayed as a form of cultural or economic gatekeeping both under authoritarian and democratic regimes. However, censorship of comics has often been justified also with the argument that comics are, in themselves, detrimental from an educational perspective because they use images rather than just written text. Thus, according to Wertham, comics were also responsible for what he termed 'linear dyslexia', the inability to read written text that developed as a consequence of 'reading images' (Hatfield 2005: 35). Visual narration has been described as a degraded form of communication, and censorship has been directed against not only the contents of comics but also against the comics form itself. Thus, censorship of comics also relates to the power struggle over the cultural capital of the comics form, seen as inferior regardless of their contents.

A distinction can be drawn between a 'regulatory' and a 'constitutive' (or 'structural') model of censorship: the regulatory model sees 'censorship as deliberate policy put into practice by those in power' (Müller 2004: 5), as 'illegitimate government action' (Strange, Green, and Brook 2000: 269). The constitutive model, 'derived from Michel Foucault's understanding of power and Pierre Bourdieu's account of censorship' (Kuhiwczak and Merkle 2011: 362), sees censorship as 'a constant discursive presence associated with power relations' (Kuhiwczak and Merkle 2011: 362). According to this model, censorship, defined in terms of discourse 'often the dominant one, produced by a given society at a given time and expressed either through repressive cultural, aesthetic and linguistic measures or through economic means' (Billiani 2007: 2), can be seen as a mechanism regulating power relations in a community, by means of laws (preventive censorship and post-fact legal sanctions) but also by social pressure, in the form of (anticipation of) physical, psychological or economic sanctions.

In authoritarian countries censorship is usually enforced by legislating institutions and by official bodies both to prevent translation and to punish publishers and translators, but sometimes also through extra-legal actions, including harming and killing. In liberal democracies censorship is instead more often a prerogative of the market, as political (including governmental) stakeholders may put pressure on publishers, which then exercise self-censorship to prevent anticipated economic losses, such as those deriving from not displaying the CCA seal on a comic book cover in the USA. Finally, censorship may be the outcome of self-restraint and control on the part of individual publishers and translators to prevent the (extra)legal or even physical consequences of institutional or economic censorship.

Disney comic stories, the largest share of which has been published in translation from and into several languages, make for an interesting case study to exemplify different types of censorship practices and policies, ranging from outright institutional censorship, with a government banning the translation and importation of the foreign comics, to economic censorship and self-censorship.

31.2   Historical Perspectives: Disney Comics in Translation

Mickey Mouse first appeared in the 1928 cartoon Steamboat Willy and, following the success of the animated movies from 1930, it featured in syndicated comics strips distributed to American newspapers by the King Features Syndicate.[1] The humorous strips with the Disney signature featuring anthropomorphic characters, together with the fantastic adventures of realistically drawn strips such as Alex Raymond's *Flash Gordon* and Lee Falk's *Mandrake*, were instrumental in the development of European comics industries and cultures. Disney's 'funny animals' comics were among the most popular among those printed in the new type of comics magazines sold in European and Latin American newsstands. In Europe Mickey Mouse stories appeared in several publications bearing its name on the cover, such as *Topolino* in Italy (1932), *Le Journal de Mickey* in France (1934), *Mickey* in Spain (1935) and *Mickey Mouse Weekly* in the UK (1936). Since then, Disney comics have been published in over 70 countries and are still among the most well-known and bestselling comics around the world.

Though Mickey Mouse is the iconic mascot of the Walt Disney Company, comics have always been only a marginal product for the US-based multinational, primarily seen as supporting the core business of films, theme parks and merchandising. In the USA, newspaper comic strips and comic books were two separate enterprises. Newspaper strips were very popular until the 1950s, but declined in the following decades until, in 1995, their production, already outsourced in 1990 to Kings Features Syndicates, was discontinued. Since then, only reprints were published, until in 2006 all Disney comic strips disappeared from American newspapers. While the daily and weekly strips were produced by the Disney Studio, in 1932 Disney started to oversee the publication of comic books outsourced to licensed partners, in the USA and abroad, though always maintaining control over their production. Initially outsourced comics were published only as collections of daily strips and later with stories specifically created in parallel with the newspaper strips. While featuring the same characters, from those populating the worlds of Mickey Mouse and Donald Duck to the vast array of anthropomorphic animals and human characters coming from other Disney popular animated cartoons and movies, the production of comic books developed along different lines from that of daily and Sunday newspaper strips. As opposed to Mickey Mouse strips, which included both long stories in continuity and short gags, Donald Duck strips were always of the latter kind, and longer stories featuring this character were only published in comic books. Disney comic strips were part of the distinct genre of 'funny animal comics', which appeared next to comic strips belonging to more adventurous genres addressed to a readership that included adult readers, whereas comic books were addressed to a younger readership. In 1939 Disney licensed the publication of Mickey Mouse magazines to Western Printing, in partnership with Dell Publishing, who took care of the US distribution. In the 1940s and 1950s Disney comic books were extremely popular in the US. In 1953 the main magazine published by Western and Dell, *Walt Disney's Comics and Stories*, sold over three million copies for each issue. Like with comic strips, the popularity of Disney comic books, magazines, and giveaways for companies, produced by Disney Studio and Western Printing and drawn by either freelance or contracted artists, declined from the 1960s, until in 1984 production was officially discontinued. In 1986 a new publisher, Gladstone, started publishing comic books containing a mix of reprints of classic US stories, stories originally published in other countries and translated into English, and a few new stories created in the USA. Gladstone managed to make comic books a lucrative business again, and in 1990 the Walt Disney Company decided to publish comic books through its own subsidiary. This only lasted until 1993, however, and Disney comics, thereafter published by other licensees, have increasingly become a niche product in the USA, mostly issued in collector's editions.

While in the USA their popularity began to wane in the 1960s, Disney comics became increasingly popular in the rest of the world. From the outset, Disney comics outside the USA have consisted of a mix of licensed stories specifically produced in each country of publication, translated US stories (and self-conclusive strips), stories produced for the international market by a variety of international authors, as well as other stories originally produced for the local market in other countries. Already in the 1950s, internal production of Disney comics in the USA was unable to meet the demand for translations abroad. In 1962, for instance, about 1100 new pages were produced in the USA, as compared to 2600 in Italy, while the 'total monthly circulation of Disney comics throughout the world was given [...] at 50 million, covering 50 countries and 15 different languages' (Kunzle 1991: 19). Thus, the Publications Department of Disney Studio decided to launch a new project, the Overseas Comic Book Program, thereafter commonly known as the Studio Program, with the aim of producing 1500 new pages a year, to be sent to licensees abroad. The Studio Program was conceived as an international project, involving German, Italian, Dutch, Brazilian, and Danish writers and artists already working for licensees outside of the USA. From the 1970s, however, most Studio Program stories were written in the USA and drawn by artists working for the Jaime Diaz Studio in Buenos Aires, Argentina, until in 1990 Disney discontinued the project, while attempting for a short time to publish directly through its imprints. After a few years Disney outsourced again the production of comics at home and abroad, and international production has since taken place elsewhere.

Since the 1950s most Disney comics have been produced outside of the USA by authors working for major European publishers, such as Mondadori in Italy, Hachette in France, Gutenberghus (Egmont since 1992) in Denmark (Egmont acquired a license for the Scandinavian countries, but also publishes local versions of Disney comics through its subsidiaries in 30 different countries, including China, Russia, Turkey, South Africa, the UK and the US) and Editora/Grupo Abril in Brazil. Italy has historically been the main centre of production of Disney comics creating most of the new stories published, and reprinted, in the country. At the height of their success, in the 1990s, just before the advent of manga, Disney comics accounted for about half of all comics sold in Italy (Castelli 1995) and about 70% of all Disney stories produced worldwide (Tosti 2011: 126). While Disney comics are, as a whole, on a downward path, in 2012 Italian productions still accounted for two thirds of all new Disney comics (Lepore 2012: 11). In Italy, the Walt Disney Company took charge of the running of Disney periodicals directly from 1988 to 2013, when the license was given to Panini, which also publishes Disney comics in Brazil, Chile, France, Germany, Greece, Mexico and Spain.[2]

A large share of Disney comics has always been made up of reprints, both of originally produced and translated stories. These include reprints of classic American stories, from those by Floyd Gottfredson, who from 1930 continued to draw and supervise Mikey Mouse daily strips and Sunday pages until 1975, to those featuring Donald Duck, a character that since 1938 had slowly risen to threaten Mickey Mouse's popularity, in the strips drawn by Al Taliaferro and then in the celebrated stories by Carl Barks. It should be noted, however, that the first story featuring Donald Duck, scripted and drawn by Federico Pedrocchi, appeared in a magazine bearing the character's name (*Paperino e altre avventure*) published in Italy in 1937 by Mondadori. Since the 1960s other non-American stories, characters and authors have ascended to Disney comics stardom and contributed to the design and character of contemporary incarnations of Disney comics, ranging from the Great Disney Parodies written by Guido Martina in the 1960s in Italy, to the Scrooge McDuck saga created by the American author Don Rosa from the 1980s (mostly for Gutenberghus/ Egmont, according to Bryan 2021, 185–201), to stories by authors such as the Italians Romano Scarpa, Giorgio Cavazzano and Silvia Ziche, the Chilean Victor José Arriagada Rios (Vicar), the Dutch Daan Jippes and many others. Different characters are created, developed or preferred in different countries, which have established their own 'Disney' cultures. Some characters, like the 'beatnik' type Fethry Duck, created by the Studio Program for international distribution, and Rockerduck, a millionaire rival of Scrooge created by Carl Barks, never caught on and are barely known in the USA. Conversely, in a story published in Dutch translation Ludwig von Drake, a scientist created by Al Taliaferro, was replaced by Donald Duck (Kaindl 1999: 279). Stories containing indigenous characters, sometimes inspired by popular local real or fictional people,

Censorship of Comics in Translation

may be less likely to be translated abroad, though some characters have become very popular in Disney comics all over the world. These include the originally Italian Paperinik, whose stories have been translated and created in several languages. The 'Duck Avenger', Donald Duck's super heroic alter ego, subsumes several characters from Italian popular culture, including written literature, comics, TV and films, as well as from US superhero comics (Zanettin 2022).

It was not until the 1980s that Disney started to acknowledge the names of the actual creators of its comics. Until then most readers in the world would read stories written and drawn in their own country thinking they were translations of stories created by Walt Disney himself. Since all Disney comics were attributed to the company founder, they could be said to be pseudotranslations (Bosco Tierno 2015). Instead, they have been translated not only from English into other languages, but also into English from other languages and between these other languages. Some stories have only been published in one country (either in the USA or elsewhere) and have never been translated. Other stories have only been published in translation, originating both in the USA or elsewhere but without ever having been published in the country where they had been produced. For instance, a story may be first published in France and then in Chile and Mexico in translation, but not elsewhere, or it may be produced in the USA but only published in Italy, Germany or the UK. A Dutch artist might draw a story written by an American writer and commissioned by the Studio Program for the international market, which is subsequently translated into Spanish, Italian and Finnish, but not into French; a French artist might draw a story written by a British or Italian writer and commissioned by Egmont for the north European market, which is never published in the UK or in Italy. In some cases, American writers would provide foreign artists with only a short one-page script, as in several stories drawn by the Italian Romano Scarpa. The stories that have been translated into other languages were in some cases translated directly, e.g., from Italian into English or Brazilian Portuguese, in other cases indirectly, i.e., using a translation as the source language or English as a relay language. For example, 'When Gladstone I (sic!) in the 1980s got ready to publish its first Italian story [...] they couldn't actually acquire it in Italian at that moment, due to (at the time) the poor communication between various publishers [...]. So: the Gladstone English version [...] was actually translated into English from a German version, localised in the Fuchs tradition by Gudrun Penndorf' (David Gerstein, Disney writer, editor and translator for IDW and before for Egmont), 2017, https://featherysociety.proboards.com/thread/418/localisat ion-tradition?page=2). Stories produced for Egmont, by contrast, are always written in English, often by non-native speakers. As one user of The Feathery Society, a Disney comics English fan forum puts it, 'Egmont scripts are written in English by people for which, in most cases, English is not their first language, and these stories are not primarily written for an English audience anyway' (https://featherysociety.proboards.com/thread/418/localisation-tradition?page=4; see also https://featherysociety.proboards.com/thread/1369/which-language-access-disney-comics). Sometimes the drawings and the dialogues are sent separately, or dialogues and sound effects can be written in pencil in the balloons. Local editors localise and re-create the dialogues for local audiences out of the English script, and often freely 'adapt' them to go with the pictures. The images themselves may be changed to suit local rules, and sometimes panels and pages are added or deleted.

Internet forums, wikis, blogs and other types of publications are a rich source of information about translation policies and practices concerning Disney comics. These sites are populated by knowledgeable groups of fans, often also interacting with (or themselves also being) translators, editors and authors. They contain an extensive record of the sometimes-incensed discussions on the work of individual translators, national traditions, local publishers and corporate guidelines. One topic that has recurrently come up is that of translation and localisation (on comics translation as localisation, see Zanettin 2008). Several users and practitioners distinguish, in fact, between

493

'translation', by which they mean 'literal translation', and localisation, which also includes the distinct stage of 're-dialoguing'. US translators, in particular, seem more likely to refer to themselves as 'dialogue creators' rather than 'simply' translators and they are, in fact, acknowledged as such on the comic book cover of some American editions. The publication of imported Disney comics may thus be a two-step process, involving, first, a literal translation, which in some cases can be provided by an MT system, and then dialogue writing, which may involve adding jokes and changing the text to make it sound 'more natural'.

Stories are localised by foreign licensees who, 'for instance, delete scenes considered offensive or inappropriate to the national sensibility […], have dialogues more or less accurately translated, more or less freely adapted, and add local color (in the literal sense: the pages arrive at the foreign press ready photographed onto black and white transparencies ("mats"), requiring the addition of color as well as dialogue in the local idiom)' (Kunzle 1991: 10). Different colour schemes, in fact, apply to how characters are dressed in different countries and/or by different publishers, though sometimes these colours may get carried over in translated stories (see https://featherysoci ety.proboards.com/thread/12/character-worldwide-colour-schemes). National productions have developed into somewhat distinct 'Disney comics dialects', whose features were often largely established by translation. As far as the verbal text is concerned, in Germany, for example, a local tradition was established by the translations of Erika Fuchs, who translated all Disney stories between 1951 and 1988 (Bryan 2021: 105–41). Fuchs's 'often free renderings and refined transla- tion solutions—ducks quoting from literary classics—have become a part of the German language usage itself, to such an extent that an 'Erikativ', the German word to refer to verbs shortened to their stem, not only to imitate sounds—onomatopoeia—but also to represent soundless events, was coined after the famous translator' (Bosco Tierno 2015: 274). Such 'dialects' were established in Denmark by the translations of Sonja Rindom, who translated all Disney stories from 1949 to 1982 (Grun and Dollerup 2003: 203), and in Italy by the translations of Guido Martina, who translated US stories in the 1950s and 1960s while using the same literary language and sometimes antiquated vocabulary found in the dialogues of the Disney stories he originally wrote himself.

Stories that are now part of the Disney canon are continuously 'updated' (Zanettin 2008) when reprinted and retranslated, both intra- and inter-lingually. Some characters are given a name only in translation, while in other cases names carry across from one translation to the other. For instance, '[t]he Phantom Blot's identity is revealed at the end of Gottfredson's 'Mickey Outwits the Phantom Blot'. We get to see the face of the man under the hood, but his name remains a mystery. Not so in the German translation, where the unmasked Blot is known by the name of Plattnase ('Flatnose'). This name was carried over as Platneus in the Dutch pocketbooks, since the translators relied on the German version. According to German tradition, Plattnase is actually an impostor! This serves as an explanation to reconcile two different approaches to the Phantom Blot. In Egmont stories, the Phantom Blot is never seen without his hood and Mickey doesn't know his identity. In Italian stories, the Phantom Blot frequently appears unmasked. The Germans decided that whenever Plattnase appears, he is only pretending to be the Phantom Blot!'. Furthermore, 'in many older French translations, they gave unmasked Phantom Blot a different name, as if he was a separate character. Called either "Jo Crisse" or "Jo Larapine"' (https://featherysociety.proboards. com/thread/1139/named-translation). The same story may be reprinted in the language of first pub- lication as well as in translations several times, and each time either or both the dialogues and the drawings may be revised and edited, some pages may be cut or redrawn, so that different versions may appear at different times in the same or different countries. In fact, revisions may be at times quite extensive, so that rather different versions of the same story may appear. Reprints, both in English and in translation, may have different lettering, while inscriptions and onomatopoeias may be changed, added or subtracted, and a story may be printed in black and white or with different colours. Different publication formats involve changes in layout and size, so that comics originally published in the standard Italian pocketbook format in three rows are adapted to the standard North American and North European format in four rows, and vice versa.

Translation strategies and approaches have varied significantly in the course of almost one hundred years, depending on the translating country, the time of translation and the readership addressed. For instance, according to an anonymous user of the Feathery Society forum, translations into American English and German tend to rewrite the dialogues, while translations into Portuguese or Italian tend to be more literal (see https://featherysociety.proboards.com/thr ead/418/localisation-tradition?page=4). However, translations from English into Italian can also be translated quite liberally, while Italian stories may be translated into English more literally in collector's editions. After some stories or authors have been canonised through several reprints, they may be re-translated with an almost philological intent, while the source dialogues of other stories may be used only as a script. Some translations may even go as far as to change part of the plot, at times with the translator collaborating with the author of the original dialogues. Reprints, both in the original language of production and in translation, like newly published stories (in translation or not), are continuously monitored and changes are routinely implemented in order to adapt them to the new cultural context and current sensibility.

31.3   Core Issues

31.3.1   Institutional Censorship

Disney comics may be used to illustrate censorship in its most commonly understood institutional sense as the prohibition by a government to import, translate and print a foreign product. One of the most apparent examples is the ban imposed on comics in Germany until the end of WWII. At a time when other European countries, both liberal and authoritarian, were using American comics as the main fodder to set up a new industry, comics were reviled by the Nazi regime as degenerate sub-cultural products. Nazi culture objected to the representation of people as mice. The second volume of Art Spiegelman's *Maus* has as its epigraph a quotation from a newspaper article, printed in Germany in the mid-1930s, that reads: 'Mickey Mouse is the most miserable ideal ever revealed [...]. Healthy emotions tell every independent young man and every honorable youth that the dirty and filth-covered vermin, the greatest bacteria carrier in the animal kingdom, cannot be the ideal type of animal [...]. Away with Jewish brutalisation of the people! Away with Mickey Mouse! Wear the Swastika cross!' (in Spiegelman, 1991: 3). After a brief appearance in 1930, Disney comics disappeared from newspapers, to reappear only in 1951, when they were published by the German division of the Danish publishing house Gutenberghus. Still, comics were looked upon with suspicion, and subjected to censorship by a 1953 law which prohibited the distribution of 'harmful material' and by the Federal Department for Writings Harmful to Young Persons (*Bundesprüfstelle für jugendgefährdende Schriften*), established in 1954 (McCabe 2016). Initially German Disney comic books and magazines replicated the Scandinavian editions, which mostly contained translated American stories, though from the 1970s they also included Italian and international productions, as well as local stories. A local comics culture developed only towards the end of the century, being influenced more by Japanese manga than by American comics.

In the Soviet Union, like in Nazi Germany, comics were banned and in the Eastern bloc they generally did not have an easy life. In Russia Disney comics were first published in 1989 by Egmont Russia, being translations of stories produced in Denmark and Italy. While both the Nazi and communist regimes perceived comics as a vehicle of corruption and applied a blanket censorship to the comics form, quite different policies were adopted in Italy during the Fascist era. Like France and Spain, Italy embraced the new form of graphic narrative, but made it an object of social control. From 1935 all publishers were required to deposit at the Ministry of the Interior three copies of all books and magazines before publication. Some attempts were also made to restrict the share of pages containing comics (on educational grounds) and to put a quota on imported comics (on economic grounds) in national magazines (Zanettin 2017). In response, publishers resorted to self-censorship, considerably altering foreign comics by editing or deleting all verbal and visual elements that could potentially attract the attention of the censors. Publishers collaborated under threat of publication requisition, negotiating with the regime what could and could not be published, and increasingly reduced the number of foreign stories. In 1938 a Ministerial circular banned foreign comics (almost) completely, as well as all stories 'inspired by foreign production'. In practice, the regime tolerated for a while the publication of some foreign materials, while publishers circumvented the ban by attributing translated stories to non-existent Italian authors, or even by having some stories entirely redrawn and rewritten using the American sources as loose scripts. The names of the characters could be altered to make them sound Italian, and the plot could be changed to transform two unmarried characters into brother and sister. Bare legs could be covered by drawing a longer shirt, Anglo-American blond hair could be painted Italian black, and hips of skeletons could be deleted from a panel. (For a more detailed analysis of these examples, see Zanettin (2017). On comics and censorship in Italy between 1949 and 1953 see Meda (2002) and on censorship of Italian crime comics, the 'fumetti neri' from the 1960s, see also the ruling of the Italian senate [Repubblica italiana 1965]). Foreign comics were thus adapted to stay within the limits of acceptability established by unofficial political and moral guidelines as a form of preventive self-censorship. The self-imposed guidelines of publishers and translators in Fascist Italy (as well as in Francoist Spain), like those of publishers and translators in 1950s France, the UK, Australia or the USA, mostly applied to visual and verbal representations of love, nudity and sex, violence and death.

A notable exception to the 1938 ban was Disney comics. The circular dictated the 'Complete abolition of all foreign import material, with the exception of creations by Walt Disney, which stand out from the others for their artistic value and substantial morality' (in Gadducci, Gori and Lama 2011: 187, my translation). The exception for Disney comics was made for various cultural, political and economic reasons. It is well-known that Mussolini and his family enjoyed Disney characters, that Mussolini had personally welcomed Walt Disney in Rome in 1935 (and, it was rumoured, also in 1938), and reportedly Mussolini himself did not approve the ban on Disney comics in a list submitted to him (Gadducci, Gori and Lama 2011: 187–200). Furthermore, Disney's licensee in Italy was Mondadori, the main Italian publisher, which openly supported Fascism and acted almost as its official publisher. It was certainly not in favour of stopping a lucrative publishing venture (Rundle 2010). However, in 1942 the last Disney story appeared in an impoverished *Topolino* magazine, and in 1943 the magazine itself closed, reopening only in 1945 after the end of the hostilities. According to Becattini (2019: 15), it was Hitler himself who, enraged after hearing that a Mickey Mouse comics story made fun of Nazi leaders, requested not only that the story not be published in Italy, but also that the magazine itself be discontinued, and Mussolini complied. While in Germany state censorship stifled the birth of a comics industry, Italian institutional censorship and mechanisms of self-censorship favoured local production and laid the basis for the development of a local comics culture (Antonutti 2013; Sinibaldi 2016; Zanettin 2017).

A more recent case of institutional censorship is that of Disney comics published in Arabic in the MENA region (Zitawi 2004; 2008b; 2008a). The publication of Disney stories is here mostly managed by Disney-Jawa, a joint venture between Disney and the Saudi Jawa family, which issues licenses to Arabic publishing houses that produce and distribute the translations. Under Saudi law Disney-Jawa is compelled, like all authors, publishers and distributors, to provide the Ministry of Information with two copies of the intended publication for clearance prior to its publication, and more copies after publication. Disney-Jawa supervises the stories translated by its licensees, the main two of which are Al-Futtaim/ITP in the UAE, and Al-Qabas in Kuwait, after which it sends the stories to the Ministry of Information, which checks every story page and either concedes or bans publication, or requires minor changes to be implemented before publication. In order to prevent official censorship, translated Disney stories are first edited by the publishers and then revised by the Disney-Jawa editor in what can be considered a case of self-censorship (see below).

31.3.2 Self-censorship

Like in the case of institutional censorship, and regardless of whether it involves original or translated comics, a first type of self-censorship is simply non-publication. Both in the USA and elsewhere some commissioned stories deemed to go against values of 'decency' (moral or aesthetic) have never been published, others have never been reprinted and others have only been published after substantial changes to either dialogues or drawings or to both. Editorial control over comics published with the Disney signature can be exerted by both Disney Studio and local licensees. For instance, in the USA in the 1940s and 1950s the editors at Disney Studio in Burbank rejected several stories by Carl Barks and requested that others be partly redrawn. For instance, the Donald Duck story 'Treat of trick', written and drawn by Carl Barks in 1952, was deemed by American Disney editors to contain horror and sexual innuendos not suitable for Disney comics, and the author was asked to redraw some of the pages, while others were removed from the story. The original version of the story was first printed in the Netherlands in 1978, and with time, four recognisably different versions have been printed, containing 23, 32, 33 or 33 and a half pages, respectively (Manetti 2002; see also www.seriesam.com/barks/detc_ccus_wdc0064-u01.html). Similarly, in Italy Mario Gentilini, the director of the main Disney magazine, *Topolino*, rejected and required changes to be made to stories written by Guido Martina, who sometimes inserted in the stories rather graphic scenes of violence. The often-praised parody of Dante's Inferno by Martina and Bioletto (*L'inferno di Topolino*, 1948) was cleansed in later Italian reprints of some panels showing sinners in hell being sliced alive. The original version was only reprinted in a collector's edition in Italy, while other countries only published the sanitised version, mostly after the year 2000.

Though all Disney stories take place in the realm of fantasy, they often contain visual and verbal features pointing to the context in which they are produced, from background scenarios to cultural references. For instance, 1930s US stories were often set in rural America, while stories created by German authors in the 1960s and 1970s for the Studio Program had a distinct Bavarian flavour. Different countries also have different target readers and different cultural preferences. For instance, while Brazilian Mickey Mouse stories veer towards slapstick comedy, both American and Italian stories tend to be adventurous (see https://featherysociety.proboards.com/thread/1132/disney-comics-italian-countries).

> Even when foreign editors do not find it convenient to commission stories locally, they can select the type of story, and combination of stories ('story mix') which they consider suited to particular public taste and particular marketing conditions, in the country or countries they are serving [...] Expressed preferences of foreign editors reveal certain broad

differences in taste. Brazil and Italy tend towards more physical violence, more blood and guts; Chile […] tended (like Scandinavia, Germany and Holland), to more quiet adventures, aimed (apparently) at a younger age group. (Kunzle 1991: 10–11)

When selecting stories for publication in translation, licensees discard those that are deemed too much in conflict with local values or which would require too much editing to be amended.

Flows of translation and retranslation vary, as different countries favour the importation of Disney comics from some countries more than others. Apparently, for instance, 'Portugal has the highest rate of Italian translated stories outside of Italy, as well as having the highest rate of Brazilian stories outside of Brazil. You'll find even fewer Egmont and Dutch stories there, however' (see https://featherysociety.proboards.com/thread/1369/which-language-access-disney-comics). Stories created in Italy, which may contain violent imagery (e.g., references to killing or harming someone, images of weapons) are mostly not imported in the USA or in the Netherlands, though some Italian authors may also work on different types of stories for Egmont.

Some of the editorial changes that affect both original and translated stories can and have been described as acts of (self-)censorship. In the USA, while Disney never adhered to the Comics Code Authority, as if its compliance was taken for granted, Disney comics were always supervised, or self-censored, in order to prevent the publication of elements not in line with images and values that might have endangered their economic value. The Walt Disney Company has strict corporate guidelines, which prescribe, for instance, that American translations must be in plain, simple English, as opposed to the spoken/dialectal English of early American comics (see https://featherysociety.proboards.com/thread/823/another-thread-localisation-disney-solicits?page=3), and which have evolved over time (for instance, to expunge stories which may be seen as containing racial stereotypes). The Walt Disney Company can also have a say in stories published abroad. In a 1990 Italian story Mickey Mouse was shown in one panel taking off his shoes while sitting on the bed of his new girlfriend (in what turns out to be a dream), and this was used by a satirical magazine as supposed evidence that 'Topolino tromba' (Mickey Mouse has sex). The (hypothetical) breaking of the sexual taboo by a Disney character had some echo in the media, and the incident transpired in Burbank, where apparently a ban was issued. As a consequence, the story was never reprinted, neither in Italy nor elsewhere (Glide Manno 2020).

Some Disney stories are created primarily for national markets, though they may later be sold to foreign publishers, in which case dialogues and pictures of the translated stories are localised. Other stories, like those by the Studio Program or by Egmont, are created primarily for the international market. Stories created for international distribution are internationalised before being localised, i.e., Disney editors try to make sure that no culture-bound images or language (e.g., puns) are present (see https://featherysociety.proboards.com/thread/823/another-thread-localisation-disney-solicits?page=4) and try to avoid possibly controversial topics, e.g., references to religion and the supernatural. International productions, designed to make the publication of these stories more palatable to international licensees, may thus be said to be regulated by preventive economic self-censorship. Finally, modifications may be carried out by foreign licensees in order to prevent institutional censorship and/or to adapt the comics to local sensibilities.

When a story is, in fact, published in translation, both dialogues and images can be radically modified, or even completely replaced. While self-censorship also affects the creation of original comics, when different editions of the same story (in translation or not) are seen side by side, it becomes possible to observe what is deemed censorable. Visual alterations that involve the deletion, redrawing, retouching of images, panels or pages are especially apparent and 'visible'. Changes to both verbal and visual elements may be required from the author or implemented by local editors. These changes may concern cultural artifacts and conventions such as currency denomination but are also often related to areas such as sexuality, violence, religion and death. For instance, several stories by Don Rosa, written in English but first published in Denmark (in translation), were partly rewritten and redrawn when published in the USA. Some panels were added, some were deleted, and others were retouched. In one story guns were removed and replaced by pointing fingers. In another a bullet hole in the forehead of a man (in a picture) was removed. In a third story several panels portraying a horrific gigantic flea were removed, while in a fourth story some panels were added (in this case to fit a different publication format). Such changes can arguably be seen as instances of censorship and are in fact defined as such by Grünke (2001). However, the boundary between censorship and decency, 'good taste' and 'bad taste', 'free speech' and 'hate speech' are always shifting and relative to personal values and ideologies. What some see as acts of censorship others may see as legitimate interventions aimed at protecting corporate values or simply as personal aesthetic choices. As one American translator, Joe Torcivia, explains, he had some 'epic disagreements' with a fan 'over translations and more-so [over] what he calls "Censorship" and I term "Editorial Prerogative"' (see https://featherysociety.proboards.com/thr ead/418/localisation-tradition?page=4).

American and European Disney comics also undergo changes when published in countries which, like the predominantly Muslim Indonesia and Arab-speaking countries of the MENA (Middle East and North Africa) region, have markedly different cultural backgrounds and assumptions regarding what is perceived as appropriate or 'decent'. Similar to what happens in America and Europe, these changes can be, and have been, described as motivated by self-censorship, publishing guidelines or translator preferences. The first Disney stories in the MENA region were published in Egypt in 1958 by the publisher Dar Al-Hilal, in magazines that contained both stories created in Egypt and in translation, as well as non-Disney comics. Since 1993, however, Disney-Jawa has been the main distributor of Disney comics in the area, supervising the translation and distribution of stories produced mostly in France, the Netherlands, Italy and Denmark. Comics licensed by Disney-Jawa to Arab publishers are systematically monitored by the editors and, like in the USA, some of them are rejected and others are returned requiring modifications. Approved stories are then submitted to the Saudi Ministry of Information for final approval (see previous section). A list of taboo topics, references to which are consistently deleted, include romantic and sexual allusions, magic and supernatural occurrences, religion, the human body and images of pigs (Zitawi 2004; 2008a; 2008b). For instance, an Italian story submitted by the publisher Al-Qabas in Kuwait was rejected by Disney-Jawa's chief editor because it dealt with magic, even though the publisher had tried to edit out all visual and verbal references to it. In Disney-Jawa publications nostrils are consistently deleted from the nose of pig characters, and women's bodies are consistently covered, so that female characters wearing a bathing suit are blackened from neck to ankle. Conversely, in stories published by Dar Al-Hilal in Egypt, where there is no explicit regulatory body, it was left to the publisher to decide what could or could not be published without provoking the reaction of the regime or of religious organisations. The Dar Al-Hilal Disney license expired in 2003 (Zitawi 2004: 95). On the one hand, both verbal and visual editing is less pronounced in Egypt than in publications distributed in more conservative countries in the Arabic peninsula as far as religion and sexuality are concerned, and verbal references to romantic involvement were also not edited by Dar Al-Hilal. On the other hand, Uncle Scrooge's top hat is usually deleted in Egypt (seen as either a sign of 'Jewishness' or of Western culture) but not in translations supervised by Disney-Jawa (Zitawi 2008a: 144). Zitawi (2008b) does not construe these changes in terms of censorship,

The Routledge Handbook of Translation and Censorship

but rather describes them within the framework of Brown and Levinson's (1987) politeness theory. Zitawi sees official censorship as one component of a 'composite speaker', which includes Disney-Jawa, the Saudi Ministry of Information, licensed publishers and translators. Together, according to Zitawi, they act to minimise face-threatening acts in Disney comics in the form of negative images and stereotypical representations of Arabs, verbal and/or visual representations of taboo topics and potentially offensive forms of address.

The policies followed by the Egyptian publisher can be compared to those in place in Indonesia, which are instead described by Yuliasri (2017) in terms of censorship. Disney comics have been translated in Indonesia since 1974, and are currently published by Gramedia, the country's largest publisher. Like in Egypt, there is no official censoring body in Indonesia, so that '[c]ensorship is not imposed by the government, but is the responsibility of the translators (and publishers)' (Yuliasri 2017: 110). Gramedia also conforms to market censorship; for example, it withdrew from bookstores the Indonesian translation of Marjane Satrapi's *Persepolis* (George and Liew 2021: 192). As opposed to Zitawi's extensive analysis of both images and dialogues, Yuliasri only describes changes to the verbal text, showing how translations are edited in order to make them conform to perceived cultural norms of acceptability, 'i.e., for educational and good moral values, which is also reflected in "decent" language' (Yuliasri 2017: 107). Edits include omissions; for instance, mentions of 'god' are deleted, as are translations of verbal sarcasm and insults, and generalisations, for instance 'pigs' are turned into 'farm animals' in translation. During an interview, a senior editor who supervises all translations, confirmed that 'decency' was prioritised over clarity and the preservation of humour, and that the dialogues were rewritten or adapted in order to favour 'Indonesian' values of 'collectivity and harmony' over 'Western' values of 'individuality and privacy' (Yuliasri 2017: 109). These references to moral values and decency echo similar calls that frame 1950s self-censorship in the Americas, Europe and Australia.

31.4   Current Debates

Comics in translation and the translation of comics offer no small field of research for studies in translation and censorship. Research focusing on this topic is, however, still limited. Apart from those previously cited in this chapter, studies that explicitly focus on censorship in translated comics include Rahimi (2015) on the translation into Persian of Hergé's Tintin albums before and after the 1978–79 Iranian Revolution (see also Kenevisi and Sanatifar 2016); Yean Fun Chow, Hasuria Che Omar and Wan Rose Eliza Abdul Rahman (2021) on the translation of manga in Malaysia; and Polli (2019, 2021, 2022) on the translation of underground American comix in Italy.

The case study presented here offers only a general introduction to translation and censorship in the world of Disney comics, based mostly on anecdotal evidence and without touching on important aspects such as issues of copyright, censorship and ideological bias also in favour of, rather than against, Disney comics (see e.g., Dorfman and Mattelart 1972; Dorfman 2018; Krause 2022; F. Gadducci and Tavosanis 2000). Disney comics are (primarily) aimed at children; therefore, this chapter also does not touch on topics related to censorship of translated adult (only) comics including, for instance, pornographic comics, graphic novels and political cartoons, not to mention the several genres of the largest comics industry in the world, Japanese manga. For reasons of space, only two of these possible areas of research are briefly mentioned, i.e., pornographic comics and political cartoons.

The case of Japanese erotic comics imported into Italy makes for an interesting case of reverse censorship. Though various attempts were made in Japan to regulate the production

Censorship of Comics in Translation

of *hentai* (erotic manga), including a major campaign launched in 1990 that involved 'everybody from left-wing feminists to right-wing conservatives' (Sabin 2003: 208), no legislation was enacted to prevent their publication. However, Article 175 of the Japanese Criminal Code forbids the publication of obscene materials. Specifically, depictions of sexual intercourse and pubic hair are considered obscene, and the vast majority of hentai publishers abide by the law and whiten out details of sexual intercourse even in explicit, full-screen frames of sexual acts. In Italy pornographic comics had been sold in newsstands since the 1960s and include the explicit depiction of sexual organs and intercourse. Thus, when erotic manga were introduced in translation in Italy, in several cases publishers went to the extreme of editing the pictures to remove censorship in the original artwork, i.e., by having missing details of genitalia re-drawn in the panels.

The translation of political cartoons is certainly another topic of interest for censorship scholars. Even within a community sharing the same language, not to mention when a cartoon is reprinted in another country in translation, there is no one-to-one correspondence between a cartoonist's chosen signifiers and what they can be taken to signify, since even drawings that are straightforwardly denotative can be prone to misinterpretation, as exemplified by the real life stories of cartoonists and comic artists recounted in words and drawings by George and Liew (2021). As the two authors put it,

> [w]hile cartooning as a mode of communication could be said to be a universal language, each cartoon uses symbolic signs whose intended connotations are based on conventions that are culturally specific. The clever metaphor falls flat when it confronts readers who don't share the same stock of cultural references the cartoonist takes for granted (George and Liew 2021: 396).

The fact that images do not presuppose knowledge of written language to be (mis)interpreted contributes to the possibility of alternative readings. A well-known example is that of the cartoons showing the prophet Muhammad published in a Danish newspaper in 2005. When these political cartoons, that were already controversial in their original context, were reprinted in other countries, new interpretative contexts were supplied. Thus, in the Netherlands,

> the defense of the cartoons was embraced mostly by the secularist and anti-immigrant right. In France the cartoons were incorporated in a rather different political landscape: the discussion focused on freedom of the press and the position of religion in the public sphere, therefore the cartoons were published also in left-wing newspapers such as *Liberation*. In the USA, where religion has a more central position in public life than in Europe, the cartoons weren't published in any of the important newspapers. And in societies with predominant Muslim populations, public responses (sometimes sponsored by national governments) were generally angry and indignant, even though responses between Muslim nations varied widely. (Davies et al. 2008: 9)

The assassination of 12 people working at the satirical magazine Charlie Hebdo in Paris in 2015 can be seen as 'the climax of the orgy of outrage' (George and Liew 2021: 3) that began with the publication of the Danish cartoons, and as an extreme example of violent censorship directed against ideological-political-religious taboo topics. The Paris massacre sparked a debate about the fine line between freedom of expression and hate speech, which has far from subsided.

Further Reading

George, Cherian and Liew, Sonny. 2021. *Red Lines. Political Cartoons and the Struggle Against Censorship.* Cambridge, MA, and London: M.I.T. Press.
A comprehensive report—between graphic narrative and scholarly research—on censorship of political cartoons around the world.

Green, Jonathan and Karolides, Nicholas J. 2005. *Encyclopedia of Censorship, New Edition.* New York: Facts on File.
Contains details of censorship legislation and social campaigns against comics in the main entry on 'Comic Books Censorship' but also elsewhere in the volume, focusing on English-speaking countries.

Hajdu, David. 2009. *The Ten-Cent Plague: The Great Comic-Book Scare and How It Changed America.* New York: Macmillan.
A detailed account of the comics controversy and censorship in the USA in the 1950s.

Sabin, Roger. 2003. *Adult Comics: An Introduction.* London and New York: Routledge.
An historical introduction to comics for adult readers, which illustrates the complex relationship between the comics industry and censorship, with particular reference to the British and US contexts.

Zanettin, Federico. 2017. 'Translation, Censorship and the Development of European Comics Cultures', *Perspectives: Studies in Translation Theory and Practice*, 26(6): 868–84.
An historical overview of the role played by translation in the development of national traditions of graphic storytelling in Europe between the 1930s and the 1950s, highlighting institutional censorship policies and self-censorship practices.

Notes

1 Unless otherwise noted, all information concerning Disney comics is derived from the encyclopedic history of Disney comics compiled by Alberto Becattini (2019; for a previous English version see Becattini 2016), and from an interview held on 4 April 2022 in Lucca, Italy (Becattini 2022). Alberto Becattini is a Disney fan, historian, translator and editor, who collaborated with several Italian and international Disney licensees and authors.

2 The most comprehensive bibliographic resource which documents all Disney comics published worldwide is the I.N.D.U.C.K.S. online database, which as of 2022 had indexed, by title, author, country of original and other publication, etc. over 150,000 stories from 73 countries (https://featherysociety.proboards.com/), Scrooge MacDuck Wiki—The Unified Disney Comics Wiki (https://scrooge-mcduck.fandom.com/), Vintage Comics (https://vintagecomics.forumcommunity.net/), McDrake International (http://bb.mcdrake.nl/engdisney/index.php), Papersera.net (www.papersera.net/forum/), Ventenni Paperoni www.ventennipaperoni.com, and translator blogs (e.g., https://tiahblog.blogspot.com/ by Joe Torcivia, translating into English for the US publisher IDW), among others.

References

Antonutti, Isabelle. 2013. 'Fumetto et Fascisme: la naissance de la Bande Dessinée Italienne', *Comicalités. Études de Culture Graphique*, 1–30. https://doi.org/10.4000/comicalites.1306

Becattini, Alberto. 2016. *Disney Comics: The Whole Story.* S.l.: Theme Park Press.

Becattini, Alberto. 2019. *Disney a fumetti. Storie, autori e personaggi, 1930–2018.* Reggio Emilia: ANAFI.

Becattini, Alberto. 2022. I fumetti Disney in traduzione. Interview by Federico Zanettin. Audio recorded.

Billiani, Francesca. 2007. 'Assessing Boundaries. Censorship and Translation. An Introduction', in F. Billiani (ed.), *Modes of Censorship in Translation: National Contexts and Diverse Media.* Manchester: St Jerome, 1–25.

Bosco Tierno, Caterina. 2015. 'Translation, Pseudotranslation and Adaptation of Disney Comics in Italian Language and Culture', in N. Mälzer (ed.), *Comics – Übersetzungen Und Adaptionen.* Berlin: Frank & Timme, 268–79.

Brown, Penelope and Levinson, Stephen. 1987. *Politeness: Some Universals in Language Usage.* Cambridge: Cambridge University Press.

Bryan, Peter Cullen. 2021. *Creation, Translation, and Adaptation in Donald Duck Comics: The Dream of Three Lifetimes*. Cham, Switzerland: Springer International Publishing.

Castelli, Alfredo. 1995. 'America on My Mind', *afnews.info Volume 1: 1995/2021* (blog). www.afnews.info/wordpress/speciali/propage/comesidiventaautoredifumetti/america-on-my-mind-by-alfredo-castelli/

Chow, Yean Fun, Che Omar, Hasuria and Abdul Rahman, Wan Rose Eliza. 2021. 'Manga Translation and Censorship Issues in Malaysia', *KEMANUSIAAN The Asian Journal of Humanities*, 28(1): 1–21. https://doi.org/10.21315/kajh2021.28.1.1

Comics Magazine Association of America. 1955. Comic Book Code of 1954. United States Government Printing Office. Wikisource. https://en.wikisource.org/wiki/Comic_book_code_of_1954

Davies, Christie, Kuipers, Giselinde, Lewis, Paul, Martin, Rod A., Oring, Elliott and Raskin, Victor. 2008. 'The Muhammad Cartoons and Humor Research: A Collection of Essays', in P. Lewis (ed.), *Humor. International Journal of Humor Research*, 21(1): 1–46. https://doi.org/10.1515/HUMOR.2008.001

Dorfman, Ariel. 2018. 'How We Roasted Donald Duck, Disney's Agent of Imperialism', *The Guardian*, 5 October 2018, sec. Books. www.theguardian.com/books/2018/oct/05/ariel-dorfman-how-we-roasted-donald-duck-disney-agent-of-imperialism-chile-coup

Dorfman, Ariel and Mattelart, Armand. 1972. *Pare leer el Pato Donald*. Siglo XXI Editores. Buenos Aires.

Gadducci, Fabio, Gori, Leonardo and Lama, Sergio. 2011. *Eccetto Topolino: lo scontro culturale tra fascismo e fumetti*. Eboli: NPE.

Gadducci, Fabio and Tavosanis, Mirko. 2000. *Casa Disney. Autori e diritto d'autore*. Bologna: PuntoZero.

George, Cherian and Liew, Sonny. 2021. *Red Lines. Political Cartoons and the Struggle Against Censorship*. Cambridge, MA, and London: M.I.T. Press.

Glide Manno, Antonio. 2020. 'Topolino tromba! La storia proibita dalla Disney', *Ventenni Paperoni* (blog). 25 June 2020. www.ventennipaperoni.com/2020/06/25/topolino-tromba/

Green, Jonathan and Karolides, Nicholas J. 2005. *Encyclopedia of Censorship, New Edition*. New York: Facts on File.

Grun, Maria and Dollerup, Cay. 2003. '"Loss" and "Gain" in Comics', *Perspectives*, 11(3): 197–216. https://doi.org/10.1080/0907676X.2003.9961474

Grünke, Alexander. 2001. 'Changed and Censored Stories', Duckhunt. All About the Works of Disney Artist Keno Don Rosa. 21 October 2001. www.duckhunt.de/censorship/

Hatfield, Charles. 2005. *Alternative Comics: An Emerging Literature*. Jackson: University Press of Mississipi.

Kaindl, Klaus. 1999. 'Thump, Whizz, Poom: A Framework for the Study of Comics under Translation'. *Target*, 11(2): 263–288. https://doi.org/10.1075/target.11.2.05kai

Kenevisi, Mohammad Sadegh and Sanatifar Mohammad Saleh. 2016. 'Comics Polysystem in Iran: A Case Study of the Persian Translations of Les Aventures de Tintin', *TranscUlturAl*, 8(2): 174–204. https://doi.org/10.21992/T9DK98

Krause, Till. 2022. 'I diritti di Topolino'. Translated by Susanna Karasz. *Internazionale*, 18 March 2022.

Kuhiwczak, Piotr and Merkle, Denise. 2011. 'Translation Studies Forum: Translation and Censorship', *Translation Studies*, 4(3): 358–73. https://doi.org/10.1080/14781700.2011.589657

Kunzle, David. 1991. 'Introduction to the English Edition', in A. Dorfman and A. Mattelart (eds.), *How to Read Donald Duck*. New York: I.G. Editions, 11–23.

Lepore, Mario. 2012. 'Storia e storie. Introduzione', in A. Becattini, L. Boschi, L. Gori and A. Sani (eds.), *I Disney Italiani*. Roma: NPE, I, 10–11.

Manetti, Francesco. 2002. 'Dolcetto scherzetto: traversie di una storia', *Paperino. Carl Bark's Comic Art*, 16. Milano: Edizioni If, 88–90.

McCabe, Caitlin. 2016. '"Smut and Trash:" A Brief History of Comics Censorship in Germany', *Comic Book Legal Defense Fund* (blog). 9 September 2016. http://cbldf.org/2016/09/smut-and-trash-a-brief-history-of-comics-censorship-in-germany/

Meda, Juri. 2002. 'Vietato ai minori. Censura e fumetto nel secondo dopoguerra tra il 1949 e il 1953', *Schizzo 10 'Idee'*, 72: 73–88.

Merkle, Denise. 2018. 'Translation and Censorship', in F. Fernández and J. Evans (eds.), *The Routledge Handbook of Translation and Politics*. London and New York: Routledge, 238–53.

Moor, Nicole. 2012. *The Censor's Library: Uncovering the Lost History of Australia's Banned Books*. St Lucia: University of Queensland Press.

Müller, Beate. 2004. 'Censorship and Cultural Regulation: Mapping the Territory', in B. Müller (ed.), *Censorship & Cultural Regulation in the Modern Age*. Amsterdam and New York: Rodopi, 1–31.

Patrick, Kevin. 2011. 'A Design for Depravity: Horror Comics and the Challenge of Censorship in Australia, 1950–1986', *Script & Print*, 35(3): 133–56.

Polli, Chiara. 2019. 'Translating the Untold: Greg Iron's Raw War Comics and the Challenge to American Mythologies', in C. Polli and A. Binelli (eds.), *Rielaborazioni del mito nel fumetto contemporaneo*. Trento: Università degli Studi di Trento, 179–208.

Polli, Chiara. 2021. 'Isotopy as a Tool for the Analysis of Comics in Translation: The Italian "Rip-Off" of Gilbert Shelton's Freak Brothers', *Punctum. International Journal of Semiotics*, 7(2): 17–43.

Polli, Chiara. 2022. 'Subversive Sixties in Ink: Underground Comix, Censorship, and Translation Between the United States and Italy', *TTR: Traduction, Terminologie, Rédaction*, 35(2): 129–60.

Rahimi, Mina Zand. 2015. 'Ideologically Driven Strategies in the Translation of Comics Before and After the Islamic Revolution', *International Journal of English Language and Translation Studies*, 3(4): 42–9.

Repubblica italiana. 1965. FUMETTI NERI- Sentenza N. 52/65 R. Sen.

Rundle, Christopher. 2010. *Publishing Translations in Fascist Italy*. Oxford: Peter Lang.

Sabin, Roger. 2003. *Adult Comics: An Introduction*. London and New York: Routledge.

Sergi, Joe. 2012. 'A History of Censorship: Richard Felton Outcault and the Yellow Kid'. Comic Book Legal Defense Fund. http://cbldf.org/2012/07/a-history-of-censorship-richard-felton-outcalt-and-the-yellow-kid/

Sinibaldi, Caterina. 2016. 'Between Censorship and Innovation: The Translation of American Comics During Italian Fascism', *New Readings*, 16: 1–21.

Spiegelman, Art. 1991. *Maus. A Survivor's Tale*. New York: Pantheon Books.

Strange, Jeffrey J., Green, Melanie C. and Brook, Timothy C. 2000. 'Censorship and the Regulation of Expression', in E. F. Borgatta and R. J. V. Montgomery (eds.), *Encyclopedia of Sociology*, Second Edition, Volume 1. New York: McMillan, 267–81.

Tosti, Andrea. 2011. *Topolino e il fumetto Disney italiano: storia, fasti, declino e nuove prospettive*. Latina: Tunué.

Wertham, Fredric. 1954. *Seduction of the Innocent. The Influence of Comic Books on Today's Youth*. New York: Rinehart & Company.

Yuliasri, Issy. 2017. 'Translators' Censorship in English-Indonesian Translation of Donald Duck Comics', *Indonesian Journal of Applied Linguistics*, 7(1): 105–16. https://doi.org/10.17509/ijal.v7i1.6863

Zanettin, Federico. 2008. 'The Translation of Comics as Localization. On Three Italian Translations of La Piste Des Navajos', in F. Zanettin (ed.), *Comics in Translation*. Manchester: St Jerome, 200–19.

Zanettin, Federico. 2017. 'Translation, Censorship and the Development of European Comics Cultures', *Perspectives: Studies in Translation Theory and Practice*, 26(6): 868–84. https://doi.org/10.1080/09076 76X.2017.1351456

Zanettin, Federico. 2018. 'Translating Comics and Graphic Novels', in S.-A. Harding and O. Carbonell i Cortés (eds.), *The Routledge Handbook of Translation and Culture*. London and New York: Routledge, 445–60.

Zanettin, Federico. 2022. 'Global Comic Book Heroes: Intra- and Inter-Cultural Translations of Tintin, Asterix, and Paperinik Comics', *New Readings*, 18: 52–69.

Zitawi, Jehan. 2004. 'The Translation of Disney Comics in the Arab World: A Pragmatic Perspective'. PhD, Manchester: University of Manchester. https://ethos.bl.uk/OrderDetails.do?uin=uk.bl.ethos.488196

Zitawi, Jehan. 2008a. 'Contextualizing Disney Comics Within the Arab Culture', *Meta: Journal Des Traducteurs*, 53(1): 139–53. https://doi.org/10.7202/017979ar

Zitawi, Jehan. 2008b. 'Disney Comics in the Arab Culture(s): A Pragmatic Perspective', in F. Zanettin (ed.), *Comics in Translation*. Manchester: St Jerome, 152–71.

32
CENSORSHIP IN VIDEO GAME LOCALISATION

Ugo Ellefsen

32.1 Core issues and Topics

32.1.1 Introduction

The first hurdle encountered when discussing censorship in video game localisation is defining 'video game localisation' itself, which is composed of two terms, 'video games' and 'localisation', and then defining what is meant by the word 'censorship'. The following discussion of terminology will take a layered approach.

A primary definition of video games would consider the medium as a digital software product that 1) relies on either text or images to convey its interactions with users, 2) is supported by a variety of platforms, such as consoles, phones or personal computers, and 3) involves one or multiple players connected through physical or networked environments (Frasca 2001: 4). The implied interactions and feedback loops between code, machine and humans are mediated through a plethora of interfaces, controllers, keyboards, touch screens, monitors and so on. To encompass the wide variety of artefacts that fall under the video game moniker, Miguel Bernal-Merino has relied on the term 'Multimedia Interactive Entertainment Software' (MIES), which includes a broad range of products from preinstalled games on computers or phones to gambling machines and products that are considered 'adult entertainment' (2014). The inclusion of 'multimedia' in Bernal-Merino's term also addresses the multimodal aspect of video games, considered as such 'because [video games] combine a linguistic system with a pictographic or an audio and visual one, and these different semiotic systems are creatively interwoven to achieve a somehow more lifelike, illuminating or even cathartic communication experience with the receivers of the product' (Bernal-Merino 2014: 46). This concept of 'multimodality' is crucial in assessing potential content modification issues and censorship considering that, beyond textual content as a first level of source cultural material to be translated, non-textual yet culturally relevant elements might require some level of adaptation to be exportable. Beyond their multimodality, a relevant dichotomy in the ontology of video games concerns whether games should be considered commodities or works of art. This dichotomy is especially pertinent to a discussion of censorship because censoring agents and regulatory bodies will often apply different rules to content alteration depending on whether content is defined as art or a commodity. Moreover, such considerations evolve and, eventually,

DOI: 10.4324/9781003149453-39

regulations and norms adapt to new ontological classifications. While the artistic value of video games is often asserted in academia, the industry has been relying on the ambiguous ontology of video games to defend its decisions and legal posture, especially in matters of censorship. It asks regulatory bodies to soften restrictions in some regions, while promoting approaches to public and structural censorship as necessary for the commercialisation of products in other locales.

It is generally assumed that video games are embedded in production processes that are part of the culture industry and so face the same challenges as other sectors within this specific segment of industry, such as newspapers, television or music, namely 'the high risk involved in producing content, the tension between creativity and profit, the high production and low reproduction costs, the semi-public good nature of games and the artificial construction of scarcity in the market' (Kerr 2017: 5–6). As such, the logic behind localising video games and censoring them tend to follow (local) market rules and norms.

As for localisation, the broad use and general acceptance of the term, especially within the industry, presuppose that the task is different from translation. Localisation is defined as a form of adaptation related to the global commercialisation of software (Esselink 2000), a process that combines 'language and technology to produce a product that can cross cultural, and language barriers' (Esselink 2003: 4). Often, the term departs from its technological connection and its relationship to the digital. In this broader context, it is used to define tasks that encompass various instances of linguistic and cultural transfer of a given content during the process of globalisation to make it local in character so as to facilitate its sale outside of its culture of origin. Within academia, the debate over whether localisation in its wider sense is merely another form of translation applied to industrial processes is ongoing (Bernal-Merino 2014). To explain how video game localisation as a task differs in several respects from translation, scholarly works have relied on terminology such as 'transcreation', which is a language and culture transfer task that entails potential departure from the source text for the sake of preserving the 'look and feel' of the original experience as opposed to fidelity to source content (Fry 2003 in O'Hagan and Mangiron 2013: 198). Moreover, when paired with video games, localisation is often perceived as a very *skopos*-based form of language transfer, in which adequate user experience matters more than equivalence-based textual fidelity (O'Hagan and Mangiron 2013). This flexibility as a justification for extra-linguistic manipulation is central to our understanding of censorship and the alterations, removals or additions of content implied by this definition of video game localisation. Moreover, due to the complexity of localisation endeavours and the multiple agents involved in producing a video game for one or more target locales, authors often rely on a definition of 'games' as created and localised through shared authorship (Bernal-Merino 2014) or collaborative authorship (Mandiberg 2017). Thus, any entity, whether it be a member of the production team, a regulatory body or even the audience, can become an agent in the process of video game creation and localisation.

From the previous discussion, a connection begins to emerge between localisation as a specific activity and as a form of acceptable source-culture-content-modification for the purpose of adequate global commercialisation. This connection between the flexibility offered to the 'localiser' and the potential alteration of the source material seems to be part of normative and acceptable work processes, not unlike in other areas of translational activity (Brunette 2002). As such, it becomes particularly difficult to determine whether a specific divergence from the source material can be included in the definition of 'censorship'. This definitional vagueness results from the tendency to consider video game localisation as a form of adaptation or transcreation for a type of content often perceived first as a product destined for mass consumption, and second as a form of art. Censorship found in video game localisation is mainly enacted by regulatory and government bodies, but it is also industry-imposed through developers, publishers or platform holders, and finally, it can be enacted by translators or language service providers and as such is defined as self-censorship (O'Hagan and Mangiron 2013: 224–26). Because of the status of video games as complex cultural artefacts, akin to literary productions, the definition of censorship used for this chapter will rely on Brownlie's taxonomy of public censorship, structural censorship and self-censorship (Brownlie 2007: 205). Self-censorship— as enacted by translators themselves —does take place in video games localisation, but it is difficult to document without access to specific materials and even then, nondisclosure agreements prevent localisers from freely discussing their practice. Therefore, this chapter will focus on public censorship, as 'imposed by authorities through implicit laws' (Brownlie 2007: 205), and structural censorship, where censorship is enacted 'through the structure of society itself, […] on the structure of the field which discourse circulates, […] without explicit laws' (Brownlie 2007: 205–206). This taxonomy allows us to uncover both overt and covert forms of censorship, and it becomes especially relevant in a discussion of censorship in video game localisation because the definition of censorship seems to change in response to commercial versus legal imperatives. Any form of ban on the distribution of a video game product, or source content alteration during the intralinguistic, interlinguistic, intersemiotic or inter-platform transfer, whether it be enforced by structures, internal forces or forces external to the context of production within the source and target cultures or within professional circles and numerous intermediaries, will be considered a form of censorship for the purposes of this examination of what censorship in video game localisation 'looks and feels' like. These parameters for investigation provide us with the means necessary to address both audience and producer definitions of censorship.

32.1.2 *Cultural Distance and Culturalisation*

As mentioned above, video game localisation extends beyond pure linguistic content; it is therefore important to assess how the intercultural transfer of a given video game may require changes to the core gameplay, to non-textual or to purely linguistic features. The scope of changes also lies in the perceived 'cultural distance' between the source and target cultures.

Early in the intercultural movement of games between Japan and the US, some localised versions underwent major changes to game mechanics once they crossed geopolitical borders. A notable example is *Final Fantasy IV* (Square 1991), which was labelled *Final Fantasy II* for the US market, since only the first game had been released in English. The game received significant cuts in gameplay features because the Japanese source game was deemed too complicated for American audiences. Along with simpler potential strategies offered to players, a dancing woman in the North American game was graphically modified, depicting her wearing clothes instead of a bikini. Certain graphics in the next North American episode of the series (*Final Fantasy III* in the US, *Final Fantasy VI* in Japan (Square 1994)) were also censored; for example, sprites were modified to cover their partial nudity. The case of 'mature themes', such as the depiction of nudity and sexual language, appears to be one of the common content elements addressed in video game localisation censorship between Japan and the United States, with American localisers appearing to perceive Japanese nudity and sexual content as excessive (Carlson and Corliss 2011).

Religion is another topic that requires a certain amount of content awareness and alteration to enable exportation to foreign locales. Japanese games, such as *Castlevania* (Konami 1986) or *Dragon Warrior III* (Chunsoft 1986), which depicted Christian crosses, or games such as *Lufia*

II (Neverland 1995), which relied on occult symbols like pentagrams as part of magic rituals, were censored in their US versions. Beyond the graphic display of potentially sensitive religious themes, other details required modification for export. Another example can be found in the general-audience-rated game *LittleBigPlanet* (Media Molecule 2008), which became famous for including potential religious misrepresentation and so serves as a cautionary tale for developers. The 2D platform game, which was about to be released, featured a background music track called *Tapha Niang* by Toumani Diabate, a Malian musician. The track included lyrics that referenced Surah 29 verse 57, and Surah 55 verse 26 of the Qur'an; however, these references had gone unnoticed by Sony's content assessors. The official release of the game had to be recalled and re-released after the developer applied a corrective patch to avoid a ban in certain locales. Another example of the relationship between religion and censorship will be discussed in the following section on applied public censorship.

As even subtle content changes can have a substantial impact on sales, a perceived cultural distance between source(s) and target(s) cultures justifies a significant number of changes and departures from the source content. A core issue in the censorship of video games in the process of localisation involves identifying what is censored, which is often difficult to do, given that censoring agents (developers, publishers, platform holders, language service providers and translator themselves) often obfuscate the processes involved and rely on unclear terminology.

Industry-led endeavours aimed at international commercialisation through risk mitigation play a central role in the globalisation and localisation strategy called 'culturalisation'. The intercultural transfers implied by culturalisation auditing as an assessment of foreign target culture audience reception extend far beyond language and may require the modification of game assets such as graphics, sounds and elements of gameplay. The goal of culturalisation is to protect and facilitate the sale of video game products at the international level to avoid state-issued policy control over distribution, as well as additional costs or financial losses. Due to the significant budgets required to develop modern games, market them and ensure their international viability, along with maximising profits, the risk of being banned or reclassified by regulatory organisations is taken very seriously by game developers.

32.1.3 *Applied Public Censorship and National Policies*

Public censorship in the form of a ban on sales and policy-informed changes to content and access is generally what comes to mind when discussing censorship in the video game industry. Three geopolitical spaces (China, Iran and Germany) will be discussed to illustrate the sensitivities of authorities to certain content that lead to public censorship and the types of content modification that result.

32.1.3.1 *China*

The People's Republic of China is considered an especially sensitive space for game developers since there is no room for negotiation regarding imported content (Edwards 2011). Nevertheless, China as a gaming industry market cannot be disregarded since it is considered almost on par with the US in terms of revenue generation (Wijman 2023). To understand the specificities of China as a market, we will summarise its video game history along with the regulatory bodies there that oversee video game content.

From 2000 to 2015, access to video game content through the importation of video game consoles into China was banned, which was justified by the authorities as a measure to protect

Censorship in Video Game Localisation

'public morals', although outsiders were quick to label the legislation as economic protectionism (Liboriussen et al. 2015). Consequently, most of the hardware-bound video game content consumed in mainland China was either from the 'gray' market or developed in China. With the democratisation of the internet in the early 2000s, foreign online games entered Chinese territory. In those early days, legislators had no proper means of addressing content distribution. To monitor the flow of content coming into China, the government assigned the task to two different departments: the General Administration of Press and Publication of the Peoples' Republic of China (GAPP) and the Ministry of Culture of the Peoples' Republic of China (MOC). This bipartite system allows for checks and balances, but it can also delay the release of games on Chinese territory by up to 22 months in some instances (Zhang 2012). In keeping with modern standardised procedures, the GAPP assesses the suitability of games pre-release while the MOC oversees games post-release (Zhang 2012). The content monitored by the GAPP and the MOC includes:

1 content that opposes the basic principles established in the Constitution
2 content that endangers the unification, sovereignty and territorial integrity of the State
3 content that divulges secrets of the State, harming national security, or impairing the honour and interests of the State
4 content that incites the enmity, discrimination of nationalities, jeopardising the unity amongst the various ethnic groups, or violating the customs and habits of minority nationalities
5 content that spreads cults or superstitions
6 content that disturbs the social order and destroys social stability
7 content that incites pornography, gambling, violence or instigating a crime
8 content that insults or libels others, or violates the lawful rights and interests of others
9 content that endangers social moralities or fine national cultural traditions
10 other content that is prohibited by current laws and administrative regulations or by the State. (MOC 2011; quoted in Zhang 2012).

Instead of being sold as modified, games are occasionally banned from sale when content alteration fails to meet the content requirements mentioned above. For example, from its original release in 2002 to its most current version, the World War II-based strategy game franchise *Heart of Irons* (Paradox Development Studios) has been banned from sale in China for 'distorting history and damaging China's sovereignty and territorial integrity' (Sheng and Zhu 2004, quoted in Zhang 2012). The game allows players to assume the role of political leaders, including those of fascist states, and does not include regions such as Tibet and Taiwan as part of Greater China on the world map (Zhang 2012).

While localisation generally entails some amount of content modification across locales, for the Chinese market specifically, game developers may have to significantly redesign in-game graphical assets to ensure approval by the authorities. This was the case for the Chinese release of the 2012 game *Diablo III* (Blizzard Entertainment), which required attenuation of violence: blood was coloured black instead of red, exposed skeletons were covered with flesh and wound marks were removed. Overall, it is estimated that 18% of the total graphical assets of the game has been altered to comply with official Chinese regulations (3DM Games 2015, quoted in Dong and Mangiron 2018). This can be costly for game developers, but given the size of the Chinese market, the modifications are considered worthwhile, offering a significant return on investment. The Chinese government has also put in place regulated processes to ensure proper localisation and to position itself as a partner with the industry. To facilitate localisation and avoid pitfalls, game publishers that are willing to enter the Chinese market are legally bound to cooperate with local companies to

509

ensure compliance with national regulations (Kerr 2017). This partnership between non-Chinese publishers and local developers has been highly profitable for companies such as Tencent, which went from a local company in 2012 to the most profitable video game company in the world in 2013 in terms of revenue generation (Kerr 2017).

32.1.3.2 Iran

Iran as a geopolitical space is also considered a sensitive foreign market because there is no separation of church and state (Edwards 2011), and Islam is the predominant religion. Iran is estimated to have a population of gamers totalling 28 million, which is not a negligible market for developers (Khoshsaligheh and Ameri 2020). The following subsection will summarise the Iranian context in which the regulatory body overseeing video game content operates and outlines its general functioning principles.

In 2010, the Iran National Foundation of Computer Games, an affiliate organisation of the Iranian Ministry of Culture and Islamic Guidance, announced the creation of an Islamic video game rating system and created an authority called the Entertainment Software Rating Association (ESRA) (Šisler 2013). This organisation is responsible for game content assessment, but, as opposed to other rating boards, the organisation does not base its content classification solely on age but also on 'the culture, society and the special values of Islam' (Alexander 2010). Generally, in the Middle East, and specifically in Muslim majority countries such as Iran, the policies in place support a de-westernisation of game development (Šisler 2013) and of localisation by extension. The list of content considered harmful by the organisation includes 187 items, although they can be categorised around seven principal themes: graphic representation of violence, tobacco and drug use, sexual stimuli, fear, religious value violation, violation of social norms and 'hopelessness' (ESRA Booklet in Piasecki and Malekpour 2016). The ESRA relies on three committees to assess the suitability of a specific video game content: sociological, psychological and Islamic assessments are produced by the committees, which act as a check and balance system and also provide a process for content assessment.

The ESRA will often require that developers change some content to suit the target audience in order to gain access to the Iranian market or to authorise sale on Iranian territory. Only a game that is judged to have been modified in an undetectable way, with quality assets for example, will be rated acceptable by the ESRA (Piasecki and Malekpour 2016): common forms of censorship include adding clothing to cover body parts or changing animations so that characters do not bow down to idols (Piasecki and Malekpour 2016). While the changes are supposed to be invisible, recent audience research has shown that Iranian gamers are generally aware that the games have been censored so they seek source language versions of the game (Khoshsaligheh and Ameri 2020). Censorship can even be mechanically problematic and 'game-breaking' for Iranian players when it obfuscates crucial information that is required for the completion of specific elements of gameplay. In the Iranian version of *Grand Theft Auto San Andreas* (Rock Star North 2004), for example, one mission involves eliminating a character who can be recognised because he is seen kissing a female character in a scene. Due to governmental policies on displays of sexuality, the kissing scene was removed. As a result, Iranian players have expressed dissatisfaction that they are unable to identify and eliminate the character in question, and thus complete the mission (Afzali and Zahiri 2021). It is important to note here that some of the games officially distributed in Iran have not been localised since the country has not signed any international copyright agreements. As such, official distribution rights being tied to copyright and intellectual property have prevented official localisations from making their way into the Iranian market. Because ESRA is a recent

Censorship in Video Game Localisation

organisation in the history of video game publishing in Iran, the market has historically relied on 'hacked' localised versions. As such, a significant portion of international games sold in Iran has been modified and censored by hacker groups and sold unofficially through gray-market channels (Piasecki and Malekpour 2016).

32.1.3.3   Germany

Officially, according to the *Unterhaltungssoftware Selbstkontrolle* (USK), the German rating board, no censorship takes place in Germany because freedom of expression is protected under Article 5 paragraph 1 of German Basic Law (USK 2023). Nevertheless, Germany is known for imposing strict rules on video game content, which is often decried by stakeholders within the video game industry as 'unneeded censorship' (Stöcker 2009). USK's justifications are rooted in the historical debate over video game violence and the particular impact of violence on younger audiences. This justification allows the government to alter content given that 'the right to freedom of expression "is limited [...] by statutory provision for the protection of children and young persons", i.e., by the provisions made in the German Children and Young Persons' Protection Act' (USK 2023). Due to Germany's focus on games as commodities and their potential impact on younger audiences, two important video game themes have been considered problematic for German lawmakers: violence, a common theme for rating boards all over the world, as well as Nazi symbolism and representations of the Third Reich.

To comply with the rules put in place by USK, video game developers have been constantly modifying games where humans are enacting violence or being subjected to it. This has led developers to design assets for specific markets such as Germany, where the blood of enemies or protagonists is changed into a green liquid to pretend that players were killing aliens, zombies or robots (Chandler and O'Malley 2011). The infamously violent racing game *Carmaggedon* (Stainless Games 1997) underwent a significant change to comply with USK's policy on representations of violence: it had to turn the various human pedestrians who could be run over by the players into zombies. Major modifications, such as those pertaining to depictions of violence in video games whose core narrative revolves around acts of violence, signify that most Germans played a different game than the rest of the world. The game may even have a different name. In fact, there are cases where the German censored version has been sold as the European version of a game to comply with stricter German content control policies, to reduce potential version changes in other locales of the EEA, and to ensure standardised content and quality control. The case of the popular Konami franchise *Contra* (1987), where Bill Ryzer and Lance Bean, action hero type characters, fight against a variety of human and non-human enemies, is known in Europe as *Probotector* (1990). European localisation of the game changed the main protagonists into robots named RC011 and RD008, and all the human enemies found in the North American and Japanese versions have been changed into robots as well.

In addition to gratuitous violence, German policymakers have also censored Nazi symbolism in video games. Until 2018, the *Strafgesetzbuch* Criminal Code section 86a banned radical political content, such as German communist political organisations, and historically significant symbols, such as swastikas, in video games, often resulting in considerable modification of video game content. The justification for censorship was that video games are toys rather than an artform, such as films. In 1994, the German release of *Wolfenstein 3D* (ID software 1992) was banned because of its Nazi imagery. In 1998 a high German court ruled that video games for younger audiences could not represent Nazi symbols or the Third Reich so as to protect young minds 'vulnerable for ideological manipulation by national socialist ideas' (Orland 2018). Considering the extent to which western video games rely on World War II as a setting and on Nazis as antagonists, the measure was deemed very restrictive and required significant changes to content. A common practice for developers was to avoid Germany as a market or to change Nazi symbolism, such as swastikas, to different symbols so that the USK would allow the game to be sold on German territory. The German version of the 2017 game *Wolfenstein II: The New Colossus* (Machine Games) changed not only swastikas into other more generic symbols but also recorded new dubbing tracks. Thus, when enemies refer to their leader in German as '*mein Fürher*' in the source version, the German version refers to him as '*mein Kanzler*' (my chancellor). Since April 2018, Germany's attorney general has allowed video games to be considered forms of art and ruled that the 1998 judgment was outdated due to the absence of a rating board at that time. This change in the interpretation of the law is a major milestone for the game development industry. It shows that regulations can change based on evolving ontological concerns, and that the activity of rating boards and regulatory bodies can facilitate the acceptance of content at the legal level as opposed to enacting public censorship.

32.2 Historical Perspectives

The history of video games is embedded in discussions on how games influence users, with a focus on video games as commodities rather than works of art. The perception of video games as 'kids' toys' has been an ongoing theme in the discourse around games and so, many elements of criticism directed at video games explore their impact on younger audiences with the 'moral panic' themes of violence, psychological and social disorders, and addiction at the forefront (Paul 2012). Prior to the democratisation of home consoles, games were often played in arcades, which raised concerns as illicit drugs were rumoured to circulate in these places (Kocurek 2015; Williams 2003). Examples abound of how intercultural transfer along with the potential to expose young minds to questionable morals and dangerous behaviour led the industry to consider modifying its intellectual properties by anticipating potential problems and moving beyond purely linguistic concerns. Amongst the famous early changes in the translation of video games, one can cite the famous game Pac-Man by Namco (1980), which was originally named 'Puck Man' in Japan but was eventually renamed in the West to avoid potential vandalisation of the arcade system's marquee into the F-word expletive (Bernal-Merino 2014). While this form of content modification can hardly be considered a form of censorship per se, it shows awareness of potential problems pertaining to the linguistic idiosyncrasies of the target locale. It is also an example of how the video game development industry has always operated in risk mitigation mode. As such, a discussion of censorship within the video game industry must consider the potential impact of the medium on audiences, which can lead to the creation of rating boards as agents of content assessment in the process of video game international commercialisation.

There seems to be a persistent dichotomy between the revenue generated by the medium and its techno-positivist outcomes, such as video games being more likely to prepare kids for a career in the STEM fields of Science Technology Engineering and Mathematics fields (Chess 2017), and public outcry directed to the medium from concerned citizens and various lobby groups throughout the history of video game development. These points of conflict are important in informing our understanding of how censorship in video game localisation has emerged and illustrate how these events are connected to commercial distribution. Moreover, they inform later processes in video game commercialisation and localisation. Since its inception in the 1970s, the video game industry has shared a history with the military industrial complex as games were originally developed using military technology research laboratories, on equipment designed for military

Censorship in Video Game Localisation

purposes (Dyer-Whiteford and De Peuter 2009). However, it was only through the expansion of the industry a few years later, in 1982, that the Surgeon General of the United States of America declared video games to be potentially linked to dangerous and aggressive behaviours (Kline et al. 2003: 247) and that more control should be exerted over content and distribution channels. This event marks one of the first attempts by policymakers to address the impact of video games on the public, especially younger audiences. In parallel with these concerns over content, the US video game market experienced a video game crash in the mid-1980s, which was attributed to market saturation and low content control as games of all kinds were being developed with poor quality-assurance processes. This crash coincided with the release of the Nintendo Entertainment System (NES) outside of Japan. The company's American branch, Nintendo of America (NOA), has been instrumental in implementing content control procedures to ensure that console games would be free of potentially offensive content so that they could achieve broad-based worldwide commercial success. NOA is in fact responsible for much of the content that has been exported by the company outside of Japan since the American English localised version was often used as a pivot version for all other locales. Thus, most of the games distributed in the West in the mid-1980s had already been subjected to NOA's content filtering policies. Banned content included sexually suggestive content and nudity; graphic violence (illustrations of death, domestic violence, or abusive violence in sports games); linguistic ethnic, racial, religious, nationalistic or sexual stereotypes; profanity or obscenity in any form; the presence and promotion of illegal drugs, smoking materials and alcohol; and subliminal political messages or overt political statements (Schwartz and Schwartz 1994). By focusing on offering family-friend products, Nintendo allowed video games to re-enter households with minimal public outcry. The strategy paid dividends as Nintendo became the leading video game console maker for a whole generation of products. The family-friendly approach also left space for other products to fill the market void for less general audience entertainment. Nintendo's positioning as a general audience and kid-friendly company was especially profitable for SEGA, another Japanese video game company that also entered the Western market in 1985. During the 1990s, SEGA's marketing strategy positioned the company as more 'mature' and 'male teen-oriented' (Dyer-Whiteford and De Peuter 2009).

The 16-bit console and updated hardware on Personal Computers (PC) in the 1990s provided developers with enhanced graphic technology and augmented processing power, which allowed game developers to expand themes and representational possibilities. This technological leap led to the release of *Mortal Kombat* (Midway 1992), *Night Trap* (Digital Pictures 1992) and *Doom* (ID Software 1993) in 1993, games that, at the time, were considered crude, with graphic, realistic depictions of violence. As part of the different marketing strategies in place during the 'console war' between Nintendo and SEGA, games such as *Mortal Kombat*, which could originally be played in arcades, did not display any blood or gore on the Super Nintendo Entertainment System (SNES), while the SEGA platform version of the game allowed it. In fact, *Mortal Kombat* on the SNES is a case of inter-platform censorship where the source game is ported to a console with stricter content-control policy. The commercial success of the non-censored SEGA version eventually convinced Nintendo to allow more graphic displays of violence, and the second product of the *Mortal Kombat* (Midway 1992) franchise was similarly bloody and violent on both the Nintendo and the SEGA platforms. In fact, 'issues of violence, rating, and censorship became inextricably entwined in the power struggle between the two companies (Nintendo and SEGA) and were exploited by both as weapons for strategic advantage' (Kline, Dyer-Whiteford and De Peuter 2003: 134). This change in policy ultimately resulted in the 1993 US Congressional Hearings on Video Games to address the issue of violence in video games. The outcome of the hearings led the still expanding video game industry to react to potential government control over

The Routledge Handbook of Translation and Censorship

content by looking for solutions internally. Game developer representatives eventually devised supra-regional industry-defined assessment of content in a push to avoid looming state regulations. While the United Kingdom has, since 1989, used a rating board called the European Leisure Software Publishers Association (ELSPA), which extended the work undertaken by the British Board Film Classification (BBFC), the 1993 US congressional hearings led to the creation of Entertainment Software Rating Board (ESRB) for the United States, Canada and Mexico along with the USK for Germany in 1994, the *Tokutei Hieiri Katsudō Hōjin Konpyūta Entāteinmento Rētingu Kikō* (CERO) in Japan in 2002, and the Pan-European Game Information System (PEGI) in Europe in 2003. These classification systems rely on age-appropriate assessment of content, which varies based on what the supra-regional entity considers as culturally or socially sensitive or potentially troublesome politically (Kerr 2017).

Rating boards are essential in identifying the targets of potential censorship in video games as they assess what constitutes adequate content for a given locale. Thus, any discussion of censorship in video game localisation needs to consider the first layer of content-filtering spearheaded at a regional or national level. Rating boards exert significant control over censorship within locales. For example, a game that aims to receive a 'general' audience rating with no age restrictions might be subjected to more rigorous censorship; this is also the case for most types of content as translations seek to reach broader markets (Merkle 2010). In other words, in order to cater to what is considered the most sensitive audience of a given larger group of consumers (e.g., children), content must be censored with the strictest rules in mind. Thus, a rating board classification can make or break the sale of a given game in a specific locale.

However, not all countries have designed an exhaustive content classification system, and so in 2013 an association of six major national and regional rating authorities created the *International Age Rating Coalition* (IARC) to work towards rating standardisation. The IARC provides developers with a comprehensive survey containing a checklist of 'yes' or 'no' questions to identify specific types of content in the game. The answers generate a table of different ratings for all IARC members rating boards. The process streamlines the publication of a video game for a given locale and allows developers to foresee rating issues and address them upfront.

Because rating boards are creations of the industry and involve industrial stakeholders, they are considered to be self-regulation mechanisms. Nevertheless, the 2007–2009 post-financial crisis context has facilitated, especially in Europe, the emergence of governmental regulatory measures (Kerr 2017). These measures are often put in place to protect younger audiences from problematic marketing strategies and addiction to games. In 2018, Belgian courts ruled that loot boxes, which are randomly distributed in-game products and can be purchased with real-world currency, are a form of gambling that should not be marketed to minors (Gerken 2018). This ruling has led major video game companies, such as Electronic Arts, to remove the monetisation mechanism from the Belgian versions of their games. In fact, the industry has currently moved past the autoregulation model and moved towards a hybrid model where regulation is both enforced internally and in partnership with governments, para-national or para-regional organisations.

32.3 New Debates

Improved access to source material has increased audience awareness of video game localisation practices, which has led to some public backlash at certain companies. While NOA is notorious for significantly altering Japanese games for the English-speaking market, the availability of 'original' Japanese games and the potential for comparisons with the target versions has generated reactions from a vocal fringe of the gaming community. As a result, player groups are demanding that

Censorship in Video Game Localisation

companies 'stop localising, and start translating' (Diño 2017), since they feel that the removal of certain elements of gameplay is a type of censorship. This situation has generated enough traction in the world of video game journalism to spread into Game Studies academic discourse.

For example, depiction of non-heterosexual relationships and representation of homosexual characters in Japanese and Western games have sparked significant debate in game localisation circles over the last several years. One notable case involves the localisation of the Nintendo 3DS game *Fire Emblem Fates* (Intelligent System 2015), which was the first to introduce gay marriage as part of a Nintendo release. The positive representation was overshadowed by homophobic narratives and cinematic scenes (Kerr 2017). As a type of role-play strategy game in a fantasy world, *Fire Emblem Fates* also introduced relationship mechanics where players could interact with characters to develop an intimate narrative and connections with a character of their choosing. The Japanese version of the game featured a mini game called 'skinship' in which players could, with the help of the Nintendo 3DS stylus and the touch screen interface of the portable console, interact and 'touch' characters' heads and 'pet' them to increase their relationship status. The Japanese to English-as-a-pivot-language localisation team decided to remove the problematic content, along with the previously mentioned homophobic dialogues and scenes, as the touching mechanics were perceived to be overly sexual (Mandiberg 2017). This created a significant outcry from a certain group of gamers, which considered these alterations to be an egregious form of censorship. The Twitter hashtag #TorrentialDownpour has been used to comment on and protest this act of censorship, and the whole movement has been embedded in the 'Gamer Gate' controversy taking place among audience members, industry stakeholders and game journalists (Mandiberg 2017).

Another example of recent player outcry relates to the 2018 release of a worldwide patch for the 2015 online game *Rainbow Six Siege* (Ubisoft Montréal). The original game had not yet been released for the Chinese market and, in anticipation of that release, some graphic assets were adjusted to be compliant with Chinese policies pertaining to depictions of violence, sexuality and gambling. Icons such as skulls or knives were changed to less graphic representations of violence, and background scenes were altered to remove depictions of gambling, violence and sexuality. As patches are often released in a unified fashion, they correct issues across all locales, and so the 2018 patch applied the Chinese alterations to games everywhere. The change was picked up by a community that had been playing the game for three years prior to these changes. Western player outcry against this perceived censorship forced Ubisoft to backtrack on the changes and, instead of publishing one version for all locales, the publisher decided to develop at least one version for the Chinese market and a different one for the Western market. To the extent that publishing two versions demands extra work, concerns for the future of video game development have been gravitating around the idea that because the Chinese market now has as many players as the American market does, game developers might adapt their games to Chinese policies. Consequently, in the long term, game development may adopt a 'safer' approach to content creation. Industry experts fear that this 'safer' approach could lead to creative stagnation (Batchelor 2018). The previously mentioned example of games such as the *Contra/Probotector* franchise, which were localised and sold in other locales of the European Economic Area, shows that this is a potential outcome to consider as the industry fully embraces its global ambitions.

Globalised networked distribution channels not only facilitated the distribution of content designed for specific locales across geopolitical lines but also contributed to the creation of extra-commercial pathways for content distribution and alteration. The case of fan translation (also called 'translation hacking') and ROM-Hacking are good examples of an extra-commercial distribution channel of translated material. Fan translations do not have to abide by strict content

515

control policies since they are distributed outside mainstream commercial channels. As such, fan translations and ROM-Hacking have historically been an effective way to circumvent censorship (Muñoz-Sánchez 2009). This has led an increasing number of gamers, especially PC gamers who can more easily modify their games, to rely on unofficial fan-made patches applied to reverse censorship measures and access a version of the game that is closer to the original source content (Kerr 2017). Interestingly, the industry has picked up the idea of applying a patch to alter game content to reach a broader audience while retaining the potential shock value of graphic depictions of violence for a niche audience of older players. For example, the game *Total War: Warhammer II* (Creative Assembly 2017) is sold with an ESRB rating of T (for Teen) in North America. Provided they pay more and meet the age requirement, North American players can acquire the *Blood for the Blood God II* downloadable content, which is rated M (for mature) due to the graphic depiction of gore and violence in the game. This marketing strategy approaches censorship and culturalisation issues globally, ensuring that even the most sensitive locales will receive a game that suits their specific needs while allowing players to engage with more problematic themes, provided they pay the price and acquire the rights to download the content. In this case, censorship is applied upstream rather than downstream as an afterthought for localisation. More specifically, adding violence as downloadable content monetises the culturalisation and censorship processes. Such approaches to censorship show that localisation is moving continually closer to development and user experience concerns as 'translation as an afterthought' becomes a relic of the past.

Further Reading

Bernal-Merino, Miguel Á. 2014. *Translation and Localisation in Video Games: Making Entertainment Software global*. London and New York: Routledge.
This monograph is a seminal text in video game localisation and in Translation Studies as it defines the place of the discipline within a Translation Studies framework. In addition, it provides an overview of specific components of a video game that require translation. Moreover, the work tackles the industrial process of video game localisation, which is of paramount importance to the discussion on culturalisation and censorship.

Kerr, Aphra. 2017. *Global Games: Production, Circulation and Policy in the Networked Era*. New York: Taylor & Francis.
This book is an exhaustive examination of video game production as an industry, through an investigation of the various flows and nodes of the production process, to unravel the different movement of capital, ideas and people, and the various spaces that participate in making global games local.

O'Hagan, Minako, and Mangiron, Carme. 2013. *Game Localisation: Translating for the Global Digital Entertainment Industry*. Amsterdam and Philadelphia: John Benjamins Publishing.
This pioneering book defines most of the tenets of video game localisation, with an emphasis on cultural awareness, transcreation and Japanese to English translation movements. The book explains the specificities of video game localisation within a Translation Studies framework, bridging the gap between commercial translation processes and academia.

References

Afzali, Katayoon and Zahiri, Mahboobeh. 2021. 'A netnographic exploration of Iranian videogame players translation needs: The case of in-game texts', *The Translator*, 28(1):74–94.
Alexander, Leigh. 2010. 'Middle East's Game Industry Creates Islam-Centric Game Ratings'. www.gamedeveloper.com/pc/middle-east-s-game-industry-creates-islam-centric-game-ratings, November 30 (Accessed: 25 September 2023).

Batchelor, James. 2018. 'On Ubisoft's Pandering to Unreasonable Players'. www.gamesindustry.biz/articles/ 2018-11-21-on-ubisofts-pandering-to-unreasonable-players (Accessed: 25 September 2023).

Bernal-Merino, Miguel Á. 2014. *Translation and Localisation in Video Games: Making Entertainment Software Global*. London and New York: Routledge.

Brownlie, Siobhan. 2007. 'Examining self-censorship: Zola's *Nana* in English translation', in R. Looby (ed.), *Modes of Censorship and Translation. National Contexts and Diverse Media*. Manchester: St Jerome, 205–34.

Brunette, Louise. 2002. 'Normes et censure: ne pas confondre.' *TTR* 15(2): 223–233. https://doi.org/10.7202/ 007486ar

Carlson, Rebecca and Corliss, Jonathan. 2011. 'Imagined commodities: Video game localization and mythologies of cultural difference', *Games and Culture*, 6(1): 61–82.

Chandler, Heather Maxwell and O'Malley Deming, Stephanie. 2011. *The Game Localization Handbook*. Burlington, MA: Jones & Bartlett Publishers.

Chess, Shira. 2017. *Ready Player Two: Women Gamers and Designed Identity*. Minnesota: University of Minnesota Press.

Diño, Gino. 2017. 'Japanese Game Fans to Nintendo: We Want Translated, Not Localized Games'. https://slator.com/features/japanese-game-fans-to-nintendo-we-want-translated-not-localized-games/ (Accessed: 25 September 2023).

Dong, Luo and Mangiron, Carme. 2018. 'Journey to the East: Cultural adaptation of video games for the Chinese market', *The Journal of Specialised Translation*, 29: 149–68.

Dyer-Witheford, Nick and De Peuter, Greig. 2009. *Games of Empire: Global Capitalism and Video Games*. Minnesota: University of Minnesota Press.

Edwards, Kate M. 2011. 'Culturalization: The geopolitical and cultural dimension of game content', *TRANS: revista de traductología*, 15: 19–28.

Esselink, Bert. 2000. *A Practical Guide to Localization*. Amsterdam and Philadelphia: John Benjamins Publishing.

Esselink, Bert. 2003. 'The evolution of localization', *The Guide from Multilingual Computing & Technology: Localisation*, 14(5): 4–7.

Frasca, Gonzalo. 2001. 'Videogames of the Oppressed: Videogames as a Means for Critical Thinking and Debate'. Master's thesis. School of Literature, Communication, and Culture, Georgia Institute of Technology.

Gerken, Tom. 2018, April 26. 'Video Game Loot Boxes Declared Illegal Under Belgium Gambling Laws'. www.bbc.com/news/technology-43906306 (Accessed: 25 September 2023).

Kerr, Aphra. 2017. *Global games: Production, Circulation and Policy in the Networked Era*. New York: Taylor & Francis.

Khoshsaligheh, Masood and Ameri, Saeed. 2020. 'Video game localisation in Iran: a survey of users' profile, gaming habits and preferences', *The Translator*, 26(2): 190–208.

Kline, Stephen, Dyer-Witheford, Nick and De Peuter, Greig. 2003. *Digital Play: The Interaction of Technology, Culture, and Marketing*. Montreal: McGill-Queen's Press.

Kocurek, Carly A. 2015. *Coin-Operated Americans: Rebooting Boyhood at the Video Game Arcade*. Minnesota: University of Minnesota Press.

Liboriussen, Bjarke, White, Andrew and Wang, Dan. 2015. 'The ban on gaming consoles in China: Protecting national culture, morals, and industry within an international regulatory framework', in J. DeWinte and S. Conway (eds.), *Video Game Policy: Production, Distribution and Consumption*. New York: Routledge, 230–43.

Mandiberg, Stephen. 2017. 'Fallacies of game localization: Censorship and# TorrentialDownpour', *The Journal of Internationalization and Localisation*, 4(2): 162–82.

Merkle, Denise. 2010. 'Censorship', in Y. Gambier and L. Van Dorslaer (eds.), *Handbook of Translation Studies*. New York: John Benjamins, 18–21.

O'Hagan, Minako and Mangiron, Carme. 2013. *Game Localisation: Translating for the Global Digital Entertainment Industry*. Amsterdam: John Benjamins Publishing.

Orland, Kyle. 2018, 10 August. 'Germany Says Games with Nazi Symbols can Get "Artistic" Exception to Ban'. https://arstechnica.com/gaming/2018/08/german-ratings-board-starts-allowing-nazi-symbols-in-video-games/ (Accessed: 25 September 2023).

Paul, Christopher. 2012. *Wordplay and the Discourse of Video Games: Analyzing Words, Design, and Play*. New York: Routledge.

Piasecki, Stefan and Malekpour, Setareh. 2016. 'Morality and religion as factors in age rating computer and video games: ESRA, the Iranian games age rating system', *Online – Heidelberg Journal of Religions on the Internet*, 11.

Sánchez, Pablo Muñoz. 2009. 'Video game localisation for fans by fans: The case of romhacking', *The Journal of Internationalization and Localisation*, 1(1): 168–85.

Schwartz, Steven and Schwartz, Janet. 1994. *Parent's Guide to Video Games*. Rocklin, CA: Prima Lifestyles.

Šisler, Vit. 2013. 'Video game development in the Middle East: Iran, the Arab world, and beyond', in N. Hunteman and B. Aslinger (eds.), *Gaming Globally: Production, Play and Place*. New York: Palgrave Macmillan, 251–71.

Stöcker, Christian. 2009, 19 August. 'Electronic Arts fordert Ablösung der Game-Selbstkontrolle'. www.spiegel.de/netzwelt/games/jugendschutz-electronic-arts-fordert-abloesung-der-game-selbstkontrolle-a-643815.html (Accessed: 25 September 2023).

Unterhaltungssoftware Selbstkontrolle (USK). 2023. 'Can Age Rating Amount to Censorship?' https://usk.de/en/the-usk/faqs/censorship/ (Accessed: 25 September 2023).

Wijman, Tom. 2023, August. 'Newzoo's Games Market Revenue Estimates and Forecasts by Region and Segment for 2023'. https://newzoo.com/resources/blog/games-market-estimates-and-forecasts-2023 (Accessed 25 September 2023).

Williams, Dmitri. 2003. 'The video game lightning rod', *Information Communication & Society*, 6(4): 523–50.

Zhang, Xiaochun. 2012. 'Censorship and digital games localisation in China', *Meta*, 57(2): 338–50.

Ludography

Blizzard Entertainment. 2012. *Diablo III*, Blizzard Entertainment, Windows, OS X, Playstation 3, Xbox 360, Playstation 4, Xbox One, Nintendo Switch.

Chunsoft. 1986. *Dragon Warrior*, Enix, Nintendo, NES.

Creative Assembly. 2017. *Total War: Warhammer II*, Windows, Linux, Mac OS.

Digital Pictures. 1992. *Night Trap*, SEGA, SEGA CD.

ID Software. 1992. *Wolfenstein 3D*, ID Software, DOS, Arcade, PC-98, SNES, Jaguar.

ID Software. 1993. *Doom*, ID Software, MS-DOS.

Intelligent Systems. 2015. *Fire Emblem Fates*, Nintendo.

Konami. 1986. *Castlevania*, Konami, Famicom/NES, Arcade, C64, Amiga, MS-Dos.

Konami. 1987. *Contra*, Konami, Arcade, Famicom/NES.

Konami. 1990. *Probotector*. Nintendo Entertainment System. Konami.

Machine Games. 2017. *Wolfenstein II: The New Colossus*, Bethesda Softworks, Windows, Playstation 4, Xbox One, Nintendo Switch.

Media Molecule. 2008. *LittleBigPlanet*. PlayStation 3. Sony Computer Entertainment.

Midway. 1992. *Mortal Kombat*, Midway, Arcade, Amiga, Game Boy, MS-DOS, SEGA CD, Game Gear, Genesis, Master System, Super NES.

Namco. 1980. *Pac-Man*, Namco, Midway, Arcade.

Neverland. 1995. *Lufia II: Rise of the Sinistrals*, Taito, Natsume, Nintendo, Super NES.

Paradox Development Studio. 2002. *Heart of Irons*, Strategy First, Atari, SA, indows, Mac OS, OS X.

Rockstar North. 2004. *Grand Theft Auto: San Andreas*, Rockstar Games, Playstation 2, Microsoft Windows, Xbox, Mac OS X, Xbox 360, Playstation 3.

Square. 1991. *Final Fantasy IV*, Square, Super Nintendo.

Square. 1994. *Final Fantasy VI*, Square, Super Nintendo.

Stainless Games. 1997. *Carmaggedon*, Interplay Productions/Sales Curve Interactive, MS-DOS, Windows, Mac OS, Nintendo 64.

Ubisoft Montréal. 2015. *Rainbow Six Siege*, Ubisoft, Windows, Playstation 4, Playstation 5, Xbox One, Xbox Series X/S.

INDEX

Aaltonen, Sirkku 384
Aarma, Liivi 111–13
Abassi, Salah 19
Abbas, Amin 24
Abdel Fattah, Ashraf 20–1
Abdel-Rahim, Said 18
Abderrahmane, Taha 31
Abellán, Manuel Luis 399, 409, 415, 435, 439, 441–2, 444–5
Abiz, Alireza 50
abortion 399, 406, 436, 444
Abrams vs. United States 344
Abu Sadira, Essam 18
Abu Shadi, Ali 23
Adamaite, Undīne 146
Addley, Esther 330
Adventures of Huckleberry Finn 284
Afzali, Katayoon 510
Ahačič, Kozma 155
Ahn, Hyung-Ju 347
Akbariyani, Mohammad Hashem 50
Aktener, Ilgın 88
Albachten, Özlem Berk 291–2, 423
Albonetti, Pietro 355
Alexander, Leigh 510
Alfieri, Vittorio 388
Alhajri, Ayed 30
Alieri, Dino 367
Alkan, Mehmet 80–1
Alkhunaizi, Hind 29
Allan, Keith 420
Alsharhan, Alanoud 22–3
Althusser, Louis 2
Alvstad, Cecilia 477, 479, 481–3
Ameri, Saeed 510

American Library Association (ALA) 1–2, 297, 300
Andaluz Pinedo, Olaia 410
Animal Farm 18, 101–4, 106, 120, 148, 181, 187, 208, 281
Anthelme, Paul 316
anti-fascism 198, 377
antisemitism 42, 101, 357, 377, 468
Antochi, Roxana-Mihaela 270, 273
Antonutti, Isabelle 496
Apīnis, Aleksejs 140
Apolliniare, Guillaume 88
Arabacı, Caner 82
Arabian Nights 4, 24
Arabisation 31
archival materials 77, 151, 201–3, 209, 217, 222, 238, 274, 281, 285, 333
archival research 3, 172, 210, 217, 284–5, 360, 365, 417
archives 72, 144, 171–2, 193, 254–5, 269, 285, 355, 391, 415, 423; private 374, 421, 423, 445
Arianism 459, 462
Ariès, Philippe 477
Asseraf, Arthur 15
Assis Rosa, Alexandra 424
atheism 74, 89, 284, 402
Atwood, Blake 54
audiovisual translation 4, 21–2, 30, 414–16, 421–2, 435; *see also* translation
Augenspiegel 42
Austro-Hungarian Empire 165, 216, 263, 338
authoritarianism 25, 29, 208, 218
Avramescu, Tiberiu 267, 271
Al-Azami, Muhammad M. 459–60
Azevedo, Cândido de 372

Index

Baath Party 19
Babits, Mihály 209
Bachleitner, Norbert 5, 155, 157
Bacon: Francis 130; Joséphine 310
Bader, Barbara 482
Baer, Brian James 75, 121–2, 149, 266, 345, 395, 422–4, 467
Báez, Fernando 127–8
Baghiu, Ştefan 265–7, 269, 274
Bajc, Gorazd 160
Bak, János 213
Baker, Trudy 380
Bakhtin, Mikhail 122, 478, 482
Baltic Germans 110–16, 120
Balyko, Anastasiia 75
Bamford, Julian 292
Bandia, Paul 80
Bandín, Elena 408, 410, 415
Banham, Martin 15
Barata, José de Oliveira 386, 393
Barck, Simone 193–4, 201, 203
Barenbaum, Iosif 65, 72
Barrale, Natascia 420–1
Bart, István 211, 213
Barthes, Roland 332
Barton, John 464
Basalamah, Salah 20, 25, 30–1
Basen, Ira 337
Bassler, Gerhard 142
Bastin, Georges 136
Batchelor, James 515
Bates, John M. 223, 225–7, 230, 232–3, 236
Bathrick, David 196
Baumgarten, Stefan 2
Bautista Cordero, Rosa María 415
Beauregard, Claude 336–40
Becattini, Alberto 496, 502
Bednarczyk, Anna 225
Beletskii, Aleksandr 168, 171
Bennett, Karen 416
Bentham, Jeremy 5
Bérenger, Jean 156
Berkowitz, Eric 1
Bernal-Merino, Miguel 505–6, 512
Bernstein, Henri 217
Bernstein, Karen 314
Bertrand, Karine 311
Bettelheim, Bruno 485
Biały, Paulina 225
Bible 38, 71, 109, 111–13, 120–1, 155–7, 169, 173, 457, 459–63, 465–9
Bible translations 459, 463–4, 466–7
bilingualism 279, 312, 317
Billiani, Francesca 110, 190, 285, 322, 356, 365, 368, 414, 416, 422, 455

Bilodid, Ivan 248
Bilokin, Serhii 244–5, 254–5
Birett, Herbert 43
Black Beauty 19
Blium, Arlen 67, 73–4
Blizzard Entertainment 509
Blum, Hanna 192, 195–6, 198–200, 202
Boase-Beier, Jean 185, 400
Boéri, Julie 20
Böhm, Karl 197
Bohn, Henry 4
Bolshevism 338
Bompiani, Valentino 353, 359–65, 368
Bonsaver, Guido 359, 363–4, 368
Booth, Arthur John 69
Booth, Marilyn 18
Boriak, Bennadii 168–70, 172
Börner, Hein 197
Borodo, Michal 476
Bosco Tierno, Caterina 493–4
Bouchard, Gérard 27
Boulogne, Pieter 45
Bourdieu, Pierre 5–8, 14, 95, 110, 117, 222, 306, 310, 423–4, 455–6, 470–1
Bourrie, Mark 337–41, 348
Bowden, John 460–1
Bowen, Wayne 26
boycotting 1, 331, 464, 466
Boyd, Neil 307
Bradburn, Jamie 342
Braden, Allison 331
Brandenberger, David 255
Brawn, Steph 29
Brems, Elke 291
Breuer, Dieter 42
Breuer, Matthew 193
Briedis, Raimonds 148
Brilla, Fritz 197
Brodie, Geraldine 384
Brontë, Charlotte 267, 435
Brontë, Emily 440, 449
Brownlie, Siobhan 507
Brunette, Louise 506
Bryan, Peter Cullen 492, 494
Brzezińska, Bogna 225–8, 231
Budnik, Magdalena 225
Budrowska, Kamila 223–5, 230, 232, 234–5
Bunn, Matthew 2, 37, 44, 99
Burgat, François 26
Burghardt, Oswald 253–4
Burnett, Frances Hodgson 209
Burnett, Stephen 42
Burridge, Kate 420
Burt, Richard 322
Burton, Richard 4, 314
Butler, Donald 315

520

Index

Butler, Judith 2, 422
Bystydzieńska, Grazyna 225–6, 232, 234

Cabrera, Ana 384–5, 387, 390
Cadera, Susanne M. 423
Caetano, Marcelo 371–2
Callaham, David 330
Calvinism 215, 261, 463
Campillo Arnaiz, Laura 415, 419
Campoamor, Clara 376
Camus, Albert 54, 119, 209, 237, 248, 373
Camus Camus, Maria del Carmen 400, 404–5, 410, 435
capitalism 100, 106, 131, 145, 147, 180, 199, 229, 274, 332, 342
Carlson, Rebecca 507
Carmichael, Cathie 154
Carmichael, Joel 378
Carnation Revolution 371, 374, 376, 379
Carpenter, Kenneth 40
Carroll, Lewis 209
Carvalho, Manuela 385, 394, 396
Casanova, Julián 118, 413, 441
Castelli, Alredo 492
catechism 111, 113
Catherine II (the Great) 66–7, 114, 174
Catholicism 43, 45, 128–9, 132, 136, 155–7, 308, 313, 316, 463, 469
Cecchi, Emilio 362–3, 365, 368
censors 3–4, 38–40, 66–70, 111–18, 120–1, 143–9, 185–7, 223–4, 226–9, 231–7, 266–71, 316–17, 337–40, 372–82, 389–90, 392–6, 415–21, 434–6, 442–5, 467–9; appointed 3; chief 3, 337; imperial 158, 171; local 158, 340; official 269, 408; secular 66, 70
censorship 1–9, 13–25, 27–32, 49–59, 80–4, 109–22, 147–51, 154–62, 179–90, 222–6, 264–76, 336–48, 371–82, 413–24, 432–5, 455–9, 467–71, 495–502, 505–8, 510–16; book 109, 157, 222, 374, 446; colonial 97; covert 18, 20, 29, 193, 321–2, 333; economic 16, 44, 263, 268, 490; editorial 270, 294, 416; epistemic 30; institutional 7, 210, 223, 232, 401; legal 315; military 67, 342; moral 224, 322, 401; overt 184, 188; partial 436, 442
censorship board 100, 114–15, 211, 405, 409, 441, 443, 449
censorship bodies 69, 72, 81, 224, 340, 407, 442
Censorship Bureau 52, 279–80, 316, 401
censorship commission 372, 378–9, 385, 390, 392
censorship committees 114, 167, 170, 390, 392–3
censorship legislation 8, 216, 306, 336, 338, 502
censorship methods 24, 207, 229
censorship norms 29, 50, 53, 57, 59, 61, 401–2
censorship office 21, 43, 51, 53, 157–9, 169–70, 223, 226, 228, 234, 346–7

censorship policies 68, 89, 179, 187, 243, 254, 367, 421, 442; institutional 502; state-centered 89
censorship practices 8, 28–9, 32, 66, 77, 127, 137, 207, 215, 222, 224
censorship process 193, 199, 201, 203, 422, 441, 445, 449, 462, 464, 516
censorship regulations 19, 37, 339, 401
censorship restrictions 3, 168, 246, 343, 346, 348, 386, 400, 403, 455
censorship system 8, 14, 110, 113, 182, 184, 187, 238, 262, 264, 270–1, 417–18, 422
Chabbak, Salma 22
Chan, Red 188–9, 291
Chandler, Heather Maxwell 511
Chang, Nam Fung 188
Charles, William H. 309
Chen, Zhongyi 180
Cherevatenko, Leonid 249
Cherkaska, Hanna 246
Chernetsky, Vitaly 172
Cherniakov, Borys Ivanovych 248
Chess, Shira 512
children's literature 17–19, 55, 194, 224–5, 228–30, 238, 244, 282–4, 292–4, 301, 475–86
Chilton, Bruce 458–9
Choldin, Marianna T. 68, 76
Chow, Yean Fun 500
Chunsoft 507
Chvatík, Květoslav 323
cinema 49, 51, 57–9, 263–4, 395, 401, 403, 405–7, 409–10, 416–17, 419, 421
Cisquella, Georgina 403
Clark: Jaime 419; Katerina 145
Clavelin, Guillaume 133
Coats, Karen 298
Cohen, Mark 8, 306–7, 310–11
Cohen, Robin 26
Cold War 95, 98–100, 102, 104, 106, 192, 273, 322, 324–5, 328, 331–3, 475
colonialism 96, 99, 106, 249, 371, 374, 378, 381
Comănescu, Denisa 270, 272, 275
comics 8, 315, 358, 481, 484–5, 489–93, 495–500, 502
Comics Code Authority 490, 498
Comics Magazine Association 489
commercialism 320
communism 86, 90, 98, 100–1, 187, 217, 229, 231–2, 265, 269, 271–2, 275, 323
communist censorship 222, 264, 269, 271, 274–6
Communist Manifesto 85–6
conservatism 215, 401
Constitutional Revolution of 1906 (Iran) 50
Copilaş, Emanuel 274
Corliss, Jonathan 507
Cornea, Paul 263

Index

Cornellá, Jordi 409, 423
Corobca, Liliana 265–6, 268, 275
Cotter, Sean 265
Counter-Reformation 156, 463
Couvée, Petra 2
Craig, Ian S. 394, 415
Creasman, Allyson 38–9
Cullen, Poppy 99
cultural policies 118, 142–3, 193, 195, 202, 207, 230, 234, 254, 366
culture planning 273
Cvirn, Janez 157–9, 161
Czigány, Lóránt 215
Czigányik, Zsolt 212, 217

Dahl, Roald 14, 16
Daneshvar, Esfaindyar 57
Daniell, David 460–1
D'Annunzio, Gabriele 117
Danylenko, Andrii 165–9, 172, 174
Darnton, Robert 195
Davidson, Jared 343
Davies, Christie 501
Dawkins, Richard 89
Debs vs. United States 344
Declaration of the Rights of Man and of the Citizen 126–7
Decleva, Enrico 354
Dehdarian, Roja 50
De Jonge, Henk J. 462
De Kuyper, Arie 465
Delabastita, Dirk 294–5, 297
Delille, Maria Manuela Gouveia 388, 394
Delisle, Jean 339
Demirel, Fatmagül 81–2
Dench, Judi 328–9
Denize, Eugen 265–6
De Peuter, Greig 513
Depman, Jaan 116
Derzhavyn, Volodymyr 253–4
Devictor, Agnès 58
Dewhirst, Martin 3
Deželak Barič, Vida 280
diaspora 26–8, 55, 60, 97, 250, 253, 467
Díaz-Cintas, Jorge 416
Dibrova, Volodymyr 172
dictatorship 18, 76, 159, 374, 400–3, 407–9, 414, 418–19, 421, 433, 443; military 100, 264, 371, 373
Diderot, Denis 40, 66, 70, 72, 130–1
Dietz, Bettina 41
Digard, Jean-Pierre 50
Dimitriu, Rodica 264, 266–9, 272–3
D'Ina, Gabriella 368
Diño, Gino 515
Disney 119, 328, 490–500, 502

Ditmajer, Nina 156, 161–2
Dobrovol'skii, Lev 69–71
Doğaner, Yasemin 83
Dollerup, Cay 273, 494
Dolores, Carmen 385
Domańska, Ewa 231
Dong, Luo 509
Dorfman, Ariel 500
Dotsenko, Rostyslav 169
Dović, Marijan 156–7, 159, 161, 283
Dragomanov, Michel 171
Dreimane, Jana 144
Drewett, Michael 422
Drnovšek, Marjan 159
dubbing 4, 21, 23–5, 317, 405–6, 416
Dunnett, Jane 358, 364, 368
Durand, Pascal 275
Dussel, Enrique 30
Dwyer, Tessa 4
Dyer-Whiteford, Nick 513
Dymel-Trzebiatowska, Hanna 225
Dzera, Oksana 172, 243, 256
Dziuba, Ivan 249, 254

Eastern Orthodoxy 65, 469
Eberharter, Markus 236
Echeverri, Álvaro 136
Edwards, Kate M. 508, 510
Ege, Süleyman 86
Ehasalu, Epp 111
Eiris, Ariel 136
Eisler, Jerzy 224
El-Amrani, Issandr 18
Eliade, Mircea 264
Ellis, Havelock 5
Elouardaoui, Ouidyane 23–4
Éluard, Paul 378
Emerson, Caryl 482
emigration 74, 149, 159, 345, 385
Encyclopédie 40, 130–1
Endzelīns, Jānis 146
Engels, Friedrich 118, 145, 216, 380
Enlightenment 4, 30–1, 39, 44, 126, 128, 132, 136, 157, 215, 232; French 114, 157; German 40; post- 322
Epstein, B. J. 422, 424
Ergun, Emek 424
erotica 413
erotic content 39, 150, 159, 208, 413, 415, 419
Ersland, Anlaug 300–1, 303
Esleben, Jörg 42
Esposito, Edoardo 362–3
Esselink, Bert 506
Essentialist Theatre Manifesto 388
Estado Novo 384

euphemism 4, 7, 22, 295, 403, 456
Evans, Janet 479
extremism 14, 26, 28, 75, 299
Eyüboğlu, Sabahattin 85–6

Fabre, Giorgio 356, 364, 367–8
Fabrikant, Nikolai 166, 168, 171, 173
Fadda, Sebastiana 388
fascism 144, 150, 199, 358, 368, 382, 435
Federazione Nazionale Fascista 368
feminism 30, 50, 440, 443, 445, 449
Fendler, Ute 41
Ferme, Valerio 368
Ferreira, José Medeiros 377
Feuillebois-Pierunek, Eve 56
field theory 5, 7
Figarski, Władysław 229
Filati, Rita 3
Filewood, Alan 391
film *see* cinema
film censorship 59, 307, 317, 333, 401, 405, 416
Findley, Carter Vaughn 88
Finn, Peter 2
Fischer, Caroline 26, 112–13
Fiset, Louis 343, 346–7
Fish, Stanley 307
Fitos, Stephan 39
Flesher, Paul V. M. 458–9
Foreign Bible Society 169, 467–8
formalism 198–9
Foss, Sonja K. 455
Foucault, Michel 1–3, 5–6, 222, 322, 332–3, 423, 455, 490
Fournier, Théo 210
Fox, Myron 346
Fraiberg, Selma 480
Franco, Francisco 376, 399–401, 409, 414–19, 421, 423, 432, 449
Franco Aixelá, Javier 410, 415, 418–19
Francoism 375, 402–4, 406–7, 415, 417–21, 424, 433–5, 440, 443, 445, 448–9
Francoist Spain 358, 367, 373, 376, 382, 400, 409, 417, 422, 432–5, 440
Frankenstein 293, 297–8
Frasca, Gonzalo 505
Freeman, Charles 458
Freifeld, Alice 216
French Revolution 66, 68–9, 71, 85, 114, 116, 121, 126, 130, 132, 136, 215
Freund, Hilger 37
Friedberg, Maurice 145–6
Friedman, Vanessa 332
Frohwerk vs. United States 344
Frycie, Stanisław 225
Fylypovych, Pavlo 166, 168, 171, 254

Gabrič, Aleš 160–1, 281–5
Gadducci, Fabio 358, 368, 496, 500
Gagnon, Charles 341
Gallego Roca, Miguel 416, 421
galley proofs 360, 435–6, 441–3, 446; *see also* proofs
Gamal, Muhammad 21–3
Gambier, Yves 18
García de Sena, Manuel 136
García Lorca, Federico 423
García Márquez, Gabriel 54, 74, 248
Gardocki, Wiktor 225
Garrosa García, María-Jesús 129–30
Gaszyńska-Magiera, Małgorzata 231
gay 330, 419, 422–3
Géher, István 211
Gentzler, Edwin 344
Gerdmar, Anders 466
Gerken, Tom 514
German occupation 110, 118, 120, 139, 142, 145, 263, 279, 281, 284
Gerstein, David 493
Gessen, Masha 3
Ghanoonparvar, Mohammad 51–3, 55
Giardino, Vittorio 315
Gibbels, Elisabeth 37, 43–5
Gikambi, Hezekiel 103
Gili Roig, Gustavo 403–4
Gill, Ann 455
Giovanopoulos, Anna-Christina 194, 199–200
Glavlit 71–3, 118–19, 141–2, 147–9, 265–6, 343
Glide Manno, Antonio 498
Godayol, Pilar 415, 434–5, 439, 442, 445
Godeša, Bojan 279–80, 284
Gombár, Zsófia 208, 210, 214–15, 217
Gomes, Joaquim Cardoso 373
Gómez Castro, Cristina 382, 399, 406–7, 409, 415–18, 422, 445–6
Gömöri, George 215
Goodenough, Ward 127
Gori, Leonardo 496
Goriaeva, Tat'iana 72, 225
Gouanvic, Jean-Marc 14, 87
Gow, James 154
Gramsci, Antonio 233
Great Terror 244, 246, 249, 258, 440
Greco, Lorenzo 367
Greek Orthodoxy 65, 462
Greenblatt, Stephen 16
Greene, Graham 415
Greer, Bradford 465
Grégoire, Henri 41
Greilich, Susanne 40–1
Griffiths, James 23, 466
Groulx, Gilles 342
Grünke, Alexander 499

Index

Guerrero, Javier 134–5
Guimard, Paul 213
Günyol, Vedat 85–6
Gutiérrez Lanza, Camino 407, 410, 416–17, 446

Habermas, Jürgen 27–8
habitus 2, 5–6, 14, 95, 110, 322
Habsburg Monarchy 154–6, 158, 161–2, 173, 218, 262
Hade, Daniel 479
Hadjivayanis, Ida 103
Hamšík, Dušan 320, 323–5
Hannah, Emily 415
Hantzsch, Viktor 40
Harry Potter 18–19
Härtner, Bernd 197
Hartvig, Gabriella 217
Hatfield, Charles 490
Havel, Václav 321, 325–7, 332–3, 389
Hayashi, Brian Masaru 346–7
Haynes, Joanna 477–8
Hébert, Pierre 307, 313, 315–17
Heikkilä-Halttunen, Päivi 478, 480–1
heliocentrism 66
Hemingway, Ernest 74, 147, 180, 209, 236, 267, 280, 359–60, 373
Henry, Neil 103
Henzi, Sarah 311
Herr, Richard 129–31
Hiedel, Lembe 119
Highway, Tomson 311
Hillmann, Michael G. 55
Hispanic America 127–8, 132, 136
Hitler, Adolf 149, 377, 414, 416, 496
Hofeneder, Philipp 202
Hofstein, David 246
Hohol, Mykola 167, 246, 252
Holman, Michael 185, 400
Holme, Constance 432
Holmes, James 5
Holmes, Oliver Wendall 344
Holquist, Michael 4, 478, 482
Homestead Act of 1862 344
homosexuality 19, 75, 148, 217, 399, 417–19, 423–4, 444, 515
Hordynsky, Yaroslav 169
Horrell, J. Scott 466
Houdassine, Ismaël 317
Hoyer, Svennik 145
Hrytsenko, Pavlo 170
Hrytsiv, Nataliia 256
Hudson, David L. 342, 344
Huggan, Graham 322
Huizinga, Jan 477
humanism 146, 378
Hurcombe, Martin 376

Hurtley, Jacqueline 406, 435, 440, 443, 445
Hutchinson, Allen C. 307

immigration 308, 338, 344–6
imperialism 15, 198, 246, 322
Index Librorum Prohibitorum 38, 45, 156, 215, 463
Index of Information Not to Be Covered in the Open Press 343
Index Translationum 252, 354
indigenisation 31, 244, 255, 466
indigenous populations 127–8, 132, 308
indigenous publications 80–2, 88, 306
internationalism 150, 246, 254, 266
internment camps 338, 346–7
interpreting 96, 201–3, 312, 342, 348, 464, 482
Ionescu, Gelu 267, 269, 271
Iranian Revolution 26, 500
İrtem, Süleyman Kani 81
Isaievych, Yaroslav 167
Islam 15, 19, 21, 27, 49, 54, 58, 97, 102, 456, 460, 510
Islamic law 24, 54
Islamic Republic 26, 50–3, 56–9
Islamic Revolution 57, 60, 83
Islamism 83
Issakov, Sergei 115
Italian occupation 279, 284
Ito, Robert 330
Izmozik, Vladlen 67
Izwaini, Sattar 21

Jacquemond, Richard 17
Jager, Benedikt 194, 198
Jäger, Manfred 193
Jakobson, Roman 8, 291, 482
Jane Eyre 267, 435, 440
Jané-Lligé, Jordi 421
Jannsen, Johan Woldemar 115
Jansen, Ea 115
Jansen, Sue 317, 320–2, 331–2
Jendis, Mareike 479, 481–2, 484
Jenny, Beat Rudolf 40
Jin, Xingrao 180
Joachimsthaler, Jürgen 43
Johansen, Paul 111
Johnson, Alice 18
Johnston, David 384
Jones, Rachel 380
Jones, Toby 26
Jones, William 42
journalism 7, 30, 133, 244, 317, 337, 436
Judaism 42, 456, 458, 460–2, 499
Julio, Teresa 435
Juvan, Marko 158, 161

Index

Kahanovych, Naum 245–6, 254
Kaindl, Klaus 422, 424, 492
Kalnychenko, Oleksandr 167, 246, 252, 254
Kamen, Henry 128–9
Kamovnikova, Natalia 73, 75
Kansu Yetkiner, Neslihan 89
Kappeler, Andreas 165
Karakışla, Yavuz Selim 81
Karimi-Hakkak, Ahmad 51–2, 54, 56–7, 59–60
Karst, Roman 236
Karulis, Konstantīs 141
Kasekamp, Andres 110
Katouzian, Homa 51
Keane, John 321
Kelemen, Roland 216
Kemény, G. Gábor 216
Kenevisi, Mohammad Sadegh 500
Kerr, Aphra 506, 510, 514–16
Kerversau, François-Marie de 133
Keshen, Jeff 337
Keul, István 215
Khalifa, Abdel-Wahab 17, 24
Khoptiar, Alla 170
Khorrami, Mohammad Mehdi 51–3, 61
Khoshsaligheh, Masood 510
Khosravi, Fariborz 51, 55
Khvylia, Andrii 245
Kirsten, Jens 194, 199
Kissinger, Henry 183, 186
Kıvılcımlı, Hikmet 83–4
Kline, Stephen 513
Kobets, Svitlana 255
Kobuch, Agatha 43–4
Koçak, Nalan 24
Kochur, Hryhorii 169, 248–51
Kocurek, Carly A. 512
Kofman, Jan 216
Kohn, Janos 261–2
Kolomiyets, Lada 166, 243–5, 252, 255–6
Konami 507, 511
Konca, İrem 83–8
Kondek, Stanisław Adam 230
Kortländer, Bernd 41
Koskinen, Kaisa 480, 483–4
Kövér, György 209
Kovhaniuk, Stepan 254
Krause, Till 500
Kress, Gunther 482
Krevetsky, Ivan 166, 169, 171–3
Kubaichuk, Victor 245
Kubo, Sakae 469
Kuhiwczak, Piotr 6, 96, 186, 210, 225, 293, 303, 324, 490
Kulyk, Ivan 253–4
Kundera, Milan 212, 320–1, 323–5
Kunzle, David 492, 494, 498

Kuszelewska, Stanisława 233
Kuznetsova, Ekaterina 74, 147
Kynge, James 332

Lafarga, Francisco 129–30
Lafargue, Paul 71
Lafond, Pierrette 316
Lal, Priya 98, 101, 477
Lamarche, Gara 322
Lanckoronska, Maria 40
Lange, Anne 119, 121, 147
Larraz, Fernando 399, 442
Larson, Richard 18
Lasa Álvarez, Begoña 415, 419
Lator, László 212–13, 218
Lawrence, D.H. 96
Lázaro, Alberto 409–10
Lázaro Lafuente, Alberto 415, 419
Lecky, William 69
Leder, Andrzej 232
Lee Masters, Edgar 360
Lefevere, André 127, 263, 322, 456, 479, 482
Le Grand, Eva 323
Lehotay, Veronika 216
Lehtonen, Maija 480
Lem, Stanisław 238
Leonardi, Vanessa 294
Lepore, Mario 492
lesbian 435
Levasseur, Jean 313
Lever, Yves 313, 316–17
Lewis, Joanna 99
Lewis, Sinclair 209
LGBTQ+ 217, 317, 330
Liboriussen, Bjarke 509
libraries 2, 52, 55, 65–8, 72–3, 75–6, 141, 143, 147, 149–51, 197–8, 203, 264–5; monastic 161; public 2, 73, 86, 198, 209, 217, 266, 279–81, 284–85; royal 2
Liebknecht, Nathalie 43
Likhachev, Dmitrii 65
Limane, Lilija 140
Linder, Daniel 410, 415, 418
Lindfords, Berth 101
Liseling-Nilsson, Sylvia 478, 480, 483–4
literacy 2, 23, 96, 115, 245
literalism 254, 257, 324, 465, 469, 494
literary translation 17–18, 73–4, 76, 160–1, 173, 193–4, 200–3, 207, 222–3, 226, 238, 247–53, 255–7, 292, 303–4
literature, young adult *see* children's literature
Ljubljana 155–8, 279–81, 283
Llompart Pons, Auba 301
Llopis Mestre, Sara 435, 443
Lobejón Santos, Sergio 408, 410, 419, 421, 445–6
localisation 31, 493–4, 505–10, 512–13, 515–16
Loff, Manuel 376

Index

Löffler, Dietrich 195–8, 203
Lokatis, Siegried 193–6, 201, 203
Lolita 181, 187–8
Looby, Robert 217, 225–7, 229–30, 232–3, 236–7
Lorenss, Davids Herberts 149
Loseff, Lev 3, 122
Löser, Freimut 38
Lotman, Juri 99
Lotman, Piret 111
Luchuk, Olha 169
Luckyj, George S. N. 166
Lukash, Mykola 247–9, 251, 254, 256
Lumans, Valdis 143
Lumbard, Joseph 460
Lüsebrink, Hans-Jürgen 40–1
Luther, Martin 38, 112, 215, 460–1, 463
Lutheranism 111–15, 155–6

MacCulloch, Diarmaid 459–60
Mackay, Robert Simson 309
Macrea-Toma, Ioana 267, 269–71
Madeira, Cláudia 394
Makaryk, Irena 171
Maksimenkov, Leonid 73
Maksudyan, Nazan 88
Małczak, Leszek 225
Malekpour, Setareh 510–11
Maluf, Ramez 23
Mamdani, Mahmood 100
Manacorda, Giuliano 368
Manasterska-Wiącek, Edyta 225
Mandiberg, Stephen 506, 515
Manetti, Francesco 497
manga 315, 492, 495, 500–1
Mangiron, Carme 506–7, 509
manipulation 8, 20, 121, 147, 258, 261, 295, 297, 378, 386, 389; emotional 478; extra-linguistic 506; ideological 119, 292–4, 297, 303, 511; textual 5, 85, 149, 464, 470, 478
Manipulation School 261
Mann, Bryan K. 315
Maráczi, Géza 217
Marais, Kobus 8, 470
March Revolution of 1848 155, 158, 162, 285
Marinetti, Cristina 354, 384
market censorship 8, 268, 275–6, 317, 320–1, 330–3, 424, 466, 500
marketing 322, 409, 423, 477, 497, 513–14, 516
Markovits, Györgyi 216
Marquette, Catherine 362–4, 368
Marsh, James H. 309
Marshall, Alex 331
Martínez Bretón, Juan Antonio 401
Martínez Martín, Jesús A. 406
Martínez Pleguezuelos, Antonio 416, 423
Martín Ruano, M. Rosario 419

Marx, Karl 69, 84, 99, 116, 118, 145, 216, 314, 332, 380
Marx-Aveling, Eleanor 43
Marxism 83–4, 373, 380
Marxism-Leninism 119, 192, 202, 257, 378–80
Marxismo 380
Masenko, Larysa 254
Massardier-Kenney, Françoise 434–5
Matin-Asgari, Afshin 51
Matkowska, Ewa 225
Mattelart, Armand 500
Matthiesen, Toby 26
Mayer, Franziska 39
Mazrui, Alamin 95, 101, 103
McCabe, Caitlin 495
McCarthy, Mary 415, 435
McCullough, Colleen 415, 417
McDonald, Grantley 462
McDonough Dolmaya, Julie 336, 341
McKirdy, Euan 23
McLaughlin, Martin 3
McLean, Matthew 40
McMahon, Liv 29
McRae, John 292, 340
Mdallel, Sabeur 19
Meda, Juri 496
Medina, João 377
Mehawej, Isabelle 30
Mein Kampf 140, 149
Mendelssohn, Moses 42
Merino, Raquel 367, 404, 415–18
Merkle, Denise 5, 8, 13–14, 16–19, 185, 313, 322, 333, 414, 416, 423–4, 455–6, 464–5, 467, 489–90
Meseguer Cutillas, Purificación 410, 415
meta-censorship 332, 468–70
Metse, Kristi 114
Meydani, Assaf 210
Meyer, Richard 13
Meylaerts, Reine 8
MI5 337
Michelangelo 5
Michelove, Peter A. 1
Mickey Weekly Magazine 19
Middle Ages 37–8, 42, 44, 65
Mignolo, Walter 30
Mihályi, Gábor 211
Mikolič Južnič, Tamara 160
Milani, Abbas 55
Miller, Arthur 56, 314, 391
Miller, Henry 87, 208, 314, 415
Miller-Naudé, Cynthia 456, 465, 467, 470
Milton, John 80, 120, 180, 307, 325, 409
Mistral, Gabriela 377
Mix, York-Gothart 40, 491
Miyakovsky, Volodymyr 167, 171
Mizuno, Takeya 346

Mlakar, Boris 280, 284
Mnakri, Moufida 30
modernism 117, 232, 264, 271, 388–9, 480
Mojsak, Kajetan 225, 228, 232, 234, 236–7
Möldre, Aile 116–20
Monas, Sydney 1
Moniz, Maria Lin 190, 377, 381–2, 414, 416, 418
Montejo Gurruchaga, Lucia 440, 442
Monticelli, Daniele 116–17, 119–21, 142, 144
Monzón Rodríguez, Sofia 410, 415
Moor, Nicole 489
Moore, James D. 458, 471
morality 5, 58, 70, 74, 110, 117, 157, 184, 374, 378, 417; official 407; religious 97; sexual 416–19, 424
morals 53, 58, 68, 81, 371, 512
Morel, Auguste 314
Moreno, Amparo 435
Moreno, Mariano 136
Moreno Tovar, Manuel 297
Morissette, Isabelle 342
Morris, Peter 316
Morson, Gary Saul 482
Moser, Michael 172
Moskalenko, Mykhailo 165, 172, 250–1
Mo'taqedi, Robabeh 51
Motyl, Alexander J. 255
Mroczek, Eva 457
Müller, Beate 222, 456, 465, 490
Mulsow, Martin 39
multilingualism 20, 110, 115, 166, 173, 336, 338
Muncy, Robyn 345
Munday, Jeremy 8, 433
Muñoz-Basols, Javier 3
Murris, Karin 477–8
Mussolini, Benito 160, 355, 358, 363–5, 367, 496
Mwaura, Peter 99
Mykytenko, Oleh 247, 251

Nabokov, Vladimir 148, 181, 187–8
Nagel, Michael 42
Nahaylo, Bohdan 254
Namaste, Viviane 317
Nandris, Grigore 65
Nash, Mary 443
Nassar, Nourhan 21
nationalism 19, 76, 244–5, 263, 267, 354
National Socialism 373, 376–9
Naudé, Jacobus A. 456, 460–1, 463, 465–7, 470
Navabi, Davoud 52
Nazi occupation 120, 142
Nazism 358, 511
Negoițescu, Ion 271, 275
Neț, Mariana 262–3
Neubauer, John 208
Neubert, Gunter 202

newspapers 80–2, 84, 115, 158, 160, 255, 257–8, 262, 264, 266, 338–9, 345, 489, 491; foreign-language 337, 344–5; immigrant 345–6; official 145, 248, 346; political 262
New York Times 331, 343
Niane, Ballé 60
Ní Chuilleanáin, Eiléan 332, 414, 416
Nicoli, Miriam 42, 44
Nida, Eugene A. 466
Niedre, Jānis 142, 146
Nikitenko, Aleksandr Vasilievich 3–5
Nodelman, Perry 475, 485
non-periodical publications 43, 215, 227, 372
non-translation 2, 4, 41, 104, 106, 183–4, 272, 321–2
Nord, Christiane 127
Nordland, Rod 18
Noss, Philip A. 459
Nottola, Francesca 359
Novoe Russkoe Slovo 345
Novykova, Maryna 249
Nygård, Severi 484–5

Obichkin, Gennadii 71
obscenity 8, 86–8, 90, 140, 184–5, 216, 306, 308–10, 314, 413, 419–20
O'Callaghan, Daniel 42
October Crisis of 1970 (Canada) 336, 341–2
October Manifesto 140
Oginga Odinga, Jaramogi 98–9, 104
Ogrin, Matija 157, 161–2
Oikari, Raija 211
Oittinen, Riitta 478, 481–2, 485
Olesen, Alexa 328, 332
Olohan, Maeve 202
Olshanskaya, Nataliya 255
O'Malley, Stephanie 511
Onyshko, Anatolii 251
Order in Council (OIC) 337
Orel Kos, Silvana 284
Orland, Kyle 511
Ortega Sáez, Marta 382, 415, 420, 435, 440
Orthodox Church 70, 114, 116
orthodoxy 68, 113, 457, 464; doctrinal 460; political 416; religious 419
Orwell, George 18, 101–4, 106, 146, 148, 150, 181, 187, 208, 210, 237–8
O'Sullivan: Carol 4, 6, 414; Emer 45
Otis, Alan 339
Ott: Dana 96, 100; Wolfgang 228
Ovsiienko, Vasyl 255
Owen, Robert 69
Owen, Ruth 194, 200
Özalp, N. Ahmet 292
Özek, Çetin 88
Özmen, Ceyda 89

Index

Paatsi, Vello 115
Pâcleanu, Ana-Maria 267, 271–2
Padlock Law 338
Pahlavi Dynasty 51, 58
Paine, Thomas 45, 136
Paker, Saliha 81–2
Pakhomov, Nikolai 65–6
Palamarchuk, Dmytro 248, 250
Paloheimo, Martti 148
Panchón Hidalgo, Marian 435
Pann, Lilia 74
Partridge, Eric 295–6
Pastar, Andrej 158
Paszkowska-Wilk, Anna 225
Patrick, Kevin 489
patriotism 246, 342, 345, 480
Patrusheva, Natalia 68–9
Paul, Toomas 112
Pavese, Cesare 360, 365
Pavese, Claudio 360–6, 368
Pawlicki, Aleksander 223
Pedersen, Daniel 477–8
Pegenaute, Luis 399
Penas Ibáñez, María Azucena 291
Peoples' Republic of China 98–9, 180–4, 508–9
Perepadia, Antatol 248, 251
Peres del Puerto, Ángela 402
perestroika 119–20, 148, 249
periodicals 1–3, 40, 42, 68, 126, 130–2, 136, 140, 279–80, 356, 372
Perry, Samuel L. 468–9
Petcu, Marian 261–4, 268
Peter I (the Great) 66, 110, 174
Petersen, Karen 307
Petrillo, Gianfranco 359
Piasecki, Stefan 510–11
Pierre, Michel 484–5
Pikalo, Matjaz 283
Pillière, Linda 301
Pimentel, Irene Flunser 377
Poirier, Agnes 307
Pokorn, Nike K. 145, 159, 161, 281–5, 345, 479, 484, 486
Pollak, Seweryn 225, 235
Polli, Chiara 500
polyglot 141, 248, 256, 461
Pop, Doru 274
Popa, Ioana 271
pornography 14, 39, 86, 208, 307–9, 315, 378–80, 413, 500, 509
Porto, Carlos 391
post-colonialism 25, 97, 225, 231, 252, 292, 322
Post-Socialist Period 283, 476
Post-Soviet Period 148, 173, 250, 252
Potvin, Maryse 27
Pound, Ezra 73, 147, 363

Pravda 246
Press Freedom Index 62
Pribytkov, Viktor 72
Price, Byron 342
Priidel, Endel 109, 119
Procyk, Anna 167
proofreading 52, 89, 147, 149, 225
proofs 129, 217, 249, 267, 360–1, 395, 464
Protestantism 128, 155
Pruzsinszky, Sándor 215–16
pseudotranslations 404–5, 407, 417–18, 467–8, 493
Puhar, Alenka 281
Pullman, Philip 293, 300–3
pulp literature 140–1
Purcell, Gillis 338–9
Pylypchuk, Dmytro 244

Qi, Lintao 5
Qiblawi, Tamara 26
Quasimodo, Salvatore 248
Al-Qudah, Isra 21, 23
queer 5, 330, 418, 422–4
Qur'ān 20, 81, 97, 459–60, 465, 508
Qurayshī 460

Raabe, Paul 38
Raag, Raimo 111
Rabadán, Rosa 415–17, 419
racism 284, 311, 375, 381, 389, 416, 483; structural 331
radio 20, 85, 147, 151, 160, 252, 338, 340–1, 344, 372, 375; public 19
Radman, Saba 60
Rădulescu, Anda 272
Radyk, Oleh 249
Rahbaran, Shiva 57–9
Rahimi, Mina Zand 500
Rajabzadeh, Ahmad 51–4
Rajalin, Marita 480
Rajch, Marek 43, 225–8, 231–3
Ralian, Antoaneta 269, 272, 274
Raliv, M. 170
Rambsy, Kenton 274
Rancière, Jacques 2
Rayner, Fran 392
realism 58, 159, 198, 236, 322, 378–9, 388, 483; critical 265
Rebello, Luiz Francisco 386, 388, 392, 394
Reed, Betsy 18
Reed, John 72–3
Reformation 111, 114, 126, 128, 460, 463
Regina vs. Butler 309, 315
Reimo, Tiiu 114–15
Reisp, Branko 156
Reiss, Katherina 478
Remy, Johannes 172

Index

Renaissance 82, 248
Repe, Bozo 280
residential schools 310–11
retranslation 4, 17, 50, 85–7, 254, 256, 283–4, 423–4, 475–6, 483–4, 486
retranslation hypothesis 483
Reuchlin, Johannes 42
Révész, Sándor 214
rewriting 127, 291–5, 297, 304, 322, 328, 384, 389–90, 478, 481, 483
Reyent, Oleksandr 172
Reynolds, Matthew 4, 341, 414, 456, 461
Režek, Mateja 161, 283–4
Riba, Caterina 415, 435
Rioux, Philippe 317
Al-Riqābah 14
Ristuccia, Cristiano Andrea 354
Röben de Alencar Xavier, Wiebke 41
Robinson Crusoe 72, 145, 170, 267, 272
Robinson, Douglas 30, 170, 256, 460
Rodrigues, Graça Almeida 372, 395–6
Rodrigues, Tiago 394–5
Rodríguez, Jaime 131, 136
Rogoż, Michal 225
Roig-Sanz, Diana 354
Rojas Claros, Francisco 442
Rojas-Lizana, Isolda 415
Rojo, Ana 415, 418
Roman Catholic Church 27, 156–7, 159, 281–2, 306, 315, 400–2, 443, 445, 459–63, 469
Romek, Zbigniew 223, 229
Rosas, Ana Elizabeth 347, 371, 377, 379
Ross, Kristiina 112
Rossi, Miriam 75
Roszkowska, Anna 235
Roszkowski, Wojciech 216
Rotroff, Heidi 201
Rousseau, Jean Jacques 81, 136
Rowling, J. K. 18
Rozwadowska, Kinga 225
Rubin, Andrew N. 102
Rudnytska, Nataliia 170, 173, 244, 253, 256
Rudzītis, Helmars 141
Rukavina, Steve 27
Rumland, Marie-Kristin 197
Runcan, Miruna 273
Rundle, Christopher 150, 354–5, 358–9, 367, 416, 496
Runesson, Anders 458
Rushdie, Salman 17, 61, 189
Russell, Bertrand 119, 216, 373
Russian occupation 7, 171, 262
Russian Orthodox Church 65–6
Russian Revolution 71–2, 85, 103–4, 110, 115–16, 167, 378
Ryder, Bruce 313

Saada, Anne 40
Sabin, Roger 501
Sadr, Hamid-Reza 58
Saiegh, Marc 14
Salagī, Mohammad 54, 57
Salama-Carr, Myriam 190
Salazar, Oliveira 210, 332, 358, 367, 371–2, 374–5, 377–9, 386, 390–1, 396, 416
Salevsky, Heidemarie 202
Salinas, Ann O'Toole 96, 100
Salu, Herbert 113
Salupere, Malle 109, 115–16
Sánchez Reboredo, José 408
Sands, Farran Norris 298
Sanmartí, Carme 415, 435
Santaemilia, José 415, 420, 423
Santos, Boaventura 30, 128, 384–6, 394–5
Sanz Gallego, Guillermo 415
Sanz-Moreno, Raquel 415–16, 422
Sapiro, Gisèle 6
Sappho 5, 413
Saramago, José 373, 375
Sartre, Jean-Paul 54, 56, 73, 228, 281, 373, 394
Sâsâiac, Andi 268, 275
Sashegyi, Oszkár 215
Sasvari, Tom 310
Savchenko, Fedir 168, 171
Savchyn, Valentyna 256
Saviotti, Gino 388
Schaefer vs. United States 344–5
Schäfer, Hans Dieter 143
Schandl, Veronika 212, 217
Schaub, Michael 18
Scheer, Tamara 216
Schenk vs. United States 344
Schmidt, Johann Lorenz 42
Schmitz, Manfred 202
Schneiderman, David 308–10
Schniedewind, William M. 458
Scholz, László 214
Schreck, Joachim 201
Schubbe, Elimar 198
Schütz, Hans J. 38, 42
Schwartz, Alexandra 300
Schwartz, Lowell 16, 513
Schwartzel, Erich 328–30, 334
Scotton, James F. 96–7
Second Vatican Council 400, 402
Sedley, Charles 308
Segal, Lynne 315
self-censorship 5–8, 15–16, 22–3, 29–31, 73, 75–6, 90, 185–8, 190, 200–1, 210–12, 271–2, 328–9, 367–8, 408, 416–21, 439–40, 464–5, 496–500, 507; epistemological 31; pre-emptive 6, 188, 356, 417; preventive 496, 498; processes of 88, 272; translatorial 150, 185, 188

Index

Serrano Fernández, Luis 410
Seruya, Teresa 190, 375–7, 381, 414, 416, 418
sexuality 300–1, 303, 374, 378–80, 413–14, 416–24, 481, 484, 499, 510, 515
Shafak, Elif 88–9
Shakespeare, William 101, 169, 173, 180, 262, 267, 272, 293–7, 382, 389, 392, 415, 419
Shandra, Valentyna 168, 172
Shavit, Zohar 481
Shelley, Mary 180, 293, 297–9
Sherry, Samantha 75, 109, 121, 144
Shevelov, George Y. 169, 254
Shmiher, Taras 172, 243, 254, 256
Shomrakova, Inga 72
Sigel, Lisa 413
The Simpsons 21
Singh, Sikander 41
Sinibaldi, Caterina 368, 496
Sipos, Anna Magdolna 210
Šisler, Vit 510
Skipton, David M. 1, 3, 342–3
Skopečková, Eva 292–3
Ślarzyńska, Małgorzata 225
Smelik, Willem F. 459
Smolik, Marijan 284
Smolnikar, Breda 283
Smulski, Jerzy 230–3, 237
Smyth, Sarah 255
Snoj, Janz 284
socialism 73, 102–3, 106, 140, 145, 187, 198–9, 202, 208, 267, 272; late 253
socialist realism 72, 119, 198, 207–8, 224, 230, 250, 265, 269, 271, 274
social translation 25–30
Sohár, Anikó 211, 213–14, 218
Sokhan, Pavlo 166
Solberg, Ida Hove 144
Solzhenitsyn, Aleksandr 119, 147, 208, 237, 320
Somacarrera, Pilar 415, 418
Sonina, Elena 71
Sousa, Alexandre Barros de 388, 390
Sova, Dawn B. 420
Soviet occupation 139, 141–2, 144, 146–8, 192, 213, 229
Spanish Catholic Church 402, 418
Spanish Index 1
Specht, Walter F. 469
Spiegelman, Art 495
Špirk, Jaroslav 322, 332
Staats Zeitung 344
Stainless Games 511
Stalin, Joseph 73, 101, 145, 244, 255, 257, 477
Stalinism 103, 119–20, 149, 207–8, 230, 265–6, 475–6
Stalinist period 119, 146, 225–6, 230, 232–4, 273–4
Stallybrass, Oliver 324–5

Staniów, Bogumila 225
Stanton, Sarah 15
The Stars and Stripes 346
Steele, Jennifer Elaine 2
Stein, Peter 41, 69
Steinbeck, John 147, 180, 236, 267, 282, 360, 364
Stewart, Philip 17, 341
Stewart-Murray, Katharine 376
Stine, Philip C. 466
Stöcker, Christian 511
Stolt, Birgit 483
Strikha, Maksym 165–7, 169–70, 172–3, 244, 246–7, 249, 251–2, 254, 256
Strober, Maya 30
Strods, Heinrihs 141–2, 144, 147–8
structural censorship 5–8, 37, 44–5, 89, 110, 306, 424, 465, 470, 506–7
Studen, Andrej 160
Studynsky, Kyrylo 169
Sturge, Kate 143, 358, 416
Stus, Vasyl 250–1
subtitling 4, 21–4, 316–17, 405, 416
Suleiman, Yasir 15–16
Sullivan, Karen 294, 415
Sun, Jodie Yuzhou 99
Sun, Zhili 180–1
Süren, Merve Sevtap 297
Sutherland, John 423
Sutter Fichtner, Paula 156
Švent, Rozina 283
Svetina, Peter 284
Svitanok 248
Svitlychny, Ivan 250–1
Svoljšek, Petra 159
Swindler, William 348
Swoboda, Victor 254
Szili, József 209

Tabaire, Bernard 97
taboo 19, 22, 73–4, 147, 150, 189–90, 193, 414, 417, 419–20, 424, 443, 480–1, 498–501
Tafenau, Kai 112
Tageblatt 344
Tagg, Lori 344
Tahir Gürçağlar, Sehnaz 83
Takács, Ferenc 212, 218
Talattof, Kamran 55, 57
Talvoja, Kädi 146
Tammer, Enno 109, 119
Tan, Zaixi 183, 189–90, 332
Tanganyika 96–7, 100–2, 106
Tapper, Jake 21
Tapper, Richard 57–8
Tarnopolosky, Walter S. 308–10
Tavosanis, Mirko 500
Taylor, Charles 27

Index

Taylor, Miriam 27
television 100, 252, 435, 506
Telo, António José 377
Teodorowicz-Hellman, Ewa 481
terrorism 20, 29, 69, 72, 75, 90, 159, 253, 317
Tervaharju, Minttu 477
Thawabteh, Mohammad 22
Thomas, Deb 314
Thomson-Wohlgemuth, Gabriele 194–6, 198–9, 201, 203, 214, 476–7, 479–81, 483, 486
Tidy, Joe 29
Timokhina, M.V. 74
Tito, Josip Broz 280, 282–3
Toledano, Carmen 415, 419–21
Topuz, H. 81
Torop, Peeter 122
Toska, Zehra 82
Tosti, Andrea 492
totalitarianism 76, 103, 208, 333
Tóth, Gyula 214
Toury, Gideon 110, 121, 267, 273, 404, 433
TRACE Research Group 6, 367, 406–7, 410, 416–18, 435
Tranfaglia, Nicola 354, 359
Trupej, Janko 284
Truskolaska-Kopeć, Emilia 225
Tsvetaeva, Marina 147
Tymoczko, Maria 121, 185, 187, 210, 212
Tyndale, William 38, 461–3
typesetting 141, 235
Tyšš, Igor 365

Ubisoft 515
Ulbricht, Walter 192–3, 201
Ulrichsen, Kristian 20
Unāms, Zanis 141–3
Unamuno, Miguel de 144, 377
United Nations 264, 309, 341
Uras, Umut 24
Uras Yılmaz, Arsun 297
Uribe-Urán, Victor 128, 132
Uricaru, Ioana 4
Uşaklıgil, Halid Ziya 81
Üstünsöz, İrem 86–8

Vajdová, Libuša 270
Valdeón, Roberto 128, 422
Vandaele, Jeroen 367
van Doorslaer, Luc 291, 294
van Leeuwen, Theo 482
Van Wagenen, Julianne 366
Varga: Alajosné 213; Sándor 211
Vatican 129, 381
Vatican II 459
Vatican's Index 316
Veinberga, Sandra 140

Veisbergs, Andrejs 139
Venuti, Lawrence 102, 320, 322, 478, 483
Vermeer, Hans 478
Veskimägi, Kaljo-Olev 109, 119
Vianu, Lidia 274
video game history 508, 511–12
video game industry 508, 511–13
video game localisation 505–16
video games 8, 317, 505–8, 511–14, 516
Vidmar, Luka 156–8, 161
Vittoria, Albertina 354, 359
Vittorini, Elio 360–7
Vladimirov, Leonid 343
Vogel, Ezra F. 183
Volceanov, George 272
Volmar, Victor 23
Voltaire 66, 70, 114, 129, 131, 133, 215
von Flotow, Luise 414
Vose, Robin 2
Vrinceanu, Alexandra 267
Vsesvit 172, 247–9
Vulpius, Ricarda 172

Wagner, Rob 18
War Measures Act of 1914 306, 308, 314, 337–8, 341
Warsaw Uprising 236
Weiss, Hellmuth 111
Weiss, Peter 394
Wells, Stanley 180, 295
Wertham, Frederic 489–90
Wertheimer Bible 42
Wicksteed, Charles 69
Wiegand, Wayne A. 2
Wiesner, Luis 134–5
Wijman, Tom 508
Wilde, Oscar 117, 226, 232, 415
Willis, Michael 26
Willis, Ted 389
Wilson, Amrit 100
Winiarska-Górska, Izabela 225
Winkelbauer, Thomas 156
Wolf, Michaela 5, 13, 15–16, 158–9, 161, 168, 270, 294, 424
Wolfenstein 3D 511
Wolfenstein II 512
women writers 432–4, 445, 449
Woods, Michelle 8, 324, 334, 395, 424, 456, 464, 466, 468
World War I 43, 140, 263, 285, 314, 336–7, 342–3, 348, 359, 480
World War II 230–1, 233, 236, 246, 264, 272, 274, 336, 338–9, 342–3, 346–8, 373–4, 379, 382, 475–8
Woźniak, Monika 225
Woźniak-Łabieniec, Marzena 224

Index

Wu, Xi 180
Wurm, Carsten 201
Wüst, Wolfgang 38
Wuthering Heights 230, 449
Wycliffe, John 461

Yahiaoui, Rashid 21
Yang, Luo 194, 199
Yılmaz, Mustafa 83
Yugoslavia 154–5, 159, 161, 266, 279–80, 282–5, 479, 486
Yuliasri, Issy 500
Yurchak, Aleksei 4
Yuzefovich, Mikhail 167

Zabuzhko, Oksana 256
Zaccaria, Giuseppe 368
Zahiri, Mahboobeh 510
Zalar, Jeffrey T. 40

Zalizniak, Andrei 65
Zanders, Viesturs 141
Zanettin, Federico 484–5, 489, 493–4, 496
Zaragoza, Gora 414–16, 432, 435, 443
Zarych, Elzibeta 225
Zauberga, Ieva 147
Zavala, Iris M. 434
Zelenov, Mikhail 64
Zellis, Kaspars 143
Zelmenis, Gints 140–1
Zethsen, Karen Korning 292
Zeveleva, Olga 7
Zhang, Xiachun 509
Zhirkov, Gennadii 65–9
Zitawi, Jehan 19, 496, 499–500
Žnideršič, Martin 282
Zorivchak, Roksolana 254
Źrałka, Edyta 225
Zuckermayer, Carl 160